Designing and Patternmaking for Stretch Fabrics

Designing and Patternmaking for Stretch Fabrics

Keith Richardson

International Academy of Design and Technology
Toronto, Ontario

Fairchild Books, Inc.
New York

Director of Sales and Acquisitions: Dana Meltzer-Berkowitz

Executive Editor: Olga T. Kontzias

Acquisitions Editor: Joseph Miranda

Senior Development Editor: Jennifer Crane

Art Director: Adam B. Bohannon

Production Manager: Ginger Hillman

Cover Design: Adam B. Bohannon

Second Printing, 2008

Library of Congress Catalog Card Number: 2007935039

ISBN: 978-1-56367-479-2

GST R 133004424

Printed in the United States of America

TP12

For Margaret

CONTENTS

INTRODUCTION

In the past, the garment industry was segmented into different categories such as daywear, eveningwear, and swimwear. The industry was also divided into houses that manufactured knits and those that manufactured woven fashions. However, in order to remain competitive in the current marketplace, today, all designers and manufacturers must incorporate stretch fabrics in their collections. A large portion of modern collections are created from stretch and knit fabrics. Almost all tops, sweaters, swimsuits, and dresses in a designer collection are created utilizing knit fabrics. The modern designer must understand the use of knit fabrics and the specific patternmaking procedures required to make knit garments.

Most new stretch designers and patternmakers mistakenly believe that stretch and knit garments must be extremely close-fitting and tight. While this is often the case, it is not always truc. Stretch garments can also be loose, draped, shirred, oversized, and fluid. Cowl necks, draped effects, ruffles, and flow can easily and very effectively be created through the use of knit fabrics. It is the character of the fabric to be fluid and liquid, and it is for this reason that many designers and manufacturers use stretch fabrics in their collections. Most beginners also assume that stretch garments are not "designer." However, Sonia Rykiel, Azzedine Alaia, Missoni, Norma Kamali, and Stephen Burrows, are examples of designers who have built entire collections and empires based primarily on knit fabrics.

Throughout this text, the terms "stretch fabric" and "knit fabric" are used interchangeably. The characteristic that makes fabric stretch is knitting that is not done like your grandmother while she sat on the porch in her favorite rocking chair, but instead with huge industrial machines that replicate the exact same stitches she used to make that holiday sweater. The new designer can't imagine that your favorite T-shirt, hoodie, or your comfy fleece track pants were created by knitting with either small or large needles.

The Intended Audience

This book is intended for students of fashion, current designers that need refresher lessons or updated knowledge of designing and patternmaking for stretch, and the experienced home sewer who requires patternmaking knowledge for stretch fabrics. This book assumes that the reader has a basic understanding of sewing and will be able to construct these garments with industrial equipment. It does not show very many sewing and construction techniques.

This text is unique in that is develops different slopers for each different stretch ratio, thus allowing the patternmaker to focus on the realization of the design and not the mathematics necessary to compensate for the stretch factors of knit fabrics. The largest ratio is drafted and the other stretch ratios, being smaller, are outlined on the larger sloper.

This book is intended as an introduction to the principles and practices of stretch patternmaking and not every imaginable style is illustrated. To gain a more thorough knowledge of the subject matter it is imperative that the student practice and apply the principles explained in this book. Eventually, the patternmaking will become instinctual.

This book also cannot foresee the constant and evolving changes inherent in the fashion industry and, consequently, the styles illustrated throughout this text are not chosen for their fashion importance, but rather as a teaching tool to illustrate the many different patterndrafting techniques the student should understand. The styles created throughout this text are not shown as examples of current fashion. Instead, they are intended to instruct the patternmaker and designer how to use their own creativity to develop their own unique styles.

This textbook is different from other books in that it studies and explains each garment type, rather than garment parts. The student is able to go to the section for T-shirts, and find out how to draft the sloper, create the pattern, and use the relevant garment details, rather than sifting through chapters trying to find the information necessary. Often, this textbook is repetitive because it has been created so that students may turn to the chapter they are interested in and be able to complete a project without having to flip though many chapters and each every page looking for a neckline that may only apply to a T-shirts.

How This Book Is Organized

Each area of study will begin with the draft of a sloper/block, which is a basic template of the garment, and then proceed to illustrate different patterns within the subject area. The final portion of each area of study will focus on advanced patternmaking practices of the subject matter. This will be followed by an exercise, garment, to test the designer's knowledge of the subject matter, and a short quiz to determine that you fully understand the concepts of the project. Each project will incorporate two different seam finishes, so that by the time the student has completed the ten projects required for the course, the student will have a thorough understanding of stretch fabrics.

About the Diagrams and Illustrations

Please note the diagrams and illustration are not in the correct proportions. The reader cannot measure the illustrations because they are not accurate. All measurements will be indicated and should be followed as taken from the measurement charts provided. Any of the measurements given may be substituted with personal measurements for the development of personal slopers and patterns or for custom designs.

Legend

The following will be used throughout the text and may be used as a guide to the illustrations.

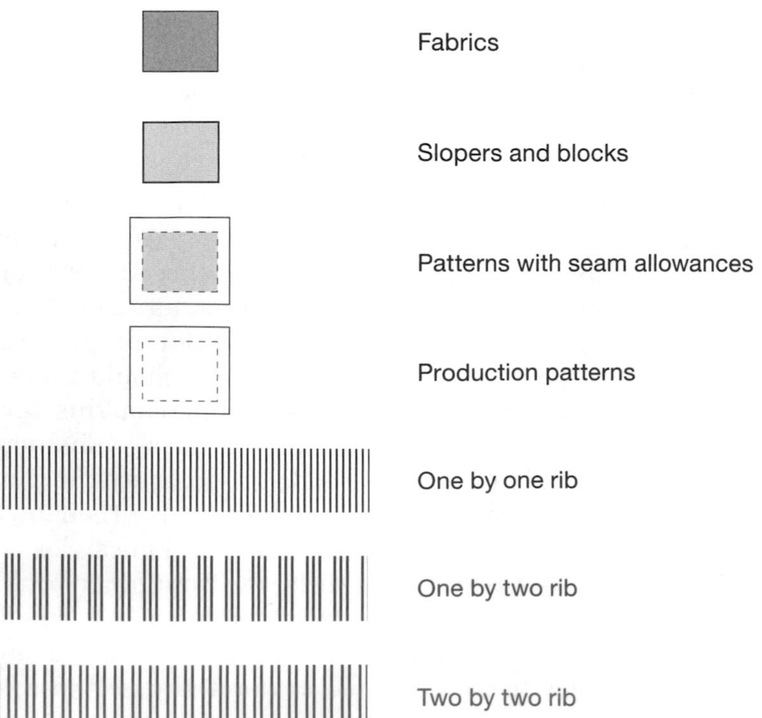

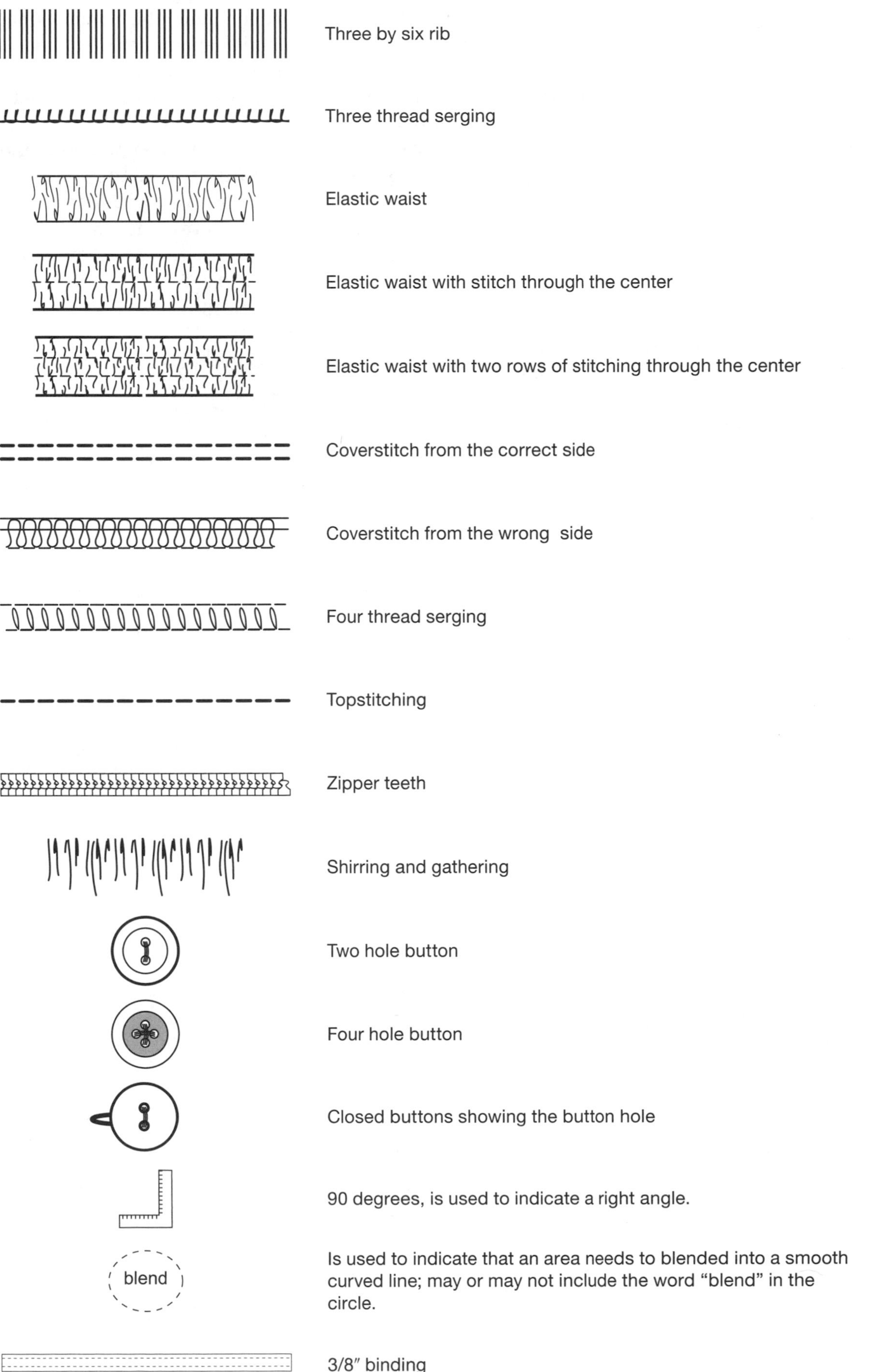
Three by six rib
Three thread serging
Elastic waist
Elastic waist with stitch through the center
Elastic waist with two rows of stitching through the center
Coverstitch from the correct side
Coverstitch from the wrong side
Four thread serging
Topstitching
Zipper teeth
Shirring and gathering
Two hole button
Four hole button
Closed buttons showing the button hole
90 degrees, is used to indicate a right angle.
blend
Is used to indicate that an area needs to blended into a smooth curved line; may or may not include the word "blend" in the circle.
3/8″ binding

Pattern Labeling

All patterns should be created full open. However, for clarity and space the patterns in this text are often created on the fold. All patterns should be labeled with grain lines, style number, and the stretch ratio.

Sewing

As mentioned earlier, this book is about making patterns for use with stretch fabrics—not sewing. This text presupposes you have the ability to put the garment together with the equipment you have and is intended for the professional designers with industrial equipment. Although most of the instructions are intended for the industrial sewer, the home sewer will also benefit from the information contained.

Stretch fabrics may seem complicated and confusing in the beginning, but they become easier and easier to understand with each completed project. Practice serging a few seams, attaching elastic, and cover stitching a few hems before beginning any project. Eventually your understanding of stretch fabric will become instinctual and effective.

ACKNOWLEDGMENTS

The author would like to thank the following for their patience help and understanding during the preparation of this text: colleagues, coworkers, and, especially, the students of the International Academy of Design, whose help and constant questions have been the driving force of this book. In addition, thank you to James Fowler for submitting this series of handouts to Fairchild Books and to Lori Stilwell, my original knitting instructor. To friends, Alan Thomas Smith, Stephen Wong, and Suzanne Boyd, thank you so much for your patience, support, and understanding while I was writing this text. Also, special thanks to the authors of all other fashion and garment textbooks, whose writing and teaching have educated me and inspired me to embark on this journey. And, thank you to Margaret, for a lifetime of love.

Designing and Patternmaking for Stretch Fabrics

CHAPTER 1

Stretch Terms and Jargon

Objective

Because of the former segmentation of the garment industry, into eveningwear, knitwear, and swimwear, the stretch industry has its own terminology and jargon. The stretch designer and patternmaker must understand the specific terms in order to communicate ideas, details, and specifications to manufacturers and contractors.

This chapter introduces the reader to the terminology and jargon that is specific to stretch design, patternmaking, and construction. After reading this chapter the reader should be able to identify stretch ratios, the direction of stretch, and understand the stretch patternmaking process.

It is important to know these terms before studying any of the other chapters, as this terminology will be used throughout the text.

All Knit Fabrics Are Created on Knitting Machines

It doesn't matter whether your fabric is a lightweight, sheer jersey knit such as in many designer T-shirts, or a bulky knitted sweater. They are all knitted on knitting machines. Fine knits for T-shirts are created on knitting machines with very fine needles and yarn, while bulky fabrics are created on thicker-gauged machines with larger needles and bulky yarn. The knit fabric that you purchase is knit. Your favorite T-shirt is knit. Your winter toque is knit. And while there are many different sizes of needles and yarn, as well as combinations of stitches, they are all knit on some variation of the basic knitting machine.

Direction of Stretch

The first and most important aspect of understanding knit fabrics is understanding the direction of the stretch, and how the direction should be used when creating garments.

stretches across the fabric

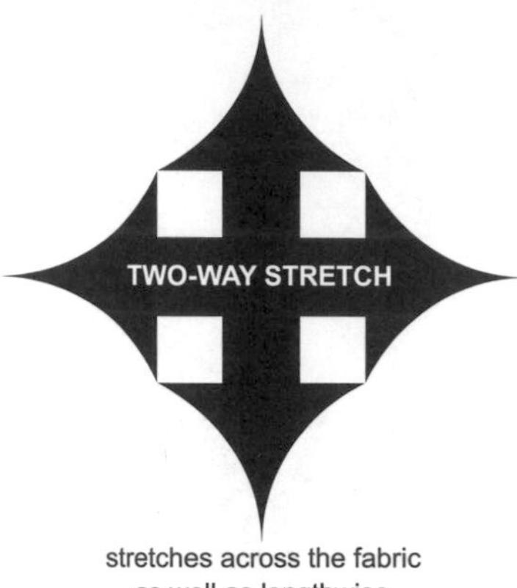

stretches across the fabric as well as lengthwise

stretches across the fabric as well as lengthwise and has spandex added

ONE-WAY STRETCH

One-way stretch is fabric that only stretches across the fabric, and the stretch is entirely derived from the stitches used when creating the fabric. Garments should be made with the stretch going around the body.

TWO-WAY STRETCH

Two-way stretch is fabric that stretches across as well as up and down; the stretch is derived from the yarn and the stitches.

FOUR-WAY STRETCH

Four-way stretch is fabric that stretches across as well as up and down the fabric, and has supplementary stretch added through spandex/Lycra® being added to the fibers before knitting.

Most knits stretch more in one direction than the other, and many knits stretch in only one direction: crosswise. The experienced patternmaker always utilizes the built-in stretch of knits, with the direction of stretch encircling the figure when knits are used for dresses, jackets, pants, skirts, tops, and sleeves. However, the greatest degree of stretch should go up and down the torso for bodysuits, catsuits, leotards, or any other garment that passes through the crotch, to allow for maximum mobility. One-way-stretch knits are rarely used for these garments because of the discomfort created in the crotch when the customer raises her arms.

Two-way-stretch and four-way-stretch patterns are identical, meaning, the same patterns may be used interchangeably. However, garments made with two-way stretch will often sag on the body, at the knees, elbows, and crotch, because the fabric does not have any memory, or elasticity, and will not return to its original shape after it's worn.

Also note that one-way-stretch patterns may be used with four-way-stretch fabrics, as long as the garment does not need lengthwise reductions. For example, a one-way-stretch skirt may be cut using a four-way-stretch fabric, because there is nothing holding the skirt down at the bottom hem (referred to as an anchor). Thus, the lengthwise direction of stretch is not utilized at all.

Distinctive and separate four-way-stretch patterns are only necessary when the stretch of the garment is anchored through the crotch, such as with catsuits, bodysuits, leotards, one-piece swimsuits, and other garments that pass through the crotch.

Why Knit Fabrics Stretch

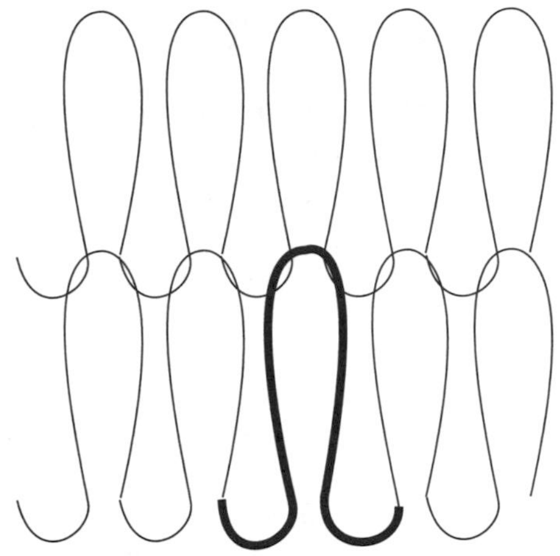

Knit fabrics are created by interlooping yarn; each loop is caught in the row above, and is anchored to the stitches beside it. As the fabric stretches, the loops expand.

Stable-knit fabrics stretch because the knitted loops will expand horizontally. Because the yarn itself does not stretch, the fabric will not stretch in the lengthwise direction.

Two-way-stretch fabrics stretch because the yarn that is used to knit them is textured and crimped in a spiral formation. It uncoils as it stretches, and thus will stretch in both directions—across, and up and down.

Four-way-stretch fabrics have a core yarn of spandex, latex, or Lycra® with another yarn wrapped in a spiral around it. The coils loosen as the fabric stretches, and because of the elastic core, it will spring back to its original size.

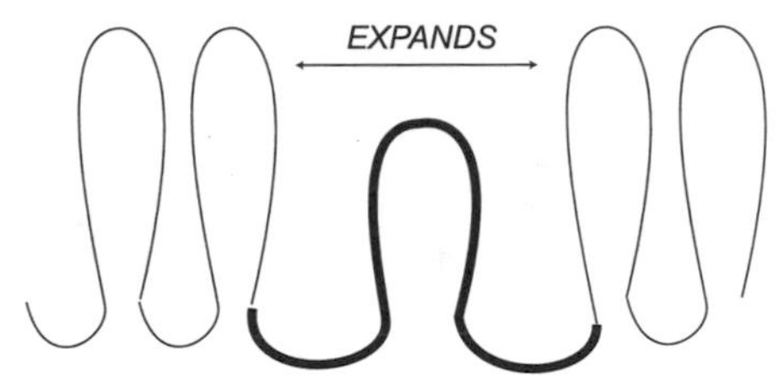

Stretch Factor

The stretch factor, or stretch ratio, is the maximum percentage that a fabric will stretch. Most knits stretch from 18 to 100 percent.

There are five different stretch factors used for designing and drafting stretch patterns.

SPANDEX

Spandex is a synthetic fabric, in which the latex yarn used for the knitting is wrapped with another yarn. Spandex will give the fabric excellent memory, and the ability to stretch a lot more than yarn without spandex.

LYCRA VS. SPANDEX

Lycra® is a trademarked name for spandex. People incorrectly use the terms spandex and Lycra interchangeably. Lycra is a version of spandex, created by DuPont.

LATEX

Latex is a natural elastic or rubber core yarn, with other yarns wrapped around it. It is a natural fiber used to create spandex.

ELASTANE

Canadian or other name for "spandex."

Stretch Ratios

It is also important to understand that different knit fabrics stretch different amounts, and each stretch ratio must have its own set of slopers.

Stable knits	18%–25%	5″ stretches to 6¼″	Stable knits have very little stretch, and will need garment ease to allow for movement when worn. Stable knits are often created oversized to allow for garment ease. Examples of stable knits are Polarfleece®, sweat fabrics, etc.
Moderate knits	26%–50%	5″ stretches to 7¼″	This type will stretch more than stable knits. Examples include T-shirt fabric, interlocks, jerseys, etc.
Stretchy knits	51%–75%	5″ stretches to 8¾″	Examples of stretch knits include velour, stretch terry, and some T-shirt fabrics, etc.
Super-stretch knits	76%–100%	5″ stretches to 10″	Excellent stretch and recovery make this fabric suitable for catsuits, bodysuits, leotards, and swimwear, etc. (for example, fibers blended with spandex or latex). The elastic fibers of this type of knit can stretch many times their original length and width and return to the original measurement. Examples include spandex, nylon spandex, cotton spandex, jumbo spandex.
Rib knits	Up to 100%	5″ stretches up to 10″	Known as the traditional "knit one, purl one" wristband stitch. Rib knits depend on the knit pattern used (e.g., 1 × 1 ribs will stretch more than 2 × 2, 3 × 3, etc.). Rib knits are created by alternating stitches between the two needle beds. They appear identical on both sides of the fabric, and don't curl at the edges. Examples include cuff ribbing, waistband ribbing, and crew-neck collars.
Sweater knits	18%–50%	5″ will stretch to 7½″	Sweater knits are those types of fabrics that one would typically use to create sweaters and sweater dresses. They are usually made with a thicker yarn.
Stretchwovens	Less than 18%	5″ will stretch to 6″	Stretch woven fabrics are created by weaving Lycra® within the fabric, and should be treated as a woven fabric. However, the ease should be reduced, or removed from the slopers.

1

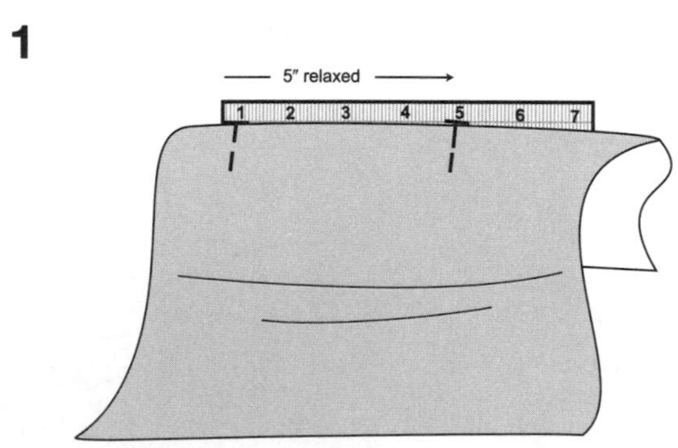

2

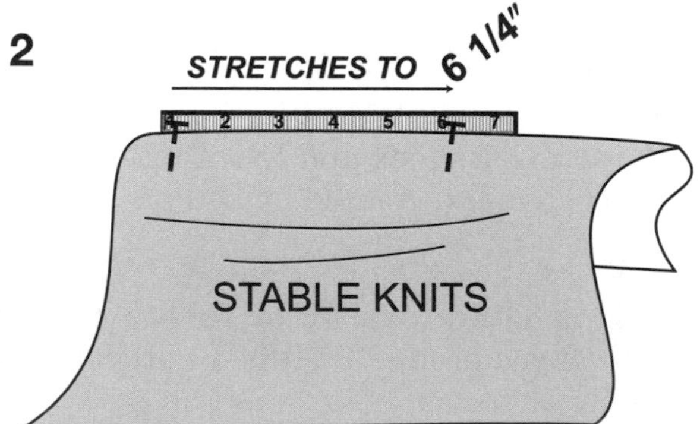

How to Determine the Stretch Ratio of Your Fabric

Take your fabric and fold it a few inches below the cut edge. Place one pin a few inches in from the selvedge and place another pin at 5″ away from the first pin.

To get an accurate measurement, always measure a few inches below the cut edge, because the cut edge often stretches.

Stretch the fabric within the pinned area. If it comfortably stretches to 6¼″, it is a stable knit, with a stretch ratio of 25 percent, and you should use the stable-knit slopers to draft any styles with this fabric.

3

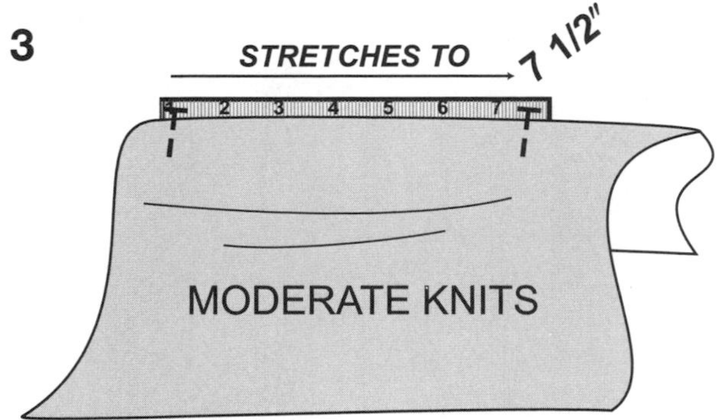

If it comfortably stretches to 7½″, it is a moderate knit, with a stretch ratio of 50 percent.

4

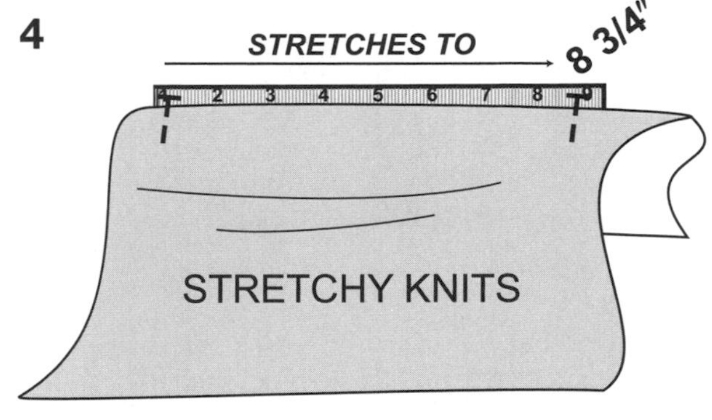

If it comfortably stretches to 8¾″, it is a stretchy knit, with a stretch ratio of 75 percent.

5

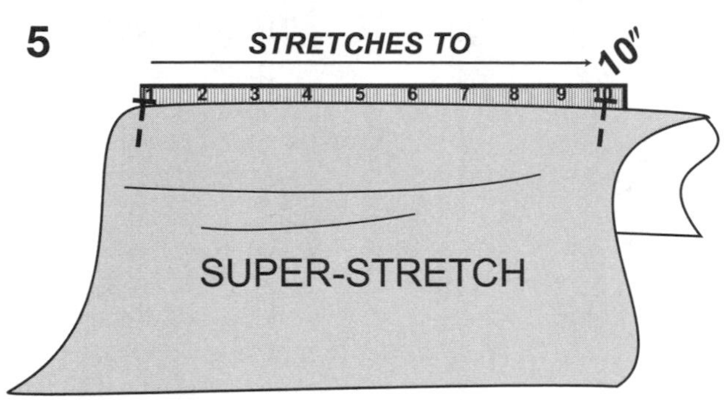

If it comfortably stretches to 10″, it is a super-stretch knit, with a stretch ratio of 100 percent.

6

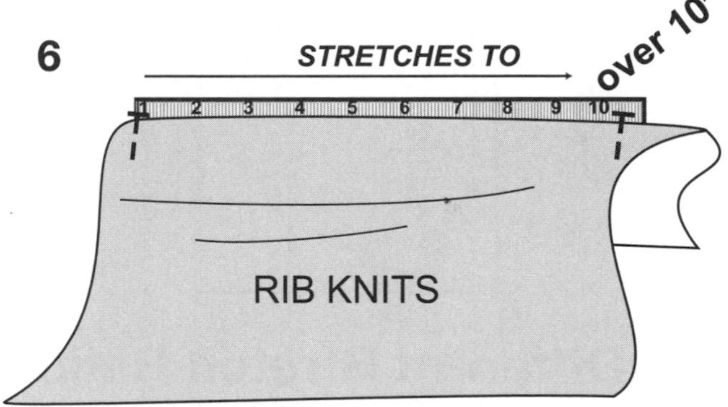

If it comfortably stretches more than 10″, it is a rib knit, with a stretch ratio of over 100 percent.

7

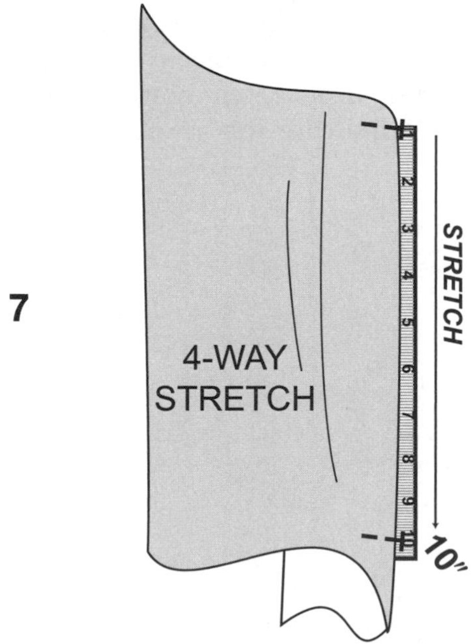

And if it stretches to 10″ or more in both directions, it is a two-way-stretch knit.

If it bounces back, returns to its original measurement when released, it is a four-way-stretch knit.

8

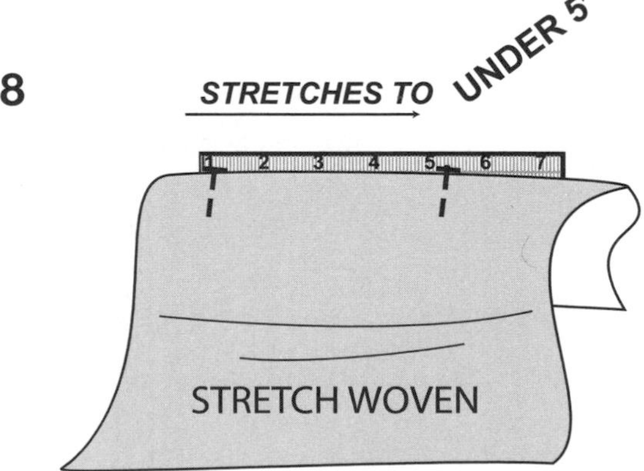

If your fabric doesn't stretch at least 25 percent, to 6¼″, then it should be treated as a stretch woven.

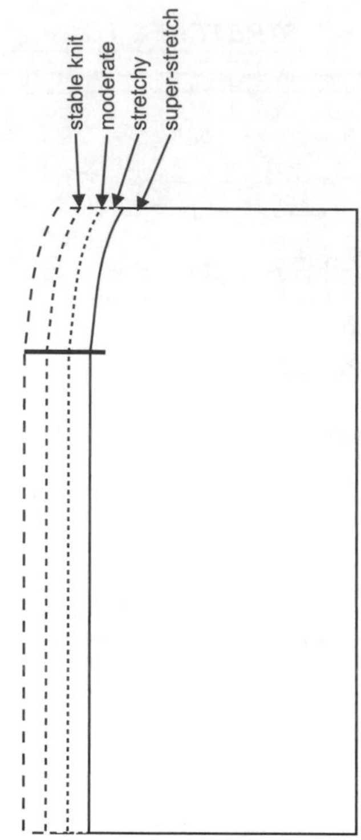

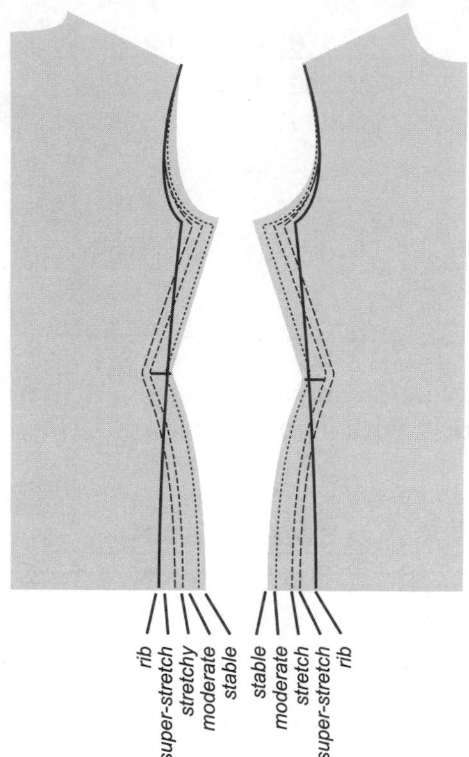

The Different Stretch Ratios and How to Use Them

All of the block drafts in this text will be drafted in the largest stretch ratio, and all subsequent ratios will be drawn on those blocks. If your fabric is a moderate stretch ratio, then trace out those lines on the blocks to begin your draft. If your fabric is super-stretch, then trace out those lines to begin your draft. Never cut off the stretch ratios, as you will definitely need them in the future. If you are working with many knit fabrics, then it is a good idea to trace out each individual stretch block on separate oak-tag. If you only use stretch fabrics occasionally, then simply indicate the stretch ratios on the block.

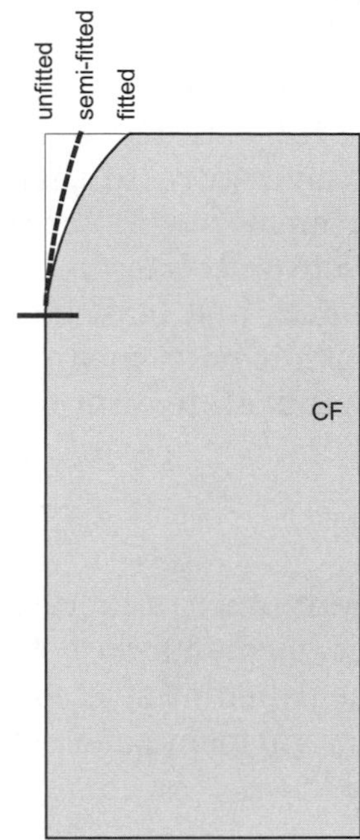

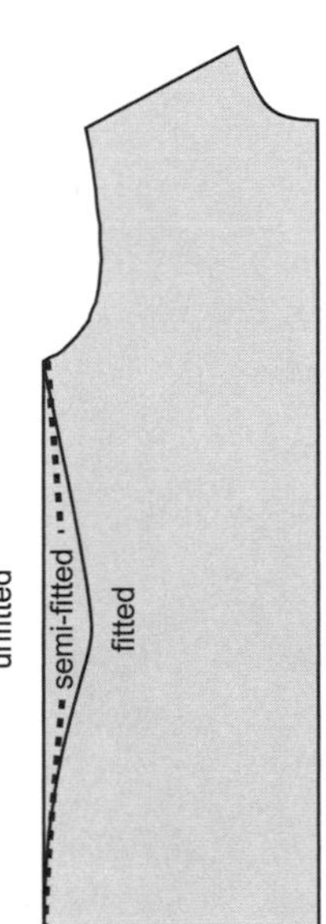

Different Stretch Fits

Knit garments can be created with different waist fits. If you require a tight fit, trace out the fitted waist. If you require an unfitted waist, trace out that waist.

If you are working with many knit fabrics, then it is a good idea to trace out each individual stretch block on separate oak-tag. If you only use stretch fabrics occasionally, then indicate the different waists on the blocks.

If you require a fitted top, then trace out the fitted waist. If you require an unfitted waist, trace out that waist.

Stretch Memory

Stretch memory is the amount that a knit will return to its original shape after being fully stretched. Fabrics with excellent memory will completely return to their original shape, whereas fabrics with poor memory will not return to their intended shape and will eventually sag on the body. With the use of Lycra®, spandex, latex, and elastane, knit fabrics are available with 100 percent memory, meaning they will completely return to their original state after being stretched.

Garment Ease

Garment ease is the amount of extra fabric required to allow for a comfortable fit. Knit garments do not require as much garment ease, because the inherent stretch of the fabric usually provides the necessary garment ease.

Negative Ease

Negative ease is the amount of extra fabric removed, or reduced, to allow for an accurate fit. Many knits are made smaller than the actual body and use the inherent stretch of knit fabrics to achieve the desired fit.

Design Ease

Design ease is the amount of extra fabric required to create a particular design. The designer may require a fit that is oversized or much larger than the body by increasing the amount of design ease. Shirring, gathering, and draped effects are all created with design ease.

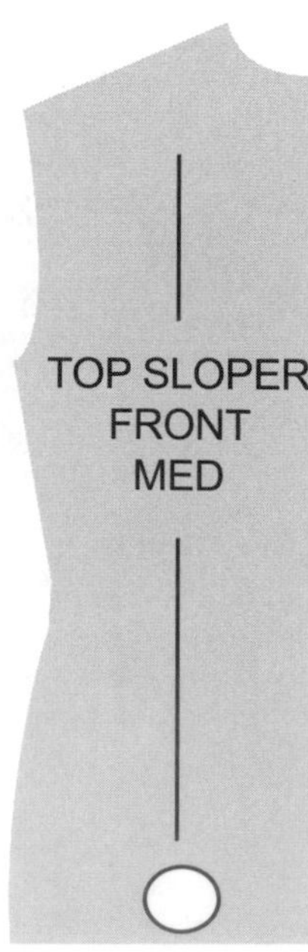

Patternmaking Terms

SLOPER

A sloper, often referred to as a "block" or "master pattern," is a template of the desired fit, like a croquis; it doesn't have any seam allowances or details. It is your basic fit, and from it, many styles can be developed. Experienced patternmakers do not start each pattern from scratch, but instead trace out the required sloper and add style lines and details as needed. It would be far too time-consuming, and expensive, to begin each pattern from raw measurements.

1

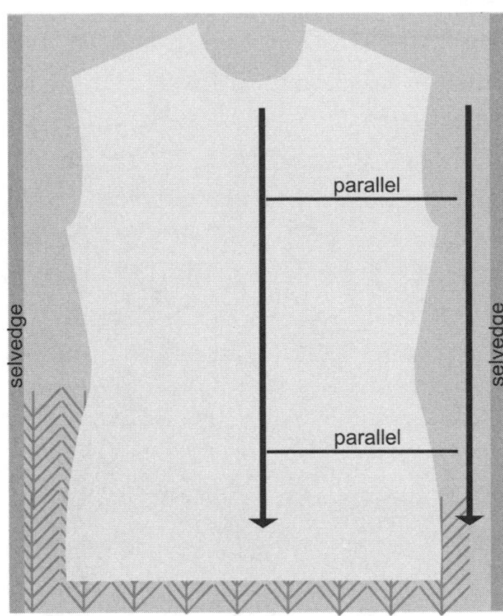

GRAIN

The direction parallel to the selvage of the fabric is referred to as the grain of the fabric. If a garment is not cut exactly on grain, it will twist on the body and be unwearable—and, ultimately, unsellable.

2

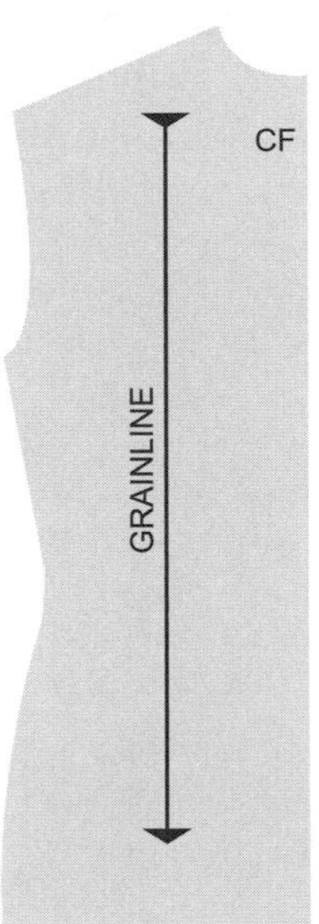

GRAINLINE

The grainline is a line on the pattern that indicates in which direction the garment will hang, and is needed to ensure that the garment is cut on grain. The grainline should always be parallel to the selvage when cutting out the garment. Since most knit fabrics have a nap, grainlines on stretch patterns should have both arrows pointing in the same direction, one direction only, as illustrated. Blocks and slopers should not have any grainlines, because a fabric has not been assigned to the design yet and you can't know in which direction it should be cut.

3

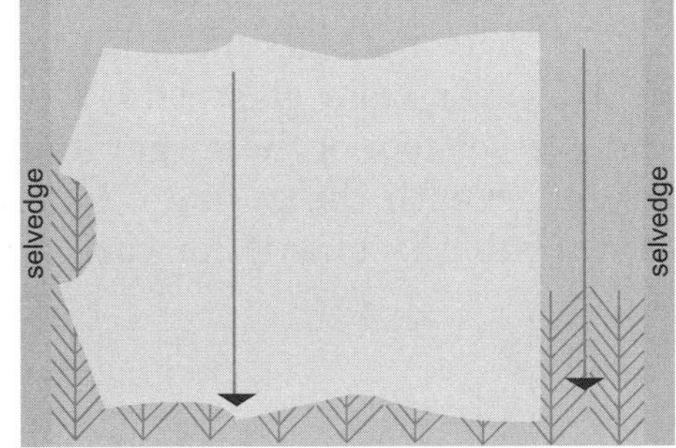

CROSS GRAIN

Cross grain is the grain that is perpendicular to the length grain. Two-way-stretch and four-way-stretch fabrics may be cut on the cross grain, since the fabric also stretches in that direction. Some fabrics such as swimwear fabrics are created so they stretch more in the lengthwise direction than the crosswise direction, and should be cut accordingly.

4

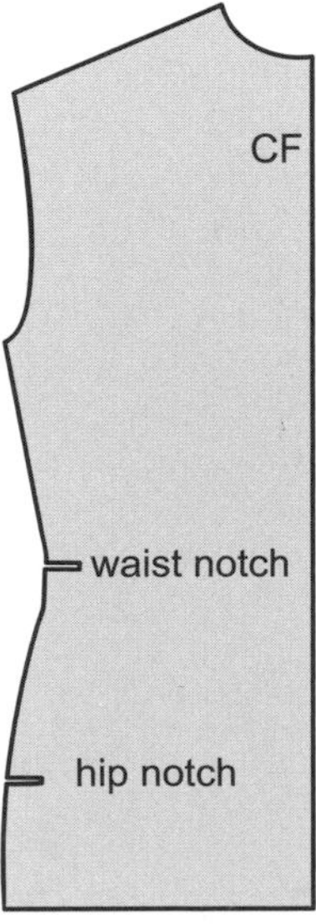

NOTCHES

Notches are small clips in the pattern that indicate where two pieces of a garment line up.

In woven patternmaking, notches may be used to indicate the seam allowances. But in stretch fabric this is not necessary, because almost all seam allowances are ⅜″. Remember to keep all notches in knit fabrics within ⅛″, or you will create holes in your garments.

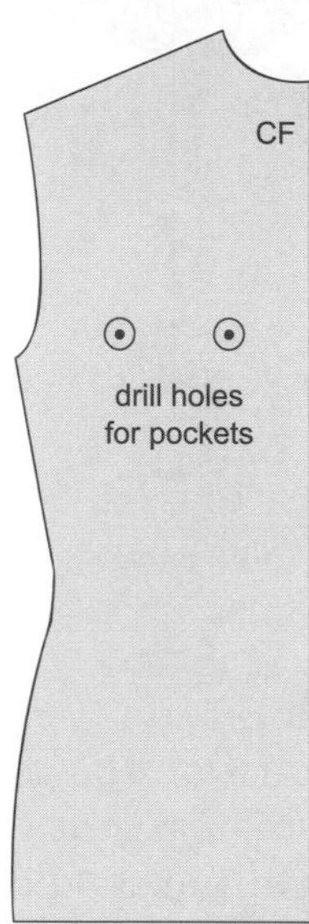

DRILL HOLES

Drill holes, or drill marks, are used to indicate placements, such as where a pocket should line up on a garment. Do not use a drill on knit fabric—it will cause the fabric to run. Mark the fabric with an awl, or chalk marks. Often, loose chalk is pushed into the drill holes of the pattern, one layer at a time, to transfer markings to the garment.

SHOULDER STAYS

Knit tops require shoulder stays, usually ¼″ twill tape to prevent the shoulders from stretching out of shape. The twill tape may be applied while serging the seams or you may use a metering device to attach the tape to the shoulders. Sleeveless garments do not require twill tape, since there is no weight pulling on the shoulders.

Sometimes clear elastic is used to stay the shoulders; it will not shrink with repeated washings. However, clear elastic has a tendency to grip the presser foot of the serger and should be placed underneath the garment to allow the feed dogs to pull the elastic forward with the garment.

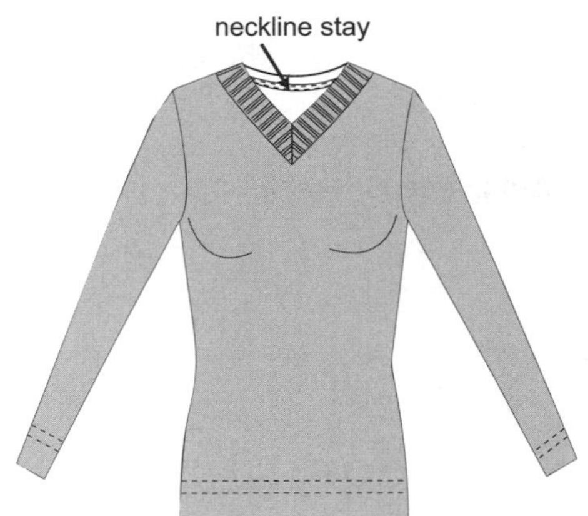

neckline and shoulder stay

NECKLINE STAYS

Many knit garments require a neckline stay, or tape to prevent the neckline from stretching. The neckline tape is only applied to the back neck, to allow the front to stretch large enough to get the garment on the body.

If there is a zipper or other opening in the front of the garment, the tape may completely encircle the neckline. This is especially the case when creating ribbed T-shirts.

As the rib collar is attached to the rib garment, it will often stretch out of shape and needs to be returned to the original size and held in place.

Sometimes the neckline stay and shoulder stay are combined into one single tape that extends from the shoulder across the back neck and along the other shoulder.

The illustration shows the single stitching line that holds the combined neckline and shoulder tape.

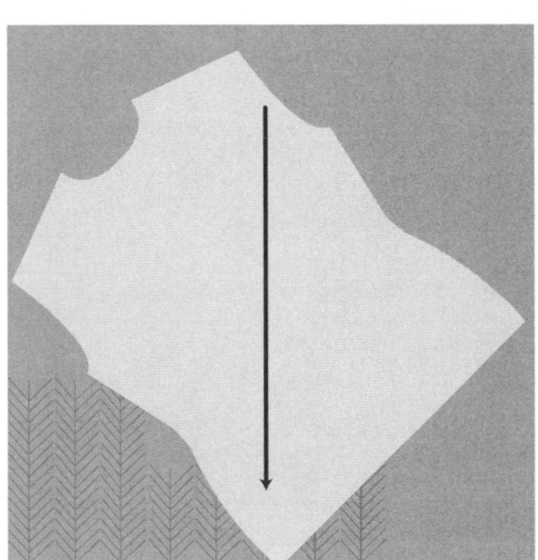

BIAS

Bias is any pattern piece cut on an angle, with true bias being the 45-degree angle to the straight grain. In woven fabrics the greatest amount of stretch is on the bias; however, in knit fabrics the greatest amount of stretch is across. Therefore, bias garments are never created with knit fabrics. Knit bias does not have any of the stretch and drape characteristics that woven bias would impart to garments.

DRAFTING

Drafting is the process of creating a pattern on paper. The sloper is traced out, the details added, and finally the necessary seam allowances and notches are added.

PATTERN

A pattern is the finished template used to cut out the garments. It includes all the details that will eventually be incorporated into the design. It also includes all the seam allowances and notches necessary for the construction of the final garment. Final patterns should always be made from oak-tag.

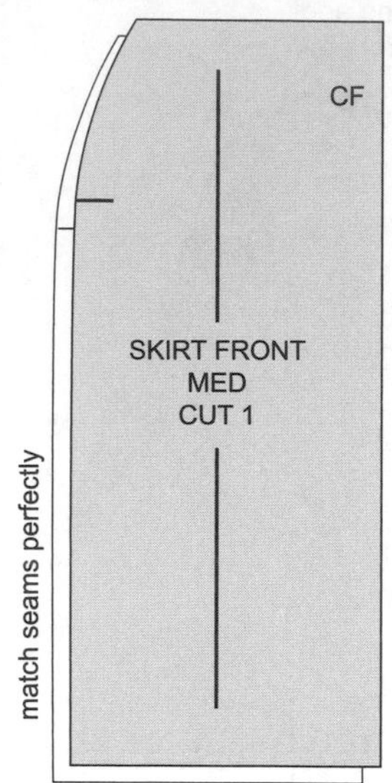

MATCHING SEAMS

Before using any pattern, all seams should be matched to ensure that they are the same length and will sew together perfectly.

When matching seams, the patterns should be on top of each other.

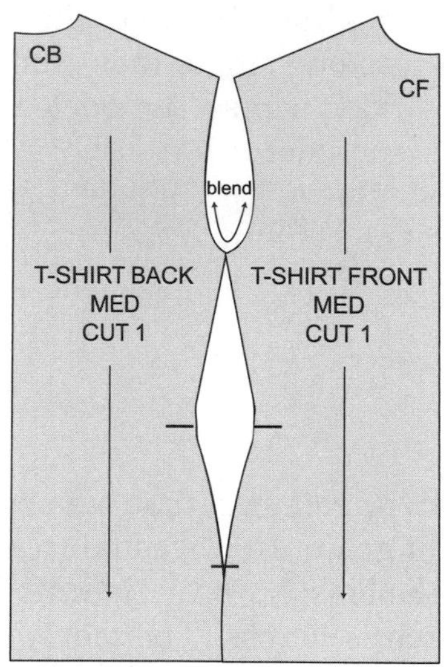

TRUEING SEAMS

Trueing seams is the process of matching all the seams of the pattern, and checking that the lengths of seams match and will sew together perfectly; that they intersect at a desirable angle; and that all notches match. To true a seam, line up the pieces as if they had been sewn and pressed open, beside each other. Check to see that all intersecting lines and seams are blended into smooth and continuous lines.

When trueing the side seams, make sure that the underarm curve is a smooth and continuous line.

Check that the hem is a smooth and continuous line.

To true the shoulders, line them up beside each other, as if they had been sewn and were pressed open. Ensure that the neckline is a smooth and continuous line.

Check that the armhole is a smooth and continuous line.

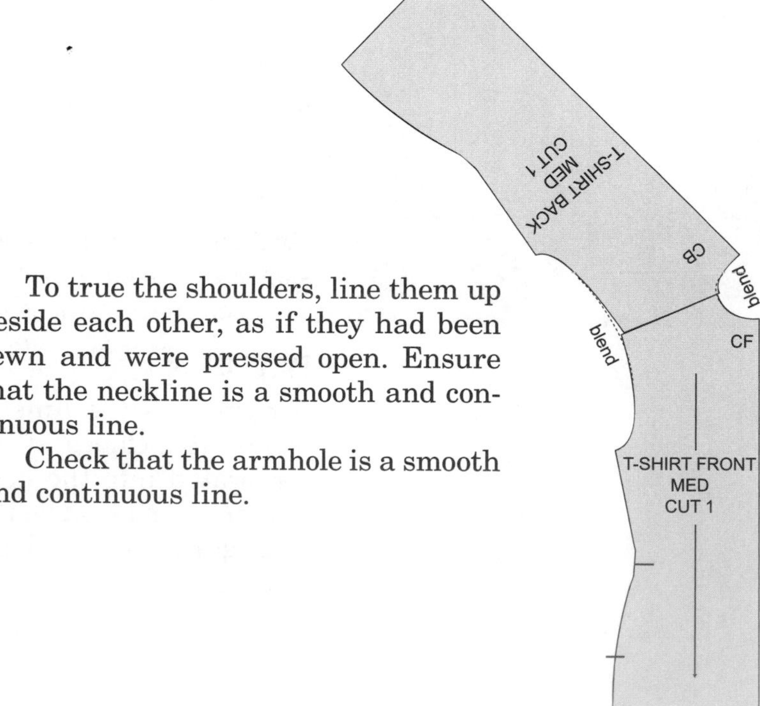

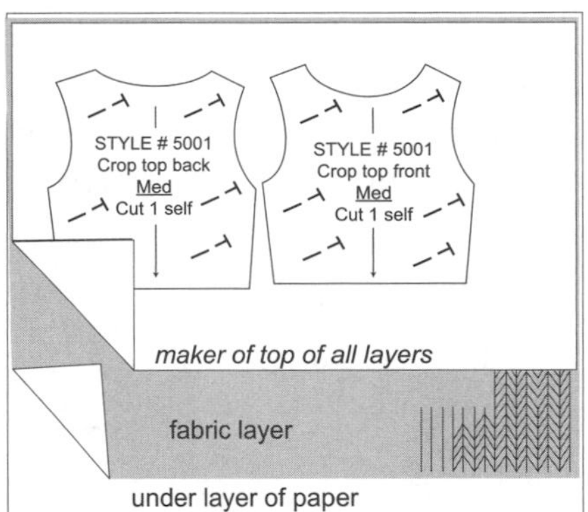

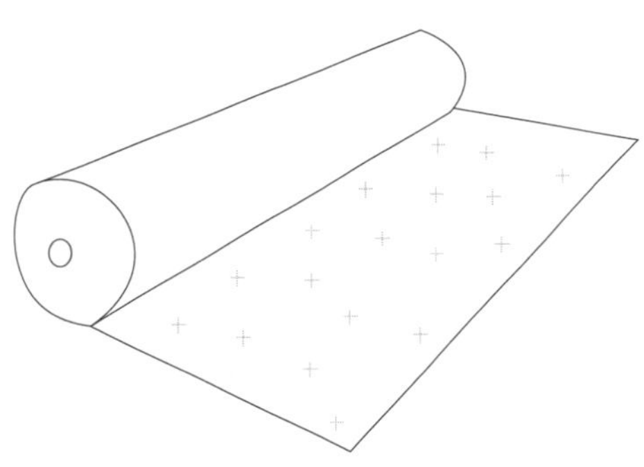

MARKER

A marker is a paper tracing of the complete pattern that is applied to the fabric and held in place with pins, weights, staples, or lightweight spray glue, and is cut together with the fabric. All markers should be made on grain so that when cut out, all the fabric pieces will be on grain. There should be a layer of paper under the fabric to aid in cutting. There should also be a layer of paper between each new color, to prevent the color above or below from staining the fabric as the blade of the cutting knife moves up and down.

MARKER PAPER

Marker paper or dot paper is specially printed with a grid and numbers for the accurate laying of pattern pieces. The marker maker can simply follow the grid to ensure that all pattern pieces are placed perfectly on grain.

MARKER TACKER

A marker tacker is a type of stapler that doesn't have the bottom attachment. It is used to staple the marker paper to the fabric lay, to hold it in place while cutting. Never staple in any of the garment pieces, but staple in areas of the fabric that will be discarded, waste fabric. Also, when cutting out, be sure not to cut a staple or you will create sparks, and greatly dull your knife blade.

SPEC SHEET

A spec sheet is a sheet created by the designer, or spec technician, containing all the information the patternmaker needs to create the pattern for a particular style. It should include:

A sketch, both front view and back view.

Fabric swatch.

All required seam allowances.

Seam finishes.

Hem allowances.

Any important construction notes.

SIZE SPECS

Size specs are the measurements of the manufacturer's target market. Each manufacturer will create garments for a particular customer, and these measurements will be indicated in the size specs. (See Chapter 2: Sizing and Measurements.)

PATTERN CARD

The pattern card, or "must," is included with all finished patterns. It lists all the pieces that "must" be cut to create the garment. All finished patterns should have a pattern must.

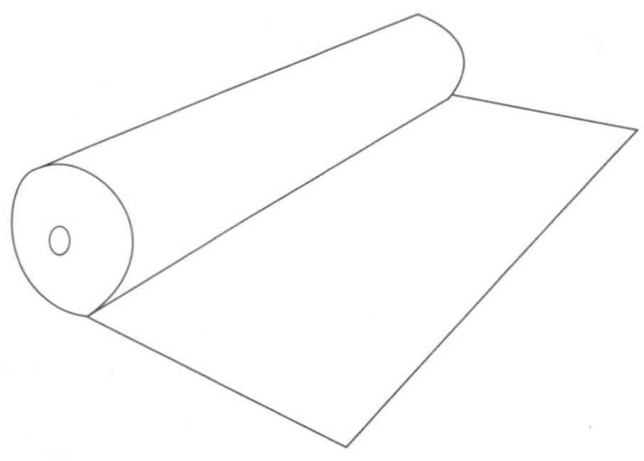

PATTERN PAPER

Pattern paper is any lightweight, inexpensive paper that may be used for drafting patterns. Do not draft directly on oak-tag, because it is difficult to fold back pleats, tucks, darts, or seam allowances for trueing.

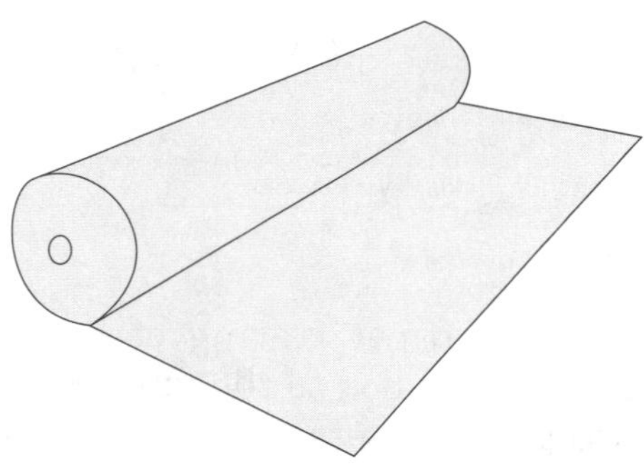

OAK-TAG

Oak-tag is a heavier weight of paper than that used for drafting. Because it is thicker and stiffer, it is much easier to trace around when making markers, and/or tracing with wax or chalk. Only final and production patterns should be traced onto oak-tag, because it is difficult to fold and crease.

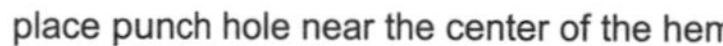

place punch hole near the center of the hem

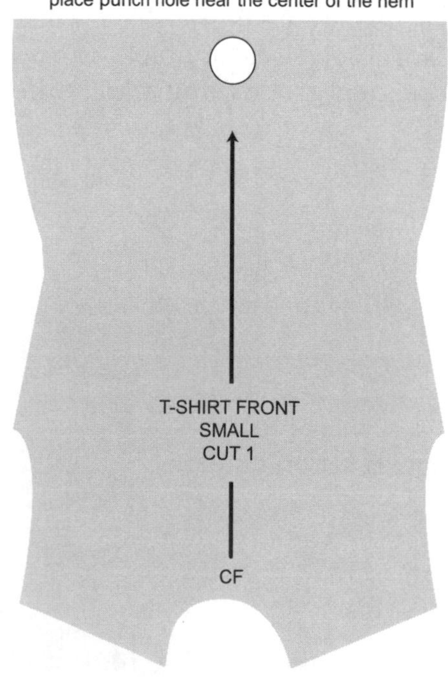

PATTERN HOOKS

All patterns should be hung on pattern hooks and stored when not in use.

When punching holes for patterns, the hem is a more desirable place to make the hole, because if the pattern rips or tears while being stored, it is much easier to replace a portion of the hem than to repair a torn-off neckline or waist. Place the punch hole near the center of the pattern pieces so they hang balanced and do not swing.

COSTING SHEET

This is a sheet created for each style in a collection, which keeps an account of the costs needed to make the garment. Each style should have its own cost sheet. Remember that the most important part of a garment is the "price tag"!

PATTERN LABELING

All patterns must be labeled with the style number, the stretch ratio, the size, a grainline, the direction of cutting, the date completed, the patternmaker's name, and pattern numbering.

Garment manufacturers identify styles by style numbers:

1000	stable knits	100	blouses/shirts	00	the last two digits (sometimes written in roman numerals to avoid confusion) should represent the various styles within the collection.
2000	moderate knits	200	dresses		
3000	stretchy knits	300	pants		
4000	super-stretch knits	400	jackets		
5000	rib knits	500	skirts		
6000	four-way-stretch knits	600	vests		

Note that there are multiple methods of creating style numbers, and the manufacturer that you work for will most likely have its own method.

PATTERN NUMBERING

All pattern pieces of a particular style should be numbered, and should also include the total number of pattern pieces needed for the garment. Use any one of these methods of numbering.

All the examples show the third pattern piece for a garment with a total of four pattern pieces needed to complete it.

Remember that the marker maker and cutter have not gone to fashion school, and do not understand patterns, so they would not realize if a pattern piece is missing.

Often, a designer will trace a pattern piece from a current style when creating a new style. What would happen if the cutter cut out thousands of garments with a pattern piece missing?

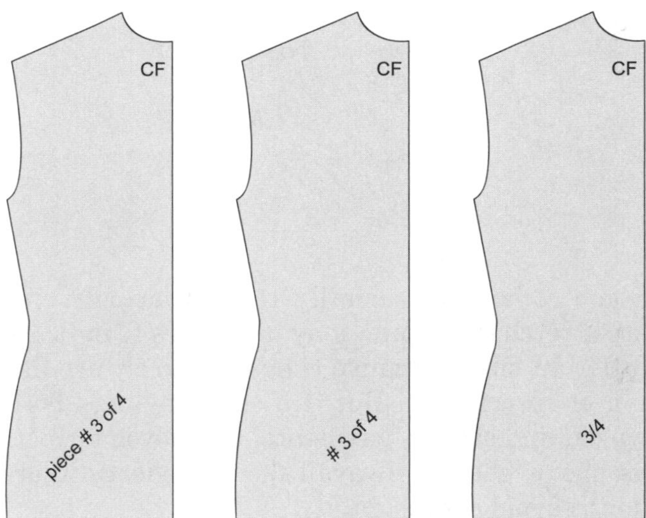

RIGHT SIDE UP

R.S.U. stands for "Right Side Up" and should be used for any asymmetrical patterns to ensure that you always cut the correct side. The example shows a top with only one shoulder, and to ensure that the back is cut with the matching shoulder, it must also be labeled "Right Side Up."

The reverse side, or the back of the pattern, should be labeled R.S.D. for "Right Side Down." Right side up and right side down patterns should always be labeled on both sides of the pattern.

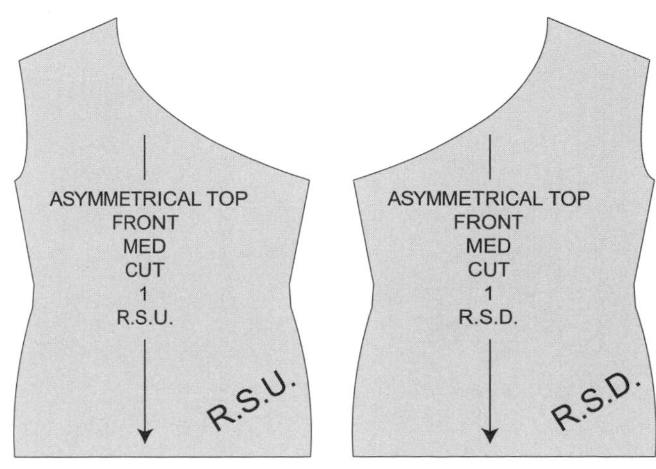

Color Coding

Black	Self or main fabric.
Red	Lining fabric.
Blue	Fusing, or interfacing. The patternmaker should list the type of fusing.
Green	Contrast or any secondary fabric, such as rib.
Purple	Other contrast fabrics, etc.
Pink	Other contrast fabrics, etc.
Brown	Other contrast fabrics, etc.

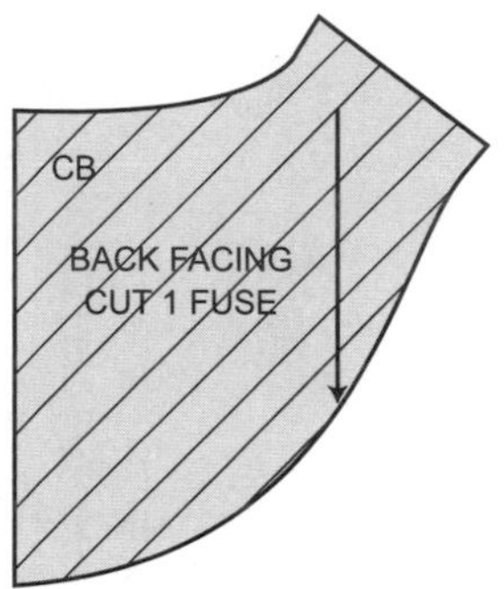

Some companies, usually those that only create stretch garments, may use colors to indicate different sizes, because they will rarely use lining or interfacing. But if a company does both woven and stretch garments, the woven format, as above, should always take precedence in order to avoid confusion.

For companies that label sizes with colors, fuse pattern pieces are indicated with diagonal lines drawn on the pattern piece.

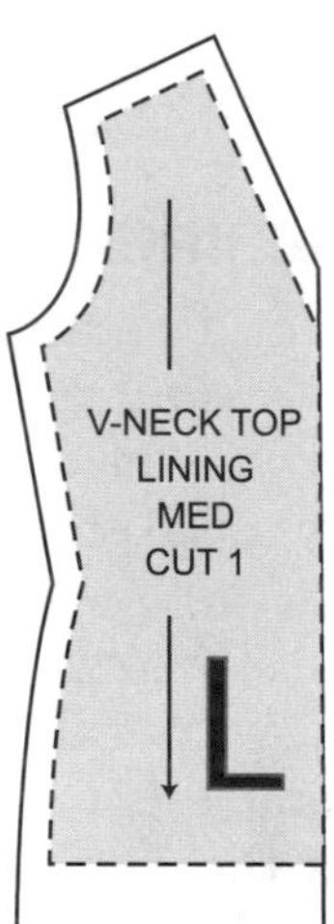

For companies that label sizes with colors, lining is indicated with a large letter “L” on the pattern.

Types of Fit

There are many different types of fit that may be used to create knit garments, and each will be illustrated throughout the text. The designer may specify the fit, or the patternmaker must use his or her own judgment and experience to determine the fit. Fashion trends will also determine the fit. Some seasons will require the fit to be very loose around the waist, while other seasons will demand that fit be much looser. Both the designer and the patternmaker must understand current fashion in order to work effectively.

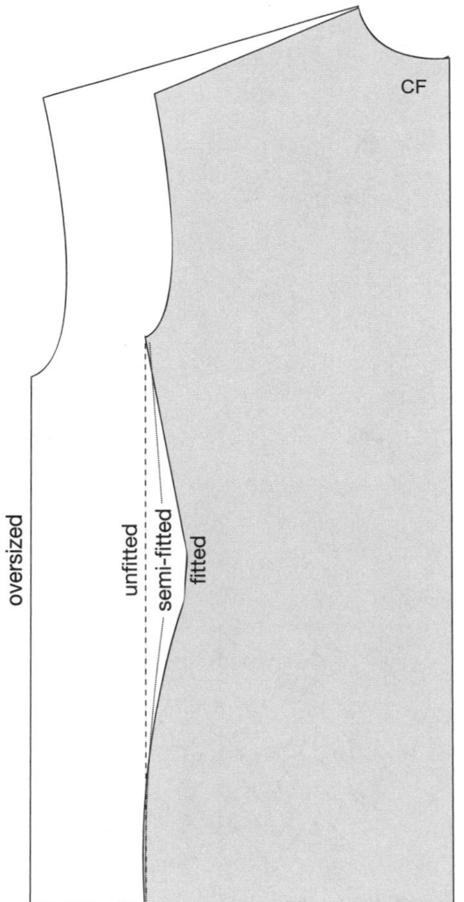

TIGHT FIT

Use the block exactly as drafted without increasing any of the measurements. Most slopers and blocks in this text will be drafted with the tight fit. While this fit may be too extreme, or too tight for the final garment, it is always easier to create a looser fit from a tight-fitting sloper than the reverse.

SEMI-FIT

A semi-fit is halfway between a tight and loose fit, slightly looser around the waist area, and is the most common fit. It appears to have a lot of shaping and will appear like a fitted silhouette, while still allowing some room around the waist.

LOOSE FIT

A loose fit goes straight down from the bust to the hips, and is generally only loose in the waist area.

OVERSIZED

Slash and spread the sloper to create a new oversized sloper (illustrated in Chapter 11, Oversized Projects). Hoodies and track suits are good examples of oversized garments. You cannot simply grade the garment into a larger size, because the neckline, cuffs, and hems would also increase in size.

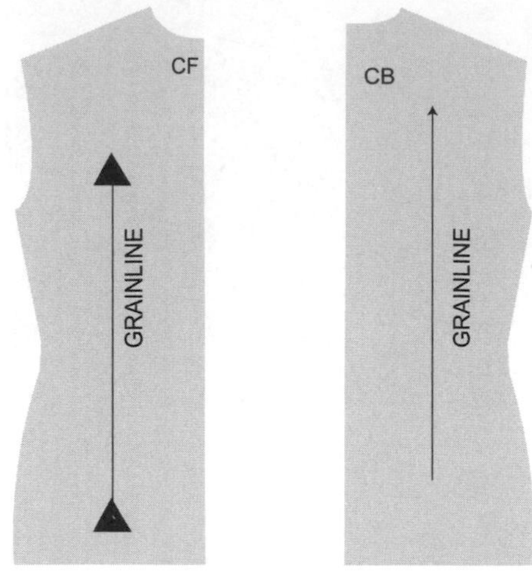

Cutting with Nap and Shine

Because of the way knits are created, all knits have a nap and many knit fabrics are finished and polished to create a shine or texture on the surface. Patternmakers must take this into consideration and label the patterns accordingly. It would not be acceptable to cut a garment with the front in one direction and the back in the other. When the customer tries on the garment, it would look as if the front and back had been cut with two different fabrics.

The patternmaker will create a grainline with arrows pointing in the same direction to indicate nap (as illustrated). Remember that because of the way knits are made, there is always a slight nap to the fabric, and it should always be cut accordingly.

Grainline with arrows pointing in one direction indicates a "napped or with shine" layout.

Knits are made by interlocking loops from one row to the next; therefore, all knits have a nap. While some fabrics show this nap more than others do, it is a good habit to always label your grainline with arrows going in one direction.

Unless you are absolutely certain that the fabric has no discernable difference, always use one directional arrow on your grainlines.

Knit fabric will look like this illustration when viewed from one direction.

And it will look like this when viewed from the other direction.

Direction of Knitting

Another thing to consider is whether or not the fabric will run, like pantyhose. Knit fabrics usually only unravel in the direction that they were knit, which is from the last row knit downward.

Consequently, when placing the pattern on the fabric, place it so that it runs upward from the hem rather than downward from the neck. The downward placement will often stretch when the garment is being pulled on, which can create a run in the fabric and make it unsellable.

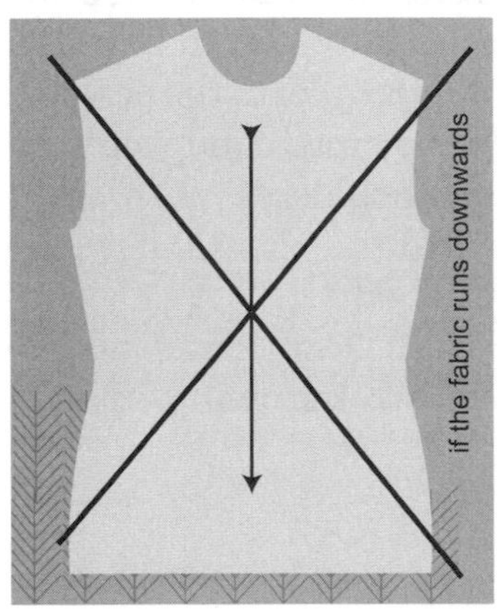

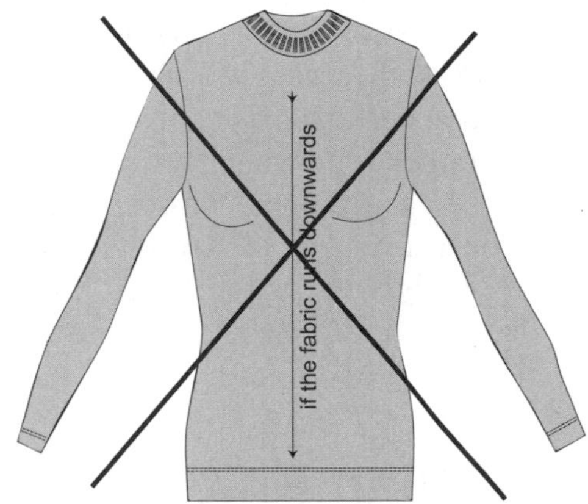

INCORRECT DIRECTION OF THE GRAINLINE

INCORRECT

This is the incorrect way of laying the pattern on the fabric. The neckline receives the most stretch and will almost always run.

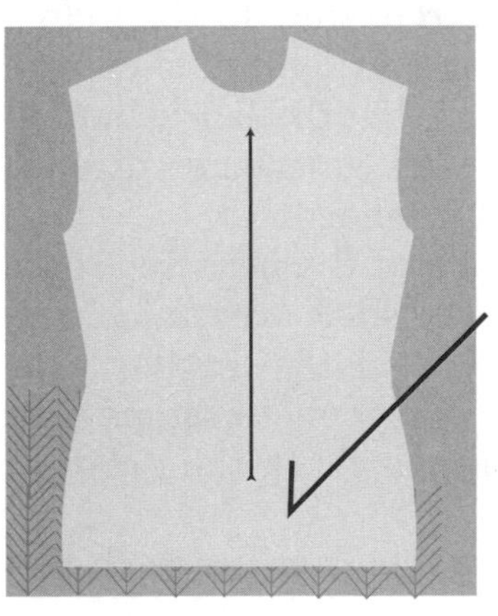
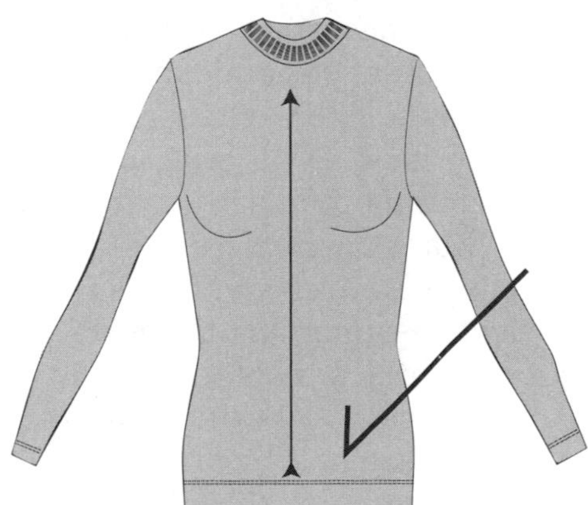

CORRECT DIRECTION OF THE GRAINLINE

CORRECT

This is the correct way of laying the pattern on the fabric. The hem receives the least amount of stress and will not run as easily.

If the fabric runs, the pattern should be labeled as "with nap," which should be indicated with single-direction arrows on the pattern.

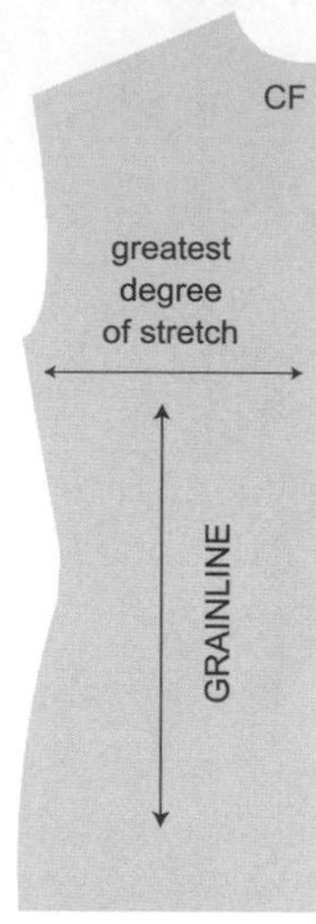

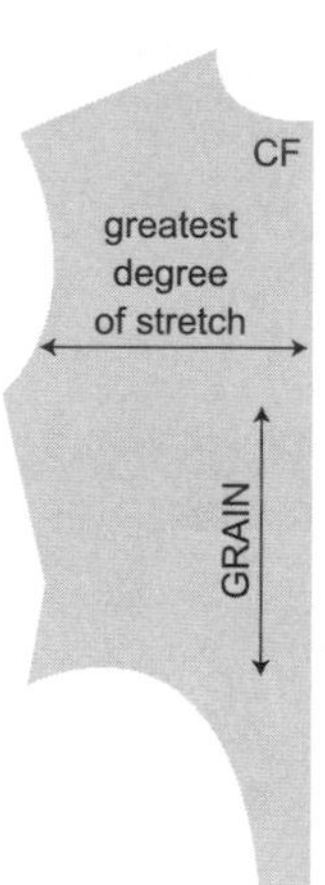

Greatest Degree of Stretch

When creating two-way-stretch and four-way-stretch garments, usually one direction stretches slightly more than the other. Experienced patternmakers will take this into consideration, and use it to their benefit.

When creating dresses and tops, the greatest direction of stretch should be utilized going around the body. But for catsuits, leotards, and bodysuits, or any garment that passes through both the crotch and the shoulders, the greatest direction of stretch should be utilized going up and down the body.

Usually the greatest degree of stretch is crosswise; however, some knit fabrics, such as swimsuit fabrics, are specially knit to have the greatest direction of stretch going lengthwise, parallel to the selvage. This is because the garments pass through the crotch and would be uncomfortable when the customer raises her shoulders.

Tops, dresses, pants, skirts, and sweaters should use the greatest degree of stretch going around the body.

Bodysuits, catsuits, or any garment that is anchored by the crotch should have the greatest degree of stretch going up and down the body.

Cutting Knits

The cutter should always let the fabric relax for 24 hours before cutting. Often the goods have been stretched when they were rolled onto a bolt, as in the case when goods are purchased from jobbers who reroll the goods too tight when they check the quality. Jobbers often stretch the fabric when rerolling it to get a better yield thereby make more money by shortchanging you! Always double-check the width of goods before purchasing. In the industry, cutters often make up the lay, leave it overnight, and cut the goods the following morning. This ensures that the fabric has relaxed back to its original length. Otherwise garments cut with stretched out fabric may be smaller than intended.

Many manufacturers slice off the ends of the bolts to create rolls of binding and trim, and sell any fabrics left over to jobbers. Never assume that the goods are a standard width. Circular knitted fabrics are sometimes cut open, and you cannot assume that the fabric has been cut on grain. So always check the grain to make sure it is accurate.

Never allow the fabric to hang off the table. It will stretch and result in inaccurate cutting.

Knit garments are constructed with very small seam allowances, usually ¼″ or ⅜″, so it is necessary to keep all notches to a minimum and within the seam allowance, usually ⅛″. Otherwise you will create holes in the garment.

Wax or clay chalk is best for marking knit. Wax marks will steam out of natural fibers, but will leave stains on synthetics. Clay marks easily can be brushed away. It is always best to cut a garment with a paper marker.

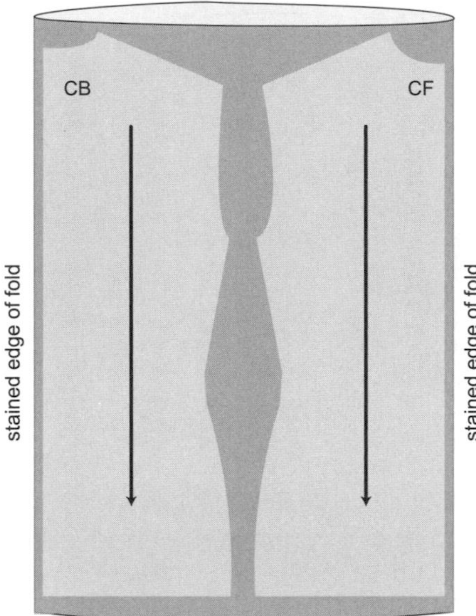

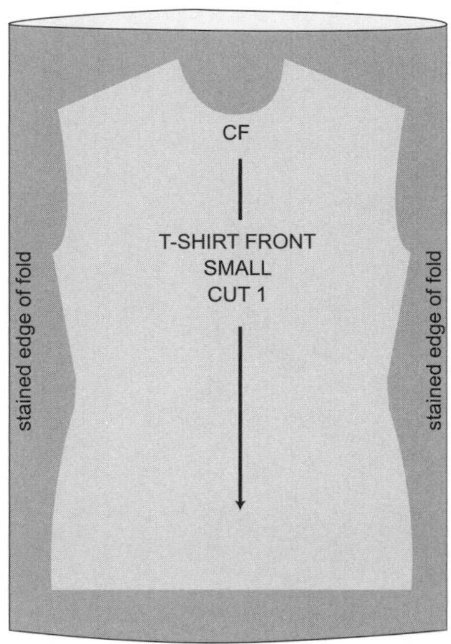

Cutting Tubular Goods

When using tubular knits, never place any pattern on the fold. It is often dirty or stained. If a knit has a pressed-in fold or crease, it is probably permanent and you will need to refold the fabric to avoid placing a permanent crease in the center front or center back of your garment. To avoid these problems, manufacturers never use the fold of the fabric, but instead cut all patterns full and open. This, however, forces them to cut an even number of garments only, which may not be practical for the student or small manufacturer who may only want a single garment, or an odd number. So it is necessary to refold the goods when cutting the front and back of a garment. However, you may use the original fold when cutting out the sleeves, because the crease will be discarded.

Manufacturers cut patterns full open so that a blemish is not used in any part of the garment, but discarded as waste.

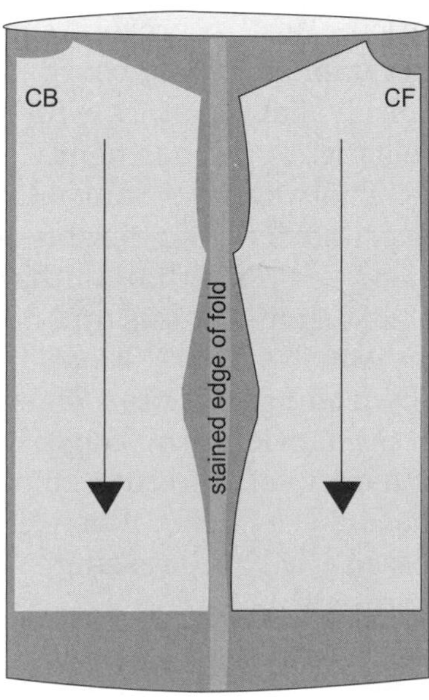

For a single item of clothing, refold the tubular fabric so the stain or crease is in the center of the tube and will not be used in the garment.

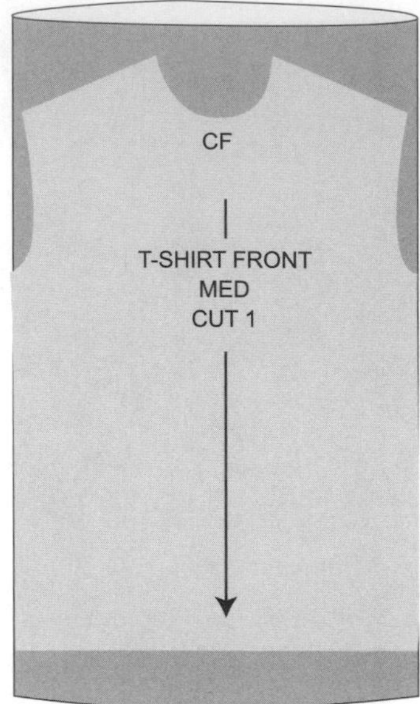

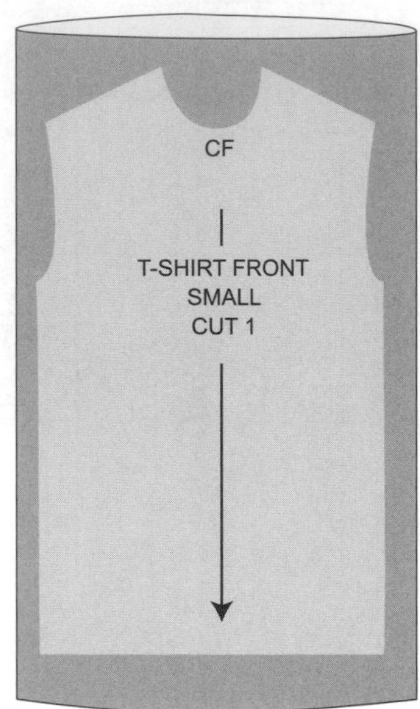

Garments without Side Seams

Occasionally, knit tops are manufactured without any side seams. This is only available if the tubular fabric is exactly the same width as the garment. Manufacturers rarely create all sizes of T-shirt without side seams—usually only Medium size because it is the most common. Because the side seams will be hidden under the arm, any permanent creasing will not show as much. If a company chooses to manufacture all of its tops without side seams, it will have to order fabric in exactly the widths needed for all sizes.

When cutting the Small size garment, it will be necessary to have side seams, or the manufacturer will have to order fabric in the exact width.

Pressing Knits

Knit fabrics don't press very effectively and are usually not pressed during construction. Most pressing is done when the garment is complete, to block and shape it and make the hems lie flat, as well as to relax the stitching and elastic.

Knits fail to take a sharp crease. The way that a knitted fabric presses depends primarily on its fiber content and stitch formation.

Acrylic is extremely sensitive to heat damage and should never be touched by the iron. Nylon and acetate are easily damaged by ironing, so be careful not to leave the iron on the fabric for any duration of time. Always test a scrap of fabric before ironing the actual garment.

Knit fabrics are frequently pressed on a vacuum table. This is an ironing board with a powerful vacuum installed. The vacuum helps prevent the garment from sliding off the ironing board, as well as cools the garment immediately, which helps set the seams and block the garment.

Most knit tops are pressed flat, and it is preferable to store them flat and folded rather than on hangers, which will stretch the shoulders and necklines out of shape.

Elastic should be steamed to help it to relax. Often elastic is stretched out of shape during the construction process and steaming helps it return to its original size.

Fusible interfacing still requires dry pressing.

Needles and Thread

Most knit fabrics can be sewn using a universal-point needle, which has a slightly rounded tip that is suitable for sewing knits. It is usually better to use a ballpoint needle, which has a rounded tip that penetrates the fabric without puncturing the fabric yarns.

Knit garments need strong and elastic seams, so always use good-quality polyester or cotton-wrapped polyester thread.

WOOLLY NYLON

Woolly nylon is a multifilament thread that is puffy when relaxed but gets thin when stretched. It is often used on one or two loopers of the serger to create a soft and elastic seam, especially for dance and gymnastic garments in which harsh seams can create calluses on the wearer. Woolly nylon thread can also be used in the bottom looper of the cover-stitch machine or collarette machine. This thread is rarely used in the needles, because of its tendency to bunch up and the difficulty it poses in threading the needles.

Interfacing

Knit garments don't require as much interfacing as woven garments, because the interfacing will prevent the fabric from stretching. Sometimes a garment may need to be interfaced to prevent certain areas from stretching, such as the seam allowances for zippers, facings, and front plackets for buttonholes.

Styles with facings are not meant to stretch at the facing edge, and need to be cut larger for the head to pass through. Facings and interfacings may only be used on garments that have a large enough neckline to fit over the head without stretching or styles that have a zipper or button closing.

Tricot interfacing has a crosswise stretch and no lengthwise stretch. For best results, use tricot fusing so it stretches as needed. Sometimes the designer will need to control the lengthwise stretch and sometimes the crosswise stretch. Tricot interfacing can also be used to stabilize zipper seam allowances to prevent stretching during application.

Tricot fusing is an excellent choice for most knit fabrics, because knit fabrics are not flat compared to woven fabrics, and tricot fusing can stretch into the minute crevices of the fabrics. It therefore gives better adhesion and won't pucker or bubble the way that a Pellon or a woven fusing might.

Block Fusing

Loosely knit fabrics are occasionally "block" fused with tricot. Block fusing is when the goods are entirely fused before being cut out. They are used to stabilize a loosely knit or woven fabric.

Zippers

Knit garments rarely need zippers, because most garments can often be stepped into or pulled over the head. However, the designer will sometimes use zippers as a design detail, such as a center front zipper in a hooded sweatshirt, or exposed teeth zippers in track pants, or welt zippers for neckline openings or pockets.

Always try to eliminate functional zippers if the fabric has enough stretch and the garment can be stepped into or pulled over the head. This may not always be possible with catsuits and other garments that pass through the crotch. If a zipper is necessary, use invisible zippers, since they don't have any topstitching on the outside, which makes them easy to sew in knit fabrics because topstitching will stretch the fabric. The key to invisible zipper applications is to use a zipper that is at least 1½ inches longer than the zipper opening, or to change the length of the opening to be 1½ inches shorter than the zipper. If you use a zipper that is the same length as the opening, it is not possible to sew the very bottom of the zipper because the slider gets in the way. With a longer zipper you can place the excess length at the bottom of the zipper. Use a ½-inch seam allowance for invisible zippers.

Shrinkage

Shrinkage refers to the reduction in width and length of the garment, or both, that happens when a fabric is washed or dry-cleaned. There are different methods of compensating for shrinkage, and each depends on the way the fabric was dyed and its ultimate use.

How to Compensate a Pattern for Shrinkage

PRESHRINKING

The fabric can be purchased preshrunk or prewashed to shrink before cutting out the garment. Also, the manufacturer can send the fabric out to be "sponged" or preshrunk.

COMPACTING

The fabrics are compressed at the mill, the amount equal to the shrinkage. The manufacturer can cut and sew these garments knowing that when washed they will return to their intended size.

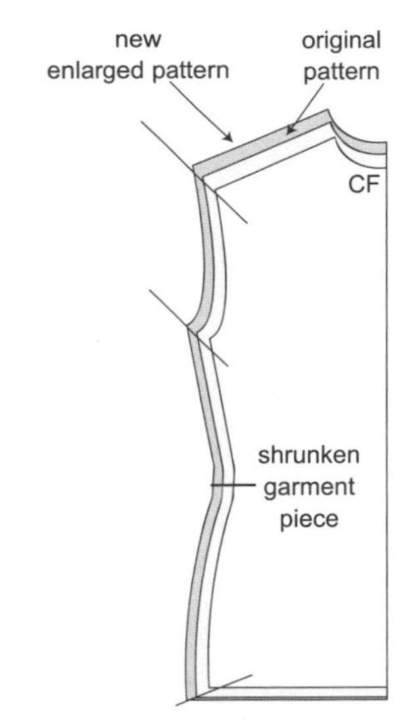

PATTERN COMPENSATION

The patternmaker simply cuts out all of the garment pieces, washes and dries them, then places them back on the original pattern to measure the shrinkage. The new pattern is enlarged to compensate. This method is used for garments that will be dyed, or washed after construction.

SANFORIZED

Sanforized is a trademarked process of shrinking the fabric. Fabrics bearing this trademark will not shrink more than 1 percent because they have been subjected to a method of compressive shrinkage.

RESIDUAL SHRINKAGE

Residual shrinkage indicates the percentage of shrinkage that occurs in the fabric after its first washing.

PROGRESSIVE SHRINKAGE

Progressive shrinkage is the shrinkage that may occur in a garment upon each subsequent washing.

Testing for Shrinkage

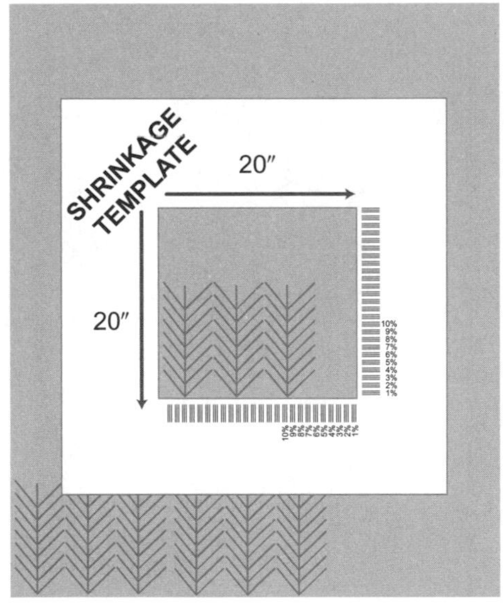

You should shrink test every fabric by drawing a 20″ × 20″ square in the center of the fabric—always in the center because there is usually some variation towards the edges, especially if the goods have been split open or treated in some way. Create a cardboard template of the square for testing every single dye lot.

Do this, also, to check torque on the goods, that annoying thing that happens if you buy a cheap T-shirt and your seams end up twisting after washing. Many times goods will be rejected if they have more than 5 percent torque and 5 percent shrinkage.

Some fabrics are worse than others for torque, such as jersey knits and any variation like eyelets or anything with a drop needle like poor boy ribs. Interlocks are terrible for shrinkage. Even after compacting, interlock fabrics can have 5 to 6 percent shrinkage.

After washing and drying the square, measure how much the fabric has shrunk in length and width and make a new pattern based on these percentages. Do this with every lot of fabric. You must make multiple patterns if there is a lot of variation in the dye lots; for example, there may be a pattern for a top with shrinkage of 6 percent length and 2 percent width, and another for the same top with shrinkage of 4 percent length and 1 percent width.

Alternatively, you can wash a garment that has been made from the goods that have not been tested initially, then measure the overall garment shrinkage in various areas. For example, the center front length may shrink more than the armhole because the armhole has all that thread in the seams to keep it from shrinking or stretching. You must compensate for this in the pattern for the final garment. So if the overall shrinkage is 6 percent, put the majority of it in the area from the bottom of the armhole to the hem.

Shrinkage Template

A 20-inch template is used because it is easy to multiply by 5 to get the percentages.

Dyeing Knits

The method of dyeing will affect the amount of shrinkage and also the method and amount of compensation used to correct the fit.

STOCK DYEING

The raw materials, the fibers, are dyed before being spun into yarn. They will have the most amount of shrinkage but also will produce the most color saturation. Stock dyeing is called "solution" dyeing when synthetic fibers are involved. One advantage of dyeing raw fiber stock is that different colors or shades can later be spun together to create complex yarns.

SOLUTION DYEING

Some manmade fibers are dyed by adding colors to the polymer before they are spun. These colors are fast and durable. Solution dyeing is also called dope-dyeing.

YARN DYEING

The yarn is dyed before knitting and will have a lot of shrinkage but also great color saturation. Yarn dyeing allows fabric to be created from yarns of different color, allowing Jacquards, Fair Isles, plaids, brocades, and other knit-in designs. Space dyeing, a variation of yarn dyeing, is a technique in which yarns are dyed at intervals along their length. One problem with yarn dying is "barre," in which some areas of the yarn might be slightly different shades of the same color and not obvious when unknitted. But when knitted, these areas might coincidently line up to create blocks of an obviously different shade.

PIECE DYEING

The fabric is dyed after knitting, which results in less shrinkage of the completed garment. Problems associated with piece dyeing including uneven shrinkage and uneven dye saturation. Piece dyeing is also called vat dyeing.

GARMENT DYEING

The garment is dyed after cutting and sewing. Many manufacturers stock undyed garments, called greige goods, and will dye them as needed according the customer's tastes and wants. The manufacturer must compensate for any shrinkage so that the completed garment will shrink very little. The designer must take into consideration the fact that threads, trims, and zippers must also shrink and dye similarly.

DYE LOTS

Every fabric when dyed is given a dye lot number. If two bolts of fabric have the same dye lot number, it is because they were both dyed at the same time, in the same dye solution. The next bolt of fabric may have a different dye lot number, because it was dyed in a different bath. Each dye lot varies slightly in color, and garments cannot be cut from different dye lots. Different dye lots often shrink differently as well, and every one must be tested for shrinkage.

GREIGE GARMENTS

Undyed fabrics are called "greige." Often garments are manufactured greige, and not dyed or colored until after being sewn. This way the manufacturer may stock the needed garments and not dye them until they are certain that any color is popular. This greatly reduces the production lead-time. The greige garment may be dyed any color the designer wants.

Ready to Dye

Natural cotton, after weaving and washing, is an off-white color, a light shade of ecru or cream. Normally, if the fabric is to be dyed, it goes straight to the dyer at that point. If it is to be sold as bleached fabric or made into "white" clothing, it is first bleached, then washed, then often treated with optic whiteners and washed again. Optic whiteners are kind of like a white dye. While technically there is no such thing as a white dye, the optic whiteners occupy, on a molecular level, the same spaces as dyes do. Therefore, unbleached fabrics are said to take dyes better than white or optically whitened fabric.

PREPARED FOR DYEING (PFD) GARMENTS

PFD garments have had no whiteners added and are actually an off-white in color. They must be sewn with cotton thread (so the stitching dyes the same color), and are usually cut oversize based on the understanding that the garment is going to be dyed and will shrink.

This usually means:

a. There are no starches, sizing, or finishes applied to the fabric that could interfere with the dyeing.
b. The garment is sewn with cotton thread.
c. The item is cut oversize to allow for shrinkage.

Exercise #1: Study a Knit Garment

Each student brings one stretch garment to class and studies that garment to determine its characteristics, then prepares a report on this garment covering:

The direction(s) it stretches.

Whether it is a one-way, two-way, or four-way-stretch garment.

The stretch ratio.

Whether or not it has memory.

Its design ease, negative ease, garment ease.

The estimated amount of garment and design ease in the garment.

Whether the fit is tight, semi-fit, unfitted, or oversized.

The direction of the knitting stitches.

The fabric's nap or shine (or lack thereof).

The greatest direction of stretch (for four-way-stretch fabrics).

The kind of seam and hem finishes, and equipment used.

How it was dyed.

Test Your Knowledge of the Material in This Chapter

1. What is a one-way-stretch fabric?
2. What is a two-way-stretch fabric?
3. What is a four-way-stretch fabric?
4. Define the term "stretch factor."
5. Define the term "stretch memory."
6. Define the term "direction of stretch."
7. What is a sloper or block?
8. What is a spec sheet?
9. What is a costing sheet?
10. What is a pattern must?
11. What are the three different methods to create a sweater?
12. What is a rib knit?

CHAPTER 2

Sizing and Measurements

About This Chapter

You may have noticed that you do not fit the same size garment from one manufacturer to another or from one country to the next. While this might be confusing at times, some of the reasons for it become obvious when you look at the following chapter. There is no true standard size or industry rule, and each designer must fit a company's size specifications to their target market and company requirements. A designer with a very young market will have tighter-fitting clothing, because younger customers have tighter, slimmer bodies, and generally they like to show them off. Some American manufacturers offer garments with larger and higher busts, because of the proliferation of breast implants, which affects size specifications.

The student designer or beginner may have trouble grasping the sizing concepts. The main idea to understand is that a designer may place any size tag that he/she desires into a garment. However, some simple guides do apply; see the charts that follow.

Sizing Categories

Clothing sizes depend on both height and figure type.

Note that some of the size ranges overlap, because most knit manufacturers create a range of five sizes. In woven, these sizes will only fit a small percentage of the population, but in knit, the ranges will overlap, because alphabet sizes—Extra Small (XS), Small (S), Medium (M), Large (L), and Extra Large (XL)—skip every other size.

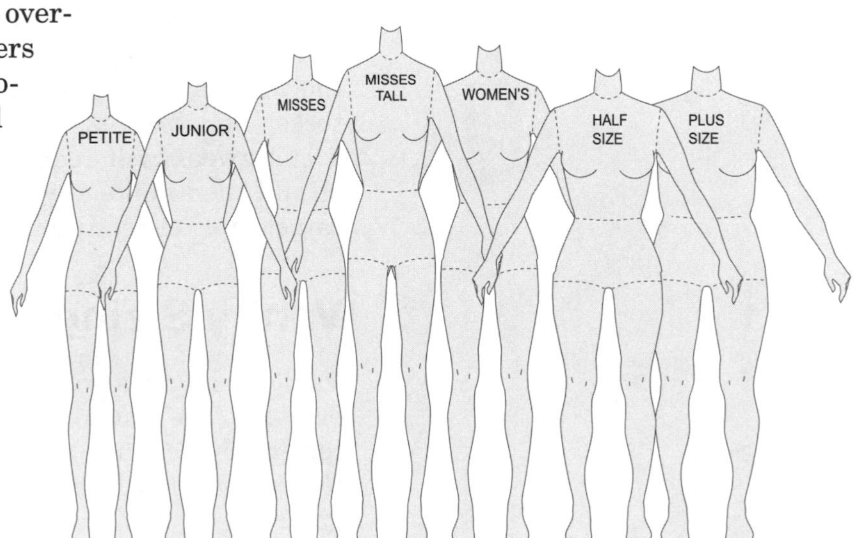

Petite	2P–14P	4′11″ to 5′4″	Women with a small frame with a slightly smaller bust and hip than the junior size range. Proportioned for women 4′11″ to 5′4″ tall, with shorter arms, legs, and overall garment length, cut smaller across the back as well.
Junior	5-7-9-11-13-15	5′2″ to 5′6″	Odd-numbered sizing for young women with a high bust, small waist, narrow bottom, and a slender figure.
Misses	6-8-10-12-14-16-18	5′5″ to 5′8″	Even-numbered sizing for the average-proportioned body type. Most designer collections are created in this size range.
Misses Tall	6-8-10-12-14-16-18	5′8″ to 6′1″	Even-numbered sizing for taller women of average proportions.
Women's	16W–32W	5′5″ to 5′9″	Well-proportioned women with a fuller stomach and a lower bustline, and extra weight in the upper arms and upper back. A 16W or 18W has broader fit through the top than a Misses 16 or 18.
Half Size	14½–30½	Under 5′5″	Half Sizes were a popular subdivision of the Misses category (starting at 14½ and going up to 30½). But this size has been replaced by Women and Petite sizing. Any size with a ½ in the sizing is for older and shorter women with a heavier body type. A Half Size is somewhat shorter than a Misses size and a bit fuller and rounder.
Plus Size	16–34	5′5″ to 5′9″	This size range is for larger or full-figured women. Plus Size clothing is fuller through the waist, back, thighs, and arms.
Metric Sizing	Roughly equivalent to the bust measurement, because if the bust fits, most waist, hip, and length alterations are easy to complete.		

Size Changes

Size labels are often changed and may not correspond to these charts. Some of the reasons become clear when viewing the next section.

Designer Fitting

Often designers will change or customize their slopers to accommodate the particular fit of their customers. If the designer has a very young customer, he or she may reduce the hip measurement to accommodate smaller and higher buttocks, and breasts; or designers who work primarily with eveningwear will require a much tighter fit. Each designer should then make any changes to size specifications that the target market requires.

Vanity Sizing

Vanity sizing is also referred to as size shifting. Often designers will place a smaller label in the garment to flatter the customer, who is much more likely to buy a garment with a label that makes her think that she has lost weight, rather than gained.

Eveningwear

Eveningwear will always fit tighter than other categories of clothing, and it is much more expensive to alter a sequined or beaded evening gown.

Catalogue

Catalogue clothes are labeled smaller, or created larger, so that they will generate fewer returns. The customer will live with a garment that's a little too big, but will always return a garment that is too tight.

French Sizing

French women prefer to wear clothing that is a lot tighter than North American women do.

Italian Sizing

Italian women prefer clothing that is very snug at the hip and buttocks.

German Sizing

German women are a lot taller and larger than most women from other countries, and the clothing designed in Germany is therefore larger than that of many other countries.

American Sizing

Americans tend to be more muscular than other countries, with larger backs and smaller waists; therefore, the clothes must be able to accommodate these bodies. In addition, more Americans work than their European counterparts, and they need to be able to move in their clothing.

European New Sizing

1-2-3 sizing category that is roughly equivalent to American S-M-L.

One Size Fits All

There is no such thing as "one size fits all" no matter how much spandex is used! Clothing labeled as one size fits all, in fact, doesn't fit anyone properly.

SIZE COMPARISON CHART

Use this chart to compare sizing of different categories and different countries.

Misses

Knit size	Extra Small		Small		Medium		Large		Extra Large		Extra Extra Large	
Size	**0**	**2**	**4**	**6**	**8**	**10**	**12**	**14**	**16**	**18**	**20**	**22**
Bust	30 1/2	31 1/2	32 1/2	33 1/2	34 1/2	35 1/2	37	38 1/2	40	41 1/2	43 1/2	45 1/2
Waist	22 1/2	23 1/2	24 1/2	25 1/2	26 1/2	27 1/2	29	30 1/2	32	33 1/2	35 1/2	37 1/2
Hips	33 1/2	34 1/2	35 1/2	36 1/2	37 1/2	38 1/2	40	41 1/2	43	44 1/2	46 1/2	48 1/2
Crotch depth	10 1/2	10 5/8	10 3/4	10 7/8	11	11 1/8	11 1/4	11 3/8	11 1/2	11 5/8	11 3/4	11 7/8

Petite

Knit size	Extra Small		Small		Medium		Large		Extra Large		Extra Extra Large	
Size	**0p**	**2p**	**4p**	**6p**	**8p**	**10p**	**12p**	**14p**	**16p**	**18p**	**20p**	**22p**
Bust	31 1/2	32 1/2	33 1/2	34 1/2	35 1/2	37	38 1/2	40	41 1/2	43	45	47
Waist	23 1/2	24 1/2	25 1/2	26 1/2	27 1/2	29	30 1/2	32	33 1/2	35	37	39
Hips	34 1/2	35 1/2	36 1/2	37 1/2	38 1/2	40	41 1/2	43	44 1/2	46	48	50
Crotch depth	10 1/8	10 1/4	10 3/8	10 1/2	10 5/8	10 3/4	10 7/8	11	11 1/8	11 1/4	11 3/8	11 1/2

Junior

Knit size	Extra Small		Small		Medium		Large		Extra Large		Extra Extra Large	
Size	**3**	**5**	**7**	**9**	**11**	**13**	**15**	**17**	**19**	**21**	**23**	**24**
Bust	32	33	34	35	36	37.5	39	40.5	42	43.5	45.5	47.5
Waist	25	26	27	28	29	30.5	32	33.5	35	36.5	38.5	40.5
Hips	35	36	37	38	39	40.5	42	43.5	45	46.5	48.5	50.5
Crotch depth	10.24	10.365	10.49	10.615	10.74	10.865	10.99	11.115	11.24	11.365	11.49	11.615

Misses Tall

Knit size	Extra Small		Small		Medium		Large		Extra Large		Extra Extra Large	
Size	**0**	**2**	**4**	**6**	**8**	**10**	**12**	**14**	**16**	**18**	**20**	**22**
Bust	32 1/2	33 1/2	34 1/2	35 1/2	36 1/2	38	39 1/2	41	42 1/2	44	45 1/2	47
Waist	24 1/2	25 1/2	26 1/2	27 1/2	28 1/2	30	31 1/2	33	34 1/2	36	37 1/2	39
Hips	35 1/2	36 1/2	37 1/2	38 1/2	39 1/2	41	42 1/2	44	45 1/2	47	48 1/2	50
Crotch depth	11 1/4	11 3/8	11 1/2	11 5/8	11 3/4	11 7/8	12	12 1/8	12 1/4	12 3/8	12 1/2	12 5/8

Women's

Knit size	Extra Small		Small		Medium		Large		Extra Large		Extra Extra Large	
Size	**16 w**	**18 w**	**20 w**	**22 w**	**24 w**	**26 w**	**28 w**	**30 w**	**32 w**	**34 w**	**16 w**	**24**
Bust	43	45	47	49	51	53	55	57	59	61	63	65
Waist	35	37	39	41	43	45	47	49	51	53	55	57
Hips	46	48	50	52	54	56	58	60	62	64	66	68
Crotch depth	11 3/4	13 3/4	15 3/4	17 3/4	19 3/4	21 3/4	23 3/4	25 3/4	27 3/4	29 3/4	31.75	33.75

(continued)

(continued)

Half Sizes												
Knit size	**Extra Small**		**Small**		**Medium**		**Large**		**Extra Large**		**Extra Extra Large**	
Size	**14½**	**16½**	**18½**	**20½**	**22½**	**24½**	**26½**	**28½**	**30½**	**32½**	**34½**	**24**
Bust	41	43	45	47	49	51	53	55	57	59	61	63
Waist	32½	34½	36½	38½	40½	42½	44½	46½	48½	50½	52.5	54.5
Hips	44	46	48	50	52	54	56	58	60	62	64	66
Crotch depth	11⅛	13⅛	15⅛	17⅛	19⅛	21⅛	23⅛	25⅛	27⅛	29⅛	31.125	33.125
Plus Sizes												
Knit size	**Extra Small**		**Small**		**Medium**		**Large**		**Extra Large**		**Extra Extra Large**	
Size	**16**	**18**	**20**	**22**	**24**	**26**	**28**	**30**	**32**	**34**	**36**	**38**
Bust	41	43	45	47	49	51	53	55	57	59	61	63
Waist	33	35	37	39	41	43	45	47	49	51	53	55
Hips	44	46	48	50	52	54	56	58	60	62	64	66
Crotch depth	11⅝	13⅝	15⅝	17⅝	19⅝	21⅝	23⅝	25⅝	27⅝	29⅝	31⅝	33⅝
Other Sizing												
Metric	**32**		**34**	**36**	**38**	**40**	**42**	**44**	**46**	**48**	**50**	**52**
France	0	2	4	6	8	10	12	14	6	8	10	12
Italy	2	0	2	4	6	8	0	12	14	16	18	20
Germany	−4	−2	0	2	4	6	8	10	12	14	16	18
Vanity sizing	−6	−4	−2	0	2	4	6	8	10	12	14	16
European equivalent to S-M-L	0		1		2		3		4		5	

How to Take Measurements

The measurements included are in the Misses size range, so that students can compare their own measurements with those taken from the dress-form. Compare your measurements with the ones provided to determine the size of your dress-form, and to check if you are taking measurements correctly.

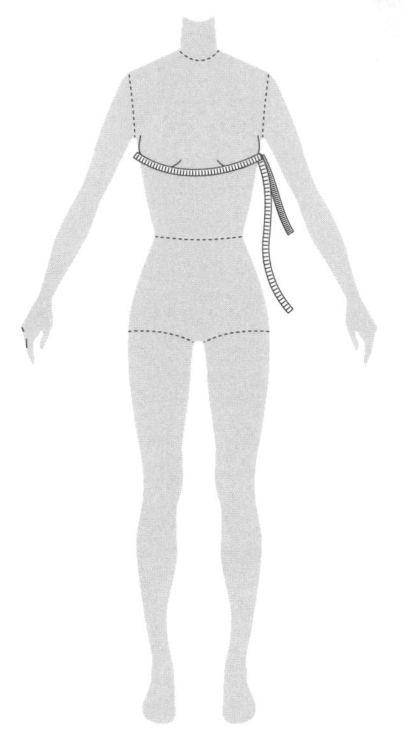

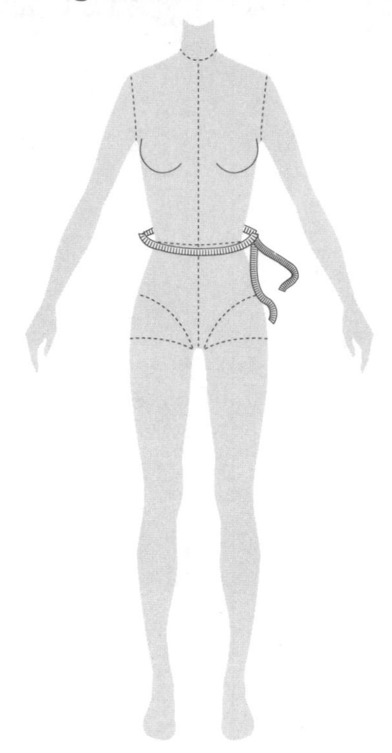

#1 BUST

Stand on the side of the model with the arms down, and measure all the way around the fullest part of the chest. Then have the model take a deep breath and let it out, while you hold the tape measure. Record the largest measurement.

#2 WAIST

Measure around the smallest part of the waist. Do not pull the tape too tight, but keep it comfortably relaxed.

#1 BUST

Size	Extra Small		Small		Medium		Large		Extra Large		Extra Extra Large	
Misses	30 4/8	31 4/8	32 4/8	33 4/8	34 4/8	35 4/8	37	38 4/8	40	41 4/8	43 4/8	45 4/8
Petite	31 8/16	32 8/16	33 8/16	34 8/16	35 8/16	37	38 8/16	40	41 8/16	43	45	47
Junior	32	33	34	35	36	37 8/16	39	40 8/16	42	43 8/16	45 8/16	47 8/16
Misses tall	32 8/16	33 8/16	34 8/16	35 8/16	36 8/16	38	39 8/16	41	42 8/16	44	45 8/16	47
Women's	43	45	47	49	51	53	55	57	59	61	63	65
Half size	41	43	45	47	49	51	53	55	57	59	61	63
Plus size	41	43	45	47	49	51	53	55	57	59	61	63

Your company's measurement may differ and may be changed to suit your particular target customer.

#2 WAIST

Size	Extra Small		Small		Medium		Large		Extra Large		Extra Extra Large	
Misses	22 1/2	23 1/2	24 1/2	25 1/2	26 1/2	27 1/2	29	30 1/2	32	33 1/2	35 1/2	37 1/2
Petite	23 1/2	24 1/2	25 1/2	26 1/2	27 1/2	29	30 1/2	32	33 1/2	35	37	39
Junior	24	25	26	27	28	29	30 1/2	32	33 1/2	35	36 1/2	38 1/2
Misses tall	24 1/2	25 1/2	26 1/2	27 1/2	28 1/2	30	31 1/2	33	34 1/2	36	37 1/2	39
Women's	35	37	39	41	43	45	47	49	51	53	55	57
Half size	32 1/2	34 1/2	36 1/2	38 1/2	40 1/2	42 1/2	44 1/2	46 1/2	48 1/2	50 1/2	52 1/2	54 1/2
Plus size	33	35	37	39	41	43	45	47	49	51	53	55

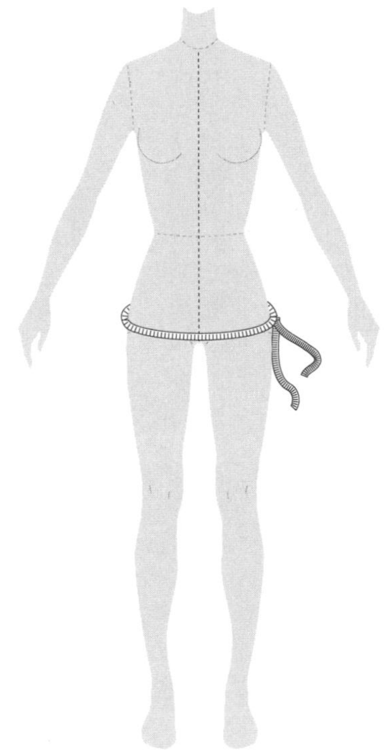

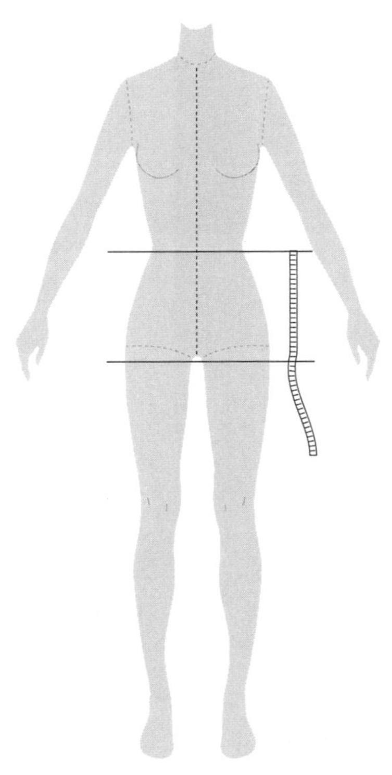

#3 HIP

Measure around the widest part of the hip, slide the tape up and down to make sure that you record the largest measurement.

The hip is approximately 7–8″ down from the waist.

#4 CROTCH DEPTH

The crotch depth measurement may be taken in three ways:

1. When standing, from the front waist to the back waist, passing through the entire crotch area. Divide that number by 2.
2. With the customer seated, take the measurement from the top of the chair seat up to the waist level.
3. Use an "L" square ruler and measure from the crotch up to the waist level.

#3 HIP

Size	Extra Small		Small		Medium		Large		Extra Large		Extra Extra Large	
Misses	33 4/8	34 4/8	35 4/8	36 4/8	37 4/8	38 4/8	40	41 4/8	43	44 4/8	46 4/8	48 4/8
Petite	34 8/16	35 8/16	36 8/16	37 8/16	38 8/16	40	41 8/16	43	44 8/16	46	48	50
Junior	35	36	37	38	39	40 8/16	42	43 8/16	45	46 8/16	48 8/16	50 8/16
Misses tall	35 4/8	36 4/8	37 4/8	38 4/8	39 4/8	41	42 4/8	44	45 4/8	47	48 4/8	50
Women's	46	48	50	52	54	56	58	60	62	64	66	68
Half size	44	46	48	50	52	54	56	58	60	62	64	66
Plus size	44	46	48	50	52	54	56	58	60	62	64	66

#4 CROTCH DEPTH

Size	Extra Small		Small		Medium		Large		Extra Large		Extra Extra Large	
Misses	9 7/8	10	10 1/8	10 2/8	10 3/8	10 4/8	10 5/8	10 6/8	10 7/8	11	11 1/8	11 2/8
Petite	10 2/16	10 4/16	10 6/16	10 8/16	10 10/16	10 12/16	10 14/16	11	11 2/16	11 4/16	11 3/8	11 1/2
Junior	10 4/16	10 6/16	10 8/16	10 10/16	10 12/16	10 14/16	11	11 2/16	11 4/16	11 6/16	11 8/16	11 10/16
Misses tall	11 2/8	11 3/8	11 4/8	11 5/8	11 6/8	11 7/8	12	12 1/8	12 2/8	12 3/8	12 4/8	12 5/8
Women's	11 6/8	13 6/8	15 6/8	17 6/8	19 6/8	21 6/8	23 6/8	25 6/8	27 6/8	29 6/8	31 6/8	33 6/8
Half size	11 2/16	13 2/16	15 2/16	17 2/16	19 2/16	21 2/16	23 2/16	25 2/16	27 2/16	29 2/16	31 2/16	33 2/16
Plus size	11 10/16	13 10/16	15 10/16	17 10/16	19 10/16	21 10/16	23 10/16	25 10/16	27 10/16	29 10/16	31 10/16	33 10/16

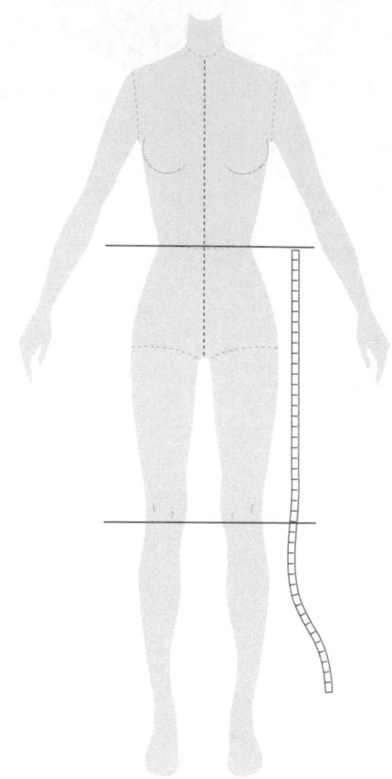

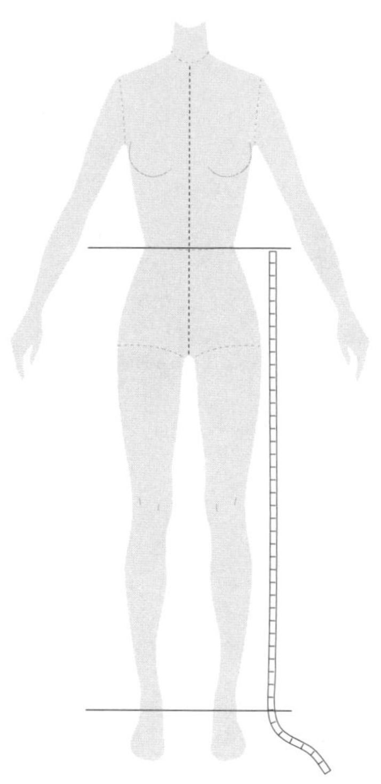

#5 WAIST TO KNEE

From the side seam, hold the tape at the waist and measure to the knee level.

#6 WAIST TO ANKLE

From the side seam, hold the tape at the waist and measure to the bottom of the ankle bone.

#5 WAIST TO KNEE

	Extra Small		Small		Medium		Large		Extra Large		Extra Extra Large	
Size	**2**	**4**	**6**	**8**	**10**	**12**	**14**	**16**	**18**	**20**	**22**	**24**
Misses	20 1/8	23	23 1/8	23 2/8	23 3/8	23 4/8	23 5/8	23 6/8	23 7/8	24	24 1/8	24 2/8
Petite	21 3/8	21 1/2	21 5/8	21 3/4	21 7/8	22	22 1/8	22 1/4	22 3/8	22 1/2	22 5/8	22 3/4
Junior	22 7/8	23	23 1/8	23 2/8	23 3/8	23 4/8	23 5/8	23 6/8	23 7/8	24	24 1/8	24 2/8
Misses tall	24 5/8	24 6/8	24 7/8	25	25 1/8	25 2/8	25 3/8	25 4/8	25 5/8	25 6/8	25 7/8	26
Women's	24	24 1/8	24 2/8	24 3/8	24 4/8	24 5/8	24 6/8	24 7/8	25	25 1/8	25 2/8	25 3/8
Half size	22 3/8	22 4/8	22 5/8	22 6/8	22 7/8	23	23 1/8	23 2/8	23 3/8	23 4/8	23 5/8	23 6/8
Plus size	24	24 1/8	24 2/8	24 3/8	24 4/8	24 5/8	24 6/8	24 7/8	25	25 1/8	25 2/8	25 3/8

#6 WAIST TO ANKLE

	Extra Small		Small		Medium		Large		Extra Large		Extra Extra Large	
Size	**2**	**4**	**6**	**8**	**10**	**12**	**14**	**16**	**18**	**20**	**22**	**24**
Misses	38 2/8	38 4/8	38 6/8	39	39 2/8	39 4/8	39 6/8	40	40 2/8	40 4/8	40 6/8	41
Petite	36 5/8	36 7/8	37 1/8	37 3/8	37 5/8	37 7/8	38 1/8	38 3/8	38 5/8	38 7/8	39 1/8	39 3/8
Junior	38 2/8	38 4/8	38 6/8	39	39 2/8	39 4/8	39 6/8	40	40 2/8	40 4/8	40 6/8	41
Misses tall	40 7/8	41 1/8	41 3/8	41 5/8	41 7/8	42 1/8	42 3/8	42 5/8	42 7/8	43 1/8	43 3/8	43 5/8
Women's	38 5/8	38 6/8	38 7/8	39	39 1/8	39 2/8	39 3/8	39 4/8	39 5/8	39 6/8	39 7/8	40
Half size	37 2/8	37 3/8	37 4/8	37 5/8	37 6/8	37 7/8	38	38 1/8	38 2/8	38 3/8	38 4/8	38 5/8
Plus size	39 5/8	39 6/8	39 7/8	40	40 1/8	40 2/8	40 3/8	40 4/8	40 5/8	40 6/8	40 7/8	41

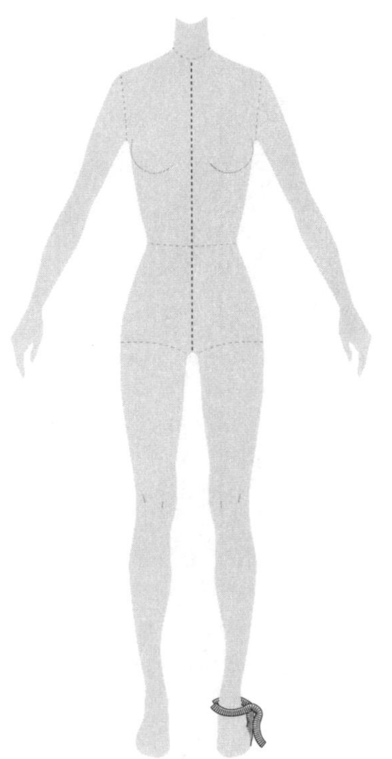

#7 ANKLE

Wrap the tape around the ankle and record the measurement.

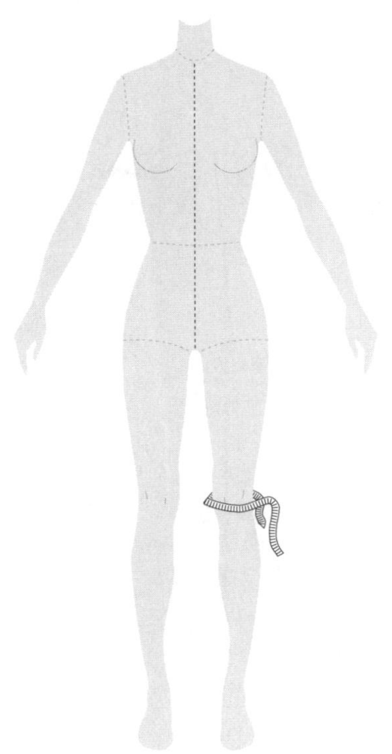

#8 KNEE

Wrap the tape around the knee and record the measurement.

#7 ANKLE

	Extra Small		Small		Medium		Large		Extra Large		Extra Extra Large	
Size	**2**	**4**	**6**	**8**	**10**	**12**	**14**	**16**	**18**	**20**	**22**	**24**
Misses	7 5/8	7 6/8	7 7/8	8	8 1/8	8 2/8	8 3/8	8 4/8	8 5/8	8 6/8	8 7/8	9
Petite	6 5/8	6 6/8	6 7/8	7	7 1/8	7 2/8	7 3/8	7 4/8	7 5/8	7 6/8	7 7/8	8
Junior	7 7/8	8 1/8	8 3/8	8 5/8	8 7/8	9 1/8	9 3/8	9 5/8	9 7/8	10 1/8	10 3/8	10 5/8
Misses tall	7 7/8	8	8 1/8	8 2/8	8 3/8	8 4/8	8 5/8	8 6/8	8 7/8	9	9 1/8	9 2/8
Women's	10	10 2/8	10 4/8	10 6/8	11	11 2/8	11 4/8	11 6/8	12	12 2/8	12 4/8	12 6/8
Half size	9 5/8	9 7/8	10 1/8	10 3/8	10 5/8	10 7/8	11 1/8	11 3/8	11 5/8	11 7/8	12 1/8	12 3/8
Plus size	9 5/8	9 7/8	10 1/8	10 3/8	10 5/8	10 7/8	11 1/8	11 3/8	11 5/8	11 7/8	12 1/8	12 3/8

#8 KNEE

	Extra Small		Small		Medium		Large		Extra Large		Extra Extra Large	
Size	**2**	**4**	**6**	**8**	**10**	**12**	**14**	**16**	**18**	**20**	**22**	**24**
Misses	13 1/8	13 3/8	13 5/8	13 7/8	14 1/8	14 3/8	14 5/8	14 7/8	15 1/8	15 3/8	15 5/8	15 7/8
Petite	13 2/8	13 4/8	13 6/8	14	14 2/8	14 4/8	14 6/8	15	15 2/8	15 4/8	15 6/8	16
Junior	13 5/8	13 7/8	14 1/8	14 3/8	14 5/8	14 7/8	15 1/8	15 3/8	15 5/8	15 7/8	16 1/8	16 3/8
Misses tall	13 5/8	13 7/8	14 1/8	14 3/8	14 5/8	14 7/8	15 1/8	15 3/8	15 5/8	15 7/8	16 1/8	16 3/8
Women's	18 1/8	18 2/8	18 3/8	18 4/8	18 5/8	18 6/8	18 7/8	19	19 1/8	19 2/8	19 3/8	19 4/8
Half size	17 2/8	17 3/8	17 4/8	17 5/8	17 6/8	17 7/8	18	18 1/8	18 2/8	18 3/8	18 4/8	18 5/8
Plus size	18 1/8	18 2/8	18 3/8	18 4/8	18 5/8	18 6/8	18 7/8	19	19 1/8	19 2/8	19 3/8	19 4/8

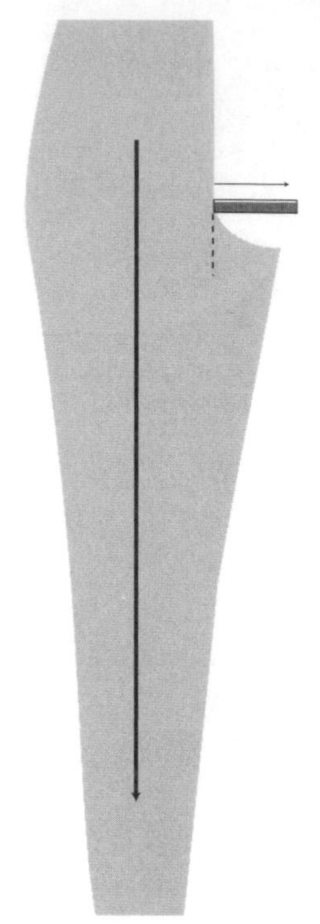

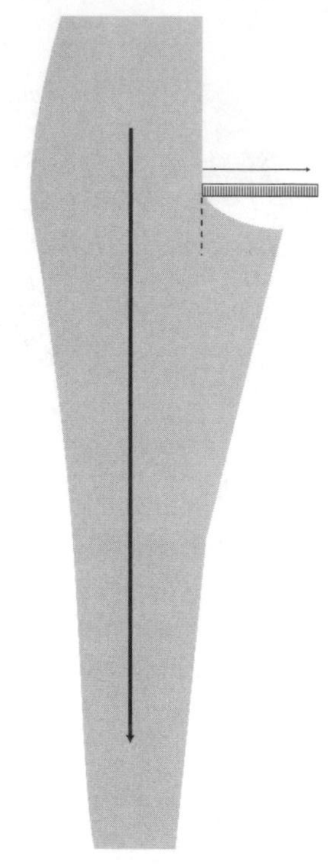

#9 FRONT CROTCH EXTENSION

The front crotch extension is not a direct body measurement, but is necessary for drafting pants.

The front crotch measurement is one-third of the front hip draft measurement.

#10 BACK CROTCH EXTENSION

The back crotch extension is not a direct body measurement, but is necessary for drafting pants.

The back crotch measurement is one-fourth of the front hip measurement.

#9 FRONT CROTCH EXTENSION

	Extra Small		Small		Medium		Large		Extra Large		Extra Extra Large	
Size	**2**	**4**	**6**	**8**	**10**	**12**	**14**	**16**	**18**	**20**	**22**	**24**
Misses	2 1/8	2 1/8	2 2/8	2 2/8	2 3/8	2 3/8	2 4/8	2 5/8	2 6/8	2 6/8	2 7/8	3
Petite	2 1/8	2 2/8	2 2/8	2 3/8	2 3/8	2 4/8	2 5/8	2 6/8	2 6/8	2 7/8	3	3 1/8
Junior	2 2/8	2 2/8	2 3/8	2 3/8	2 4/8	2 4/8	2 5/8	2 6/8	2 7/8	2 7/8	3	3 1/8
Misses tall	2 2/8	2 2/8	2 3/8	2 3/8	2 4/8	2 5/8	2 5/8	2 6/8	2 7/8	3	3	3 1/8
Women's	2 7/8	3 1/8	3 3/8	3 5/8	3 7/8	4 1/8	4 3/8	4 5/8	4 7/8	5 1/8	5 3/8	5 5/8
Half size	2 6/8	3	3 2/8	3 4/8	3 6/8	4	4 2/8	4 4/8	4 6/8	5	5 2/8	5 4/8
Plus size	2 6/8	3	3 2/8	3 4/8	3 6/8	4	4 2/8	4 4/8	4 6/8	5	5 2/8	5 4/8

#10 BACK CROTCH EXTENSION

	Extra Small		Small		Medium		Large		Extra Large		Extra Extra Large	
Size	**2**	**4**	**6**	**8**	**10**	**12**	**14**	**16**	**18**	**20**	**22**	**24**
Misses	2 6/8	2 7/8	3	3	3 1/8	3 2/8	3 3/8	3 4/8	3 5/8	3 6/8	3 7/8	4
Petite	2 7/8	3	3	3 1/8	3 2/8	3 3/8	3 4/8	3 5/8	3 6/8	3 7/8	4	4 1/8
Junior	2 7/8	3	3 1/8	3 1/8	3 2/8	3 3/8	3 4/8	3 5/8	3 6/8	3 7/8	4	4 2/8
Misses tall	3	3	3 1/8	3 2/8	3 2/8	3 3/8	3 4/8	3 5/8	3 6/8	3 7/8	4	4 1/8
Women's	3 7/8	4	4 1/8	4 3/8	4 4/8	4 5/8	4 7/8	5	5 1/8	5 3/8	5 4/8	5 5/8
Half size	3 5/8	3 7/8	4	4 1/8	4 3/8	4 4/8	4 5/8	4 7/8	5	5 1/8	5 3/8	5 4/8
Plus size	3 5/8	3 7/8	4	4 1/8	4 3/8	4 4/8	4 5/8	4 7/8	5	5 1/8	5 3/8	5 4/8

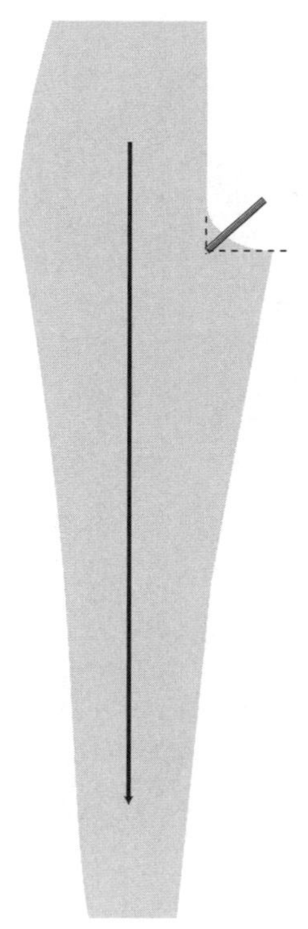

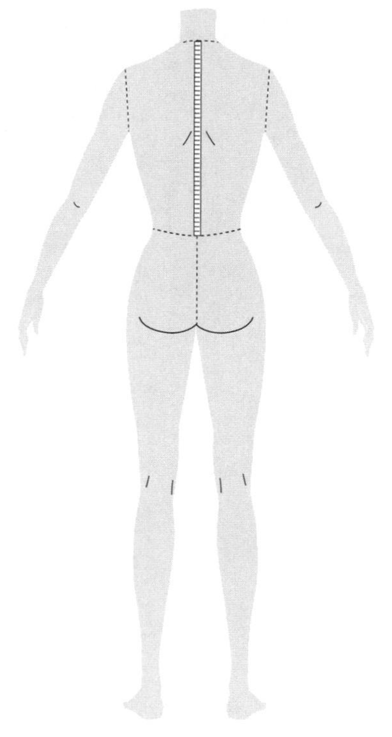

#11 CROTCH ANGLE

The crotch angle is not a direct body measurement, but is necessary for drafting pants.

The crotch angle is one-half of the front crotch extension.

#12 NAPE TO WAIST

The nape is the point where the neck intersects with the back.

Measure straight down from the nape to the waist at the center back.

#11 CROTCH ANGLE

Size	Extra Small		Small		Medium		Large		Extra Large		Extra Extra Large	
Misses	1	1 1/8	1 1/8	1 1/8	1 1/8	1 2/8	1 2/8	1 2/8	1 3/8	1 3/8	1 4/8	1 4/8
Petite	1 1/8	1 1/8	1 1/8	1 1/8	1 2/8	1 2/8	1 2/8	1 3/8	1 3/8	1 4/8	1 4/8	1 5/8
Junior	1 1/8	1 1/8	1 1/8	1 2/8	1 2/8	1 2/8	1 3/8	1 3/8	1 3/8	1 4/8	1 4/8	1 5/8
Misses tall	1 1/8	1 1/8	1 1/8	1 2/8	1 2/8	1 2/8	1 3/8	1 3/8	1 3/8	1 4/8	1 4/8	1 5/8
Women's	1 4/8	1 1/8	1 3/8	1 4/8	1 5/8	1 7/8	2	2 1/8	2 3/8	2 4/8	2 5/8	2 7/8
Half size	1 3/8	1 1/8	1 2/8	1 3/8	1 5/8	1 6/8	1 7/8	2 1/8	2 2/8	2 3/8	2 5/8	2 6/8
Plus size	1	1 1/8	1 2/8	1 4/8	1 5/8	1 6/8	2	2 1/8	2 2/8	2 4/8	2 5/8	2 6/8

#12 NAPE TO WAIST

Size	Extra Small		Small		Medium		Large		Extra Large		Extra Extra Large	
Misses	15 3/8	15 5/8	15 7/8	16 1/8	16 3/8	16 5/8	16 7/8	17 1/8	17 3/8	17 5/8	17 7/8	18 1/8
Petite	14 6/8	15	15 2/8	15 4/8	15 6/8	16	16 2/8	16 4/8	16 6/8	17	17 2/8	17 4/8
Junior	15 3/8	15 5/8	15 7/8	16 1/8	16 3/8	16 5/8	16 7/8	17 1/8	17 3/8	17 5/8	17 7/8	18 1/8
Misses tall	16 7/8	17 1/8	17 3/8	17 5/8	17 7/8	18 1/8	18 3/8	18 5/8	18 7/8	19 1/8	19 3/8	19 5/8
Women's	16 5/8	16 7/8	17 1/8	17 3/8	17 5/8	17 7/8	18 1/8	18 3/8	18 5/8	18 7/8	19 1/8	19 3/8
Half size	15 4/8	15 6/8	16	16 2/8	16 4/8	16 6/8	17	17 2/8	17 4/8	17 6/8	18	18 2/8
Plus size	17	15 4/8	15 6/8	16	16 2/8	16 4/8	16 6/8	17	17 2/8	17 4/8	17 6/8	18

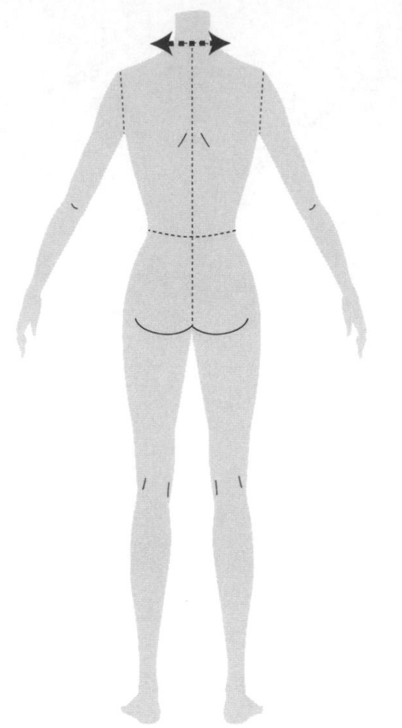

#13 BACK NECKLINE

The back neckline is not a direct measurement, but is calculated as one-sixth of the total neckline measurement.

#14 BACK NECK RISE

The back neck rise is not a direct body measurement, but is calculated as one-eighteenth of the neckline measurement.

#13 BACK NECKLINE

Size	Extra Small		Small		Medium		Large		Extra Large		Extra Extra Large	
Misses	2 3/8	2 3/8	2 3/8	2 4/8	2 4/8	2 1/2	2 1/2	2 1/2	2 1/2	2 5/8	2 5/8	2 5/8
Petite	2 2/8	2 3/8	2 3/8	2 3/8	2 3/8	2 3/8	2 3/8	2 1/2	2 1/2	2 1/2	2 1/2	2 1/2
Junior	2 3/8	2 5/8	2 5/8	2 6/8	2 6/8	2 6/8	2 7/8	2 7/8	3 4/8	0	2 3/8	2 3/8
Misses tall	2 1/2	2 1/2	2 1/2	2 1/2	2 1/2	2 1/2	2 5/8	2 5/8	2 5/8	2 5/8	2 5/8	2 5/8
Women's	3	3 2/8	3 4/8	3 6/8	4	4 2/8	4 4/8	4 6/8	5	5 2/8	5 4/8	5 6/8
Half size	2 3/4	3	3 2/8	3 1/2	3 3/4	4	4 1/2	4 1/2	4 6/8	5	5 2/8	5 4/8
Plus size	2 3/4	3	3 1/4	3 1/2	3 3/4	4	4 1/4	4 1/2	4 3/4	5	5 1/2	5 1/2

#14 BACK NECK RISE

Size	Extra Small		Small		Medium		Large		Extra Large		Extra Extra Large	
Misses	3/4	3/4	3/4	7/8	7/8	7/8	7/8	7/8	7/8	7/8	7/8	7/8
Petite	3/4	3/4	3/4	3/4	3/4	3/4	3/4	7/8	7/8	7/8	7/8	7/8
Junior	3/4	7/8	7/8	7/8	7/8	7/8	1	1	1 1/8	0	3/4	3/4
Misses tall	7/8	7/8	7/8	7/8	7/8	7/8	7/8	7/8	7/8	7/8	7/8	7/8
Women's	1	1 3/8	1 3/8	1 3/8	1 3/8	1 1/2	1 1/2	1 1/2	1 1/2	1 1/2	1 1/2	1 5/8
Half size	7/8	1 3/8	1 3/8	1 3/8	1 3/8	1 3/8	1 3/8	1 4/8	1 4/8	1 4/8	1 1/2	1 1/2
Plus size	7/8	1 3/8	1 3/8	1 3/8	1 3/8	1 3/8	1 3/8	1 1/2	1 1/2	1 1/2	1 1/2	1 1/2

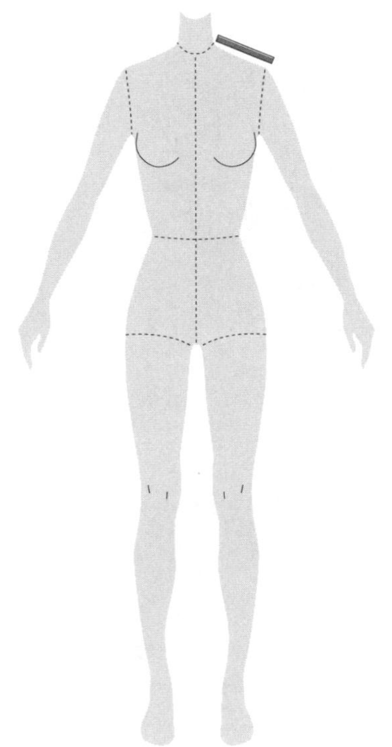

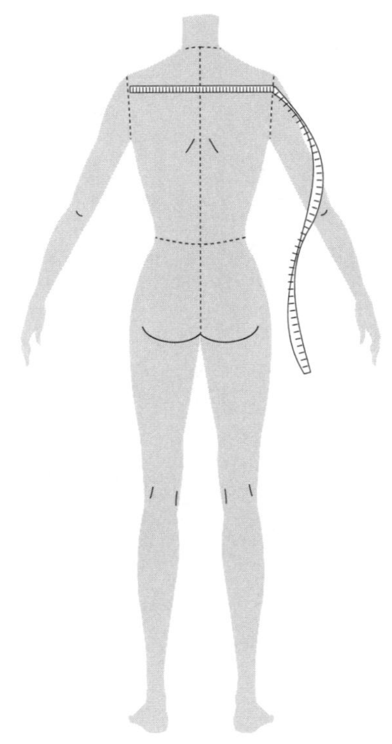

#15 SHOULDER LENGTH

Measure from the point that the neck and shoulders intersect to the point where the shoulder and arms intersect.

Where exactly are the shoulders?

Place your hand on the bone at the top of your shoulder. Pivot the arm. If you have the correct location on the bone, your arm should pivot around this point.

#16 ACROSS BACK

Measure between the two bones at the top of the armhole, and since the draft will be completed as one-quarter of the body, you need to divide this measurement in half.

#15 SHOULDER LENGTH

Size	Extra Small		Small		Medium		Large		Extra Large		Extra Extra Large	
Misses	5	5 1/8	5 1/4	5 1/2	5 3/4	6	6 1/4	6 1/2	6 3/4	7	7 1/4	7 4/8
Petite	4 7/8	5	5	5 1/8	5 1/8	5 2/8	5 3/8	5 4/8	5 5/8	5 6/8	5 7/8	6
Junior	4 7/8	5	5 1/8	5 2/8	5 3/8	5 4/8	5 5/8	5 6/8	5 7/8	6	6 1/8	6 2/8
Misses tall	4 7/8	5	5	5 1/8	5 1/8	5 2/8	5 3/8	5 4/8	5 5/8	5 6/8	5 7/8	6
Women's	5 5/8	5 6/8	5 3/4	5 7/8	5 7/8	6	6	6 1/8	6 1/8	6 1/4	6 1/4	6 3/8
Half size	5 1/2	5 5/8	5 5/8	5 3/4	5 3/4	5 7/8	5 7/8	6	6	6 1/8	6 1/8	6 2/8
Plus size	5 4/8	5 5/8	5 5/8	5 3/4	5 3/4	5 7/8	5 7/8	6	6	6 1/8	6 1/8	6 2/8

#16 ACROSS BACK

Size	Extra Small		Small		Medium		Large		Extra Large		Extra Extra Large	
Misses	6 7/8	7	7 1/8	7 2/8	7 3/8	7 4/8	7 5/8	7 6/8	7 7/8	8	8 1/8	8 3/8
Petite	7 2/8	7 3/8	7 4/8	7 5/8	7 6/8	7 7/8	8	8 1/8	8 2/8	8 3/8	8 4/8	8 5/8
Junior	7 2/8	7 3/8	7 5/8	7 6/8	8	8 1/8	8 3/8	8 4/8	8 6/8	8 7/8	9 1/8	9 2/8
Misses tall	7 4/8	7 5/8	7 6/8	8	8 1/8	8 3/8	8 4/8	8 6/8	8 7/8	9 1/8	9 2/8	9 4/8
Women's	8 5/8	8 6/8	8 7/8	9	9 1/8	9 2/8	9 3/8	9 4/8	9 5/8	9 6/8	9 7/8	10
Half size	8 3/8	8 4/8	8 5/8	8 6/8	8 7/8	9	9 1/8	9 2/8	9 3/8	9 4/8	9 5/8	9 6/8
Plus size	8 3/8	8 4/8	8 5/8	8 6/8	8 7/8	9	9 1/8	9 2/8	9 3/8	9 4/8	9 5/8	9 6/8

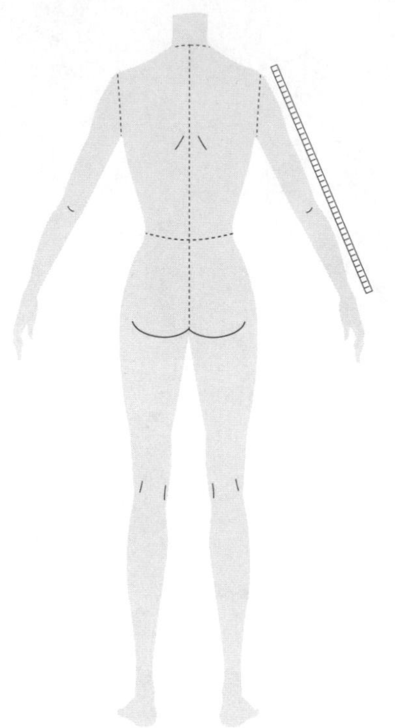

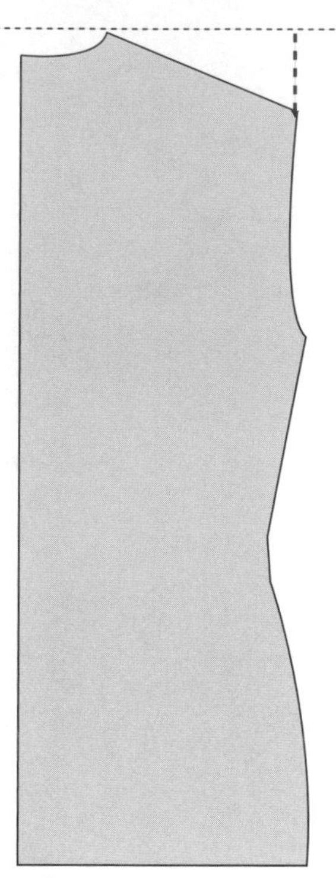

#17 SLEEVE LENGTH

Measure from the top of the sleeve to the wrist.

Measure from the shoulder bone to the elbow and continue down to the wrist.

#18 SHOULDER PITCH

Also called shoulder angle.

The shoulder pitch is not a direct body measurement, but is calculated as one-eleventh of the nape to waist measurement.

#17 SLEEVE LENGTH

Size	Extra Small		Small		Medium		Large		Extra Large		Extra Extra Large	
Misses	22 5/8	22 6/8	22 7/8	23	23 1/8	23 2/8	23 3/8	23 4/8	23 5/8	23 6/8	23 7/8	24
Petite	21 2/8	21 3/8	21 4/8	21 5/8	21 6/8	21 7/8	22	22 1/8	22 2/8	22 3/8	22 4/8	22 5/8
Junior	23 3/8	23 4/8	23 5/8	23 6/8	23 7/8	24	24 1/8	24 2/8	24 3/8	24 4/8	24 5/8	24 6/8
Misses tall	24 3/8	24 4/8	24 5/8	24 6/8	24 7/8	25	25 1/8	25 2/8	25 3/8	25 4/8	25 5/8	25 6/8
Women's	23 7/8	24	24 1/8	24 2/8	24 3/8	24 4/8	24 5/8	24 6/8	24 7/8	25	25 1/8	25 2/8
Half size	22 2/8	22 3/8	22 4/8	22 5/8	22 6/8	22 7/8	23	23 1/8	23 2/8	23 3/8	23 4/8	23 5/8
Plus size	32 1/8	32 2/8	32 3/8	32 4/8	32 5/8	32 6/8	32 7/8	33	33 1/8	33 2/8	33 3/8	33 4/8

#18 SHOULDER PITCH

Size	Extra Small		Small		Medium		Large		Extra Large		Extra Extra Large	
Misses	1 3/8	1 3/8	1 4/8	1 4/8	1 4/8	1 4/8	1 4/8	1 4/8	1 5/8	1 5/8	1 5/8	1 5/8
Petite	1 3/8	1 3/8	1 3/8	1 3/8	1 3/8	1 4/8	1 4/8	1 4/8	1 4/8	1 4/8	1 5/8	1 5/8
Junior	1 4/8	1 4/8	1 5/8	1 5/8	1 5/8	1 5/8	1 5/8	1 6/8	1 6/8	1 6/8	1 6/8	1 6/8
Misses tall	1 4/8	1 4/8	1 5/8	1 5/8	1 5/8	1 5/8	1 5/8	1 6/8	1 6/8	1 6/8	1 6/8	1 6/8
Women's	1 4/8	1 5/8	1 6/8	1 7/8	2	2 1/8	2 2/8	2 3/8	2 4/8	2 5/8	2 6/8	2 7/8
Half size	1 3/8	1 4/8	1 5/8	1 6/8	1 7/8	2	2 1/8	2 2/8	2 3/8	2 4/8	2 5/8	2 6/8
Plus size	1 4/8	1 5/8	1 6/8	1 7/8	2	2 1/8	2 2/8	2 3/8	2 4/8	2 5/8	2 6/8	2 7/8

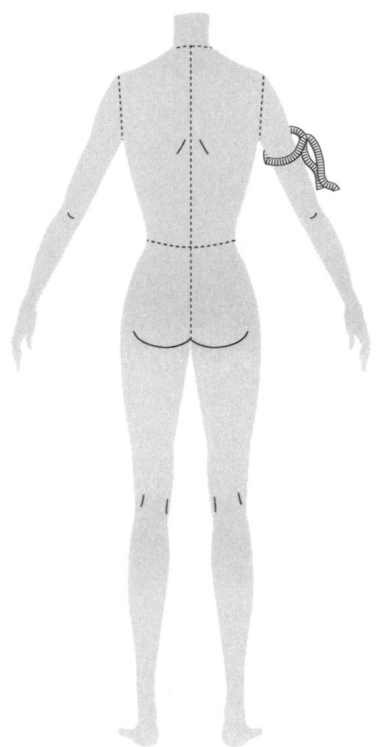

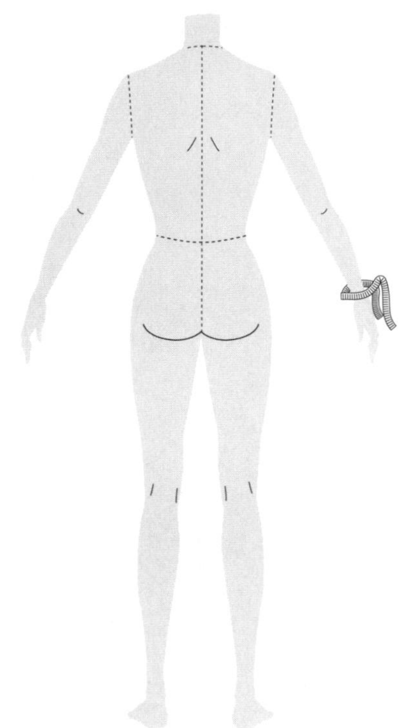

#19 BICEP CIRCUMFERENCE

Wrap tape around the fullest part of the bicep. This measurement is helpful when drafting the sleeve to check that the sleeve will be large enough to accommodate a larger bicep.

#20 WRIST CIRCUMFERENCE

Wrap tape around the wrist. This measurement is helpful when drafting the sleeve to check that the wrist will be large enough to accommodate the hand.

#19 BICEP CIRCUMFERENCE

Size	Extra Small		Small		Medium		Large		Extra Large		Extra Extra Large	
Misses	10	10 3/8	10 6/8	11 1/8	11 4/8	11 7/8	12 2/8	12 5/8	13	13 3/8	13 6/8	14 1/8
Petite	10 3/8	10 6/8	11 1/8	11 4/8	11 7/8	12 2/8	12 5/8	13	13 3/8	13 6/8	14 1/8	14 4/8
Junior	10 6/8	11 1/8	11 4/8	11 7/8	12 2/8	12 5/8	13	13 3/8	13 6/8	14 1/8	14 4/8	14 7/8
Misses tall	10 5/8	11	11 3/8	11 6/8	12 1/8	12 4/8	12 7/8	13 2/8	13 5/8	14	14 3/8	14 6/8
Women's	14 4/8	14 7/8	15 2/8	15 5/8	16	16 3/8	16 6/8	17 1/8	17 4/8	17 7/8	18 2/8	18 5/8
Half size	13 6/8	14 1/8	14 4/8	14 7/8	15 2/8	15 5/8	16	16 3/8	16 6/8	17 1/8	17 4/8	17 7/8
Plus size	13 6/8	14 1/8	14 4/8	14 7/8	15 2/8	15 5/8	16	16 3/8	16 6/8	17 1/8	17 4/8	17 7/8

#20 WRIST CIRCUMFERENCE

Size	Extra Small		Small		Medium		Large		Extra Large		Extra Extra Large	
Misses	5 1/8	5 4/8	5 7/8	6 2/8	6 5/8	7	7 3/8	7 6/8	8 1/8	8 4/8	8 7/8	9 2/8
Petite	5 6/8	6 1/8	6 4/8	6 7/8	7 2/8	7 5/8	8	8 3/8	8 6/8	9 1/8	9 4/8	9 7/8
Junior	5 7/8	6	6 1/8	6 2/8	6 3/8	6 4/8	6 5/8	6 6/8	6 7/8	7	7 1/8	7 2/8
Misses tall	5 7/8	6 2/8	6 5/8	7	7 3/8	7 6/8	8 1/8	8 4/8	8 7/8	9 2/8	9 5/8	10
Women's	7 1/8	7 4/8	7 7/8	8 2/8	8 5/8	9	9 3/8	9 6/8	10 1/8	10 4/8	10 7/8	11 2/8
Half size	6 6/8	7 1/8	7 4/8	7 7/8	8 2/8	8 5/8	9	9 3/8	9 6/8	10 1/8	10 4/8	10 7/8
Plus size	6 6/8	7 1/8	7 4/8	7 7/8	8 2/8	8 5/8	9	9 3/8	9 6/8	10 1/8	10 4/8	10 7/8

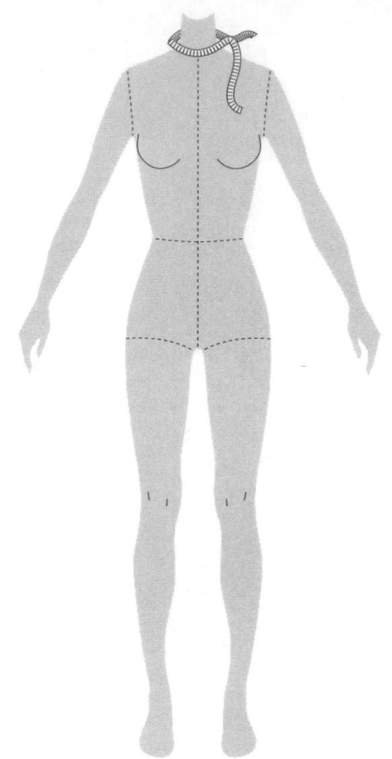

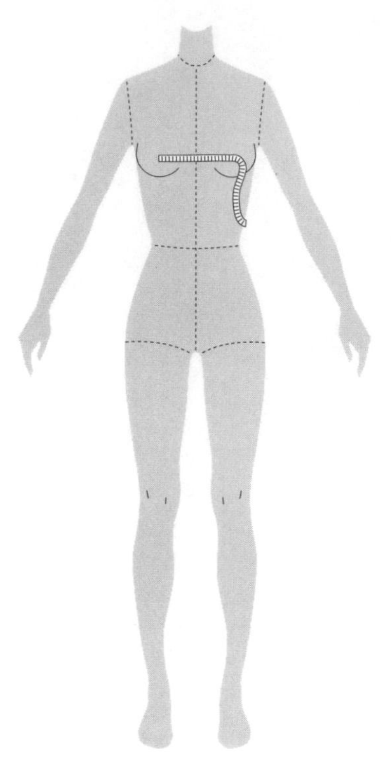

#21 NECK CIRCUMFERENCE

Wrap measuring tape around base of neck, and measure but do not pull the tape too tight.

#22 BUST SPAN

Measure from apex to apex across the front chest. Drafting tube tops may be useful.

#21 NECK CIRCUMFERENCE

	Extra Small		Small		Medium		Large		Extra Large		Extra Extra Large	
Size	**2**	**4**	**6**	**8**	**10**	**12**	**14**	**16**	**18**	**20**	**22**	**24**
Misses	14 3/8	14 4/8	14 5/8	14 6/8	14 7/8	15	15 1/8	15 2/8	15 3/8	15 4/8	15 5/8	15 6/8
Petite	13 6/8	13 7/8	14	14 1/8	14 2/8	14 3/8	14 4/8	14 5/8	14 6/8	14 7/8	15	15 1/8
Junior	14 5/8	14 7/8	15 2/8	15 4/8	15 7/8	16 1/8	16 4/8	16 6/8	17 1/8	17 3/8	17 6/8	18
Misses tall	14 5/8	14 6/8	14 7/8	15	15 1/8	15 2/8	15 3/8	15 4/8	15 5/8	15 6/8	15 7/8	16
Women's	17 2/8	17 5/8	18	18 3/8	18 6/8	19 1/8	19 4/8	19 7/8	20 2/8	20 5/8	21	21 3/8
Half size	16 6/8	17 1/8	17 4/8	17 7/8	18 2/8	18 5/8	19	19 3/8	19 6/8	20 1/8	20 4/8	20 7/8
Plus size	16 6/8	17 1/8	17 4/8	17 7/8	18 2/8	18 5/8	19	19 3/8	19 6/8	20 1/8	20 4/8	20 7/8

#22 BUST SPAN

Size	Extra Small		Small		Medium		Large		Extra Large		Extra Extra Large	
Misses	6 4/8	6 5/8	6 6/8	6 7/8	7	7 1/8	7 2/8	7 4/8	7 5/8	7 7/8	8 1/8	8 3/8
Petite	6 5/8	6 6/8	6 7/8	7	7 1/8	7 2/8	7 4/8	7 5/8	7 7/8	8	8 2/8	8 3/8
Junior	6 5/8	6 6/8	6 7/8	7	7 1/8	7 2/8	7 3/8	7 4/8	7 5/8	7 6/8	7 7/8	8
Misses tall	6 6/8	6 7/8	7	7 1/8	7 2/8	7 3/8	7 5/8	7 6/8	8	8 1/8	8 3/8	8 4/8
Women's	8	8 1/8	8 2/8	8 3/8	8 4/8	8 5/8	8 6/8	8 7/8	9	9 1/8	9 2/8	9 3/8
Half size	7 6/8	7 7/8	8	8 1/8	8 2/8	8 3/8	8 4/8	8 5/8	8 6/8	8 7/8	9	9 1/8
Plus size	7 6/8	7 7/8	8	8 1/8	8 2/8	8 3/8	8 4/8	8 5/8	8 6/8	8 7/8	9	9 1/8

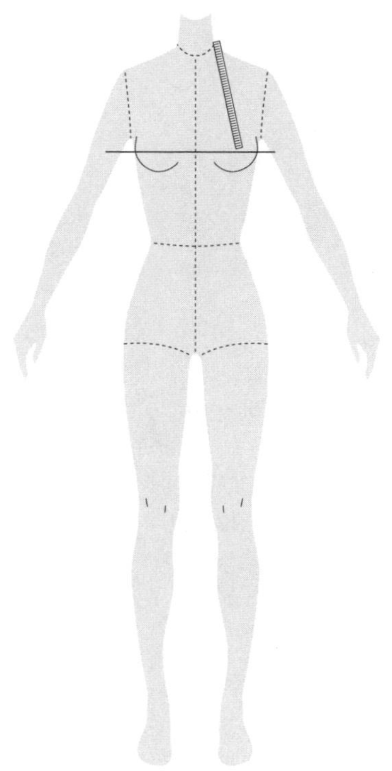

#23 BUST LEVEL

Measure from the shoulder point down to fullest part of bust. This measurement is helpful when determining the bust apex, and will be useful when drafting low-cut tops.

#23 BUST LEVEL

Size	Extra Small		Small		Medium		Large		Extra Large		Extra Extra Large	
Misses	9 7/8	10	10 1/8	10 2/8	10 3/8	10 4/8	10 5/8	10 6/8	10 7/8	11	11 1/8	11 2/8
Petite	9 3/8	9 4/8	9 5/8	9 6/8	9 7/8	10	10 1/8	10 2/8	10 3/8	10 4/8	10 5/8	10 6/8
Junior	9 7/8	10 1/8	10 3/8	10 5/8	10 7/8	11 1/8	11 3/8	11 5/8	11 7/8	12 1/8	12 3/8	12 5/8
Misses tall	10 6/8	10 7/8	11	11 1/8	11 2/8	11 3/8	11 4/8	11 5/8	11 6/8	11 7/8	12	12 1/8
Women's	12 2/8	12 4/8	12 6/8	13	13 2/8	13 4/8	13 6/8	14	14 2/8	14 4/8	14 6/8	15
Half size	11 3/8	11 5/8	11 7/8	12 1/8	12 3/8	12 5/8	12 7/8	13 1/8	13 3/8	13 5/8	13 7/8	14 1/8
Plus size	11 7/8	12 1/8	12 3/8	12 5/8	12 7/8	13 1/8	13 3/8	13 5/8	13 7/8	14 1/8	14 3/8	14 5/8

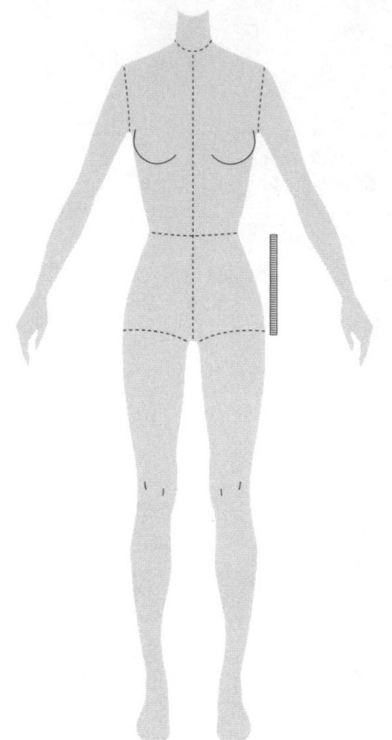

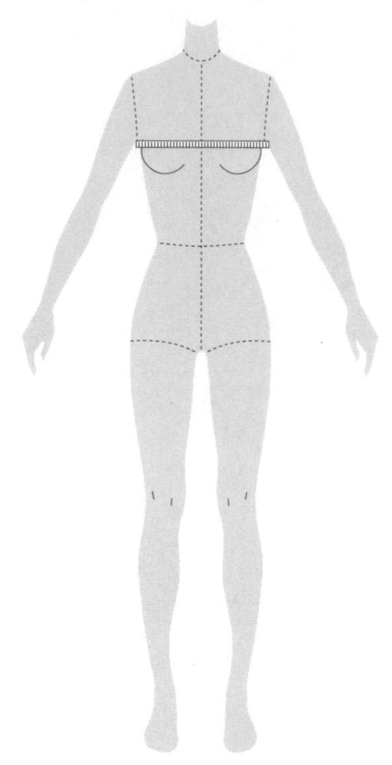

#24 HIP DEPTH

Measure the distance from the waist to the fullest part of the hip. May be used to check hip placement and hip notches.

#25 HIGHEST PART OF CHEST OR BUST

Measure around the highest part of the chest, directly under arms. Note: This is above the fullest part of the chest.

#24 HIP DEPTH

Size	Extra Small		Small		Medium		Large		Extra Large		Extra Extra Large	
Misses	33 4/8	34 4/8	35 4/8	36 4/8	37 4/8	38 4/8	40	41 4/8	43	44 4/8	46 4/8	48 4/8
Petite	34 8/16	35 8/16	36 8/16	37 8/16	38 8/16	40	41 8/16	43	44 8/16	46	48	50
Junior	35	36	37	38	39	40 8/16	42	43 8/16	45	46 8/16	48 8/16	50 8/16
Misses tall	35 4/8	36 4/8	37 4/8	38 4/8	39 4/8	41	42 4/8	44	45 4/8	47	48 4/8	50
Women's	46	48	50	52	54	56	58	60	62	64	66	68
Half size	44	46	48	50	52	54	56	58	60	62	64	66
Plus size	44	46	48	50	52	54	56	58	60	62	64	66

#25 HIGHEST PART OF CHEST OR BUST

Size	Extra Small		Small		Medium		Large		Extra Large		Extra Extra Large	
Misses	32	33	34	35	36 1/2	38	39 1/2	41	43	45	32	33
Petite	32	33	34	35	36 1/2	38	39 1/2	41	42 1/2	44	32	33
Junior	32	33	34	35	36 1/2	38	39 1/2	41	42 1/2	44	32	33
Misses tall	33	34	35	36	37 1/2	39	40 1/2	42	43 1/2	45	33	34
Women's	42	43	44	45	46 1/2	48	49 1/2	51	52 1/2	54	42	43
Half size	42	43	44	45	46 1/2	48	49 1/2	51	52 1/2	54	42	43
Plus size	43	45	47	49	51	53	55	57	59	61	43	45

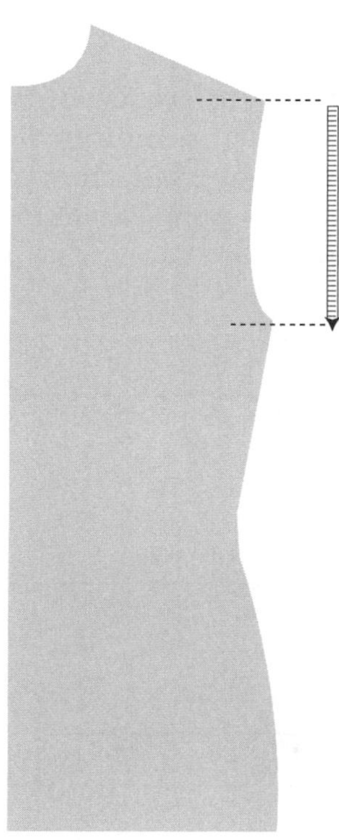

#26 ARMHOLE DEPTH

The armhole depth is not a direct body dimension, but is taken from the sloper draft. Measure the distance from the shoulder straight down to the bottom of the armhole.

#26 ARMHOLE DEPTH

	Extra Small		Small		Medium		Large		Extra Large		Extra Extra Large	
Size	**2**	**4**	**6**	**8**	**10**	**12**	**14**	**16**	**18**	**20**	**22**	**24**
Misses	6 7/8	7	7 1/8	7 2/8	7 3/8	7 4/8	7 5/8	7 6/8	7 7/8	8	8 1/8	8 2/8
Petite	6 5/8	6 6/8	6 7/8	7	7 1/8	7 2/8	7 3/8	7 4/8	7 4/8	7 5/8	7 6/8	7 7/8
Junior	6 7/8	7	7	7 1/8	7 2/8	7 3/8	7 4/8	7 5/8	7 4/8	8 7/8	8 1/8	8 2/8
Misses tall	7 5/8	7 6/8	7 7/8	8	8 1/8	8 2/8	8 3/8	8 4/8	8 5/8	8 5/8	8 6/8	8 7/8
Women's	7 3/8	7 1/8	7 2/8	7 2/8	7 3/8	7 4/8	7 5/8	7 6/8	7 7/8	7 7/8	8	8 1/8
Half size	6 7/8	6 5/8	6 5/8	6 6/8	6 7/8	7	7 1/8	7 2/8	7 2/8	7 3/8	7 4/8	7 5/8
Plus size	7 5/8	6 4/8	6 4/8	6 5/8	6 6/8	6 7/8	7	7 1/8	7 1/8	7 2/8	7 3/8	7 4/8

Cup Sizes

Cup size is determined by the difference between the bust measurement and the upper bust measurement. This chart shows different bust measurements, but all upper chest measurements are 36″ for illustration purposes only.

#27 CUP SIZE

If the upper chest is 36″

Bust	36½	37	38	39	40	41	42	43	44	45
Upper chest	36″	36″	36″	36″	36″	36″	36″	36″		
Difference	½	1	2	3	4	5	6	7	8	9
Difference	Up to ½″	½″ to 1¼	1½ to 2¼	2½″ to 3¼	4¼	5¼	6¼	7¼	8¼	9¼
Cup size	AA	A	B	C	D	DD/E	DDD/F	G	H	I

#28 CUP RADIUS

Estimate the diameter of the breast.

	Extra Extra Small	Extra Small	Small	Medium	Large	Extra Large	Extra Extra Large
Stable	2⅛	2¼	2⅜	2½	2⅝	2¾	2⅞
Moderate	2⅛	2¼	2⅜	2½	2⅝	2¾	2⅞
Stretchy	2	2⅛	2¼	2⅜	2½	2⅝	2¾
Super	1⅞	2	2⅛	2¼	2⅜	2½	2⅝
Rib	1¾	1⅞	1⅞	2	2⅛	2¼	2⅜

How to Determine Your Own Size Range

The first step in starting your own label or your own company is to determine your size range and size specs. There are two basic ways to get sizing information. One is to buy it, and the other is to design it yourself, usually by reverse engineering of your competitor's products.

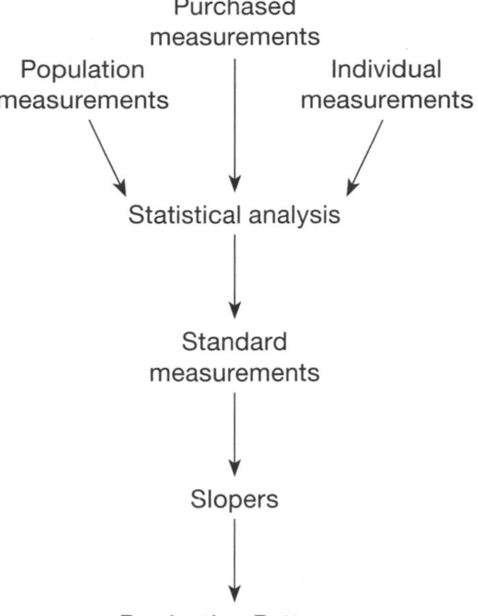

POPULATION MEASUREMENTS

May be obtained from the American Bureau of Standards and Measurements, which lists measurements based on age groups, and is updated every November.

http://www.astm.org

INDIVIDUAL MEASUREMENTS

Individual measurements of sample customers, or fit models and dress-forms, should be taken.

STATISTICAL ANALYSIS

Analyze the measurements taken, along with those purchased, and compare them to decide on the appropriate measurements for you target market. Create grade tables based on your analysis.

SLOPERS

Develop a measurement chart for your company, or use one of the measurement charts provided in this text, before creating your company's slopers.

PRODUCTION PATTERNS

Production patterns should be drafted to the company size specs. Often, designer samples are created in model's proportions, for showroom sales and fashion shows. These measurements do not fit the average consumer and should be corrected for production patterns. This is the responsibility of the spec technician.

COMPETITORS

You can purchase garments from your competitors and take the measurements directly from the garment.

FRACTIONS TO DECIMALS CONVERSION CHART

If you use a computer program, such as Gerber, to create slopers and patterns, it will be necessary to convert fraction to decimals in order to enter measurements into the computer.

To figure it out on your own calculator, or computer, simply divide the number 1 by the denominator.

So, for example, if you need to find the number for one-eighth, divide the number 1 by 8 and you will get the result of 0.125.

Halves	Quarters	Eighths	Sixteenths	Thirty-Seconds	Decimal Equivalent
				1/32	0.03125
			1/16	2/32	0.0625
				3/32	0.09375
		1/8	2/16	4/32	0.125
				5/32	0.15625
			3/16	6/32	0.1875
				7/32	0.21875
	1/4	2/8	4/16	8/32	0.25
				9/32	0.28125
			5/16	10/32	0.3125
				11/32	0.34375
		3/8	6/16	12/32	0.375
				13/32	0.40625
			7/16	14/32	0.4375
				15/32	0.46875
1/2	2/4	4/8	8/16	16/32	0.5
				17/32	0.53125
			9/16	18/32	0.5625
				19/32	0.59375
		5/8	10/16	20/32	0.625
				21/32	0.65625
			11/16	22/32	0.6875
				23/32	0.71875
	3/4	6/8	12/16	24/32	0.75
				25/32	0.78125
			13/16	26/32	0.8125
				27/32	0.84375
		7/8	14/16	28/32	0.875
				29/32	0.90625
			15/16	30/32	0.9375
				31/32	0.96875
2/2	4/4	8/8	16/16	32/32	1.0

Test Your Knowledge of the Material in This Chapter

1. Why don't clothes from one manufacturer fit the same as from another manufacturer?
2. What are the "true sizings" or industry guidelines for sizing garments?
3. What type of customers are Junior sizes intended for?
4. What type of customers are Plus sizes intended for?
5. What is vanity sizing?
6. What is catalogue sizing?
7. How much is the bust difference between size 10 and size 12?
8. How much is the bust difference between size 10 and size 8?
9. How much is the bust difference between Small and Medium?
10. How much is the bust difference between Medium and Large?

Exercise #2

Create a personal measurement chart with the associated reductions, for future drafts.

#		Personal Measurement	Divide by	Stable knits −0%	Moderate knits −2%	Stretchy knits −3.5%	Super-stretch knits −5%	Rib knits −10%	Two- & Four-way knits −5% both directions
Multiply By				*100	*.98	*.965	*.95	.90	*.09
1	Bust		4						
2	Waist		4						
3	Hip		4						
4	Crotch depth		N/A	No length reduction					
5	Waist to knee		N/A	No length reduction					
6	Waist to ankle		N/A	No length reduction					
7	Ankle		4						
8	Knee		4						
9	Front crotch	One quarter of hip measurement							
10	Back crotch	One-third of hip measurement							
11	Crotch angle	One half of front crotch extension							
12	Nape to waist		N/A						
13	Back neck	From size chart closest to your size	N/A						
14	Back neck rise	From size chart closest to your size	N/A						
15	Shoulder		N/A	No reduction					
16	Across back		2						
17	Sleeve length		N/A						
18	Shoulder pitch	From an appropriate chart	N/A						
19	Bicep								
20	Wrist								
21	Neck								
22	Bust span								
23	Bust level								
24	Hip depth								
25	Upper bust								

CHAPTER 3

Principles of Pattern-Drafting

About This Chapter

This chapter introduces the reader to the principles and practices of stretch patternmaking. While previous patternmaking experience will help in understanding these concepts, the occasional, or new, patternmaker will greatly benefit from seeing how stretch patternmaking differs from conventional patternmaking. In many ways, stretch patternmaking is simpler.

Flat Patternmaking

Flat patternmaking is the process of creating templates used to cut out the final garments. Patternmaking is the process of creating a two-dimensional template for a three-dimensional garment, by tracing out the sloper on a blank sheet of paper, then manipulating by slash and spread and adding garment details to create a final pattern.

Sloper

A sloper is a template of basic styles, without any seam allowances or style details. Many different patterns can be made from a single sloper. Because a sloper is your master pattern, it should not be changed or altered unless you wish to make those same alterations to all future styles. Slopers should be traced out on lightweight drafting paper, and then changed into the style that you wish to create.

Patterns

A pattern is an outline, or a template, of the intended style that is used when cutting out the fabric. All patterns should include seam allowances to allow the pieces to be sewn together; notches to help match seams together; a grainline and any necessary drill holes; plus all necessary labeling and instructions. All final patterns should be made of oak-tag, and all drafts and working patterns should be made of lightweight drafting paper. There are two methods of creating patterns: flat patternmaking and draping.

How Patterns Are Used

Patterns are used to cut out a garment. Every garment needs a pattern, regardless of the stories you hear about someone's grandmother "who never uses a pattern." In those cases, you can be sure the garments are ill-fitting and unprofessional, and must indeed look it.

Pattern Development

All patterns are developed by tracing out the appropriate sloper, manipulating through slash and spread, and applying the design details to the paper draft, and then finally adding all of the necessary seam allowances.

Draping Knits

Draping is a method by which the fabric is placed on the fitting Judy and the garment is cut and molded to the style. Draping is difficult, if not impossible, with stretch fabrics, because it is extremely difficult to maintain the same amount of stretch when draping the separate front and back of the garment. Often the side seams of draped garments will twist around the body, because the seams are not identical and were not equalized effectively. To get around this problem, drape the front of the garment, and use that drape to create the back of the garment by changing the neckline and the armholes of the draft, or the reverse: drape the back of the style, and draft the back, from that drape.

The Differences between Woven and Stretch Patterns

Since all woven fabrics are basically the same, and don't stretch, they only need a single set of slopers. With stretch fabrics, however, there are many different stretch ratios. Consequently, each stretch fabric needs an appropriate sloper.

Besides the different seam finishes and seam allowances needed to create stretch patterns, there is one huge difference between stretch and woven patterns. Each stretch fabric requires a different sloper. Stable-knit fabrics, which stretch up to 25 percent, require slopers created for that particular fabric. While this seems like you would need hundreds of different slopers, in fact there are only six different sloper sets:

Stable knit	stretches up to 25%
Moderate-stretch knit	stretches up to 50%
Stretchy knit	stretches up to 75%
Super-stretch knit	stretches up to 100%
Two-way-stretch and four-way-stretch knit	stretches up to 100% in both directions
Rib knit	stretches over 100%

This manual takes a unique approach to drafting slopers, in that the largest-sized sloper is created and on each piece the other stretch ratios are indicated. This method saves a lot of time when drafting slopers, and uses far less supplies, which is especially helpful to the student, or beginning patternmaker.

How Patternmaking Works

In order to create a pattern, you must trace out the appropriate sloper on a fresh sheet of lightweight paper; complete any slash and spread, draw in the details, add the necessary seam allowances, and finally trace the lightweight pattern onto oak-tag, or hard paper, and label and notch the pattern accordingly. Before any pattern can be considered complete, you must true and check every seam, check every notch, blend every curve, and then label the pattern. Also remember that fitting and corrections are part of the patternmaking process.

When adding seam allowances, create all final patterns in oak-tag, or hard pattern paper.

Principles of Patternmaking

There are six principles of knit patternmaking that will be explained and illustrated throughout this chapter:

1. Ease
2. Adding a style line
3. Slash and spread to add fullness, flare, gathering, and ease, and pivoting
4. Reductions for binding, banding, trim, and elastic
5. Circles for skirts and ruffles
6. Fitting and corrections

Seam Allowances

None of the calculations used to create the slopers or blocks in this manual include seam allowances, nor, for that matter, should any sloper or block. Seams should only be added to the final pattern pieces; otherwise you would soon find yourself confused as to whether they'd been added or not. The amount of seam allowance you add depends on the type of machine you use, which in turn is determined by the type of fabric and seam finish.

When drafting patterns for stretch garments, keep in mind that seams also affect the way the garment stretches. A simple serged seam along the side of a garment doesn't really affect much, but consider, for example, using a topstitched seam along that same side seam. Such a seam would be a nice decorative feature, but all that bulk acts as an anchor line and will not allow the fabric to stretch as much along its length as would a simple serged seam. So you need to allow extra length, which might in turn affect the fit of the rest of the garment.

A topstitched seam also tends to hold in a straight line, so be aware that you might need to allow a little extra in garment length or find yourself with a bunch of 45-degree puckers down one side of the seam. You can use this to your advantage or you can be constantly chasing yourself in circles trying to work out why something doesn't fit the way you hoped it would. The closer or tighter the fit and the smaller the garment, the more you need to build excess into small allowances for unforeseen circumstances. This usually isn't a problem when working with standard sizes, but when making custom garments, these considerations might be critical.

The seam allowances are determined by the type of knits, and consequently the type of serger. The patternmaker must know which machine to use in order to apply the correct seam allowances.

Knit	Ratio	Serger	Seam allowance	Hem Allowance
Stable knit	25%	4-thread or 5-thread if the fabric is very thick	3/8″ or 1/2″	1″ for straight, 1/2″ for curved
Moderate knit	50%	4-thread	3/8″	1″ for straight, 1/2″ for curved
Rib knit	100%	4-thread	3/8″	1″ for straight, 1/2″ for curved
Super-stretch knit	100%	4-thread or 3-thread for very fine knits	3/8″ or 1/4″	1″ for straight, 1/2″ for curved
Loosely knitted super-stretch knit	100%	4-thread	3/8″	
Sweater knits (cut and sew)	18–50%	4-thread or 5-thread if loosely knitted	3/8″ or 1/2″	1 1/2″ for straight, 1/2″ for curved
Fully-fashioned sweaters	18–50%	Single needle, crochet, linking Single-stitch seam allowance	1/8″	
Custom garments	When making custom fit garments use 1/2″ seams to baste the garment together for the first fitting using a straight-stitch machine. The excess can be cut away later using a serger.		1/2″	

Drafting Hems

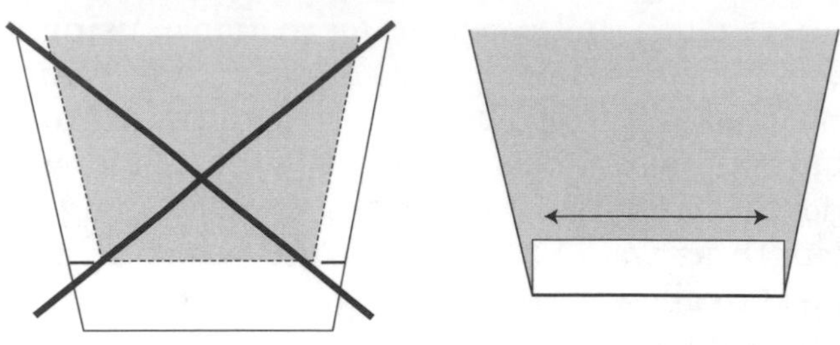

This is an incorrect hem allowance because when the fabric folds up, it will be too short to sew.

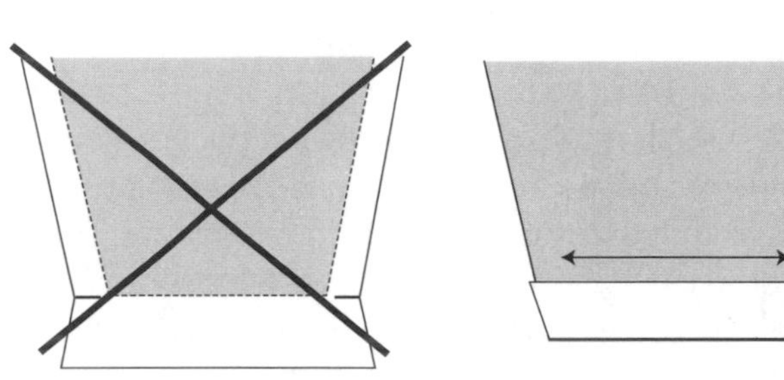

This is an incorrect hem allowance because when the fabric folds up, it will get larger and stretch out from sewing.

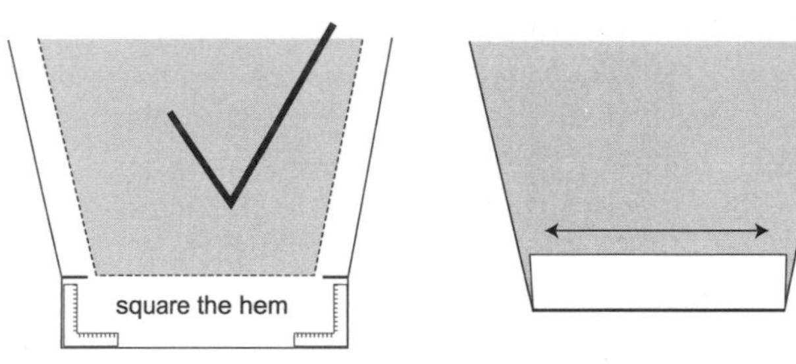

Create the correct hem allowance by drawing a line parallel to the bottom of the pant, then squaring up at the sides. This hem allowance is slightly smaller, and will not stretch out when sewing and actually will help pull the hem in slightly.

Understanding the Sewing of Hems

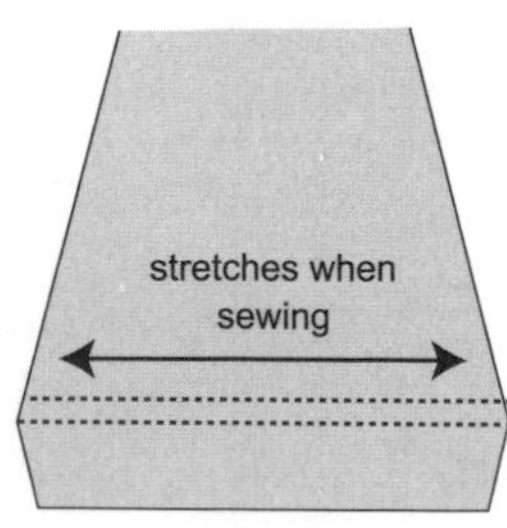

1″ HEM

All straight hems must have at least a 1″ hem allowance.

Cover-stitching causes the seam to stretch out. By using a 1″ hem allowance, the folded edge will remain intact while the stitched edge stretches out and may be easily pressed back into shape.

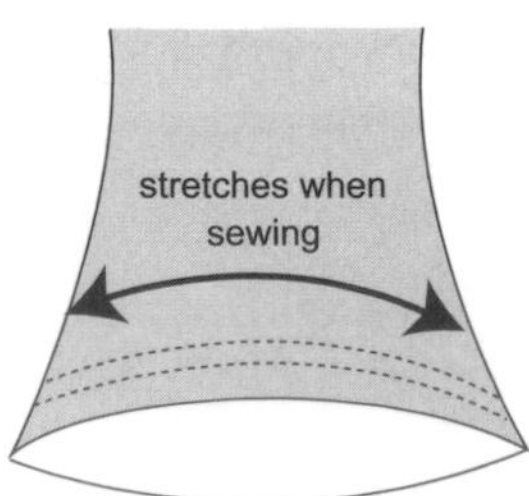

½″ HEM

A ½″ hem will cause the edge to stretch out.

There is no choice but to use a ½″ hem allowance on a curved edge, but a stretched edge is less obvious on a curved hem and easier to shrink back to shape while pressing.

Different Ways to Sew a Stretch Hem

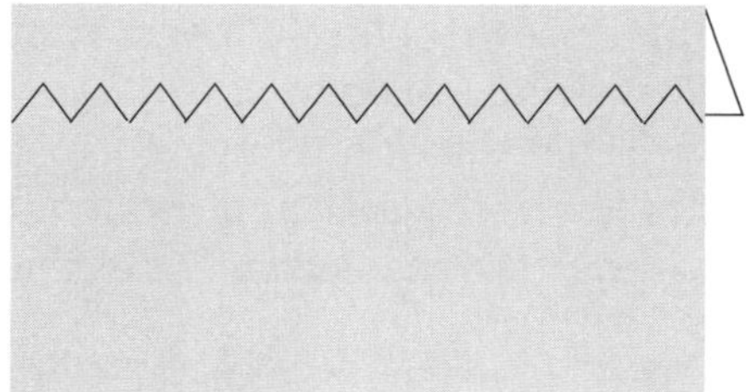

ZIGZAG MACHINE

A zigzag machine may be used to hem a stretch garment.

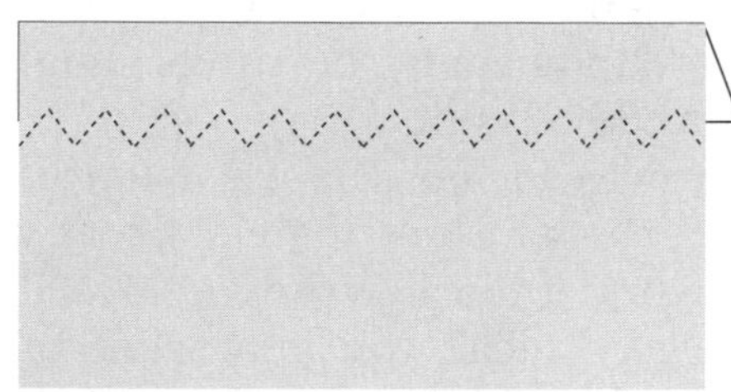

MARCEL STITCH

A marcel stitch is a straight stitch in a zigzag pattern. Stretch this seam slightly while sewing.

STRAIGHT-STITCH MACHINE

Sew this hem using a large stitch length and stretch the seam as you sew. When the seam has been stretched during sewing, it will have large floats on the right side of the garment. A stretched seam will not lie flat, but instead will be wavy and stretched. If the seam is not stretched beyond the amount the wearer will stretch it, it will pop when worn.

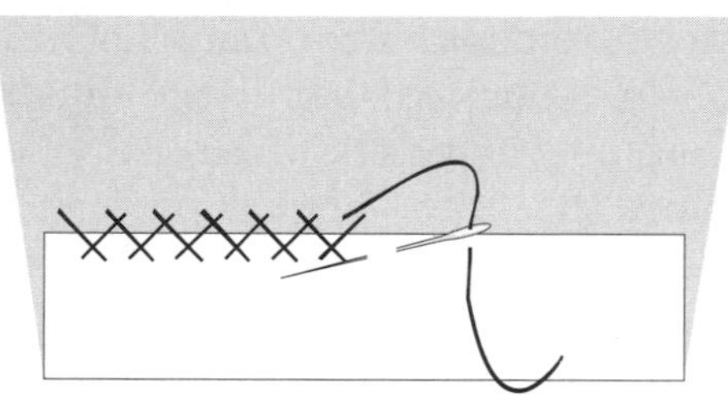

HAND HEM

A hand hem is used when a blind hemmer is not available or when the designer wants to create a truly invisible hem.

The needle travels from right to left, but the sewing is actually going left to right. Keep the stitches smaller than 3/8″. Back-tack every third stitch, to reinforce the hem. Hide stitches under the serge when creating delicate garments, such as sweaters.

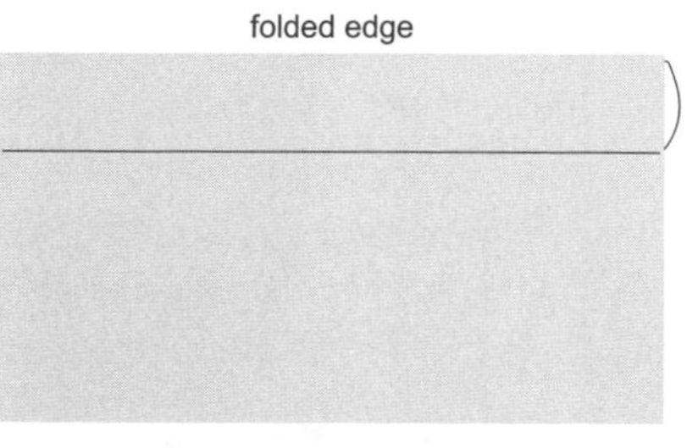

SERGED-ON BAND

A serged-on band is a separate strip of fabric that is folded in half and serged to the raw edge of the fabric. Serged-on bands can be done on almost any seam; the band width can vary from 1/4″ to 3″ and may also be used on necklines to create crew-neck collars.

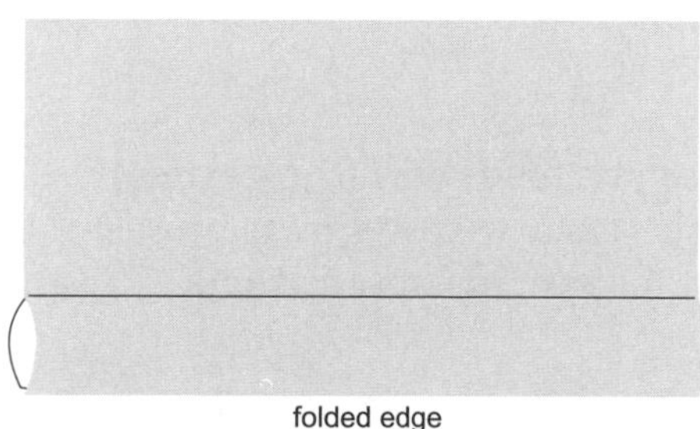

TUBULAR HEM

A tubular hem looks like a serged-on band but is really a folded-up hem, created using the serger. This hem can only be applied to straight hems.

Since the cover-stitch cannot pivot around a corner, it is necessary to hem the front and back of the skirt before sewing the side seams.

ELASTIC

Elastic may be used to finish a raw edge. It also will help keep any outside edge tight and close to the body, and hem leg openings snug on bathing suits and bodysuits.

Allowances for elastic are usually 1⁄16 inch more than the width of the elastic. If you have several layers of fabric wrapping over the elastic (not a good idea), you may want to allow a little more, about 1⁄32 inch extra per layer of fabric being wrapped.

ELASTIC FOR WAIST

Whenever using elastic that is larger than 1 inch, always remove 1 inch from the sample waist measurement. That may not seem like enough of a reduction, but if the elastic is too tight it will aggravate the wearer.

Measure the Judy—not the pattern (e.g., medium size waist = 26½″; then 26½″–1″ = 25½″).

The ends of the elastic must also be sewn together, so add seam allowances to the ends (½ inch each side).

Remember that different manufacturers use different seam allowances on the end, so always label the waist of the pattern with the finished (after sewn) elastic measurement (e.g., 1″ × 25½″ = finished elastic).

For lowered waist or hip huggers, measure the Judy at the lowered waist and reduce that measurement–never the measurement of the pattern.

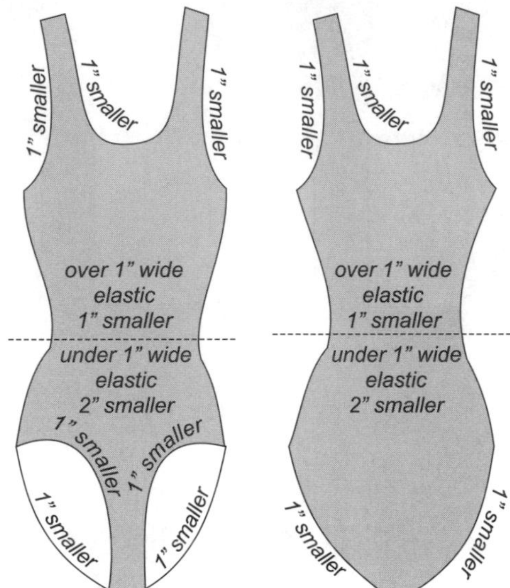

Elastic Reductions

Waist elastic	Less than 1″ wide, cut the elastic 2″ smaller than the waist. More than 1″ wide, cut the elastic 1″ smaller than the waist.	Cutout armholes	Cut the elastic ½″ smaller than the armhole measurement.
		Regular armholes	Cut the elastic the same as the armhole measurement.
Front neckline	Cut the elastic 1″ smaller than the front neckline measurement.	Front leg opening	Cut the elastic 1″ smaller than the front leg opening measurement.
Back neckline	Cut the elastic 1″ smaller than the back neckline measurement.	Back leg opening	Cut the elastic 1″ smaller than the back leg opening measurement.

Types of Elastic

Stretch garments need elastic that stretches with the garment. There are various types of elastic, each with its own properties and characteristics designed for specific applications.

INSERT ELASTIC

Insert elastic is intended to be covered by the fashion fabric, and can be inserted or stitched into a casing or a channel. Insert elastic can be either knitted or braided. It may be topstitched through the center of a waistband to prevent it from rolling and folding in half, or collapsing.

NON-ROLL ELASTIC

Non-roll, or roll-ban, elastic is insert elastic that is usually braided and resists rolling and folding over when stretched. It does not need to be stitched through the center.

SWIMWEAR ELASTIC

Swimwear elastic is specially treated to resist chlorine and salt water.

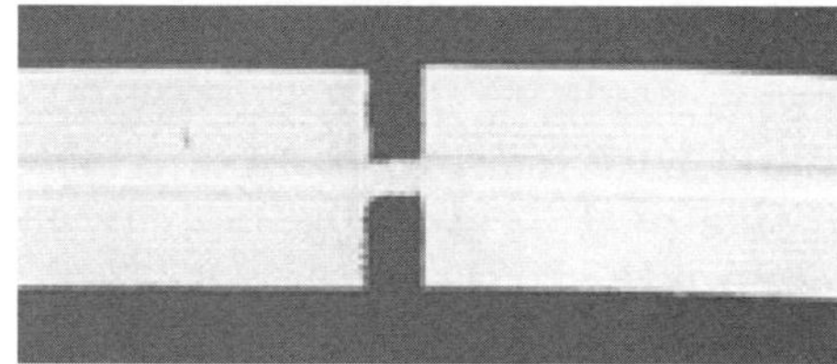

DRAWSTRING ELASTIC

This elastic has a braided cord knitted into the center of the elastic, which will expand to become a drawstring. Never pull the cord out, as it is impossible to get it back into the elastic.

FELT-BACKED ELASTIC

This elastic has a soft, plushy backing that is comfortable next to the skin.

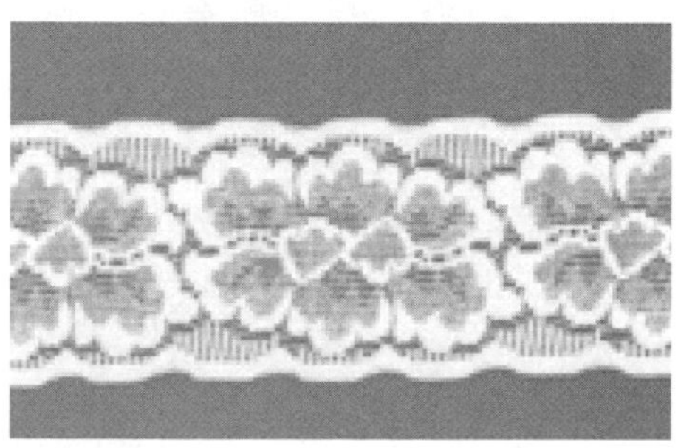

LACE ELASTIC

Lace elastic may be used to give a decorative finish.

RUBBER SWIMWEAR ELASTIC

Rubber swimwear elastic has a tendency to stick to the presser foot. Always place this elastic under the garment, against the feed dogs, so the teeth can grab the elastic and pull it through the serger.

LINGERIE ELASTIC

Basic lingerie elastic comes in a variety of widths and colors and is typically used as an insert elastic.

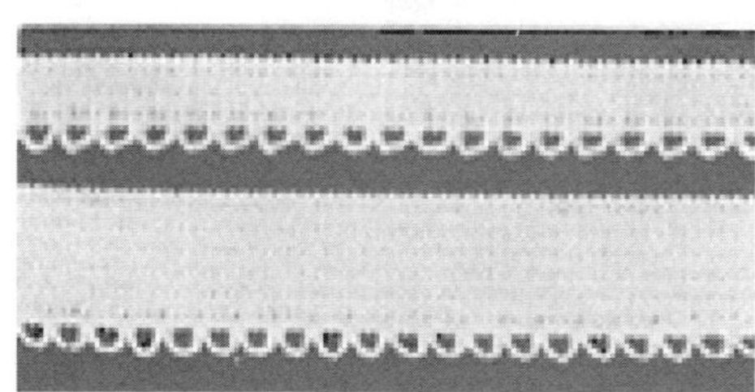

PICOT ELASTIC

Picot elastic has a small lacy finish on one edge, and is used to reduce panty lines.

It is used on lingerie and undergarments, because the small picot adds a decorative finish and reduces bulk, thereby reducing panty lines from showing through outerwear.

Sew this elastic to the right side of the garment, then flip and cover-stitch.

Elastic Used to Create Shirring and Gathering

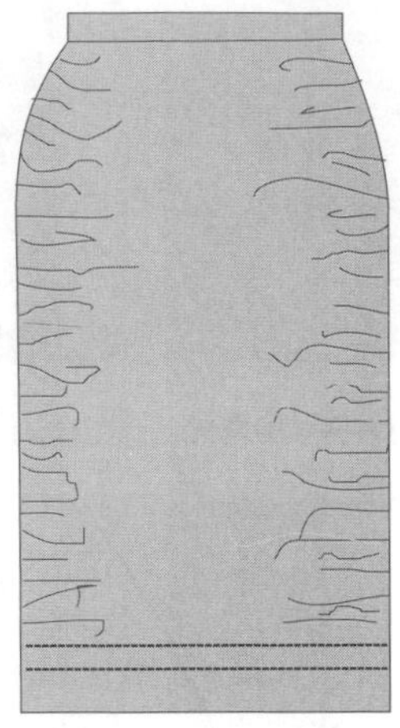

GATHERED SIDE SEAMS

Clear elastic may be used to gather or shirr any part of a garment. Remember to serge the seams before sewing the elastic with the straight stitch. If you try to attach the elastic while serging at the same time, it will be much too difficult.

A skirt, top, pant, or dress style may be created with gathering on both sides. Lengthen the original pattern, and simply stretch elastic in the seam allowance and sew with a straight stitch.

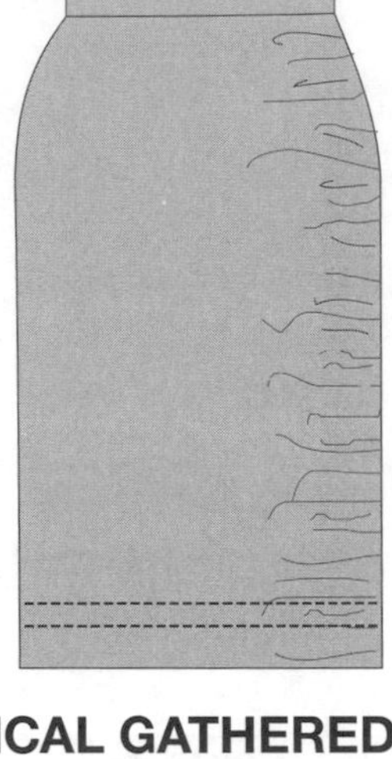

ASYMMETRICAL GATHERED SIDE SEAMS

Draft a skirt with a drawstring or gathering on only one side with a straight hem by slashing and spreading the pattern on one side.

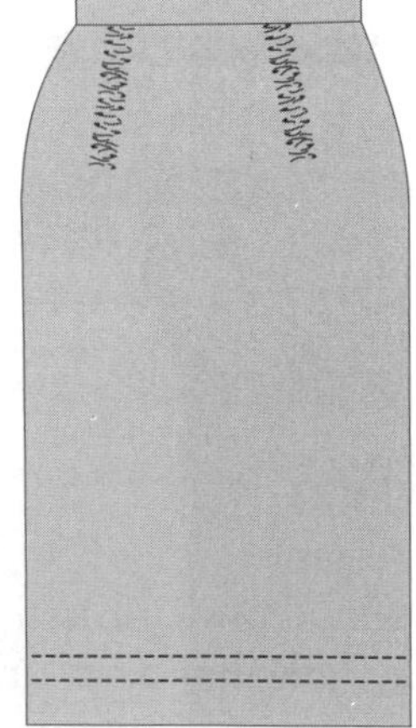

SKIRT WITH ELASTIC GATHERING DETAIL

Gathering details may be added as a detail, using the slash and spread technique.

Stretch and sew clear elastic to create the gathering detail.

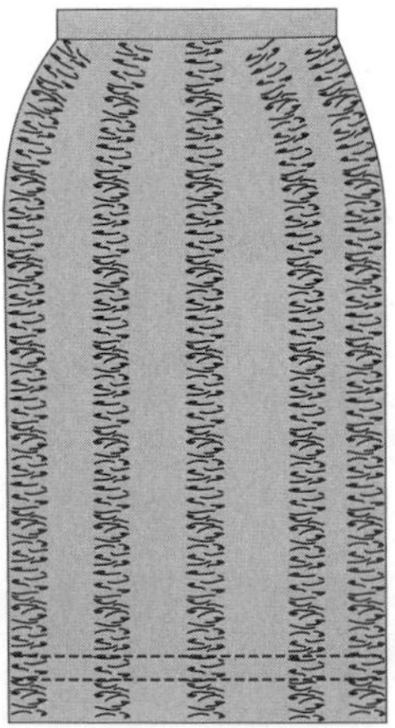

VERTICALLY GATHERED SKIRT

Gathering details may be added to the entire length of skirt, using the slash and spread technique.

Stretch clear elastic to create the gathering detail.

Binding

Binding may be used to finish necklines, armholes, leg openings, and the bottom of cycling tops but is rarely used on regular hems of tops and dresses, because it tends to be a bit stiff and heavy for a hem. It may be sewn manually with the cover-stitch machine, or automatically with a binding turner.

COLLARETTE

This attachment for a cover-stitch machine will attach a collar easily.

When used for necklines, one shoulder must be left open until after the collar is attached.

Collarette may be sewn automatically with a turner, manually by basting, or serging and then cover-stitching.

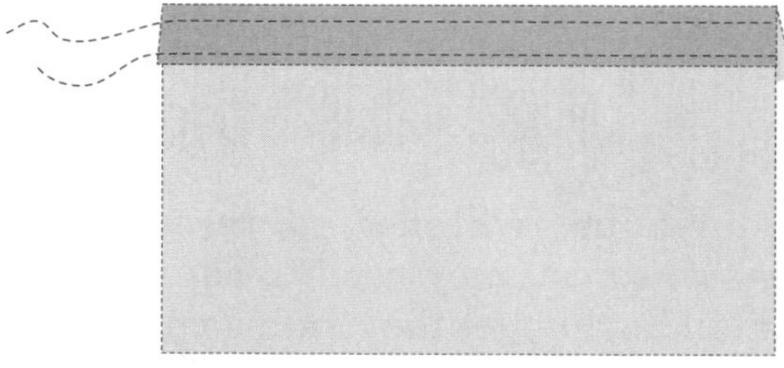

BINDING REDUCTIONS

The binding must be reduced to create a tight finish. Reduce the length of the binding by one-sixth of the original measurement.

$$\frac{F+B}{6} \times 5$$

Front armhole + back armhole = ? Then divide by 6 = ? Then multiply by 5 = ?

9″ + 9″ = 18 / 6 = 5 × 5 = 15″

Example:

If the original measurement is 6″, then the reduced binding should be 5″.

If the original measurement is 12″, then the reduced binding should be 10″.

If the original measurement is 18″, then the reduced binding should be 15″.

(front + back) divided by 6, then multiplied by 5

Even though the machine will apply the correct amount of binding, stretched at the right tension, it is necessary to label the pattern, armhole, neckline, etc., with the binding measurement. This will determine how much binding to cut, or order for production.

BINDING WITH THE COVER-STITCH MANUALLY

Sometimes a sample room may not have the turner that is needed for binding. In such a case it is still possible to create binding manually using the cover-stitch.

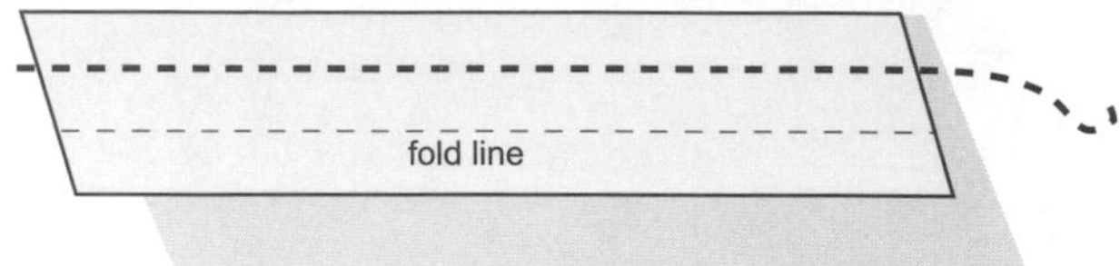

Baste the binding using a large stitch, on the straight-stitch machine, and don't apply any back-tacks. This is temporary basting that will be popped after the binding is complete.

Fold the binding over the raw edge, and cover-stitch in place.

Use the cover-stitch to finish the raw edge on the inside of the garment. When complete, remember to pop and snap all the basting stitches, or they will pop and snap when the customer tries on the garment. She then will think she has torn it and not purchase it.

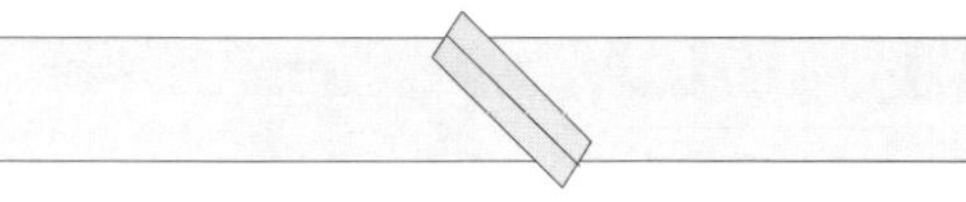

PIECING BINDING

Piece plain knits diagonally.

Pieced binding will not go through the turner easily, so you may need to cut multiple widths of binding, or get the binding cut.

BINDING WITH A TURNER

Note that the pattern should be labeled with the length of binding, so that the production manager will know how much binding to cut, or order.

Cut the binding 1⅛″ wide for a ⅜″ finished binding. Look for the cut and finished measurements engraved on the turner. The turner will be engraved with the cutting measurement as well as the finished (after sewn) measurement.

When binding with a turner, it is not necessary to calculate the reductions because the machine will automatically stretch the binding the correct amount. Remember that the binder cannot bind in a complete circle, so one shoulder must be left open when binding the neckline until after all the binding is complete. When binding armholes, leave the side seams open until after the binding is complete.

BANDING

Banding may also be used to pull portions of the garment closer and tighter to the body. Do not raise and take in an armhole of a tank top if banding is to be applied. The banding will tighten the armhole because it is smaller than the armhole and stretched to fit when sewing.

Make the finishing banding smaller than the opening by reducing the armhole measurement by 1/6 th of the total length measurement.

Banding must be created smaller than the edge to which it will be applied. This helps keep the banding flat and keep the garment edge tight.

Banding must be reduced to create a tight finish. Reduce the length or the band by 1/6 th of the original measurement.

measure armhole
measure neckline

Banding Reductions:

If the original measurement is 6″, then the reduced band should be 5″.

If the original measurement is 12″, then the reduced band should be 10″.

If the original measurement is 18″, then the reduced band should be 15″.

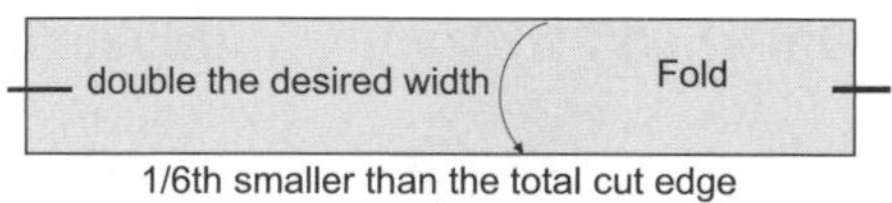

Draft the band double the desired width, because it will fold in half.

BANDING WITH A COLLARETTE

When banding with a banding attachment, called a collarette turner, it isn't necessary to calculate the reductions because the machine will automatically stretch the banding the correct amount. Remember that the collarette cannot sew in a complete circle, so one shoulder must be left open until after the entire collar is complete. When banding armholes, leave the side seams open until after the banding is complete.

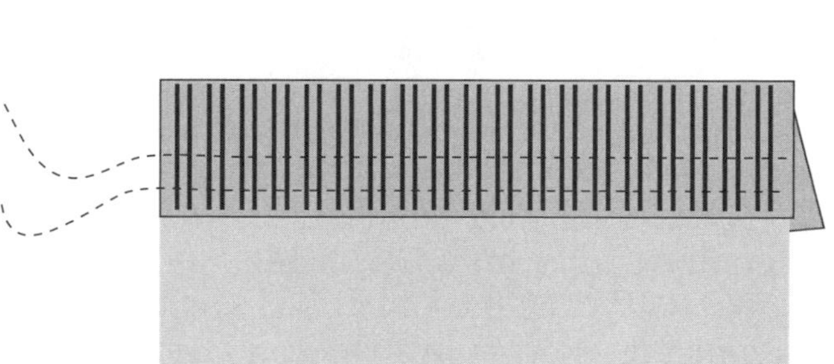

Ribbed Finishes

A serged-on cuff may be used on the wrist of a garment to pull the sleeve tighter and snugger to the body. The same principles may be used to create a serged-on rib waist on a sweatshirt, or a serged-on waist for pants and skirts. Make the ribbed cuff smaller than the customer's wrist, not simply smaller than the pattern, which might be oversized.

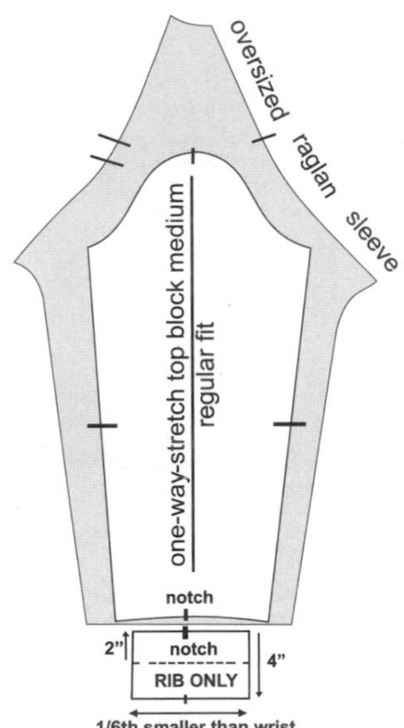

In order for the cuff to fit snugly on the wrist, it must be smaller and tighter than the wrist and stretched to fit.

The width of the cuff can be whatever the designer desires, but the length must be one-sixth smaller than the wrist. When using an oversized sloper, make the cuff smaller than the customer's wrist, not just smaller than the widened pattern.

If the ribbed cuffs will be finished at 2″ wide, and folded in half, then draft them 4″ wide.

To determine the length of the cuffs: Reduce the cuff measurement by one-sixth of the original (regular fit) sleeve.

We still want the cuffs to fit tightly on the same customer; her wrist did not get any thicker, just the sleeve.

The ribbed waist will be finished at 2″ wide and folded in half, making it 4″ wide.

To determine the length of the waist: Reduce it by one-sixth of the original (regular fit) waist, or hip.

We still want the waistband to fit tightly on the same customer; her waist did not get any thicker, just the top because she's wearing it with a looser fit.

The ribbed waist will be stretched to fit the oversized top, in order to pull it in snugly to the body.

Make sure to label the waistband as "rib only."

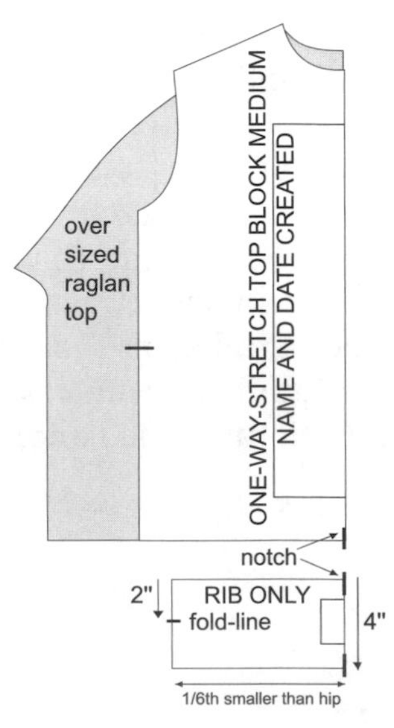

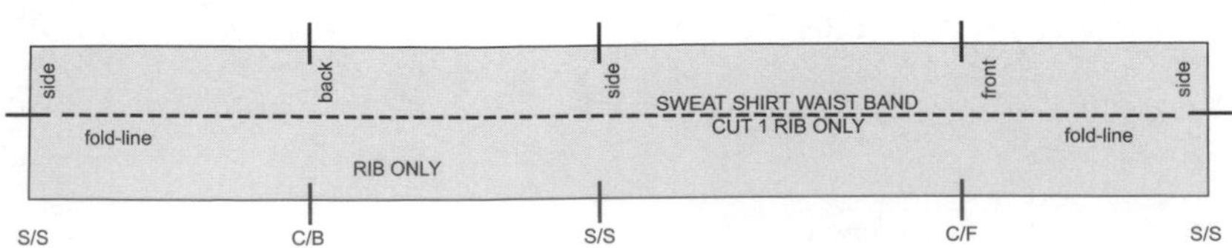

The waistband should only have one seam, at either of the side seams.

Notch the waistband at the center/front, center/back, and the side/seams.

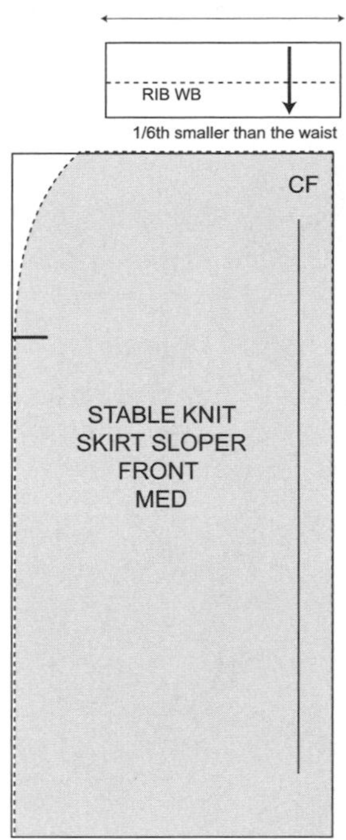

RIBBED WAISTBAND FOR SKIRTS OR PANTS

The same rib reduction principles may be used to create a serged-on rib waist on a sweatshirt, or a serged-on waist for pants and skirts.

Make the ribbed cuff smaller than the customer's wrist, not simply smaller than the block or pattern, which might be oversized.

Ease

Ease is the amount that a pattern is larger, or in the case of knit fabrics, smaller, than the body. Some garments must be made larger than the body to allow movement and comfort. Stretch garments are often cut smaller than the body measurements, since comfort and movement are provided through the inherent stretch of the fabric. There are different types of ease used when creating patterns:

Negative Ease Negative ease is the amount that the garment is made smaller than the body. Because knit fabrics stretch to accommodate body types, it is desirable to create the garments slightly smaller than the actual body. Negative ease can also refer to the amount of extra fabric removed, or reduced, to allow for an accurate fit. Many knits are made smaller than the actual body and use the inherent stretch to achieve the desired fit.

Garment Ease Garment ease is the amount of extra fabric required to allow for a comfortable fit. Knit garments do not require as much garment ease, since the inherent stretch of the fabric usually provides the necessary garment ease.

Design Ease Design ease is the amount of extra fabric required to create a particular design; for example, shirring, gathering, and draped effects. The designer may effect a fit that is oversized or much larger than the body by increasing the amount of design ease.

Ease at the Waist of Skirts and Pants

FITTED WAIST

For a fitted waist (only applicable if the fabric will stretch enough to be pulled on over the hips), simply use the sloper as drafted, and add seam allowances, hems, and other details required.

To check, place the crosswise fold of the fabric a few inches below the cut edge on the waist of your fabric, and place pins marking the amount of the waist of your sloper/patterns. Hold tight and check to see if this amount will stretch to the width of the hips. If the fabric does not stretch enough, use the unfitted waist; and if that is too large, use the semi-fitted waist.

UNFITTED WAIST

Use loosely fitted waist draft when the fabric does not stretch enough to allow the waist to be pulled on over the hips, such as with stable and moderate knits. For example, the waist of a stable-knit skirt is only 26½″, while the hip is 36½″; the fabric will not stretch enough to allow the skirt to be pulled on over the hips. 26½″ + 25% (6¾″) = 33¼″, which is not enough to pull on over 36½″ hips.

SEMI-FITTED WAIST

For a semi-fitted waist, find the middle of the fitted waist and the loose waist and draw a new hip, using the variform hip curve. Alternatively, increase the waist by any amount that will allow the waist to fit over the hips.

Creating Style Lines to Flatter the Wearer

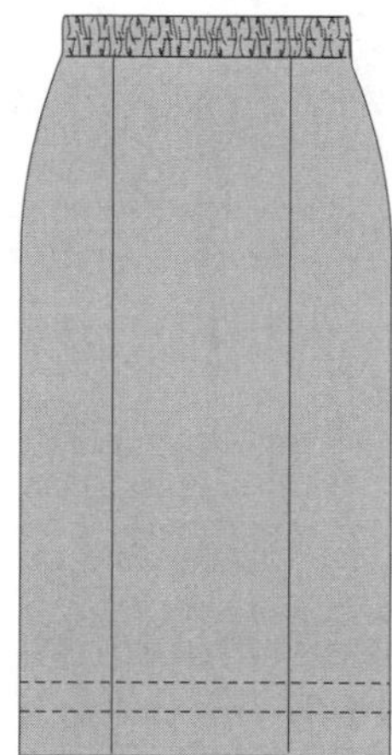

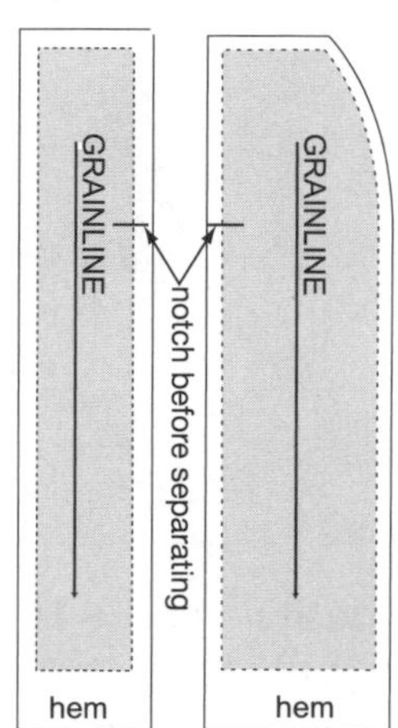

CREATING STYLE LINES

Style lines should be used to create specific designs. Style lines may be horizontal, across the garment, vertical, up and down the garment, or on the bias, i.e., diagonally through the garment.

Different designs may be created by rearranging the style lines. By using style lines for trumpet skirts, godets and pleats, fullness may be added to the hem.

Simply slash the draft and trace the two pieces separately. Notch and separate the two pieces, for construction. Add seam allowances, hem, grainlines, and labeling.

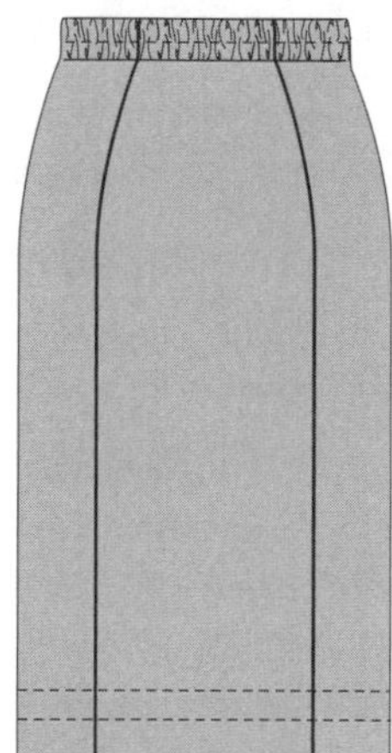

VERTICAL STYLE LINES

Finding the perfect style line takes time, practice, and experience. Different style line placement creates different design effects.

By making the seam line parallel to the side seam, you can create a sexier design that makes the wearer look thinner as the eye is forced to travel the length of the seam upward.

Also, by dividing the skirt visually into three sections, the eye will assume all three pieces are equal and judge the wearer thinner.

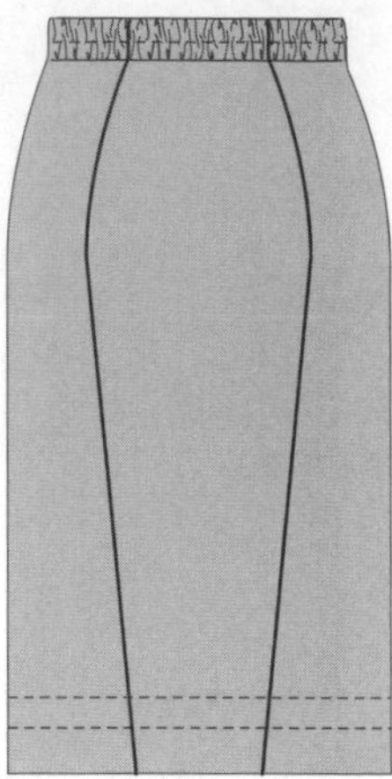

This style line will make the wearer's hips appear narrow, but will add weight to the thigh.

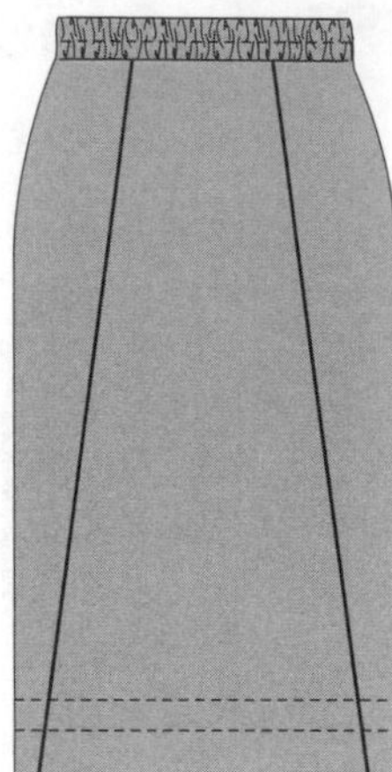

This style line will minimize the hips, but add visual weight to the thigh area.

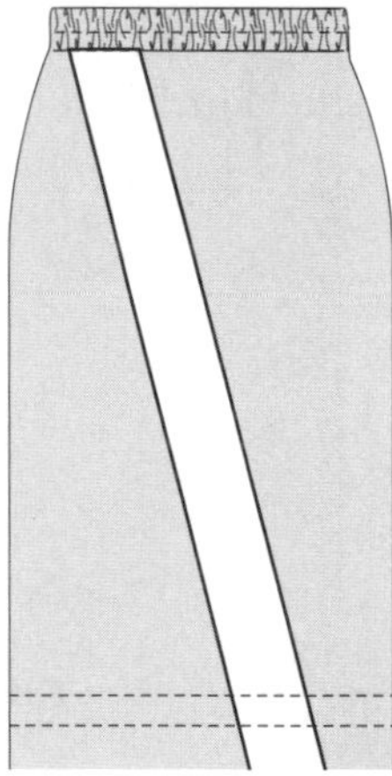

A contrast detail will draw the eye upward, and create a thinner look.

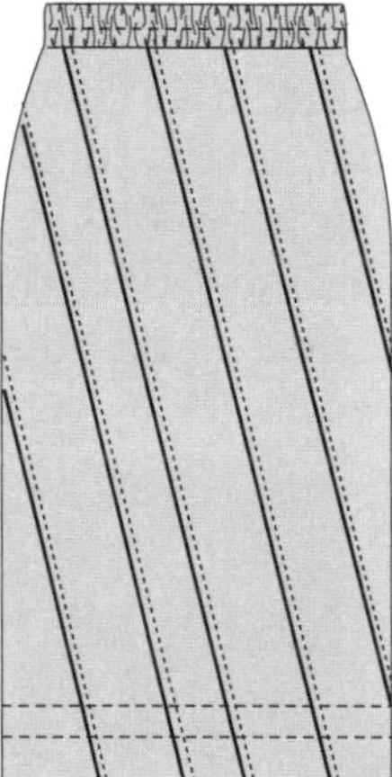

Topstitching, pin tucks, and diagonal lines will exaggerate this effect, to make the wearer look taller and slimmer.

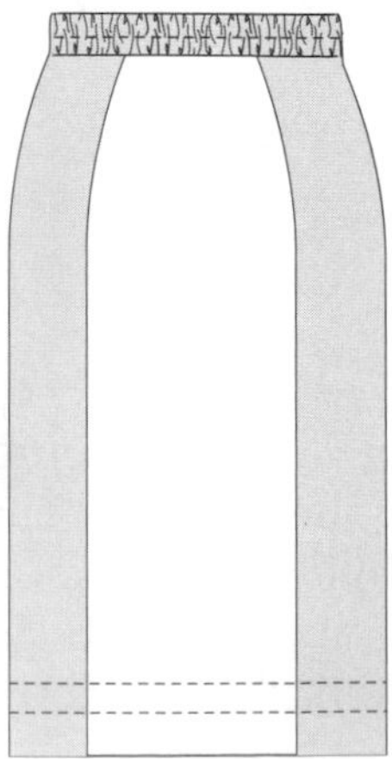

Placing a darker color on the side panels will make them almost invisible and create the illusion of a taller, thinner person.

HORIZONTAL STYLE LINES

STYLE #3-002 POINTED YOKE

Horizontal lines widen the figure, so often the style line is broken up or angled in some manner to help make the customer appear thinner.

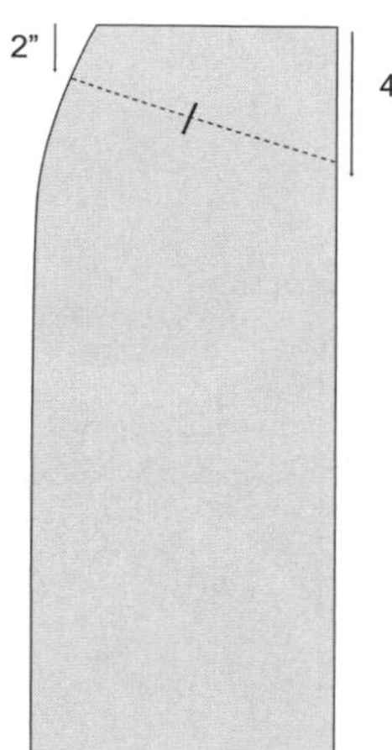

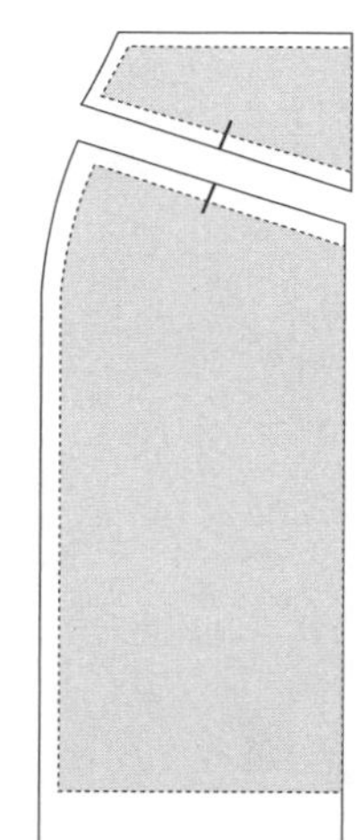

Draw in the yoke style line, illustrated at 2″ down at the side seam, and 4″ down the center fold, but it may be any measurement the designer requires.

Notch and trace out the separate pieces. Add the necessary seam allowances.

Asymmetrical style lines may also be created by drafting the pattern open.

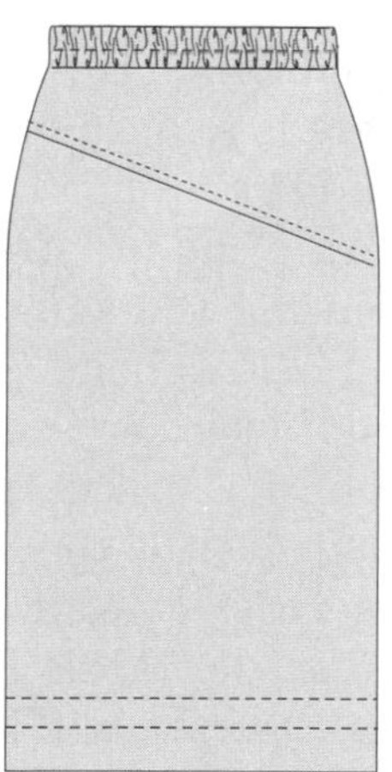

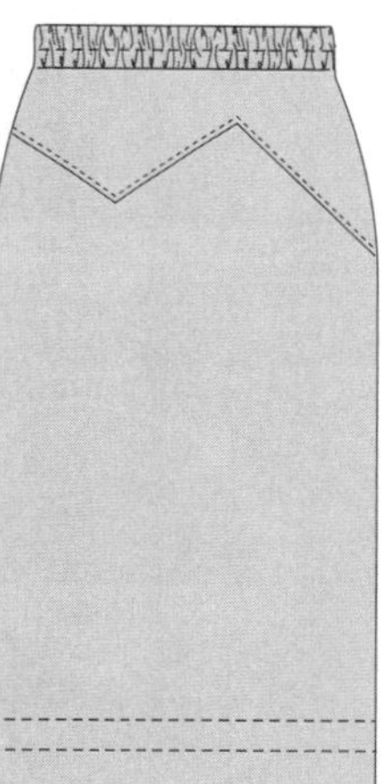

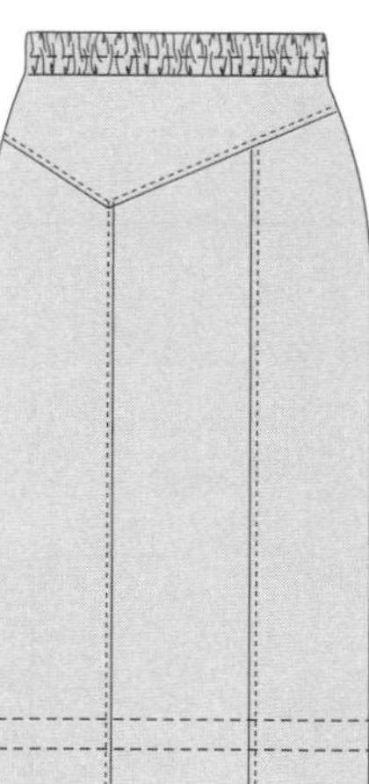

Variations of horizontal style lines.

Pattern Labeling

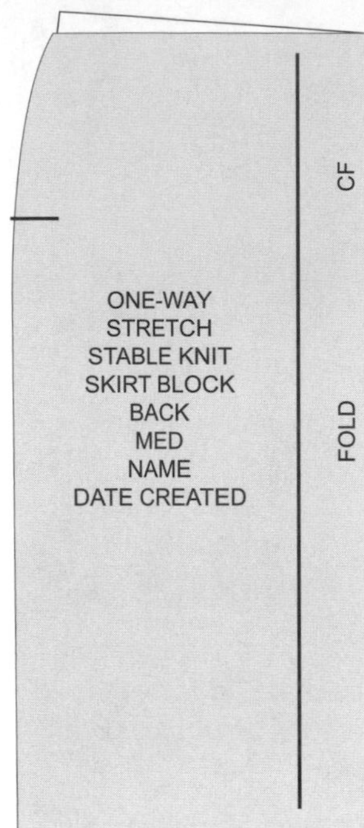

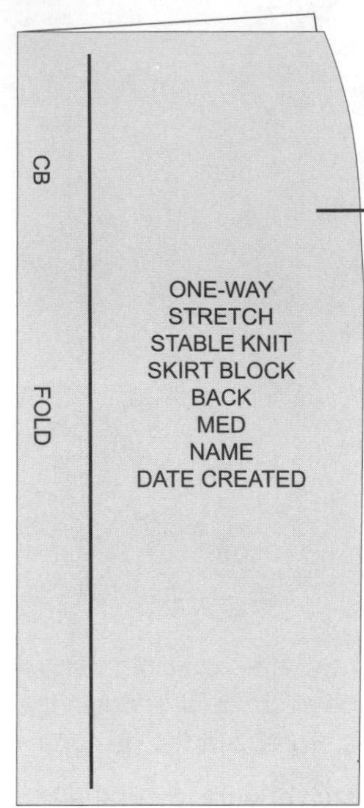

All final patterns should be on folded oak-tag, butterfly style, and should include:

- All necessary seam allowances.
- All necessary notches.
- The grainline, with arrows in one direction only because of the nap of knit fabrics.
- The type of stretch, or the stretch ratio to ensure that the patterns are only used for the particular stretch they were intended for.
- A style number if it is a pattern, or labeled as "BLOCK" or "SLOPER."
- The name of the particular pattern piece, such as "FRONT" or "BACK."
- The size—Small, Medium, Large, etc.
- The date created, to ensure that you are using the most current version of the pattern.
- The name of the patternmaker.

Grainlines

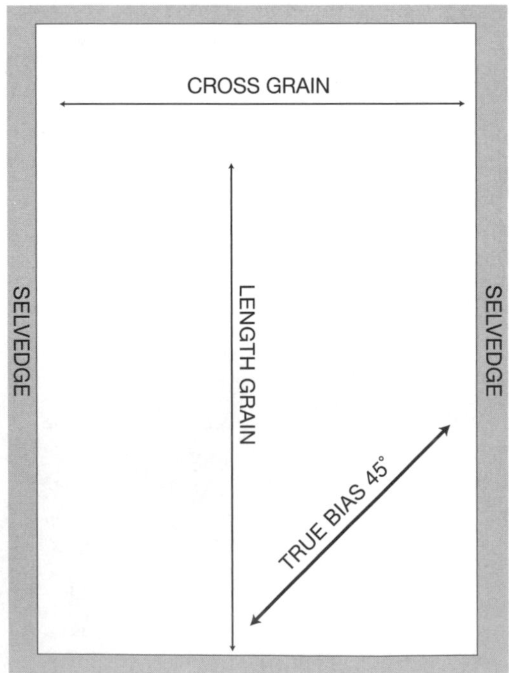

Each pattern should have a grainline indicated. If you notice on each of your pattern pieces, there is a large arrow. On a stretch pattern, the grainline should be in the middle of the piece, whenever possible. The grainline for stretch patterns should have both arrows pointing the same direction, indicating a "with nap" cutting instruction.

All fabrics have three grains: lengthwise, crosswise, and bias. The lengthwise grain runs parallel to the edges of the fabric, which are also called selvedges. It is the most stable direction of the fabric and has very little, if any, stretch. The crosswise grain runs across the fabric from selvedge to selvedge. The fabric store salesperson will have cut your fabric on the crosswise grain. The crosswise direction of knit fabrics has a lot of stretch. The bias grain is the direction formed if you fold a perfect square of fabric in half. It is the diagonal side of the triangle. This direction has very little stretch in knit fabrics.

It is extremely important that the arrow on your fabric be placed on the lengthwise grain of the fabric. This ensures that your garment will hang straight and will not twist around the body when being worn. When you lay out the pattern pieces, always measure from the arrow to the selvedge edge of the marker paper at both ends of the arrow to be sure that the piece is on the "straight of grain."

MAKING A MARKER FOR CUTTING

Once you have a final pattern and fabric ready, it is time to lay out the pattern pieces, make a marker, and cut out your garment. All garments, including first samples, should be cut out using a marker. A marker is a tracing of the pattern on special marking paper that has printed lines and/or numbers used for lining up the grainline.

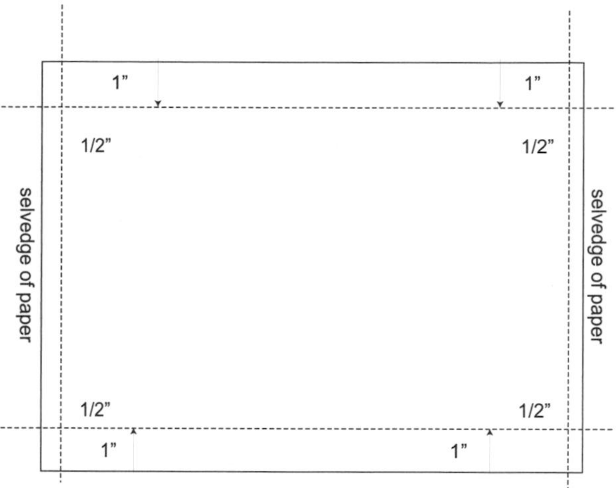

Preparing the marker paper:

Draw a line across the top edge of the marker 1″ below the cut edge. This is in case the fabric, which will be underneath, is not straight.

Draw a line ½″ in from the sides of the marker paper. This is so that the selvedge will not be in the final garment.

All markers waste 1″ of fabric at each end of the marker, and ½″ on each side.

Tracing the pattern pieces:

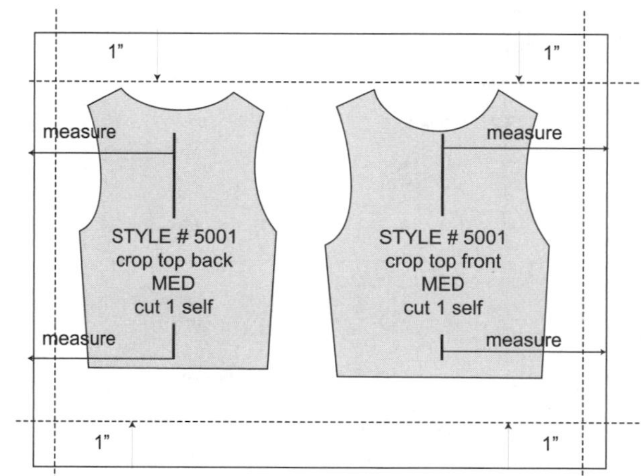

Trace all the pattern pieces (right side up), making sure to include every notch and any drill marks.

Measure each piece from the grainline to ensure that each pattern piece is perfectly on grain (parallel to the selvedge), or use the printed grid to ensure that every piece is parallel to the selvedge.

Circle every drill hole so the cutter will know whether it is really a drill mark and not just an incidental mark on the paper.

This is the incorrect way to trace out the pattern pieces. The garment will end up OFF-grain, and will twist around the body when worn.

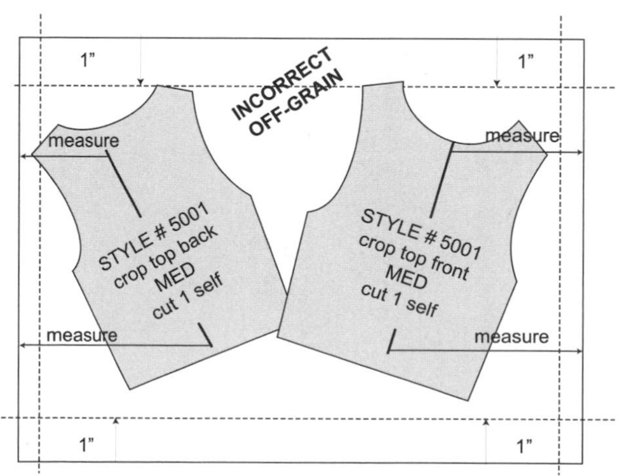

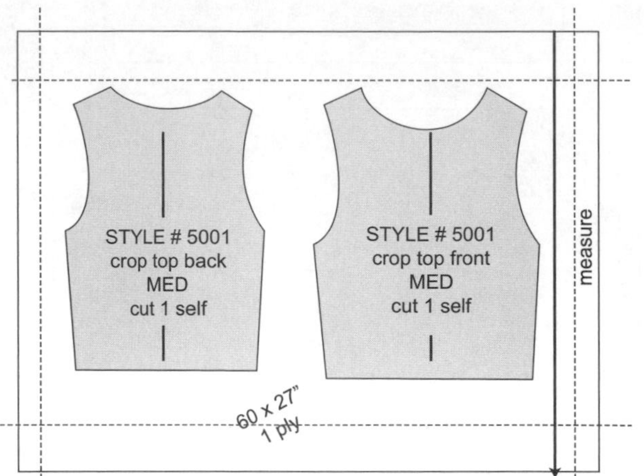

Measure the length and width of the marker paper so you know how much fabric you will need and how long to lay each ply of the fabric for each garment.

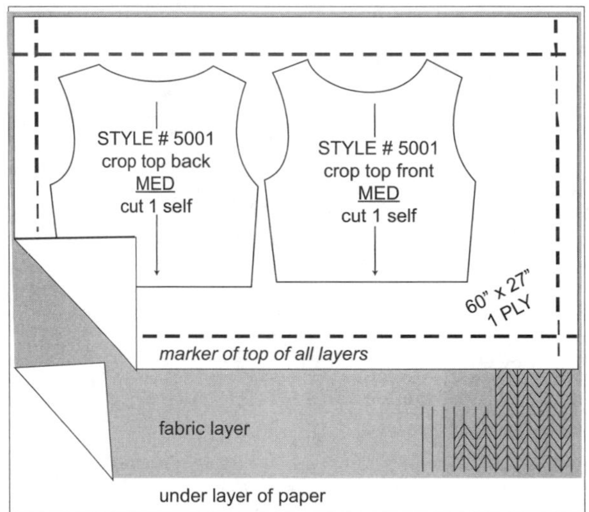

Place a length of paper underneath the fabric, on the cutting table, and then place the fabric, lining up all selvedges. Place the marker on top of all layers.

It is also necessary to place one layer of paper between each color if cutting more than one color, because the fibers and colors will migrate when using an industrial cutting knife.

DO NOT place the marker crookedly on the fabric. This will cause the garment to hang OFF-grain and twist on the body.

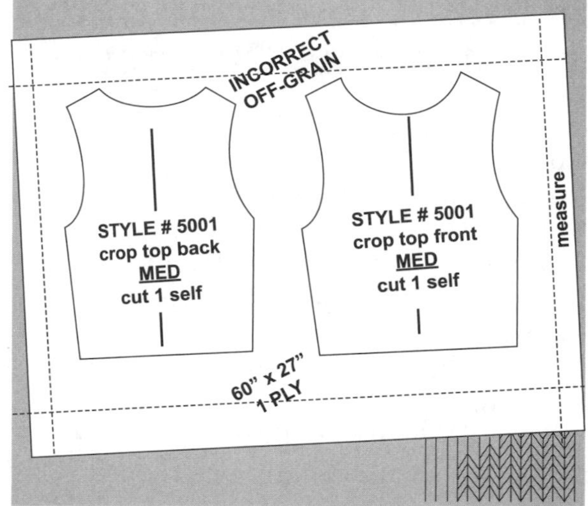

Pin the layer together and cut all layers, including paper, together.

Or if the lay is very thick, use weights to hold the marker to the fabric.

Or use a stapler in the discarded areas of the marker.

Or use marker spray glue to hold the marker down.

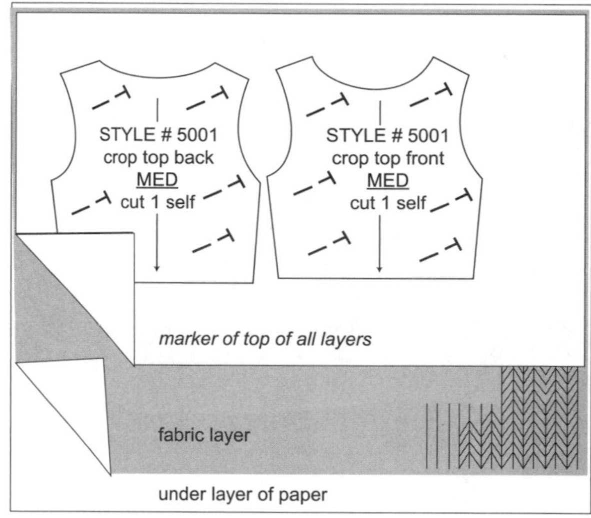

Keep the layers of paper with the bundles until ready to sew, at the machine, so that if you have forgotten a notch, the operator will be able to check the marker. The marker is the only way to differentiate between sizes, so the operator will sew the corresponding sizes of pieces together.

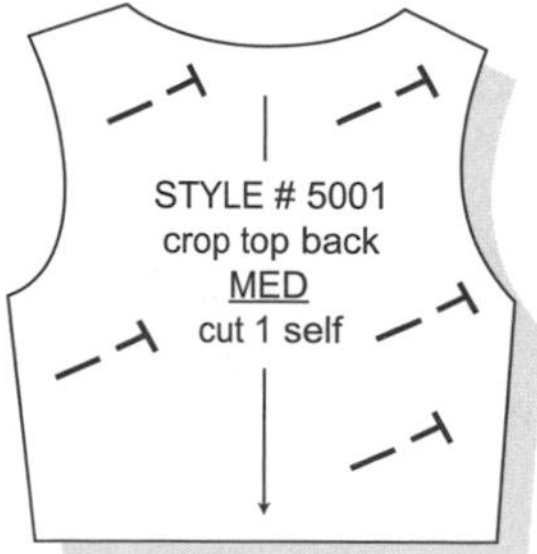

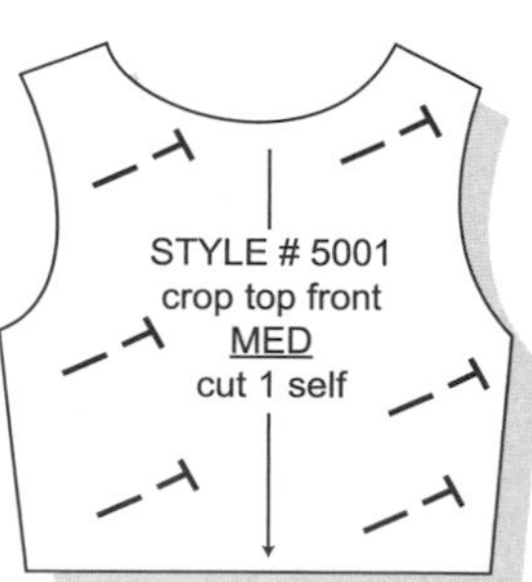

Test Your Knowledge of the Material in This Chapter

1. What is a sloper?
2. What is a pattern?
3. What are patterns used for?
4. What is the difference between woven patternmaking and stretch patternmaking?
5. Explain the technique of "matching of seams."
6. Explain what is meant by the term "trueing seams."
7. How much should binding be reduced?
8. How much should banding be reduced?
9. What is negative ease?
10. What is garment ease?
11. What is design ease?
12. What are the seam allowances on slopers?
13. When should you use one-way-stretch slopers?
14. Why should you exaggerate the size of a garment?
15. Which direction are measurements reduced for one-way-stretch?

CHAPTER 4

Slopers and Reductions

About This Chapter

This chapter illustrates the different measurements and stretch reductions used in the development of stretch slopers and blocks.

To begin, choose the stretch ratio that applies to your particular fabric, then choose the appropriate measurements from this chapter.

Follow the directions in the next chapters using measurements and reductions from this chapter.

Sloper Reductions

This section illustrates the different stretch reductions used in the development of stretch slopers and blocks.

A COMPLETE SET OF PROFESSIONAL SLOPERS INCLUDES:

	Stable knit	**Moderate knit**	**Stretchy**	**Super-stretch**	**Two- & Four-way stretch**	**Rib knit**
	0–25% stretch	**25–50% stretch**	**50–75% stretch**	**75–100% stretch**	**100% in both directions**	**over 100% stretch**
Reduction for stretch	0% smaller for across measurements	2% smaller for across measurements	3.5% smaller for across measurements	5% smaller for across measurements	10% smaller both directions	10% smaller for across measurements
Multiply your measurement by	*0	*.98	*.96.5	*.95	*.90	*.90 in both directions
Skirt	Yes	Yes	Yes	Yes	Same as super-stretch	Yes
Pant	Yes	Yes	Yes	Yes	Same as super-stretch	Yes
Top	Yes	Yes	Yes	Yes	Same as super-stretch	Yes
Dresses	Yes	Yes	Yes	Yes	Same as super-stretch	Yes
Oversized top	Yes	Yes	Yes	Yes	Yes	Yes
Catsuits	N/A	N/A	N/A	N/A	Yes	N/A
Leotard	N/A	N/A	N/A	N/A	Yes	N/A
Bikini	N/A	N/A	N/A	N/A	Yes	N/A

Slopers

A sloper or master block is a template of the desired fit, like a croquis; it never has any seam allowances or details. The experienced patternmaker will never start each draft from scratch but instead will trace the sloper then add details and seam allowances to create a pattern. By using a sloper with a perfected fit, the patternmaker must only make small adjustments to the finished pattern rather than making extensive fitting corrections to each pattern.

MISSES STABLE KNIT REDUCTIONS

Zero percent smaller in crosswise direction without any reductions in lengthwise direction.
Use these measurements when drafting slopers for fabrics that stretch from 0% to 25%.

		Multiply your across measurements by	Extra Small	Small	Medium	Large	Extra Large
			2	6	10	14	18
1	Bust	0 for stable knits	31 1/2	33 1/2	35 1/2	38 1/2	41 1/2
2	Waist	0 for stable knits	23 1/2	25 1/2	27 1/2	30 1/2	33 1/2
3	Hip	0 for stable knits	34 1/2	36 1/2	38 1/2	41 1/2	44 1/2
4	Crotch depth	No reduction	10	10 1/4	10 1/2	10 3/4	11
5	Waist to knee	No reduction	23	23 1/4	23 1/2	23 3/4	24
6	Waist to ankle	No reduction	38 1/2	39	39 1/2	40	40 1/2
7	Ankle	0 for stable knits	7 3/4	8	8 1/4	8 1/2	8 3/4
8	Knee	0 for stable knits	13 3/8	13 7/8	14 3/8	14 7/8	15 3/8
9	Front crotch	0 for stable knits	2 1/8	2 1/4	2 3/8	2 5/8	2 3/4
10	Back crotch	0 for stable knits	2 7/8	3	3 1/4	3 1/2	3 3/4
11	Crotch angle	0 for stable knits	1	1 1/8	1 1/4	1 1/4	1 3/8
12	Nape to waist	No reduction	15 5/8	16 1/8	16 5/8	17 1/8	17 5/8
13	Back neck	No reduction	2 3/8	2 1/2	2 1/2	2 1/2	2 5/8
14	Back neck rise	0 for stable knits	3/4	7/8	7/8	7/8	7/8
15	Shoulder length	No reduction	5 1/8	5 1/2	6	6 1/2	7
16	Across back	0 for stable knits	7	7 1/4	7 1/2	7 3/4	8
17	Sleeve length	No reduction	22 3/4	23	23 1/4	23 1/2	23 3/4
18	Shoulder pitch	0 for stable knits	1 3/8	1 1/2	1 1/2	1 1/2	1 5/8
19	Bicep	0 for stable knits	10 3/8	11 1/8	11 7/8	12 5/8	13 3/8
20	Wrist	0 for stable knits	5 1/2	6 1/4	7	7 3/4	8 1/2
21	Neck	0 for stable knits	14 1/2	14 3/4	15	15 1/4	15 1/2
22	Bust span	0 for stable knits	6 5/8	6 7/8	7	7 1/2	7 7/8
23	Bust level	No reduction	10	10 1/4	10 1/2	10 3/4	11

Reductions for Stretch

STRETCH RATIOS

Each knit fabric has a different stretch ratio, and each garment must be drafted accordingly. The chart below illustrates the reductions needed to draft slopers, and eventually patterns, for each fabric.

Stable knits	5″ stretches to 6¼″	18% to 25% stretch	Reduce by 0%	Use the measurements exactly as recorded
Moderate knits	5″ stretches to 7½″	26% to 50% stretch	Reduce by 2%	Multiply your across measurements by 0.98
Stretchy knits	5″ stretches to 8¾″	51% to 75% stretch	Reduce by 3%	Multiply your across measurements by 0.97
Super-stretch knits	5″ stretches to 10″	76% to 100% stretch	Reduce by 5%	Multiply your across measurements by 0.95
Rib knits	5″ stretches over 10″	Over 100% stretch	Reduce by 10%	Multiply your across measurements by 0.90
Four-way-stretch knits	5″ stretches to 10″ in both directions	100% stretch in both directions	Reduce by 5% across; Reduce by 10% lengthwise	Multiply your measurements by 0.90 in both directions

Any fabric that stretches less than 18% should be treated as a stretch woven and should have the ease removed.

MISSES MODERATE REDUCTIONS

Two percent smaller in crosswise direction without any reductions in lengthwise direction.
Use these measurements when drafting slopers for fabrics that stretch from 25% to 50%.
Multiply your across measurements by 0.98, 2% smaller, except for the shoulder measurement, because the final garment will have twill tape to stabilize the seam and prevent it from stretching.

		Multiply by	Extra Small	Small	Medium	Large	Extra Large
			2	6	10	14	18
1	Bust	× .98	31⅞	33¾	36¼	39¼	42⅝
2	Waist	× .98	24	26	28⅜	31⅜	34¾
3	Hip	× .98	34¾	36¾	39¼	42⅛	45⅝
4	Crotch depth	No reduction	10⅛	10⅜	10⅝	10⅞	11⅛
5	Waist to knee	No reduction	23⅛	23⅜	23⅝	23⅞	24⅛
6	Waist to ankle	No reduction	38¾	39¼	39¾	40¼	40¾
7	Ankle	× .98	7¾	8	8¼	8½	8¾
8	Knee	× .98	13⅜	13⅞	14⅜	14⅞	15⅜
9	Front crotch	× .98	2⅛	2¼	2½	2⅝	2⅞
10	Back crotch	× .98	2⅞	3	3¼	3½	3 6/8
11	Crotch angle	× .98	1	1⅛	1¼	1⅜	1⅜
12	Nape to waist	No reduction	15⅞	16⅜	16⅞	17⅜	17⅞
13	Back neck	No reduction	2⅜	2½	2½	2 4/8	2⅝
14	Back neck rise	× .98	¾	⅞	⅞	⅞	⅞
15	Shoulder length	No reduction	5¼	5¾	6¼	6¾	7¼
16	Across back	× .98	7	7⅓	7⅝	7⅞	8
17	Sleeve length	No reduction	22⅞	23⅛	23⅜	23⅝	23⅞
18	Shoulder pitch	× .98	1⅜	1½	1½	1½	1⅝
19	Bicep	× .98	10½	11¼	12	12¾	13½
20	Wrist	× .98	5¾	6½	7¼	8	8¾
21	Neck	× .98	14¼	14½	14¾	15	15¼
22	Bust span	× .98	6½	6¾	7⅛	7½	8
23	Bust level	No reduction	10	10⅙	10⅜	10⅝	11

MISSES STRETCHY KNIT REDUCTIONS

Three percent smaller in crosswise direction without any reductions in lengthwise direction.
Use these measurements when drafting slopers for fabrics that stretch from 50% to 75%.
Multiply your across measurements by 0.97, 3% smaller, except for the shoulder measurement, because the final garment will have twill tape to stabilize the seam and prevent it from stretching.

		Multiply by	Extra Small	Small	Medium	Large	Extra Large
			2	6	10	14	18
1	Bust	× .97	31 1/2	33 1/2	35 7/8	38 3/4	42 1/4
2	Waist	× .97	23 3/4	25 3/4	28 1/8	31	34 3/8
3	Hip	× .97	34 3/8	36 3/8	38 3/4	41 3/4	45 1/8
4	Crotch depth	No reduction	10 1/8	10 3/8	10 5/8	10 7/8	11 1/8
5	Waist to knee	No reduction	23 1/8	23 3/8	23 5/8	23 7/8	24 1/8
6	Waist to ankle	No reduction	38 3/4	39 1/4	39 3/4	40 1/4	40 3/4
7	Ankle	× .97	7 5/8	7 7/8	8 1/8	8 3/8	8 5/8
8	Knee	× .97	13 1/4	13 3/4	14 1/8	14 5/8	15 1/8
9	Front crotch	× .97	2 1/8	2 1/4	2 3/8	2 5/8	2 7/8
10	Back crotch	× .97	2 7/8	3	3 1/4	3 1/2	3 3/4
11	Crotch angle	× .97	1	1 1/8	1 1/4	1 1/4	1 3/8
12	Nape to waist	No reduction	15 7/8	16 3/8	16 7/8	17 3/8	17 7/8
13	Back neck	No reduction	2 3/8	2 1/2	2 1/2	2 1/2	2 5/8
14	Back neck rise	× .97	3/4	7/8	7/8	7/8	7/8
15	Shoulder length	No reduction	5 1/4	5 3/4	6 1/4	6 3/4	7 1/4
16	Across back	× .97	7	7 3/8	7 5/8	7 7/8	8
17	Sleeve length	No reduction	22 7/8	23 1/8	23 3/8	23 5/8	23 7/8
18	Shoulder pitch	× .97	1 3/8	1 1/2	1 1/2	1 1/2	1 5/8
19	Bicep	× .97	10 3/8	11 1/8	11 7/8	12 5/8	13 3/8
20	Wrist	× .97	5 3/4	6 3/8	7 1/7	7 7/8	8 5/8
21	Neck	× .97	14 1/8	14 3/8	14 5/8	14 7/8	15
22	Bust span	× .97	6 1/2	6 3/4	7	7 3/8	7 7/8
23	Bust level	No reduction	9 7/8	10	10 1/4	10 1/2	10 3/4

MISSES SUPER-STRETCH KNIT REDUCTIONS

Five percent smaller in crosswise direction without any reductions in lengthwise direction.
Use these measurements when drafting slopers for fabrics that stretch from 75% to 100%.
Multiply your across measurements by 0.95, 5% smaller, except for the shoulder measurement, because the final garment will have twill tape to stabilize the seam and prevent it from stretching.

		Multiply by	Extra Small	Small	Medium	Large	Extra Large
			2	6	10	14	18
1	Bust	× .95	30 7/8	32 3/4	35 1/8	38	41 3/8
2	Waist	× .95	23 2/8	25 1/8	27 1/2	30 3/8	33 3/4
3	Hip	× .95	33 6/8	35 5/8	38	40 7/8	44 1/8
4	Crotch depth	No reduction	10 1/8	10 3/8	10 5/8	10 7/8	11 1/8
5	Waist to knee	No reduction	23 1/8	23 3/8	23 5/8	23 7/8	24 1/8
6	Waist to ankle	No reduction	38 3/4	39 1/4	39 3/4	40 1/4	40 3/4
7	Ankle	× .95	7 1/2	7 3/4	8	8 1/4	8 3/8
8	Knee	× .95	13	13 3/8	13 7/8	14 3/8	14 7/8
9	Front crotch	× .95	2 1/8	2 1/4	2 3/8	2 1/2	2 3/4
10	Back crotch	× .95	2 3/4	3	3 1/8	3 3/8	3 5/8
11	Crotch angle	× .95	1	1 1/8	1 1/4	1 2/8	1 3/8
12	Nape to waist	No reduction	15 7/8	16 3/8	16 7/8	17 3/8	17 7/8
13	Back neck	No reduction	2 3/8	2 1/2	2 1/2	2 1/2	2 5/8
14	Back neck rise	× .95	3/4	7/8	7/8	7/8	7/8
15	Shoulder length	No reduction	5 1/4	5 3/4	6 1/4	6 3/4	7 1/4
16	Across back	× .95	7	7 3/8	7 5/8	7 7/8	8
17	Sleeve length	No reduction	22 7/8	23 1/8	23 3/8	23 5/8	23 7/8
18	Shoulder pitch	× .95	1 3/8	1 3/8	1 1/2	1 1/2	1 1/2
19	Bicep	× .95	10 1/4	11	11 5/8	12 3/8	13
20	Wrist	× .95	5 5/8	6 1/4	7	7 3/4	8 3/8
21	Neck	× .95	13 7/8	14	14 1/4	14 1/2	14 3/4
22	Bust span	× .95	6 3/8	6 5/8	6 7/8	7 1/4	7 5/8
23	Bust level	No reduction	9 5/8	9 7/8	10	10 1/3	10 4/7

MISSES RIB KNIT REDUCTIONS

Ten percent smaller in crosswise direction without any reductions in lengthwise direction.
Use these measurements when drafting slopers for fabrics that stretch 100% and over.
Multiply your across measurements by 0.90, 10% smaller, except for the shoulder measurement, because the final garment will have twill tape to stabilize the seam and prevent it from stretching.

		Multiply by	Extra Small	Small	Medium	Large	Extra Large
			2	6	10	14	18
1	Bust	× .90	29 1/4	31	33 1/4	36	39 1/8
2	Waist	× .90	22	23 7/8	26 1/8	28 3/4	32
3	Hip	× .90	32	33 3/4	36	38 3/4	41 7/8
4	Crotch depth	No reduction	10 1/8	10 3/8	10 5/8	10 7/8	11 1/8
5	Waist to knee	No reduction	23 1/8	23 3/8	23 5/8	23 7/8	24 1/8
6	Waist to ankle	No reduction	38 3/4	39 1/4	39 3/4	40 1/4	40 3/4
7	Ankle	× .90	7	7 3/8	7 1/2	7 3/4	8
8	Knee	× .90	12 1/4	12 3/4	13 1/8	13 5/8	14
9	Front crotch	× .90	2	2 1/8	2 1/4	2 3/8	2 5/8
10	Back crotch	× .90	2 5/8	2 7/8	3	3 1/4	3 1/2
11	Crotch angle	× .90	1	1	1 1/8	1 1/4	1 1/4
12	Nape to waist	No reduction	15 7/8	16 3/8	16 7/8	17 3/8	17 7/8
13	Back neck	No reduction	2 3/8	2 1/2	2 1/2	2 1/2	2 5/8
14	Back neck rise	× .90	3/4	7/8	7/8	7/8	7/8
15	Shoulder length	No reduction	5 1/4	5 3/4	6 1/4	6 3/4	7 1/4
16	Across back	× .90	7	7 3/8	7 5/8	7 7/8	8
17	Sleeve length	No reduction	22 7/8	23 1/8	23 3/8	23 5/8	23 7/8
18	Shoulder pitch	× .90	1 1/4	1 3/8	1 3/8	1 3/8	1 1/2
19	Bicep	× .90	9 5/8	10 3/8	11	11 3/4	12 3/8
20	Wrist	× .90	5 1/4	6	6 5/8	7 3/8	8
21	Neck	× .90	13 1/8	13 3/8	13 1/2	13 3/4	14
22	Bust span	× .90	6	6 1/4	6 1/2	6 7/8	7 1/4
23	Bust level	No reduction	9 1/8	9 3/8	9 5/8	9 3/4	10

MISSES FOUR-WAY-STRETCH KNIT REDUCTIONS

Ten percent smaller in crosswise direction and 10% smaller in the lengthwise direction.
Use these measurements when drafting slopers for fabrics that stretch 100% in both directions.
Multiply your measurements by 0.90, 10% smaller, in both directions, except for the shoulder measurement, because the final garment will have twill tape to stabilize the seam and prevent it from stretching. Note that four-way stretch has memory and will return to the original shape; therefore, twill tape is not necessary to stabilize the shoulders.

		Multiply by	Extra Small	Small	Medium	Large	Extra Large
			2	6	10	14	18
1	Bust	× .90	29 1/4	30 1/8	31	32	33 1/4
2	Waist	× .90	22	23	23 7/8	24 3/4	26 1/8
3	Hip	× .90	32	32 7/8	33 3/4	34 5/8	36
4	Crotch depth	× .90	9 1/8	9 1/4	9 3/8	9 1/2	9 5/8
5	Waist to knee	× .90	20 7/8	22	22 1/4	22 3/8	22 1/2
6	Waist to ankle	× .90	34 7/8	37	37 1/4	37 1/2	37 3/4
7	Ankle	× .90	7	7 1/4	7 3/8	7 3/8	7 1/2
8	Knee	× .90	12 1/4	12 1/2	12 3/4	13	13 1/8
9	Front crotch	× .90	2	2	2 1/8	2 1/8	2 1/4
10	Back crotch	× .90	3	3	3 1/8	3 1/4	3 1/3
11	Crotch angle	× .90	1	1	1	1	1 1/8
12	Nape to waist	× .90	14 1/4	15 3/8	15 1/2	15 3/4	16
13	Back neck	No reduction	2 3/8	2 1/2	2 1/2	2 1/2	2 1/2
14	Back neck rise	No reduction	6/8	7/8	7/8	7/8	7/8
15	Shoulder length	No reduction	5 1/4	5 1/2	5 3/4	6	6 1/4
16	Across back	No reduction	7	7 2/8	7 3/8	7 4/8	7 5/8
17	Sleeve length	No reduction	22 7/8	23	23 1/8	23 1/4	23 3/8
18	Shoulder pitch	No reduction	1 4/8	1 1/2	1 1/2	1 1/2	1 1/2
19	Bicep	× .90	9 5/8	10	10 3/8	10 6/8	11
20	Wrist	× .90	5 2/8	5 5/8	6	6 2/8	6 5/8
21	Neck	No reduction	14 5/8	14 6/8	14 7/8	15	15
22	Bust span	× .90	6	6 1/8	6 1/4	6 3/8	6 1/2
23	Bust level	× .90	9 1/8	9 3/4	9 7/8	10	10

JUNIOR SIZE REDUCTIONS

Zero percent smaller in crosswise direction without any reductions in lengthwise direction.
Use these measurements when drafting slopers for fabrics that stretch from 0% to 25%.
Use your measurements exactly as recorded without any reductions.

		Multiply your across measurements by	Extra Small	Small	Medium	Large	Extra Large
			2	6	10	14	18
1	Bust	0 for stable knits	32	34	36	39	42
2	Waist	0 for stable knits	25	27	29	32	35
3	Hip	0 for stable knits	35	37	39	42	45
4	Crotch depth	No reduction	10 1/4	10 1/2	10 3/4	11	11 1/4
5	Waist to knee	No reduction	22 7/8	23 1/8	23 3/8	23 5/8	23 7/8
6	Waist to ankle	No reduction	38 1/4	38 3/4	39 1/4	39 3/4	40 1/4
7	Ankle	0 for stable knits	7 7/8	8 3/8	8 7/8	9 3/8	9 7/8
8	Knee	0 for stable knits	13 5/8	14 1/8	14 5/8	15 1/8	15 5/8
9	Front crotch	0 for stable knits	2 1/4	2 3/8	2 1/2	2 5/8	2 7/8
10	Back crotch	0 for stable knits	3	3	3 1/4	3 1/2	3 3/4
11	Crotch angle	0 for stable knits	1	1 1/8	1 1/4	1 3/8	1 3/8
12	Nape to waist	No reduction	15 3/8	15 7/8	16 3/8	16 7/8	17 3/8
13	Back neck	No reduction	2 3/8	2 5/8	2 3/4	2 7/8	3 1/2
14	Back neck rise	0 for stable knits	3/4	7/8	1	1	1 1/8
15	Shoulder length	No reduction	4 7/8	5	5 3/8	5 5/8	5 7/8
16	Across back	0 for stable knits	7 1/4	7 5/8	8	8 3/8	8 6/8
17	Sleeve length	No reduction	23 3/8	23 5/8	23 7/8	24 1/8	24 3/8
18	Shoulder pitch	0 for stable knits	1 3/8	1 4/8	1 1/2	1 1/2	1 5/8
19	Bicep	0 for stable knits	10 3/4	11 1/2	12 1/4	13	13 3/4
20	Wrist	0 for stable knits	5 7/8	6 1/8	6 3/8	6 5/8	6 7/8
21	Neck	0 for stable knits	14 5/8	15 1/4	15 7/8	16 1/2	17
22	Bust span	0 for stable knits	6 5/8	6 7/8	7	7 3/8	7 5/8
23	Bust level	No reduction	9 7/8	10 3/8	10 7/8	11 3/8	11 7/8

JUNIOR SIZE MODERATE REDUCTIONS

Two percent smaller in crosswise direction without any reductions in lengthwise direction.
Use these measurements when drafting slopers for fabrics that stretch from 25% to 50%.
Multiply your across measurements by 0.98, 2% smaller, except for the shoulder measurement, because the final garment will have twill tape to stabilize the seam and prevent it from stretching.

		Multiply by	Extra Small	Small	Medium	Large	Extra Large
			2	6	10	14	18
1	Bust	× .98	31 3/8	33 3/8	35 1/4	38 1/4	41 1/8
2	Waist	× .98	24 1/2	26 1/2	28 3/8	31 3/8	34 1/4
3	Hip	× .98	34 1/4	36 1/4	38 1/4	41 1/8	44 1/8
4	Crotch depth	No reduction	10 1/4	10 1/2	10 3/4	11	11 1/4
5	Waist to knee	No reduction	22 7/8	23 1/8	23 3/8	23 5/8	23 7/8
6	Waist to ankle	No reduction	38 1/4	38 3/4	39 1/4	39 3/4	40 1/4
7	Ankle	× .98	7 3/4	8 1/4	8 3/4	9 1/4	9 5/8
8	Knee	× .98	13 3/8	13 7/8	14 3/8	14 7/8	15 3/8
9	Front crotch	× .98	2 1/8	2 1/4	2 3/8	2 5/8	2 3/4
10	Back crotch	× .98	2 7/8	3	3 1/8	3 3/8	3 5/8
11	Crotch angle	× .98	1	1 1/8	1 1/5	1 2/7	1 3/8
12	Nape to waist	No reduction	15 3/8	15 7/8	16 3/8	16 7/8	17 3/8
13	Back neck	No reduction	2 3/8	2 5/8	2 3/4	2 7/8	3 1/2
14	Back neck rise	× .98	3/4	7/8	1	1	1 1/8
15	Shoulder length	No reduction	4 7/8	5	5 3/8	5 5/8	5 7/8
16	Across back	× .98	7 1/4	7 5/8	8	8 3/8	8 6/8
17	Sleeve length	No reduction	23 3/8	23 5/8	23 7/8	24 1/8	24 3/8
18	Shoulder pitch	× .98	1 3/8	1 3/8	1 1/2	1 1/2	1 1/2
19	Bicep	× .98	10 1/2	11 1/4	12	12 3/4	13 1/2
20	Wrist	× .98	5 3/4	6	6 1/4	6 1/2	6 3/4
21	Neck	× .98	14 1/4	14 7/8	15 1/2	16 1/8	16 3/4
22	Bust span	× .98	6 3/7	6 5/8	7	7 1/8	7 3/8
23	Bust level	No reduction	9 5/8	10 1/8	10 5/8	11 1/8	11 5/8

JUNIOR SIZE STRETCHY KNIT REDUCTIONS

Three percent smaller in crosswise direction without any reductions in lengthwise direction.
Use these measurements when drafting slopers for fabrics that stretch from 50% to 75%.
Multiply your across measurements by 0.97, 3% smaller, except for the shoulder measurement, because the final garment will have twill tape to stabilize the seam and prevent it from stretching.

		Multiply by	Extra Small	Small	Medium	Large	Extra Large
			2	6	10	14	18
1	Bust	× .97	31	33	35	37 5/6	40 3/4
2	Waist	× .97	24 1/4	26 1/4	28 1/8	31	34
3	Hip	× .97	34	35 7/8	37 7/8	40 3/4	43 5/8
4	Crotch depth	No reduction	10 1/4	10 1/2	10 3/4	11	11 1/4
5	Waist to knee	No reduction	22 7/8	23 1/8	23 3/8	23 5/8	23 7/8
6	Waist to ankle	No reduction	38 1/4	38 3/4	39 1/4	39 3/4	40 1/4
7	Ankle	× .97	7 5/8	8 1/8	8 5/8	9	9 5/8
8	Knee	× .97	13 1/4	13 3/4	14 1/8	14 5/8	15 1/8
9	Front crotch	× .97	2 1/8	2 1/4	2 3/8	2 1/2	2 3/4
10	Back crotch	× .97	2 7/8	3	3 1/7	3 3/8	3 5/8
11	Crotch angle	× .97	1	1 1/8	1 1/5	1 2/7	1 3/8
12	Nape to waist	No reduction	15 3/8	15 7/8	16 3/8	16 7/8	17 3/8
13	Back neck	No reduction	2 3/8	2 5/8	2 3/4	2 7/8	3 1/2
14	Back neck rise	× .97	3/4	7/8	1	1	1 1/8
15	Shoulder length	No reduction	4 7/8	5	5 3/8	5 5/8	5 7/8
16	Across back	× .97	7 1/4	7 5/8	8	8 3/8	8 3/4
17	Sleeve length	No reduction	23 3/8	23 5/8	23 7/8	24 1/8	24 3/8
18	Shoulder pitch	× .97	1 1/3	1 3/8	1 1/2	1 1/2	1 1/2
19	Bicep	× .97	10 3/8	11 1/8	11 7/8	12 5/8	13 3/8
20	Wrist	× .97	5 3/4	6	6 1/8	6 3/8	6 5/8
21	Neck	× .97	14 1/8	14 3/4	15 3/8	16	16 1/2
22	Bust span	× .97	6 3/8	6 5/8	6 7/8	7	7 3/8
23	Bust level	No reduction	9 5/8	10	10 1/2	11	11 1/2

JUNIOR SUPER-STRETCH KNIT REDUCTIONS

Five percent smaller in crosswise direction without any reductions in lengthwise direction.
Use these measurements when drafting slopers for fabrics that stretch from 75% to 100%.
Multiply your across measurements by 0.95, 5% smaller, except for the shoulder measurement, because the final garment will have twill tape to stabilize the seam and prevent it from stretching.

		Multiply by	Extra Small	Small	Medium	Large	Extra Large
			2	6	10	14	18
1	Bust	× .95	30 3/8	32 1/4	34 1/4	37	39 7/8
2	Waist	× .95	23 3/4	25 5/8	27 1/2	30 3/8	33 1/4
3	Hip	× .95	33 1/4	35 1/8	37	39 7/8	42 3/4
4	Crotch depth	No reduction	10 1/4	10 1/2	10 3/4	11	11 1/4
5	Waist to knee	No reduction	22 7/8	23 1/8	23 3/8	23 5/8	23 7/8
6	Waist to ankle	No reduction	38 1/4	38 3/4	39 1/4	39 3/4	40 1/4
7	Ankle	× .95	7 1/2	8	8 3/8	9	9 3/8
8	Knee	× .95	13	13 3/8	13 7/8	14 3/8	14 7/8
9	Front crotch	× .95	2	2 1/4	2 3/8	2 1/2	2 5/8
10	Back crotch	× .95	2 3/4	3	3	3 3/8	3 5/8
11	Crotch angle	× .95	1	1	1 1/8	1 1/4	1 3/8
12	Nape to waist	No reduction	15 3/8	15 7/8	16 3/8	16 7/8	17 3/8
13	Back neck	No reduction	2 3/8	2 5/8	2 3/4	2 7/8	3 1/2
14	Back neck rise	× .95	3/4	7/8	1	1	1 1/8
15	Shoulder length	No reduction	4 7/8	5	5 3/8	5 5/8	5 7/8
16	Across back	× .95	7 1/4	7 5/8	8	8 3/8	8 3/4
17	Sleeve length	No reduction	23 3/8	23 5/8	23 7/8	24 1/8	24 3/8
18	Shoulder pitch	× .95	1 3/8	1 3/8	1 3/8	1 1/2	1 1/2
19	Bicep	× .95	10 1/4	11	11 5/8	12 3/8	13
20	Wrist	× .95	5 5/8	5 7/8	6	6 1/4	6 1/2
21	Neck	× .95	13 7/8	14 3/8	15	15 5/8	16 1/4
22	Bust span	× .95	6 1/4	6 1/2	6 3/4	7	7 1/8
23	Bust level	No reduction	9 3/8	9 7/8	10 3/8	10 3/4	11 1/4

JUNIOR RIB KNIT REDUCTIONS

Ten percent smaller in crosswise direction without any reductions in lengthwise direction.
Use these measurements when drafting slopers for fabrics that stretch 100% and over.
Multiply your across measurements by 0.90, 10% smaller, except for the shoulder measurement, because the final garment will have twill tape to stabilize the seam and prevent it from stretching.

		Multiply by	Extra Small	Small	Medium	Large	Extra Large
			2	6	10	14	18
1	Bust	× .90	28 3/4	30 5/8	32 3/8	35 1/8	37 3/4
2	Waist	× .90	22 1/2	24 1/4	26 1/8	28 3/4	31 1/2
3	Hip	× .90	31 1/2	33 1/4	35 1/8	37 3/4	40 1/2
4	Crotch depth	No reduction	10 1/4	10 1/2	10 3/4	11	11 1/4
5	Waist to knee	No reduction	22 7/8	23 1/8	23 3/8	23 5/8	23 7/8
6	Waist to ankle	No reduction	38 1/4	38 3/4	39 1/4	39 3/4	40 1/4
7	Ankle	× .90	7	7 1/2	8	8 1/2	8 7/8
8	Knee	× .90	12 1/4	12 3/4	13 1/8	13 5/8	14
9	Front crotch	× .90	2	2	2 1/4	2 3/8	2 1/2
10	Back crotch	× .90	2 5/8	2 3/4	3	3 1/8	3 3/8
11	Crotch angle	× .90	1	1	1	1 1/6	1 1/4
12	Nape to waist	No reduction	15 3/8	15 7/8	16 3/8	16 7/8	17 3/8
13	Back neck	No reduction	2 3/8	2 5/8	2 3/4	2 7/8	3 1/2
14	Back neck rise	× .90	3/4	7/8	1	1	1 1/6
15	Shoulder length	No reduction	4 7/8	5	5 3/8	5 5/8	5 7/8
16	Across back	× .90	7 1/4	7 5/8	8	8 1/3	8 3/4
17	Sleeve length	No reduction	23 3/8	23 5/8	23 7/8	24 1/8	24 3/8
18	Shoulder pitch	× .90	1 1/4	1 2/7	1 1/3	1 3/8	1 3/7
19	Bicep	× .90	9 5/8	10 3/8	11	11 3/4	12 3/8
20	Wrist	× .90	5 1/4	5 1/2	5 3/4	6	6 2/8
21	Neck	× .90	13 1/8	13 5/8	14 1/4	14 3/4	15 3/8
22	Bust span	× .90	6	6 1/8	6 3/8	6 5/8	6 3/4
23	Bust level	No reduction	8 7/8	9 3/8	9 3/4	10 1/4	10 3/4

JUNIOR FOUR-WAY-STRETCH KNIT REDUCTIONS

Ten percent smaller in crosswise direction and 10% smaller in the lengthwise direction.
Use these measurements when drafting slopers for fabrics that stretch 100% in both directions.
Multiply your measurements by 0.90, 10% smaller, in both directions, except for the shoulder measurement, because the final garment will have twill tape to stabilize the seam and prevent it from stretching.

		Multiply by	Extra Small	Small	Medium	Large	Extra Large
			2	6	10	14	18
1	Bust	× .90	28 3/4	29 3/4	30 5/8	31 1/2	32 3/8
2	Waist	× .90	22 1/2	23 3/8	24 1/4	25 1/4	26 1/8
3	Hip	× .90	31 1/2	32 3/8	33 1/4	34 1/4	35 1/8
4	Crotch depth	× .90	9 3/4	9 7/8	10	10	10 2/8
5	Waist to knee	× .90	21 3/4	21 7/8	22	22	22 1/4
6	Waist to ankle	× .90	36 3/8	36 5/8	36 7/8	37	37 1/4
7	Ankle	× .90	7	7 3/8	7 1/2	7 3/4	8
8	Knee	× .90	12 1/4	12 1/2	12 3/4	13	13 1/8
9	Front crotch	× .90	2	2	2	2 1/8	2 1/4
10	Back crotch	× .90	3	3	3	3 1/8	3 1/4
11	Crotch angle	× .90	1	1 1/8	1 1/8	1 1/4	1 1/4
12	Nape to waist	× .90	14 5/8	14 7/8	15	15 3/8	15 1/2
13	Back neck	No reduction	2 3/8	2 5/8	2 5/8	2 3/4	2 3/4
14	Back neck rise	No reduction	3/4	7/8	7/8	7/8	1
15	Shoulder length	No reduction	4 7/8	5	5	5 1/4	5 3/8
16	Across back	No reduction	7 1/4	7 3/8	7 5/8	7 3/4	8
17	Sleeve length	No reduction	23 3/8	23 1/2	23 5/8	23 3/4	23 7/8
18	Shoulder pitch	No reduction	1 3/8	1 3/8	1 1/2	1 1/2	1 1/2
19	Bicep	× .90	9 5/8	10	10 3/8	10 3/4	11
20	Wrist	× .90	5 1/4	5 3/8	5 1/2	5 5/8	5 3/4
21	Neck	No reduction	14 5/8	14 7/8	15 1/4	15 1/2	15 7/8
22	Bust span	× .90	6	6	6 1/8	6 1/4	6 3/8
23	Bust level	× .90	9 3/8	9 5/8	9 7/8	10	10 3/8

Petite Size Reductions

PETITE STABLE KNIT REDUCTIONS

Zero percent smaller in crosswise direction without any reductions in lengthwise direction.
Use these measurements when drafting slopers for fabrics that stretch from 0% to 25%.
Multiply your across measurements by 1, 0% smaller, except for the shoulder measurement, because the final garment will have twill tape to stabilize the seam and prevent it from stretching.

		Multiply by	Extra Small	Small	Medium	Large	Extra Large
			2	6	10	14	18
1	Bust	× 0	31 1/2	33 1/2	35 1/2	38 1/2	41 1/2
2	Waist	× 0	23 1/2	25 1/2	27 1/2	30 1/2	33 1/2
3	Hip	× 0	34 1/2	36 1/2	38 1/2	41 1/2	44 1/2
4	Crotch depth	No reduction	10 1/8	10 3/8	10 5/8	10 7/8	11 1/8
5	Waist to knee	No reduction	21 3/8	21 5/8	21 7/8	22 1/8	22 3/8
6	Waist to ankle	No reduction	36 5/8	37 1/8	37 5/8	38 1/8	38 5/8
7	Ankle	× 0	6 5/8	6 7/8	7 1/8	7 3/8	7 5/8
8	Knee	× 0	13 1/4	13 3/4	14 1/4	14 3/4	15 1/4
9	Front crotch	× 0	2 1/8	2 1/4	2 3/8	2 5/8	2 3/4
10	Back crotch	× 0	2 7/8	3	3 1/4	3 1/2	3 3/4
11	Crotch angle	× 0	1	1 1/8	1 1/4	1 2/8	1 3/8
12	Nape to waist	No reduction	14 3/4	15 1/4	15 3/4	16 1/4	16 3/4
13	Back neck	No reduction	2 1/4	2 3/8	2 3/8	2 3/8	2 1/2
14	Back neck rise	× 0	3/4	3/4	6/8	3/4	7/8
15	Shoulder length	No reduction	4 7/8	5	5 1/8	5 3/8	5 5/8
16	Across back	× 0	7 1/4	7 4/8	7 3/4	8	8 1/4
17	Sleeve length	No reduction	21 1/4	21 1/2	21 3/4	22	22 1/4
18	Shoulder pitch	× 0	1 3/8	1 3/8	1 3/8	1 1/2	1 1/2
19	Bicep	× 0	10 3/8	11 1/8	11 7/8	12 5/8	13 3/8
20	Wrist	× 0	5 3/4	6 1/2	7 1/4	8	8 3/4
21	Neck	× 0	13 3/4	14	14 1/4	14 1/2	14 3/4
22	Bust span	× 0	6 5/8	6 7/8	7	7 4/8	7 7/8
23	Bust level	No reduction	9 3/8	9 5/8	9 7/8	10 1/8	10 3/8

PETITE SIZE MODERATE KNIT REDUCTIONS

Two percent smaller in crosswise direction without any reductions in lengthwise direction.
Use these measurements when drafting slopers for fabrics that stretch from 25% to 50%.
Multiply your across measurements by 0.98, 2% smaller, except for the shoulder measurement, because the final garment will have twill tape to stabilize the seam and prevent it from stretching.

		Multiply by	Extra Small	Small	Medium	Large	Extra Large
			2	6	10	14	18
1	Bust	× .98	30 7/8	32 7/8	34 3/4	37 3/4	40 5/8
2	Waist	× .98	23	25	27	29 7/8	32 7/8
3	Hip	× .98	33 3/4	35 3/4	37 3/4	40 5/8	43 5/8
4	Crotch depth	No reduction	10 1/8	10 3/8	10 5/8	10 7/8	11 1/8
5	Waist to knee	No reduction	21 3/8	21 5/8	21 7/8	22 1/8	22 3/8
6	Waist to ankle	No reduction	36 5/8	37 1/8	37 5/8	38 1/8	38 5/8
7	Ankle	× .98	6 1/2	6 3/4	7	7 2/8	7 1/2
8	Knee	× .98	13	13 3/8	14	14 3/8	14 7/8
9	Front crotch	× .98	2 1/8	2 1/4	2 1/4	2 1/2	2 3/4
10	Back crotch	× .98	2 7/8	3	3 1/8	3 3/8	3 5/8
11	Crotch angle	× .98	1	1 1/8	1 1/8	1 1/4	1 3/8
12	Nape to waist	No reduction	14 3/4	15 1/4	15 3/4	16 1/4	16 3/4
13	Back neck	No reduction	2 1/4	2 3/8	2 3/8	2 3/8	2 1/2
14	Back neck rise	× .98	3/4	3/4	3/4	3/4	7/8
15	Shoulder length	No reduction	4 7/8	5	5 1/8	5 3/8	5 5/8
16	Across back	× .98	7 1/4	7 1/2	7 6/8	8	8 1/4
17	Sleeve length	No reduction	21 1/4	21 1/2	21 3/4	22	22 1/4
18	Shoulder pitch	× .98	1 3/8	1 3/8	1 3/8	1 1/2	1 1/2
19	Bicep	× .98	10 1/8	11	11 5/8	12 3/8	13 1/8
20	Wrist	× .98	5 5/8	6 3/8	7 1/8	7 7/8	8 5/8
21	Neck	× .98	13 1/2	13 3/4	14	14 1/4	14 1/2
22	Bust span	× .98	6 3/8	6 5/8	7	7 1/4	7 5/8
23	Bust level	No reduction	9 1/4	9 3/8	9 5/8	10	10 1/8

PETITE STRETCHY KNIT REDUCTIONS

Three percent smaller in crosswise direction without any reductions in lengthwise direction.
Use these measurements when drafting slopers for fabrics that stretch from 50% to 75%.
Multiply your across measurements by 0.97, 3% smaller, except for the shoulder measurement, because the final garment will have twill tape to stabilize the seam and prevent it from stretching.

		Multiply by	Extra Small	Small	Medium	Large	Extra Large
			2	6	10	14	18
1	Bust	× .97	30 1/2	32 1/2	34 3/8	37 3/8	40 1/4
2	Waist	× .97	22 3/4	24 3/4	26 5/8	29 5/8	32 1/2
3	Hip	× .97	33 1/2	35 3/8	37 3/8	40 1/4	43 1/8
4	Crotch depth	No reduction	10 1/8	10 3/8	10 5/8	10 7/8	11 1/8
5	Waist to knee	No reduction	21 3/8	21 5/8	21 7/8	22 1/8	22 3/8
6	Waist to ankle	No reduction	36 5/8	37 1/8	37 5/8	38 1/8	38 5/8
7	Ankle	× .97	6 3/8	6 5/8	7	7 1/8	7 3/8
8	Knee	× .97	12 3/4	13 1/4	13 3/4	14 1/4	14 3/4
9	Front crotch	× .97	2	2 1/4	2 3/8	2 1/2	2 3/4
10	Back crotch	× .97	2 3/4	3	3 1/8	3 3/8	3 5/8
11	Crotch angle	× .97	1	1 1/8	1 1/8	1 1/4	1 3/8
12	Nape to waist	No reduction	14 3/4	15 1/4	15 3/4	16 1/4	16 3/4
13	Back neck	No reduction	2 1/4	2 1/4	2 3/8	2 3/8	2 1/2
14	Back neck rise	× .97	3/4	3/4	3/4	3/4	7/8
15	Shoulder length	No reduction	4 7/8	5	5 1/8	5 3/8	5 5/8
16	Across back	× .97	7 1/4	7 4/8	7 3/4	8	8 1/4
17	Sleeve length	No reduction	21 1/4	21 1/2	21 3/4	22	22 1/4
18	Shoulder pitch	× .97	1 1/4	1 3/8	1 3/8	1 3/8	1 1/2
19	Bicep	× .97	10	10 3/4	11 1/2	12 1/4	13
20	Wrist	× .97	5 5/8	6 1/4	7	7 3/4	8 1/2
21	Neck	× .97	13 3/8	13 5/8	13 7/8	14	14 1/4
22	Bust span	× .97	6 3/8	6 5/8	6 7/8	7 1/4	7 5/8
23	Bust level	No reduction	9	9 3/8	9 5/8	9 7/8	10

PETITE SUPER-STRETCH KNIT REDUCTIONS

Five percent smaller in crosswise direction without any reductions in lengthwise direction.
Use these measurements when drafting slopers for fabrics that stretch from 75% to 100%.
Multiply your across measurements by 0.95, 5% smaller, except for the shoulder measurement, because the final garment will have twill tape to stabilize the seam and prevent it from stretching.

		Multiply by	Extra Small	Small	Medium	Large	Extra Large
			2	6	10	14	18
1	Bust	× .95	30	31 7/8	33 3/4	36 5/8	39 3/8
2	Waist	× .95	22 3/8	24 1/4	26 1/8	29	31 7/8
3	Hip	× .95	32 3/4	34 5/8	36 5/8	39 3/8	42 1/4
4	Crotch depth	No reduction	10 1/8	10 3/8	10 5/8	10 7/8	11 1/8
5	Waist to knee	No reduction	21 3/8	21 5/8	21 7/8	22 1/8	22 3/8
6	Waist to ankle	No reduction	36 5/8	37 1/8	37 5/8	38 1/8	38 5/8
7	Ankle	× .95	6 1/4	6 1/2	6 3/4	7	7 1/4
8	Knee	× .95	12 1/2	13	13 1/2	14	14 3/7
9	Front crotch	× .95	2	2 1/8	2 1/4	2 1/2	2 5/8
10	Back crotch	× .95	2 3/4	2 7/8	3	3 2/8	3 1/2
11	Crotch angle	× .95	1	1	1 1/8	1 1/4	1 3/8
12	Nape to waist	No reduction	14 3/4	15 1/4	15 3/4	16 1/4	16 3/4
13	Back neck	No reduction	2 1/4	2 3/8	2 3/8	2 3/8	2 1/2
14	Back neck rise	× .95	3/4	3/4	3/4	3/4	7/8
15	Shoulder length	No reduction	4 7/8	5	5 1/8	5 3/8	5 5/8
16	Across back	× .95	7 1/4	7 1/2	7 3/4	8	8 1/4
17	Sleeve length	No reduction	21 1/4	21 1/2	21 3/4	22	22 1/4
18	Shoulder pitch	× .95	1 1/4	1 3/8	1 3/8	1 3/8	1 1/2
19	Bicep	× .95	9 7/8	10 5/8	11 2/8	12	12 3/4
20	Wrist	× .95	5 1/2	6 1/8	6 7/8	7 5/8	8 3/8
21	Neck	× .95	13	13 1/4	13 1/2	13 3/4	14
22	Bust span	× .95	6 1/4	6 1/2	6 3/4	7	7 3/8
23	Bust level	No reduction	9	9 1/8	9 3/8	9 5/8	9 7/8

PETITE RIB KNIT REDUCTIONS

Ten percent smaller in crosswise direction without any reductions in lengthwise direction.
Use these measurements when drafting slopers for fabrics that stretch 100% and over.
Multiply your across measurements by 0.90, 10% smaller, except for the shoulder measurement, because the final garment will have twill tape to stabilize the seam and prevent it from stretching.

		Multiply by	Extra Small	Small	Medium	Large	Extra Large
			2	6	10	14	18
1	Bust	× .90	28 3/8	30 1/8	32	34 5/8	37 3/8
2	Waist	× .90	21 1/8	23	24 3/4	27 1/2	30 1/8
3	Hip	× .90	31	32 7/8	34 5/8	37 3/8	40
4	Crotch depth	No reduction	10 1/8	10 3/8	10 5/8	10 7/8	11 1/8
5	Waist to knee	No reduction	21 3/8	21 5/8	21 7/8	22 1/8	22 3/8
6	Waist to ankle	No reduction	36 5/8	37 1/8	37 5/8	38 1/8	38 5/8
7	Ankle	× .90	6	6 1/4	6 3/8	6 5/8	6 7/8
8	Knee	× .90	11 7/8	12 3/8	12 3/4	13 1/4	13 5/8
9	Front crotch	× .90	2	2	2 1/8	2 3/8	2 1/2
10	Back crotch	× .90	2 5/8	2 3/4	2 7/8	3 1/8	3 3/8
11	Crotch angle	× .90	1	1	1	1 1/6	1 1/4
12	Nape to waist	No reduction	14 3/4	15 1/4	15 3/4	16 1/4	16 3/4
13	Back neck	No reduction	2 1/4	2 3/8	2 3/8	2 3/8	2 1/2
14	Back neck rise	× .90	3/4	3/4	3/4	3/4	7/8
15	Shoulder length	No reduction	4 7/8	5	5 1/8	5 3/8	5 5/8
16	Across back	× .90	7 1/4	7 1/2	7 3/4	8	8 1/4
17	Sleeve length	No reduction	21 1/4	21 1/2	21 3/4	22	22 1/4
18	Shoulder pitch	× .90	1 1/4	1 1/4	1 1/4	1 3/8	1 3/8
19	Bicep	× .90	9 3/8	10	10 3/4	11 3/8	12
20	Wrist	× .90	5 1/8	5 7/8	6 1/2	7 1/4	7 7/8
21	Neck	× .90	12 3/8	12 5/8	12 7/8	13	13 1/4
22	Bust span	× .90	6	6 1/8	6 3/8	6 3/4	7
23	Bust level	No reduction	8 1/2	8 5/8	8 7/8	9 1/8	9 3/8

PETITE FOUR-WAY-STRETCH KNIT REDUCTIONS

Ten percent smaller in crosswise direction and 10% smaller in the lengthwise direction.
Use these measurements when drafting slopers for fabrics that stretch 100% in both directions.
Multiply your across measurements by 0.90, 10% smaller, except for the shoulder measurement, because the final garment will have twill tape to stabilize the seam and prevent it from stretching.

		Multiply by	Extra Small	Small	Medium	Large	Extra Large
			2	6	10	14	18
1	Bust	× .90	28 3/8	29 1/4	30 1/8	31	32
2	Waist	× .90	21 1/8	22	23	23 7/8	24 3/4
3	Hip	× .90	31	32	32 7/8	33 3/4	34 5/8
4	Crotch depth	× .90	9 5/8	9 3/4	9 7/8	10	10
5	Waist to knee	× .90	20 1/4	20 3/8	20 1/2	20 5/8	20 3/4
6	Waist to ankle	× .90	34 3/4	35	35 1/4	35 1/2	35 3/4
7	Ankle	× .90	6	6	6 1/4	6 1/4	6 3/8
8	Knee	× .90	11 7/8	12	12 3/8	12 1/2	12 3/4
9	Front crotch	× .90	2	2	2	2 1/8	2 1/8
10	Back crotch	× .90	2 7/8	3	3	3 1/8	3 1/4
11	Crotch angle	× .90	1	1 1/8	1 1/8	1 1/8	1 2/8
12	Nape to waist	× .90	14	14 1/4	14 1/2	14 3/4	15
13	Back neck	No reduction	2 1/4	2 3/8	2 3/8	2 3/8	2 3/8
14	Back neck rise	No reduction	3/4	3/4	3/4	3/4	3/4
15	Shoulder length	No reduction	4 7/8	5	5	5	5 1/8
16	Across back	No reduction	7 1/4	7 3/8	7 1/2	7 5/8	7 3/4
17	Sleeve length	No reduction	21 1/4	21 3/8	21 1/2	21 5/8	21 3/4
18	Shoulder pitch	No reduction	1 3/8	1 3/8	1 3/8	1 3/8	1 3/8
19	Bicep	× .90	9 3/8	9 5/8	10	10 3/8	10 6/8
20	Wrist	× .90	5 1/8	5 1/2	5 7/8	6 1/4	6 1/2
21	Neck	No reduction	13 3/4	13 7/8	14	14 1/8	14 1/4
22	Bust span	× .90	6	6	6 1/8	6 1/4	6 3/8
23	Bust level	× .90	9	9	9 1/8	9 1/4	9 3/8

Misses Tall Reductions

MISSES TALL STABLE KNIT REDUCTIONS

Zero percent smaller in crosswise direction without any reductions in lengthwise direction.
Use these measurements when drafting slopers for fabrics that stretch from 0% to 25%.
Multiply your across measurements by 0.95, 5% smaller, except for the shoulder measurement, because the final garment will have twill tape to stabilize the seam and prevent it from stretching.

		Multiply by	Extra Small	Small	Medium	Large	Extra Large
			2	6	10	14	18
1	Bust	× .95	32 1/2	34 1/2	36 1/2	39 1/2	42 1/2
2	Waist	× .95	24 1/2	26 1/2	28 1/2	31 1/2	34 1/2
3	Hip	× .95	35 1/2	37 1/2	39 1/2	42 1/2	45 1/2
4	Crotch depth	No reduction	11 1/4	11 1/2	11 3/4	12	12 1/4
5	Waist to knee	No reduction	24 5/8	24 7/8	25 1/8	25 3/8	25 5/8
6	Waist to ankle	No reduction	40 7/8	41 3/8	41 7/8	42 3/8	42 7/8
7	Ankle	× .95	7 7/8	8 1/8	8 3/8	8 5/8	8 7/8
8	Knee	× .95	13 5/8	14 1/8	14 5/8	15 1/8	15 5/8
9	Front crotch	× .95	2 1/4	2 3/8	2 1/2	2 5/8	2 7/8
10	Back crotch	× .95	3	3 1/8	3 1/4	3 1/2	3 3/4
11	Crotch angle	× .95	1 1/8	1 1/8	1 1/4	1 3/8	1 3/8
12	Nape to waist	No reduction	16 7/8	17 3/8	17 7/8	18 3/8	18 7/8
13	Back neck	No reduction	2 4/8	2 1/2	2 1/2	2 5/8	2 5/8
14	Back neck rise	× .95	7/8	7/8	7/8	7/8	7/8
15	Shoulder length	No reduction	4 7/8	5	5 1/8	5 3/8	5 5/8
16	Across back	× .95	7 1/2	7 3/4	8 1/8	8 1/2	8 7/8
17	Sleeve length	No reduction	24 3/8	24 5/8	24 7/8	25 1/8	25 3/8
18	Shoulder pitch	× .95	1 1/2	1 5/8	1 5/8	1 5/8	1 3/4
19	Bicep	× .95	10 5/8	11 3/8	12 1/8	12 7/8	13 5/8
20	Wrist	× .95	5 7/8	6 5/8	7 3/8	8 1/8	8 7/8
21	Neck	× .95	14 5/8	15	15 1/8	15 3/8	15 5/8
22	Bust span	× .95	6 3/4	7	7 1/4	7 5/8	8
23	Bust level	No reduction	10 3/4	11	11 1/4	11 1/2	11 3/4

MISSES TALL MODERATE KNIT REDUCTIONS

Two percent smaller in crosswise direction without any reductions in lengthwise direction.
Use these measurements when drafting slopers for fabrics that stretch from 25% to 50%.
Multiply your across measurements by 0.98, 2% smaller, except for the shoulder measurement, because the final garment will have twill tape to stabilize the seam and prevent it from stretching.

		Multiply by	Extra Small	Small	Medium	Large	Extra Large
			2	6	10	14	18
1	Bust	× .98	31 7/8	33 3/4	35 3/4	38 3/4	41 5/8
2	Waist	× .98	24	26	28	30 7/8	33 3/4
3	Hip	× .98	34 3/4	36 3/4	38 3/4	41 5/8	44 5/8
4	Crotch depth	No reduction	11 1/4	11 1/2	11 3/4	12	12 1/4
5	Waist to knee	No reduction	24 5/8	24 7/8	25 1/8	25 3/8	25 5/8
6	Waist to ankle	No reduction	40 7/8	41 3/8	41 7/8	42 3/8	42 7/8
7	Ankle	× .98	7 3/4	8	8 1/4	8 1/2	8 3/4
8	Knee	× .98	13 3/8	13 7/8	14 3/8	14 7/8	15 3/8
9	Front crotch	× .98	2 1/8	2 1/4	2 3/8	2 5/8	2 3/4
10	Back crotch	× .98	2 7/8	3	3 1/4	3 1/2	3 3/4
11	Crotch angle	× .98	1	1 1/8	1 1/4	1 1/4	1 3/8
12	Nape to waist	No reduction	16 7/8	17 3/8	17 7/8	18 3/8	18 7/8
13	Back neck	No reduction	2 1/2	2 1/2	2 1/2	2 5/8	2 5/8
14	Back neck rise	× .98	7/8	7/8	7/8	7/8	7/8
15	Shoulder length	No reduction	4 7/8	5	5 1/8	5 3/8	5 5/8
16	Across back	× .98	7 1/2	7 3/4	8 1/8	8 1/2	8 7/8
17	Sleeve length	No reduction	24 3/8	24 5/8	24 7/8	25 1/8	25 3/8
18	Shoulder pitch	× .98	1 1/2	1 1/2	1 5/8	1 5/8	1 5/8
19	Bicep	× .98	10 3/8	11 1/8	11 8/9	12 5/8	13 3/8
20	Wrist	× .98	5 3/4	6 1/2	7 1/4	8	8 3/4
21	Neck	× .98	14 3/8	14 5/8	14 7/8	15 1/8	15 3/8
22	Bust span	× .98	6 1/2	6 3/4	7	7 3/8	7 3/4
23	Bust level	No reduction	10 1/2	10 3/4	11	11 1/4	11 1/2

MISSES TALL STRETCHY KNIT REDUCTIONS

Three percent smaller in crosswise direction without any reductions in lengthwise direction.
Use these measurements when drafting slopers for fabrics that stretch from 50% to 75%.
Multiply your across measurements by 0.97, 3% smaller, except for the shoulder measurement, because the final garment will have twill tape to stabilize the seam and prevent it from stretching.

		Multiply by	Extra Small	Small	Medium	Large	Extra Large
			2	6	10	14	18
1	Bust	× .97	31½	33½	35⅜	38⅜	41¼
2	Waist	× .97	23¾	25¾	27⅝	30½	33½
3	Hip	× .97	34⅜	36⅜	38⅜	41¼	44⅛
4	Crotch depth	No reduction	11¼	11½	11¾	12	12¼
5	Waist to knee	No reduction	24⅝	24⅞	25⅛	25⅜	25⅝
6	Waist to ankle	No reduction	40⅞	41⅜	41⅞	42⅜	42⅞
7	Ankle	× .97	7⅝	7⅞	8⅛	8⅜	8⅝
8	Knee	× .97	13¼	13¾	14⅛	14⅝	15⅛
9	Front crotch	× .97	2⅛	2¼	2⅜	2⅝	2¾
10	Back crotch	× .97	2⅞	3	3¼	3⅜	3⅝
11	Crotch angle	× .97	1	1⅛	1¼	1¼	1⅜
12	Nape to waist	No reduction	16⅞	17⅜	17⅞	18⅜	18⅞
13	Back neck	No reduction	2½	2½	2½	2⅝	2⅝
14	Back neck rise	× .97	⅞	⅞	⅞	⅞	⅞
15	Shoulder length	No reduction	4⅞	5	5⅛	5⅜	5⅝
16	Across back	× .97	7½	7¾	8⅛	8½	8⅞
17	Sleeve length	No reduction	24⅜	24⅝	24⅞	25⅛	25⅜
18	Shoulder pitch	× .97	1½	1½	1⅝	1⅝	1⅝
19	Bicep	× .97	10¼	11	11¾	12½	13¼
20	Wrist	× .97	5¾	6⅜	7⅛	7⅞	8⅝
21	Neck	× .97	14¼	14½	14¾	15	15¼
22	Bust span	× .97	6½	6¾	7	7⅜	7¾
23	Bust level	No reduction	10⅜	10⅝	10⅞	11	11⅜

MISSES TALL SUPER-STRETCH KNIT REDUCTIONS

Five percent smaller in crosswise direction without any reductions in lengthwise direction.
Use these measurements when drafting slopers for fabrics that stretch from 75% to 100%.
Multiply your across measurements by 0.95, 5% smaller, except for the shoulder measurement, because the final garment will have twill tape to stabilize the seam and prevent it from stretching.

		Multiply by	Extra Small	Small	Medium	Large	Extra Large
			2	6	10	14	18
1	Bust	× .95	30⅞	32¾	34⅝	37½	40⅜
2	Waist	× .95	23¼	25⅛	27	30	32¾
3	Hip	× .95	33¾	35⅝	37½	40⅜	43¼
4	Crotch depth	No reduction	11¼	11½	11¾	12	12¼
5	Waist to knee	No reduction	24⅝	24⅞	25⅛	25⅜	25⅝
6	Waist to ankle	No reduction	40⅞	41⅜	41⅞	42⅜	42⅞
7	Ankle	× .95	7½	7¾	8	8¼	8⅜
8	Knee	× .95	13	13⅜	13⅞	14⅜	14⅞
9	Front crotch	× .95	2⅛	2¼	2⅜	2½	2¾
10	Back crotch	× .95	2¾	3	3⅛	3⅜	3⅝
11	Crotch angle	× .95	1	1⅛	1⅛	1¼	1⅜
12	Nape to waist	No reduction	16⅞	17⅜	17⅞	18⅜	18⅞
13	Back neck	No reduction	2½	2½	2½	2⅝	2⅝
14	Back neck rise	× .95	⅞	⅞	⅞	⅞	⅞
15	Shoulder length	No reduction	4⅞	5	5⅛	5⅜	5⅝
16	Across back	× .95	7½	7¾	8⅛	8½	8⅞
17	Sleeve length	No reduction	24⅜	24⅝	24⅞	25⅛	25⅜
18	Shoulder pitch	× .95	1½	1½	1½	1⅗	1⅝
19	Bicep	× .95	10	10¾	11½	12¼	13
20	Wrist	× .95	5⅝	6¼	7	7¾	8⅜
21	Neck	× .95	14	14⅛	14⅜	14⅝	14⅞
22	Bust span	× .95	6⅜	6⅝	6⅞	7⅛	7½
23	Bust level	No reduction	10⅛	10⅜	10⅝	10⅞	11⅛

MISSES TALL RIB KNIT REDUCTIONS

Ten percent smaller in crosswise direction without any reductions in lengthwise direction.
Use these measurements when drafting slopers for fabrics that stretch 100% and over.
Multiply your across measurements by 0.90, 10% smaller, except for the shoulder measurement, because the final garment will have twill tape to stabilize the seam and prevent it from stretching.

		Multiply by	Extra Small	Small	Medium	Large	Extra Large
			2	6	10	14	18
1	Bust	× .90	29 1/4	31	32 7/8	35 1/2	38 1/4
2	Waist	× .90	22	23 7/8	25 5/8	28 1/3	31
3	Hip	× .90	32	33 3/4	35 1/2	38 1/4	41
4	Crotch depth	No reduction	11 1/4	11 1/2	11 3/4	12	12 1/4
5	Waist to knee	No reduction	24 5/8	24 7/8	25 1/8	25 3/8	25 5/8
6	Waist to ankle	No reduction	40 7/8	41 3/8	41 7/8	42 3/8	42 7/8
7	Ankle	× .90	7	7 3/8	7 1/2	7 3/4	8
8	Knee	× .90	12 1/4	12 3/4	13 1/8	13 5/8	14
9	Front crotch	× .90	2	2 1/8	2 1/4	2 3/8	2 1/2
10	Back crotch	× .90	2 5/8	2 7/8	3	3 1/4	3 3/8
11	Crotch angle	× .90	1	1	1 1/8	1 1/4	1 1/4
12	Nape to waist	No reduction	16 7/8	17 3/8	17 7/8	18 3/8	18 7/8
13	Back neck	No reduction	2 1/2	2 1/2	2 1/2	2 5/8	2 5/8
14	Back neck rise	× .90	7/8	7/8	7/8	7/8	7/8
15	Shoulder length	No reduction	4 7/8	5	5 1/8	5 3/8	5 5/8
16	Across back	× .90	7 1/2	7 3/4	8 1/8	8 1/2	8 7/8
17	Sleeve length	No reduction	24 3/8	24 5/8	24 7/8	25 1/8	25 3/8
18	Shoulder pitch	× .90	1 3/8	1 3/8	1 1/2	1 1/2	1 1/2
19	Bicep	× .90	9 5/8	10 1/4	11	11 5/8	12 1/4
20	Wrist	× .90	5 1/4	6	6 5/8	7 3/8	8
21	Neck	× .90	13 1/4	13 3/8	13 5/8	13 7/8	14
22	Bust span	× .90	6	6 1/4	6 1/2	6 3/4	7 1/8
23	Bust level	No reduction	9 5/8	9 7/8	10	10 1/4	10 1/2

MISSES TALL FOUR-WAY-STRETCH KNIT REDUCTIONS

Ten percent smaller in crosswise direction and 10% smaller in the lengthwise direction.
Use these measurements when drafting slopers for fabrics that stretch 100% in both directions.
Multiply your measurements by 0.90, 10% smaller, in both directions.

		Multiply by	Extra Small	Small	Medium	Large	Extra Large
			2	6	10	14	18
1	Bust	× .90	29 1/4	30 1/8	31	32	32 7/8
2	Waist	× .90	22	23	23 7/8	24 3/4	25 5/8
3	Hip	× .90	32	32 7/8	33 3/4	34 5/8	35 1/2
4	Crotch depth	× .90	10 3/4	10 3/4	11	11	11 1/8
5	Waist to knee	× .90	23 3/8	23 1/2	23 5/8	23 3/4	23 7/8
6	Waist to ankle	× .90	38 7/8	39	39 1/4	39 1/2	39 3/4
7	Ankle	× .90	7	7 1/4	7 3/8	7 3/8	7 1/2
8	Knee	× .90	12 1/4	12 1/2	12 3/4	13	13 1/8
9	Front crotch	× .90	2	2	2 1/8	2 1/8	2 2/8
10	Back crotch	× .90	3	3	3 1/8	3 1/4	3 2/8
11	Crotch angle	× .90	1 1/8	1 1/8	1 1/8	1 1/4	1 1/4
12	Nape to waist	× .90	16	16 1/4	16 1/2	16 3/4	17
13	Back neck	No reduction	2 1/2	2 1/2	2 1/2	2 1/2	2 1/2
14	Back neck rise	No reduction	7/8	7/8	7/8	7/8	7/8
15	Shoulder length	No reduction	4 7/8	5	5	5	5 1/8
16	Across back	No reduction	7 1/2	7 5/8	7 3/4	8	8 1/8
17	Sleeve length	No reduction	24 3/8	24 1/2	24 5/8	24 3/4	24 7/8
18	Shoulder pitch	No reduction	1 1/2	1 1/2	1 5/8	1 5/8	1 5/8
19	Bicep	× .90	9 5/8	10	10 1/4	10 5/8	11
20	Wrist	× .90	5 1/4	5 5/8	6	6 1/4	6 5/8
21	Neck	No reduction	14 5/8	14 3/4	15	15	15 1/8
22	Bust span	× .90	6	6 1/8	6 1/4	6 3/8	6 1/2
23	Bust level	× .90	10 1/8	10 1/4	10 3/8	10 1/2	10 5/8

Women's Size Reductions

WOMEN'S STABLE KNIT REDUCTIONS

Zero percent smaller in crosswise direction without any reductions in lengthwise direction.
Use these measurements when drafting slopers for fabrics that stretch from 0% to 25%.
Multiply your across measurements by 1, 0% smaller, except for the shoulder measurement, because the final garment will have twill tape to stabilize the seam and prevent it from stretching.

		Multiply by	Extra Small	Small	Medium	Large	Extra Large
			2	6	10	14	18
1	Bust	× 0	43	47	51	55	59
2	Waist	× 0	35	39	43	47	51
3	Hip	× 0	46	50	54	58	62
4	Crotch depth	No reduction	11 3/4	15 3/4	19 3/4	23 3/4	27 3/4
5	Waist to knee	No reduction	24	24 1/4	24 1/2	24 3/4	25
6	Waist to ankle	No reduction	38 5/8	38 7/8	39 1/8	39 3/8	39 5/8
7	Ankle	× 0	10	10 1/2	11	11 1/2	12
8	Knee	× 0	18 1/8	18 3/8	18 5/8	18 7/8	19 1/8
9	Front crotch	× 0	2 7/8	3 3/8	3 7/8	4 3/8	4 7/8
10	Back crotch	× 0	3 7/8	4 1/8	4 1/2	4 7/8	5 1/8
11	Crotch angle	× 0	1 1/2	1 3/8	1 5/8	2	2 3/8
12	Nape to waist	No reduction	16 5/8	17 1/8	17 5/8	18 1/8	18 5/8
13	Back neck	No reduction	3	3 1/2	4	4 1/2	5
14	Back neck rise	× 0	1	1 3/8	1 3/7	1 1/2	1 1/2
15	Shoulder length	No reduction	5 5/8	5 3/4	5 7/8	6	6 1/8
16	Across back	× 0	8 5/8	8 7/8	9	9 3/8	9 5/8
17	Sleeve length	No reduction	23 7/8	24 1/8	24 3/8	24 5/8	24 7/8
18	Shoulder pitch	× 0	1 1/2	1 3/4	2	2 1/4	2 1/2
19	Bicep	× 0	14 1/2	15 1/4	16	16 3/4	17 1/2
20	Wrist	× 0	7 1/8	7 7/8	8 5/8	9 3/8	10 1/8
21	Neck	× 0	17 1/4	18	18 3/4	19 1/2	20 1/4
22	Bust span	× 0	8	8 1/4	8 1/2	8 3/4	9
23	Bust level	No reduction	12 1/4	12 3/4	13 1/4	13 3/4	14 1/4

WOMEN'S MODERATE KNIT REDUCTIONS

Two percent smaller in crosswise direction without any reductions in lengthwise direction.
Use these measurements when drafting slopers for fabrics that stretch from 25% to 50%.
Multiply your across measurements by 0.98, 2% smaller, except for the shoulder measurement, because the final garment will have twill tape to stabilize the seam and prevent it from stretching.

		Multiply by	Extra Small	Small	Medium	Large	Extra Large
			2	6	10	14	18
1	Bust	× .98	42 1/8	46	50	53 7/8	57 7/8
2	Waist	× .98	34 1/4	38 1/4	42 1/8	46	50
3	Hip	× .98	45	49	53	56 7/8	60 3/4
4	Crotch depth	No reduction	11 3/4	15 3/4	19 3/4	23 3/4	27 3/4
5	Waist to knee	No reduction	24	24 1/4	24 1/2	24 3/4	25
6	Waist to ankle	No reduction	38 5/8	38 7/8	39 1/8	39 3/8	39 5/8
7	Ankle	× .98	9 3/4	10 1/4	10 3/4	11 1/4	11 3/4
8	Knee	× .98	17 3/4	18	18 1/4	18 1/2	18 3/4
9	Front crotch	× .98	2 7/8	3 1/4	3 3/4	4 1/4	4 3/4
10	Back crotch	× .98	3 3/4	4	4 3/8	4 3/4	5
11	Crotch angle	× .98	1 3/8	1 1/4	1 5/8	2	2 1/4
12	Nape to waist	No reduction	16 5/8	17 1/8	17 5/8	18 1/8	18 5/8
13	Back neck	No reduction	3	3 1/2	4	4 1/2	5
14	Back neck rise	× .98	1	1 3/8	1 3/8	1 1/2	1 1/2
15	Shoulder length	No reduction	5 5/8	5 3/4	5 7/8	6	6 1/8
16	Across back	× .98	8 5/8	8 7/8	9	9 3/8	9 5/8
17	Sleeve length	No reduction	23 7/8	24 1/8	24 3/8	24 5/8	24 7/8
18	Shoulder pitch	× .98	1 1/2	1 3/4	2	2 1/4	2 1/2
19	Bicep	× .98	14 1/4	15	15 5/8	16 3/8	17 1/8
20	Wrist	× .98	7	7 3/4	8 1/2	9 1/4	10
21	Neck	× .98	16 7/8	17 5/8	18 3/8	19	19 3/4
22	Bust span	× .98	7 7/8	8	8 3/8	8 5/8	8 7/8
23	Bust level	No reduction	12	12 3/8	13	13 3/8	14

WOMEN'S STRETCHY KNIT REDUCTIONS

Three percent smaller in crosswise direction without any reductions in lengthwise direction.
Use these measurements when drafting slopers for fabrics that stretch from 50% to 75%.
Multiply your across measurements by 0.97, 3% smaller, except for the shoulder measurement, because the final garment will have twill tape to stabilize the seam and prevent it from stretching.

		Multiply by	Extra Small	Small	Medium	Large	Extra Large
			2	6	10	14	18
1	Bust	× .97	41¾	45⅝	49½	53⅜	57¼
2	Waist	× .97	34	37⅞	41¾	45⅝	49½
3	Hip	× .97	44⅝	48½	52⅜	56¼	60⅛
4	Crotch depth	No reduction	11¾	15¾	19¾	23¾	27¾
5	Waist to knee	No reduction	24	24¼	24½	24¾	25
6	Waist to ankle	No reduction	38⅝	38⅞	39⅛	39⅜	39⅝
7	Ankle	× .97	9¾	10⅛	10⅝	11⅛	11⅝
8	Knee	× .97	17⅝	17⅞	18	18¼	18½
9	Front crotch	× .97	2¾	3¼	3¾	4¼	4¾
10	Back crotch	× .97	3¾	4	4⅜	4¾	5
11	Crotch angle	× .97	1⅜	1¼	1⅝	2	2¼
12	Nape to waist	No reduction	16⅝	17⅛	17⅝	18⅛	18⅝
13	Back neck	No reduction	3	3½	4	4½	5
14	Back neck rise	× .97	1	1⅜	1⅜	1½	1½
15	Shoulder length	No reduction	5⅝	5¾	5⅞	6	6⅛
16	Across back	× .97	8⅝	8⅞	9	9⅜	9⅝
17	Sleeve length	No reduction	23⅞	24⅛	24⅜	24⅝	24⅞
18	Shoulder pitch	× .97	1½	1¾	2	2¼	2½
19	Bicep	× .97	14	14¾	15½	16¼	17
20	Wrist	× .97	7	7⅝	8⅜	9	9⅞
21	Neck	× .97	16⅝	17⅜	18⅛	18⅞	19⅝
22	Bust span	× .97	7¾	8	8¼	8½	8¾
23	Bust level	No reduction	11⅞	12¼	12¾	13¼	13¾

WOMEN'S SUPER-STRETCH KNIT REDUCTIONS

Five percent smaller in crosswise direction without any reductions in lengthwise direction.
Use these measurements when drafting slopers for fabrics that stretch from 75% to 100%.
Multiply your across measurements by 0.95, 5% smaller, except for the shoulder measurement, because the final garment will have twill tape to stabilize the seam and prevent it from stretching.

		Multiply by	Extra Small	Small	Medium	Large	Extra Large
			2	6	10	14	18
1	Bust	× .95	40⅞	44⅝	48½	52¼	56
2	Waist	× .95	33¼	37	40⅞	44⅝	48½
3	Hip	× .95	43¾	47½	51¼	55	58⅞
4	Crotch depth	No reduction	11¾	15¾	19¾	23¾	27¾
5	Waist to knee	No reduction	24	24¼	24½	24¾	25
6	Waist to ankle	No reduction	38⅝	38⅞	39⅛	39⅜	39⅝
7	Ankle	× .95	9½	10	10½	11	11⅜
8	Knee	× .95	17¼	17½	17¾	18	18⅛
9	Front crotch	× .95	2¾	3¼	3⅝	4⅛	4⅝
10	Back crotch	× .95	3⅝	4	4¼	4⅝	5
11	Crotch angle	× .95	1⅜	1¼	1⅝	1⅞	2¼
12	Nape to waist	No reduction	16⅝	17⅛	17⅝	18⅛	18⅝
13	Back neck	No reduction	3	3½	4	4½	5
14	Back neck rise	× .95	1	1⅜	1⅜	1½	1½
15	Shoulder length	No reduction	5⅝	5¾	5⅞	6	6⅛
16	Across back	× .95	8⅝	8⅞	9	9⅜	9⅝
17	Sleeve length	No reduction	23⅞	24⅛	24⅜	24⅝	24⅞
18	Shoulder pitch	× .95	1½	1¾	2	2⅛	2⅜
19	Bicep	× .95	13¾	14½	15¼	16	16⅝
20	Wrist	× .95	6¾	7½	8¼	9	9⅝
21	Neck	× .95	16⅜	17	17¾	18½	19⅛
22	Bust span	× .95	7⅝	7⅞	8	8⅜	8½
23	Bust level	No reduction	11⅝	12	12½	13	13½

WOMEN'S RIB KNIT REDUCTIONS

Ten percent smaller in crosswise direction without any reductions in lengthwise direction.
Use these measurements when drafting slopers for fabrics that stretch 100% and over.
Multiply your across measurements by 0.90, 10% smaller, except for the shoulder measurement, because the final garment will have twill tape to stabilize the seam and prevent it from stretching.

		Multiply by	Extra Small	Small	Medium	Large	Extra Large
			2	6	10	14	18
1	Bust	× .90	38 3/4	42 1/4	45 7/8	49 1/2	53 1/8
2	Waist	× .90	31 1/2	35 1/8	38 3/4	42 1/4	45 7/8
3	Hip	× .90	41 3/8	45	48 5/8	52 1/4	55 3/4
4	Crotch depth	No reduction	11 3/4	15 3/4	19 3/4	23 3/4	27 3/4
5	Waist to knee	No reduction	24	24 1/4	24 1/2	24 3/4	25
6	Waist to ankle	No reduction	38 5/8	38 7/8	39 1/8	39 3/8	39 5/8
7	Ankle	× .90	9	9 1/2	10	10 3/8	10 3/4
8	Knee	× .90	16 3/8	16 1/2	16 3/4	17	17 1/4
9	Front crotch	× .90	2 5/8	3	3 1/2	4	4 3/8
10	Back crotch	× .90	3 1/2	3 3/4	4	4 3/8	4 5/8
11	Crotch angle	× .90	1 1/4	1 1/8	1 1/2	1 3/4	2
12	Nape to waist	No reduction	16 5/8	17 1/8	17 5/8	18 1/8	18 5/8
13	Back neck	No reduction	3	3 1/2	4	4 1/2	5
14	Back neck rise	× .90	1	1 3/8	1 3/8	1 1/2	1 1/2
15	Shoulder length	No reduction	5 5/8	5 3/4	5 7/8	6	6 1/8
16	Across back	× .90	8 5/8	8 7/8	9	9 3/8	9 5/8
17	Sleeve length	No reduction	23 7/8	24 1/8	24 3/8	24 5/8	24 7/8
18	Shoulder pitch	× .90	1 3/8	1 5/8	1 7/8	2	2 1/4
19	Bicep	× .90	13	13 3/4	14 3/8	15	15 3/4
20	Wrist	× .90	6 3/8	7	7 3/4	8 1/2	9 1/8
21	Neck	× .90	15 1/2	16 1/8	16 7/8	17 1/2	18 1/8
22	Bust span	× .90	7 1/4	7 3/8	7 5/8	7 7/8	8
23	Bust level	No reduction	11	11 3/8	11 7/8	12 3/8	12 3/4

WOMEN'S FOUR-WAY-STRETCH KNIT REDUCTIONS

Ten percent smaller in crosswise direction and 10% smaller in the lengthwise direction.
Use these measurements when drafting slopers for fabrics that stretch 100% in both directions.
Multiply your measurements by 0.90, 10% smaller, in both directions.

		Multiply by	Extra Small	Small	Medium	Large	Extra Large
			2	6	10	14	18
1	Bust	× .90	38 3/4	40 1/2	42 1/4	44 1/8	45 7/8
2	Waist	× .90	31 1/2	33 1/4	35 1/8	36 7/8	38 3/4
3	Hip	× .90	41 3/8	43 1/4	45	46 3/4	48 5/8
4	Crotch depth	× .90	11 1/8	13	15	16 7/8	18 3/4
5	Waist to knee	× .90	22 3/4	23	23	23 1/8	23 1/4
6	Waist to ankle	× .90	36 3/4	36 7/8	37	37	37 1/8
7	Ankle	× .90	9	9 1/4	9 1/2	9 5/8	10
8	Knee	× .90	16 3/8	16 3/8	16 1/2	16 5/8	16 3/4
9	Front crotch	× .90	2 5/8	2 7/8	3	3 1/4	3 1/2
10	Back crotch	× .90	3 7/8	4	4 1/8	4 3/8	4 1/2
11	Crotch angle	× .90	1 1/2	1 1/7	1 3/8	1 1/2	1 5/8
12	Nape to waist	× .90	15 3/4	16	16 1/4	16 1/2	16 3/4
13	Back neck	No reduction	3	3 1/4	3 1/2	3 3/4	4
14	Back neck rise	No reduction	1	1 3/8	1 3/8	1 3/8	1 3/8
15	Shoulder length	No reduction	5 5/8	5 3/4	5 3/4	5 7/8	5 7/8
16	Across back	No reduction	8 5/8	8 3/4	8 7/8	9	9
17	Sleeve length	No reduction	23 7/8	24	24 1/8	24 1/4	24 3/8
18	Shoulder pitch	No reduction	1 1/2	1 5/8	1 3/4	2	2
19	Bicep	× .90	13	13 3/8	13 3/4	14	14 3/8
20	Wrist	× .90	6 3/8	6 3/4	7	7 3/8	7 3/4
21	Neck	No reduction	17 1/4	17 5/8	18	18 3/8	18 3/4
22	Bust span	× .90	7 1/4	7 3/8	7 3/8	7 1/2	7 5/8
23	Bust level	× .90	11 5/8	11 7/8	12	12 2/8	12 1/2

Plus Size Reductions

PLUS STABLE KNIT REDUCTIONS

Zero percent smaller in crosswise direction without any reductions in lengthwise direction.
Use these measurements when drafting slopers for fabrics that stretch from 0% to 25%.
Use your measurements exactly as recorded without any reductions.

		Multiply by	1X	2X	3X	4X	5X
			16	20	24	28	32
1	Bust	× 0	41	45	49	53	57
2	Waist	× 0	33	37	41	45	49
3	Hip	× 0	44	48	52	56	60
4	Crotch depth	No reduction	11 5/8	15 5/8	19 5/8	23 5/8	27 5/8
5	Waist to knee	No reduction	24	24 1/4	24 1/2	24 3/4	25
6	Waist to ankle	No reduction	39 5/8	39 7/8	40 1/8	40 3/8	40 5/8
7	Ankle	× 0	9 5/8	10 1/8	10 5/8	11 1/8	11 5/8
8	Knee	× 0	18 1/8	18 3/8	18 5/8	18 7/8	19 1/8
9	Front crotch	× 0	2 3/4	3 1/4	3 3/4	4 1/4	4 3/4
10	Back crotch	× 0	3 5/8	4	4 3/8	4 5/8	5
11	Crotch angle	× 0	1	1 1/4	1 5/8	2	2 1/4
12	Nape to waist	No reduction	17	15 3/4	16 1/4	16 3/4	17 1/4
13	Back neck	No reduction	2 3/4	3 1/4	3 3/4	4 1/4	4 3/4
14	Back neck rise	× 0	1	1 3/8	1 3/8	1 3/8	1 1/2
15	Shoulder length	No reduction	5 1/2	5 5/8	5 3/4	5 7/8	6
16	Across back	× 0	8 3/8	8 5/8	8 7/8	9 1/8	9 3/8
17	Sleeve length	No reduction	32 1/8	32 3/8	32 5/8	32 7/8	33 1/8
18	Shoulder pitch	× 0	1 1/2	1 3/4	2	2 1/4	2 1/2
19	Bicep	× 0	13 3/4	14 1/2	15 1/4	16	16 3/4
20	Wrist	× 0	6 3/4	7 1/2	8 1/4	9	9 3/4
21	Neck	× 0	16 3/4	17 1/2	18 1/4	19	19 3/4
22	Bust span	× 0	7 3/4	8	8 1/4	8 1/2	8 3/4
23	Bust level	No reduction	11 7/8	12 3/8	12 7/8	13 3/8	13 7/8

PLUS MODERATE KNIT REDUCTIONS

Two percent smaller in crosswise direction without any reductions in lengthwise direction.
Use these measurements when drafting slopers for fabrics that stretch from 25% to 50%.
Multiply your across measurements by 0.98, 2% smaller, except for the shoulder measurement, because the final garment will have twill tape to stabilize the seam and prevent it from stretching.

		Multiply by	1X	2X	3X	4X	5X
			16	20	24	28	32
1	Bust	× .98	40 1/8	44 1/8	48	52	55 7/8
2	Waist	× .98	32 3/8	36 1/4	40 1/8	44 1/8	48
3	Hip	× .98	43 1/8	47	51	54 7/8	58 3/4
4	Crotch depth	No reduction	11 5/8	15 5/8	19 5/8	23 5/8	27 5/8
5	Waist to knee	No reduction	24	24 1/4	24 1/2	24 3/4	25
6	Waist to ankle	No reduction	39 5/8	39 7/8	40 1/8	40 3/8	40 5/8
7	Ankle	× .98	9 3/8	10	10 3/8	11	11 3/8
8	Knee	× .98	17 3/4	18	18 1/4	18 1/2	18 3/4
9	Front crotch	× .98	2 3/4	3 1/8	3 5/8	4 1/8	4 5/8
10	Back crotch	× .98	3 5/8	4	4 1/4	4 5/8	5
11	Crotch angle	× .98	1	1 1/4	1 5/8	2	2 1/4
12	Nape to waist	No reduction	17	15 3/4	16 1/4	16 3/4	17 1/4
13	Back neck	No reduction	2 3/4	3 1/4	3 3/4	4 1/4	4 3/4
14	Back neck rise	× .98	1	1 3/8	1 3/8	1 3/8	1 1/2
15	Shoulder length	No reduction	5 1/2	5 5/8	5 3/4	5 7/8	6
16	Across back	× .98	8 3/8	8 5/8	8 7/8	9 1/8	9 3/8
17	Sleeve length	No reduction	32 1/8	32 3/8	32 5/8	32 7/8	33 1/8
18	Shoulder pitch	× .98	1 1/2	1 3/4	2	2 1/4	2 1/2
19	Bicep	× .98	13 1/2	14 1/5	15	15 5/8	16 3/8
20	Wrist	× .98	6 5/8	7 3/8	8	8 7/8	9 1/2
21	Neck	× .98	16 3/8	17 1/8	17 7/8	18 5/8	19 3/8
22	Bust span	× .98	7 5/8	7 7/8	8	8 3/8	8 5/8
23	Bust level	No reduction	11 5/8	12 1/8	12 5/8	13 1/8	13 5/8

PLUS STRETCHY KNIT REDUCTIONS

Three percent smaller in crosswise direction without any reductions in lengthwise direction.
Use these measurements when drafting slopers for fabrics that stretch from 50% to 75%.
Multiply your across measurements by 0.97, 3% smaller, except for the shoulder measurement, because the final garment will have twill tape to stabilize the seam and prevent it from stretching.

		Multiply by	1X	2X	3X	4X	5X
			16	20	24	28	32
1	Bust	× .97	39 3/4	43 5/8	47 1/2	51 3/8	55 1/4
2	Waist	× .97	32	35 7/8	39 3/4	43 5/8	47 1/2
3	Hip	× .97	42 5/8	46 1/2	50 1/2	54 1/3	58 1/4
4	Crotch depth	No reduction	11 5/8	15 5/8	19 5/8	23 5/8	27 5/8
5	Waist to knee	No reduction	24	24 1/4	24 1/2	24 3/4	25
6	Waist to ankle	No reduction	39 5/8	39 7/8	40 1/8	40 3/8	40 5/8
7	Ankle	× .97	9 3/8	9 7/8	10 1/4	10 3/4	11 1/4
8	Knee	× .97	17 5/8	17 7/8	18	18 1/4	18 1/2
9	Front crotch	× .97	2 5/8	3 1/8	3 5/8	4 1/8	4 5/8
10	Back crotch	× .97	3 1/2	3 7/8	4 1/4	4 1/2	4 7/8
11	Crotch angle	× .97	1	1 1/4	1 5/8	2	2 1/4
12	Nape to waist	No reduction	17	15 3/4	16 1/4	16 3/4	17 1/4
13	Back neck	No reduction	2 3/4	3 1/4	3 3/4	4 1/4	4 3/4
14	Back neck rise	× .97	1	1 3/8	1 3/8	1 3/8	1 1/2
15	Shoulder length	No reduction	5 1/2	5 5/8	5 3/4	5 7/8	6
16	Across back	× .97	8 3/8	8 5/8	8 7/8	9 1/8	9 3/8
17	Sleeve length	No reduction	32 1/8	32 3/8	32 5/8	32 7/8	33 1/8
18	Shoulder pitch	× .97	1 1/2	1 3/4	2	2 1/4	2 1/2
19	Bicep	× .97	13 3/8	14	14 3/4	15 1/2	16 1/4
20	Wrist	× .97	6 1/2	7 1/4	8	8 3/4	9 1/2
21	Neck	× .97	16 1/4	17	17 3/4	18 3/8	19 1/8
22	Bust span	× .97	7 1/2	7 3/4	8	8 1/4	8 1/2
23	Bust level	No reduction	11 1/2	12	12 1/2	13	13 1/2

PLUS SUPER-STRETCH KNIT REDUCTIONS

Five percent smaller in crosswise direction without any reductions in lengthwise direction.
Use these measurements when drafting slopers for fabrics that stretch from 75% to 100%.
Multiply your across measurements by 0.95, 5% smaller, except for the shoulder measurement, because the final garment will have twill tape to stabilize the seam and prevent it from stretching.

		Multiply by	1X	2X	3X	4X	5X
			2	6	10	14	18
1	Bust	× .95	39	42 3/4	46 1/2	50 3/8	54 1/8
2	Waist	× .95	31 3/8	35 1/8	39	42 3/4	46 4/8
3	Hip	× .95	41 3/4	45 5/8	49 3/8	53 1/4	57
4	Crotch depth	No reduction	11 5/8	15 5/8	19 5/8	23 5/8	27 5/8
5	Waist to knee	No reduction	24	24 1/4	24 1/2	24 3/4	25
6	Waist to ankle	No reduction	39 5/8	39 7/8	40 1/8	40 3/8	40 5/8
7	Ankle	× .95	9 1/8	9 5/8	10	10 5/8	11
8	Knee	× .95	17 1/4	17 1/2	17 3/4	18	18 1/8
9	Front crotch	× .95	2 5/8	3	3 5/8	4	4 1/2
10	Back crotch	× .95	3 1/2	3 3/4	4 1/8	4 3/8	4 3/4
11	Crotch angle	× .95	1	1 1/4	1 1/2	1 7/8	2 1/8
12	Nape to waist	No reduction	17	15 3/4	16 1/4	16 3/4	17 1/4
13	Back neck	No reduction	2 3/4	3 1/4	3 3/4	4 1/4	4 3/4
14	Back neck rise	× .95	1	1 3/8	1 3/8	1 3/8	1 1/2
15	Shoulder length	No reduction	5 1/2	5 5/8	5 3/4	5 7/8	6
16	Across back	× .95	8 3/8	8 5/8	8 7/8	9 1/8	9 3/8
17	Sleeve length	No reduction	32 1/8	32 3/8	32 5/8	32 7/8	33 1/8
18	Shoulder pitch	× .95	1 1/2	1 3/4	2	2 1/8	2 3/8
19	Bicep	× .95	13	13 3/4	14 1/2	15 1/5	16
20	Wrist	× .95	6 3/8	7 1/8	7 7/8	8 1/2	9 1/4
21	Neck	× .95	16	16 5/8	17 3/8	18	18 3/4
22	Bust span	× .95	7 3/8	7 5/8	7 7/8	8	8 3/8
23	Bust level	No reduction	11 1/4	11 3/4	12 1/4	12 3/4	13 1/8

PLUS RIB KNIT REDUCTIONS

Ten percent smaller in crosswise direction without any reductions in lengthwise direction.
Use these measurements when drafting slopers for fabrics that stretch 100% and over.
Multiply your across measurements by 0.90, 10% smaller, except for the shoulder measurement, because the final garment will have twill tape to stabilize the seam and prevent it from stretching.

		Multiply by	1X	2X	3X	4X	5X
			2	6	10	14	18
1	Bust	× .90	36 7/8	40 1/2	44 1/8	47 3/4	51 1/4
2	Waist	× .90	29 3/4	33 1/4	36 7/8	40 1/2	44 1/8
3	Hip	× .90	39 5/8	43 1/4	46 3/4	50 3/8	54
4	Crotch depth	No reduction	11 5/8	15 5/8	19 5/8	23 5/8	27 5/8
5	Waist to knee	No reduction	24	24 1/4	24 1/2	24 3/4	25
6	Waist to ankle	No reduction	39 5/8	39 7/8	40 1/8	40 3/8	40 5/8
7	Ankle	× .90	8 5/8	9 1/8	9 5/8	10	10 1/2
8	Knee	× .90	16 3/8	16 1/2	16 3/4	17	17 1/4
9	Front crotch	× .90	2 1/2	3	3 3/8	3 7/8	4 1/4
10	Back crotch	× .90	3 1/4	3 5/8	3 7/8	4 1/4	4 1/2
11	Crotch angle	× .90	7/8	1 1/8	1 1/2	1 3/4	2
12	Nape to waist	No reduction	17	15 3/4	16 1/4	16 3/4	17 1/4
13	Back neck	No reduction	2 3/4	3 1/4	3 3/4	4 1/4	4 3/4
14	Back neck rise	× .90	1	1 3/8	1 3/8	1 3/8	1 1/2
15	Shoulder length	No reduction	5 1/2	5 5/8	5 3/4	5 7/8	6
16	Across back	× .90	8 3/8	8 5/8	8 7/8	9 1/8	9 3/8
17	Sleeve length	No reduction	32 1/8	32 3/8	32 5/8	32 7/8	33 1/8
18	Shoulder pitch	× .90	1 3/8	1 5/8	1 7/8	2	2 1/4
19	Bicep	× .90	12 3/8	13	13 3/4	14 3/8	15
20	Wrist	× .90	6	6 3/4	7 3/8	8	8 3/4
21	Neck	× .90	15	15 3/4	16 3/8	17 1/8	17 3/4
22	Bust span	× .90	7	7 1/4	7 3/8	7 5/8	7 7/8
23	Bust level	No reduction	10 3/4	11 1/8	11 5/8	12	12 1/2

PLUS FOUR-WAY-STRETCH KNIT REDUCTIONS

Ten percent smaller in crosswise direction and 10% smaller in the lengthwise direction.
Use these measurements when drafting slopers for fabrics that stretch 100% in both directions.
Multiply your across measurements by 0.90, 10% smaller, in both directions.

		Multiply by	1X	2X	3X	4X	5X
			2	6	10	14	18
1	Bust	× .90	36 7/8	38 3/4	40 1/2	42 1/4	44 1/8
2	Waist	× .90	29 3/4	31 1/2	33 1/4	35 1/8	36 7/8
3	Hip	× .90	39 5/8	41 3/8	43 1/4	45	46 6/8
4	Crotch depth	× .90	11	13	14 7/8	16 3/4	18 5/8
5	Waist to knee	× .90	22 3/4	23	23	23 1/8	23 1/4
6	Waist to ankle	× .90	37 5/8	37 3/4	37 7/8	38	38 1/8
7	Ankle	× .90	8 5/8	8 7/8	9 1/8	9 1/3	9 5/8
8	Knee	× .90	16 3/8	16 3/8	16 1/2	16 5/8	16 3/4
9	Front crotch	× .90	2 1/2	2 3/4	3	3 1/8	3 3/8
10	Back crotch	× .90	3 5/8	3 7/8	4	4 1/8	4 3/8
11	Crotch angle	× .90	1	1 1/8	1 1/4	1 1/2	1 5/8
12	Nape to waist	× .90	16 1/8	14 3/4	15	15 1/4	15 1/2
13	Back neck	No reduction	2 3/4	3	3 1/4	3 1/2	3 3/4
14	Back neck rise	No reduction	1	1 3/8	1 3/8	1 3/8	1 3/8
15	Shoulder length	No reduction	5 1/2	5 5/8	5 5/8	5 3/4	5 3/4
16	Across back	No reduction	8 3/8	8 1/2	8 5/8	8 3/4	8 7/8
17	Sleeve length	No reduction	32 1/8	32 1/4	32 3/8	32 1/2	32 5/8
18	Shoulder pitch	No reduction	1 1/2	1 5/8	1 3/4	2	2
19	Bicep	× .90	12 3/8	12 3/4	13	13 3/8	13 3/4
20	Wrist	× .90	6	6 3/8	6 3/4	7	7 3/8
21	Neck	No reduction	16 3/4	17 1/8	17 1/2	17 7/8	18 1/4
22	Bust span	× .90	7	7	7 1/4	7 3/8	7 3/7
23	Bust level	× .90	11 1/4	11 1/2	11 3/4	12	12 1/4

Half Size Stable Knit Reductions

HALF SIZE STABLE KNIT REDUCTIONS

Zero percent smaller in crosswise direction without any reductions in lengthwise direction.
Use these measurements when drafting slopers for fabrics that stretch from 0% to 25%.
Use your measurements exactly as recorded without any reductions.

		Multiply by	Extra Small	Small	Medium	Large	Extra Large
			14 1/2	**18 1/2**	**22 1/2**	**26 1/2**	**30 1/2**
1	Bust	× 0	41	45	49	53	57
2	Waist	× 0	32 1/2	36 1/2	40 1/2	44 1/2	48 1/2
3	Hip	× 0	44	48	52	56	60
4	Crotch depth	No reduction	11 1/8	15 1/8	19 1/8	23 1/8	27 1/8
5	Waist to knee	No reduction	22 3/8	22 5/8	22 7/8	23 1/8	23 3/8
6	Waist to ankle	No reduction	37 1/4	37 1/2	37 3/4	38	38 1/4
7	Ankle	× 0	9 5/8	10 1/8	10 5/8	11 1/8	11 5/8
8	Knee	× 0	17 1/4	17 1/2	17 3/4	18	18 1/4
9	Front crotch	× 0	2 3/4	3 1/4	3 3/4	4 1/4	4 3/4
10	Back crotch	× 0	3 5/8	4	4 3/8	4 5/8	5
11	Crotch angle	× 0	1 3/8	1 1/4	1 3/5	2	2 1/4
12	Nape to waist	No reduction	15 1/2	16	16 1/2	17	17 1/2
13	Back neck	No reduction	2 3/4	3 1/4	3 3/4	4 1/4	4 3/4
14	Back neck rise	× 0	1	1 3/8	1 3/8	1 3/8	1 1/2
15	Shoulder length	No reduction	5 1/2	5 5/8	5 3/4	5 7/8	6
16	Across back	× 0	8 3/8	8 5/8	8 7/8	9 1/8	9 3/8
17	Sleeve length	No reduction	22 1/4	22 1/2	22 3/4	23	23 1/4
18	Shoulder pitch	× 0	1 3/8	1 5/8	2	2 1/8	2 3/8
19	Bicep	× 0	13 3/4	14 1/2	15 1/4	16	16 3/4
20	Wrist	× 0	6 3/4	7 1/2	8 1/4	9	9 3/4
21	Neck	× 0	16 3/4	17 1/2	18 1/4	19	19 3/4
22	Bust span	× 0	7 3/4	8	8 1/4	8 1/2	8 3/4
23	Bust level	No reduction	11 3/8	11 7/8	12 3/8	12 7/8	13 3/8

HALF SIZE MODERATE KNIT REDUCTIONS

Two percent smaller in crosswise direction without any reductions in lengthwise direction.
Use these measurements when drafting slopers for fabrics that stretch from 25% to 50%.
Multiply your across measurements by 0.98, 2% smaller, except for the shoulder measurement, because the final garment will have twill tape to stabilize the seam and prevent it from stretching.

		Multiply by	Extra Small	Small	Medium	Large	Extra Large
			14 1/2	**18 1/2**	**22 1/2**	**26 1/2**	**30 1/2**
1	Bust	× .98	40 1/8	44 1/8	48	52	55 7/8
2	Waist	× .98	31 7/8	35 3/4	39 3/4	43 5/8	47 1/2
3	Hip	× .98	43 1/8	47	51	54 7/8	58 3/4
4	Crotch depth	No reduction	11 1/8	15 1/8	19 1/8	23 1/8	27 1/8
5	Waist to knee	No reduction	22 3/8	22 5/8	22 7/8	23 1/8	23 3/8
6	Waist to ankle	No reduction	37 1/4	37 1/2	37 3/4	38	38 1/4
7	Ankle	× .98	9 3/8	10	10 3/8	11	11 3/8
8	Knee	× .98	17	17 1/8	17 3/8	17 5/8	17 7/8
9	Front crotch	× .98	2 3/4	3 1/8	3 5/8	4 1/8	4 5/8
10	Back crotch	× .98	3 5/8	4	4 1/4	4 5/8	5
11	Crotch angle	× .98	1 3/8	1 1/4	1 1/2	1 7/8	2 1/4
12	Nape to waist	No reduction	15 1/2	16	16 1/2	17	17 1/2
13	Back neck	No reduction	2 3/4	3 1/4	3 3/4	4 1/4	4 3/4
14	Back neck rise	× .98	1	1 3/8	1 3/8	1 3/8	1 1/2
15	Shoulder length	No reduction	5 1/2	5 5/8	5 3/4	5 7/8	6
16	Across back	× .98	8 3/8	8 5/8	8 7/8	9 1/8	9 3/8
17	Sleeve length	No reduction	22 1/4	22 1/2	22 3/4	23	23 1/4
18	Shoulder pitch	× .98	1 3/8	1 5/8	1 7/8	2 1/8	2 3/8
19	Bicep	× .98	13 1/2	14 1/4	15	15 5/8	16 3/8
20	Wrist	× .98	6 5/8	7 3/8	8	8 7/8	9 1/2
21	Neck	× .98	16 3/8	17 1/8	17 7/8	18 5/8	19 3/8
22	Bust span	× .98	7 5/8	7 7/8	8	8 3/8	8 5/8
23	Bust level	No reduction	11 1/8	11 5/8	12 1/8	12 5/8	13 1/8

HALF SIZE STRETCHY KNIT REDUCTIONS

Three percent smaller in crosswise direction without any reductions in lengthwise direction.
Use these measurements when drafting slopers for fabrics that stretch from 50% to 75%.
Multiply your across measurements by 0.97, 3% smaller, except for the shoulder measurement, because the final garment will have twill tape to stabilize the seam and prevent it from stretching.

		Multiply by	Extra Small	Small	Medium	Large	Extra Large
			14 1/2	**18 1/2**	**22 1/2**	**26 1/2**	**30 1/2**
1	Bust	× .97	39 3/4	43 5/8	47 1/2	51 3/8	55 1/4
2	Waist	× .97	31 1/2	35 3/8	39 2/8	43 1/8	47
3	Hip	× .97	42 5/8	46 1/2	50 1/2	54 3/8	58 1/4
4	Crotch depth	No reduction	11 1/8	15 1/8	19 1/8	23 1/8	27 1/8
5	Waist to knee	No reduction	22 3/8	22 5/8	22 7/8	23 1/8	23 3/8
6	Waist to ankle	No reduction	37 1/4	37 1/2	37 3/4	38	38 1/4
7	Ankle	× .97	9 3/8	9 7/8	10 1/4	10 3/4	11 1/4
8	Knee	× .97	16 3/4	17	17 1/4	17 1/2	17 3/4
9	Front crotch	× .97	2 5/8	3 1/8	3 5/8	4 1/8	4 5/8
10	Back crotch	× .97	3 1/2	3 7/8	4 1/4	4 1/2	4 7/8
11	Crotch angle	× .97	1 3/8	1 1/4	1 1/2	1 7/8	2 1/4
12	Nape to waist	No reduction	15 1/2	16	16 1/2	17	17 1/2
13	Back neck	No reduction	2 3/4	3 1/4	3 3/4	4 1/4	4 3/4
14	Back neck rise	× .97	1	1 3/8	1 3/8	1 3/8	1 1/2
15	Shoulder length	No reduction	5 1/2	5 5/8	5 3/4	5 7/8	6
16	Across back	× .97	8 3/8	8 5/8	8 7/8	9 1/8	9 3/8
17	Sleeve length	No reduction	22 1/4	22 1/2	22 3/4	23	23 1/4
18	Shoulder pitch	× .97	1 3/8	1 5/8	1 7/8	2 1/8	2 3/8
19	Bicep	× .97	13 3/8	14	14 3/4	15 1/2	16 1/4
20	Wrist	× .97	6 1/2	7 1/4	8	8 3/4	9 1/2
21	Neck	× .97	16 1/4	17	17 3/4	18 3/7	19 1/8
22	Bust span	× .97	7 1/2	7 3/4	8	8 1/4	8 1/2
23	Bust level	No reduction	11	11 1/2	12	12 1/2	13

HALF SIZE SUPER-STRETCH KNIT REDUCTIONS

Five percent smaller in crosswise direction without any reductions in lengthwise direction.
Use these measurements when drafting slopers for fabrics that stretch from 75% to 100%.
Multiply your across measurements by 0.95, 5% smaller, except for the shoulder measurement, because the final garment will have twill tape to stabilize the seam and prevent it from stretching.

		Multiply by	Extra Small	Small	Medium	Large	Extra Large
			14 1/2	**18 1/2**	**22 1/2**	**26 1/2**	**30 1/2**
1	Bust	× .95	39	42 3/4	46 1/2	50 3/8	54 1/8
2	Waist	× .95	30 7/8	34 5/8	38 1/2	42 1/4	46
3	Hip	× .95	41 3/4	45 5/8	49 3/8	53 1/4	57
4	Crotch depth	No reduction	11 1/8	15 1/8	19 1/8	23 1/8	27 1/8
5	Waist to knee	No reduction	22 3/8	22 5/8	22 7/8	23 1/8	23 3/8
6	Waist to ankle	No reduction	37 1/4	37 1/2	37 3/4	38	38 1/4
7	Ankle	× .95	9 1/8	9 5/8	10	10 5/8	11
8	Knee	× .95	16 3/8	16 5/8	16 7/8	17	17 3/8
9	Front crotch	× .95	2 5/8	3	3 5/8	4	4 1/2
10	Back crotch	× .95	3 1/2	3 3/4	4 1/8	4 3/8	4 3/4
11	Crotch angle	× .95	1 1/4	1 1/4	1 1/2	1 7/8	2 1/8
12	Nape to waist	No reduction	15 1/2	16	16 1/2	17	17 1/2
13	Back neck	No reduction	2 3/4	3 1/4	3 3/4	4 1/4	4 3/4
14	Back neck rise	× .95	1	1 3/8	1 3/8	1 3/7	1 1/2
15	Shoulder length	No reduction	5 1/2	5 5/8	5 3/4	5 7/8	6
16	Across back	× .95	8 3/8	8 5/8	8 7/8	9 1/8	9 3/8
17	Sleeve length	No reduction	22 1/4	22 1/2	22 3/4	23	23 1/4
18	Shoulder pitch	× .95	1 3/8	1 5/8	1 7/8	2	2 1/4
19	Bicep	× .95	13	13 3/4	14 1/2	15 1/4	16
20	Wrist	× .95	6 3/8	7 1/8	7 7/8	8 1/2	9 1/4
21	Neck	× .95	16	16 5/8	17 3/8	18	18 3/4
22	Bust span	× .95	7 3/8	7 5/8	7 7/8	8	8 3/8
23	Bust level	No reduction	10 3/4	11 1/4	11 3/4	12 1/4	12 3/4

HALF SIZE RIB KNIT REDUCTIONS

Ten percent smaller in crosswise direction without any reductions in lengthwise direction.
Use these measurements when drafting slopers for fabrics that stretch 100% and over.
Multiply your across measurements by 0.90, 10% smaller, except for the shoulder measurement, because the final garment will have twill tape to stabilize the seam and prevent it from stretching.

		Multiply by	Extra Small	Small	Medium	Large	Extra Large
			14 1/2	**18 1/2**	**22 1/2**	**26 1/2**	**30 1/2**
1	Bust	× .90	36 7/8	40 1/2	44 1/8	47 3/4	51 1/4
2	Waist	× .90	29 1/4	32 7/8	36 1/2	40	43 5/8
3	Hip	× .90	39 5/8	43 1/4	46 3/4	50 3/8	54
4	Crotch depth	No reduction	11 1/8	15 1/8	19 1/8	23 1/8	27 1/8
5	Waist to knee	No reduction	22 3/8	22 5/8	22 7/8	23 1/8	23 3/8
6	Waist to ankle	No reduction	37 1/4	37 1/2	37 3/4	38	38 1/4
7	Ankle	× .90	8 5/8	9 1/8	9 1/7	10	10 1/2
8	Knee	× .90	15 1/2	15 3/4	16	16 1/4	16 3/8
9	Front crotch	× .90	2 1/2	3	3 3/8	3 7/8	4 1/4
10	Back crotch	× .90	3 1/4	3 5/8	3 7/8	4 1/4	4 1/2
11	Crotch angle	× .90	1 1/4	1 1/7	1 3/8	1 3/4	2
12	Nape to waist	No reduction	15 1/2	16	16 1/2	17	17 1/2
13	Back neck	No reduction	2 3/4	3 1/4	3 3/4	4 1/4	4 3/4
14	Back neck rise	× .90	1	1 3/8	1 3/8	1 3/8	1 1/2
15	Shoulder length	No reduction	5 1/2	5 5/8	5 3/4	5 7/8	6
16	Across back	× .90	8 3/8	8 5/8	8 7/8	9 1/8	9 3/8
17	Sleeve length	No reduction	22 1/4	22 1/2	22 3/4	23	23 1/4
18	Shoulder pitch	× .90	1 1/4	1 1/2	1 3/4	2	2 1/4
19	Bicep	× .90	12 3/8	13	13 3/4	14 3/8	15
20	Wrist	× .90	6	6 3/4	7 3/8	8	8 3/4
21	Neck	× .90	15	15 3/4	16 3/8	17 1/8	17 3/4
22	Bust span	× .90	7	7 1/4	7 3/8	7 5/8	7 7/8
23	Bust level	No reduction	10 1/4	10 3/4	11 1/8	11 5/8	12

HALF SIZE FOUR-WAY-STRETCH KNIT REDUCTIONS

Ten percent smaller in crosswise direction and 10% smaller in the lengthwise direction.
Use these measurements when drafting slopers for fabrics that stretch 100% in both directions.
Multiply your measurements by 0.90, 10% smaller, in both directions.

		Multiply by	Extra Small	Small	Medium	Large	Extra Large
			14 1/2	**18 1/2**	**22 1/2**	**26 1/2**	**30 1/2**
1	Bust	× .90	36 7/8	38 3/4	40 1/2	42 1/4	44 1/8
2	Waist	× .90	29 1/4	31	32 7/8	34 5/8	36 1/2
3	Hip	× .90	39 5/8	41 3/8	43 2/8	45	46 3/4
4	Crotch depth	× .90	10 5/8	12 1/2	14 3/8	16 1/4	18 1/8
5	Waist to knee	× .90	21 1/4	21 3/8	21 1/2	21 5/8	21 3/4
6	Waist to ankle	× .90	35 3/8	35 1/2	35 5/8	35 3/4	35 7/8
7	Ankle	× .90	8 5/8	8 7/8	9 1/8	9 3/8	9 5/8
8	Knee	× .90	15 1/2	15 5/8	15 3/4	15 7/8	16
9	Front crotch	× .90	2 1/2	2 3/4	3	3 1/7	3 3/8
10	Back crotch	× .90	3 5/8	3 7/8	4	4 1/8	4 3/8
11	Crotch angle	× .90	1 3/8	1	1 1/4	1 3/8	1 5/8
12	Nape to waist	× .90	14 3/4	15	15 1/4	15 1/2	15 5/8
13	Back neck	No reduction	2 3/4	3	3 1/4	3 1/2	3 6/8
14	Back neck rise	No reduction	1	1 3/8	1 3/8	1 3/8	1 3/8
15	Shoulder length	No reduction	5 1/2	5 5/8	5 5/8	5 3/4	5 3/4
16	Across back	No reduction	8 3/8	8 1/2	8 5/8	8 3/4	8 7/8
17	Sleeve length	No reduction	22 1/4	22 3/8	22 1/2	22 5/8	22 3/4
18	Shoulder pitch	No reduction	1 3/8	1 1/2	1 5/8	1 3/4	2
19	Bicep	× .90	12 3/8	12 3/4	13	13 3/8	13 3/4
20	Wrist	× .90	6	6 3/8	6 3/4	7	7 3/8
21	Neck	No reduction	16 3/4	17 1/8	17 1/2	17 7/8	18 1/4
22	Bust span	× .90	7	7	7 1/4	7 1/3	7 3/8
23	Bust level	× .90	10 3/4	11	11 1/4	11 1/2	11 3/4

Men's Regular Size Reductions

MEN'S REGULAR STABLE KNIT REDUCTIONS

Zero percent smaller in crosswise direction without any reductions in lengthwise direction.
Use these measurements when drafting slopers for fabrics that stretch from 0% to 25%.
Use your measurements exactly as recorded without any reductions.

		Multiply by	Extra Small	Small	Medium	Large	Extra Large
			32	36	40	44	48
1	Chest	× 0	32	36	40	44	48
2	Waist	× 0	26	30	34	38	42
3	Hip	× 0	34	38	42	46	50
4	Crotch depth	No reduction	9 5/8	9 7/8	10 1/8	10 3/8	10 5/8
5	Waist to knee	No reduction	21 7/8	22 1/8	22 3/8	22 5/8	22 7/8
6	Waist to ankle	No reduction	39 1/8	39 5/8	40 1/8	40 5/8	41 1/8
7	Ankle	× 0	8 3/8	14 3/8	14 7/8	15 3/8	15 7/8
8	Knee	× 0	14	14 1/2	15	15 1/2	16
9	Front crotch	× 0	2 1/8	2 3/8	2 5/8	2 7/8	3 1/8
10	Back crotch	× 0	2 7/8	3 1/8	3 1/2	3 7/8	4 1/8
11	Crotch angle	× 0	1	1 1/4	1 3/8	1 1/2	1 5/8
12	Nape to waist	No reduction	19 1/4	19 3/4	20 1/4	20 3/4	21 1/4
13	Back neck	No reduction	2 3/8	2 3/8	2 3/8	2 1/2	2 1/2
14	Back neck rise	× 0	3/4	3/4	3/4	7/8	7/8
15	Shoulder length	No reduction	6	6 1/4	6 1/2	6 3/4	7
16	Across back	× 0	8 1/4	8 3/4	9 1/4	9 3/4	10 1/4
17	Sleeve length	No reduction	24 5/8	24 7/8	25 1/8	25 3/8	25 5/8
18	Shoulder pitch	× 0	1 3/4	1 3/4	1 7/8	1 7/8	2
19	Bicep	× 0	11 1/4	12	12 3/4	13 1/2	14 1/4
20	Wrist	× 0	6 1/2	7 1/4	8	8 3/4	9 1/2
21	Neck	× 0	14	14 1/4	14 1/2	14 3/4	15
22	Chest span	× 0	5	6	6 3/8	7	7 3/8
23	Chest level	No reduction	9 7/8	9 4/5	9 7/8	9 7/8	9 7/8

MEN'S REGULAR MODERATE KNIT REDUCTIONS

Two percent smaller in crosswise direction without any reductions in lengthwise direction.
Use these measurements when drafting slopers for fabrics that stretch from 25% to 50%.
Multiply your across measurements by 0.98, 2% smaller, except for the shoulder measurement, because the final garment will have twill tape to stabilize the seam and prevent it from stretching.

		Multiply by	Extra Small	Small	Medium	Large	Extra Large
			32	36	40	44	48
1	Chest	× .98	31 3/8	35 1/4	39 1/4	43 1/8	47
2	Waist	× .98	25 1/2	29 3/8	33 3/8	37 1/4	41 1/8
3	Hip	× .98	33 3/8	37 1/4	41 1/8	45	49
4	Crotch depth	No reduction	9 5/8	9 7/8	10 1/8	10 3/8	10 5/8
5	Waist to knee	No reduction	21 7/8	22 1/8	22 3/8	22 5/8	22 7/8
6	Waist to ankle	No reduction	39 1/8	39 5/8	40 1/8	40 5/8	41 1/8
7	Ankle	× .98	8 1/4	14	14 5/8	15	15 1/2
8	Knee	× .98	13 3/4	14 2/8	14 3/4	15 1/4	15 5/8
9	Front crotch	× .98	2	2 3/8	2 5/8	2 7/8	3
10	Back crotch	× .98	2 3/4	3 1/8	3 3/8	3 3/4	4
11	Crotch angle	× .98	1	1 1/8	1 1/4	1 3/8	1 1/2
12	Nape to waist	No reduction	19 1/4	19 3/4	20 1/4	20 3/4	21 1/4
13	Back neck	No reduction	2 3/8	2 3/8	2 3/8	2 1/2	2 1/2
14	Back neck rise	× .98	3/4	3/4	3/4	7/8	7/8
15	Shoulder length	No reduction	6	6 1/4	6 1/2	6 3/4	7
16	Across back	× .98	8 1/4	8 3/4	9 1/4	9 3/4	10 1/4
17	Sleeve length	No reduction	24 5/8	24 7/8	25 1/8	25 3/8	25 5/8
18	Shoulder pitch	× .98	1 3/4	1 3/4	1 3/4	1 7/8	1 7/8
19	Bicep	× .98	11	11 3/4	12 1/2	13 1/4	14
20	Wrist	× .98	6 3/8	7 1/8	7 7/8	8 5/8	9 1/4
21	Neck	× .98	13 3/4	14	14 1/4	14 1/2	14 3/4
22	Chest span	× .98	4 3/4	5 1/4	5 3/4	6 1/4	6 3/4
23	Chest level	No reduction	9 5/8	9 5/8	9 5/8	9 5/8	9 5/8

MEN'S REGULAR STRETCHY KNIT REDUCTIONS

Three percent smaller in crosswise direction without any reductions in lengthwise direction.
Use these measurements when drafting slopers for fabrics that stretch from 50% to 75%.
Multiply your across measurements by 0.97, 3% smaller, except for the shoulder measurement, because the final garment will have twill tape to stabilize the seam and prevent it from stretching.

		Multiply by	Extra Small	Small	Medium	Large	Extra Large
			32	36	40	44	48
1	Chest	× .97	31	35	38¾	42⅝	46½
2	Waist	× .97	25¼	29	33	36⅞	40¾
3	Hip	× .97	33	36⅞	40¾	44⅝	48½
4	Crotch depth	No reduction	9⅝	9⅞	10⅛	10⅜	10⅝
5	Waist to knee	No reduction	21⅞	22⅛	22⅜	22⅝	22⅞
6	Waist to ankle	No reduction	39⅛	39⅝	40⅛	40⅝	41⅛
7	Ankle	× .97	8⅛	14	14⅜	15	15⅜
8	Knee	× .97	13⅝	14	14½	15	15½
9	Front crotch	× .97	2	2¼	2½	2¾	3
10	Back crotch	× .97	2¾	3	3⅜	3¾	4
11	Crotch angle	× .97	1	1⅛	1¼	1⅜	1½
12	Nape to waist	No reduction	19¼	19¾	20¼	20¾	21¼
13	Back neck	No reduction	2⅜	2⅜	2⅜	2½	2½
14	Back neck rise	× .97	¾	¾	¾	⅞	⅞
15	Shoulder length	No reduction	6	6¼	6½	6¾	7
16	Across back	× .97	8¼	8¾	9¼	9¾	10¼
17	Sleeve length	No reduction	24⅝	24⅞	25⅛	25⅜	25⅝
18	Shoulder pitch	× .97	1¾	1¾	1¾	1⅞	1⅞
19	Bicep	× .97	11	11⅝	12⅜	13	13⅞
20	Wrist	× .97	6¼	7	7¾	8½	9¼
21	Neck	× .97	13⅝	13⅞	14	14¼	14½
22	Chest span	× .97	4¾	5¾	6¾	7⅝	8⅝
23	Chest level	No reduction	9½	9½	9½	9½	9½

MEN'S REGULAR SUPER-STRETCH KNIT REDUCTIONS

Five percent smaller in crosswise direction without any reductions in lengthwise direction.
Use these measurements when drafting slopers for fabrics that stretch from 75% to 100%.
Multiply your across measurements by 0.95, 5% smaller, except for the shoulder measurement, because the final garment will have twill tape to stabilize the seam and prevent it from stretching.

		Multiply by	Extra Small	Small	Medium	Large	Extra Large
			32	36	40	44	48
1	Chest	× .95	30⅜	34¼	38	41¾	45⅝
2	Waist	× .95	24¾	28½	32¼	36⅛	39⅞
3	Hip	× .95	32¼	36⅛	39⅞	43¾	47½
4	Crotch depth	No reduction	9⅝	9⅞	10⅛	10⅜	10⅝
5	Waist to knee	No reduction	21⅞	22⅛	22⅜	22⅝	22⅞
6	Waist to ankle	No reduction	39⅛	39⅝	40⅛	40⅝	41⅛
7	Ankle	× .95	8	13⅝	14⅛	14⅝	15
8	Knee	× .95	13¼	13¾	14¼	14¾	15¼
9	Front crotch	× .95	2	2¼	2½	2¾	3
10	Back crotch	× .95	2¾	3	3⅜	3⅝	4
11	Crotch angle	× .95	1	1⅛	1¼	1⅜	1½
12	Nape to waist	No reduction	19¼	19¾	20¼	20¾	21¼
13	Back neck	No reduction	2⅜	2⅜	2⅜	2½	2½
14	Back neck rise	× .95	¾	¾	¾	⅞	⅞
15	Shoulder length	No reduction	6	6¼	6½	6¾	7
16	Across back	× .95	8¼	8¾	9¼	9¾	10¼
17	Sleeve length	No reduction	24⅝	24⅞	25⅛	25⅜	25⅝
18	Shoulder pitch	× .95	1⅝	1¾	1¾	1¾	1⅞
19	Bicep	× .95	10¾	11⅜	12⅛	12⅞	13½
20	Wrist	× .95	6⅛	6⅞	7⅝	8⅜	9
21	Neck	× .95	13¼	13½	13¾	14	14¼
22	Chest span	× .95	4⅝	5⅝	6½	7½	8½
23	Chest level	No reduction	9⅜	9½	9¼	9⅓	9⅓

MEN'S REGULAR RIB KNIT REDUCTIONS

Ten percent smaller in crosswise direction without any reductions in lengthwise direction.
Use these measurements when drafting slopers for fabrics that stretch 100%and over.
Multiply your across measurements by 0.90, 10% smaller, except for the shoulder measurement, because the final garment will have twill tape to stabilize the seam and prevent it from stretching.

		Multiply by	Extra Small	Small	Medium	Large	Extra Large
			32	36	40	44	48
1	Chest	× .90	28 3/4	32 3/8	36	39 5/8	43 1/4
2	Waist	× .90	23 3/8	27	30 5/8	34 1/4	37 3/4
3	Hip	× .90	30 5/8	34 1/4	37 3/4	41 3/8	45
4	Crotch depth	No reduction	9 5/8	9 7/8	10 1/8	10 3/8	10 5/8
5	Waist to knee	No reduction	21 7/8	22 1/8	22 3/8	22 5/8	22 7/8
6	Waist to ankle	No reduction	39 1/8	39 5/8	40 1/8	40 5/8	41 1/8
7	Ankle	× .90	7 1/2	13	13 3/8	13 7/8	14 1/4
8	Knee	× .90	12 5/8	13	13 1/2	14	14 3/8
9	Front crotch	× .90	2	2 1/8	2 3/8	2 5/8	2 7/8
10	Back crotch	× .90	2 1/2	2 7/8	3 1/8	3 1/2	3 3/4
11	Crotch angle	× .90	1	1	1 1/8	1 1/4	1 3/8
12	Nape to waist	No reduction	19 1/4	19 3/4	20 1/4	20 3/4	21 1/4
13	Back neck	No reduction	2 3/8	2 3/8	2 3/8	2 1/2	2 1/2
14	Back neck rise	× .90	3/4	3/4	3/4	7/8	7/8
15	Shoulder length	No reduction	6	6 1/4	6 1/2	6 3/4	7
16	Across back	× .90	8 1/4	8 3/4	9 1/4	9 3/4	10 1/4
17	Sleeve length	No reduction	24 5/8	24 7/8	25 1/8	25 3/8	25 5/8
18	Shoulder pitch	× .90	1 5/8	1 5/8	1 5/8	1 3/4	1 3/4
19	Bicep	× .90	10 1/8	10 6/8	11 1/2	12 1/8	12 7/8
20	Wrist	× .90	5 7/8	6 1/2	7 1/4	7 7/8	8 1/2
21	Neck	× .90	12 5/8	12 7/8	13	13 1/4	13 1/2
22	Chest span	× .90	4 3/8	5 1/2	6 1/4	7 1/8	8
23	Chest level	No reduction	8 7/8	8 7/8	8 7/8	8 7/8	8 7/8

MEN'S REGULAR FOUR-WAY-STRETCH KNIT REDUCTIONS

Ten percent smaller in crosswise direction and 10% smaller in the lengthwise direction.
Use these measurements when drafting slopers for fabrics that stretch 100% in both directions.
Multiply your measurements by 0.90, 10% smaller, in both directions.

		Multiply by	Extra Small	Small	Medium	Large	Extra Large
			32	36	40	44	48
1	Chest	× .90	28 3/4	30 5/8	32 3/8	34 1/4	36
2	Waist	× .90	23 3/8	25 1/4	27	28 6/8	30 5/8
3	Hip	× .90	30 5/8	32 3/8	34 1/4	36	37 6/8
4	Crotch depth	× .90	9 1/8	9 1/4	9 3/8	9 1/2	9 5/8
5	Waist to knee	× .90	20 3/4	20 7/8	21	21 1/8	21 1/4
6	Waist to ankle	× .90	37 1/8	37 3/8	37 5/8	37 7/8	38 1/8
7	Ankle	× .90	7 1/2	12 3/4	13	13 1/8	13 3/8
8	Knee	× .90	12 5/8	12 7/8	13	13 1/4	13 1/2
9	Front crotch	× .90	2	2	2 1/8	2 1/4	2 3/8
10	Back crotch	× .90	2 7/8	3	3 1/8	3 3/8	3 1/2
11	Crotch angle	× .90	1	1 1/8	1 1/4	1 1/4	1 1/3
12	Nape to waist	× .90	18 1/4	18 1/2	18 3/4	19	19 1/4
13	Back neck	No reduction	2 3/8	2 3/8	2 3/8	2 3/8	2 3/8
14	Back neck rise	No reduction	3/4	3/4	3/4	3/4	3/4
15	Shoulder length	No reduction	6	6 1/8	6 1/4	6 3/8	6 1/2
16	Across back	No reduction	8 1/4	8 1/2	8 3/4	9	9 1/4
17	Sleeve length	No reduction	24 5/8	24 3/4	24 7/8	25	25 1/8
18	Shoulder pitch	No reduction	1 3/4	1 3/4	1 3/4	1 7/8	1 7/8
19	Bicep	× .90	10 1/8	10 1/2	10 3/4	11 1/8	11 1/2
20	Wrist	× .90	5 7/8	6 1/4	6 1/2	6 7/8	7 1/4
21	Neck	No reduction	14	14 1/8	14 1/4	14 3/8	14 1/2
22	Chest span	× .90	4 3/8	4 3/4	5 1/4	5 3/4	6 1/4
23	Chest level	× .90	9 3/8	9 1/4	9 1/4	9 3/8	9 1/4

Men's Short Size Reductions

MEN'S SHORT STABLE KNIT REDUCTIONS

Zero percent smaller in crosswise direction without any reductions in the lengthwise direction.
Use these measurements when drafting slopers for fabrics that stretch from 0% to 25%.
Use your measurements exactly as recorded without any reductions.

		Multiply by	Extra Small	Small	Medium	Large	Extra Large
			32 S	**36 S**	**40 S**	**44 S**	**48 S**
1	Chest	× 0	32	36	40	44	48
2	Waist	× 0	26	30	34	38	42
3	Hip	× 0	32	36	40	44	48
4	Crotch depth	No reduction	9	9 1/4	9 1/2	9 3/4	10
5	Waist to knee	No reduction	20 1/2	20 3/4	21	21 1/4	21 1/2
6	Waist to ankle	No reduction	36	36 1/2	37	37 1/2	38
7	Ankle	× 0	8	14	14 1/2	15	15 1/2
8	Knee	× 0	13 5/8	14 1/8	14 5/8	15 1/8	15 5/8
9	Front crotch	× 0	2	2 1/4	2 1/2	2 3/4	3
10	Back crotch	× 0	2 5/8	3	3 3/8	3 5/8	4
11	Crotch angle	× 0	1	1 1/8	1 1/4	1 3/8	1 1/2
12	Nape to waist	No reduction	18 1/8	18 5/8	19 1/8	19 5/8	20 1/8
13	Back neck	No reduction	2 1/4	2 1/4	2 3/8	2 3/8	2 3/8
14	Back neck rise	× 0	3/4	3/4	7/9	4/5	4/5
15	Shoulder length	No reduction	5 7/8	6 1/8	6 3/8	6 5/8	6 7/8
16	Across back	× 0	8	8 1/2	9	9 1/2	10
17	Sleeve length	No reduction	23	23 1/4	23 1/2	23 3/4	24
18	Shoulder pitch	× 0	1 5/8	1 3/4	1 3/4	1 3/4	1 7/8
19	Bicep	× 0	10 1/2	11 1/4	12	12 3/4	13 1/2
20	Wrist	× 0	6 1/4	7	7 3/4	8 1/2	9 1/4
21	Neck	× 0	13 1/2	13 3/4	14	14 1/4	14 1/2
22	Chest span	× 0	5	5 3/8	6	6 3/8	7
23	Chest level	No reduction	9 1/2	9 3/4	10	10 1/4	10 1/2

MEN'S SHORT MODERATE KNIT REDUCTIONS

Two percent smaller in crosswise direction without any reductions in lengthwise direction.
Use these measurements when drafting slopers for fabrics that stretch from 25% to 50%.
Multiply your across measurements by 0.98, 2% smaller, except for the shoulder measurement, because the final garment will have twill tape to stabilize the seam and prevent it from stretching.

		Multiply by	Extra Small	Small	Medium	Large	Extra Large
			32 S	**36 S**	**40 S**	**44 S**	**48 S**
1	Chest	× .98	31 3/8	35 1/4	39 1/4	43 1/8	47
2	Waist	× .98	25 1/2	29 3/8	33 3/8	37 1/4	41 1/8
3	Hip	× .98	31 3/8	35 1/4	39 1/4	43 1/8	47
4	Crotch depth	No reduction	9	9 1/4	9 1/2	9 3/4	10
5	Waist to knee	No reduction	20 1/2	20 3/4	21	21 1/4	21 1/2
6	Waist to ankle	No reduction	36	36 1/2	37	37 1/2	38
7	Ankle	× .98	8	13 3/4	14 1/4	14 3/4	15 1/4
8	Knee	× .98	13 3/8	13 7/8	14 3/8	14 7/8	15 3/8
9	Front crotch	× .98	2	2 1/4	2 1/2	2 3/4	3
10	Back crotch	× .98	2 5/8	3	3 1/4	3 5/8	4
11	Crotch angle	× .98	1	1 1/8	1 1/4	1 3/8	1 1/2
12	Nape to waist	No reduction	18 1/8	18 5/8	19 1/8	19 5/8	20 1/8
13	Back neck	No reduction	2 1/4	2 1/4	2 3/8	2 3/8	2 3/8
14	Back neck rise	× .98	3/4	3/4	3/4	3/4	3/4
15	Shoulder length	No reduction	5 7/8	6 1/8	6 3/8	6 5/8	6 7/8
16	Across back	× .98	8	8 1/2	9	9 1/2	10
17	Sleeve length	No reduction	23	23 1/4	23 1/2	23 3/4	24
18	Shoulder pitch	× .98	1 5/8	1 5/8	1 3/4	1 3/4	1 3/4
19	Bicep	× .98	10 1/4	11	11 3/4	12 1/2	13 1/4
20	Wrist	× .98	6 1/8	6 7/8	7 5/8	8 3/8	9
21	Neck	× .98	13 1/4	13 1/2	13 3/4	14	14 1/4
22	Chest span	× .98	4 3/4	5 1/4	5 3/4	6 1/4	6 3/4
23	Chest level	No reduction	9 1/4	9 1/2	9 3/4	10	10 1/4

MEN'S SHORT STRETCHY KNIT REDUCTIONS

Three percent smaller in crosswise direction without any reductions in lengthwise direction.
Use these measurements when drafting slopers for fabrics that stretch from 50% to 75%.
Multiply your across measurements by 0.97, 3% smaller, except for the shoulder measurement, because the final garment will have twill tape to stabilize the seam and prevent it from stretching.

		Multiply by	Extra Small	Small	Medium	Large	Extra Large
			32 S	36 S	40 S	44 S	48 S
1	Chest	× .97	31	35	38 3/4	42 5/8	46 1/2
2	Waist	× .97	25 2/8	29	33	36 7/8	40 3/4
3	Hip	× .97	31	35	38 3/4	42 5/8	46 1/2
4	Crotch depth	No reduction	9	9 1/4	9 1/2	9 3/4	10
5	Waist to knee	No reduction	20 1/2	20 3/4	21	21 1/4	21 1/2
6	Waist to ankle	No reduction	36	36 1/2	37	37 1/2	38
7	Ankle	× .97	7 7/8	13 5/8	14	14 1/2	15
8	Knee	× .97	13 1/4	13 3/4	14 1/8	14 5/8	15 1/8
9	Front crotch	× .97	2	2 1/8	2 3/8	2 5/8	3
10	Back crotch	× .97	2 5/8	3	3 1/4	3 1/2	3 7/8
11	Crotch angle	× .97	1	1	1 1/4	1 3/8	1 1/2
12	Nape to waist	No reduction	18 1/8	18 5/8	19 1/8	19 5/8	20 1/8
13	Back neck	No reduction	2 1/4	2 1/4	2 3/8	2 3/8	2 3/8
14	Back neck rise	× .97	3/4	3/4	3/4	3/4	3/4
15	Shoulder length	No reduction	5 7/8	6 1/8	6 3/8	6 5/8	6 7/8
16	Across back	× .97	8	8 1/2	9	9 1/2	10
17	Sleeve length	No reduction	23	23 1/4	23 1/2	23 3/4	24
18	Shoulder pitch	× .97	1 5/8	1 5/8	1 5/8	1 3/4	1 3/4
19	Bicep	× .97	10 1/8	11	11 5/8	12 3/8	13
20	Wrist	× .97	6	6 3/4	7 1/2	8 1/4	9
21	Neck	× .97	13	13 3/8	13 5/8	13 7/8	14
22	Chest span	× .97	4 3/4	5 1/4	5 3/4	6 1/4	6 3/4
23	Chest level	No reduction	9 1/4	9 1/2	9 3/4	10	10 1/8

MEN'S SHORT SUPER-STRETCH KNIT REDUCTIONS

Five percent smaller in crosswise direction without any reductions in lengthwise direction.
Use these measurements when drafting slopers for fabrics that stretch from 75% to 100%.
Multiply your across measurements by 0.95, 5% smaller, except for the shoulder measurement, because the final garment will have twill tape to stabilize the seam and prevent it from stretching.

		Multiply by	Extra Small	Small	Medium	Large	Extra Large
			32 S	36 S	40 S	44 S	48 S
1	Chest	× .95	30 3/8	34 1/4	38	41 3/4	45 5/8
2	Waist	× .95	24 3/4	28 1/2	32 1/4	36 1/8	39 7/8
3	Hip	× .95	30 3/8	34 1/4	38	41 3/4	45 5/8
4	Crotch depth	No reduction	9	9 1/4	9 1/2	9 3/4	10
5	Waist to knee	No reduction	20 1/2	20 3/4	21	21 1/4	21 1/2
6	Waist to ankle	No reduction	36	36 1/2	37	37 1/2	38
7	Ankle	× .95	7 5/8	13 1/4	13 3/4	14 1/4	14 3/4
8	Knee	× .95	13	13 3/8	13 7/8	14 3/8	14 7/8
9	Front crotch	× .95	1 7/8	2 1/8	2 3/8	2 5/8	2 7/8
10	Back crotch	× .95	2 1/2	2 7/8	3 1/8	3 1/2	3 3/4
11	Crotch angle	× .95	1	1	1 1/4	1 1/3	1 3/8
12	Nape to waist	No reduction	18 1/8	18 5/8	19 1/8	19 5/8	20 1/8
13	Back neck	No reduction	2 1/4	2 1/4	2 3/8	2 3/8	2 3/8
14	Back neck rise	× .95	3/4	3/4	3/4	3/4	3/4
15	Shoulder length	No reduction	5 7/8	6 1/8	6 3/8	6 5/8	6 7/8
16	Across back	× .95	8	8 1/2	9	9 1/2	10
17	Sleeve length	No reduction	23	23 1/4	23 1/2	23 3/4	24
18	Shoulder pitch	× .95	1 5/8	1 5/8	1 5/8	1 3/4	1 3/4
19	Bicep	× .95	10	10 3/4	11 3/8	12 1/8	12 7/8
20	Wrist	× .95	6	6 5/8	7 3/8	8	8 3/4
21	Neck	× .95	12 7/8	13	13 1/4	13 1/2	13 3/4
22	Chest span	× .95	4 5/8	5 1/8	5 5/8	6 1/8	6 1/2
23	Chest level	No reduction	9	9 1/4	9 1/2	9 3/4	10

MEN'S SHORT RIB KNIT REDUCTIONS

Ten percent smaller in crosswise direction without any reductions in lengthwise direction.
Use these measurements when drafting slopers for fabrics that stretch 100% and over.
Multiply your across measurements by 0.90, 10% smaller, except for the shoulder measurement, because the final garment will have twill tape to stabilize the seam and prevent it from stretching.

		Multiply by	Extra Small	Small	Medium	Large	Extra Large
			32 T	36 T	40 T	44 T	48 T
1	Chest	× .90	28 3/4	32 3/8	36	39 5/8	43 1/4
2	Waist	× .90	23 3/8	27	30 5/8	34 2/8	37 3/4
3	Hip	× .90	28 3/4	32 3/8	36	39 5/8	43 1/4
4	Crotch depth	No reduction	9	9 1/4	9 1/2	9 3/4	10
5	Waist to knee	No reduction	20 1/2	20 3/4	21	21 1/4	21 1/2
6	Waist to ankle	No reduction	36	36 1/2	37	37 1/2	38
7	Ankle	× .90	7 1/4	12 5/8	13	13 1/2	14
8	Knee	× .90	12 1/4	12 3/4	13 1/8	13 5/8	14
9	Front crotch	× .90	1 3/4	2	2 1/4	2 1/2	2 3/4
10	Back crotch	× .90	2 3/8	2 3/4	3	3 1/4	3 5/8
11	Crotch angle	× .90	7/8	1	1 1/8	1 1/4	1 3/8
12	Nape to waist	No reduction	18 1/8	18 5/8	19 1/8	19 5/8	20 1/8
13	Back neck	No reduction	2 1/4	2 1/4	2 3/8	2 3/8	2 3/8
14	Back neck rise	× .90	3/4	3/4	3/4	3/4	3/4
15	Shoulder length	No reduction	5 7/8	6 1/8	6 3/8	6 5/8	6 7/8
16	Across back	× .90	8	8 1/2	9	9 1/2	10
17	Sleeve length	No reduction	23	23 1/4	23 1/2	23 3/4	24
18	Shoulder pitch	× .90	1 1/2	1 1/2	1 5/8	1 5/8	1 5/8
19	Bicep	× .90	9 1/2	10 1/8	10 3/4	11 1/2	12 1/8
20	Wrist	× .90	5 5/8	6 1/4	7	7 5/8	8 3/8
21	Neck	× .90	12 1/8	12 3/8	12 5/8	12 7/8	13
22	Chest span	× .90	4 3/8	5	5 3/8	5 3/4	6 1/4
23	Chest level	No reduction	8 1/2	8 3/4	9	9 1/4	9 1/2

MEN'S SHORT FOUR-WAY-STRETCH KNIT REDUCTIONS

Ten percent smaller in crosswise direction and 10% smaller in the lengthwise direction.
Use these measurements when drafting slopers for fabrics that stretch 100% in both directions.
Multiply your measurements by 0.90, 10% smaller, in both directions.

		Multiply by	Extra Small	Small	Medium	Large	Extra Large
			32 S	36 S	40 S	44 S	48 S
1	Chest	× .90	28 3/4	30 5/8	32 3/8	34 1/4	36
2	Waist	× .90	23 3/8	25 1/4	27	28 3/4	30 5/8
3	Hip	× .90	28 3/4	30 5/8	32 3/8	34 1/4	36
4	Crotch depth	× .90	8 1/2	8 5/8	8 3/4	9	9
5	Waist to knee	× .90	19 1/2	19 5/8	19 3/4	19 7/8	20
6	Waist to ankle	× .90	34 1/4	34 1/2	34 5/8	35	35 1/8
7	Ankle	× .90	7 1/4	12 3/8	12 5/8	12 7/8	13
8	Knee	× .90	12 1/4	12 1/2	12 3/4	13	13 1/8
9	Front crotch	× .90	1 6/8	2	2	2 1/8	2 1/4
10	Back crotch	× .90	2 5/8	2 7/8	3	3 1/8	3 3/8
11	Crotch angle	× .90	1	1	1 1/8	1 1/4	1 1/4
12	Nape to waist	× .90	17 1/4	17 1/2	17 3/4	18	18 1/8
13	Back neck	No reduction	2 1/4	2 1/4	2 1/4	2 3/8	2 3/8
14	Back neck rise	No reduction	3/4	3/4	3/4	3/4	3/4
15	Shoulder length	No reduction	5 7/8	6	6 1/8	6 1/4	6 3/8
16	Across back	No reduction	8	8 1/4	8 1/2	8 3/4	9
17	Sleeve length	No reduction	23	23 1/8	23 1/4	23 3/8	23 1/2
18	Shoulder pitch	No reduction	1 5/8	1 5/8	1 3/4	1 3/4	1 3/4
19	Bicep	× .90	9 1/2	9 3/4	10 1/8	10 1/2	10 3/4
20	Wrist	× .90	5 5/8	6	6 1/4	6 5/8	7
21	Neck	No reduction	13 1/2	13 5/8	13 3/4	13 7/8	14
22	Chest span	× .90	4 3/8	4 3/4	5	5 1/8	5 3/8
23	Chest level	× .90	9	9 1/8	9 1/4	9 3/8	9 1/2

Men's Tall Size Reductions

MEN'S TALL STABLE KNIT REDUCTIONS

Zero percent smaller in crosswise direction without any reductions in lengthwise direction.
Use these measurements when drafting slopers for fabrics that stretch from 0% to 25%.
Use your measurements exactly as recorded without any reductions.

		Multiply by	Extra Small	Small	Medium	Large	Extra Large
			32 T	**36 T**	**40 T**	**44 T**	**48 T**
1	Chest	× 0	32	36	40	44	48
2	Waist	× 0	27	31	35	39	43
3	Hip	× 0	32	36	40	44	48
4	Crotch depth	No reduction	10	10 1/4	10 1/2	10 3/4	11
5	Waist to knee	No reduction	23 1/8	23 3/8	23 5/8	23 7/8	24 1/8
6	Waist to ankle	No reduction	40	40 1/2	41	41 1/2	42
7	Ankle	× 0	8	14	14 1/2	15	15 1/2
8	Knee	× 0	13 5/8	14 1/8	14 5/8	15 1/8	15 5/8
9	Front crotch	× 0	2	2 1/4	2 1/2	2 3/4	3
10	Back crotch	× 0	2 5/8	3	3 3/8	3 5/8	4
11	Crotch angle	× 0	1	1 1/8	1 1/4	1 3/8	1 1/2
12	Nape to waist	No reduction	20 1/8	20 5/8	21 1/8	21 5/8	22 1/8
13	Back neck	No reduction	2 1/4	2 1/4	2 3/8	2 3/8	2 3/8
14	Back neck rise	× 0	3/4	3/4	3/4	3/4	3/4
15	Shoulder length	No reduction	5 7/8	6 1/8	6 3/8	6 5/8	6 7/8
16	Across back	× 0	8	8 1/2	9	9 1/2	10
17	Sleeve length	No reduction	26	26 1/4	26 1/2	26 3/4	27
18	Shoulder pitch	× 0	1 7/8	1 7/8	2	2	2
19	Bicep	× 0	10 1/2	11 1/4	12	12 3/4	13 1/2
20	Wrist	× 0	6 1/4	7	7 3/4	8 1/2	9 1/4
21	Neck	× 0	13 1/2	13 3/4	14	14 1/4	14 1/2
22	Chest span	× 0	5	5 3/8	6	6 3/8	7
23	Chest level	No reduction	9 3/4	10	10 1/4	10 1/2	10 3/4

MEN'S TALL MODERATE KNIT REDUCTIONS

Two percent smaller in crosswise direction without any reductions in lengthwise direction.
Use these measurements when drafting slopers for fabrics that stretch from 25% to 50%.
Multiply your across measurements by 0.98, 2% smaller, except for the shoulder measurement, because the final garment will have twill tape to stabilize the seam and prevent it from stretching.

		Multiply by	Extra Small	Small	Medium	Large	Extra Large
			32 T	**36 T**	**40 T**	**44 T**	**48 T**
1	Chest	× .98	31 3/8	35 1/4	39 1/4	43 1/8	47
2	Waist	× .98	26 1/2	30 3/8	34 1/4	38 1/4	42 1/8
3	Hip	× .98	31 3/8	35 1/4	39 1/4	43 1/8	47
4	Crotch depth	No reduction	10	10 1/4	10 1/2	10 3/4	11
5	Waist to knee	No reduction	23 1/8	23 3/8	23 5/8	23 7/8	24 1/8
6	Waist to ankle	No reduction	40	40 1/2	41	41 1/2	42
7	Ankle	× .98	8	13 3/4	14 1/4	14 3/4	15 1/4
8	Knee	× .98	13 3/8	13 7/8	14 3/8	14 7/8	15 3/8
9	Front crotch	× .98	2	2 1/4	2 1/2	2 3/4	3
10	Back crotch	× .98	2 5/8	3	3 1/4	3 5/8	4
11	Crotch angle	× .98	1	1 1/8	1 1/4	1 3/8	1 1/2
12	Nape to waist	No reduction	20 1/8	20 5/8	21 1/8	21 5/8	22 1/8
13	Back neck	No reduction	2 1/4	2 2/8	2 3/8	2 3/8	2 3/8
14	Back neck rise	× .98	3/4	3/4	6/8	6/8	6/8
15	Shoulder length	No reduction	5 7/8	6 1/8	6 3/8	6 5/8	6 7/8
16	Across back	× .98	8	8 1/2	9	9 1/2	10
17	Sleeve length	No reduction	26	26 1/4	26 1/2	26 3/4	27
18	Shoulder pitch	× .98	1 3/4	1 7/8	1 7/8	2	2
19	Bicep	× .98	10 1/4	11	11 3/4	12 1/2	13 1/4
20	Wrist	× .98	6 1/8	6 7/8	7 5/8	8 3/8	9
21	Neck	× .98	13 1/4	13 1/2	13 3/4	14	14 1/4
22	Chest span	× .98	4 3/4	5 1/4	5 3/4	6 1/4	6 3/4
23	Chest level	No reduction	9 1/2	9 3/4	10	10 1/4	10 1/2

MEN'S TALL STRETCHY KNIT REDUCTIONS

Three percent smaller in crosswise direction without any reductions in lengthwise direction.
Use these measurements when drafting slopers for fabrics that stretch from 50% to 75%.
Multiply your across measurements by 0.97, 3% smaller, except for the shoulder measurement, because the final garment will have twill tape to stabilize the seam and prevent it from stretching.

		Multiply by	Extra Small	Small	Medium	Large	Extra Large
			32 T	36 T	40 T	44 T	48 T
1	Chest	× .97	31	35	38 3/4	42 5/8	46 1/2
2	Waist	× .97	26 1/4	30	34	37 7/8	41 6/8
3	Hip	× .97	31	35	38 3/4	42 5/8	46 1/2
4	Crotch depth	No reduction	10	10 1/4	10 1/2	10 3/4	11
5	Waist to knee	No reduction	23 1/8	23 3/8	23 5/8	23 7/8	24 1/8
6	Waist to ankle	No reduction	40	40 1/2	41	41 1/2	42
7	Ankle	× .97	7 7/8	13 5/8	14	14 1/2	15
8	Knee	× .97	13 1/4	13 3/4	14 1/8	14 5/8	15 1/8
9	Front crotch	× .97	2	2 1/8	2 3/8	2 5/8	3
10	Back crotch	× .97	2 5/8	3	3 1/4	3 1/2	3 7/8
11	Crotch angle	× .97	1	1	1 1/4	1 3/8	1 1/2
12	Nape to waist	No reduction	20 1/8	20 5/8	21 1/8	21 5/8	22 1/8
13	Back neck	No reduction	2 1/4	2 1/4	2 3/8	2 3/8	2 3/8
14	Back neck rise	× .97	3/4	3/4	3/4	3/4	3/4
15	Shoulder length	No reduction	5 7/8	6 1/8	6 3/8	6 5/8	6 7/8
16	Across back	× .97	8	8 1/2	9	9 1/2	10
17	Sleeve length	No reduction	26	26 1/4	26 1/2	26 3/4	27
18	Shoulder pitch	× .97	1 3/4	1 7/8	1 7/8	2	2
19	Bicep	× .97	10 1/8	11	11 5/8	12 3/8	13
20	Wrist	× .97	6	6 3/4	7 1/2	8 1/4	9
21	Neck	× .97	13	13 3/8	13 5/8	13 7/8	14
22	Chest span	× .97	4 3/4	5 1/4	5 3/4	6 1/4	6 3/4
23	Chest level	No reduction	9 1/2	9 3/4	10	10 1/8	10 3/8

MEN'S TALL SUPER-STRETCH KNIT REDUCTIONS

Five percent smaller in crosswise direction without any reductions in lengthwise direction.
Use these measurements when drafting slopers for fabrics that stretch from 75% to 100%.
Multiply your across measurements by 0.95, 5% smaller, except for the shoulder measurement, because the final garment will have twill tape to stabilize the seam and prevent it from stretching.

		Multiply by	Extra Small	Small	Medium	Large	Extra Large
			32 T	36 T	40 T	44 T	48 T
1	Chest	× .95	30 3/8	34 1/4	38	41 3/4	45 5/8
2	Waist	× .95	25 5/8	29 1/2	33 1/4	37	40 7/8
3	Hip	× .95	30 3/8	34 1/5	38	41 3/4	45 5/8
4	Crotch depth	No reduction	10	10 1/4	10 1/2	10 3/4	11
5	Waist to knee	No reduction	23 1/8	23 3/8	23 5/8	23 7/8	24 1/8
6	Waist to ankle	No reduction	40	40 1/2	41	41 1/2	42
7	Ankle	× .95	7 5/8	13 1/4	13 3/4	14 1/4	14 3/4
8	Knee	× .95	13	13 3/8	13 7/8	14 3/8	14 7/8
9	Front crotch	× .95	1 7/8	2 1/8	2 3/8	2 5/8	2 7/8
10	Back crotch	× .95	2 1/2	2 7/8	3 1/6	3 1/2	3 6/8
11	Crotch angle	× .95	1	1	1 1/4	1 1/4	1 3/8
12	Nape to waist	No reduction	20 1/8	20 5/8	21 1/8	21 5/8	22 1/8
13	Back neck	No reduction	2 1/4	2 1/4	2 3/8	2 3/8	2 3/8
14	Back neck rise	× .95	3/4	3/4	3/4	3/4	3/4
15	Shoulder length	No reduction	5 7/8	6 1/8	6 3/8	6 5/8	6 7/8
16	Across back	× .95	8	8 1/2	9	9 1/2	10
17	Sleeve length	No reduction	26	26 1/4	26 1/2	26 3/4	27
18	Shoulder pitch	× .95	1 3/4	1 3/4	1 7/8	1 7/8	2
19	Bicep	× .95	10	10 3/4	11 3/8	12 1/8	12 7/8
20	Wrist	× .95	6	6 5/8	7 3/8	8	8 3/4
21	Neck	× .95	12 7/8	13	13 1/4	13 1/2	13 3/4
22	Chest span	× .95	4 5/8	5 1/8	5 5/8	6	6 1/2
23	Chest level	No reduction	9 1/4	9 1/2	9 3/4	10	10 1/4

MEN'S TALL RIB KNIT REDUCTIONS

Ten percent smaller in crosswise direction without any reductions in lengthwise direction.
Use these measurements when drafting slopers for fabrics that stretch 100% and over.
Multiply your across measurements by 0.90, 10% smaller, except for the shoulder measurement, because the final garment will have twill tape to stabilize the seam and prevent it from stretching.

		Multiply by	Extra Small	Small	Medium	Large	Extra Large
			32 T	36 T	40 T	44 T	48 T
1	Chest	× .90	28 3/4	32 3/8	36	39 5/8	43 1/4
2	Waist	× .90	24 1/4	28	31 1/2	35 1/8	38 3/4
3	Hip	× .90	28 3/4	32 3/8	36	39 5/8	43 1/4
4	Crotch depth	No reduction	10	10 1/4	10 1/2	10 3/4	11
5	Waist to knee	No reduction	23 1/8	23 3/8	23 5/8	23 7/8	24 1/8
6	Waist to ankle	No reduction	40	40 1/2	41	41 1/2	42
7	Ankle	× .90	7 1/4	12 5/8	13	13 1/2	14
8	Knee	× .90	12 1/4	12 3/4	13 1/8	13 5/8	14
9	Front crotch	× .90	1 3/4	2	2 1/4	2 1/2	2 3/4
10	Back crotch	× .90	2 3/8	2 3/4	3	3 1/4	3 5/8
11	Crotch angle	× .90	7/8	1	1 1/8	1 1/4	1 3/8
12	Nape to waist	No reduction	20 1/8	20 5/8	21 1/8	21 5/8	22 1/8
13	Back neck	No reduction	2 1/4	2 1/4	2 3/8	2 3/8	2 3/8
14	Back neck rise	× .90	3/4	3/4	3/4	3/4	3/4
15	Shoulder length	No reduction	5 7/8	6 1/8	6 3/8	6 5/8	6 7/8
16	Across back	× .90	8	8 1/2	9	9 1/2	10
17	Sleeve length	No reduction	26	26 1/4	26 1/2	26 3/4	27
18	Shoulder pitch	× .90	1 5/8	1 3/4	1 3/4	1 3/4	1 3/4
19	Bicep	× .90	9 1/2	10 1/8	10 3/4	11 1/2	12 1/8
20	Wrist	× .90	5 5/8	6 1/4	7	7 5/8	8 3/8
21	Neck	× .90	12 1/8	12 3/8	12 5/8	12 7/8	13
22	Chest span	× .90	4 3/8	4 7/8	5 3/8	5 3/4	6 1/4
23	Chest level	No reduction	8 3/4	9	9 1/4	9 1/2	9 5/8

MEN'S TALL FOUR-WAY-STRETCH KNIT REDUCTIONS

Ten percent smaller in crosswise direction and 10% smaller in the lengthwise direction.
Use these measurements when drafting slopers for fabrics that stretch 100% in both directions.
Multiply your measurements by 0.90, 10% smaller, in both directions.

		Multiply by	Extra Small	Small	Medium	Large	Extra Large
			32 T	36 T	40 T	44 T	48 T
1	Chest	× .90	28 3/4	30 5/8	32 3/8	34 1/4	36
2	Waist	× .90	24 1/4	26 1/8	28	29 3/4	31 1/2
3	Hip	× .90	28 3/4	30 5/8	32 3/8	34 1/4	36
4	Crotch depth	× .90	9 1/2	9 5/8	9 3/4	9 7/8	10
5	Waist to knee	× .90	22	22	22 1/4	22 1/3	22 1/2
6	Waist to ankle	× .90	38	38 1/4	38 1/2	38 3/4	39
7	Ankle	× .90	7 1/4	12 3/8	12 5/8	12 7/8	13
8	Knee	× .90	12 1/4	12 1/2	12 3/4	13	13 1/8
9	Front crotch	× .90	1 3/4	2	2	2 1/8	2 1/4
10	Back crotch	× .90	2 5/8	2 7/8	3	3 1/8	3 3/8
11	Crotch angle	× .90	1	1	1 1/8	1 1/4	1 1/4
12	Nape to waist	× .90	19 1/8	19 3/8	19 5/8	19 7/8	20
13	Back neck	No reduction	2 1/4	2 1/4	2 1/4	2 3/8	2 3/8
14	Back neck rise	No reduction	3/4	3/4	3/4	3/4	3/4
15	Shoulder length	No reduction	5 7/8	6	6 1/8	6 1/4	6 3/8
16	Across back	No reduction	8	8 1/4	8 1/2	8 3/4	9
17	Sleeve length	No reduction	26	26 1/8	26 1/4	26 3/8	26 1/2
18	Shoulder pitch	No reduction	1 7/8	1 7/8	1 7/8	1 7/8	2
19	Bicep	× .90	9 1/2	9 3/4	10 1/8	10 1/2	10 3/4
20	Wrist	× .90	5 5/8	6	6 1/4	6 5/8	7
21	Neck	No reduction	13 1/2	13 5/8	13 3/4	13 7/8	14
22	Chest span	× .90	4 3/8	4 5/8	4 7/8	5	5 3/8
23	Chest level	× .90	9 1/4	9 3/8	9 1/2	9 5/8	9 3/4

CHAPTER 5

Skirts

About This Chapter

This chapter begins with the development of the skirt sloper, since it is the easiest of all styles. Draft the skirt by following the instructions, using the measurements provided, or by substituting measurements from the charts in the previous chapter. You may create all of the different stretch skirt slopers—stable knit, moderate knit, stretchy knit, and super-stretch knit—or simply create the largest ratio, stable kit, and draw the other ratios in colored markers.

In addition, this chapter demonstrates the drafting process for different patterns, such as A-line skirt, slightly gathered waist, full gathered waist, and dirndl skirt; center back slit, side-seam slit, drawstring side-seam, and gathered side-seams. Although all these patterns are labeled "one-way stretch," they may be used interchangeably with two-way-stretch and four-way-stretch fabrics because a skirt does not pass over the shoulders or through the crotch, therefore not utilizing any of the lengthwise stretch. For maximum mobility and a tight fit, one-way-stretch garments should always be cut with the stretch going around the body.

There are five principles of knit patternmaking that are explained and illustrated throughout this chapter:

1. Negative ease
2. Adding a style line
3. Slash and spread to add fullness, flare, gathering, and ease
4. Circles for skirts and ruffles
5. Reductions for binding, banding, trim, and elastic
6. After studying this chapter, the student will have a general knowledge of stretch patternmaking.

Skirt Slopers

The skirt sloper is simply a front and back that are identical. Woven patternmakers may wonder, how this is possible. Understand that stretch-knit fabrics will always stretch to conform to the front and back areas of the body. You may also wonder why the waist is drafted straight. Understand also that the curve of the waist will happen because of the compression of the fabric.

Note that as the skirt is stretched across, it will shorten in the waist, and excess that is not shortened by stretching will compress to create an artificial curved waist. This is because the tendency of knits is to mold to the body.

One-Way-Stretch Skirt Sloper (Stable Knit)

The following draft is shown for the skirt sloper and is illustrated in Misses Medium, but the measurements for Small, Large, and Extra Large are also included for future drafts. Also, note that personal measurements may be substituted in the Standard Measurement column, to create a personal sloper, or you may substitute Misses measurements for other size ranges, such as Petite, Junior, Half Size, Plus Size, etc.

The front and back skirt sloper will be drafted on top of each other; then notched, traced, separated, and labeled. Slopers/blocks should always be made of oak-tag, green board, or block plastic.

The experienced patternmaker will complete all the sets of skirt slopers for each stretch ratio. Before starting any draft, determine the stretch ratio of the fabric and select the appropriate sloper. However, for clarity, time, and to save materials, the draft in this chapter is completed in stable knit, and the other stretch ratios are indicated on the slopers in contrasting colored markers.

Note that a particular company's size specs may fall between sizes. The draft should be drafted accordingly.

MEASUREMENTS NEEDED FOR STABLE KNIT SKIRTS

Use the Misses stable-knit measurements for the basic skirt draft, since it is the largest, then indicate the different stretch ratios on the sloper with contrasting colored markers.

#		Standard Medium measurements	Reduce by	New measurement	Divide by panels	Extra Extra Small	Extra Small	Small	Medium	Large	Extra Large	Extra Extra Large
2	Waist	27 1/2	0%	28 1/4	4	22 1/2	23 1/2	25 1/2	27 1/2	30 1/2	33 1/2	37 1/2
3	Hip	38 1/2	0%	39 1/4	4	33 1/2	34 1/2	36 1/2	38 1/2	41 1/2	44 1/2	48 1/2
4	Crotch depth	10 5/8	No length reduction			10 1/2	10 5/8	10 1/2	10 5/8	10 7/8	11 1/8	11 3/8
5	Waist to knee	23	No length reduction			22 7/8	23	22 7/8	23	23 1/4	23 1/2	23 3/4
6	Waist to ankle	38 1/2	No length reduction			38 1/4	38 1/2	38 1/4	38 1/2	39	39 1/2	40

Skirt Sloper Draft

Since the front will be drafted on top of the back, the measurements need to be divided into four.

#		Extra Extra Small	Extra Small	Small	Medium	Large	Extra Large	Extra Extra Large
2	1/4 of waist	5 5/8	5 7/8	6 3/8	6 7/8	7 5/8	8 3/8	9 3/8
3	1/4 of hip	8 3/8	8 5/8	9 1/8	9 5/8	10 3/8	11 1/8	12 1/8
4	Crotch depth	10 1/2	10 5/8	10 4/8	10 5/8	10 7/8	11 1/8	11 3/8
	1/3 of crotch depth	3 1/2	3 1/2	3 1/2	3 1/2	3 5/8	3 3/4	3 3/4

For your sample size and stretch ratios, choose measurements from the appropriate chart from the previous chapter. For an explanation of reductions and measurements used, see Chapter 4, Slopers and Reductions.

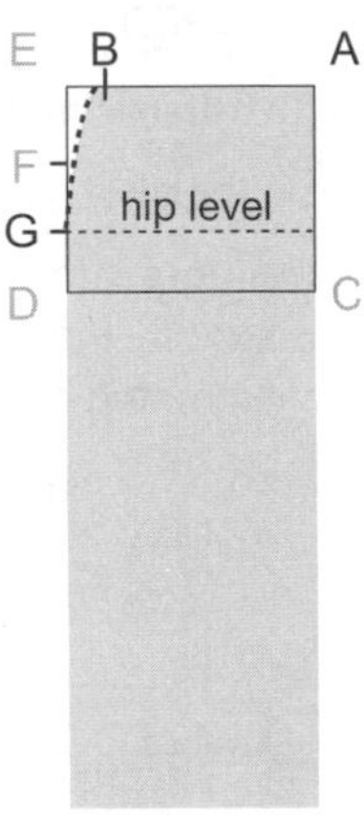

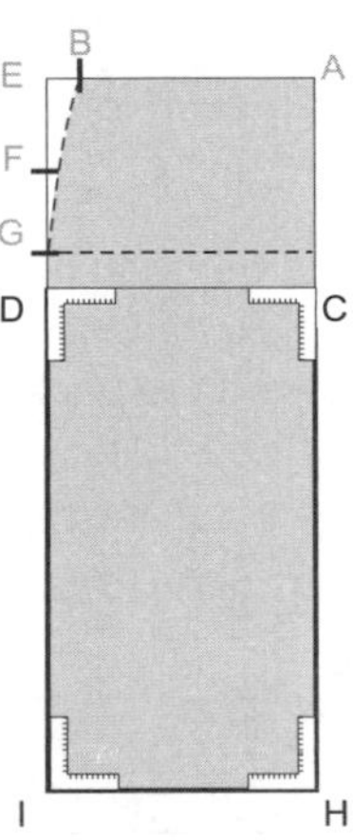

A-B = square across the waist measurement (#2 from chart).

A-C = crotch depth square down (#4 from chart).

C-D = hip measurement squared across (#3 from chart).

D-E = squared up to waist level, it's just a temporary guideline and should not meet up with B, but should square up to E.

Divide E-F into thirds, as illustrated:

E-F = one-third of E-D.

F-G = one-third of E-D.

G-D = one-third of E-D.

At B-G for industry sizes (one-third of E-D), draw a curved hip line using a variform curve, placing approximately #4 of the ruler (variform curved ruler) at the waist and blending into the side seam to draw the hip curve.

The shape of the hips may change depending on the target market, the age group, and size specs of your customer.

Since there is no such thing as "stretch muslin" to test the fit, you must create a custom style using the actual fabric. This may not be practical for the home sewer, student, or for a custom designer, who may only want to purchase enough fabric for one garment.

In order to do this you must exaggerate the fit through the hip area and simply serge off the excess after the fitting.

Draw the hip curve to the higher mark and correct the hip shape in fitting.

Do not spend a lot of time and effort drawing this hip curve, as it will eventually be serged off.

A-H = waist to knee (#4 from chart), or any length required.

A-H = waist to ankle (#6 from chart).

C-H = square down.

D-I = square down.

H-I = square across.

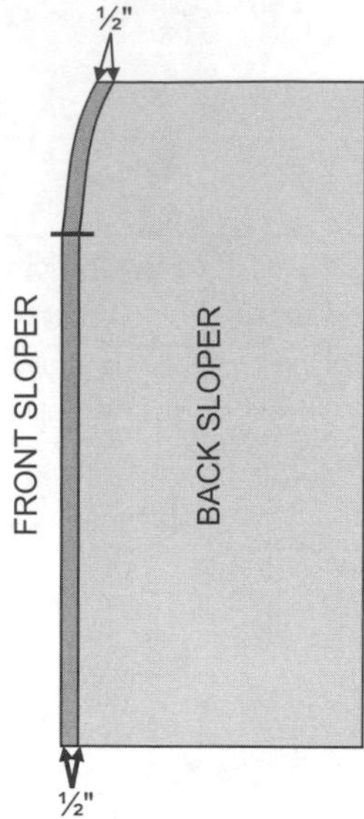

Remove ¼″ from the back side-seam of the draft.

Add ¼″ to the front side-seam of the draft.

Trace the hip notch to both pieces.

This is so the back is larger than the front; and, when viewed from the front, you cannot see the side seams, as they will be slightly toward the back.

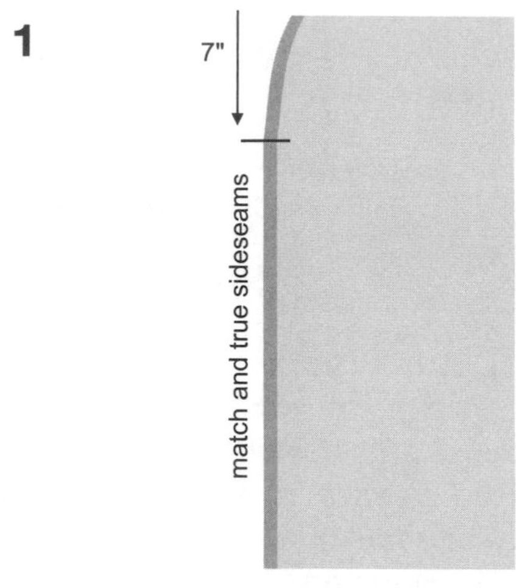

TRUEING THE SKIRT SLOPER

Place a hip notch at G (two-thirds from waist to crotch).

Trace separately and true the skirt slopers.

Place the front and back side-seams on top of each other and ensure that they are exactly the same shape and length, and that all notches match perfectly.

A perfect sloper is required for a perfect garment.

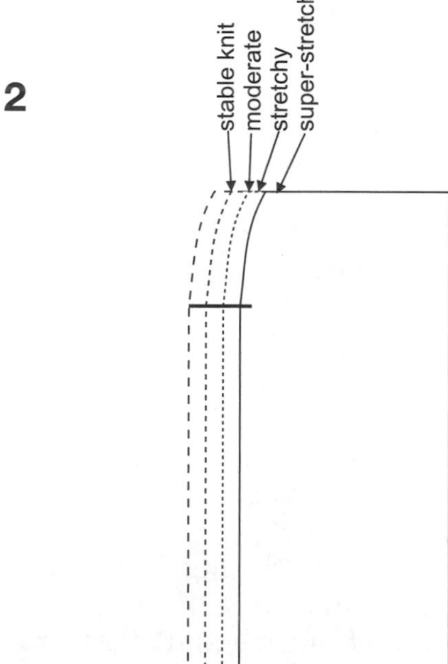

For clarity, time, and to save materials, the student designer may create the sloper for stable knits and trace the other fabrications using the measurements already provided.

	Stable Knit	Moderate Knit	Stretchy Knit	Super-Stretch Knit	Rib Knit
Waist	0	−⅛	−¼	−⅛	−¼
Hip	0	−⅛	−¼	−⅛	−¼

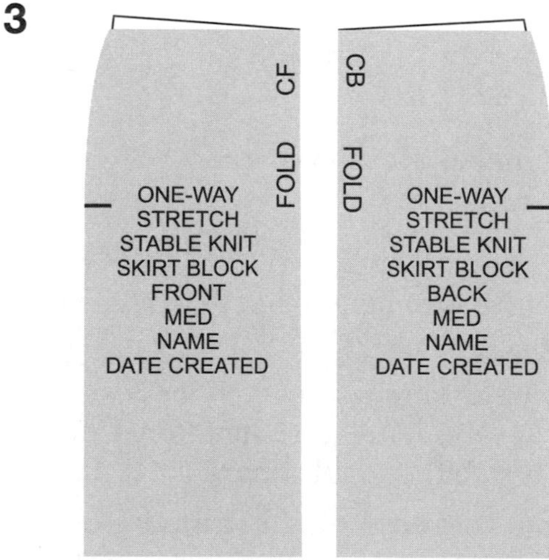

Label the slopers correctly and include whether they are the front piece or the back piece.

Label the slopers with the type of stretch—"one-way stretch"—and the degree, or type, of stretch.

Label with your name and the date created.

No grainline for blocks. It is not necessary to label the skirt "one-way" stretch, as that is implied when labeled "stable-knit."

Label the side seams with the other stretch ratios (see next).

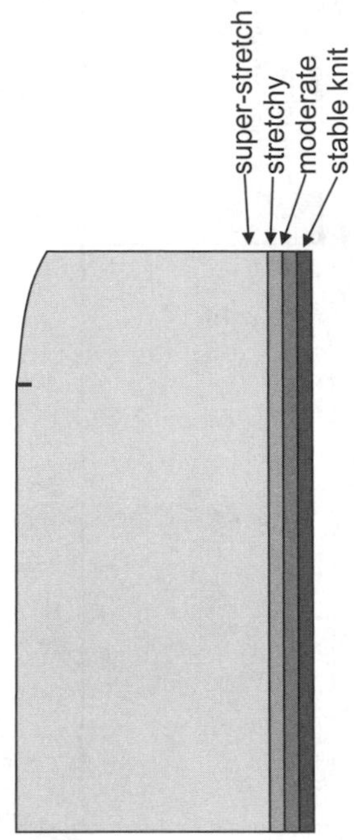

COMPARE SLOPERS

If you have created a complete set of slopers in all stretch ratios, compare and check the side seams.

Line up all four sets of skirt slopers at the side seams and check that the differences between slopers match, and that all curves are exactly the same.

Repeat for the back.

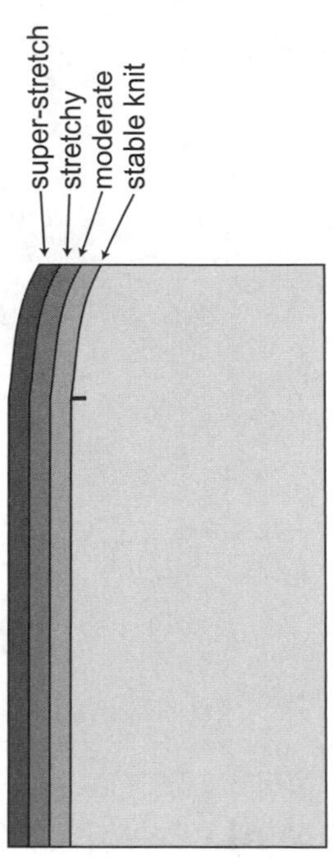

Line up all four sets of skirt slopers at the center front and check that the differences between slopers match, and that all curves are exactly the same.

Repeat for the back.

Skirt Equipment

The seam allowances needed depend on the type of fabric used and equipment used (see Chapter 3, Principles of Pattern-Drafting).

Stable Knits	Use $^3/_8$″ or ½″ seam allowances for thicker fabrics, or loosely knitted, because if the fabric is very thick, the serge will just pull off if too small	4-thread serger or 5-thread serger
Moderate Knits	Use $^3/_8$″ seam allowances	4-thread serger
Stretchy and Super-Stretch Knits	Use ¼″ or $^3/_8$″ seam allowances	4-thread serger or 3-thread serger

Seam Allowances For Skirts

Side seams	$^3/_8$″	4-thread serger
Straight hems	1″	Cover-stitch
Curved hems	½″	Cover-stitch
Waist edge (depends on the style of waist finish)	¼″	For elastic in a casing
	None	For elastic serged to waist
	$^3/_8$″	For separate waistband
	$^3/_8$″	For underwear finish
	$^3/_8$″	For ribbed waistband
	None	For $^3/_8$″ binding
Waistbands	Same width as the elastic	
Slit	1″ fold back facing/hem	Straight stitch

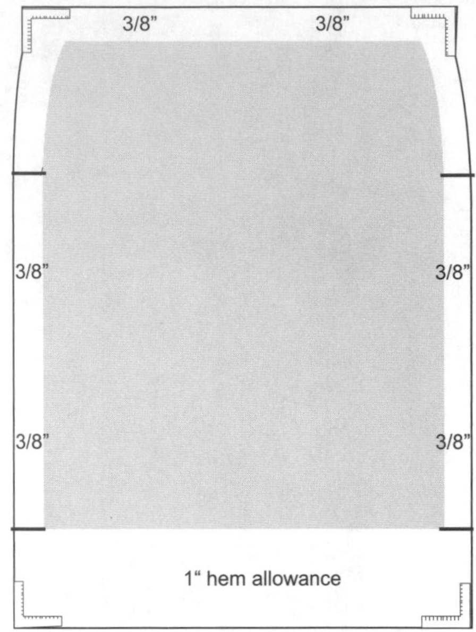

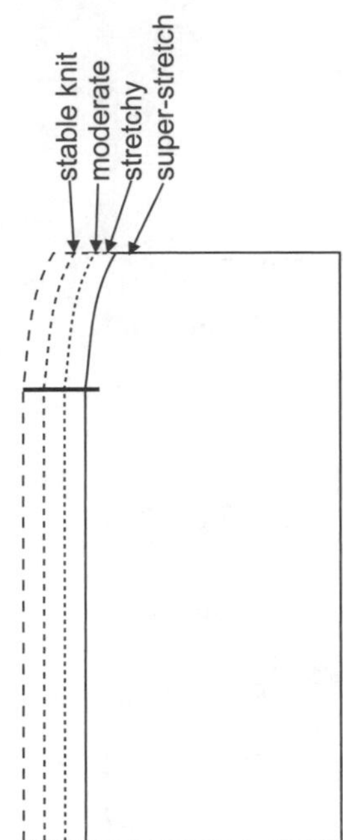

ADDING SEAM ALLOWANCES TO SKIRTS

All patterns need seam allowances for assembly. The amount of seam allowance is determined by the seam allowance in the previous chart.

To complete the pattern, trace out the draft or sloper. For a simple style, add the necessary seam allowances as illustrated, label the pattern as illustrated, and add the grainline.

Always true the pattern by checking every seam allowance before cutting it out in fabric.

Check the lengths of every seam that will be sewn together.

Check the notch placement, and that all notches match perfectly.

Check that all intersecting and crossing lines form a smooth and continuous line.

Check that all seams are squared.

Trace out the appropriate sloper front and back. The stretch ratio depends on your fabric choice:

- Stable knit
- Moderate knit
- Stretchy knit
- Super-stretch knit
- Rib knit

Decide on the fit of the waist you require, or desire:

- Fitted waist
- Semi-fitted waist
- Unfitted waist

Waist Volume

Depending on the season and the silhouette currently in fashion, you may add fullness to the waist of a skirt or pants. Each technique provides slightly different results. This section demonstrates the various techniques used to add fullness at the waist of skirts. The principles may be applied to pants and other garments as well. For instructions on how to draft a separate waistband, see Chapter 6.

For waist finishes that are attached to the skirt pattern, such as casings and elastic finishes, see the following:

Medium waist = $26\frac{1}{2}$" + 25%.

Stable-knit stretch ratio = $33\frac{1}{2}$", which is not enough to pull over the hips; $36\frac{1}{2}$" unless you use a zipper, or some kind of opening at the waist.

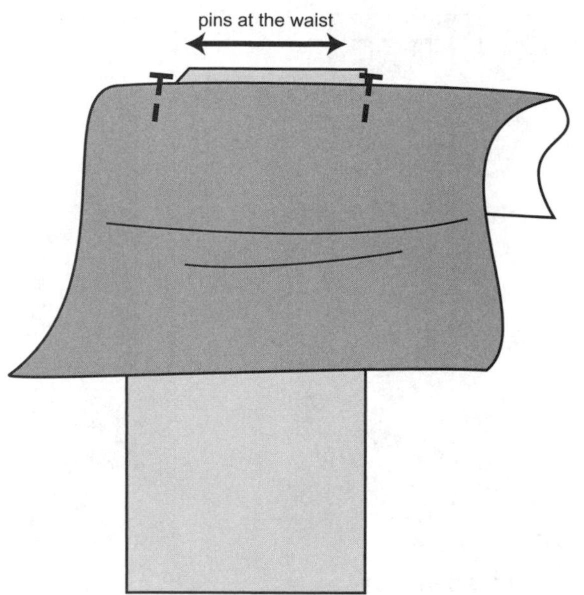

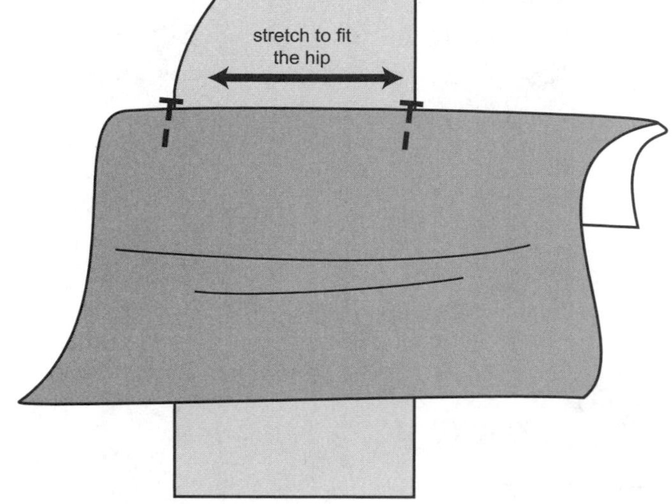

HOW TO TEST IF YOUR SKIRT WILL PULL ON WITHOUT A ZIPPER

Fold your fabric a few inches down from the cut edge and lay it on top of the skirt draft, at the waist. Place one pin at the side seam and another at the center front.

Stretch the waist and see if it will reach the draft, at the hip level.

If it stretches enough, then you may use the fitted waist. If not, then you must check to see if the semi-fitted waist will stretch enough to fit over the hips. If not, then you must use the unfitted waist.

If you fuse a waistband or facing, the skirt will still not pull on and a zipper or other opening will be needed.

WAIST FIT

There are different waist fits that must be considered when drafting skirts.

FITTED WAIST

For a fitted waist (applicable only if the fabric will stretch enough to be pulled on over the hips), use the sloper as drafted, and add seam allowances, hems, and other details required.

To check, place the crosswise fold of the fabric a few inches below the cut edge on the waist of your fabric, and place pins marking the amount of the waist of your sloper/patterns. Hold tight and see if this amount will stretch to the width of the hips. If not, use the unfitted waist. If that is too large, use the semi-fitted waist.

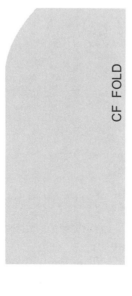

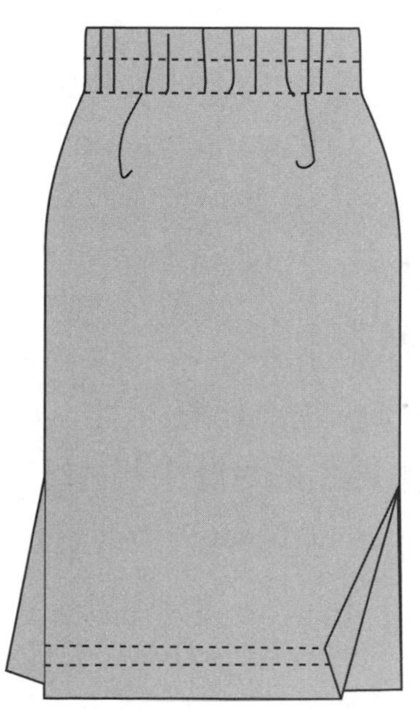

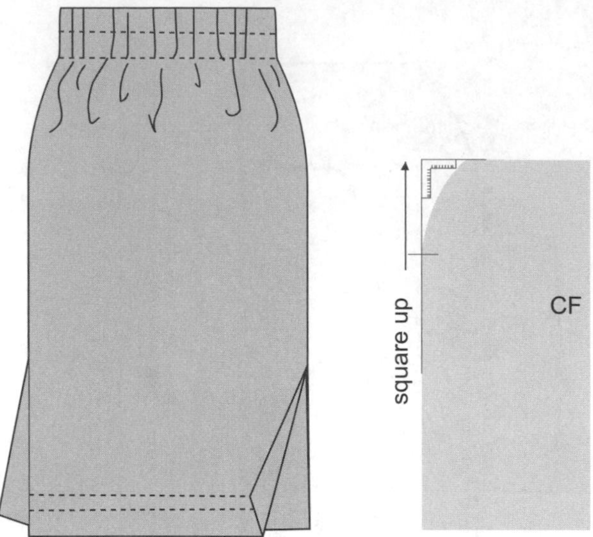

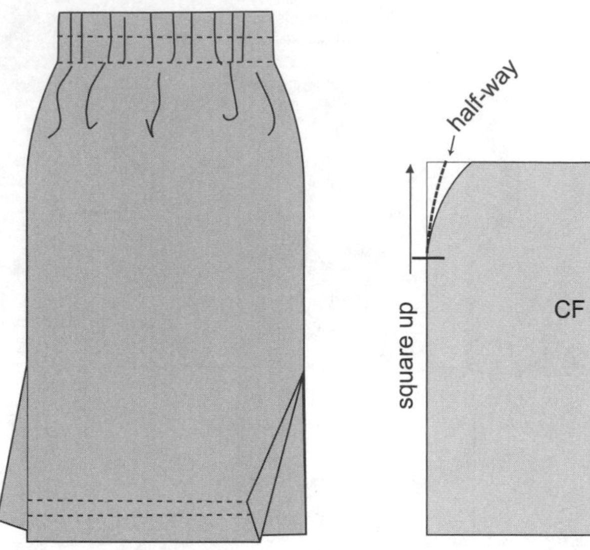

UNFITTED WAIST

Use the loosely fitted waist draft when the fabric does not stretch enough to allow the waist to be pulled on over the hips, such as with stable and moderate knits.

For example, the waist of a stable-knit skirt is only 26½″, while the hip is 36½″. The fabric will not stretch enough to allow the skirt to be pulled on over the hips:

26½″ + 25% (6¾″) = 33¼″, too small for hips of 36½″.

Increase the waist by extending the side seams straight up, which will result in a larger waist that can be pulled in with gathering or elastic.

SEMI-FITTED WAIST

For semi-fitted waist, find the middle of the fitted waist and the unfitted waist and draw a new hip, using the variform hip curve. Alternatively, increase the waist by any amount that will allow the waist to fit over the hips.

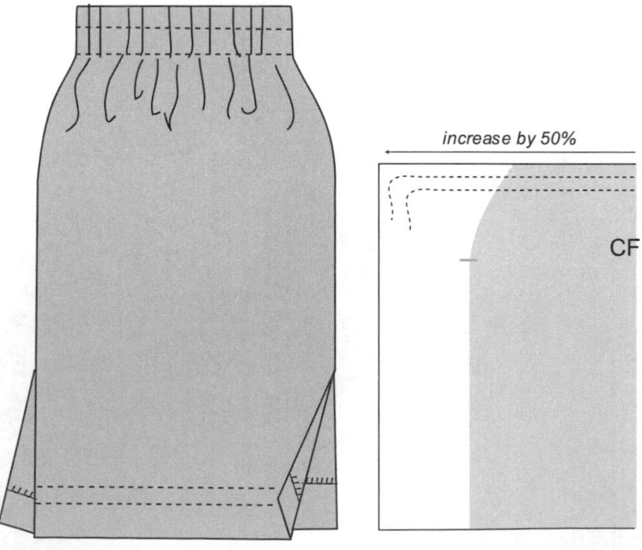

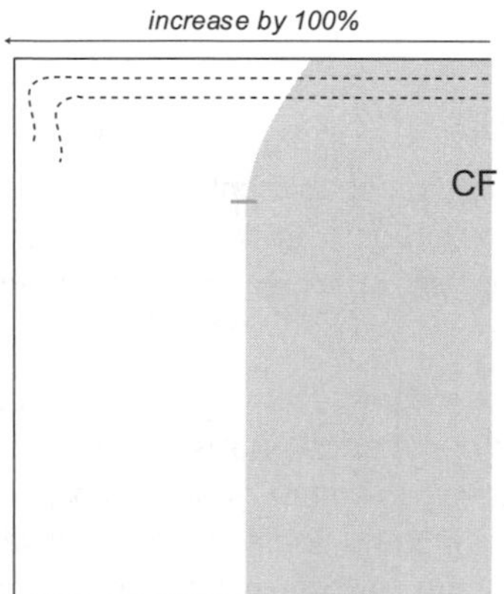

Additional Waist Gathering

Your design may require additional gathering at the waist.

For light gathering, increase the original waist measurement by 50%.

For medium gathering, double the original measurement (increase by 100%).

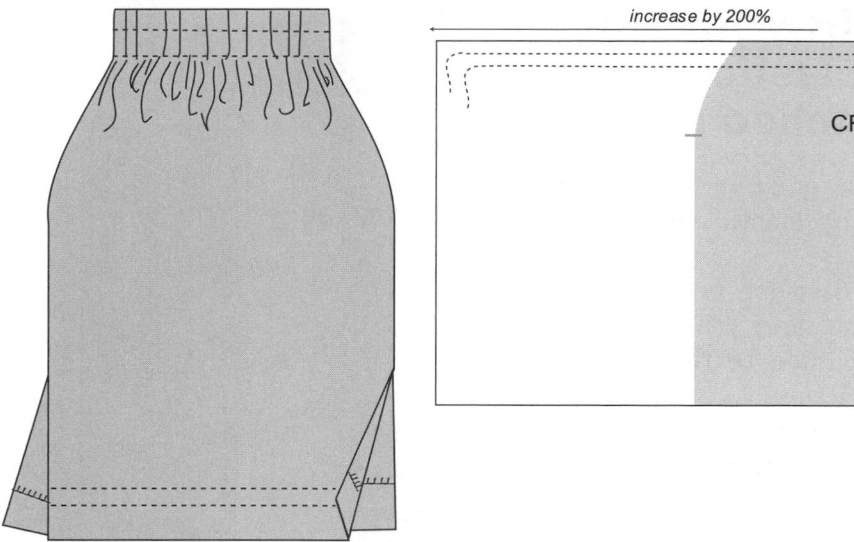

Very heavy or exaggerated gathering may triple the original measurement (increase by up to 300%).

This may be too much gathering for heavy or regular-weight fabrics.

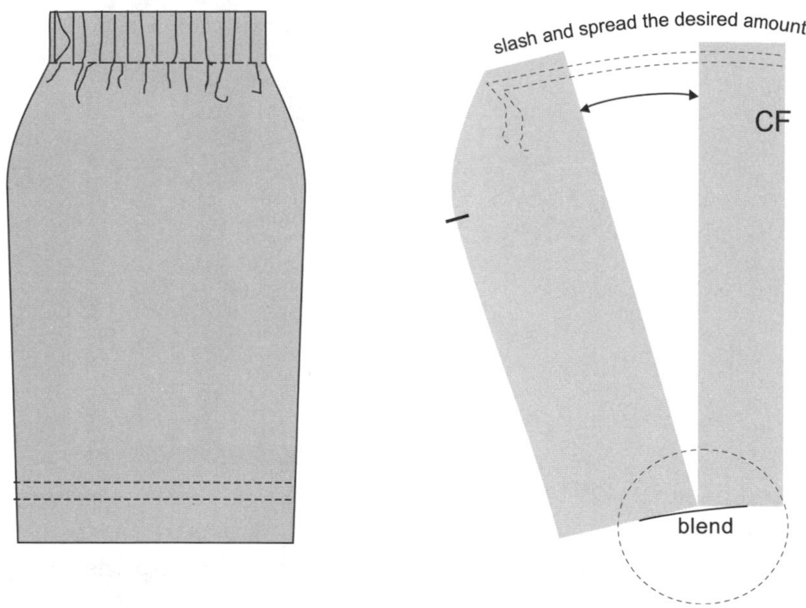

Waist Gathering Without Increasing the Width at the Hem

The previous draft increases the hem circumference as well as the waist. Follow these instructions if you wish to increase the waist and not the hem.

Slash and spread to create added fullness at the waist.

Increase by 50% of the original waist, up to as much as double the original waist measurement.

Remember to blend the hem into a smooth and continuous line.

Style #5-001 Basic Skirt With Side Slits, Patch Pockets, Elastic in a Casing, and Cover-Stitched Hem

This basic style teaches about basic skirt patterns, patch pockets, slits, details, elastic in a casing, elastic stretch ratios, and cover-stitched hems.

Complete this pattern as illustrated for practice before attempting to draft any other styles, and construct using the sewing instructions in the companion textbook, *Stretch Construction*.

Compare your skirt blocks and sample with the mark sheets in the Appendix before handing them in.

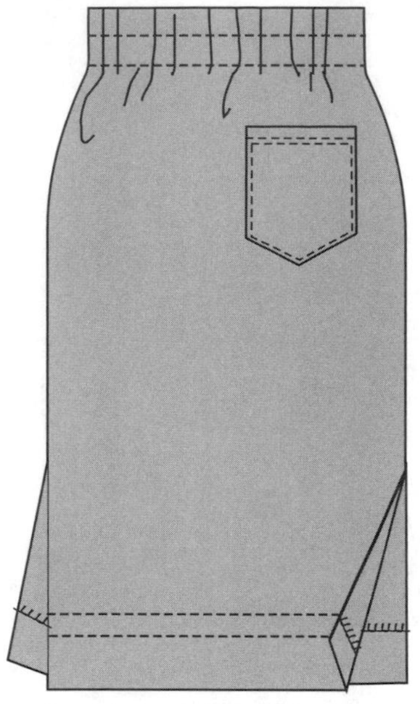

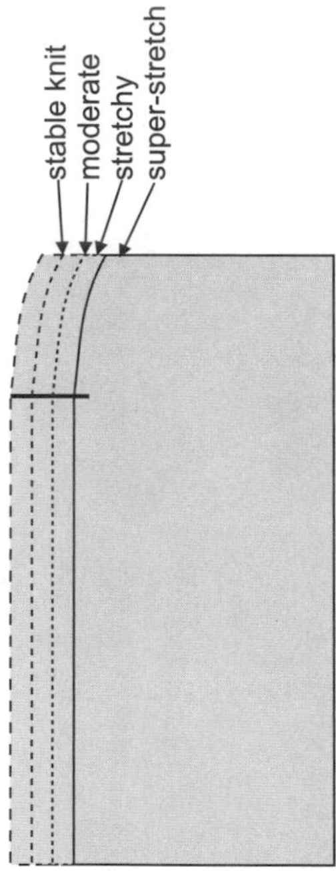

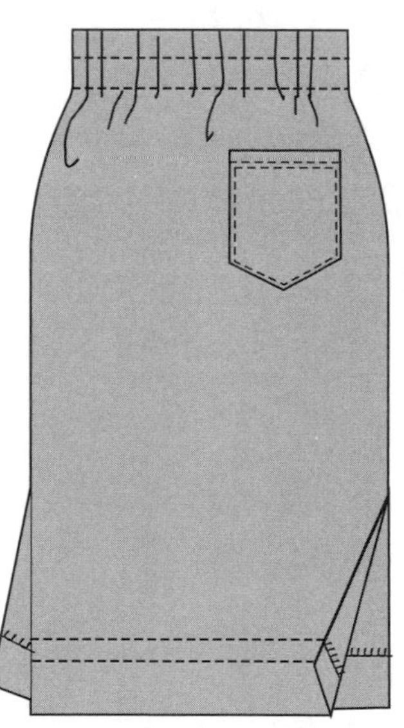

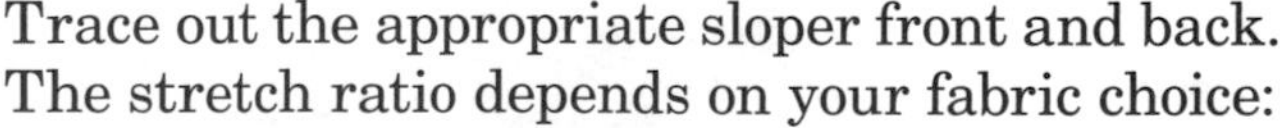

Trace out the appropriate sloper front and back. The stretch ratio depends on your fabric choice:

- Stable knit
- Moderate knit
- Stretchy knit
- Super-stretch knit
- Rib knit

Decide on the fit of the waist you require, or desire.

- Fitted waist
- Semi-fitted waist
- Unfitted waist

PATCH POCKETS

A patch pocket may be placed anywhere on the skirt, pant, top, sweater, or T-shirt, but will be explained on the back of this skirt, 2½″ below the waist.

1

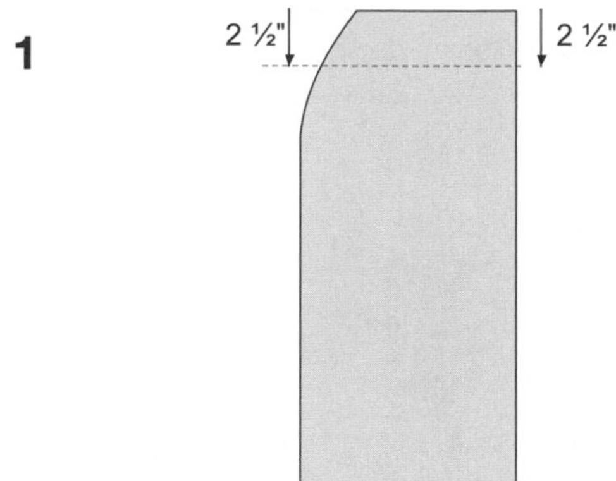

Draw a guideline 2½″ below the natural waist. It may be lower if required or if used for lowered waists, or any place that the design requires.

2

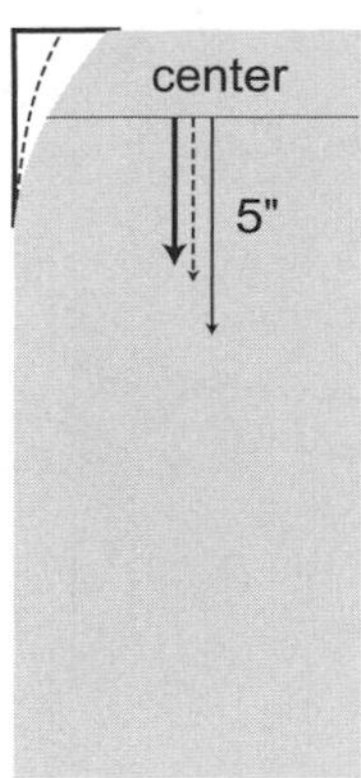

Find the center of the guideline, from hip to center back, and measure down the depth of the pocket for 5″.

If using the semi-fitted or unfitted waist, the guideline will be wider and you should use the center of that new line.

3

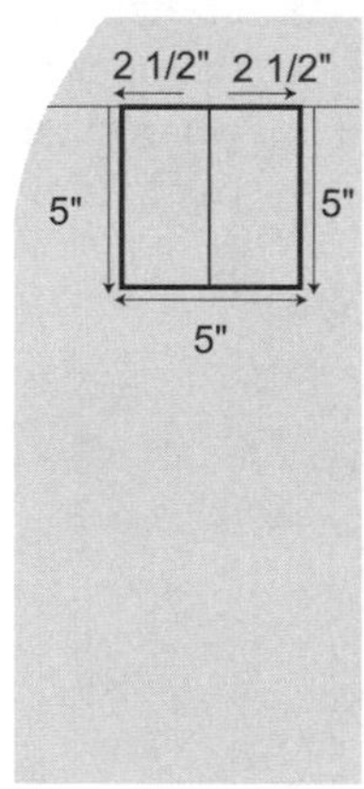

Make the pocket 5″ wide, centered on the vertical guideline, 2½″ on each side of the guideline. Alternatively, use any measurement that you require.

4

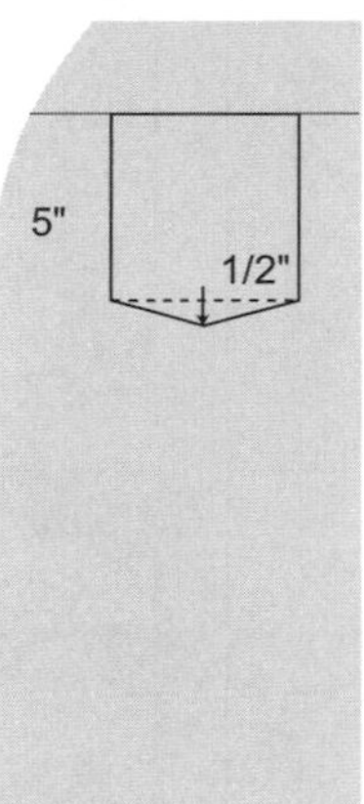

The pocket may be used straight across the bottom or may be angled. For an angled bottom, measure down an additional ½″ to create the bottom of the pocket.

5

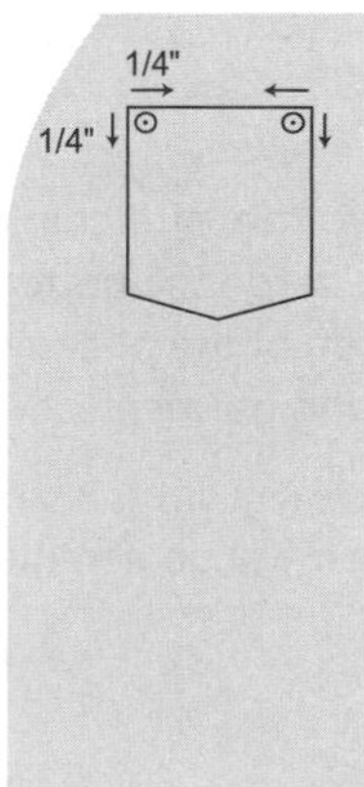

Mark the drill marks ¼″ in from the edges at the top of the pocket, and measure down ¼″ from the top edges of the pocket.

6

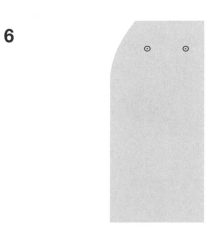

Drill holes are created by actually drilling a small hole in the garment, and must be inside the pocket or your garment will have visible holes.

Only the complete skirt should have the drill marks, not the pocket draft.

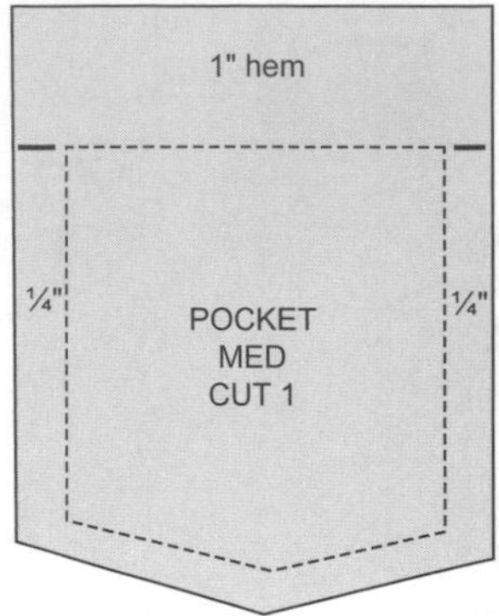

Add a 1″ hem at the top of the pocket and ⅜″ seam allowances on all other sides.

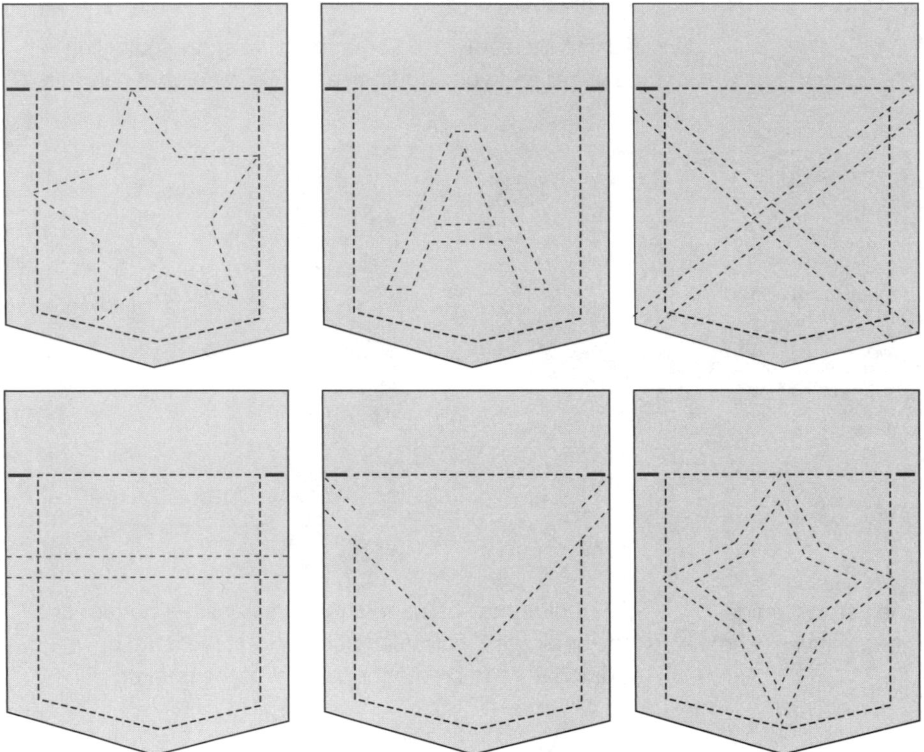

Create any design on your pocket.

The stitching used for designs will prevent the pocket from stretching out of shape. Note that the pocket will need tricot fusing when stitching a design; remember to trim away all excess tricot.

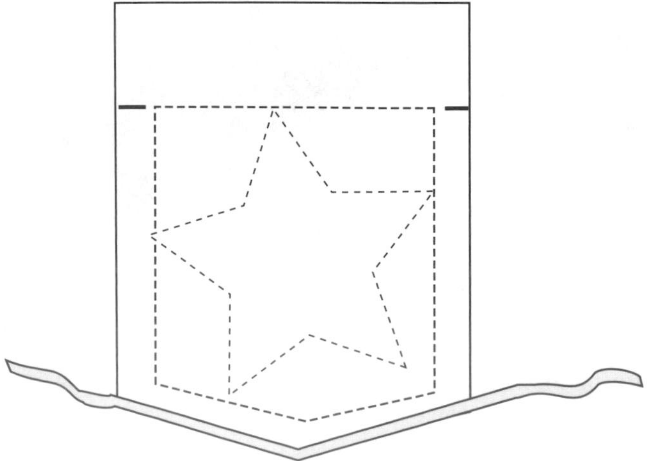

To prevent the pocket from stretching out of shape when sewing it to the skirt, serge the bottom of the pocket with twill tape, on the inside of the pocket, for one-way stretch, before applying it to the garment.

However, if using four-way stretch, serge the twill tape to all three sides. The top will be hemmed with the coverstitch machine.

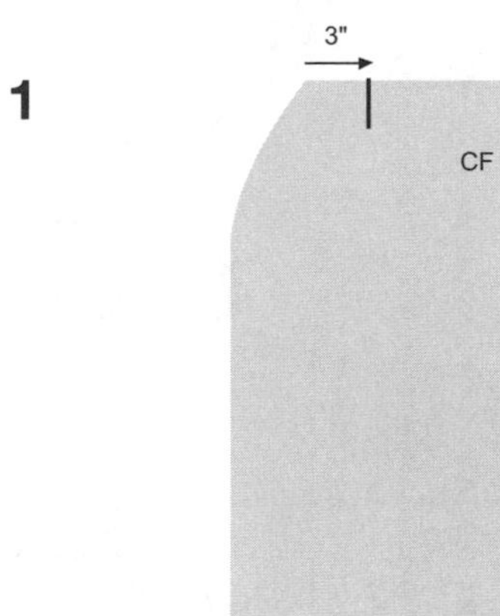

SLASH POCKETS WITH 1″ ANCHOR

Place a mark on the waist 3″ in from the side seam.

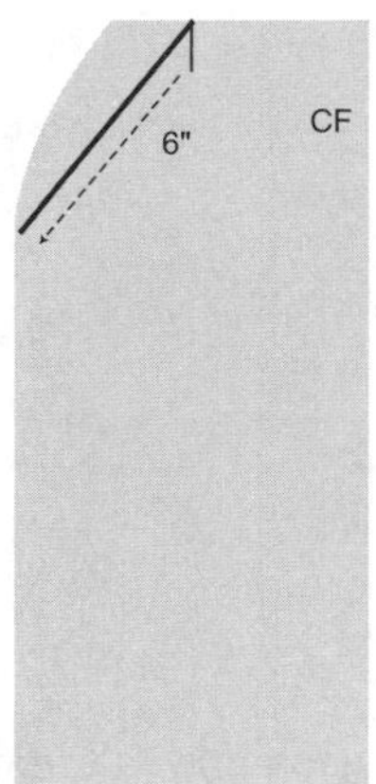

Create a 6″ pocket line going from the 3″ mark to wherever 6″ of length lands on the side seam.

You can create a pocket as small as 5½″ for very small hands and up to 7″ for large hands.

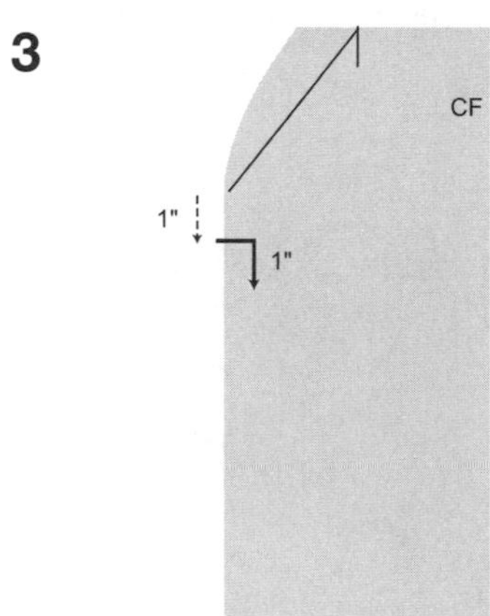

Square in for 1″. Measure down 1″ for the pocket anchor.

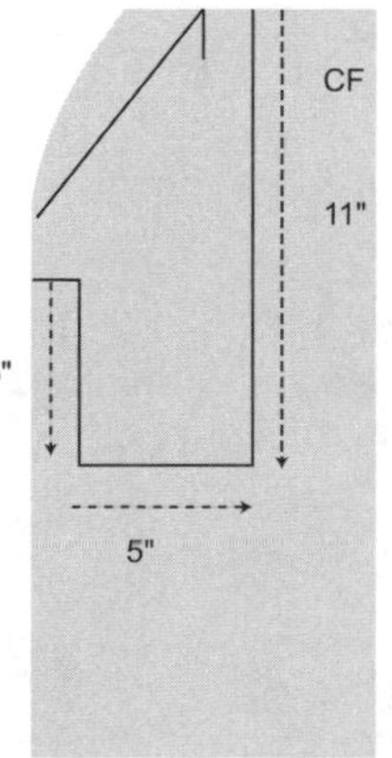

Draw the pocket bag 11″ down and at least 5″ wide. Shape as illustrated. The pocket bag can be enlarged, made deeper, but it is not a good idea to make it any shorter, because when the customer sits down the contents will fall out of her pocket.

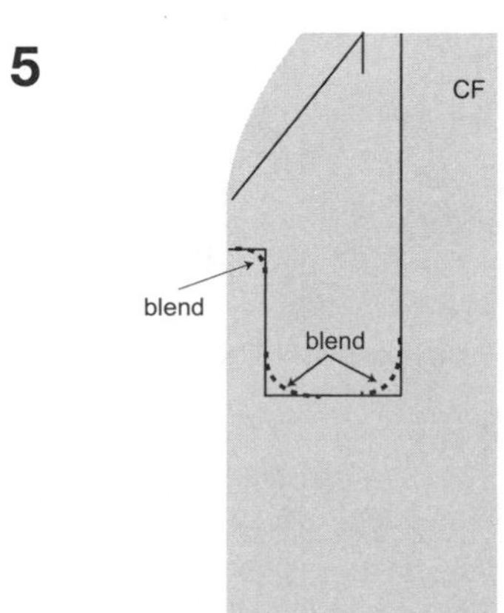

Blend into a curved pocket bag for easier assembly, so the operator can serge in one step all the way around instead of having to pivot at the corners when serging.

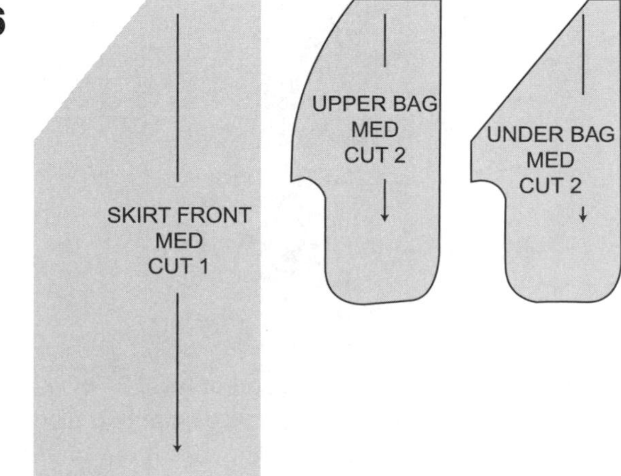

Trace and separate the pocket pieces, and label as illustrated.

7

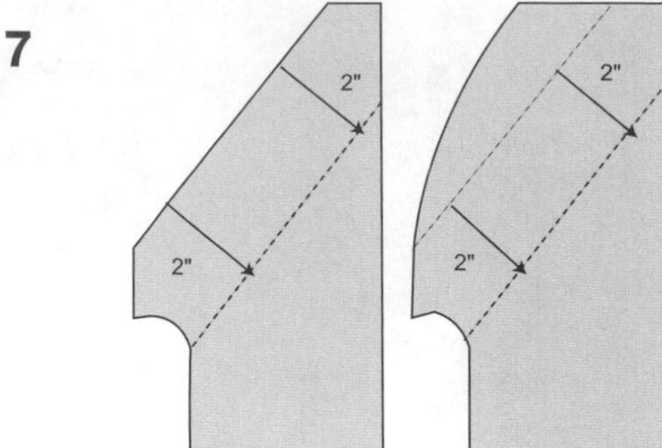

The pocket bags are customarily cut from self, but may be cut in lightweight fabric or tricot lining if a pocket facing is created.

Draw the facing line onto the under pocket, 2″ in from the cut edge, and trace it through to the upper pocket.

8

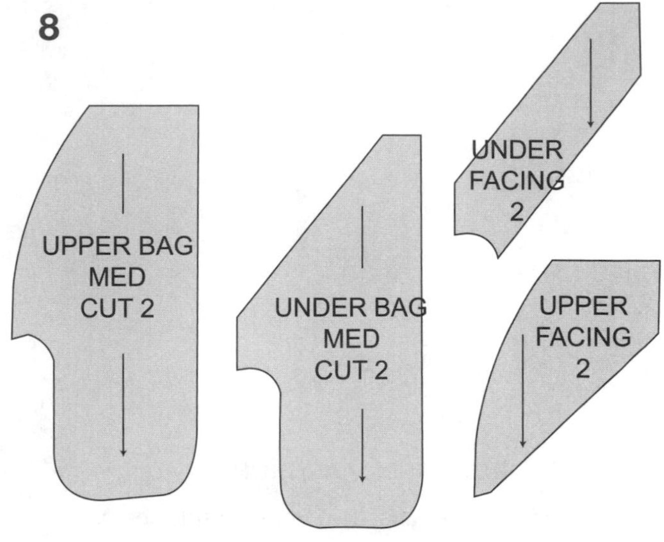

Trace out the pattern pieces as illustrated.

1

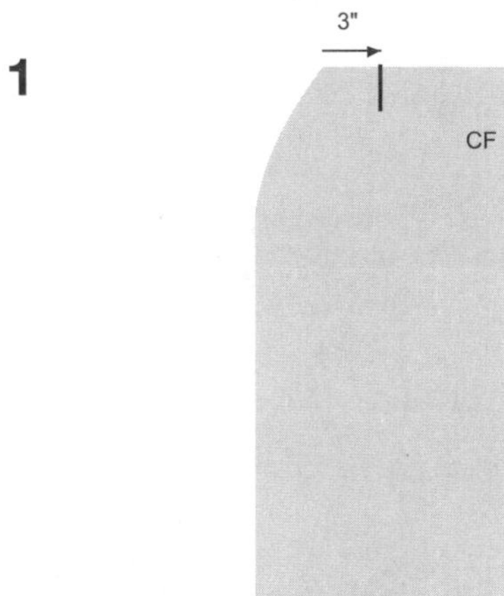

SLASH POCKET WITH FULL ANCHOR

Place a mark on the waist 3″ in from the side seam.

2

Create a 6″ pocket line going for the 3″ mark to wherever it lands on the side seam. You can create a pocket as small as 5½″ for very small hands and up to 7″ for large hands.

3

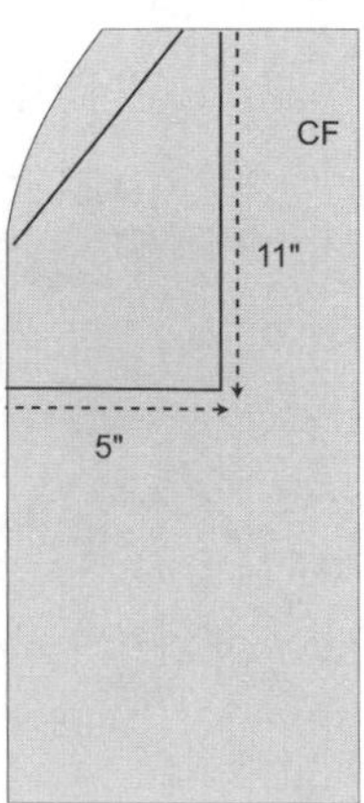

Draw the pocket bag 11″ down and at least 5″ wide. Shape as illustrated. The pocket bag can be enlarged, made deeper, but it is not a good idea to make it any shorter, because when the customer sits down the contents will fall out of her pocket.

4

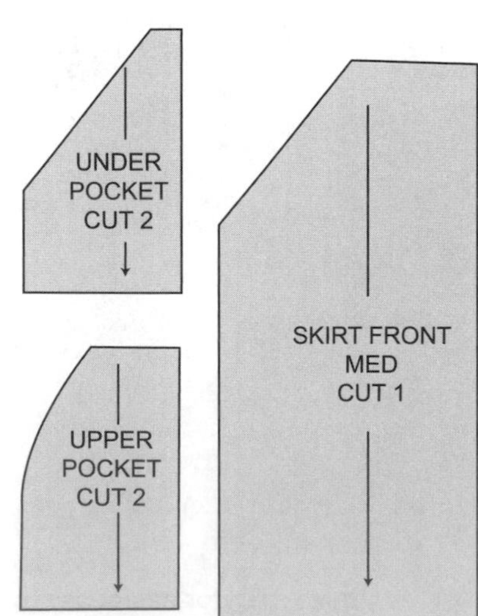

Trace out the pocket bag as illustrated.

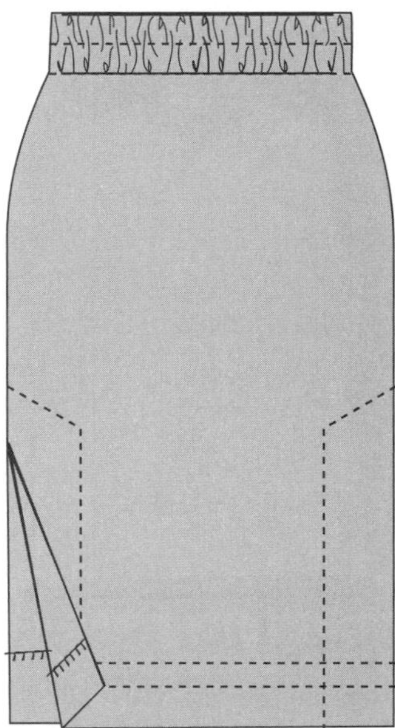

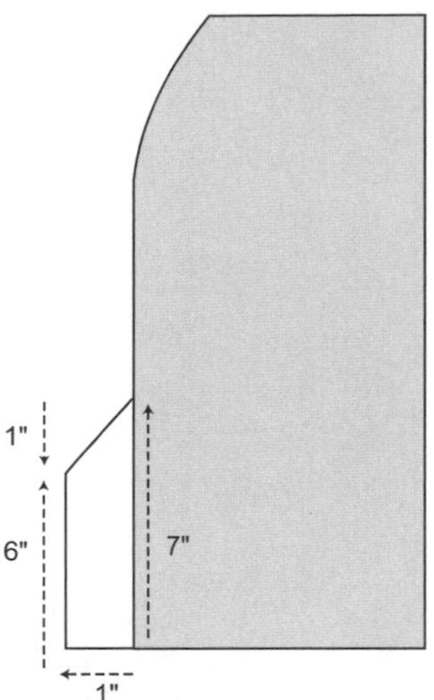

Side-Seam Slits

Skirts may be created with a slit on one side or both sides of the side seams.

The side-seam slit is created the same as the center back slit; however, it must be added to the front side-seam as well as the back side-seam of the pattern.

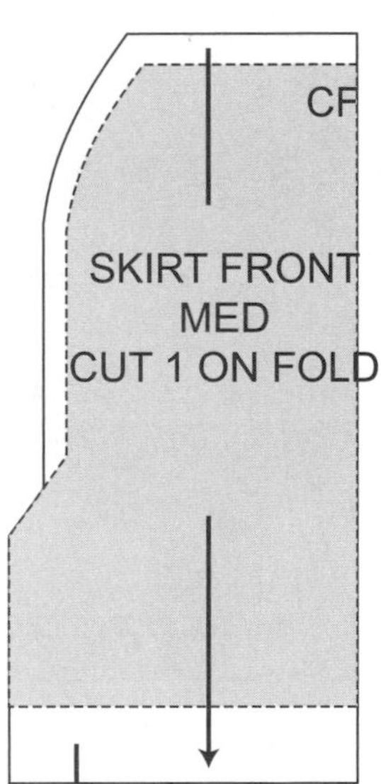

Add the necessary seam allowances to the pattern and add a notch to indicate the fold line of the slit.

You don't add an extra seam allowance to the slit, as it is already added.

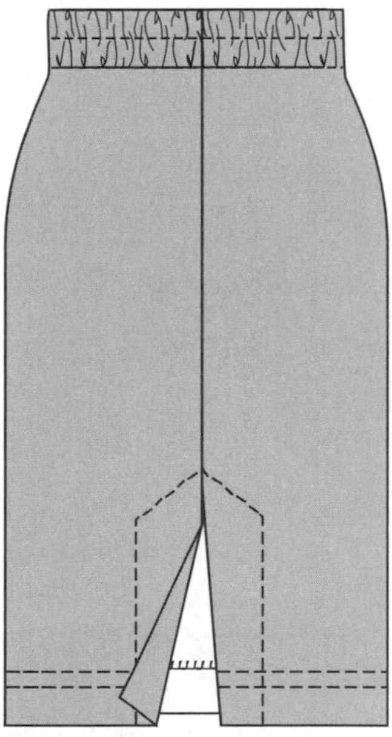

CENTER BACK SLIT

Slits should be used to allow movement and increase mobility in straight, narrow skirts that extend below the knee.

This draft requires a seam line, which is shown in the center back, but may be any place the design requires.

Draft a slit on center back, center front, or side front.

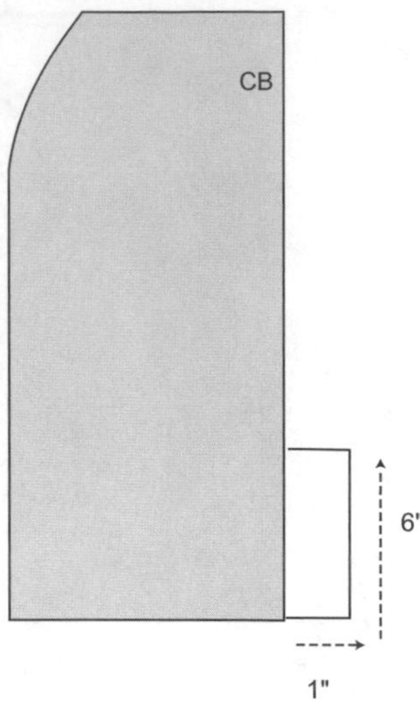

Trace out the appropriate skirt sloper.

Create a center back slit of any length, illustrated here at 6″.

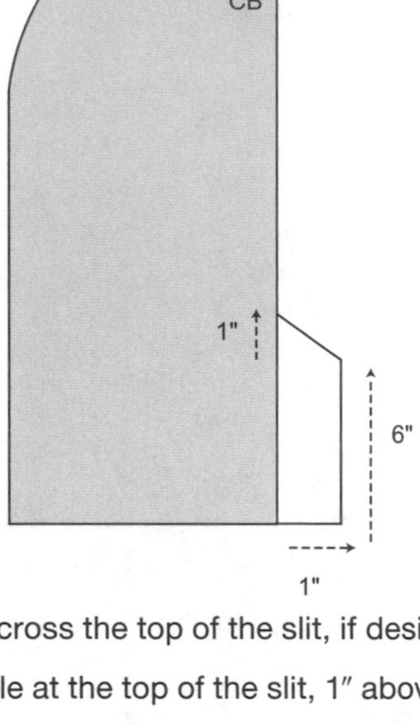

May be straight across the top of the slit, if desired.

Create a bias angle at the top of the slit, 1″ above the slit, if desired.

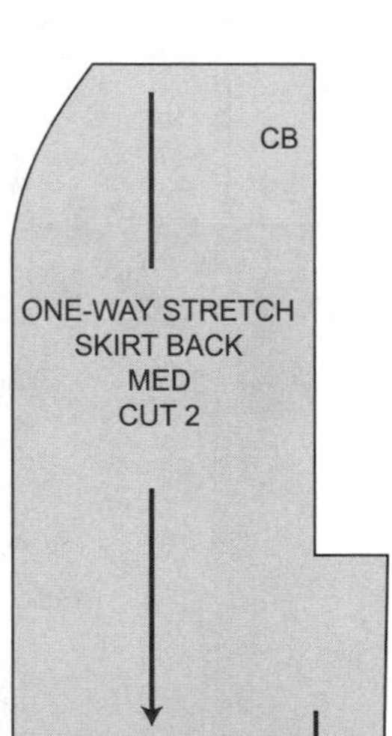

Complete the draft as illustrated.

It is not necessary to include the drill hole to indicate the end of sewing; you can easily stop sewing at the level parallel to the angle in the slit.

If the slit is not sewn down for at least 1″, it will not lie flat or remain closed. (See construction notes.)

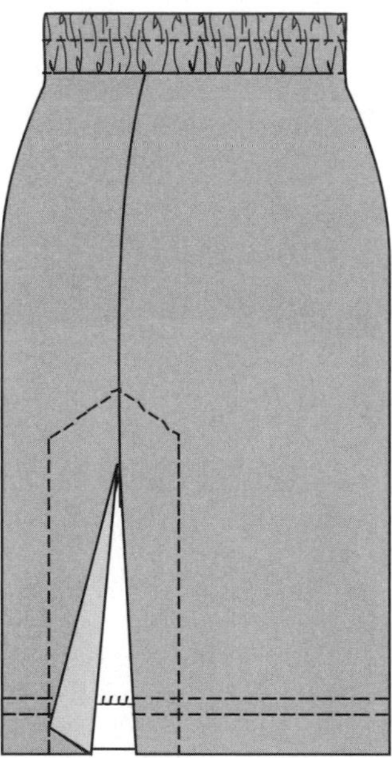

SIDE-FRONT SLIT

Create a slit on the side front by following the same instructions.

Draft the slit on either side or both sides.

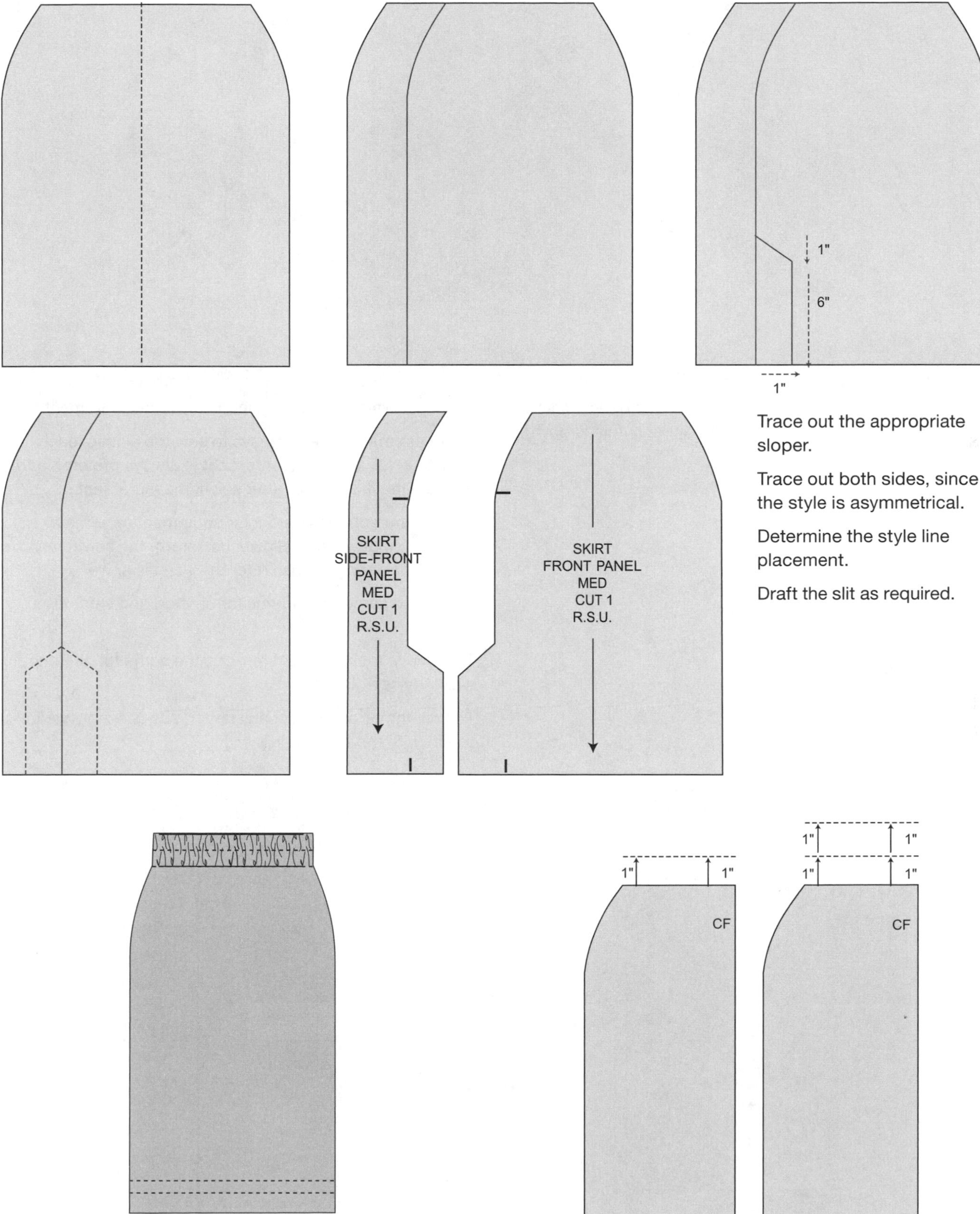

Trace out the appropriate sloper.

Trace out both sides, since the style is asymmetrical.

Determine the style line placement.

Draft the slit as required.

ELASTIC IN A CASING

There are many different ways to attach elastic at the waist. This method is the easiest, and simplest for beginners to understand.

Draw a guideline up from the waist, an amount equal to the width of the elastic (illustrated at 1″ for 1″ wide elastic).

Measure up an additional amount for the foldback. This is the area that will be inside when the waist is folded down.

Label the waist with the finished elastic measurement.

There are many different ways to sew the elastic, each with different seam amounts, so it is always preferable to indicate the finished, or after sewn, measurement.

If the manufacturer's particular equipment requires a larger or smaller seam allowance, inform the sewer what length of elastic you wish after the waist is sewn.

Follow the same procedures for unfitted and semi-fitted waists.

The elastic measurement remains the same for all three waist styles.

The customer did not get any larger; she is simply wearing a skirt with more gathering.

COVER-STITCHED HEM

Cover-stitched hems are the best and most professional choice for the hem. The cover-stitch will allow the hem to stretch.

Use at least a 1″ hem allowance for straight hems. This will give an added amount of weight to the hem, and hold it down without creating a heavy hem.

For curved hems, use a ½″ hem allowance.

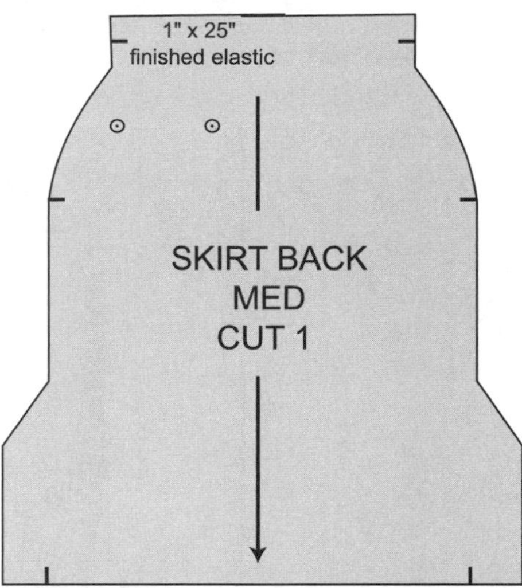

Seam Allowances For Style #5-001

Illustration shows the final style before any seam allowances have been added. Note that all production patterns should be cut full, unfolded, as illustrated.

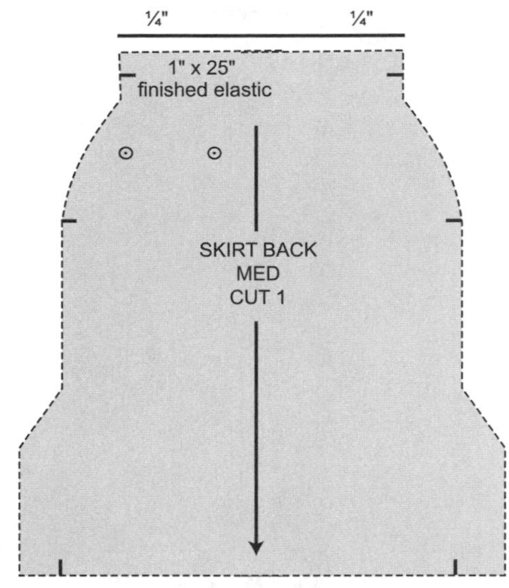

WAIST

Add 1/4″ seam allowances to the top edge of the waist, for serging, or turn under.

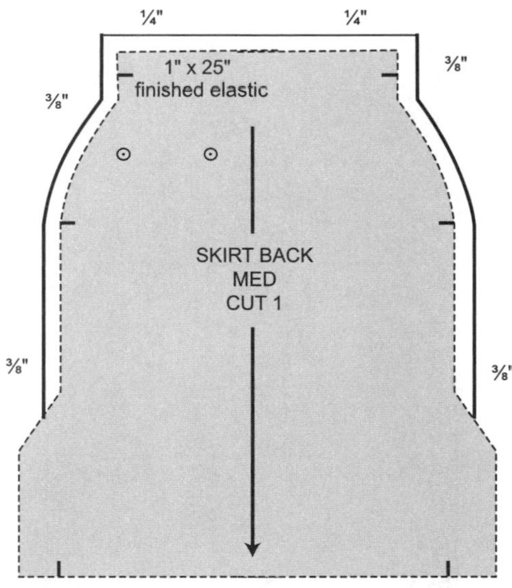

SIDE SEAMS

Add 3/8″ seam allowances for 4-thread serger.

Keep the curves exactly parallel to the original.

SLITS

The slits do not need any seam allowances added; the foldback has already been added.

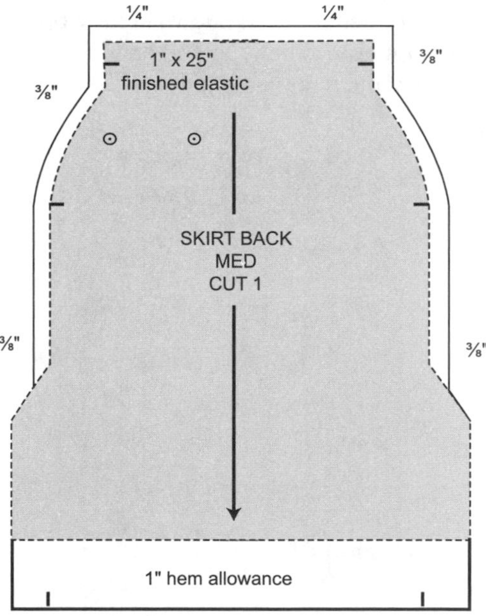

HEM

Add 1″ hem allowance for a straight hem.

The completed pattern should look like the illustration, before the necessary labeling.

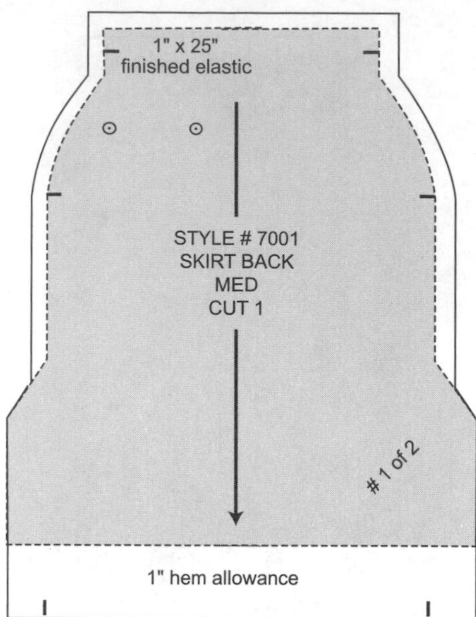

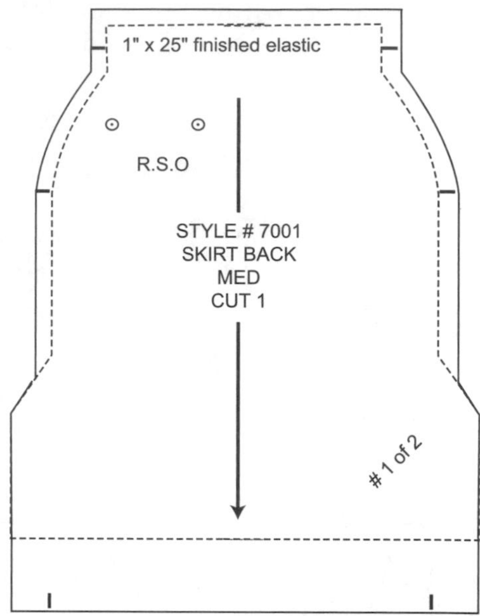

PATTERN LABELING

Label the pattern as indicated. Include the drill marks for the pocket placement, the style number, the part of the garment, the size, and how many to be cut.

Label the waist with the finished elastic measurements.

Number your pattern pieces as illustrated to correspond to the pattern card, piece number 1 of 2.

Complete the pattern card as shown in the Appendix, and paste, glue, or staple to oak-tag and hang on the pattern hook, in front of the completed pattern.

Each pattern piece should be traced out on oak-tag for production.

Many patternmakers like to have as little information as possible on the pattern, and take pride in having a clean, neat pattern; however, it is often preferable to indicate as much information on the pattern as possible, for easier production.

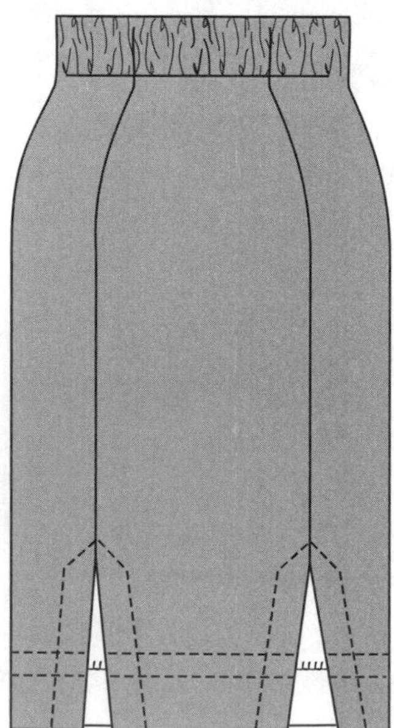

STYLE #5-002 SKIRT WITH LOWERED WAIST AND SIDE-FRONT SLITS

This style teaches how to lower a skirt waist, and the elastic reductions necessary for lowered waists, panel seams, slits, and elastic in a casing.

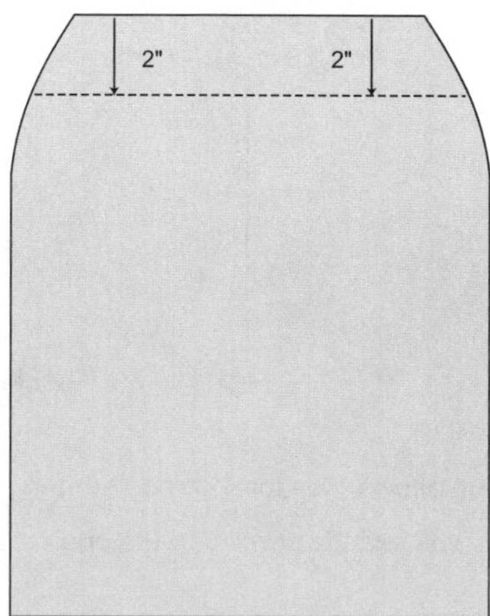

Lower the waist any amount required, but illustrated here at 2″ below the natural waist.

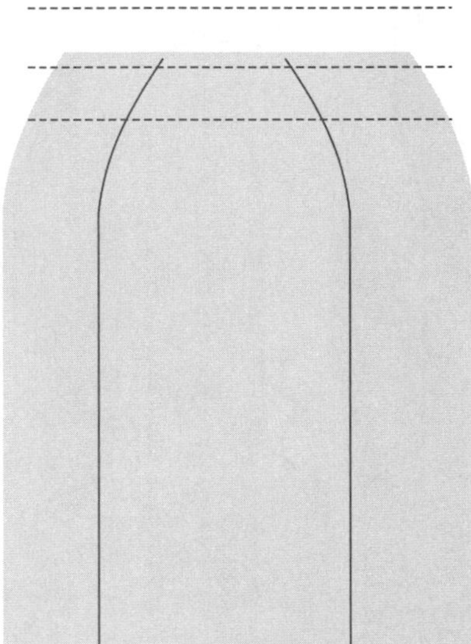

For the casing, use $1\frac{1}{2}''$ elastic, so draw a guideline $1\frac{1}{2}''$ above the newly lowered waist.

Then square up an additional $1\frac{1}{2}''$ for the part of the casing that folds down.

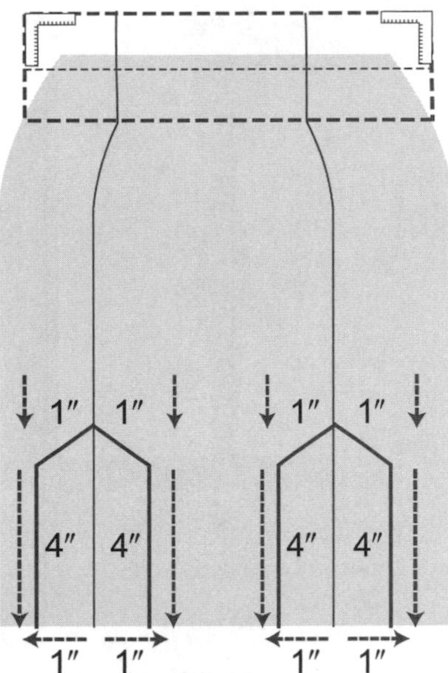

Create panel seams as desired.

It is much sexier and flattering to make the seams parallel to the original side seam, rather than having a square, boxy panel.

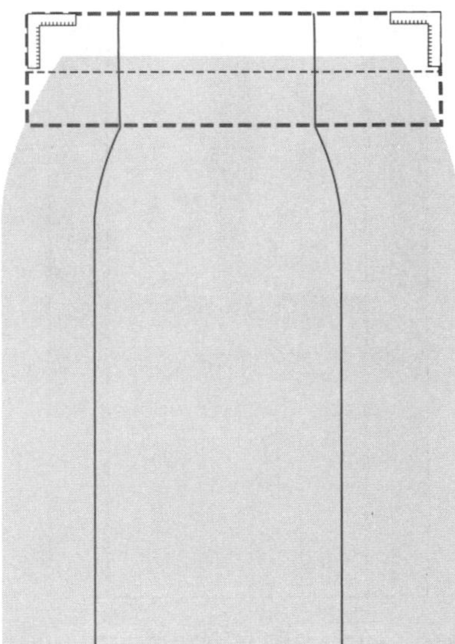

Square down to create the sides of the waist.

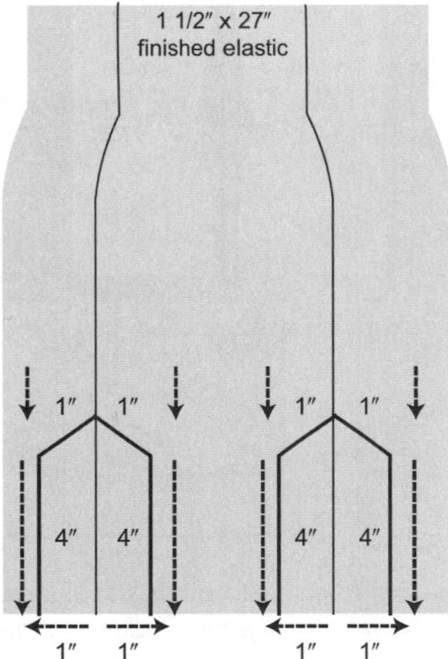

Label the waist with the finished elastic measurement.

Note that the elastic should be the measurement of the model or the dress form, at the new waist minus 1″.

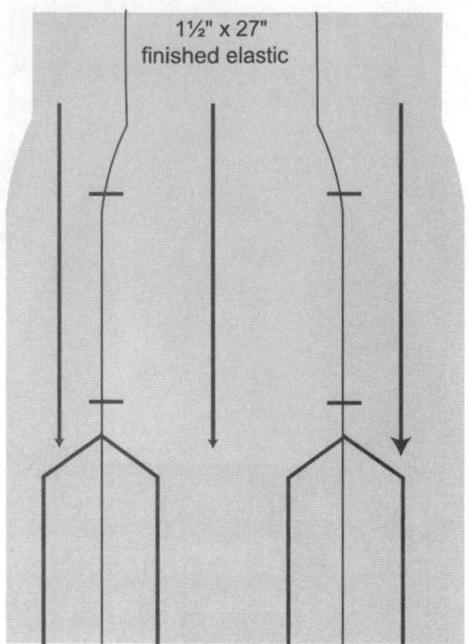

Draw a grainline on the side panel.

Notch the pieces for easier construction.

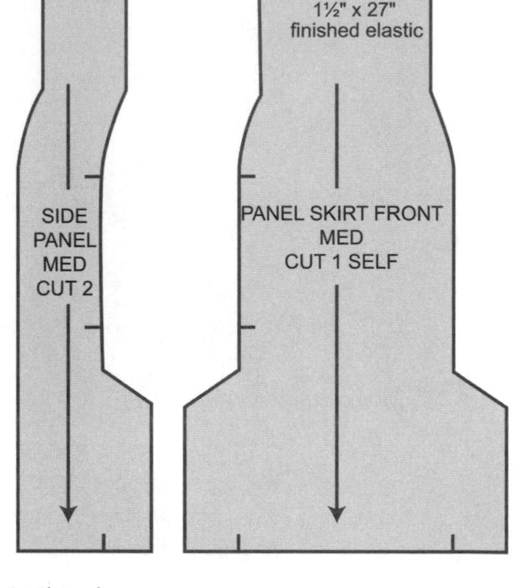

Separate the pieces.

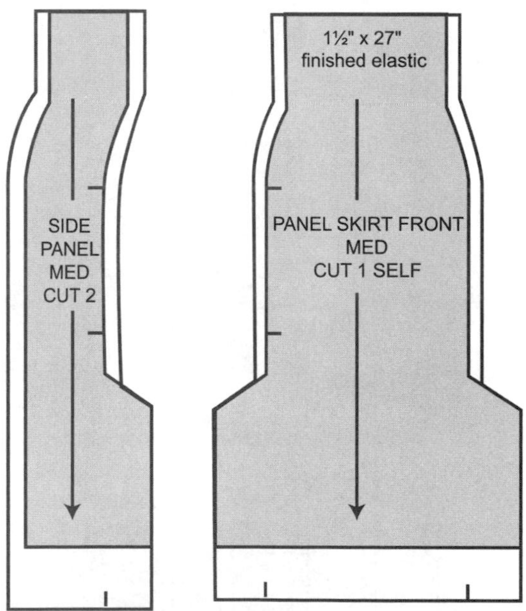

Add the necessary seam allowances as illustrated. Note that no seam allowance has been added to the slit, since it is already a hem allowance, or facing.

Also note that the seam allowance has not been added to the waist edge, since the elastic will be serged to the raw edge, folded over, and cover-stitched. The raw edge and the elastic line up perfectly, and no seam allowance in necessary for this application.

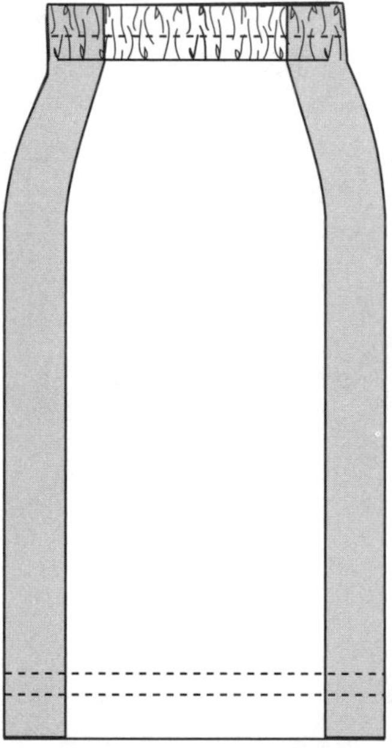

STYLE #5-003 SKIRT WITH LOWERED WAIST AND SIDE STRIPES IN CONTRASTING COLOR

This skirt design shows how to draft a single side stripe, or racing stripe, without a side seam.

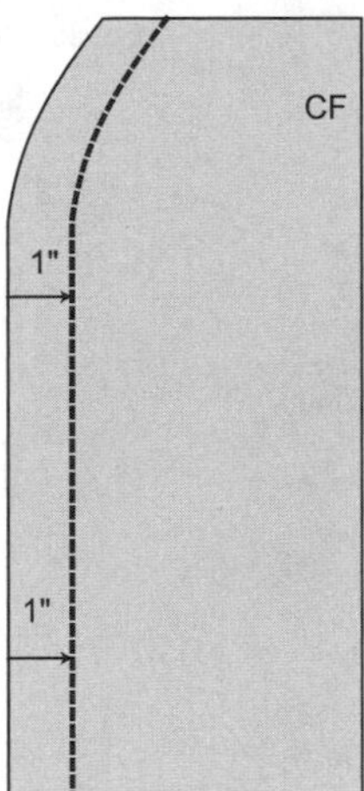

Trace out the sloper and draw in the side-seam stripe.

The maximum width without a side seam should not be more than 3″ total or 1½″ on each side.

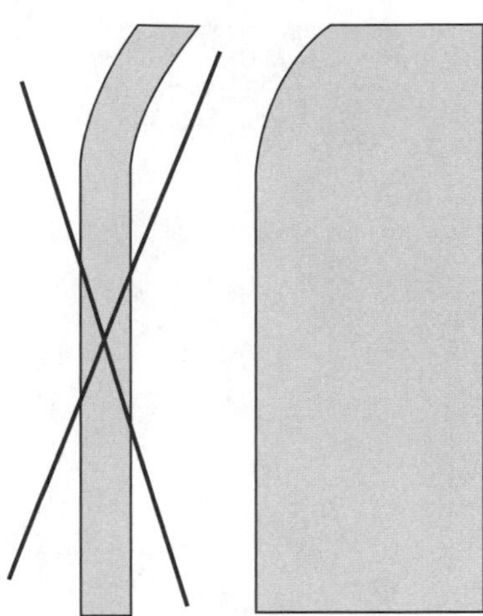

Trace and separate the pieces.

Do not cut two side panels, but instead create a single panel.

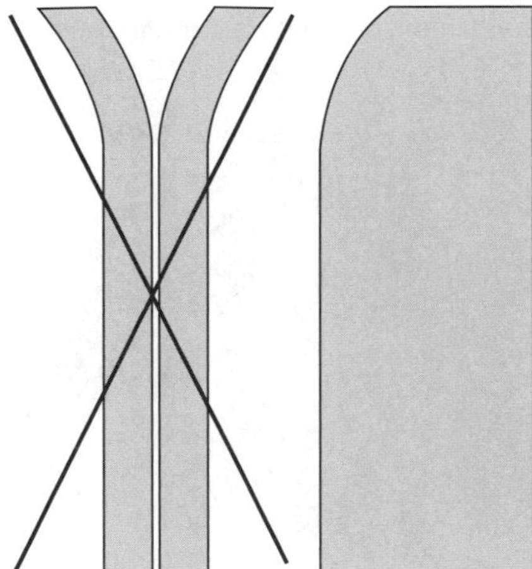

Instead of creating two side panels that require a side seam, combine the two panels.

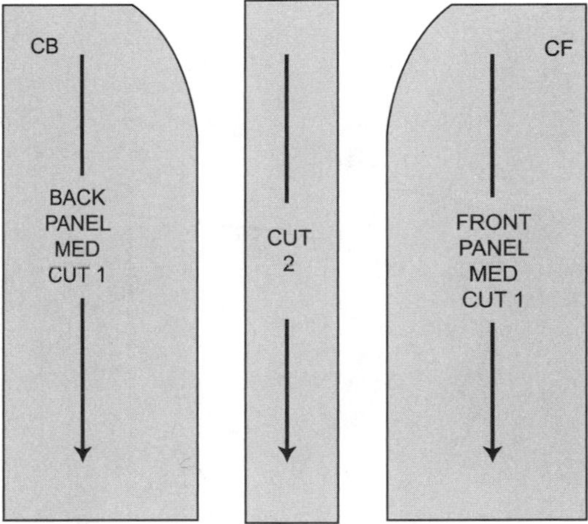

Draft a straight pattern piece that is the same length as the seams.

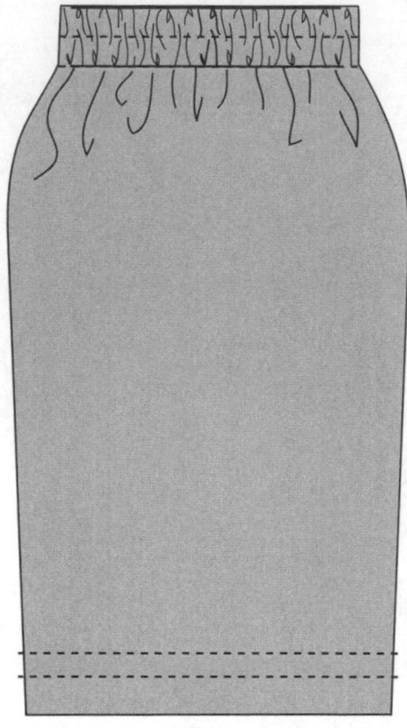

STYLE #5-004 PEGGED-WAIST SKIRT

A pegged-waist skirt may be created by enlarging the original waist, which can be pulled in with elastic or gathering.

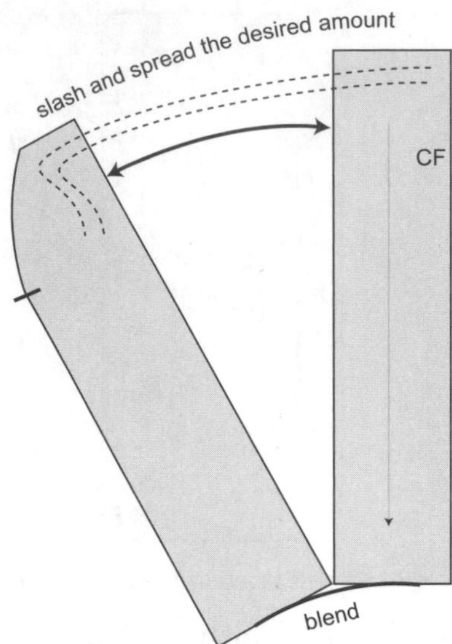

Slash and spread to create added fullness at the waist. (Refer to section on gathering ratios.)

Increase by 50% of the original waist, up to as much as double the original waist measurement.

Blend the hem into a smooth and continuous line.

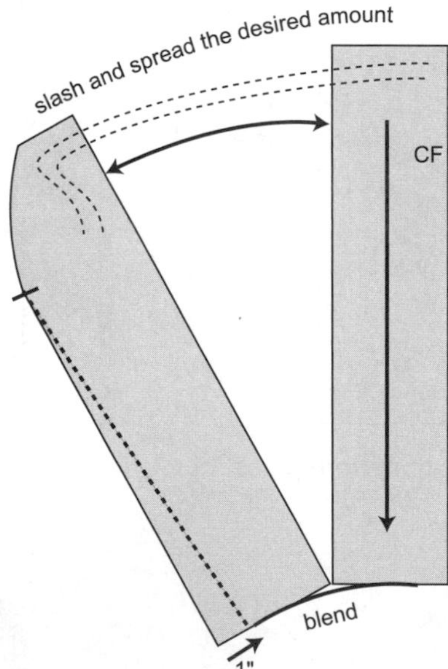

To exaggerate the pegged effect, decrease the hem by 4″ circumference, or 1″ from each side seam.

A slit will be necessary if the skirt is below the knee.

STYLE #5-005 FULL SKIRT

To create a full gathered skirt, use a combination of both techniques illustrated above.

Find the center of the original block, and draw a line to the hem.

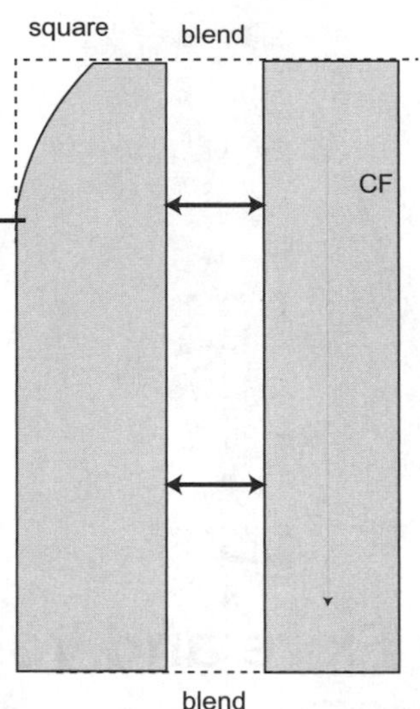

Slash and spread the waist and the hem, and enlarge anywhere from 50% to 100% of the original waist measurement.

Blend a new waist and hem.

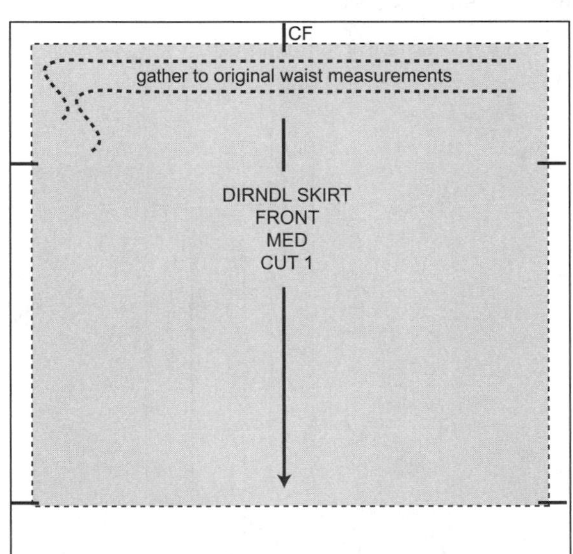

Add seam allowances and hem allowance to complete the pattern. Label the waist with the finished, already gathered, measurement. Since all knit fabrics have a nap, the grainline should have arrows pointing in the same direction as the nap.

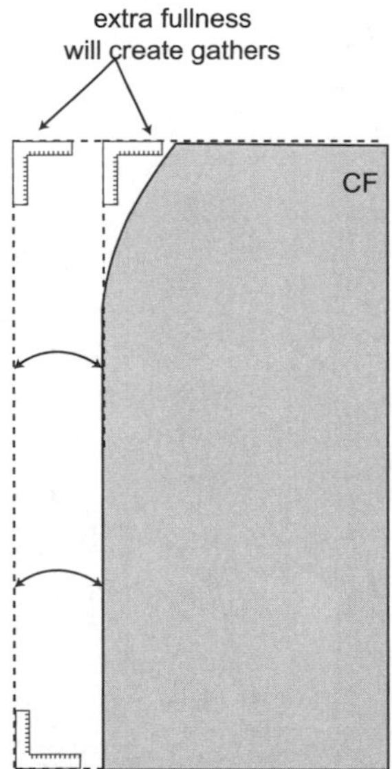

STYLE #5-006 ALTERNATE METHOD OF DRAFTING THE DIRNDL SKIRT/FULL SKIRT

Straighten out the side seam, and add fullness through the side seam of the block, usually double the measurement of the original waist. This will result in a large rectangular pattern, which will be gathered at the waist. Alternatively, use elastic in a casing to pull the waist into the original waist measurement.

Adding Flare and Volume to the Hem

STYLE #5-007 A-LINE SKIRT

Volume at the hem will add drama, movement, and fluidity to many designs.

Different A-line skirts can be created using different methods of drafting. Each will produce slightly different effects for your design.

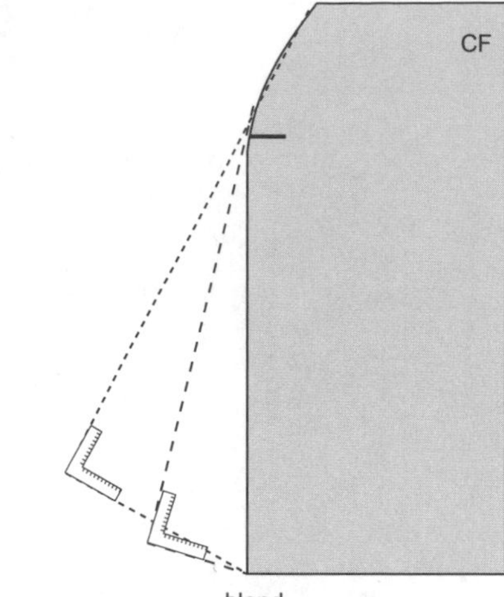

Drafting the A-line skirt with the following technique produces a skirt with the flare primarily at the sides of the skirt.

Extend the side seams outward as much as the design requires.

Keep the waist measurement the same.

Square the hem at the side seams.

Keep the side seams the same length.

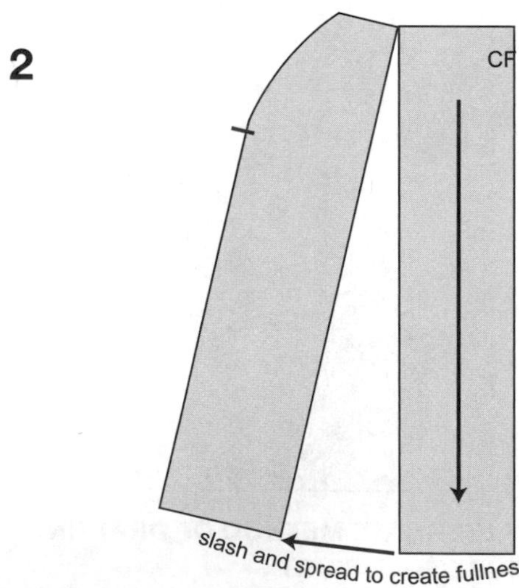

Drafting the A-line skirt with the following technique produces an A-line skirt with the flare at the front of the skirt.

Slash and spread the skirt block into an "A"-shaped line as full as the design requires.

Keep the waist measurement the same.

This draft retains the original hip curve.

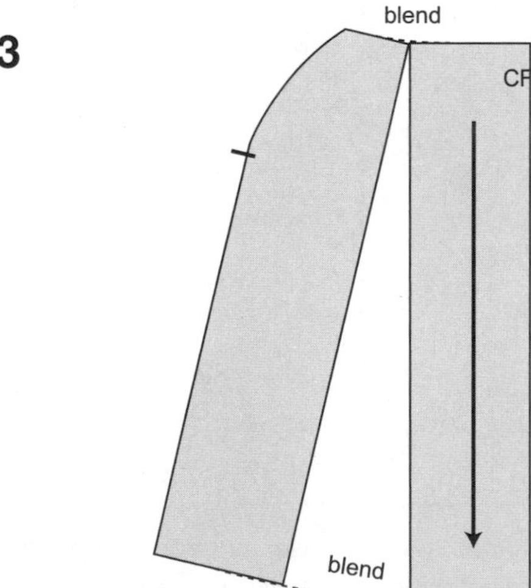

Blend the waist.

Blend the hem into a smooth, continuous line.

3

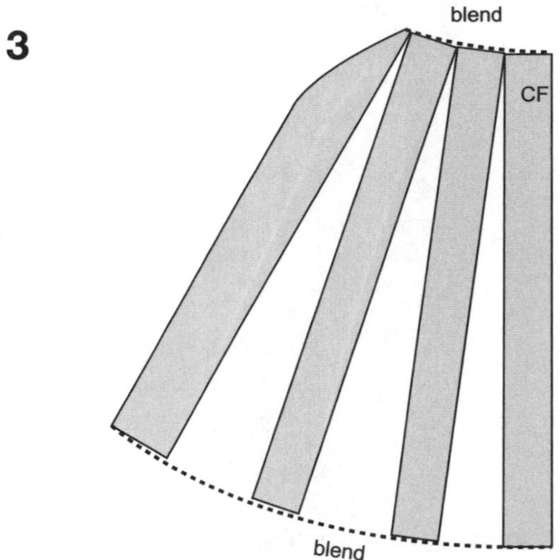

Slashing the skirt in multiple places produces a skirt pattern that has the fullness spread evenly within the front panels.

The more slashes, the more evenly the flare is spread; therefore, the more even the fullness.

Occasionally the design may even require more volume in the back than the front.

4

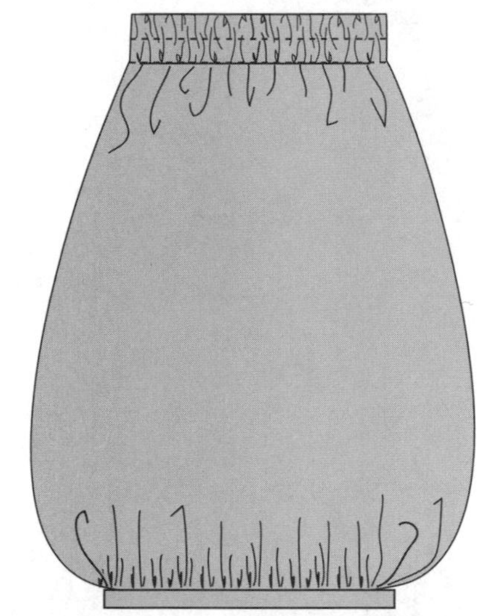

By adding a waistband or elastic to the hem, you can create a pouf skirt.

5

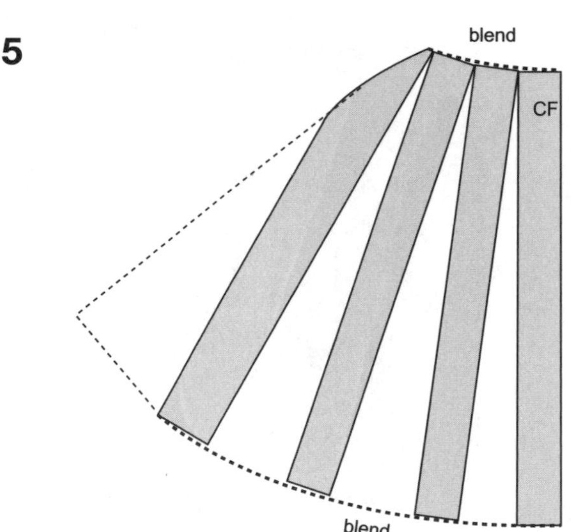

STYLE #5-008 EXAGGERATED A-LINE

Combine both of the above techniques for an exaggerated A-line skirt.

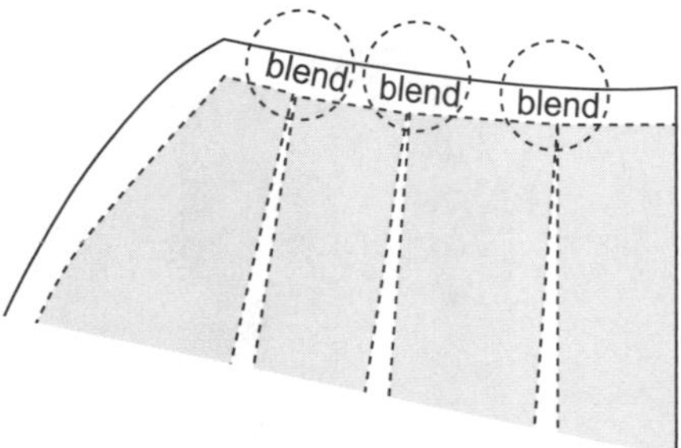

Controlling Flares

The decision of whether or not to blend the waist curve is determined by requirements of the final design. Blending the waist will force the skirt to fall evenly and softly.

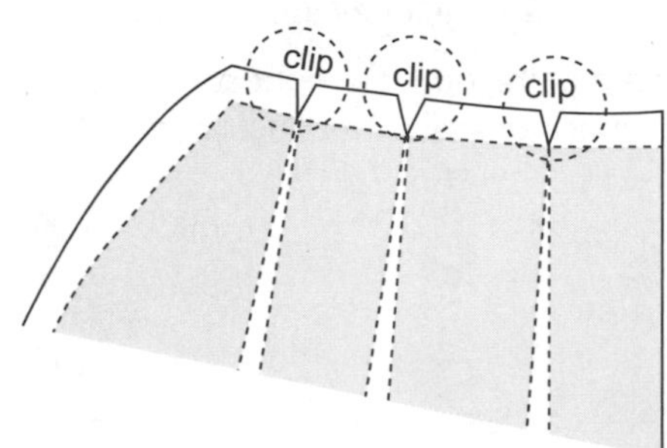

Clip the waist to force the skirt to fall in distinct folds. The tension is released and forces the skirt to fall into the folds where they are drafted, and where the clips are.

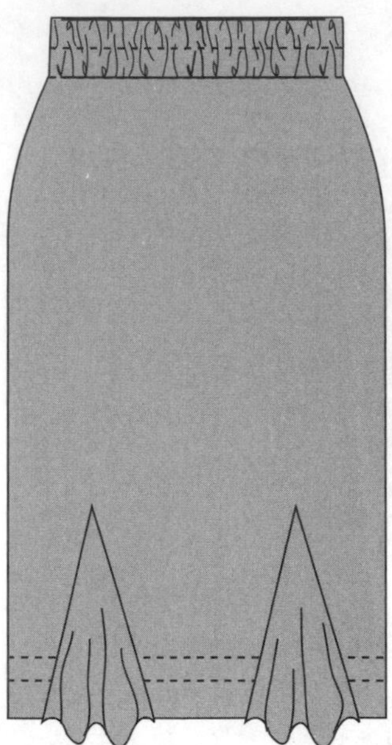

STYLE #5-009 SKIRT WITH GODETS

A godet skirt is similar to a trumpet skirt, except that the godets do not need a seam and are sewn into a slash in the hem of the skirt.

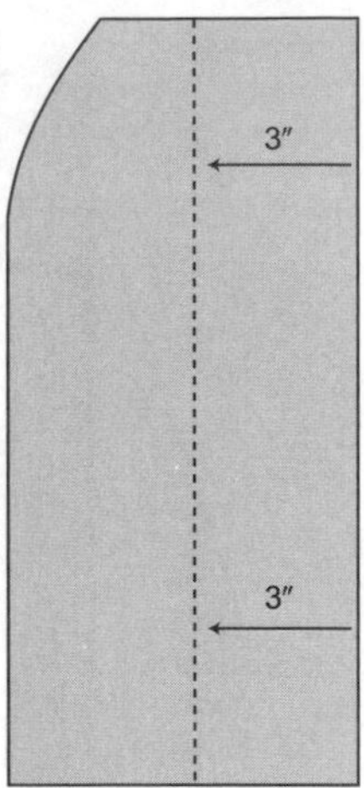

Create a temporary guideline indicating where you want the godet to be placed. (Illustrated at 3″ but may be any place the design requires.)

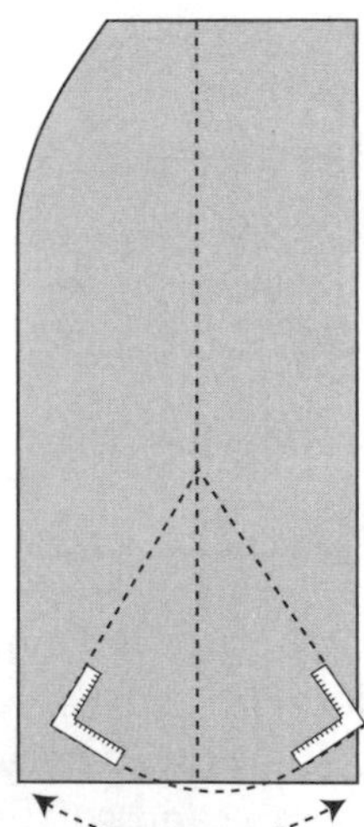

Draw the godet as large or as small as desired.

Keep the hem of the godet at right angles to the sides by using a compass or a ruler, as illustrated.

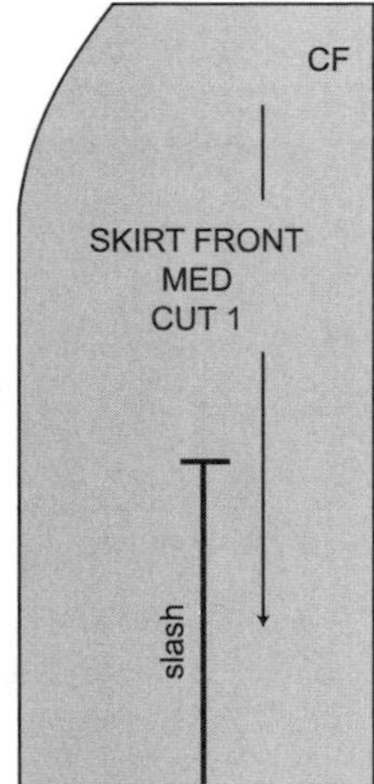

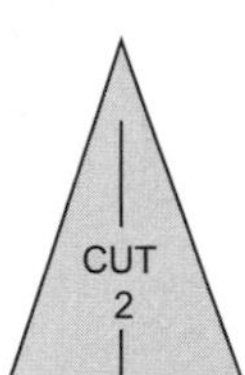

Trace out the godet pattern piece.

Since a seam allowance cannot be added to the slash, you need to add twice the seam allowance amount to the godet in order to maintain the godet size, and balance.

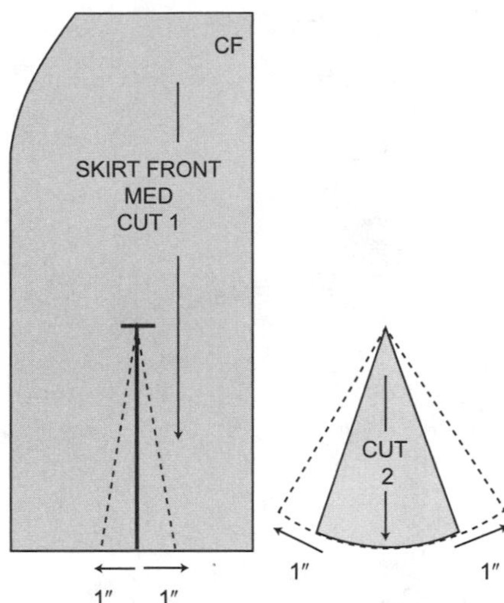

To exaggerate the appearance of the godet, and make it more visible:

Remove 1″ from the slash line at the hem.

Add 1″ to each side of the godet pattern piece, as indicated.

The sewing line decreases to almost nothing at the top of the godet.

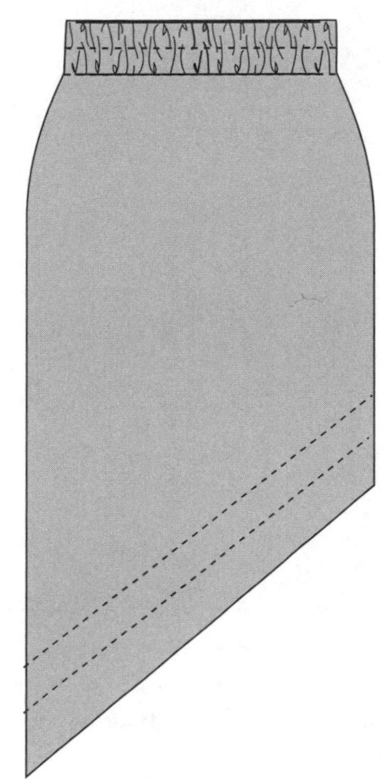

STYLE #5-010 SKIRT WITH ASYMMETRICAL HEM

Diagonal hems are created by simply shaping the hem as required.

Because the cover-stitch cannot pivot around a corner, it is necessary to hem the front and back of the skirt before sewing the side seams.

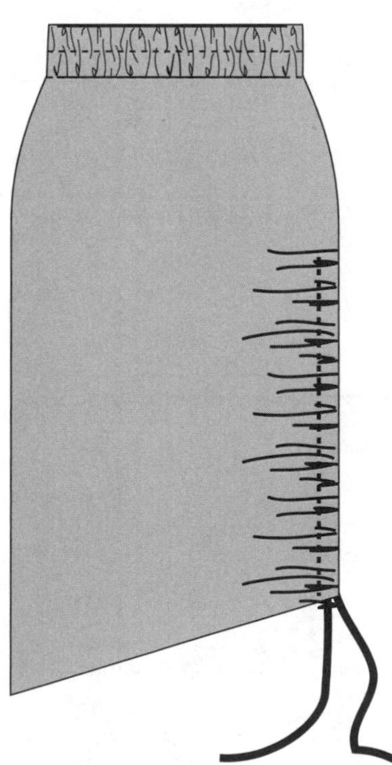

STYLE #5-011 DRAWSTRING SIDE-SEAM

An asymmetrical hem may be created by drawing up the side seam with a cord, ribbon, or string.

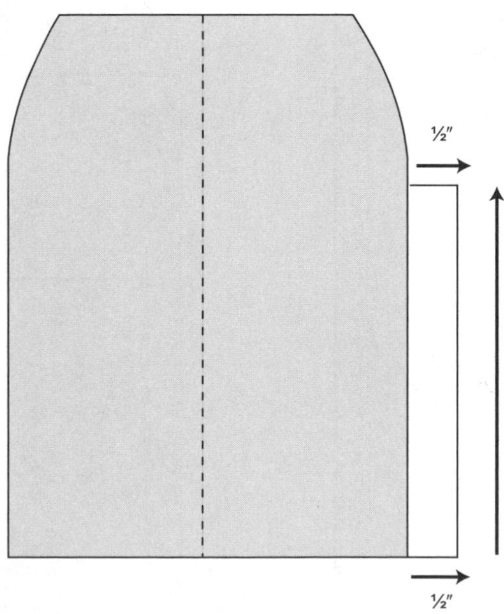

To create a drawstring at the side of the skirt, simply create a slit extension as high as you wish the drawstring to be.

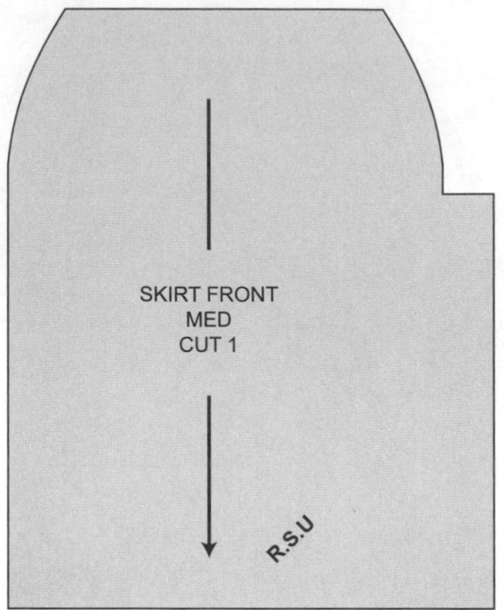

Create an equal extension on both the back and the front patterns. The drawstring extension may be applied to either side of the garment, or both sides, depending on the designer's sketch.

To construct the skirt, sew down the side seam, press the seams open, and topstitch the seams open.

Insert the string, then sew the top of the seam allowance open, catching the string.

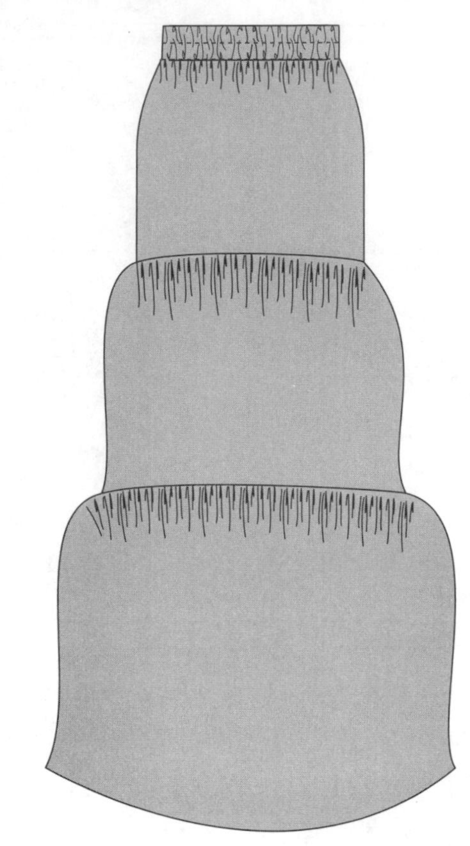

STYLE #5-012 TIERED SKIRTS

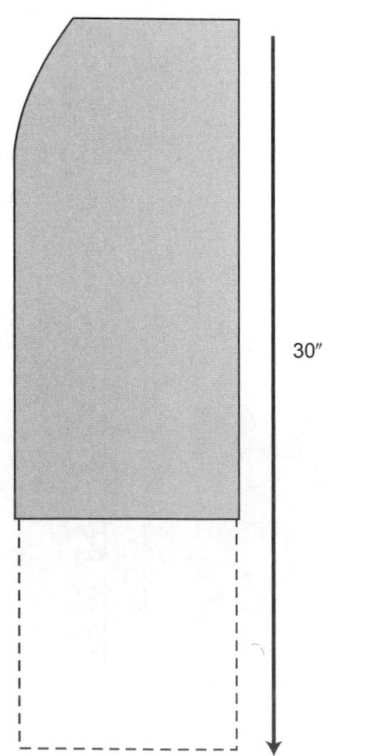

Lengthen the skirt sloper to 30″ by extending the side seams and center front straight down.

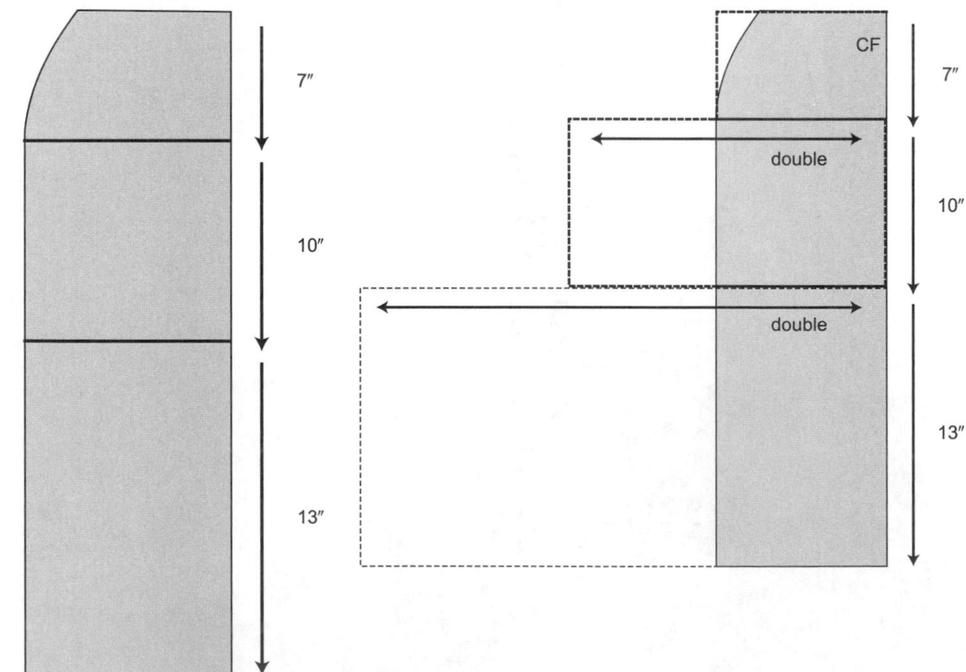

Decide on the placement of the tiers.

Tiers may be even amounts or graduated amounts, as shown.

Flare each skirt outward 1″ at the hem.

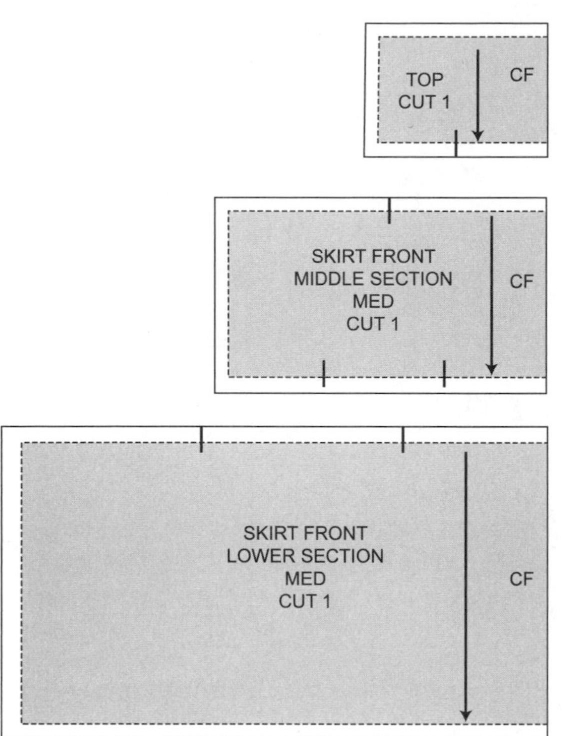

Trace out and separate the skirt tiers:

- 1 skirt that is 7″ long
- 1 skirt that is 17″ long
- 1 skirt that is 30″ long

All three skirts will attach to the same waistband.

For extra volume at the hem, add 1″ of flare to each side seam.

Because of the amount of bulk and the weight of the skirt, this draft is only suitable for lightweight fabrics.

STYLE #5-013 TIERED SKIRTS

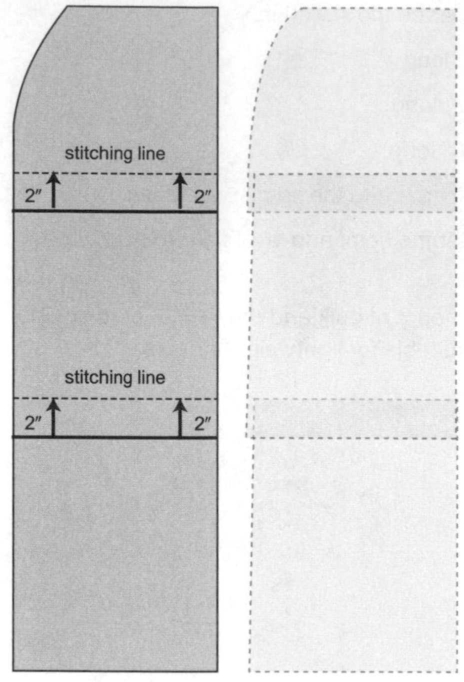

To reduce the weight of the skirt and the bulk at the waist, use a lightweight knit lining to support the tiers of the skirts.

Place the lining seam 2″ above the previous tier so it will not show.

Add 1″ flare to each side seam.

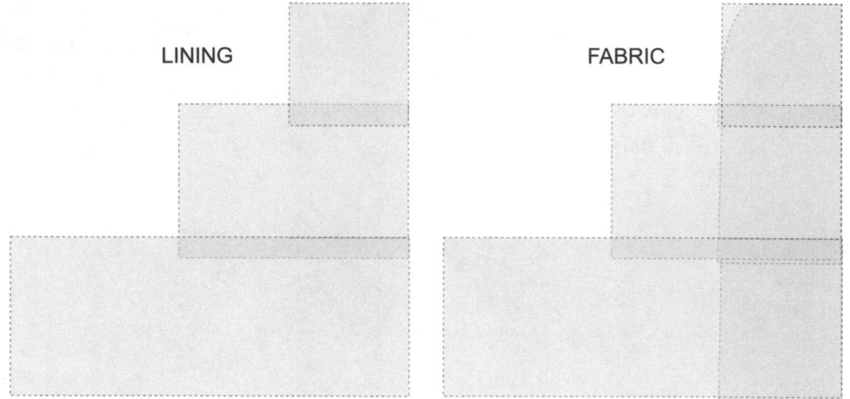

Cut the lining as described.

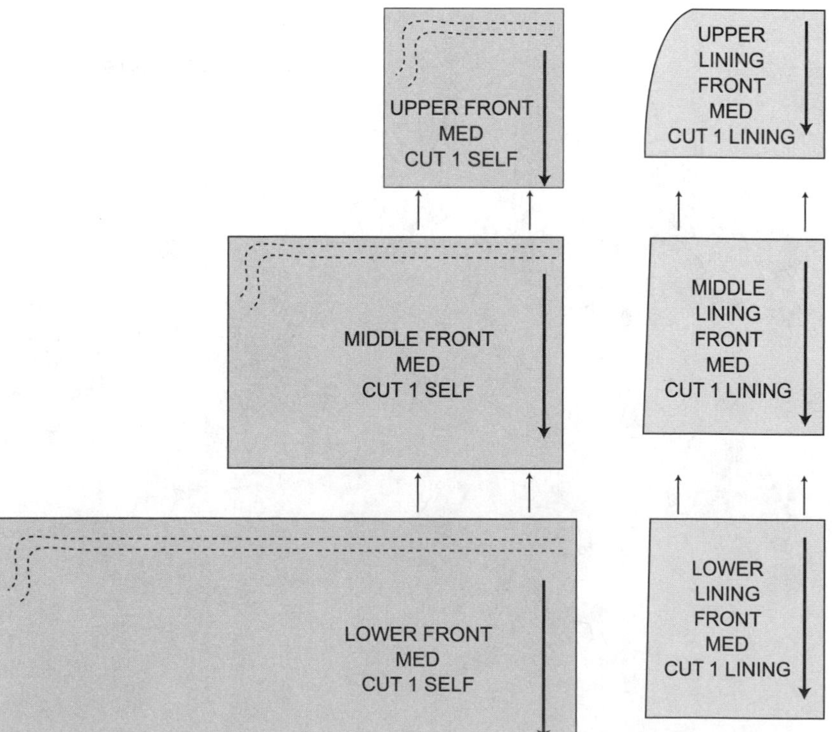

Cut the middle tier in lining and self as described.

Cut the lower tier in lining and self as described.

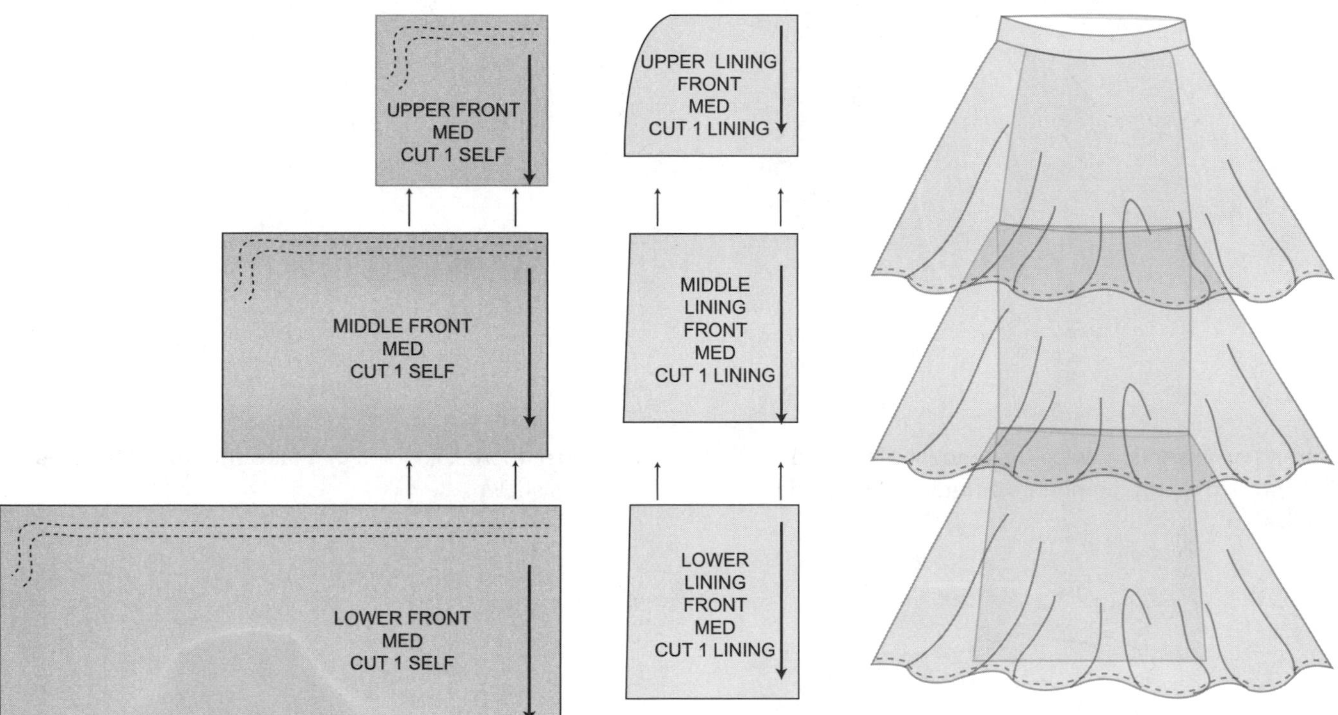

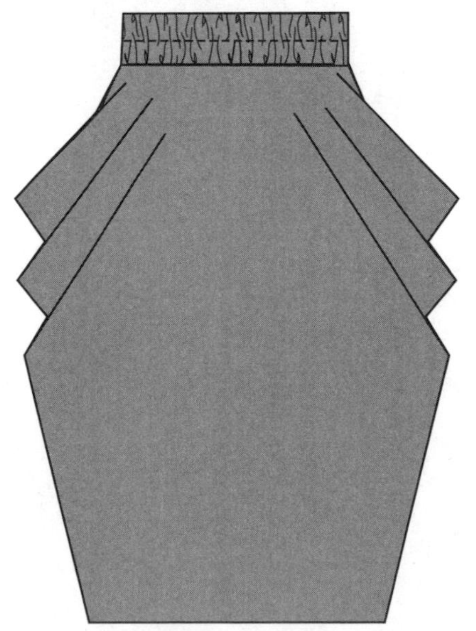

STYLE #5-014 COWL SKIRT WITH DEEP RADIATING FOLDS

Cowl skirt with deep radiating folds.

Decide on the placement of the folds.

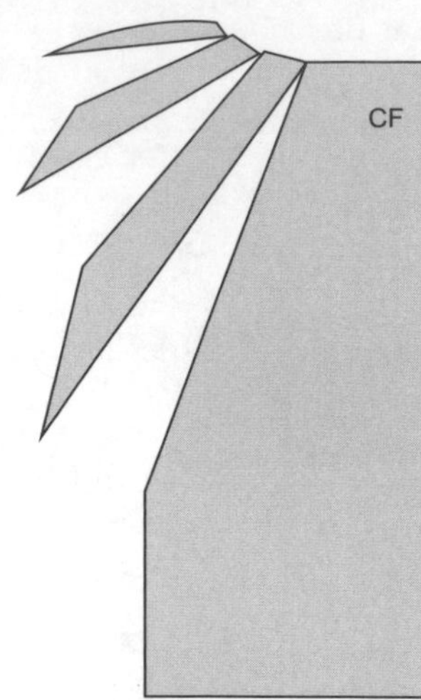

Spread each section twice the amount of the fold desired. May spread as even amounts or radiating amounts, as illustrated.

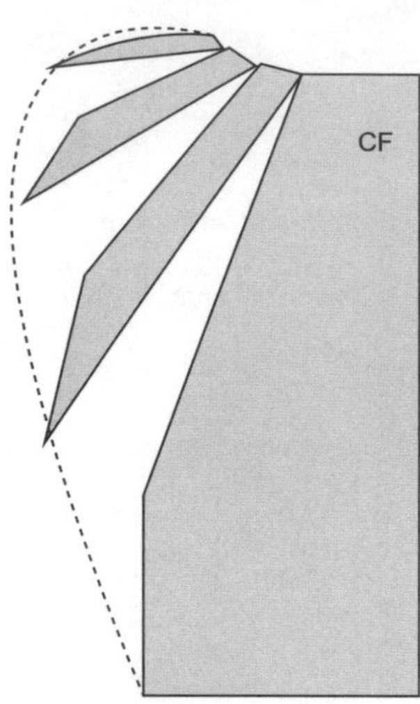

For softer, more fluid folds that fall softly, blend the side seam as shown.

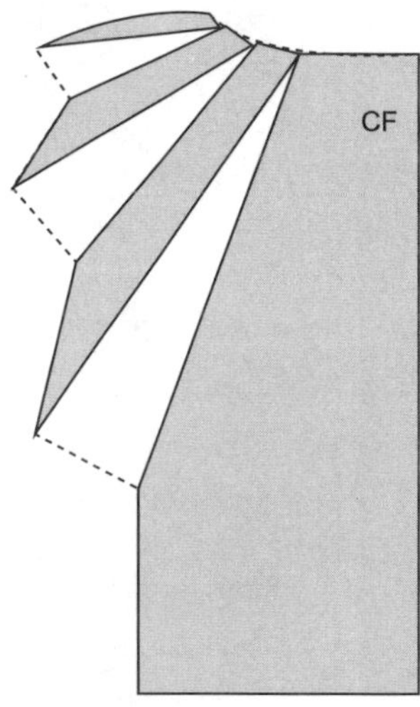

For more controlled folds, blend as indicated.

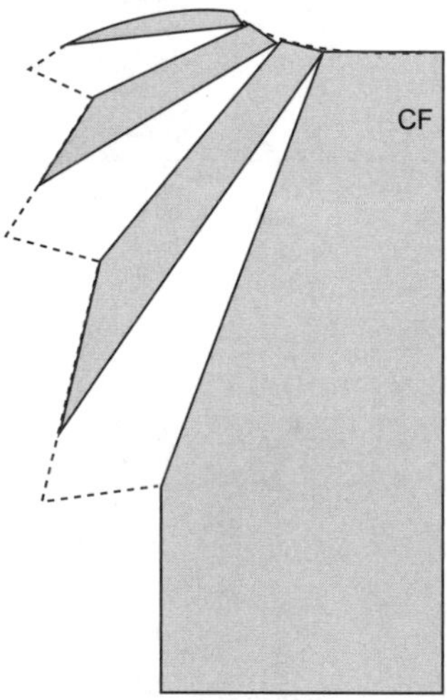

If you wish to tack the folds to the side seams, close the folds and retrace the side seam.

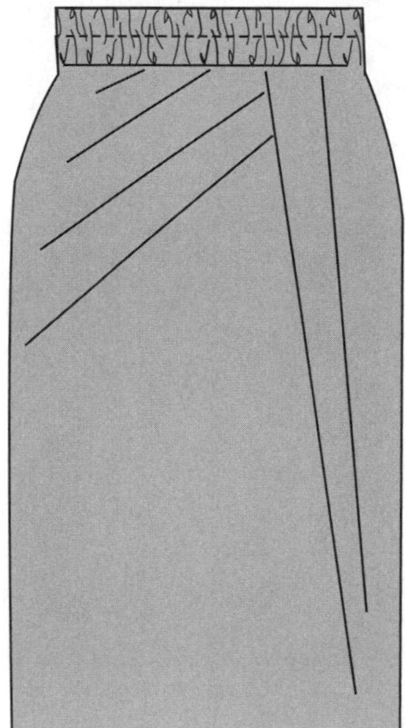

STYLE #5-015 DRAPED-EFFECT SKIRT

Sarong-effect skirts may also be created using the slash and spread technique.

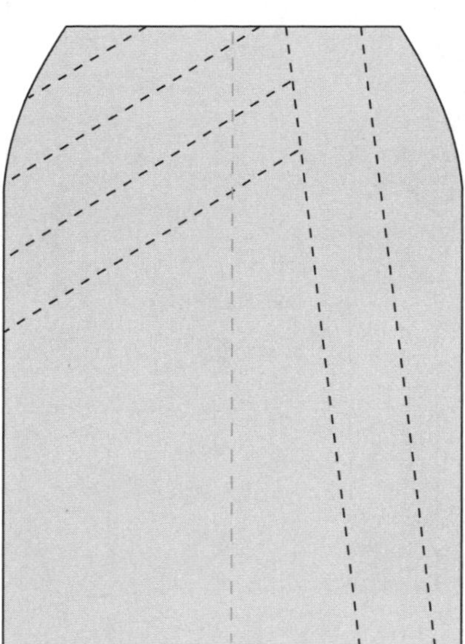

Decide on the placement of the folds.

Decide on the size of the folds.

Folds may be even amounts or radiating amounts.

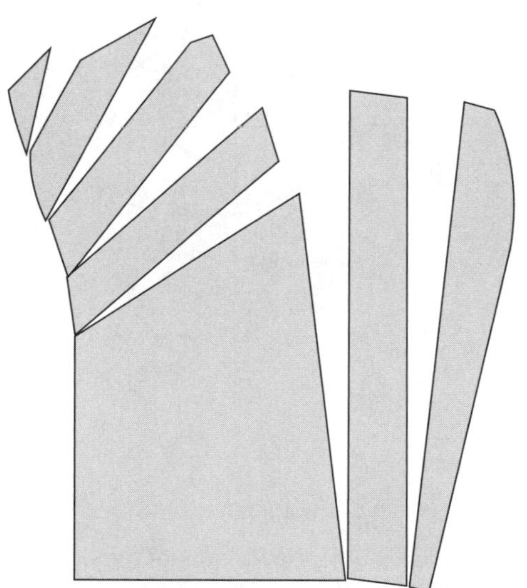

Slash and spread the folds.

Slash and spread the tucks, double the amount required.

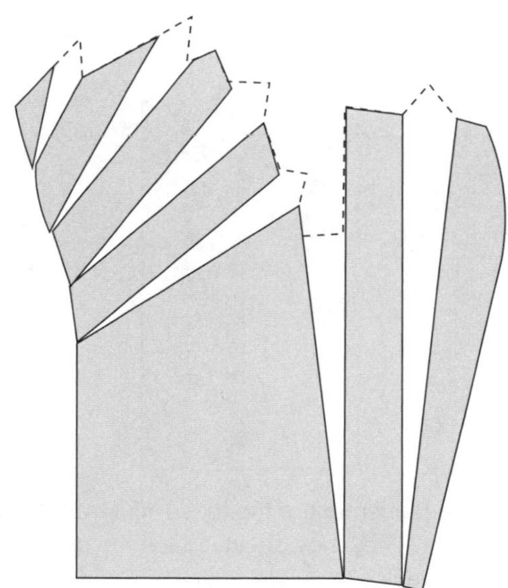

Connect all the points.

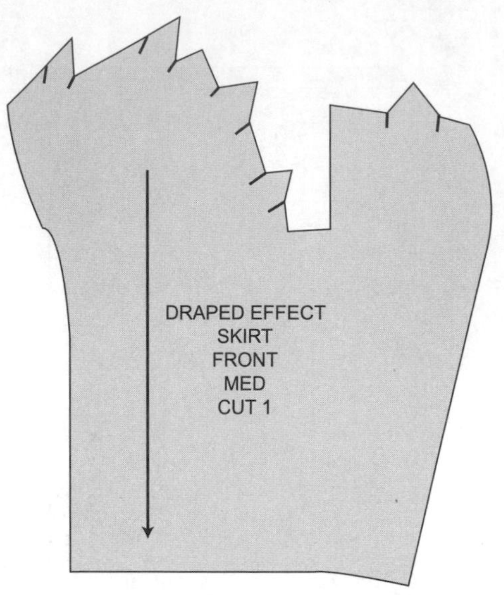

Trace out the pattern and add notches for pleat placement.

Label the pattern as indicated.

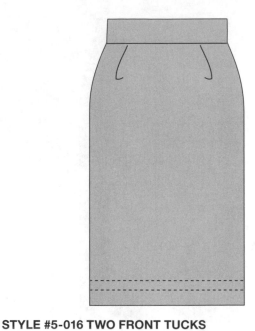

STYLE #5-016 TWO FRONT TUCKS

A single tuck may be added to the design as a style detail.

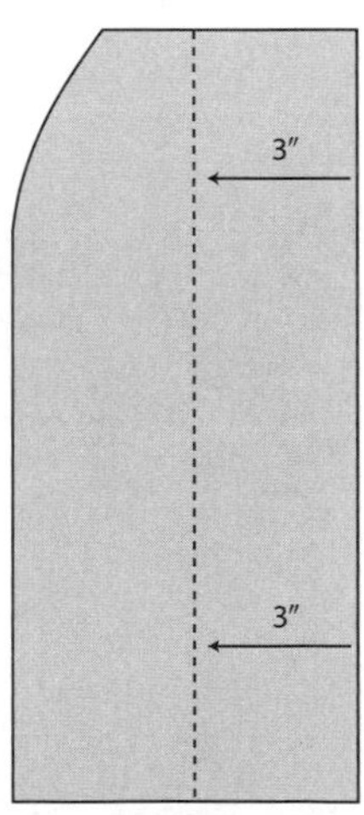

Decide on the placement of the tucks, illustrated at 3″ from the center front. They may be any place the designer or patternmaker decides.

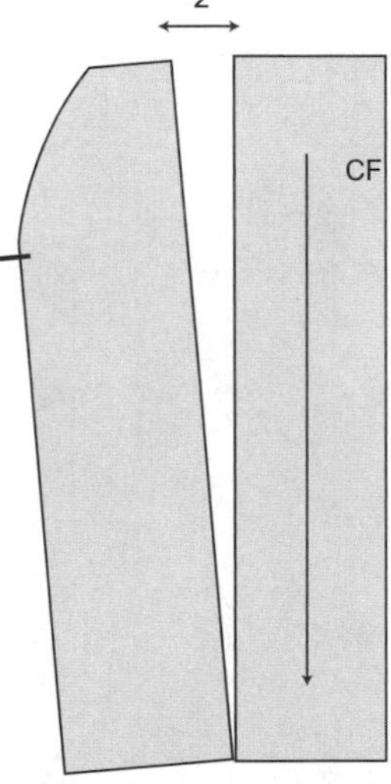

Decide on the width of the tucks.

Spread the tucks double the amount of the pleat required (illustrated at 2″ for a 1″ tuck).

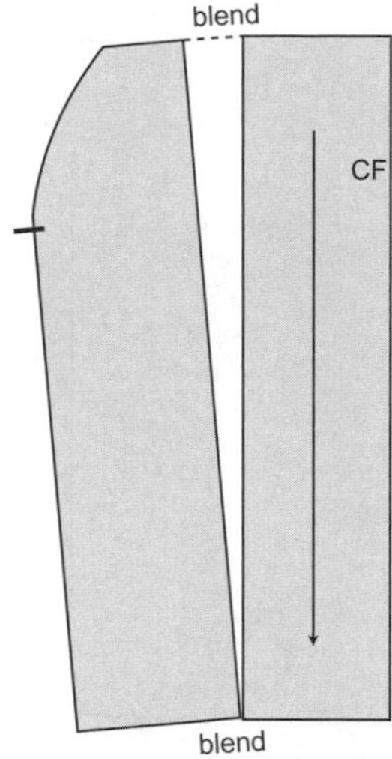

Blend a new waist.

Blend the hem.

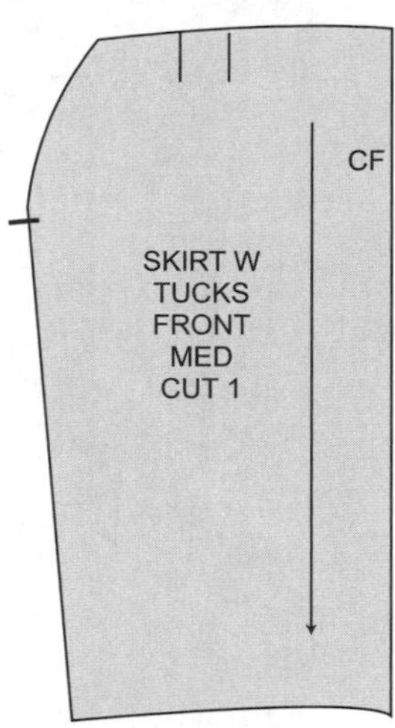

Label the pattern as indicated.

Notch the pleat placement.

Note that the technique will increase the entire width of the skirt.

For a tighter fit through the hip area, refer to the following draft: Style #5-019 Tucks for a tighter hip and thigh.

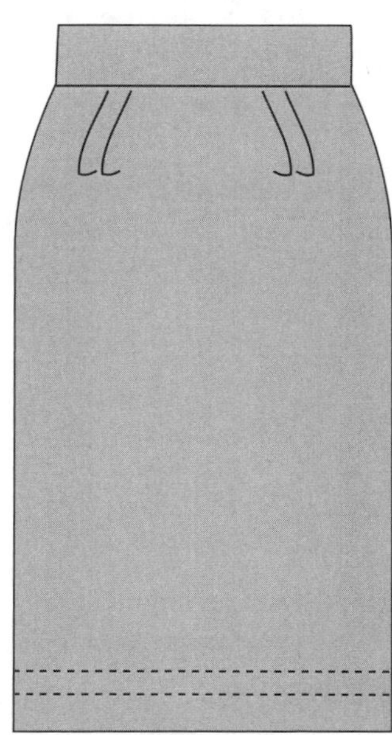

STYLE #5-017 FOUR FRONT TUCKS

A skirt with four front tucks may also be created using the slash and spread technique.

This draft will increase the entire width of the skirt, adding slight volume throughout the hip and thigh area. For a tighter fit see Style #5-019 Tucks for a tighter hip and thigh.

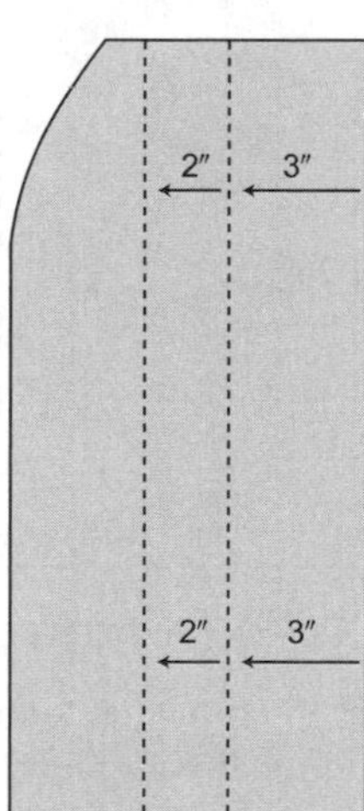

Decide on the placement of the tucks.

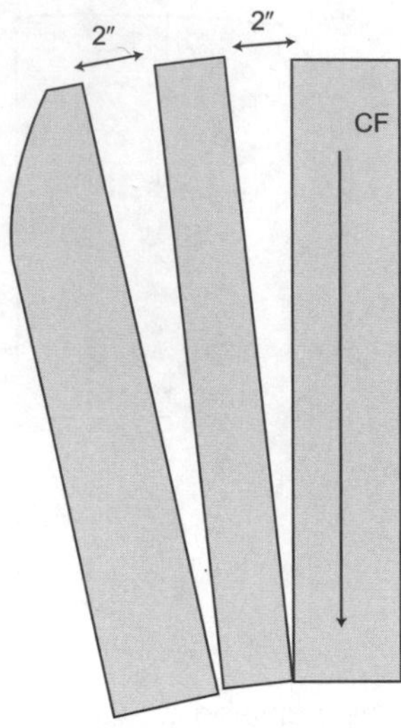

Decide on the size of the tucks.

Slash and spread the tucks.

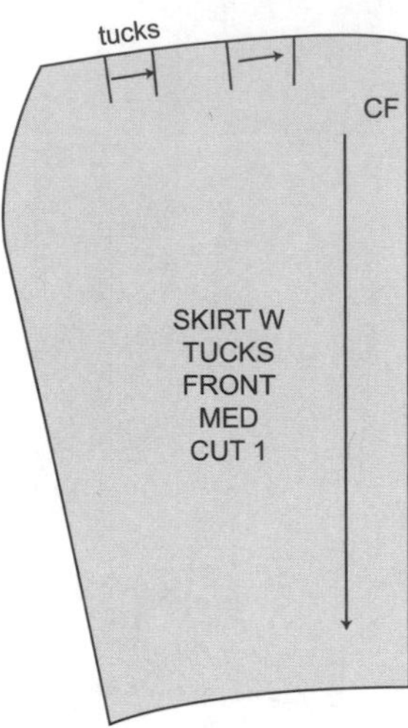

Trace out the pattern and place notches to indicate the tucks.

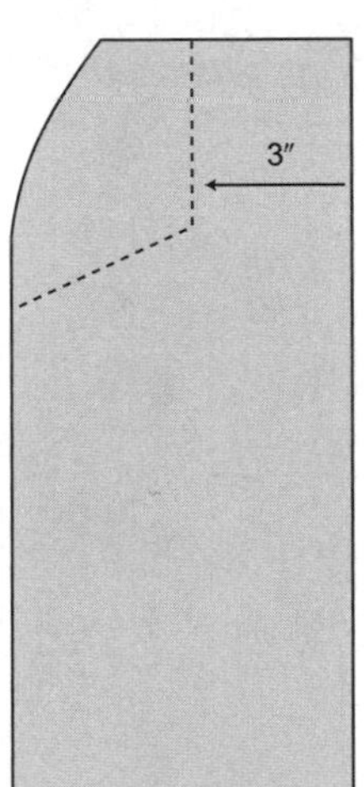

STYLE #5-018 TUCKS FOR A TIGHTER HIP AND THIGH

This draft differs from the previous technique in that the skirt is only slashed to the hip area and will not increase the entire width of the skirt, just the hip area.

However, the tucks, when sewn, will fall slightly toward the side seam.

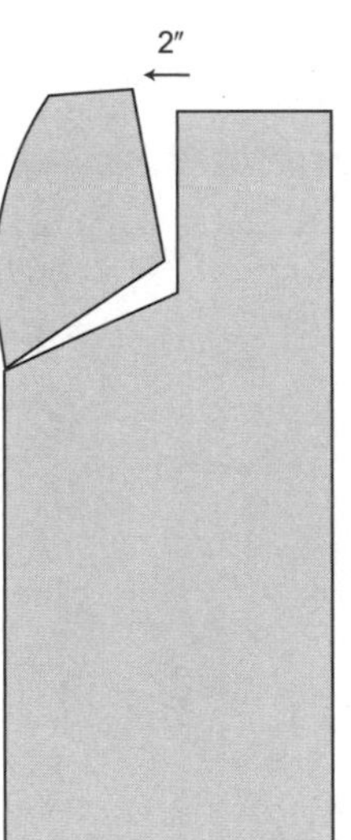

Slash and spread the desired amount.

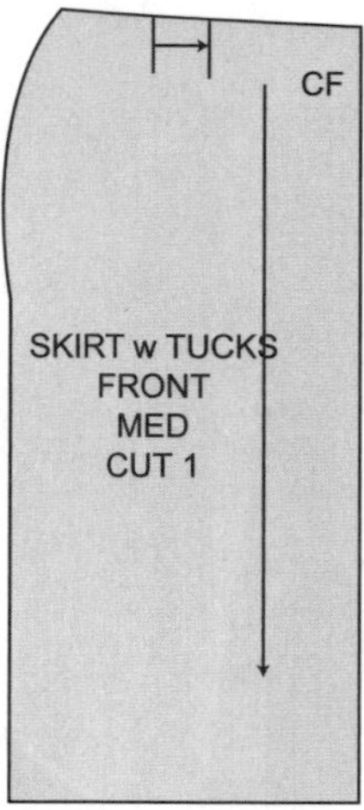

Fold and true the tucks with a tracing wheel.

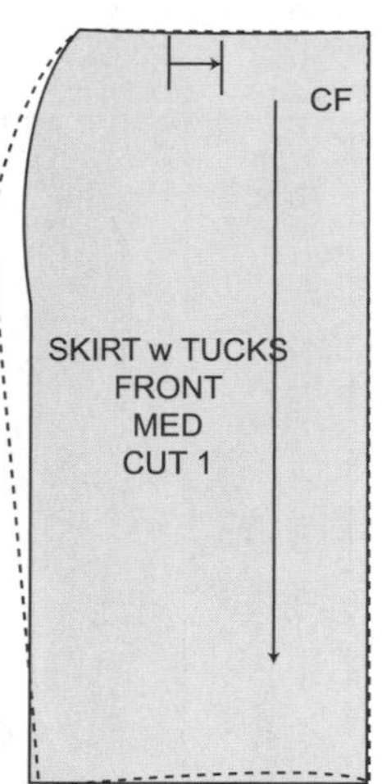

Comparing the Two Techniques

This diagram shows the difference between the two techniques. Neither is better than the other; the choice depends on the silhouette required.

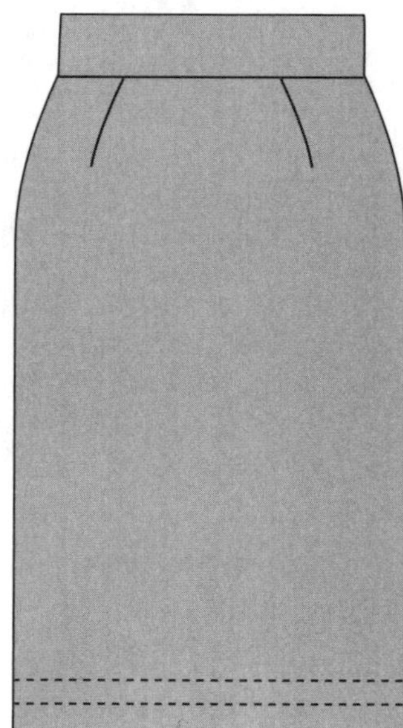

STYLE #5-019 ADDING DARTS

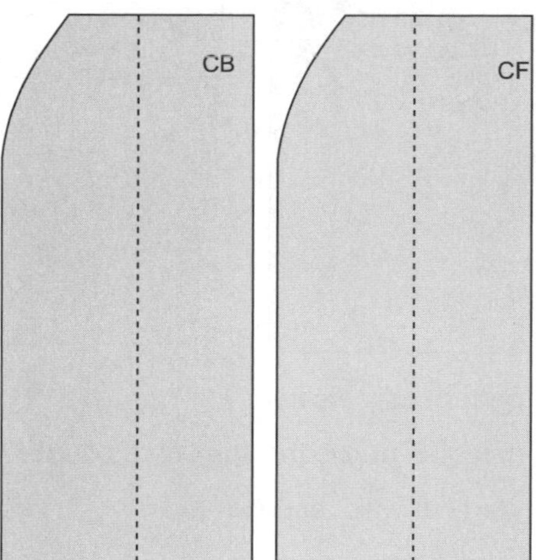

Darts are not necessary for knit garments. However, sometimes the designer may require darts for aesthetic reasons.

Place the slash line 3″ from center front.

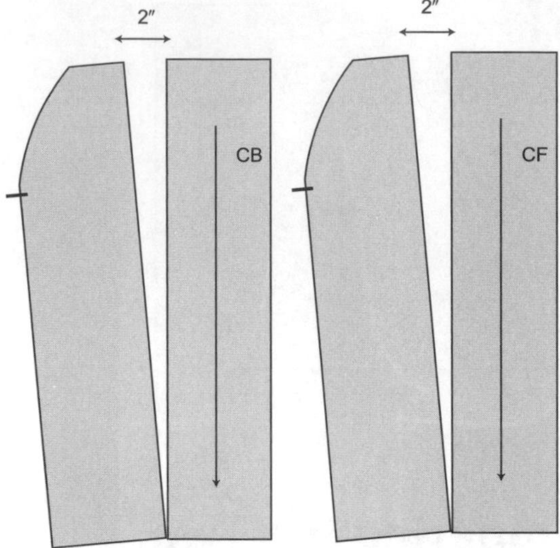

Slash and spread 2″ for a 1″ wide mouth for the dart.

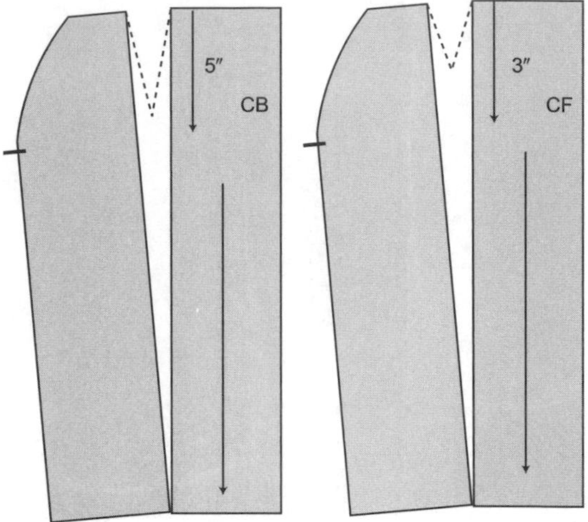

Find the center of the slash opening and draw in the dart.

Back dart 5″ down from the natural waist.

Front dart 3″ down from the natural waist.

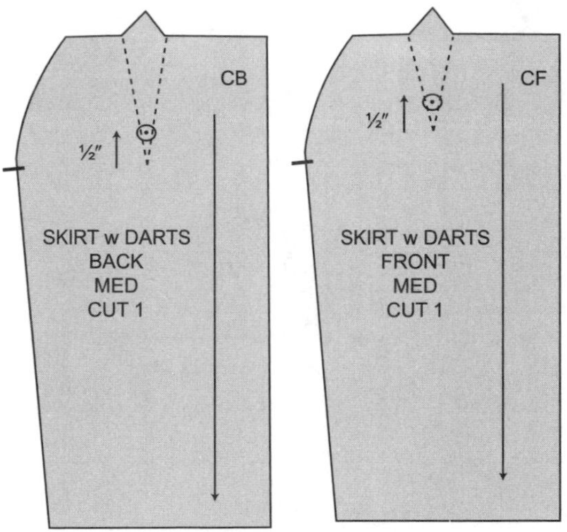

Trace out pattern as indicated.

Mark drill holes ½″ above the apex of the dart.

Notch the darts at waist and fold to true.

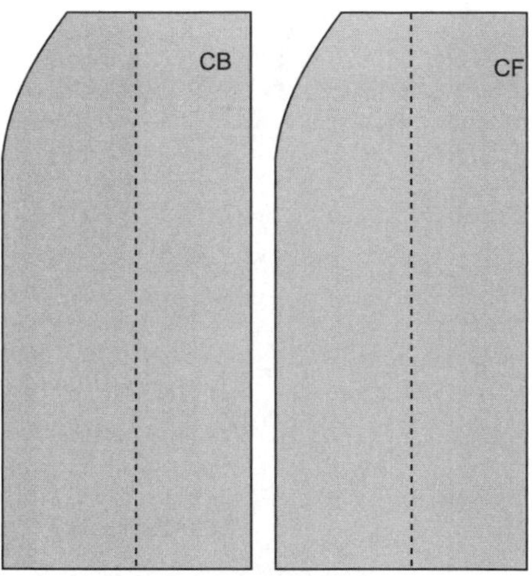

STYLE #5-020 ADDING DARTS WITHOUT INCREASING THE SIZE OF THE SKIRT

The challenge with the previous draft is that it increases the whole skirt including the area below the dart.

Use this draft when you do not want to increase the entire width of the skirt.

Place a guideline in the center of the waist.

Square down to the hem.

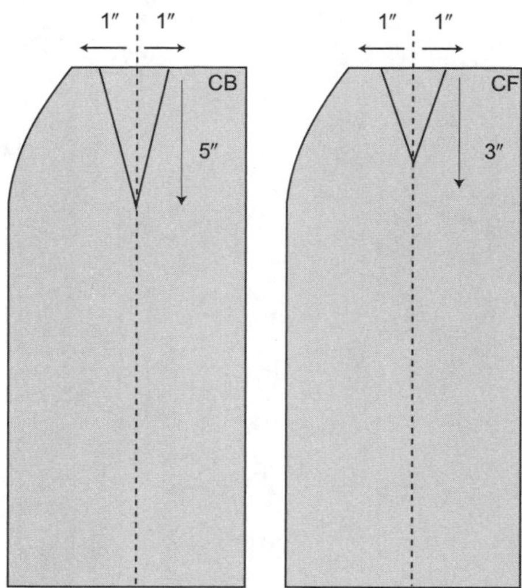

Measure 1″ on each side of the guideline.

Measure down 3″ for skirt front.

Measure down 5″ for skirt back.

Draw in the dart.

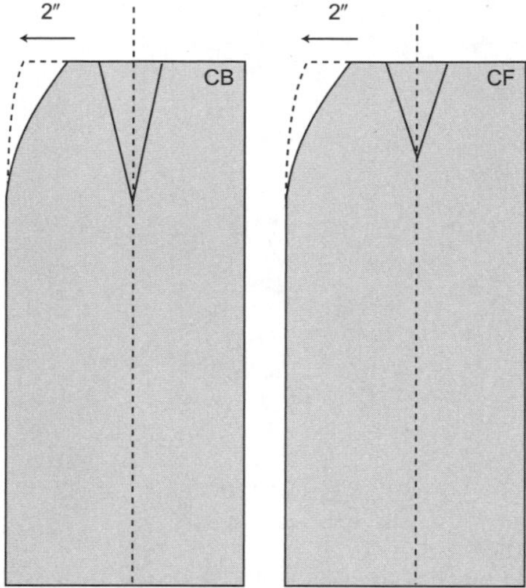

Add the amount of dart to the side seam of the skirt.

Try not to shape the side seam any lower than the bottom of dart.

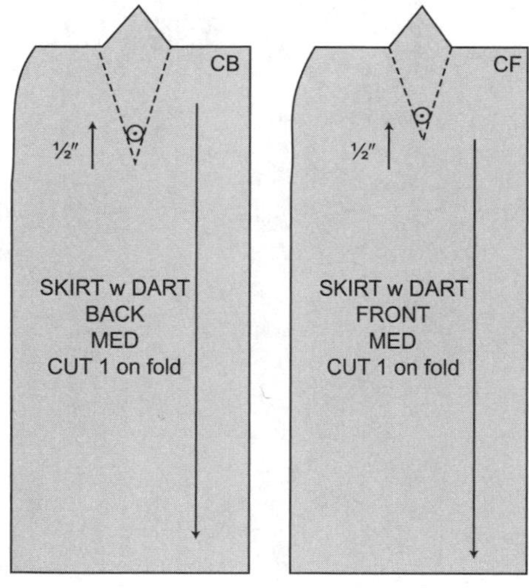

Fold and true the dart.

Place a drill mark ½″ above the apex of the dart.

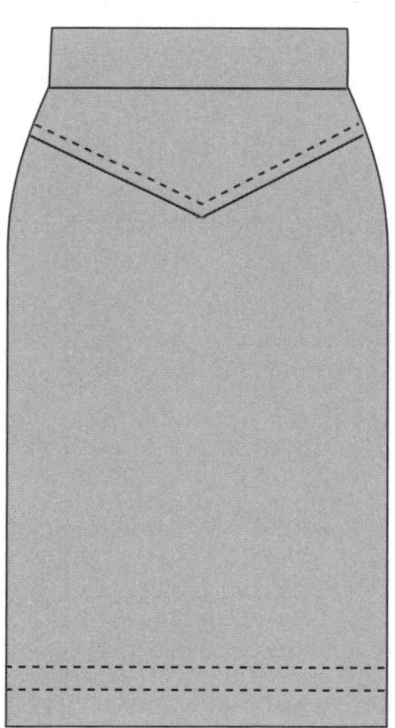

Horizontal Style Lines

STYLE #5-021 POINTED YOKE

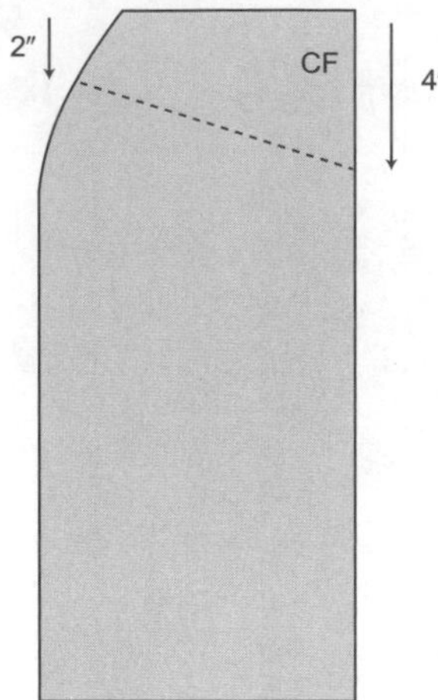

Draw in the yoke style line, illustrated at 2″ down at the side seam, and 4″ down the center front, or any measurement the design requires.

Notch, trace, and separate the pattern pieces.

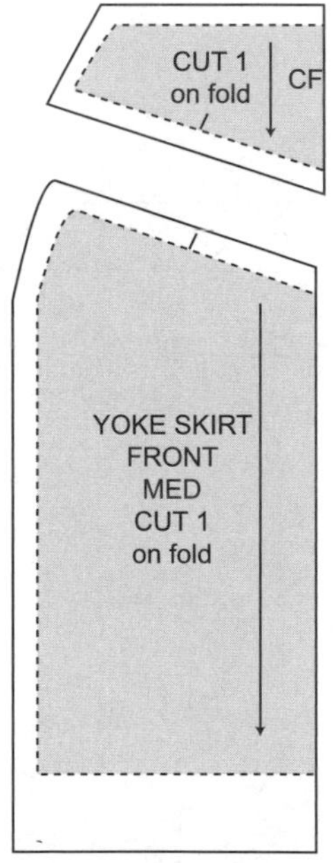

Notch and trace out the separate pieces.

Add the necessary seam allowances.

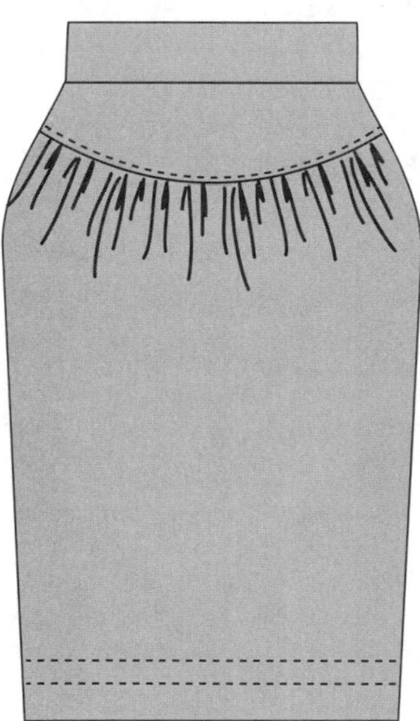

STYLE #5-022 ROUND YOKE WITH GATHERED SKIRT

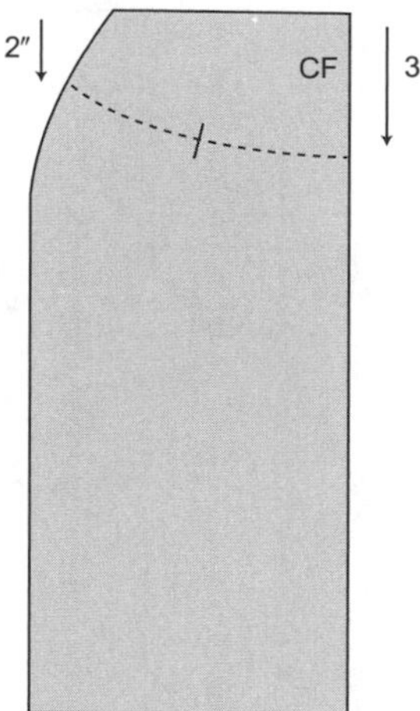

To draft a skirt with a round yoke and a gathered skirt, follow these instructions.

Measure down 1½″ on the side seam.

Measure down 3″ on the center front.

Draw in a curved yoke line.

These measurements may change as the design requires.

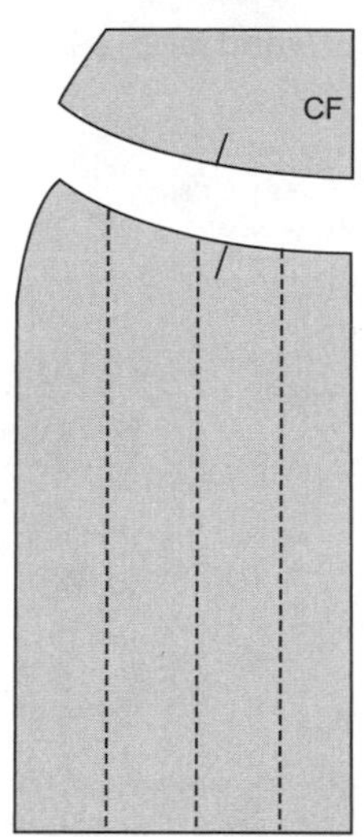

Trace and separate the pieces as indicated.

On the lower portion, divide the skirt into four sections.

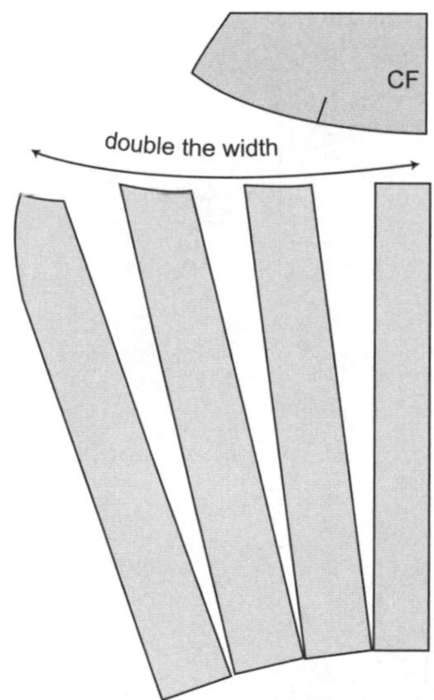

Slash the sections and spread each one until the new measurement is double the original measurement.

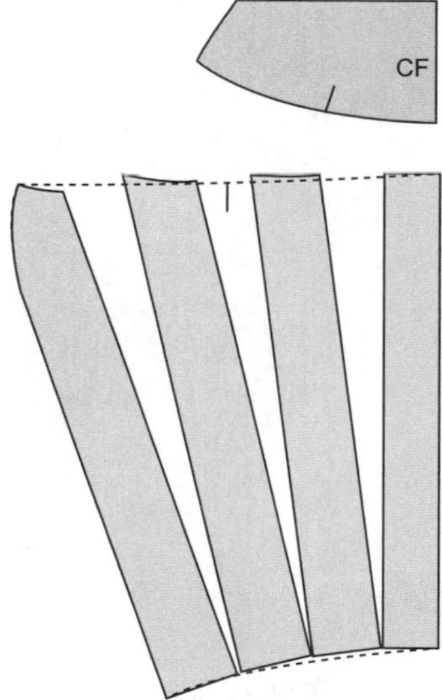

Redraw the lower portion of the skirt and place notches to line up with the yoke.

Trace out the pattern and label as indicated.

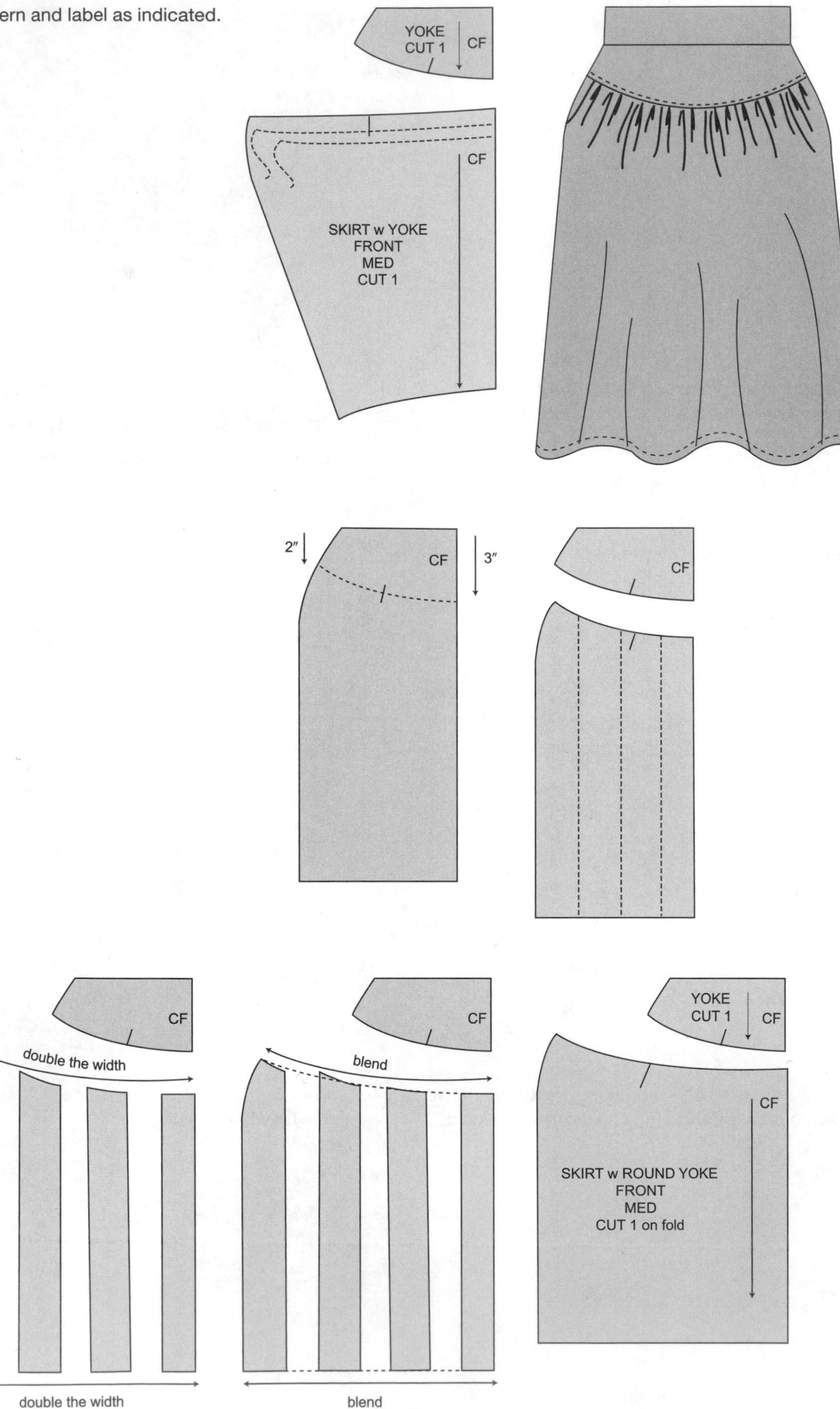

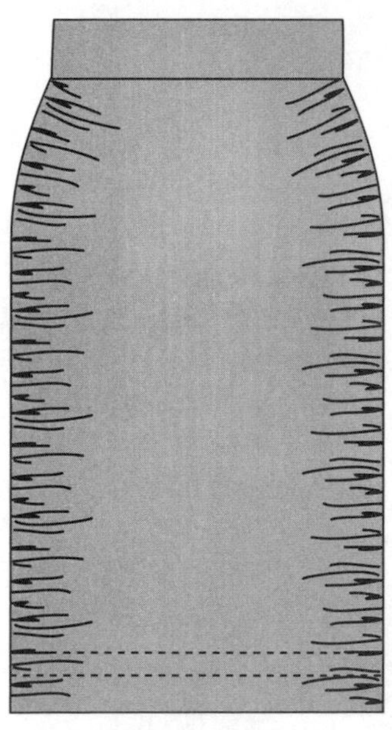

Gathered Side-Seams

Clear elastic may be used to gather or shirr any part of a garment. Remember to serge the seams before sewing the elastic with the straight stitch. If you try to attach the elastic while serging at the same time, it will be much too difficult. Always use the clear elastic since the ends will not ravel or fray.

A skirt, top, pant, or dress style may be created with gathering on both sides.

Lengthen the original pattern, and simply stretch elastic in the seams allowance and sew with a straight stitch.

It is much easier to sew the elastic with the straight stitch after the seam has been serged.

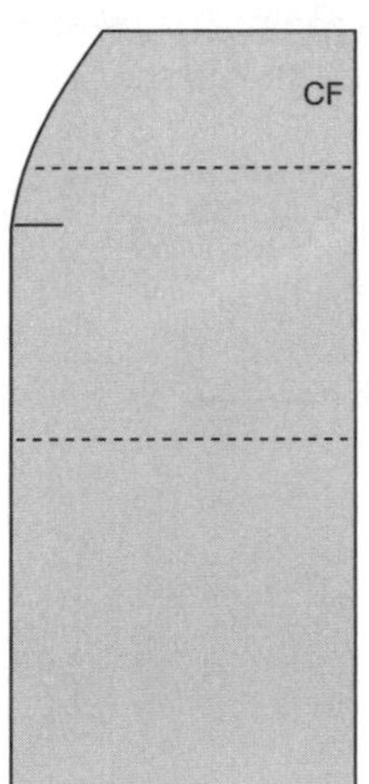

In order to keep the hip notch in proportion, slash at least once above the hip notch and once below, proportionately, as illustrated.

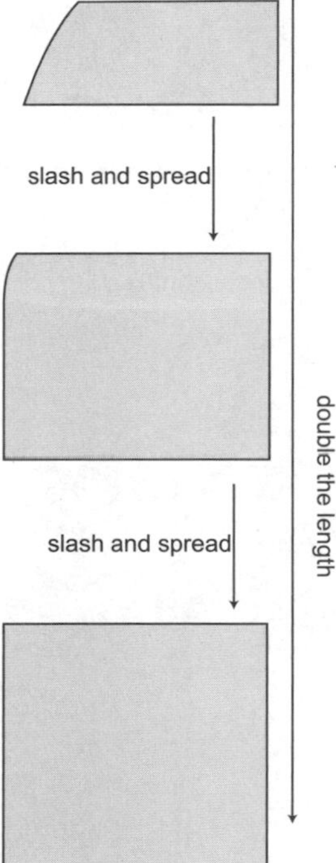

Slash and spread the section, doubling the length of the original skirt.

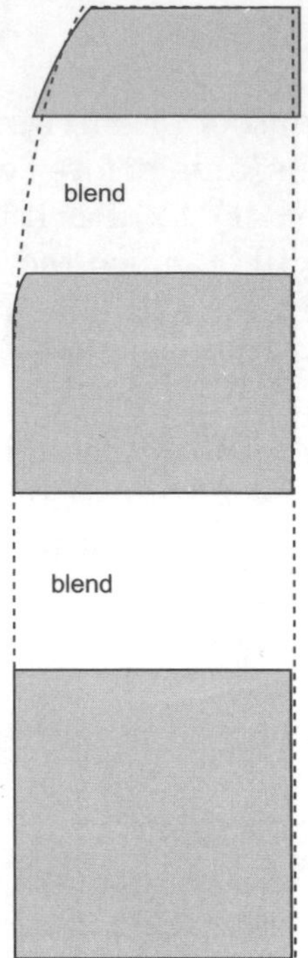

Blend a new smooth side-seam, as shown.

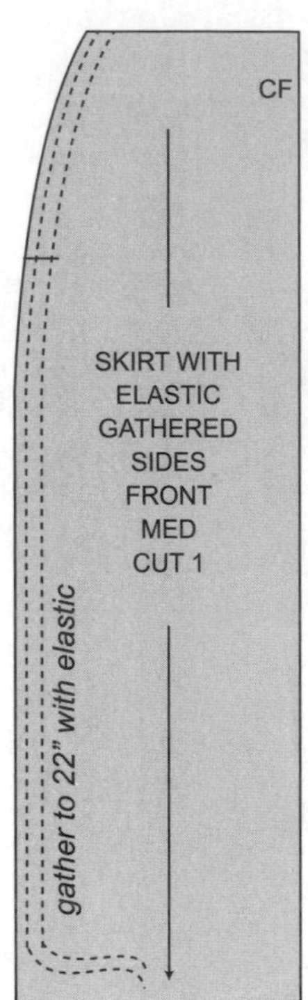

Label the pattern as illustrated. Label the side seam with the length of the original side-seam length.

Create the gathered side-seam by stretching clear rubber elastic, after serging the side seams, and sew with the straight-stitch machine. Do not stretch the elastic in the hem allowance.

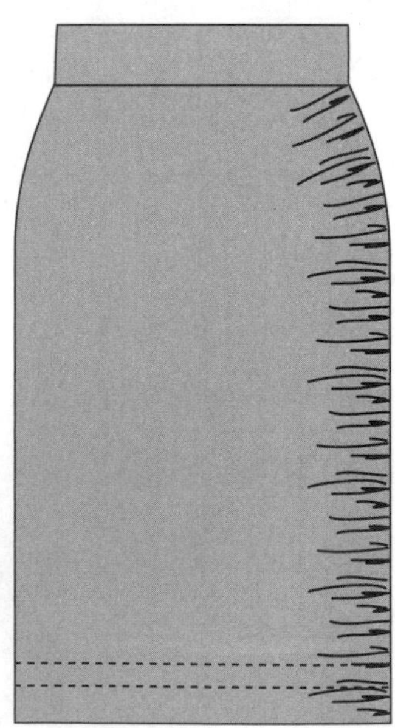

STYLE #5-023 ASYMMETRICAL GATHERED SIDE-SEAM

To draft a skirt with a drawstring or gathering on only one side, and a straight hem, follow these instructions.

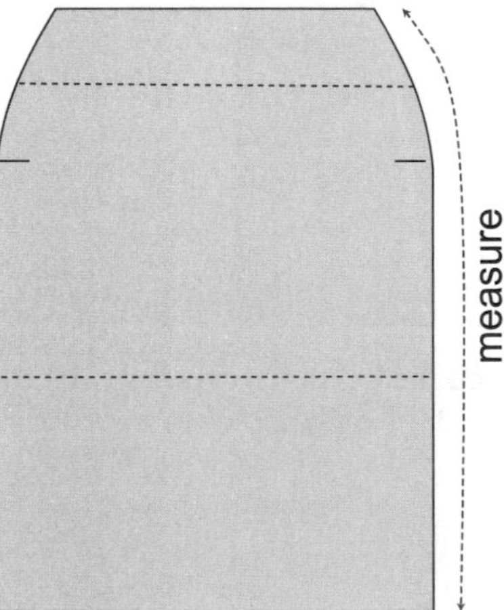

Divide the skirt at least once above the hip notch and once below the hip notch. The more slashes, the more accurate the draft and the smoother the curve.

Measure the original hip length so that you will know how long to cut the elastic.

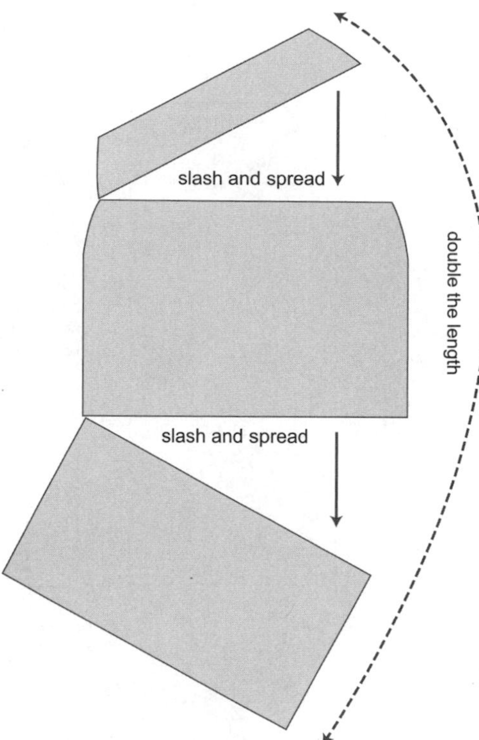

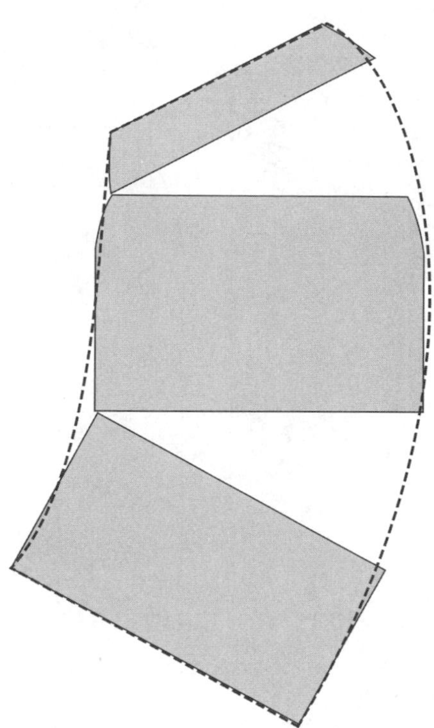

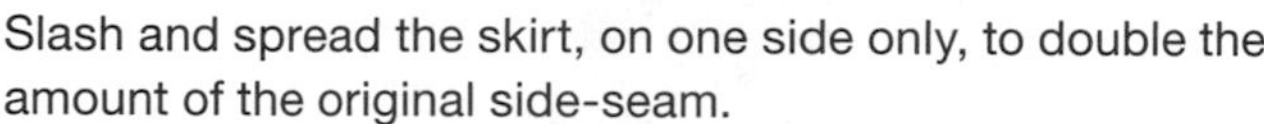

Slash and spread the skirt, on one side only, to double the amount of the original side-seam.

If the original skirt length is 22″, spread the side seam to 44″.

Blend a new side-seam as illustrated.

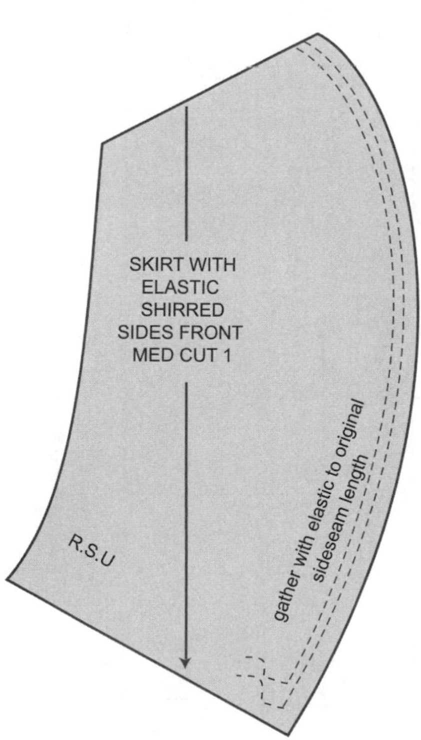

Label the pattern as illustrated. Label the side seam with the original side-seam measurement. Create the gathered side-seam by stretching clear rubber elastic when serge-ing the side-seams. Do not stretch the elastic in the hem.

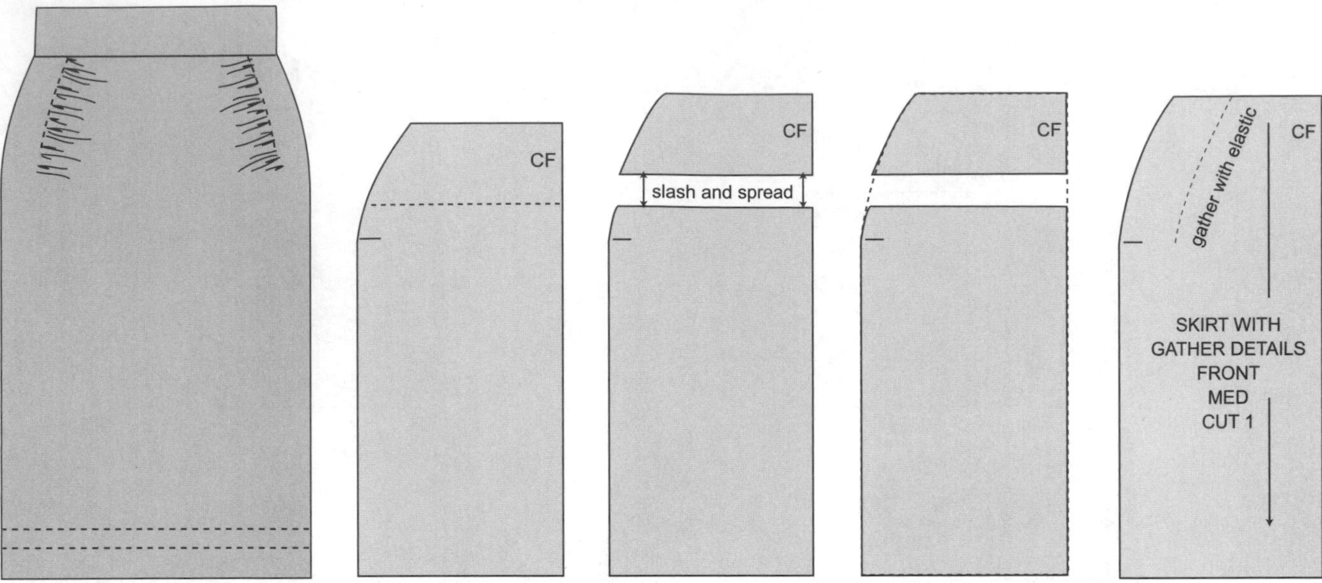

STYLE #5-024 SKIRT WITH ELASTIC GATHERING DETAIL

Gathering details may be added as a style accent, using the slash and spread technique.

Stretch and sew clear elastic to create the gathering detail.

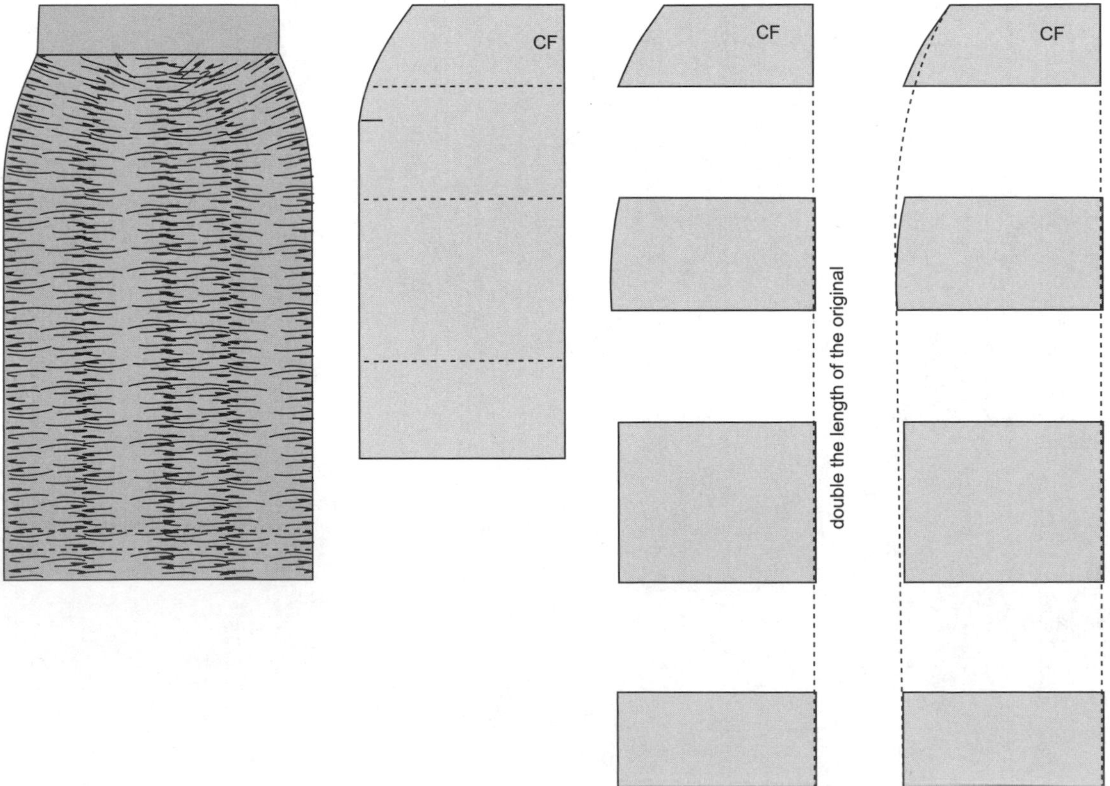

STYLE #5-025 VERTICALLY GATHERED SKIRT

Gathering details may be added to the entire length of the skirt, using the slash and spread technique.

Stretch clear elastic to create the gathering detail, or use an elastic thread in the bobbin of a straight-stitch sewing machine.

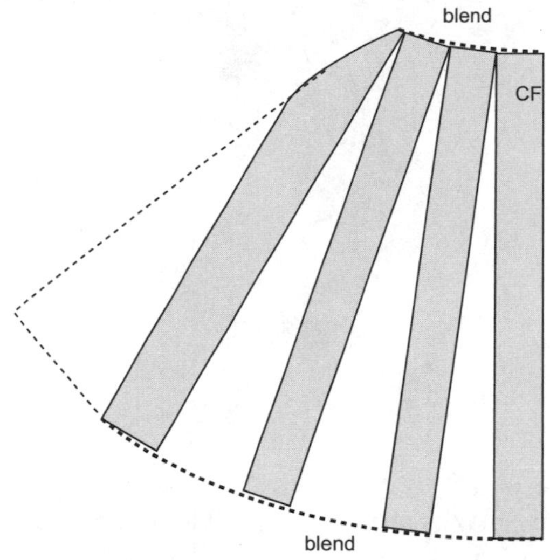

Circle Skirts and Circular Ruffles

STYLE #5-026 SLASH AND SPREAD CIRCLE SKIRT

Create a circle skirt by slashing and spreading the skirt to a 90-degree side seam.

This draft will retain the hip curve.

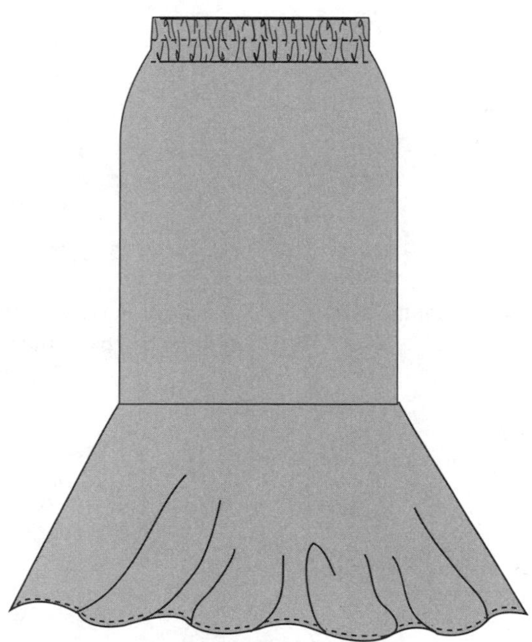

SKIRT WITH CIRCULAR FLOUNCE

A full circle skirt may be added to the hem of a skirt by following these instructions.

Draft a circle skirt to fit the hem measurements.

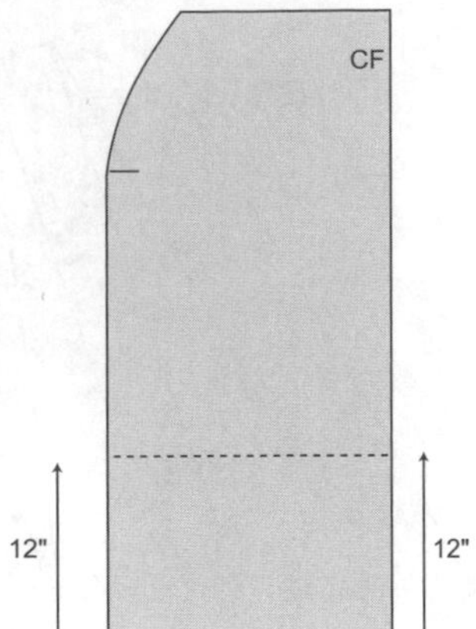

Shorten the skirt by the length of the finished ruffle (illustrated at 12″ but may be any measurement the design requires).

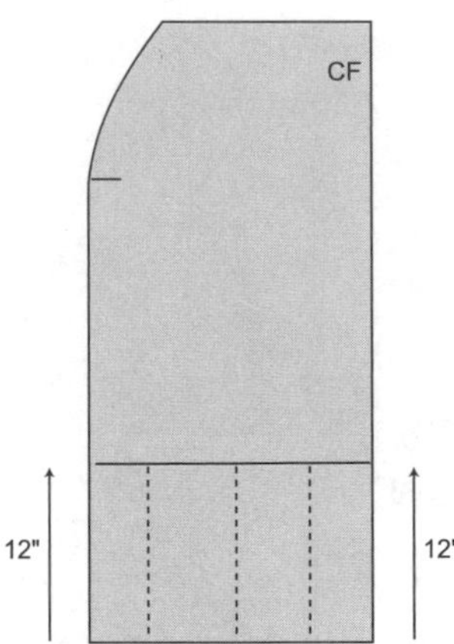

Measure the width of the skirt at the hem, illustrated at 9″.

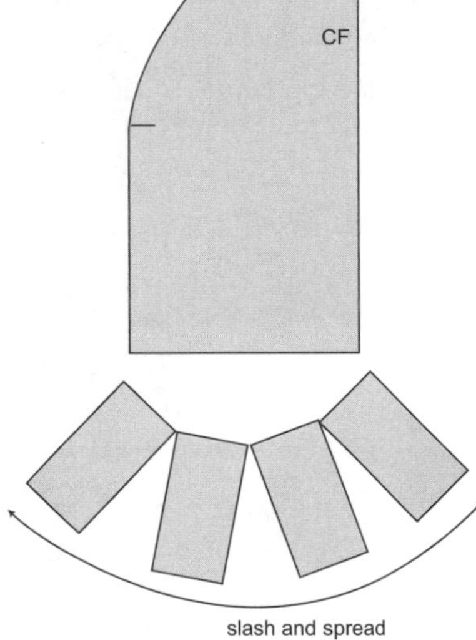

Draft a circle skirt using the measurements from the skirt.

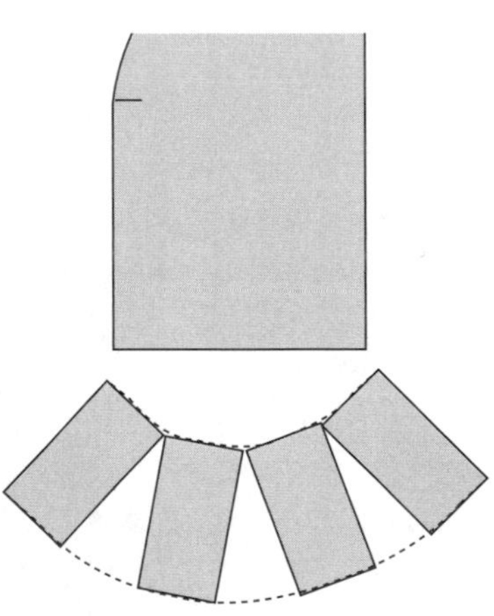

For a fuller flounce, slash and spread in more places to lengthen the circumference of the hem.

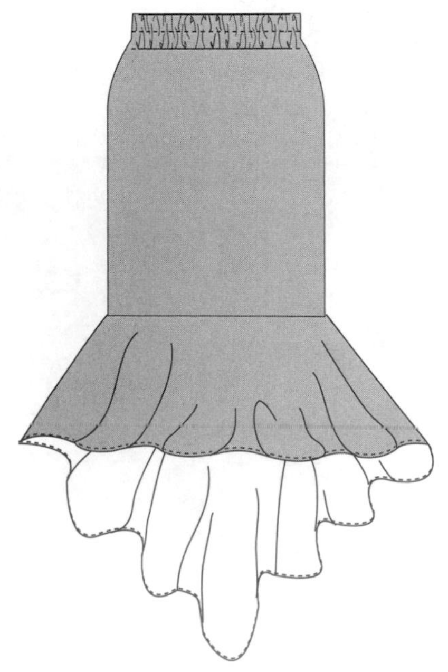

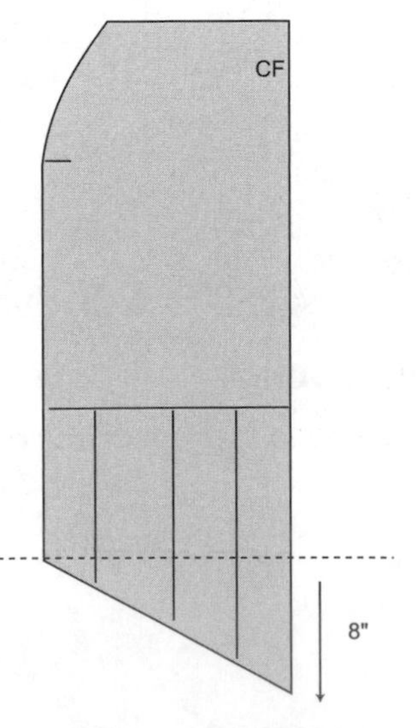

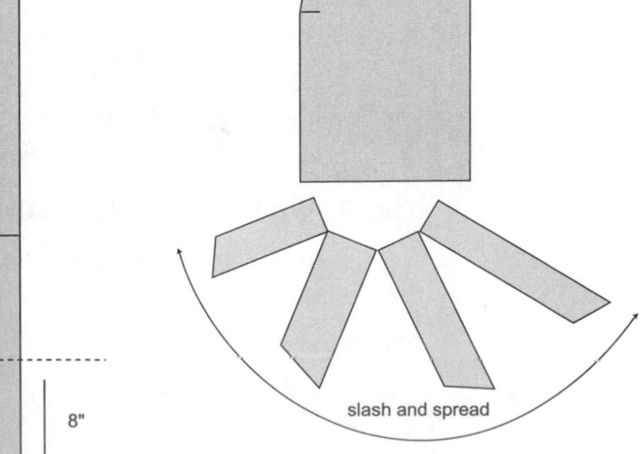

STYLE #5-027 FISHTAIL

Create an asymmetrical flounce for a dramatic skirt.

1

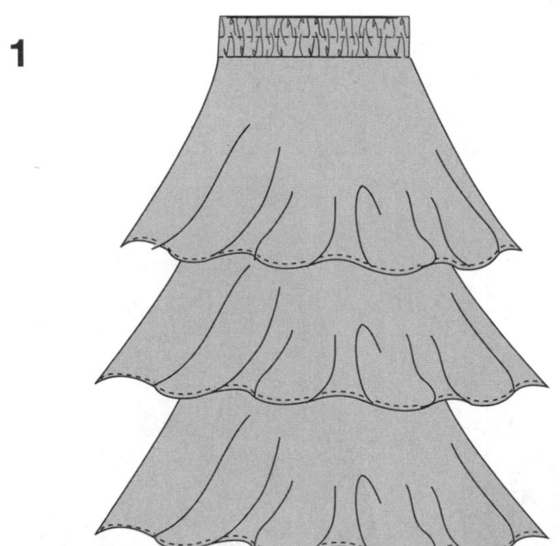

2

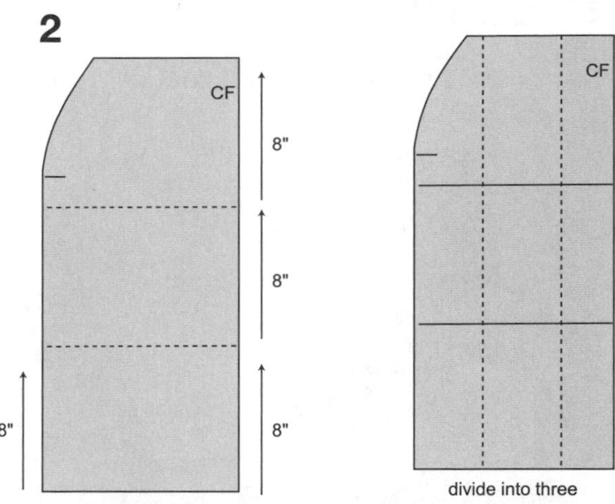

Determine the placement of the tiers.

Shorten the skirt the amount of the bottom tier.

Divide each section into thirds, or more if greater fullness is desired.

STYLE #5-028 LAYERED CIRCLE SKIRTS

Create a straight skirt with multiple tiered circular flounces by following this draft.

The draft may easily be changed to create many variations of this design.

3A

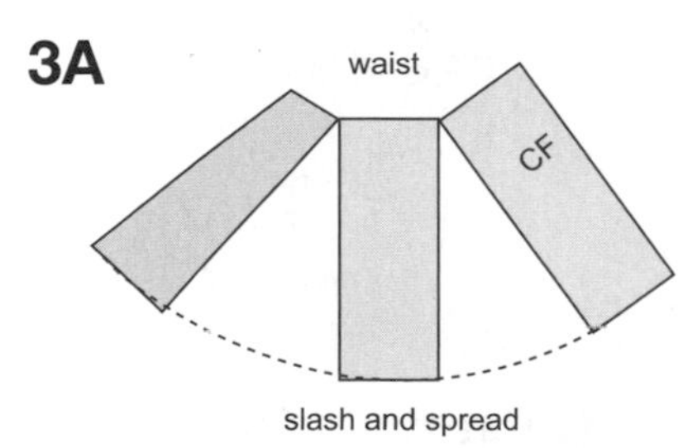

B

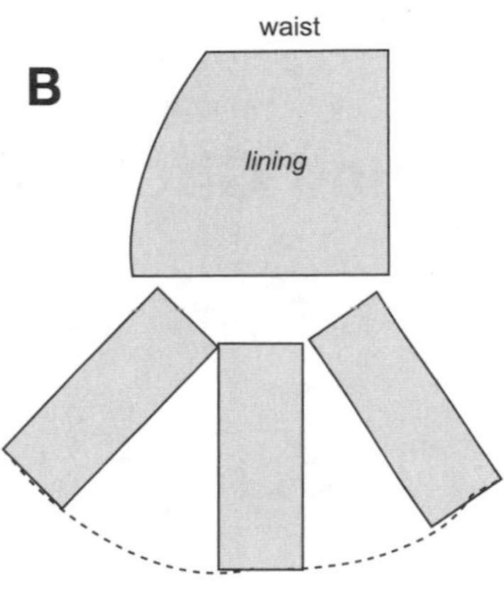

Slash and spread the top layer.

C

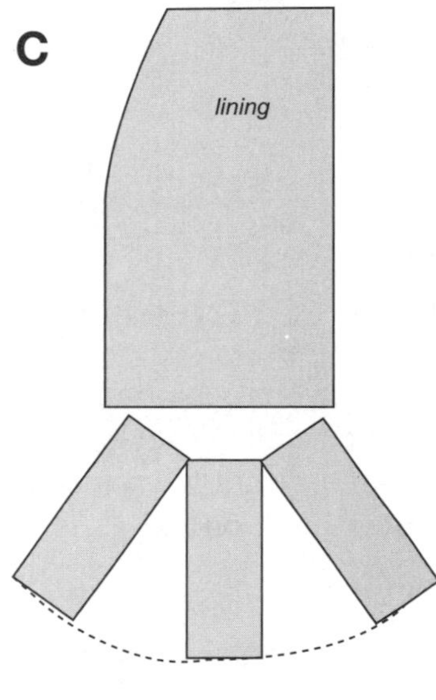

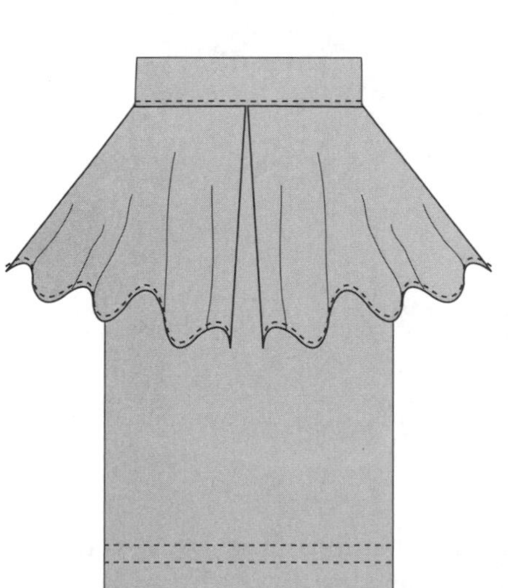

STYLE #5-029 SKIRT WITH A CIRCULAR PEPLUM ATTACHED

Using the same technique, it is also possible to draft an assortment of circular peplums and overskirts.

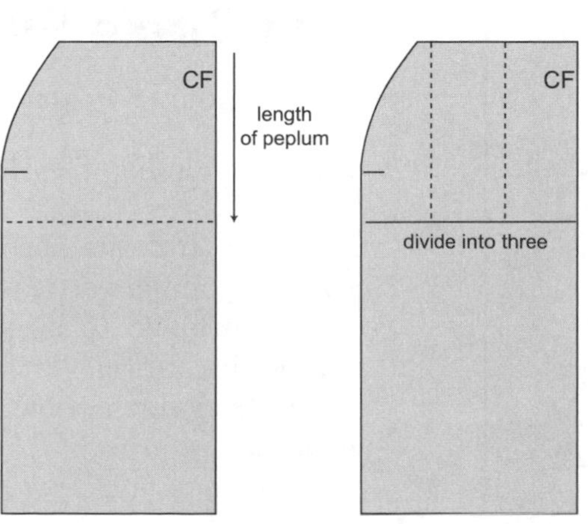

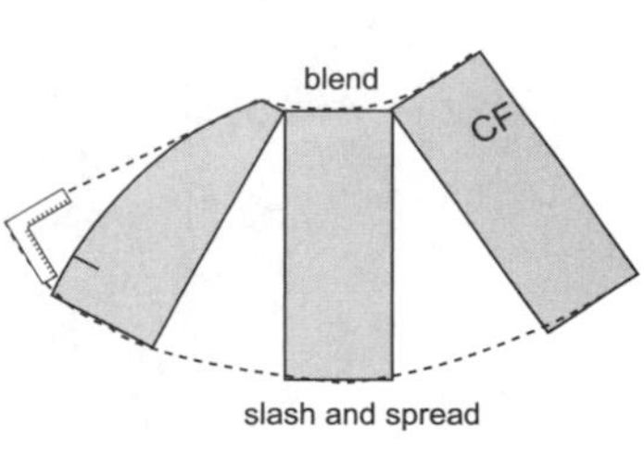

Decide on the length of peplum and draw a horizontal line.

Circle Skirts

Circle skirts are another way of creating fullness at the hem.

1

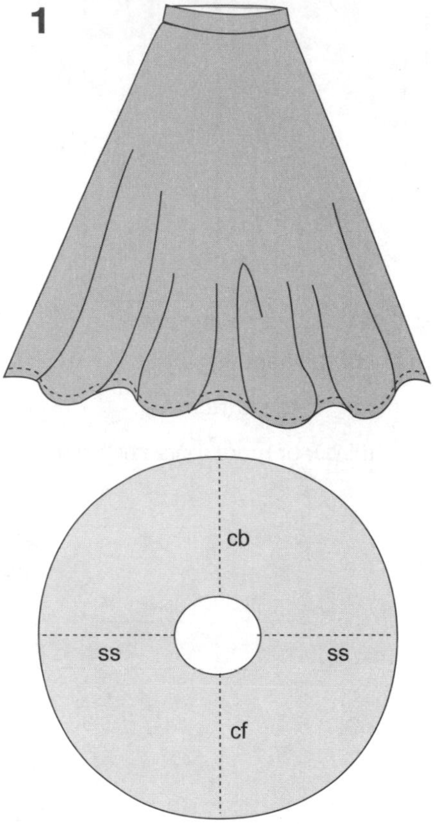

2

3

Full Circle Skirt

May be four-seamed panels or two-seamed panels, or even one-seamed panel with a seam at the center back only.

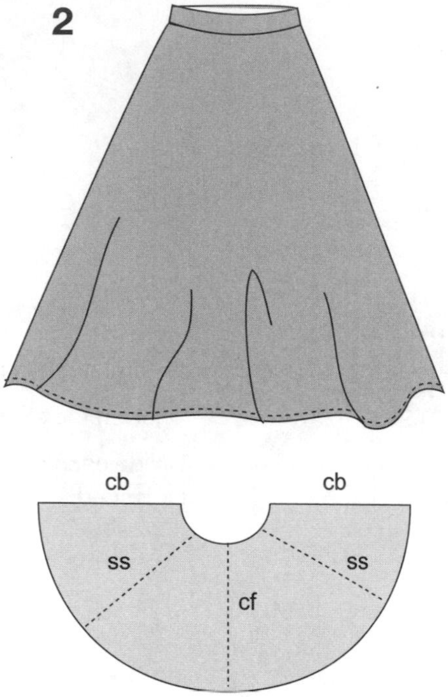

Half Circle Skirt

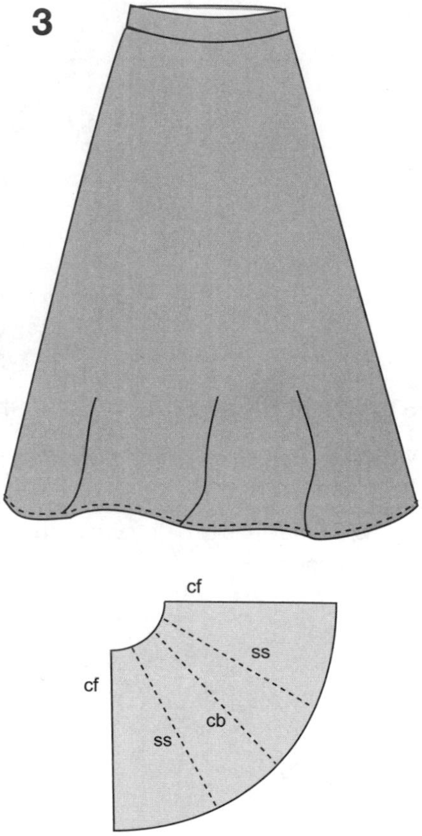

Quarter Circle Skirt

4

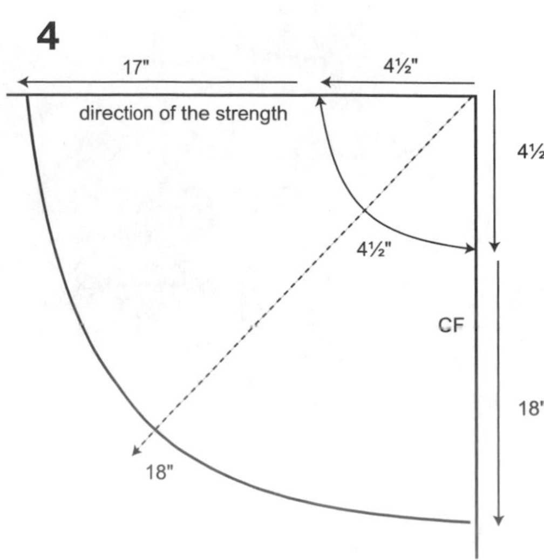

Full Circle Skirt

Example: 26½″ waist.

26½″ divided by 6 = 4½″.

Note that the across measurement has been reduced by 1″ to compensate for the fabric stretch in that direction, and may need to be shortened more depending on your particular fabric.

Skirt length shown at 18″ but may be any length the designer requires.

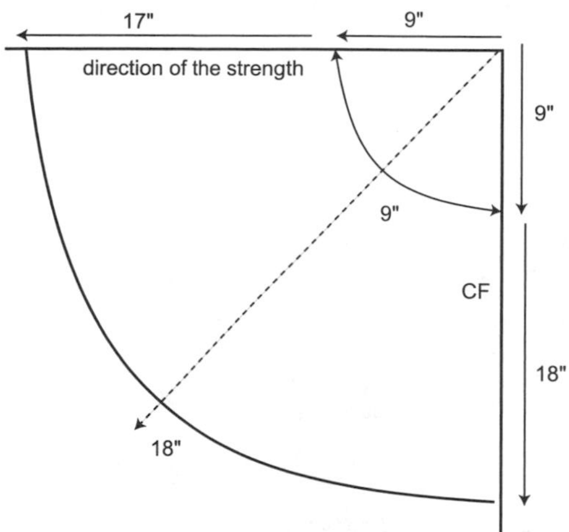

STYLE #5-030 HALF CIRCLE SKIRT

Create a half circle skirt with two panels.

Follow the same draft except use ⅔ the waist measurement.

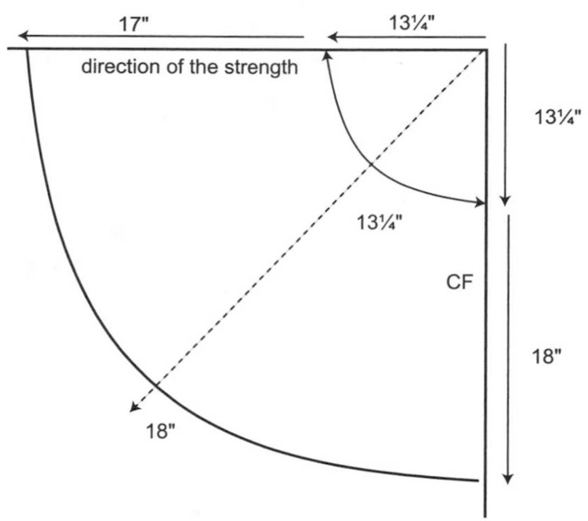

STYLE #5-031 QUARTER CIRCLE SKIRT

Create a quarter circle skirt using ⅓ the waist measurement.

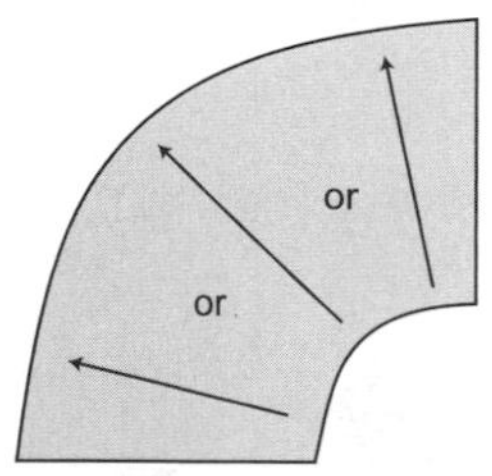

CIRCLE SKIRT GRAINLINES

You may use any one of the grainlines, as long as all pieces are cut with the same grainline.

Cut one for a quarter circle skirt, cut two for a half circle skirt, or cut four for a full circle skirt.

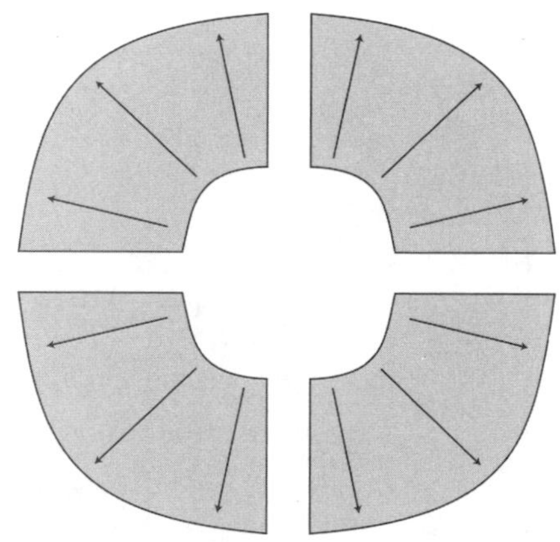

GORED CIRCLE SKIRT

Create a circle skirt with multiple panels by dividing the skirt into gores.

Add grainlines as illustrated.

Simply trace out one panel and label as "cut 4."

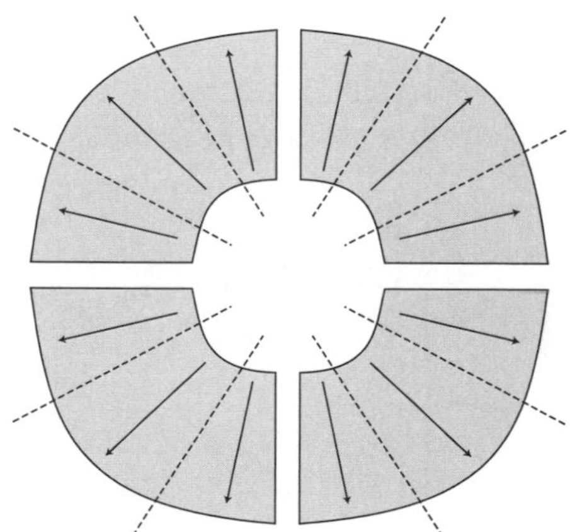

Create a circle skirt with multiple panels by dividing the skirt into multiple gores.

Add grainlines as illustrated.

Simply trace out one panel and label as "cut 12."

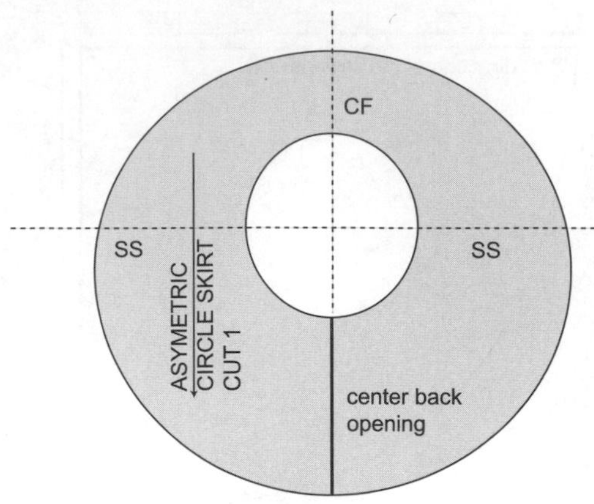

Asymmetrical Circle Skirts

An asymmetrical circle skirt may be created by moving the waist circumference to any place within the skirt.

Illustrated toward the front, which will shorten the front and lengthen the back.

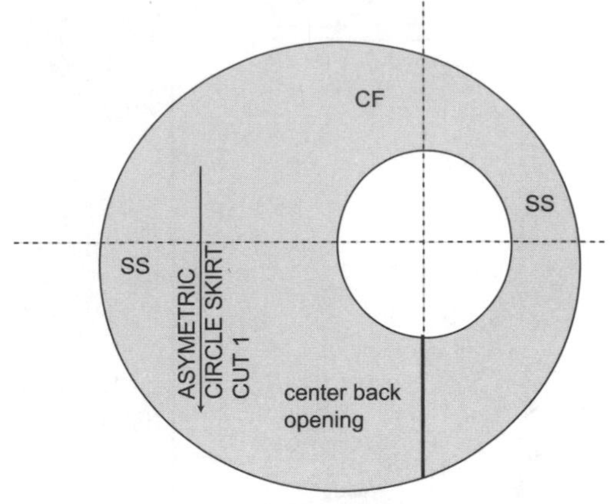

Asymmetrical Circle Skirt

Draft an asymmetrical circle skirt by drafting the waist cut out towards the side seam.

Very dramatic when added as a flounce at the bottom of a skirt.

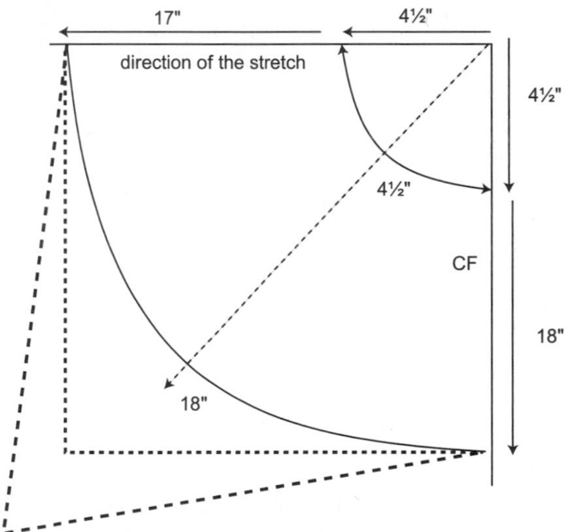

Handkerchief-Hem Circle Skirt

Create a circle skirt with a square hem by changing the shape of the hem.

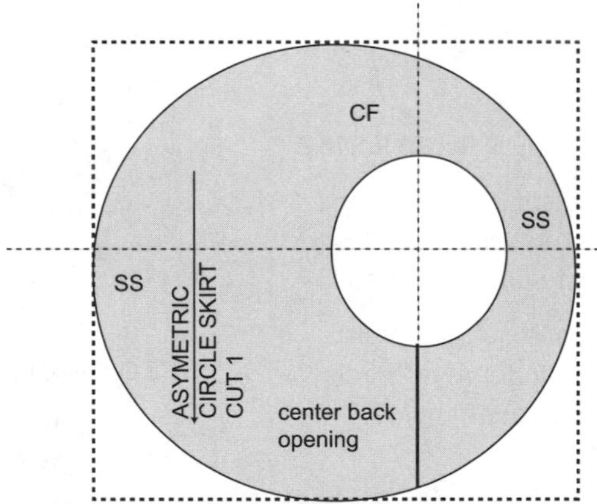

STYLE #5-032 HANDKERCHIEF-HEM ASYMMETRICAL SKIRT

Create an asymmetrical skirt with handkerchief hem, by combining both techniques.

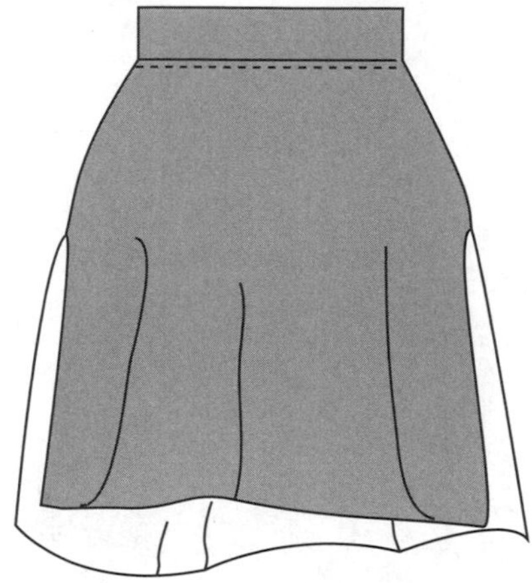

STYLE #5-033 SLASH-WAIST SKIRTS

A similar technique may be used to draft a skirt with a single straight slash as a waist opening.

For this skirt you must draft a separate waistband.

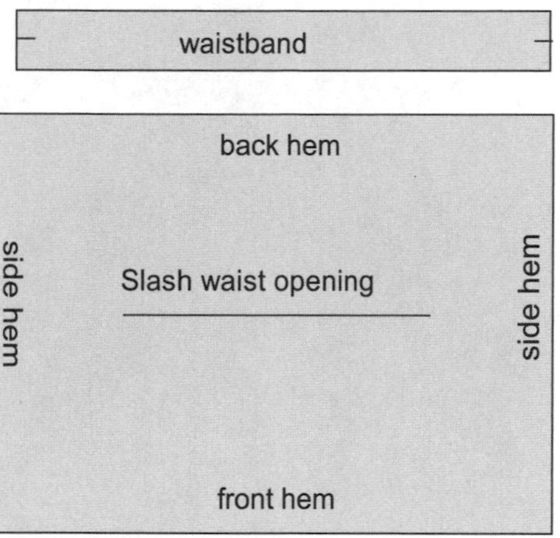

Draft a square with a waist opening in the center.

For a 26½″ waist, draw the line 13¼″ long.

Also remove the amounts equal to seam allowances from this measurement.

The slash will now be 12¼″ with four ¼″ seam allowances included.

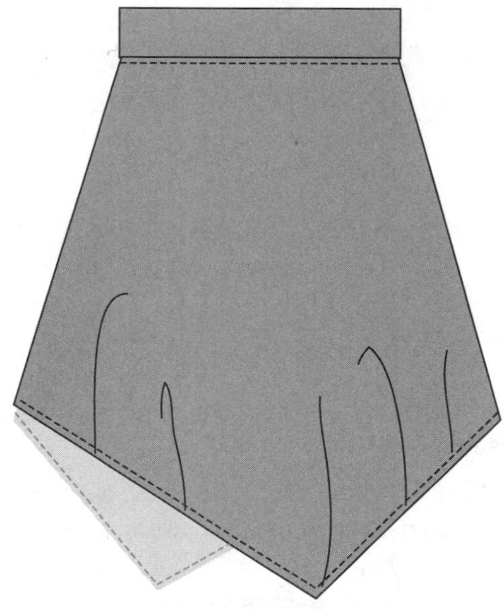

STYLE #5-034 ASYMMETRICAL SLASH-WAIST SKIRTS

Or create an asymmetrical skirt by changing the placement of the waist slash.

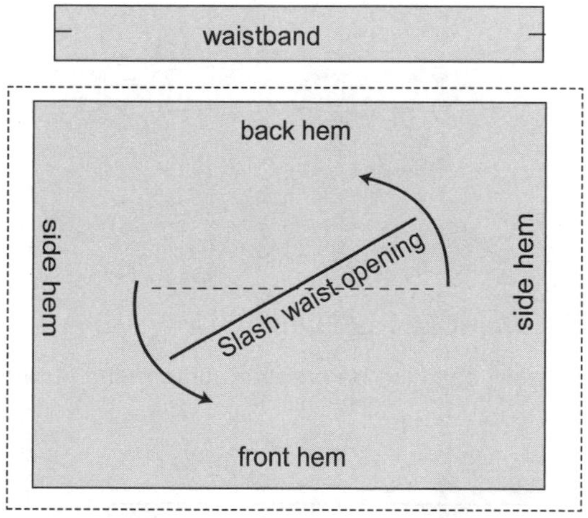

Change the placement of the waist slash by rotating it, or change the shape of the hem.

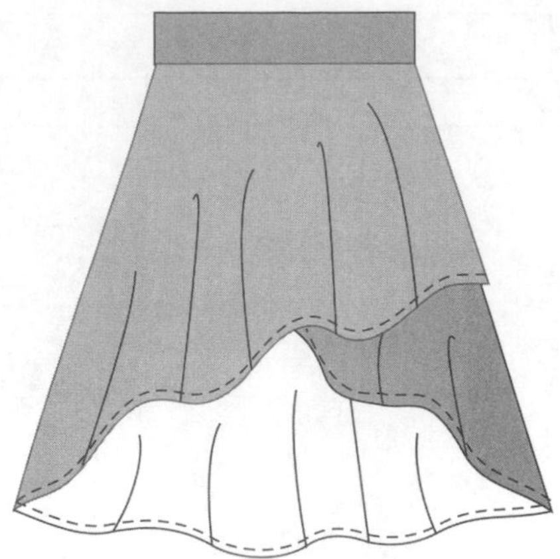

STYLE #5-035 TIERED SLASH-WAIST SKIRTS

Use two layers in lightweight fabric with offset slashes to create a variation of a tiered skirt.

STYLE #5-036 YOKED SLASH-WAIST SKIRTS

Create a yoked version, at the hipline of a skirt.

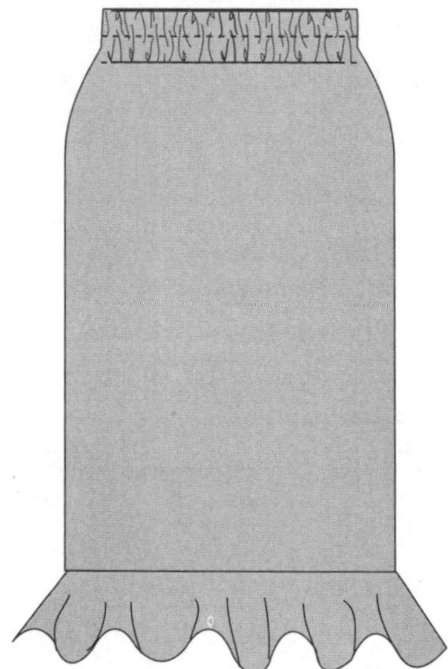

MULTIPLE CIRCLE RUFFLES

A ruffled skirt can also be created using multiple circles at the hem.

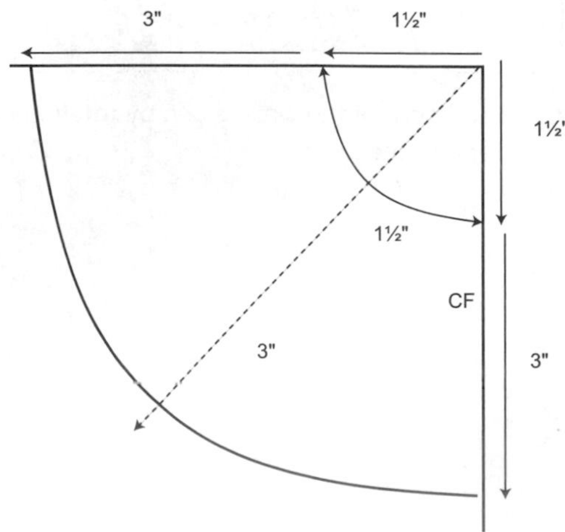

3 circles for each panel, 3″ for each circle. ⅙ of 3″ = ½″, with a ruffle length of 3″.

Measure the hem of the skirt and decide how may circles will be used.

Illustrated at 3″×3″ circles for each panel, but may be more or less fullness depending on the design.

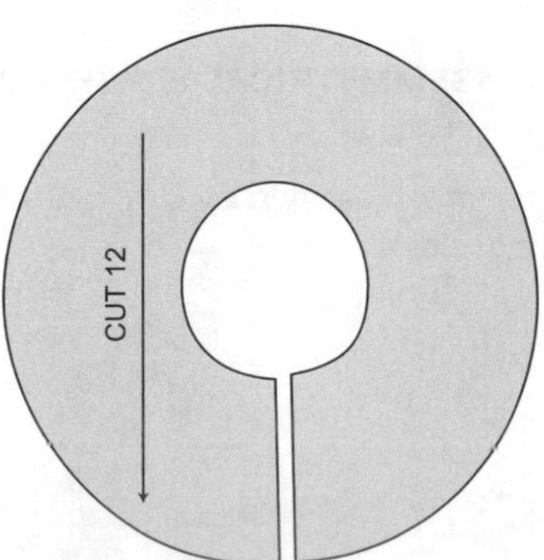

Complete the circle pattern as illustrated.

Attach all 12 circles together to form a ruffle the size of the hem.

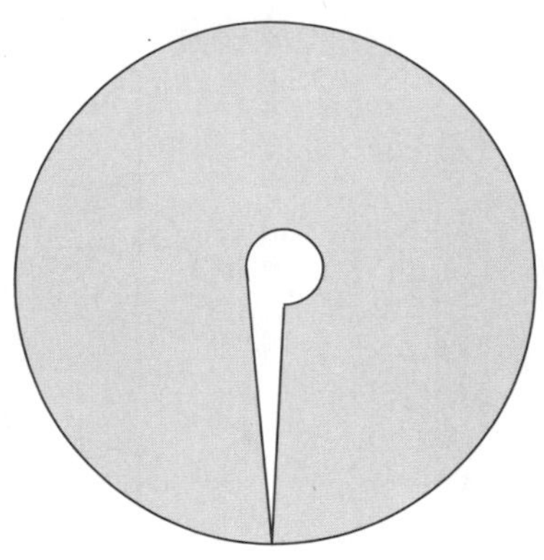

Create a circle with graduating flares.

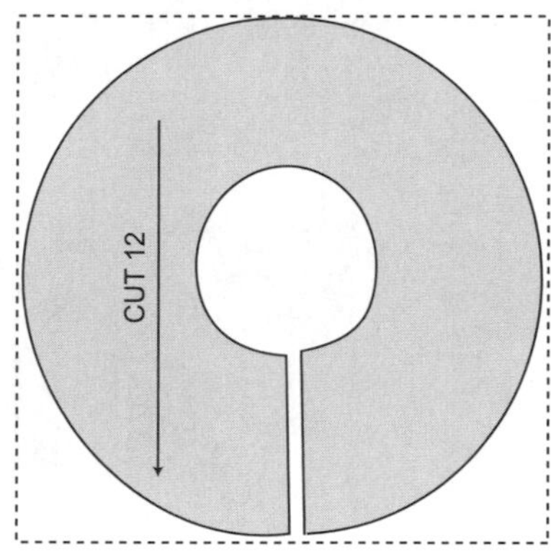

Create a ruffle with square points.

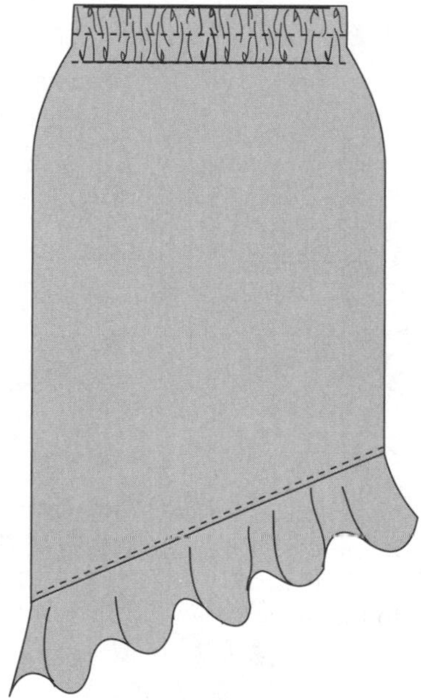

Asymmetrical Hems with Ruffles

Combine an asymmetrical hem with circular ruffles for a dramatic skirt.

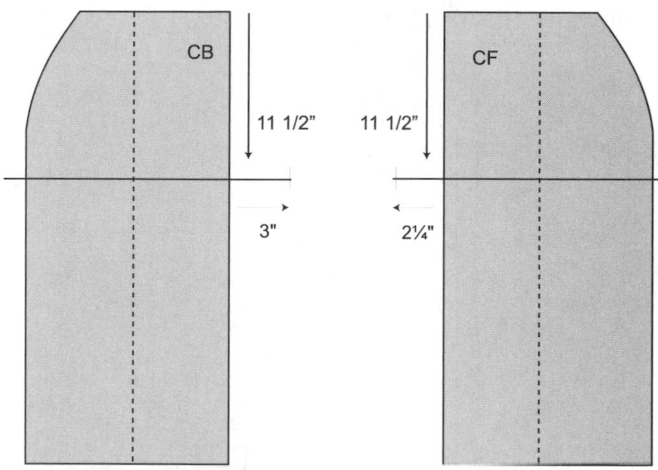

Divided Skirts

STYLE #5-037 CULOTTES

Draft the culottes with a crotch depth of 10½″ for a snug crotch, or 11½″ for a lowered, easy crotch.

Front crotch extension:

¼ of front hip measurement = 2¼″

Back crotch extension:

½ of back hip measurement = 3″

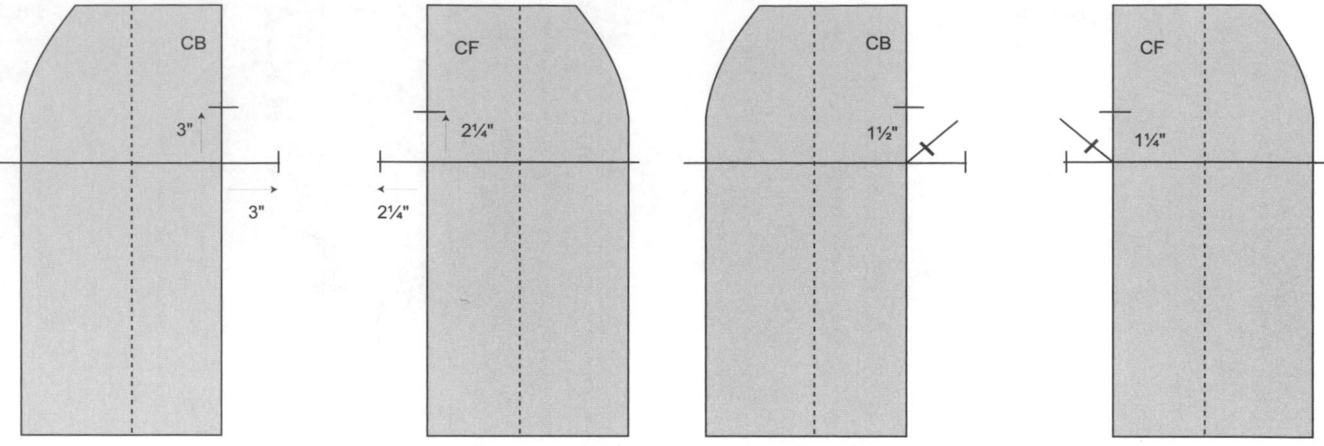

To draw a balanced crotch curve, measure equal amounts up the center front and back.

Draw an angled bias line that is half of each crotch extension.

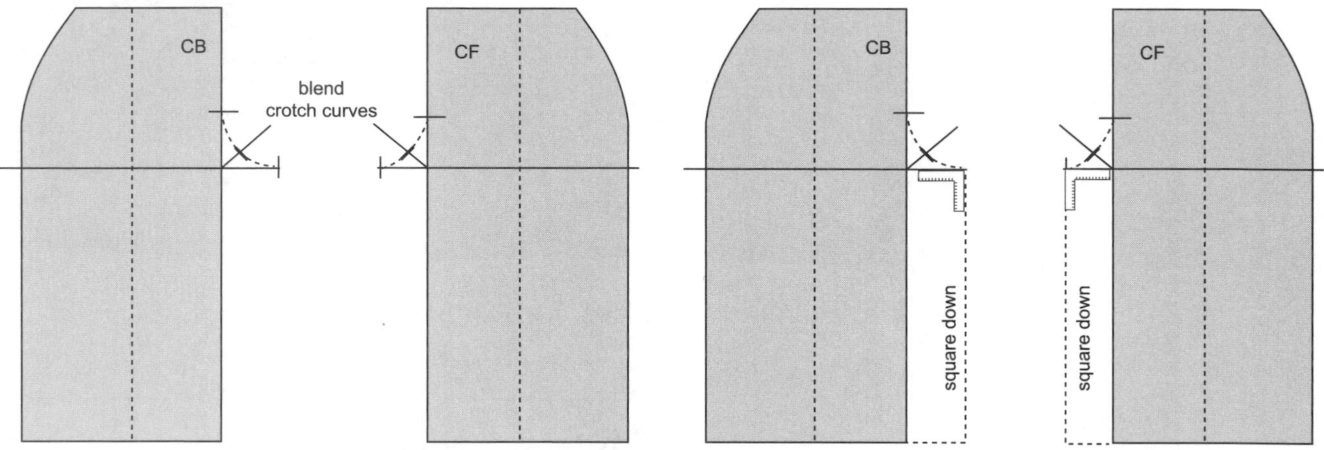

Draw in the crotch curve.

Square down to the hem.

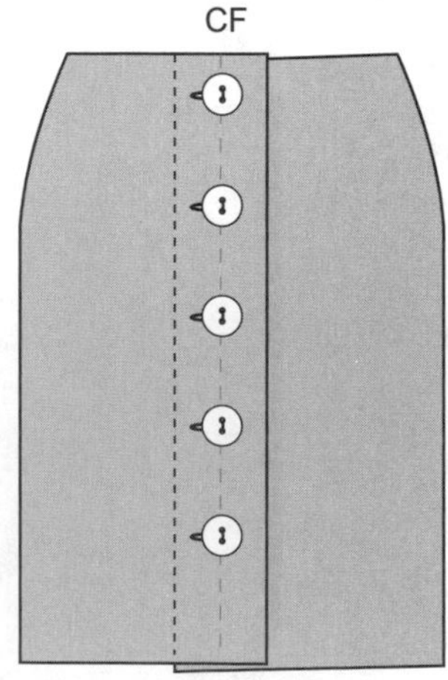

Button Closing

When drafting a button-front closing, the first decision must always be the size of the button because all measurements are taken from that size.

The front extension is always the amount of the button; e.g., a ½″ button requires a ½″ extension.

Women's and Girls garments button right over left, while Men's button left over right. This applies to tops as well as skirts, pants, jackets, etc.

Buttons are measured in units called lines.

BUTTON SIZES

Line	Inches	Line	Inches	Line	Inches
10	¼″	24-25	⅝″	40	1″
12-13	5/16″	27-28	11/16″	42-43	1 1/16″
14-15-16	⅜″	30	¾″	45	1⅛″
18	7/16″	32-33	13/16″	47-48	1 3/16
20	½″	35-36	⅞″		
22	9/16″	37-38	15/16″		

Button Profiles

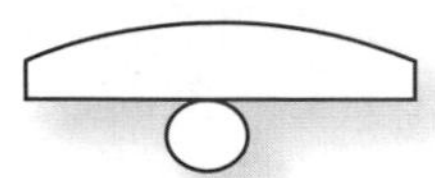

FLAT

DOME

QUARTER BALL

HALF BALL

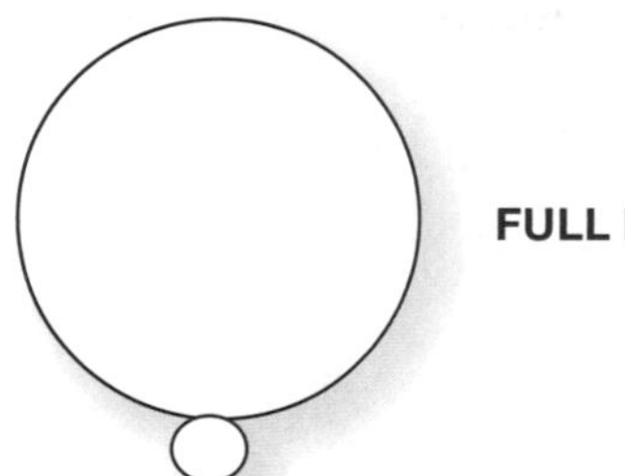

FULL BALL

Buttons

TWO HOLE

FOUR HOLE

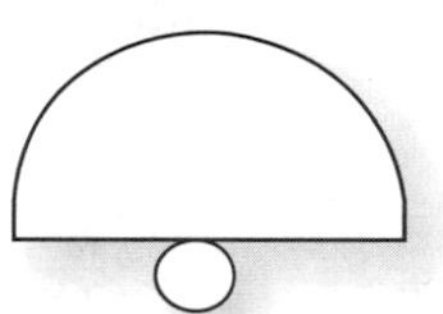

WIRE SHANK

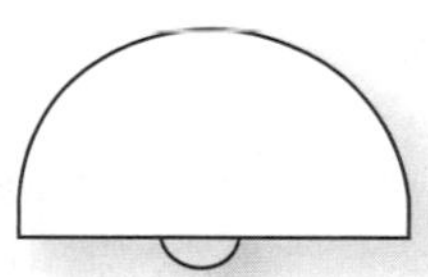

CLOTH SHANK

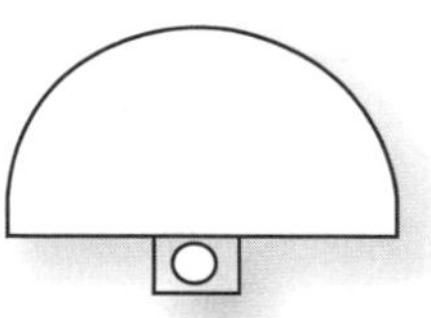

SELF SHANK

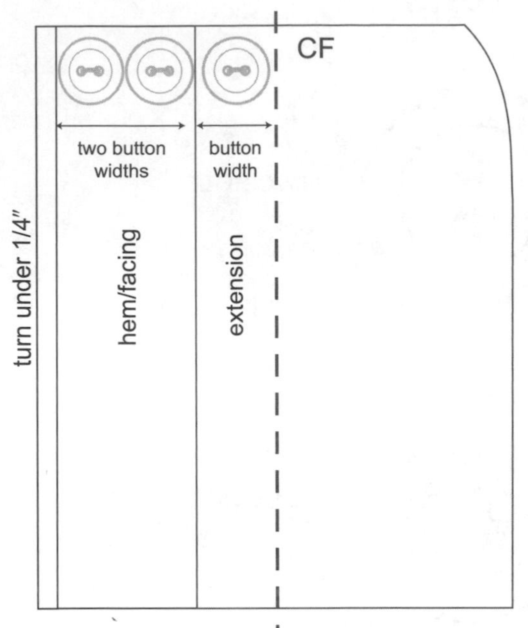

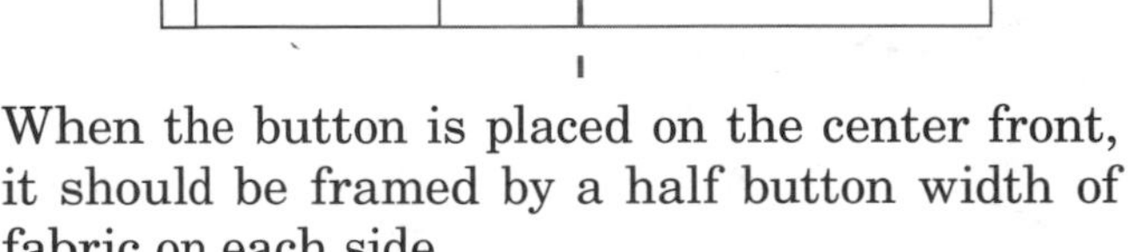

When the button is placed on the center front, it should be framed by a half button width of fabric on each side.

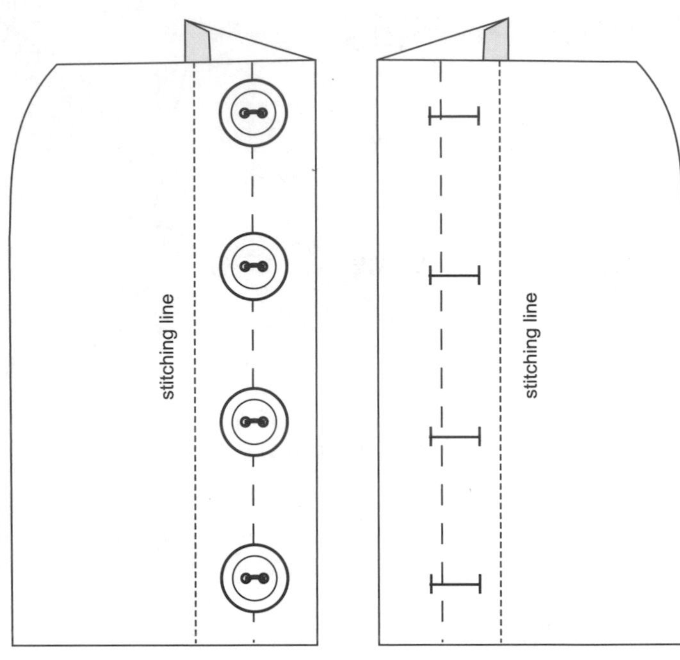

The front extension is determined by the size of the button; for example, a ½″ button requires a ½″ extension.

Draw in the extension equal to the button size. Draw in the under lap double the button size.

Draft the pattern as illustrated.

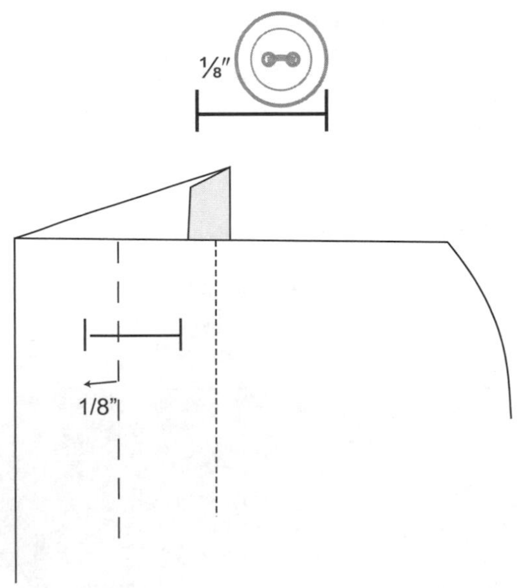

The button should be marked ⅛″ larger than the button size, to give the button enough room to open and close effectively.

And the buttonhole should be marked ⅛″ past the center front line, so that the thread from the shank, used for sewing, is accommodated and the button appears exactly on the center front.

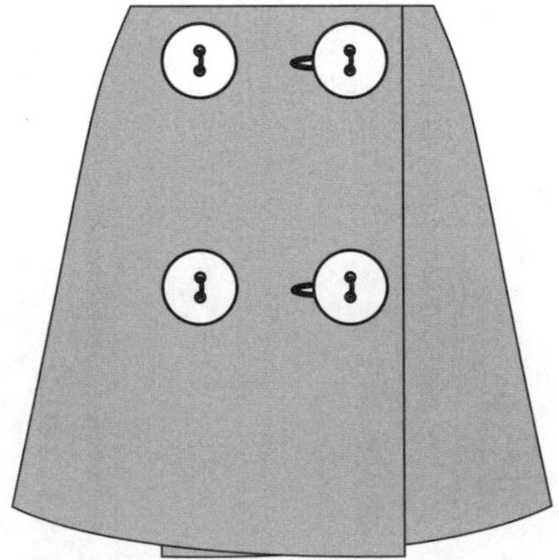

WRAP SKIRT

Drafting a double-breasted button-front skirt is very similar to the previous draft, except that the extension measurement and button placement change.

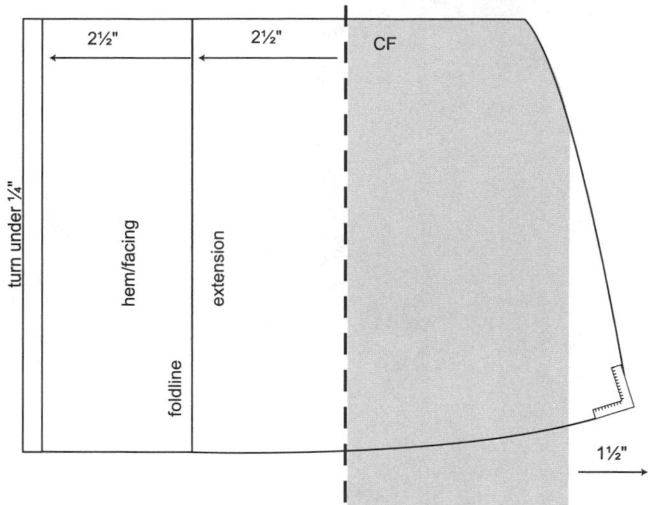

Extend the center front 2½″ for the extension.

Extend an additional 2½″ for the underlay.

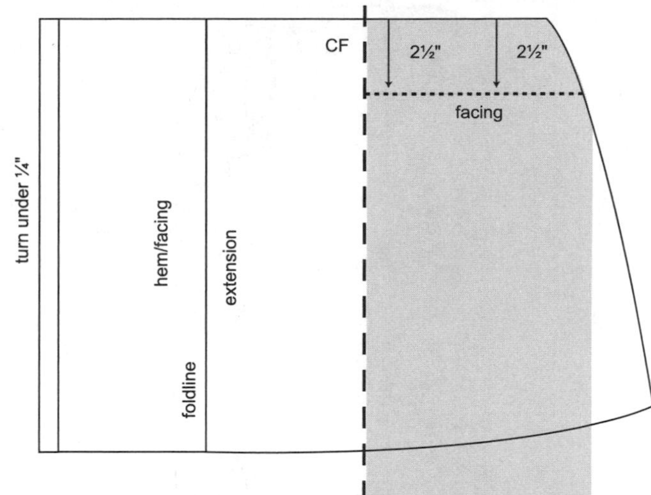

Draft the waist facing 2½″ below the waist.

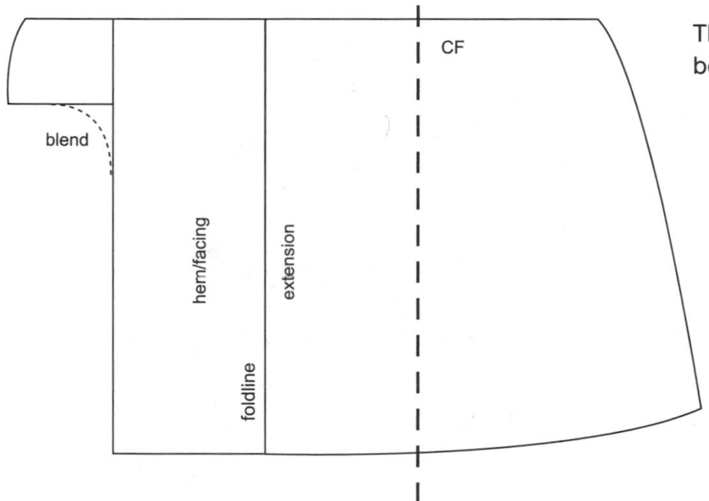

The waist may be cut as a separate pattern piece or may be joined to the front so it is a single pattern piece.

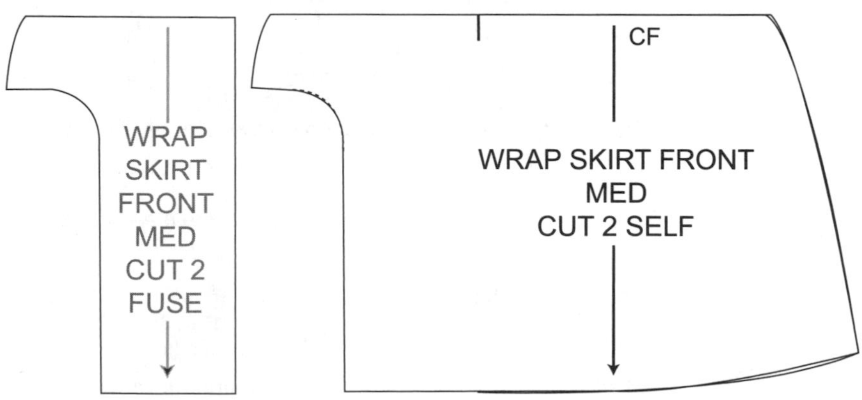

Trace out pattern as indicated.

Draft a fusing pattern piece as indicated.

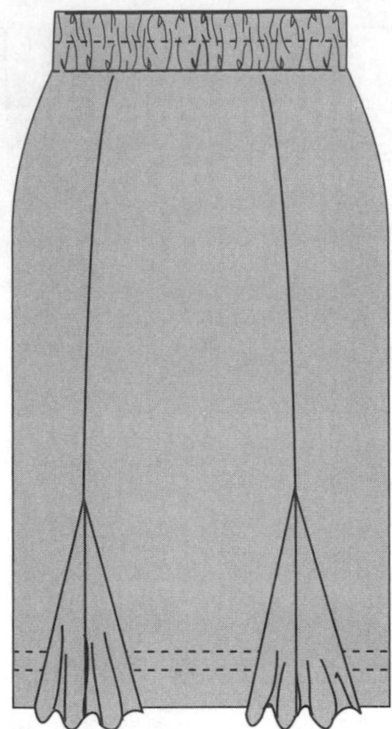

STYLE #5-038 TRUMPET SKIRT

Trumpet skirts are another way to add volume and movement to the hem of a skirt.

Trumpets may be added to any style line, shown here on front panel seams and side seams.

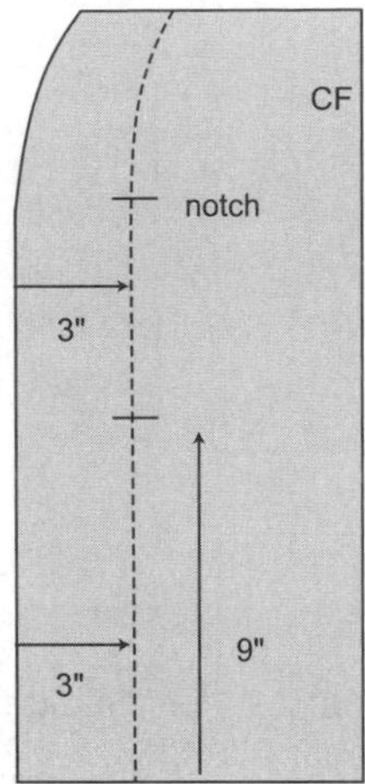

Decide on the placement of the seam line (illustrated at 3″ from the side seam, but may be any place the design requires).

Decide on the placement of the trumpet (illustrated at 9″).

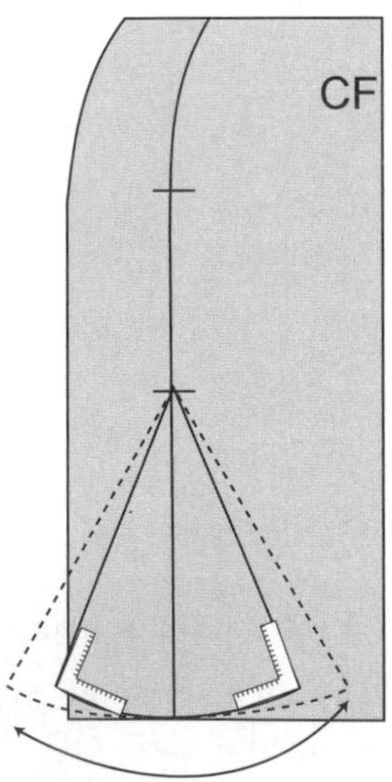

Draw in the trumpets as illustrated.

May be any place the design requires.

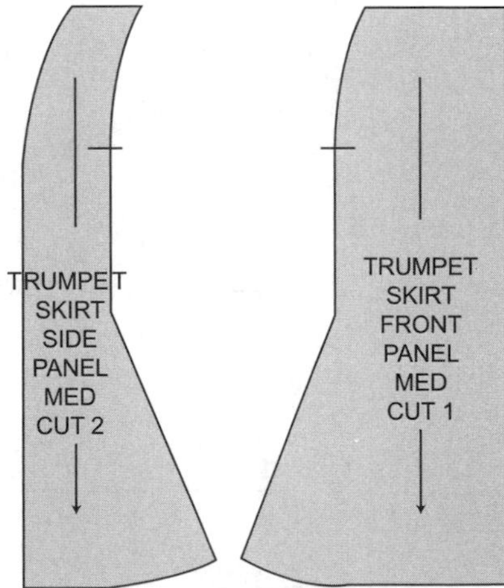

Trace out the front skirt section on the fold, as illustrated.

Blend the hem.

Blend the top of the flare, or clip to release (see section on controlling flares, above).

Label the pattern piece

Trace out the side panel, as illustrated.

Blend the hem into a smooth and continuous line.

Blend the flares, or clip, as described in section about controlling flares.

Label the pattern, as shown.

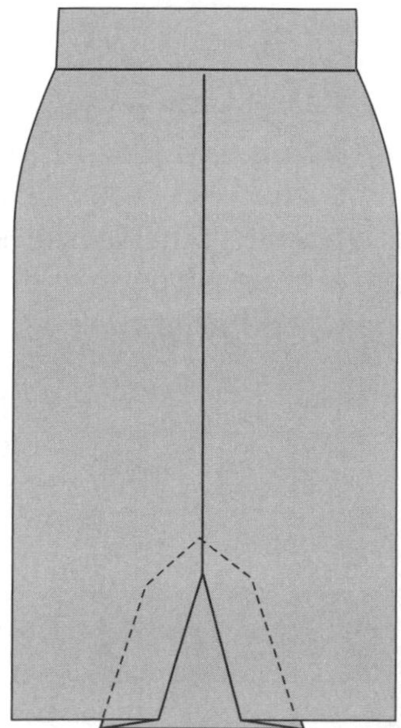

STYLE #5-039 KICK PLEAT

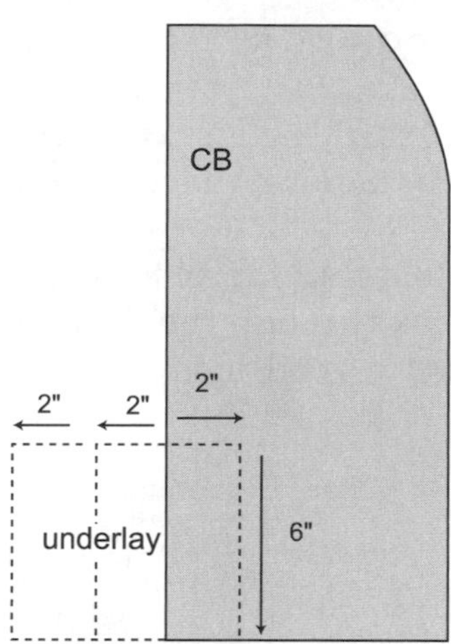

Trace out the appropriate skirt block.

Draw in the kick pleat as it will appear.

Illustrated at 2″ wide and 6″ high, but may be any size the design requires.

Trace out the underlay as indicated.

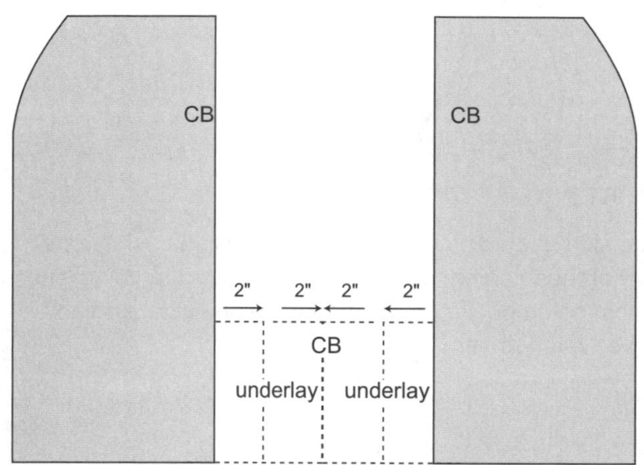

This illustration shows how the unfolded draft will appear.

The skirt pattern may be drafted as illustrated, but the amount of fabric in the center is wasted. For a more practical pattern, refer to the next.

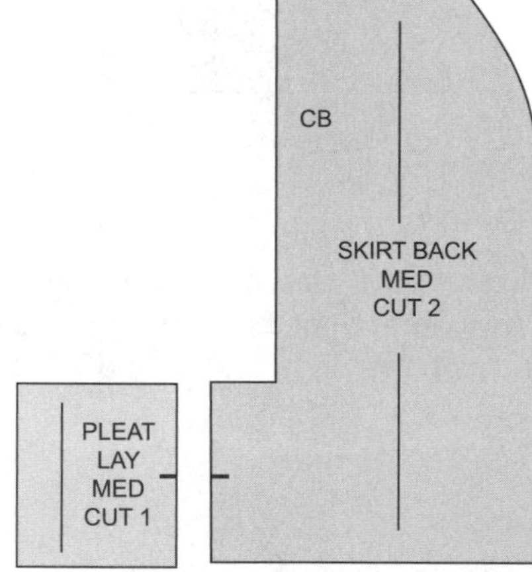

Separate the pattern pieces as illustrated for better fabric yield. Pattern may even be cut in an alternate fabric or color.

The seam will be hidden inside the pleat.

Skirt Projects

While these skirt styles are very basic, they will help you understand drafting for stretch fabrics.

Use a stable-knit fabric for the first time and gradually work through the different stretch ratios. It is also a good idea to sew the garment together to see what the fit is like, and to become familiar with knit equipment. As you work your way through this text, your drafting will become instinctive and your sewing skills will improve. Compare your slopers, patterns, and samples with the checklist provided.

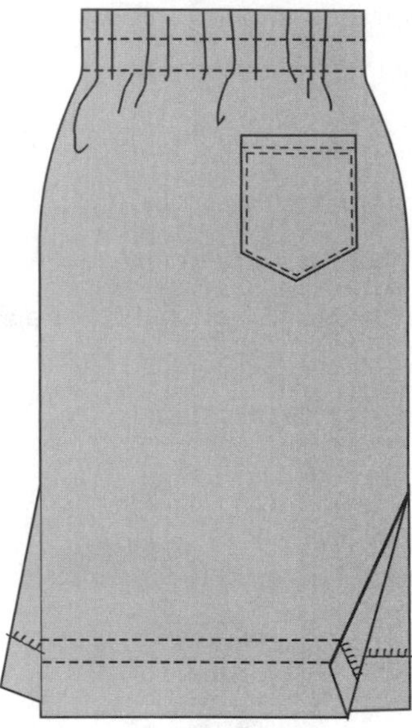

SKIRT PROJECT #1

The skirt should have a 1″ elastic waist in a casing, one row of topstitching to prevent the elastic from collapsing, with a patch pocket, slits on the sides, and a 1″ cover-stitched hem.

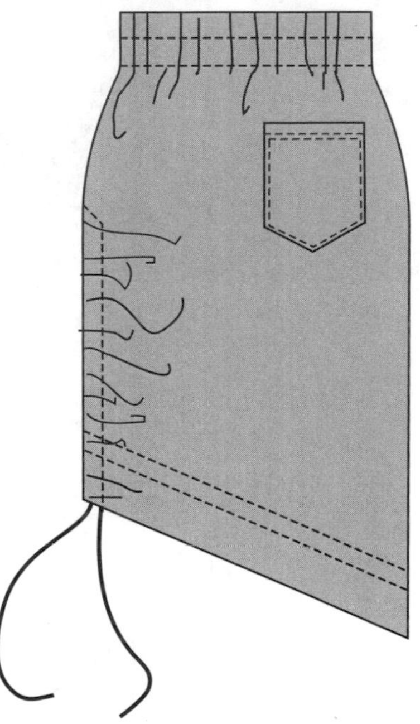

SKIRT PROJECT #2

The skirt should have a 1″ elastic waist in a casing, one row of topstitching to prevent the elastic from collapsing, with a patch pocket, a drawstring on one side, and a 1″ cover-stitched hem.

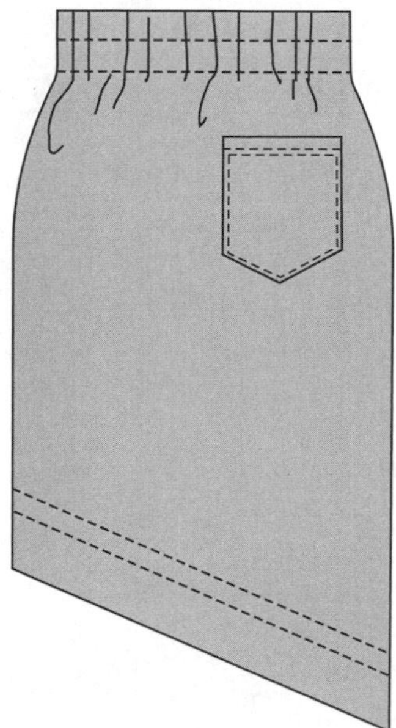

SKIRT PROJECT #3

The skirt should have a 1″ elastic waist in a casing, one row of topstitching to prevent the elastic from collapsing, with a patch pocket, and a 1″ asymmetrical cover-stitched hem.

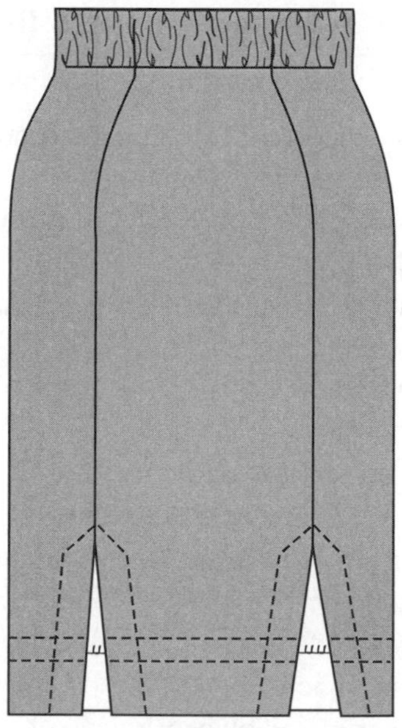

SKIRT PROJECT #4

The skirt should have a 1″ elastic waist in a casing, one row of topstitching to prevent the elastic from collapsing, with a patch pocket on the back, slits on the front panel seams, and a 1″ cover-stitched hem.

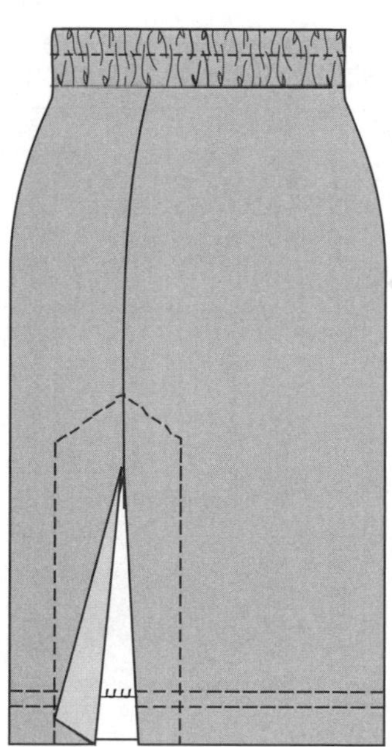

SKIRT PROJECT #5

The skirt should have a 1″ elastic waist in a casing, one row of topstitching to prevent the elastic from collapsing, with a patch pocket on the back, a slit on the side panel seam, and a 1″ cover-stitched hem.

Create a costing sheet (see Appendix A) for any skirt style that you create so you become familiar with the process of costing (remember, the most important part of the garment is the price tag!) and can see how the different costs are associated with the final price. Don't be alarmed when your price comes out extremely high; you have purchased your fabric at retail, and your labor costs are high, also. Remember, that in the industry, we cut garments a thousand at a time; consequently, the cutting costs are greatly reduced.

Compare your blocks, patterns, and sample with the checklist.

SKIRT SLOPERS CHECKLIST (NOT PATTERNS)

Check your blocks and garments to determine if you've completed the assignment correctly.

- ❐ Grainlines included on both front skirt and back skirt
- ❐ No arrows on grainlines of slopers
- ❐ Labeling in correct color (black pen or marker)
- ❐ Size Medium, Med, or M
- ❐ Labeled with all the different stretch ratios: stable knit, moderate knit, etc., along the side seams
- ❐ Labeled as "BLOCKS" or "SLOPERS" (the only way to tell this is a block is if it's labeled)
- ❐ Name on blocks
- ❐ Date on blocks
- ❐ Blocks are butterfly-folded
- ❐ Blocks cut out neatly and accurately
- ❐ Side seams are exactly the same shape when checking
- ❐ Hip notches match exactly
- ❐ The front skirt is ½″ larger than the back skirt
- ❐ No seam allowances on blocks
- ❐ No style numbers on blocks
- ❐ No waist on blocks
- ❐ No hem on blocks
- ❐ No slits on blocks
- ❐ Blocks on oak-tag
- ❐ Blocks on pattern hooks
- ❐ No pocket on blocks
- ❐ Costing sheet done correctly

SKIRT SAMPLE CHECKLIST

Check your sample to determine if you've completed the assignment correctly.

- ❐ Serged neatly and accurately
- ❐ Serged with 4-thread serger or 5-thread serger for very thick fabrics
- ❐ Serged without stretching the seams
- ❐ Perfect tension on the serger
- ❐ All loose threads trimmed
- ❐ Waist stitched evenly
- ❐ Elastic tension even all the way around, not pulling sideways
- ❐ Waist stitched in the center of sergeing, on the inside edge
- ❐ 1 row of stitching to prevent elastic from collapsing
- ❐ Hem cover-stitched evenly
- ❐ Hem cover-stitched at 1″
- ❐ Hem cover-stitched before sewing slits, so the little holes are downward
- ❐ Pocket placed correctly 2½″ below the waist, where the waist seam should be
- ❐ Top of pocket hemmed at 1″
- ❐ Pocket edges turned under ½″
- ❐ Pocket edge-stitched neatly
- ❐ Slit sewn closed for 1″ to lie flat
- ❐ Slits sewn in the center of the serge
- ❐ Slits sewn correctly and neatly
- ❐ Label sewn in the back of the garment
- ❐ Proper hanger
- ❐ Pressed neatly and handed in "store ready"!

SKIRT PATTERN CHECKLIST

Check your pattern to determine if you've completed the assignment correctly.

- ❒ Grainlines on all pattern pieces
- ❒ Arrows on grainline of patterns, pointing in one direction only
- ❒ Labeled in the correct color
- ❒ Size Medium
- ❒ Labeled with all the different stretch ratios: stable knit, moderate knit, etc.
- ❒ Labeled as "BLOCKS" or "SLOPERS" (the only way to tell this is a block is if it's labeled)
- ❒ Name on patterns
- ❒ Date on patterns
- ❒ Correct style numbers on patterns
- ❒ Patterns are butterfly-folded
- ❒ Patterns cut out neatly and accurately
- ❒ The front skirt is ½″ larger than the back skirt
- ❒ ⅜″ seam allowances on all pattern pieces, or ½″ if using very thick fabric
- ❒ The waist of the pattern is labeled with the "finished" elastic measurement, the amount after the ring is sewn closed
- ❒ Correct waist allowance on patterns, double the elastic measurement plus ¼″
- ❒ 1″ hem allowance on patterns for straight hems
- ❒ Correct slits included on pattern pieces both front and back, or as required
- ❒ Hung on pattern hooks
- ❒ Drill marks for pocket placement
- ❒ Pocket pattern included with all required seam and hem allowances
- ❒ Pattern labeled "RIGHT SIDE UP" as required for styles with a single pocket
- ❒ Hip notch
- ❒ Notch for slit foldback
- ❒ Costing sheet done correctly

Test Your Knowledge of the Material in This Chapter

1. Why is the front sloper larger than the back sloper?
2. How do you test if a skirt can be pulled on without a zipper?
3. How can you create a fitted waist for a skirt?
4. How can you create an un-fitted waist for a skirt?
5. How can you create a semi-fitted waist for a skirt?
6. How much should you increase the waist for light gathering?
7. How much should you increase the waist for medium gathering?
8. How much should you increase the waist for heavy or exaggerated gathering?
9. How can you increase the volume at the waist of a skirt?
10. How can you prevent a patch pocket from stretching while sewing it to a garment?
11. Why should you blend a pocket bag into a curve, rather than squared?
12. How can you create an A-line skirt with the volume primarily at the sides?
13. How can you create an A-line skirt with volume at the front?
14. What happens if you slash and spread the skirt multiple times, rather than just a single slash and spread?
15. What happens to the skirt's flares when you blend the waist after slashing and spreading?
16. What happens if you do not blend the skirt after slashing and spreading the waist?
17. How can you coverstitch the hem of an asymmetrical hemmed skirt?
18. How can you increase the waist for a slightly gathered waist skirt?
19. How can you increase the fullness for a gathered skirt?
20. How can you create a drawstring at the side seam of the skirt?
21. How can you create a skirt with gathers on both sides?
22. How can you create a skirt with gathering on only one side seam?

CHAPTER 6

Pants

About This Chapter

This chapter begins with the development of the one-way-stretch pant sloper, and will go on to illustrate some other pant styles. Although all these patterns are labeled "one-way stretch," they may be used interchangeably with two-way- and four-way-stretch fabrics, because the garment does not pass over the shoulders and utilize any lengthwise stretch. For maximum mobility and a tight fit, one-way-stretch garments should always be cut with the stretch going around the body. Also note that many of the skirt details, such as pockets, waistbands, and hems, may also be applied to pants.

Measurements Needed for Stable Knit Pants

Use the measurements for the Women's stable knit draft, since it is the largest, then indicate the other stretch ratios on the sloper, in contrasting color markers. (For a description of the reductions, refer to Chapter 4: Slopers and Reductions.) The measurements given here are for the Misses size range; for other measurements, refer to Chapter 4. Also note that some of the measurements are rounded off for easier drafting.

#		Standard Medium Meas.	Reduce by	New Meas.	Divide by Panels	Extra Extra Small	Extra Small	Small	Medium	Large	Extra Large	Extra Extra Large
2	Waist	27 1/2	0%	27 1/2	4	22 1/2	23 1/2	25 1/2	27 1/2	30 1/2	33 1/2	37 1/2
3	Hip	38 1/2	0%	38 1/2	4	33 1/2	34 1/2	36 1/2	38 1/2	41 1/2	44 1/2	48 1/2
4	Crotch depth	10 1/2	No length reduction			9 7/8	10	10 1/4	10 1/2	10 3/4	11	11 1/4
5	Waist to knee	23 1/2	No length reduction			20 1/8	23	23 1/4	23 1/2	23 3/4	24	24 1/4
6	Waist to ankle	39 1/2	No length reduction			38 1/4	38 1/2	39	39 1/2	40	40 1/2	41
7	Ankle	8 1/4	0%	8 1/4	8	7 5/8	7 3/4	8	8 1/4	8 1/2	8 3/4	9
8	Knee	14 3/8	0%	14 3/8	8	13 1/8	13 3/8	13 7/8	14 3/8	14 7/8	15 3/8	15 7/8
9	Front crotch	One-quarter of hip measurement				2	2 1/8	2 1/4	2 3/8	2 5/8	2 3/4	3
10	Back crotch	One-third of hip measurement				2 3/4	2 7/8	3	3 1/4	3 1/2	3 3/4	4
11	Crotch angle	One-half of front crotch extension				1	1	1 1/8	1 1/4	1 1/4	1 3/8	1 1/2

ONE-WAY-STRETCH SLOPER FRONT

This draft will use the measurements from the reduction chart in Chapter 2, and the appropriate reductions for each fabric.

A-B = waist measurement (#2 from chart).

A-C = crotch depth squared down (#4 from chart).

C-D = hip measurement squared across (#3 from chart).

D-E = square a temporary guideline straight up to the waist.

E-D = divide line into thirds.

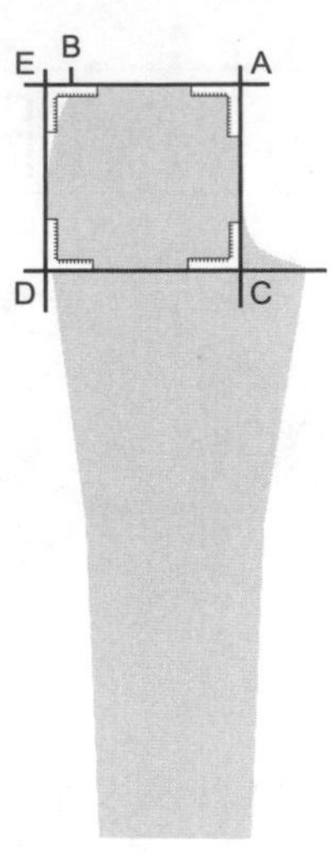

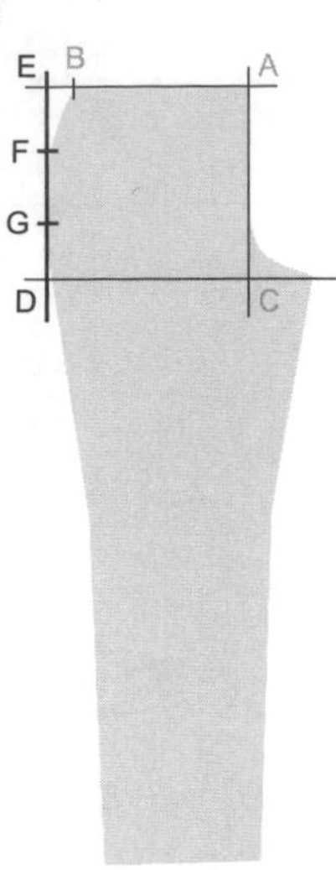

Since the front will be drafted on top of the back, the measurements need to be divided into four.

#		Extra Extra Small	Extra Small	Small	Medium	Large	Extra Large	Extra Extra Large
2	1/4 of waist	5 5/8	5 7/8	6 3/8	6 7/8	7 5/8	8 3/8	9 3/8
3	1/4 of hip	8 3/8	8 5/8	9 1/8	9 5/8	10 3/8	11 1/8	12 1/8
4	Crotch depth	10 1/2	10 5/8	10 4/8	10 5/8	10 7/8	11 1/8	11 3/8
5	Waist to knee	22 7/8	23	22 7/8	23	23 1/4	23 1/2	23 3/4
6	Waist to ankle	38 1/4	38 1/2	38 1/4	38 1/2	39	39 1/2	40
7	1/4 of ankle	22 7/8	23	23 1/4	23 1/2	23 3/4	24	24 1/4
8	1/4 of knee	38 1/4	38 1/2	39	39 1/2	40	40 1/2	41
9	Front crotch	13 1/8	13 3/8	13 7/8	14 3/8	14 7/8	15 3/8	15 7/8
10	Back crotch	2 1/8	2 1/8	2 2/8	2 3/8	2 5/8	2 6/8	3
11	Crotch angle	2 6/8	2 7/8	3	3 2/8	3 4/8	3 6/8	4
	1/3 of crotch depth	3 1/2	3 1/2	3 1/2	3 1/2	3 5/8	3 3/4	3 3/4

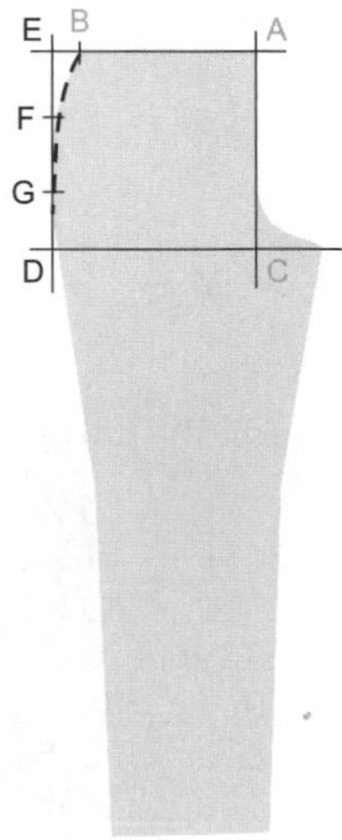

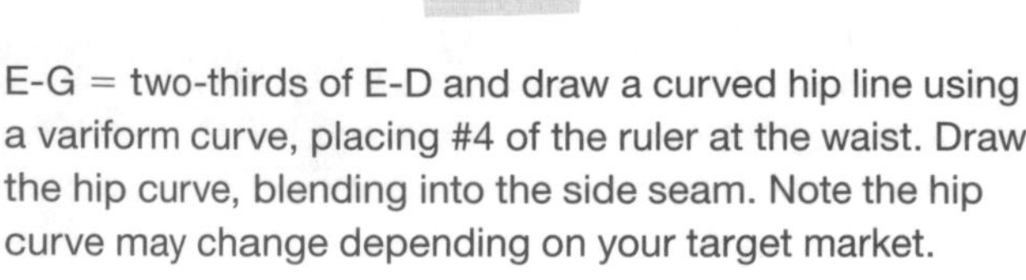
E-G = two-thirds of E-D and draw a curved hip line using a variform curve, placing #4 of the ruler at the waist. Draw the hip curve, blending into the side seam. Note the hip curve may change depending on your target market.

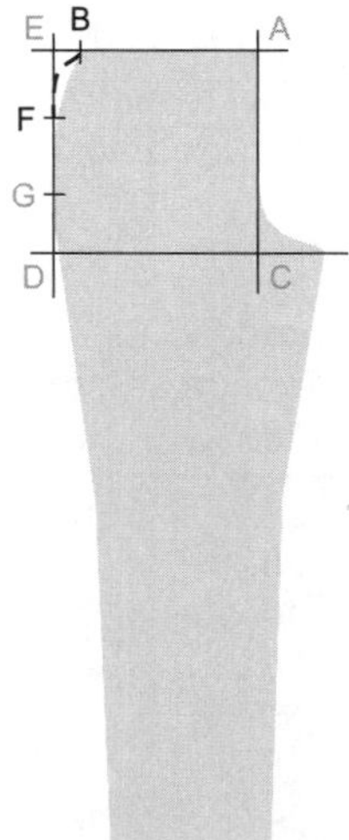

Note: For custom garments, draw the hip curve to the higher mark, to ensure that the hip is large enough to fit any customer, and correct the hip shape in fitting.

Do not fuss over the hip shape, since it may be corrected, and any excess simply serged off after fitting the garment.

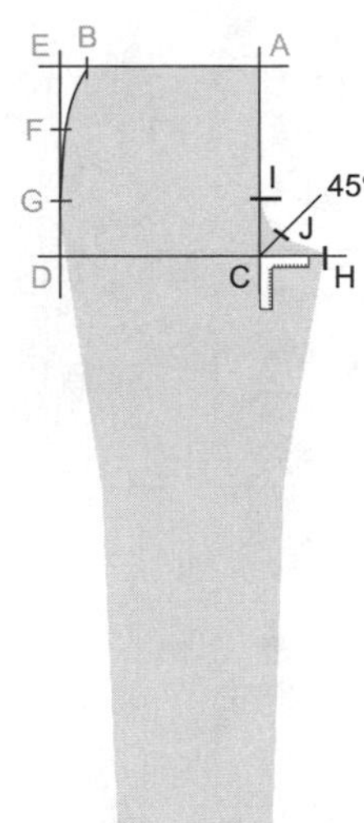

C-H = one-quarter of hip measurement C-D (#9 from chart).

C-I = one-quarter of hip measurement (#9 from chart).

At C draw a 45-degree angle and label as J.

C-J = one-half of C-H (#11 from chart).

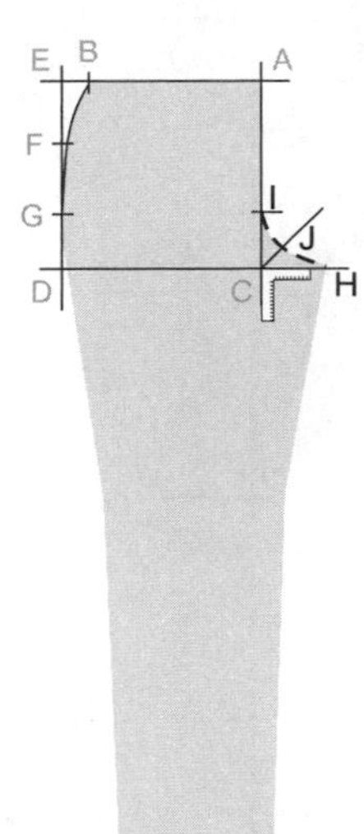

I-J-H = draw a smooth blended crotch curve.

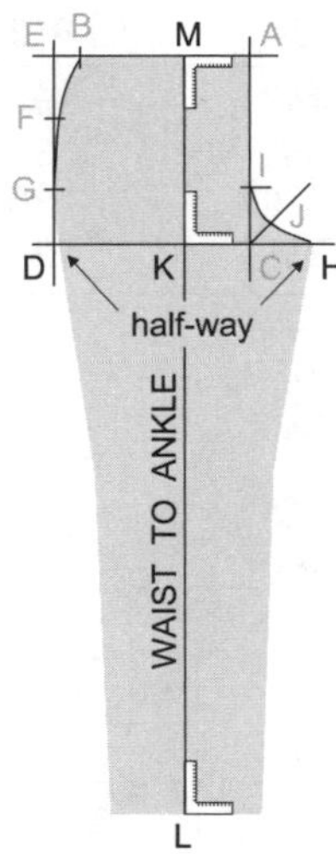

K = halfway between D and H.

K = square up to waist and label as the grainline.

M-L = square down from the waist to ankle measurement (#6 from chart).

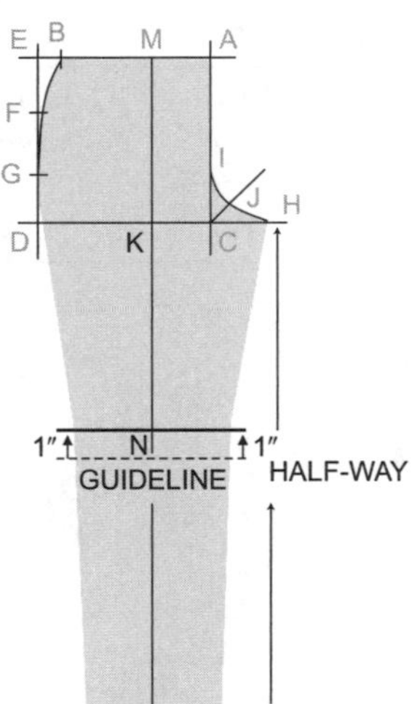

Draw a guideline halfway between K and M.

The knee line is 1″ above the guideline; label as N.

(Be careful, as there is a tendency to incorrectly locate half-way between the waist and ankle, when it should be the crotch to ankle.)

	Extra Extra Small	Extra Small	Small	Medium	Large	Extra Large	Extra Extra Large
Front Crotch extension	2	2 1/8	2 1/4	2 3/8	2 5/8	2 3/4	3
Crotch angle	1	1	1 1/8	1 1/4	1 1/4	1 3/8	1 1/2
D-H	10 1/2	10 7/9	11 2/5	12	13	14	15 1/6
Half-way	5 1/4	5 2/5	5 5/7	6	6 1/2	7	7 4/7
Waist to ankle	38 1/4	38 1/2	39	39 1/2	40	40 1/2	41
Waist to knee	13 1/5	13 1/4	13 3/8	13 1/2	13 5/8	13 3/4	13 7/8

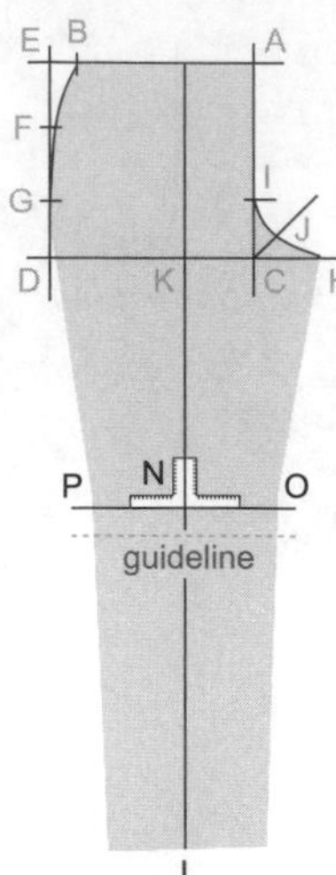

N-O = one-quarter of the knee measurement (#8 from chart).

N-P = one-quarter of the knee measurement (#8 from chart).

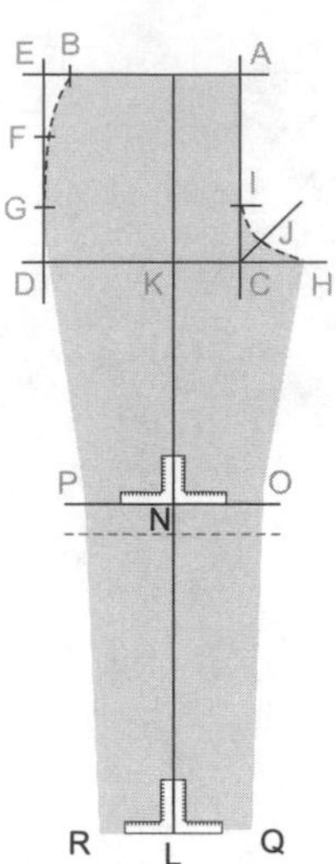

L-Q = one-quarter of the ankle measurement (#7 from chart).

L-R = one-quarter of the ankle measurement (#7 from chart).

	Extra Extra Small	Extra Small	Small	Medium	Large	Extra Large	Extra Extra Large
Total Knee	13 1/8	13 3/8	13 7/8	14 3/8	14 7/8	15 3/8	15 7/8
Quarter of knee	3 2/7	3 1/3	3 1/2	3 3/5	3 5/7	3 5/6	4
Total Ankle	7 5/8	7 3/4	8	8 1/4	8 1/2	8 3/4	9
Quarter of ankle	2	2	2	2	2 1/8	2 1/5	2 1/4

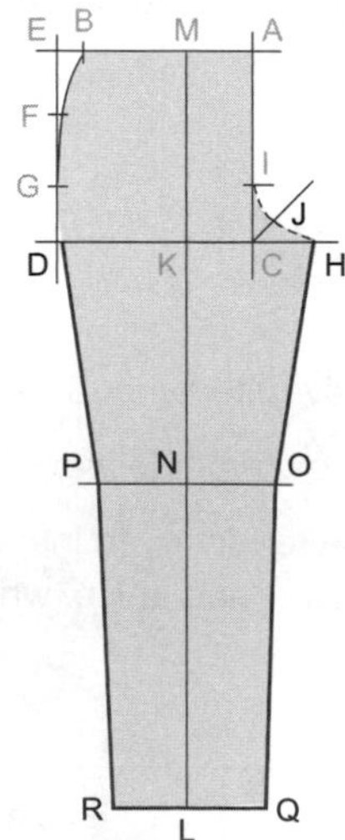

Connect H-O in a straight line.

Connect O-Q in a straight line.

Connect Q-R in a straight line.

Connect D-P in a straight line.

Connect P-R in a straight line.

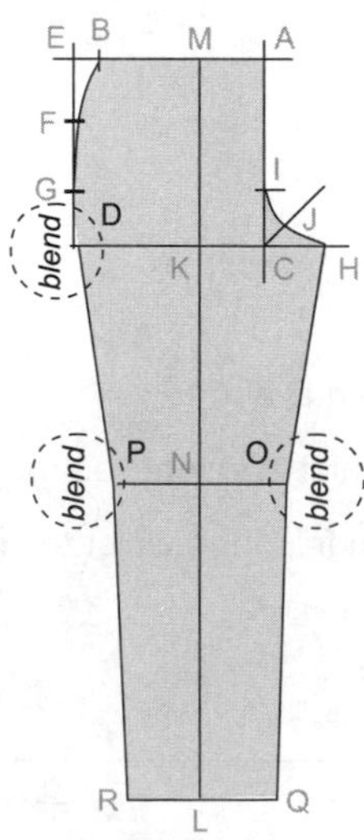

Blend the hips and knee into smooth curves, as illustrated.

PANT SLOPER BACK

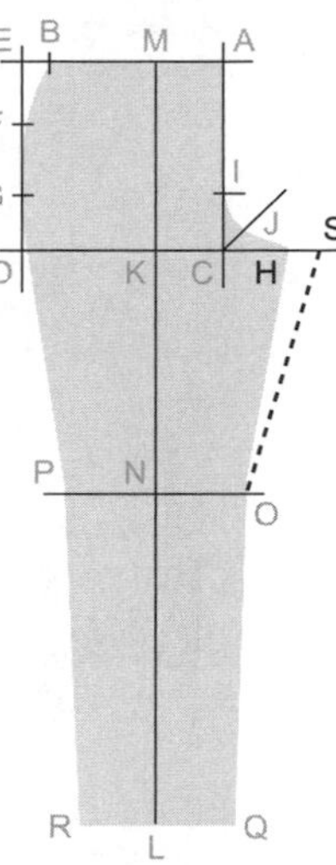

C-S = one-third of hip measurement (#10 from chart).

Since you've already added the front crotch amount, only add the additional amount because you are drafting the front on top of the back.

Connect S-O in a straight line (note that the back inseam is longer than the front inseam, and will be corrected later on).

Blend a smooth curve at O.

	Extra Extra Small	Extra Small	Small	Medium	Large	Extra Large	Extra Extra Large
Back crotch extension	$2\frac{3}{4}$	$2\frac{7}{8}$	3	$3\frac{1}{4}$	$3\frac{1}{2}$	$3\frac{3}{4}$	4
Additional amount	$\frac{3}{4}$	$\frac{3}{4}$	$\frac{3}{4}$	$\frac{3}{4}$	$\frac{7}{8}$	$\frac{7}{8}$	1

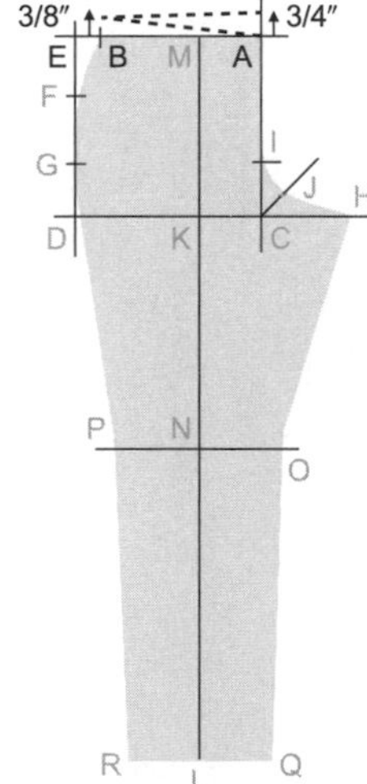

You must raise the back of the waist to allow room for sitting and bending. Skirts do not need this because they can easily slide up, whereas pants are anchored at the crotch.

Raise the side seams $\frac{3}{8}$".

Raise the center back $\frac{3}{4}$".

Do not change the center front height.

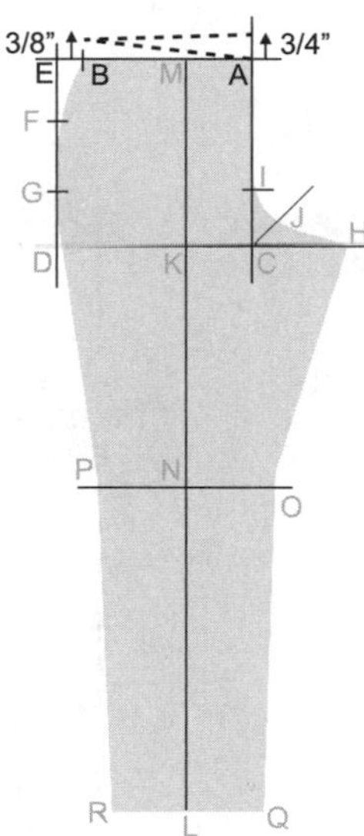

Remove $\frac{1}{4}$" from the back side seam.

Add $\frac{1}{4}$" to the front side seam.

Re-notch.

This way the front is larger than the back so that when you view it straight on, you can't see the side seams because they are slightly toward the back.

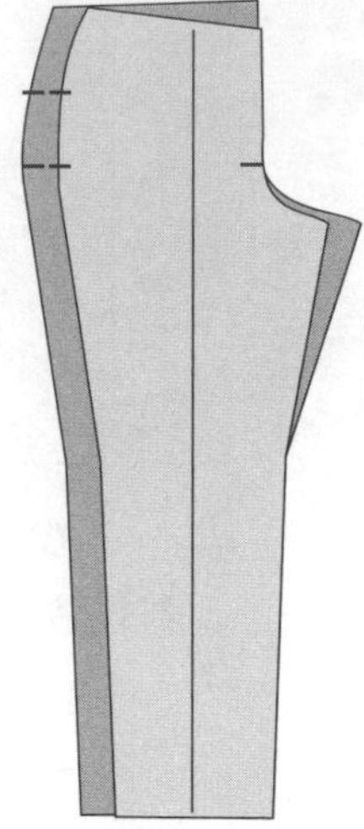

TRUEING THE PANT SLOPERS

Trace out and separate the front and back pant slopers.

Place the front sloper on top of the back sloper and match the side seams to make sure they are exactly the same.

Check notches at hips and knees.

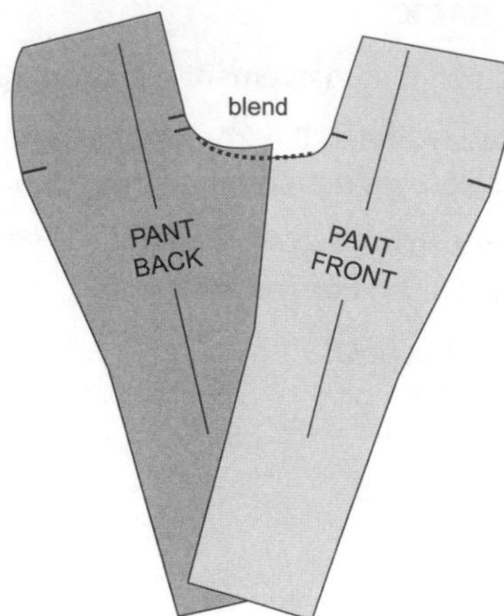

Place the inseams together the way they will be when they are finally sewn, beside each other.

Ensure that the crotch is blended into a smooth and continuous curve; it should need a slight blend, because the back inseam is slightly longer than the front inseam (about 1/8″) and must be corrected so the seams match each other perfectly.

Check that inseam knee notches match exactly, and that both of the inseams are exactly the same length.

Make sure that the hem lines up exactly, in a smooth continuous line.

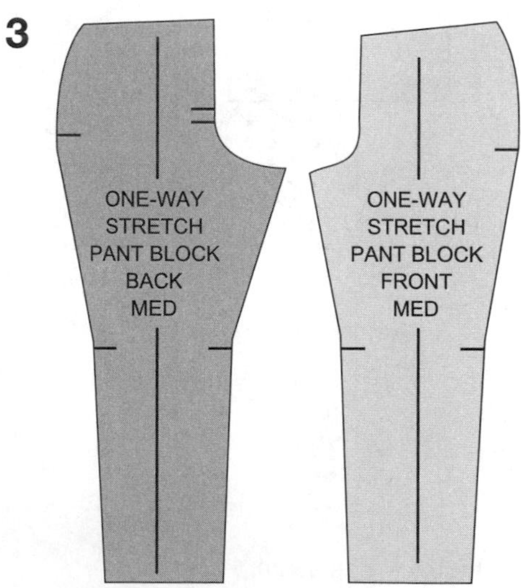

Label your slopers correctly—indicating whether they are the front piece or the back piece.

Also label the slopers with the type of stretch: "one-way stretch."

The size must also be labeled.

Label with your name and the date created.

Never place any arrows on the grainlines.

4

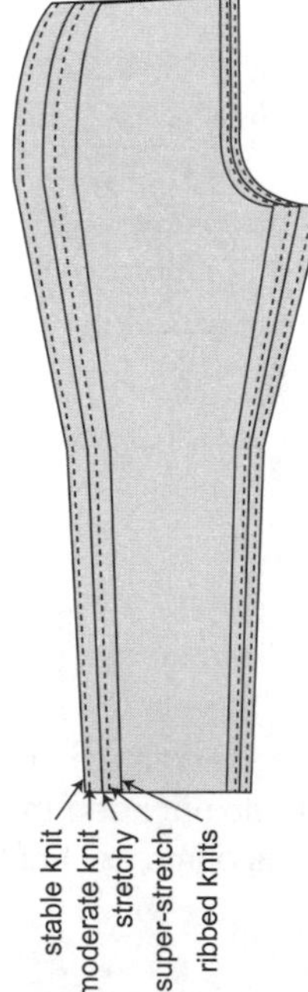

If you've drafted stable knit slopers, you can save yourself the trouble of drafting the other sloper ratios if you indicate them with lines as illustrated.

This saves save oak-tag, and allows you to carry a single sloper rather than multiple sets. The differences between the slopers must be equalized on both sides of the grainline.

Also note the illustration is exaggerated for clarity.

	Stable knit	Moderate	Stretchy knit	Super-stretch knit	Rib knit
Waist	0	−1/16	−1/8	−1/16	−1/8
Hip	0	−1/16	−1/8	−1/16	−1/8
Out-seam	0	−1/16	−1/8	−1/16	−1/8
In-seam	0	−1/16	−1/8	−1/16	−1/8

To check and correct the grainline of pants, fold the calf portion of the leg in half, then crease your paper all the way to the waist. This will be your new grainline.

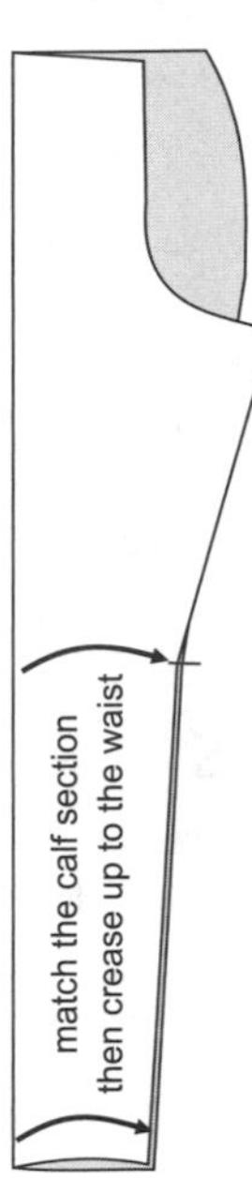

Seam Allowances For Pants

The seam allowances needed depend on the type of fabric used and equipment used.

For stable knits such as fleece and Polarfleece®	Use 1/2″ seam allowances or 3/8″	5-thread serger for very thick fabrics 4-thread serger for normal knit fabrics

If the stable knit fabric is really thick, then use 1/2″ seam allowances, because a smaller serging will not catch enough of the fabric edge to secure the seam.

Five-thread serging may be approximated by using a three-thread serger and a straight stitch.

For stretchy knits	Use 3/8″ seam allowances	4-thread serger
For moderate knits, such as T-shirt knits	Use 3/8″ seam allowances	4-thread serger
For super-stretch knits, such as spandex and 4-way stretch	Use 1/4″ seam allowances	3-thread serger
For rib knits	Use 1/4″ seam allowances	3-thread serger

Use 1″ for straight hems and 1/2″ for curved hems.

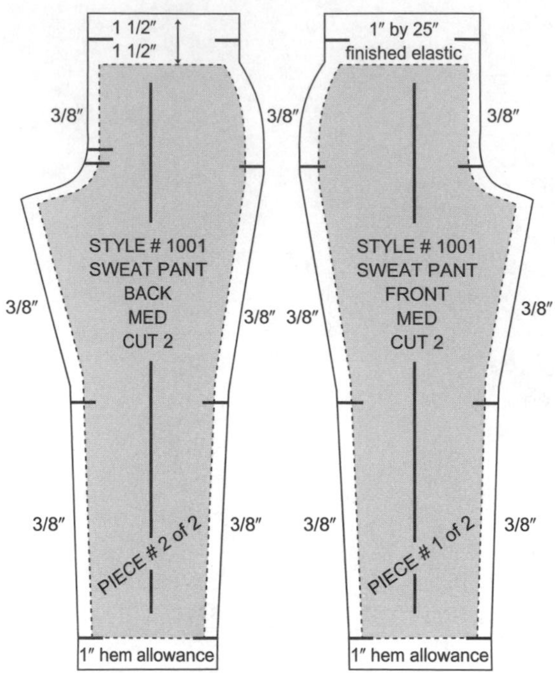

ADDING SEAM ALLOWANCES TO PANTS

Illustrated with 3/8″ seam allowances, for stable knits such as fleece for use with a four-thread serger.

Always label the waist of the pant with the finished (already sewn) elastic measurement.

Square down a hem allowance of 1″.

Extend the waist up 1½″ plus and other 1½″, total 3″ for the elastic casing.

For ½″ elastic, reduce by 2″.

For elastic over 1″ wide, reduce the measurement by 1″.

For elastic under 1″ wide, reduce the measurement by 2″.

Remember to add seam allowances to the ends of the elastic.

You don't always know what type of equipment will be used to apply the elastic, especially if the garment will be produced offshore, so you must always label the waist with the finished (already sewn) elastic measurements, including the width of the elastic.

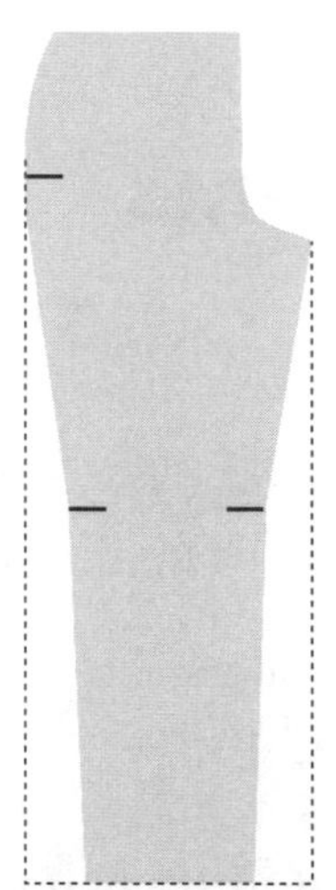

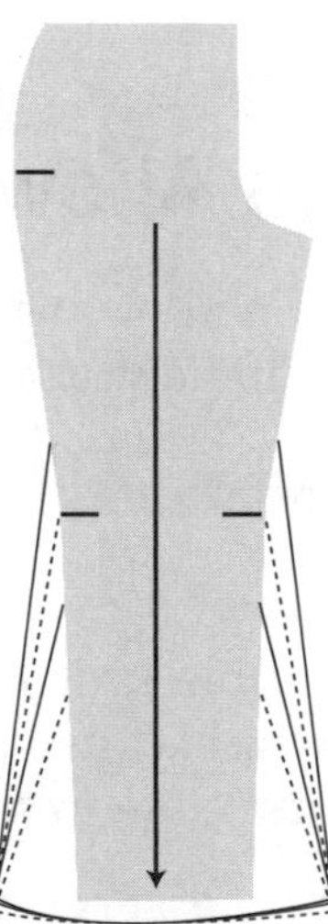

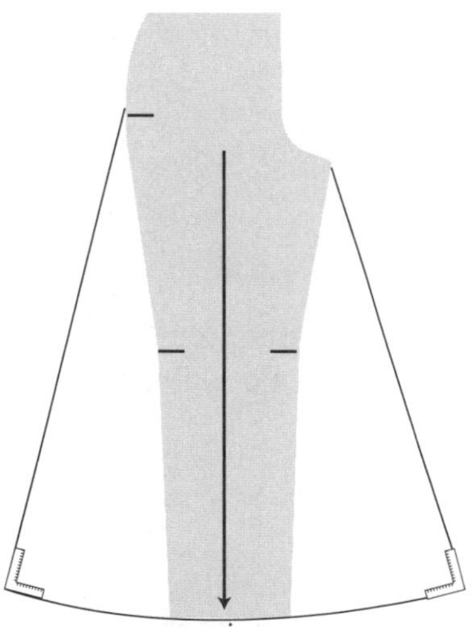

ONE-WAY-STRETCH PANT SILHOUETTE VARIATIONS

Create a stovepipe leg from the one-way-stretch pant sloper by widening the legs as illustrated.

Make the same changes to both sides of the legs. Whatever you do to one leg seam must be duplicated for the other.

Create a bell-bottom from the one-way-stretch pant sloper by widening the legs as illustrated.

Make the same changes to both sides of the legs. Whatever you do to one leg seam must be duplicated for the other leg seam.

Create a palazzo from the one-way-stretch pant sloper by widening the legs as illustrated.

Make the same changes to both sides of the legs. Whatever you do to one leg seam must be duplicated for the other leg seam.

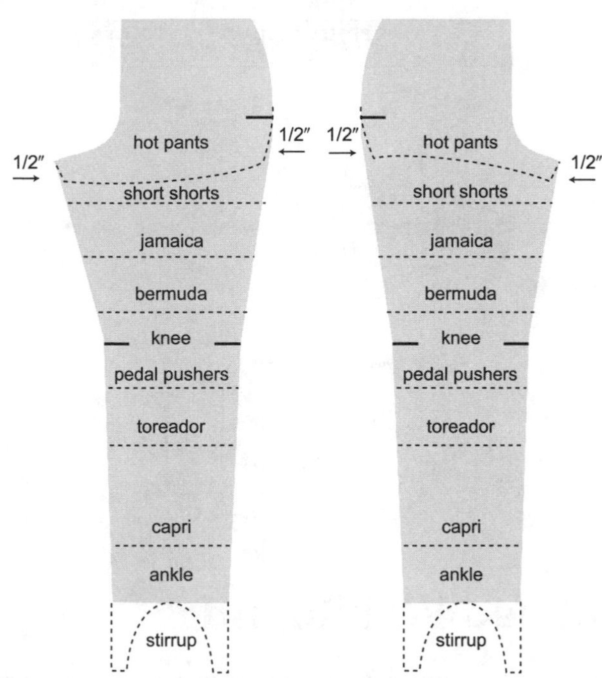

One-Way-Stretch Pant and Shorts Length Variations

Create any style of short from the one-way-stretch pant sloper.

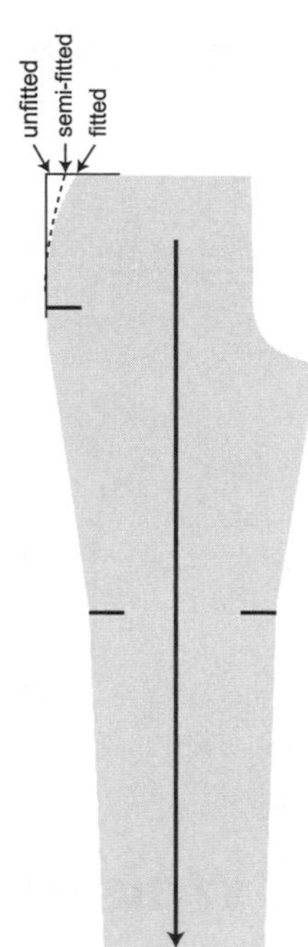

Waist Volume

Create a fitted, semi-fitted, or unfitted waist finish for any pant style.

Create unfitted by squaring a line up to the waist level.

Create semi-fitted by finding the middle of the fitted and unfitted and drawing a new curved hip.

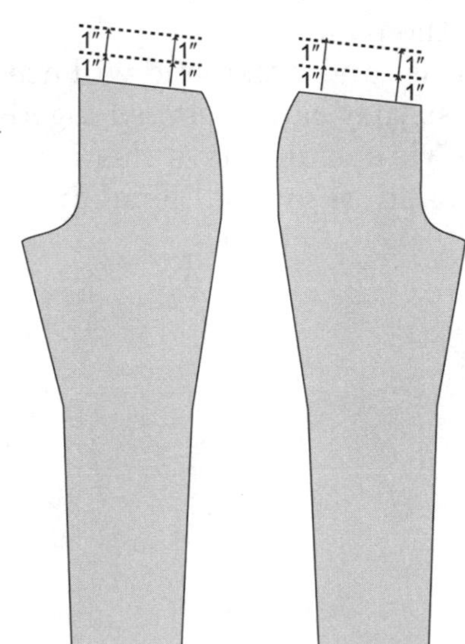

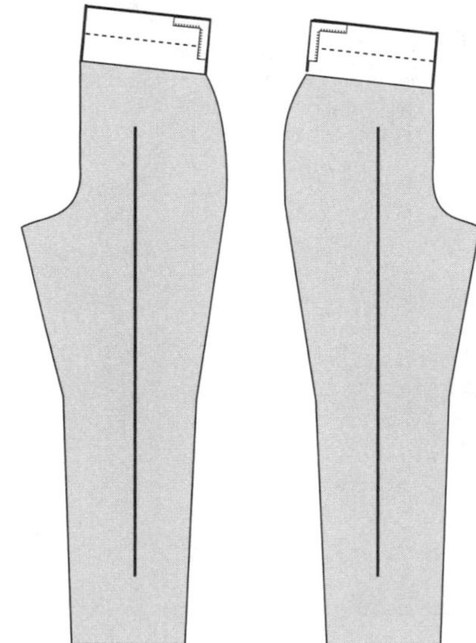

Cover-Stitched Waist Elastic

To create a cover-stitched waist:

Extend the waistband double the height of the elastic.

Illustrated at 2″ for 1″ elastic.

At the sides and end of the waist casing, square down from the top line.

This waist does not need any seam allowances at the top because the elastic will be serged to the raw edge of the waist.

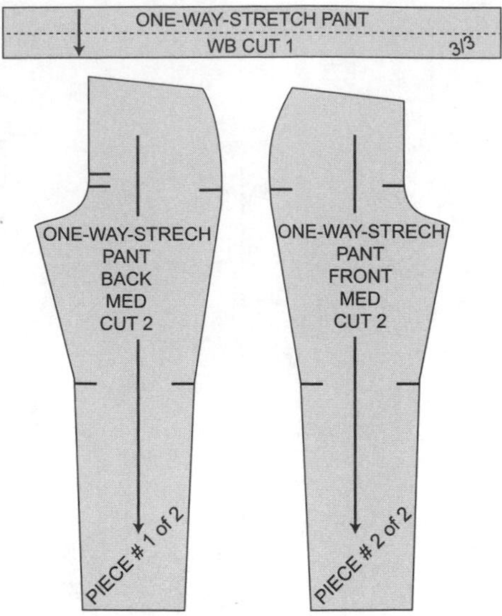

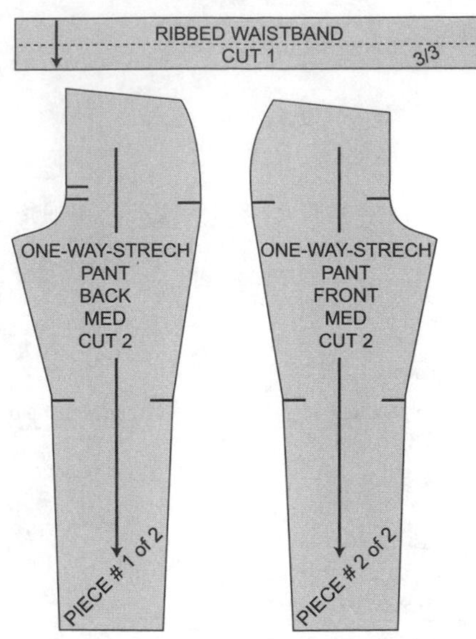

Serged-On Waistband

This waistband is a separate pattern piece.

This waistband will be folded in half and serged to the pants.

Measure twice the width of the elastic, and the length of the total waist measurement.

The waist and waistband will need seam allowances so they can be serged together. This style should also have elastic inserted into the waistband.

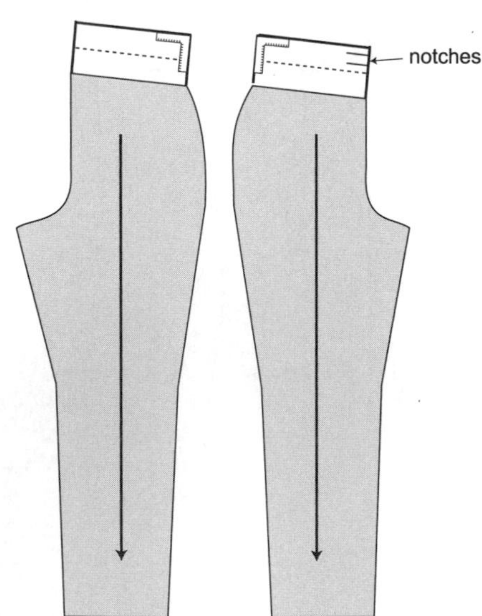

PANTS WITH DRAWSTRING ELASTIC

To create a drawstring waist:

First determine the height of the casing (above the waist) and double the measurement to allow for the foldover.

Notch the center front to create an opening for the string to pass through.

Ribbed Waistband

The ribbed waistband is a separate pattern piece.

The ribbing must be reduced in length to pull in the waist.

The waistband should have only one seam, placed at one of the sides (usually the left side), center back, or center front, if a drawstring is also inserted.

The rib should be one-sixth smaller than the rib waist measurement.

This waistband will be folded in half and serged to the pants.

The waist and waistband will need seam allowances so they can be serged together.

This style can also have elastic inserted into the waistband, or an additional drawstring.

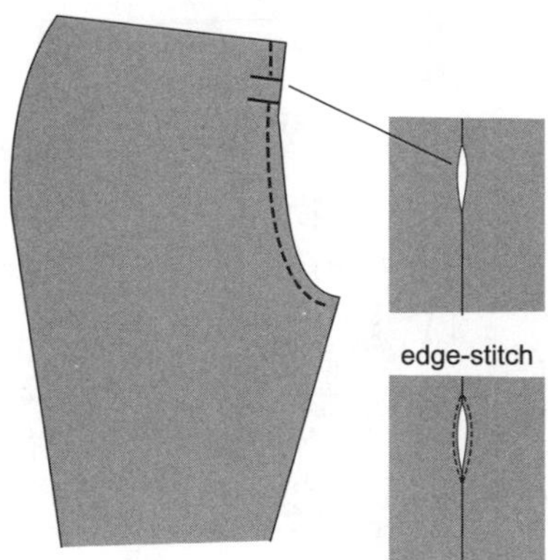

DRAWSTRING WAIST CASING

For drawstring elastic, replace the front notch with two notches 1/2″ apart to create an opening for the drawstring to pass through.

When sewing, skip over the area between the notches to create a hole in front for the string to pass through.

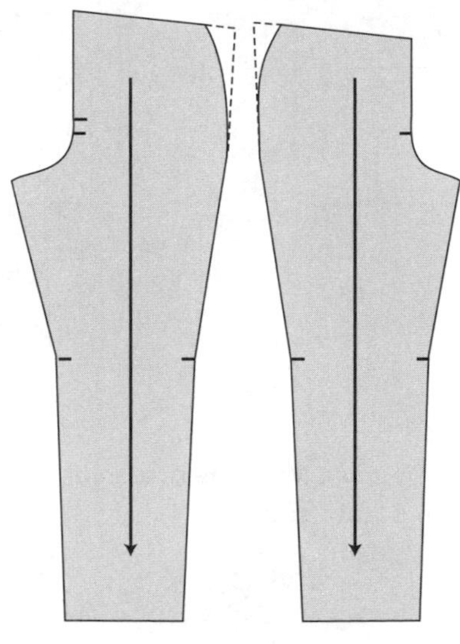

WAIST WITH ELASTIC GATHERS

To create a waist with gathered elastic, extend the waist and square down to the side seams.

This style will create a small amount of gathering at the waist. (For more on gathering, see further in the chapter.)

This waist can have any of the elastic treatments—channel, or serged-on elastic, drawstring, or separate waistband.

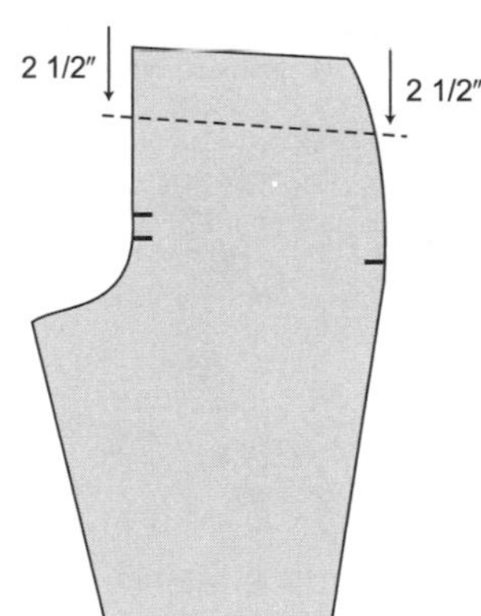

PATCH POCKETS

Measure down 2 1/2″ from the waist (but it may be placed at any level the designer wishes).

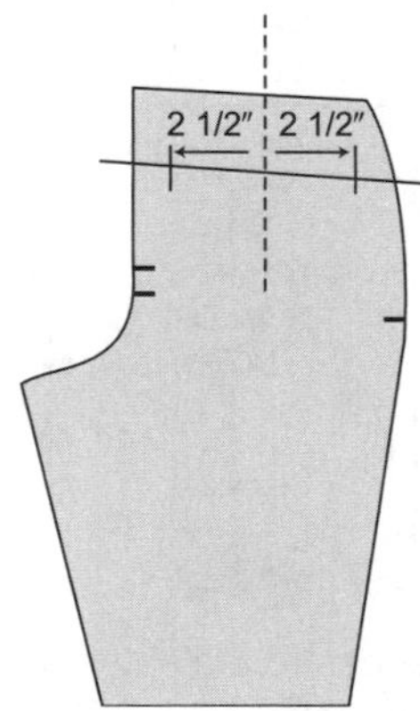

Find the center of the waist on that line and measure out 2 1/2″ in each direction, to make a pocket that is 5″ wide.

The pocket needs to be placed at the center of the waistline area, not the center of the hip, or it will appear to be falling into the hip.

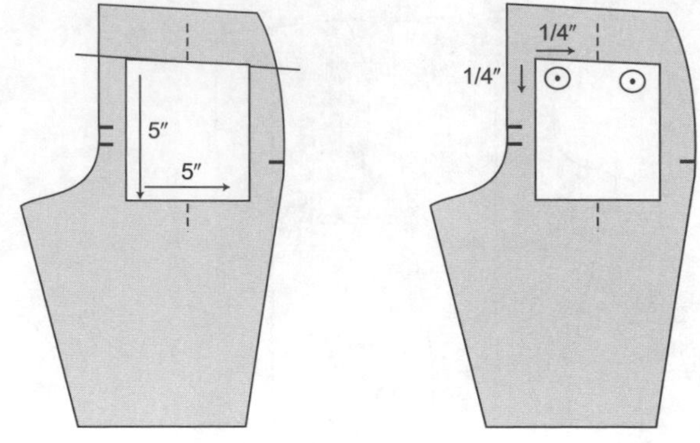

Draw the pocket 5″ down. Mark the drill holes ¼″ down, and ¼″ in from the pocket edge.

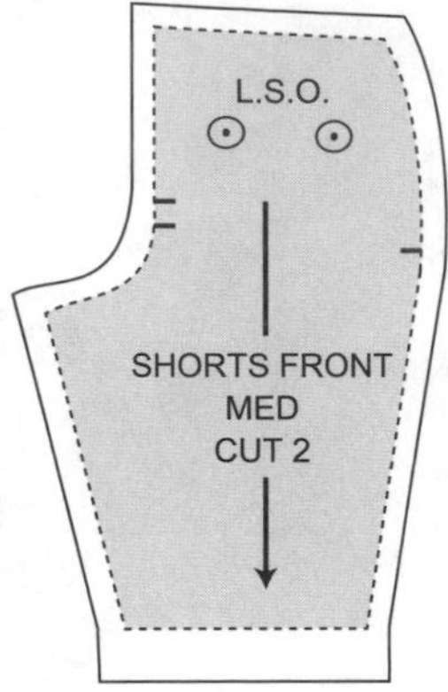

Add seam allowances and label the pattern. This pattern is labeled L.S.O. for a pocket on the "Left Side Only."

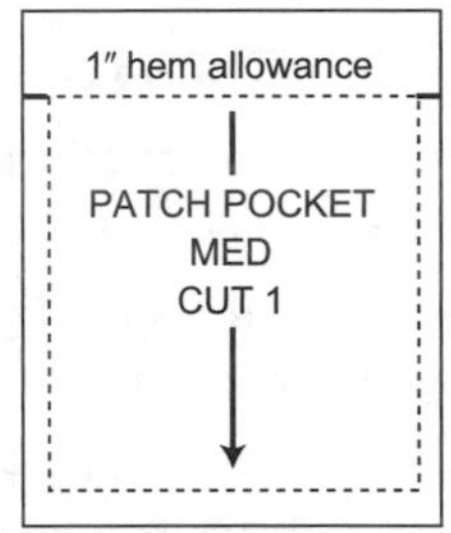

Add ¼″ seam allowances to the sides of the pocket and 1″ hem to the top of the pocket.

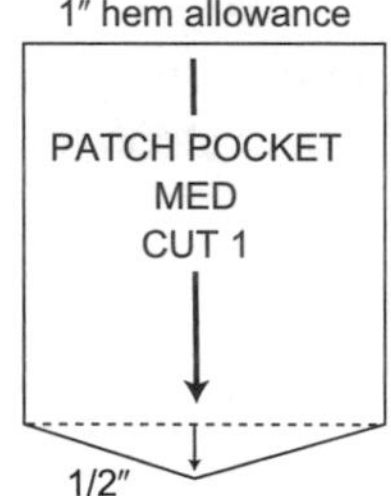

For an angled pocket, measure down ½″ at the center of the pocket and redraw.

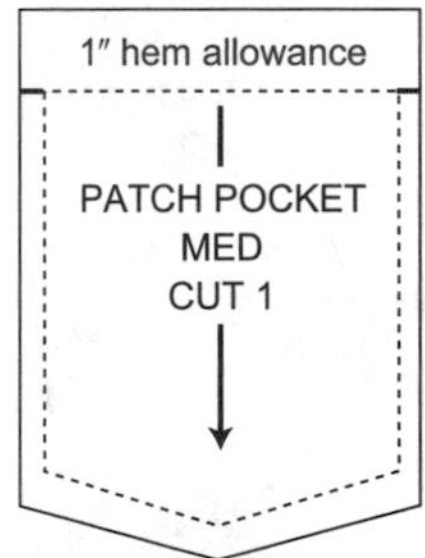

Add ¼″ seam allowances to the sides of the pocket and 1″ hem to the top of the pocket.

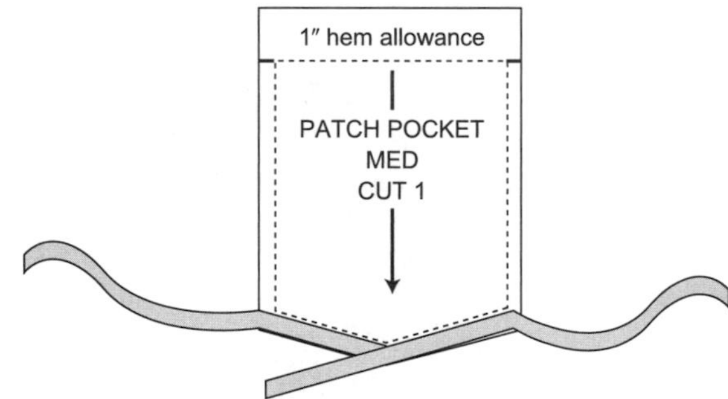

To prevent the pocket from stretching out when sewing across the bottom, serge ¼″ twill tape to the bottom edge.

If the fabric stretches in both directions, it may be necessary to serge twill tape to the sides also.

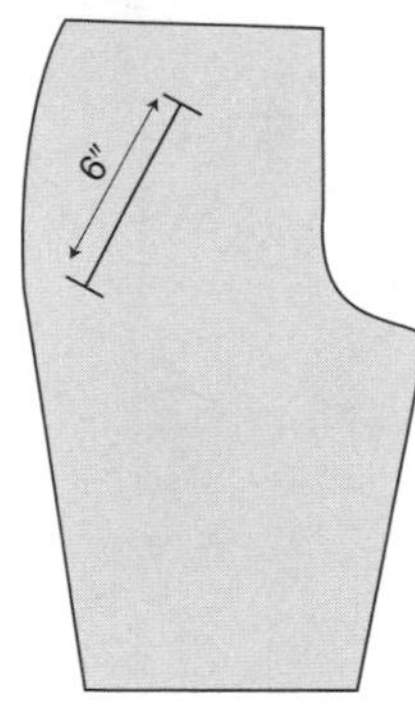

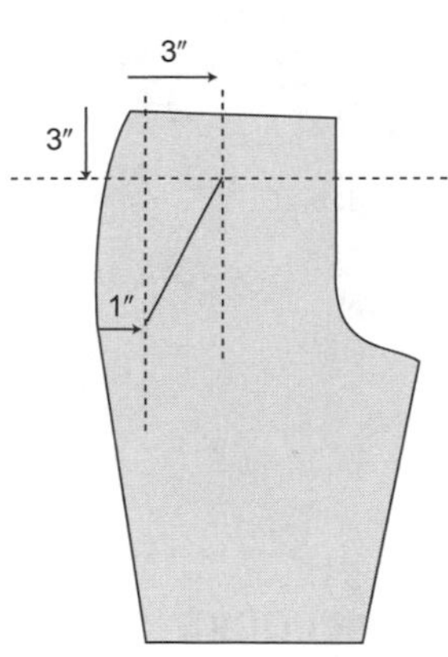

ANGLED WELT ZIPPER POCKETS

Place the pocket wherever the designer wishes.

Make the pocket 6″ wide for Medium customers.

Or use this guideline.

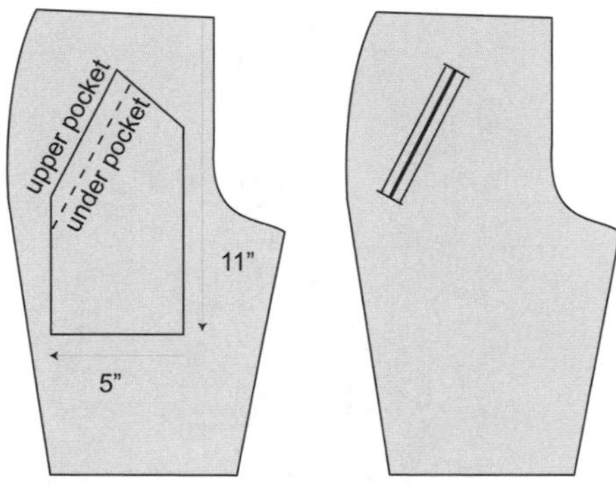

Make the pocket 11″ deep from the waist and at least 5″ wide.

Draw the welts 1/4" wide by the entire length of the pocket.

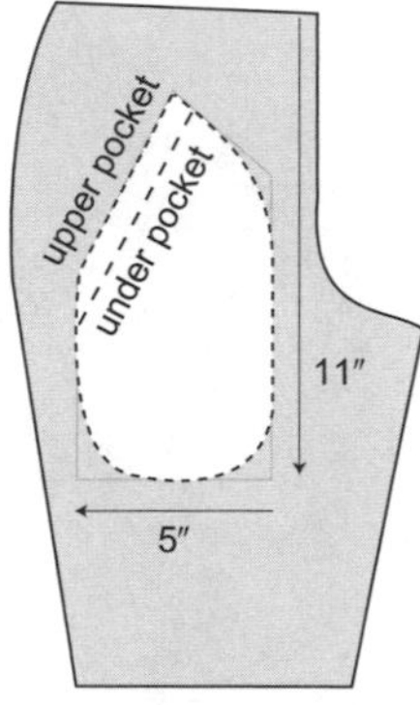

Blend the pocket bag into a curve for easier construction. You do not have to pivot at the corners and can simply serge all the way around in one easy step.

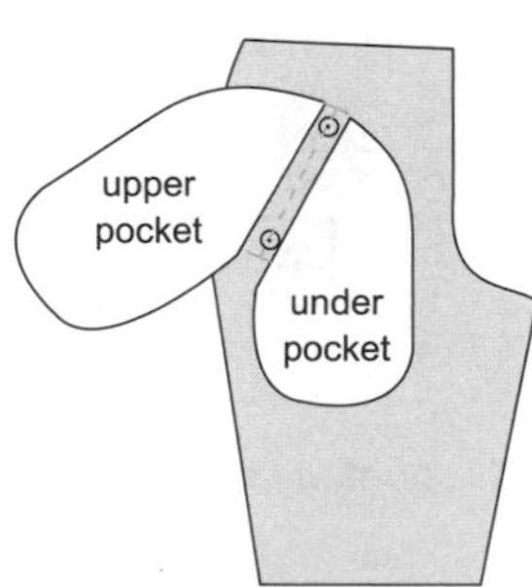

Note that the lower pocket will sew to the lower welt, and the upper pocket will sew to the upper welt, therefore the upper pocket is 1/2" larger than the lower pocket.

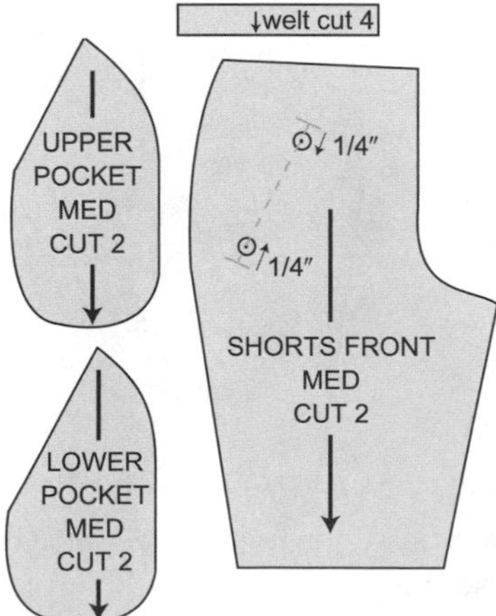

Trace and separate all the pocket pattern pieces.

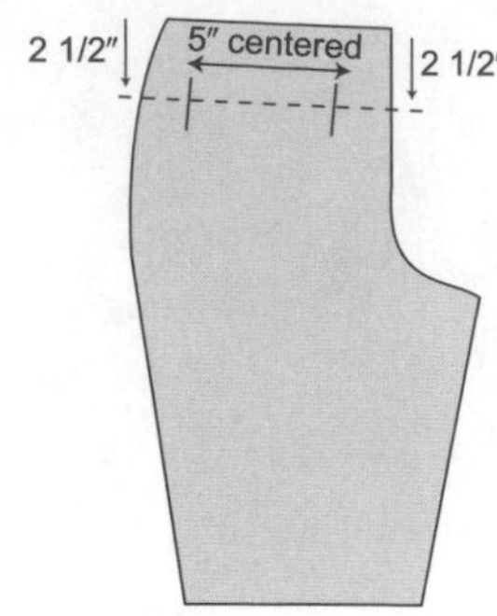

DOUBLE WELT BACK POCKETS

Measure down from the waist 2½".

Make the pocket 5" wide.

Place it centered it on the waist of the pant; do not center it on the hipline.

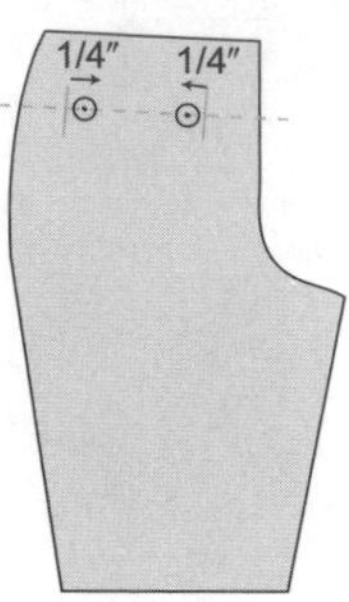

Mark the drill holes ¼" in from the ends of the pocket.

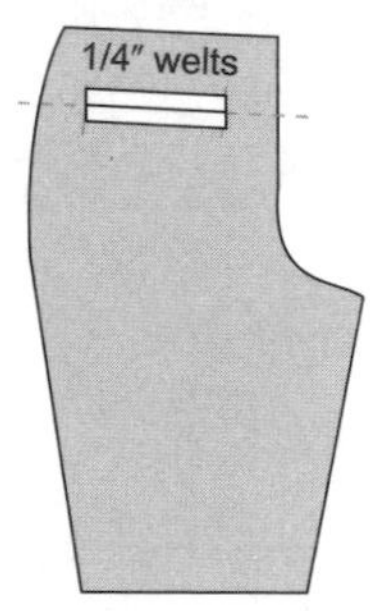

Draw the welts ¼" above and below the drill hole (cutting) line.

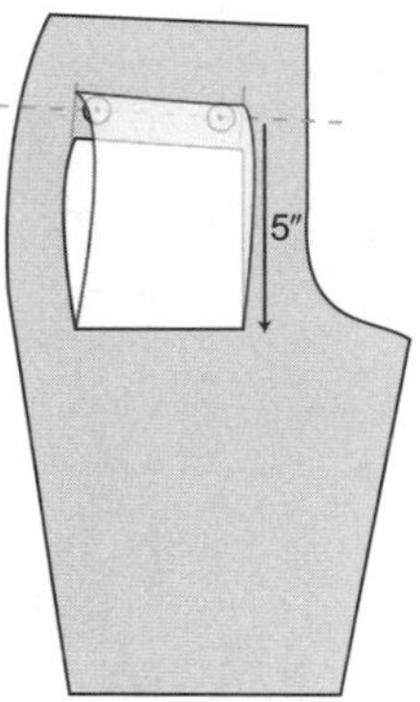

Draft the pocket bag 5" down from the drill hole (cutting) line.

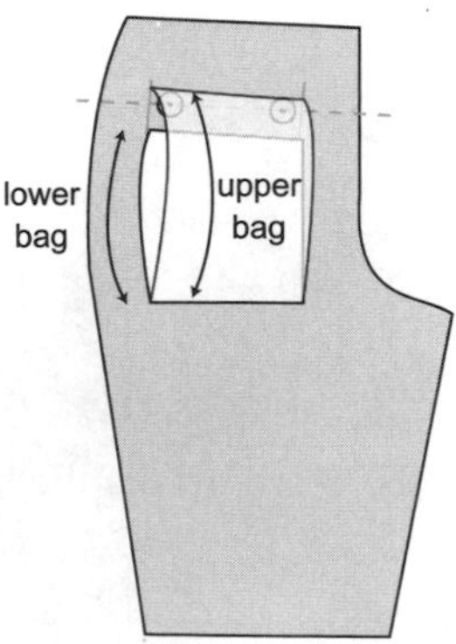

The lower pocket bag goes from the cutting line to the bottom of the pocket bag.

The upper bag goes from the top of the waist to the bottom.

Or, curve the pocket bags for easier assembly. The operator does not have to pivot the pocket pieces.

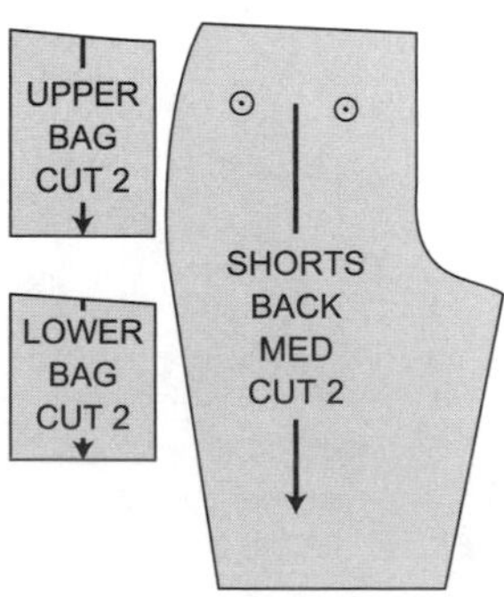

Trace out and separate the pocket bags.

Draft the welts 1" wide; they will fold in half and sew with a ¼" seam allowance and 6" long.

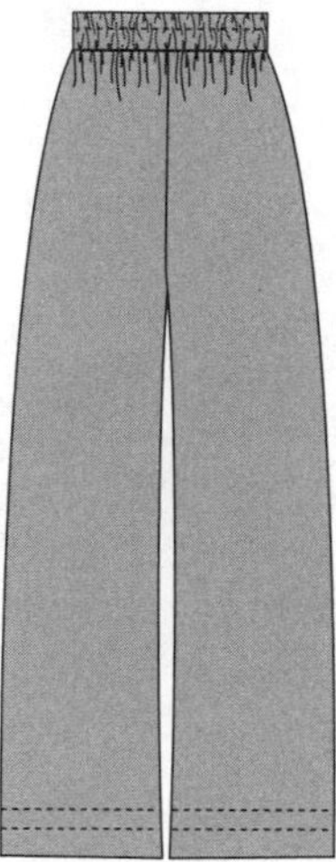

STYLE #6-001 WIDE-LEG PANTS

Wide-leg pants are very easy to draft, because all you must do is increase the width of the leg at the ankle.

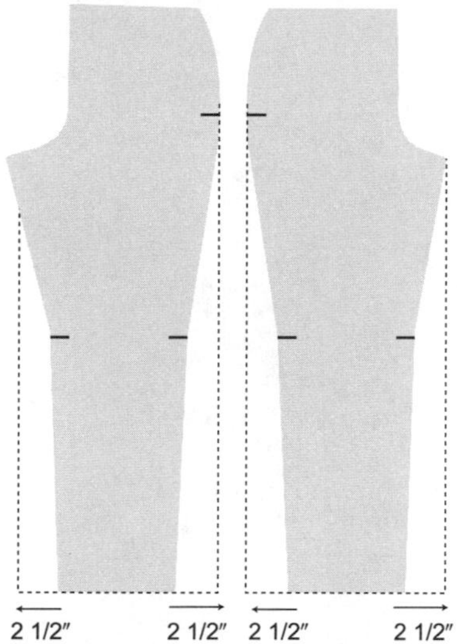

To create a wide-leg pant, square up from the hem to the front crotch, approximately 2½″ to 3″.

Increase the back leg, ankle width an equal amount to the front, and blend the back inseam at the crotch, as illustrated.

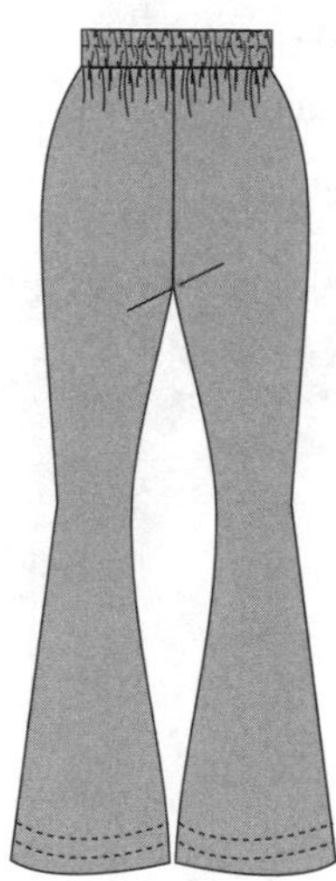

STYLE #6-002 BELL-BOTTOMS

Bell-bottom pants are easy to create, and the flare may be placed as high or as low as the designer wishes. The flare can also be as wide as the designer wishes.

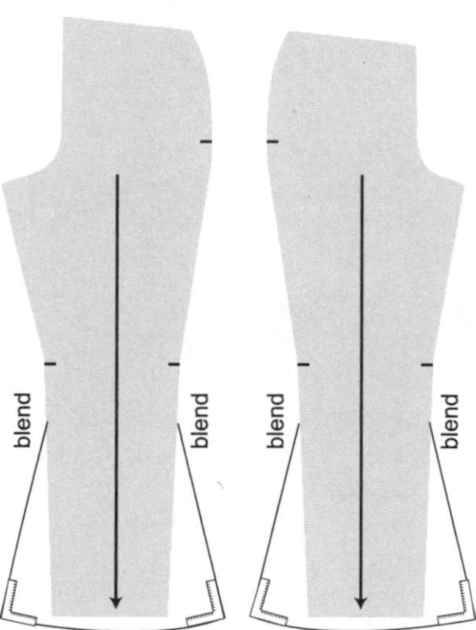

To create a bell-bottom style:

Note that the width and placement of the bell-bottom is up to the individual designer.

Keep all measurements the same, and square the side seam at the hem.

The designer may want the flare to start higher or lower than illustrated, or want the flare to be wider or narrower than illustrated.

Any variation may be created as long as all four flare heights and widths are equal to maintain balance and a correct grain.

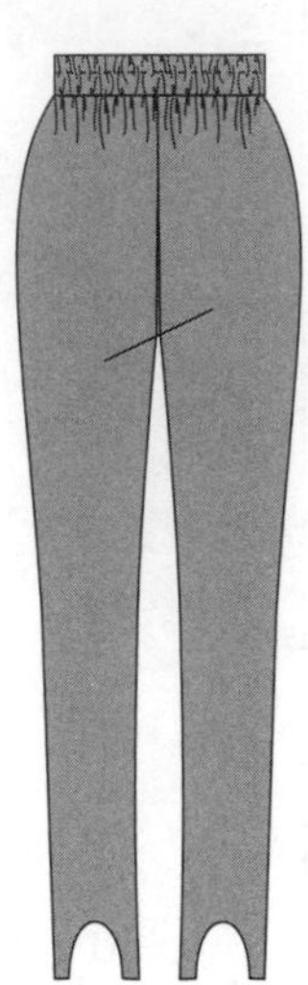

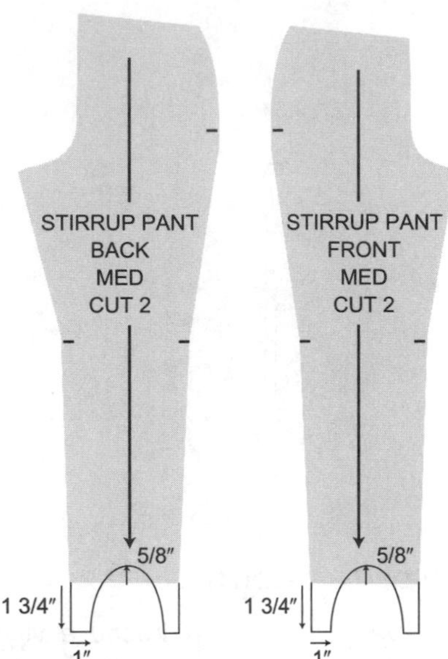

STYLE #6-003 STIRRUP PANTS

Stirrup pants, once very popular, are easy to create by making small straps that extend under the foot.

To create a pant with a stirrup:

Add seam allowances to the stirrup curved edges depending on the type of finish required.

Remember to add seam allowances to the ends (underneath the foot).

Elastic = ¼″ seam allowance.

Cover-stitched hem = ½″ seam allowance.

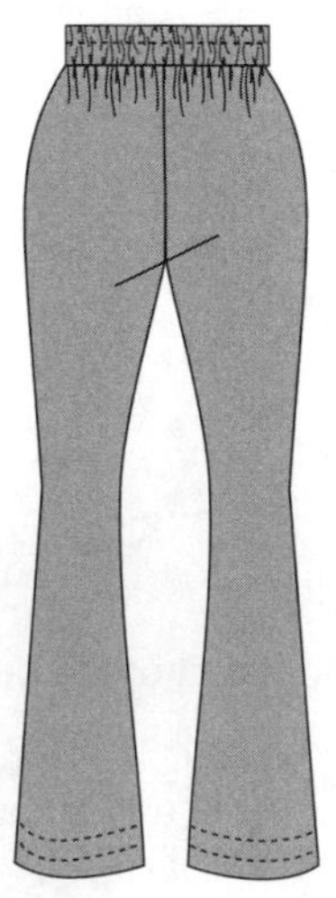

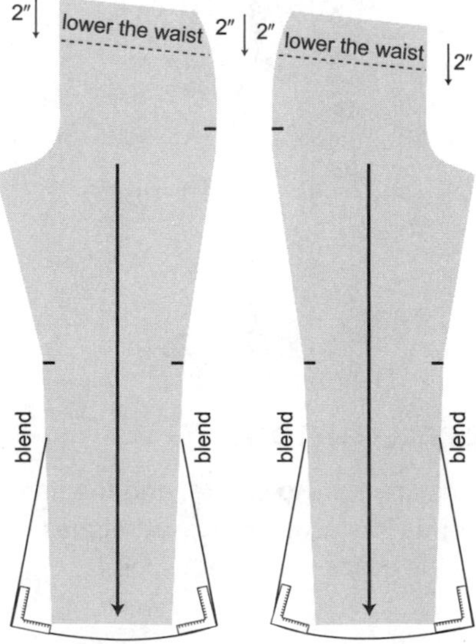

STYLE #6-004 HIP-HUGGERS

Hip-huggers, or low-rise pants, may be created by simply lowering the waist. Measure the dress-form to ensure that you do not make them too low.

Lower the waist the desired amount.

Elastic measurement should be calculated from the Judy, or the customer, at the new lower waist.

1″ smaller than the measurement of where the elastic will lie.

The designer may lower the waist any amount, as long as the front and back are equal and the elastic reduction of 1″ (for elastic more than 1″ wide) is made at the new lowered waist.

To create an elastic casing for a lowered waist:

Raise the waist double the width of the elastic and calculate the elastic length as 1″ smaller than the new lowered waist on the dress-form (for elastic that is 1″ or larger).

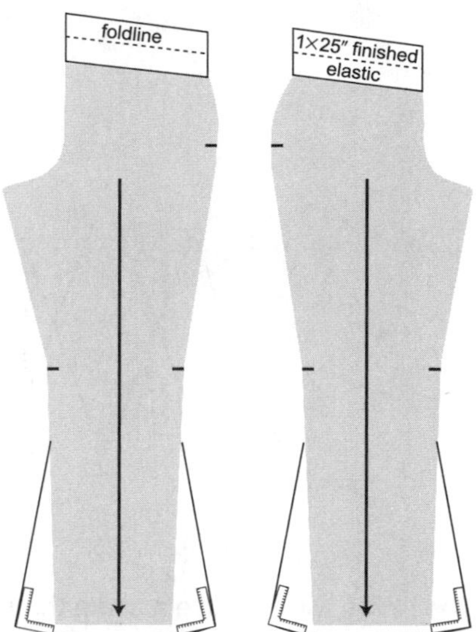

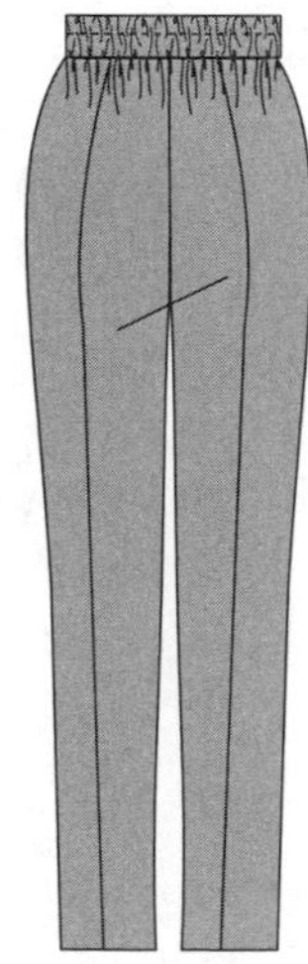

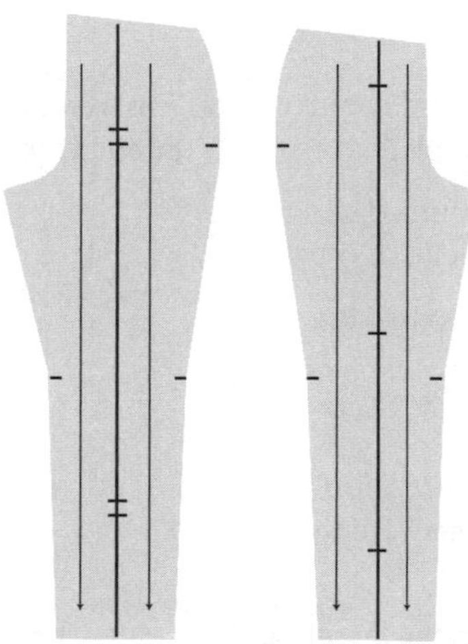

STYLE #6-005 PANTS WITH PRINCESS SEAMS

Princess or panel seams may be added to pants as a design detail or for color blocking.

Draw a line dividing the sloper in half, or even toward the sides if required.

Notch the sections for easy construction.

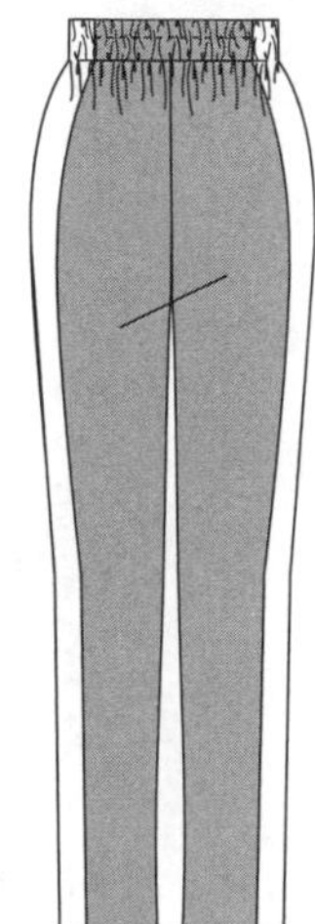

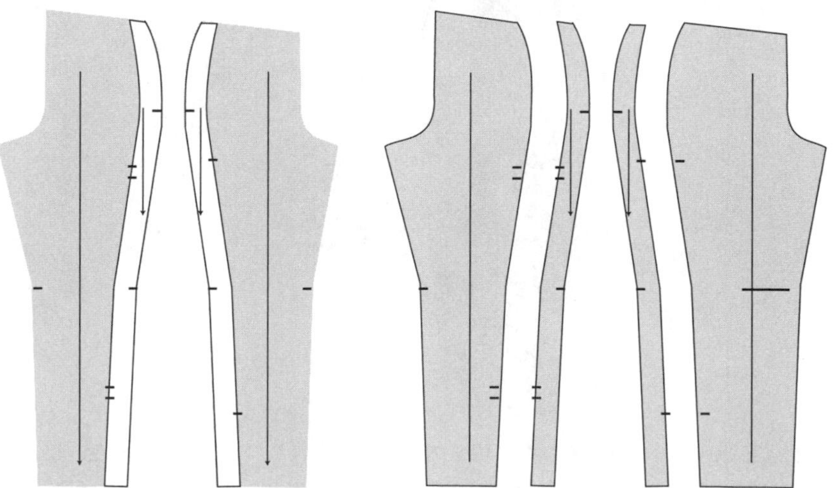

STYLE #6-006 PANTS WITH SIDE-SEAM STRIPES

Side-seam stripes can be created without any side seam, but instead the stripe should be drafted as one piece.

The pant may be created with separate pieces for the front and back, totaling four pieces.

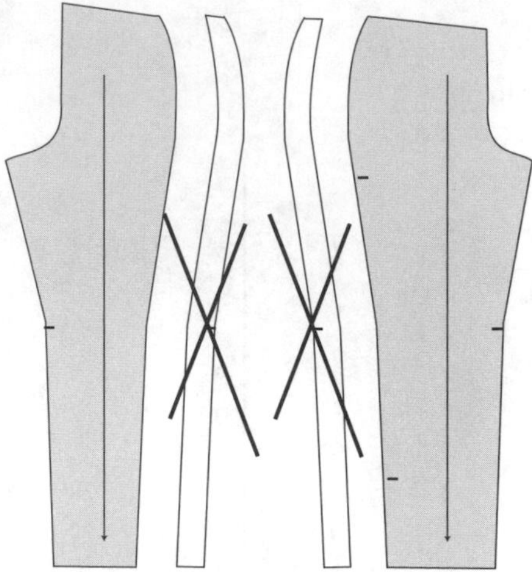

The stripe will not have a seam through the middle, but instead may be drafted as one single straight piece.

The stripe will be drafted straight instead of curved to save fabric when cutting the garment out.

From the front side seam of the sloper, remove half the amount of the stripe.

Repeat for the back.

Draft the stripe separately the length of the new side seams, the width of the total that was removed from the original.

Keep the hem straight and measure upwards the length of the seams that will be sewn together.

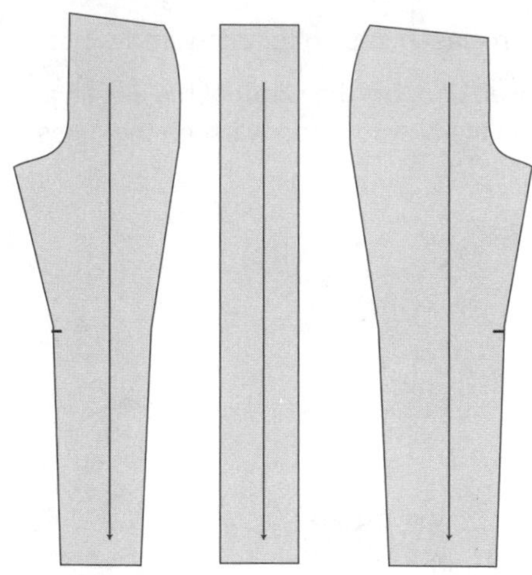

The new draft should look like the illustration and has three pieces rather than four.

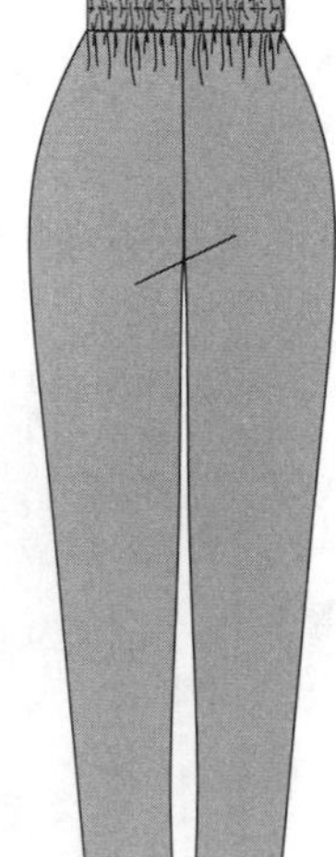

STYLE #6-008 PEGGED-WAIST PANTS

Pegged-waist pants, or pants with fullness at the waist, may be drafted with narrow hems.

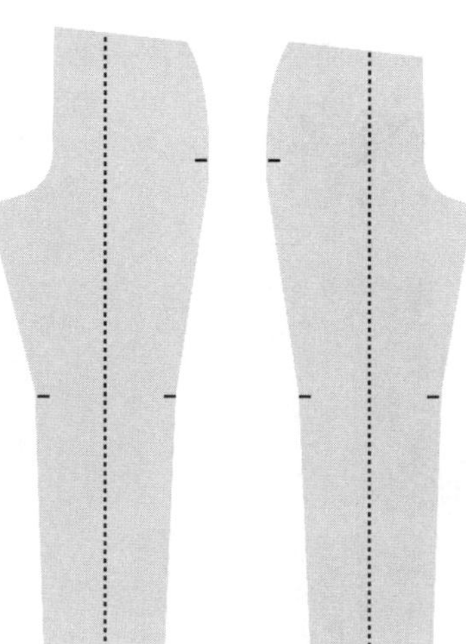

Slash and spread to create pants that are gathered at the top and remain narrow at the bottom.

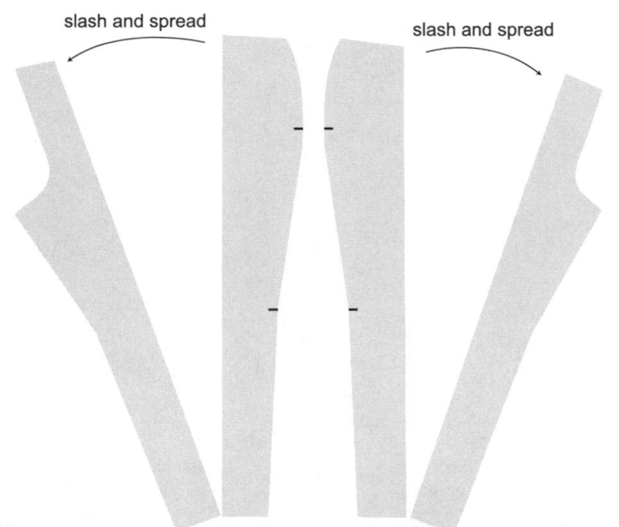

Slash the draft down the center grainline and spread any amount desired.

Gathering	Light	Medium	Heavy
Increase by	50%	100%	200%

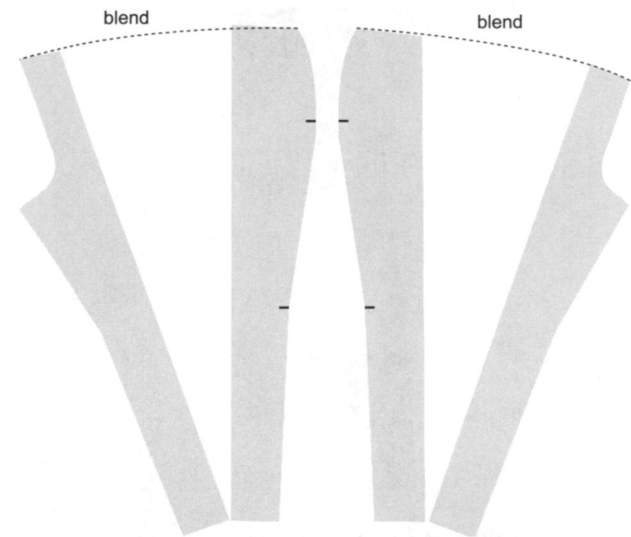

Also note that you create pants that are only gathered at the front.

Blend a new waist.

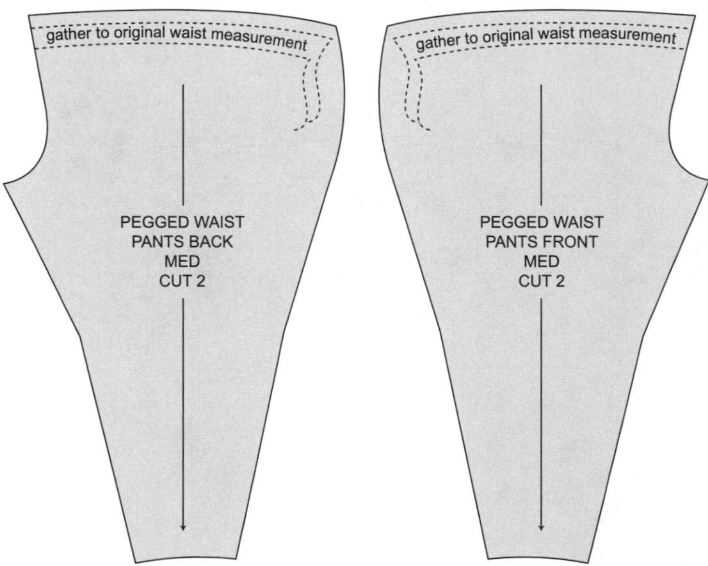

Indicate gathering on the pattern, with dashed lines as indicated.

You can also reduce the hem by 1/2″ on each side to make an even narrower hem, but check to make sure that the fabric stretches enough to get a foot through, otherwise you have to insert an invisible zipper.

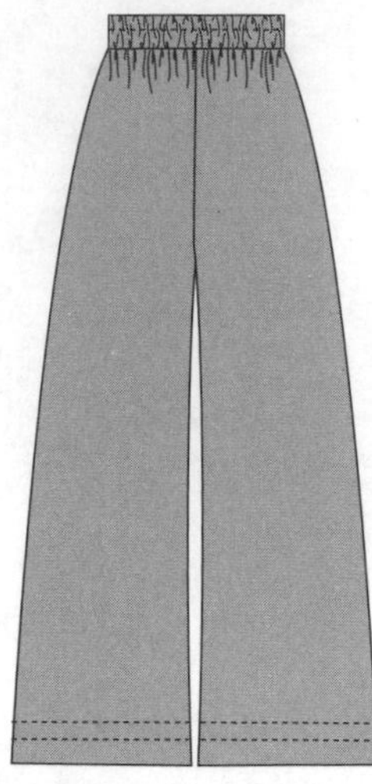

STYLE #6-009 PALAZZO PANTS

Palazzo or extreme wide-leg pants can be created by enlarging the hem volume of the pant sloper.

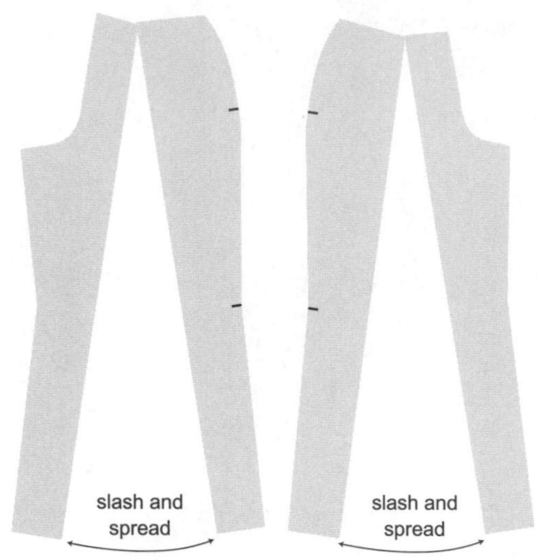

Slash and spread the hem of the pants any amount desired.

Fullness	Light	Medium	Heavy
Increase by	50%	100%	200%

Straighten out the side seams by connecting the hem to the crotch with a straight line.

Connect the hem to the hip with a straight line.

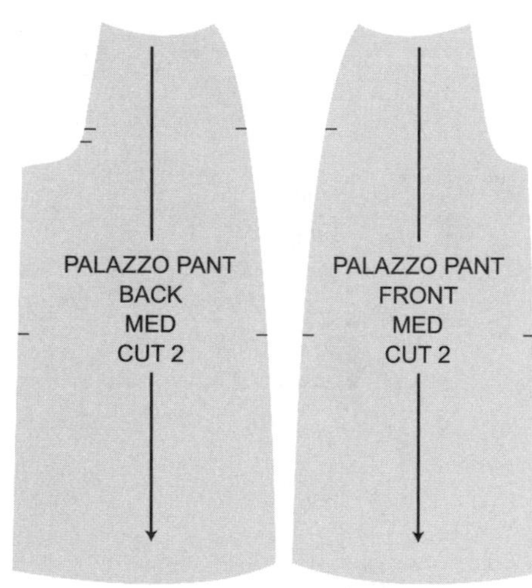

Label the pants as indicated.

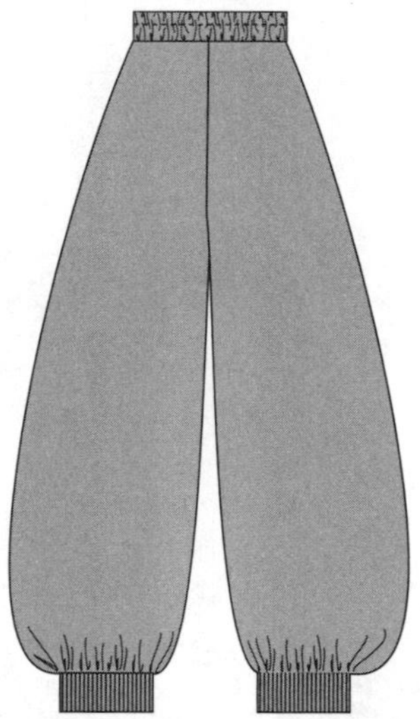

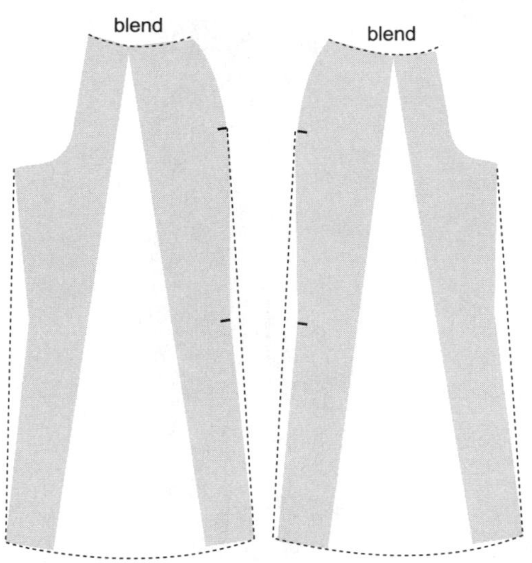

HAREM PANTS

Harem pants are created exactly like palazzo pants, except that a narrow cuff is added to the bottom to pull the pants in.

Harem pants may be created by gathering the hem and adding a ribbed cuff to the bottoms.

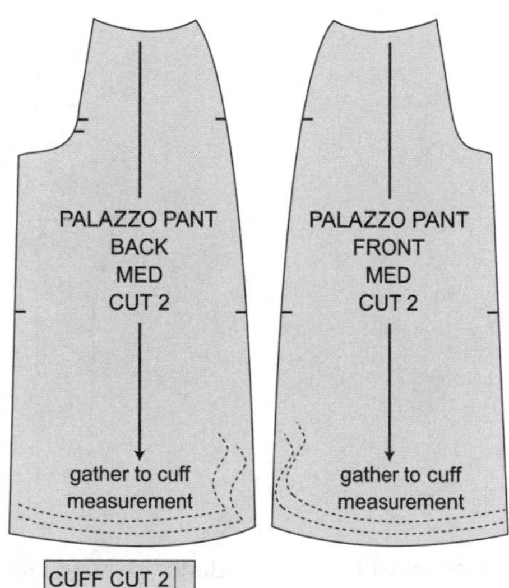

Draft a cuff the length of the original pant and 4″ high to fold into a 2″ cuff.

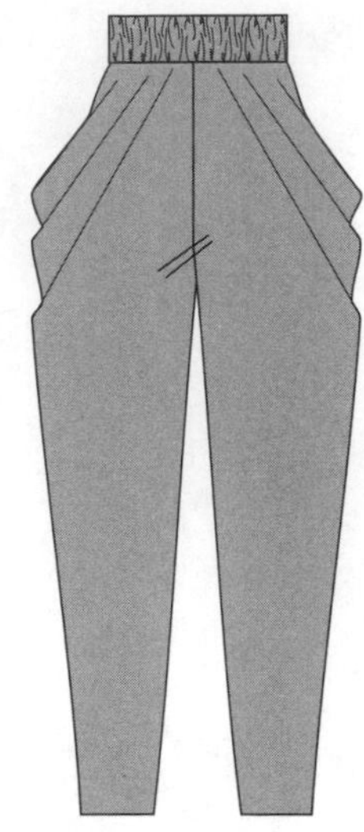

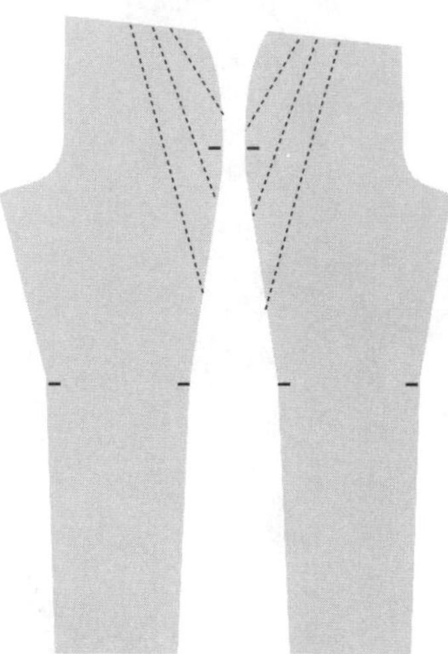

STYLE #6010 COWL-DRAPED PANTS

Cowl-draped pants are created by slashing and spreading the side seams of the pants.

Pants may be created with cowls at the side seams by following these instructions.

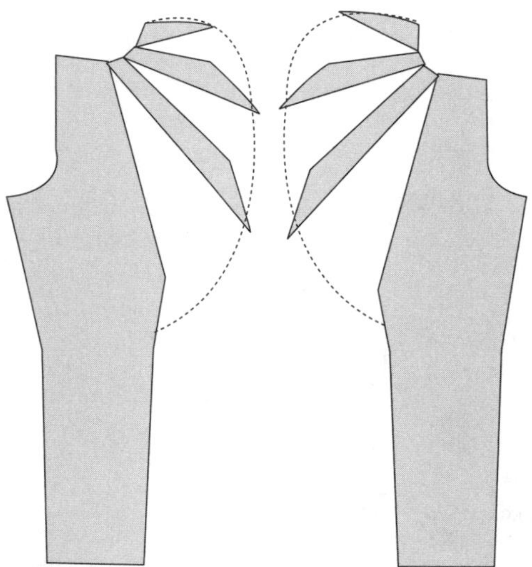

Slash and spread the sections as required, often with larger spreads for the bottom sections. Try spreading 6″ then 8″ then 10″.

Blend a new side seam.

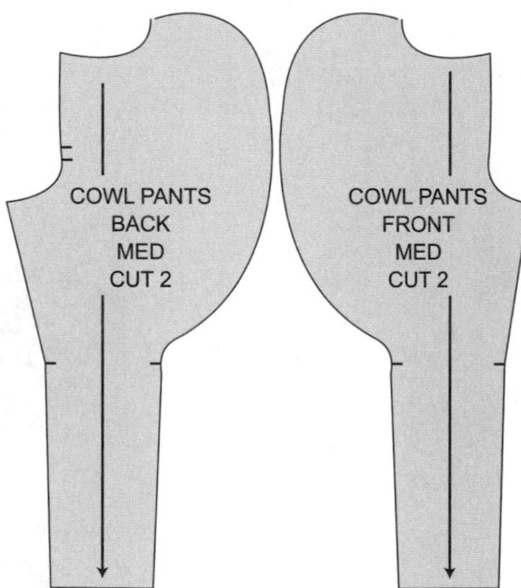

Bend the knee, add a grainline, and label your pants pattern.

When sewn, these patterns will fall into soft folds.

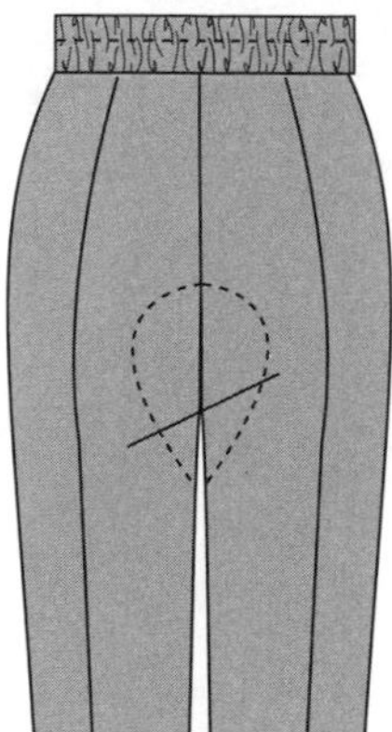

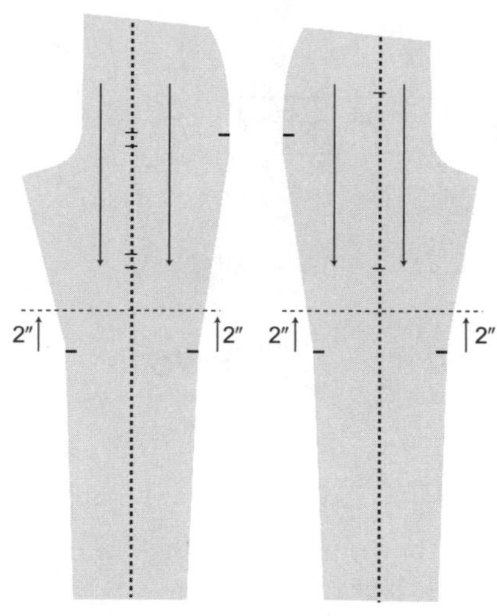

CYCLING SHORTS

This draft for cycling shorts also shows how to draft the chamois piece—another layer to protect the rider's crotch. It can be made of self- or chamois suede, and is top-stitched to the inside of the shorts.

Draw a guideline 2″ above the knee notch.

Draw vertical lines indicated the center of the panel, for panel seams.

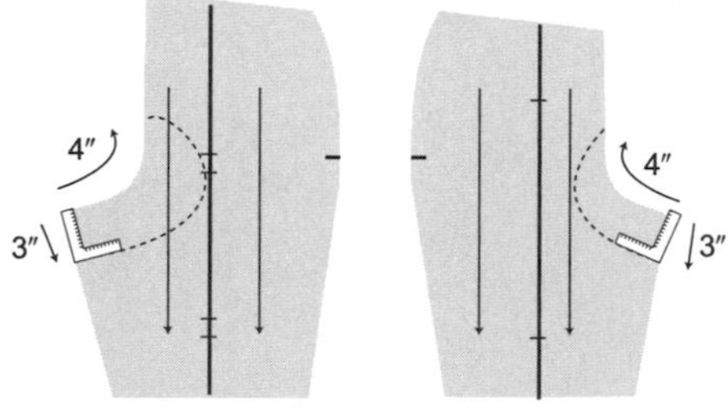

Draw the chamois 4″ above the crotch seam and 3″ below, make sure to square at the center front and back.

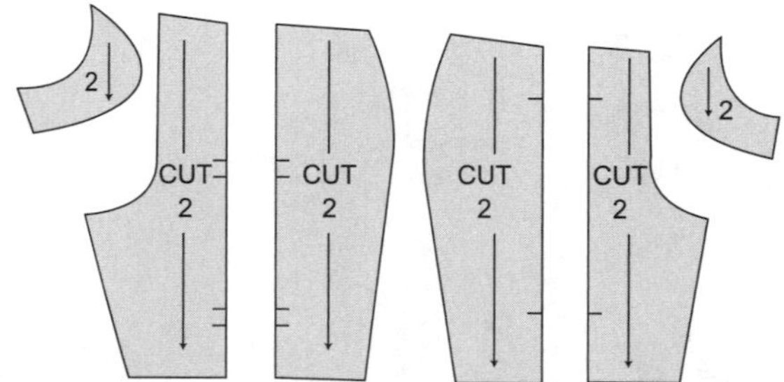

Notch and trace out all the pieces for the final pattern.

The chamois should be sewn into the inside of the shorts after the crotch seams have been shown.

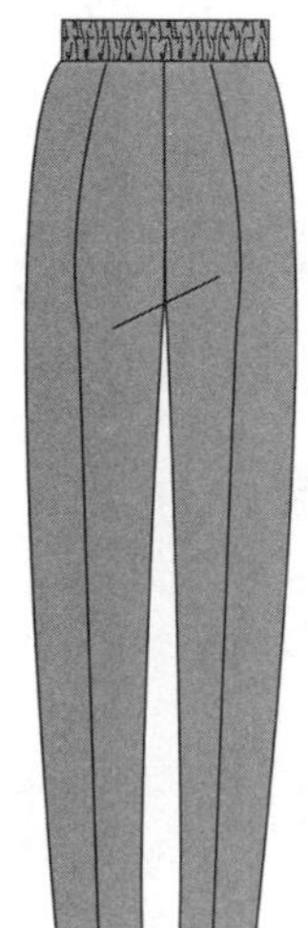

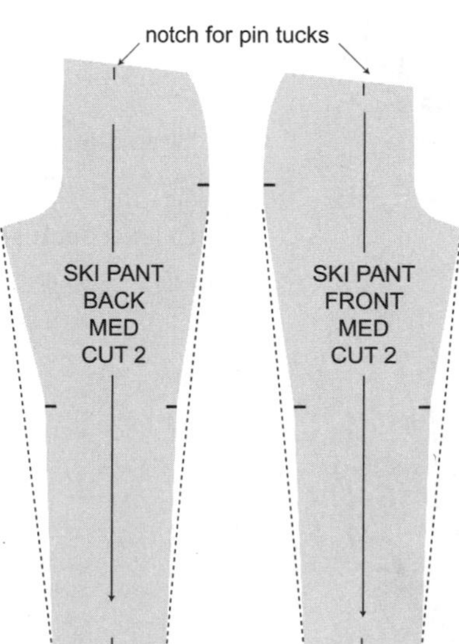

SKI PANTS

To create ski pants with a pin tuck down the front, simply straighten out the inseam and outseam as straight lines from hip to ankle and crotch to ankle.

Place a notch at the waist and hem to indicate where to sew the pin tuck.

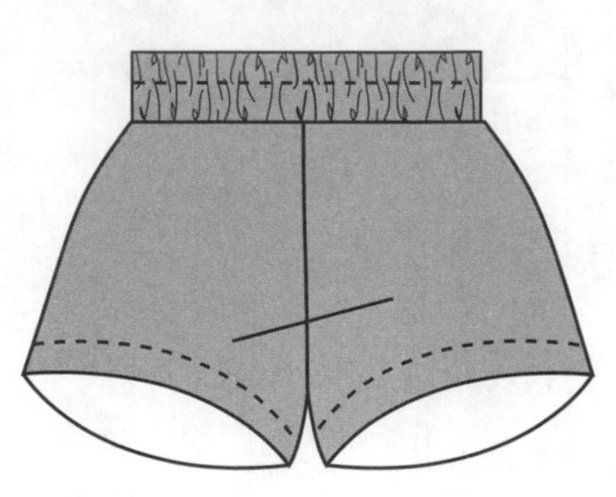

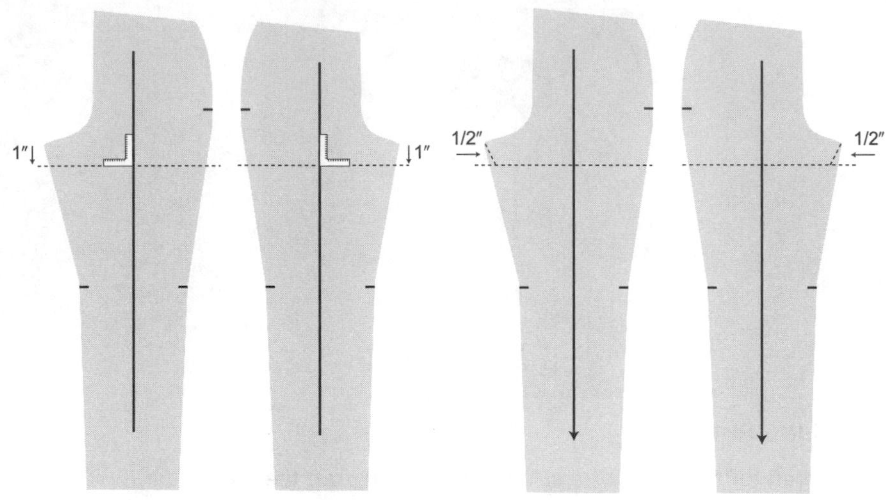

BOOTY SHORTS

Short shorts or booty shorts can be created from the basic pant sloper.

Draw the hem 1″ down from the crotch.

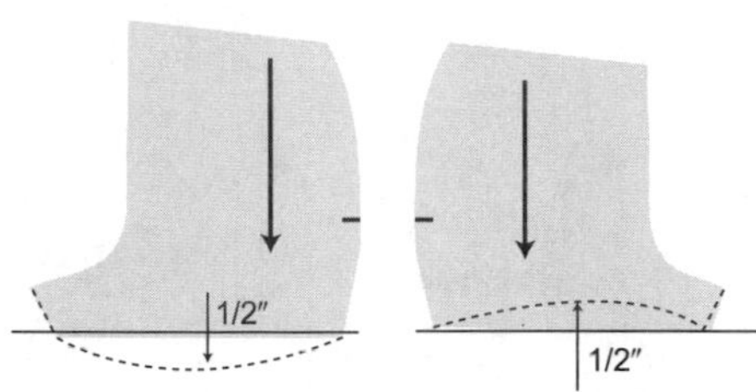

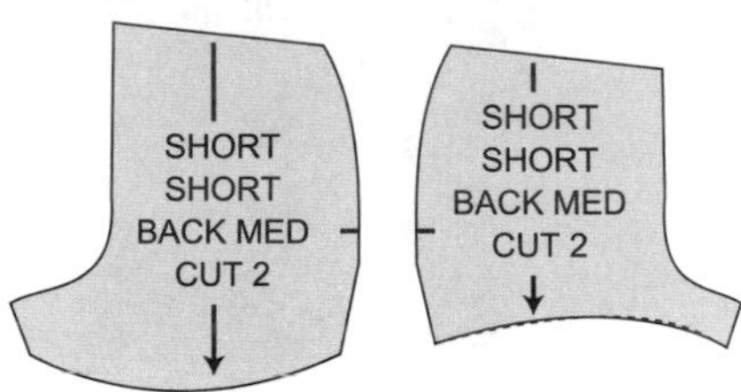

Shape the hem by raising it ½″ at the front and lowering it ½″ at the back.

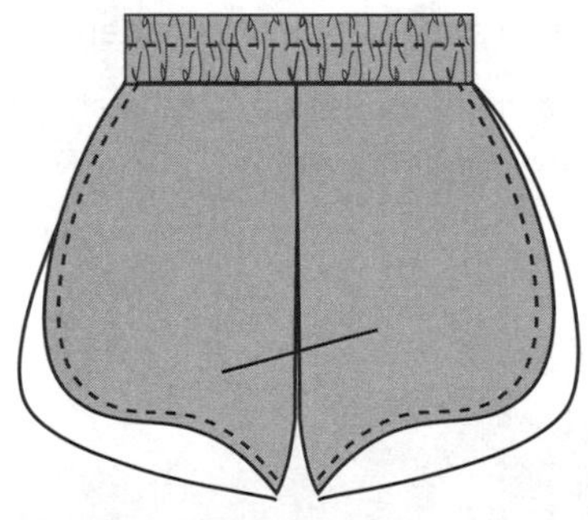

WRAP SHORTS

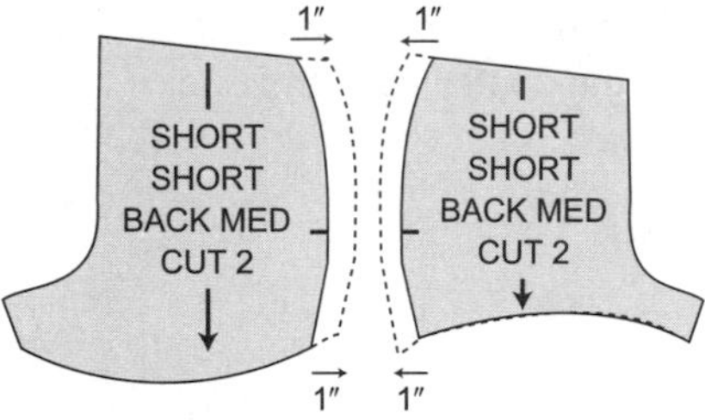

Wrap shorts are created without any side seams. They simply wrap back over the front to give complete coverage.

Extend each side seam by 1″.

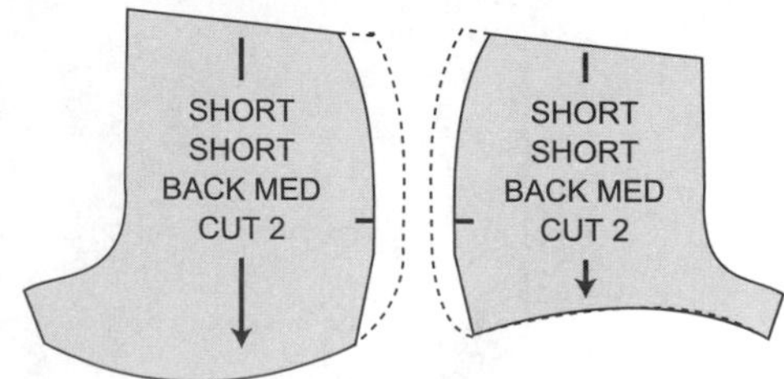

Blend a new hem and side seam into a curved line.

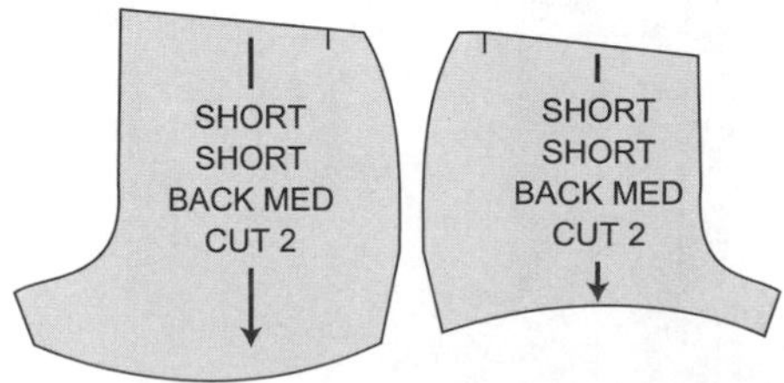

Notch the placement of the side seams for construction.

The hem and side seam should be bound with the collarette, and can remain open, or stitched down for modesty.

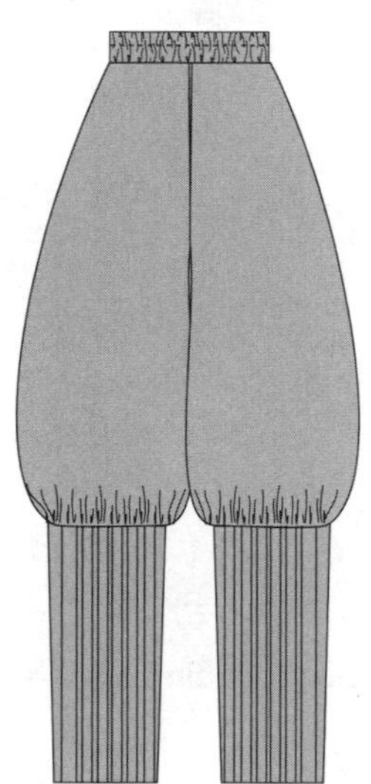

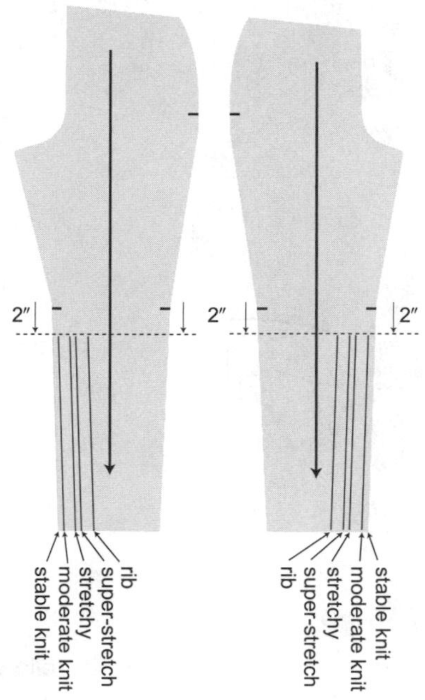

KNICKERS WITH RIBBED CUFFS

Knickers with a ribbed cuff should be drafted by tracing the upper part of the sloper in that stretch ratio, and the lower portion should be traced from the rib sloper.

Place the seam 2″ below the knee, or any amount the design requires.

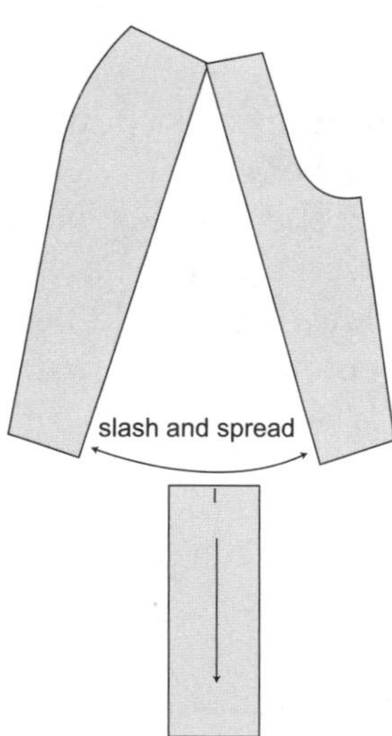

Divide the top portion and the lower portion.

Slash and spread the upper portion to increase the volume at the knee level.

Spread as much as the design requires.

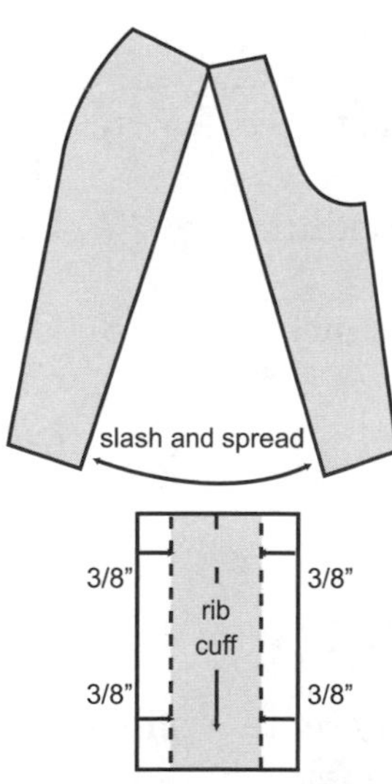

Blend the curve.

If you trace the stable knit for the lower portion, you must reduce the lower portion $^{3}/_{4}$″ as indicated.

If you trace the rib ratio for the lower portion, ignore.

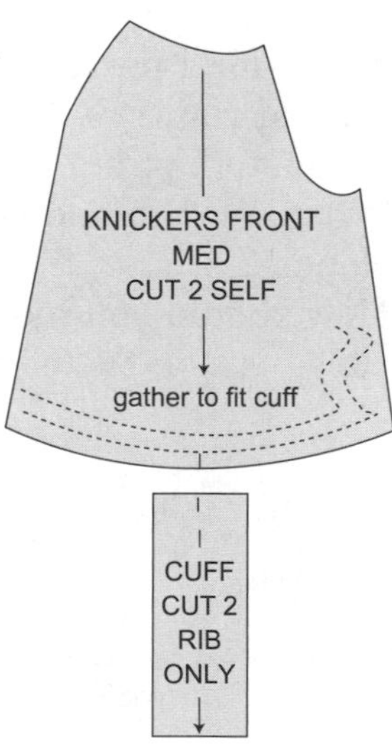

Trace and label the pattern as indicated.

Label the knee seam with gathering lines, and indicate how much to gather to.

Gathering	Light	Medium	Heavy
Increase by	50%	100%	200%

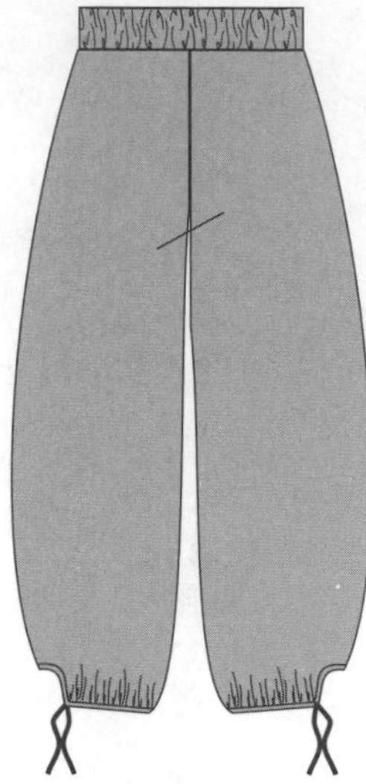

KNICKERS WITH LEG TIES

Knickers may be created with ties on the sides by following these instructions.

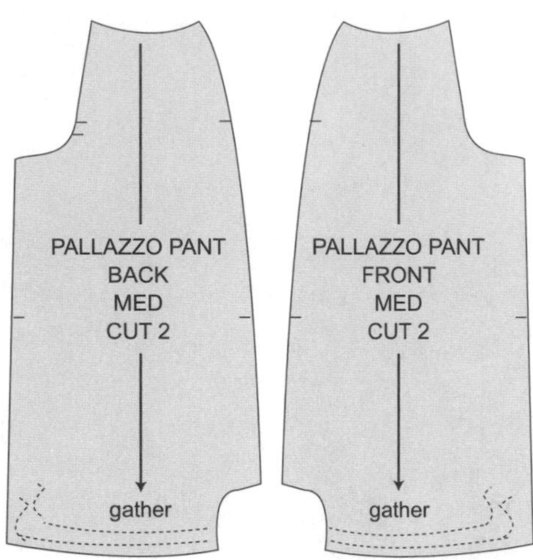

Cut out the outseam as indicated and bind with the collarette to create ties.

Test Your Knowledge of the Material in This Chapter

1. How might you draft a one-way-stretch sloper for a personal sloper?
2. Should you try to draw an exact hip curve for custom pants?
3. What color should you label your Medium slopers?
4. How should you indicate the elastic measurement on the pants pattern?
5. How much smaller should the waist elastic be?
6. When creating a lowered-waist pant, how big should the elastic be?
7. How can you prevent the elastic from collapsing, or folding over, on the wearer?
8. How much seam allowance should be used on the waist when creating pants with a serged-on elastic?

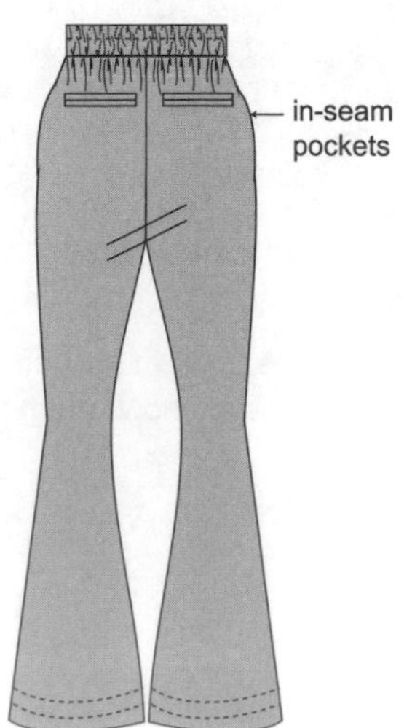

Project #1

Design and create a pair of pants using the patternmaking principles from this chapter.

Use any pant silhouette that you wish—wide leg, narrow leg, flared, or bell-bottom.

The pants must have an elastic casing waist finish, serged to the raw edge and folded over and cover-stitched, or have drawstring elastic.

Must have two pockets, which may be the same or different styles.

Must have a cover-stitched hem.

CHAPTER 7

Tops

About This Chapter

Tops are a huge portion of the fashion marketplace. They far outsell bottoms, pants, and skirts. A customer will often buy a new top for a Saturday evening, but may not want to purchase new pants or a dress as easily.

This chapter discusses tops as any garments that are worn on the top portion of the body, including tank tops, but for clarity, later chapters will discuss sweaters, oversized tops, and dresses, which are just longer tops. Many of the details noted here may be applied to them.

This chapter begins with the development of the different one-way-stretch top slopers and goes on to develop patterns for the following:

Crew-neck T-shirt

V-neck T-shirt

Mock-neck T-shirt

Raglan-sleeved T-shirt

Mock-neck top

Boatneck top

Cowl-neck top

Oversized T-shirt

One-Way-Stretch Top Sloper

This sloper will be developed on the fold, with the front on top of the back. The sloper should also be cut out full, total, folded, and butterflied on oak-tag to assist in the creation of asymmetrical designs. Also, this sloper will be developed in size Medium (Misses), for stable knits, and will draw in the different stretch ratios. If you wish to develop a personal sloper, substitute your personal measurements with those listed as "standard size," and make the appropriate reductions. Use the one-way-stretch sloper even when using four-way-stretch fabrics. Because there is nothing holding the length stretch down and anchoring it, the fabric will behave like a one-way-stretch anyway.

STABLE-KNIT TOP REDUCTIONS

Zero percent smaller in crosswise direction without any reductions in lengthwise direction.
Use these measurements when drafting slopers for fabrics that stretch from 0% to 25%.

#		Standard Medium Measurements	Reduce by	New Measurement	Divide by panels	Extra Extra Small	Extra Small	Small	Medium	Large	Extra Large	Extra Extra Large
1	Bust	35½	0%	35½	4	30½	31½	33½	35½	38½	41½	45½
2	Waist	27½	0%	27½	4	22½	23½	25½	27½	30½	33½	
3	Hip	35½	0%	36½	4	30½	31½	33½	35½	38½	41½	48½
4	Crotch depth	10½	No length reduction			9⅞	10	10¼	10½	10¾	11	11⅞
12	Nape to waist	16⅝	No length reduction			15⅜	15⅞	16⅛	16⅞	17⅛	17⅞	18⅛
13	Back neck	2½	No length reduction			2⅜	2⅜	2½	2½	2½	2⅞	2⅞
14	Back neck rise	⅞	No length reduction			¾	¾	⅞	⅞	⅞	⅞	⅞
15	Shoulder	6	No length reduction			5	5⅛	5½	6	6½	7	5⅘
16	Across back	7½	0%	7½	N/A	6⅞	7	7¼	7½	7¾	8	8⅜
18	Shoulder pitch	1½	No length reduction			1⅜	1⅜	1½	1½	1½	1⅞	1⅔

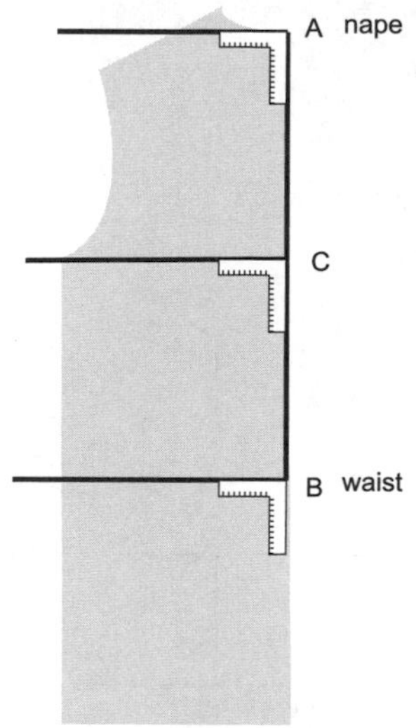

ONE-WAY-STRETCH TOP SLOPER

Select the draft with the stretch ratio of your fabric, and the size needed, from one of the previous charts.

A-B = nape to waist (#12 from chart).

A-C = halfway between A and B.

A, B, C = square out lines.

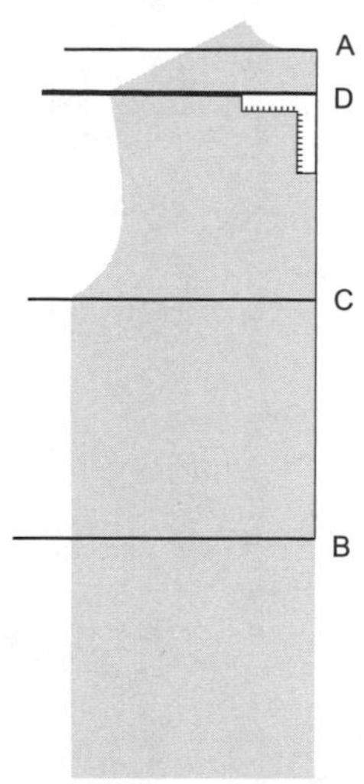

A-D = 1½″ shoulder drop (#18 from chart) and square a line across.

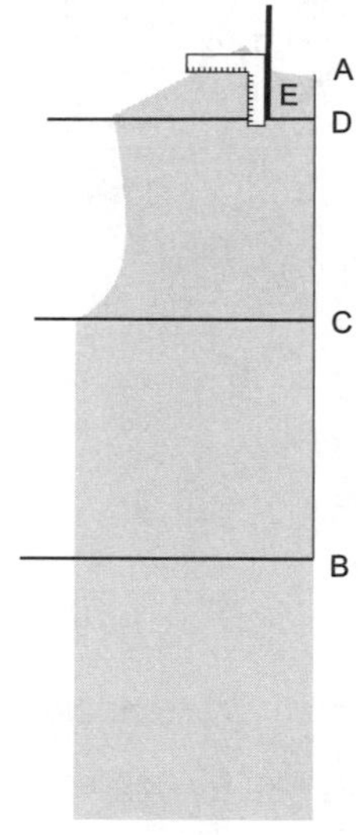

D-E = back neck (#13 from chart), square up.

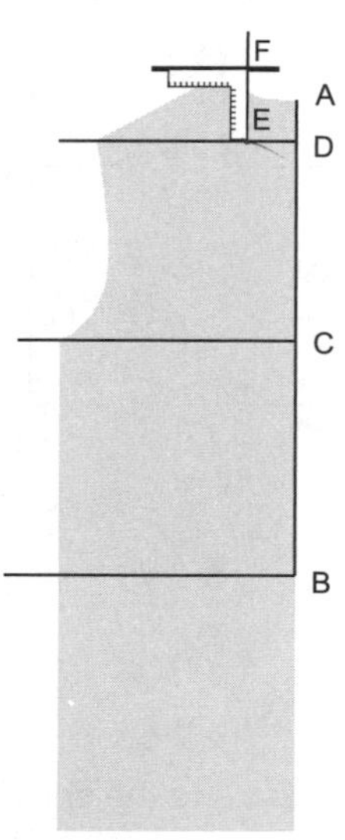

E-F = back neck rise (#14 from chart).

Since the front will be drafted on top of the back, the measurements need to be divided into four.

#		Extra Extra Small	Extra Small	Small	Medium	Large	Extra Large	Extra Extra Large
2	¼ of waist	5⅝	5⅞	6⅜	6⅞	7⅝	8⅜	9⅜
3	¼ of hip	8⅜	8⅝	9⅛	9⅝	10⅜	11⅛	12⅛
4	Crotch depth	10½	10⅝	10 4/8	10⅝	10⅞	11⅛	11⅜
	⅓ of crotch depth	3½	3½	3½	3½	3⅝	3¾	3¾
12	Nape to waist	15⅜	15⅞	16⅛	16⅞	17⅛	17⅞	18⅛
12-b	Half-way	7¾	8	8	8½	8⅝	9	9
13	Back neck	2⅜	2⅜	2½	2½	2½	2⅞	2⅞
14	Neck rise	¾	¾	⅞	⅞	⅞	⅞	⅞
18	Shoulder pitch	1⅜	1⅜	1½	1½	1½	1⅝	1⅝

1

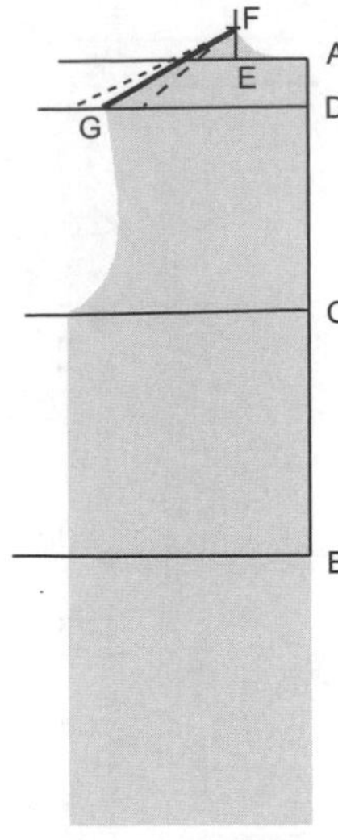

F-G = shoulder length (#15 from chart).

2

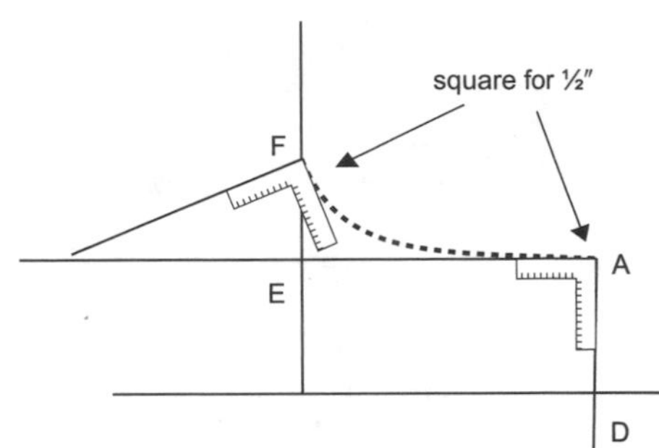

Take your ruler and line it up from point F to wherever that measurement of the shoulder length lines up on line D.

Draw in the shoulder line.

3

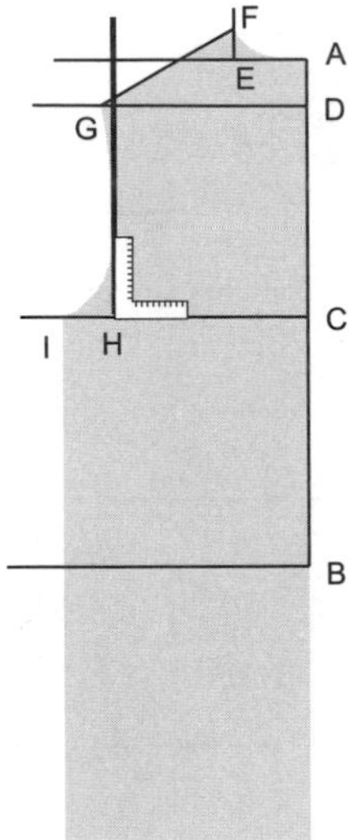

Draw in neckline as illustrated.

Square for ½″ at F, square to the shoulder line.

Square for ½″ at A, square to the center line.

Draw the line by hand, since there is no curve that perfectly replicates the curve, and then use your curves to smooth it out and neaten it up.

C-H = across back (#16 from chart), square up to shoulder, wherever it lands. Does not necessarily match with point G.

4

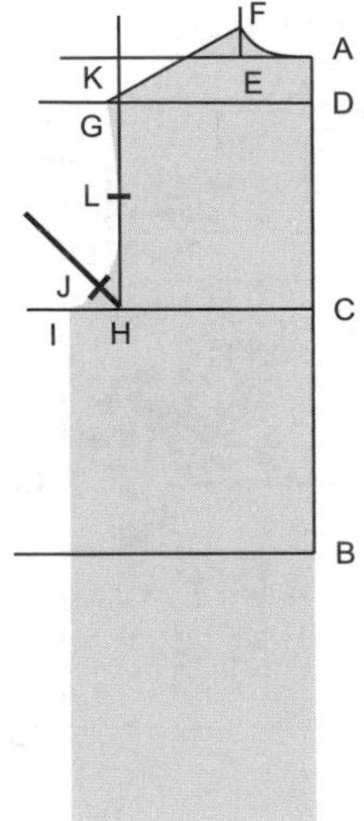

C-I = bust measurement (#1 from the chart).

H-J = ½″ on bias angle of 45 degrees.

L = halfway between K and H.

G = square a line for at least ½″ just a little past the armhole line.

	Extra Extra Small	Extra Small	Small	Medium	Large	Extra Large	Extra Extra Large
Shoulder length	5	5⅛	5½	6	6½	7	7½
Across back	6⅞	7	7¼	7½	7¾	8	8⅜
Bust	30½	31½	33½	35½	38½	41½	45½
¼ of bust	7⅞	7⅞	8⅜	8⅞	9⅞	10⅜	11⅜

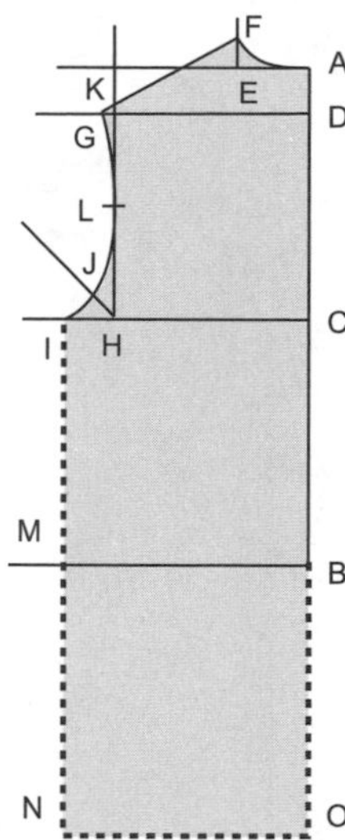

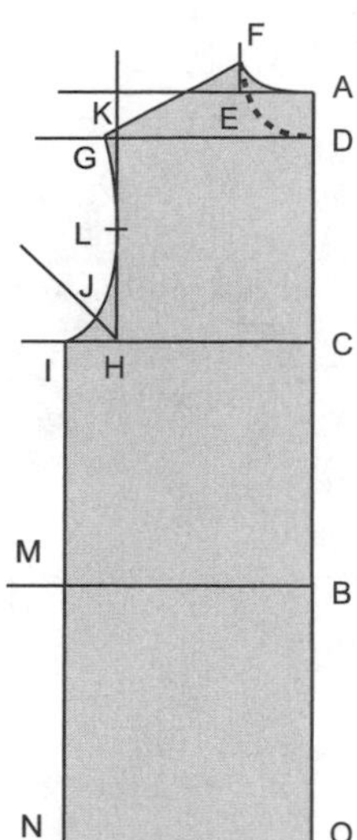

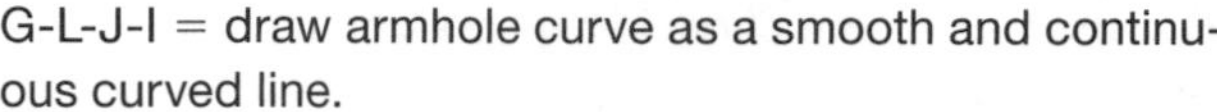

G-L-J-I = draw armhole curve as a smooth and continuous curved line.

B-M = bust (#1 from chart).

B-O = crotch depth (#4 from chart).

O-N = hip (#3 from chart).

I-M-N-O-B = connect with a straight line, as an unfitted line.

F-D = draw front neck from center front. Remember to square to the shoulder for 1/2″ at both F and D to square to the center front a point at D.

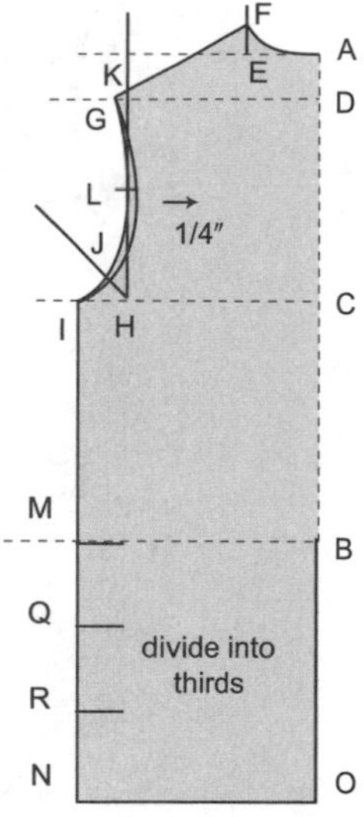

K-L = 1/4″.

G-J-L-I = draw front armhole.

Smooth out the front armhole curve.

Because the sleeve will be drafted on the fold with no difference between the front and back of the sleeve curves, you must compensate for the difference in the body. The front armhole is 1/4″ narrower than the back armhole. This is so you don't have any armhole notches on the sleeve, which will create holes when using such small seam allowances, and is only suitable for knit fabrics because they will stretch to accommodate.

Note that many T-shirt manufacturers do not bother to take in the front armhole at all, and simply create a wider back armhole for both the front of the T-shirt and the back.

Notch waist at side seam.

Trace and separate front and back.

M-N = divide into thirds.

	Extra Extra Small	Extra Small	Small	Medium	Large	Extra Large	Extra Extra Large
Bust	7 7/8	7 7/8	8 3/8	8 7/8	9 7/8	10 3/8	11 3/8
Crotch depth	9 7/8	10	10 1/4	10 1/2	10 3/4	11	11 1/4
Hip	33 1/2	34 1/2	36 1/2	38 1/2	41 1/2	44 1/2	48 1/2
1/2 of hip	8 3/8	8 7/8	9 1/8	9 7/8	10 3/8	11 1/8	12 1/8

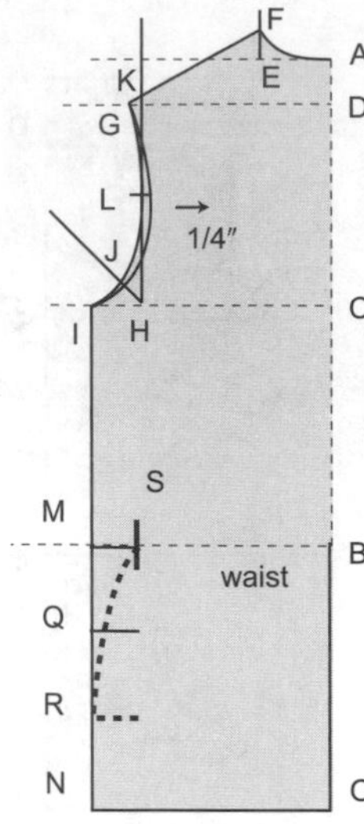

For the fitted waist:

B-S = waist measurement (#2 from chart).

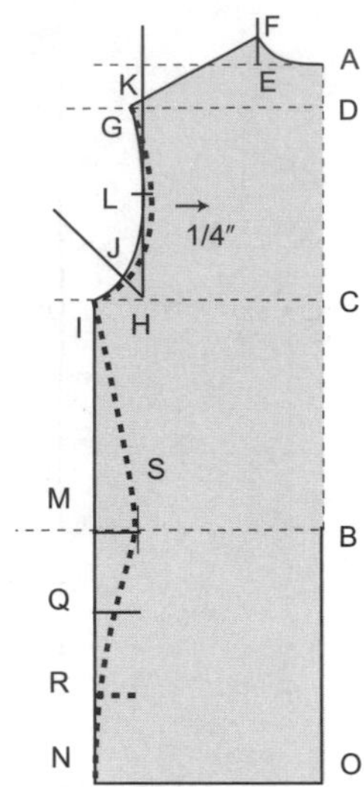

S-R = draw in the hip curve lining up #4 on the variform curve to point S.

The hip curve may change depending on your target market.

Note: This waist may be too tight and too severe for many tops.

I-S-R-N = draw a new curved side seam connecting the point and blending the curves. Blend the waist at the side seam into a curved line.

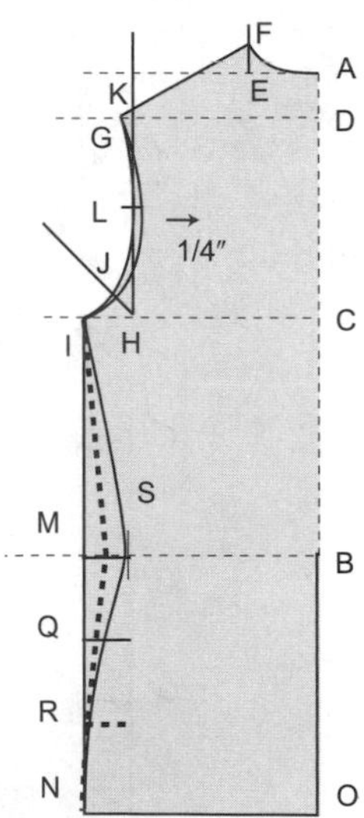

For a semi-fitted waist, draw a line halfway between the extremely fitted and the straight, unfitted waists.

	Extra Extra Small	Extra Small	Small	Medium	Large	Extra Large	Extra Extra Large
Crotch depth	$9\frac{7}{8}$	10	$10\frac{1}{4}$	$10\frac{1}{2}$	$10\frac{3}{4}$	11	$11\frac{1}{4}$
$\frac{1}{3}$ Crotch depth	$3\frac{1}{4}$	$3\frac{3}{8}$	$3\frac{3}{8}$	$3\frac{1}{2}$	$3\frac{7}{8}$	$3\frac{7}{8}$	$3\frac{3}{4}$
Waist	$22\frac{1}{2}$	$23\frac{1}{2}$	$25\frac{1}{2}$	$27\frac{1}{2}$	$30\frac{1}{2}$	$33\frac{1}{2}$	$37\frac{1}{2}$
$\frac{1}{4}$ of waist	$5\frac{7}{8}$	$5\frac{7}{8}$	$6\frac{3}{8}$	$6\frac{7}{8}$	$7\frac{7}{8}$	$8\frac{3}{8}$	$9\frac{3}{8}$

1

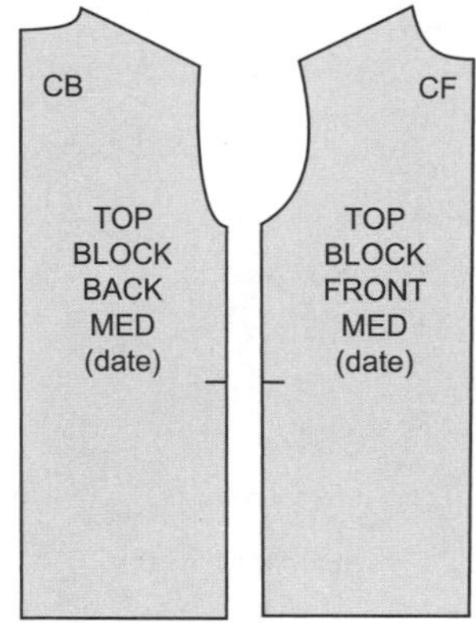

Trace and separate the front and the back top slopers.

2

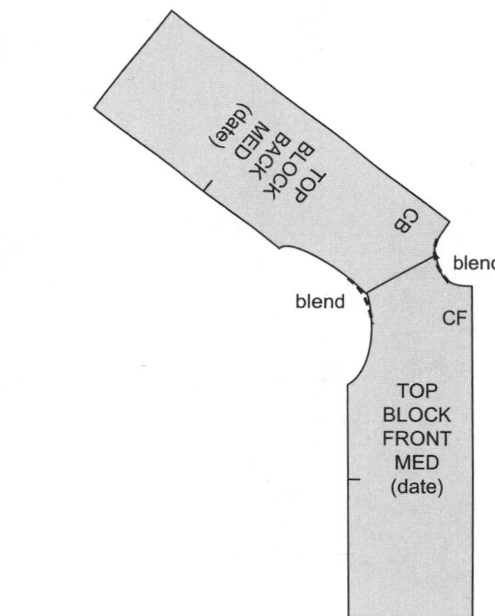

Trueing the one-way-stretch top slopers.

Place the shoulder seams together, as if they had been sewn and pressed open.

Blend a smooth armhole in a continuous line.

Blend a smooth neck in a continuous line.

Check to make sure that the shoulders are exactly the same length.

3

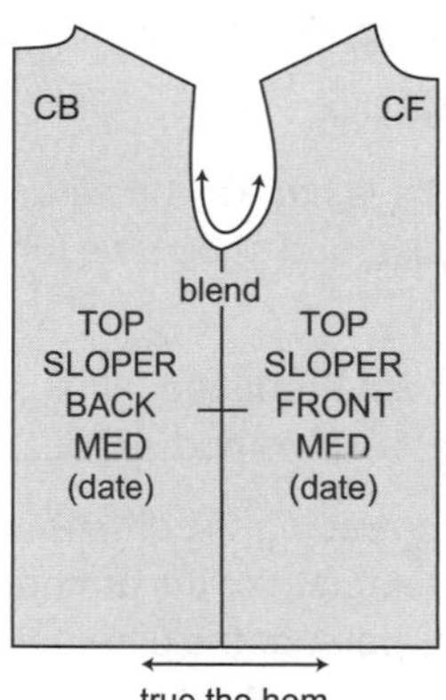

Place the side seams together, beside each other, as if they had been sewn.

Check to ensure that the side seams are exactly the same length and that the waist notches match exactly.

Blend the armhole in a smooth continuous line.

Make sure the hem is a straight line.

Make sure to correct the armhole, if needed, before drafting the sleeve.

4

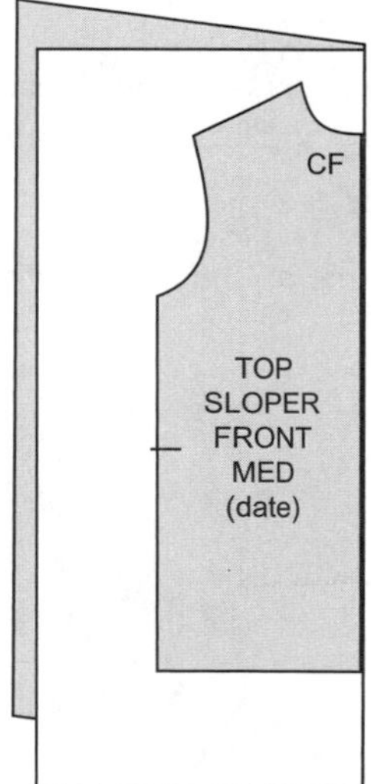

Place the paper draft on folded oak-tag.

Glue, tape, or staple into place.

Cut out all the layers at the same time.

Do not try to cut open and then fold; the edges will never line up.

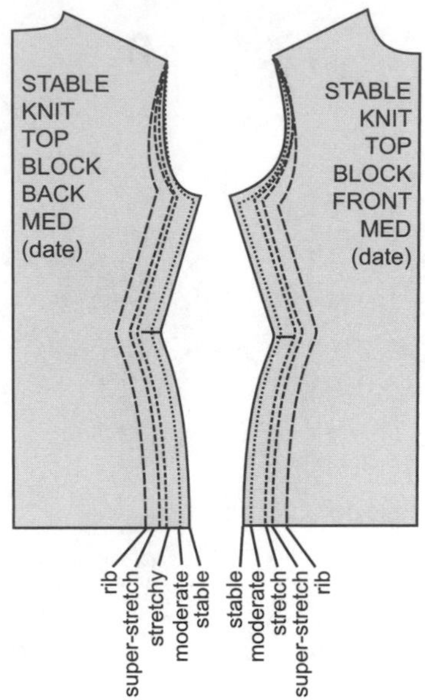

Sloper Labeling

FITTED WAIST

The fitted waist should be cut out since it is much easier to create the unfitted and semi-fitted waist from the fitted sloper, but more difficult to do the reverse.

Trace out the fitted waist and indicate the different stretch ratios.

The fitted waist may be too tight or extreme for many tops but may be necessary for dresses, especially strapless and tube dresses.

The shoulder seam isn't reduced because it will have twill tape (shoulder stay) applied and will not stretch.

UNFITTED WAIST

Label the side seams of the sloper with the additional stretch ratios.

The shoulder seam isn't reduced because it will have twill tape (shoulder stay) applied and will not stretch.

SEMI-FITTED WAIST

The semi-fitted waist is halfway between the fitted waist and the unfitted waist, and should be labeled with the different stretch ratios.

The shoulder seam isn't reduced because it will have twill tape (shoulder stay) applied and will not stretch.

The best method for tracing the different ratios of the armhole is to create a template of the armhole curve and pivot it from the shoulder point to the different ratios.

Stable knit	Moderate knit	Stretchy knit	Super-stretch knit	Rib knit
0	−1/8	−1/4	−1/8	−1/4

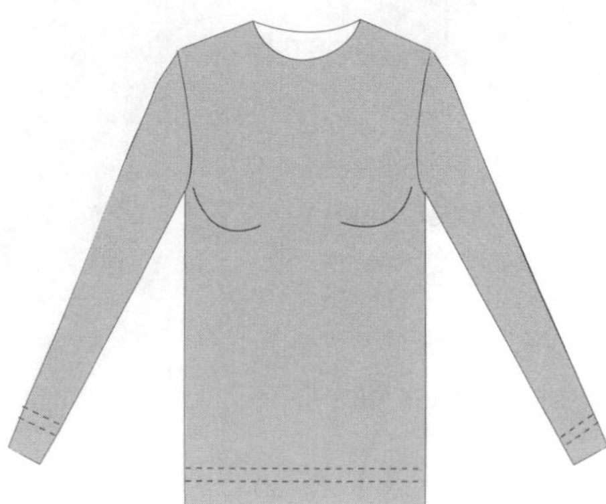

JEWEL NECKLINE

A jewel neckline is simply a round neckline, and will need a facing in order to finish the raw edge along the neckline.

In order for the neckline to be pulled on over the head, it must be enlarged to at least the head size, because once the facing is attached, it will not stretch enough.

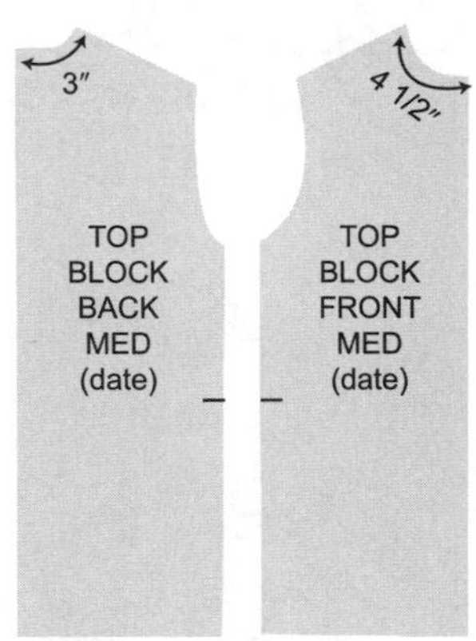

Trace out the unfitted waist of the top blocks, in the stretch ratio of you fabric.

In order for the neckline to be pulled over the head, it must be enlarged to at least 21″, unless a zipper or other opening detail is used to increase the circumference.

In this example the measurement of the total neck is 15″ and it needs to
be 21″.

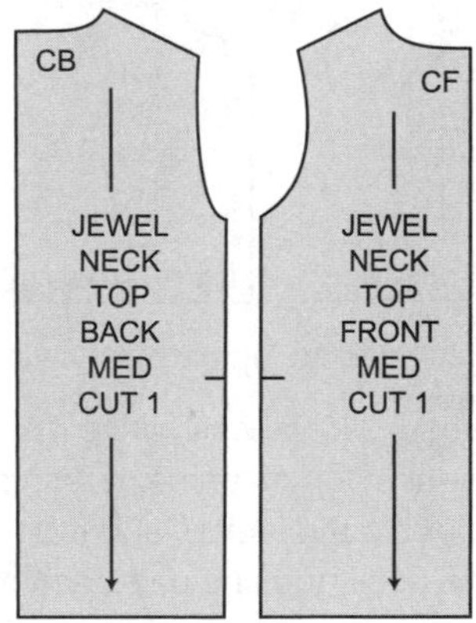

Label the pattern as indicated.

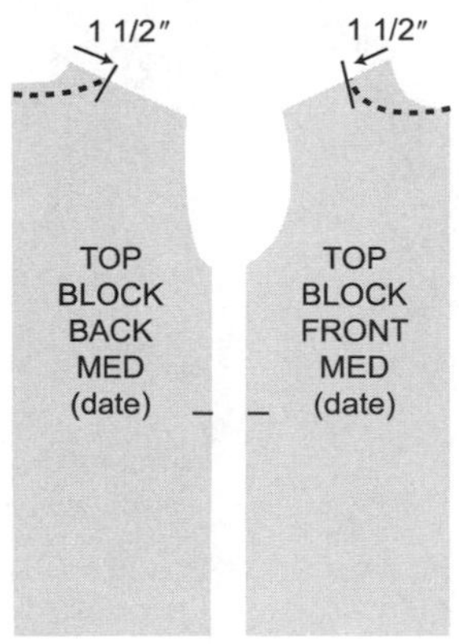

Measure the neck and subtract that amount from 21″ (minimum).

Neckline = 15″.

Subtract from 21″.

Balance = 6″.

Divide by 4 = 1½″ (two fronts and two backs).

Mark the shoulder in 1½″ from the neckline.

Reshape the neck.

Note: Sometimes the center back will be forced lower in order to maintain a smooth and balanced curve.

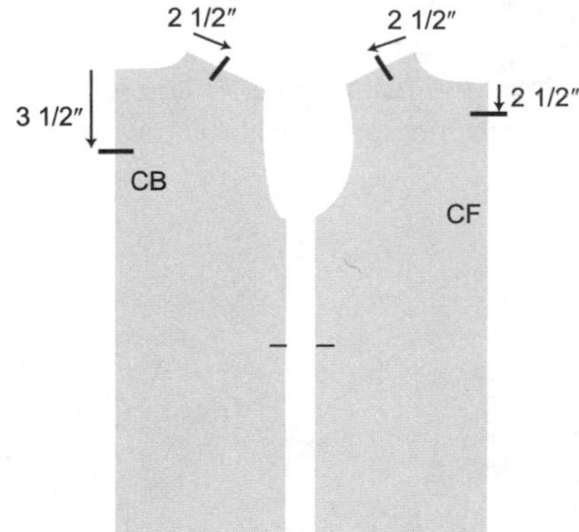

FACING FOR A JEWEL NECKLINE

Measure and mark the shoulders in 2½″ from the neck.

Measure and mark the front neckline down 2½″.

Measure and mark the center back neck down 3½″.

The center back facing is always lower than the front. It helps to keep the facing inside and creates a nice frame for the label.

1

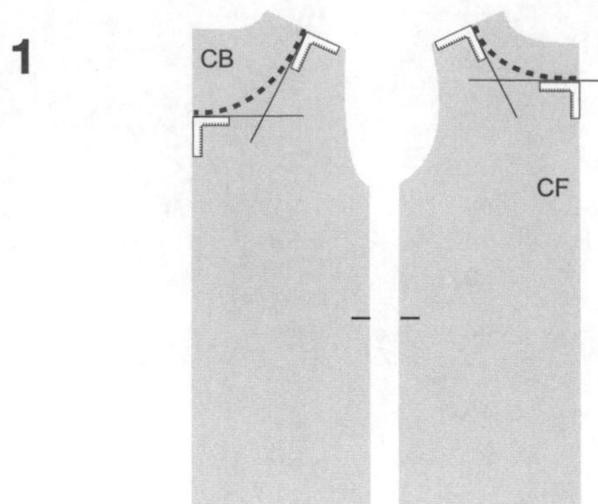

Square guidelines from the shoulder seam and center front/back.

Draw in the facing; remember to square for $\frac{1}{2}$″ at the shoulders and the necklines.

2

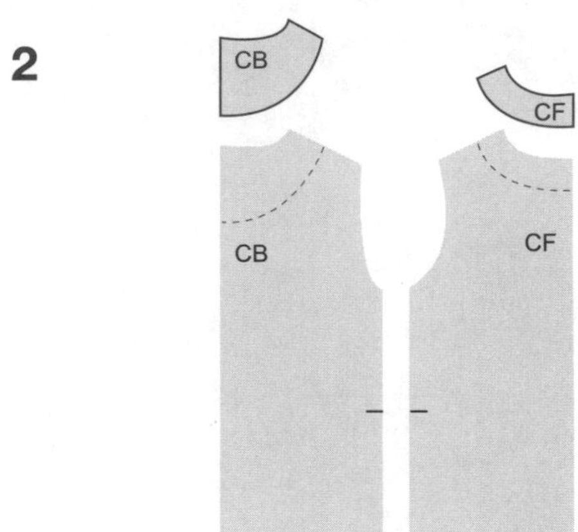

Trace out the facing on a new piece of paper.

3

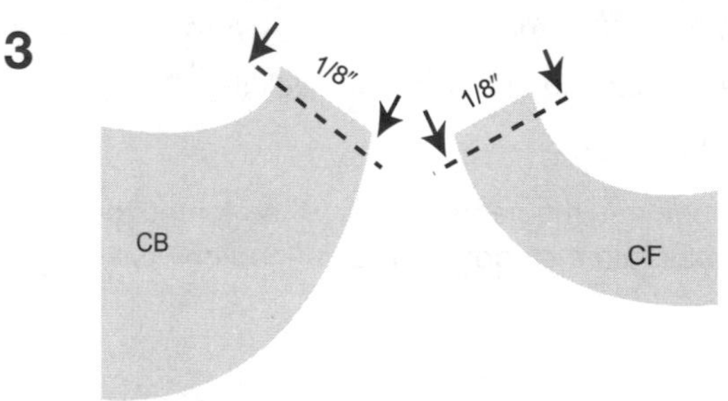

Remove $\frac{1}{8}$″ from the front shoulder line to make the facing slightly smaller so the seams will roll toward the inside of the neck facing.

4

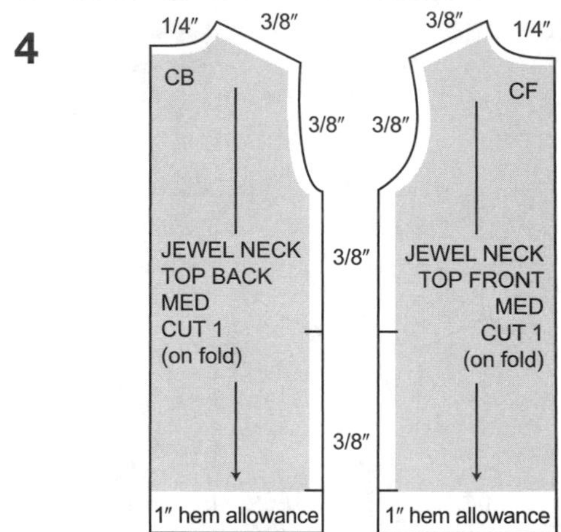

Add the seam allowances as indicated.

The neck has $\frac{1}{2}$″ seam allowances, since it should be sewn with the straight stitch machine. It won't stretch once fusing is applied to the facing, and it doesn't need to stretch because the neck opening had been made wider.

5

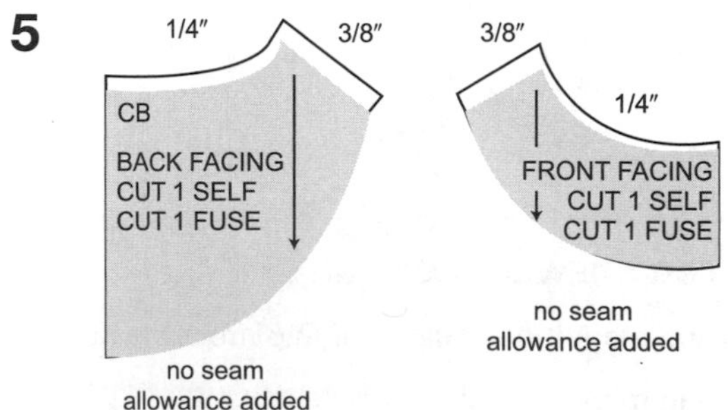

Add $\frac{1}{2}$″ seam allowances to the shoulder seams.

Add $\frac{1}{4}$″ seam allowance to the neckline edge.

No seam allowance needed for the outside edge of the facing, because it will not be sewn to anything and merely lies inside the garment.

Label the pattern:

Cut 1 self

Cut 1 fusing-tricot

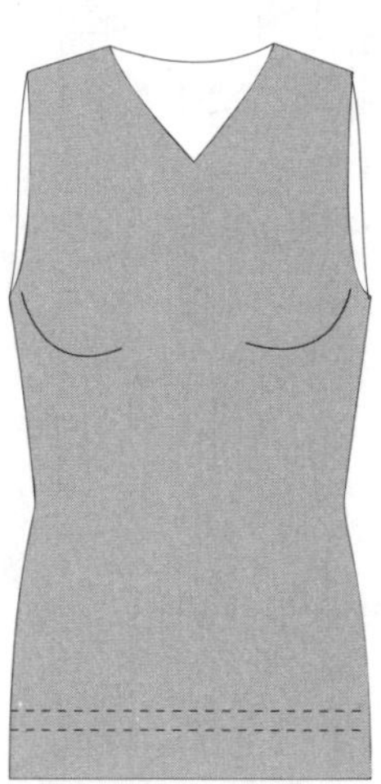

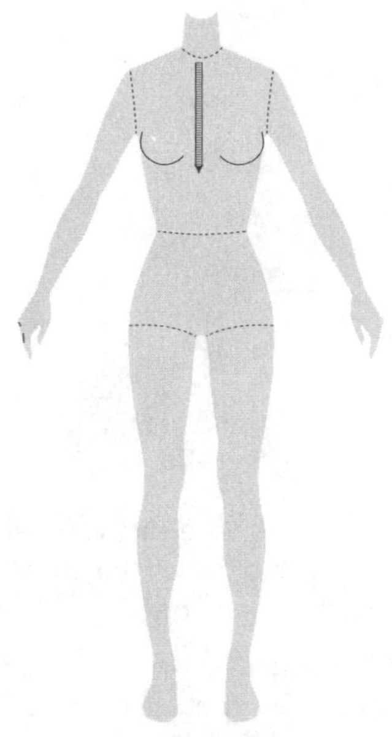

V-NECK WITH FACING

The V-neck does not have to be enlarged if the V is low enough that the head can fit through the opening.

Remember that the V-neck can be as low as your design requires.

To determine how low the V-neck will be, measure down on the dress-form, from the center front neckline downwards, and apply that measurement to the draft.

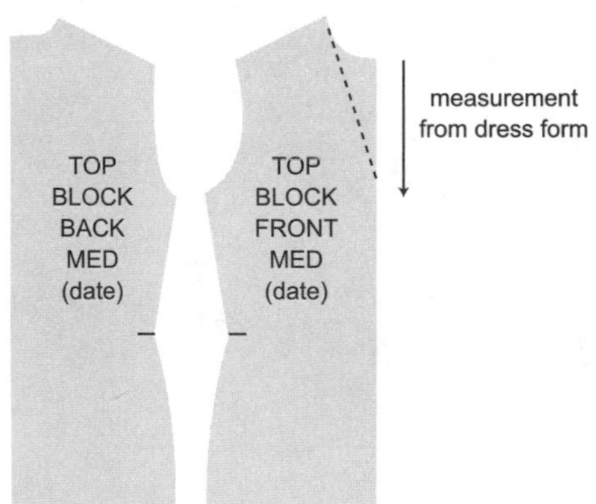

Measure down on the draft the measurement from the dress-form.

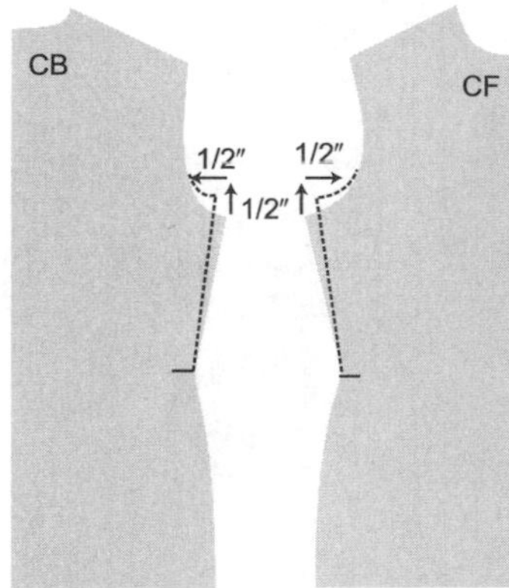

Trace out the semi-fitted waist in the stretch ratio of your fabric.

Because there is no sleeve inserted into the armhole, you must raise and take in the underarm ½″ to prevent undergarments from showing, and the sides of the breast from falling out, or showing.

Other ways to tighten this area—binding that is slightly smaller, elastic, or banding—will be discussed later in this chapter.

1

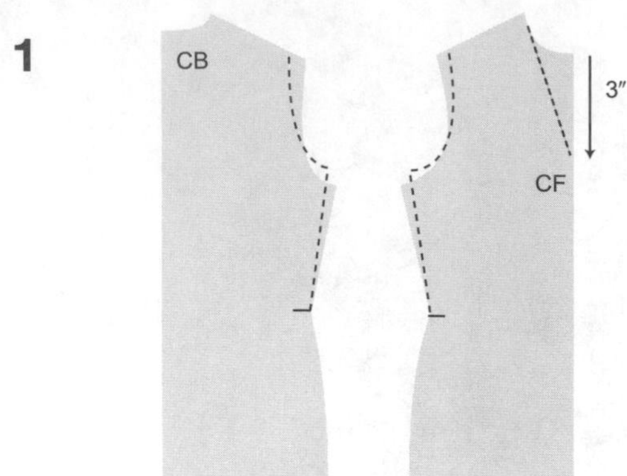

Because the garment is sleeveless, you also must bring in the shoulder a minimum of 1/2″ so the ends of the shoulder seam don't hang off the shoulders.

Remember that the armholes were drafted for sleeves to be attached. Draw a new armhole in any shape you desire.

Create a V-neck as low as you wish, illustrated here at 3″.

To determine the depth of the V-neck, simply measure down from the neck point on the dress-form to how low you wish the neck to be.

2

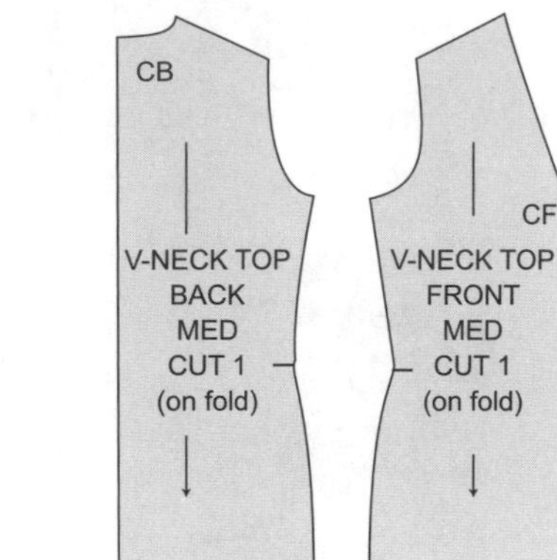

Label the pattern as indicated.

3

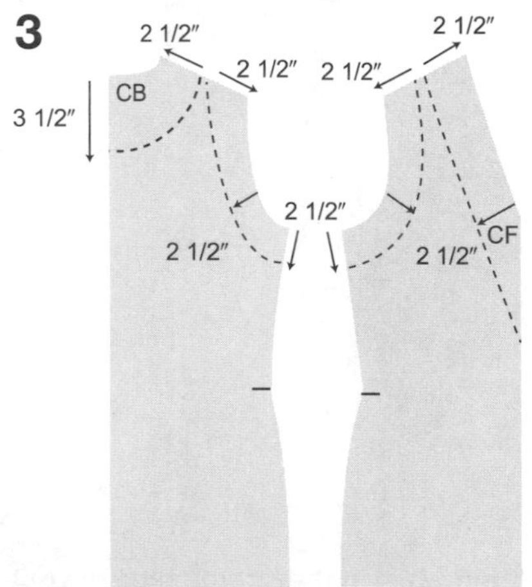

Create the facings as separate pieces as shown.

The center back facing should be 3 1/2″ low; this gives room for the label and looks more appealing when on the hanger.

All other facings should be at least 2 1/2″ wide.

4

It doesn't look very nice to see the back facing when the garment is on the hanger.

In higher-priced garments, create the back facing long enough so the facing edge is 2 1/2″ lower than the front V-neckline.

Shown here with sleeves to indicate the back facing only. If creating sleeveless garments, combine the armhole and neck facings, as will be illustrated.

Your price point and target market will determine this.

5

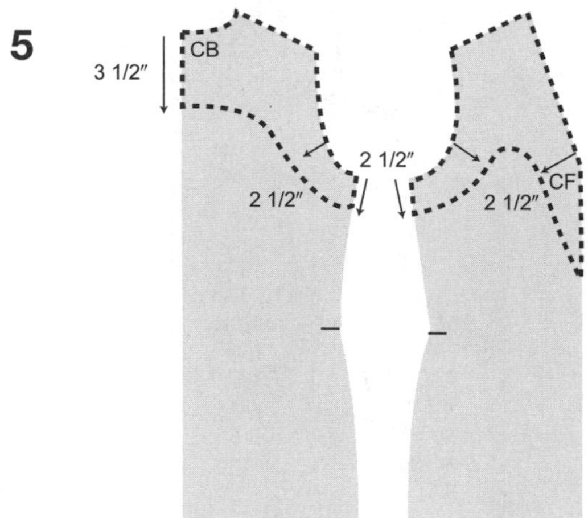

Create the facing in one piece, $2^1/_2$″ away from the neck and armholes.

Curve the lower edge shape so it doesn't show through. A straight line would show through the garment as a bold line, but if you curve it slightly it will not show through as easily when worn, especially after being pressed a few times.

A one-piece facing prevents sewing errors and is easier to cut. It also has a much better hanger appeal.

6

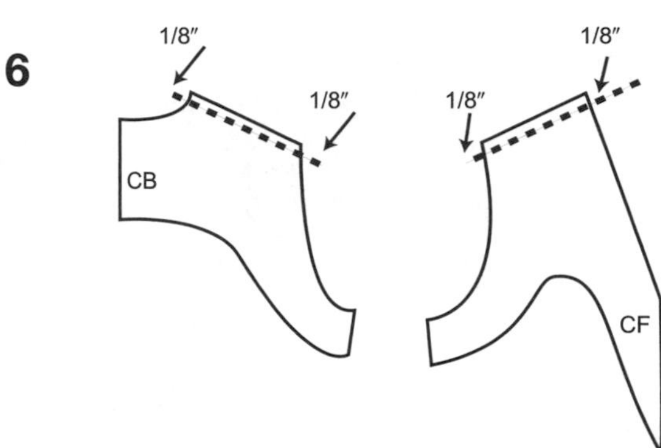

Remove ⅛″ from the shoulder seams to make the facing slightly smaller, since it is on the inside of the garment and is therefore slightly smaller. This helps to pull the seam edges slightly inward.

7

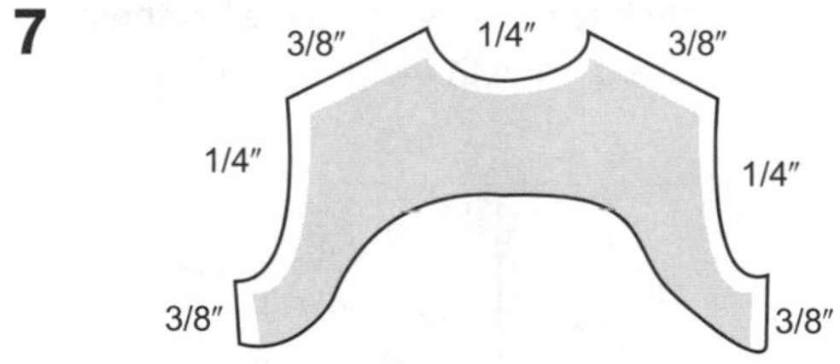

Add seam allowances to the back facing as indicated.

⅜″ for the shoulders and side seams.

¼″ for the armholes and neck.

The inside edges do not require any seam allowance because they will not be sewn to anything.

8

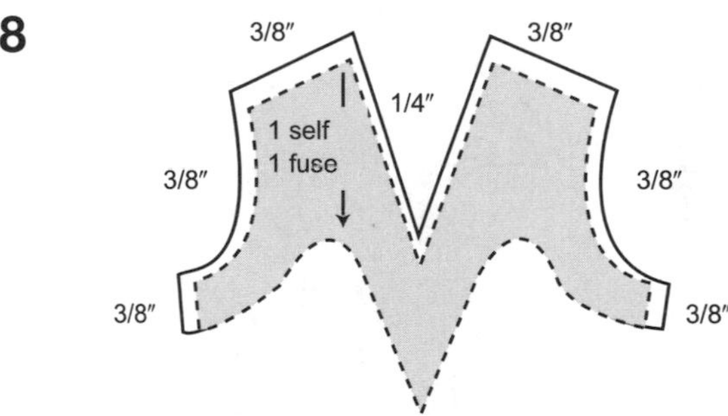

The front facing is as illustrated, in one piece.

Add seam allowances to the front facing as shown.

9

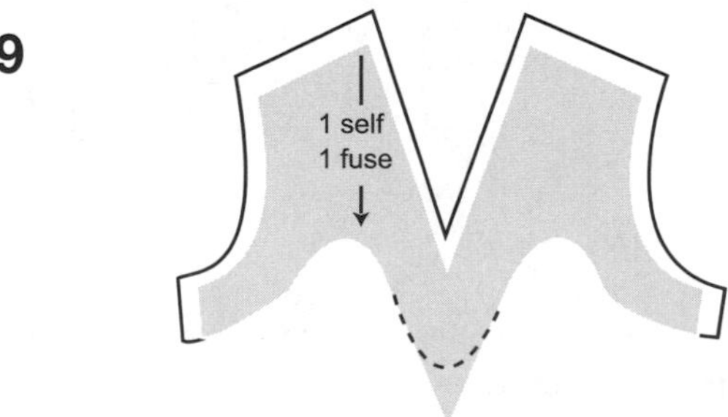

The V-point on the facing edge may be curved for easier and faster serging. This enables the operator to serge in one step, all the way around, rather than two steps, once in each direction.

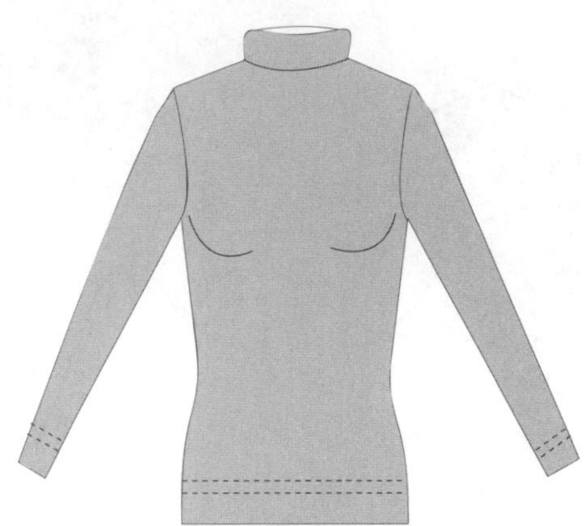

MOCK NECK

A mock neck, or mock turtleneck, T-shirt is a short turtleneck where the collar does not fold back down.

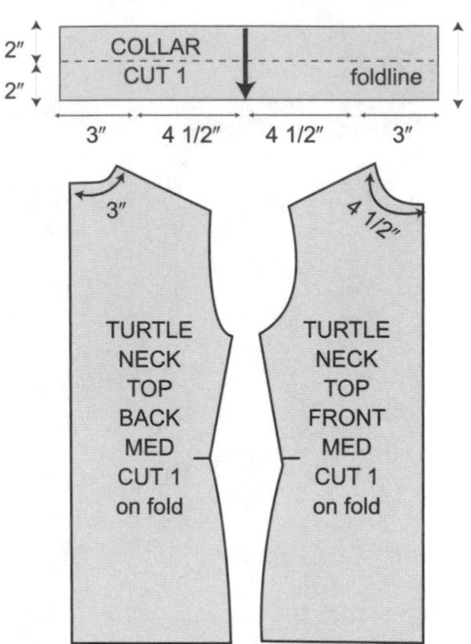

Draft the collar pattern to any height desired, but mock neck collars tend to be 3″ and under. If longer, we often refer to them incorrectly as turtlenecks.

The length is determined by the total neckline measurement, without any reductions, because the collar should stand up, not lie flat.

Note: This draft must be doubled to encircle the entire neckline. You have only measured half the draft.

The collar should only have one seam, either at the center back or, preferably, lined up with the left shoulder seam.

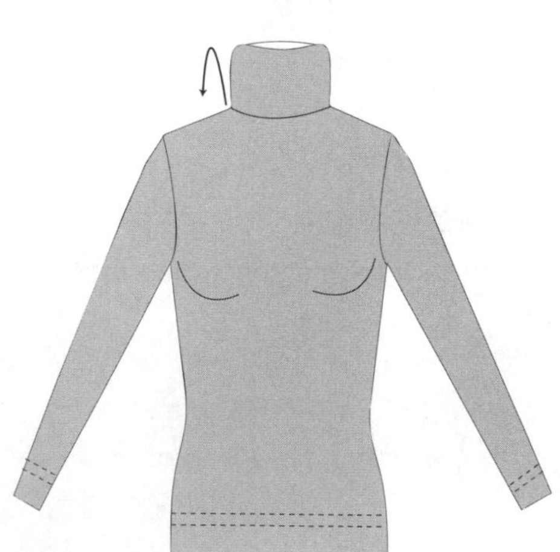

TURTLENECK

A turtleneck T-shirt has a higher collar than the mock-neck and is intended to fold down over itself.

People tend to refer to any type of mock-neck collar that is over 2½″–3″ as a turtleneck.

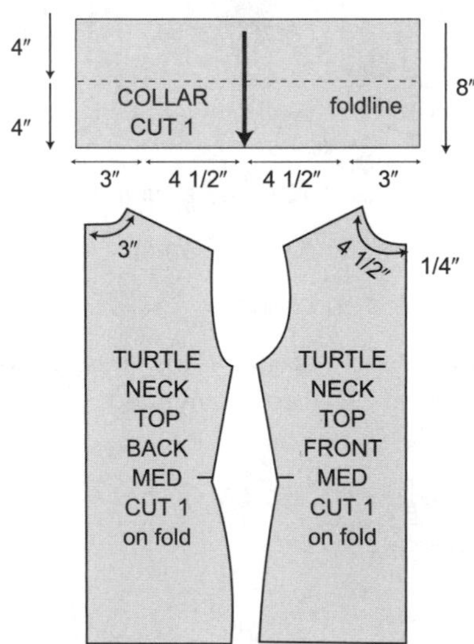

Draft the collar pattern to any height desired, but turtleneck collars are usually over 2″.

The length is determined by the total neckline measurement, without any reductions, because the collar should stand up, not lie flat.

Note: This draft must be doubled to encircle the entire neckline. You have only measured half the draft.

The collar should only have one seam, either at the center back or, preferably, lined up with the left shoulder seam.

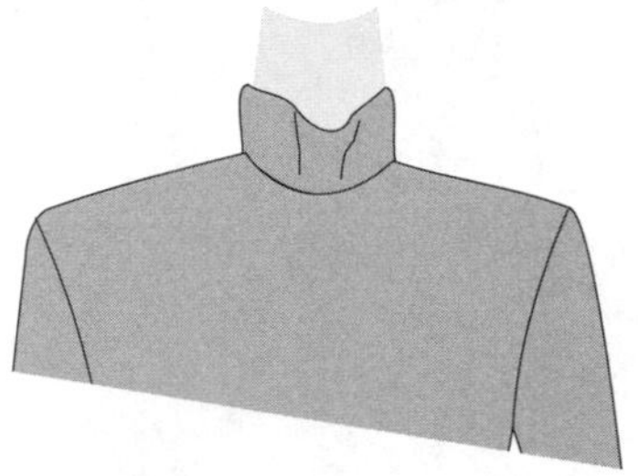

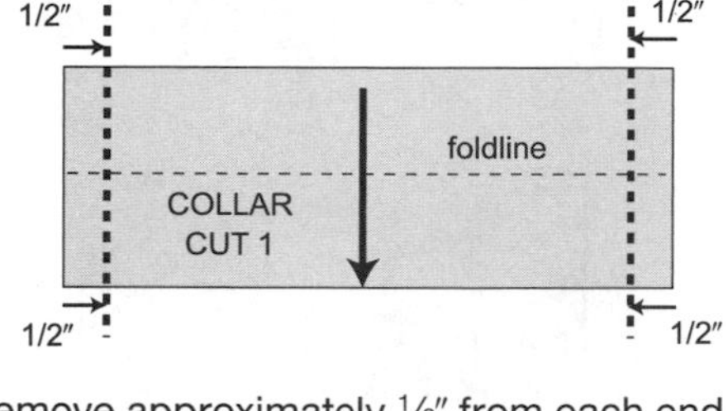

CORRECTING THE FIT OF A TURTLENECK COLLAR

Because the customer's neck is wider at the base than at the top, using the exact neckline measurement from the draft will create a collar that gapes at the top, standing away from the neck. You can leave the draft as is or make a slight correction to the fit.

To correct this, pinch out the extra amount, measure it, and remove that amount from the pattern as illustrated.

Or simply remove approximately ½″ from each end of the collar pattern.

The top of the collar is now smaller and will fit snug to the neckline.

The edge that attaches to the sweater is also smaller and must be stretched to fit into the neckline.

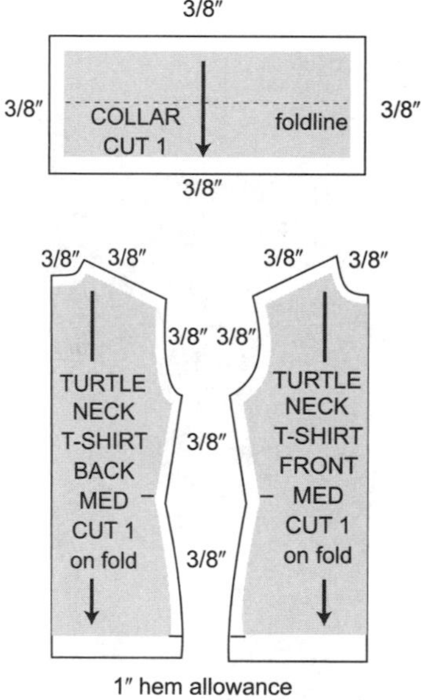

Add seam allowances and label the pattern as indicated in the Mock Necks section.

The seam of the collar should line up with either the center back or the neckline or, preferably, the left shoulder seam. Always the left, where it is less noticeable.

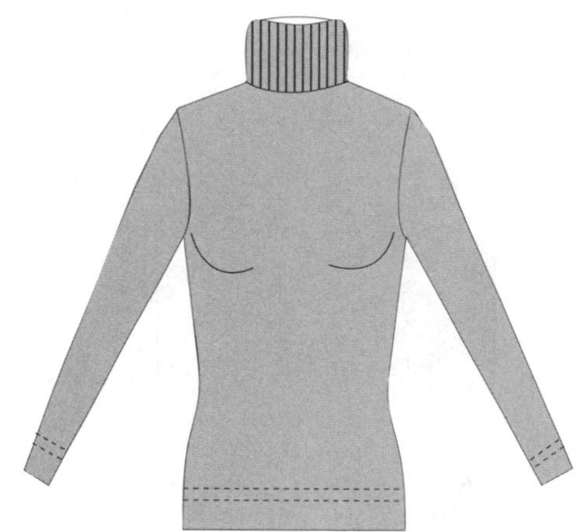

OTHER TURTLENECK COLLAR CORRECTIONS

If your fabric does not stretch enough for the collar to pull on over the head, you have several options to correct the collar. Use whichever method your collar demands.

Use a matching rib fabric, which will stretch enough to fit over the head.

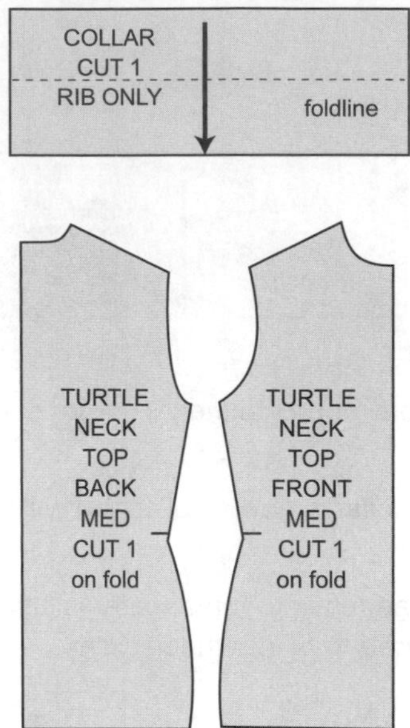

Use the same pattern piece, exactly as is, but it may not be snug enough.

Or reduce the width of the pattern by 10% for a snug fit.

Insert a zipper or other closure in the collar, so the neckline can be opened up to get the garment on and off the body.

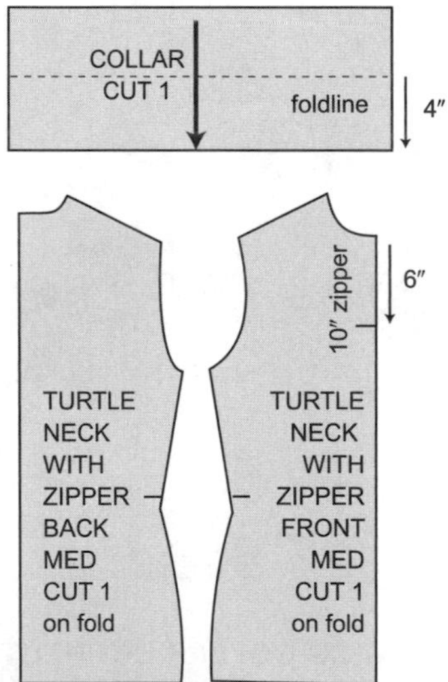

The zipper should be a total of 10″, with 4″ inserted into the collar and 6″ inserted into the front of the top.

The next illustration shows how to indicate the zipper opening.

When the zipper opening is cut out, the cutter should only cut 3″ down so the operator can cut the remaining 3″ at the machine.

Sometimes zippers may be a single tooth longer or a single tooth shorter than the actual measurement, which would leave a hole in the front, so let the sewing machine operator cut the balance of the opening while at the machine.

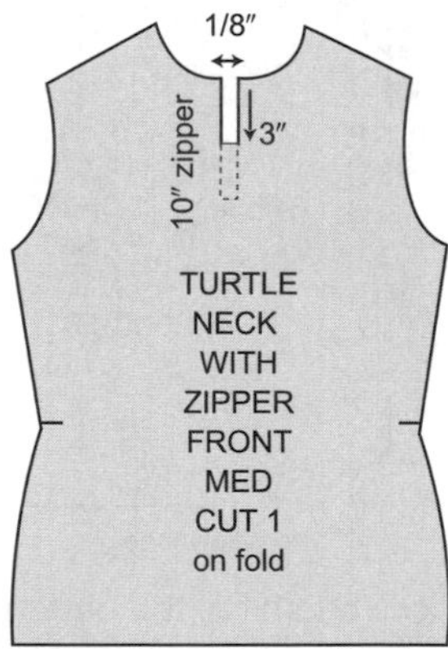

To indicate a zipper opening on the pattern, remove a slit ⅛″ wide half the length of the zipper.

The slit is made ⅛″ wide, like a notch, so the marker maker can trace into the slit area. There is room for the mechanical pencil.

Sometimes zippers may be a single tooth longer or a single tooth shorter than the actual measurement, which would leave a hole in the front, so let the sewing machine operator cut the balance.

Label the pattern with the length of zipper that should be purchased, not the length of the notch/slit, so the production manager and cutter can ensure that they have enough zippers in stock before cutting out thousands of garments.

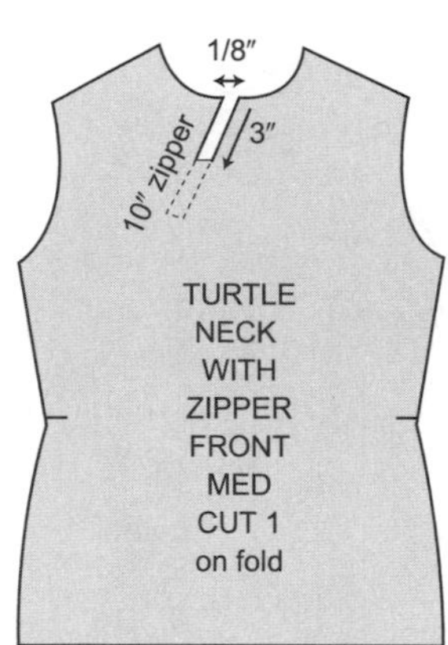

Your design may require inserting the zipper on an angle. The operators will not know that you want it cut in this direction, unless you tell them.

Indicate the slit in the place that you wish the zipper to be inserted.

Alternatively, some patternmakers use drill marks to indicate the bottom of the zipper. Drill marks aren't very dependable on knit fabric, and may create holes or runs in your garments, so they should be avoided if possible. There are times when there is no other way to indicate a detail other than with a drill mark, which should be marked with chalk.

Enlarge the collar slightly and ease it into the neckline. Use this technique for very small amounts only, otherwise your collar seam will pucker.

This will also depend on your fabric, as some knits, especially shiny ones, will visually exaggerate even the slightest amount of ease.

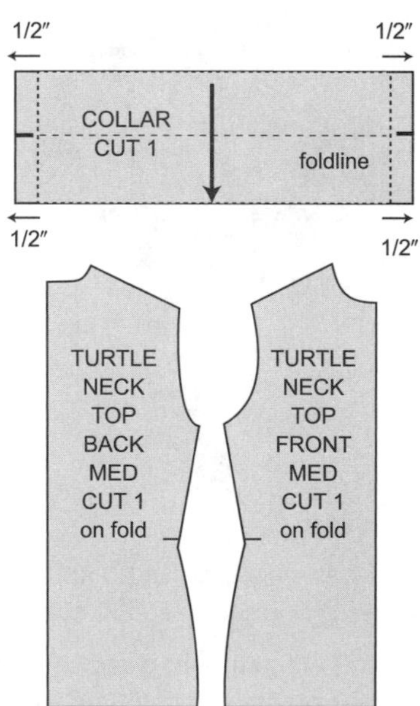

Enlarge the width of the collar, a maximum of $\frac{1}{2}$″ on each side, for a total maximum of 1″ wider.

If you make the collar any wider, it may not ease into the neckline without showing gathers and puckers.

Enlarge the neckline wider, and the collar accordingly; however, the collar will sit slightly away from the neck.

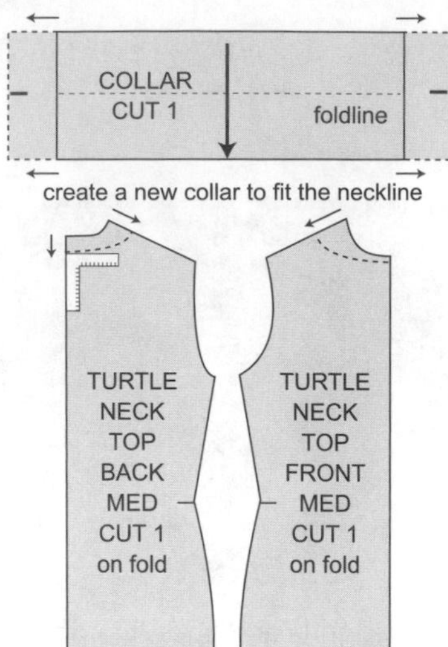

Widen the collar as much as necessary, or as much as you desire. However, have a shoulder seam of at least ½″ to prevent the top from sliding off the customer's shoulders.

In order to maintain a smooth curve on the back neckline, it may be necessary to lower the back neckline. If so, remember to keep the center back neckline square.

Create a new collar to fit the new widened neckline.

An extremely wide neckline may be created to make the top very easy to get on and off, or as a design feature.

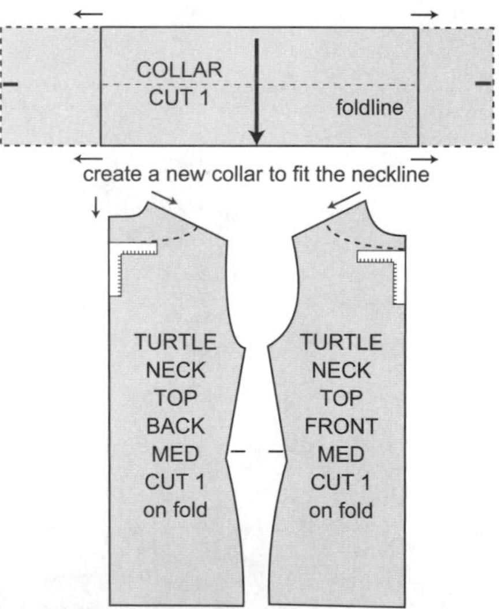

Widen the collar as much as necessary, or as much as you desire. However, have a shoulder seam of at least ½″ to prevent the top from sliding off the customer's shoulders.

In order to maintain a smooth curve on the back and front neckline, it may be necessary to lower both. If so, remember to keep the center back and center front necklines square.

Create a new collar to fit the new widened neckline.

CREW-NECK T-SHIRT

To create a crew-neck T-shirt, use rib knit for the collar in order for it to stretch enough to lie flat against the neck.

It may be difficult for the student designer to find matching jersey and rib, and you may have to use a contrast colored collar.

Knitting mills often sell matching ribs, trims, and polo collars that match the fabric. However, the student or new designer may not have access to these supplies and will have to use contrast fabrics.

Alternatively, crew-neck T-shirts can be created entirely utilizing rib fabrics: rib body and rib collar.

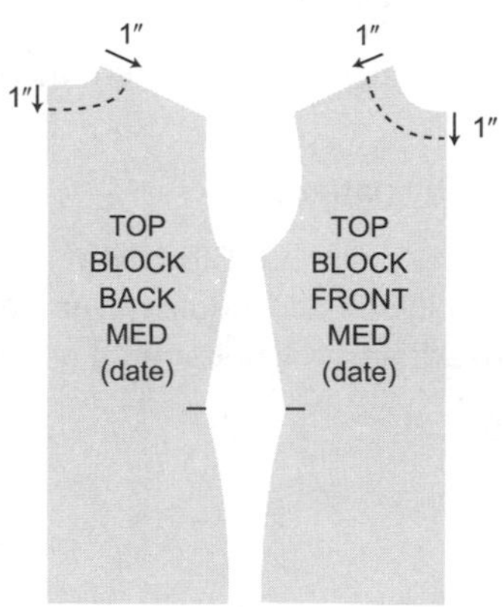

Draw the neck seam 1″ parallel to the front and back necklines, below the neckline.

Remove 1″ from the T-shirt draft parallel to and below the original neckline.

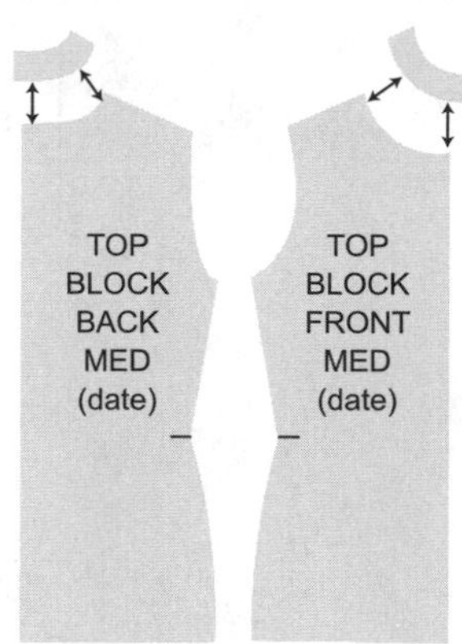

These sections will be discarded from the final patterns, and should be erased after they are measured.

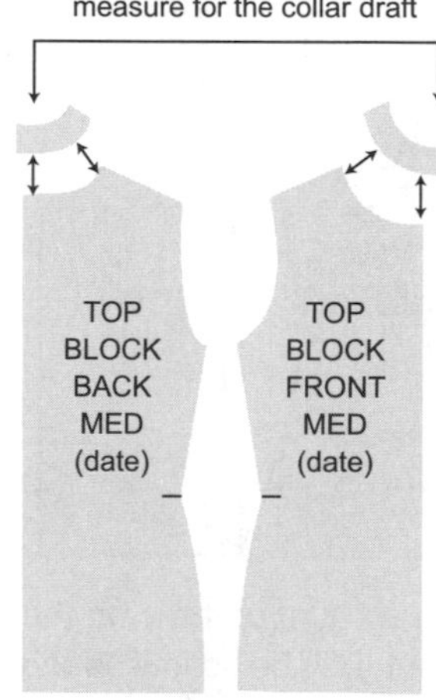

Measure and record the neck edge of the discarded pieces in order to draft the rib collar.

Measure the smaller, inside curve—the original neckline—of the block, so the final collar will lie flat.

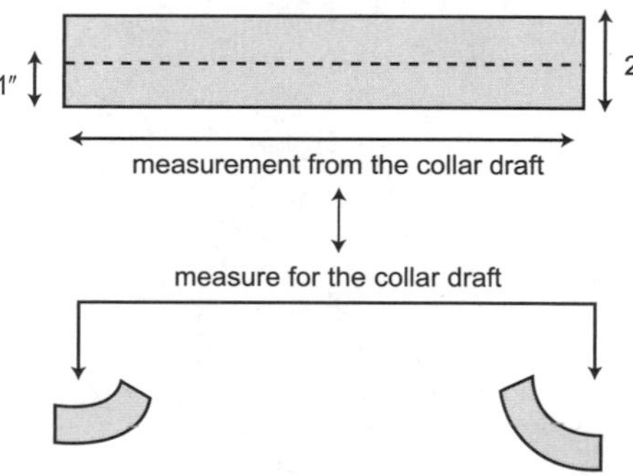

Sew the neckline measurement to draft the rib collar.

Note that the rib collar is smaller than the new neckline it will be sewn to and must be slightly stretched in order to fit.

Also note that some rib fabrics are much more stretchy than others and may need to be reduced further in order to lie flat.

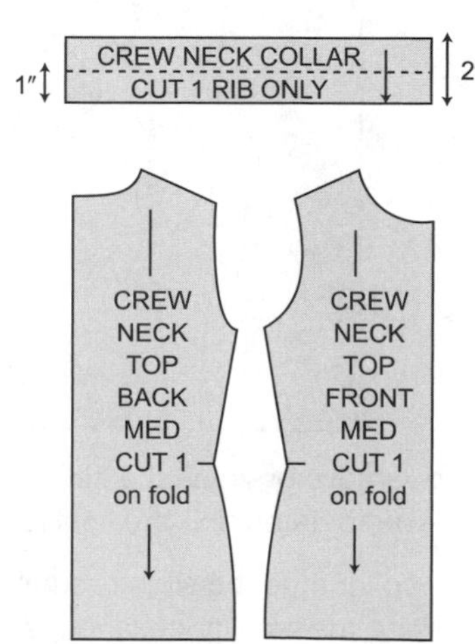

Draft the collar twice as wide as needed, since it will be folded in half and both edges sewn to the neckline.

The collar will have only one seam, at the center back, or preferably at the left shoulder.

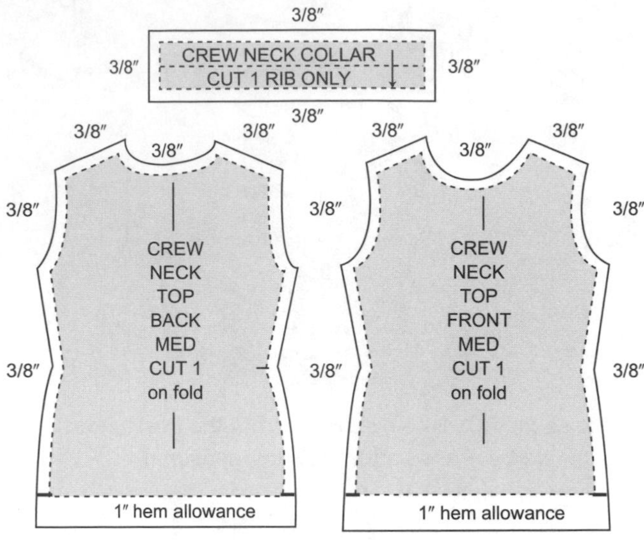

Add 3/8″ seam allowances to the pattern as illustrated, for four-thread sergers.

Add a 1″ hem to the pattern.

Be sure to label the collar as "RIB ONLY"; otherwise, the collar may be cut in self and would never stretch enough to fit over the head, and will not stretch enough to sew to the neckline.

V-NECK T-SHIRT

Determine how low you wish the V-neck to be by measuring on the dress-form from the neck down.

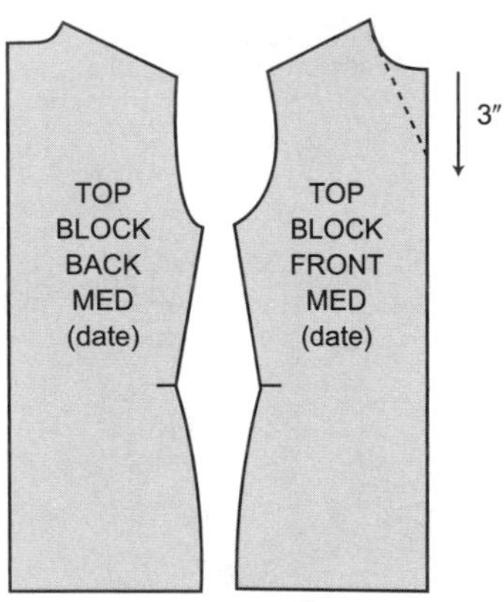

Indicate the depth amount of the V on the pattern, illustrated here at 3″ but may be as low as the design requires.

To determine how low you wish the V-neck to be, measure down the neckline of the dress-form.

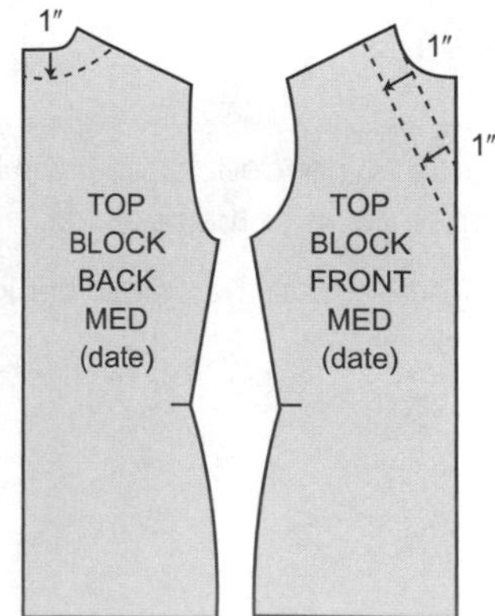

Draw the collar on the draft 1″ parallel to the neckline.

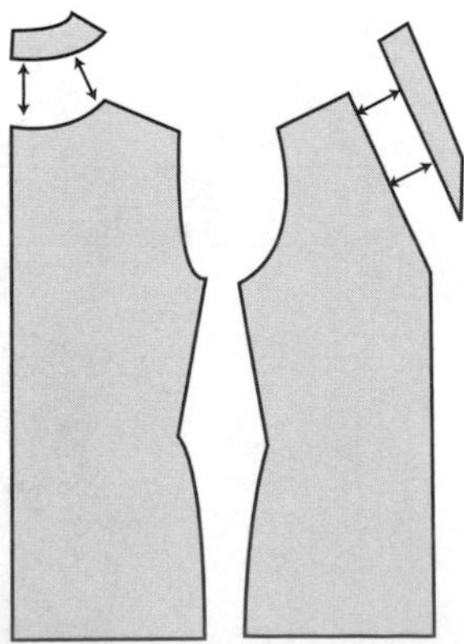

Measure, record, and remove or erase the collar portion from the draft. Measure the inside edge to determine the final length of the collar.

In order to lie flat, the collar must be slightly smaller than the neck seam. This is done by recording the smaller collar edge.

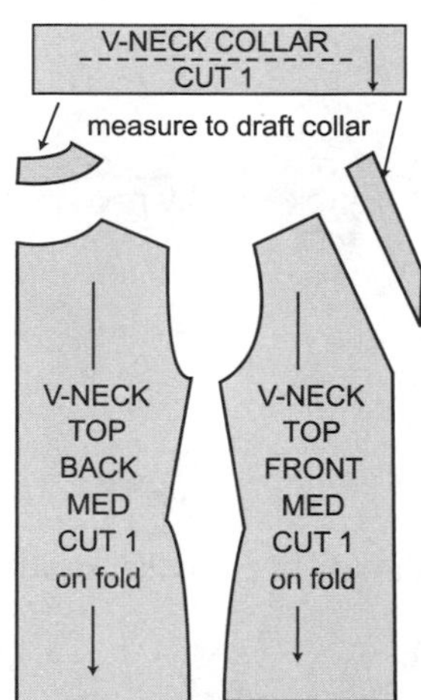

Measure the discarded piece in order to determine the length of the collar pattern.

The rib will be stretched to fit the neck opening, which will force it to lie flat.

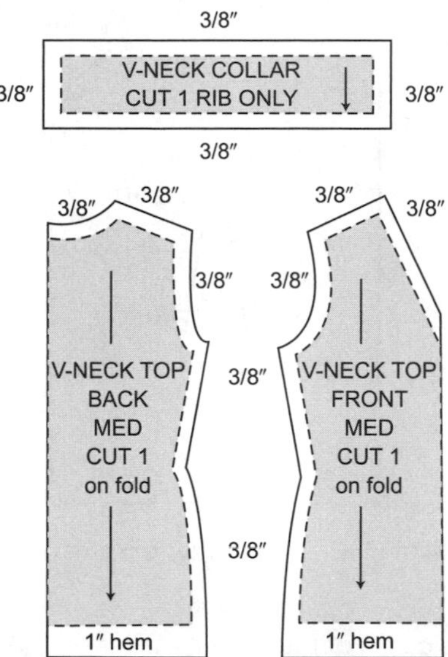

Add seam allowances and label the pattern as illustrated.

Label the collar as "RIB ONLY" to ensure that the collar does not get cut out in self fabric, which would not allow it to stretch enough to fit the neckline.

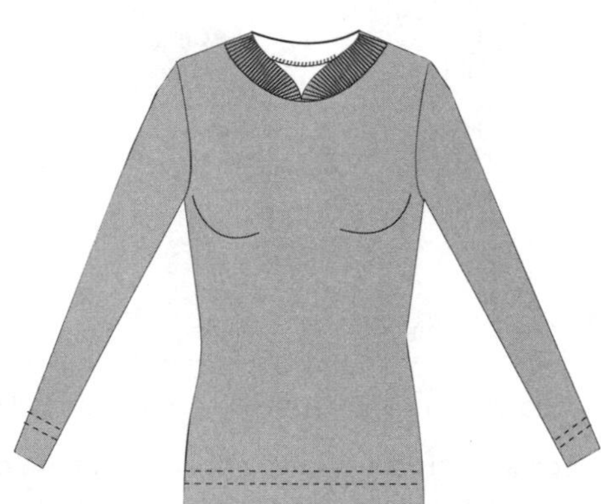

V-NECK CREW

The V-neck crew is a variation of both the crew and the V-neck.

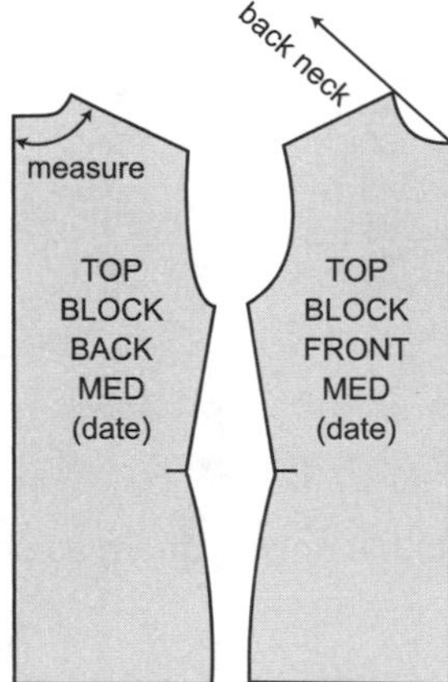

Line up the ruler with the center front and the shoulder point of the neckline.

Extend the line the length of the back neck measurement.

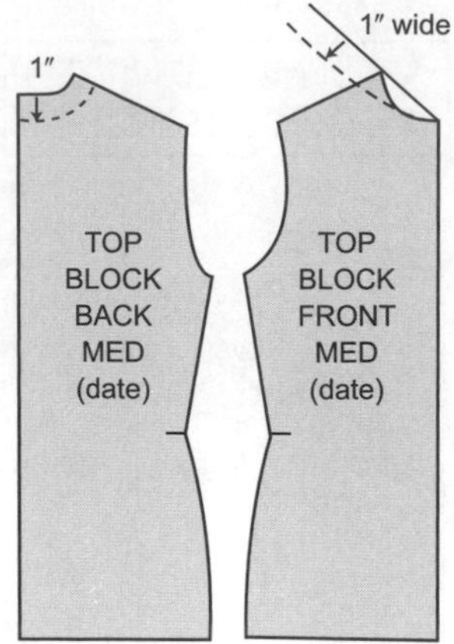

Make the collar 1″ wide and draw the line parallel to the previous line.

Blend to the curve of the front neckline.

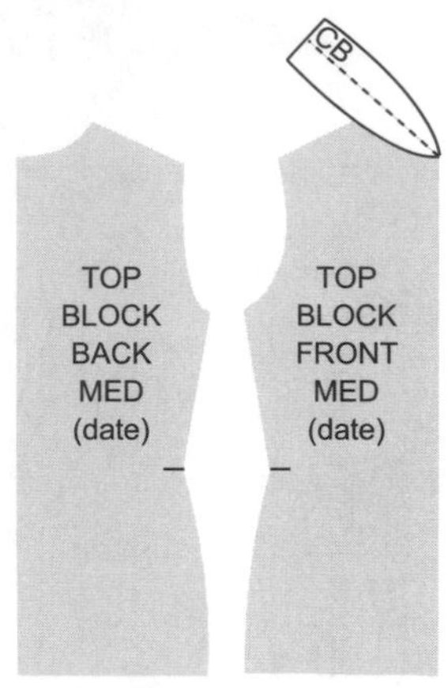

Trace out the other side of the collar draft.

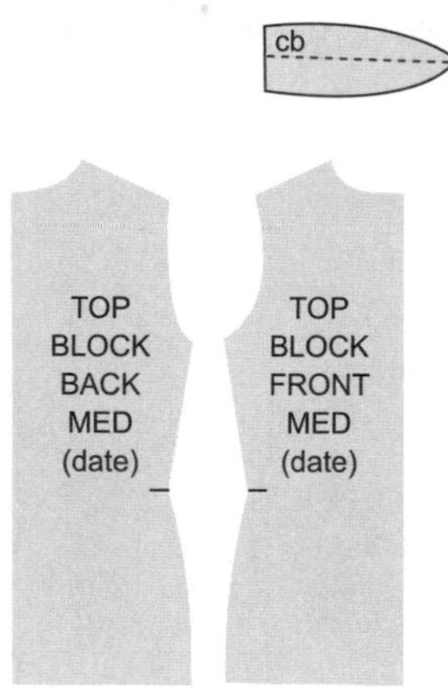

Trace and separate the collar pattern as shown.

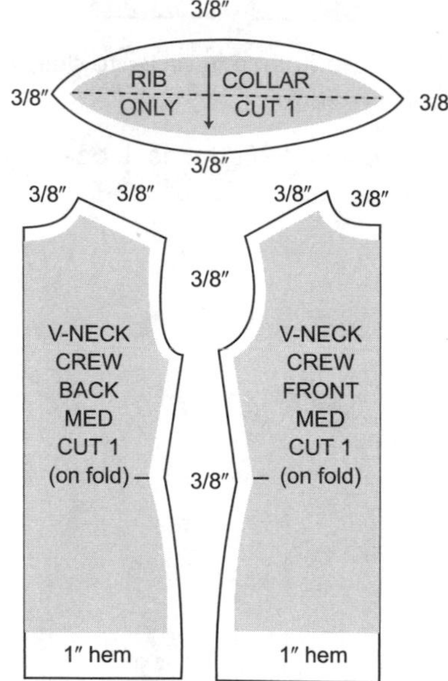

Add seam allowances and label the pattern as indicated.

Label the collar as "RIB ONLY" to ensure that the collar does not get cut out in self fabric, which would not allow it to stretch enough to fit the neckline.

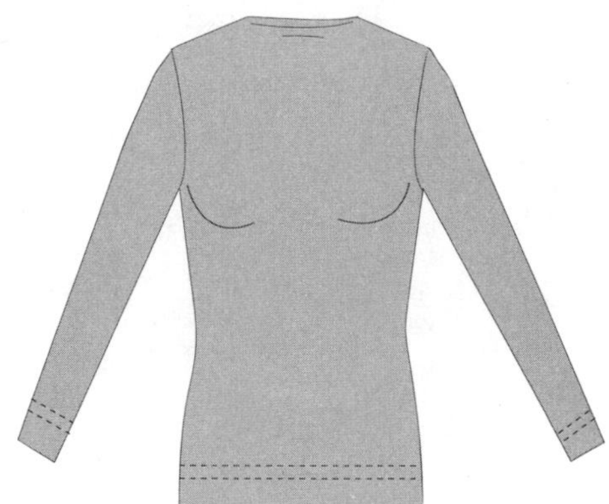

BOATNECK T-SHIRT

This boatneck is a very simple neckline to draft, and is often the basis for many cowl necklines.

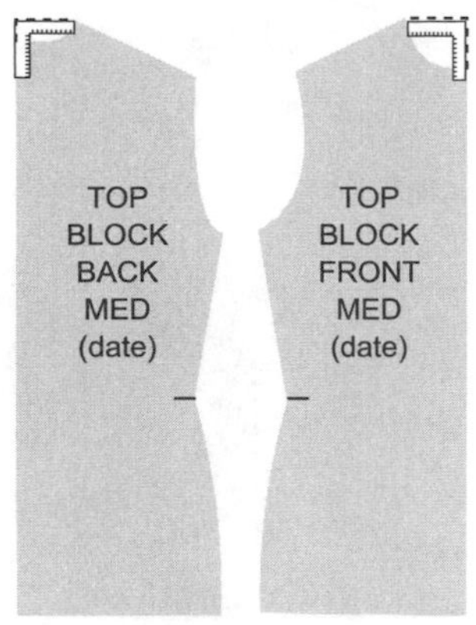

Square up the center front and back.

Square across the center front and back to line up with the shoulder point.

It appears as if this high boatneck will choke the customer, but the fabric will stretch across to allow room and comfort.

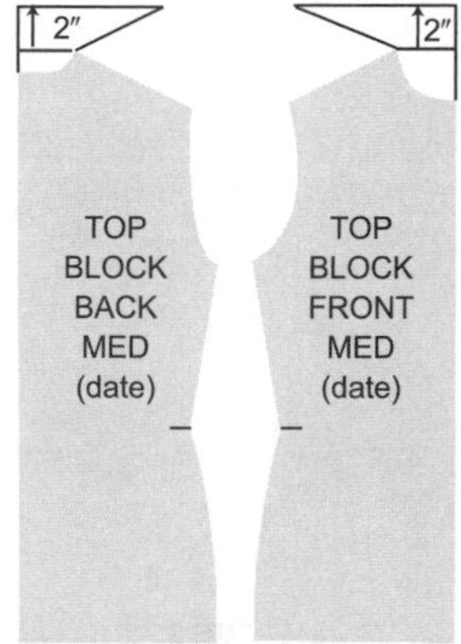

Add a 2″ hem or foldback facing to the neckline.

Fold your paper along the neckline and trace with tracing wheel to true the sides of the hem/facing so they match the shoulder line.

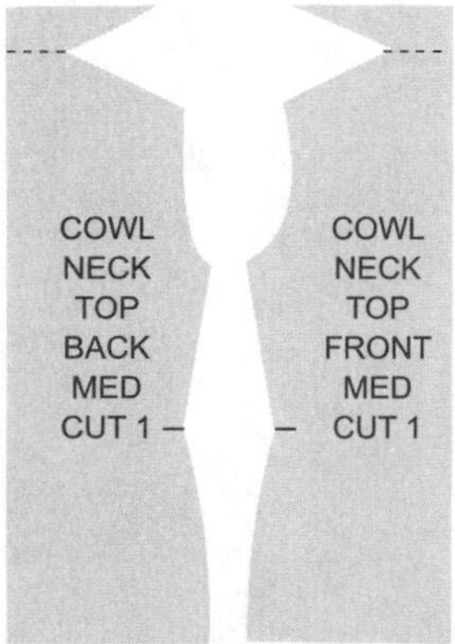

Trace out the completed pattern as illustrated.

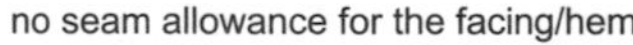

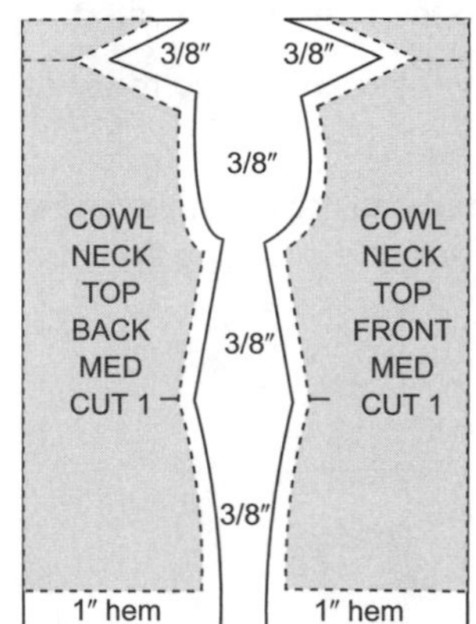

Add the required seam allowances and label as indicated.

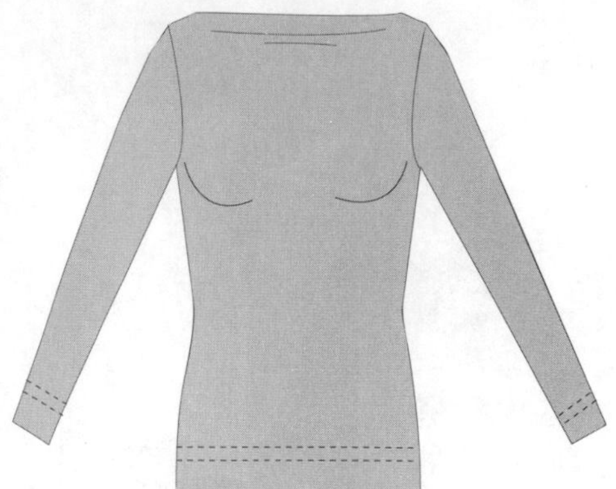

WIDE BOATNECK

The same boatneck can be drafted farther away from the neck and will not be as high as the previous draft, and may be more comfortable.

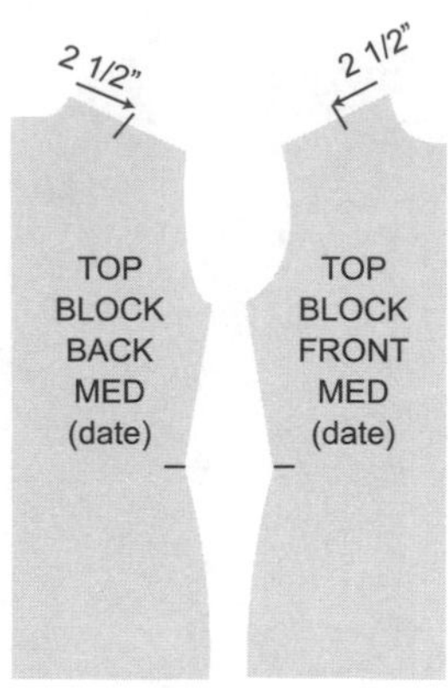

Measure in from the neck, any amount, but at least 1/2" away from the armhole so the armhole seam allowances don't show at the neckline, and especially if sleeves are to be attached.

Illustrated here at 2", but may be any amount the design requires.

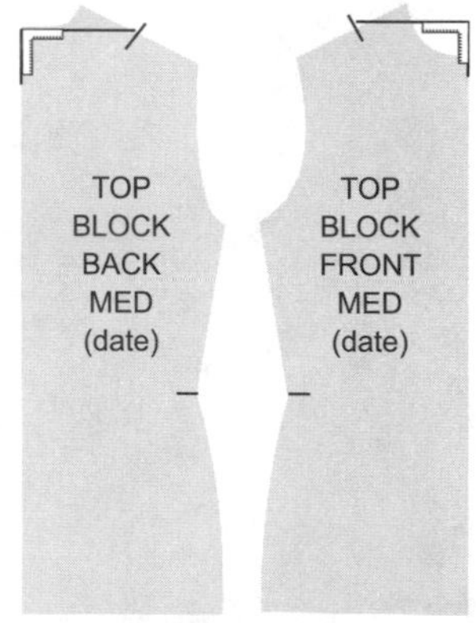

Square a line up the center front and back.

Square a line across to meet the other line.

The back neckline may have to be slightly lowered to accommodate the new boatneck.

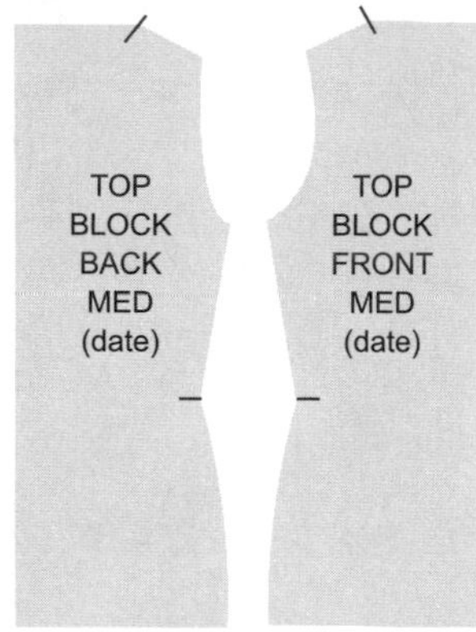

The neckline will be as illustrated, and will need a hem or facing along the neck edge.

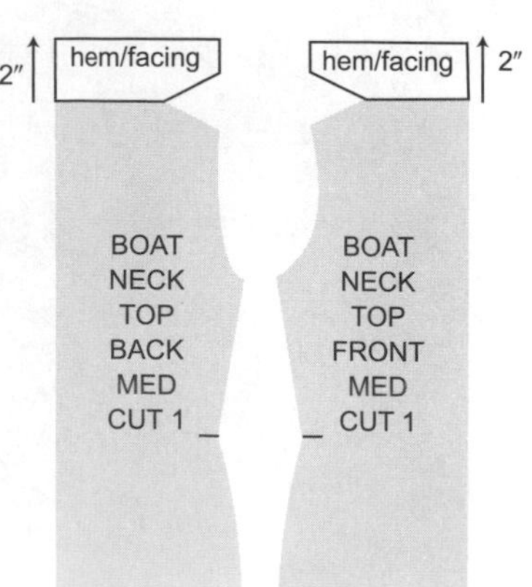

Add a 2" hem or foldback facing to the front as illustrated.

True the shoulder by folding your paper and tracing the shoulder with a tracing wheel.

With this draft, the facing will extend into the armhole, and when sewn into the sleeve seam, will prevent the facing from rolling outward.

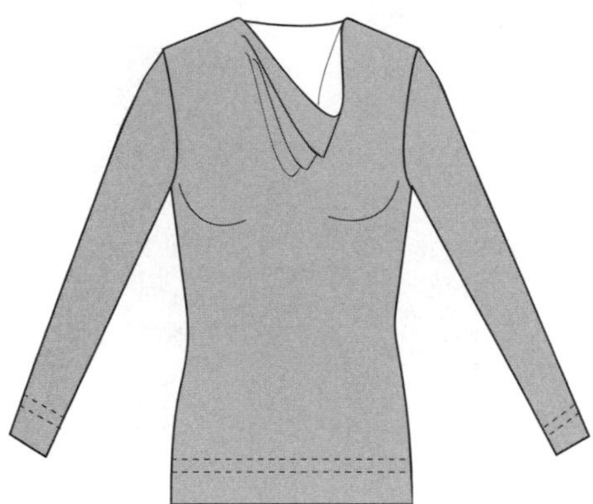

COWL NECK

By enlarging the front portion of the boatneck you can easily create a cowl neckline.

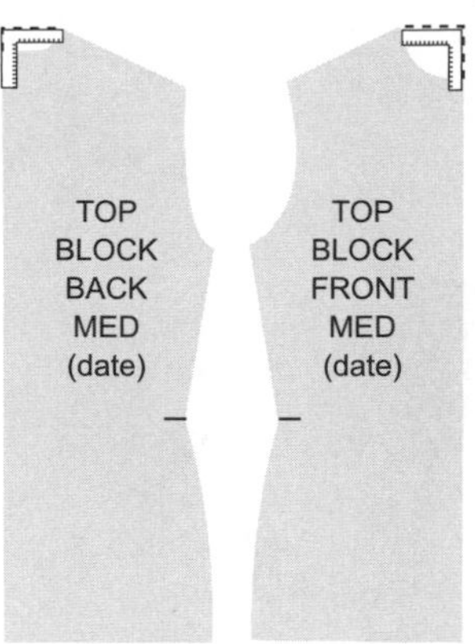

Square the back neckline up and in as for the boatneck, making sure that both lines intersect at right angles (90 degrees).

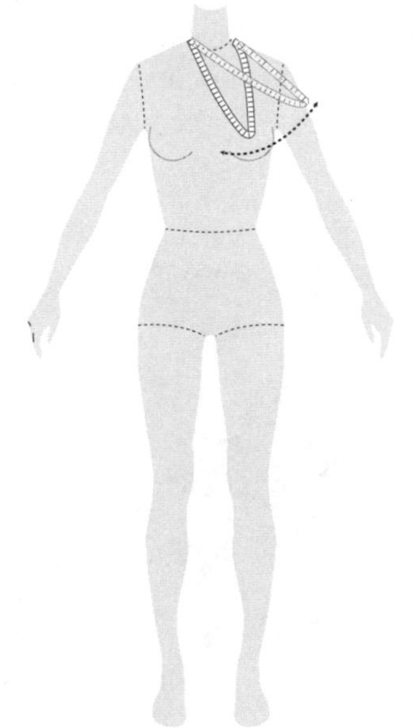

To determine the length of cowl, hold the tape measure as low as your desire and as far away from the dress-form as you desire, and record that measurement. Divide it in half to use for your draft, since you will be only drafting half of the garment.

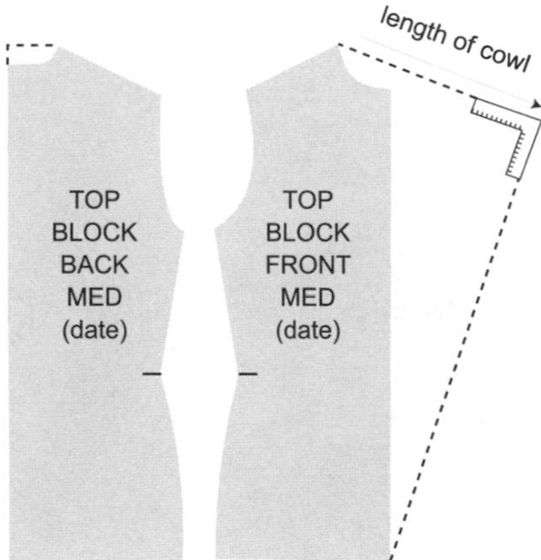

Using your “L” ruler, match the hem and the shoulder neck point as illustrated.

It must remain perfectly square at the front or your final neckline will end up having a point at the front.

Because of the cowling and extra fabric created with this style, you will need a larger hem facing than with previous drafts, in the front, as you will easily see inside the cowl.

Add 4″ hem to the front and 2″ hem at the shoulder, and draw a curved line as illustrated.

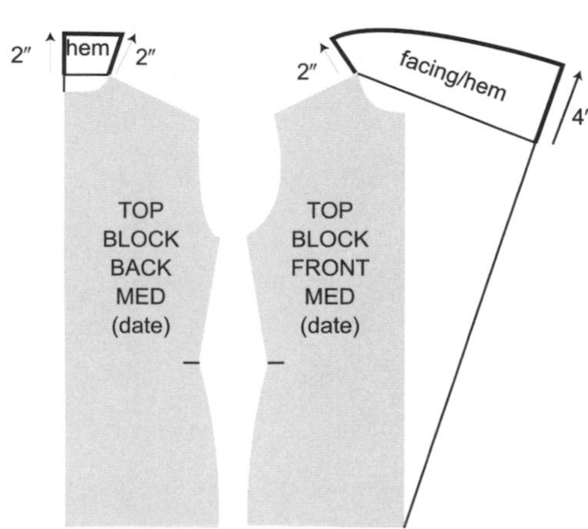

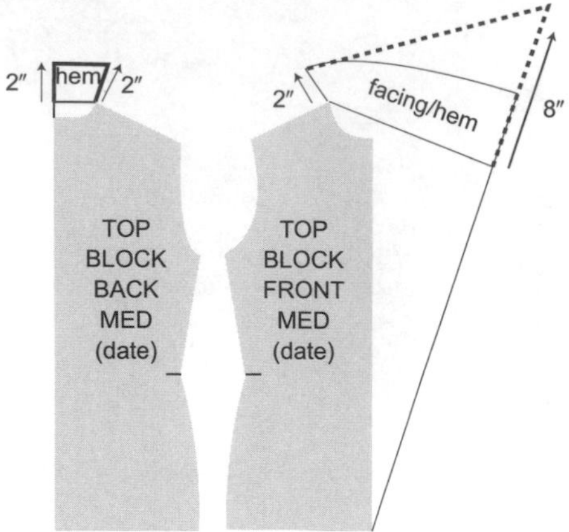

The facing can be drafted larger in the center front to prevent the facing on very fluid fabrics from rolling to the outside.

In some very high-end garments, a small weight is attached to the center front point of the facing to keep it securely inside.

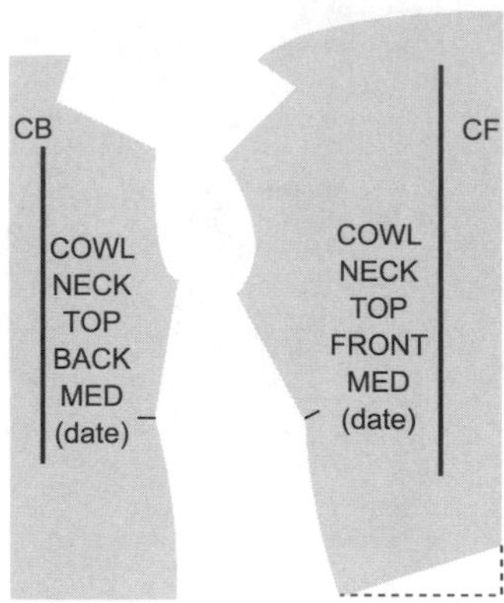

Illustration shows the completed pattern.

Note: The front hem of this draft must be corrected, straightened out, and will add length to the front of the garment. While not noticeable in a large cowl, you should use an alternative method (see later in chapter) if your design requires a straight hem or if a skirt is attached.

TUBULAR COWL

A cowl may also be created with a tubular collar attached, with a separate collar piece that is sewn to the neckline.

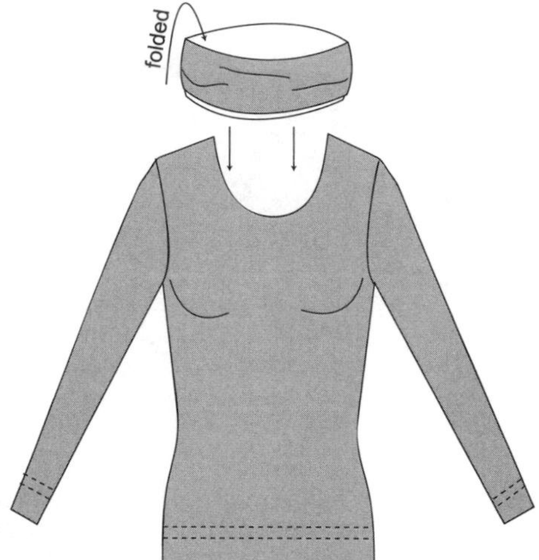

This cowl is a separate collar piece that is folded and attached to the neckline

If your tubular collar is very large, it should be sewn with wrong sides together, so the serging is on the outside and will be hidden by the large collar. If it is sewn with the serging on the inside, the seam allowances will show at the neckline.

1

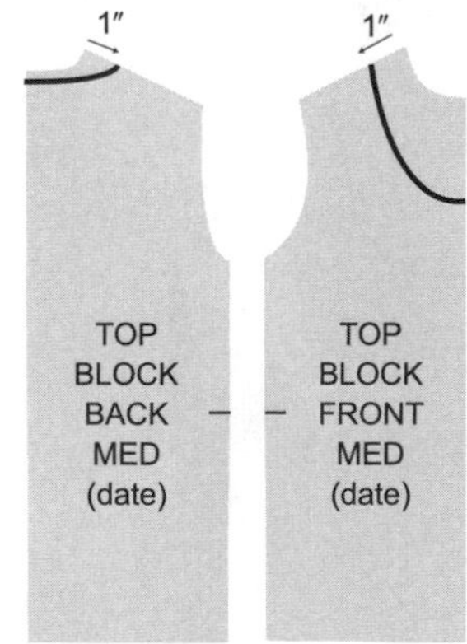

Measure how far you wish the cowl to sit from the neck, and mark.

Measure how deep you wish the cowl to be, and mark.

Draw in the neckline with curved lines.

2

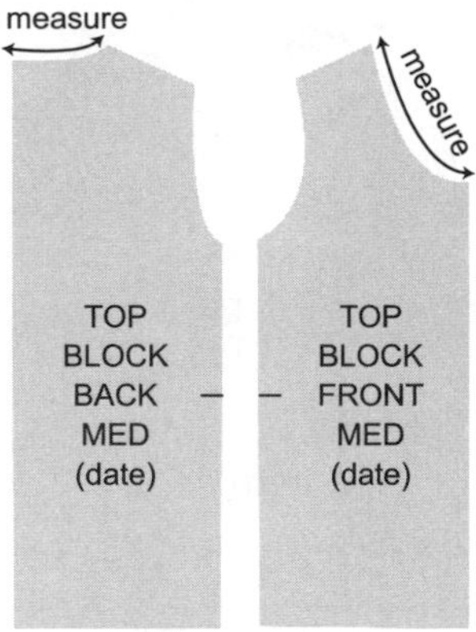

To draft the collar piece, measure the cowl design line and record the number.

3

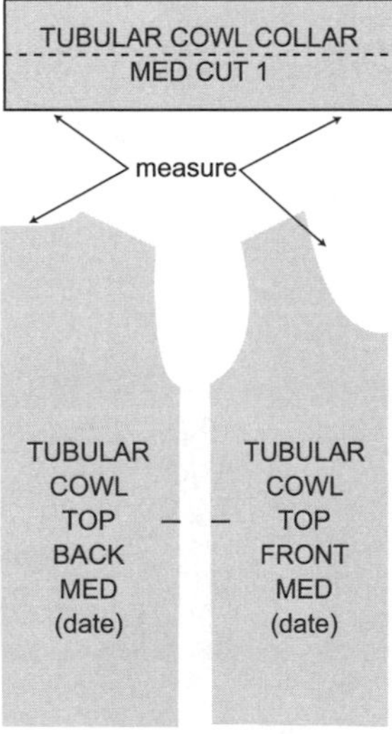

Draw the tubular cowl exactly the same length as the neckline measurements.

Make the cowl as a single pattern piece, with the seam at the center back or preferably at the left shoulder.

4

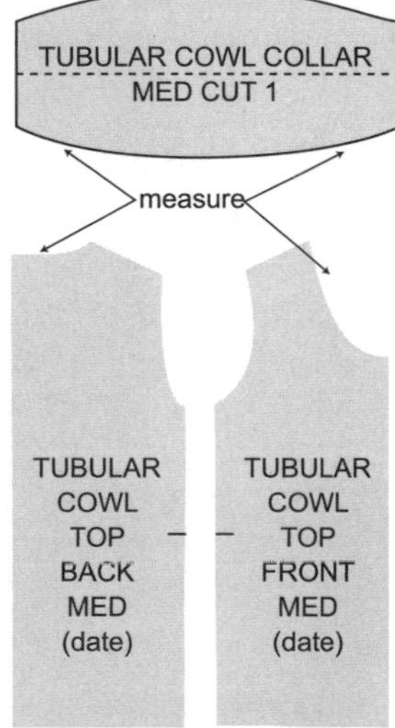

The tubular cowl can also be created with more volume at the front and less at the back as illustrated. This draft has the seam located at the center back of the top.

5

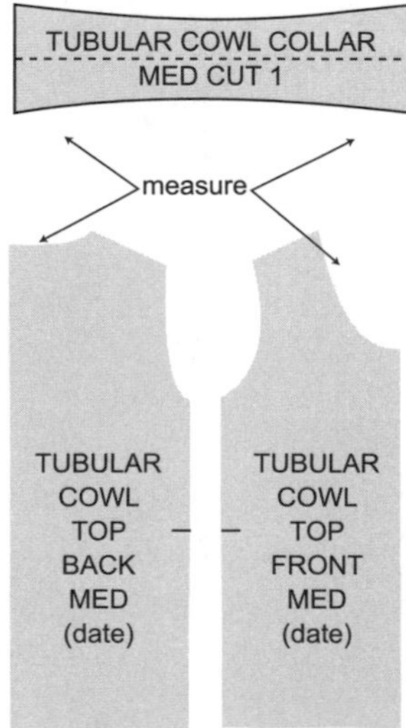

Or the cowl may be created with less volume in the front and more at the back, with the seam at the back neck.

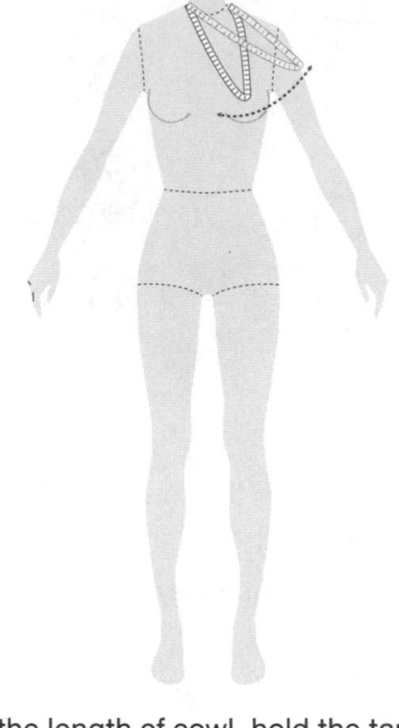

COWL NECKLINE ON A FITTED TOP

All of the previous drafts, excluding the tubular cowl, will increase the body of the garment as well as the cowl neck.

Use the following technique if you wish to create a cowl with a fitted body and don't want to increase any of the body volume.

Use this draft for longer top designs, so you don't increase volume of the body of the garment, or if you wish to attach a skirt.

To determine the length of cowl, hold the tape measure as low as your desire, and as far away from the dress-form as you desire, and record that measurement. Divide it in half to use for your draft, since you will be only drafting half of the garment.

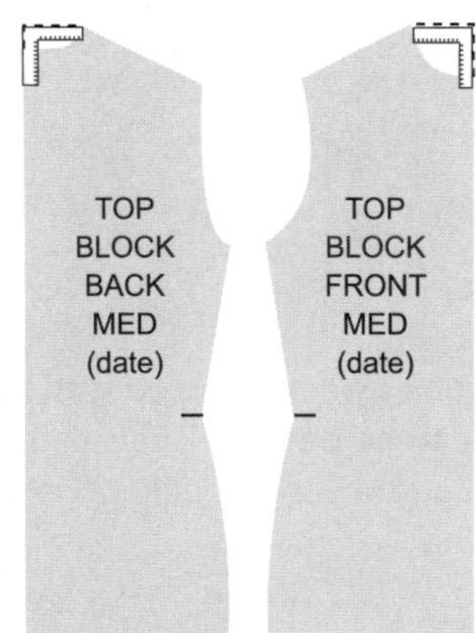

Draft the neckline as if for the tight high cowl, by squaring up and in, using the "L" ruler.

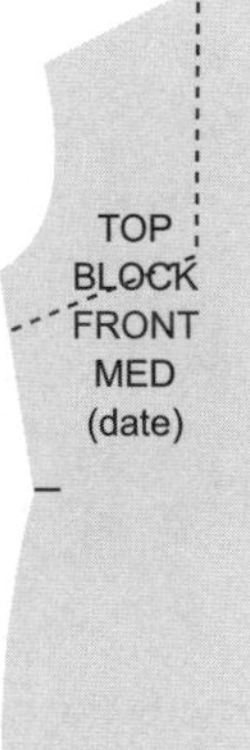

Draw slash lines from the neckline to the side seam as illustrated.

May be placed higher or lower on the side seam, depending on the amount and placement of the volume you wish to increase.

Slash and spread as illustrated.

To determine how much to spread, use the recorded measurement from the dress-form.

Square a line using the "L" square.

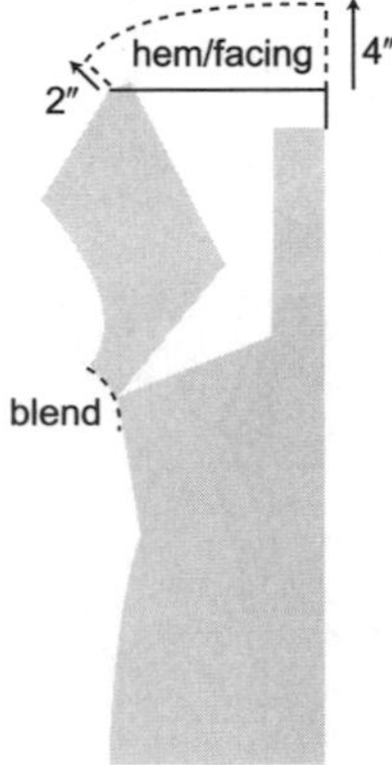

Add a 4″ hem to the front and a 2″ hem to the shoulder area, and draw a curved line.

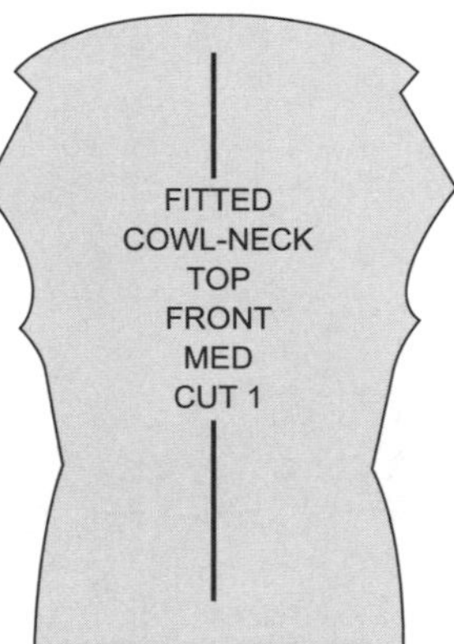

The completed pattern will add volume only to the upper part of the garment, without increasing any of the body portion.

As before, a larger facing/hem may be used if the fabric is very fluid and you wish to ensure that it does not roll outward.

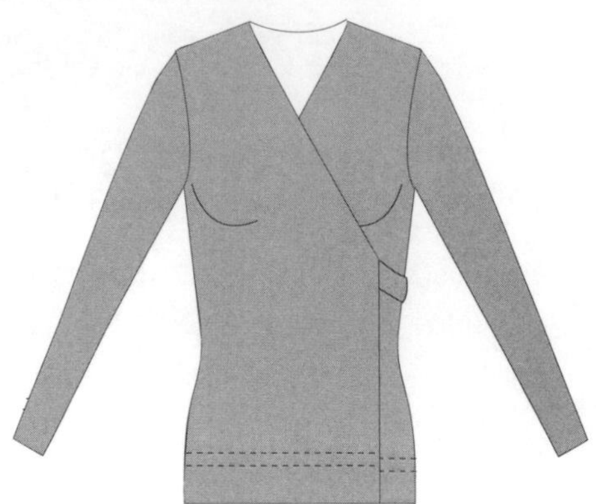

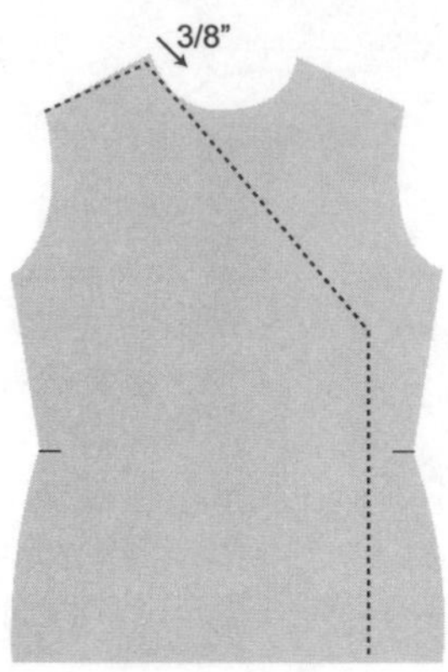

WRAP TOP

Wrap tops, being asymmetrical, must be drafted full by tracing one side of the sloper then the other side.

Remove 3⁄8" at the side seam and at the shoulders, as illustrated, to pull the top in a little closer to the body, if you intend to face the raw edges.

This is not necessary if you finish the raw edge with binding or banding, as they will be cut smaller and will pull the garment in tighter.

This is especially important if your diagonal lines are in the bust area.

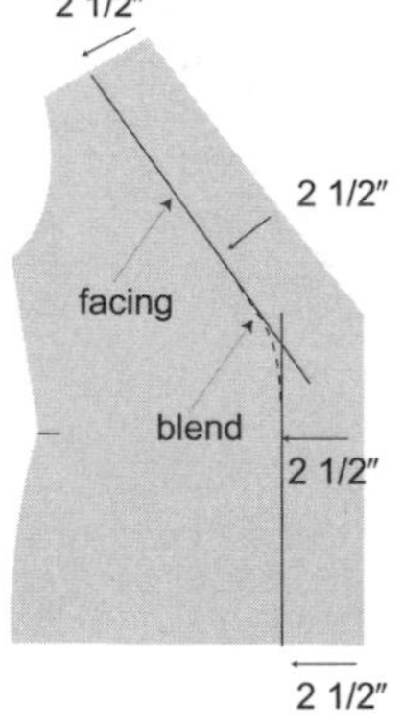

Create a facing 2½" from the front and neckline edges.

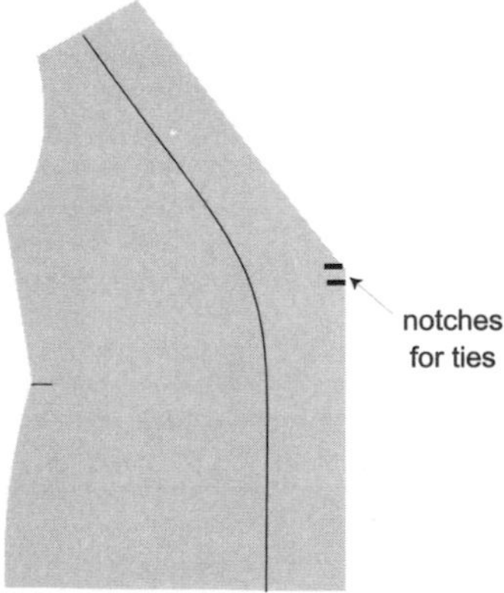

Notch the center front at the point for the ties to be inserted between the front and the facing when sewing.

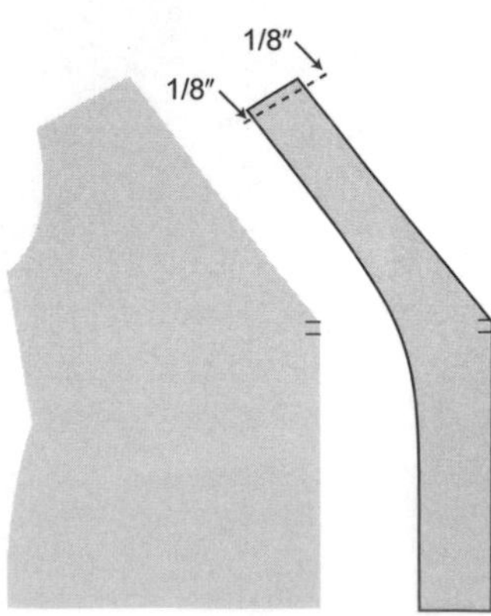

The facing needs 1⁄8" removed to make it slightly smaller than the outer garment.

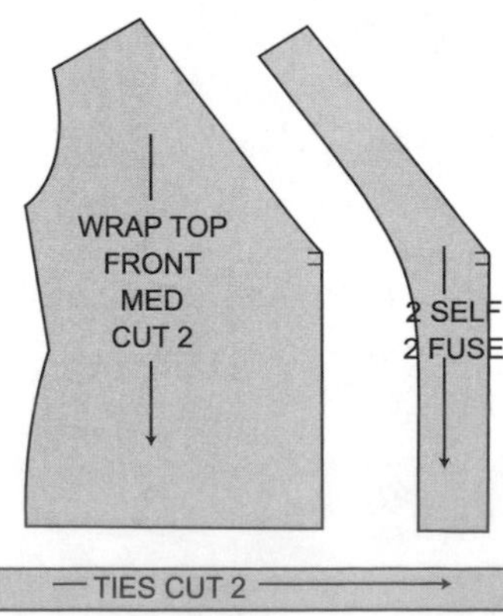

Trace and separate the pattern pieces as illustrated.

Assignment #7-1: Create A T-Shirt

To improve your understanding and knowledge of tops, draft and sew one the following garments using the instructions in this chapter.

Complete a costing sheet for your garments so you will begin to understand the costs associated with manufacturing a complete garment. Please note that your garment will be very expensive, because you will have purchased your fabric at retail, double the cost of wholesale, and your labor will be high, your sewing very slow for these initial garments. However, the exercise is still important for understanding the relationship between the different costs.

Make sure to check your T-shirt against the mark sheets, to see how well you understand the patternmaking for tops.

Cut and sew out this garment so you can see what it fits like, and how the fit can be improved.

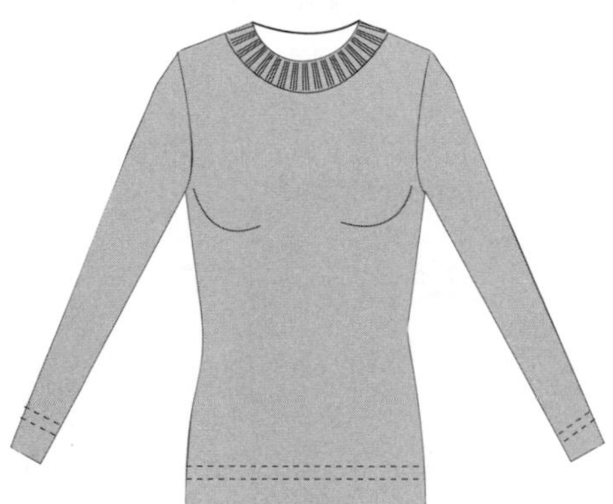

OPTION #1: CREW NECK T-SHIRT IN JERSEY WITH A RIB COLLAR

Draft this basic T-shirt with a rib collar. Note that the student or new designer may not be able to color match the jersey and rib fabrics, and that a contrast colored rib may be used.

For sleeve instructions, see Chapter 8, Sleeves.

OPTION #2: CREW-NECK T-SHIRT IN RIB WITH A RIB COLLAR

Since the student or new designer may not be able to color match the jersey and rib fabrics, you can also create the top using rib fabric for both the collar and the body of the garment.

For sleeve instructions, see Chapter 8, Sleeves.

OPTION #3: V-NECK T-SHIRT IN JERSEY WITH A RIB COLLAR

Following the drafting instructions in this chapter, create a V-neck T-shirt.

For sleeve instructions, see Chapter 8, Sleeves.

OPTION #4: V-NECK CREW T-SHIRT IN JERSEY WITH A RIB COLLAR

Following the drafting instructions in this chapter, create a combination V-neck and crew-neck T-shirt.

For sleeve instructions, see Chapter 8, Sleeves.

OPTION #5 BOATNECK T-SHIRT IN JERSEY

Following the drafting instructions in this chapter, create a boatneck T-shirt.

For sleeve instructions, see Chapter 8, Sleeves.

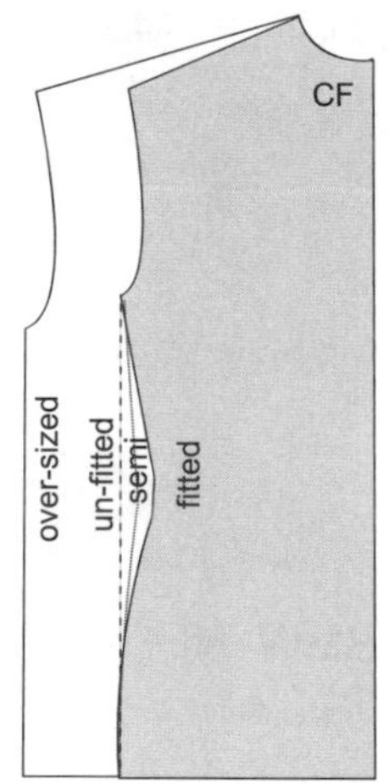

Sleeve-Less Garments

SHAPE THE SILHOUETTE AS DESIRED

Tank top designs will have finished armholes rather than sleeves. There are different methods used to finish the raw edges of the armholes, which will be illustrated throughout this chapter.

The tank top can be fitted, semi-fitted, loose, or flared depending on the designer's sketch.

Fitted:

Follows waist curve.

Semi-fitted:

Halfway between the fitted and the loose.

Unfitted:

Straight down from the underarms to the hips.

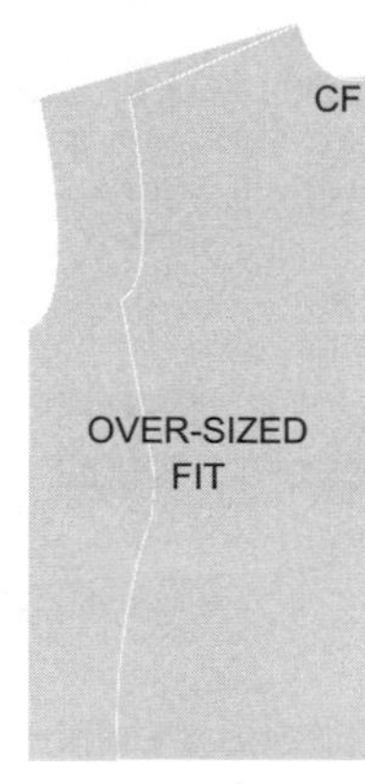

Oversized:

Use the oversized sloper (see Chapter 11, Oversized Projects).

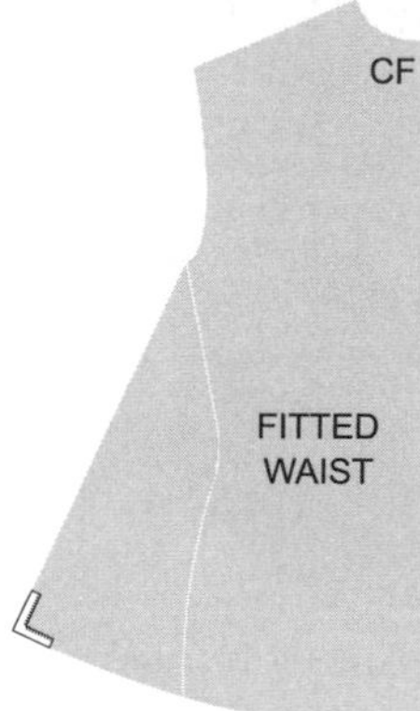

Flared:

Extend the hip out as far as desired.

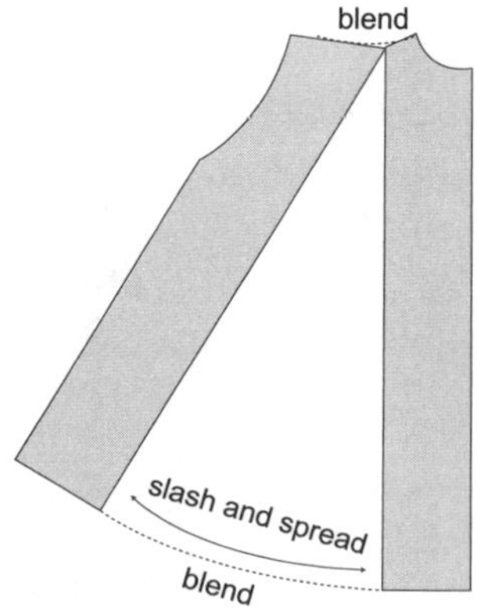

Additional volume:

Create additional volume by slashing and spreading your draft to the desired fullness.

ARMHOLE CORRECTIONS FOR SLEEVELESS GARMENTS

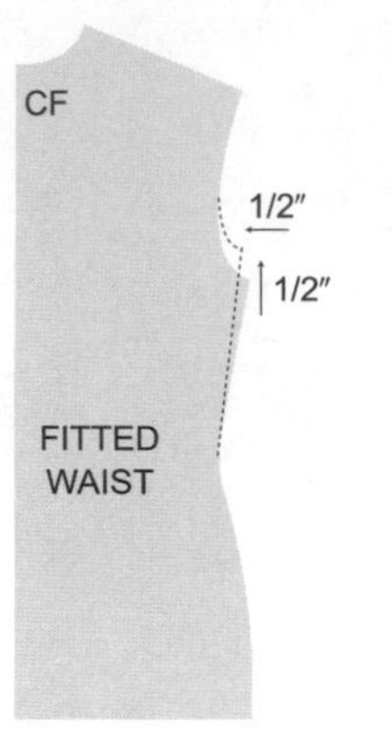

When creating sleeveless garments, the shoulder seam must be shortened by at least ½″. Remember that this sloper was created for a sleeve to be attached and the extra amount would hang over the edge, like a kind of wing.

This is not very attractive and should not be used to create cap sleeves.

UNDERARM CORRECTIONS FOR SLEEVELESS GARMENTS

This sloper was created to have sleeves attached, and the armholes are too large for a sleeveless garment.

Raise and take in the armhole at the side seam ½″ to tighten the armhole and prevent the undergarments and sides of the breast from showing.

You may also tighten the armhole by using elastic, banding, or binding methods to reduce the underarm, which will be explained further on in this text.

TANK TOP WITH FACING

This basic sleeveless garment, with armhole and neckline facings, will introduce the reader to some of the drafting and patternmaking techniques used to create tank tops.

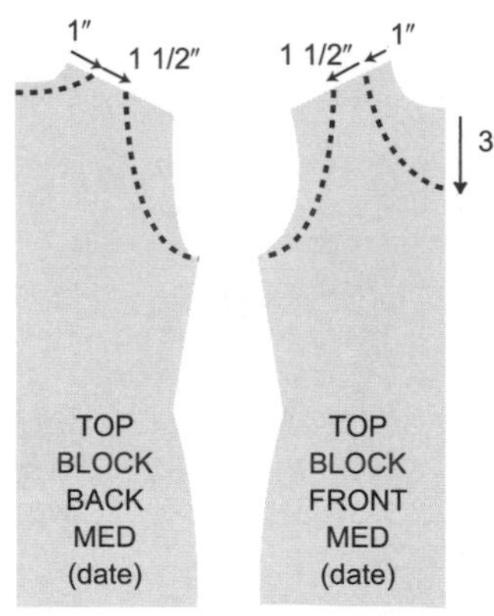

The style lines may be placed anywhere the designer wishes. Note that the shoulder straps can be very close to the neck of the wearer, or away from the neck.

Don't make the shoulder straps too close to the armhole; keep them at least ½″ away, so they don't create wings off the edge and will help keep the straps up.

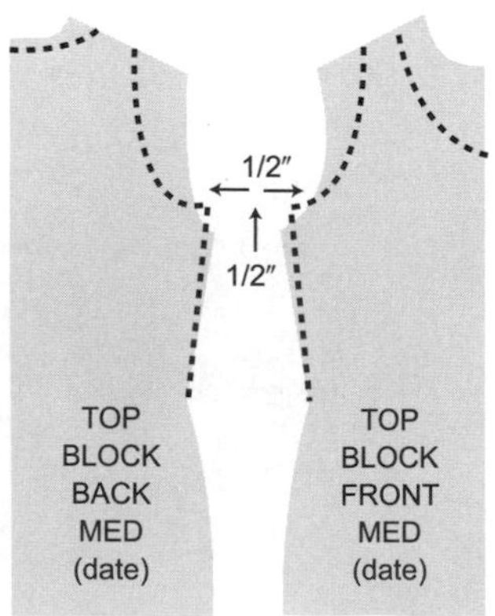

Remember that this sloper was created to have sleeves attached, and the armholes are too large for a sleeveless garment.

Raise and take in the armhole at the side seam ½″ to tighten the armhole and prevent the undergarments, and sides of the breast, from showing.

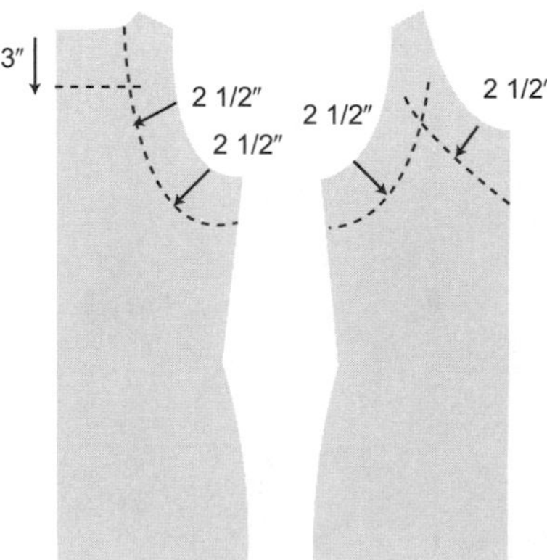

Create a 2½″ facing pattern for this garment by drawing a line parallel to the armholes and neckline.

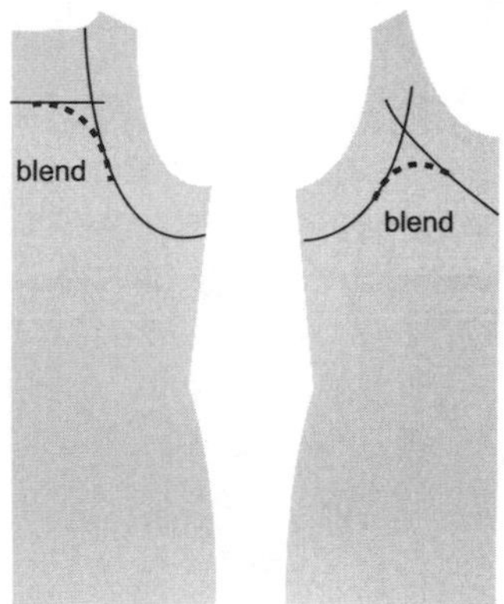

Blend the curves as illustrated.

Do not make the facing straight across, as the straight edge will easily show through the garment when being worn. A curved line will be less likely to show through.

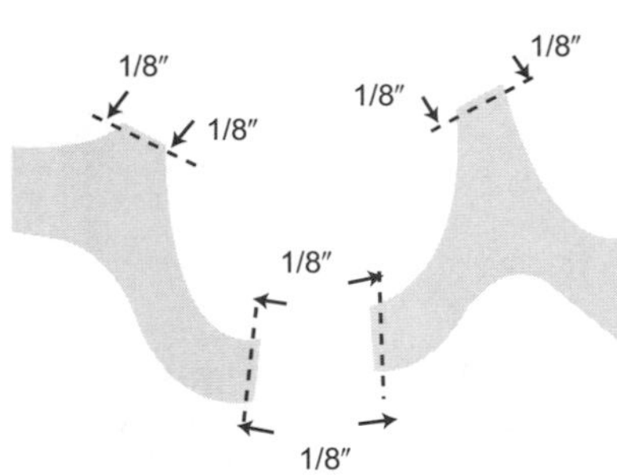

Remove ½″ from the facing to make it smaller since it will be on the inside of the garment.

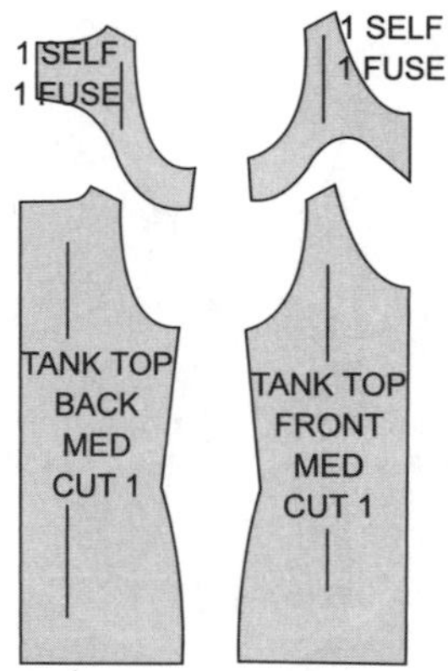

Trace, separate, and label the pattern pieces as illustrated.

V-NECK TANK TOP WITH FACING

The V-neck tank top may be created as low as the designer wishes.

To determine how low you want the V, measure down from the neck on the dress-form.

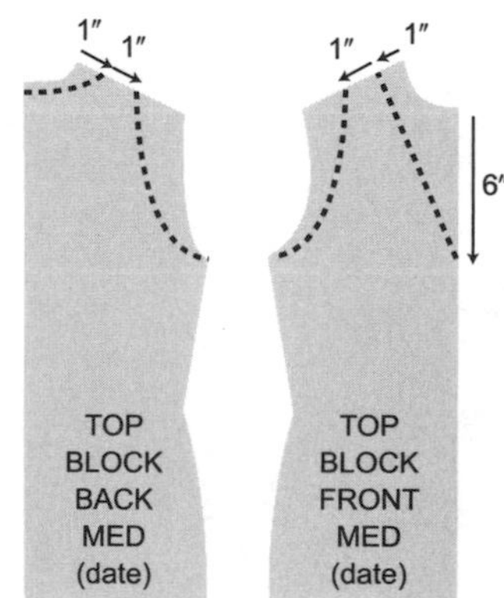

To illustrate, this garment will be created 6″ down from the neck.

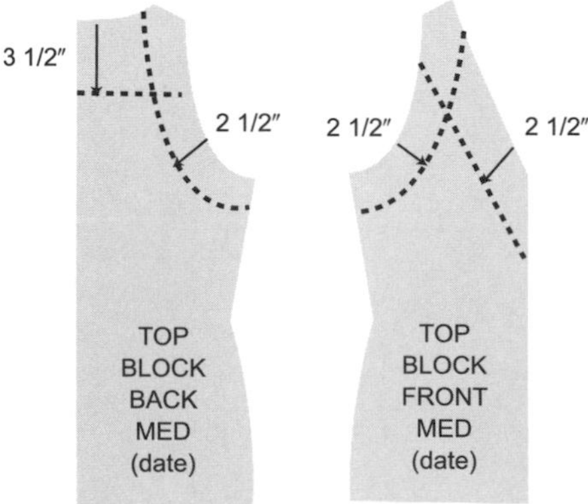

Create a 2½″ facing pattern for this garment by drawing a line parallel to the armholes and neckline.

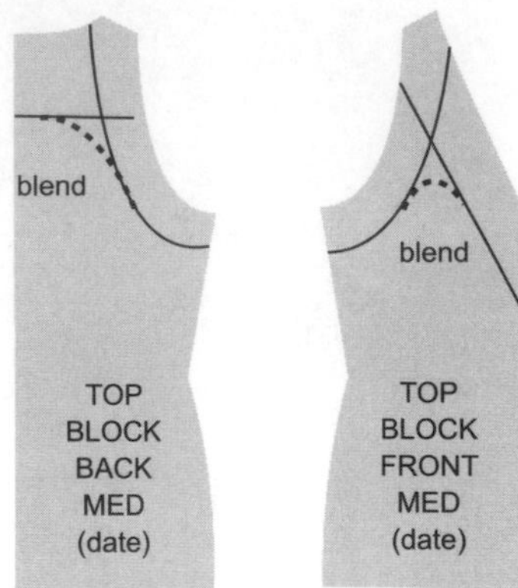

Blend the curves as illustrated.

Do not make the facing straight across, as the straight edge will easily show through the garment when being worn. A curved line will be less likely to show through.

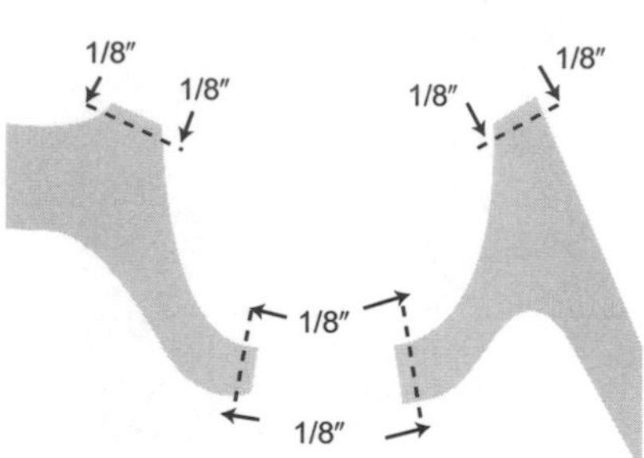

Remove ½″ from the facing to make it smaller since it will be on the inside of the garment.

High-end garments are often created with a larger back neck facing so the when on the hanger, the edge of the facing will not show. Only clean, finished self-fabric shows, which is much nicer-looking.

Note that the facing edge is curved to keep it away from the bust, thereby preventing the bust from getting heavy and lumpy if the facing moves around.

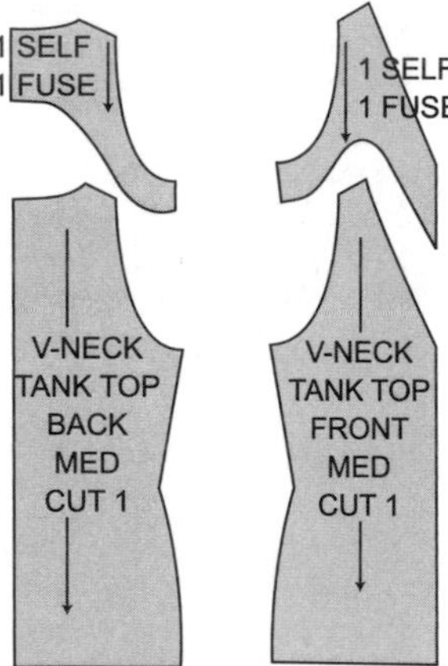

Trace, separate, and label the pattern pieces as indicated.

SQUARE-NECKED TANK TOP WITH FACING

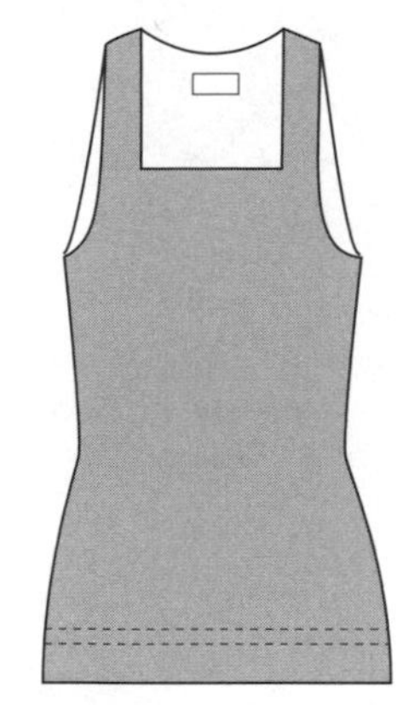

Trace out the appropriate sloper.

In order to create a flattering square neck, the width of the shoulder straps must be squared, and kept even and parallel.

Take in the armhole at the side seam ½″ to tighten the armhole, and prevent the undergarments from showing, unless you will be using elastic, banding, or binding methods to reduce the underarm.

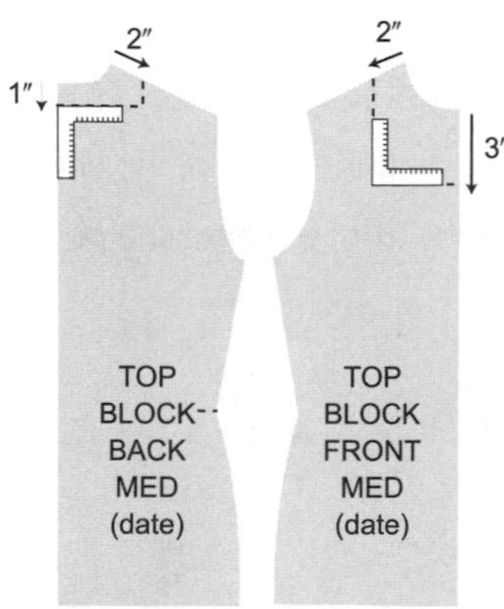

Decide how far from the neck you wish the straps to be (illustrated at 2″, but may be any measurement the designer desires).

Measure down the desired amount at the front and back neckline of the original sloper, and square a line across as illustrated at 3″ down the front and 1″ down the back, but may be any measurement the designer desires.

Remember that if you create a garment with a lowered front and back, the garment will fall off the customer.

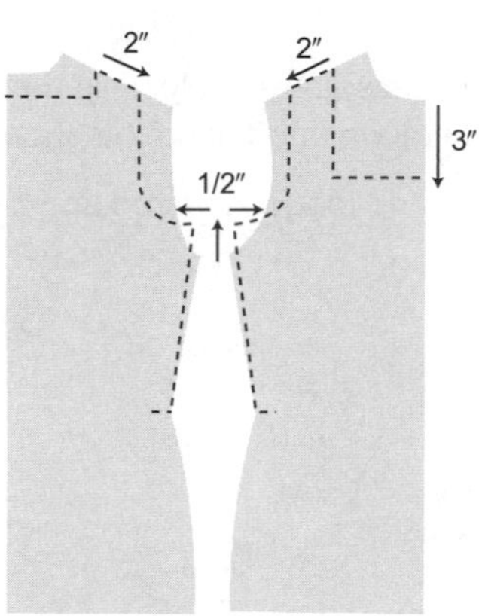

Keep the straps even and parallel to the neck, or the straps will appear wavy and uneven.

Decide how wide you wish the straps to be (illustrated at 2″, but may be any measurement the designer desires).

Raise the underarm ½″ and take it in ½″ to keep the garment tight and close to the body, and prevent the undergarment from showing.

TRUEING THE SHOULDER STRAPS

Problem-solving the straps.

At the point in the neckline where the shoulders are to match, you need a smooth neck edge to finish the raw edge.

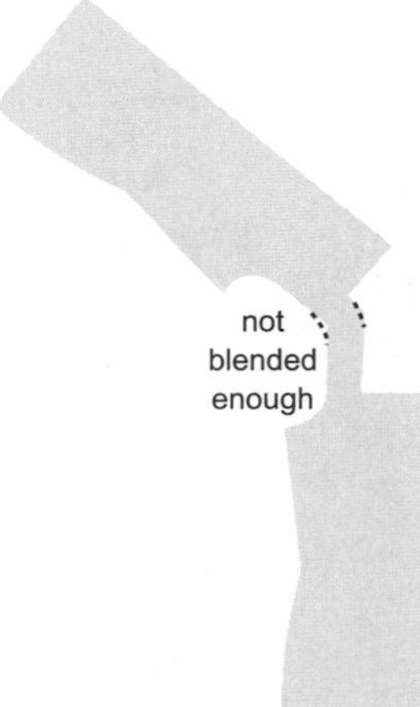

Blending it does not correct the problem; rather, it creates a slightly rounded point at the neck.

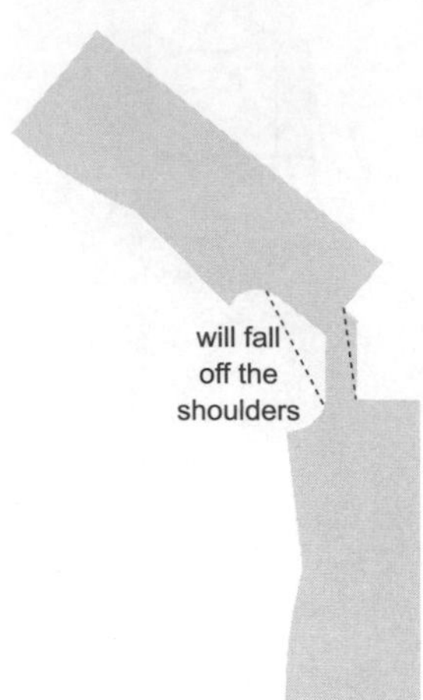

If you try to blend the square neckline in the usual manner, it will open up too much and fall off the shoulders.

Here the neckline is no longer squared and has changed shape.

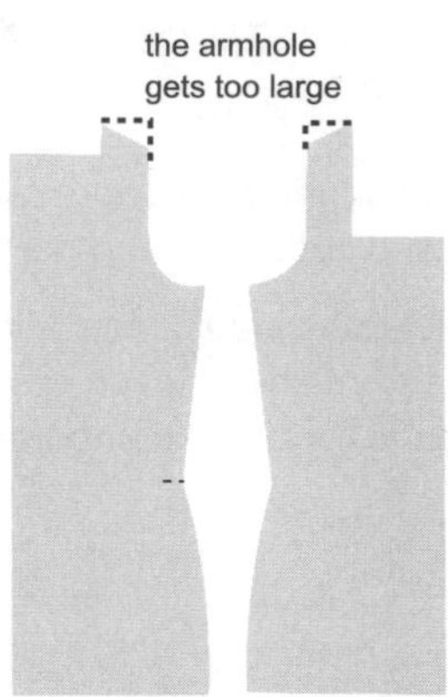

You need to square off the ends of the shoulder straps.

If you square across from the neckline point, the armhole becomes too large.

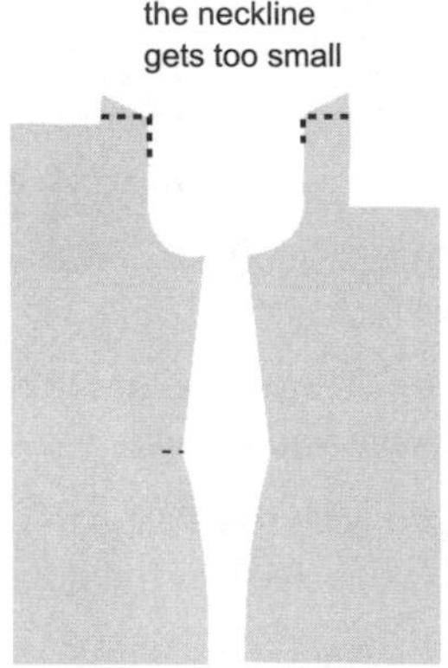

You need to square off the ends of the shoulder straps.

If you square across from the armhole point, the neckline becomes too small.

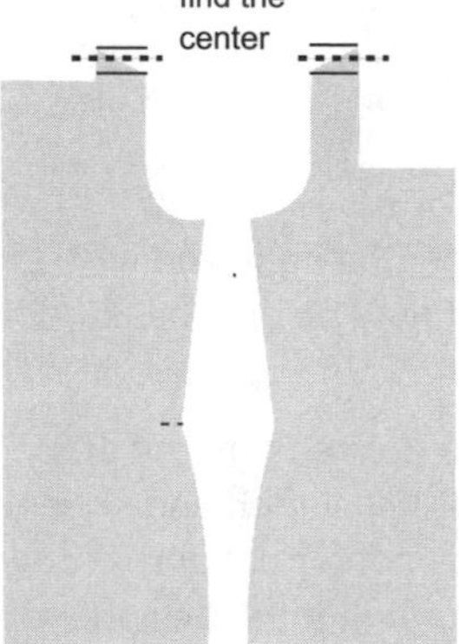

The solution is to split the difference.

Find the center of the armhole point and the neckline point and square a straight line across at that point.

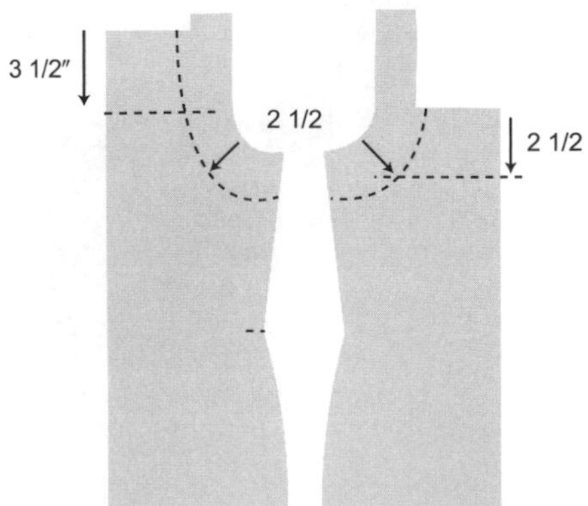

Create a 2½″ facing to clean finish the neck and armholes.

Draw the guidelines 2½″ away from and parallel to the edges.

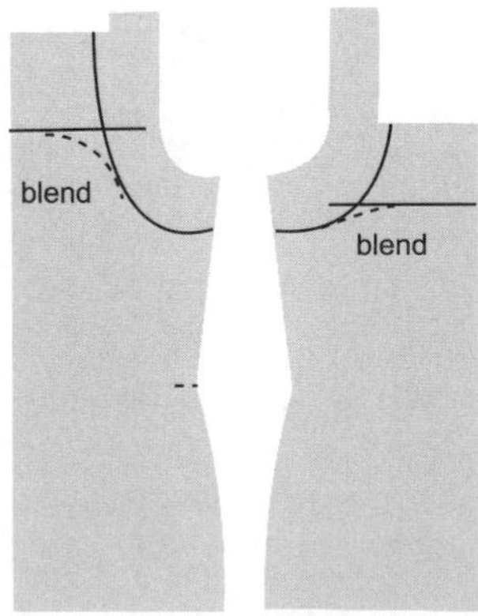

Blend the corners into smooth curves.

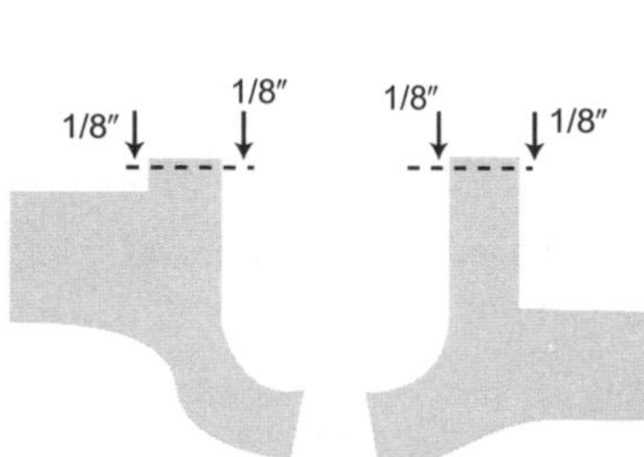

Remove $\frac{1}{8}$″ from the facing since it will be inside the garment and needs to be slightly smaller.

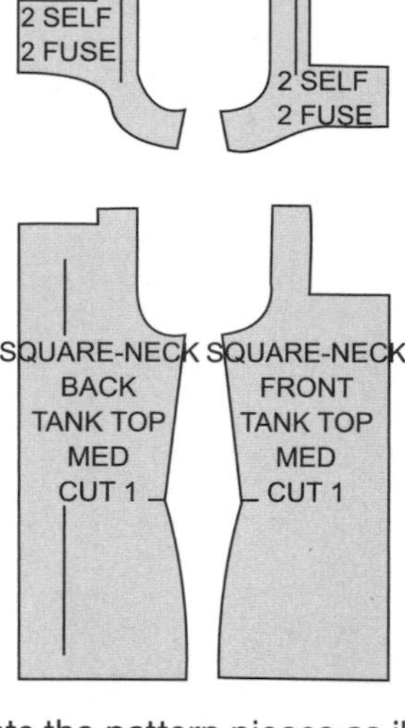

Trace and separate the pattern pieces as illustrated.

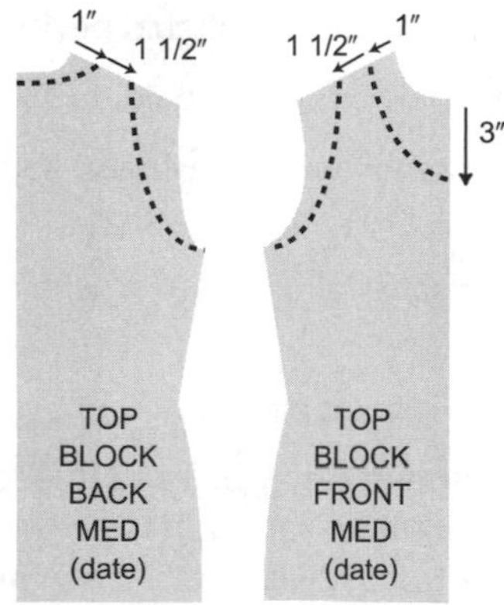

TANK TOP WITH BINDING

Binding is great way to finish the raw edges of a garment. It creates a nice, thick seam that defines the edges very well.

If you plan to use binding to finish an armhole, it is not necessary to raise and tighten the armhole as in garments with a facing. The binding is cut slightly smaller than the armhole and will pull the garment up and tighter to the body, preventing undergarments from showing.

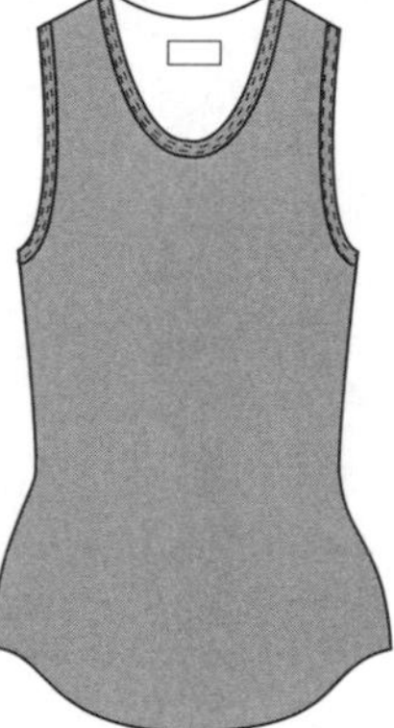

This tank top will be drafted with straps that are $1\frac{1}{2}$″ wide starting 1″ away from the neck.

The neckline will be lowered 3″.

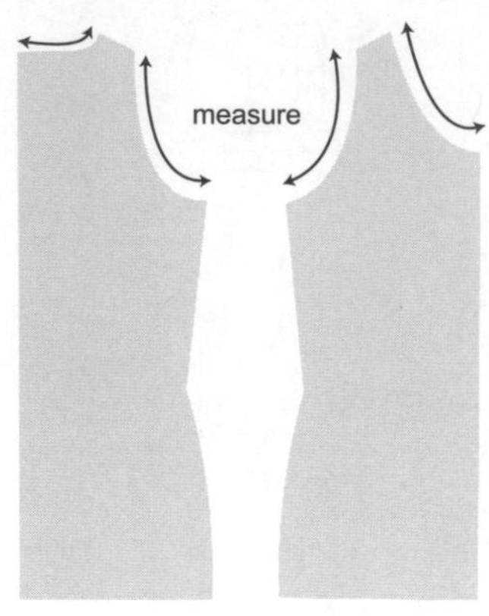

BINDING REDUCTIONS

Do not raise and take in the armhole if binding is to be applied. The binding will tighten the armhole because it is smaller than the armhole and stretched to fit during sewing.

Make the finishing binding smaller than the opening by reducing the armhole measurement by ⅙ of the total length measurement.

Add front measurement to back measurement then divide the sum by 6 and multiply by 5.

Do not add seam allowances to any edge that will have binding applied.

Alternatively, you may measure the armhole and reduce by approximately 16.5% by multiplying the measurement by 0.83.

Use 1/7 smaller for nylon spandex.

Some fabrics may need additional reduction, which you will determine with your sample.

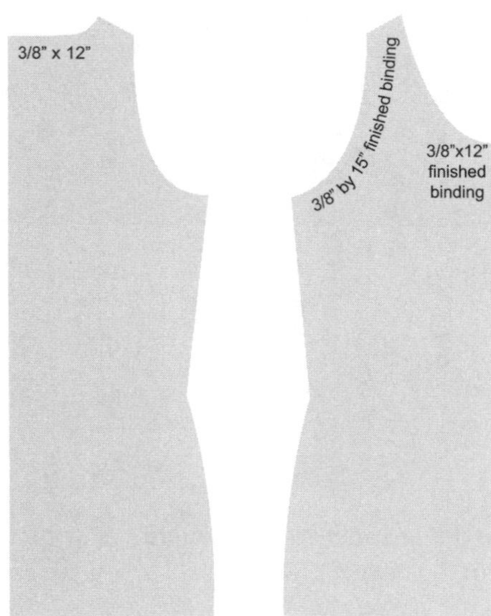

If the total armhole is 6″ then the new binding should be 5″.

If the total armhole is 12″ then the new binding should be 10″.

If the total armhole is 18″ then the new binding should be 15″.

Or 1/7 smaller for nylon spandex. Some fabrics may need additional reduction.

Label the pattern with the finished (after already sewn, with reductions) measurement.

Label the area that each binding will be applied to.

Since the manufacturer of your garments may be in another country, and to avoid confusion, binding measurements are written on the pattern in the area where they will be applied, along with the finished measurement.

Most binding is applied with a collarette that will automatically reduce the binding, and stretch it, as it is being sewn. The production manager and cutter must know how much to cut or purchase before cutting thousands of garments.

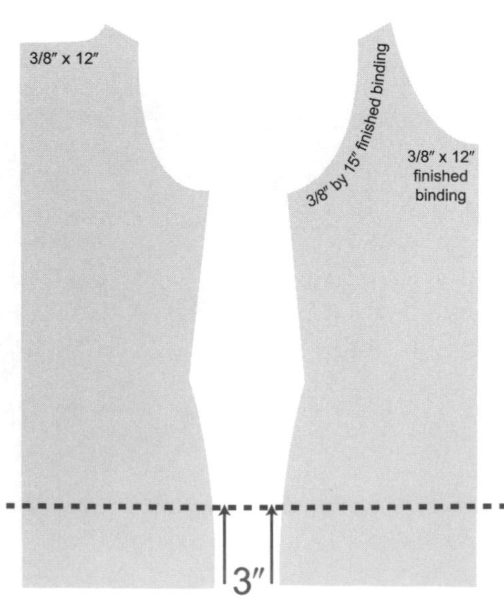

CURVED HEM

Quite often garments are created with a curved hem.

Curved hems are usually intended to be worn tucked into pants or skirts, and therefore some of the bulk in the hip area is reduced.

Straight hems are intended to be worn outside other garments.

Draw a guideline approximately 3″ above the hem, but it may be as much as the designer requires.

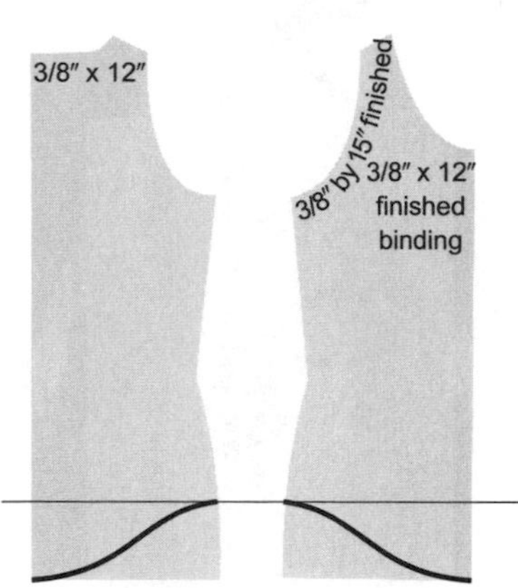

Draw in your new hemline.

Remember to keep the curves as shallow as possible so that you can cover-stitch them easily. A deep curve is too difficult to hem.

Square the front and back of the curve, otherwise you will get a point in your hem.

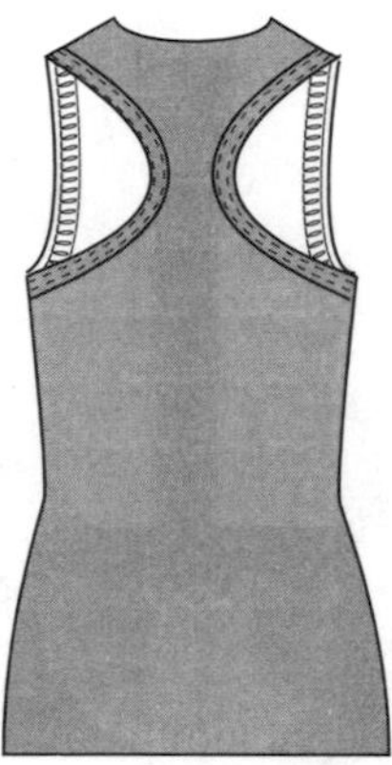

You don't have to raise and take in the armholes of a garment that will be reduced through the use of elastic, binding, or banding.

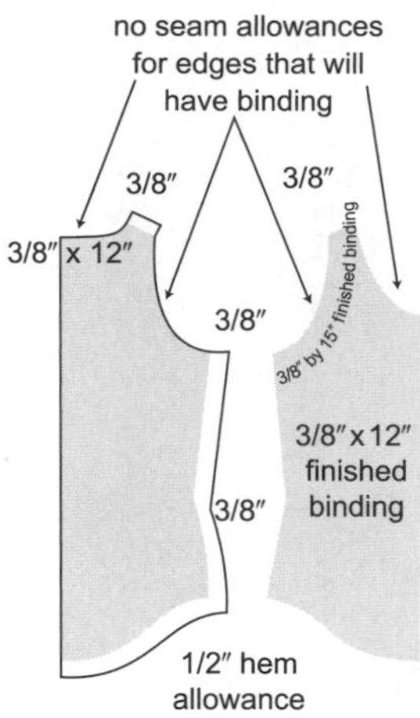

Don't add any seam allowances for edges that will have 3/8″ binding applied.

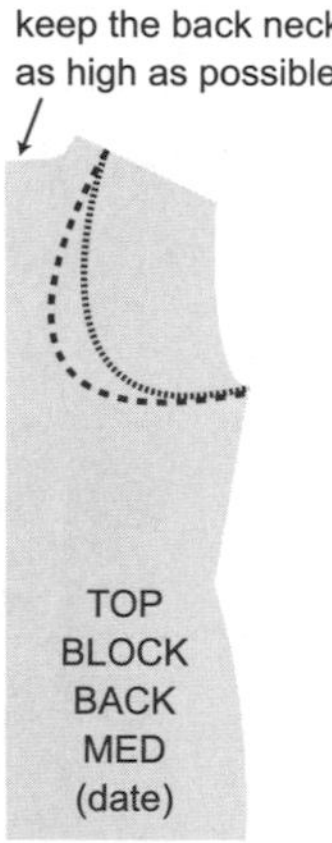

Keep the back neck very high when drafting T-back tank tops. Sometimes it may even be necessary to raise the back neck.

Make sure that the back matches the front at the side seams and the shoulders.

Do not add seam allowances to any edge that will have binding applied.

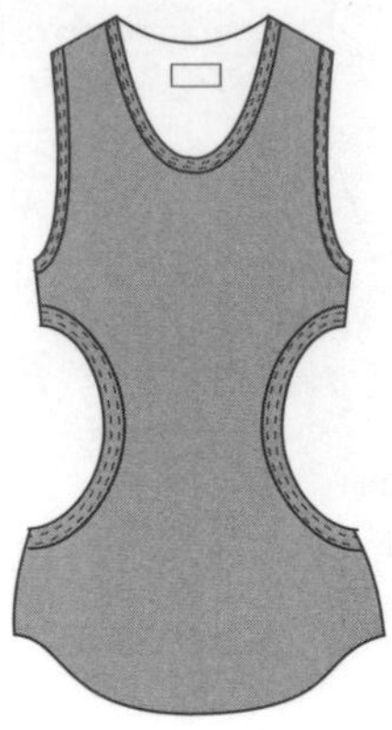

TANK TOP WITH SIDE CUT-OUTS

To create a tank top with cut-outs on the sides, leave one seam of the hole open until after the binding is applied. Check that the side seams match and line up in a smooth continuous curve.

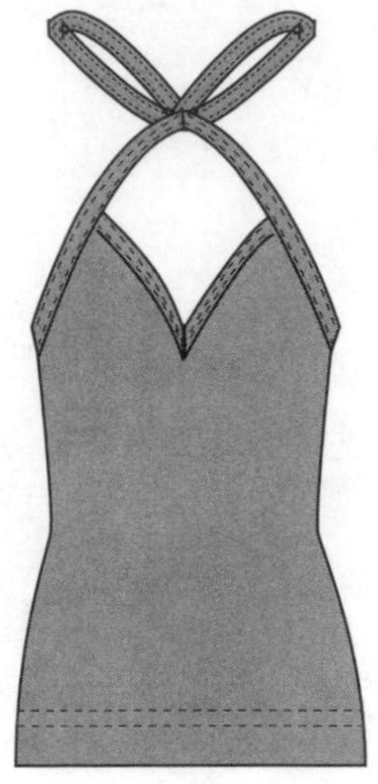

SLIP NECKLINE

A slip neckline may be created with straps that tie to each other or are attached to the back of the top.

You don't have to raise and take in the armholes or garments that will be reduced through the use of elastic, binding, or banding.

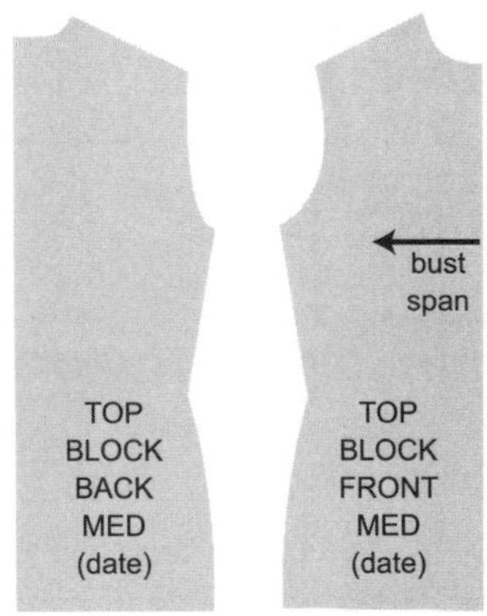

Measure across the bust span and draw a guideline.

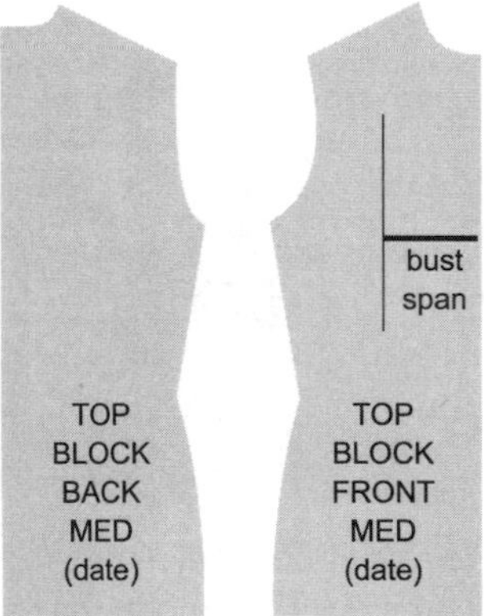

Draw a guideline parallel to the center front, squared to the bust span measurement.

Type of Knit	Extra Extra Small	Extra Small	Small	Medium	Large	Extra Large	Extra Extra Large
Stable	6 1/2	6 7/8	6 7/8	7 1/8	7 1/2	7 7/8	8 3/8
Moderate	6 3/8	6 1/2	6 3/4	7 1/8	7 1/2	7 7/8	6 3/8
Stretchy	6 3/8	6 1/2	6 3/4	7	7 3/8	7 7/8	8 1/8
Super-stretch	6 1/4	6 3/8	6 7/8	6 7/8	7 1/4	7 7/8	7 7/8
Rib	5 7/8	6	6 1/4	6 1/2	6 7/8	7 1/4	7 1/2

	Extra Extra Small	Extra Small	Small	Medium	Large	Extra Large	Extra Extra Large
Bust level	9⅞	10	10¼	10½	10¾	11	11¼

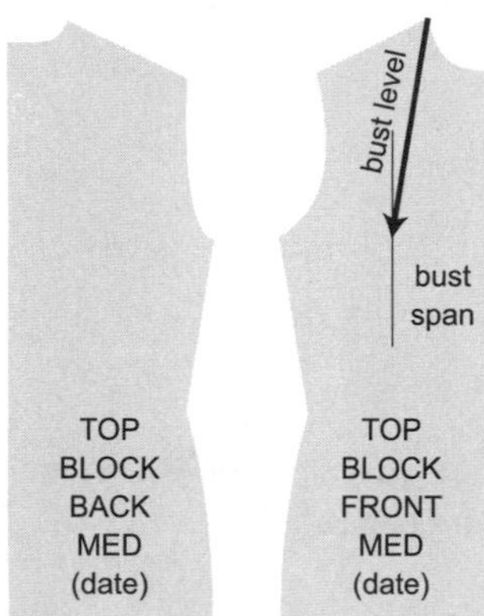

Measure down the bust level to find the apex.

The bust level is the same for all stretch ratios, since the fabric doesn't stretch in that direction, and when using a four-way stretch there is nothing holding down the fabric to stretch it in the lengthwise directions.

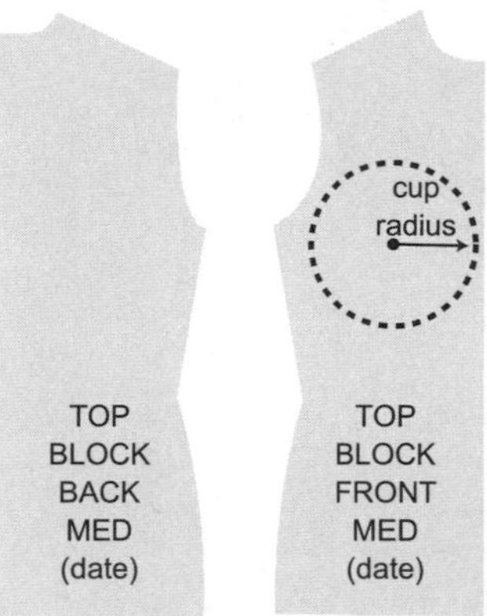

Draw the cup, using one of the radius measurements below, using a compass from the bust apex.

Type of Knit	Extra Extra Small	Extra Small	Small	Medium	Large	Extra Large	Extra Extra Large
Stable	2⅛	2¼	2⅜	2½	2⅞	2¾	2⅞
Moderate	2⅛	2¼	2⅜	2½	2⅞	2¾	2⅞
Stretchy	2	2⅛	2¼	2⅜	2½	2⅞	2¾
Super-stretch	1⅞	2	2⅛	2¼	2⅜	2½	2⅞
Rib	1¾	1⅞	1⅞	2	2⅛	2¼	2⅜

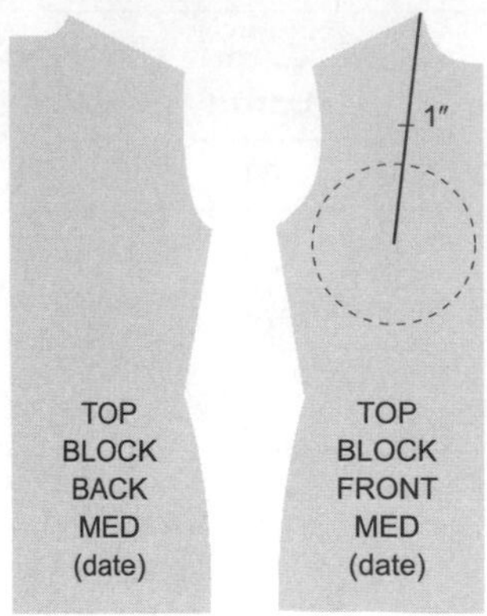

Draw a guideline from the bust apex up to the point where the shoulder meets the neck.

This guideline follows the direction of the straps, and may be changed accordingly.

Measure up 1″ on the guideline.

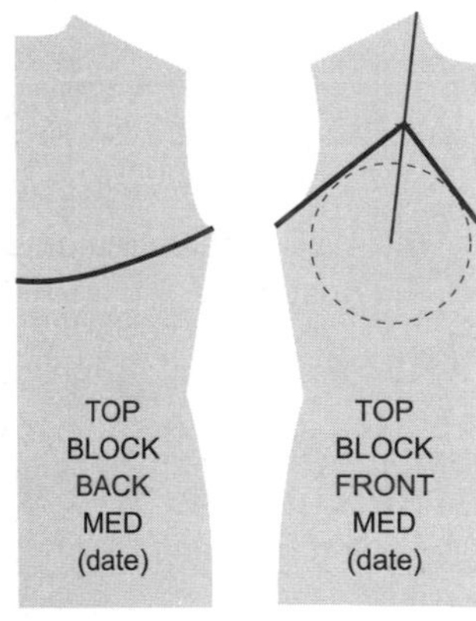

Draw in the neckline, trying not to let your lines go within the bust circle. Otherwise parts of the breast will be exposed.

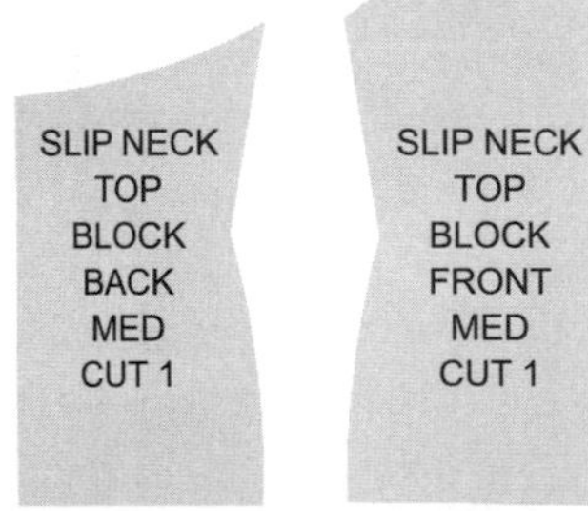

Trace and separate the pattern pieces as illustrated.

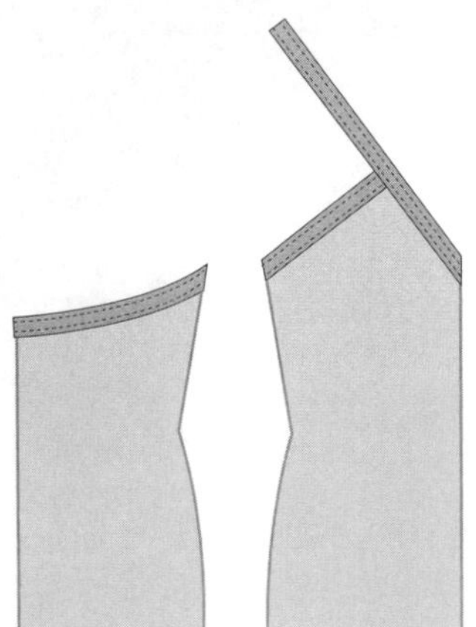

Use binding to finish off the neckline edges and to create straps or ties.

Do not add seam allowances to any edge that will have binding applied.

Attach the binding to the back and sides before attaching the front section.

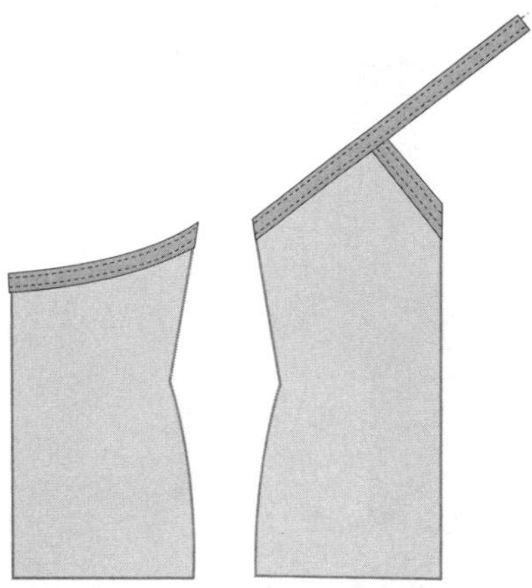

Or attach binding to the front sections before attaching the sides. This will create a different effect for the ties/straps.

When using binding to create straps, make the straps longer than necessary, and then correct and complete the measuring during fitting.

Make sure to insert twill tape in the strap portion of the binding ties to prevent them from stretching.

Bar tack the strap to the back binding for reinforcement.

Do not add seam allowances to any edge that will have binding applied.

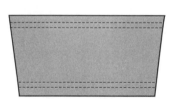

TUBE TOP

Tube tops are the easiest top to draft and sew.

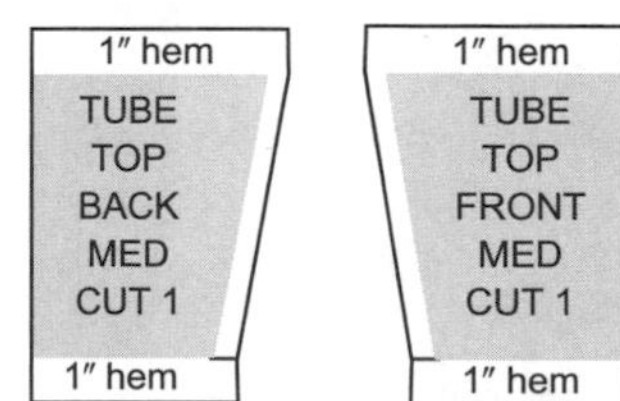

Add a 1″ hem to the top and bottom of the tube top. Note that 1″ elastic may be inserted into the top of the top to keep it secure. The elastic should be 1″ smaller in length than the top of the tube top.

Drawstring may also be added to the top by creating buttonholes for the string to pass through.

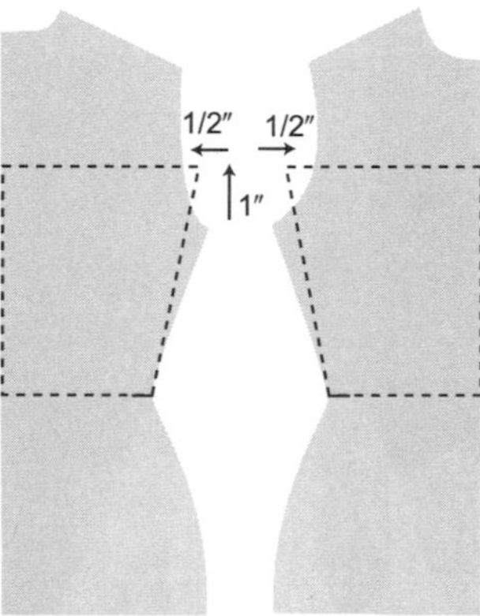

Raise the underarm 1″ and take in ½″ at the side seams for total bust coverage.

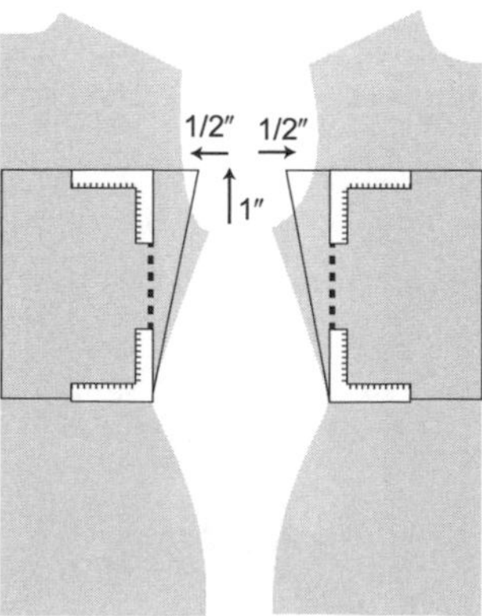

The tube top may also be created with straight side seams, by making it much tighter. In fact, a tube top can rarely be too tight.

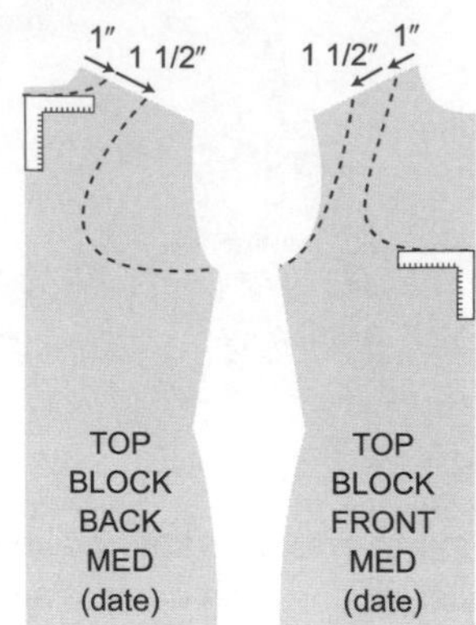

SLIT ON A CURVED SEAM

Sometimes a designer wants slits on a curved area of the garment body, such as the side seams at the hips.

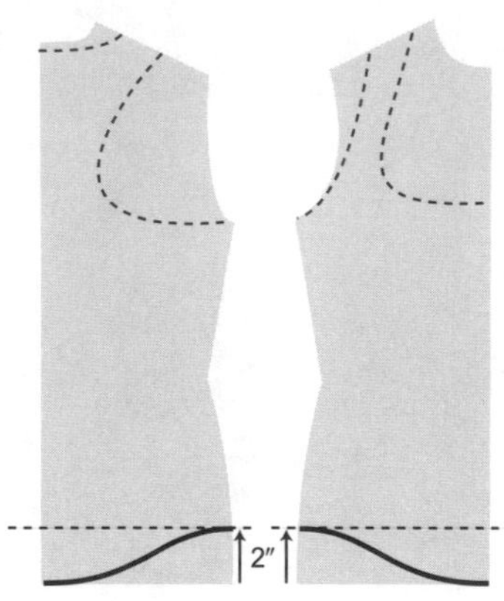

Draft the armhole and neckline curves as illustrated or as desired.

For T-backs (swim-backs), try to keep the back neck as high as possible while still maintaining a nice curved line.

For this style, raise the hem at the side seams 2″ and draw a curved hem.

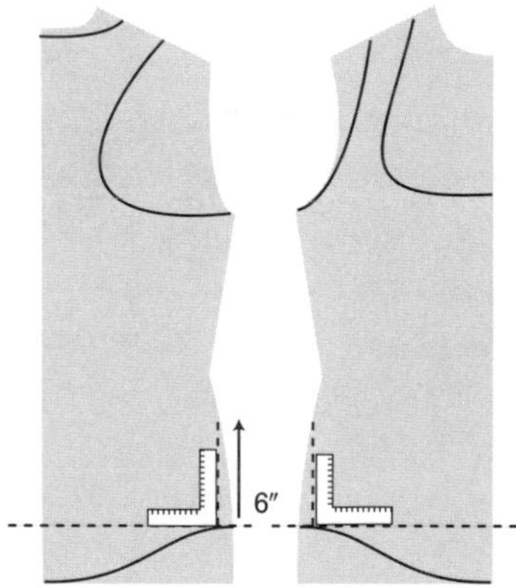

Decide on the length of the slit opening, illustrated here at 6″, but may be higher or lower as desired.

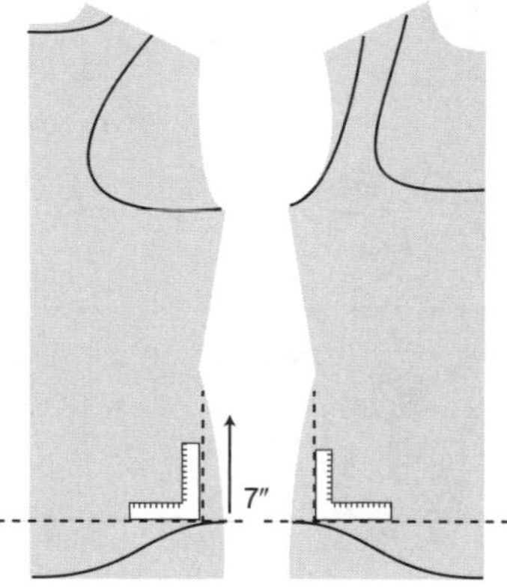

Line up your ruler on the guideline and mark 6″ wherever it lines up on the side seam, without going outside the side seam.

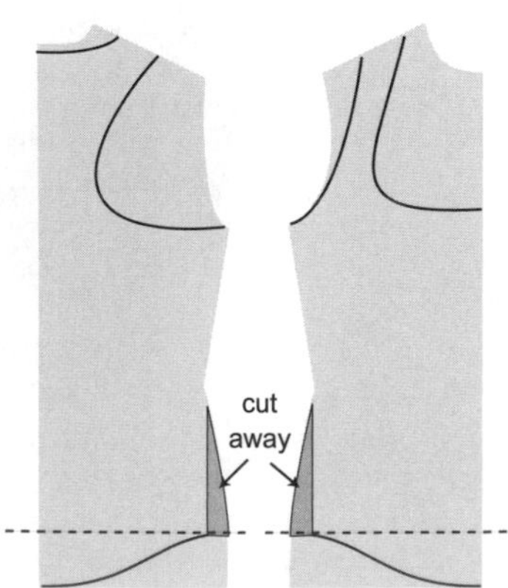

Notice that a small portion of the sides are cut off, which will expose a small amount of skin.

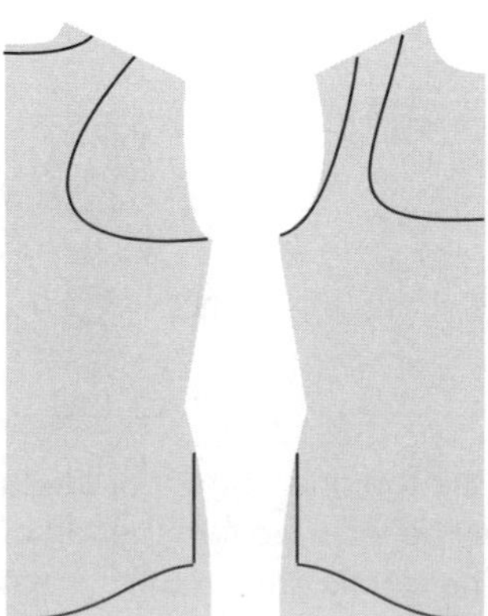

Notice that a 7″ slit will cut off the side and expose slightly more skin.

This diagram shows how the sides will be cut away and expose some skin on the side seams.

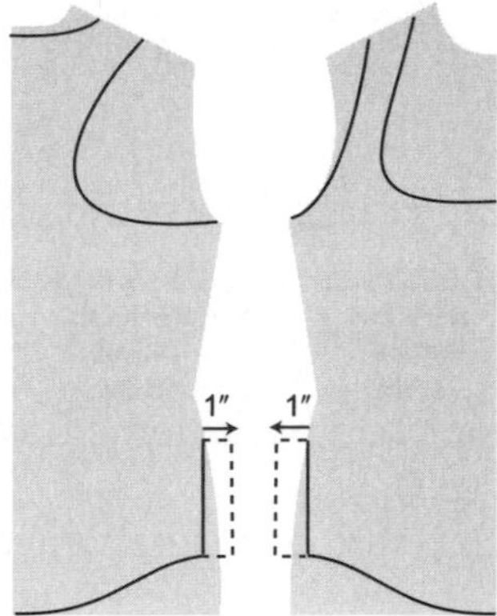

Draw in the new side seams and hem.

The style needs a 1″ foldback facing or hem.

2

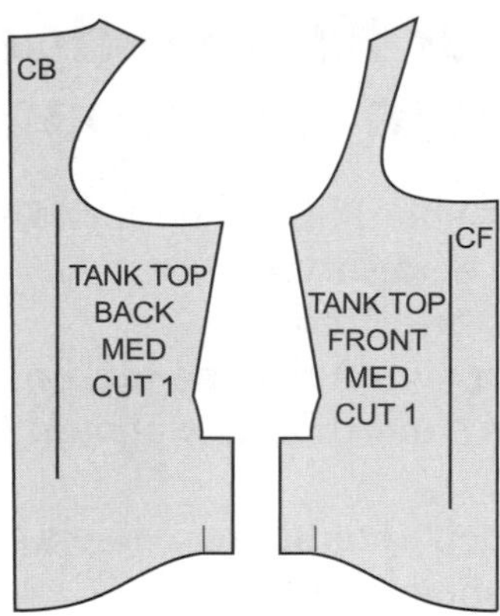

Trace out, separate, and label the new pattern as illustrated

You may place a notch at the hem to indicate where the slit facing should fold back. It is also a good idea to make the top of the facing straight across.

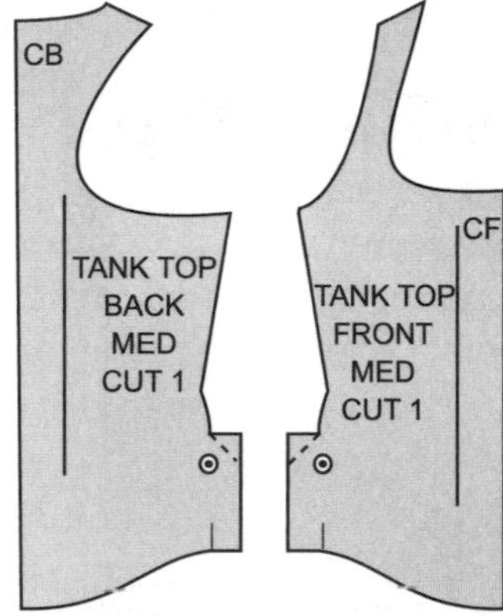

An angled line is not different enough from the side seam to tell the sewer where to stop sewing down the side seams.

But of course, if the design requires an angled line, you should include a drill mark to indicate the end of the seam.

4

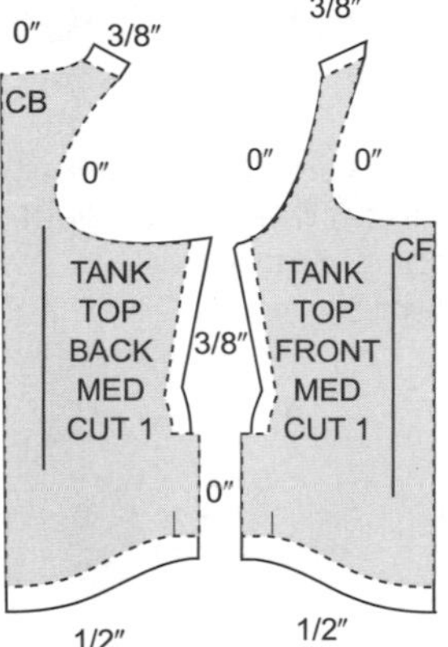

Trace out the pattern and label as indicated.

Note that there is no seam allowance added to the slit, because it is already a hem allowance.

1

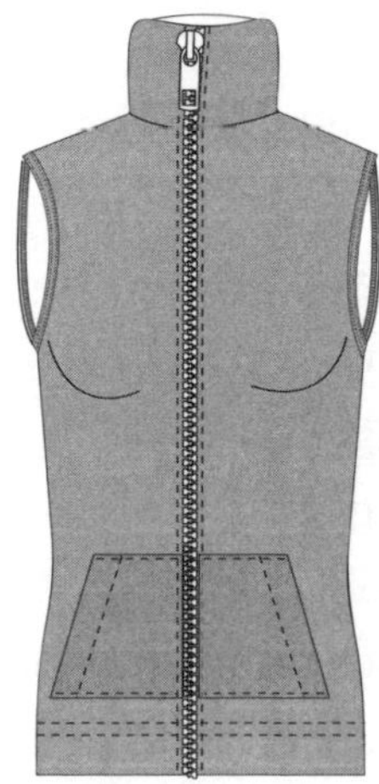

TANK TOP WITH SEPARATING ZIPPER

The width of the exposed zipper teeth will increase the size of the front, so to compensate you need to remove 1/4″ from the center front, 1/8″ from each side.

2

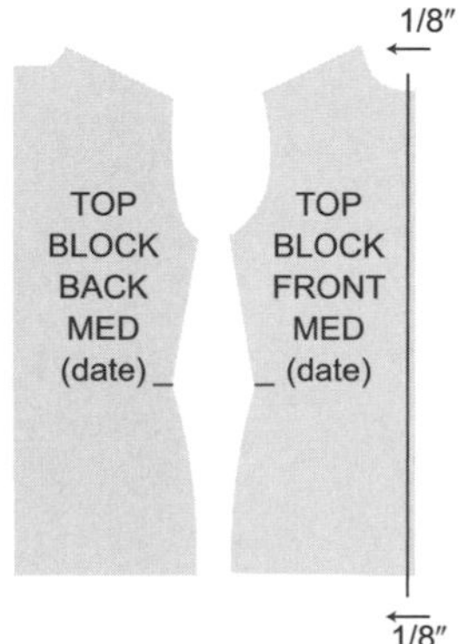

Measure the width of the zipper teeth, the amount that the zipper would increase the width, and remove half of that amount from each side of the front sloper.

Test Your Knowledge of the Material in this Chapter

1. What fit should be used for tank tops?
2. What is semi-fitted?
3. What is un-fitted?
4. How can you make the binding square?
5. How far from the neck should the straps be?
6. How much should you raise and tighten the armhole of a tank top?
7. Should you always raise and tighten the armhole of a tank top?
8. How much seam allowance should be applied to edges that will have binding applied?
9. How do you create an asymmetrical tank top?
10. How can you hem an asymmetrical hemline?
11. Do the front and back hems have to be the same curves?
12. How much is the hem allowance for curved hems?
13. How much seam allowance is needed for a separating zipper?
14. How much should banding be reduced for tank tops?

Test Your Knowledge By Creating This Tank Top

Style #	#4004	Date	July 07
Description:	One-way-stretch square-neck tank top with curved hem and slits		
Season	Spring/Summer 04	Sizes	Medium
Fabric	Interlock/jersey/T-shirt knit	Content	
Care			

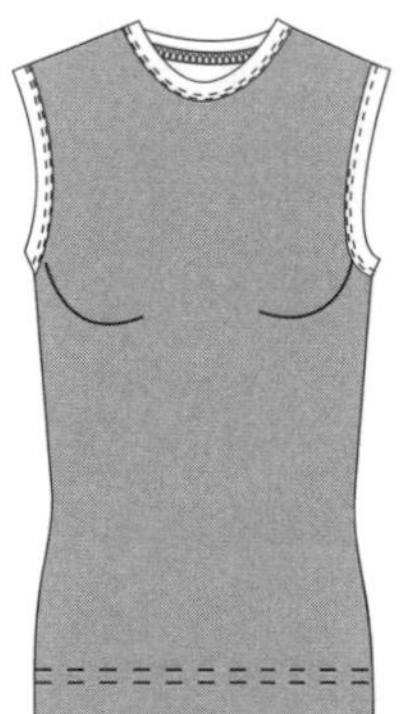

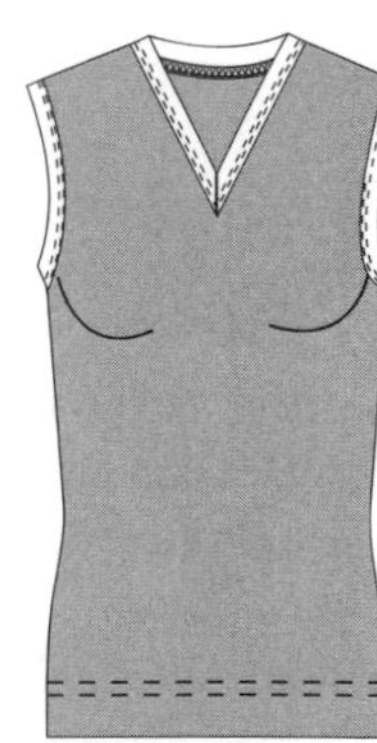

Sloper to be used	One-way-stretch top, regular fit, Medium
Neck	4″ down in front, 2″ down in back
Straps	2″ away from neck, 2″ wide
Waist	Semi-fitted
Slits	6″ high with 1″ foldback
Seam allowances	3/8″
Seam finish	Four-thread serger
Hem	Curved 3″ higher on the side seams
Hem allowance	1/2″ for curved hems
Hem finish	Cover-stitch
Armhole finish	3/8″ binding
Neck finish	3/8″ binding
Binding width	1 1/8″ cut will finish at 3/8″
Notes:	Cover-stitch hems before sewing slits.
	Sew slits closed for 1″ with straight-stitch machine.
	Little darts in neck binding to create square neckline.
	Sew slits right on the serging line.

CHAPTER 8

Sleeves

About This Chapter

This chapter develops different patterns for sleeves. The sleeve measurements are determined by the body draft; therefore, all drafting steps are the same regardless of the fabrication, except with different measurements. You can draft a sleeve for any knit garment using these instructions. This chapter starts with separate sleeves and then explains sleeve–body combinations, such as raglan sleeves, dolman sleeves, and saddle sleeves. Each fabrication should have three different sleeves with different cap heights; so, for example with the stable knit front and back, you should have three different cap heights. As with the previous chapters, you should draft the stable knit sloper and indicate the different stretch ratios for other variations.

STABLE KNIT SLEEVE REDUCTIONS

Zero percent smaller in crosswise direction without any reductions in lengthwise direction.
Use these measurements when drafting slopers for fabrics that stretch from 0% to 25%, and the other ratios will be indicated on the final slopers.

	Extra Extra Small	Extra Small	Small	Medium	Large	Extra Large	Extra Extra Large
Sleeve Length	22 5/8	22 3/4	23	23 1/4	23 1/2	23 3/4	24
Bicep	10	10 3/8	11 1/8	11 7/8	12 5/8	13 3/8	14 1/8
Bicep	5	5 1/5	5 4/7	6	6 1/3	6 2/3	7
Wrist	5 1/8	5 1/2	6 1/4	7	7 3/4	8 1/2	9 1/4
Wrist	2 4/7	2 3/4	3 1/8	3 1/2	3 7/8	4 1/4	4 5/8

CAP HEIGHT REDUCTION

The sleeve cap determines the angle that the sleeve sits into the armhole. Any cap height may be used, depending on the fit requirements of the design.

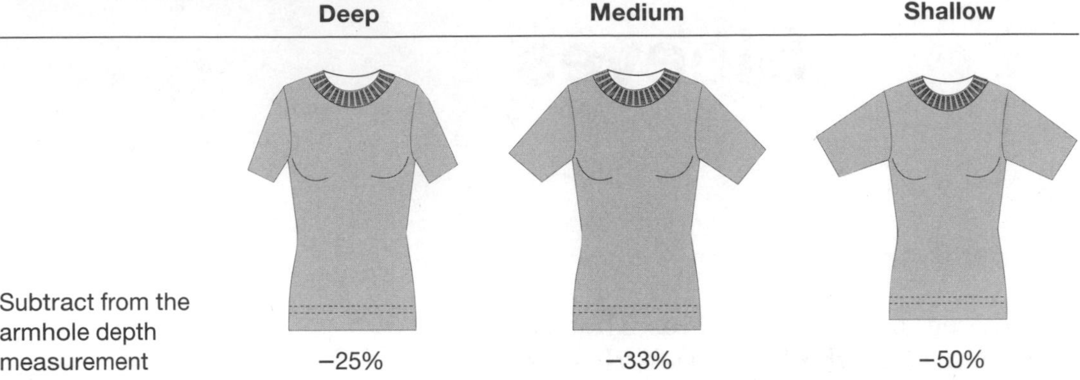

Deep
Medium
Shallow
Subtract from the armhole depth measurement
–25%
–33%
–50%

CAP MEASUREMENTS

This chart represents the different reductions based on the measurement of your armhole depth.

Armhole Depth	Deep Cap –25%	Medium Cap –33%	Shallow Cap –50%	Armhole Depth	Deep Cap –25%	Medium Cap –33%	Shallow Cap –50%
6	4½	4	3	7⅜	5½	4⅞	3¾
6⅛	4⅝	4	3	7½	5⅝	5	3¾
6¼	4¾	4⅛	3⅛	7⅝	5¾	5	3⅞
6⅜	4¾	4¼	3¼	7¾	5⅞	5⅛	3⅞
6½	4⅞	4¼	3¼	7⅞	6	5¼	4
6⅝	5	4⅜	3⅜	8	6	5¼	4
6¾	5	4½	3⅜	8⅛	6	5⅜	4
6⅞	5⅛	4½	3 4/8	8¼	6¼	5¼	4⅛
7	5¼	4⅝	3½	8⅜	6¼	5½	4¼
7⅛	5⅜	4¾	3⅝	8½	6⅜	5⅝	4¼
7¼	5¼	4¾	3⅝	8⅝	6½	5 6/8	4⅜

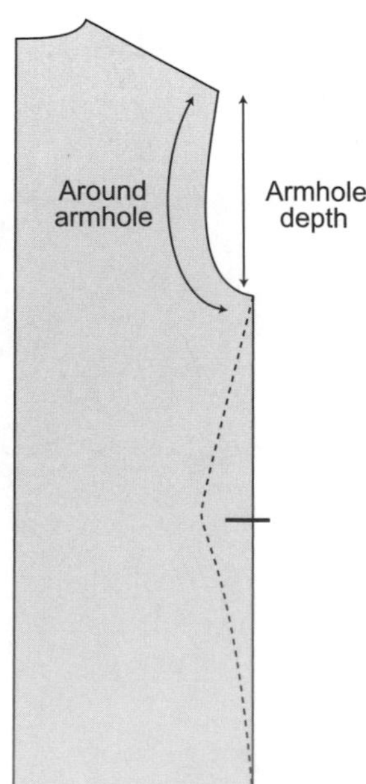

DRAFTING THE SLEEVE SLOPER

Often the patternmaker will not draft the sleeve until after the body has been fitted, to save time and effort, in case of fitting changes to the armhole.

Choose the sloper that you wish to make a sleeve for, as the measurements for the sleeve are taken from that pattern.

Decide on the type of sleeve cap that your design requires, by referring to the following diagram.

Measure armhole depth of sloper and record. Measure the total armhole circumference, both armholes, and record.

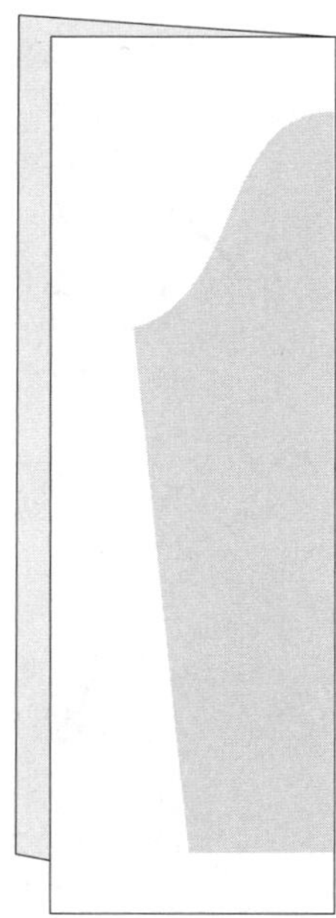

The sleeve will be drafted on a folded sheet of lightweight paper and is shown in gray so you can see and understand each step, as it applies to the draft.

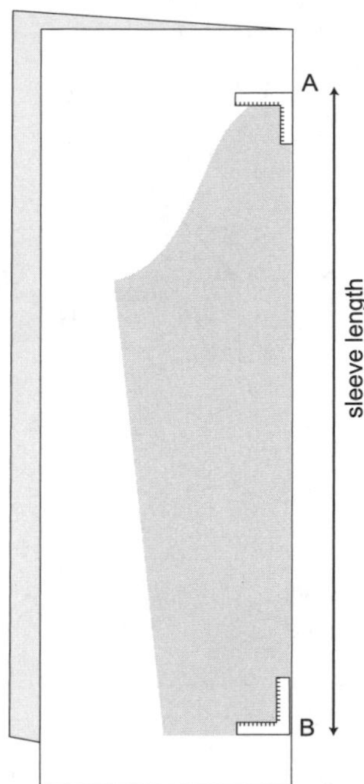

A-B = sleeve length

A-C = (armhole depth minus the amount for your particular cap height, from the chart)

Deep cap = minus 25%

Medium cap = minus 33%

Shallow cap = minus 50%

C-D = bicep line – square a line out.

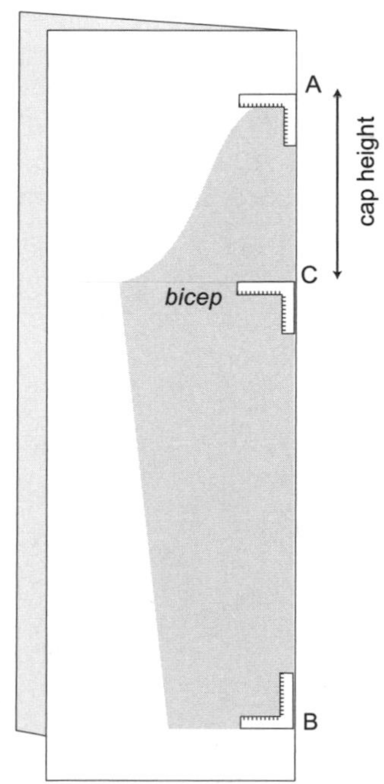

	Extra Extra Small	Extra Small	Small	Medium	Large	Extra Large	Extra Extra Large
Sleeve length	22 5/8	22 3/4	23	23 1/4	23 1/2	23 3/4	24

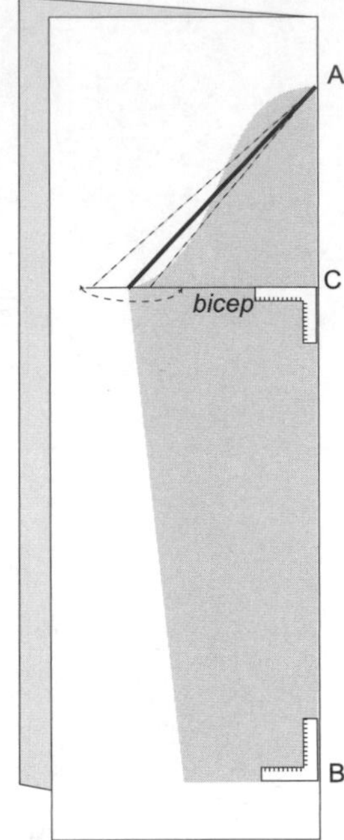

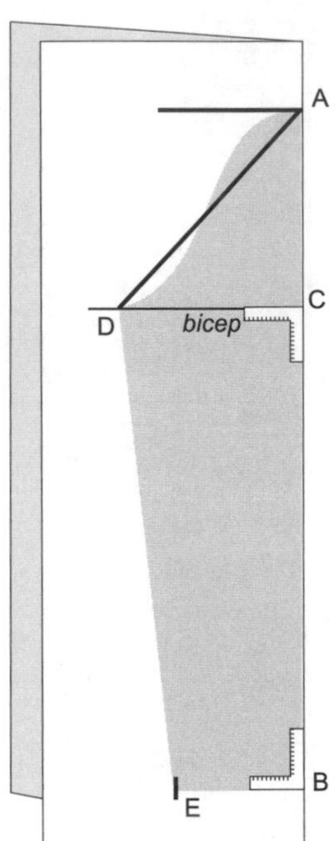

Place the ruler on point A and wherever it lines up with your armhole measurement, on the bicep line, draw a line. This determines the bicep length.

C-D = half of the total armhole measurement

Measure the front and back armhole and then divide this amount in half.

B-E = wrist

Square out ½″ from A.

Square out ½″ from D.

	Extra Extra Small	Extra Small	Small	Medium	Large	Extra Large	Extra Extra Large
Wrist	4⅜	5⅛	5⅞	6⅝	7⅜	8⅛	8⅞
Half of Wrist	2¼	2⅝	3	3⅜	3 ¾	4⅛	4½

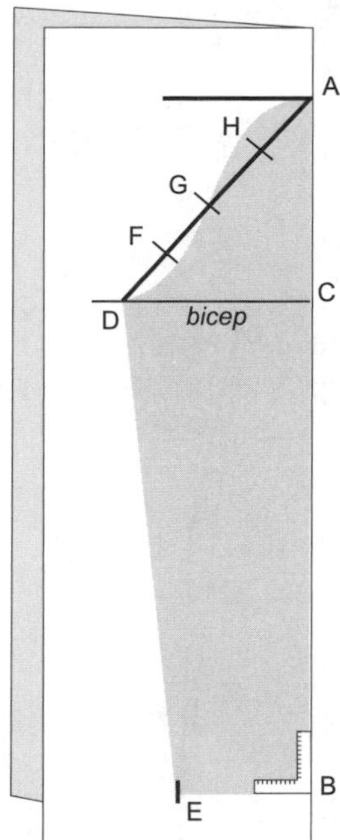

A-D divide into fourths and label F, G, and H.

Square a short guideline from each point.

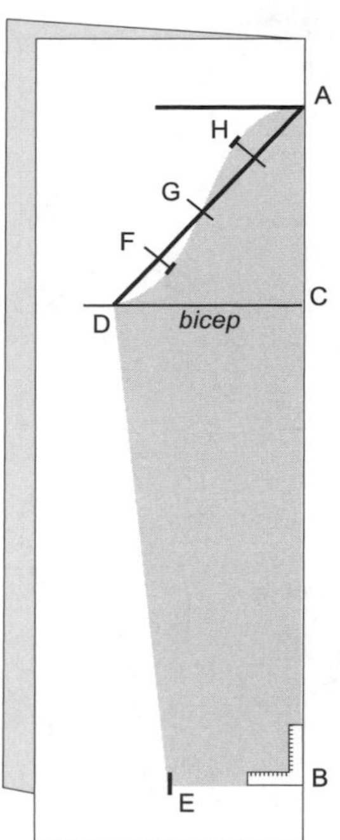

F measure down ½″.

I measure remains the same.

H measure up ½″.

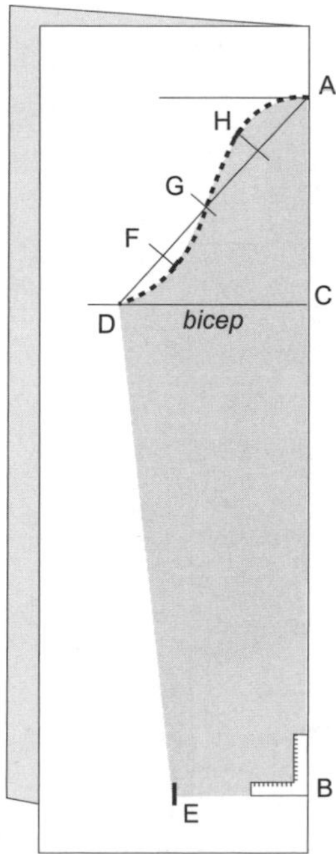

A = H = G = F = D draw the sleeve head connecting all points in a smooth and continuous line.

Remember to square for ½″ at the underarm and at the top of the sleeve head for at least ¼″.

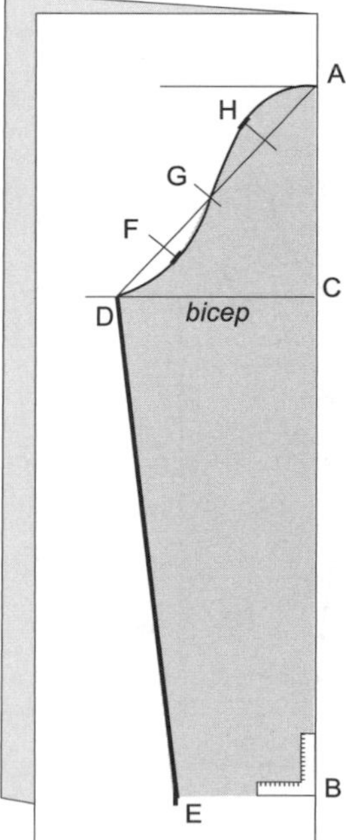

Connect point D to C to create the inseam of the sleeve.

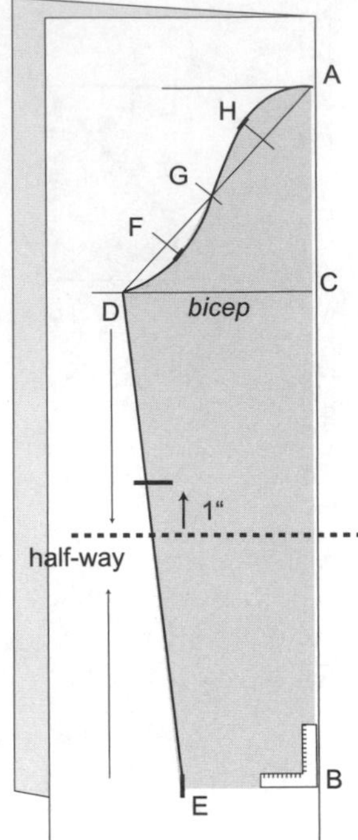

To take in the sleeve for fitted sleeve styles:

Find the half-way point of the inseam and measure 1″ up from that point.

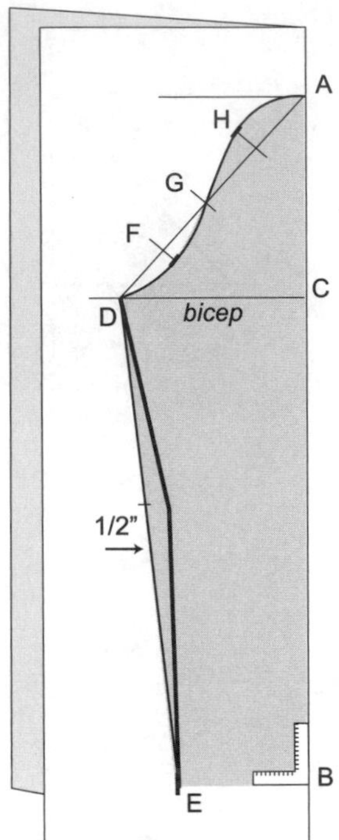

Take in the sleeve ½″ and blend a smooth inseam.

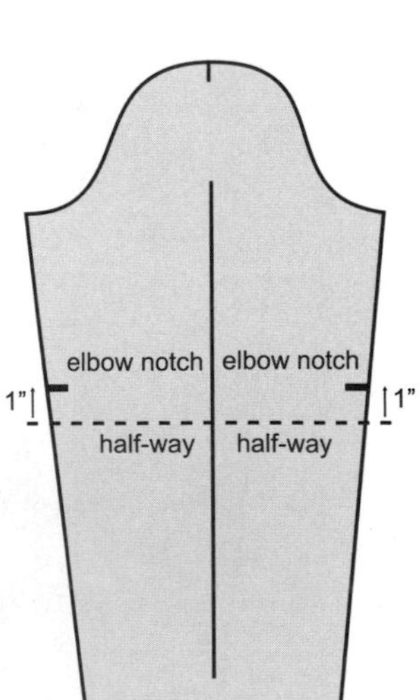

Cut out the sleeve on the fold and open up and draw in the grainline and a notch at the top of the sleeve, and an elbow notch.

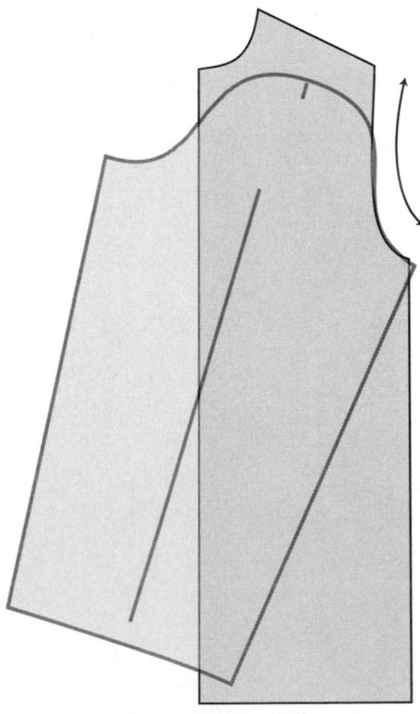

Starting at the underarm, walk the sleeve around the armhole.

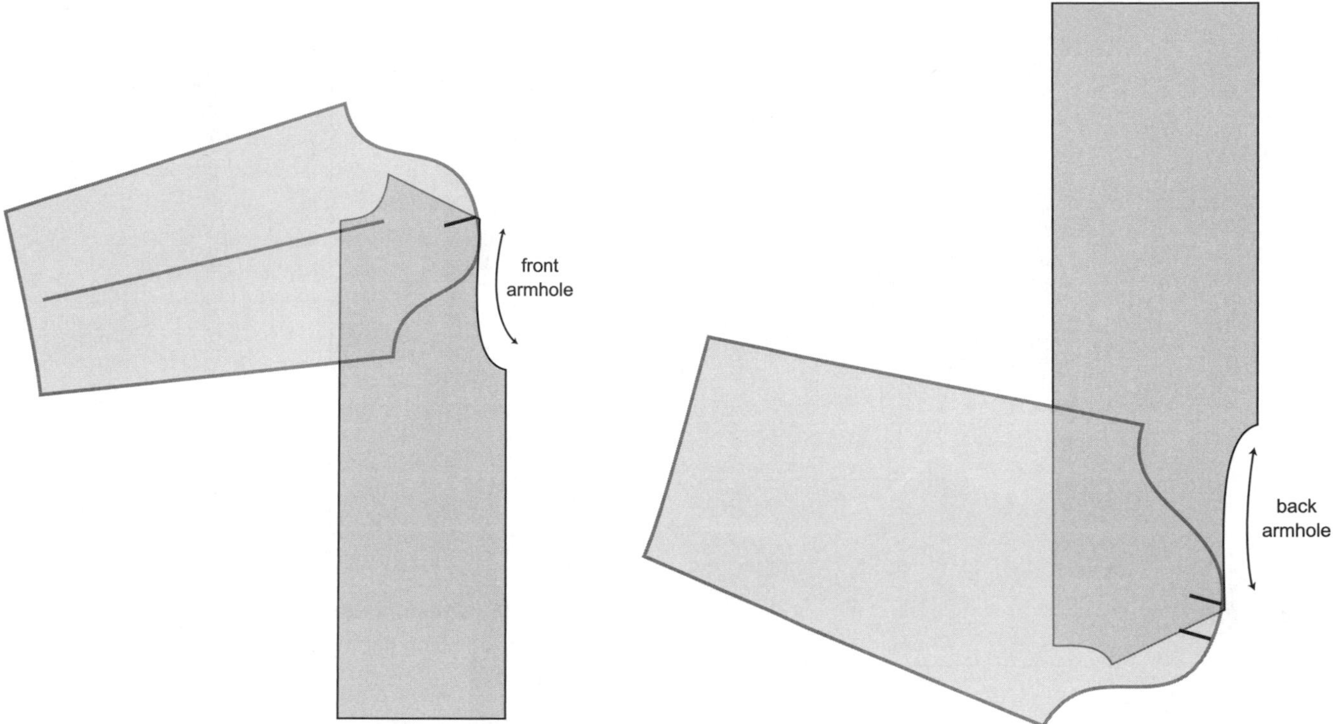

When you reach the shoulder, place a small pencil mark on the sleeve indicating by how much the sleeve is too large.

Then turn the sleeve over and walk around the other side against the back top sloper.

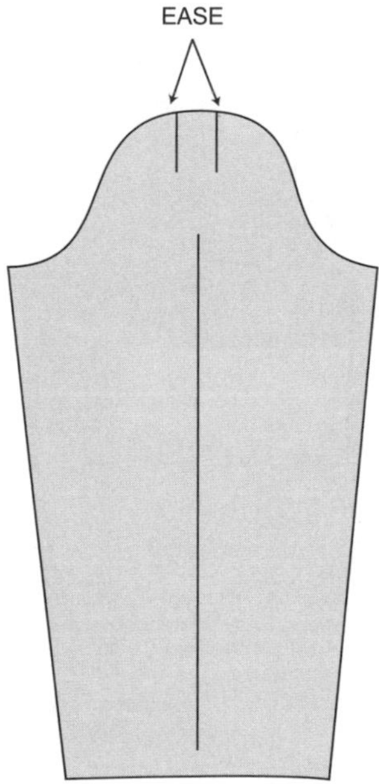

You must have two marks that indicate the amount of ease in the sleeve.

If your sleeve is bigger or smaller than the recommended ease of ½″ to ¾″, then you must correct the sleeve.

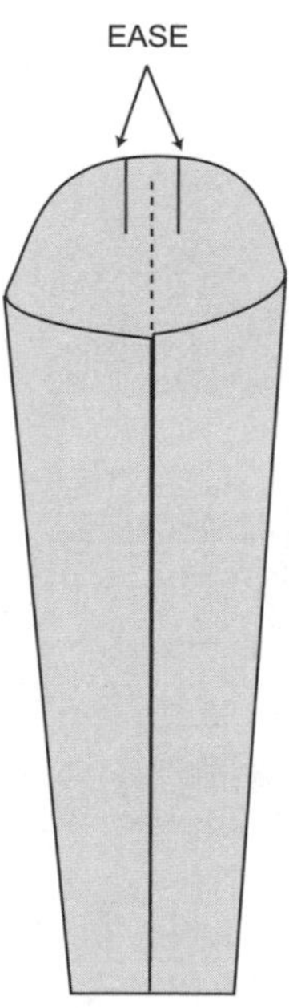

TRUEING THE SLEEVE

If your sleeve is bigger than ¾″ or smaller than ½″, then you must correct the sleeve.

You cannot add extra to the seams, because the sleeve will fit wrong; the ease must be distributed evenly throughout the sleeve as shown.

Fold side seams in towards the grainline.

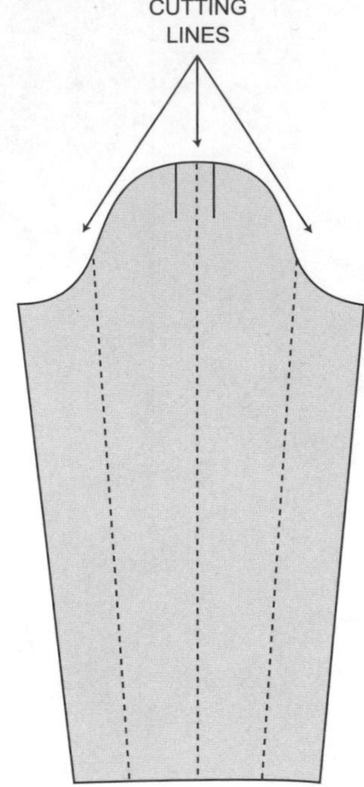

Draw in the cutting lines.

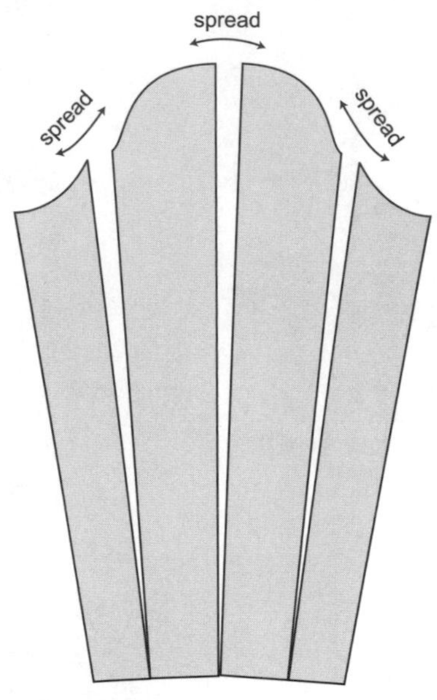

To increase the amount of ease to a minimum of ½″ and maximum of ¾″, slash and spread equally to the desired measurement.

The sleeve must always be at least ½″ bigger and at the most ¾″ larger than the armhole.

This amount is the sleeve ease, which must always be allowed to get a correct fitting sleeve.

Note: Do not change the wrist measurement.

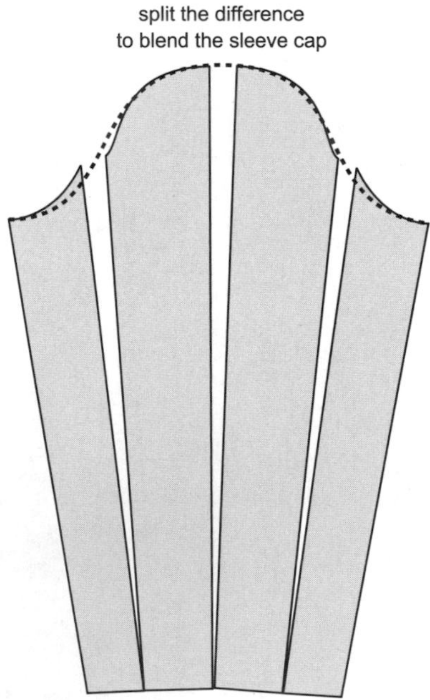

Retrace the sleeve, blending the armhole by splitting the difference between the two sides.

Recheck ease.

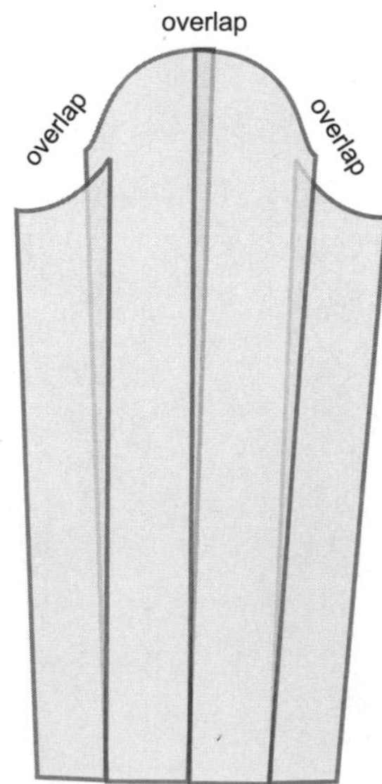

To decrease the amount of ease, slash and overlap to the desired measurement.

The sleeve must always be at least ½″ bigger and, at the most, ¾″ larger than the armhole.

This amount is the sleeve ease, which must always be allowed to get a correct fitting sleeve.

Note: Do not change the wrist measurement.

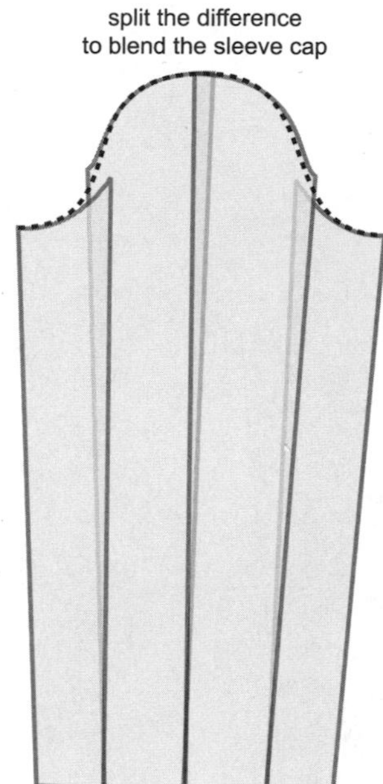

Retrace sleeve and blend the armhole by splitting the difference between the two sides.

Recheck ease.

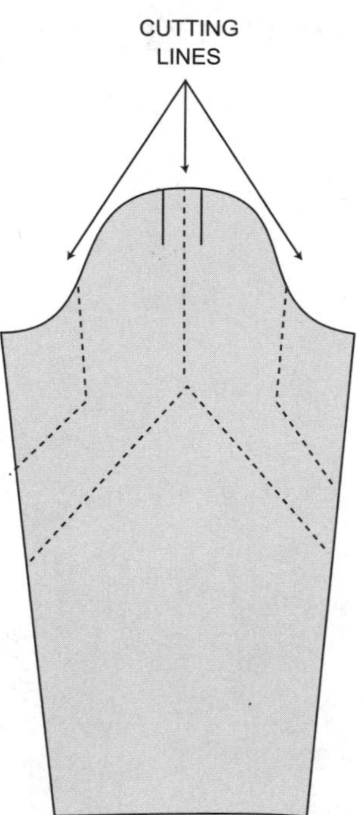

ALTERNATE METHOD OF CORRECTING SLEEVE EASE

This method of correcting the ease will not change the lower portion of the sleeve, only the sleeve cap.

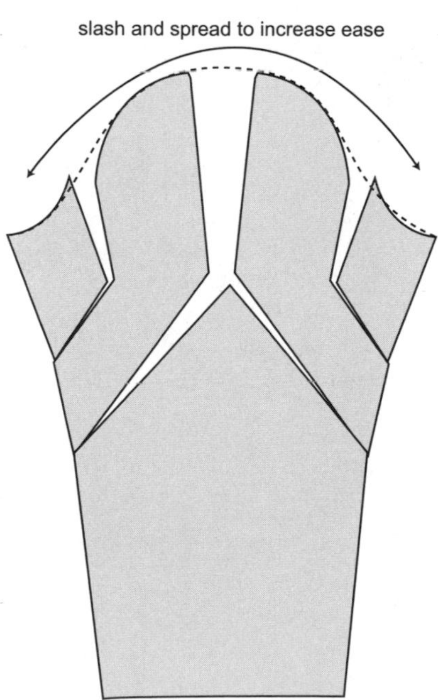

Slash and spread to increase the ease so that the total amount falls within the range of ½″ to ¾″.

Blend the new sleeve as illustrated.

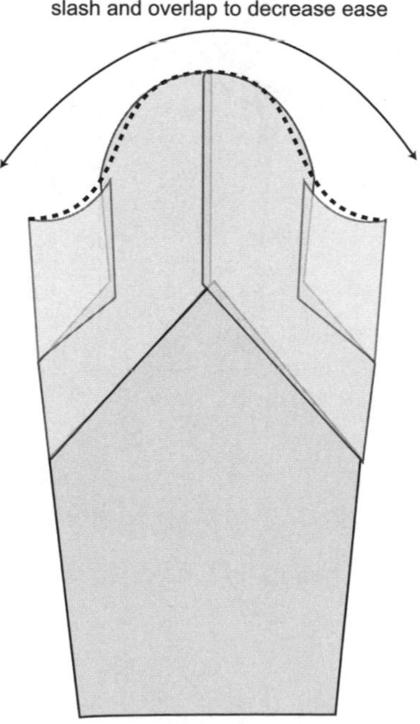

Slash and overlap to decrease the ease so that the total amount falls within the range of ½″ and ¾″. Blend the new sleeve as illustrated.

Sloper Labeling

Create all three different sleeve caps, for future use, and label as illustrated.

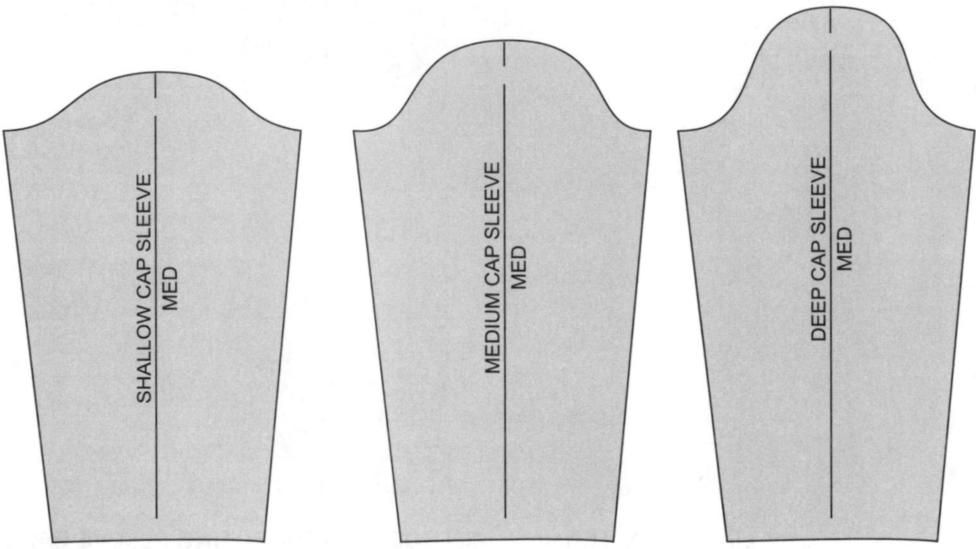

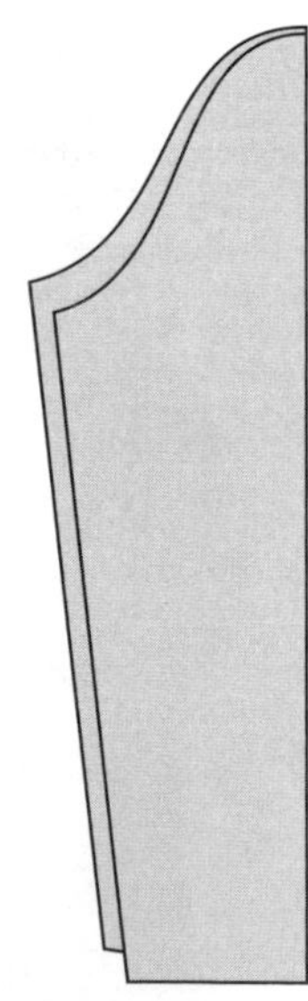

Fold the sleeve in half to find the grainline.

Flared Sleeves

Flared or bell sleeves are very popular and extremely easy to create.

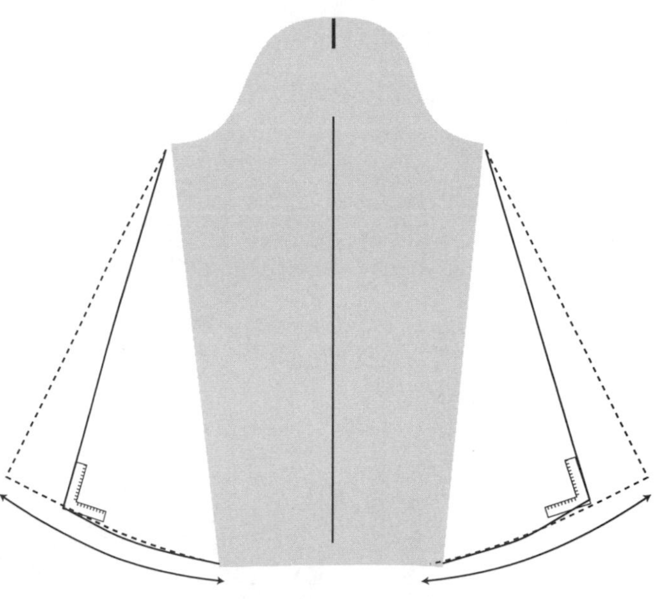

Simply extend the inseam of the sleeve the amount that you wish the sleeve to increase.

Make sure to square at the inseam.

EVENLY FLARED SLEEVES

The previous sleeve has the fullness added towards the inside. To create a sleeve that has the fullness distributed equally around the sleeve, use the following draft.

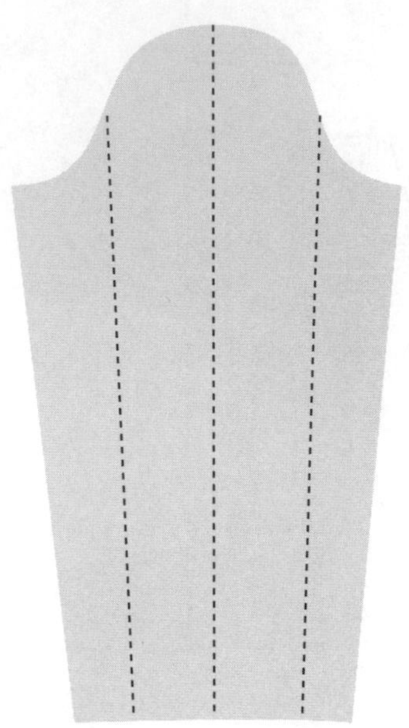

Divide the sleeve into four even sections by folding inwards towards the grainline.

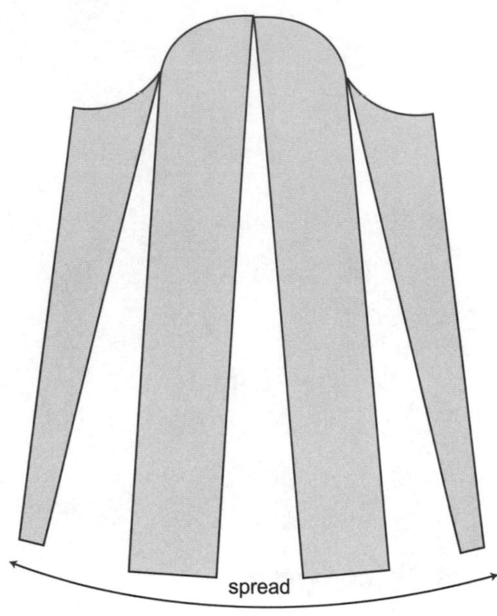

Slash and spread the sleeve to the desired fullness.

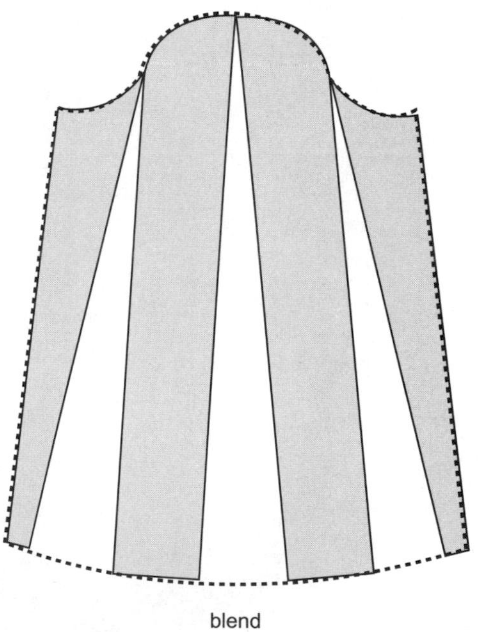

Blend the cap and hem as illustrated.

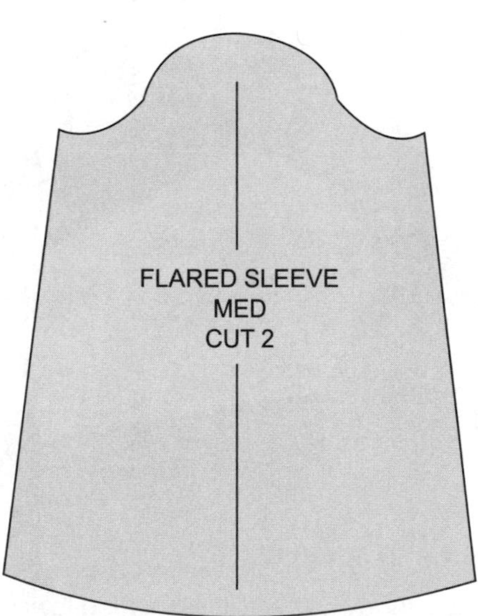

Label the new sleeve as indicated.

GATHERED SLEEVES

A sleeve with a gathered wrist may be created with the same technique.

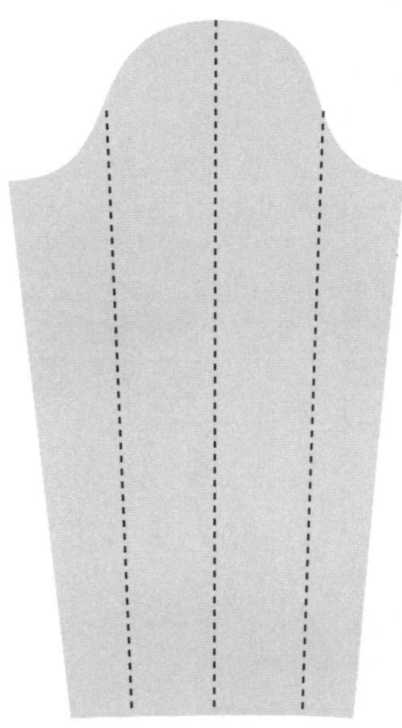

Divide the sleeve into four even sections by folding inwards towards the grainline.

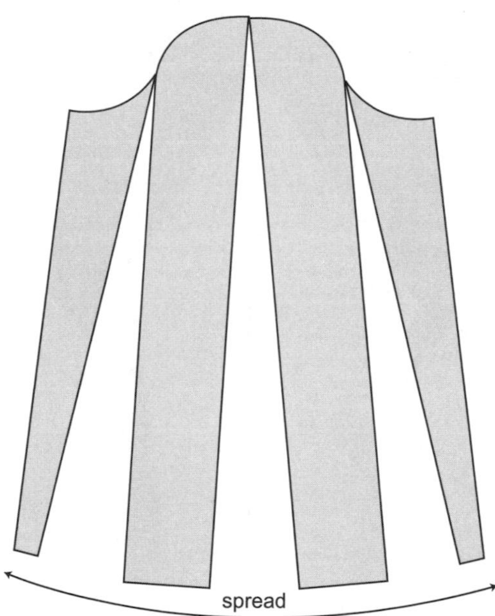

Slash and spread the sleeve to the desired fullness.

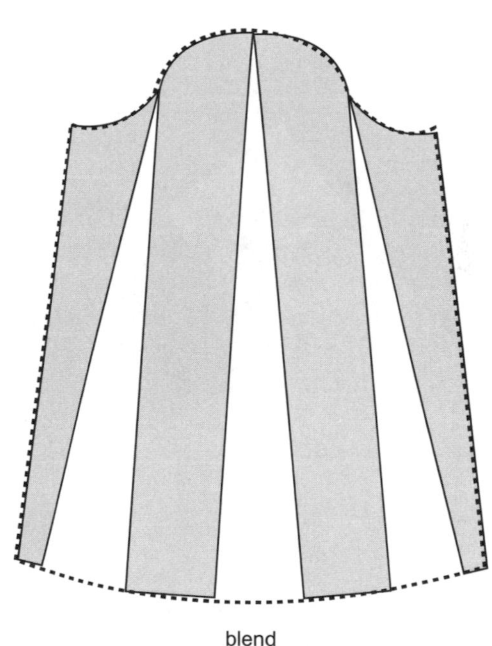

Blend the cap and hem as illustrated.

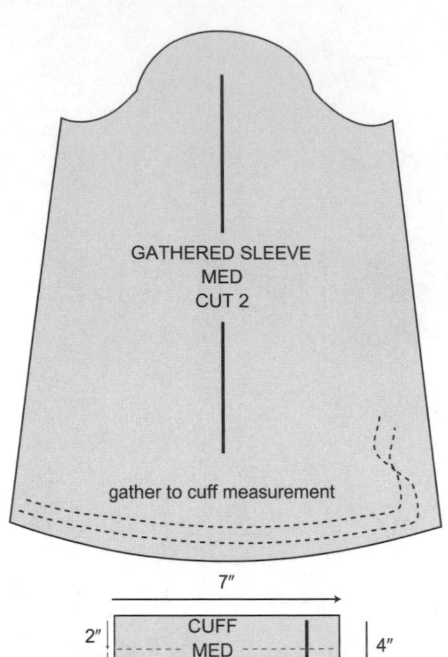

Label the new sleeve as indicated.

The wrist of the sleeve will be gathered to fit into the cuff.

Draft the cuff to fit the wrist measurement.

	Extra Extra Small	Extra Small	Small	Medium	Large	Extra Large	Extra Extra Large
Wrist	5⅛	5½	6¼	7	7¾	8½	9¼
Half of Wrist	2⅝	2¾	3⅛	3½	3⅞	4¼	4⅝

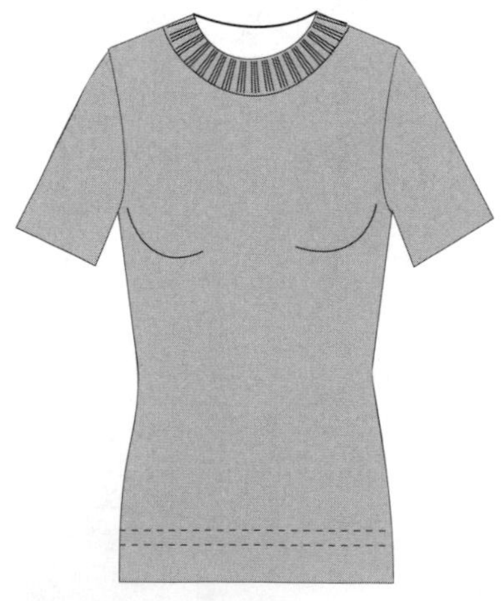

SHORT SLEEVES

Short sleeves are very easy to create.

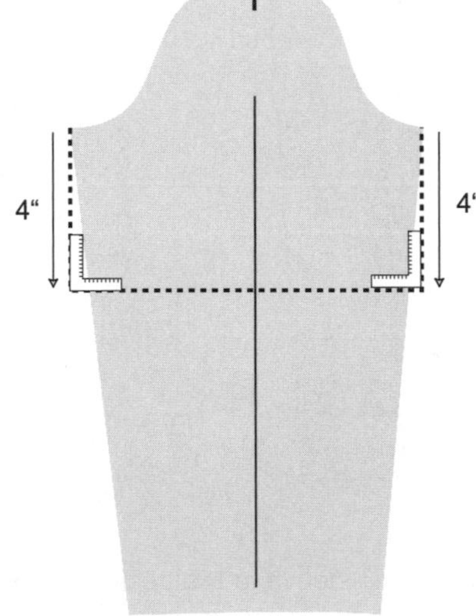

Measure down the inseam to the length your design requires.

This draft will create a little extra volume at the hem when looser styles are required.

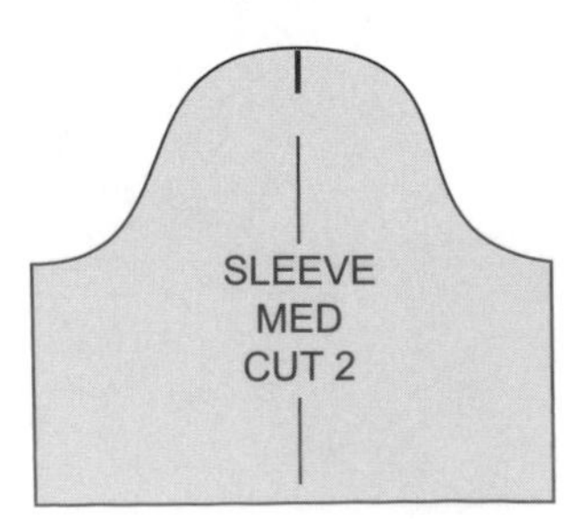

Label the short sleeve as indicated.

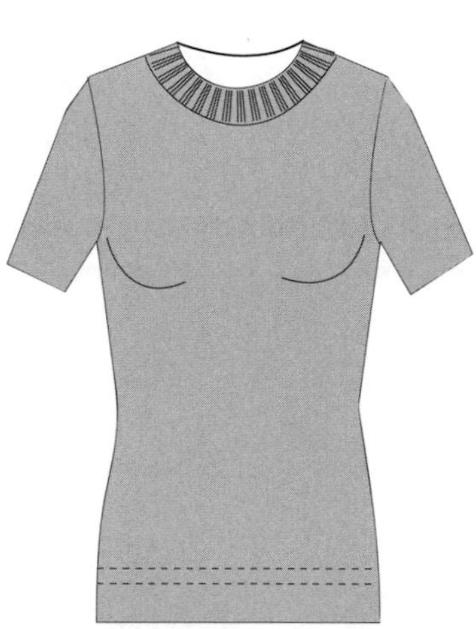

FITTED SHORT SLEEVE

The previous draft adds extra width at the bottom of the sleeve and may not be suitable for all designs.

This draft, however, is snug and fitted at the bottom.

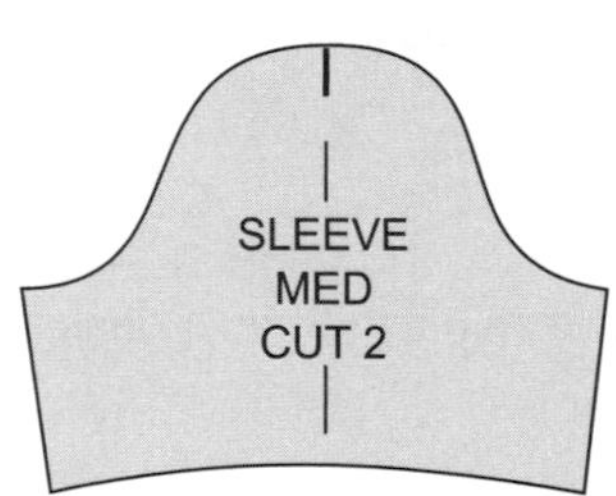

Trace out the sleeve as illustrated.

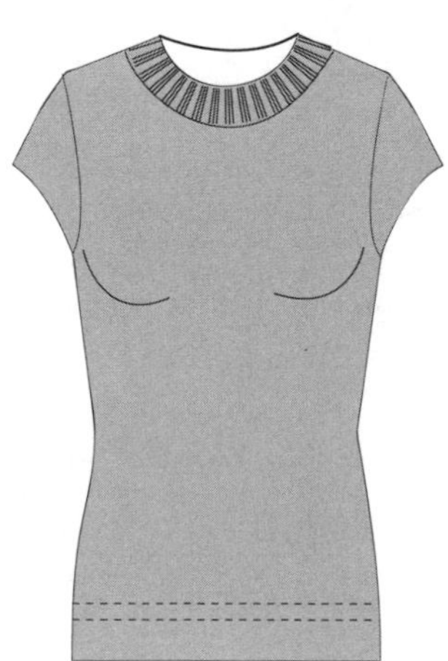

CAP SLEEVES

A cap sleeve needs to be pulled in tighter at the underarm.

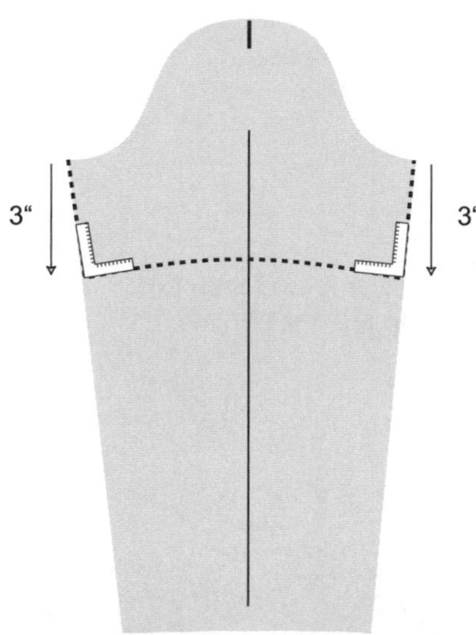

Measure down the length that your design requires and square from the side seams.

Blend a new hem.

Note: This hem is slightly curved.

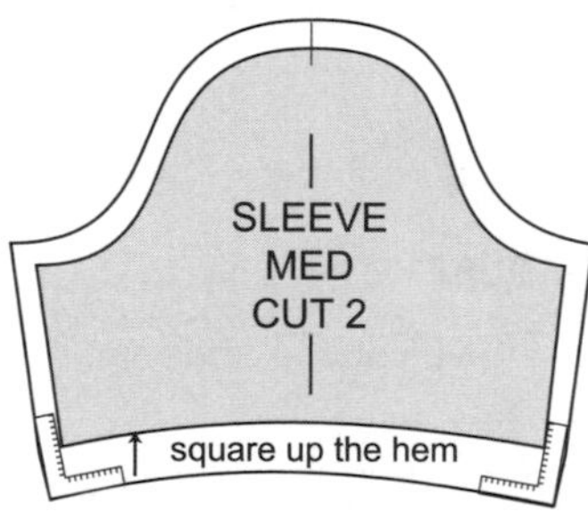

Add the necessary seam allowances to the sleeve.

Make sure to square up the hem.

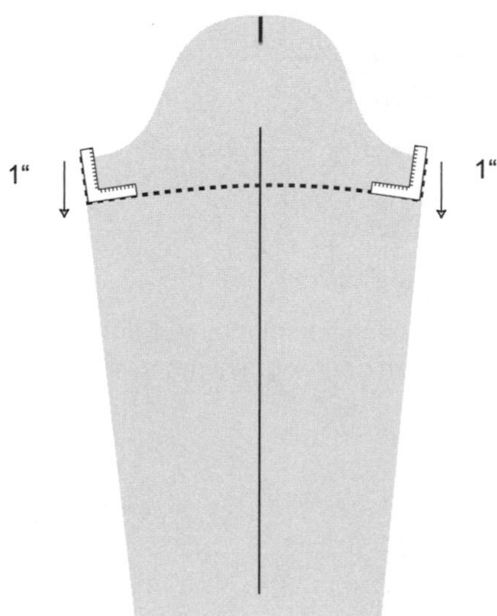

Shorten the sleeve as much as you require.

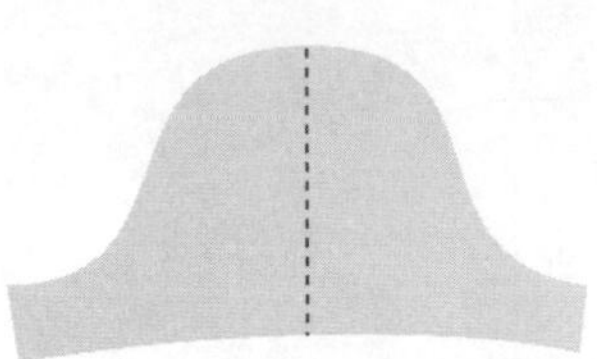

Trace out the new sleeve and then fold the sleeve in half to find the midline.

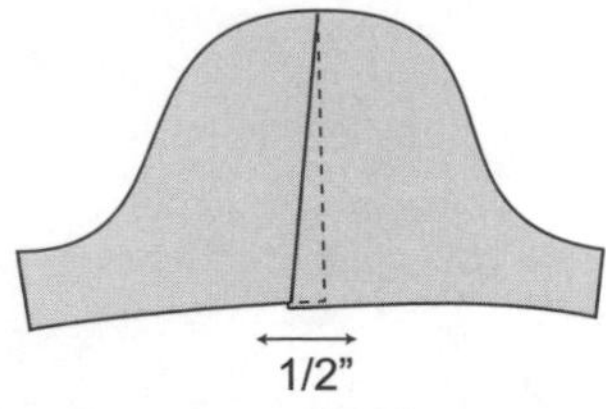

Slash and overlap the sleeve by ½″ to pull it in tighter to the body.

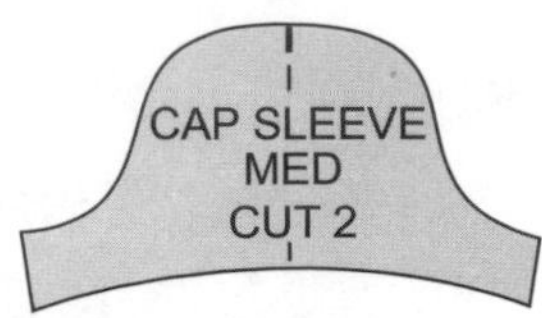

Trace out the final sleeve as illustrated.

FLARED SHORT SLEEVE

A short sleeve can have volume added to the hem.

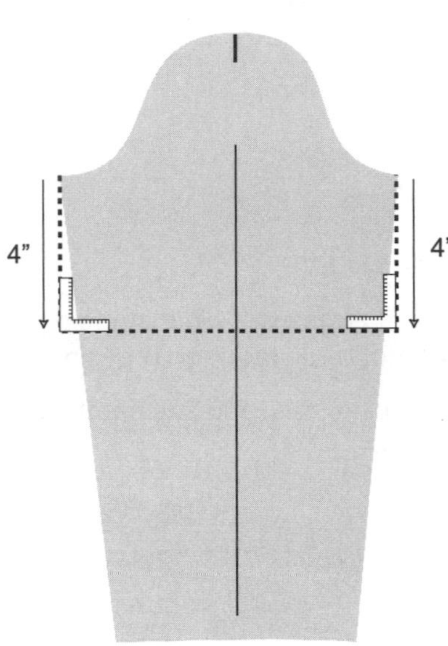

Shorten the sleeve as much as your design requires.

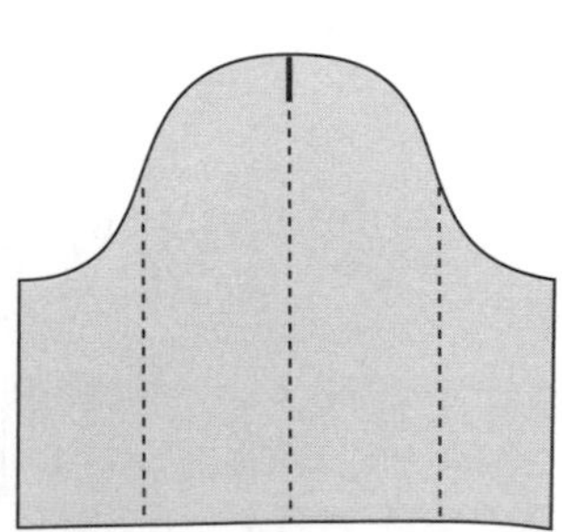

Draw in three slash lines.

To determine the slash line placement, fold the sleeve sides in towards the center grainline.

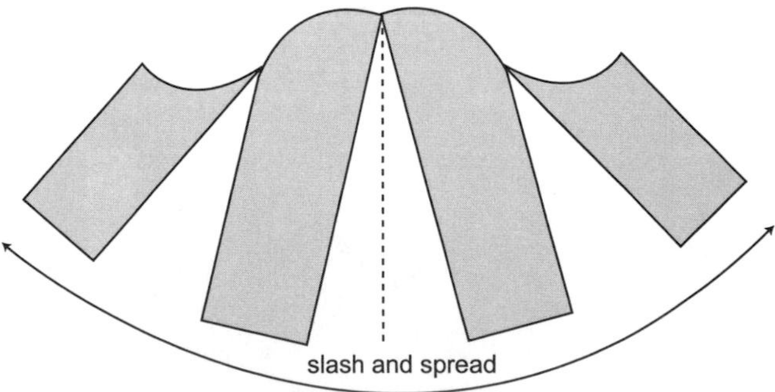

Slash and spread the sleeve any amount required.

	Light	Medium	Heavy
Spread by an additional	50%	100%	200%

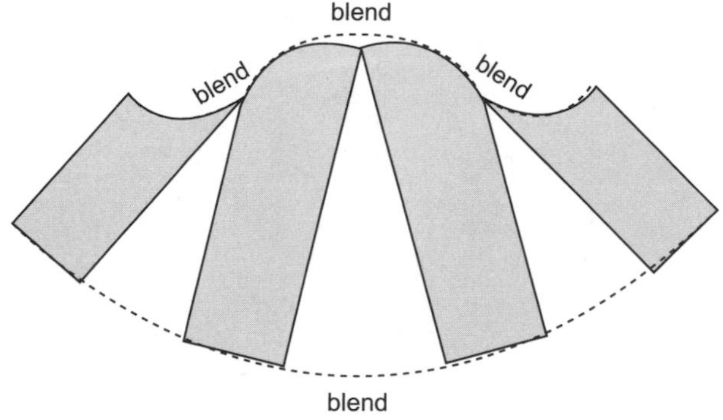

Blend the cap and the hem of the sleeve as illustrated.

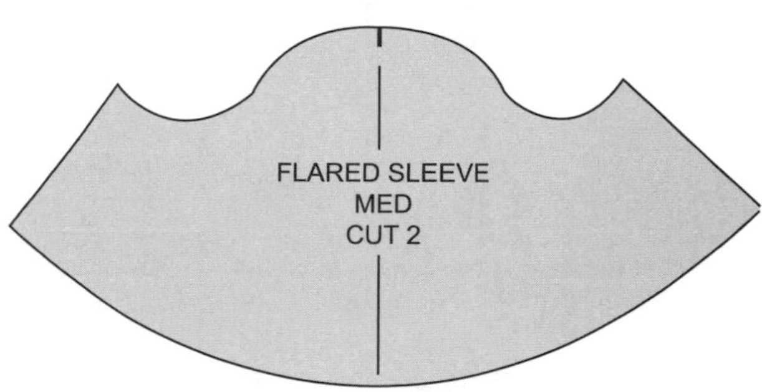

Label the final sleeve as illustrated.

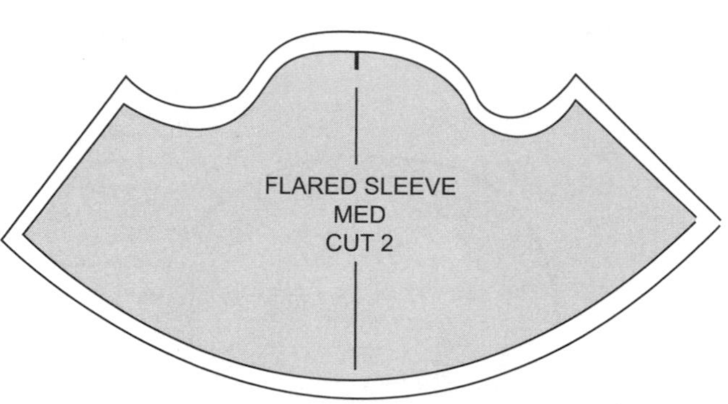

maximum 1/2" hem allowance for curved hems

The curved hem must have a very small hem allowance, maximum of ½″, in order to be hemmed smoothly.

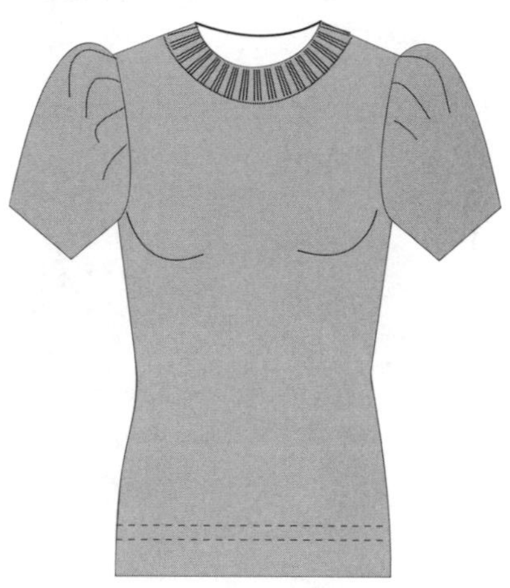

SHORT PUFFY SLEEVE

Volume can also be added to the top of the sleeve to create a puffy sleeve.

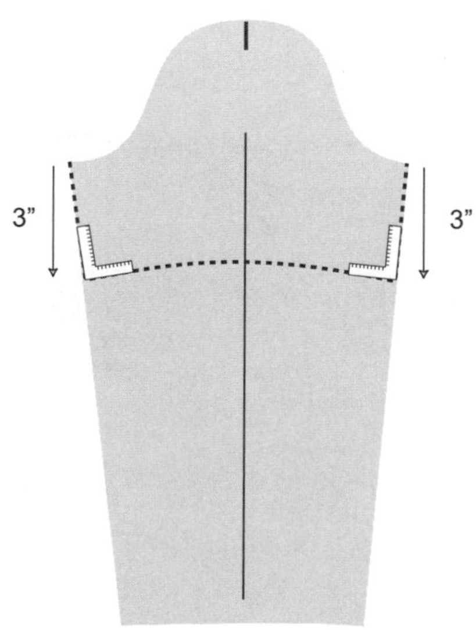

Measure down your required length, shown here at 3″, but may be any amount the designer requires.

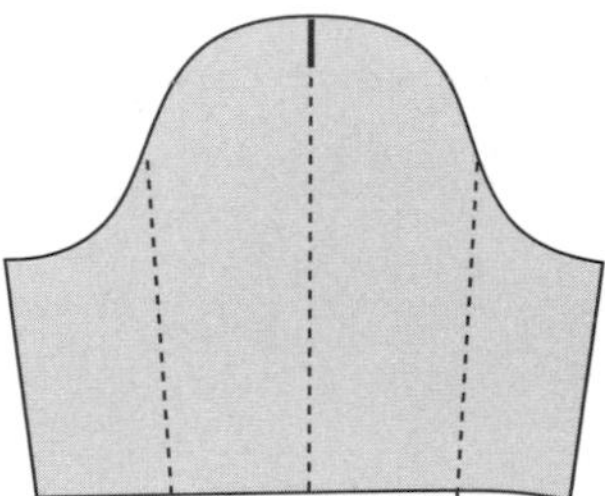

Fold the sleeve in towards the center to locate the slash lines.

Slash and spread the sleeve any amount required.

	Light	**Medium**	**Heavy**	**Very Heavy**
Spread by an additional	50%	100%	200%	300%

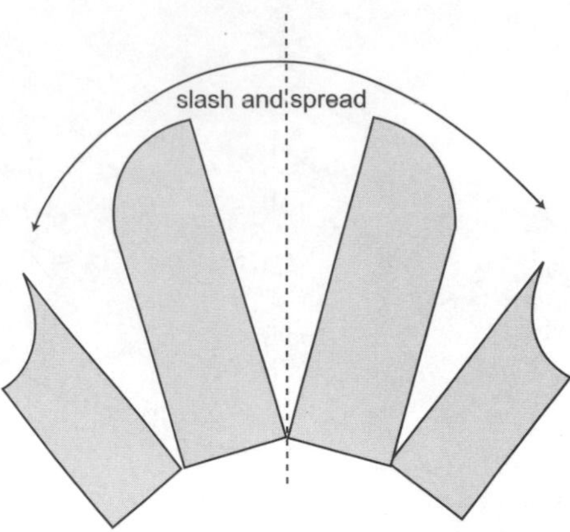

Heavy and very heavy fullness is only suitable for light and very lightweight fabrics.

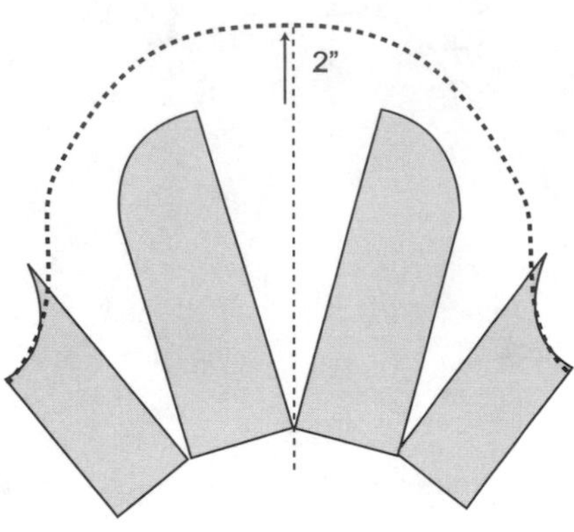

Raise the sleeve any amount required—illustrated here at 2″, for 1″ up, and 1″ back down.

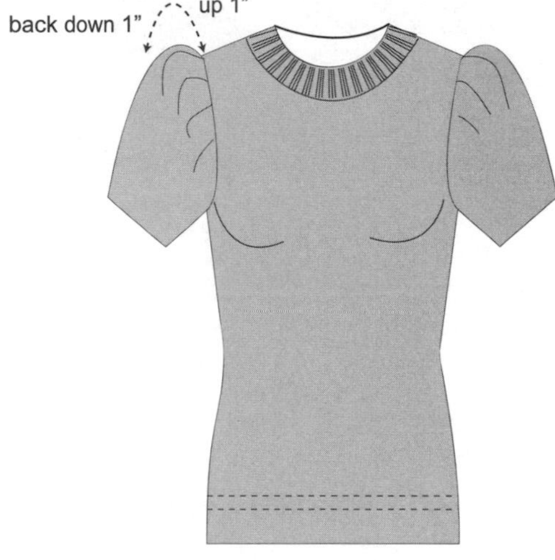

Note: The sleeve cap draft is raised 2″.

This translates into 1″ above the regular cap, and with an additional 1″ for the fabric to come back down 1″.

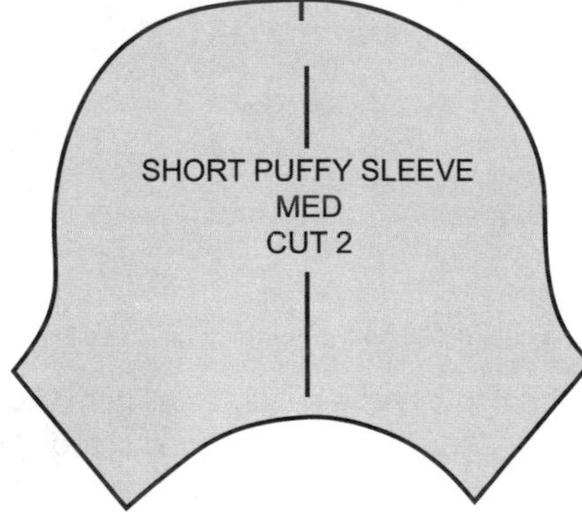

Redraw the sleeve, blending the cap and blending the hem.

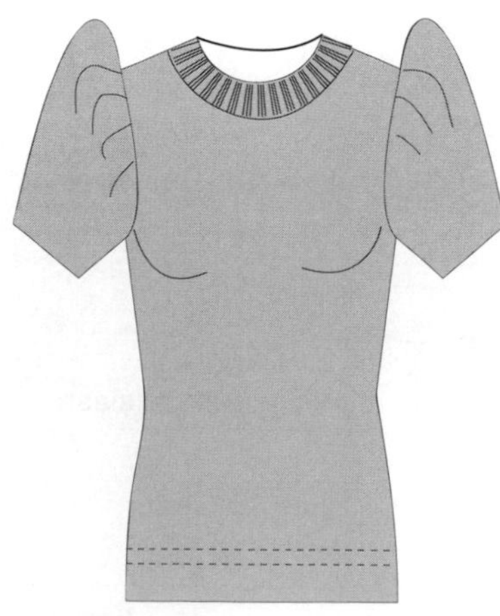

SHORT PUFFY SLEEVES, MEDIUM HEIGHT

By increasing the cap height, you can create a more dramatic puff sleeve.

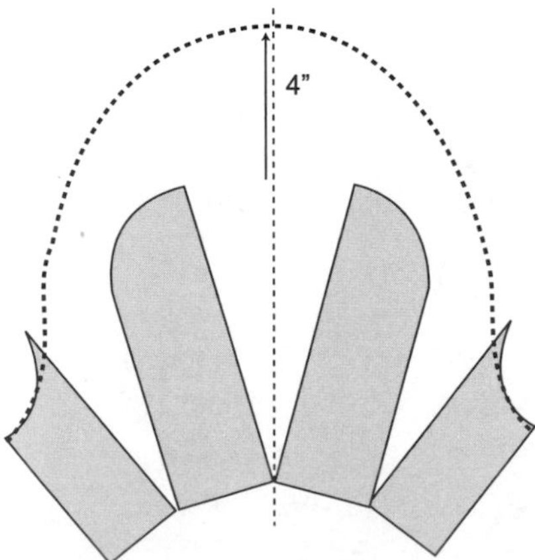

Raise the height of the cap by 4″.

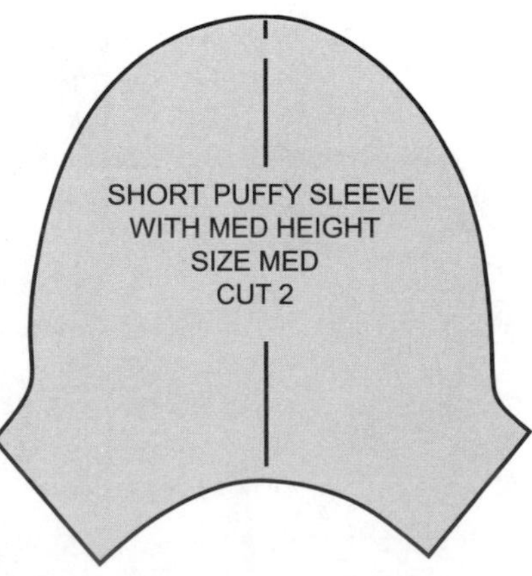

Label the sleeve as illustrated.

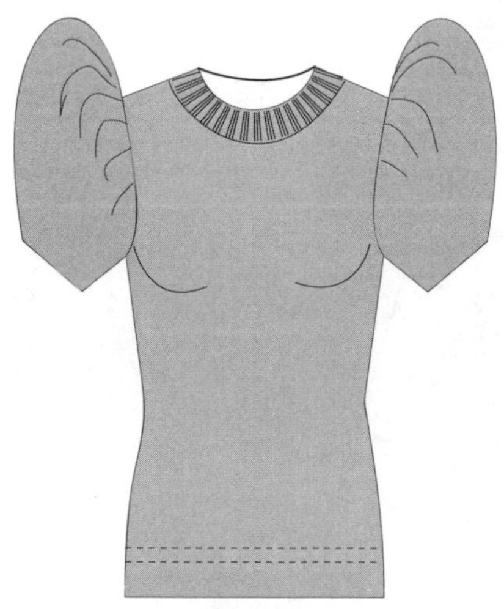

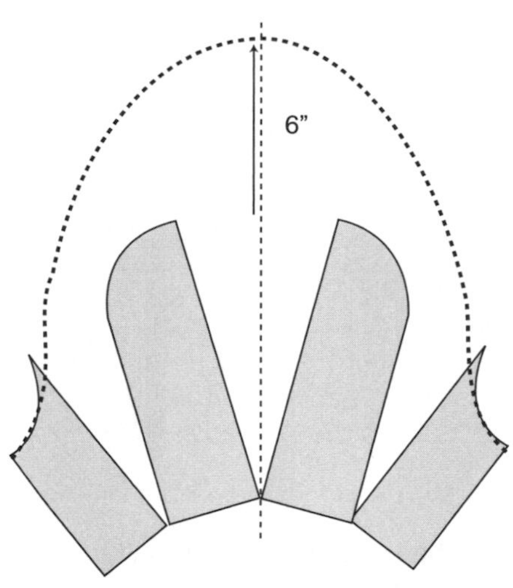

SHORT PUFFY SLEEVE, HIGHER HEIGHT

Extreme variations of this sleeve are created by following these instructions and need tulle or netting to support the sleeve.

Raise the sleeve cap 6″.

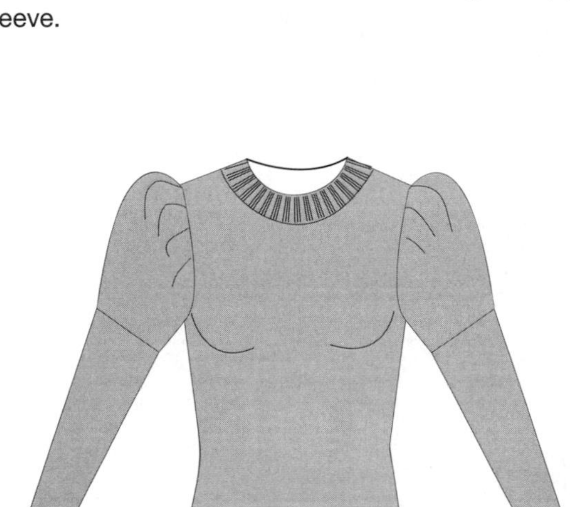

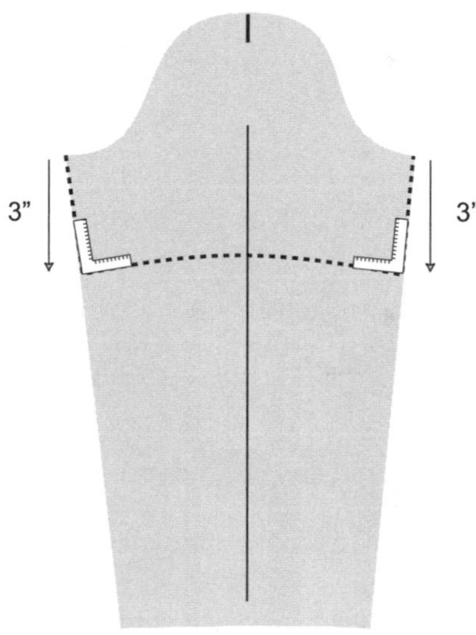

LONG SLEEVE WITH SHORT PUFFY CAP

By sewing the cap sleeve to the regular sleeve, you can create a long sleeve with a short puffy cap.

Determine the placement for your horizontal seam, illustrated here at 3″ down from the underarm, but it may be any place the designer requests.

Fold the sleeve in towards the center to locate the slash lines.

Slash and spread the sleeve any amount required.

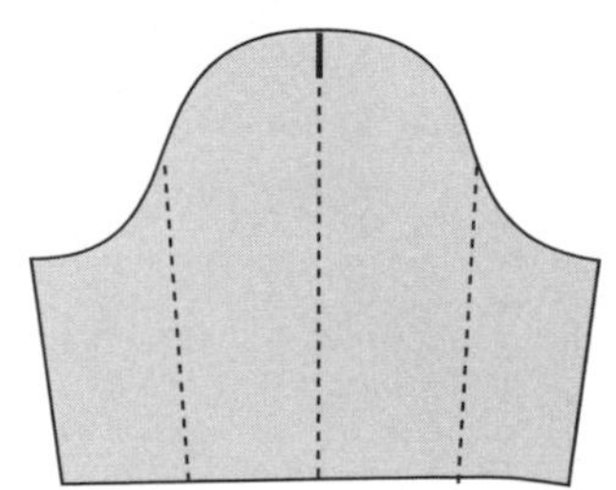

	Light	Medium	Heavy	Very Heavy
Spread by an additional	50%	100%	200%	300%

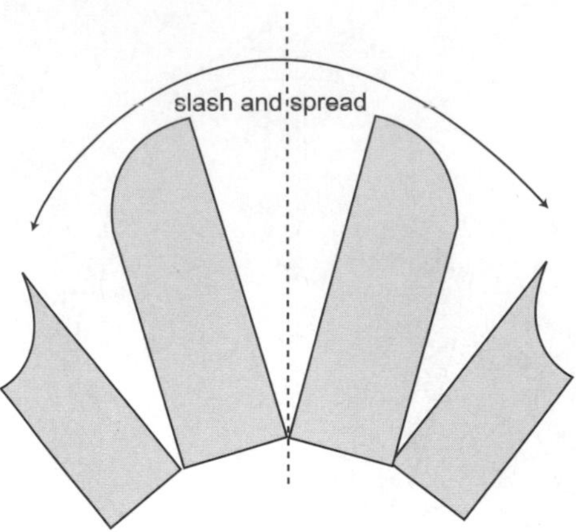

Heavy and very heavy fullness is only suitable for light and very lightweight fabrics.

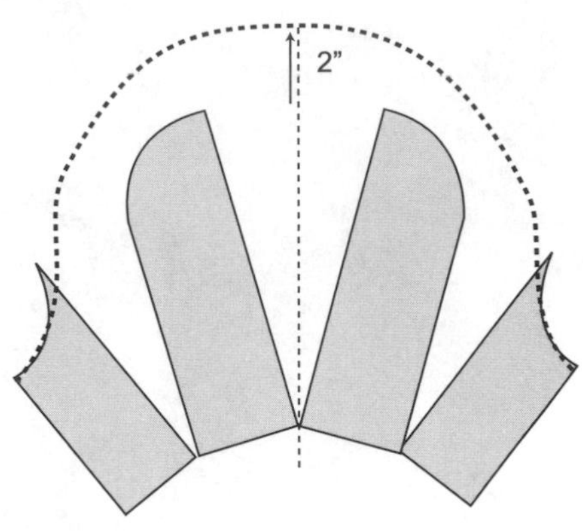

Raise the sleeve any amount required.

Illustrated here at 2″, for 1″ up, and 1″ back down.

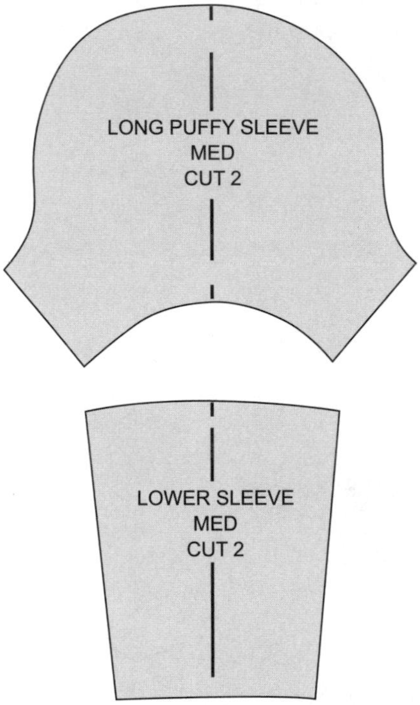

LONG PUFFY SLEEVE
MED
CUT 2

LOWER SLEEVE
MED
CUT 2

Trace, separate, and label the sleeve as illustrated.

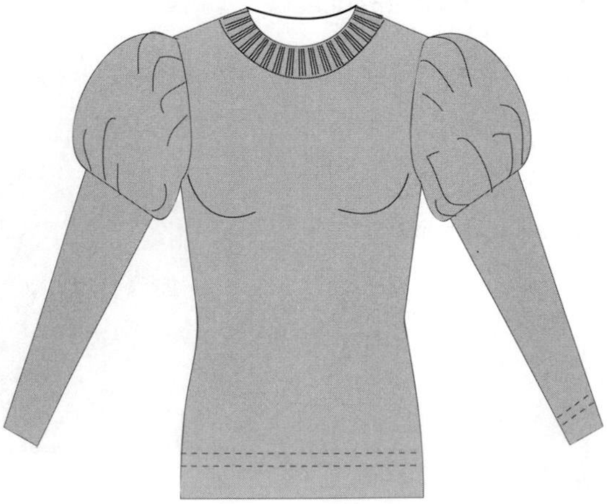

LONG SLEEVE WITH PUFFY GATHERED UPPER

This sleeve has gathering at the cap and horizontal seam.

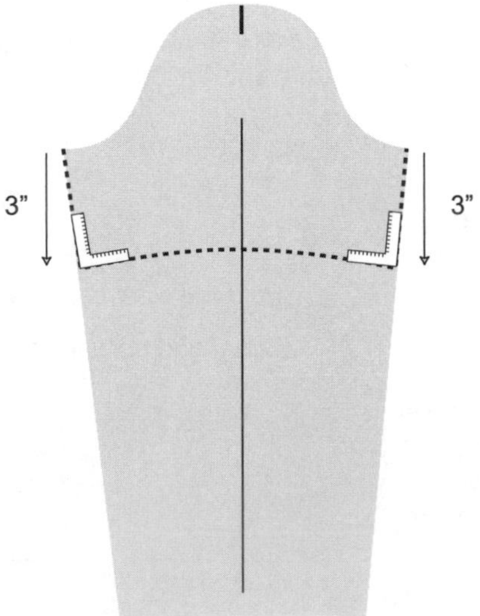

3"

3"

Measure down the amount required, illustrated here at 3″.

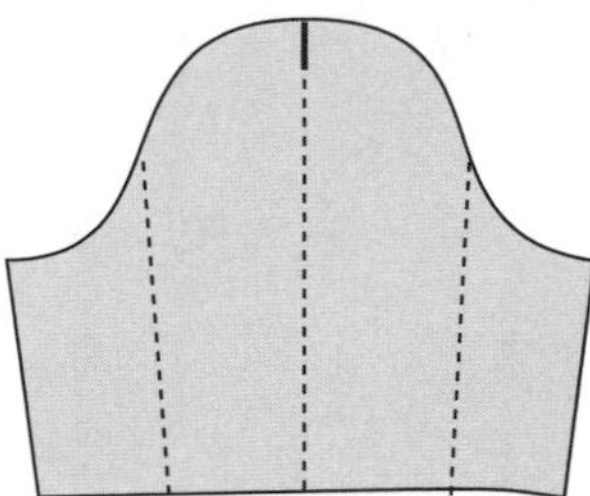

Fold the sleeve inwards towards the grainline to determine the slash lines.

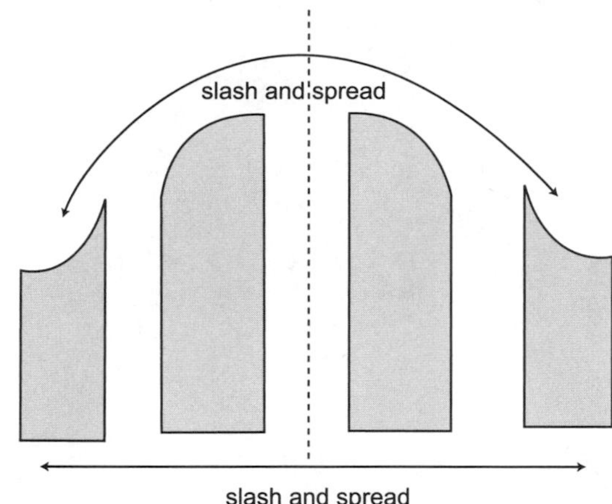

Slash and spread the sleeve, increasing the volume at the cap as well as at the horizontal seam.

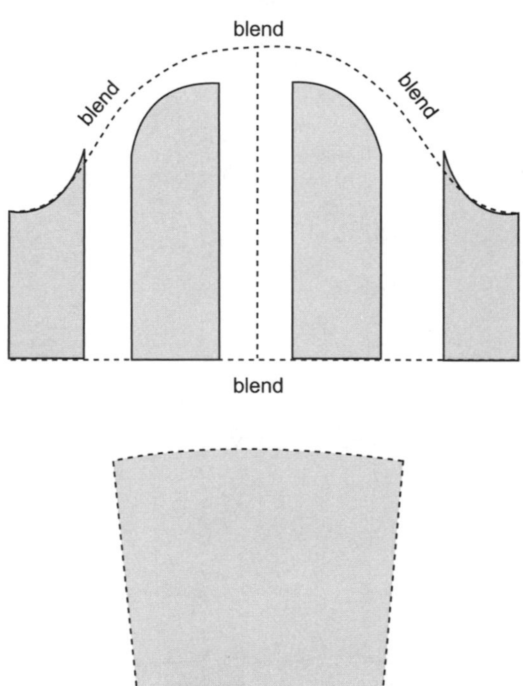

Blend the cap and horizontal seam of the sleeve.

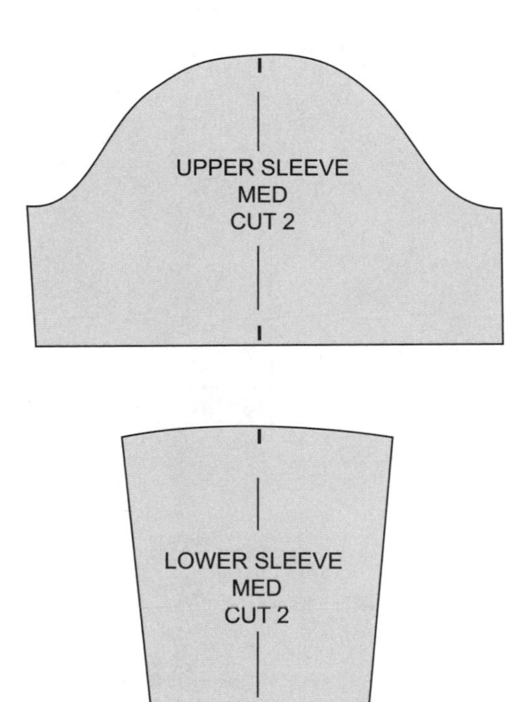

Trace, separate, and label the sleeve as illustrated.

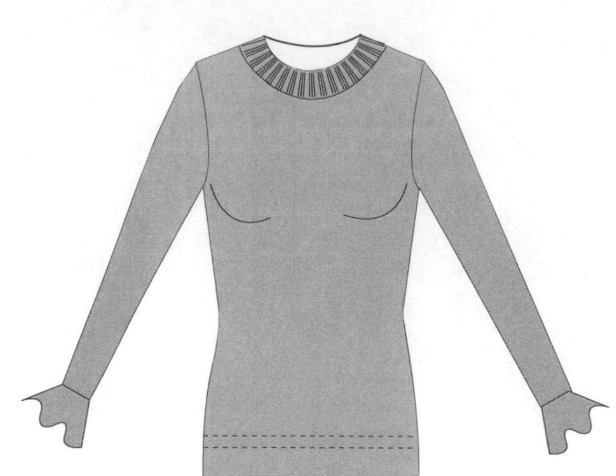

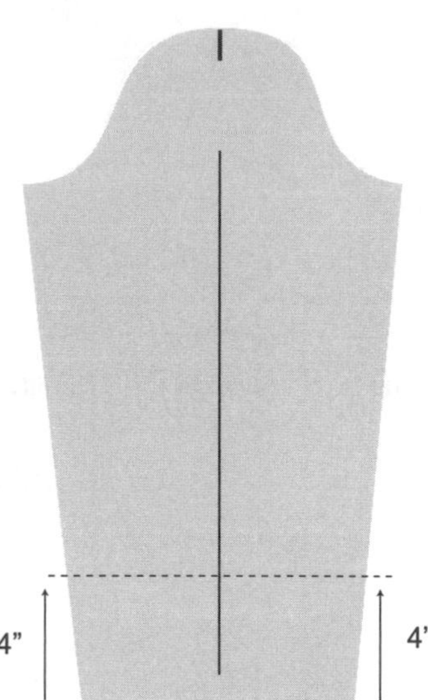

LONG SLEEVE WITH FLARED WRIST

Another way to add volume to the wrist of the sleeve is by attaching a separate circular piece to the bottom of it.

Draw a guideline wherever you wish the horizontal seam to be, illustrated here at 4″ above the wrist.

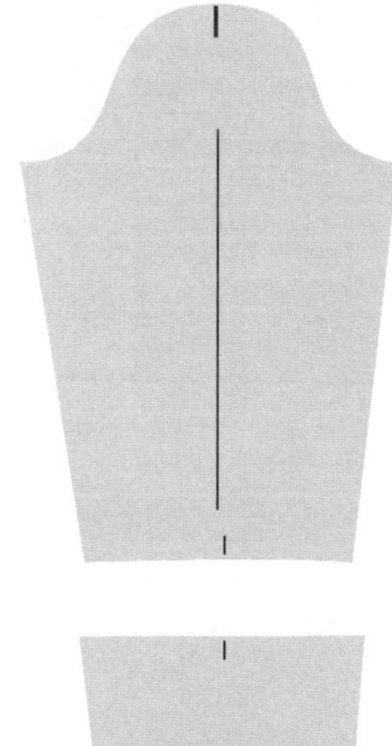

Trace and separate the pieces, remembering to notch the pieces for easy assembly.

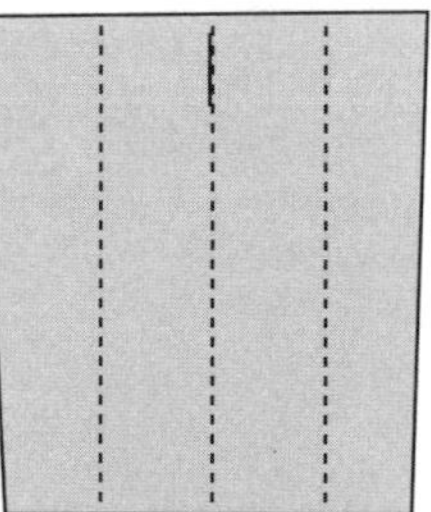

Fold the bottom portion of the sleeve inwards towards the grainline to determine the slash lines.

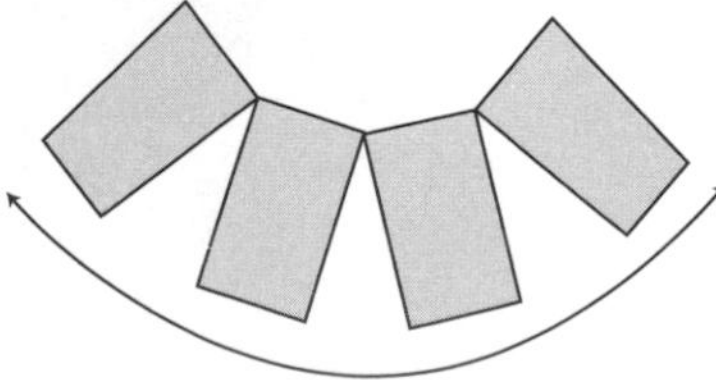

Slash and spread the hem of the sleeve as illustrated.

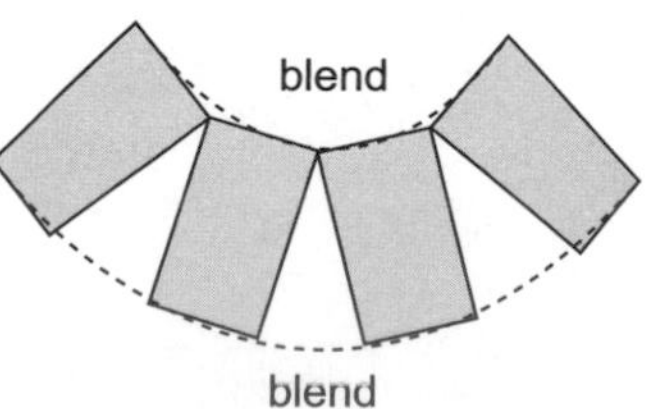

Blend the hem and the top of the piece.

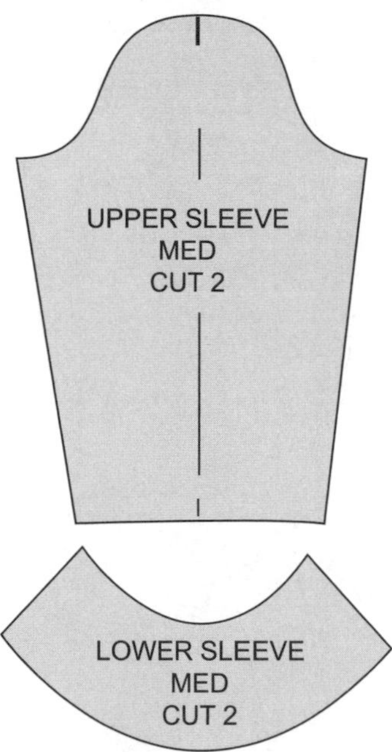

Label the pattern pieces as indicated.

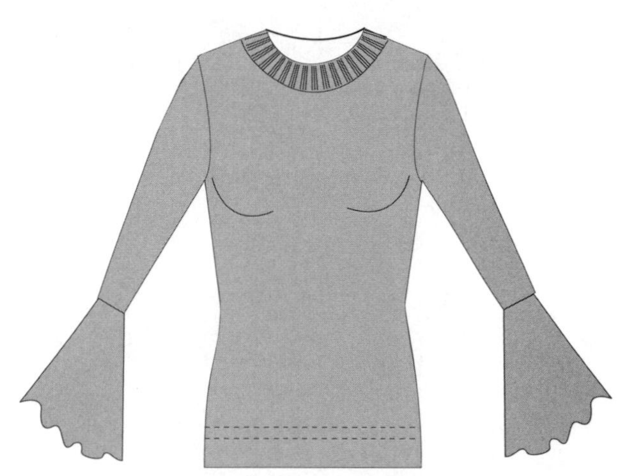

LONG SLEEVE FLARED FROM THE ELBOW DOWN

Another way to add volume to the wrist of the sleeve is by attaching a separate circular piece to the elbow of it.

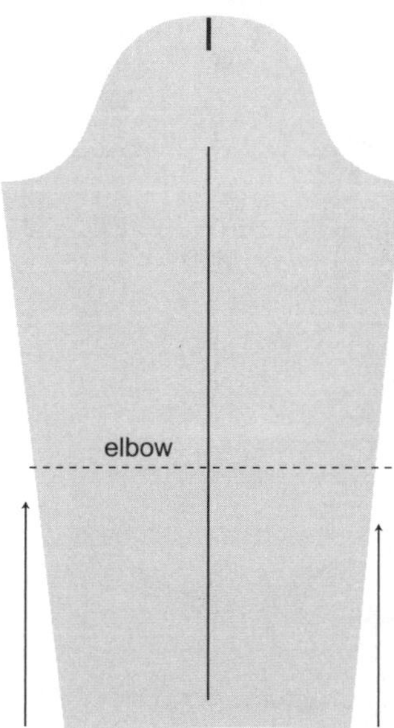

Draw a guideline wherever you wish the horizontal seam to be. It is illustrated here at the elbow notches of the sleeve.

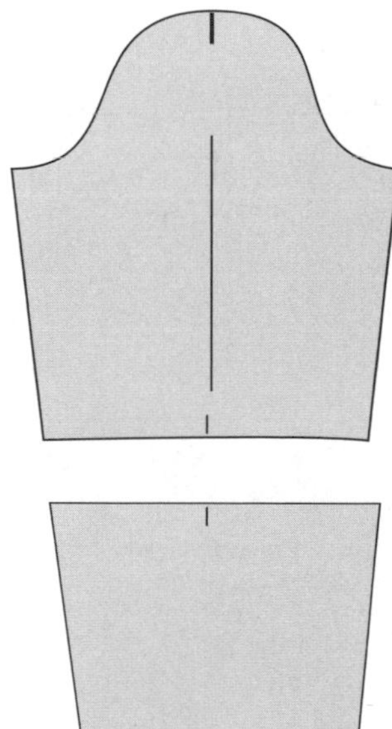

Trace and separate the pieces, remembering to notch the pieces for easy assembly.

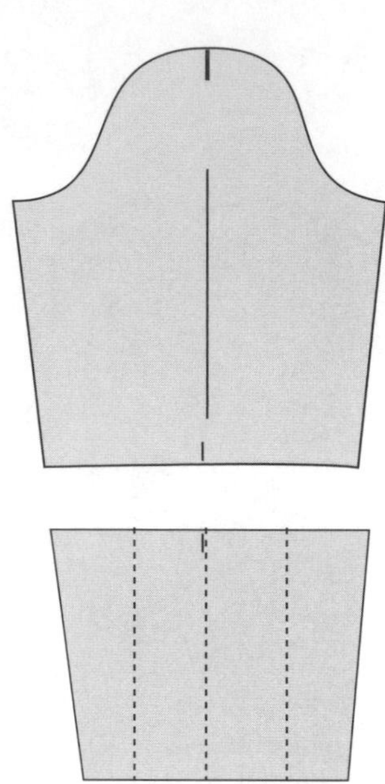

Fold the bottom portion of the sleeve inwards towards the grainline to determine the slash lines.

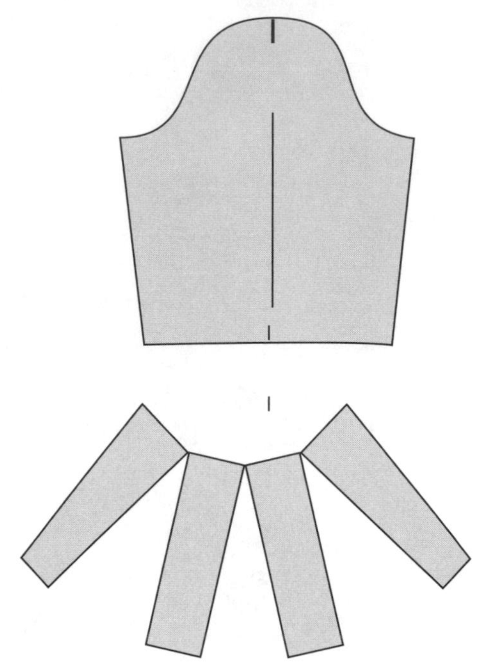

Slash and spread the hem of the sleeve as illustrated.

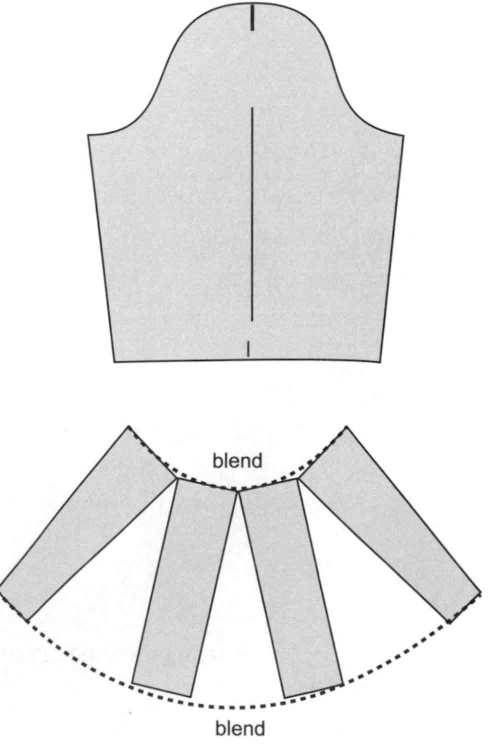

Blend the hem and the top of the piece.

The more fullness required, the more you need to spread the sleeve.

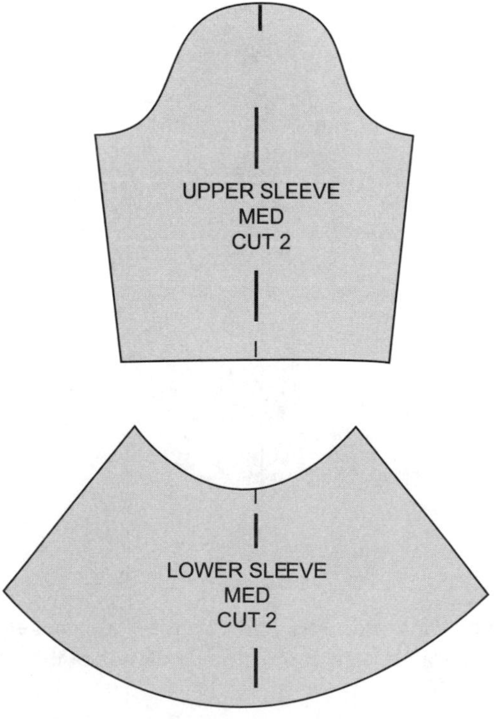

Label the pattern pieces as indicated.

Notch the sleeve for easier construction.

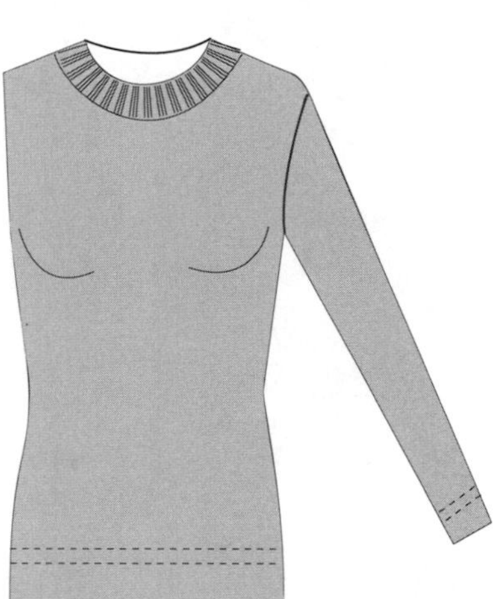

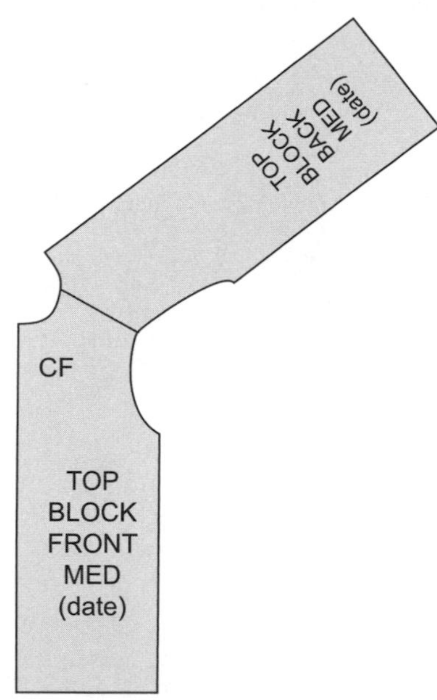

Sleeve–Body Combinations

DROPPED SHOULDER AND SLEEVES

Drop shoulder sleeves are created by moving the armhole seam away from the natural armhole.

Line up the shoulders as illustrated.

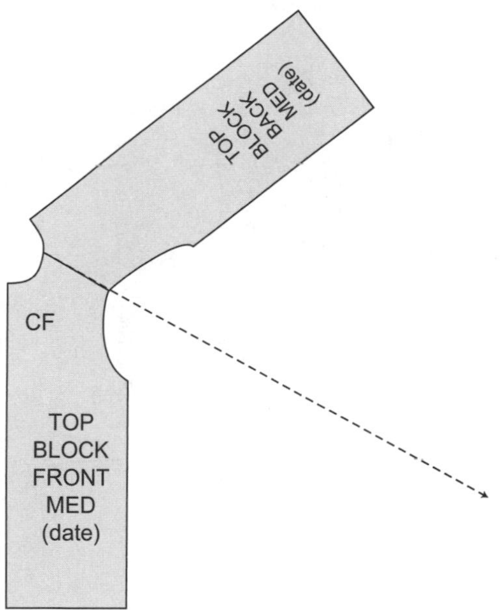

Extend a line from the shoulders equal to the length of the sleeve.

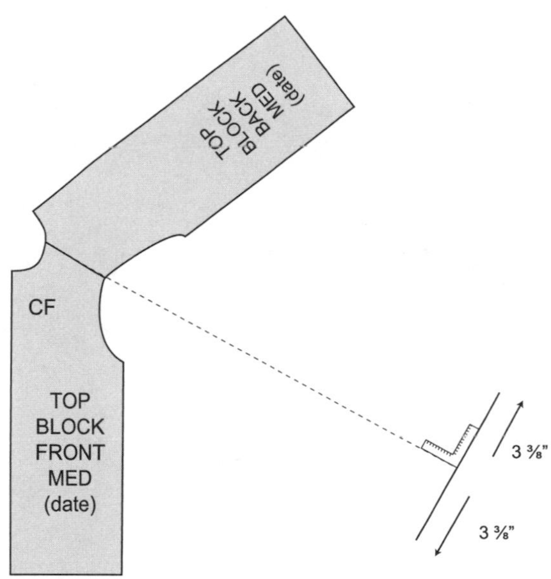

Square out in each direction an amount equal to the wrist measurement.

	Extra Extra Small	Extra Small	Small	Medium	Large	Extra Large	Extra Extra Large
Sleeve length	22 5/8	22 3/4	23	23 1/4	23 1/2	23 3/4	24
Wrist	4 3/8	5 1/8	5 7/8	6 5/8	7 3/8	8 1/8	8 7/8
Half of Wrist	2 1/4	2 5/8	3	3 3/8	3 3/4	4 1/8	4 1/2

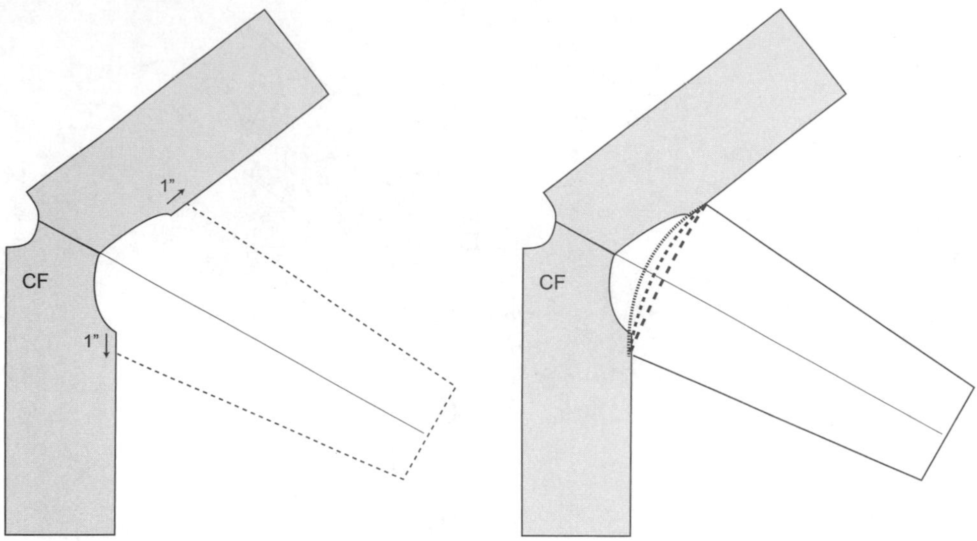

Draft the sleeve from the wrist to 1″ below the armhole.

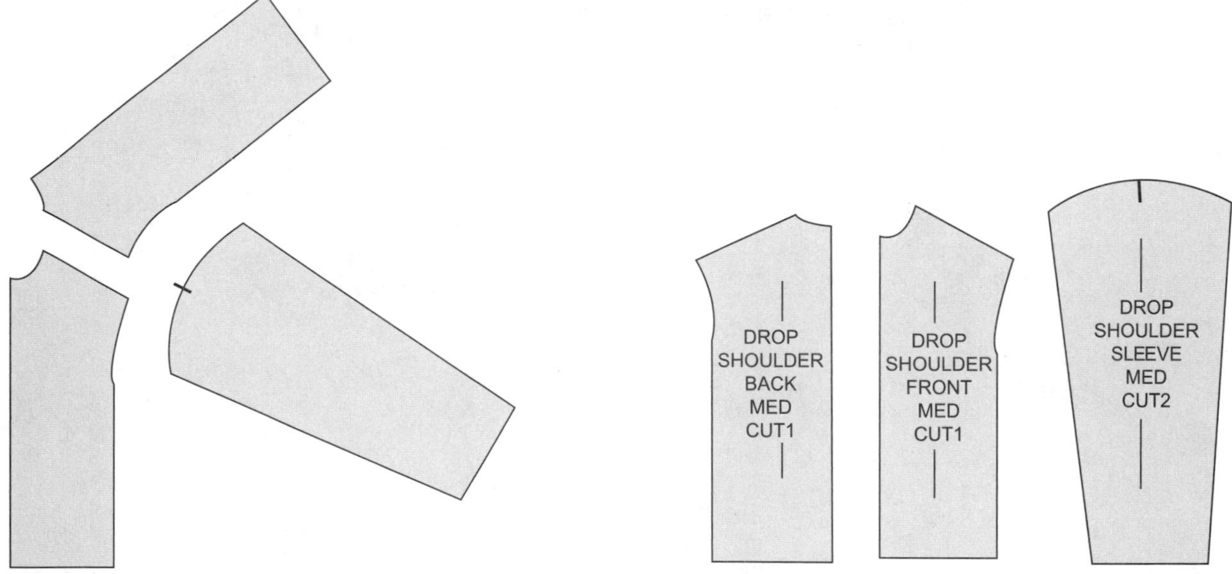

Place the new shoulder line and seam wherever you would like it.

Separate and trace the pattern pieces as illustrated.

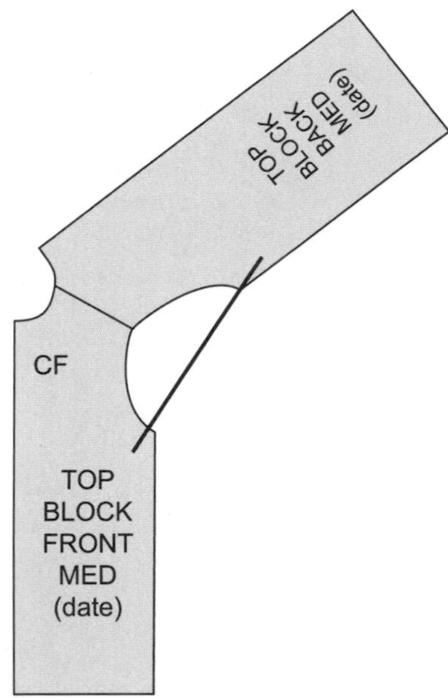

RAGLAN SLEEVES

This draft is for a raglan sleeve for stretch fabrics only.

Place the front and back top slopers together at the shoulders.

Draw a straight line through the underarm points.

Continue the line a few inches past the underarm points.

Place the sleeve sloper on the draft, matching three points:

1. The front underarm point of the sleeve lines up on the guideline.
2. The shoulder notch of the sleeve lines up with the shoulder seam.
3. The back underarm point of the sleeve lines up with the guideline.

You will have to move your sleeve around until it lines up perfectly with all three points.

Don't worry if your sleeve goes over the armhole of the body, because you will correct this in the next step.

Don't worry if your sleeve looks slightly different than this one.

Don't worry if your sleeve doesn't come as far as the arm of the body, because you will correct this in the next step.

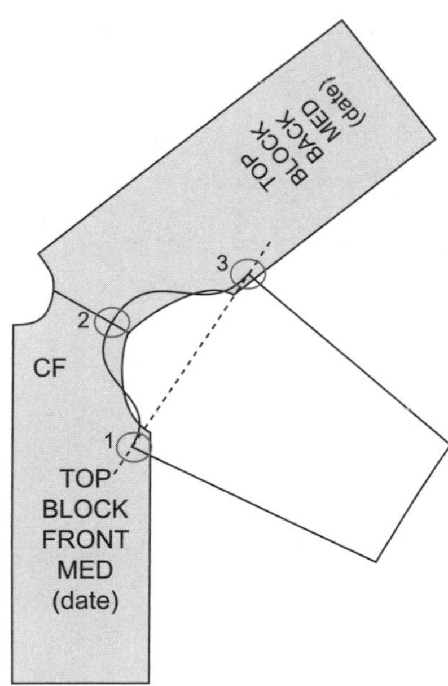

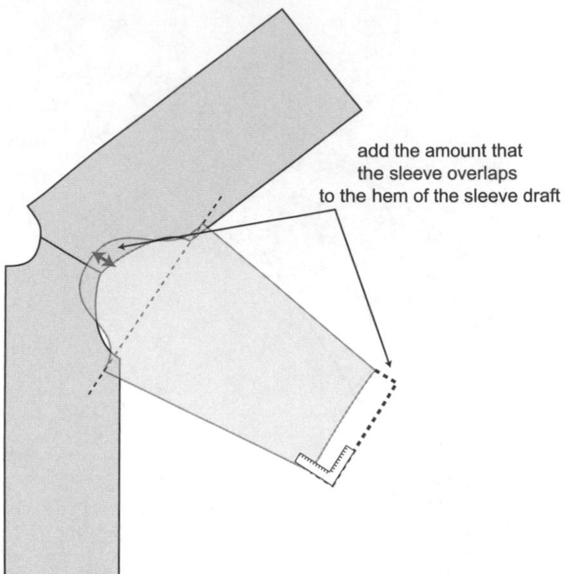

Measure the amount that the sleeve overlaps the armhole seam of the slopers and add this amount to the bottom of the sleeve to compensate for length.

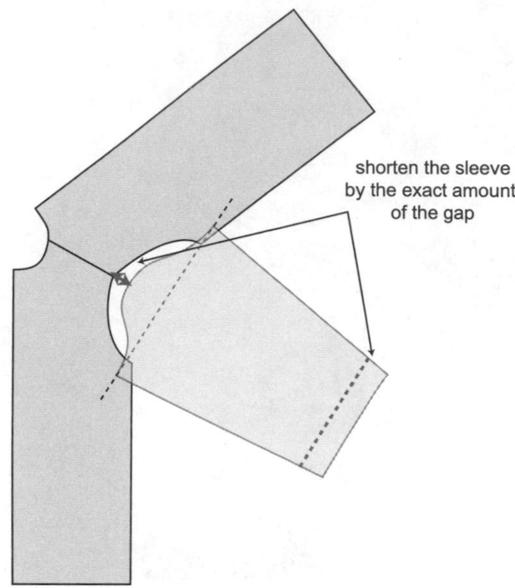

If the sleeve does not reach the armhole seams of the slopers, then the sleeve will get longer and must be shortened by that amount.

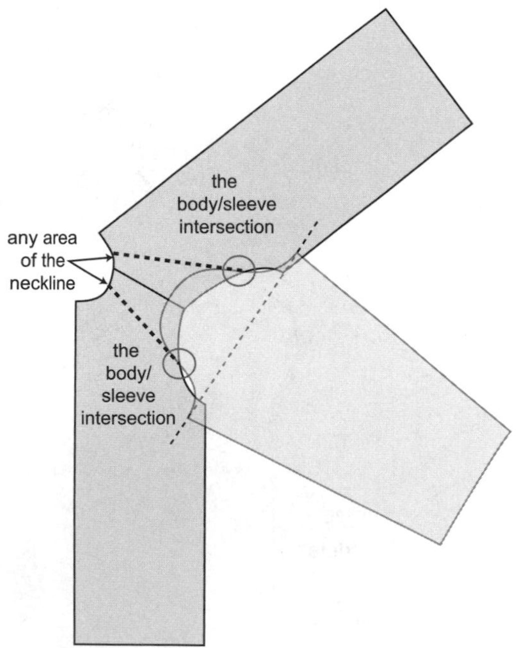

Draw the raglan seam going from any place on the neckline to the point where the sleeve and bodies intersect.

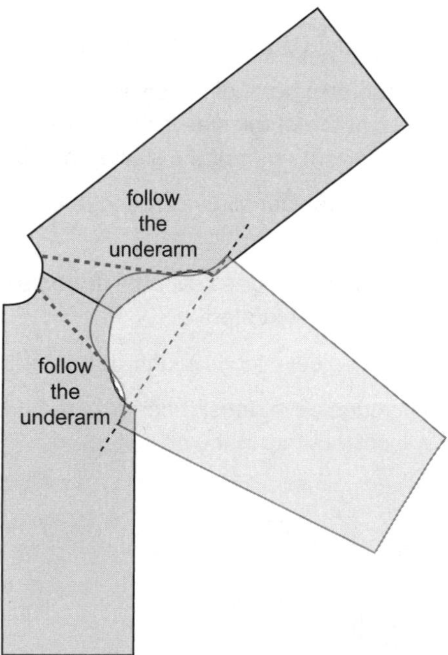

Continue the raglan style line to the underarm point.

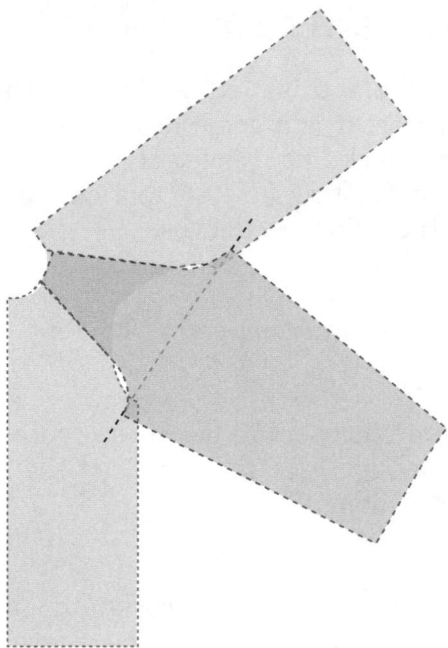

Note: The sleeve will follow one curve and the bodies will follow the opposite curves.

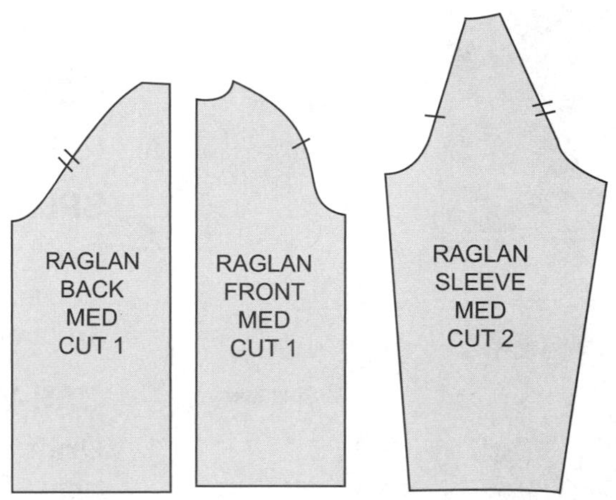

Notch the pieces for easy construction and then label, trace, and separate the pieces.

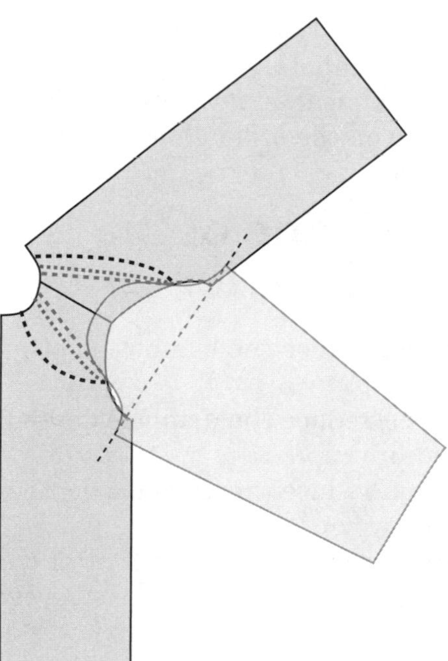

The ragline seams may be placed in any position the design requires.

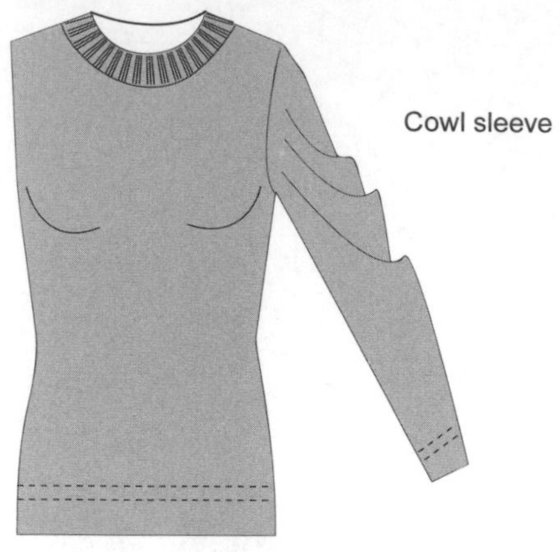
Cowl sleeve

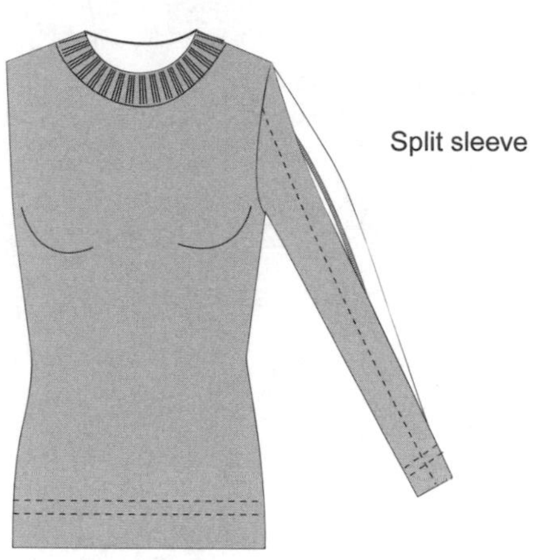
Split sleeve

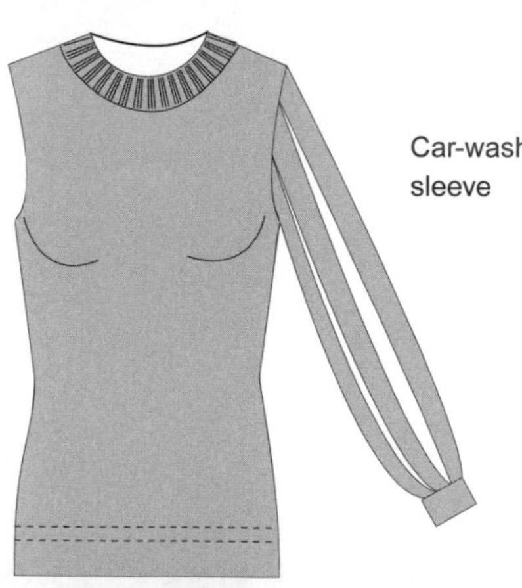
Car-wash sleeve

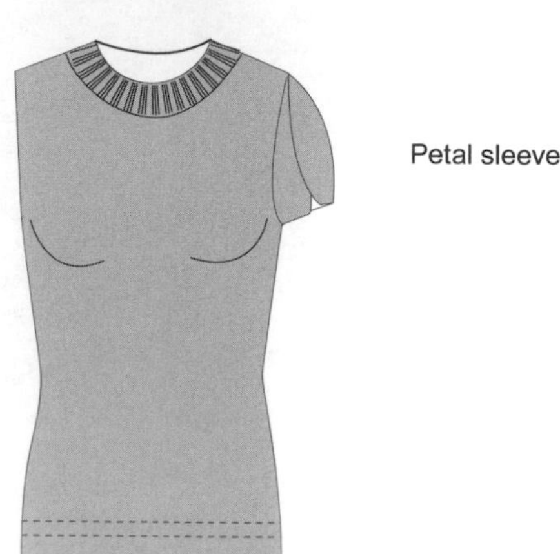
Petal sleeve

Sleeve Assignments

Using the information from this text and other chapters, draft some practice sleeves. It is a good idea to sew up these samples to see what they look like. Now that you have a little more experience pattern drafting for knit fabrics, you should be able to draft any of the following sleeves.

COWL SLEEVES

Draft a cowl sleeve, using the information in Chapter 5, Skirts.

SPLIT SLEEVES

Draft this sleeve, with a slit opening down the center of the sleeve. Sew the slit closed for 1″ at the top, 2″ at the bottom, and hem the slit with a 1″ hem allowance.

CAR-WASH SLEEVES

Draft a car-wash sleeve by splitting the sleeve into many sections. Double the width of each section so the sleeve can be clean finished by sewing the sections into tubes and turning them inside out.

PETAL SLEEVES

Draft a petal or tulip sleeve that overlaps on the front portion of the sleeve.

Draft this asymmetrical style with a short flared sleeve and binding on the other armhole.

Practice this asymmetrical style with a short capped sleeve and a slip neckline on the other side.

Test Your Knowledge of the Material in This Chapter

1. How much should you reduce the armhole depth measurement for a deep cap?
2. How much should you reduce the armhole depth measurement for a medium cap?
3. How much should you reduce the armhole depth measurement for a shallow cap?
4. Why should the patternmaker wait until after the body is fitted and corrected before drafting the sleeves?
5. How should you check the amount of ease in a sleeve cap?
6. What is the minimum amount of ease?
7. What is the maximum amount of ease?
8. How can you increase the amount of ease?
9. How can you decrease the amount of ease?
10. How can you create a flared sleeve?
11. How can you create a short sleeve?

CHAPTER 9

Sweaters

About This Chapter

Sweaters are not just for fall and winter collections, but have become an important part of every season. Lightweight sweaters are included in many collections for spring and summer. Note that some sweaters are worn directly on the skin, with only undergarments, whereas other sweaters are worn over other clothing. The designer must anticipate and design the fit of each sweater accordingly.

This chapter introduces the reader to the patternmaking techniques for creating sweaters. There are three different methods of constructing sweaters. Each sweater looks similar when viewed from the outside, but differences become apparent when you closely inspect the seam finishes.

All sweaters still need hard paper (oak-tag) patterns, and even though fully-fashioned sweaters will knit to shape, they still need an oak-tag pattern for testing fittings and blocking. Most manufacturers will knit yardage, cut the sweater sample out, and complete the fitting and any corrections before adding the expense of programming the computer to knit the pieces to shape.

There is another difference between sweaters and other knit tops. Next time you notice someone wearing a sweater, study the armhole seam. You will notice that it extends straight up to the shoulder and does not curve outwards at the top, as in T-shirts and other knit tops.

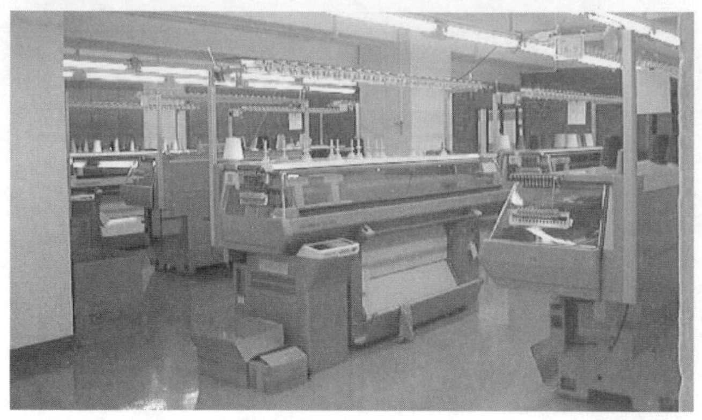

Industrial Knitting

Industrial knitting machines are capable of producing sweaters on a very large scale. Extremely fast, these machines are programmed by computer and automatically make all the necessary increases and decreases, such as stitch changes and color changes.

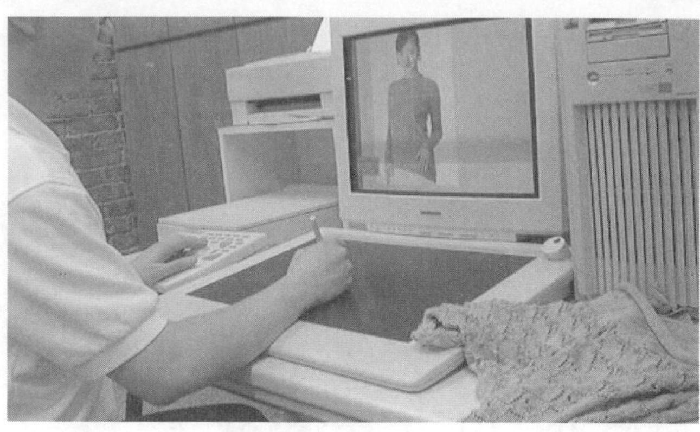

SDS-ONE

Software for an industrial knitting machines user station.

The technician uses a mouse and/or tablet to create the garment silhouette, stitch formations, increases, and decreases, which are then sent to large industrial machines for knitting.

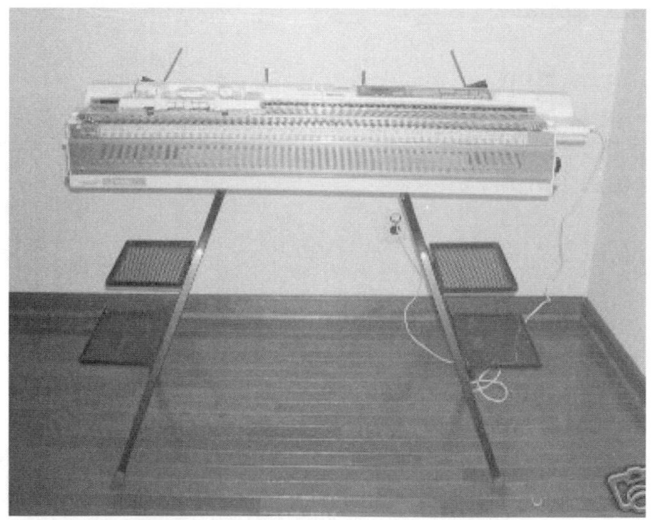

The hand knitting machine is a great tool for creating sweaters on a smaller scale, one or two, and useful for developing stitches. It is also an excellent tool for students, to teach them about knit structure, and stitch types.

The knit linker is a machine used for joining knit garment pieces together.

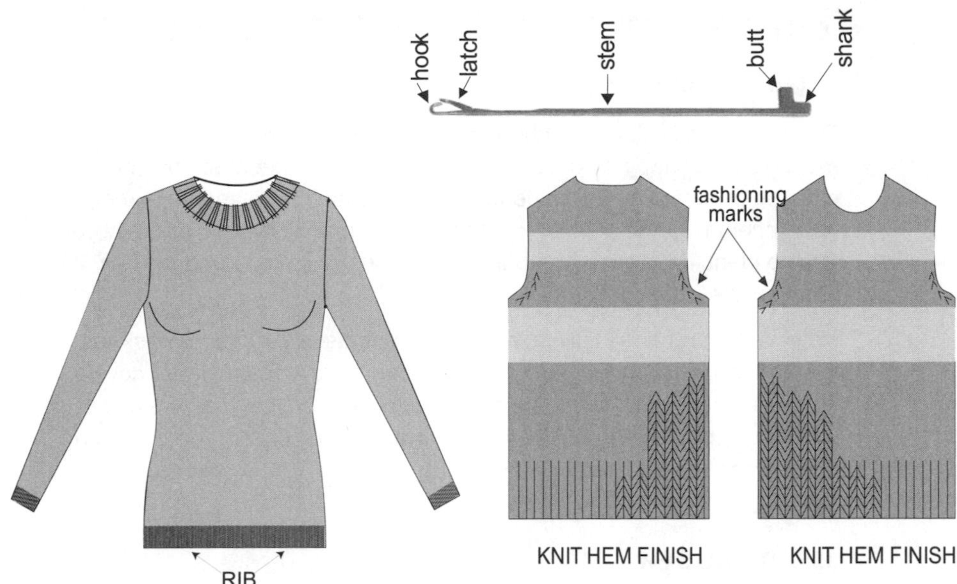

Armhole Changes For Sweater Knits

Slopers for sweaters are slightly different from slopers for other tops; for example, the armhole is knit straight up, rather than curved.

Next time you notice someone wearing a sweater, study the armhole seam, you will notice that it extends straight up to the shoulder and does not curve outwards at the top, as in t-shirt and other knit tops.

This is done for three reasons:

So that the knitter does not have to increase stitches and can simply knit straight up the armhole to the shoulder, for easier knitting, especially when knitting Fair Isle, intarsia, and other complex patterns.

So that the horizontal stretch of the fabric is reduced, therefore the armhole does not stretch out of shape when attaching the sleeves.

So that any visible stripes or ribs—remember that many sweaters are made out of rib and larger yarn that looks like vertical lines—are straightened out and it doesn't create a triangle on the top of the shoulders, when the stripes or ribs meet. This little triangle looks odd and out of place.

Note: This is only done with sweaters or garments with a visible vertical stripe or rib, so lightweight jersey fabrics for t-shirts do not require this sloper correction.

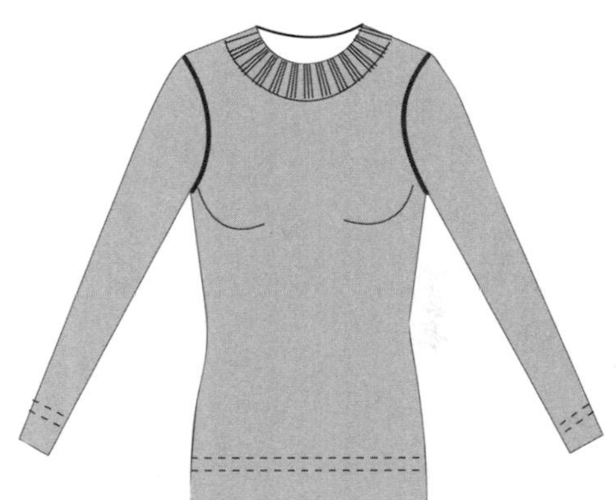

Regular curved armhole.

Sweater with straight armhole.

Three Ways to Create a Sweater

fashioning marks

KNIT HEM FINISH KNIT HEM FINISH

(1) FULLY FASHIONED

Full fashioning is like hand knitting in that the manufacturer knits the garment parts to shape by casting on and casting off stitches. This method of creating sweaters is very expensive because each size and style requires a new schematic, knit plan, or knitting instructions. Fully-fashioned sweaters can be identified by the fashioning marks on the outside and the knit linking together the inside seams.

Note: When creating "fully fashioned" garments, the trims, bands, and collars needed to finish the garment must also be fully fashioned. They can be knit as single layers; it is not necessary to fold them over, as the raw edge will already be finished by the knitting machine, by casting on or casting off the stitches.

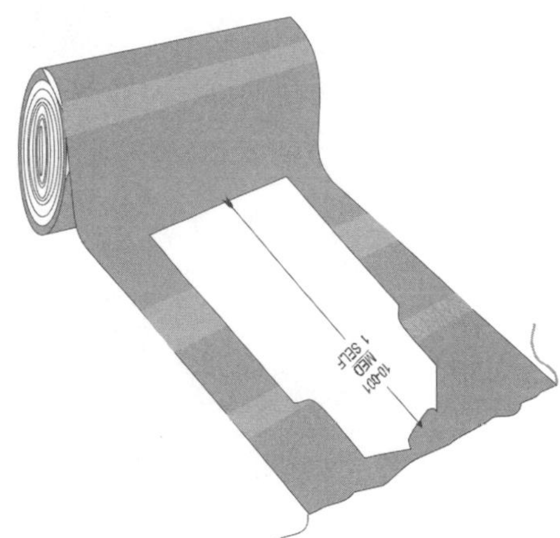

(2) CUT AND SEW

The designer purchases the knitted goods by the yard. This method of creating sweaters is the least expensive because the fabric can be purchased in bulk and used to create a variety of styles and sizes by using different oak-tag patterns.

These sweaters can be identified by sewn hems and machine serging on the inside seams.

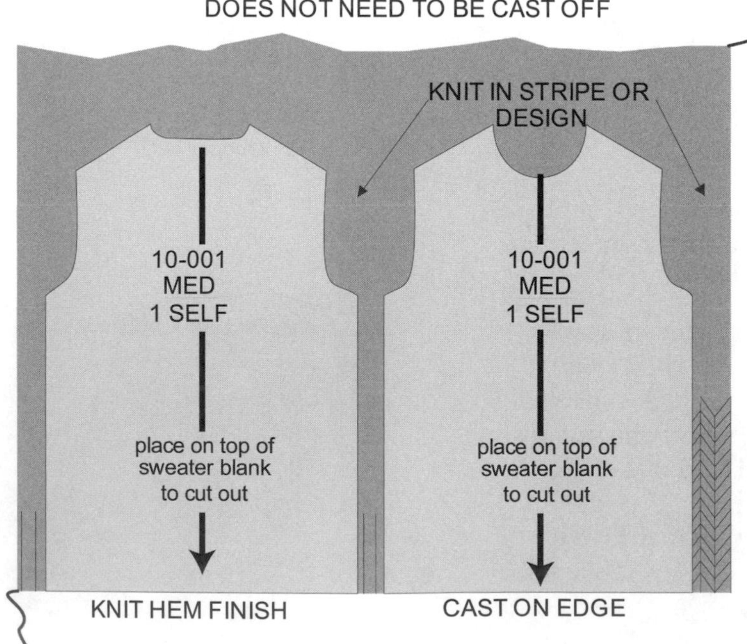

(3) SWEATER BLANKS

This is the most common method of manufacturing sweaters. The designer can create the type of knit, including hem finish, choose the yarn, and have the goods knitted only to the length of the sweater pattern needed. The manufacturer then places the oak-tag patterns on the sweater blank, lining up the bottom of the patterns with the hem of the sweater blank to cut them out. The designer can create different sizes easily using different graded oak-tag patterns. These sweaters can be identified by the knitted hems combined with the serged seams on the inside.

Note that the garment may have a ribbed, tubular, or finished hem.

The manufacturer can easily create horizontal stripes by changing the color of yarn while knitting the row, or create Fair Isle or any type of knit design that the designer imagines.

This type of sweater manufacturing is especially well suited for complex stitches such as Fair Isle, pointelle, and tuck stitches, because the complexity of the knitting is reduced and the knit technician does not have to determine increases and decreases for the armholes and neckline.

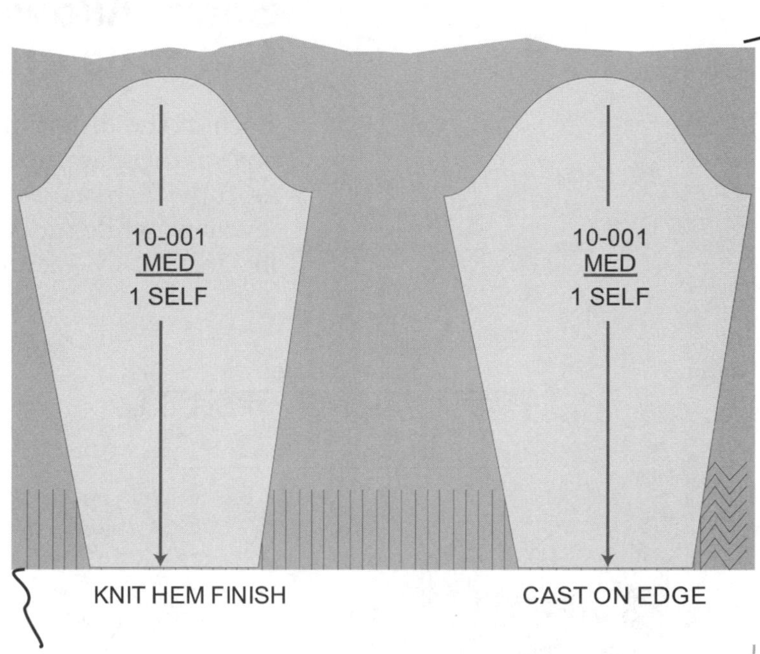

SWEATER BLANK SLEEVES

Illustration shows how sleeves are cut from sweater blanks

The extra rib, or finished hem between the sleeves may be used to cut out the collar.

Or the neckline may be re-attached to the knitting machine and the collar may be knit.

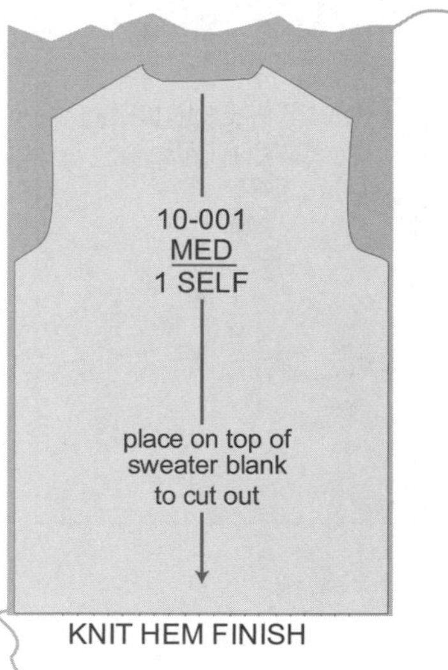

Another variation of cut and sew:

The sweater blank is knit to the exact width of the sweater panel, reducing the need for side seam finishing.

The sweater seams may be linked with a linking machine, or sewn with a straight stitch.

Theses side seams require 1/8″ seam allowance, while the shoulders and armholes require 3/8″ seam allowance, and no hem allowance needs to be added to the pattern.

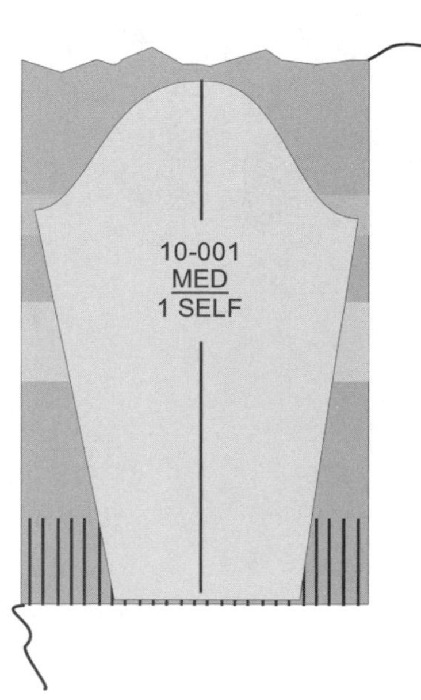

Illustration shows the alternative technique for knitting sweater blanks.

The sleeve is knitted to the widest part of the sleeve pattern, and will need to be serged to finish the raw edges of the inseam and armhole.

Alternatively, the sleeve may be shaped with increases and decreases along the inseam, while the cap may be knit straight up and left raw for cut and sew.

The sleeve requires 3/8″ seam allowance.

Seam Allowances for Different Methods of Construction

Each of the different methods of construction requires different seam allowance amounts. Seams that are finishes such as fully fashioned only need a ⅛″, or single stitch seam allowance, while any garment part that is cut out requires over locking with ⅜″ seam allowance.

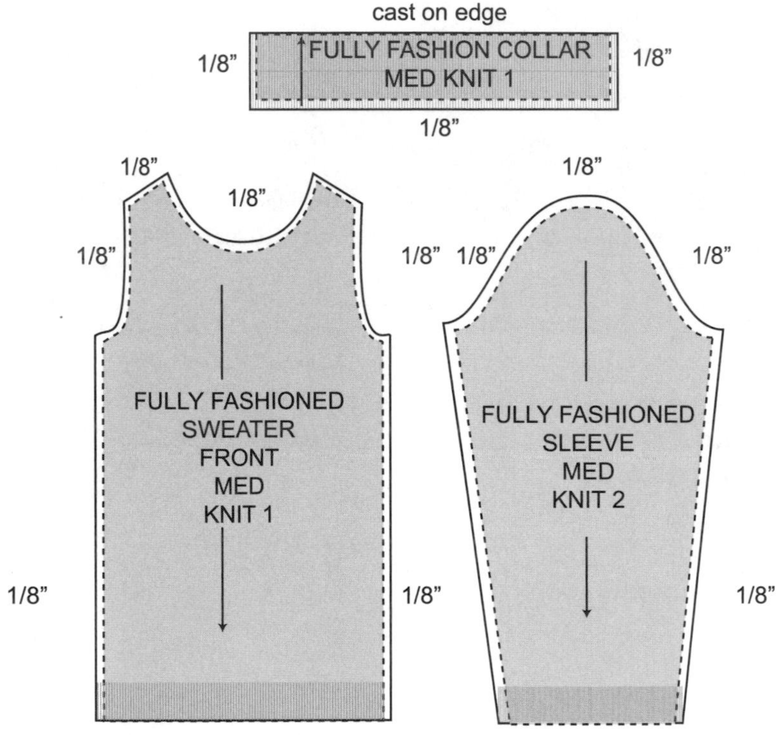

FULLY FASHIONED

Fully fashioned patterns do not need a hem allowance, since the hem is already finished on the knitting machine, and should simply be indicated on the pattern.

Seam allowances are one stitch wide, ⅛″ on all other seams, or seams that will be linked, or sewn together.

The trim should also be knit with finished edges, so trims and collars may be single layer or double layer if you require thicker trims.

Trim measurements should be indicated on the final patterns.

You may not need to create patterns for fully-fashioned collars, since the sweater will be hooked up to the knitting machine to knit the collar.

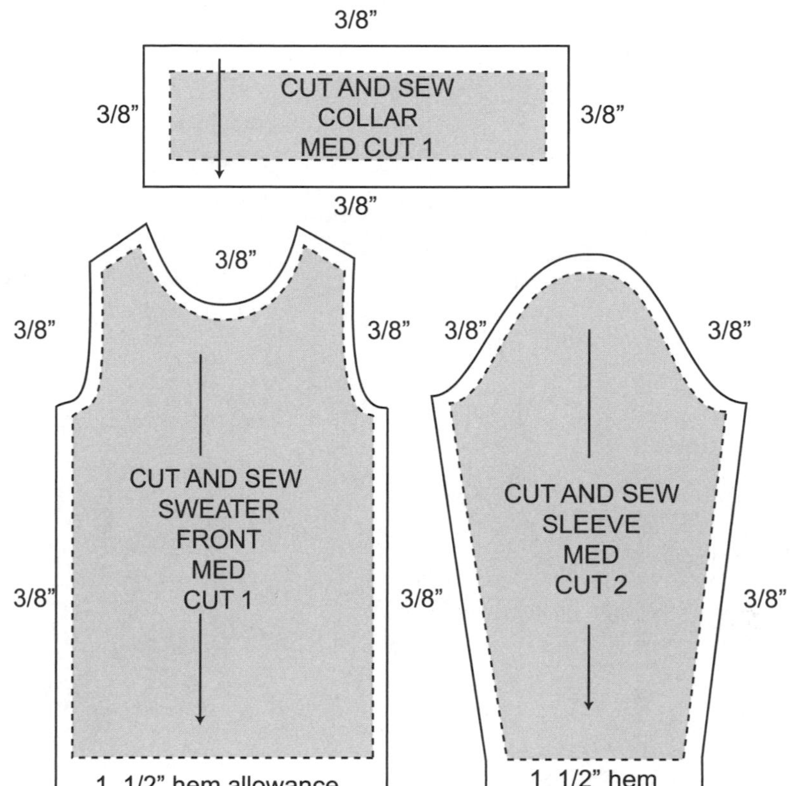

CUT AND SEW

Cut and sew sweaters need seam allowances for the over-lock machine, to finish the raw edges.

They also need a hem allowance, since the hem must be sewn by hand or machine.

All collars, trims, and bands must be doubled (folded over).

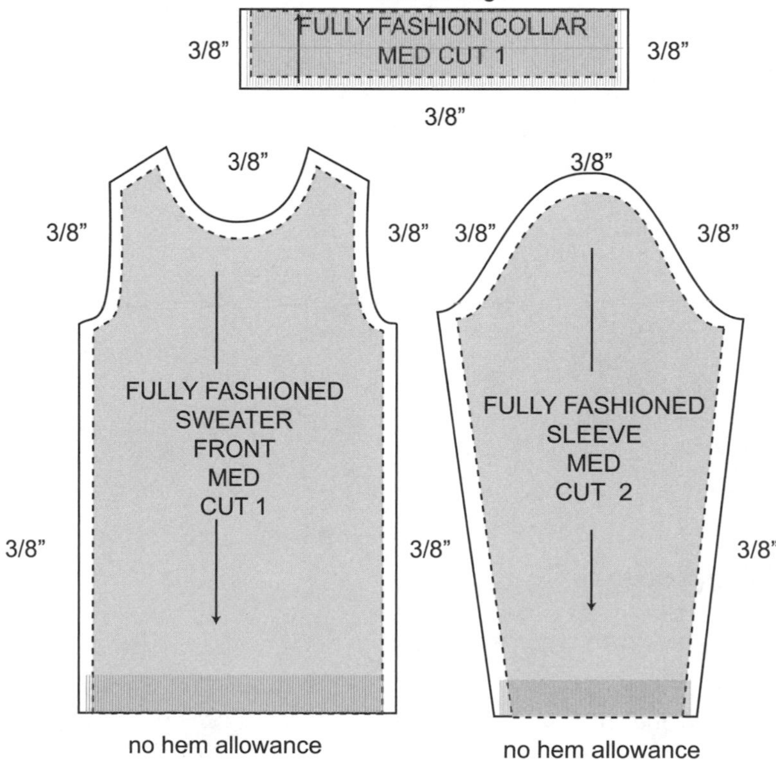

SWEATER BLANKS

Sweaters cut from sweater blanks do not need a hem allowance, because the hem finish is already included on the blank and should simply be indicated on the pattern.

If the blank is knitted the exact width of the sweater, it will need a 1/8″ seam allowance at the sides.

If the sweater blank is knit larger than the blank, then it should have a 3/8″ seam allowance for overlocking (serging).

If the trim is cut from a finished edge, it does not need to be folded over.

If the trim is cut from the body of the fabric, then it must be doubled.

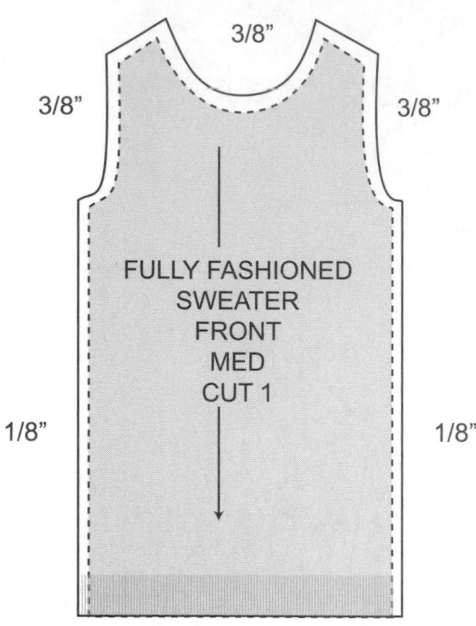

KNIT-TO-WIDTH SWEATER BLANKS

When a sweater is knit to the exact body width, it is not necessary to overlock the seams, therefore a ⅛″ seam allowance is all that is needed for the sides of the body.

The armholes, shoulders, and neckline will require a ⅜″ seam allowance, since they must be over-locked.

No hem allowance is necessary since the hem will already be finished on the knitting machine.

This type of construction is especially useful when creating Fair Isle and patterned designs, the knitter can simply focus on the patterning techniques without having to worry or fuss with the shaping techniques.

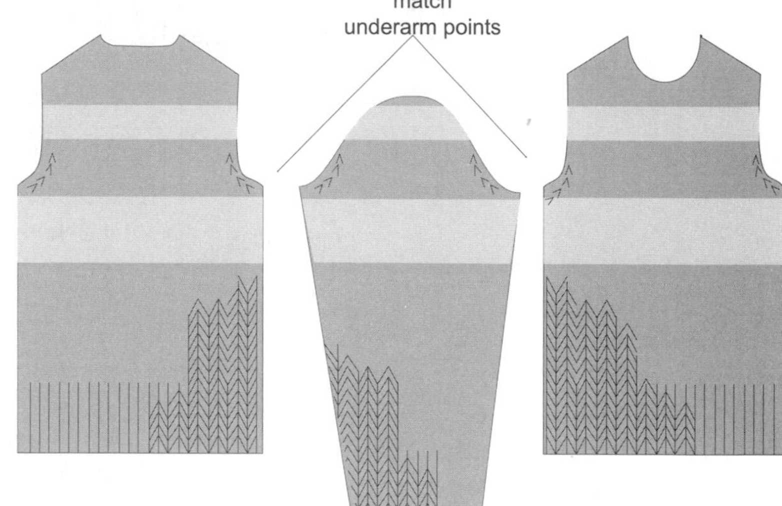

MATCHING STRIPES

To match the stripes of a knit garment, line up the underarm points.

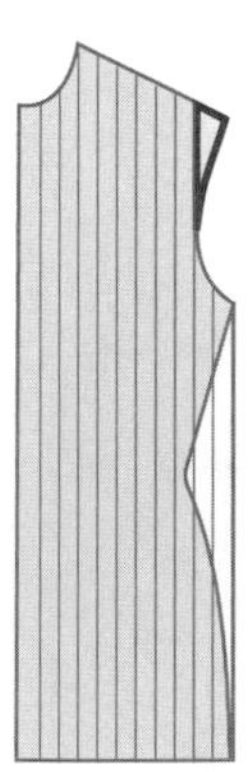

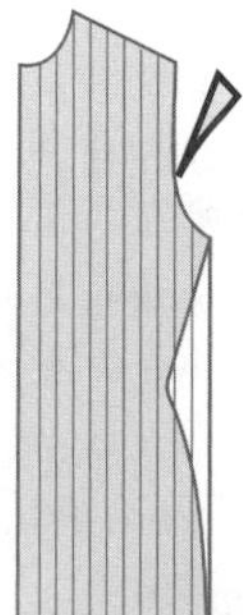

Sweater Slopers

SLOPERS FOR SWEATER KNITS

Slopers for sweaters are slightly different from slopers for other tops, for example, the armhole shaping.

Use the knit top sloper, with all three of the different sleeves and cap heights.

When using a visible stripe or rib, the designer or patternmaker must make corrections to the top slopers before they can be used for sweaters.

You must make the armhole and side seams follow the visible rib or stripe, or else the shoulder seam will look strange. The little triangle will stretch out of shape when attaching the sleeve because of the way that ribs stretch out while sewing and the sleeve will not hang correctly.

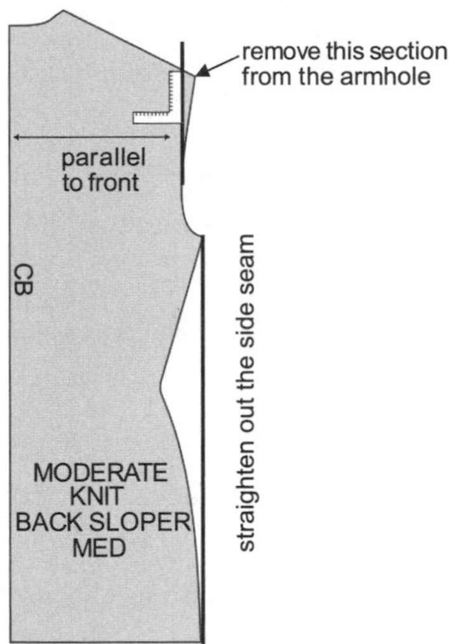

Trace the moderate knit (50% stretch) top *back* sloper (most sweater fabrics are moderate knit).

Square up the armhole parallel to the center back, from the narrowest part of the armhole straight up to the shoulder, as indicated.

Also straighten the side seams to create an unfitted garment. When using a visible stripe or rib, you don't want the rib to stretch out or have unmatched chevrons.

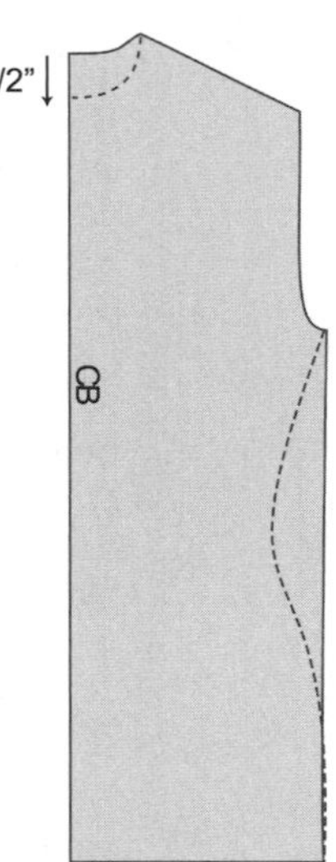

Since the shoulders and armholes are identical, you can create a back sloper and change the neckline to create the front sloper.

To create the front sloper, trace out the back sloper and change the neck by lowering it the amount of the shoulder pitch, and drawing in a new front neckline.

	Extra Extra Small	Extra Small	Small	Medium	Large	Extra Large	Extra Extra Large
NECK	1 3/8	1 3/8	1 1/2	1 1/2	1 1/2	1 5/8	1 5/8

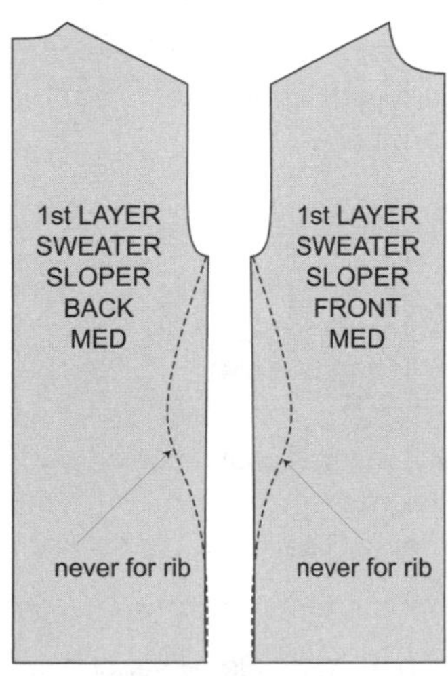

Trace and separate the sweater slopers.

Label them as "first layer," meaning that they will be worn with nothing but undergarments underneath.

You may use the fitted waist on jersey knits, but it should not be used for ribbed waists, because it will stretch out and create huge exaggerated hips when sewing the side seams.

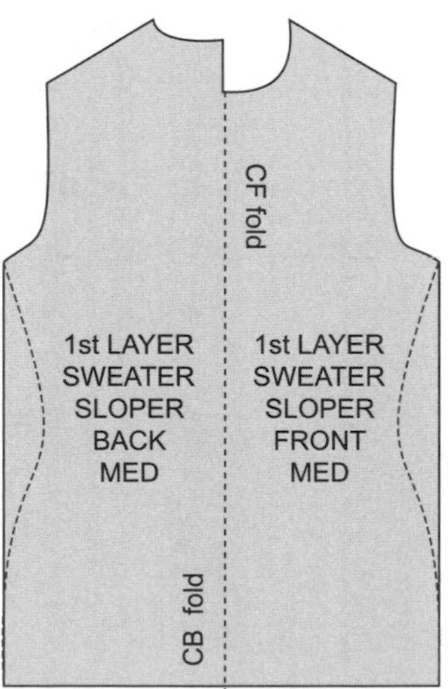

Often sweater slopers are created as illustrated to take up less materials and oak-tag.

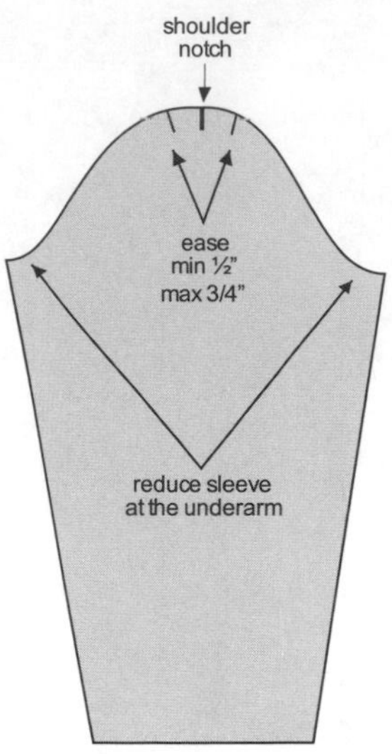

THE SWEATER SLEEVE SLOPER

The sleeve sloper must be corrected to fit the new armhole, and must reflect the slight changes.

Use the moderate knit sleeve sloper with medium cap height.

Reduce or enlarge the sleeve to fit the new armhole by removing the excess from the inseams.

Remember that ease is still necessary for the sweater sleeve.

Minimum ease = ½″ total.

Maximum ease = ¾″ total.

Mark the amount of ease required on the cap of the sleeve, with half of the ease on either side of the shoulder notch.

½″ ease is better for fully-fashioned sleeves; it makes it slightly easier to attach the sleeve with the linker.

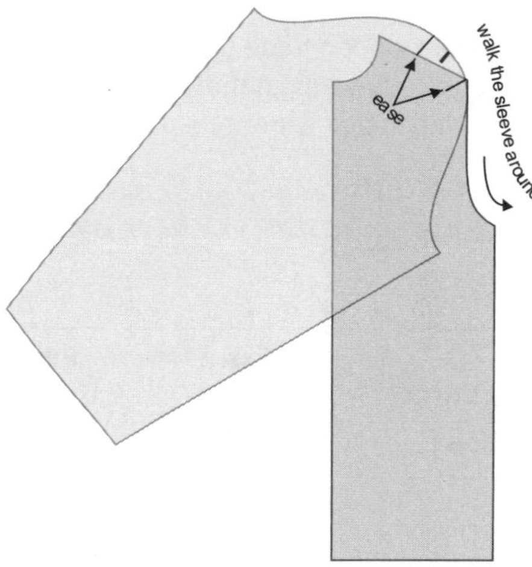

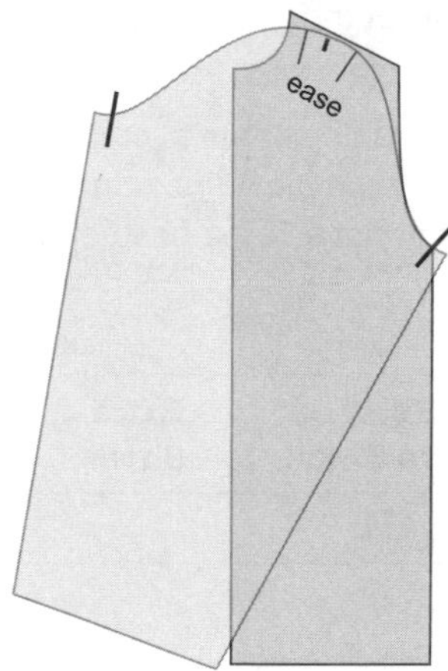

Measure and mark the ease amount equally on either side of the sleeve notch.

Start outside the ease marks, ignoring the ease amount.

Walk the sleeve around the armhole to the underarm.

When the sleeve reaches the new underarm side-seam point, mark with a pencil the amount that the sleeve extends past the armhole.

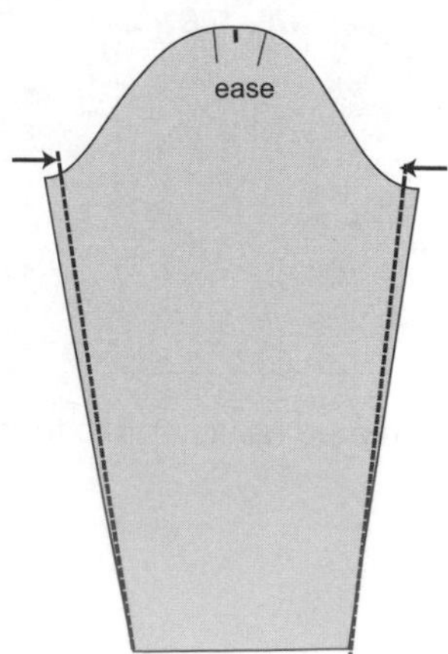

Remove the excess amount from the sleeve.

This amount of the correction is usually so small that it can safely be removed from the underarm of the sleeve. If it is large—more than ½″—it must be corrected by slash and spread (see Chapter 8, Sleeves).

Do not change the width at the wrist; rather, taper to nothing as shown.

If your sleeve happens to be smaller than the armhole, either change the amount of ease to ½″ or enlarge the sleeve so that it now fits the armhole (excluding ease).

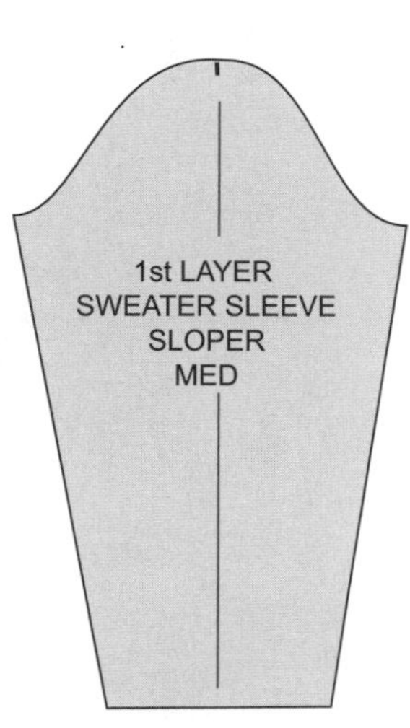

Trace and label the sweater sloper.

You may leave the faint pencil marks to indicate the ease amount, for future reference.

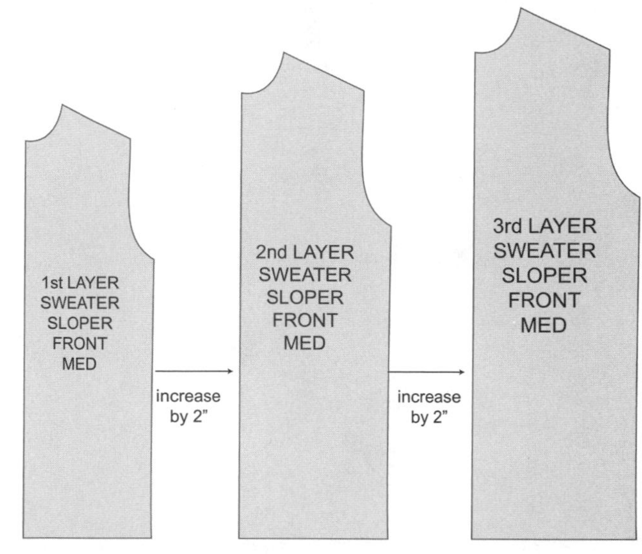

FIRST OR SECOND LAYER SLOPERS FOR SWEATERS

First layer sweater slopers create garments that have nothing except undergarments worn underneath; for example, summer-weight knits, dresses, and tops that are worn "next to the skin."

Second layer slopers or jacket slopers are used when the designer wants to create styles intended to be worn over other clothing, such as pullovers and cardigans, so the size must increase to accommodate the clothing underneath.

Third layer slopers create sweaters that are worn over other sweaters; for example, zip-front cardigans, sweater coats, and the like.

All are still size Medium; however, they are size Medium intended to be worn over other garments.

The first layer sweater sloper will be increased in width a total of 2″, or ½″ per panel, to create a second layer or jacket sloper for sweaters.

Repeat or double the measurements for third layer slopers.

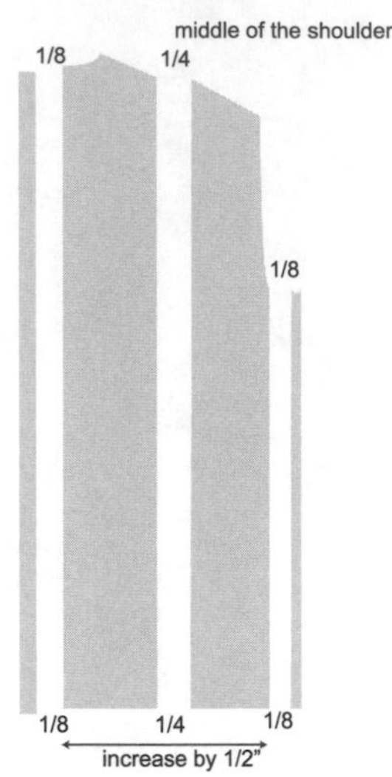

WIDTH INCREASES

Make the increases to the back sloper, and simply change the neckline to create the front sloper.

To apply the width increases:

Draw a line parallel to the side seams approximately ¾″ in from the side seam (increase by ⅛″ per panel).

Draw a vertical line through the shoulder approximately half-way (increase by ¼″ per panel).

Draw a vertical line 1″ in from the front along the neck edge (increase by ⅛″ per panel).

Slash and spread accordingly.

LENGTH INCREASE

To apply the length increases:

Draw a line parallel to the shoulder approximately ¾″ in from the shoulder (increase by ⅛ per panel).

Draw a horizontal line through the armhole area, approximately half way through the armhole (increase by ½ per panel).

For additional length increase, draw a horizontal line below the waist notch (increase by ⅛ per panel).

Slash and spread accordingly.

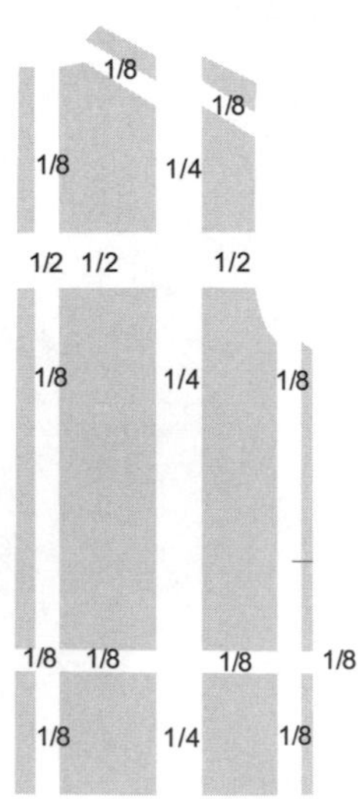

Both directions of increases should look like the illustration. Slash and spread these areas by the amounts illustrated.

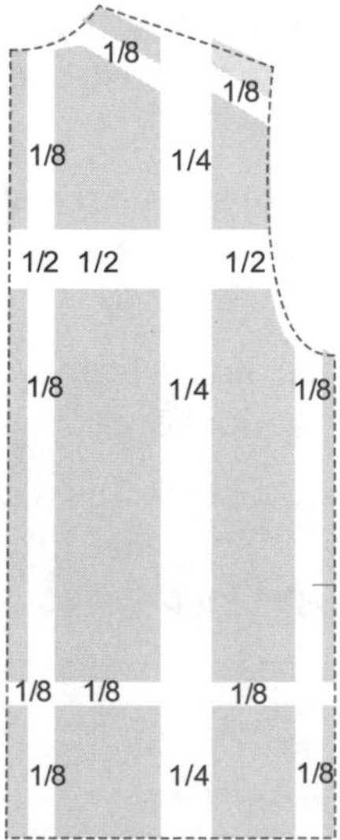

BLENDING AND TRUEING THE SLOPERS

Straighten out the shoulder by drawing a new straight line from neck to armhole and ignore any discrepancies.

Blend the armhole, neck, and underarm areas.

Label as "jacket slopers" or "second layer sloper for sweaters."

SECOND LAYER SLOPER FRONT

Draw the front neckline below the front using the chart below.

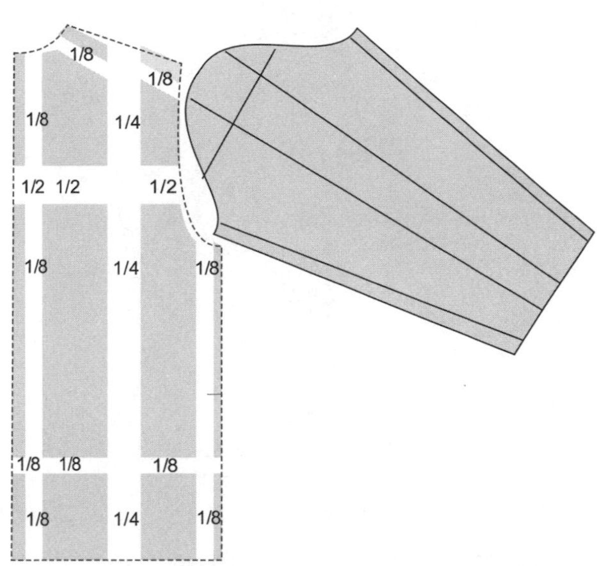

SECOND LAYER SWEATER SLEEVE SLOPERS

To find the increase areas for the sleeve, line up the sleeve with the body as illustrated, and match the increase areas accordingly.

It is possible, and easier, to increase half of the sleeve and copy to the other side, or draft it on the fold of your paper and open it up to trace onto oak-tag.

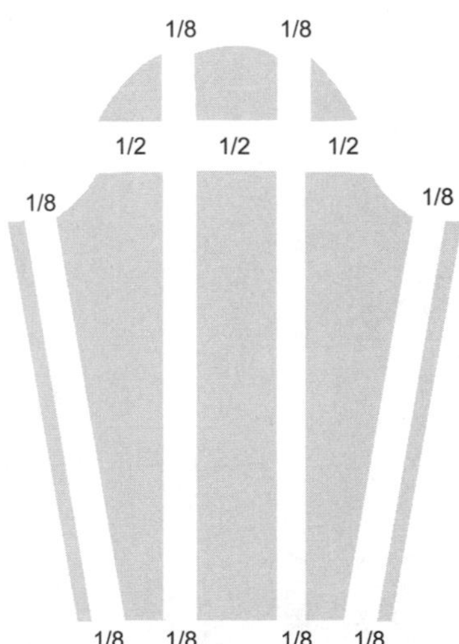

Mark the sleeve to correspond to the body, as shown.

Slash and spread once above the elbow notch.

Slash and spread once below the elbow notch.

Slash and spread the sleeve sloper as illustrated, to match the body increases.

Blend the sleeve as illustrated.

You can use the original sleeve sloper as a template to blend the curved parts of the new sleeve.

	Extra Extra Small	Extra Small	Small	Medium	Large	Extra Large	Extra Extra Large
Neckline Drop	1 ½	1 ½	1 ⅝	1 ⅝	1 ⅝	1 ¾	1 ¾

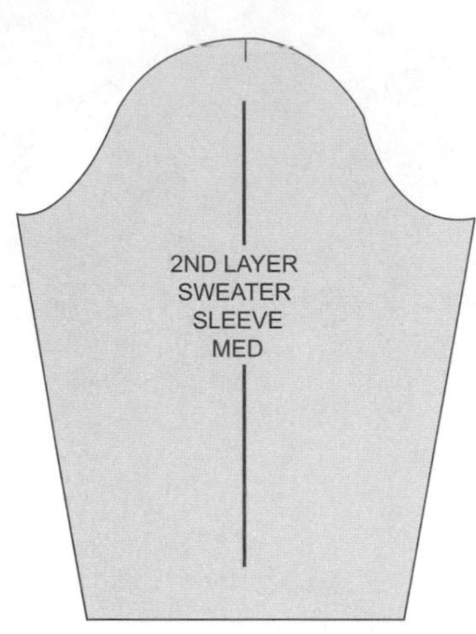

Walk the sleeve around the armhole to check for accuracy.

Label as "jacket sloper" or "second layer sloper for sweaters."

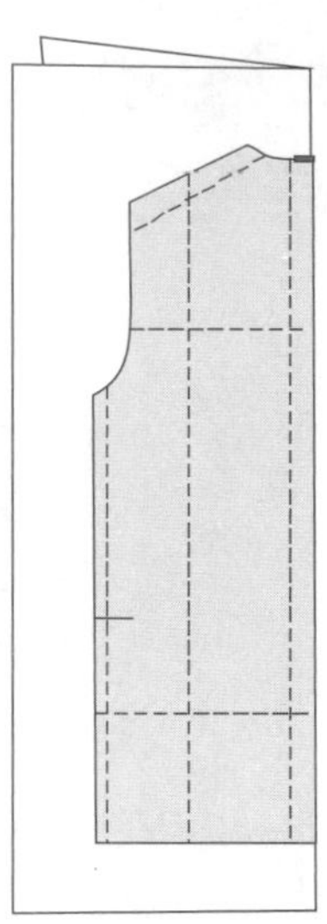

SLOPER SHIFTING TO CREATE SECOND LAYER SLOPERS

It is not always necessary to slash and spread to create second layer slopers. You may simply shift the regular sloper the required amount and trace each part as it is enlarged; see the following:

Trace out the back neck section for approximately 1″.

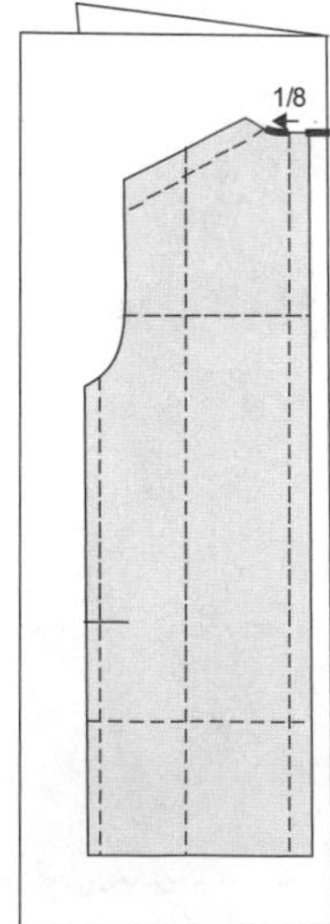

Shift the sloper to the left, ⅛″, as illustrated, and trace out the next section of the neck.

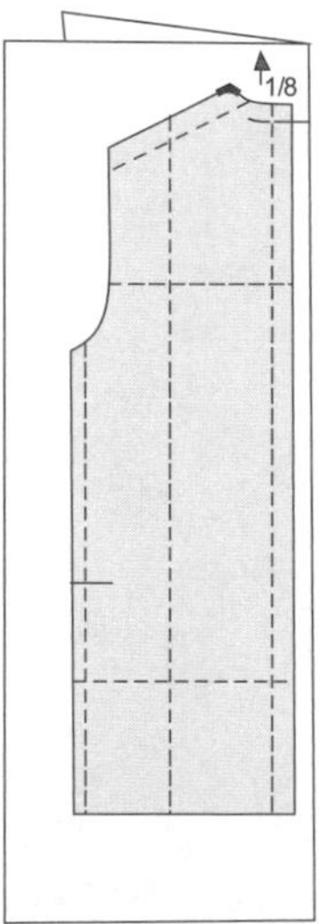

Shift the sloper up ⅛″ and trace out the next section of the neck and the corner intersection.

Because the neck will be blended with a ruler in a straight line, it is not necessary to draw the entire shoulder, just the corners.

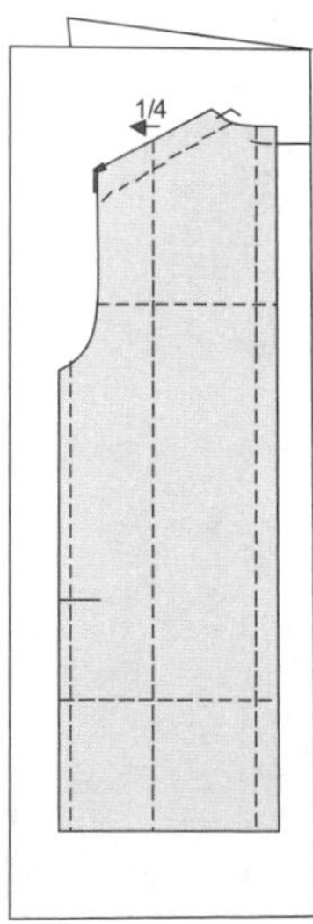

Shift the sloper out ¼″ as illustrated and trace the next section of the shoulder, the shoulder corner intersection.

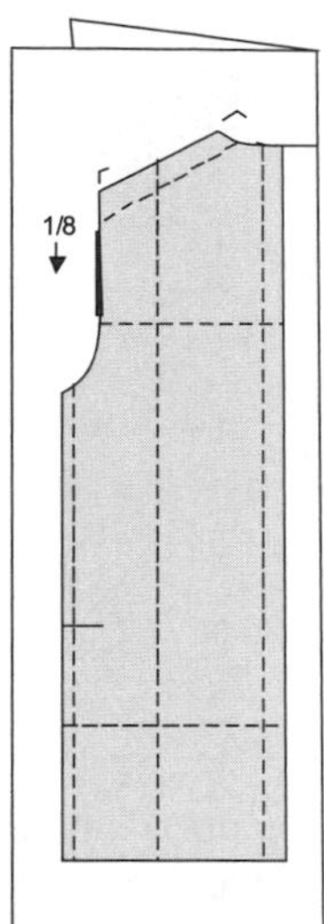

Shift the sloper down ⅛″ and trace the next section of the sloper.

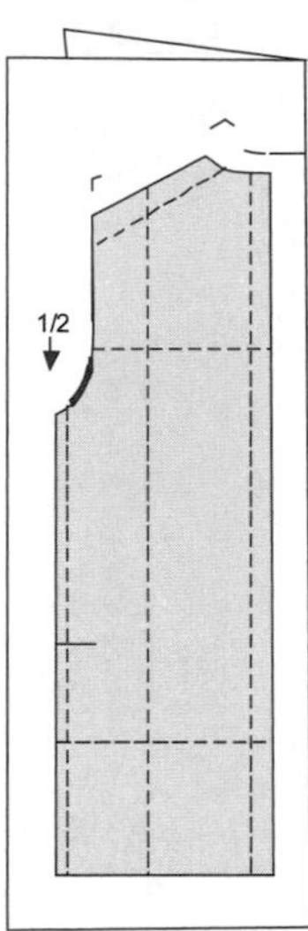

Shift the sloper down another ½″ and trace out the next sections.

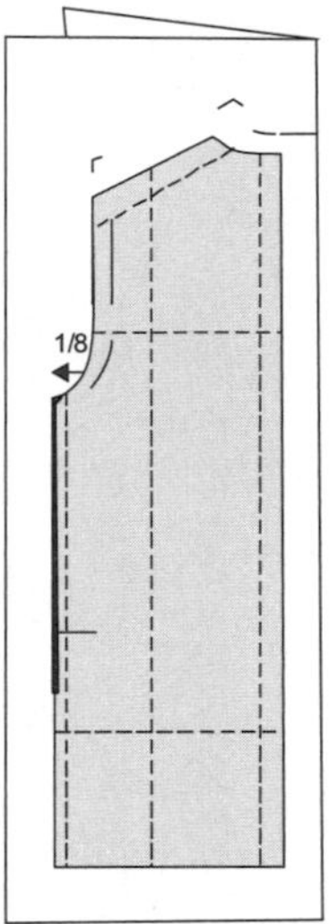

Shift the sloper out ⅛″ and trace the remainder of the underarm and the corner intersection.

Indicate the waist notch.

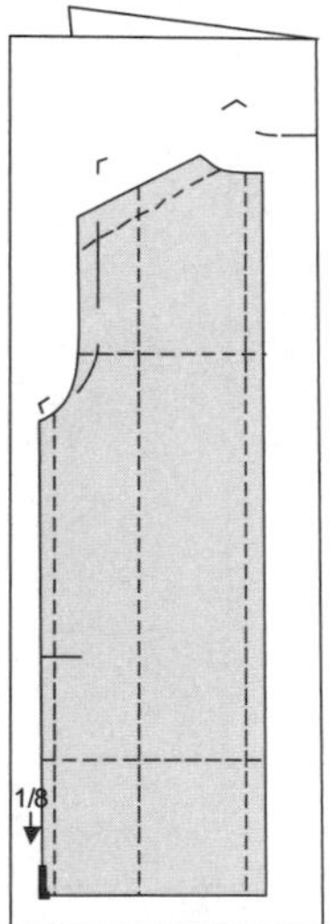

Shift the sloper down ⅛″ and trace to the hem and the hem corner intersection.

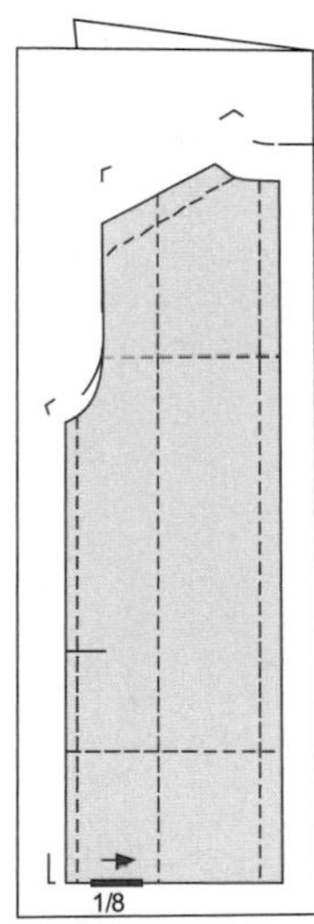

Shift the sloper back ⅛″ and trace that portion of the hem.

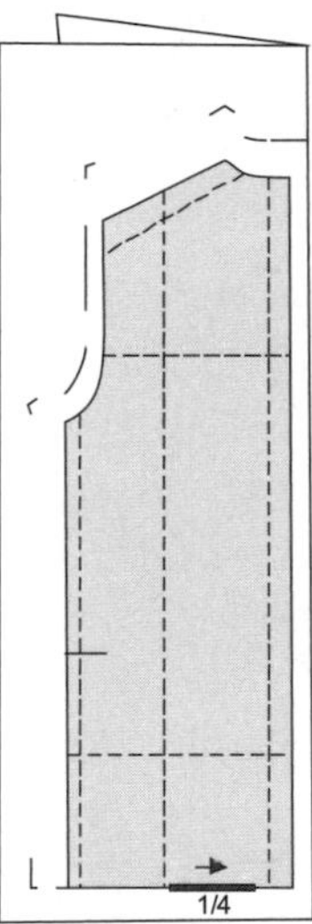

Shift the sloper back ¼″ and trace that section of the hem.

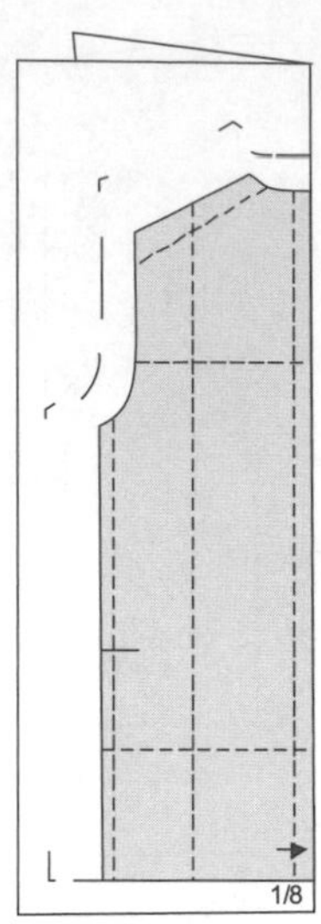

Shift the sloper over ⅛″ and trace the remaining section of the hem, and the corner.

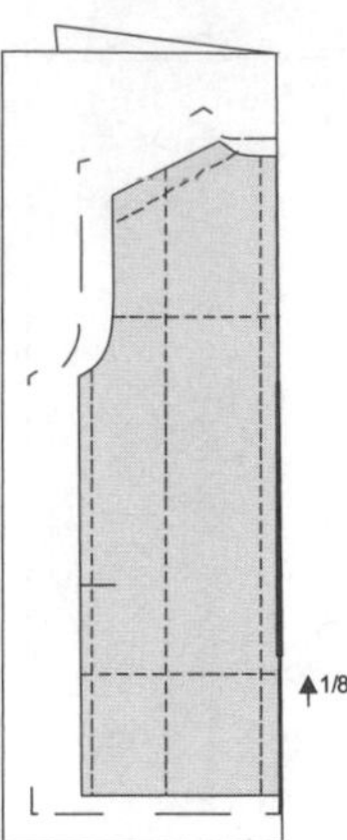

Shift the sloper back up ⅛″ and trace that portion of the center back.

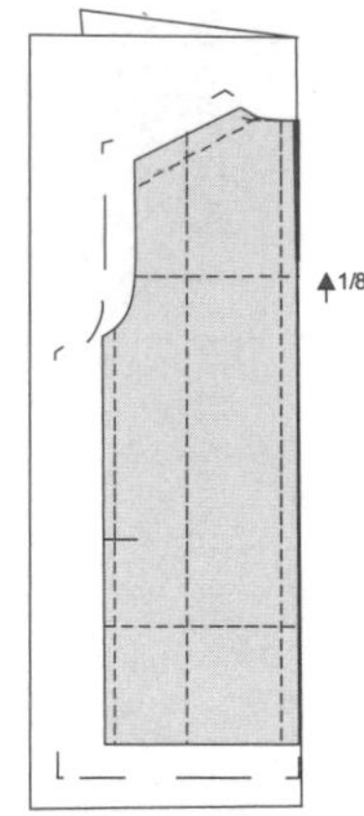

Shift the sloper up ¼″ and trace the last portion of the center back.

The sloper should have traveled a full circle and be back at the same point that it originated.

To blend:

Connect the shoulders, side seams, and hems with a straight line.

Blend the neck and underarm, using the original sloper as a curve template, so that the new sloper retains the original curves.

Note that it may look as if the neck has increased by a total of ¼″, but after blending it should have only increased by ⅜″ due to the nature of the curves.

Repeat for the front sloper.

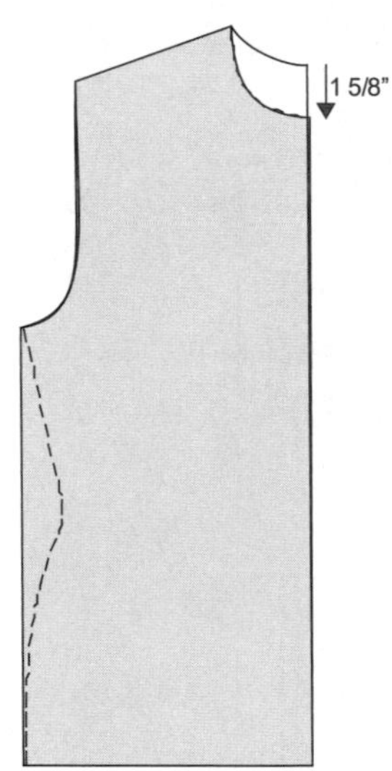

To create the front sloper:

Trace out the back sloper and make changes to the neck as illustrated.

Lower the neck 1⅜″ and bend a new neck.

Or use the original neckline as a template.

To indicate the fitted waist, trace the side seam from the original sloper.

	Extra Extra Small	Extra Small	Small	Medium	Large	Extra Large	Extra Extra Large
Neckline Drop	1½	1½	1⅝	1⅝	1⅝	1¾	1¾

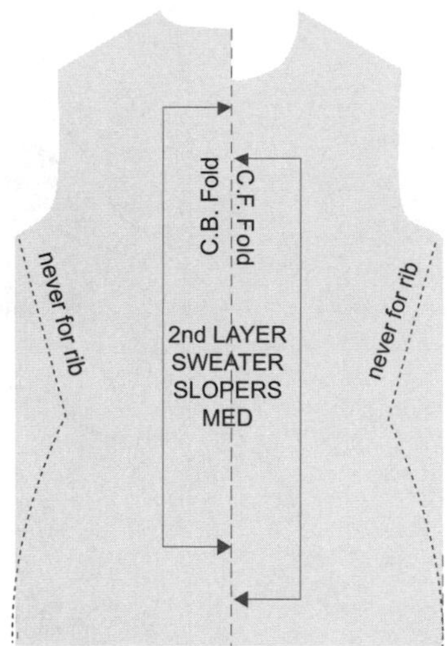

Alternate method of cutting out sweater slopers:

To save space and oak-tag, place front and back together as illustrated.

Fold on the fold line of center/front and center/back. In order to use these slopers, you must trace the back twice and the front twice, using the center as the fold line.

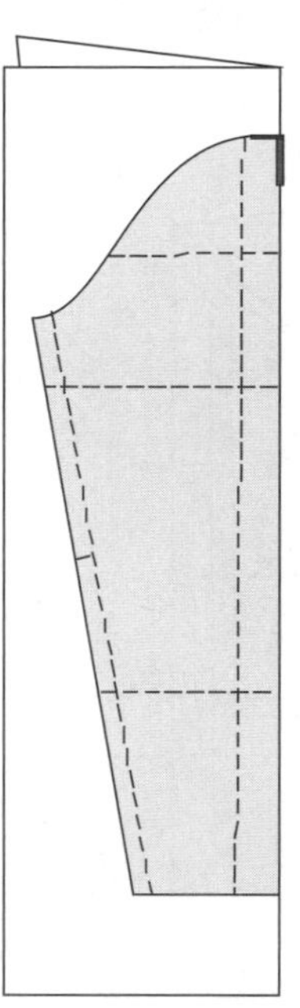

SLOPER SHIFTING TO CREATE SECOND LAYER SLEEVE SLOPERS

The sleeve sloper may be increased on the fold on light paper, as half, then opened and traced onto oak-tag.

Trace the first section of the sleeve as indicated.

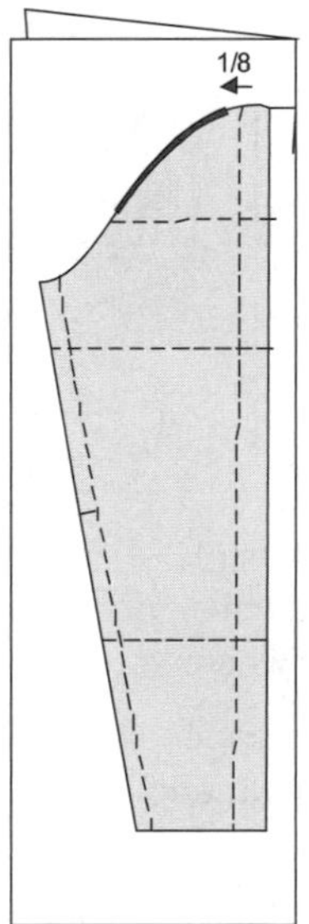

Shift the sloper out ⅛″ and trace the next section.

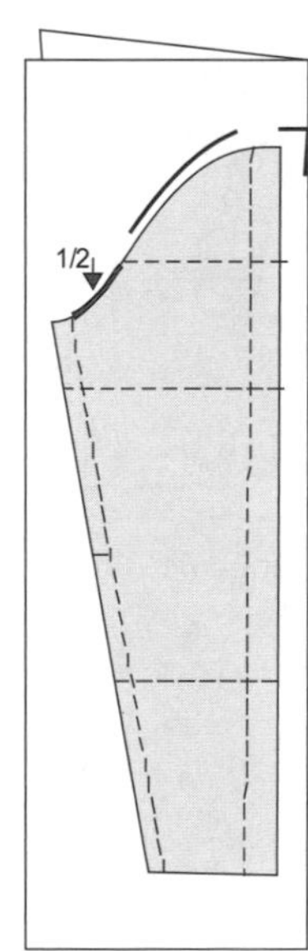

Shift the sloper down ½″ and trace next section.

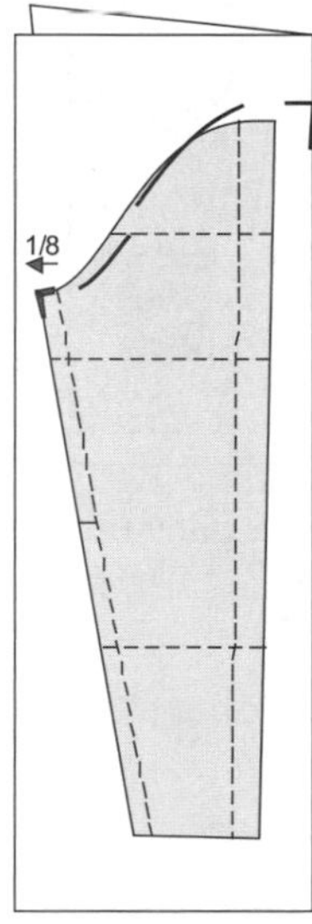

Shift the sloper out ⅛″ and trace as indicated.

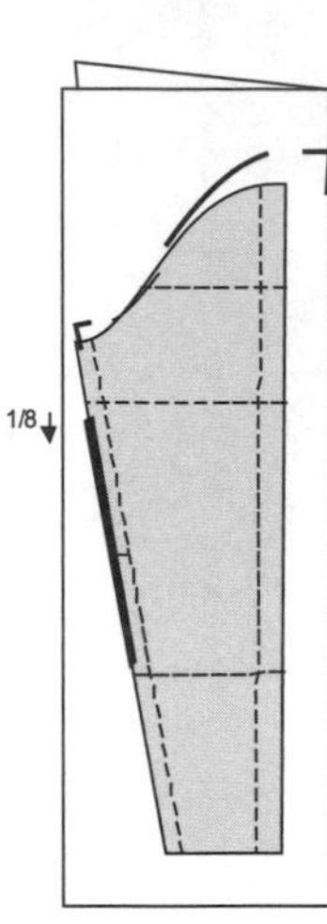

Shift the sloper down ⅛″.

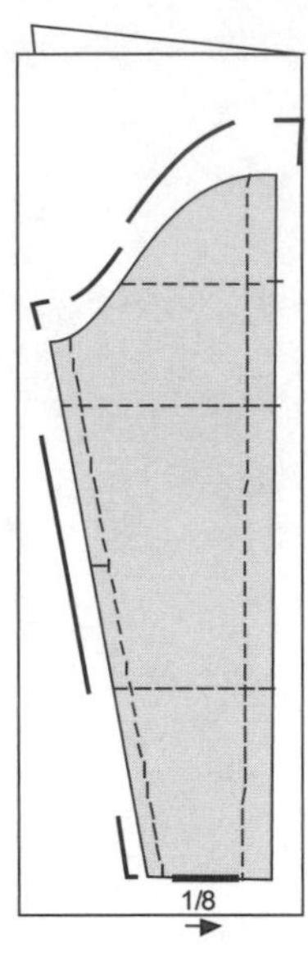

Shift the sloper back in and trace.

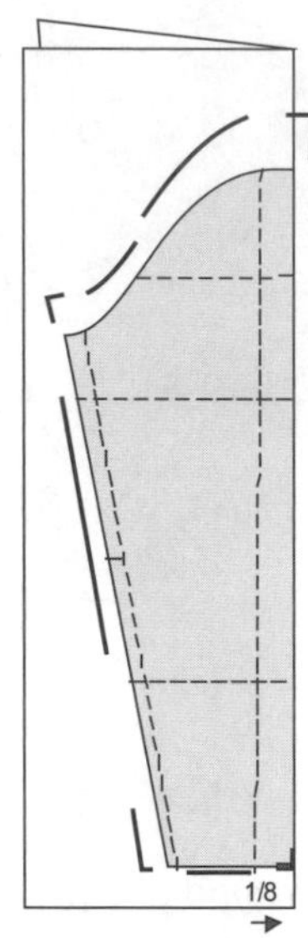

Shift the sloper in ⅛″.

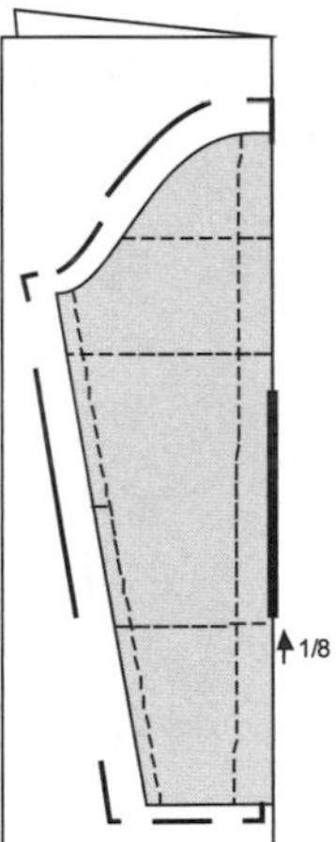

Shift the sloper back up ⅛″ and trace as indicated.

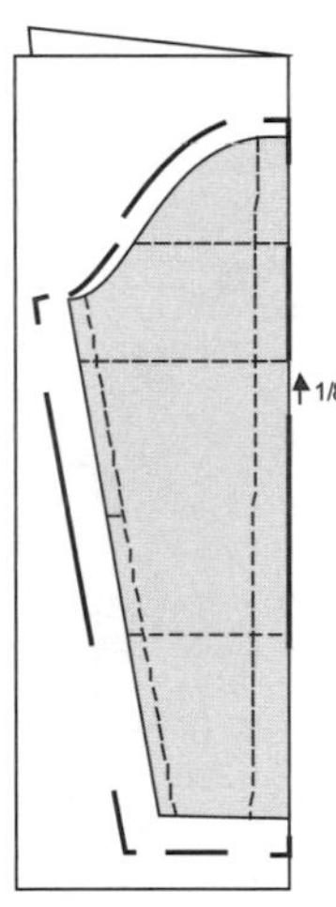

Shift the sloper up ⅛″.

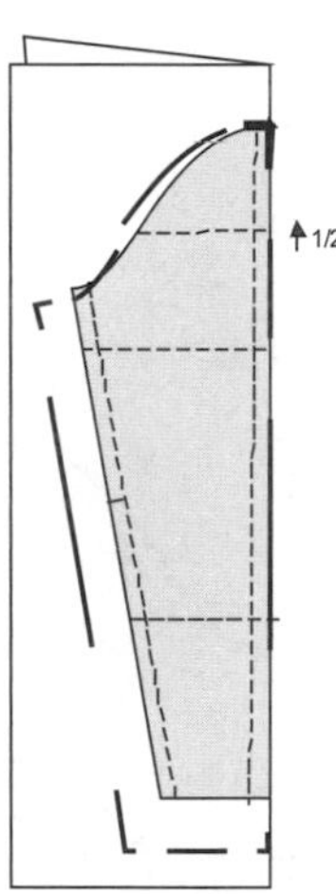

Shift the sloper up ¼″ as indicated and you should have gone a full circle and be exactly where you started.

Cut out the paper sloper on the fold, and open it up and trace again onto oak-tag.

Always cut the sleeve full/open, and do not put a crease in your sleeve sloper, as it will wear out along that edge too fast.

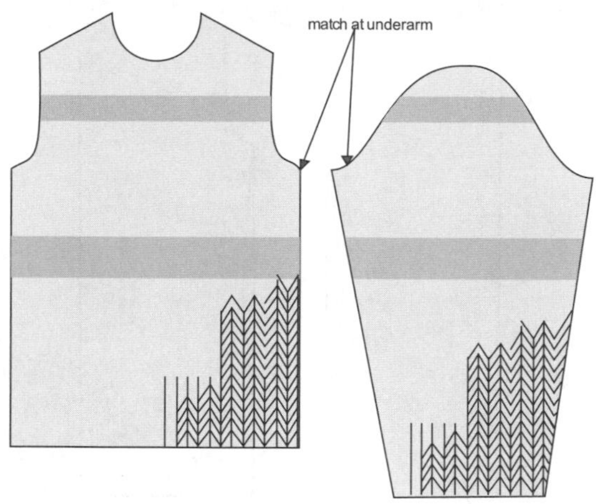

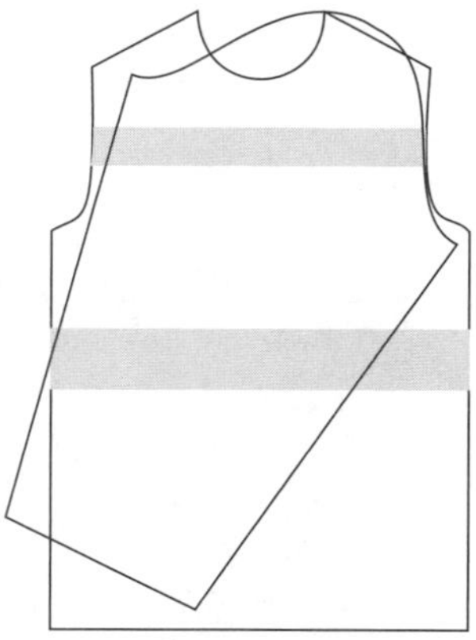

MATCHING STRIPES

Match the stripes of any design at the underarm, as illustrated.

Note: You cannot match from the bottom because the sleeve will often be much longer than the body.

To match the stripes of the body to the stripes of the sleeves, lay the front pattern on the striped fabric and draw faint lines to indicate the stripe placements.

Walk the sleeve pattern around the body pattern and match the sleeve stripe at the underarms as illustrated.

Seam Allowances for Sweaters

This manual illustrates all sweater drafts with a hem allowance, even though fully fashioned sweaters or those cut from sweater blanks do not need the hem allowance added.

This manual also illustrates all completed patterns on the fold, which is not acceptable for production patterns.

	Cut and Sew	Sweater Blanks	Fully Fashioned
Side seam	3/8″ four-thread serger	3/8″ four-thread serger	One stitch seam allowance 1/8″
Armhole and sleeves	3/8″ four-thread serger	3/8″ four-thread serger	One stitch seam allowance 1/8″
Shoulders	3/8″ four-thread serger With twill tape, or clear elastic to prevent the shoulders from stretching, for styles with sleeves only. four thread serger	3/8″ four-thread serger With twill tape, or clear elastic to prevent them from stretching, for styles with sleeves.	One stitch seam allowance 1/8″
Neckline and collars	3/8″ four-thread serger	3/8″ four-thread serger	One stitch seam allowance 1/8″
Hem	1 ½″ for hand hem or blind hem	No hem allowance needed for sweater blanks, since the hem is already knit in.	No hem allowance for fully fashioned since the hem is already knit.

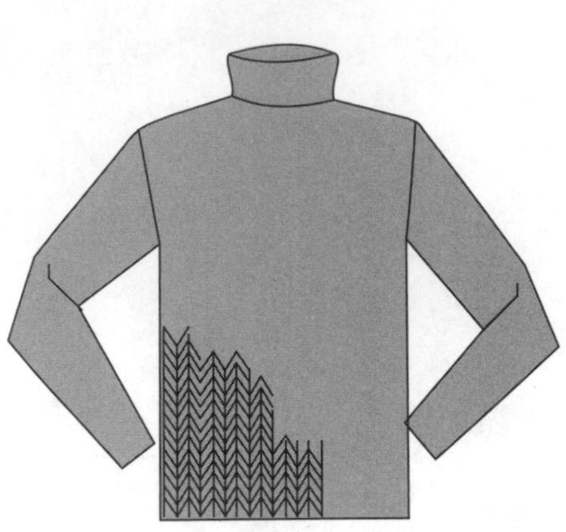

STYLE # 10-001 TURTLENECK SWEATER

A turtleneck sweater is one of the simplest of all sweater patterns to draft.

The collar is simply a long rectangle that is folded over and attached to the neck.

Turtlenecks can be created for first, second, or third layer slopers.

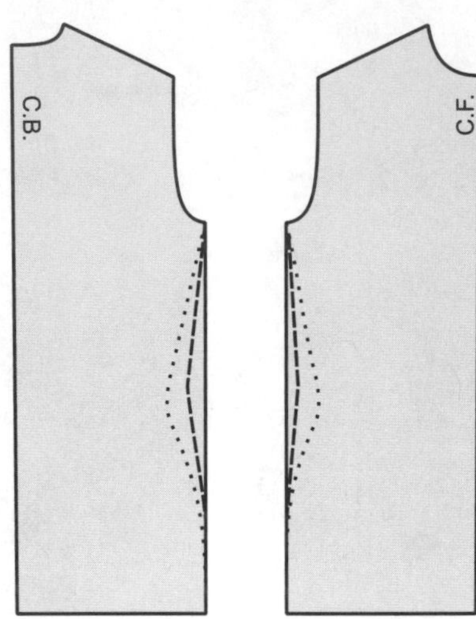

Decide whether you want a fitted, semi-fitted, or unfitted waist for your design.

You'll probably desire the unfitted waist for a pullover, so it's easier for the customer to put on and off.

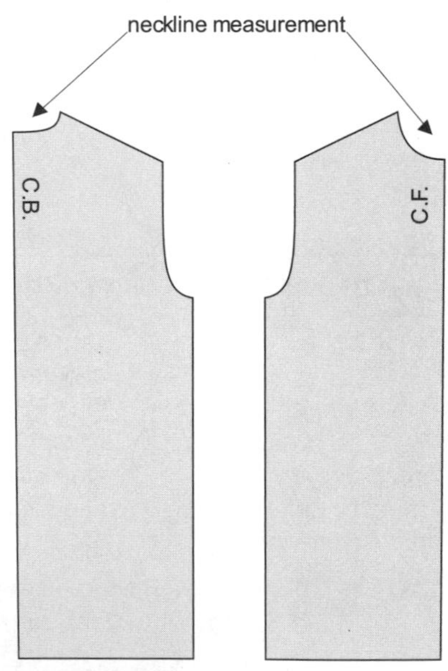

Trace out the appropriate sloper.

Measure the front and back neckline of the sloper.

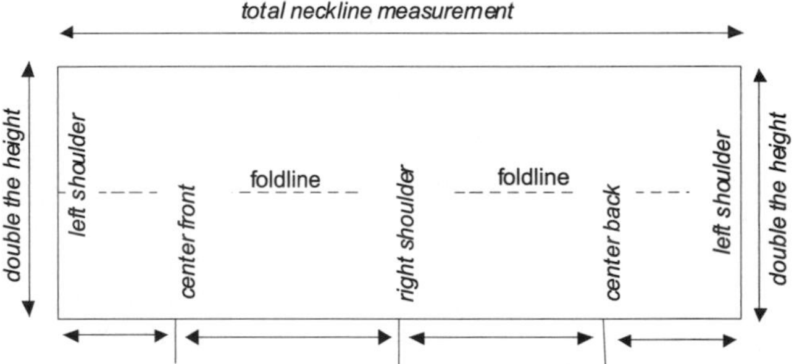

Draft the collar double the height of the required collar since it will be folded over and both raw edges will be sewn to the neckline of the sweater.

Draft the collar pattern any height desired, but remember that any collar higher than 4″ will be pushed down by the jaw.

The collar should have only one seam, either at the center back, or preferably lined up with the left shoulder seams. Therefore, the neckline measurement must be doubled, because you've only measured half of the neckline.

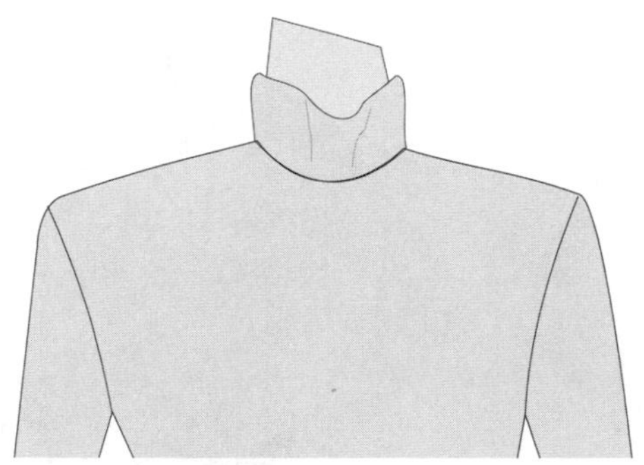

Since the neck is wider at the base than at the top, using the exact neckline measurement from the draft will create a collar that gapes at the top.

To correct this, pinch out the extra amount, measure it, and remove that amount from the pattern as illustrated.

The collar should be left with this extra fabric when inserting a zipper, since the zipper will scratch the wearer's neck.

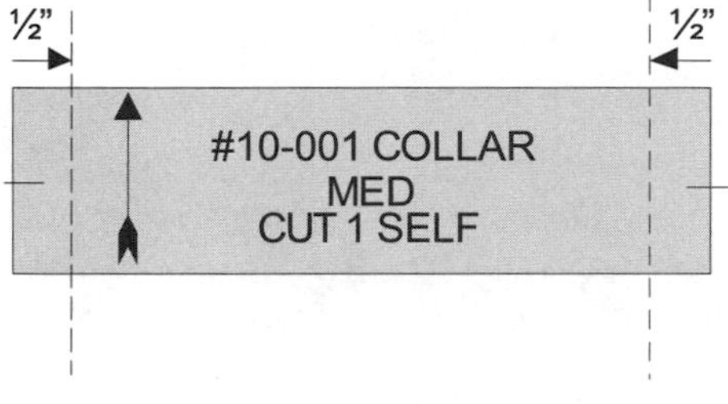

Or simply remove approximately ½" from each end of the collar pattern.

The top of the collar is now smaller and will fit snug to the neckline.

The edge that attaches to the sweater is also smaller and must be stretched to fit into the neckline of the sweater.

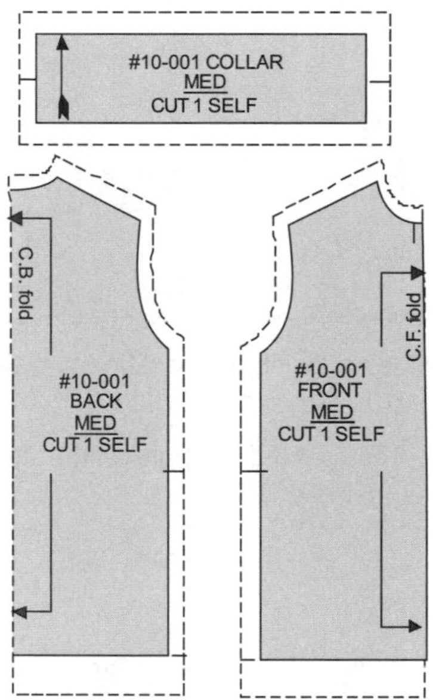

Add seam allowances and label the pattern.

Note that fully fashioned or sweaters cut from sweater blanks should not have hem allowance added.

Fully-fashioned sweaters should only have a "one-stitch" seam allowance, or ⅛".

COLLAR CORRECTIONS

If your fabric does not stretch enough for the collar to pull on over the head, then you have several adjustment options.

Insert a zipper or other closure in the collar.

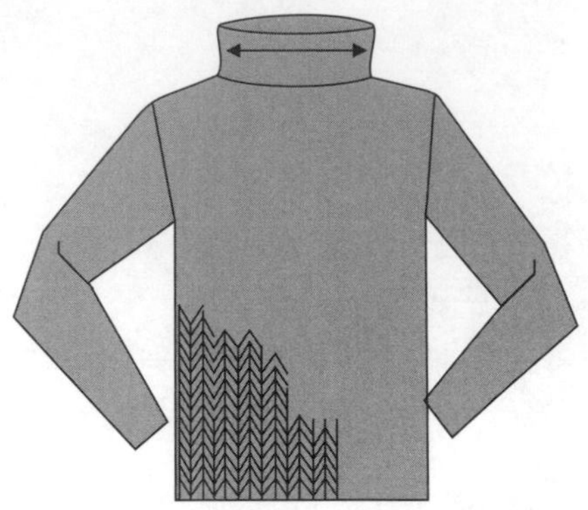

Enlarge the neckline and the collar accordingly; however, the collar will sit away from the neck.

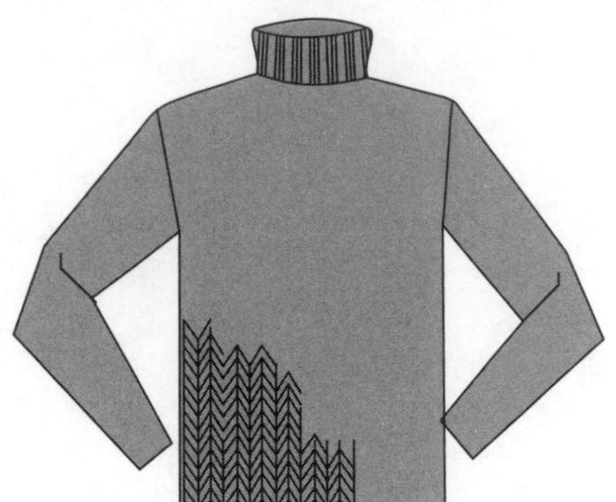

Use a contrast fabric, one that stretches more, for the collar.

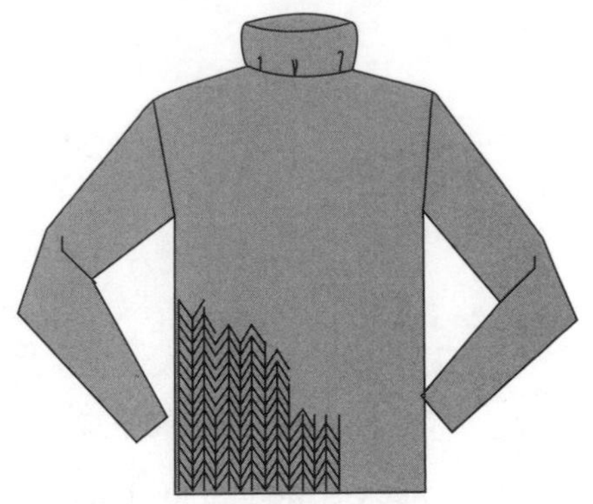

Enlarge the collar and ease it into the neckline, for very small amounts only, to avoid puckering of the collar seam.

STYLE # 10-002 SWEATER WITH OVER-SIZED TURTLENECK OR TUBULAR COLLAR

A tubular cowl neck sweater may be created by widening the neck opening and drafting a larger collar.

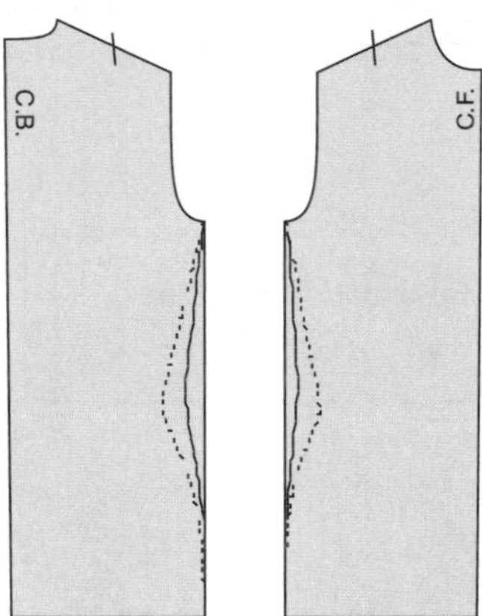

Decide how wide you wish the neckline to be and mark accordingly.

Stay at least ½″ in from the armhole so the sleeve seam allowance doesn't show.

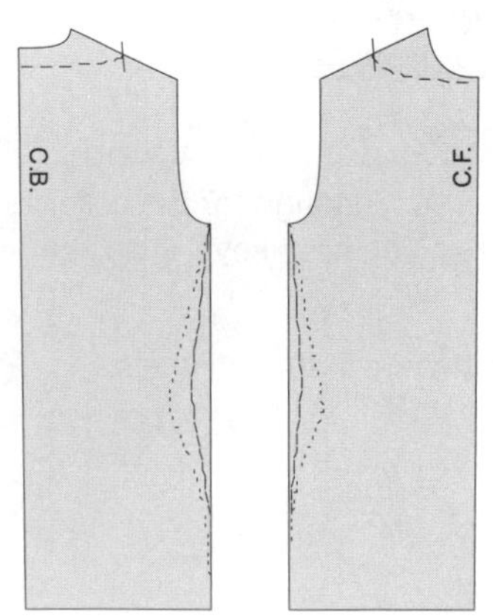

Draw in the new neckline, staying as high or close to the original neckline as possible, and square for ½″ at the shoulders, to blend.

Draw the collar according to the new measurements; no reductions are necessary.

In addition, when constructing this garment, serge the collar so the seam allowances are toward the outside of the garment, since they will be hidden by the collar and would otherwise show on the inside.

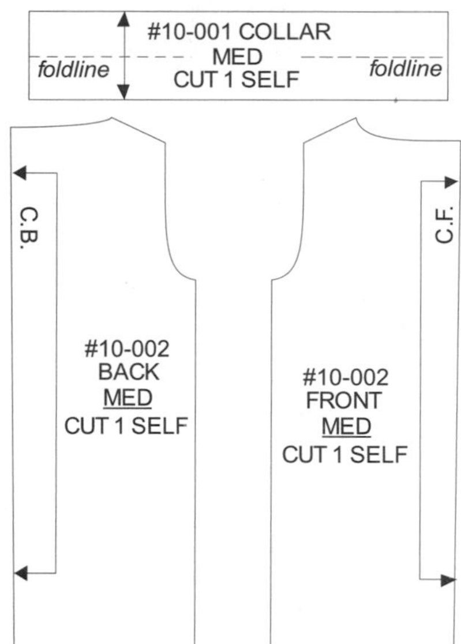

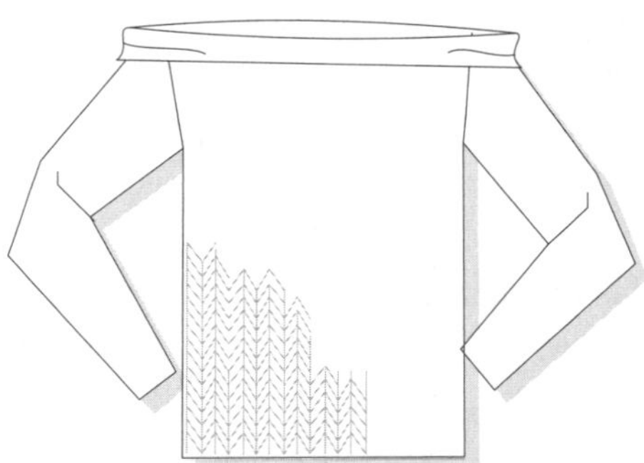

STYLE # 10-003 OFF-THE-SHOULDER SWEATER

This is an off-the-shoulder sweater.

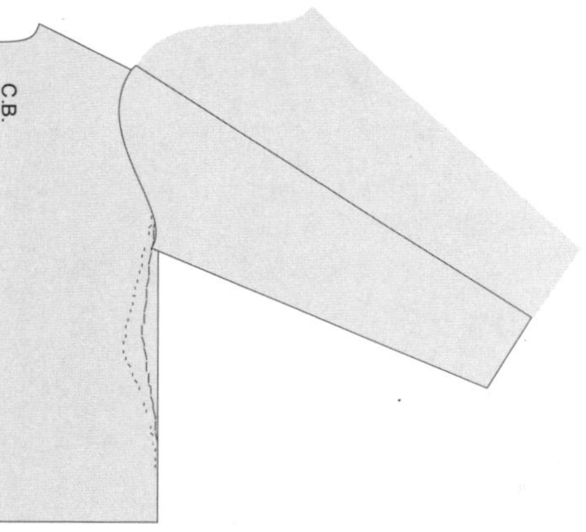

Walk the sleeve around the armhole to the shoulder seam.

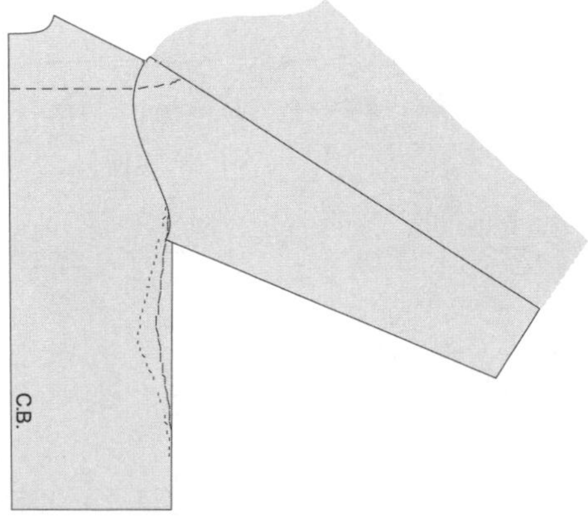

Line the sleeve up with the body.

Ignore any ease at the top of the sleeve, since that portion of the sleeve is not included in the design.

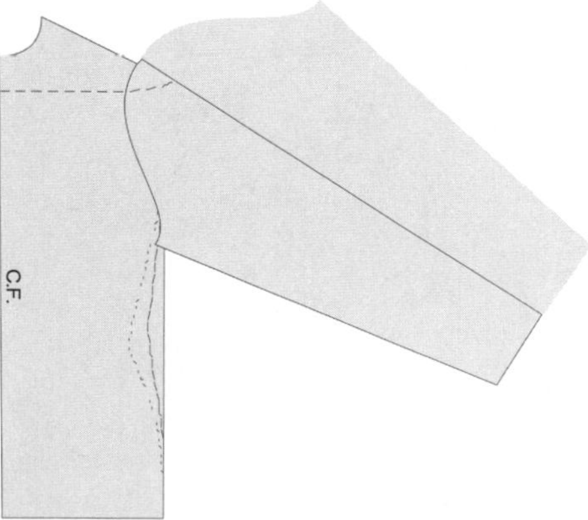

Draw in the neckline as required.

Don't draw it too low in the back; otherwise it will droop, and sag in the back.

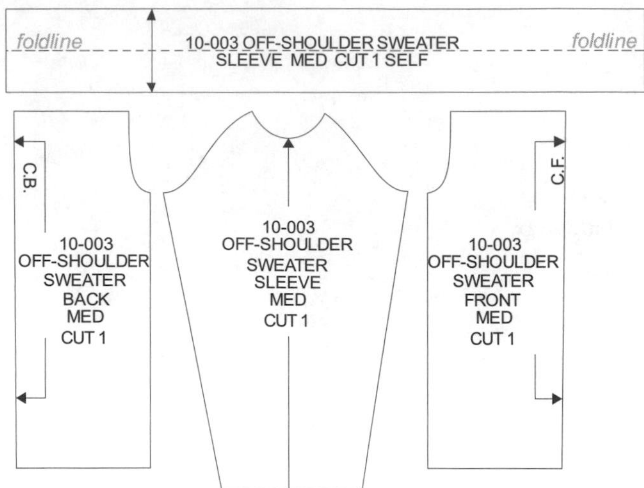

Trace and separate the pieces.

Draft the collar using the neckline measurements.

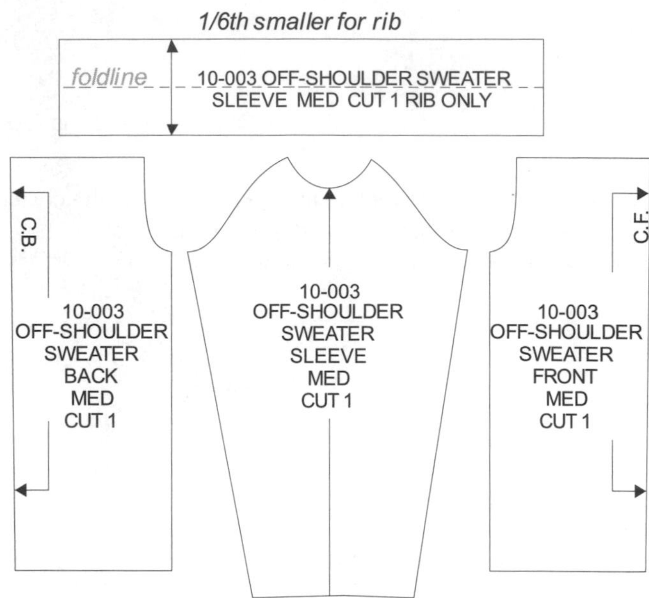

If you wish the collar to fit snugly against the arms, then reduce the collar pattern by one-sixth of the total measurement.

The collar may be knit in matching rib (one-sixth smaller), or sewn with elastic inserted into the collar to keep it snug against the body.

For fully-fashioned sweaters, mark the ribbing on the pattern pieces.

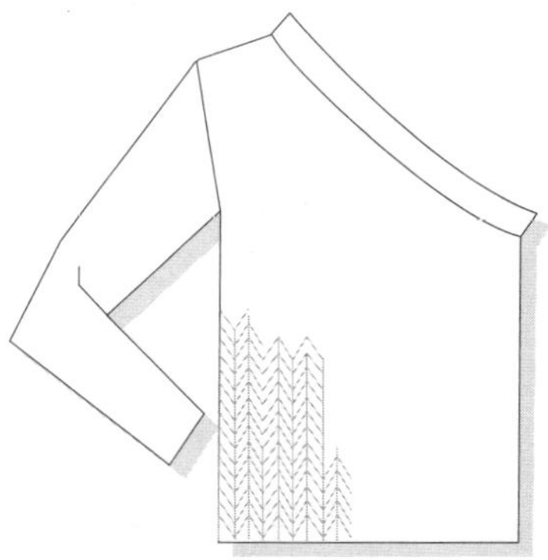

STYLE # 10-004 TUBULAR COLLAR IN ASYMMETRICAL NECKLINE

A one-shoulder sweater may be created by following these instructions.

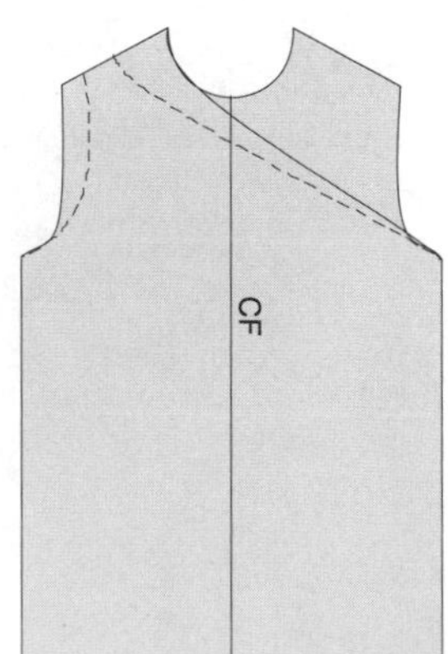

Draft any asymmetrical style with the sloper unfolded. Draw the asymmetrical neckline as required; give ample bust coverage by keeping the neckline high at the underarm.

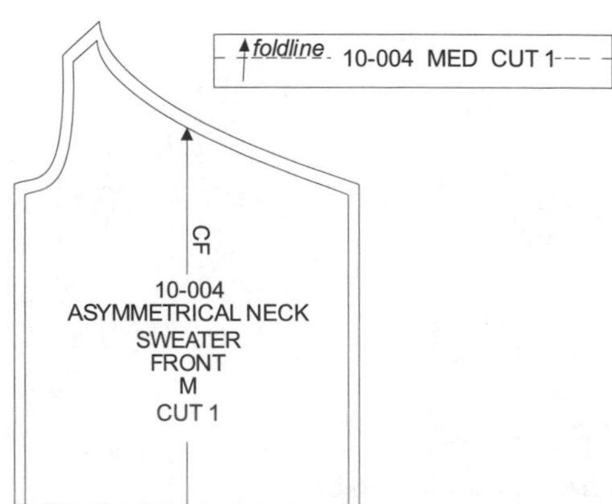

Draft the collar using the new neckline measurements.

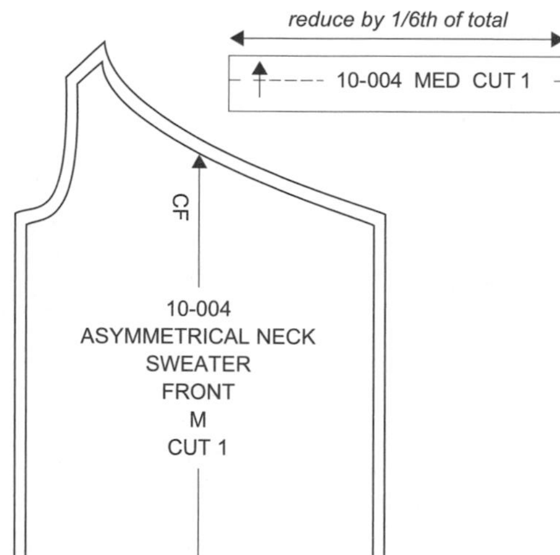

If you wish the collar to fit snug against the arms, then reduce the collar pattern by one-sixth of the total measurement.

The collar may be knit in matching rib, or sewn on with elastic inserted into the collar.

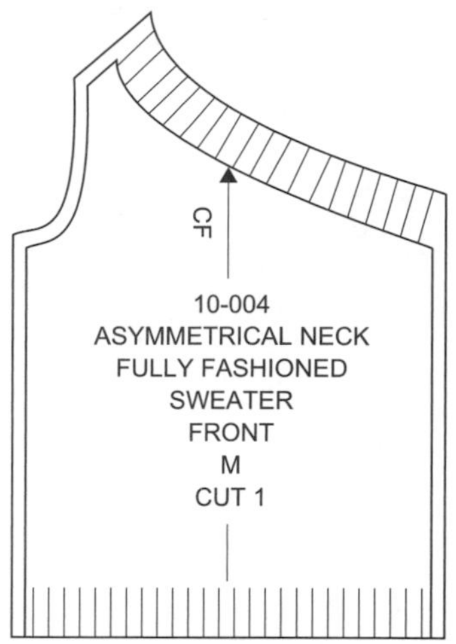

For fully-fashioned machine knit sweaters, draft the patterns with the rib finish drawn onto the pattern, as illustrated.

The rib is drawn onto the pattern and any half-scale patterns since the sweater will be knit using the knit radar, and is easier to follow in this manner.

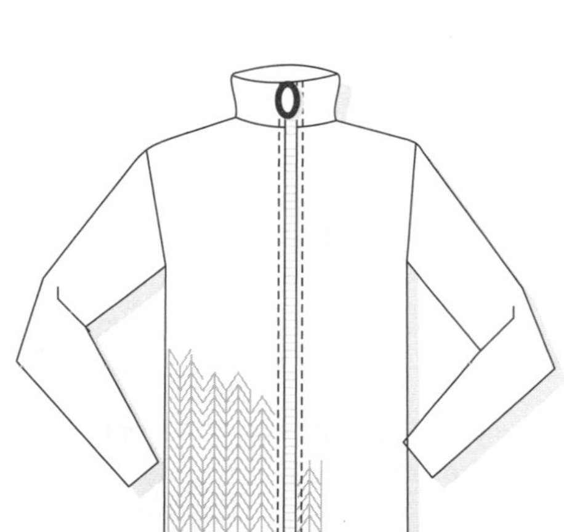

STYLE #10-005 TURTLENECK SWEATER WITH CENTER FRONT ZIPPER

Zip-front turtleneck sweaters are drafted similarly to the other turtleneck sweater.

Trace out the second layer sweater sloper, since the cardigan will most likely be worn over other clothing.

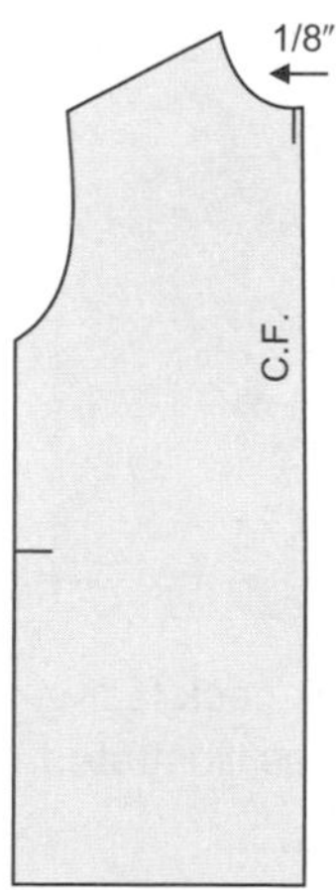

Because the width of the zipper teeth will add an extra ¼″ to the center front (⅛″ to each side of the cardigan), you must move the center front notch in by ⅛″, from the center front.

Later you will add ⅜″ seam allowance to each front but sew the front with ½″ seam allowance, thereby using up the extra ¼″.

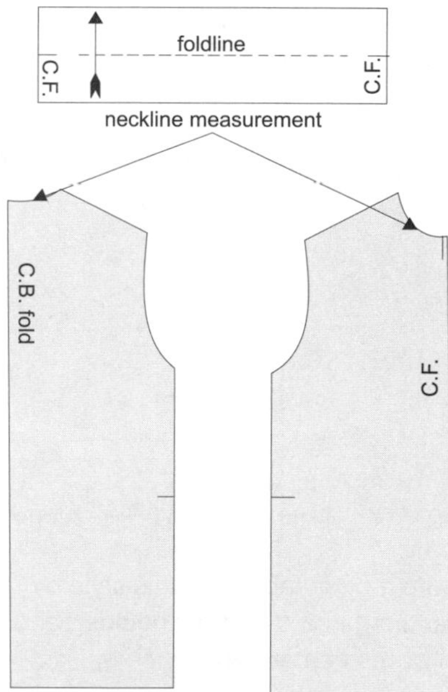

Draft the collar pattern to the height/width desired.

The length is determined by the total neckline measurement.

Do not reduce the collar like the turtleneck draft, since there is a zipper in the front that would be uncomfortable if the collar was snug.

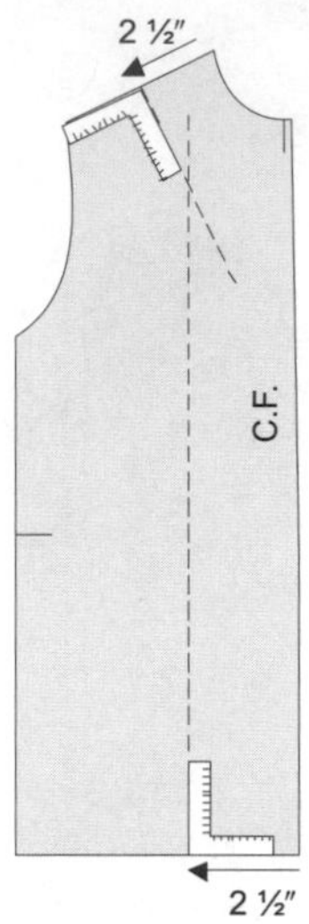

Measure in and mark the shoulder 2½″ from the neck, along the shoulder, and square down for a few inches.

Measure 2½″ in from the center front, along the hem, and square up to meet the other line.

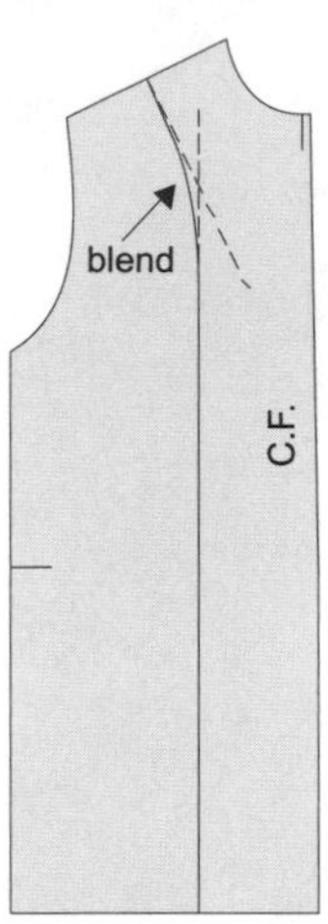

Blend a smooth curve along the facing line.

Trace out the facing on a separate piece of paper.

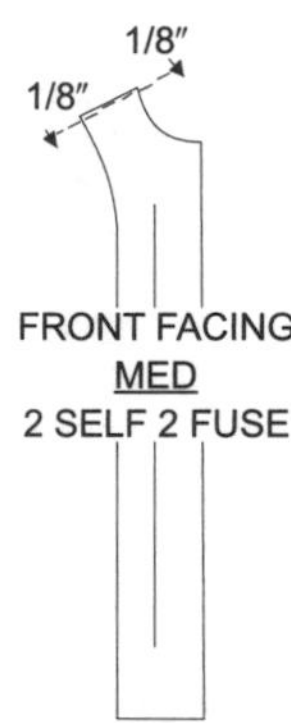

Remove ⅛″ from the shoulder of the facing as indicated.

This will make the inside facing slightly smaller than the outside, to accommodate the thickness of the fabric.

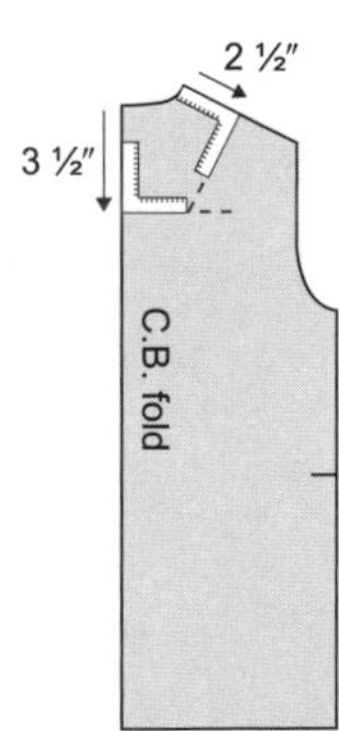

Create a back facing for this style by measuring in 2½″ at the shoulder, and 3½″ at the center back.

The back of the facing is lower to prevent it from rolling up and coming out when worn. It also provides extra room for placing the label.

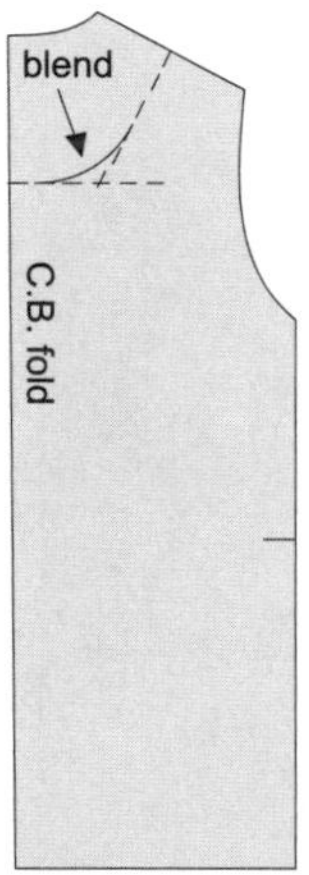

Blend the back neck facing into a smooth curve as illustrated.

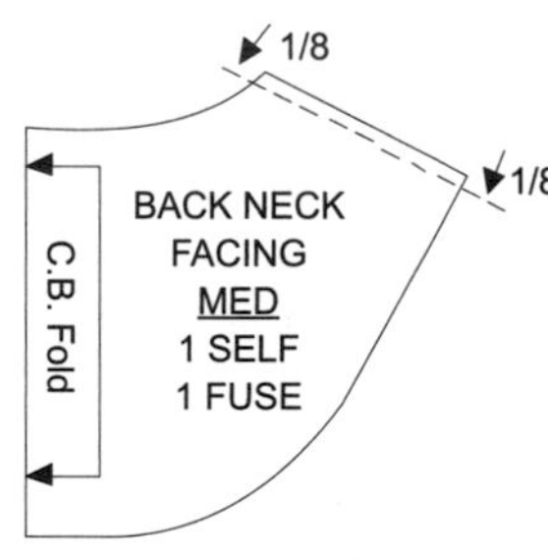

Remove ½″ from the shoulder of the facing as illustrated.

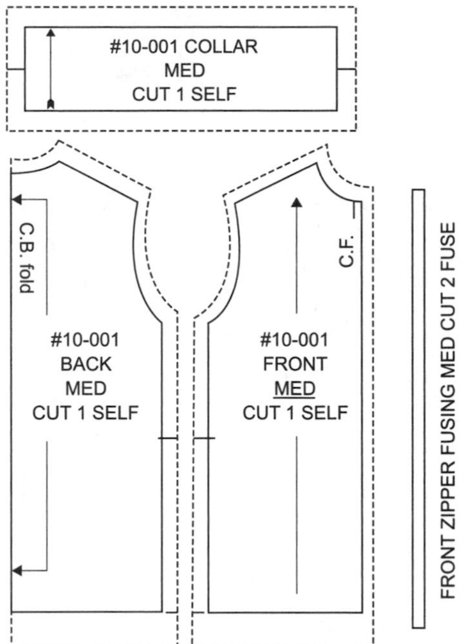

PATTERN OPTION # 1

This pattern option may be used when the designer does not want a facing.

Cut the fusing 3/8″ wide and as long as the front. This piece will prevent the front from stretching while the zipper is being attached.

This option will show the exposed zipper tape when viewed from the inside.

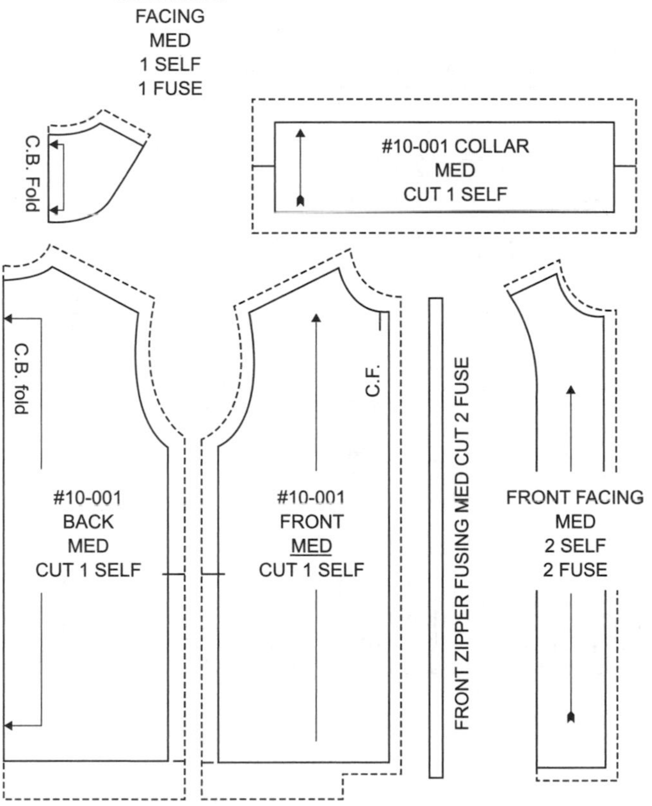

PATTERN OPTION # 2

This option shows the pattern for the same sweater but with an inside facing that clean-finishes the inside front so the zipper tape is not visible.

PATTERN OPTION # 3

This option shows the pattern with a front facing and no back facing.

The back neckline seam is finished with neckline tape.

Note the tape measurement written along the back neck of the sweater.

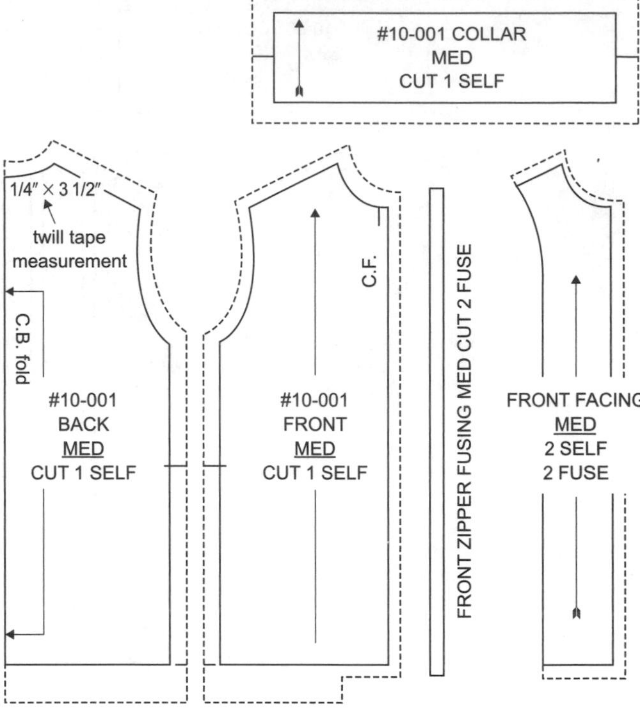

PATTERN OPTION # 4

Use this option for sweaters cut from sweater blanks.

Do not add any hem allowance, since the hem will be knit into the fabric.

The collar may be cut single layer because the top edge is finished by the knitting machine.

There is no front facing. Instead, 1″ wide knit stolling is used, and will be sewn to the inside of the zipper. Stolling should be knit double jersey to prevent it from rolling.

Draw the ribbed hem onto the fully-fashioned pattern for easier knitting.

Since most knitting starts from the hem upwards, it is easy to see the hem amount in the knitting machine, using the radar.

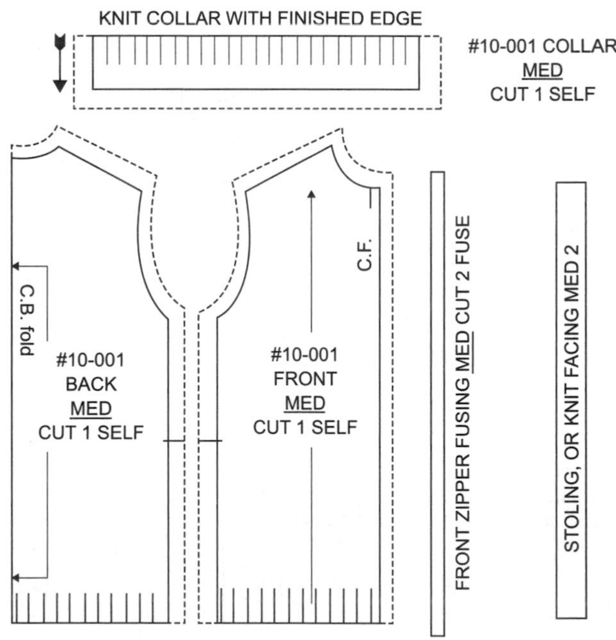

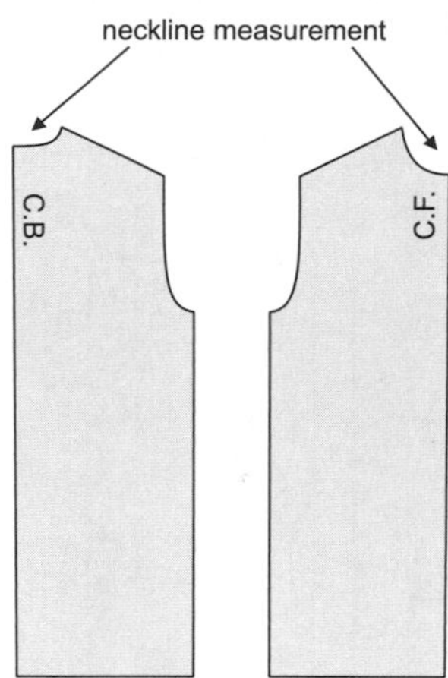

PATTERN OPTION # 5

Use this option for fully-fashioned sweaters.

This sweater requires a single-stitch seam allowance (1/8″) for linking or sewing because there are no raw edges.

The rib or hem finish is drawn onto the pattern, since it does not need to fold up.

Stolling may be knit to match the sweater, so a facing is not needed. Stolling should be knit double jersey to prevent it from rolling.

STYLE #10-006 CARDIGAN SWEATER

The following illustrates the draft for a cardigan sweater, with a 1/2″ button, thus a 1/2″ overlap.

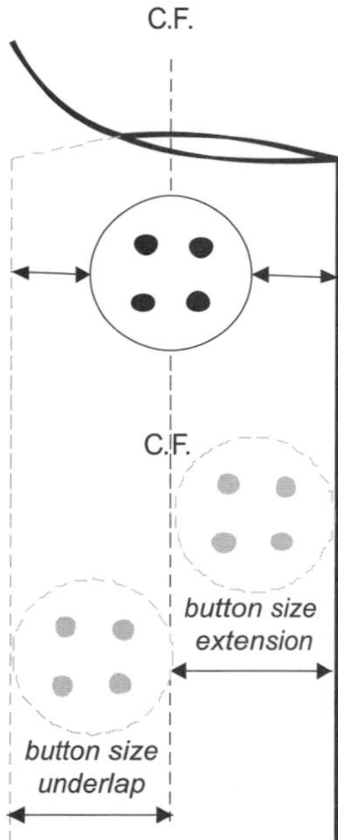

The center should always be extended the width of the button to make a "frame" equal to a half button width all the way around the button.

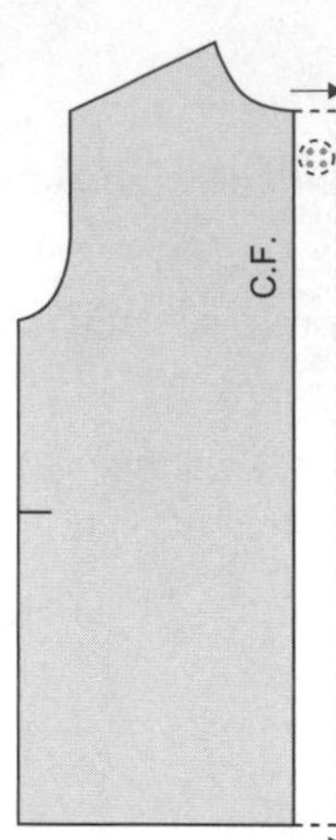

Extend the center front an amount equal to the width of the button you plan on using.

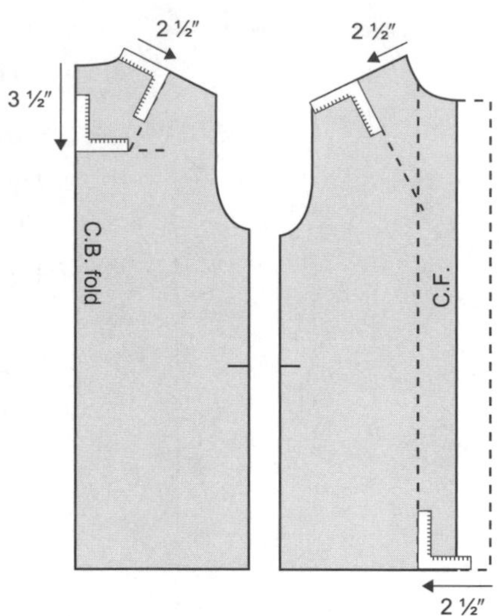

Create a facing as in Style #10-002.

2½″ in from the center front; consequently, 3½″ from the edge because of the extension.

2½″ along the shoulder.

3½″ down the center back.

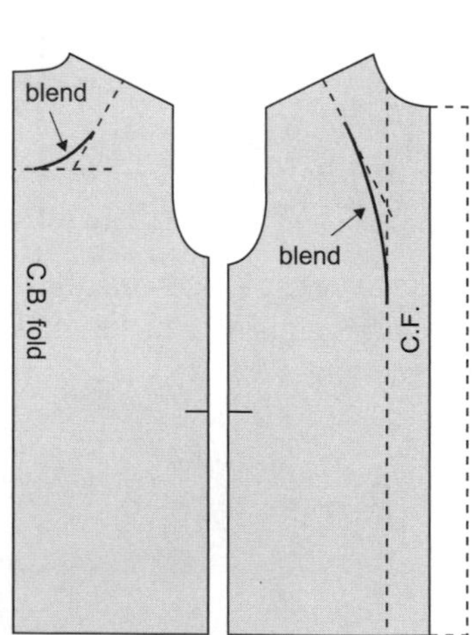

Blend the facing line into a smooth curve.

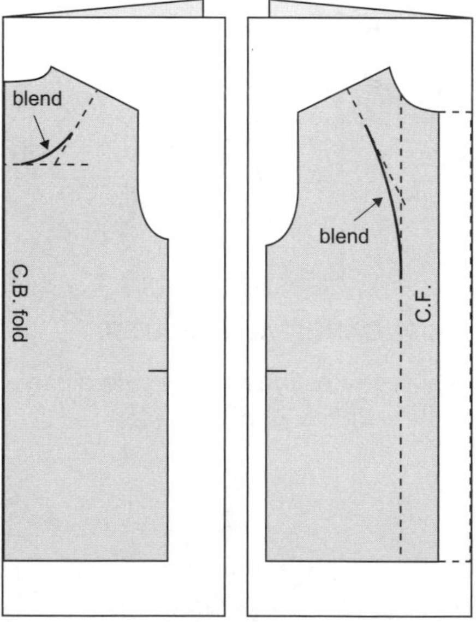

Place the front on the folded edge of a piece of paper, as illustrated, and trace the entire front. Also trace the front facing lines.

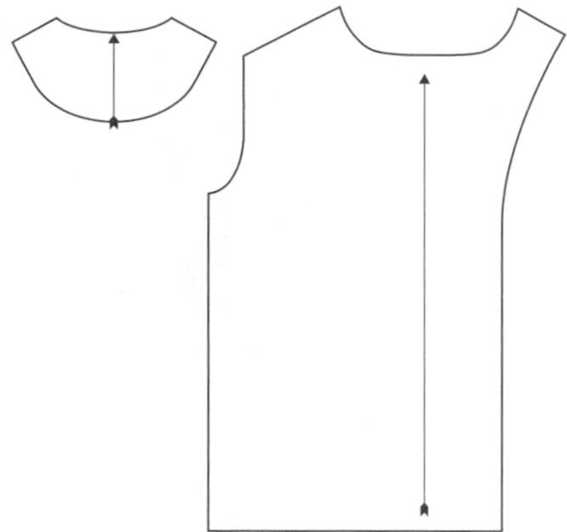

Open up the paper as illustrated.

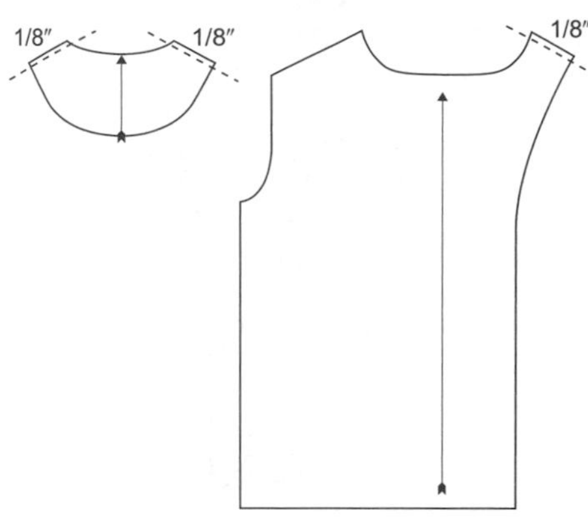

Remove ⅛″ from the shoulder edges of the facing, to account for the fact that the facing is on the inside and needs to be slightly smaller than the outside.

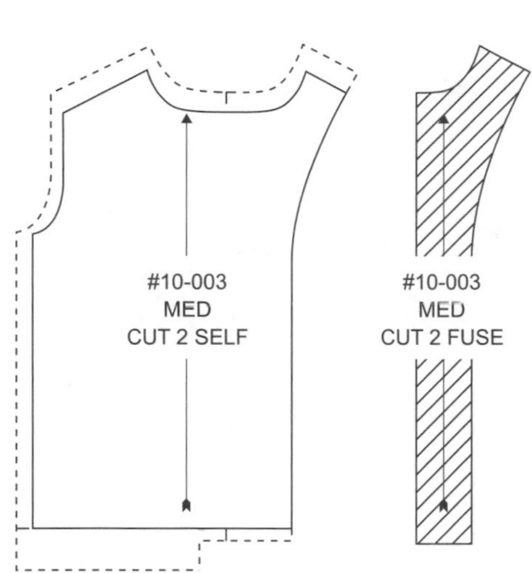

Add seam and hem allowances.

Label as indicated.

Create a new pattern piece for the fusing as indicated.

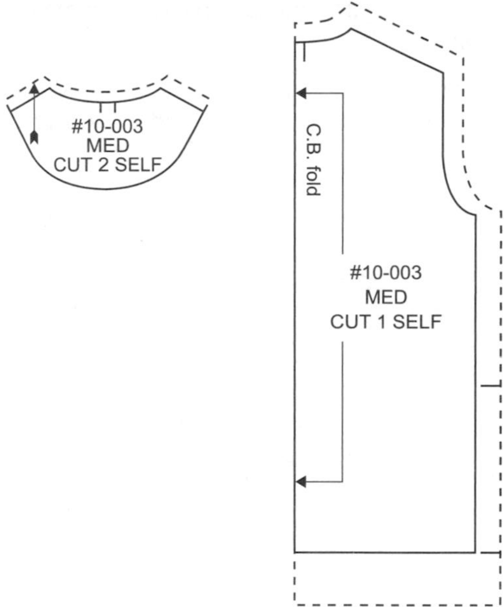

Create the back pattern pieces as illustrated.

If the pattern is cut and sewn, add a hem allowance as indicated.

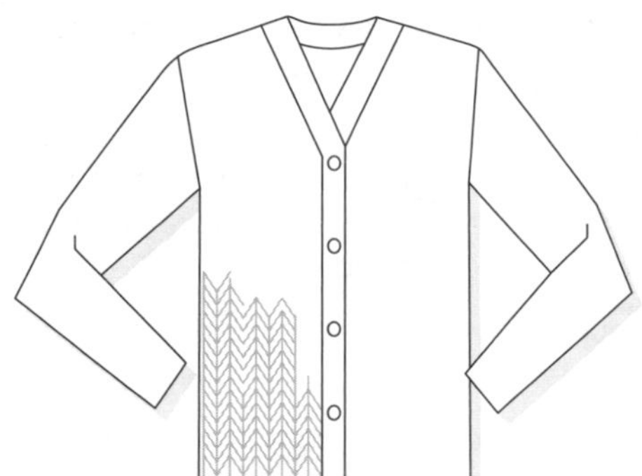

STYLE # 10-009 V-NECK CARDIGAN WITH BAND FINISHING

A similar cardigan may be drafted with a band to finish the front edges.

The band may be knit in rib, as a single layer or a double layer, or it may be cut and sewn as a double-layer.

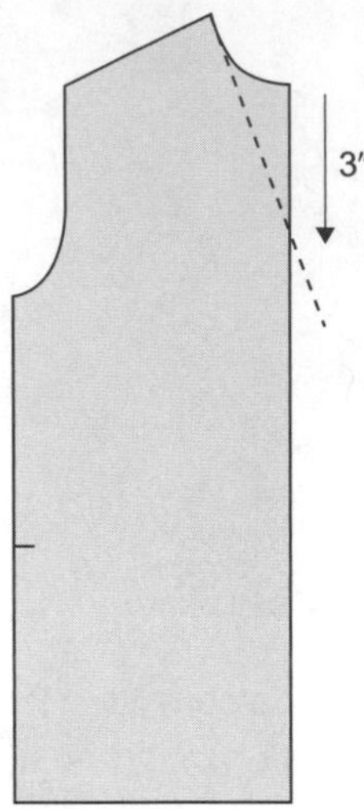

Draw in a V-neck.

The illustration shows the V extending 3″ below the original neckline, but the depth may be any measurement the designer wants.

To determine how low you wish to create the V-neck, measure down from the center front of the fitting Judy.

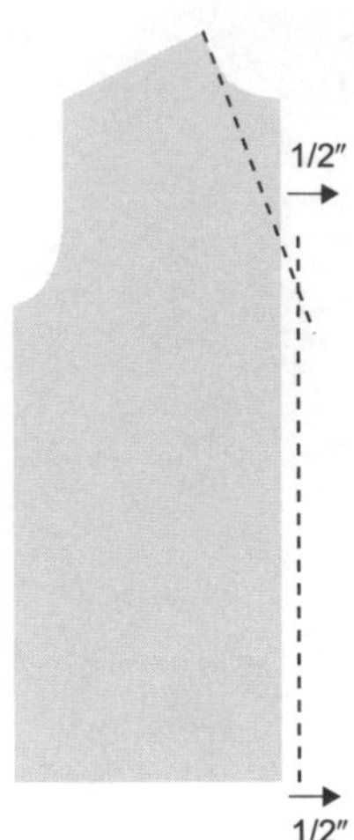

Extend the center front past the original center front by the amount equal to the width of your button.

The illustration shows ½″ for a ½″ button, but the button may be any size the designer requires, as long as the center front is extended an equal amount.

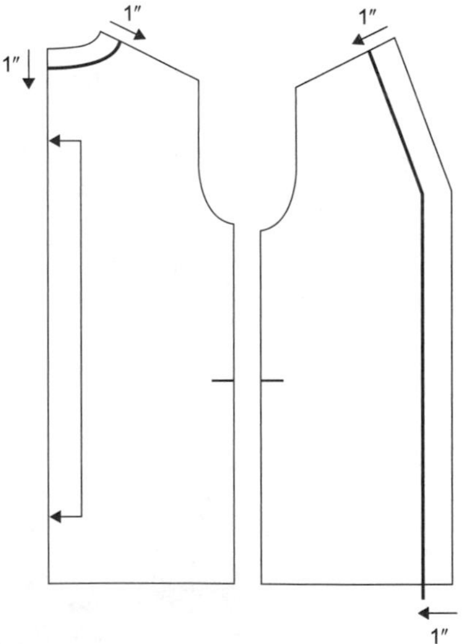

Draw in the collar with the neck band parallel to the new neckline.

Make the band double the width of the buttons (illustrated at 1″ for a ½″ button).

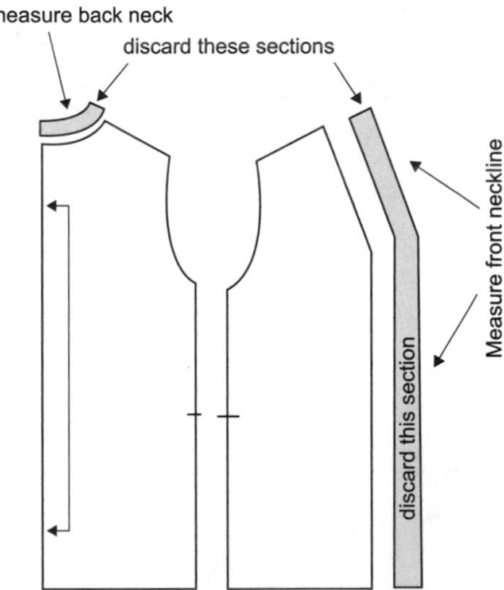

Remove and discard the band sections from the draft.

The band will be drafted as a new straight piece from the neckline measurements and will be folded in half when sewn.

To make the back neck lie flat at the back collar, and not stand up in the air, make it smaller than the back neckline and stretch it slightly to fit the neck edge.

Reduce the back neck portion of the collar by one-third of the neckline measurement.

Or simply measure the smaller, upper portion of the back neck curve and use that measurement.

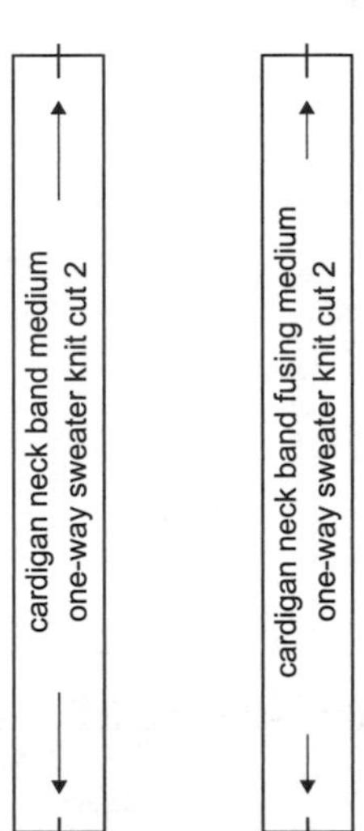

Draft the neckband pattern from the length of the total neckline, the neck edge of the discarded pieces.

Place a notch to correspond with the shoulder seam, so you will know when to start stretching the collar band.

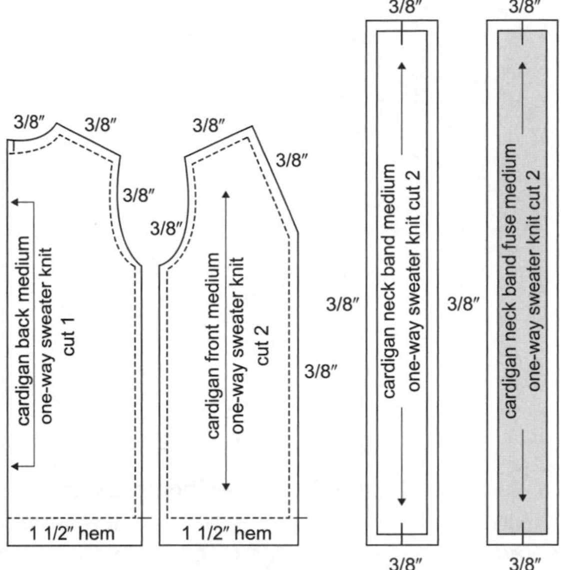

Because knit fabrics are looser than woven fabrics and easily fray and unravel, use ⅜″ seam allowances and a four-thread serger for construction.

Do not cover-stitch a sweater knit hem—it will stretch out of shape and not lie flat.

Use a blind hemmer or hand sew the hem.

Use a 1½″ hem allowance for hand hems.

Note that the band does not extend beyond the bottom of the garment, and is only as long as the outside portion of the front. It will not be folded up with the hem.

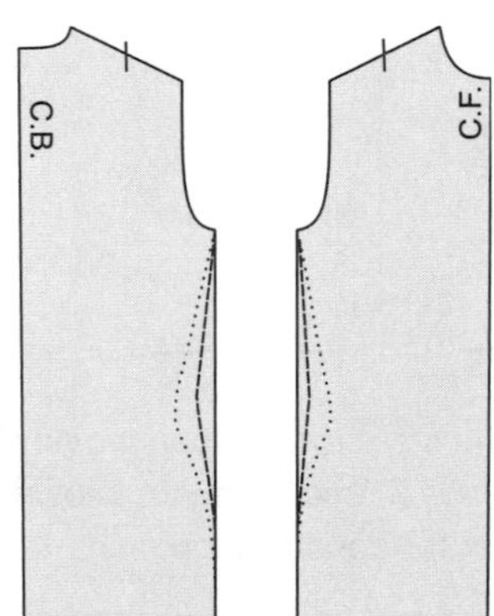

For fully fashioned sweaters, add ⅛″ seam allowance.

It is possible to knit the band as ribbed trim and link it onto the front.

Do not add hem allowance to fully-fashioned sweaters; just indicate the hem amount with a line.

STYLE # 10-010 BOAT NECK SWEATER

A boat neck is one of the simplest necklines to draft and sew.

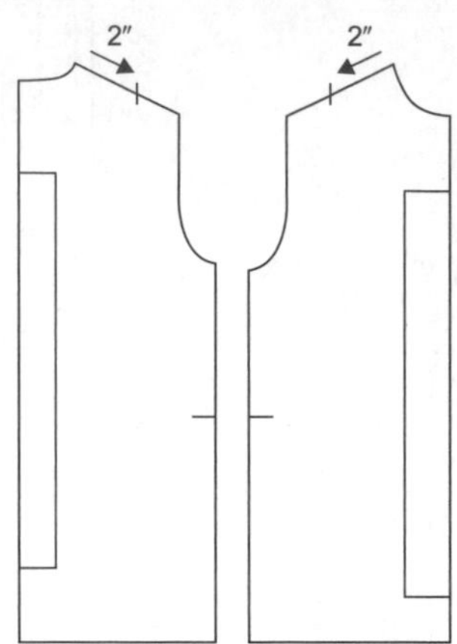

Find a placement for the ends of the boatneck and mark. The illustration shows 2″ from the neck, but it may be any measurement the designer wants, up to ½″ from the armhole, so the seam allowances will be hidden.

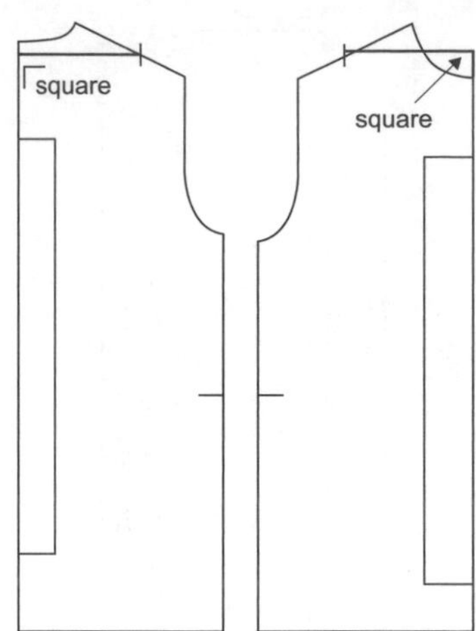

Square a line from the center front to meet the marks on the shoulder.

Note: The center front must be extended in order to draw the line, and will consequently raise the new boatneck above the neck seam. Don't worry about this choking the customer, as the fabric will stretch to allow for comfort.

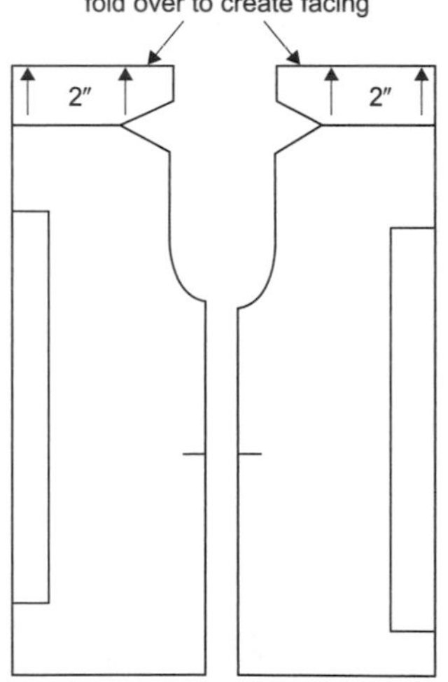

Fold the paper along the new neckline and trace the shoulder and armholes.

Unfold the paper and create a 2″ facing/hem as illustrated.

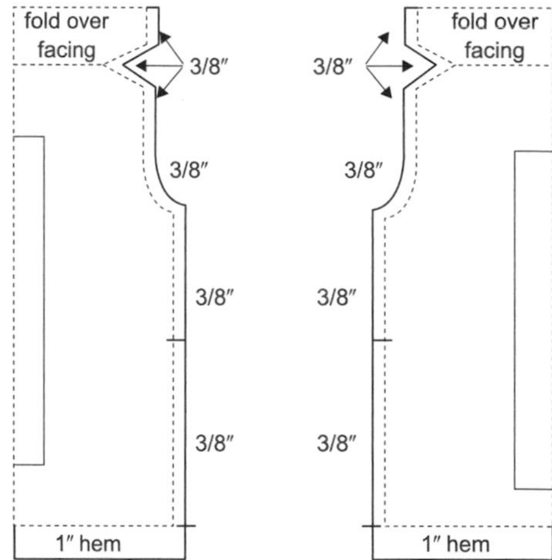

Because knit fabrics are looser than woven fabrics and easily fray and unravel, use ⅜″ seam allowances and a four-thread serger for construction.

Always use at least a 1″ hem allowance for all straight hems and ½″ for curved hems.

Do not cover-stitch a sweater knit—it will stretch.

Use a blind hemmer or hand sew the hem.

Use a 1½″ hem allowance for hand hems.

STYLE # 10-011 COWL-NECK SWEATER

Cowl necklines are created like boatnecks; however, the center front is extended to create the drape effect.

A cowl may be created on the front, the back, the sleeve or anywhere else the designer might imagine.

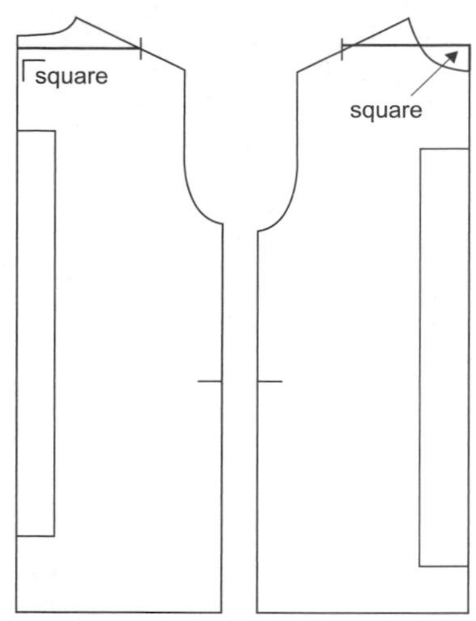

Place a mark on the shoulder of the draft.

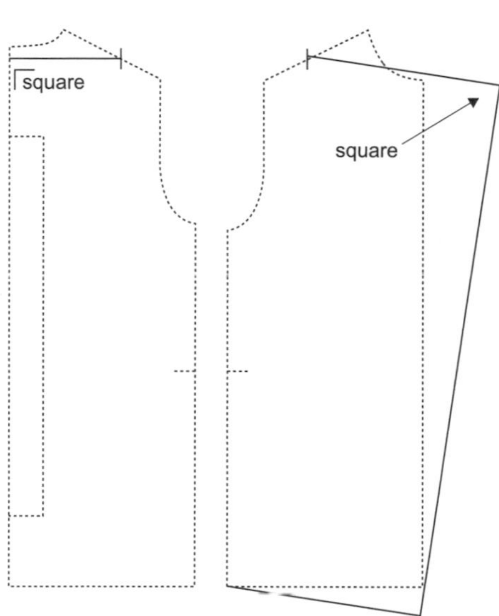

Using the L-square ruler, draw in the new neckline at the length desired.

The neckline must always be squared to the new center front.

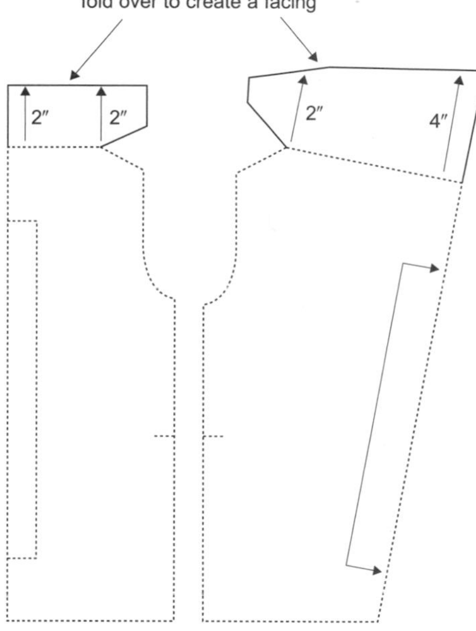

Fold the paper along the new neckline and trace the shoulder and armholes.

Unfold the paper and create a facing/hem that is 2″ on the back and shoulders but with a slightly curved line, to become 4″ on the front. This compensates for the fact that you can see inside this neckline.

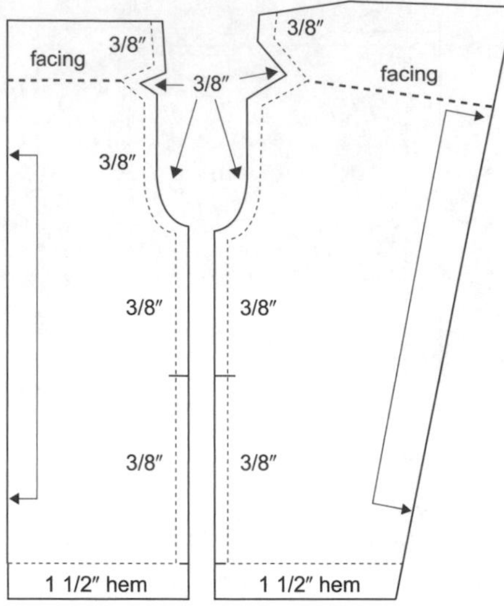

Because knit fabrics are looser than woven fabrics and easily fray and unravel, use ⅜″ seam allowances and a four-thread serger for construction.

Always use at least a 1″ hem allowance for all straight hems and ½″ for curved hems.

STYLE #10-012 CREW-NECK SWEATER

Rib knit must be used for the collar of this sweater.

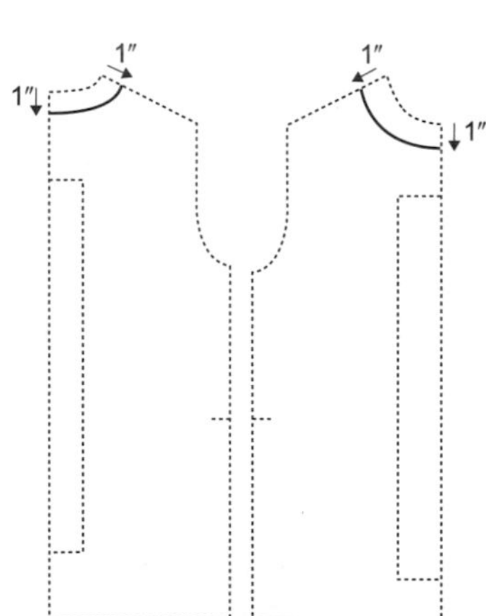

To create a crew-neck sweater with a 1″ collar, remove 1″ from the sweater draft parallel to and below the original neckline.

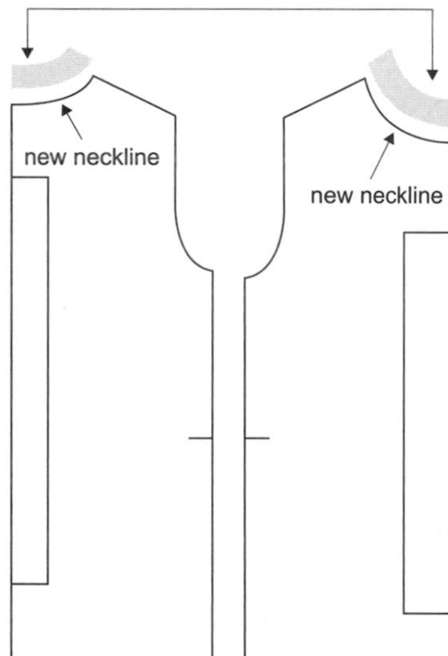

Since the collar will be drafted as a straight piece, to fold in half, remove these sections and draft the collar separately.

In order for the collar to remain flat, it must be drafted one-sixth smaller than the new neck opening.

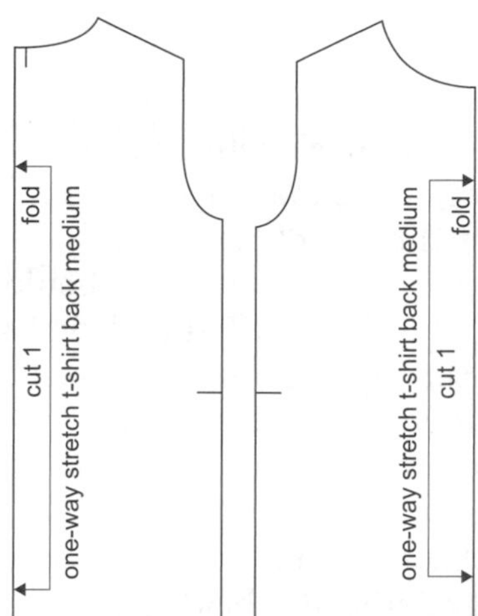

In order to lie flat, crew-neck collars can only be made from rib fabrics.

The width of the collar is 2″.

The length of the collar pattern is determined by the length of the outside edge of the original neckline (the discarded pieces), which is one-sixth smaller than the new neck opening.

Alternately, draft the collar one-sixth smaller than the cut edge of the neck opening (see section on binding and banding).

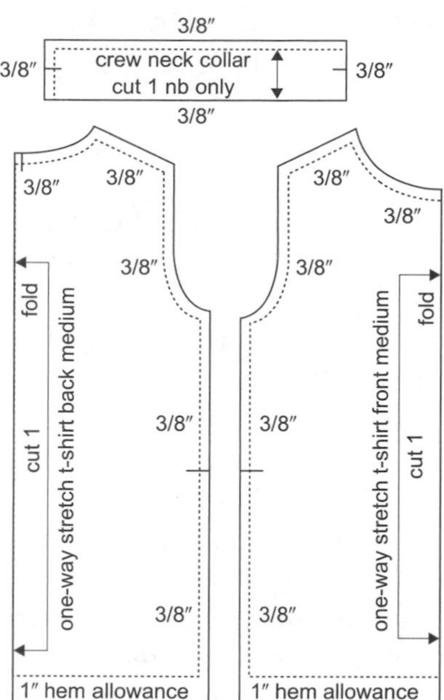

Because sweater knits fabrics are knitted a little looser than other knits, a larger seam allowance is needed so that they don't unravel, fray, or run.

Use a four-thread serger with a 3/8″ seam allowance.

For straight hems, use a minimum of 1″ hem allowance.

For curved hems, use a 1/2″ hem allowance.

Assignment #1

Create a zip front cardigan sweater with hood, and a front facing and back neck twill tape.

Use a 24″ separating zipper.

Add a 1 1/2″ hem allowance and hand hem or blind hem the sweater.

Cut and sew this garment using a purchased sweater knit.

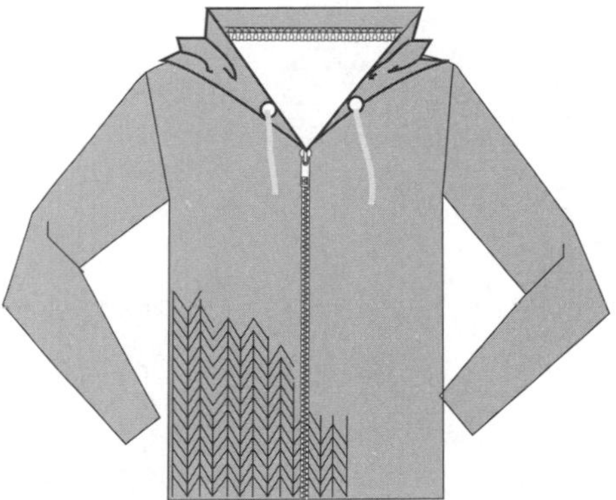

Assignment #2

Create a crew neck sweater with a 6″ zipper in the center front.

Add a 1 1/2″ hem allowance and hand hem, or blind hem the sweater.

Cut and sew this garment using a purchased sweater knit.

Test Your Knowledge of the Material in This Chapter

1. What are the three methods to create a sweater?
2. What corrections should be made to the one-way-stretch top sloper to create a sweater sloper?
3. How much ease should the sleeve of a sweater have?
4. What is a "second layer" sweater sloper?
5. How much should you enlarge the sweater sloper for second layer?
6. Can you cover-stitch the hem of a sweater knit?
7. How are the cowl necklines drafted?
8. How do you draft a turtleneck?
9. How many seams should the turtleneck collar have?
10. Will a turtleneck collar drafted with the exact neckline measurements fit snugly against the neck?
11. How much hem allowance should be added to patterns for a fully-fashioned sweater or a sweater using sweater blocks?
12. How much seam allowance is necessary on the center front for a style with separating zippers?
13. Can a fitted sloper be used to create sweaters out of ribbed fabric?
14. How can you reduce the collar pattern for a turtleneck so that it fits snugly against the neck?
15. What are "fashioning marks"?

CHAPTER 10

Dresses

About This Chapter

This chapter introduces the reader to the patternmaking techniques needed to draft stretch dresses. Because most neckline and sleeve variations are illustrated in the chapter on tops and sweaters, this chapter is brief.

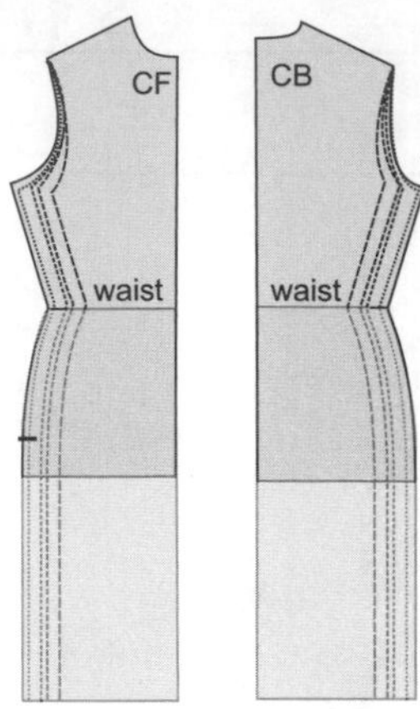

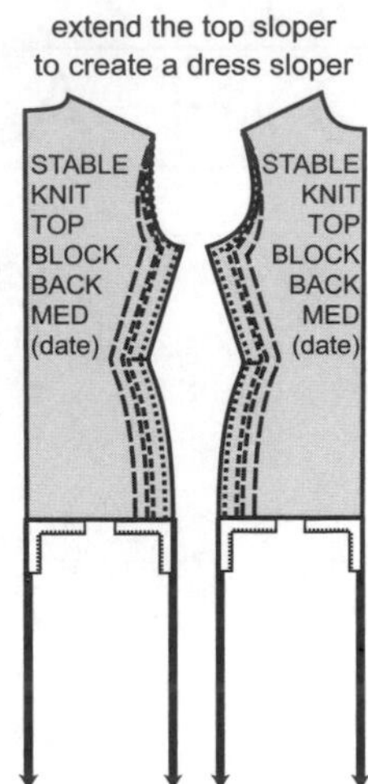

One-Way-Stretch Dress Sloper

You can attach the skirt sloper to the top sloper to create a dress sloper. All the stretch ratios remain the same.

Since we created the top sloper to hem at the crotch level, below any of the hip curves, you can simply convert a one-way-stretch top sloper into a dress sloper by extending the one-way-stretch top sloper straight down from the hip to the desired length.

Extend the stretch ratios all the way down to the hem.

	Extra Extra Small	Extra Small	Small	Medium	Large	Extra Large	Extra Extra Large
Waist to knee	22 7/8	23	23 1/4	23 1/2	23 3/4	24	24 1/4
Waist to ankle	38 1/4	38 1/2	39	39 1/2	40	40 1/2	41

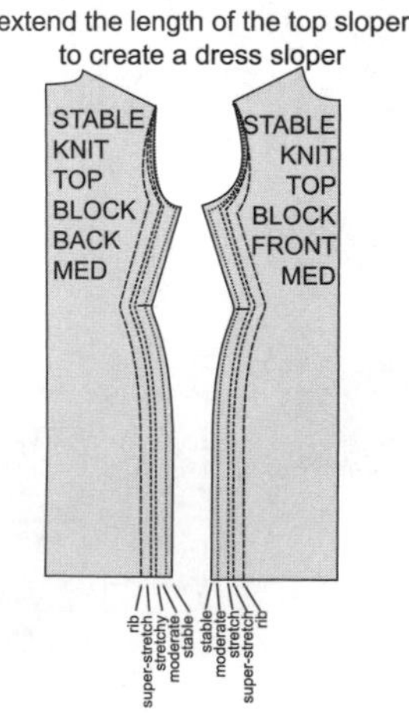

Stretch Ratios for Dresses

The stretch ratios for the dress slopers are the same as for the top slopers.

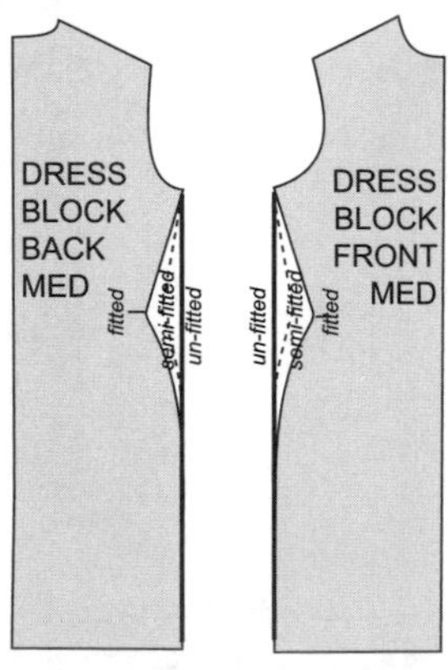

Dress Waist

The dress sloper or pattern can be made fitted, semi-fitted, or unfitted, depending on the design.

For fitted, use the draft as is.

For unfitted, square a line up from the hip to the underarm point.

For semi-fitted, find the midpoint between unfitted and fitted and draw in a new waist.

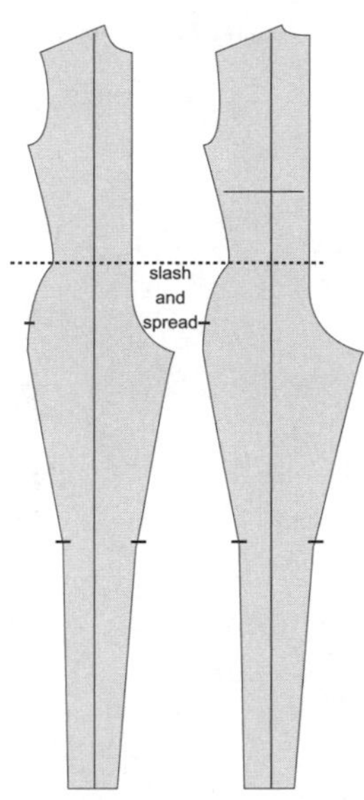

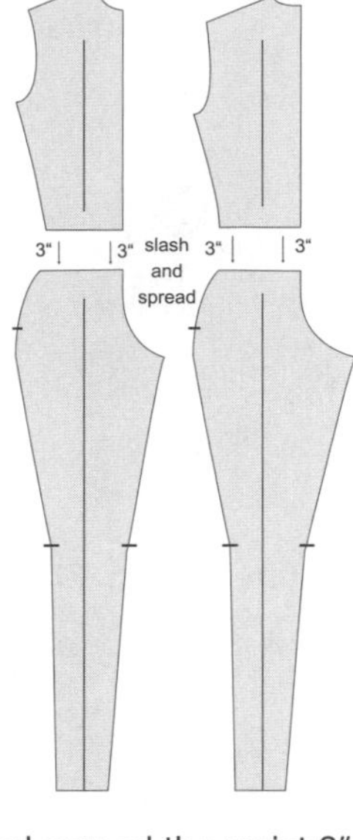

CREATING A DRESS SLOPER FROM A CATSUIT SLOPER

Because we raised the waist when creating the catsuit draft, we must lower it 1½″ for a T-shirt or a short dress.

If creating a very long dress, leave the waist shortened, because the weight of the fabric will pull the waist down.

Because you shortened the waist when drafting the catsuit sloper, you will have to increase the length if you plan to use the catsuit sloper for a dress style.

Slash and spread the waist 3″ to return it to the natural waist.

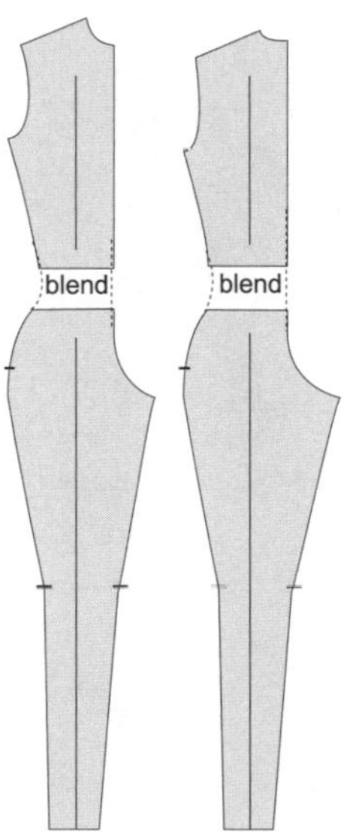

Because we raised the waist when creating the catsuit draft, we must lower it 1½″ for a T-shirt or short dress.

If creating a very long dress, leave the waist shortened, because the weight of the fabric will pull the waist down.

For a medium-length dress, you may have to lower the waist by half of the amount previously shortened. This process may take some testing.

Bend new side seams.

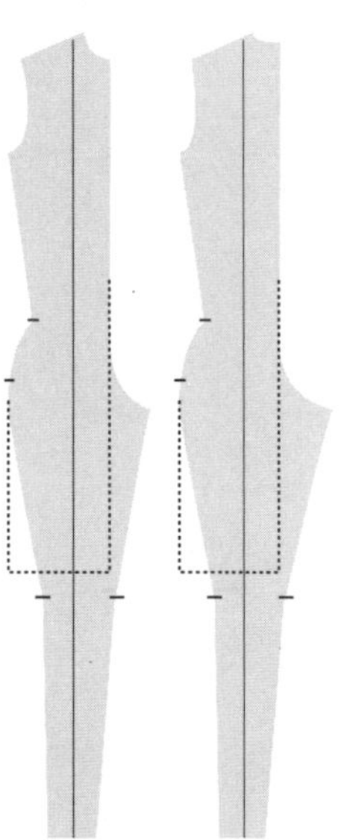

Extend the center front to the length of dress required, and square a new hem.

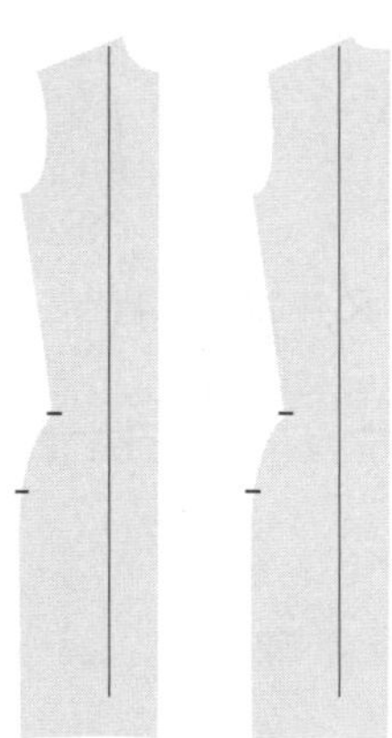

Trace out a new dress sloper.

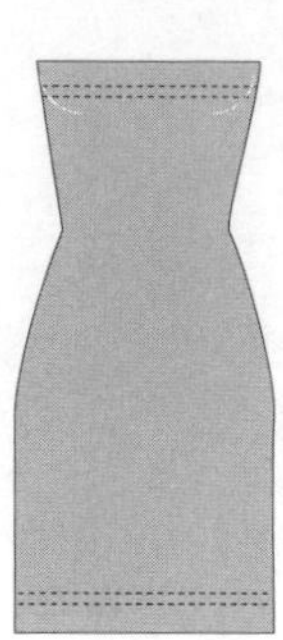

STYLE #10-001 TUBE DRESS

A tube dress is one of the easiest styles to draft.

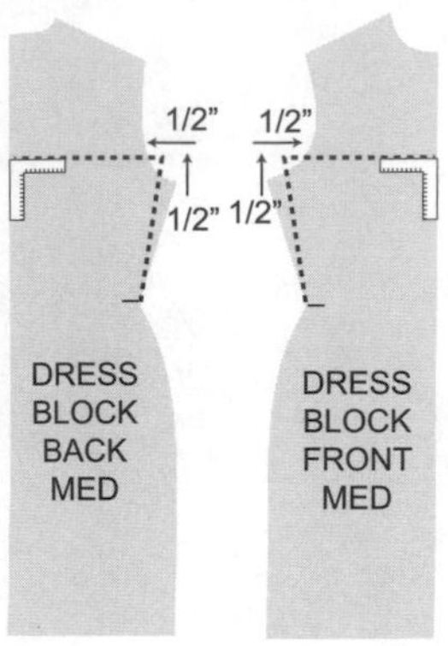

Raise the underarm by ½″.

Take in the underarm by ½″ to make the garment tighter in this area, as the original sloper was created to have sleeves. This is not necessary, however, if you use binding, elastic, or some other reducing trim.

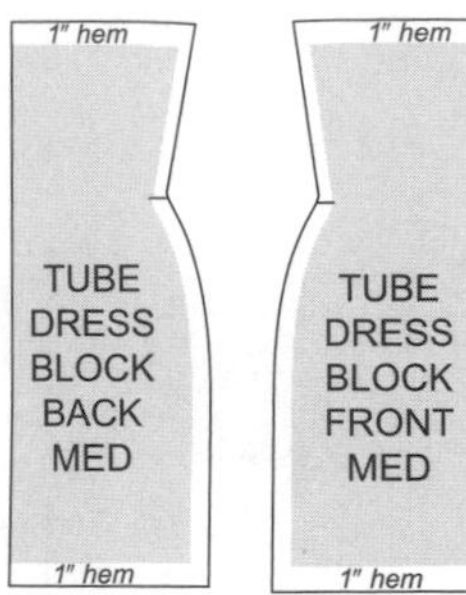

Add a 1″ hem to both top and bottom of the dress, and label as illustrated.

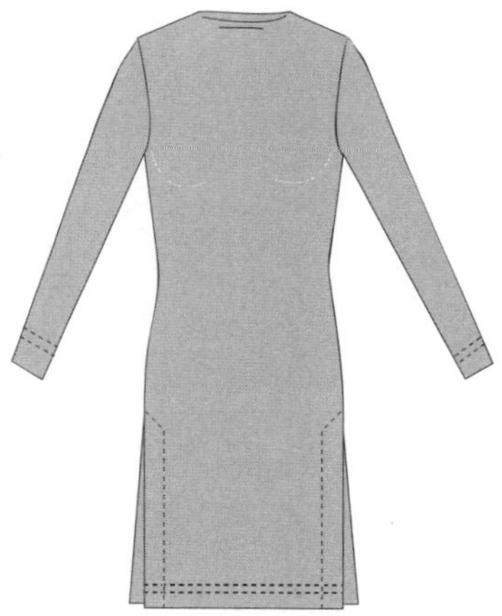

STYLE #10-002 BOATNECK DRESS

The boatneck dress is the basis for many cowl-styled dresses but can also be a style on its own.

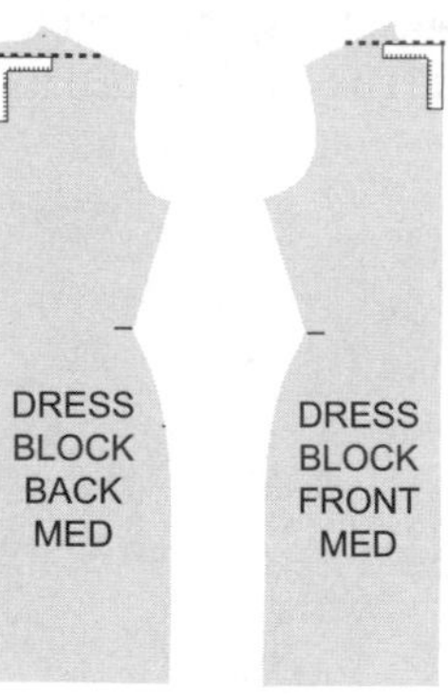

Square a line across the front where you want the neckline to be. Repeat for the back.

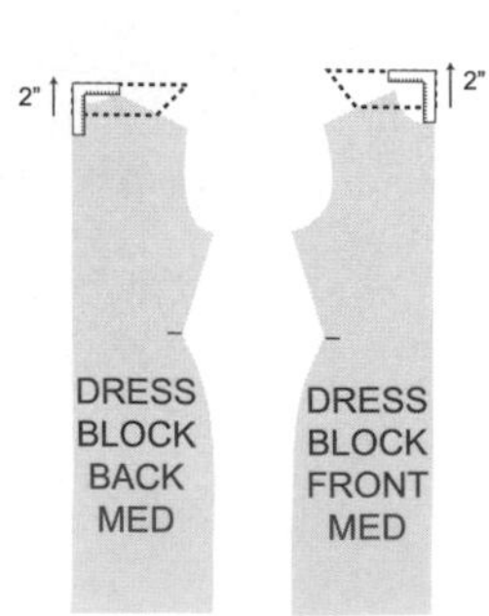

Add a 2″ facing or hem to the top edge of the dress.

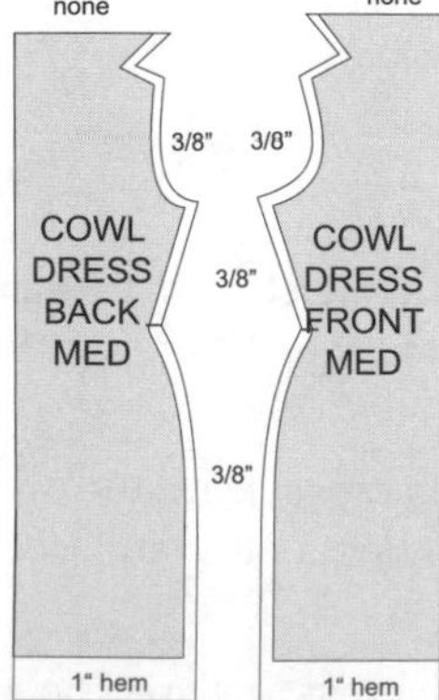

Add seam allowances as illustrated. However, you do not have to add seam allowances to the top, because the hem allowance is already added.

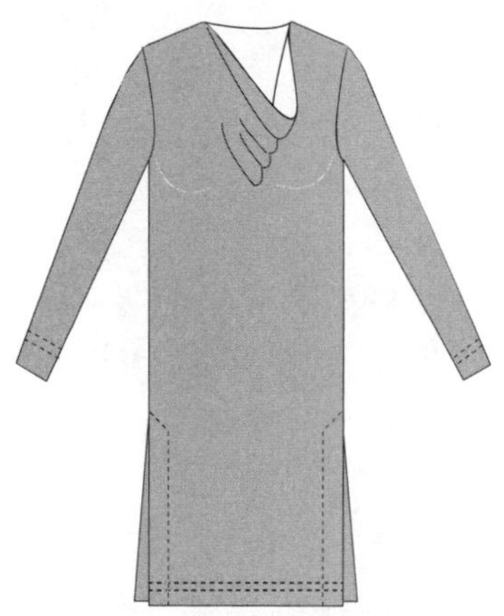

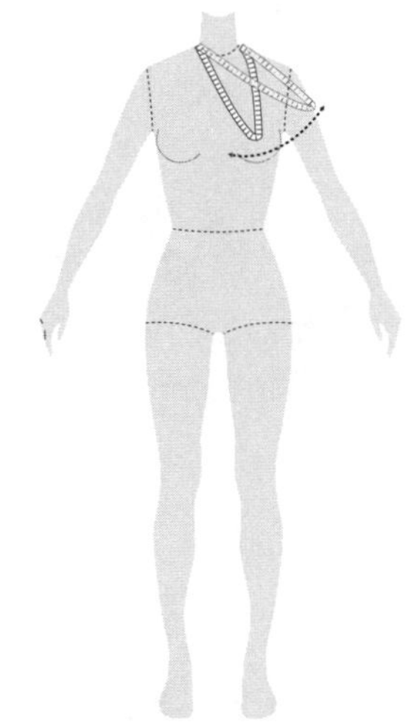

STYLE #10-003 COWL-NECK DRESS

There are different techniques used to create cowl-neck dresses. The method shown here will increase the overall width of the dress and may not be suitable for all styles.

Measure on the customer or the dress-form how low you wish the cowl to be, measuring from one side of the neck down the length of the cowl and back up to the other side of the neck. Then divide this measurement in half, because you will be working on one-half of the pattern.

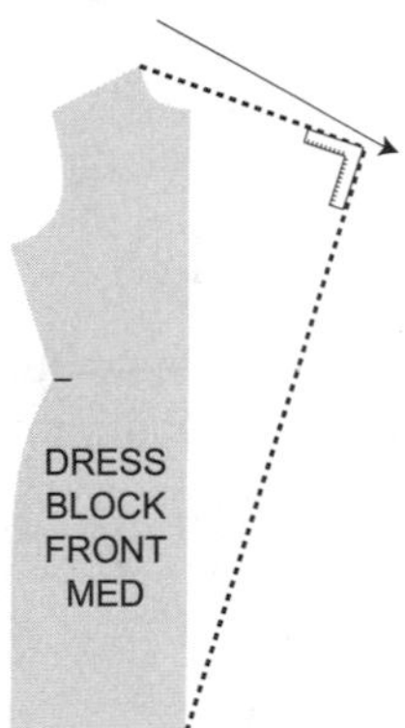

Using your measurement and an "L" square, draft the cowl to the hem of the dress, as illustrated.

Because it will be possible to see inside the cowl, you must create a larger hem/facing for the front portion of the cowl, or 4″, and curve it to the shoulder seam, 2″.

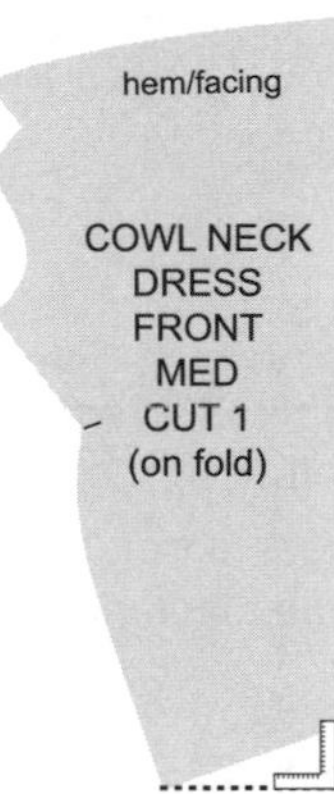

The hem of the dress must be corrected.

STYLE #10-004 ALTERNATE COWL NECK DRESS

The previous method of drafting the cowl will increase volume throughout the entire garment, resulting in a looser waist.

To create a dress that is fitted except for the cowl, use the following instructions.

Slash through the shoulder area to any area between the underarm and waist. This area will get larger, so if you want it tight, keep the slash high on the side seam.

Slash and spread the section.

Measure from the center front to determine how large you want the cowl.

Extend the center front and square across.

Make sure the new center front is perfectly square at the neck; otherwise, you will get a point at the front because it is on the fold.

Create a facing 4″ at the front and 2″ at the shoulder.

Because you will be able to see inside the front, a deeper hem/facing is needed.

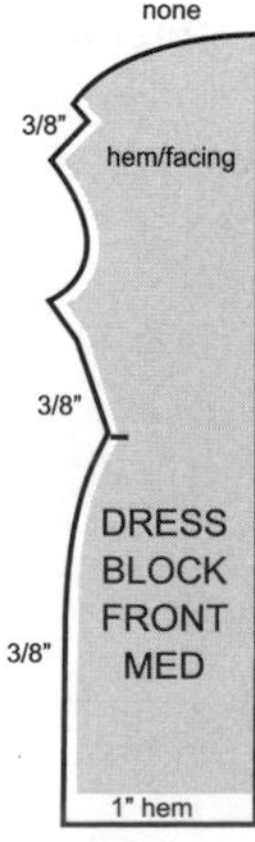

Add seam allowances to the completed pattern.

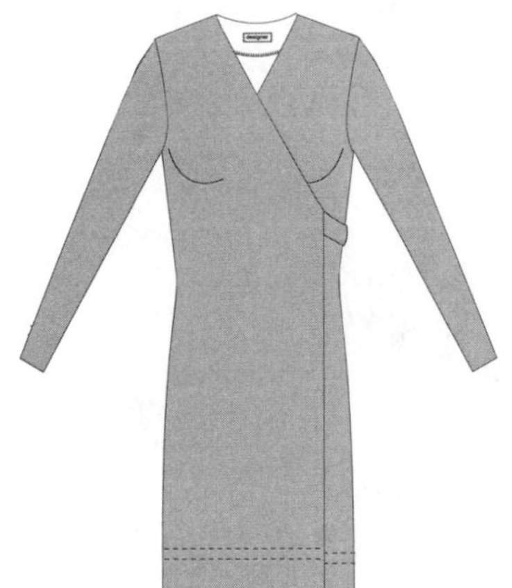

STYLE #10-005 WRAP DRESS

This wrap dress may be drafted with a self-tie that inserts into the facing edge.

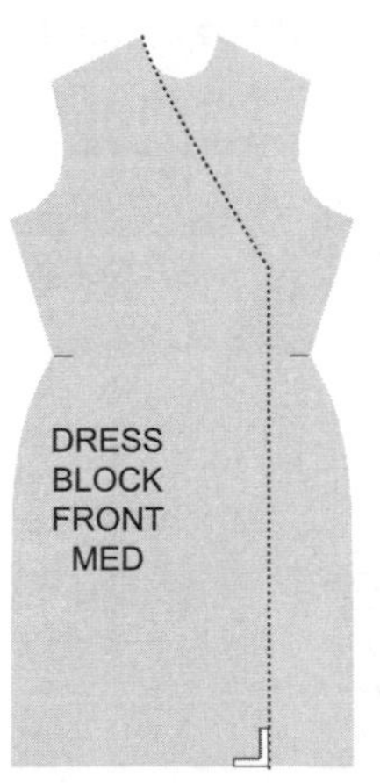

To draft a wrap dress, trace out the full sloper, both sides.

Draw in the wrap front with the V-neckline as low or as high as you wish.

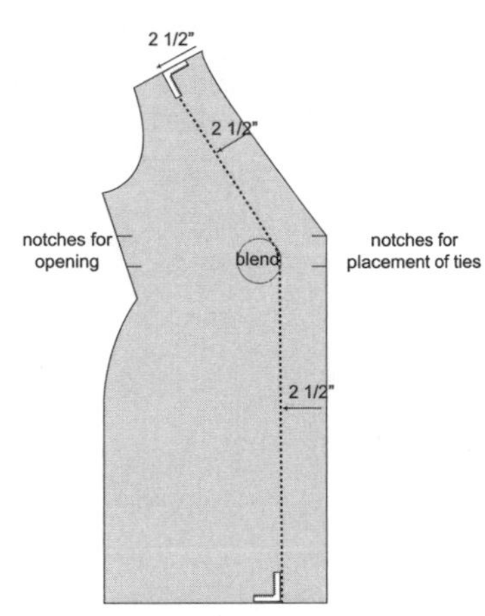

Add a $2\frac{1}{2}''$ facing to the front edge.

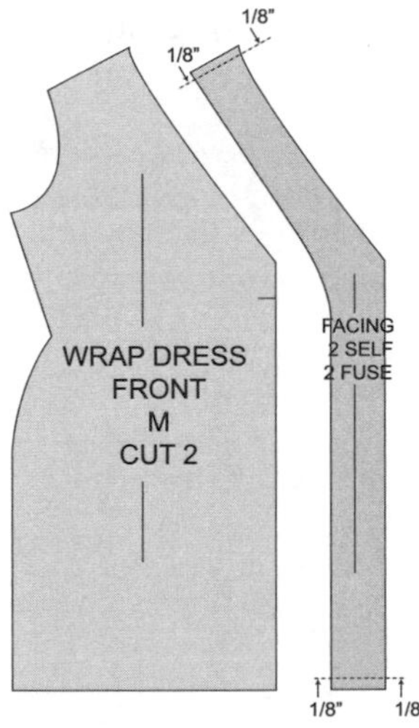

Trace and separate the pattern pieces.

Remember to reduce the facing as in previous facing drafts, by $\frac{1}{8}''$.

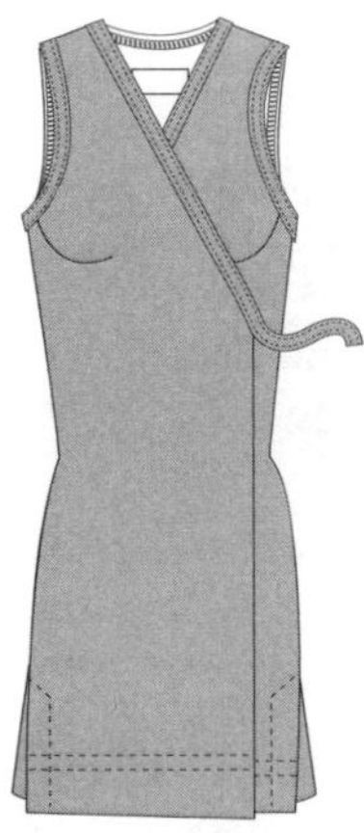

STYLE #10-006 WRAP DRESS WITH BINDING

The same dress can be created with binding for ties. The edges that will be bound do not need any seam allowances added.

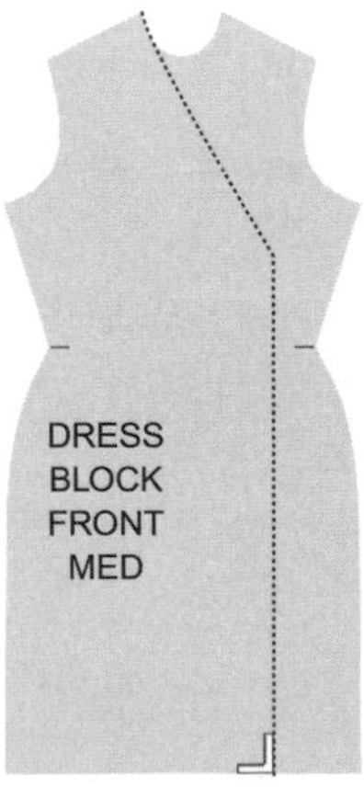

Trace both sides of the sloper for asymmetrical styles.

Place the style line where you wish to create the overlap, 2″ to $2\frac{1}{2}''$ past the center front.

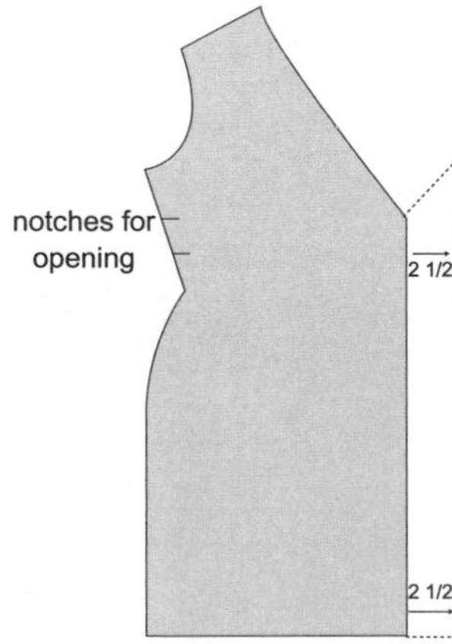

Create a hem along the front edge.

The neck edge should be finished with binding.

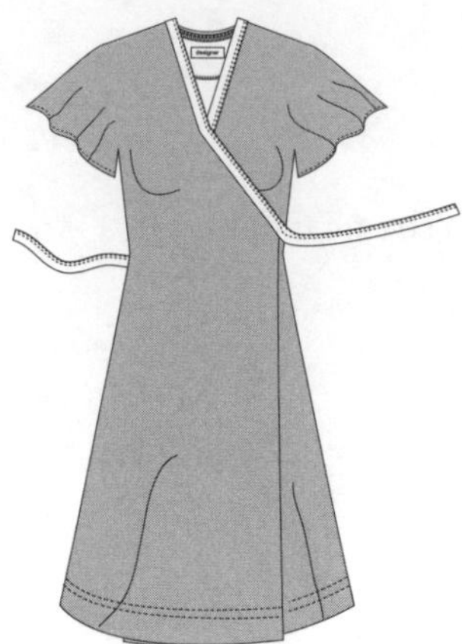

STYLE #10-007 WRAP DRESS WITH FLARED CAP SLEEVES

Create a flared-sleeve wrap dress.

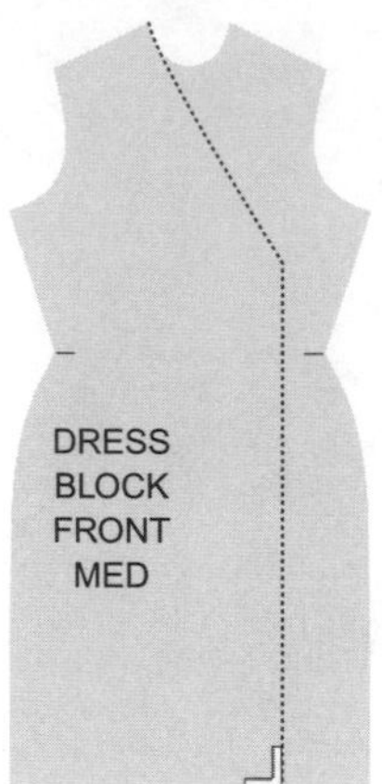

Trace both sides of the sloper for asymmetrical styles.

Place the style line where you wish to create the overlap, 2″ to 2½″ past the center front.

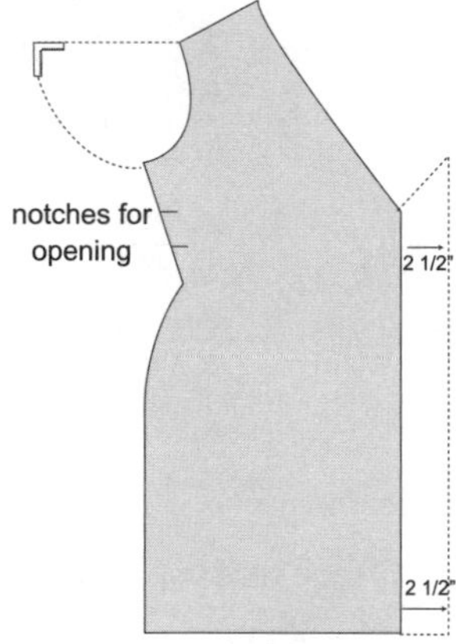

Create a 2½″ hem for the center fronts.

Create the sleeve as illustrated, remembering to keep the end squared; otherwise, you will get a peak at the tip of the sleeve.

Place notches on the side seam where the tie will come out.

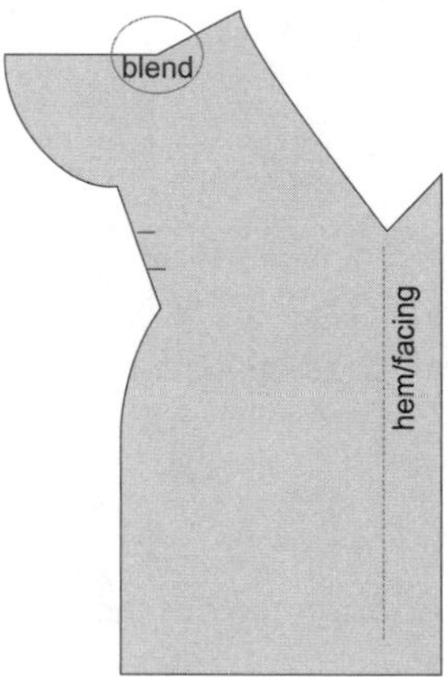

Blend the shoulder sleeve intersection.

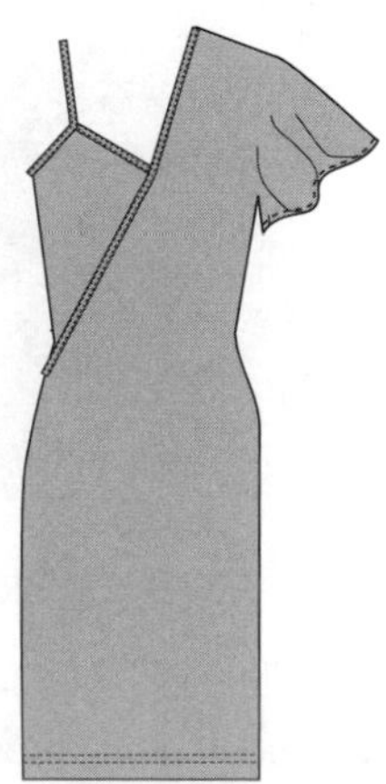

STYLE #10-008 ASYMMETRICAL-STYLED DRESS

Create an asymmetrical dress with flared cap sleeves on one side and a slip neckline on the other.

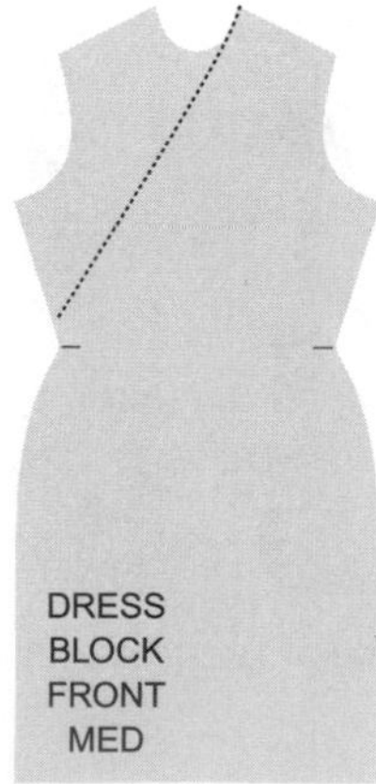

Trace both sides of the sloper for asymmetrical styles.

Place the style line where you wish to create the overlap, all the way to the side seam.

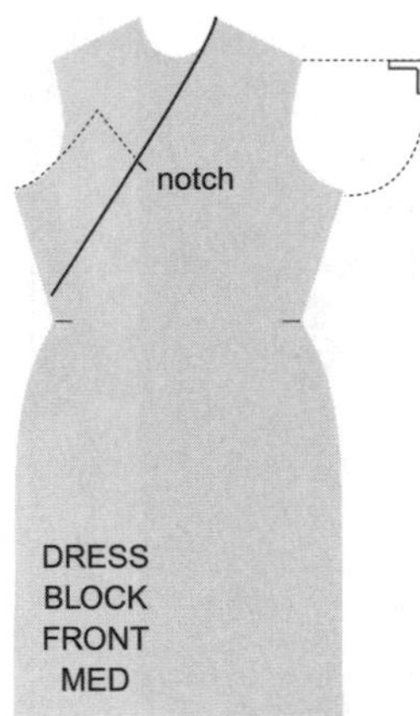

Draw in the slip neckline on the alternate side, remembering to maintain complete bust coverage.

Place a notch where the two pieces will attach to each other.

Extend the shoulder into a sleeve as illustrated.

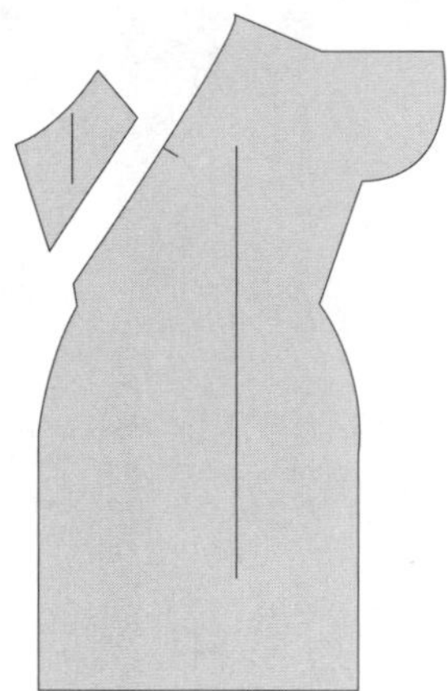

Trace and separate the piece, remembering to include the notches as necessary for matching up the pieces.

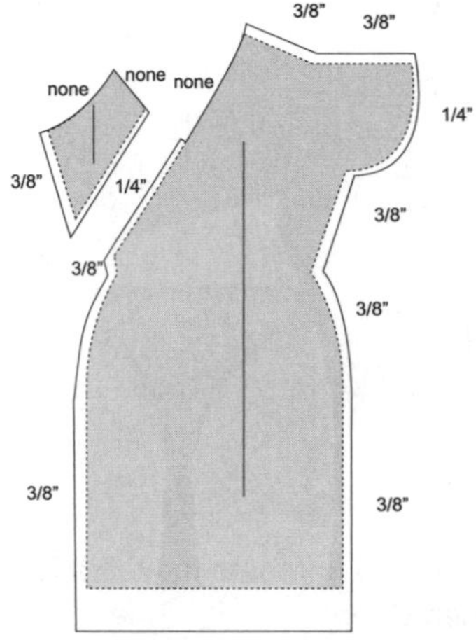

Add seam allowances to the pieces as illustrated.

There should not be any seam allowances on the neckline, because it will be finished with a ³⁄₈" wide binding.

While constructing this garment, serge the front seam towards the outside so that you can bind that edge.

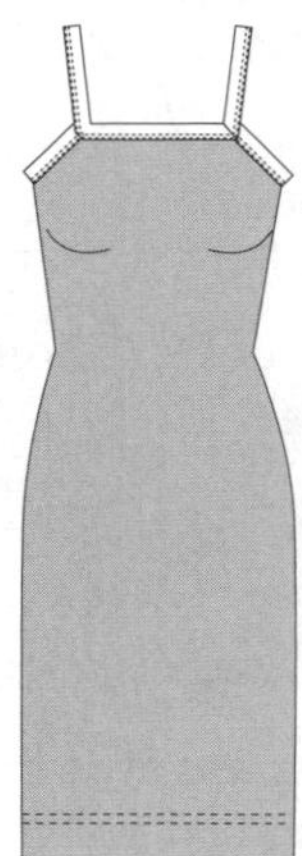

STYLE #10-009 SLIP NECKLINE DRESS

This dress has a neckline that is straight across the front.

You don't have to raise or take in the side seams if you will be using reduced binding. The binding will pull the underarms higher and tighter because it is slightly smaller.

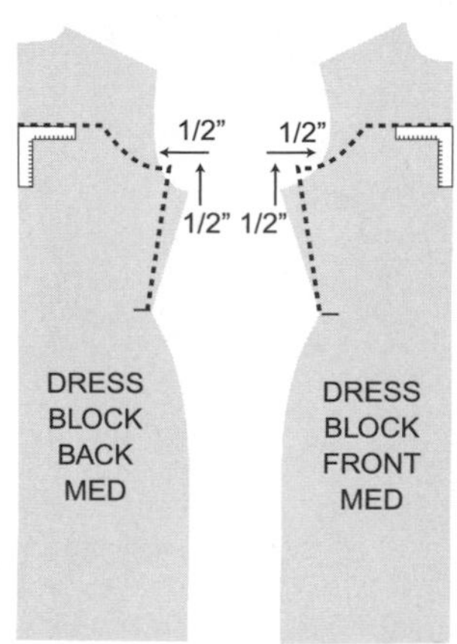

STYLE #10-010 TOP AND SKIRT COMBINATIONS

You can easily combine skirt and top patterns to create dress styles.

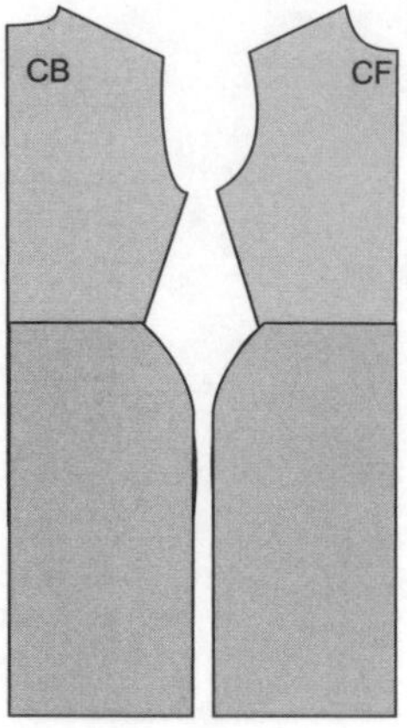

Line the slopers up as illustrated, and you will see how easy it is to match the pieces.

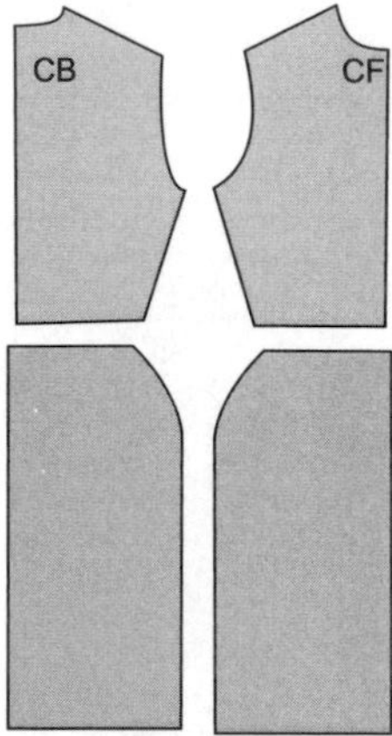

Or you can separate a dress style into separate pieces for drafting dresses with a waist seam.

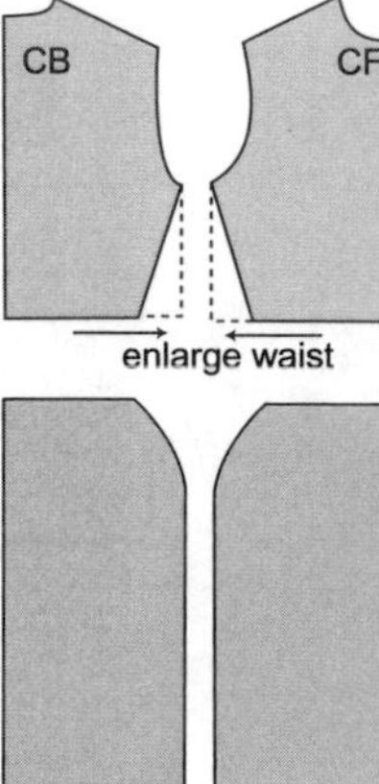

Enlarge the waist of the top to create the extra fullness required for the gathered top.

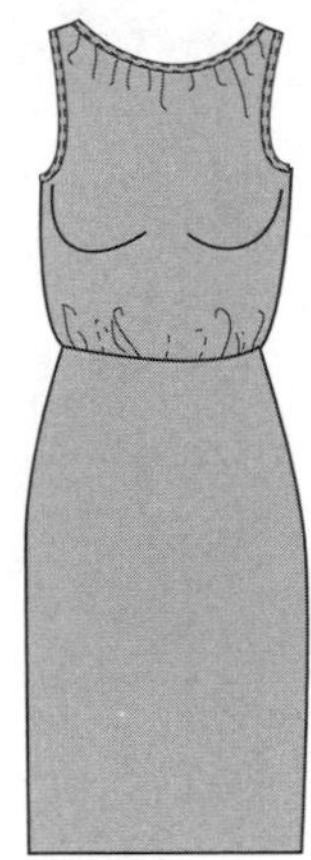

STYLE #10-011 EMPIRE-WAIST DRESS

Create an Empire-waist dress with gathered skirt.

In order to draft this skirt, which has a horizontal seam below the bust, you must first determine where the bust is on the sloper.

The first step is to find the apex of the bust.

Draw a guideline parallel to the center that is half the bust span away from the center front.

	Extra Extra Small	Extra Small	Small	Medium	Large	Extra Large	Extra Extra Large
Stable	6 1/2	6 5/8	6 7/8	7 1/8	7 1/2	7 7/8	8 3/8
Moderate	6 3/8	6 1/2	6 3/4	7 1/8	7 1/2	7 7/8	6 3/8
Stretchy	6 3/8	6 1/2	6 3/4	7	7 3/8	7 7/8	8 1/8
Super-stretch	6 1/4	6 3/8	6 5/8	6 7/8	7 2/8	7 5/8	7 7/8
Rib	5 7/8	6	6 1/4	6 1/2	6 7/8	7 1/4	7 1/2

Draw a guideline parallel to the center front but away from the front by half the bust span amount.

Measure the bust level to wherever it lands on the guideline. This is your apex.

	Extra Extra Small	Extra Small	Small	Medium	Large	Extra Large	Extra Extra Large
WBust level	9 7/8	10	10 1/4	10 1/2	10 3/4	11	11 1/4

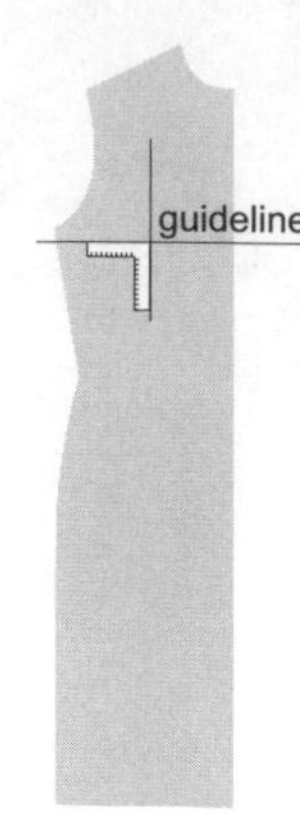

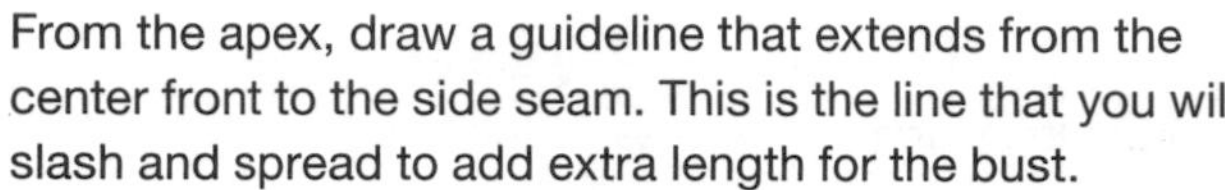

From the apex, draw a guideline that extends from the center front to the side seam. This is the line that you will slash and spread to add extra length for the bust.

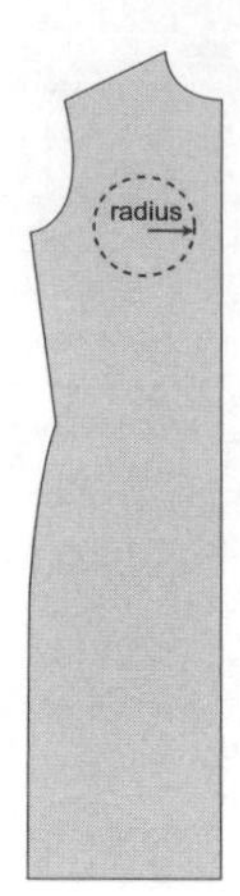

To determine the bust radius, use the chart below.

From the original bust apex, draw in the bust radius using a compass.

	Extra Extra Small	Extra Small	Small	Medium	Large	Extra Large	Extra Extra Large
Stable	$2\frac{1}{8}$	$2\frac{1}{4}$	$2\frac{3}{8}$	$2\frac{1}{2}$	$2\frac{5}{8}$	$2\frac{3}{4}$	$2\frac{7}{8}$
Moderate	$2\frac{1}{8}$	$2\frac{1}{4}$	$2\frac{3}{8}$	$2\frac{1}{2}$	$2\frac{5}{8}$	$2\frac{3}{4}$	$2\frac{7}{8}$
Stretchy	2	$2\frac{1}{8}$	$2\frac{1}{4}$	$2\frac{3}{8}$	$2\frac{1}{2}$	$2\frac{5}{8}$	$2\frac{3}{4}$
Super-stretch	$1\frac{7}{8}$	2	$2\frac{1}{8}$	$2\frac{1}{4}$	$2\frac{3}{8}$	$2\frac{1}{2}$	$2\frac{5}{8}$
Rib	$1\frac{3}{4}$	$1\frac{7}{8}$	$1\frac{7}{8}$	2	$2\frac{1}{8}$	$2\frac{1}{4}$	$2\frac{3}{8}$

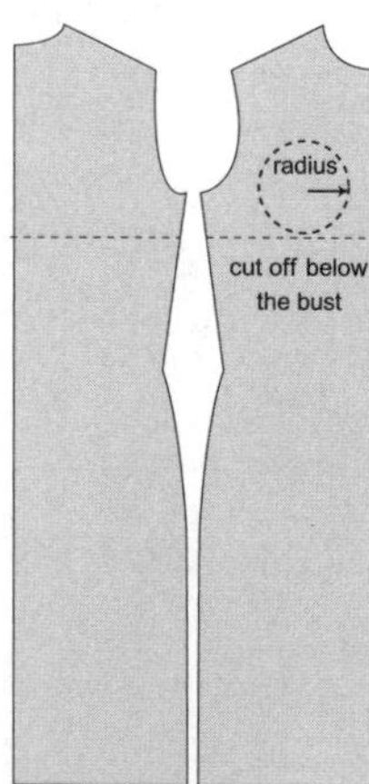

Cut and separate the upper portion from the lower portion, slightly below the bust.

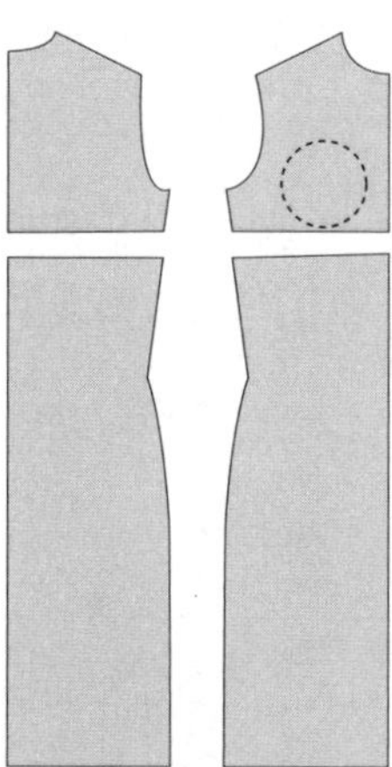

Separate the sections.

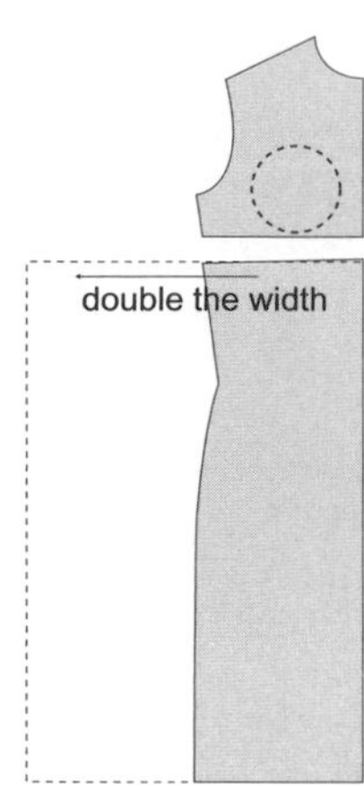

Enlarge the skirt to create the extra fullness required for the gathering.

Add 50% for light gathering.

Add 100% for medium gathering.

Add 200% for heavy gathering (only for very light fabrics).

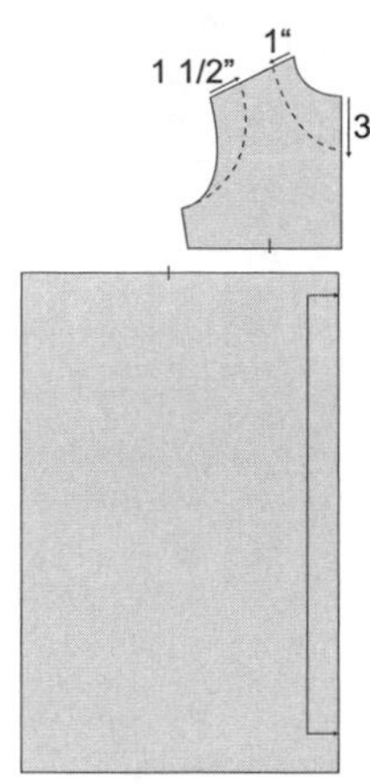

Draw in the neck and armhole style line (refer to sleeveless garments).

Make sure to notch the pattern pieces for easy assembly.

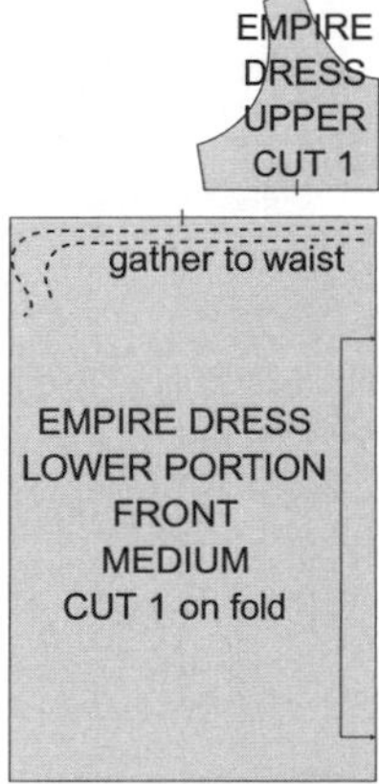

Label the pattern as illustrated.

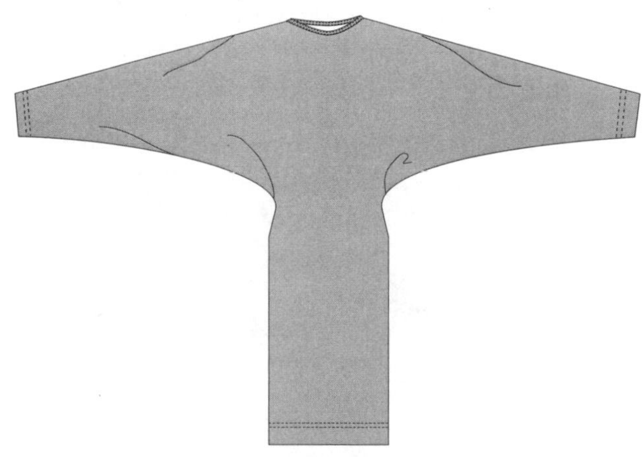

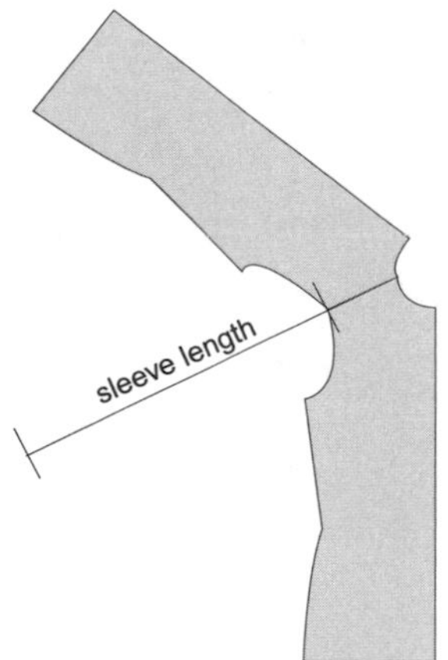

STYLE #10-012 DOLMAN-SLEEVE DRESS

It is easy to create a dolman-sleeve dress, one without any armhole seams. The pattern is simply a front piece and a back piece. Note that these styles consume a lot of fabric, and a lot of fabric is wasted, because of the large pieces.

Line up the shoulders as illustrated, and extend the shoulder line an amount equal to the length of the sleeve.

	Extra Extra Small	Extra Small	Small	Medium	Large	Extra Large	Extra Extra Large
Wrist	4 3/8	5 1/8	5 7/8	6 5/8	7 3/8	8 1/8	8 7/8
Half of wrist	2 1/4	2 5/8	3	3 3/8	3¾	4 1/8	4 1/2

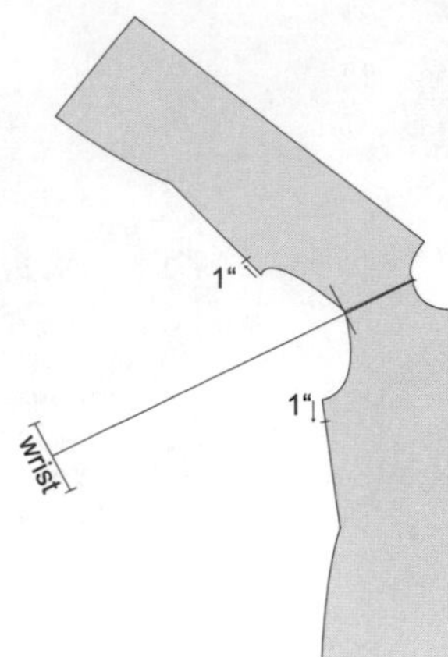

At the wrist, square a line in each direction equal to the wrist measurement.

Measure and mark down from the underarm point on the side seam (illustrated at 1″, but may be any measurement that the designer requires).

If you make the armhole too low, it will be difficult to wear this garment under many jackets and coats.

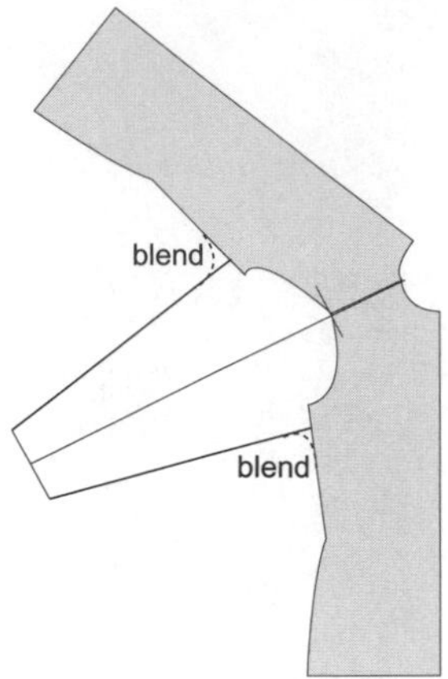

Blend a smooth curve at the underarm.

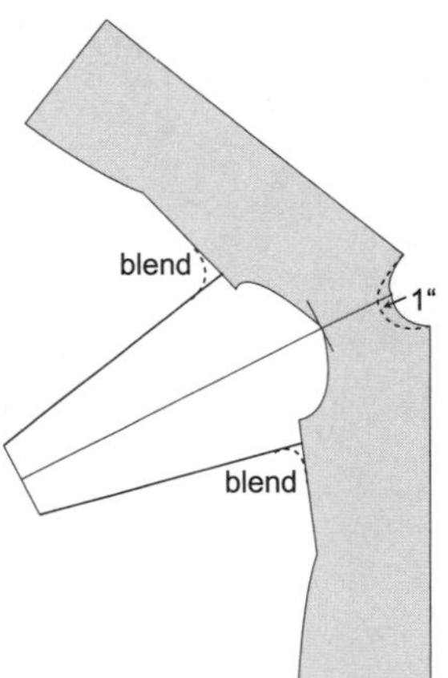

Draw in the neckline, as required by your design.

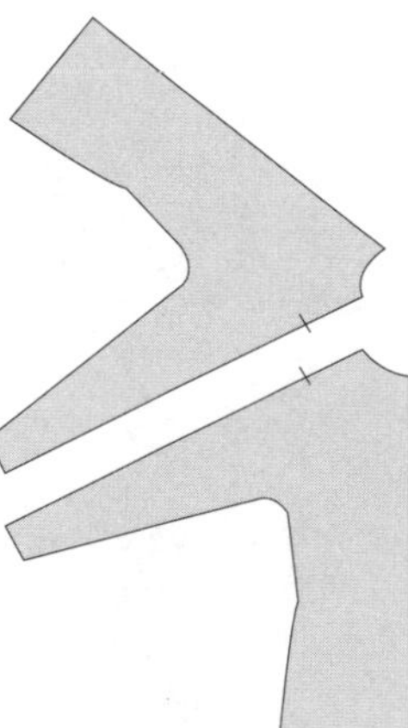

Trace and separate the pattern pieces as illustrated, remembering to notch for easy assembly. You should probably place the notches at the original shoulder point for future styling, so you will always be able to determine where the exact shoulder point is on this pattern.

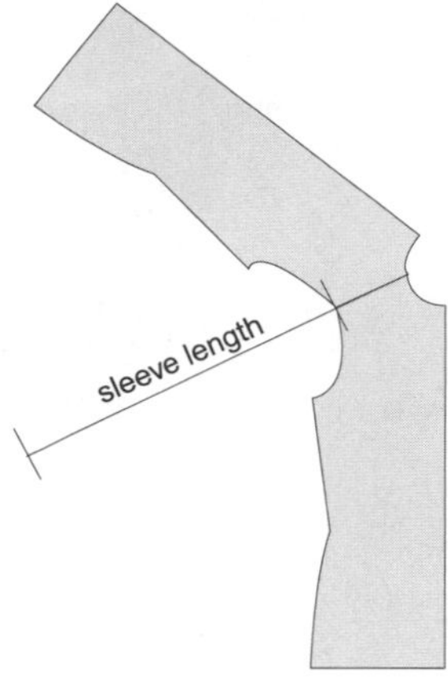

STYLE #10-013 LOWERED ARMHOLE WITH DOLMAN SLEEVE

This dolman dress has a lowered armhole, a wider wrist measurement, and an armhole seam.

Line up the shoulders as illustrated and extend the shoulder line an amount equal to the length of the sleeve.

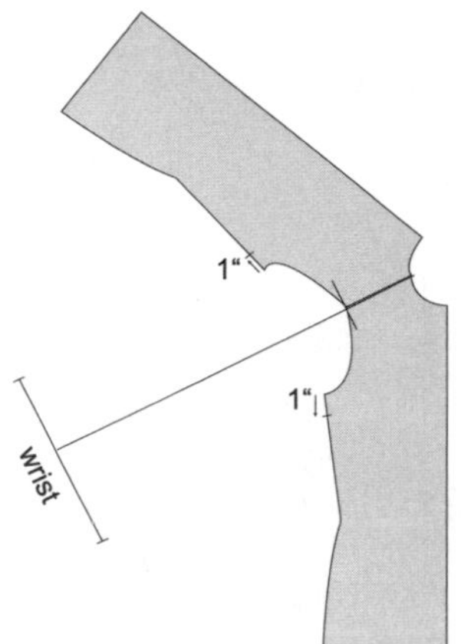

At the end of the sleeve, square a line in each direction as wide as you want the sleeve to be.

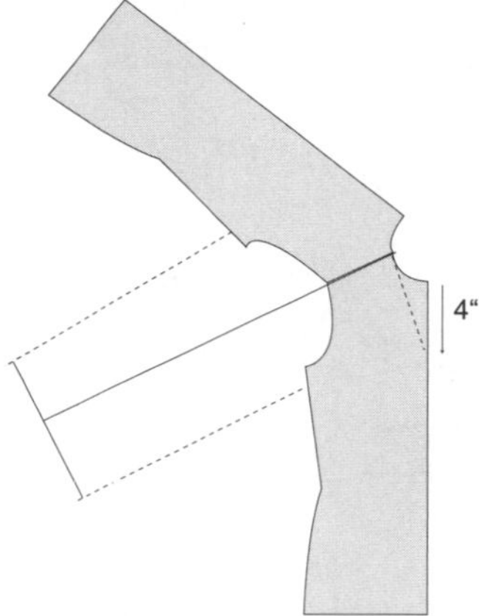

Measure and mark down from the underarm point on the side seam (illustrated at 1″, but may be any measurement that the designer requires).

If you make the armhole too low, it will be difficult to wear this garment under many jackets and coats.

	Extra Extra Small	Extra Small	Small	Medium	Large	Extra Large	Extra Extra Large
Sleeve length	22 5/8	22 7/8	23 1/8	23 3/8	23 5/8	22 5/8	22 7/8
Wrist	4 3/8	5 1/8	5 5/8	6 5/8	7 3/8	8 1/8	8 7/8
Half of wrist	2 1/4	2 5/8	3	3 3/8	3 3/4	4 1/8	4 1/2

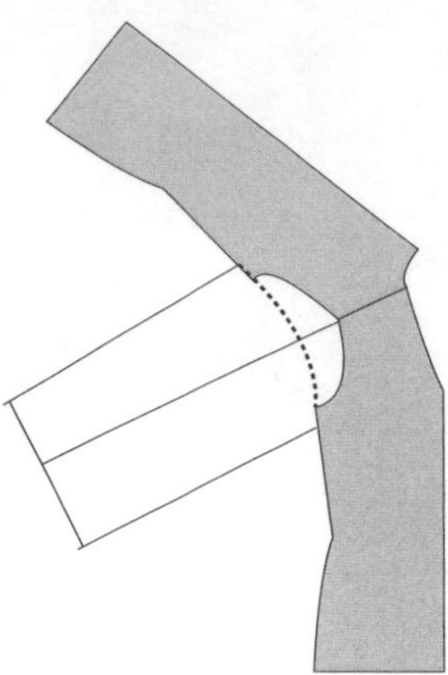

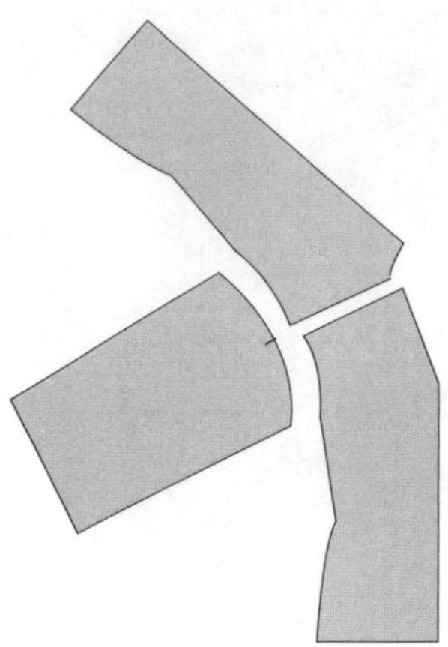

Connect the wrist to the lowered underarm point with a straight line.

Lower the front for a V-neck as illustrated.

Draw in an armhole seam as illustrated; it may be any style you wish.

Trace and separate the pattern pieces as illustrated.

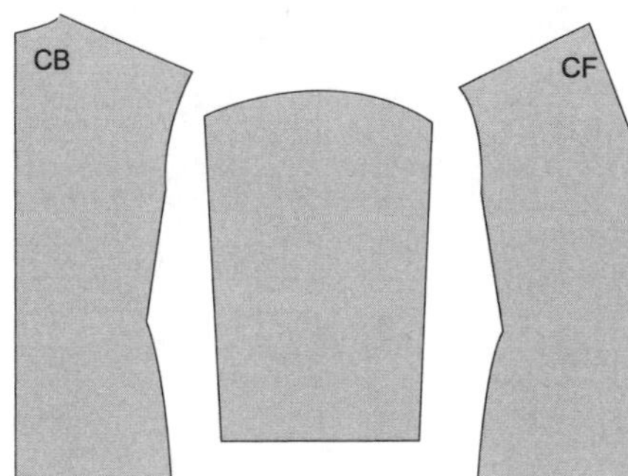

Trace and separate the pattern pieces as illustrated.

STYLE #10-014 V-NECK T-SHIRT DRESS

Same as for V-neck T-shirt, except that the dress sloper is used instead of the T-shirt sloper.

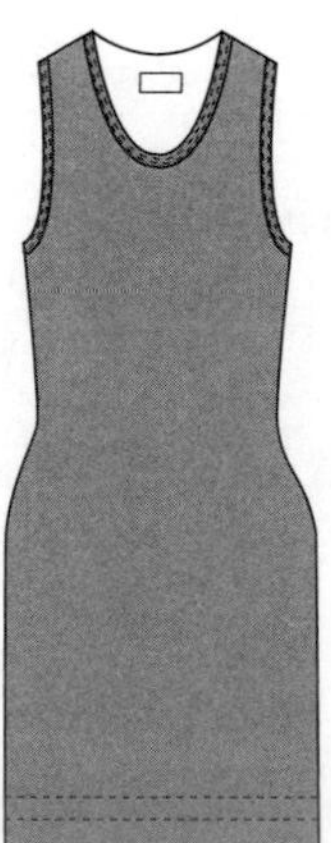

STYLE 10-015 TANK DRESS

Follow the instructions for tank tops, substituting the dress block for the top block.

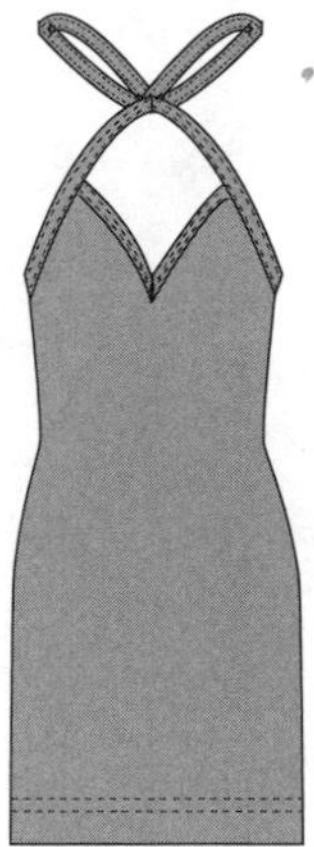

STYLE #10-016 SLIP NECKLINE

A slip neckline may be created with straps that tie to each other or are attached to the back of the top.

You don't have to raise and take in the armholes of a garment that will be reduced through the use of elastic, binding, or banding.

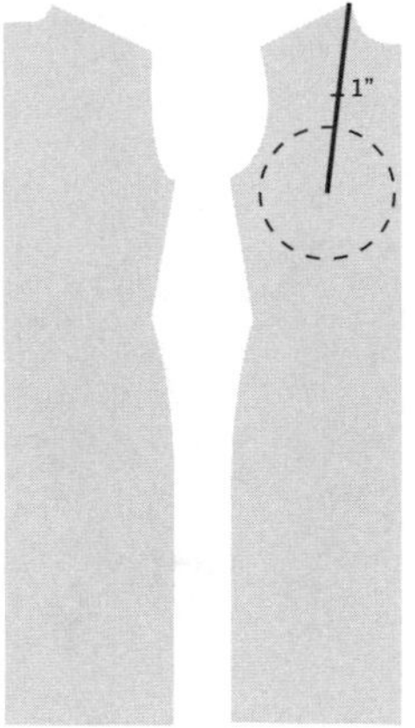

Draw a guideline from the bust apex up to the point where the shoulder meets the neck.

This guideline follows the direction of the straps, and may be changed accordingly.

Measure up 1″ on the guideline.

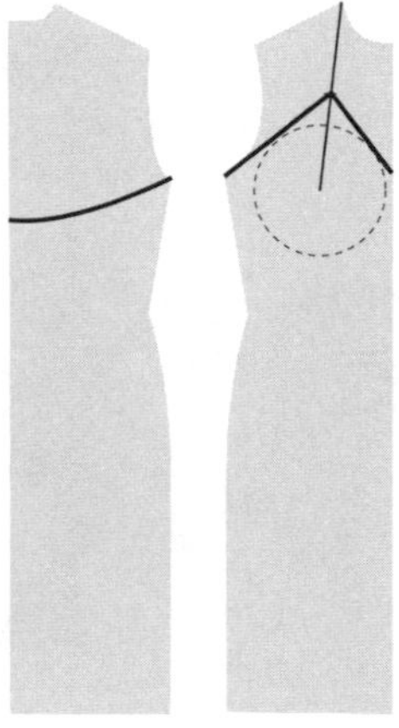

Draw in the neckline, trying not to let your lines go within the bust circle; otherwise, parts of the breast will be exposed.

Trace and separate the pattern pieces as illustrated.

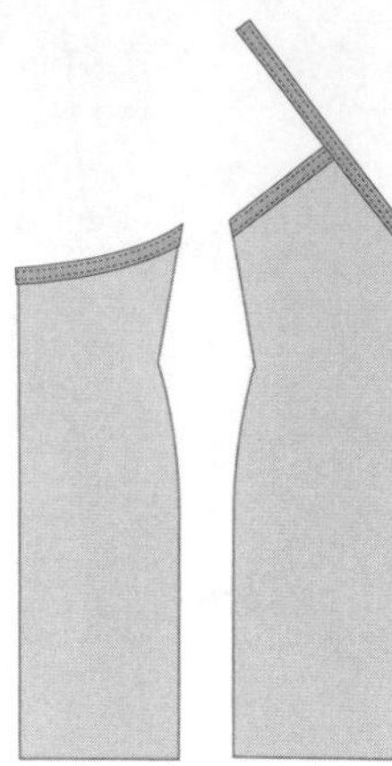

Use binding to finish off the neckline edges and to create straps or ties.

Do not add seam allowances to any edge that will have binding applied.

Attach the binding to the back and sides before attaching the front section.

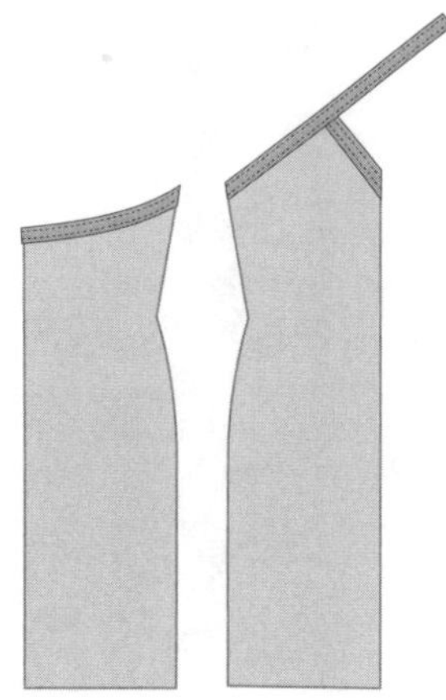

Or you may attach binding to the front sections before attaching the sides. This will create a different effect for the ties/straps.

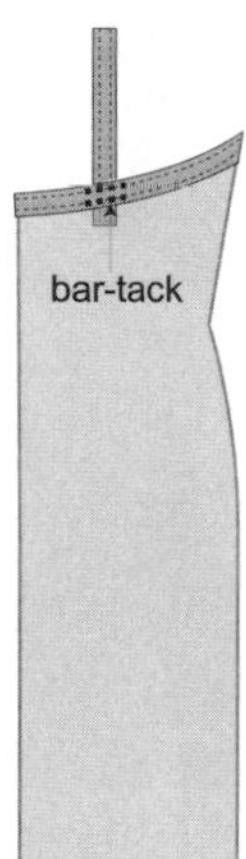

When using binding to create straps, make the straps longer than necessary, then correct and complete the measuring during fitting.

Insert twill tape in the strap portion of the binding ties to prevent them from stretching.

Bar tack the strap to the back binding for reinforcement.

Do not add seam allowances to any edge that will have binding applied.

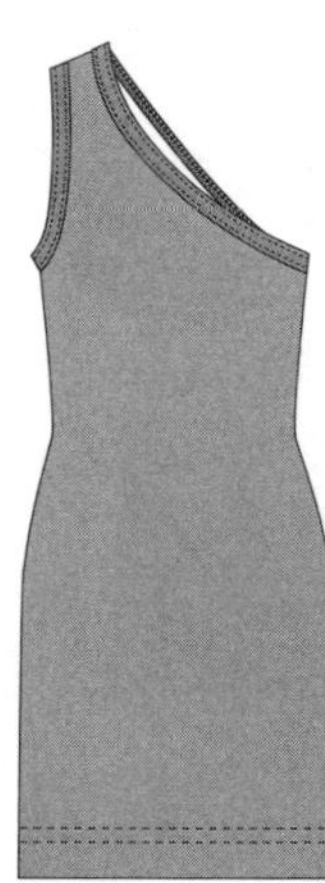

To create an asymmetrical neckline, you must trace out the sloper full, both sides open, before drafting the neckline.

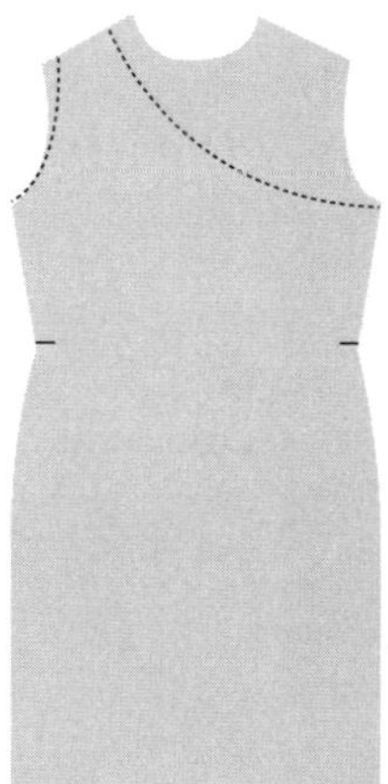

You don't have to raise and take in the armholes of a garment that will be reduced through the use of elastic, binding, or banding.

Do not add seam allowances to any edge that will have binding applied.

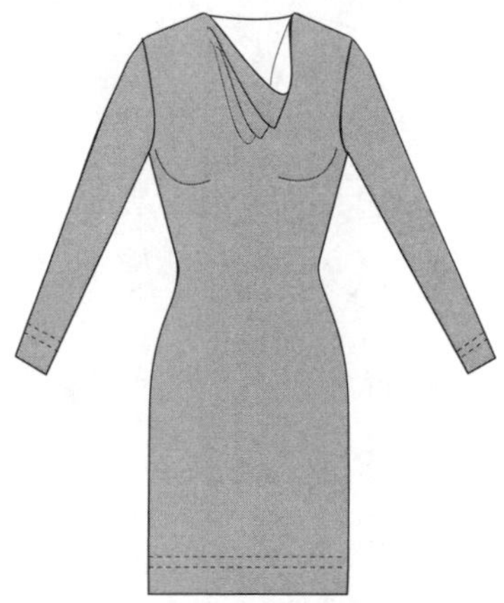

STYLE #10-017 COWL-NECK DRESS

Use this draft for longer top designs to avoid increasing the volume of the body of the garment, or if you wish to attach a skirt to the bottom of the top.

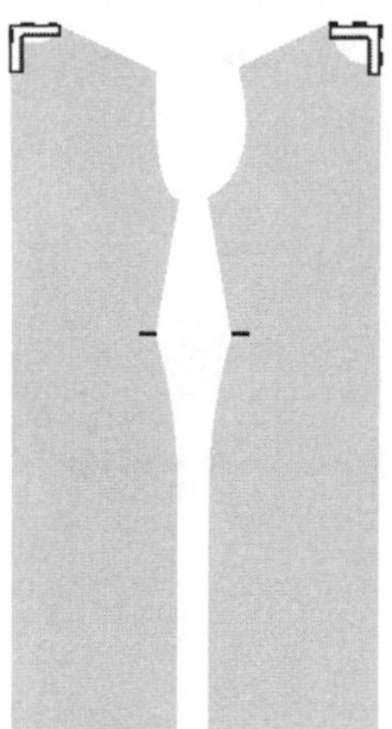

To determine the length of the cowl, hold the tape measure as low and as far away from the dress-form as your desired distance, and record that measurement. Divide that measurement in half to use for your draft, because you will only be drafting half of the garment.

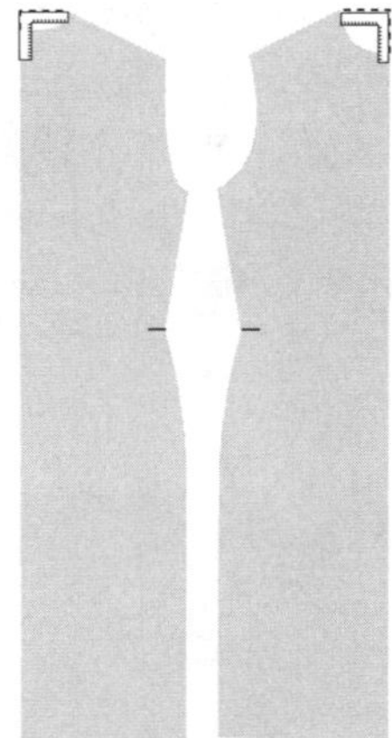

Draft the neckline as in the tight high cowl, squaring up and in using the “L” ruler.

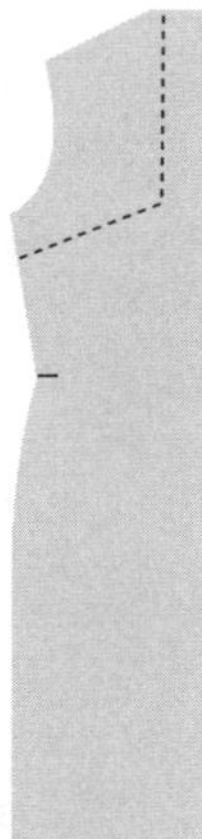

Draw slash lines from the neckline to the side seam as illustrated.

These may be placed higher or lower on the side seam, depending on the amount and placement of the volume you wish to increase.

Slash and spread as illustrated.

To determine how much to spread, use the recorded measurement from the dress-form.

Square a line using the “L” square.

Add a 4″ hem to the front and a 2″ hem to the shoulder area, and then draw a curved line as illustrated.

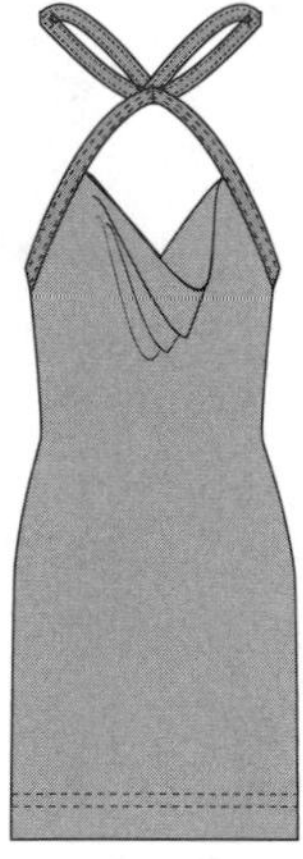

STYLE #10-018 SLIP NECKLINE WITH COWL

You may also create a slip neckline with a cowl in the front.

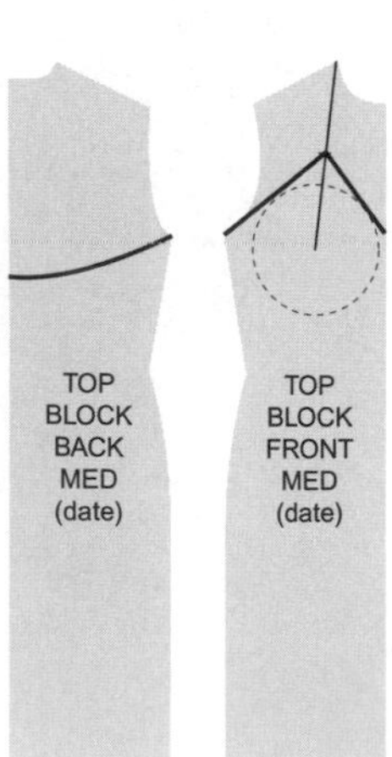

Draw in the neckline, trying not to let your lines go within the bust circle; otherwise, parts of the breast will be exposed.

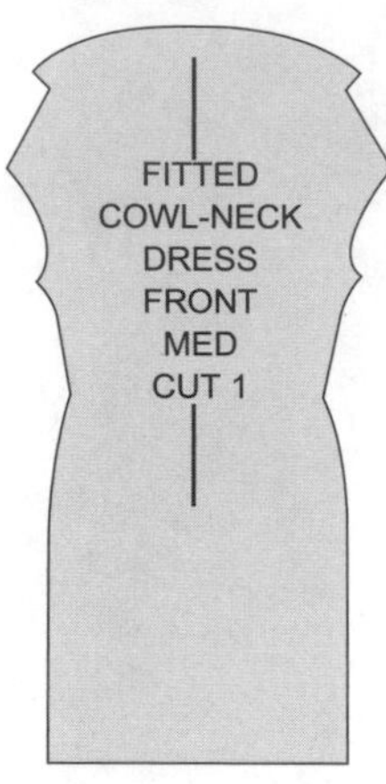

The completed pattern will add volume only to the upper part of the garment, without increasing any of the body portions.

As before, a larger hem/facing may be used if the fabric is very fluid and you wish to ensure that it does not roll outwards.

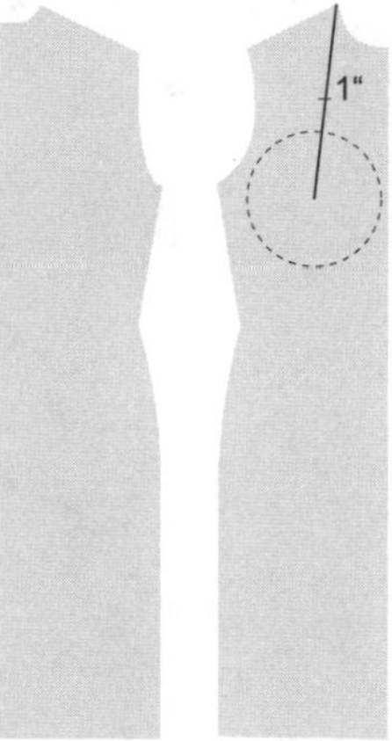

Draw a guideline from the bust apex up to the point where the shoulder meets the neck.

This guideline follows the direction of the straps, and may be changed accordingly.

Measure up 1″ on the guideline.

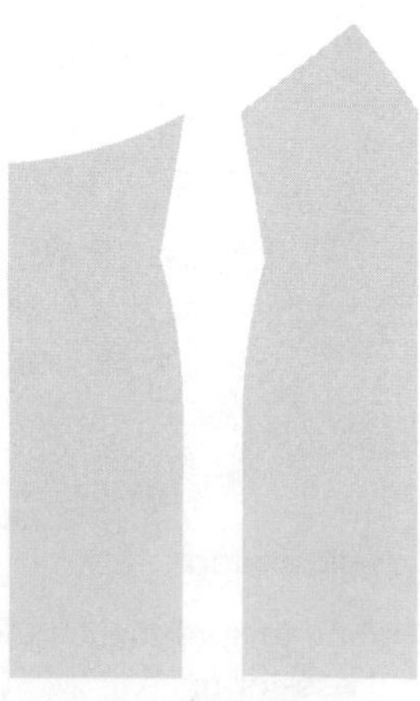

Trace and separate the pattern pieces as illustrated.

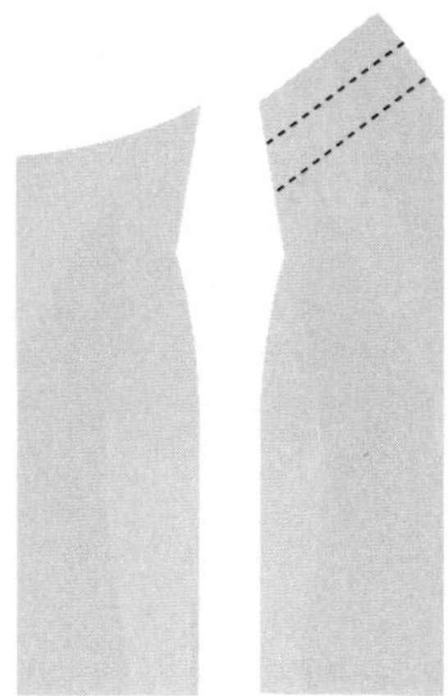

Draw in the slash lines for the cowl.

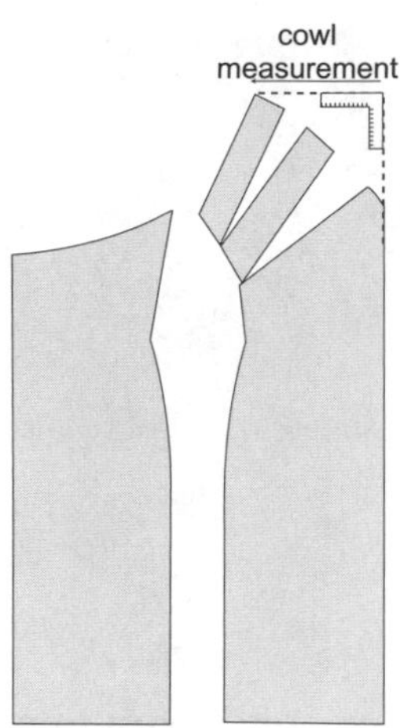

Slash and spread the sections an amount equal to the amount of cowl required.

Make sure that the center front remains squared.

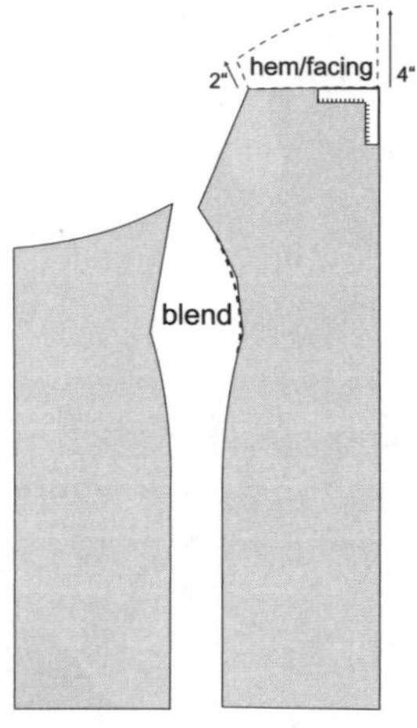

Because you can see inside of the cowl, you will require a deeper hem/facing in the front.

Add a 4″ hem to the center front and a 2″ hem at the shoulders, and then blend with a smooth curved line.

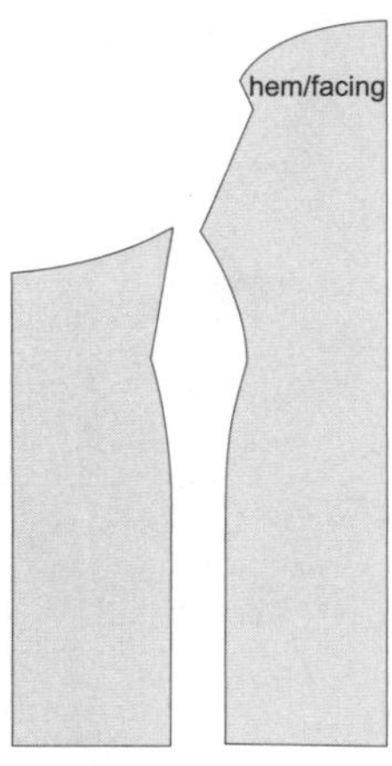

Trace the pattern as illustrated.

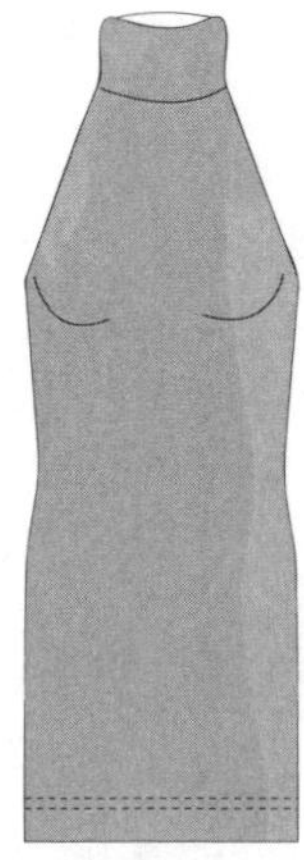

STYLE #10-019 HALTER DRESS

You can easily create a halter dress. It may be a halter in the back as well, or it can easily be created as a backless style.

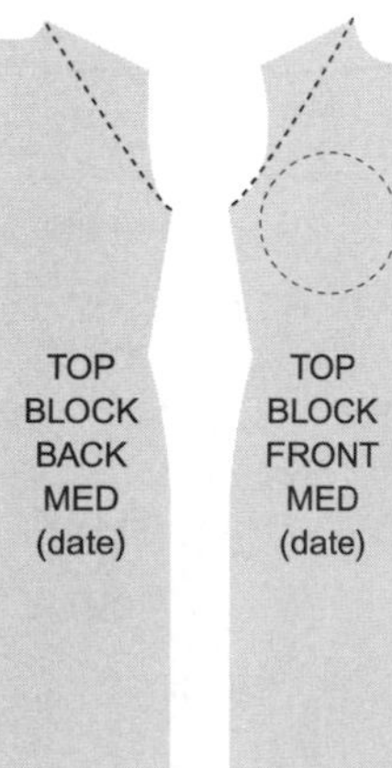

Draw in the style lines as you wish them to appear, remembering to shape them for complete bust coverage.

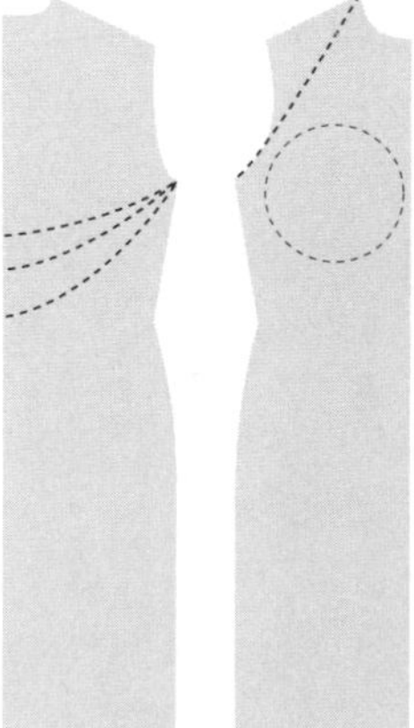

The back of this dress may also be lowered if you desire.

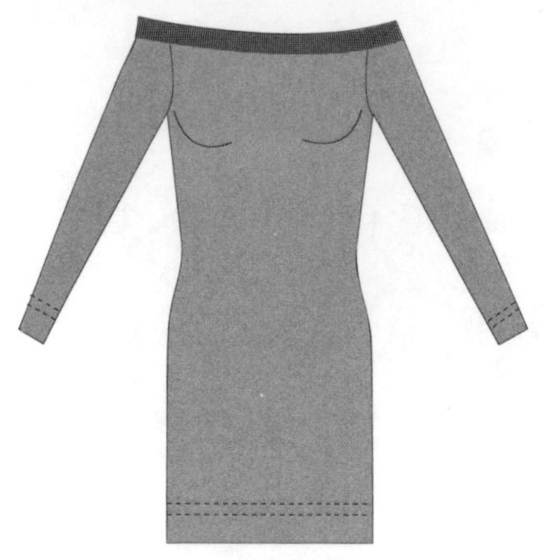

STYLE #10-020 OFF-THE-SHOULDER DRESS WITH BAND FINISH

The off-the-shoulder styled dress requires sleeve and body drafting.

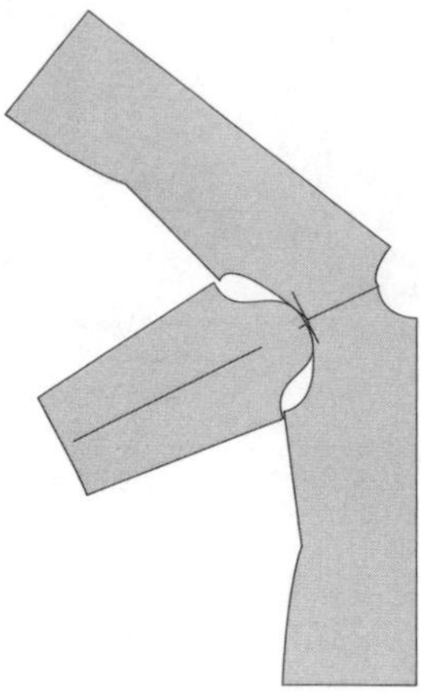

Line up the front and back dress slopers as illustrated and place the sleeve along the shoulder.

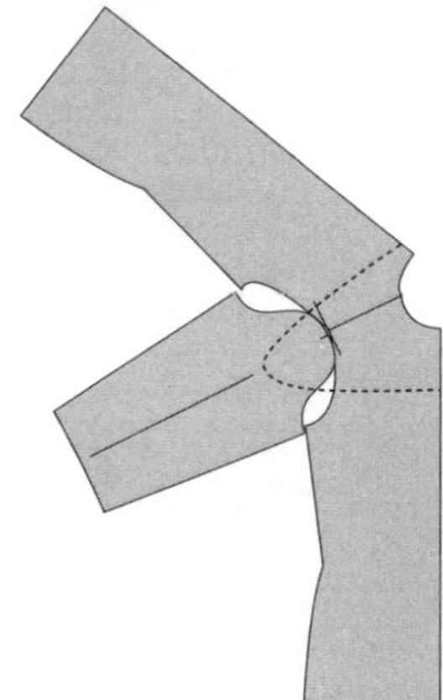

Draw in the lowered neckline as illustrated.

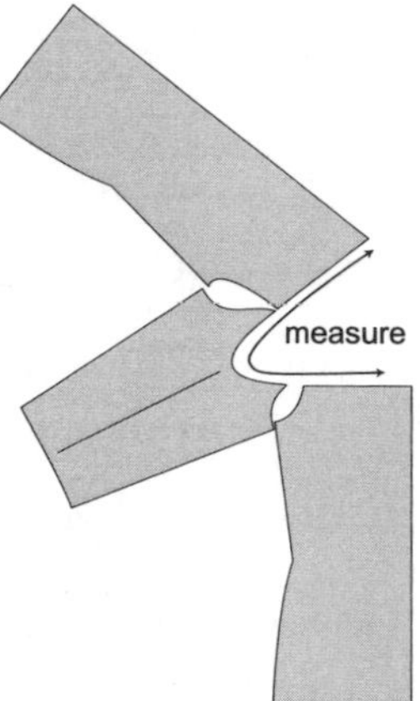

Measure the neckline in order to draft the ribbed band for the neckline.

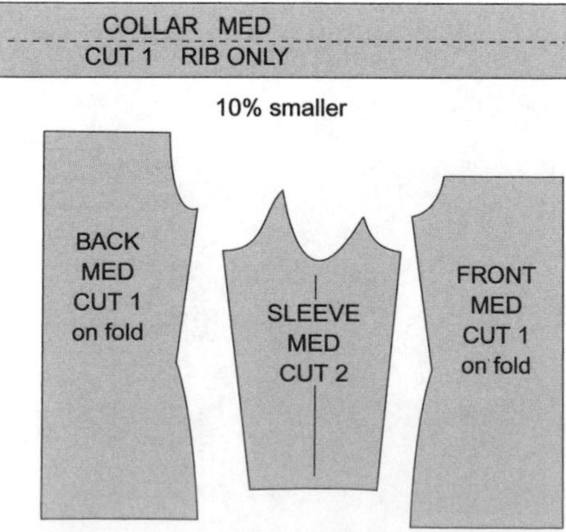

Make the rib pattern one-tenth smaller than the neckline.

Jumpsuits

ABOUT THIS SECTION

This section will explore some patternmaking details and designs for jumpsuits. These garments are not as tight as catsuits and may be used with one-way-stretch fabrics.

The jumpsuit sloper combines the top sloper and the pant sloper to create a one-piece sloper. Note that the jumpsuit has a much lower crotch than the catsuit because it is created from one-way-stretch fabric and needs some comfort and extra fabric in the crotch area.

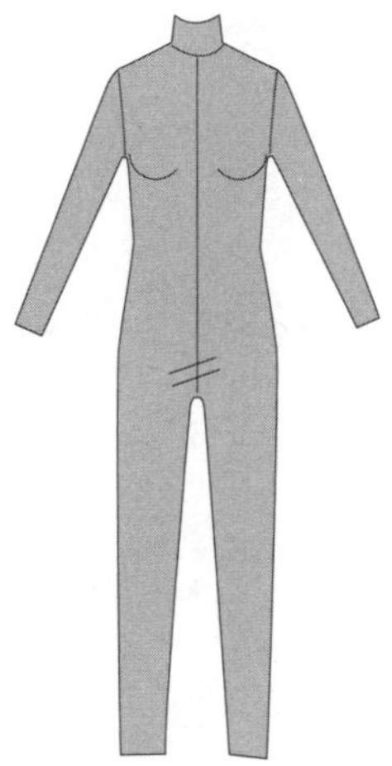

JUMPSUIT SLOPERS

This draft is for a jumpsuit, which is different from the catsuit in that it may be used for one-way-stretch fabrics. However, please note that the crotch will be much lower and looser than the catsuit because the fabric does not stretch in the lengthwise direction.

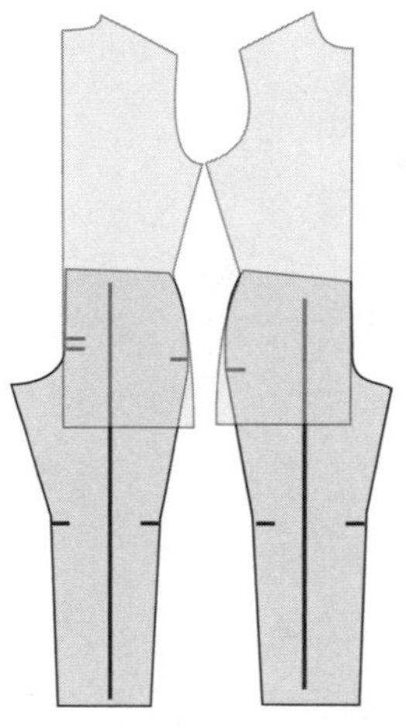

Simply attach the top sloper to the pant sloper.

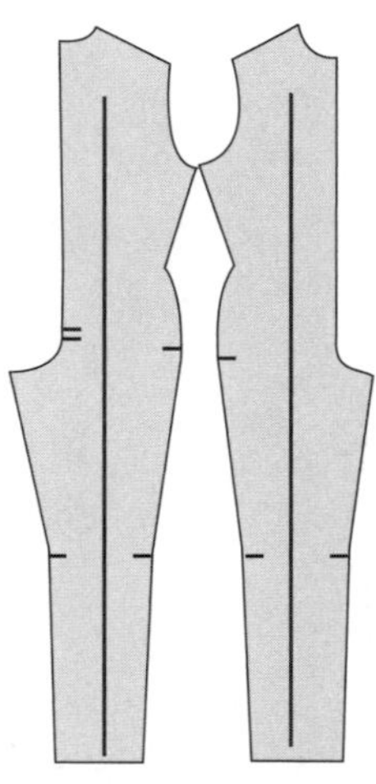

Trace out a new sloper and label as a jumpsuit.

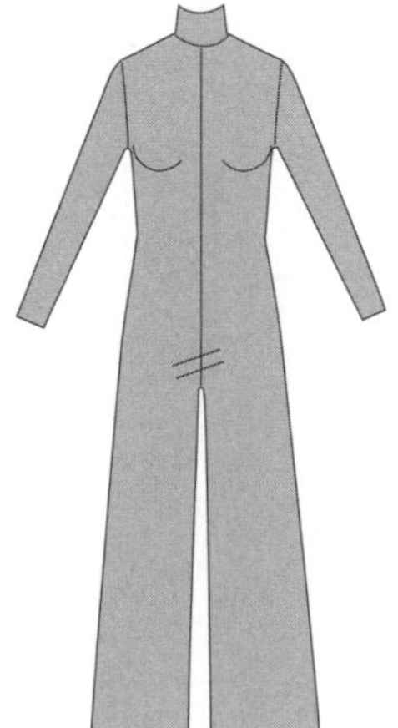

JUMPSUIT WITH WIDE LEGS

Create a jumpsuit with wide legs.

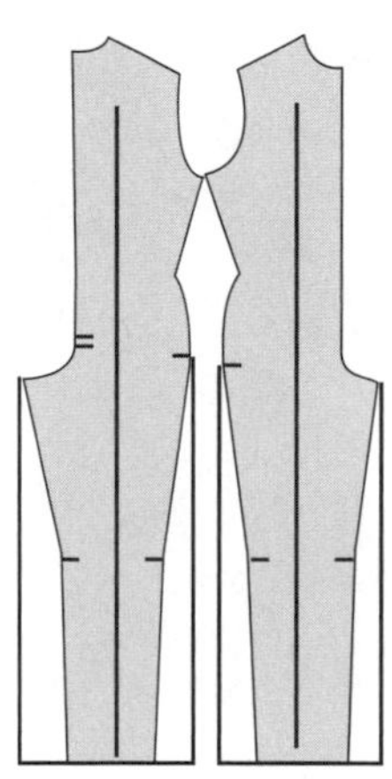

Simply square down from the crotch.

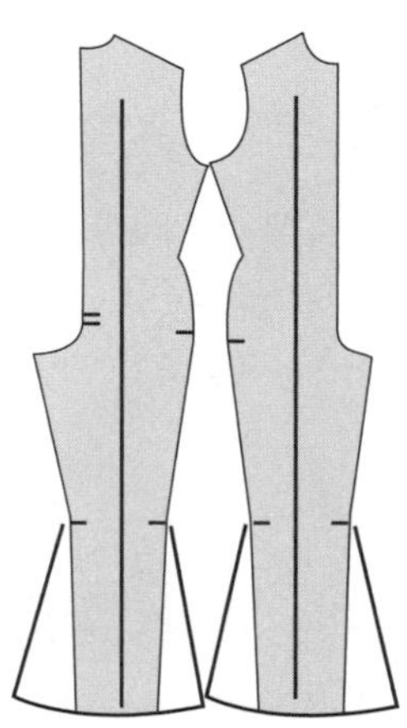

Or create a bell bottom jumpsuit.

Test Your Knowledge of the Material in this Chapter

1. How do you draft a dress from a top sloper?
2. What changes must you make to the catsuit sloper if you want to use it to create a dress sloper?
3. How can you create a dress with an unfitted waist?
4. How can you create a dress with a fitted waist?
5. How can you create a dress with a semi-fitted waist?
6. Which sloper should be used to create a dress from a four-way stretch fabric?

CHAPTER 11

Oversized Projects

About this Chapter

Occasionally a designer may require garments to be oversized, or much larger than normal garments. This chapter will introduce the reader to the concepts and patternmaking techniques used to create oversized garments, and will begin by drafting of a set of oversized top slopers. Understand that your garments may be created as large as you wish, but the size label does not change, because the customer is simply wearing them larger, looser, and baggier. To create an oversized jacket, use the jacket sloper and enlarge as much as your design requires.

Once you have created the oversized slopers, you may use any of the other details in this text on oversized styles.

OVERSIZED TOP SLOPERS

The following examples will be illustrated with and total body increase of 6″, but the designer may want a smaller increase, or a larger increase.

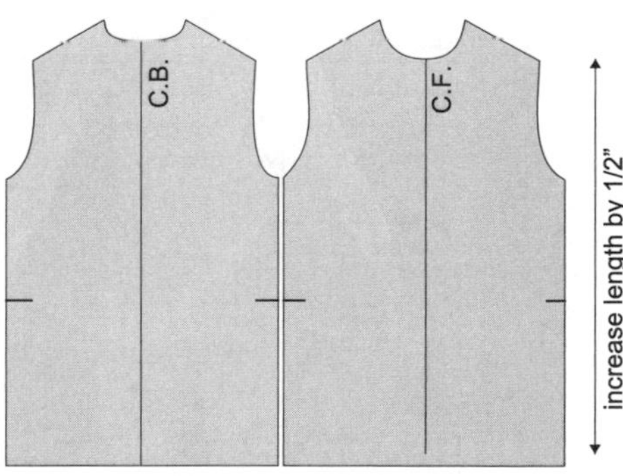

middle of the shoulder
underarm area
armhole area
increase by 3/4″
increase by 3/4″

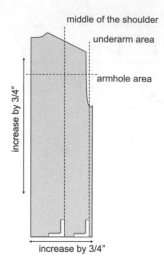

The oversized sloper is used when the designer wants to create styles that are loosely fitted or baggy.

This is still a size Medium, because the neckline has not been changed, and should be labeled "Medium Oversized."

To create a style that is 6″ larger around the circumference, extend each quarter of the pattern by 1½″, half of that through the shoulder and the other half through the underarm.

Draw a vertical line through the shoulder area to the hem and then through the underarm area to the hem.

Then draw a line horizontally through the armhole the same amount that the shoulder has increased, because you don't want an oversized project with tight armholes.

Use the straight waist, as it doesn't make sense to make an oversized fitted waist.

INCREASE CHART

Use this cart to determine the amount for each increase.

Total Body Increase	Quarter Body Increase	Shoulder Increase	Underarm Increase
1″	¼	⅛	⅛
2″	½	½	½
3″	¾	⅜	⅜
4″	1	½	½
5″	1¼	⅝	⅝
6″	1½	¾	¾
7″	1¾	⅞	⅞
8″	2	1	1
9″	2¼	1⅛	1⅛
10″	2½	1¼	1¼
11″	2¾	1⅜	1⅜
12″	3	1½	1½
13″	3¼	1⅝	1⅝
14″	3½	1¾	1¾

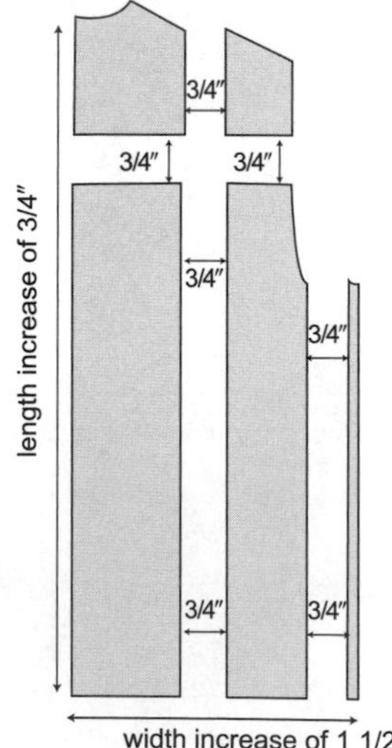

Slash and spread the body to increase the fit.

6″ divide by 4 = 1½″ for each panel of the body.

1½″ divided by 2 = ¾″ for each area that will be enlarged.

Slash and spread these two areas by ¾″ each, as illustrated.

Only the widths of the body and sleeve have changed, not the neckline, or the wrist.

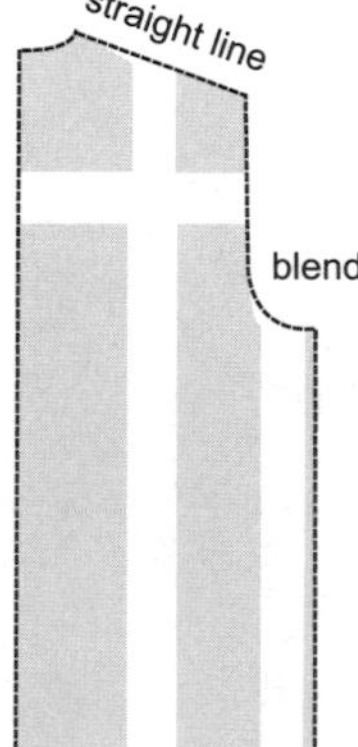

To blend:

Straighten out the shoulder by drawing a new straight line from the neck to armhole, ignoring any discrepancies.

Blend the armhole and the underarm areas.

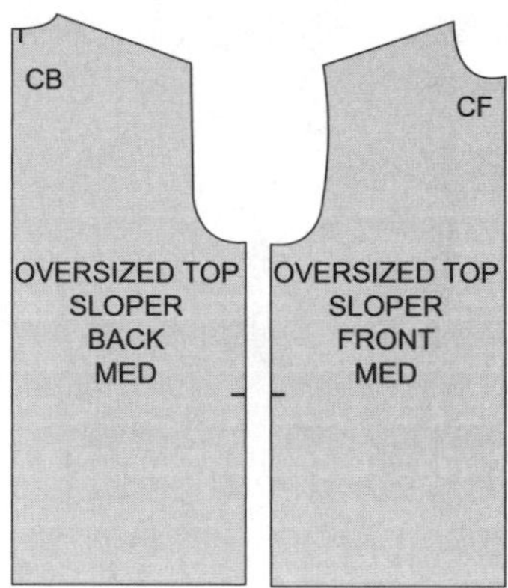

Label as "oversized slopers."

It is still Medium size, but intended to be worn looser.

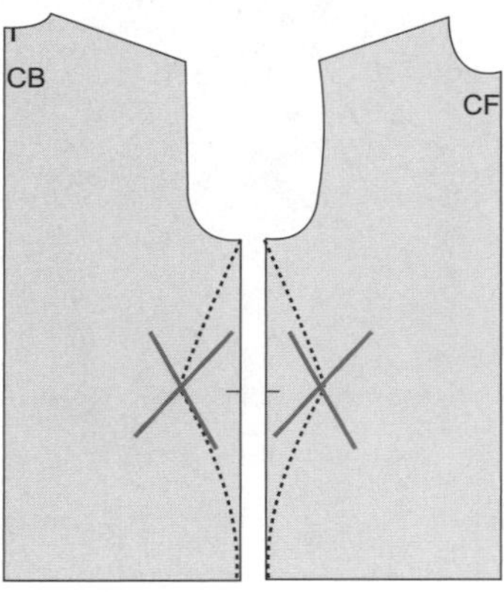

It does not make any sense to create a fitted oversized top sloper, since it is already so oversized, and the sides extend well past the waist of the customer.

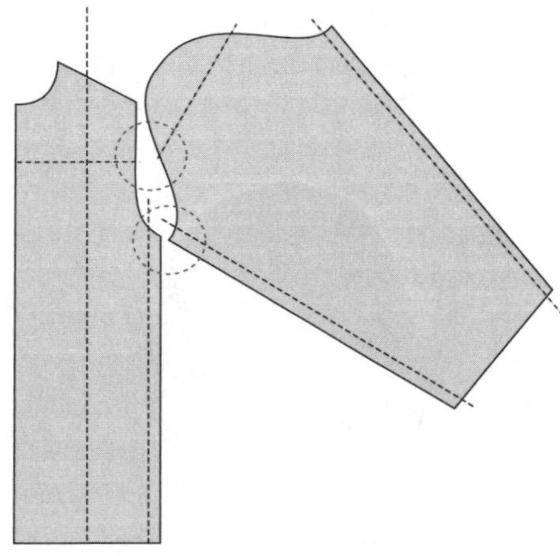

OVERSIZED SLEEVE

The sleeve must increase equally in order to fit into the body.

By looking at the illustration, it is easy to understand the placement and amounts of the increases necessary.

Make the changes necessary to ensure that the sleeve fits into the new body.

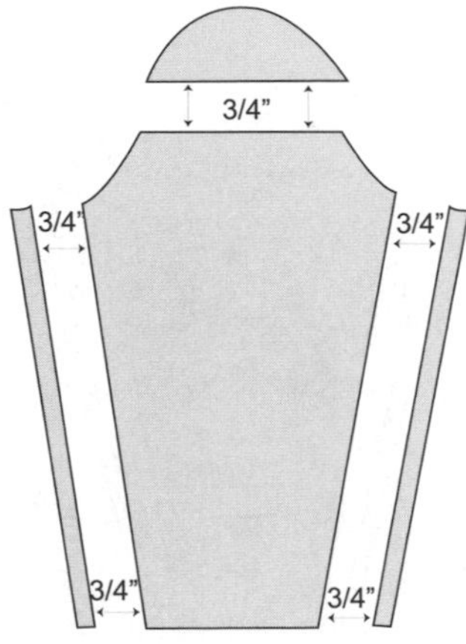

Figuring out the sleeve is simple, whatever changes have been made to the armhole must be re-created so the sleeve will fit into it.

Slash and spread the sleeve to correspond to the body, as illustrated.

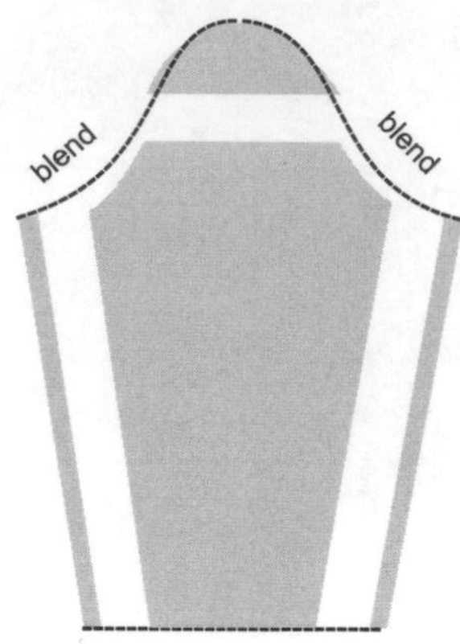

Blend the new sleeve and walk around to check for accuracy.

Remember to allow for sleeve ease.

Check the ease.

Minimum ½″ Maximum ¾″

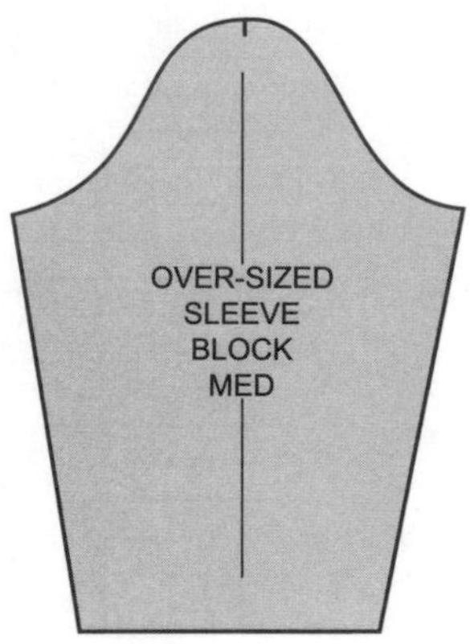

Label the sleeve as Medium Oversized Sleeve Sloper.

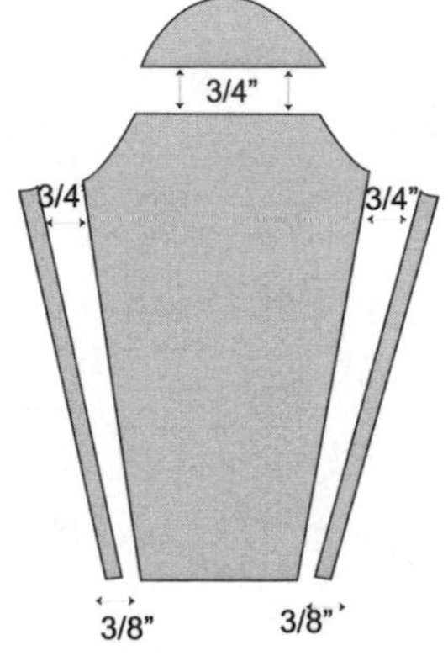

Sometimes the wrist area of the sleeve is only enlarged half as much as the balance of the sleeve.

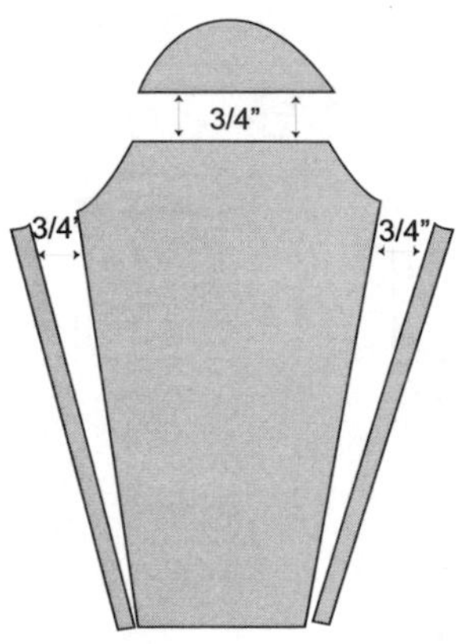

Sometimes the wrist is not enlarged at all. You must determine by your design which method to use.

OVERSIZED CREW NECK T-SHIRT

The oversized crew neck T-shirt is created the same way as the fitted crew neck, except that the oversized slopers will be used.

See Chapter 9, Tops

OVERSIZED V-NECK T-SHIRT

The oversized V-neck T-shirt is created the same way as the regular V-neck T-shirt, except that the oversized sloper is used instead of the regular sloper.

See Chapter 9, Tops

OVERSIZED HOODIE

Hoodies are a great example of oversized garments.

This draft will demonstrate an oversized hoodie.

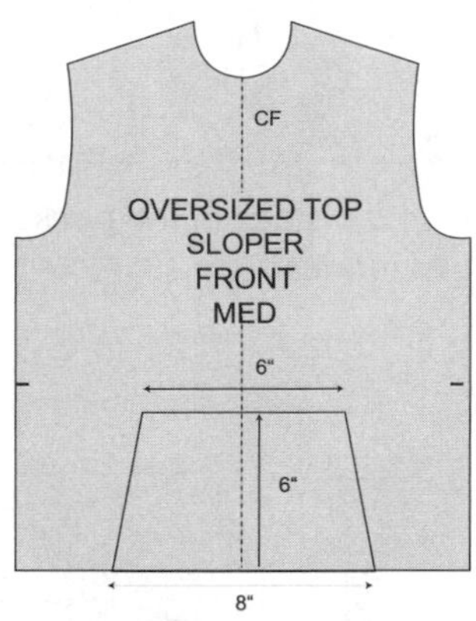

THE KANGAROO POCKET

The kangaroo pocket can be applied to many different garments, such as pants, skirts, T-shirts, and can be any size or dimension you wish.

Measure up the center front 6″.

Measure across the hem 4″ in each direction.

Measure across the top of the pocket 3″ on each side.

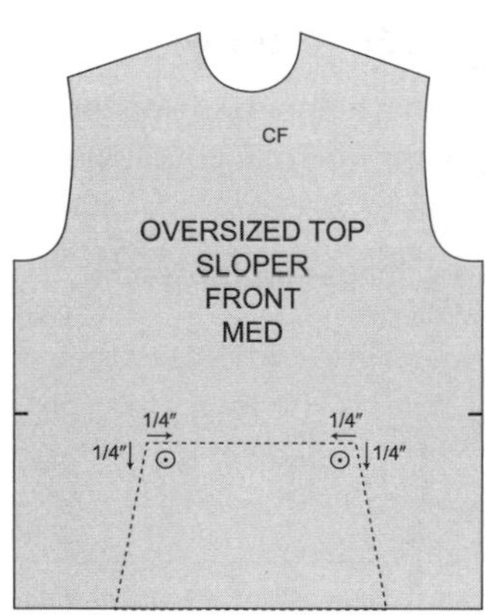

Mark the drill marks ¼″ in and ¼″ down from the line, since you don't want the marks, sometimes drilled, to show once the pocket is applied.

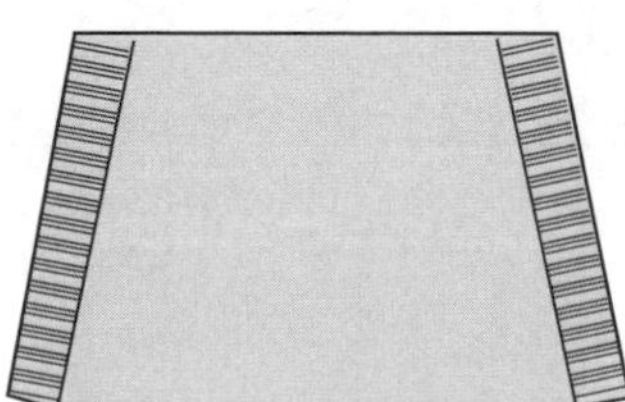

Alternately, you can use a folded rib to finish the sides of the pocket.

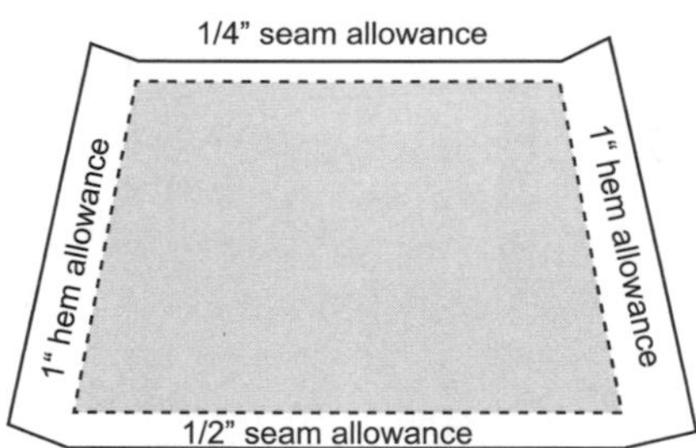

Add hem allowance and seam allowances to the pocket as illustrated.

The sides of the pocket will be hemmed with the cover stitch.

The top of the pocket will be edge-stitched in place.

The bottom of the pocket will be caught in the rib waistband.

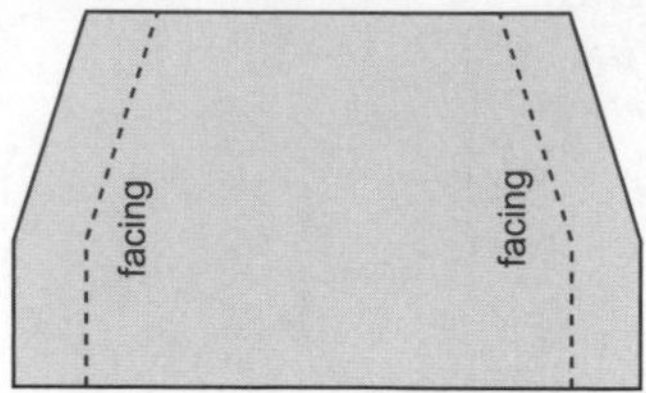

If you want to shape the sides of the pocket, you must use a facing to finish the edges.

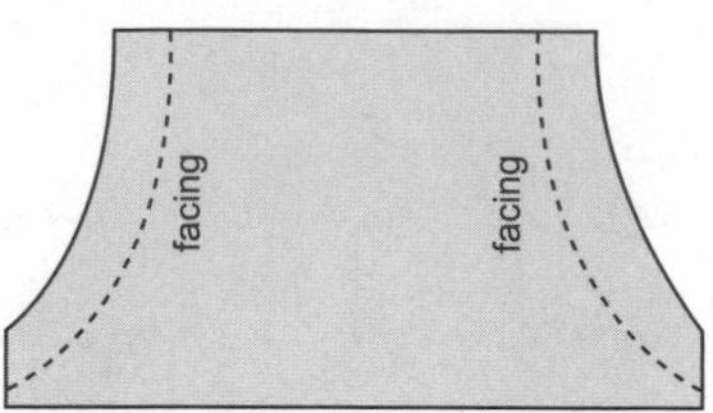

To curve the sides of the pocket, you must add a facing.

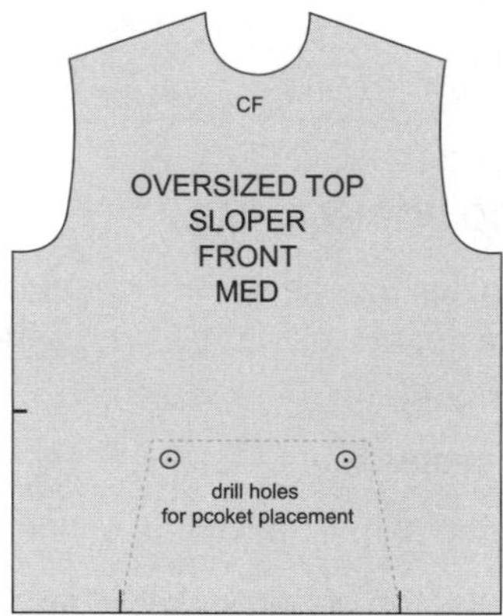

Label the front of the top as illustrated with drill marks and notches to indicate the pocket placement.

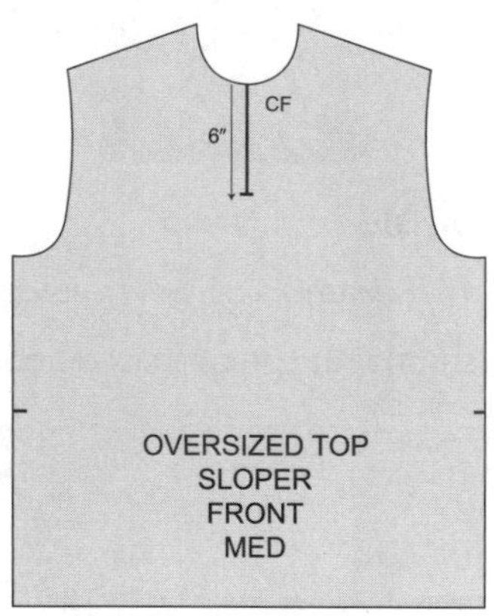

ZIPPER WITH COVERED TEETH

To create a top with a zipper opening, whereby you don't want to see the teeth, you can create welts to cover the teeth.

Measure down any length for the zipper.

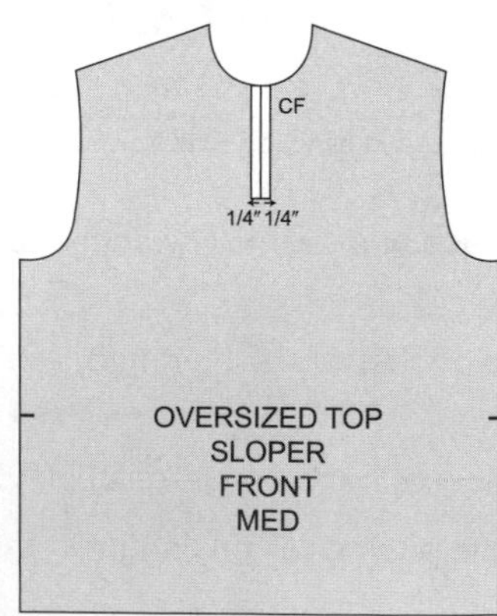

Draw parallel lines 1/4″ wide to draft the welts.

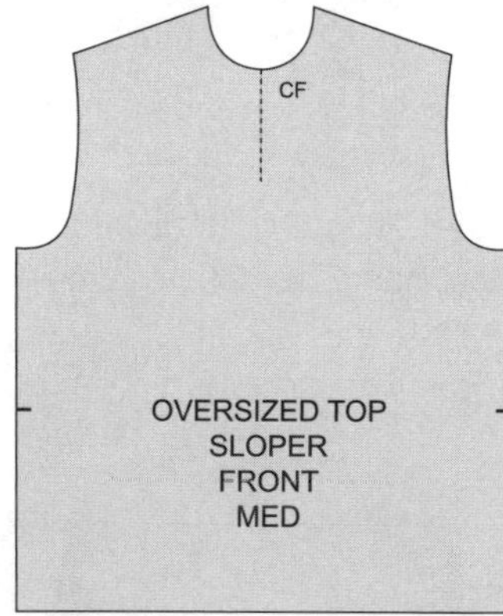

Trace and separate the pieces as illustrated.

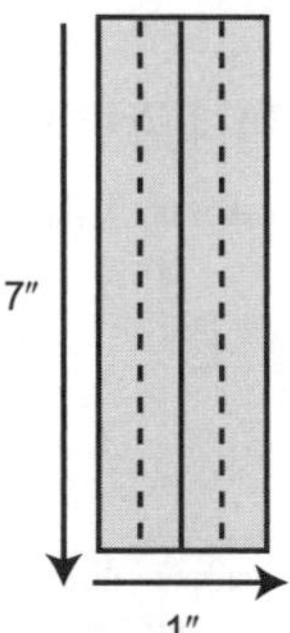

The welts drawn on the pattern can be traced on the fold as illustrated, and seam allowances added.

The long side of the welts should have 1/4″ seam allowances, and the ends should have 1/2″ seam allowances.

When folded, the welts look like the illustration.

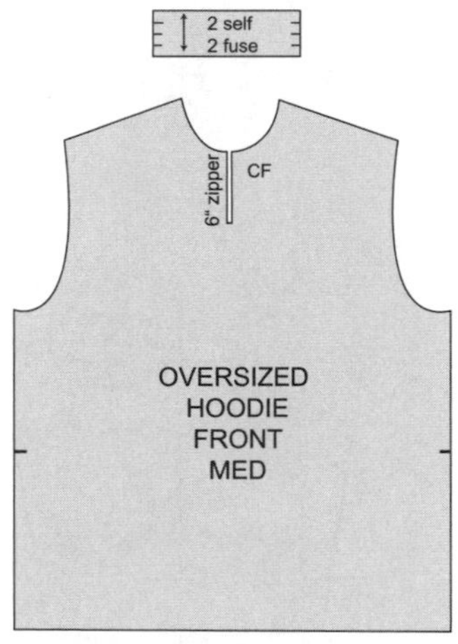

Label the pattern pieces as indicated.

The welts must be fused with tricot to prevent them from stretching when sewing and wearing.

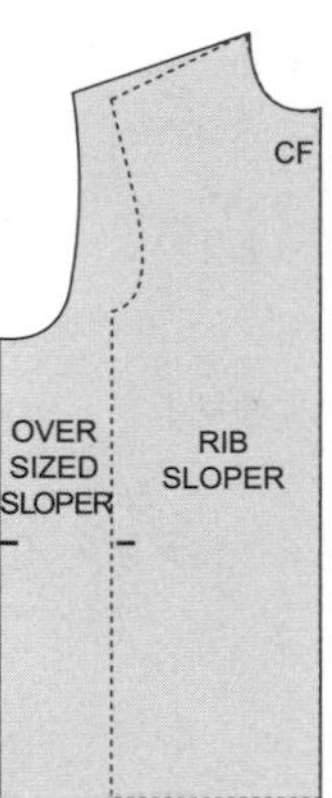

RIB WAISTBAND

The rib waistband needs to be slightly smaller than the waist. Even when creating the waistband for an oversized top, the waist is still drafted using the regular sized sloper.

It needs to be snug on the customer's waist.

The width to the waistband can be any size you wish, and will be folded over and sewn to the hem.

Use the rib sloper with built in reductions to determine the length of the waistband.

This waist must be multiplied by four to create a waistband to fit around the entire hem.

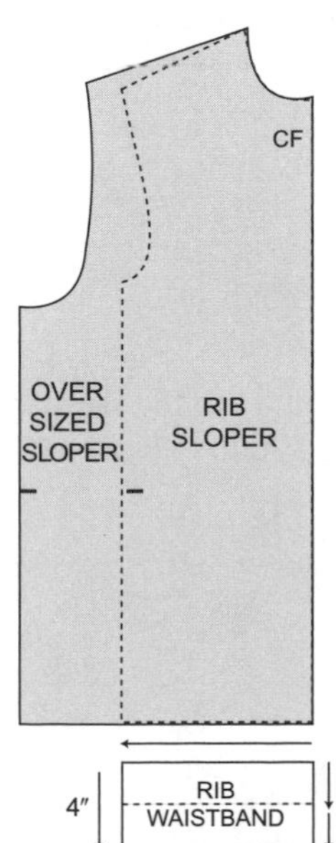

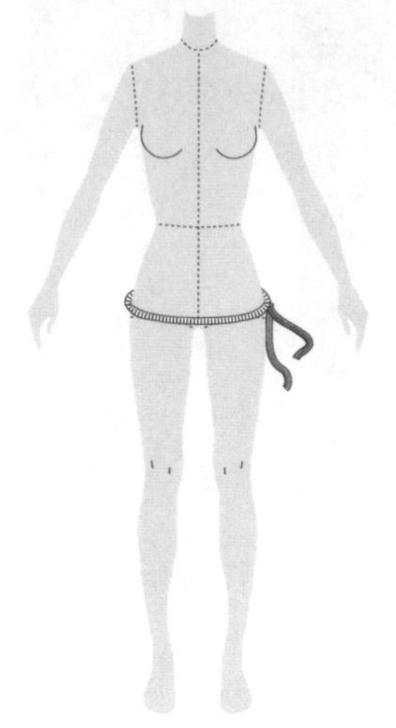

ALTERNATE METHOD OF DETERMINING RIB LENGTH

Measure the dress-form or fit the model at the area of the body where the rib will sit.

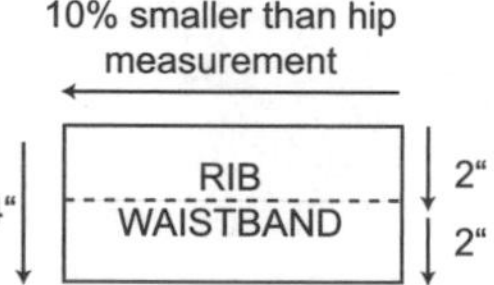

Make the rib length 10% smaller.

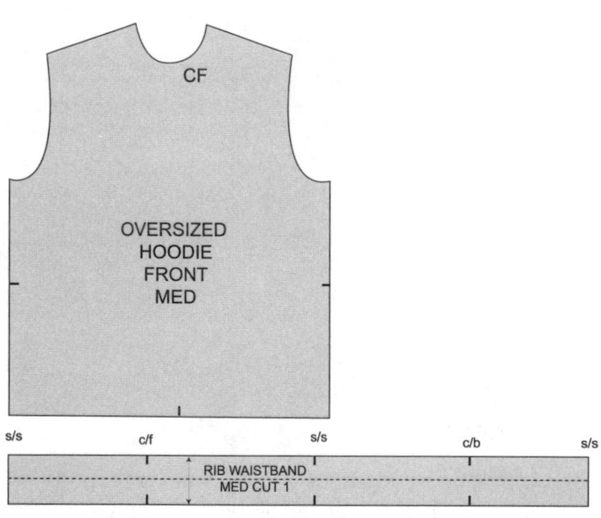

Label the pattern as illustrated.

Notch the front, back, and sideseams of the waistband for easy assembly and to ensure that you stretch the waistband to fit the top evenly.

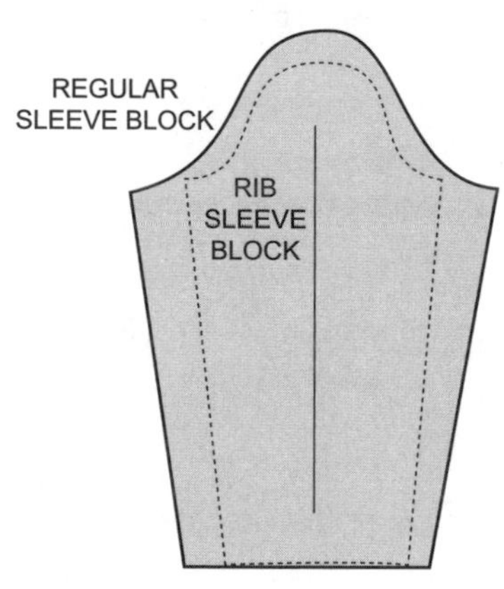

RIB CUFFS

When drafting a ribbed cut, use the regular rib sloper, so that it is snug on the customer's wrist.

Make the length to fit the regular rib sloper as wide as you wish, illustrated at 4″ which is folded in half.

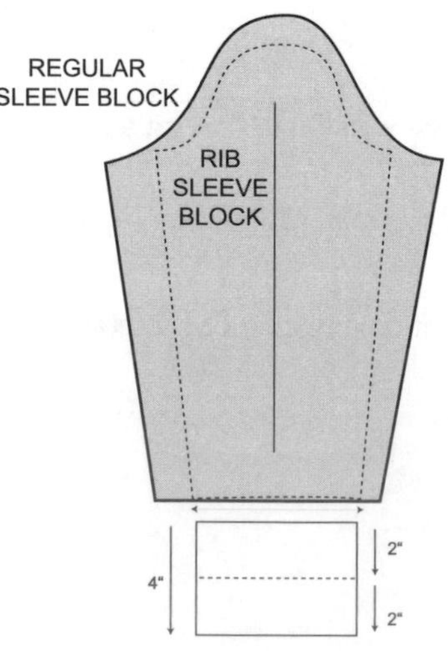

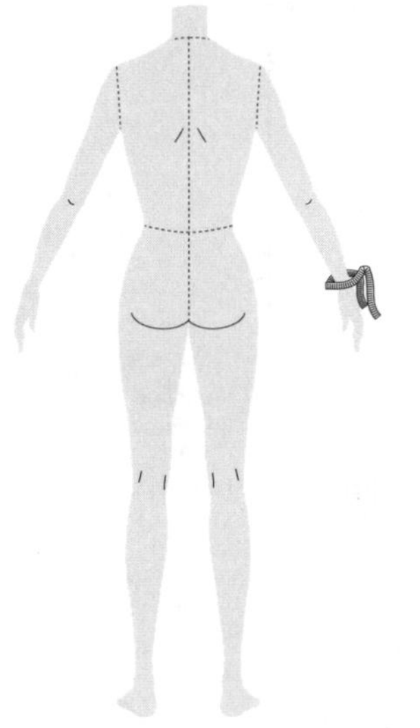

ALTERNATE METHOD OF DETERMINING CUFF RIB LENGTH

Measure the dress-form, or fit model at the area of the body where the rib will sit.

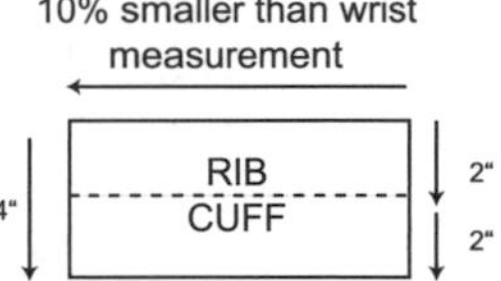

Make the rib length 10% smaller.

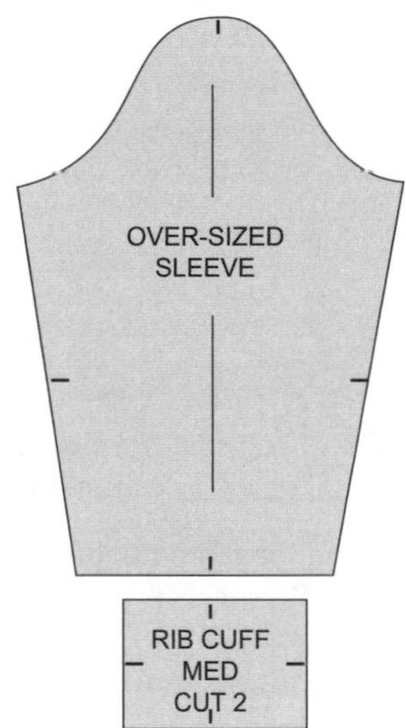

Label the pattern as illustrated.

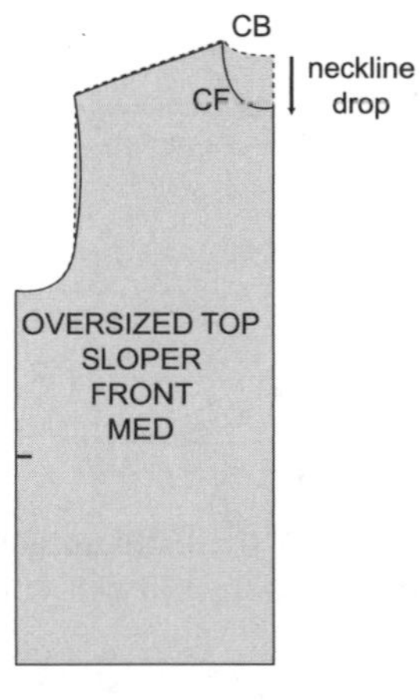

HOODS

Hoods may be created for any neckline or for regular fit, T-shirts, sweaters, tank tops, and catsuits.

Place the front sloper on top of the back sloper, matching the shoulders.

Measure the difference between the necklines; this is the amount of the neckline drop.

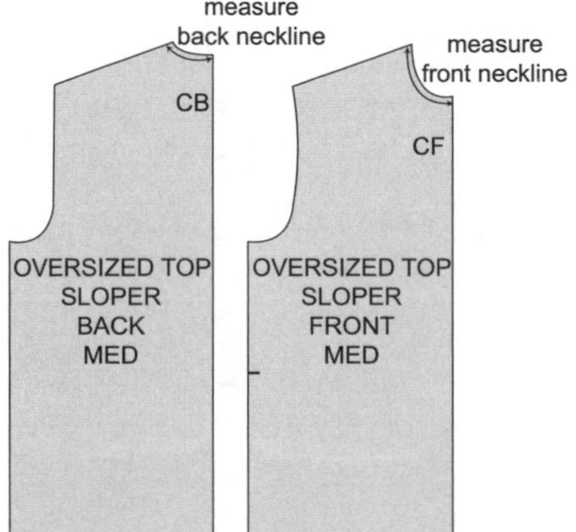

Measure the front neckline and the back neckline.

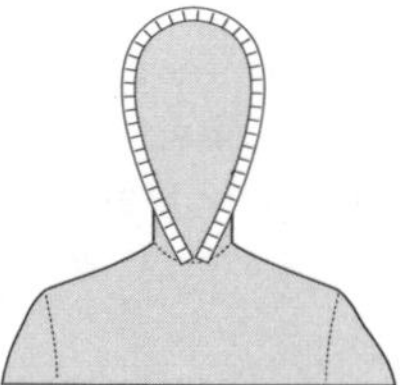

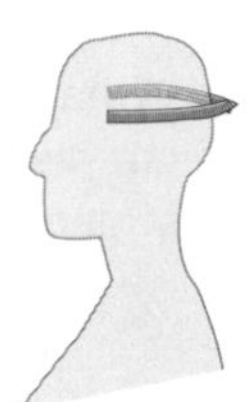

Measure from the pit of the neck, all the way around the head to the pit of the neck on the other side.

Measure around the head from eyebrow to eyebrow.

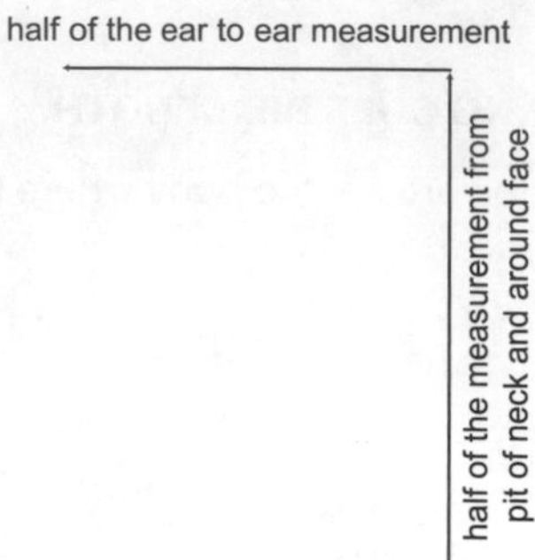

Draw intersecting lines.

From the lower point mark, measure up 15″ or desired amount.

Square a line 12″ across, or the desired amount.

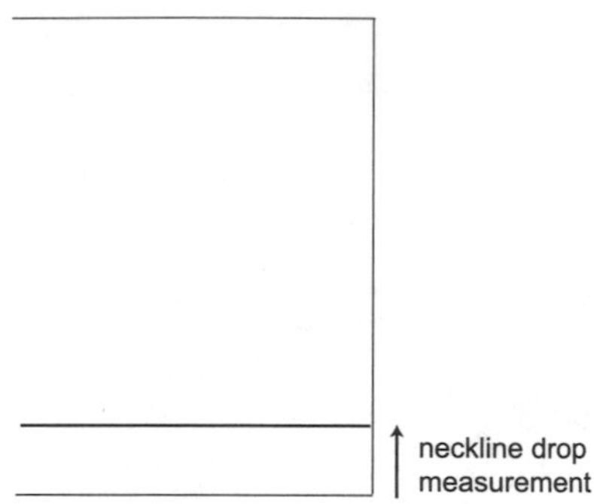

Mark a guideline above by the amount of the neckline drop.

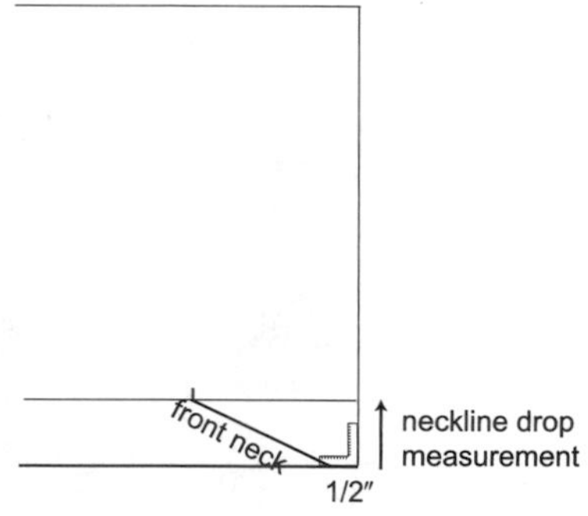

Using the measurement of the front neckline, hold the ruler on the lower line and place it wherever your front neckline lines up on the upper line.

Make sure to square the line for ½″.

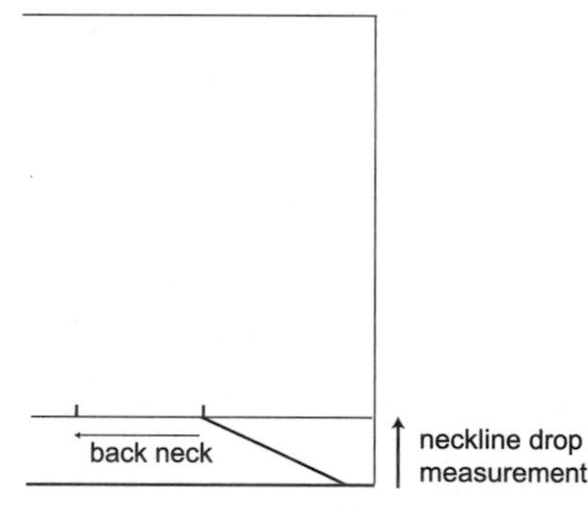

Apply the back neckline measurement along the upper line.

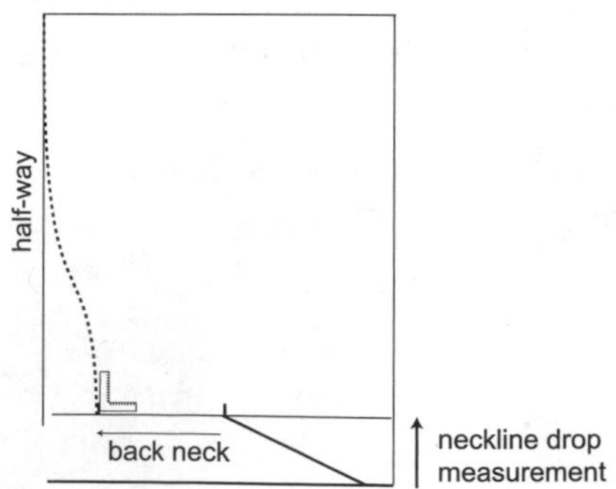

At approximately half-way along the center back, shape the hood to resemble the back of your head, making sure that the line is squared straight up for the first 1″.

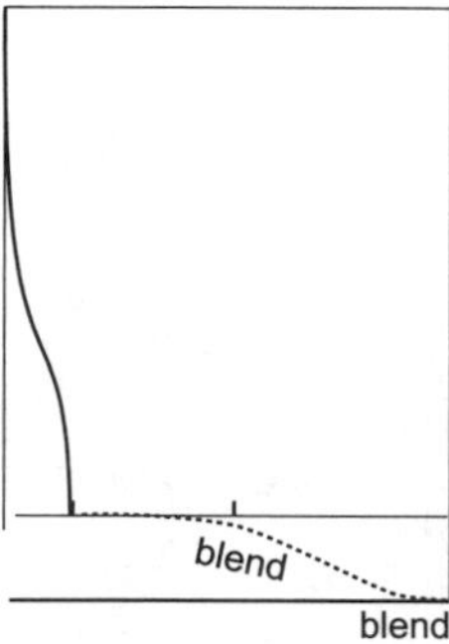

Blend the neckline into a smooth curve for easier sewing.

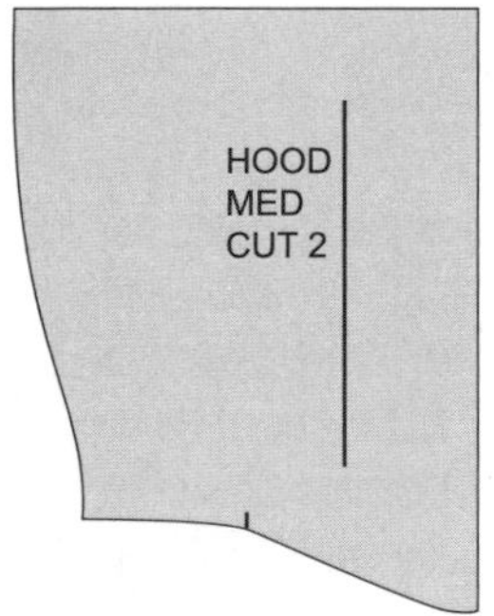

Trace and label the hood as illustrated.

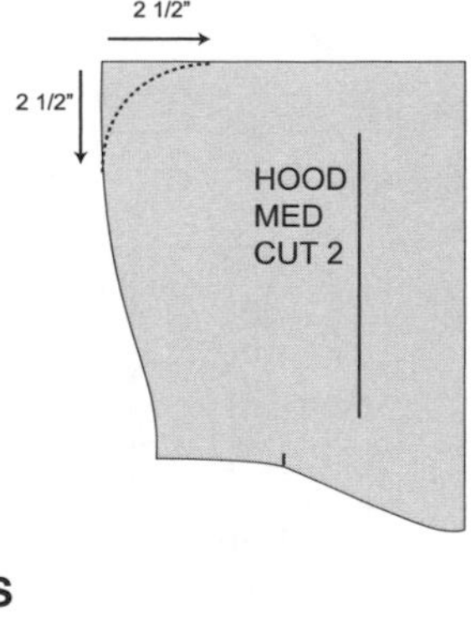

HOOD OPTIONS

To create a curved hood, measure 2½″ from the points, and draw the curve.

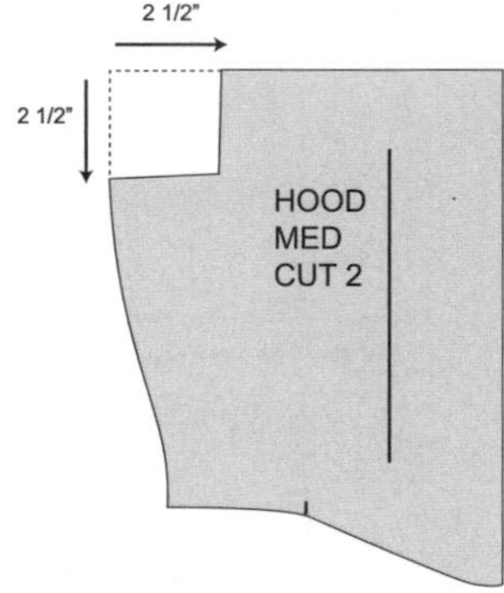

Measure in 2½″.

Measure down 2½″.

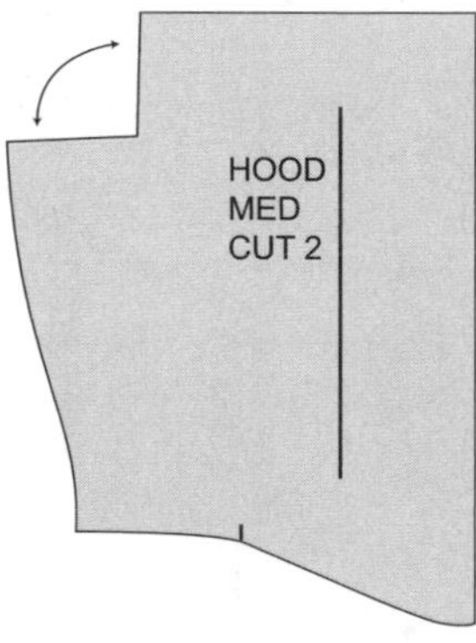

Cut out the section so that it forms a dart at the top of the back of the hood.

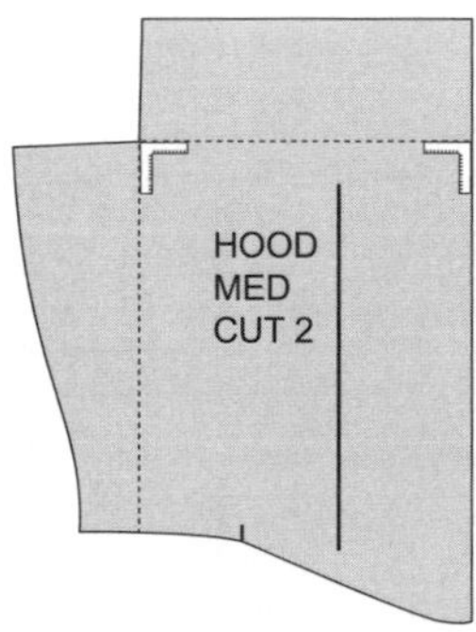

HOOD WITH PANEL SEAMS AND CENTER BACK SEAM

Square a line across and down from the 2½″ marks.

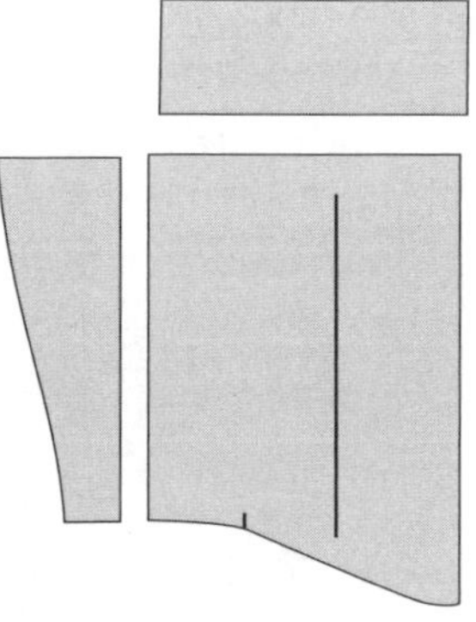

Separate the pattern pieces.

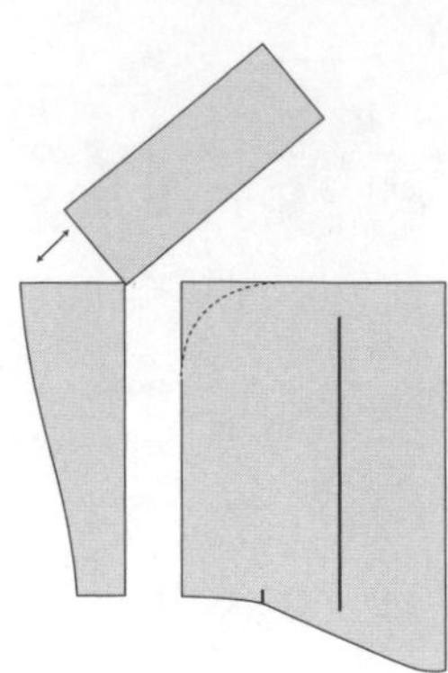

Swing the center back panels to line up with each other as illustrated and make into one single piece.

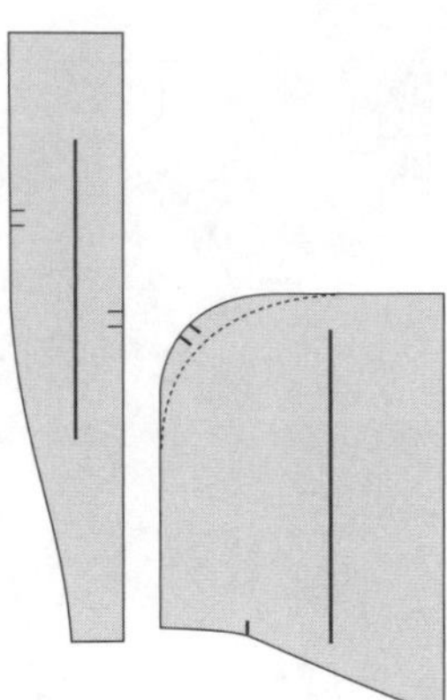

Blend the corners into a smooth curve, and you will have to reduce the length of the center back, from the top edge of the panel, so that it fits to the new curved line.

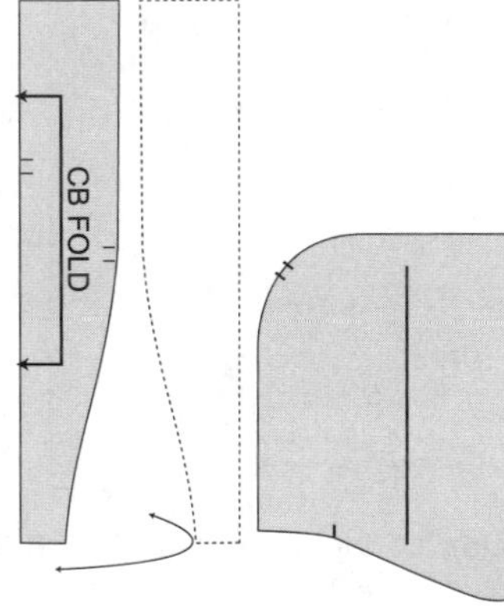

A hood pattern can be drafted without a center back seam, by reversing the center back panel and cutting it on the fold.

It will need a length correction, from the top edge, so that it fits perfectly to the curved lines.

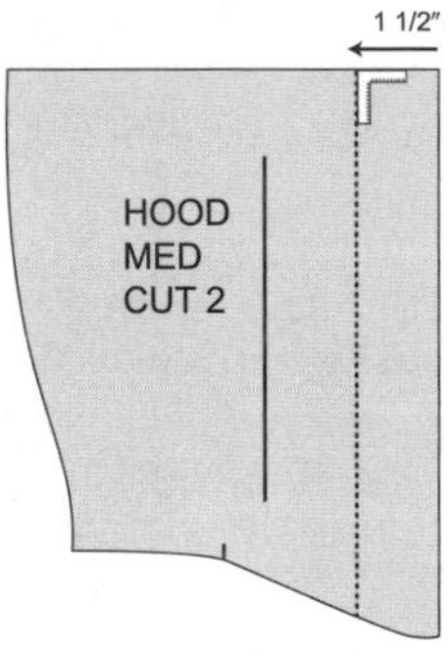

HOOD WITH RIBBING

The hood may also be drafted with ribbing to finish the edge of the hood.

Measure an amount for the rib, illustrated at $1\frac{1}{2}$", but may be larger or smaller, as the designer wishes.

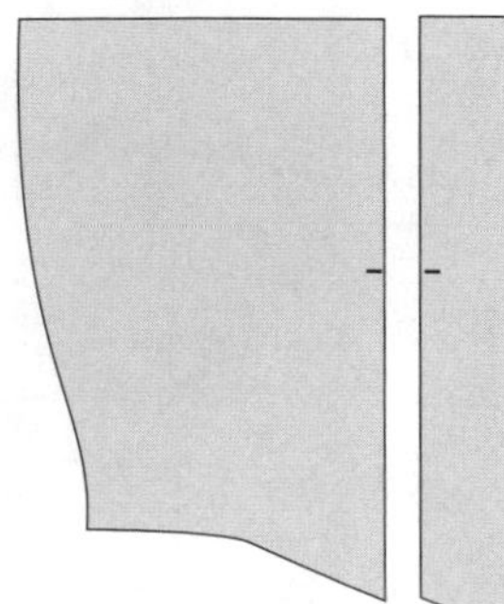

Separate the pieces.

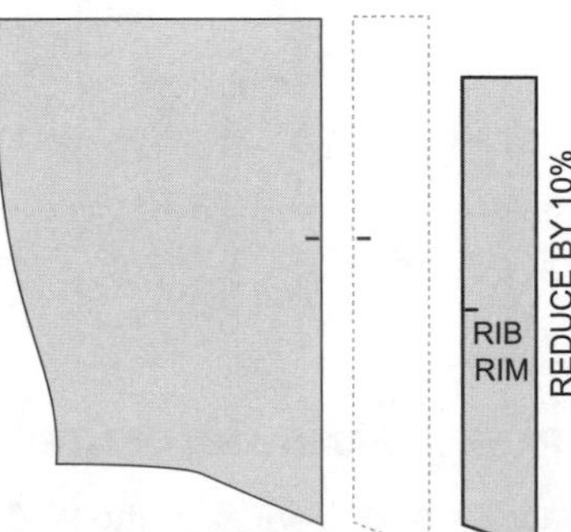

Reduce the length of the ribbing pattern piece by 10%, remove it from the top, then straight edge.

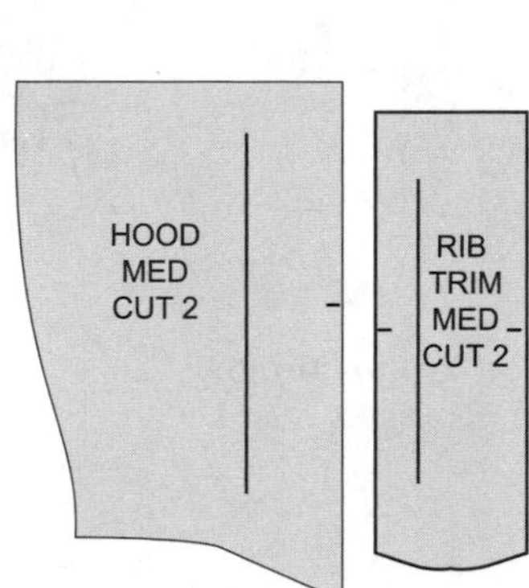

Fold and trace the pattern pieces as illustrated.

This hood has a seam in the ribbing at the top of the head, but may also be cut in a single piece.

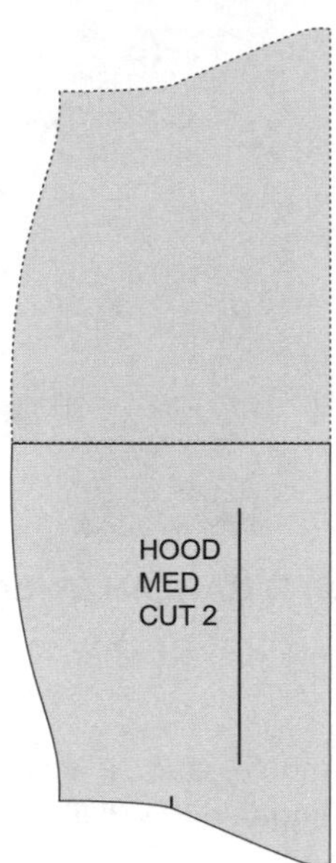

HOOD ON FOLD

The hood may be drafted with a fold at the top.

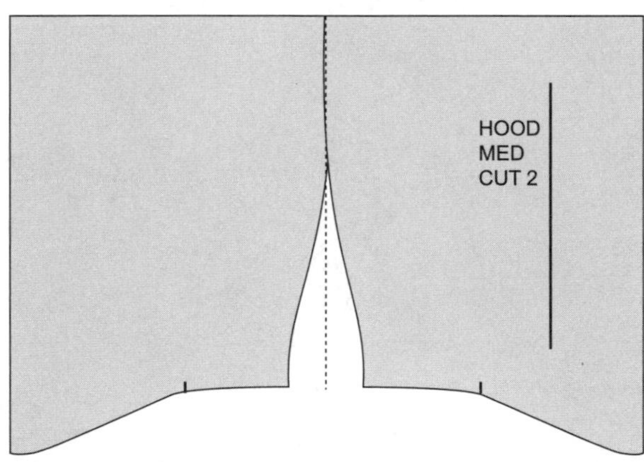

HOOD ON CENTER BACK FOLD

The hood may be drafted without a seam in the back and just a large dart. This is very useful when using striped fabrics since both sides will match at the back.

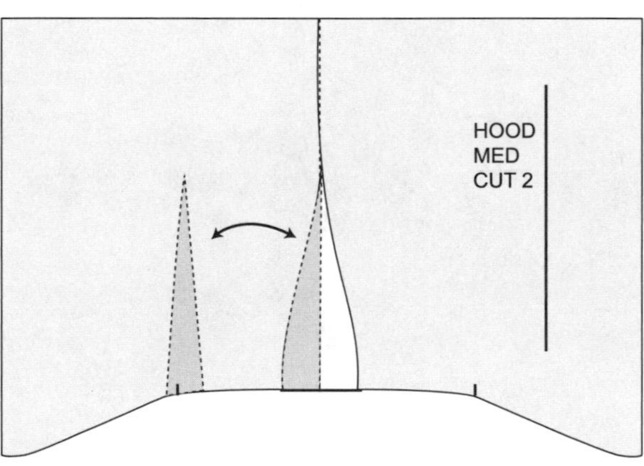

Alternatively, the dart intake amounts may be transferred to the shoulder notch, the excess, normally taken in at the center back, must be taken in as a dart at the shoulder notch.

OVERSIZED HOODED RAGLAN SWEATSHIRT

Raglan sleeves are often used when creating oversized garments.

Since there is no armhole seam, it is not as obvious that the garment is cut bigger, and will fit a larger segment of the population.

In this section, we will create the pattern for a raglan-sleeved top with a hood, ribbed cuffs, and waistband.

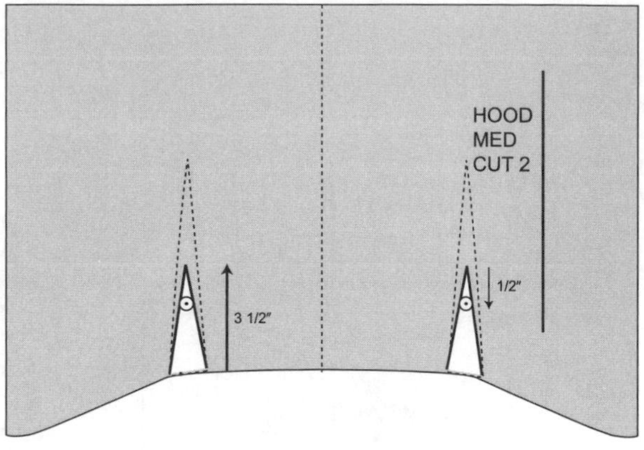

Reduce the length of the dart to 3½″.

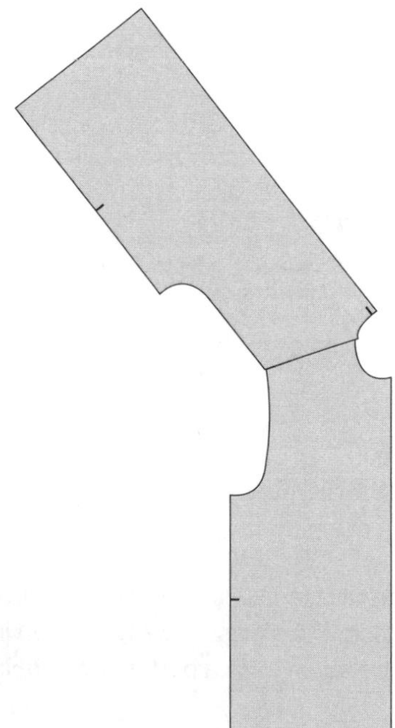

Place the front and back slopers together along the shoulders.

Draw a line connecting the underarm points.

Extend the line beyond the underarms.

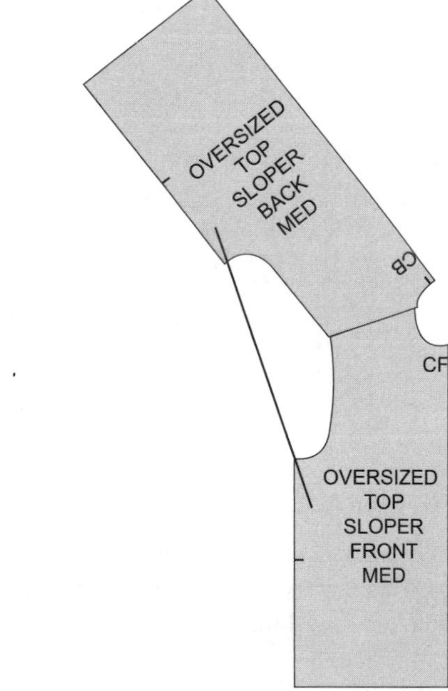

Draw a guideline from each underarm point and extend the line past the underarm point by approximately 3″.

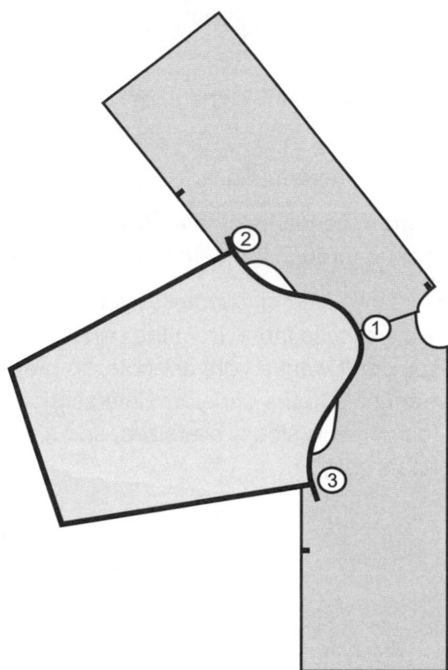

Place the sleeve on the underarm line as illustrated.

Match Point 1 to the shoulder notch on the shoulder line.

Match Point 2 to the back underarm point on the line.

Match Point 3 to the front underarm point on the line.

Note: The sleeve will overlap at the shoulder and go past the underarm points. We will correct this in the next step.

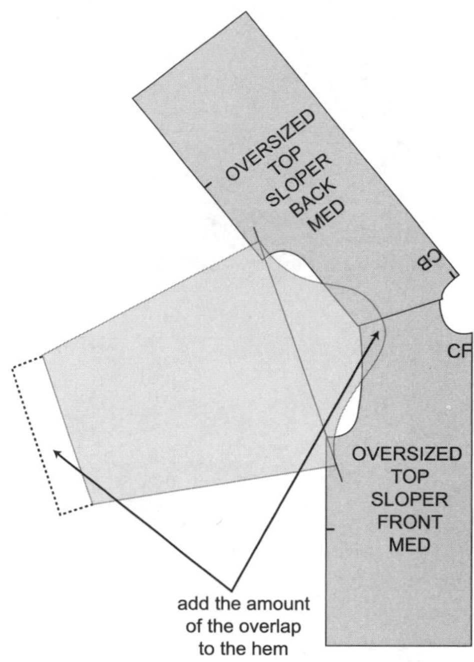

Remember to add to the length of the sleeve, the amount that the sleeve overlaps the shoulders, and to keep the length consistent, otherwise the sleeve will be too short.

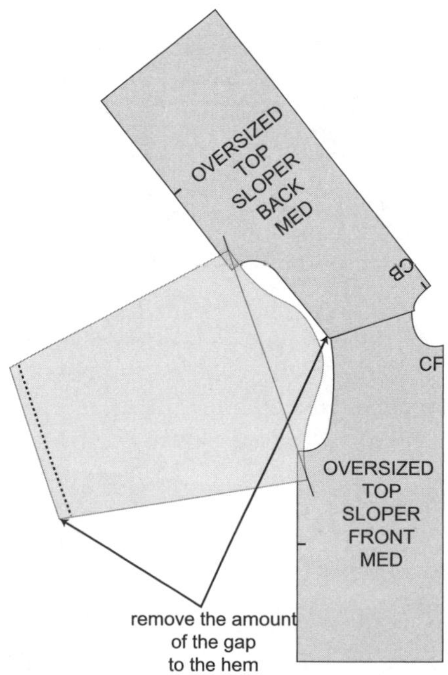

If there is a gap when the sleeve is placed on top, then this amount must be removed from the hem of the sleeve so it doesn't get any longer.

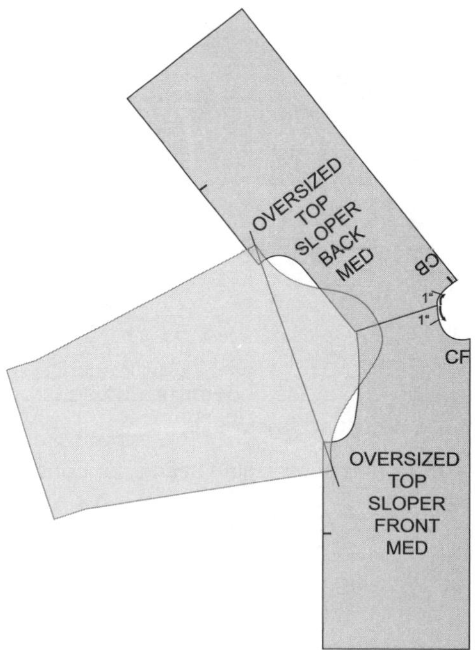

Mark the neckline 1″ from the shoulder line in both directions, or use any measurement the designer desires.

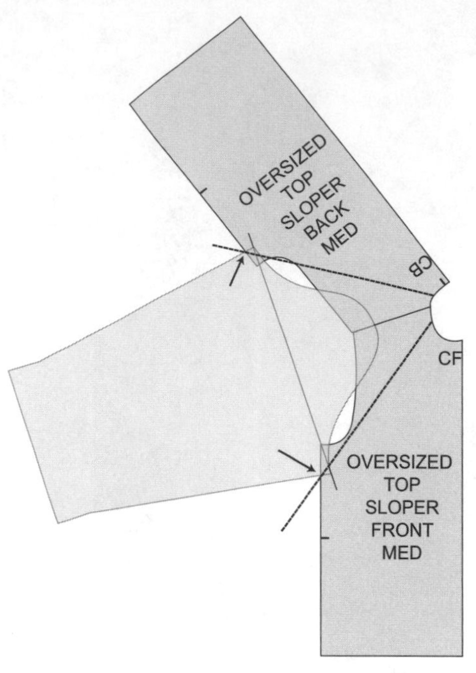

Draw a straight line from the neck point to the underarm intersections as shown.

Extend this line past 1½″ the underarm point.

Draw the raglan style line from the marks on the neck to the sleeve armhole intersection and continue through the center of the underarm point.

When drafting the fitted raglan T-shirt in Chapter 7, you followed the opposing curves to remove the excess fabric from the underarm. However, with the oversized top, you don't want a tight armhole, so draw a line straight through the new armhole to the underarm intersection. You've gone to a lot of trouble to make this sloper oversized, and should use the extra fabric for a comfortable easy fit.

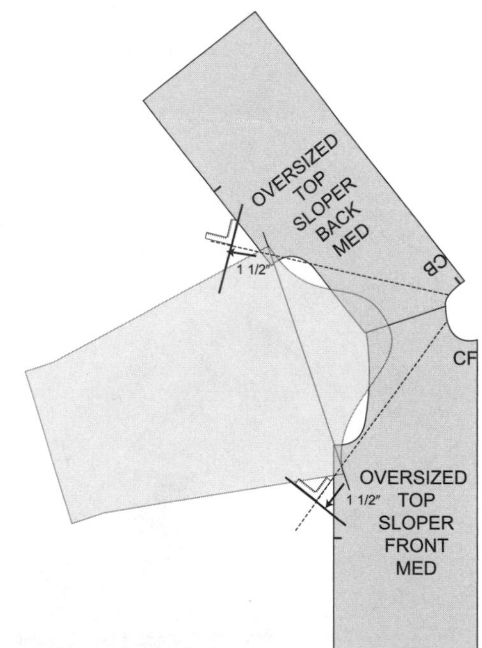

Measure down 1½″ at the underarms and square a line across to the body and the sleeve.

Notch the front and back raglan seams for construction.

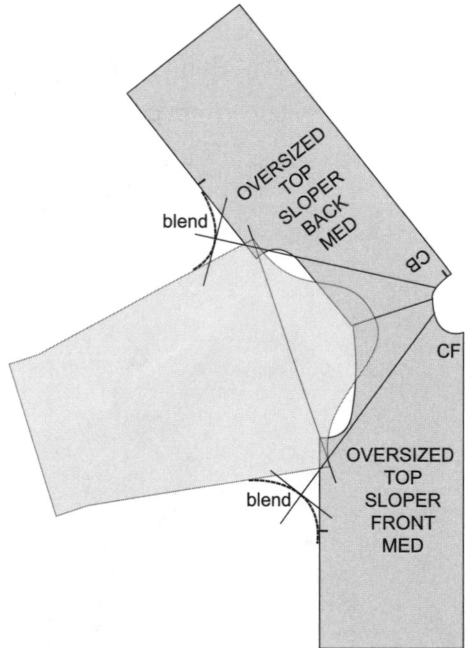

Blend a new curved underarm.

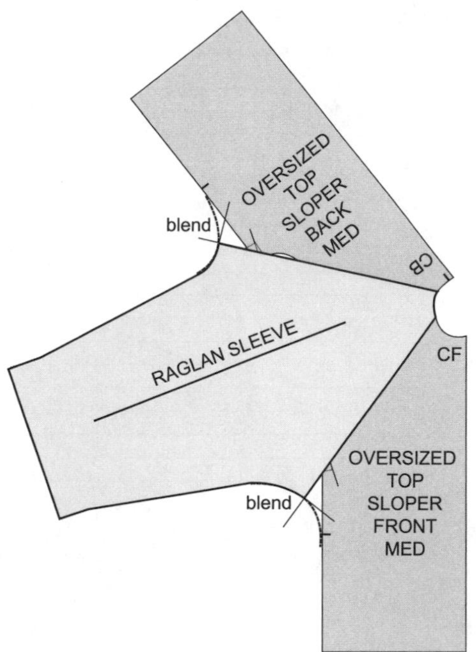

Trace out the sleeve in a contrast colored pencil or pen, so that you can see the piece clearly.

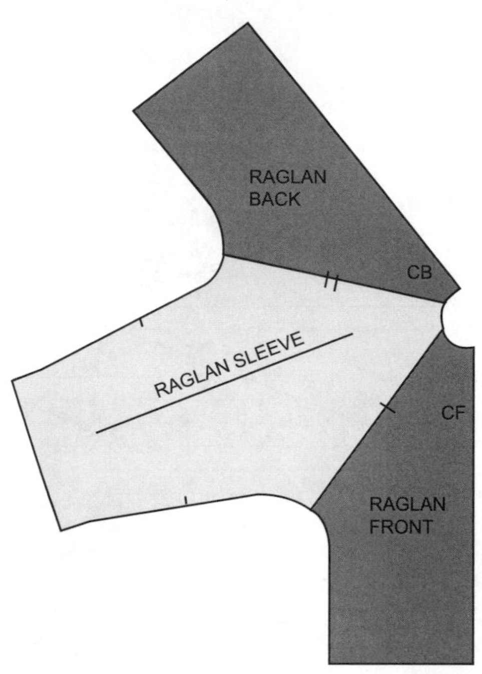

Trace out the front and back bodies in a contrast colored pencil, or pen, so that you can see the pieces clearly.

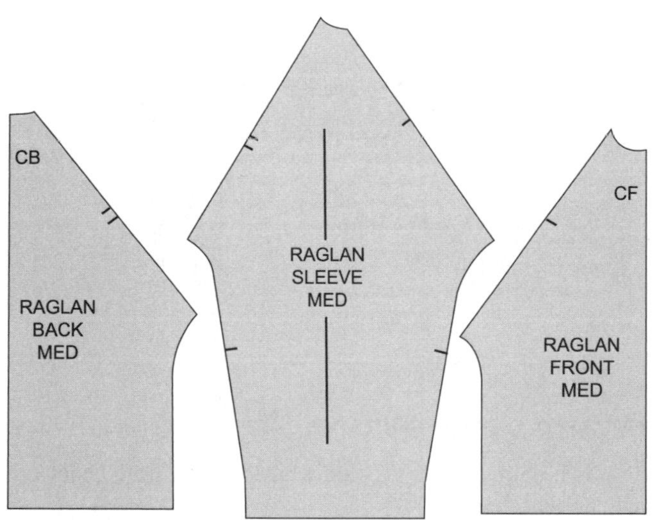

Notch, separate, and label the pattern pieces.

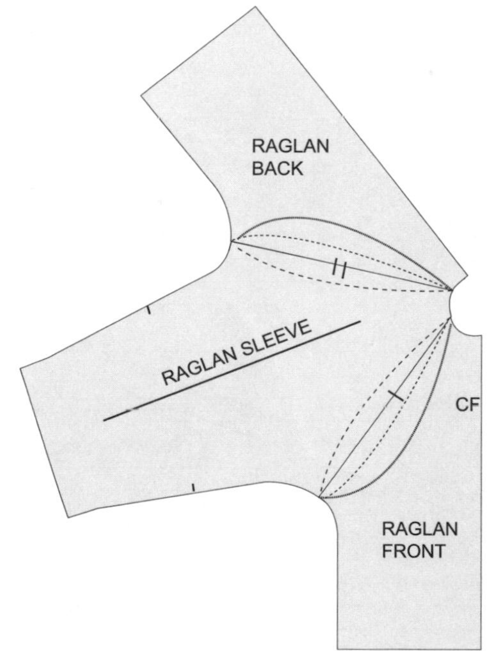

Raglan Style Options

The raglan seam may be shaped as desired.

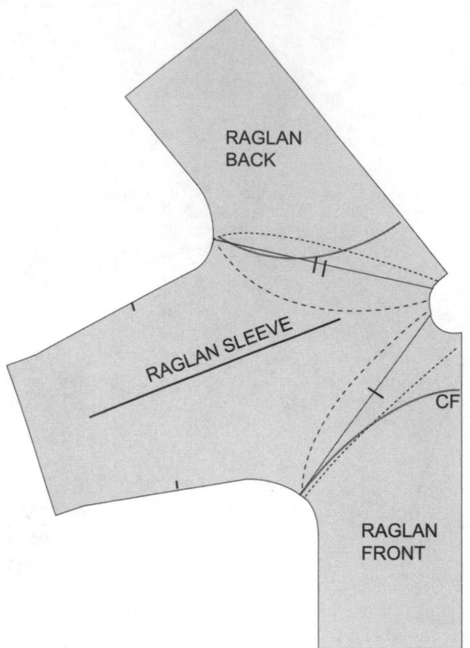

The raglan seam may be shaped as desired; it may even extend into the center front if you desire.

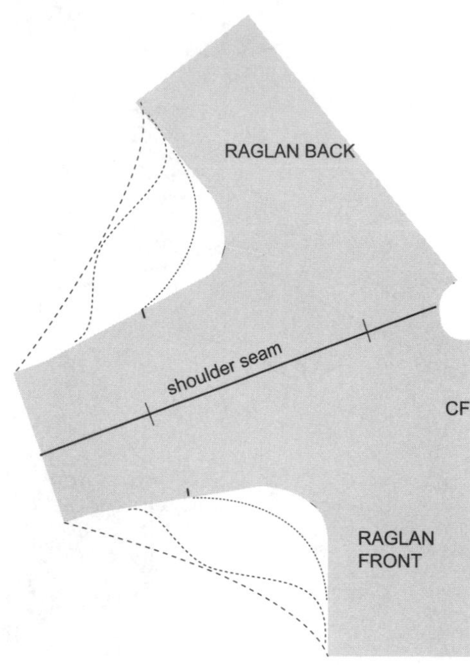

The basic raglan draft may also be used to create dolman or batwing sleeves.

Shape the underarm as desired and place a long seam down the shoulder of the garment.

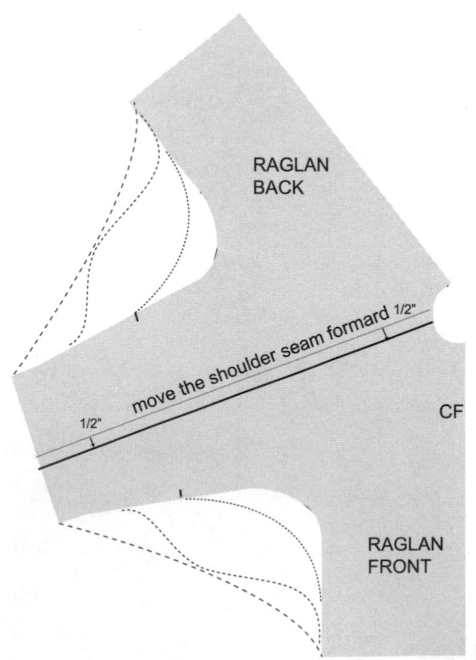

For a more comfortable fit, and to keep the sleeves from falling backwards on the customer, move the shoulder seam towards the front or the arm by ½″.

OVERSIZED POLO SHIRT

The polo shirt may be created with a knitted polo collar or a self collar.

Knit collars are purchased in different lengths:

Nevertheless, many manufacturers simply knit one size and either stretch it to fit the neckline, or ease it into a smaller neckline.

XS	13
S	14″
M	15″
L	16″
XL	17″

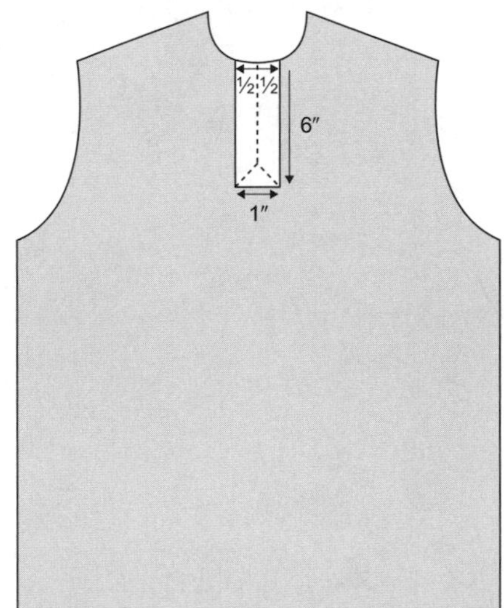

Draft the placket on top of the top draft, so you can see and understand how it all fits together.

Draft the slit as deep as you wish, illustrated here at 6″.

Then draft the placket to finish at 1″ wide.

The placket is 1″ wide and will fit into an opening of 1″ wide.

The two plackets will overlap for buttons and buttonholes.

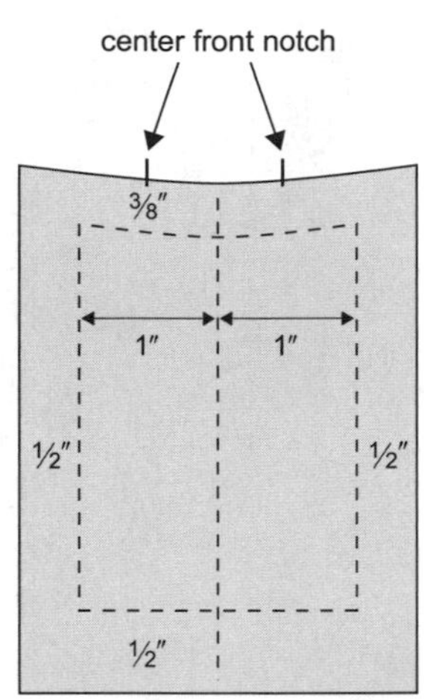

Trace out the placket as illustrated and add seam allowances.

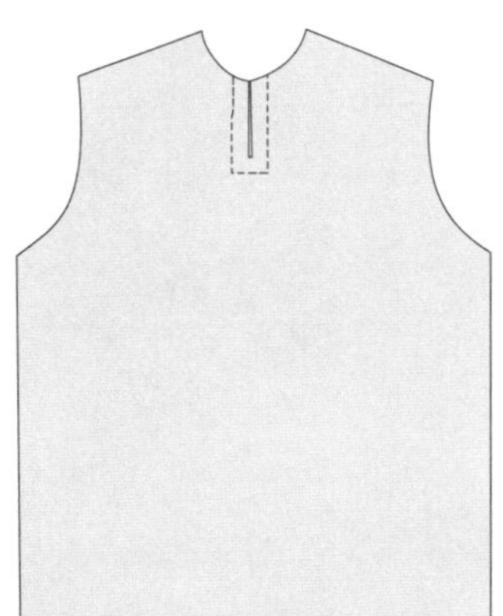

Indicate with a slit or a notch the center front placement of the placket on the front of the top.

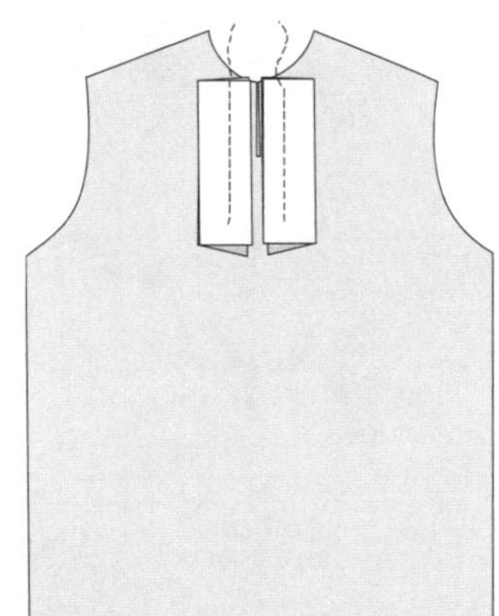

To sew:

Fuse the placket pieces to re-enforce them for buttons and buttonholes.
Fold both plackets in half.
Line up both plackets, folded, with raw edges touching.
Sew at ½″ stopping ½″ before the ends of the plackets.
Clip the slit all the way until 1′ before the end.
Clip a Y in the slit.

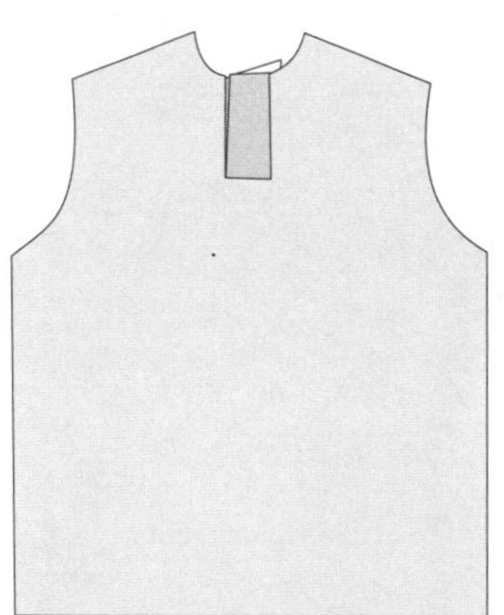

Fold each placket towards the inside.

Sew across the bottom, catching the little triangle.

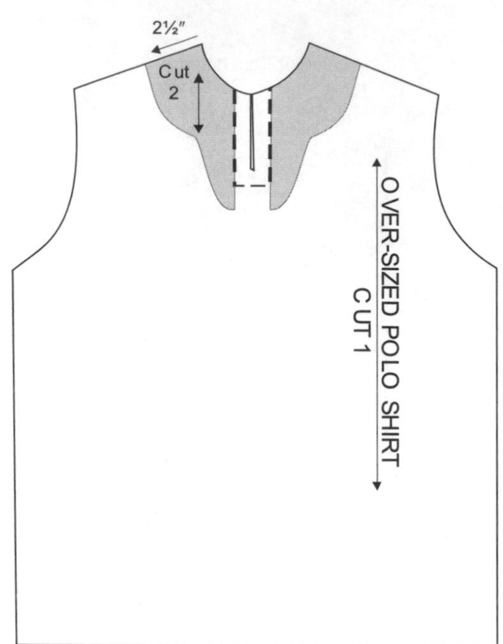

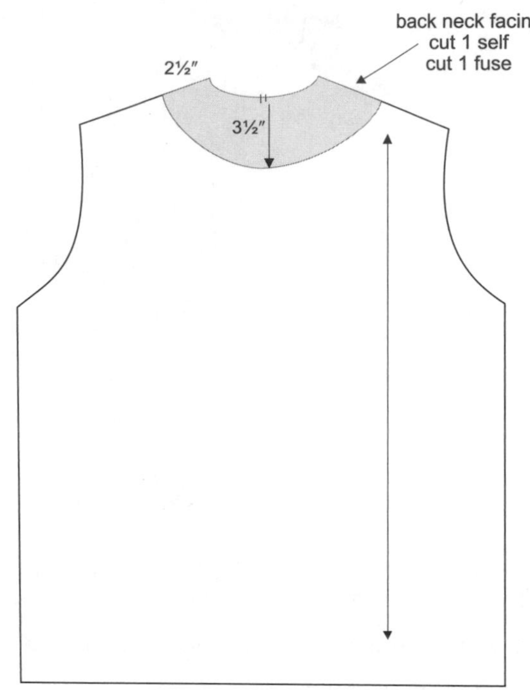

POLO COLLAR FACINGS

You may also create a facing for a style with a placket.

Make the back facing longer than the front, since it will be viewed when on the hanger.

Make the back placket 3½″ down at the center back.

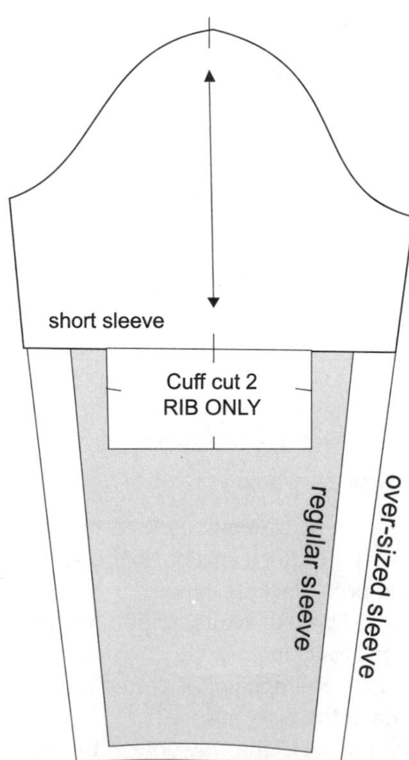

OVERSIZED SHORT SLEEVE WITH RIBBED CUFF

A rib cuff still needs to fit snugly on the arm even though the garment is oversized.

It must be made 10% smaller than the original sloper, before enlarging.

Assignment #1: Hoodie with Kangaroo Pocket

Create an oversized hoodie with set-in sleeves, an exposed teeth zipper, rib cuffs, and waistband with a kangaroo pocket.

Assignment #2: Create an Oversized Hoodie

Create an oversized raglan hoodie with a separating zipper, rib cuffs, and waistband.

Assignment #3: Create an Oversized Polo Top

Create an oversized raglan-sleeved polo top using a purchased collar with a center front button placket.

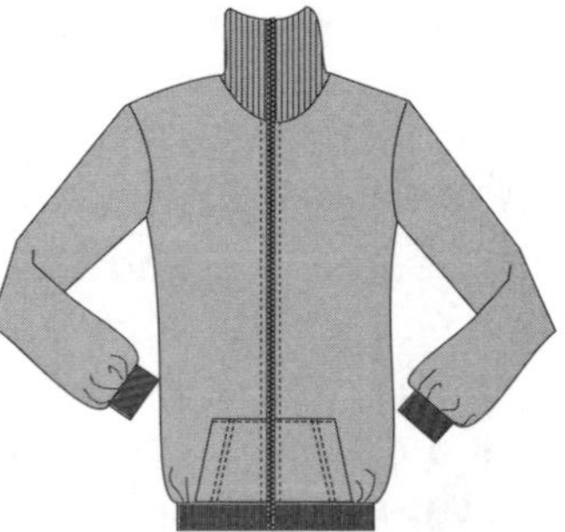

Assignment #4: Create an Oversized Turtleneck

Create an oversized turtleneck top with a separating zipper, ribbed collar, cuffs, and waistband.

Assignment #5: Create an Oversized Dolman Sleeved Top

Create a cropped oversized dolman sleeved top with rib cuffs and waistband.

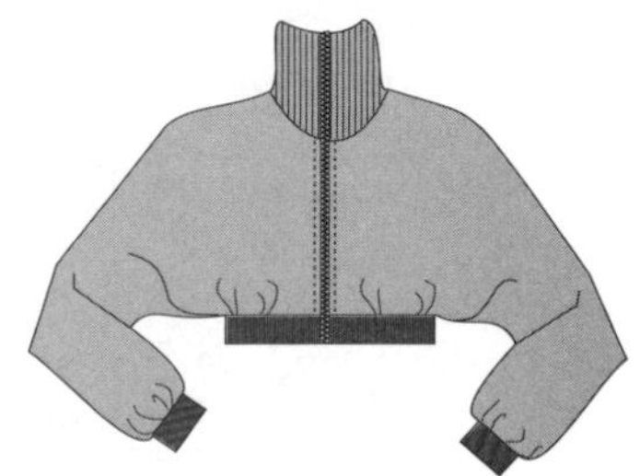

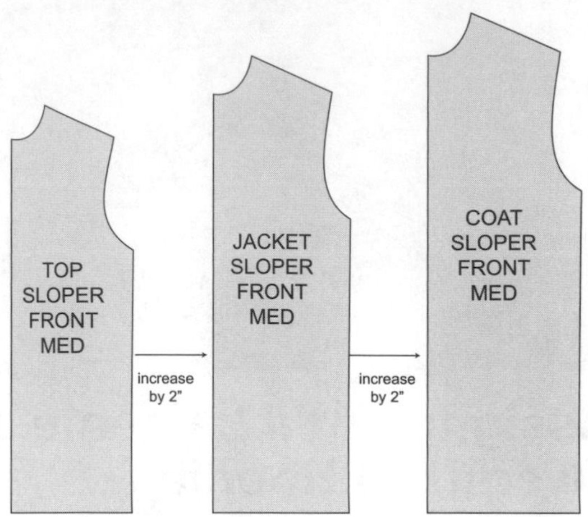

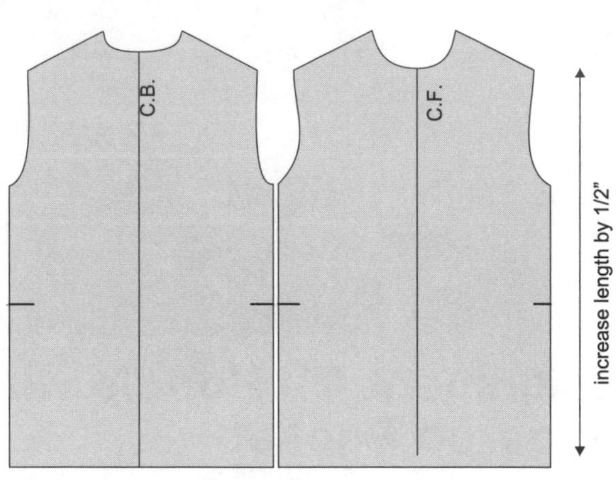

Jacket Slopers

This section will introduce the patternmaking principles used to create knit jackets and coats. The principles are similar to those already studied; however, the blocks used are slightly different. Jackets must be created slightly larger than the clothes worn underneath. The slopers must be enlarged enough to accommodate the clothes worn underneath, and knit coats must be larger than the jackets worn underneath.

Regular slopers are used to create a garment that has nothing except undergarments worn underneath. For example, summer weight knits, dresses, and tops that are worn "next to the skin."

Jacket slopers are used when the designer wants to create styles intended to be worn over other clothing, such as pullovers and cardigans. Therefore, the size must increase to accommodate the clothing underneath.

Coat slopers are used to create garments that are worn over other sweaters or jackets.

They are still all size Medium, however, they are intended to be worn over other garments.

The regular top sloper will be increased in width a total of 2″ or ½″ per panel to create a jacket sloper.

Repeat or double the measurements for coat slopers.

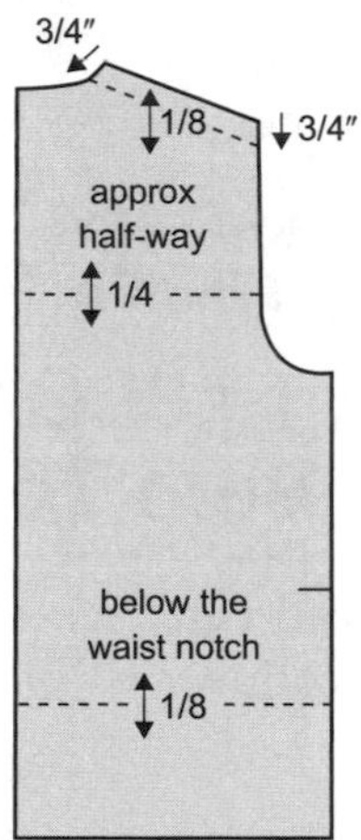

VERTICAL INCREASES

Make the increases to the back sloper and simply change the neckline to create the front sloper.

To apply the vertical increases:

Draw a line parallel to the side seams approximately ¾″ in from the side seam (increase by ⅛″ per panel).

Draw a vertical line through the shoulder approximately half-way (increase by ¼″ per panel).

Draw a vertical line 1″ in from the front along the neck edge (increase by ⅛″ per panel).

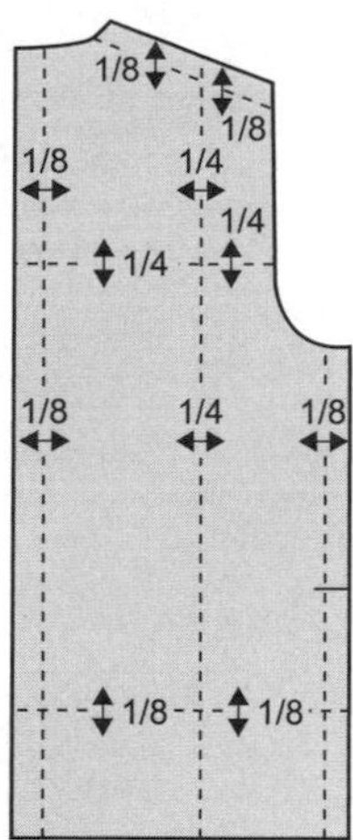

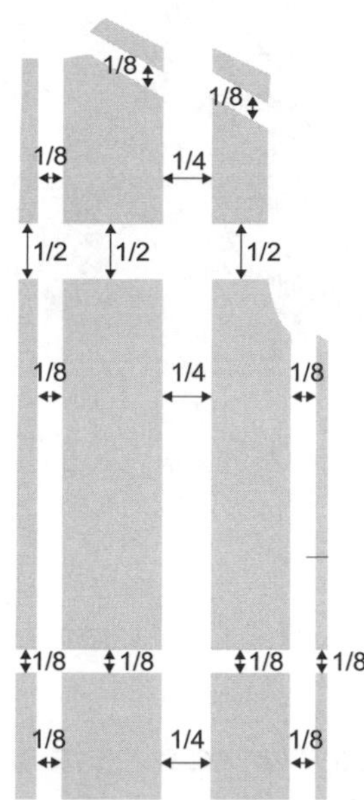

Slash and spread these areas by the amounts illustrated.

HORIZONTAL INCREASE

To apply the horizontal increases:

Draw a line parallel to the shoulder approximately ¾″ in from the shoulder (increase by ⅛ per panel).

Draw a horizontal line through the armhole area, approximately half-way through the armhole (increase by ½ per panel).

Draw a horizontal line below the waist notch (increase by ⅛ per panel).

When both directions of increases are indicated, they should look like the illustration.

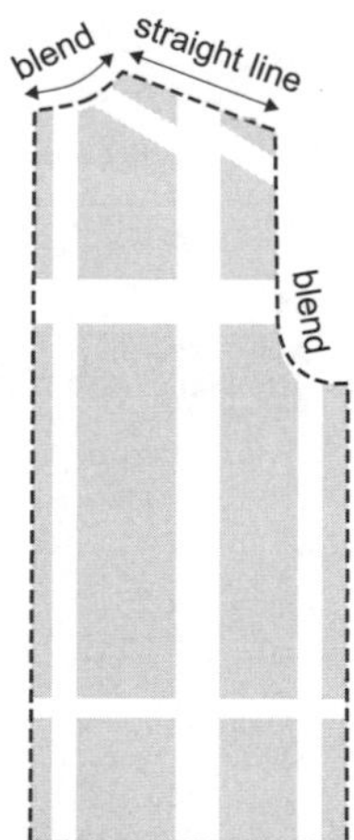

BLENDING AND TRUEING THE SLOPERS

Straighten out the shoulder by drawing a new straight line from the neck to armhole, ignoring any discrepancies.

Blend the armhole, neck, and the underarm areas.

Label as "jacket slopers" or "second layer sloper" for sweaters.

SECOND LAYER SLOPER FRONT

To create the second layer front sweater sloper, simply trace out the back sloper, when completed, and lower the front neck 1½″ and draw in a new neckline as illustrated.

Or use your front sloper and trace out the neckline.

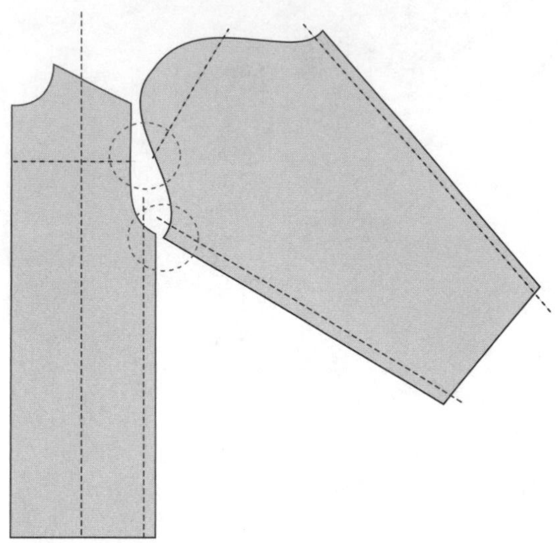

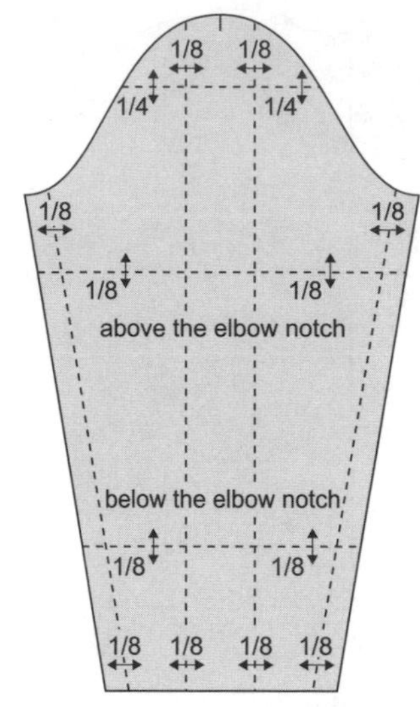

SECOND LAYER SWEATER SLEEVE SLOPERS

To find the increase areas for the sleeve, line up the sleeve with the body as illustrated and match the increase areas accordingly.

It is possible, and easier, to increase one-half of the sleeve and copy to the other side, or draft it on the fold of your paper and then open it up to trace onto oak-tag.

Mark the sleeve to correspond to the body, as illustrated.

Slash and spread once above the elbow notch.

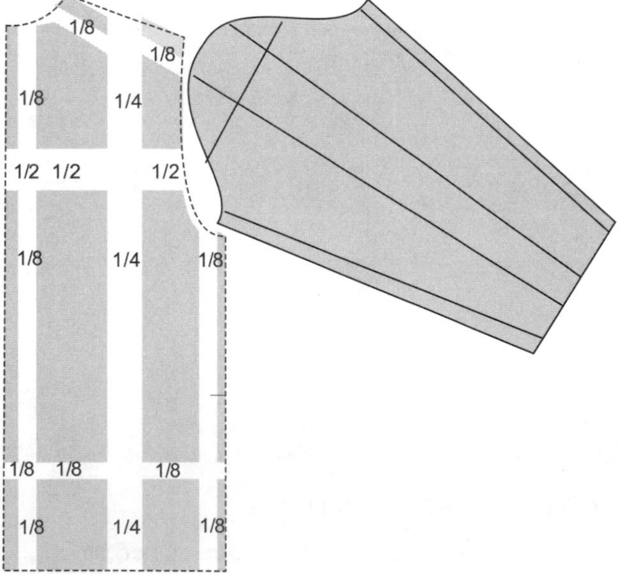

Slash and spread the sleeve sloper as illustrated to match the body increases.

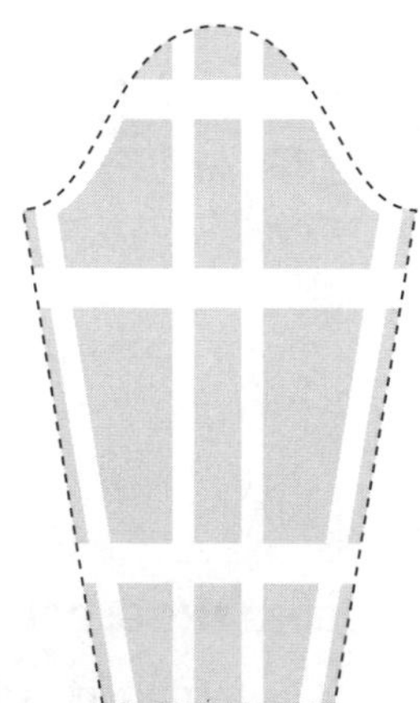

Blend the sleeve as illustrated.

You can use the original sleeve sloper as a template to blend the curved parts of the new sleeve.

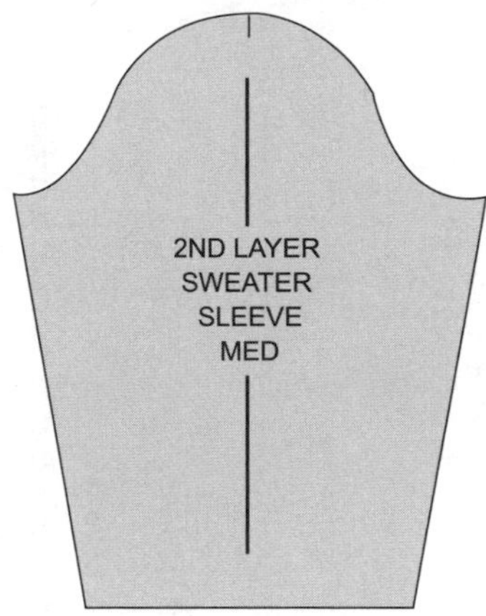

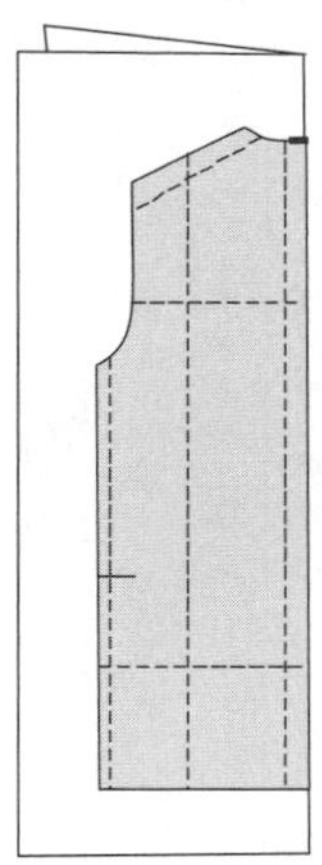

Walk the sleeve around the armhole to check for accuracy.

Label as "jacket sloper" or "second layer sloper for sweaters."

SLOPER SHIFTING TO CREATE SECOND LAYER SLOPERS

It is not always necessary to slash and spread to create second layer slopers. You can simply shift the regular sloper the required amount, and trace each part as it is enlarged. See the following:

Trace out the back neck section for approximately 1″.

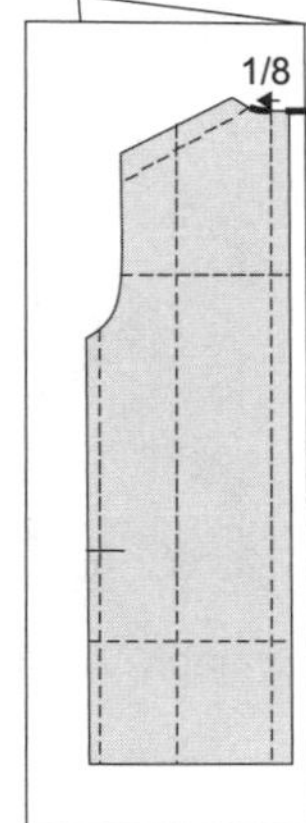

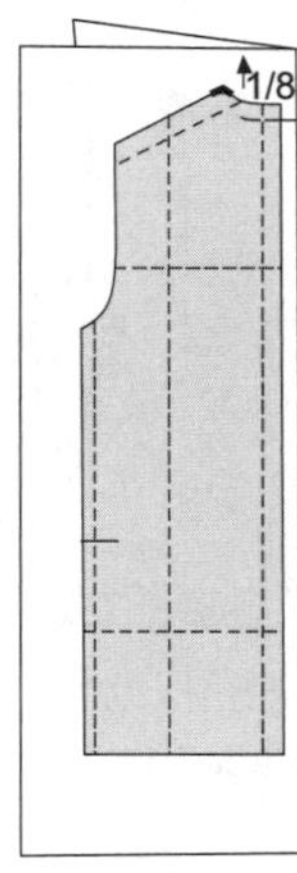

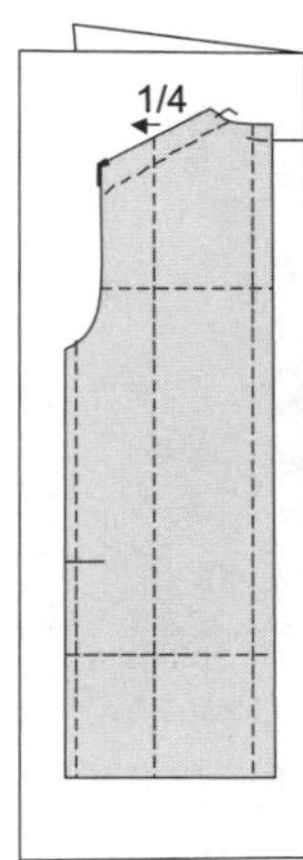

Shift the sloper to the left, ⅛″, as illustrated, and trace out the next section of the neck.

Shift the sloper up ⅛″ and trace out the next section of the neck and the corner intersection.

Because the neck will be blended with a ruler in a straight line, it is not necessary to draw the entire shoulder, just the corners.

Shift the sloper out ¼″ as illustrated and trace the next section of the shoulder, then the shoulder corner intersection.

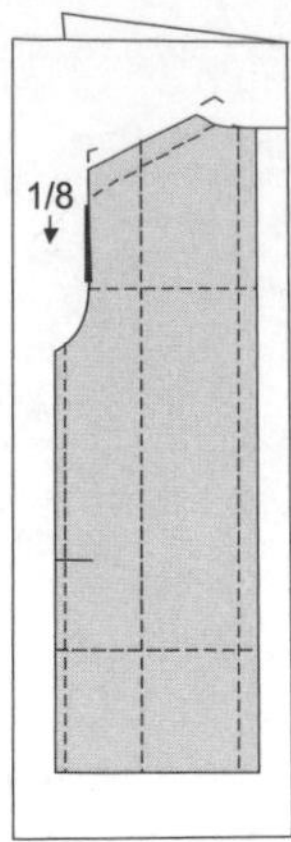

Shift the sloper down 1/8″ and trace the next section of the sloper.

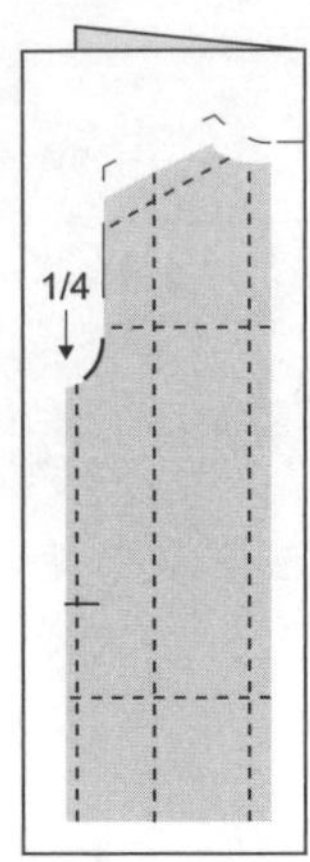

Shift the sloper down another 1/4″ and trace out the next sections.

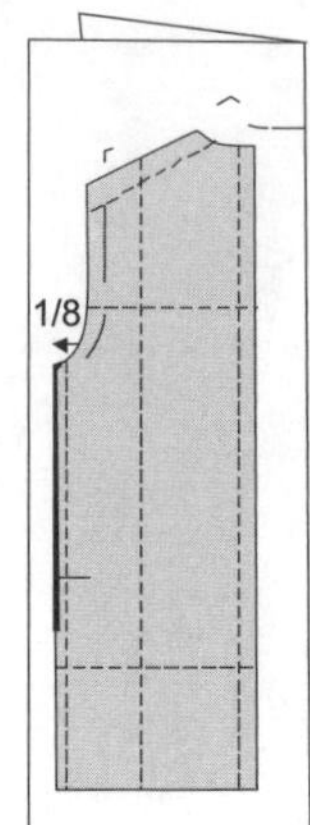

Shift the sloper out 1/8″ and trace the remainder of the underarm and the corner intersection.

Indicate the waist notch.

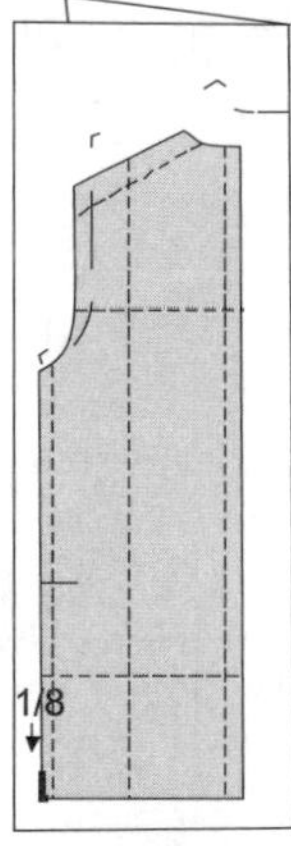

Shift the sloper down 1/8″ and trace to the hem and the hem corner intersection.

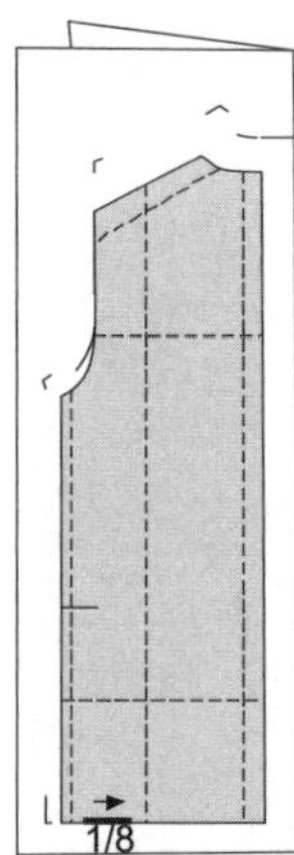

Shift the sloper back 1/8″ in the reverse direction and trace that portion of the hem.

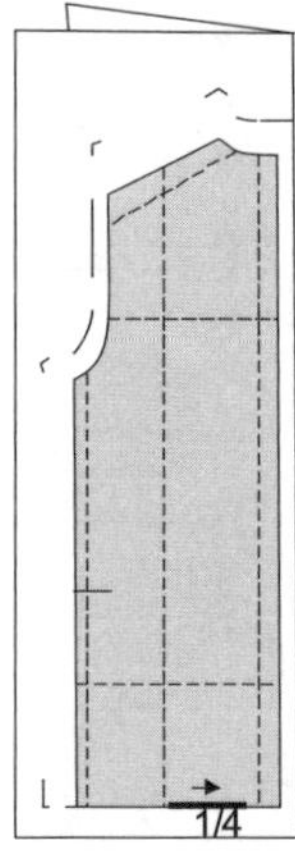

Shift the sloper back 1/4″ and trace that section of the hem.

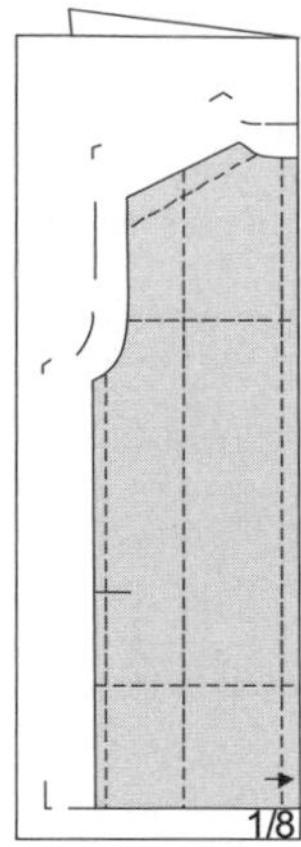

Shift the sloper over ⅛″ and trace the remaining section of the hem and the corner.

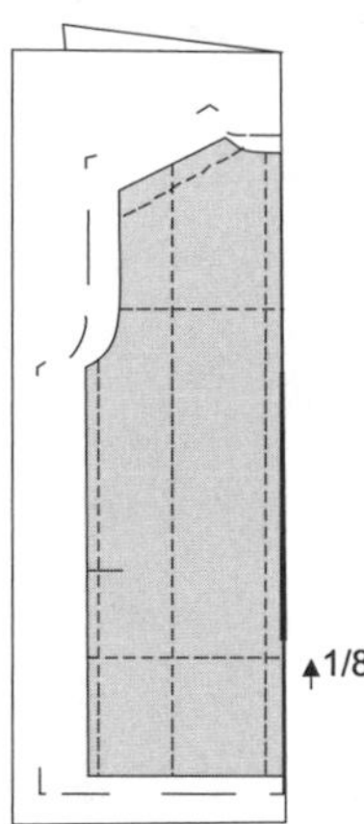

Shift the sloper back up ⅛″ and trace that portion of the center back.

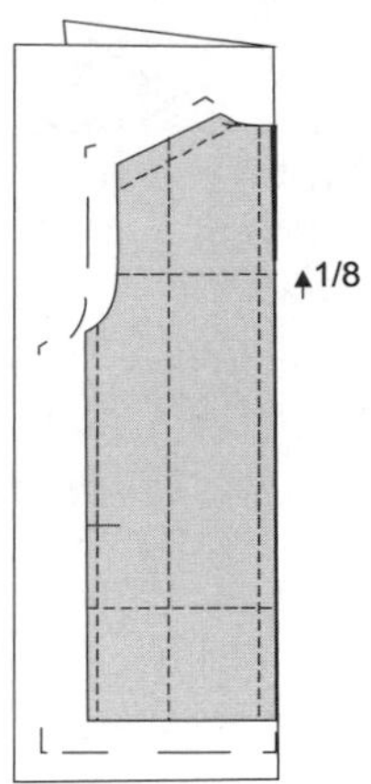

Shift the sloper up ¼″ and trace the last portion of the center back.

The sloper should have traveled a full circle and be back at the same point that it originated.

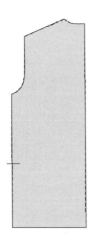

To blend:

Connect the shoulders, side seams, and hems with a straight line.

Blend the neck and underarm, using the original sloper as a curve template, so that the new sloper retains the original curves.

Note: It may look as if the neck has increased by a total of ¼″, but after blending, it should have only increased by ⅜″ due to the nature of the curves.

Repeat for the front sloper.

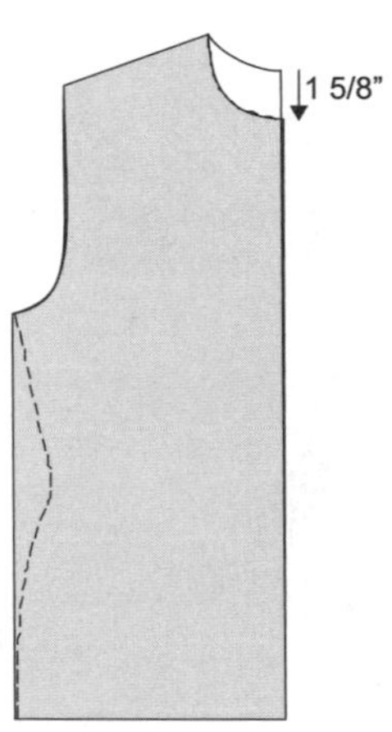

To create the front sloper:

Trace out the back sloper and make changes to the neck as illustrated.

Lower the neck 1⅝″ and bend a new neck.

Or use the original neckline as a template.

To indicate the fitted waist, trace the side seam from the original sloper.

	Extra Small	**Small**	**Medium**	**Large**	**Extra Large**
Neck drop	1 7/16	1 8/16	1 9/16	1 9/16	1 10/16

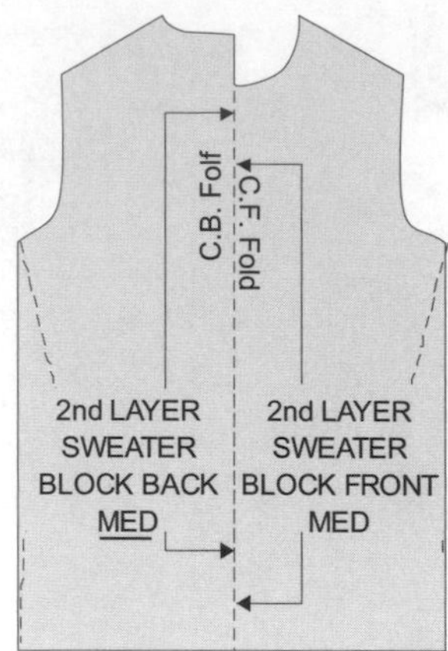

Alternate method of cutting out sweater slopers:

To save space and oak-tag, place front and back together as illustrated.

Then fold on the fold line of center/front and center/back. In order to use these slopers, you must trace the back twice and the front twice, using the center as the fold line.

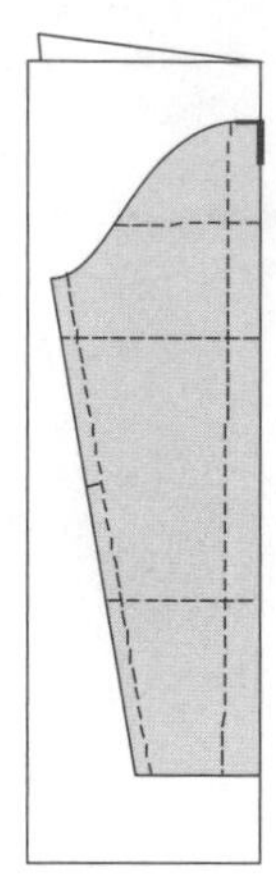

SLOPER SHIFTING TO CREATE SECOND LAYER SLEEVE SLOPERS

The sleeve sloper may be increased on the light paper fold, as half, then opened and traced onto oak-tag.

Trace the first section of the sleeve, as indicated.

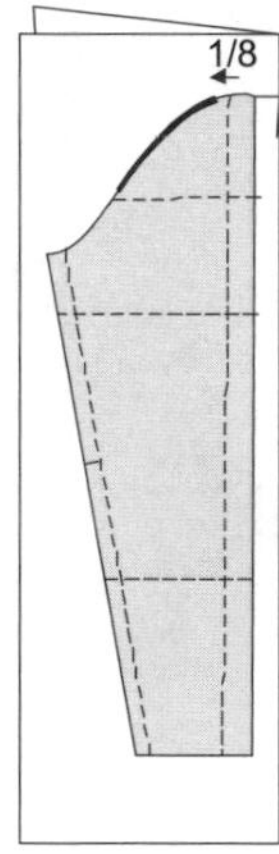

Shift the sloper out 1/8″ and trace the next section.

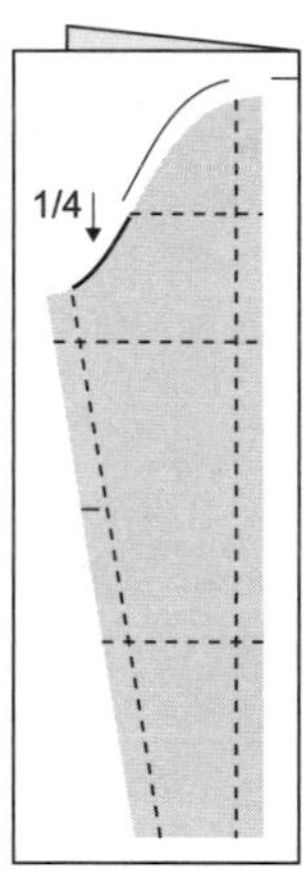

Shift the sloper down 1/4″ and trace the next section.

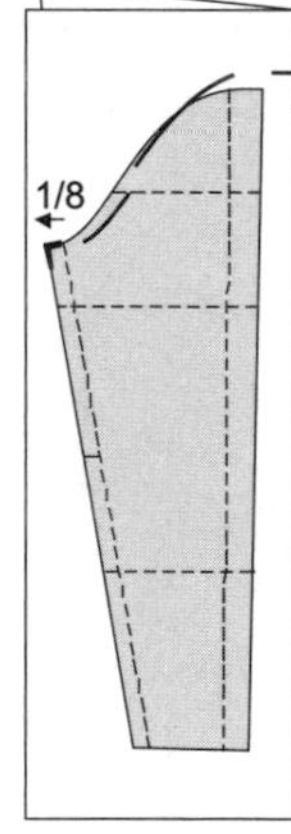

Shift the sloper out 1/8″ and trace, as indicated.

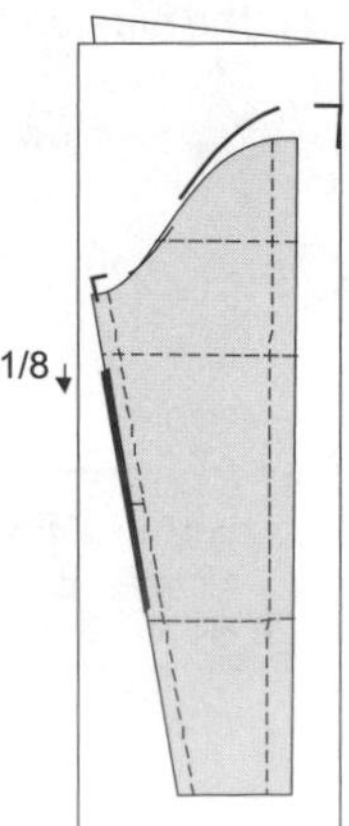

Shift the sloper down 1/8″.

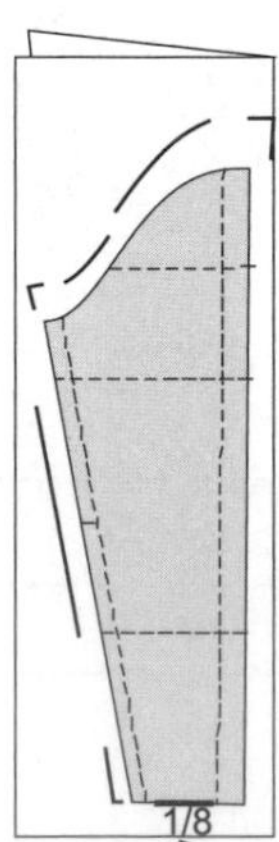

Shift the sloper back in and trace.

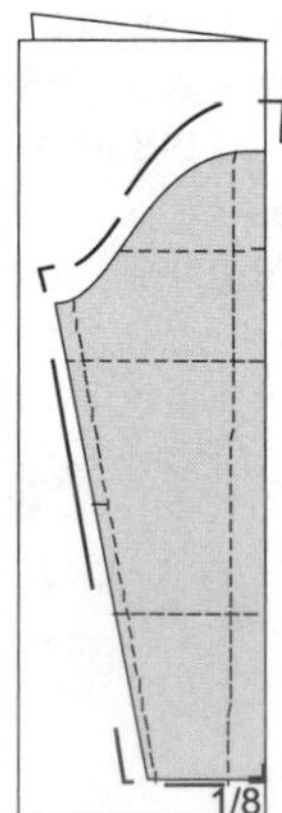

Shift the sloper in 1/8″.

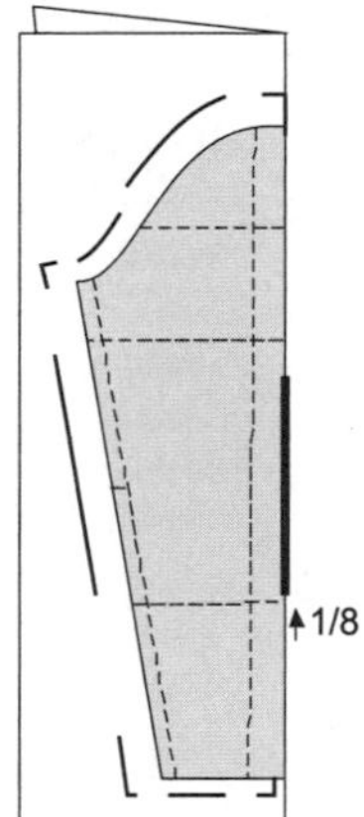

Shift the sloper back up ⅛″ and trace as indicated.

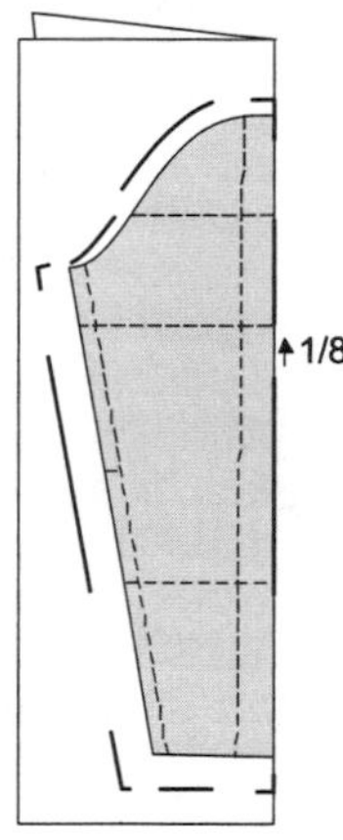

Shift the sloper up ⅛″.

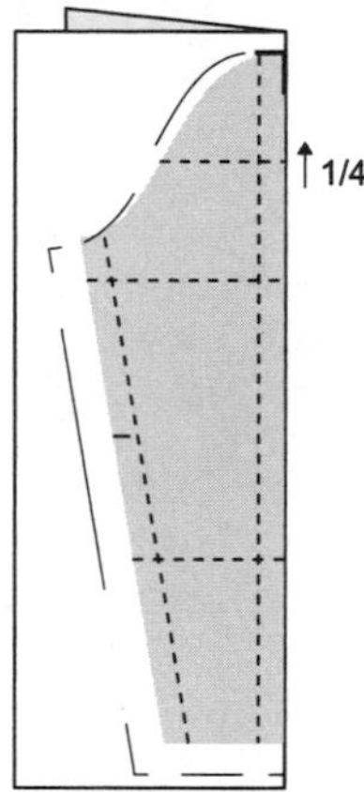

Shift the sloper up ¼″ as indicated. You should have gone full circle and be exactly where you started.

Cut out the paper sloper on the fold, open it up, and trace again onto the oak-tag.

Always cut the sleeve full/open, and do not put a crease in your sleeve sloper, as it will wear out along that edge too fast.

Assignment #6

Create your own version of Style # 10-002, zip front oversized turtleneck with a front facing and back neck twill tape.

Create a 3″ high, finished collar.

Use a 24″ separating zipper.

Add a 1½″ hem allowance and hand hem, or blind hem the sweater.

Cut and sew this garment using a purchased sweater knit.

Test Your Knowledge of the Material in this Chapter

1. How much larger should the oversized sloper be?
2. What size is the oversized sloper?
3. When should you use an oversized sloper?
4. How can you figure out how much larger to make the sleeve?
5. How can we ensure that the ribbed cuffs fit snugly?

CHAPTER 12

Four-Way-Stretch

About This Chapter

This chapter introduces the principles of two-way- and four-way-stretch fabrics. The patterns are identical for both types of stretch; the difference becomes apparent when the customer wears the garment, and areas of stretch do not return to their original shape, causing baggy knees, crotches, waists, and so forth.

stretches across the fabric

Stretches only across the fabric, and the stretch is entirely derived from the stitches used when creating the fabric. Garments should be made with the stretch going around the body.

stretches across the fabric
as well as lengthwise

Stretches across as well as up and down the fabric. The additional stretch is derived from the texturing and crimping of the yarn used to knit the fabric.

stretches across the fabric
as well as lengthwise
and has spandex added

Stretches across as well as up and down the fabric. Supplementary stretch is added to the yarn before knitting by using spandex/Lycra®.

Most knits stretch more in one direction than in the other. Many knits only stretch in the crosswise direction. When using knits for dresses, jackets, pants, skirts, and tops and sleeves, the experienced patternmaker always utilizes the built-in stretch of knits so that the direction of stretch encircles the figure. However, the greatest degree of stretch should go up and down the torso for bodysuits, catsuits, leotards, or any other garment that passes through the crotch, to allow for maximum mobility; one-way-stretch knits are rarely used for these garments, because when the customer raised her arms it would be uncomfortable in the crotch.

Two-way- and four-way-stretch patterns are created identically, meaning the same patterns may be used interchangeably.

Please note, however, that garments made with two-way-stretch will often sag on the body at the knees, elbows, and crotch because the fabric doesn't have any memory or elasticity and will not return to its original shape when worn.

Also note that one-way-stretch patterns may be used with four-way-stretch fabrics as long as the garment does not need lengthwise reductions. For example, a one-way-stretch skirt may be cut using a four-way-stretch fabric because there is nothing holding the skirt down at the bottom hem (referred to as an anchor), so the lengthwise direction of stretch is not utilized at all.

Distinct and separate four-way-stretch patterns are only necessary when the stretch of the garment is anchored through the crotch, such as with catsuits, bodysuits, leotards, and one-piece swimsuits.

Four-Way-Stretch Slopers

Rule of thumb: 5″ will stretch to 10″ or more in both directions.

Four-way-stretch garments are not just for swimsuits and activewear. The increased use of spandex in more and more knits results in more resilient fabrics that don't bag or sag when worn. When you use super-four-way-stretch fabrics, the pattern can and should be simpler because of the fabric's innate ability to mold around the body.

Many four-way-stretch fabrics don't necessarily look like activewear fabrics, so the garments created with them don't have to be activewear. Because knitted fabrics with spandex have excellent stretch and excellent memory, they allow us to create form-fitting garments that hold their shape without the need for tailoring or for zippers and other fasteners.

For maximum mobility and tight fit, four-way-stretch garments must have negative ease, meaning that they must be smaller than the actual body. When drafting for super stretch, the designer must reduce the body measurements to compensate for the stretch. While each combination of knit stitches and fiber content requires an individual solution, an average 10 percent reduction applied to vertical and horizontal measurements will result in a basic fit. Because it is much easier to take in an oversized garment than to let out a too-tight garment, note that all measurements should be exaggerated until after the fitting.

Four-Way-Stretch Reductions

Rule of thumb: 10 percent smaller in crosswise direction without any reductions in lengthwise direction; 10 percent smaller in the lengthwise direction.

Use these measurements when drafting slopers for fabrics that stretch 100 percent in both directions.

Only four-way-stretch slopers are used for garments that pass through the crotch and shoulders, in order to utilize the lengthwise stretch.

These reductions may also be used for two-way-stretch fabrics.

MEASUREMENT CHART

The following draft will use the "Misses Medium" measurements; however, for a personal sloper, substitute the measurements in the standard column or use the size range that you wish.

#	Measurement	Standard	Reduce by 5% × .90 = 10%	Extra Extra Small	Extra Small	Small	Medium	Large	Extra Large	Extra Extra Large
1	Bust	34½	× .90	28⅜	29¼	30⅛	31	32	33¼	34⅝
2	Waist	26½	× .90	21⅛	22	23	23⅞	24¾	26⅛	27½
3	Hip	37½	× .90	31	32	32⅞	33¾	34⅝	36	37⅜
4	Crotch depth	10⅜	× .90	9	9⅛	9¼	9⅜	9½	9⅝	9⅝
5	Waist to knee	23⅜	× .90	20¾	20⅞	22⅛	22¼	22⅜	22½	22⅝
6	Waist to ankle	39¼	× .90	34⅝	34⅞	37	37¼	37½	37¾	38
7	Ankle	8⅛	× .90	7	7⅛	7¼	7⅜	7⅜	7½	7⅝
8	Knee	14⅛	× .90	12	12¼	12½	12¾	13	13⅛	13⅜
9	Front crotch	2⅜	× .90	2	2	2	2⅛	2⅛	2¼	2⅜
10	Back crotch	3⅛	× .90	2⅞	3	3	3⅛	3¼	3⅜	3½
11	Crotch angle	1⅛	× .90	1	1	1	1	1⅛	1⅛	1⅛
12	Nape to waist	16⅜	× .90	14⅛	14¼	15⅜	15½	15¾	16	16¼
13	Back neck	2½	no reduction	2⅜	2⅜	2½	2½	2½	2½	2½
14	Back neck rise	⅞	no reduction	¾	¾	⅞	⅞	⅞	⅞	⅞
15	Shoulder length	5¾	no reduction	5⅛	5¼	5½	5¾	6	6¼	6½
16	Across back	7⅜	no reduction	7	7⅛	7¼	7⅜	7½	7⅝	7¾
17	Sleeve length	23⅛	no reduction	22¾	22⅞	23	23⅛	23¼	23⅜	23½
18	Shoulder pitch	1½	no reduction	1⅜	1½	1½	1½	1½	1½	1½
19	Bicep	11½	× .90	9⅜	9⅝	10	10⅜	10¾	11	11⅜
20	Wrist	6⅝	× .90	5	5¼	5⅝	6	6¼	6⅝	7
21	Neck	14⅞	no reduction	14½	14⅝	14¾	14⅞	15	15⅛	15¼
22	Bust span	7	× .90	5⅞	6	6⅛	6¼	6⅜	6½	6¾
23	Bust level	10⅜	× .90	9	9⅛	9¾	9⅞	10	10⅛	10¼
24	Upper chest	32								

Four-Way-Stretch Sloper Draft

A-B = nape to waist

	Extra Extra Small	Extra Small	Small	Medium	Large	Extra Large	Extra Extra Large
Nape to Waist	14⅛	14 ¼	15⅜	15½	15 ¾	16	16¼
Half-way	7	7⅛	7⅞	7 ¾	7⅞	8	8⅛

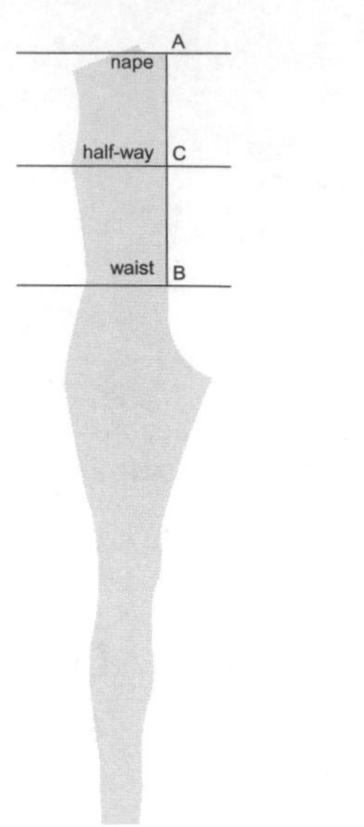

A-C = half of A-B

Square a guideline at A-B-C.

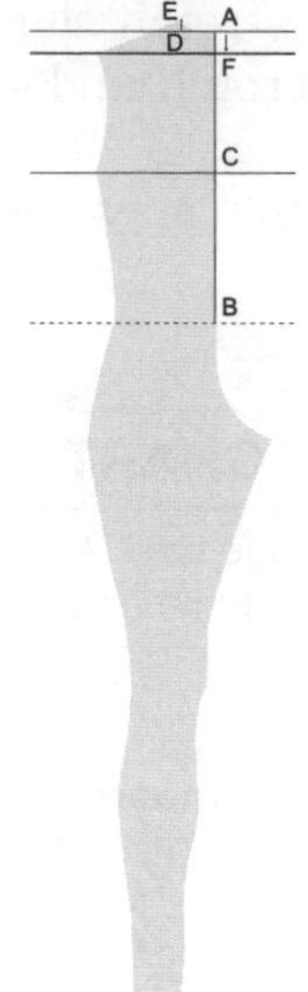

A-D = back neck

A-E = Back neck rise

A-F = shoulder pitch

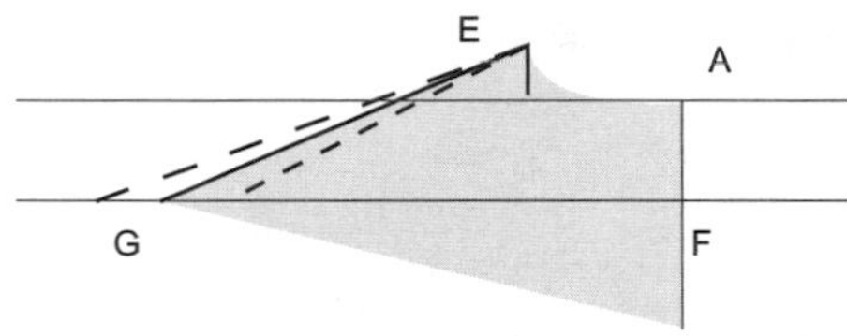

E-G = shoulder length (goes from point F to wherever that measurement lines up on line F, the shoulder pitch line).

Square a line from the shoulder at point E past line F, the shoulder pitch line.

Since the front will be drafted on top of the back, the measurements need to be divided into four.

	Extra Extra Small	Extra Small	Small	Medium	Large	Extra Large	Extra Extra Large
$\frac{1}{4}$ of waist	$5\frac{5}{8}$	$5\frac{7}{8}$	$6\frac{3}{8}$	$6\frac{7}{8}$	$7\frac{5}{8}$	$8\frac{3}{8}$	$9\frac{3}{8}$
$\frac{1}{4}$ of hip	$8\frac{3}{8}$	$8\frac{5}{8}$	$9\frac{1}{8}$	$9\frac{5}{8}$	$10\frac{3}{8}$	$11\frac{1}{8}$	$12\frac{1}{8}$
Crotch depth	$10\frac{1}{2}$	$10\frac{5}{8}$	$10\frac{4}{8}$	$10\frac{5}{8}$	$10\frac{7}{8}$	$11\frac{1}{8}$	$11\frac{3}{8}$
$\frac{1}{3}$ of crotch depth	$3\frac{1}{2}$	$3\frac{1}{2}$	$3\frac{1}{2}$	$3\frac{1}{2}$	$3\frac{5}{8}$	$3\frac{3}{4}$	$3\frac{3}{4}$

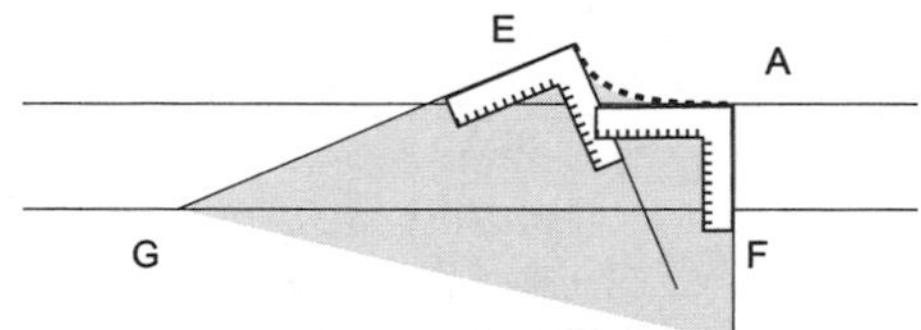

BACK NECK

Draw a curved line as illustrated. Remember to square for ½″ from E and ½″ from A. Draw free hand and clean up the line with your curved ruler.

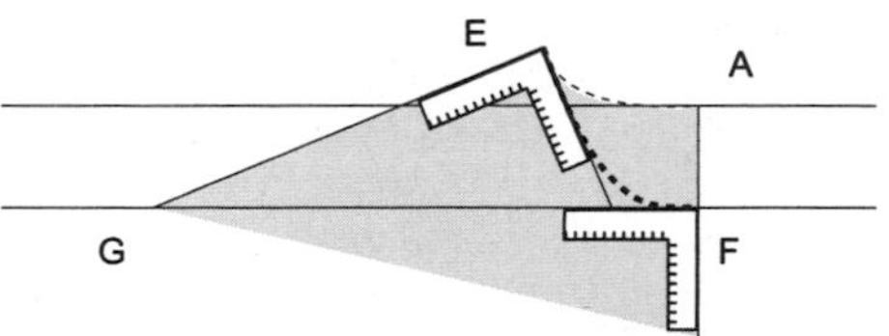

FRONT NECK

Draw a curved line as illustrated. Remember to square for ½″ from E and ½″ for F. Draw free hand and clean up the line with your curved ruler.

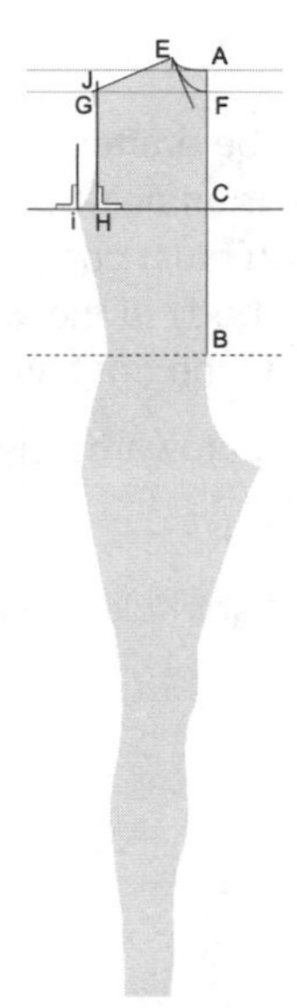

C-H = across back measurement, square up to shoulder, and label the point where it intersects the shoulder line point J (it does not meet up with point G).

C-I = bust measurement.

K = half of H-J.

H-K = ½″ on a bias angle.

	Extra Extra Small	Extra Small	Small	Medium	Large	Extra Large	Extra Extra Large
Across back	7	7⅛	7¼	7⅜	7½	7⅝	7¾
Bust	7⅛	7⅜	7½	7¾	8	8⅜	8⅝

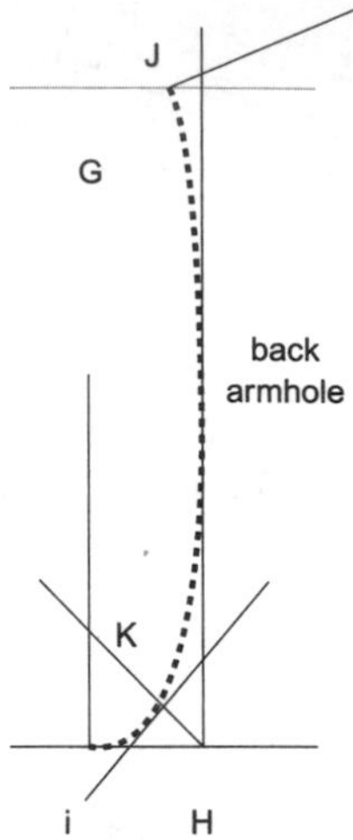

Draw the armhole by connecting points J-K-I. Draw freehand, then clean up the line with your curved ruler.

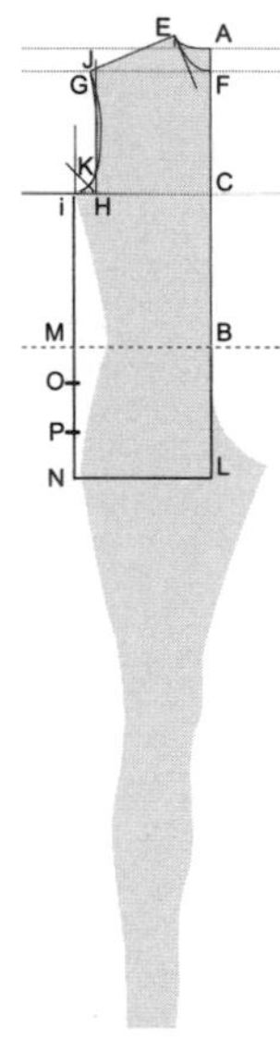

C-I = bust

B-L = crotch depth

L-M = hip

Connect all points with straight lines, B-L-N-M-I.

M-N = divide into thirds.

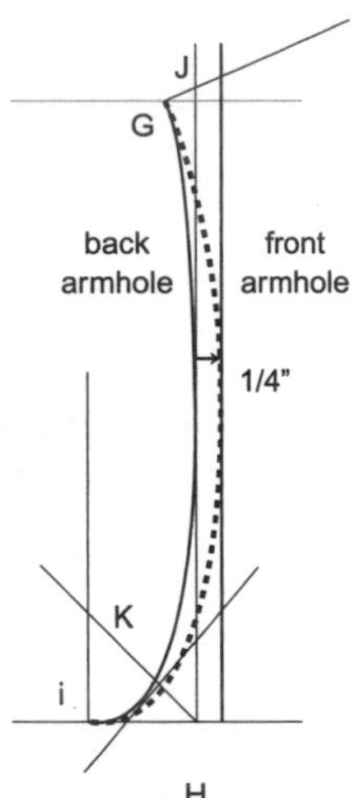

Because the sleeve will be drafted on the fold without any difference between the front and back, and consequently no armhole notches, you must compensate for the necessary difference in the body at the armhole. The back armhole is 1/4″ larger than the front armhole.

Draw a guideline of 1/4″, in towards the body.

Draw front armhole, G-K-I.

Blend and smooth front armhole curve.

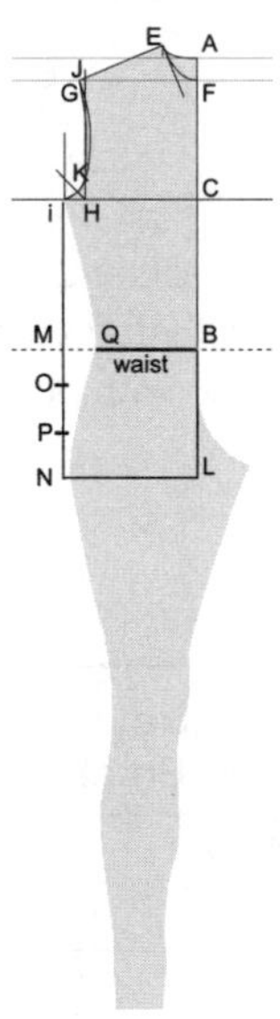

B-Q = waist measurement.

	Extra Extra Small	Extra Small	Small	Medium	Large	Extra Large	Extra Extra Large
Hip	31	32	32 7/8	33 3/4	34 5/8	36	37 3/8
Crotch depth	9	9 1/8	9 1/4	9 3/8	9 1/2	9 5/8	9 5/8
Thirds	3	3	3 1/8	3 1/8	3 1/8	3 1/4	3 1/4
Waist	21 1/8	22	23	23 7/8	24 3/4	26 1/8	27 1/2

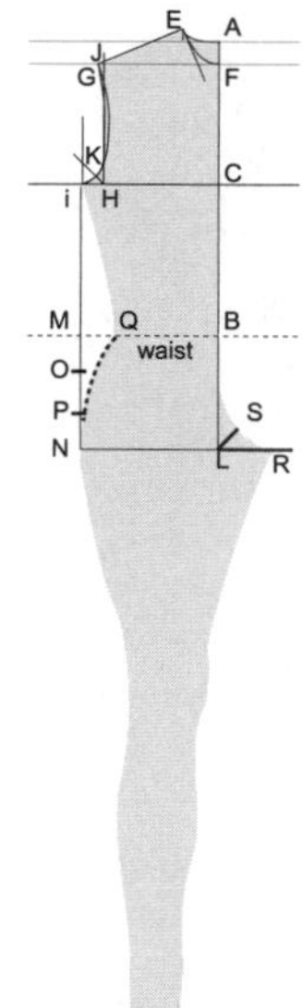

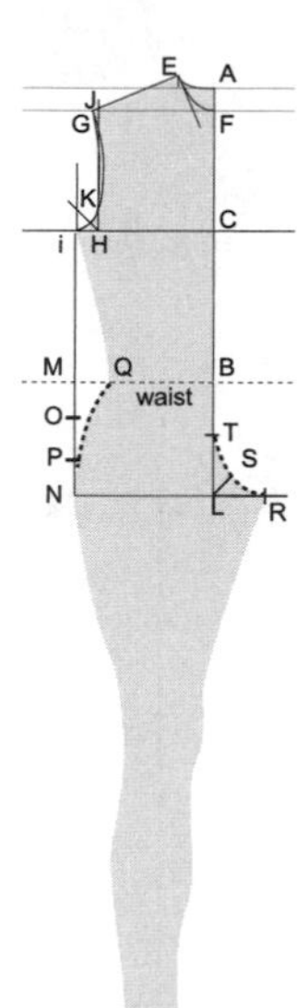

Q-P = draw a curved line

If you place #4 of the variform curve at the waist point Q, then pivot the curve until it reaches point P, you can achieve a nice hip curve. Alternatively, you can exaggerate the hip and correct it in first fitting.

L-R = front crotch extension

L-S = crotch angle, on the bias

T-S-R = To draw a balanced crotch, place a mark up the curve an amount equal to the crotch extension, and draw the curve through all three points, T-S-R.

Draw the curve by hand and clean it up using the French curves.

	Extra Extra Small	Extra Small	Small	Medium	Large	Extra Large	Extra Extra Large
Front crotch	2	2	2	2 1/8	2 1/8	2 1/4	2 3/8
Crotch angle	1	1	1	1	1 1/8	1 1/8	1 1/8
Grain	4 7/8	5	5 1/8	5 1/4	5 3/8	5 5/8	4 7/8
Waist to ankle	34 5/8	34 7/8	37	37 1/4	37 1/2	37 3/4	38
Waist to knee	20 3/4	20 7/8	22 1/8	22 1/4	22 3/8	22 1/2	22 5/8

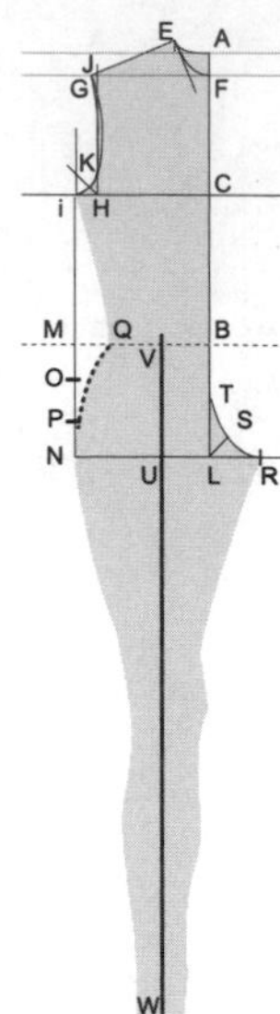

W = half way between point N and point R

Square a line up from W all the way to the waist and label point V.

At V, square down to ankle and label (waist to ankle).

V-W = waist to ankle

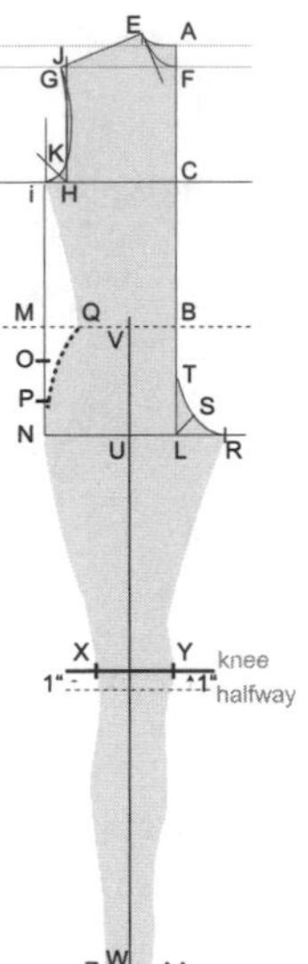

To locate the knee, find the halfway mark between point U and point W, then measure an additional 1″ up. Note that this is between the crotch and the ankle, not the waist and ankle.

X-Y = knee measurement

X-Z = knee measurement

W-AA = ankle measurement

W-BB = ankle measurement

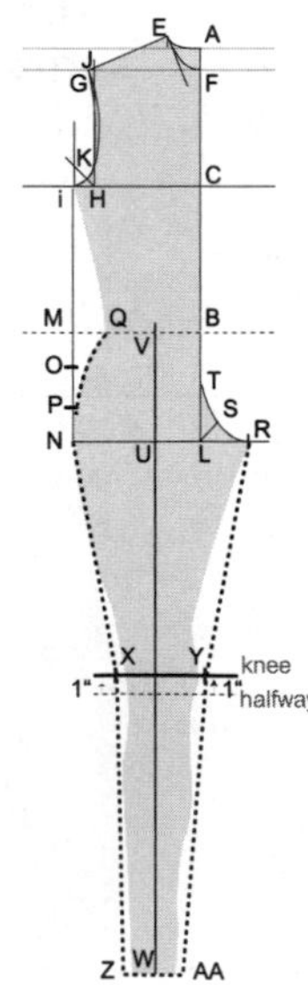

N-X-Z-AA-Y-R = connect with straight lines

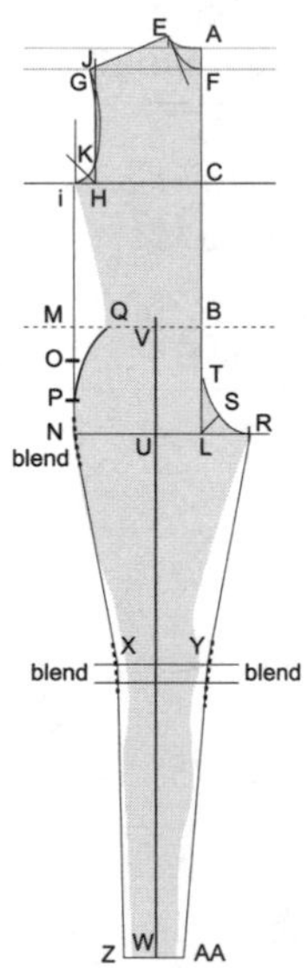

Blend the hip (point N) and knee curves (points X and Y).

	Extra Extra Small	Extra Small	Small	Medium	Large	Extra Large	Extra Extra Large
Knee	3	3 1/8	3 1/8	3 1/8	3 1/4	3 1/4	3 3/8
Ankle	1 3/4	1 3/4	1 3/4	1 7/8	1 7/8	1 7/8	1 7/8
Back crotch	2 7/8	3	3	3 1/8	3 1/4	3 3/8	3 1/2
Front crotch	2	2	2	2 1/8	2 1/8	2 1/4	2 3/8
Additional	7/8	1	1	1	1	1 1/8	1 1/8

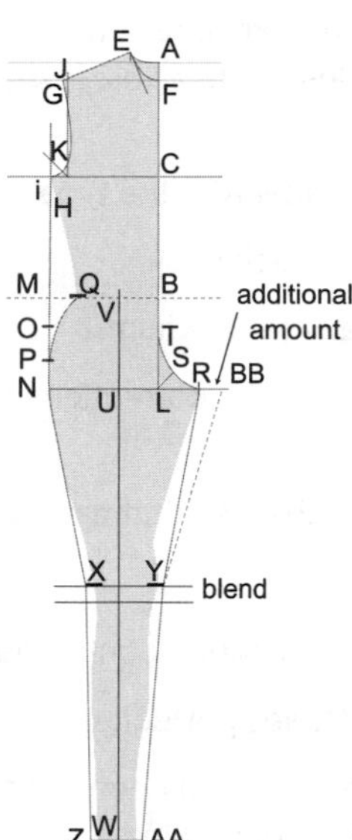

R-BB = additional amount

Because this draft is on top of the front dart, and you've already added the front crotch amount, it is only necessary to add the additional amount to equal the back crotch total.

BB-Y = connect with a straight line

At Y, blend a smooth curve.

Place notches at waist, hip, and knees.

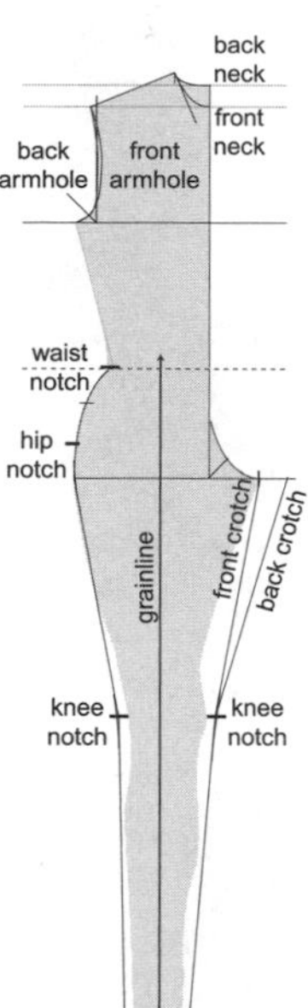

Illustration shows how the front and back are interrelated and which lines are required.

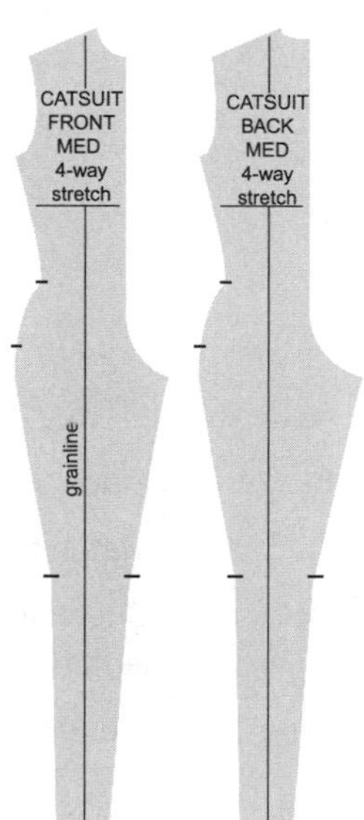

Trace and separate the front from the back.

Label the slopers with two (2) grain lines, because it may be cut either way.

To correct the fit throughout the hips, waist, and legs, you must make up a sample garment and test the fit on a model or dress-form.

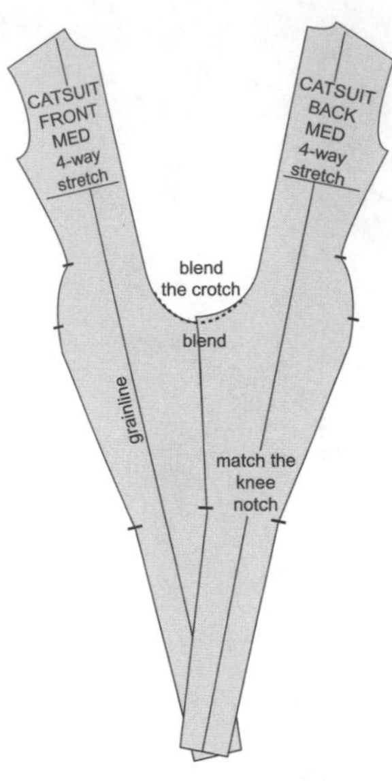

TRUEING THE CATSUIT SLOPERS

Trace out separate pattern pieces and true them, checking that all seams match and are accurate at the shoulders, armholes, underarms, inseam, crotch, outseam, and neckline.

Label the pattern pieces, remembering to label with the type of stretch.

Notch at the waist, hips, knees, and center back neck.

Also remember to label all pieces with black for Medium.

This sloper must be cut, sewn, and fitted with the corrections indicated on the block.

Place the back and front inseams together the way that they will be when sewn.

Match from the knee notch upwards.

Check to see that the crotch is blended in a smooth, continuously curved line.

Ensure that from the knee notch down matches perfectly.

Normally when we blend, we split the difference between the two points. However, in this instance, the front crotch is correct and the back crotch must be lowered by a very small amount to match it.

Note that some designers prefer to leave the excess in the pattern as ease in the back thigh area.

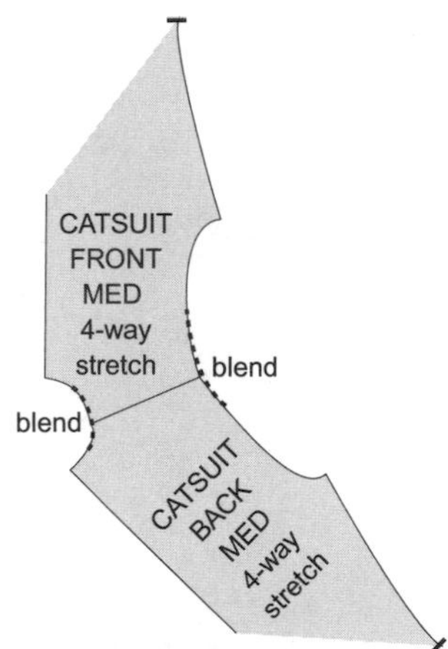

Place the shoulder seams together as they will be when sewn.

Blend a smooth armhole in a continuous line.

Blend a smooth neck.

Check to ensure that the shoulders are exactly the same length.

If there is any discrepancy, split the difference between the two, taking some away from the larger side and adding to the smaller side.

Blend as necessary.

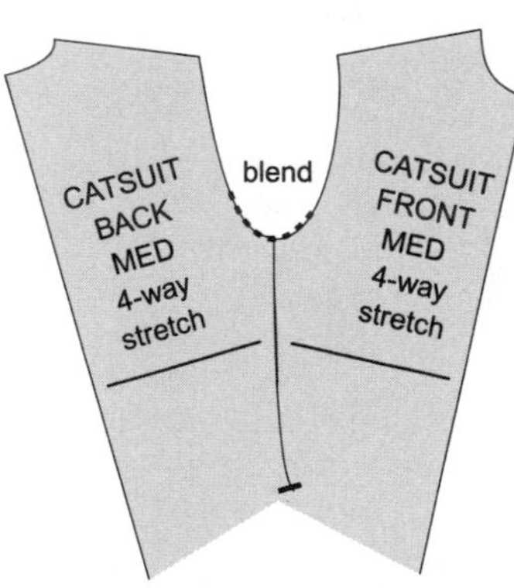

Place the side seams together as they will be when sewn.

Match from the waist notch upwards.

Check to ensure that the side seams are exactly the same length and that the notches match.

Blend the armhole in a smooth, continuously curved line.

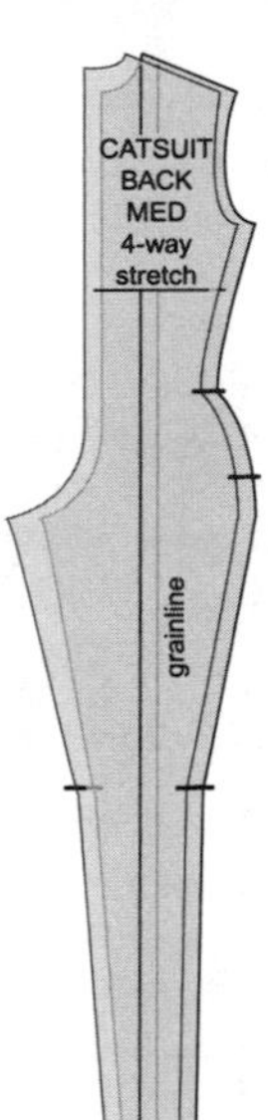

Checking the Side Seams

Place the front and back catsuit slopers on top of each other, check to see that the side seams are exactly the same and that every notch matches exactly.

Four-Way-Stretch Seam Allowances

Four-way-stretch fabrics should be serged with a three-thread serger, as the fabric needs to stretch a lot more than other fabrics. If a three-thread serger is not available, a four-thread will work.

Shoulder	1/4″ or 3/8″
	Twill tape is not necessary in the shoulders if the fabric has memory (meaning that it will return to its original measurement after being stretched).
Side seams	1/4″ or 3/8″
Armholes	1/4″ or 3/8″
Neckline	1/4″ or 3/8″
Hem	1″ for straight hems
	1/2″ for curved hems
Zipper	1/2″ seams for invisible zipper application

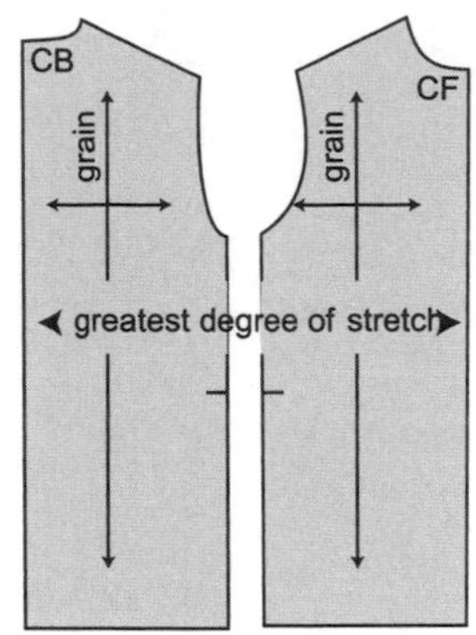

Greatest Degree of Stretch

When creating two-way- and four-way-stretch garments, usually one direction stretches slightly more than the other. Experienced patternmakers consider this and use it to their benefit.

When creating dresses and tops, the greatest direction of stretch should be utilized going around the body. However, for catsuits, leotards, and bodysuits, or any garment that passes through the crotch and the shoulders, the greatest direction of stretch should be utilized going up and down the body.

Usually the greatest degree of stretch is crosswise; however, some knit fabrics, such as swimsuit fabrics, are specially knit to have the greatest direction of stretch going lengthwise, parallel to the selvage. This is because these garments pass through the crotch and would be uncomfortable when the customer raises her shoulders.

Tops, dresses, pants, skirts, and sweaters should use the greatest degree of stretch going around the body.

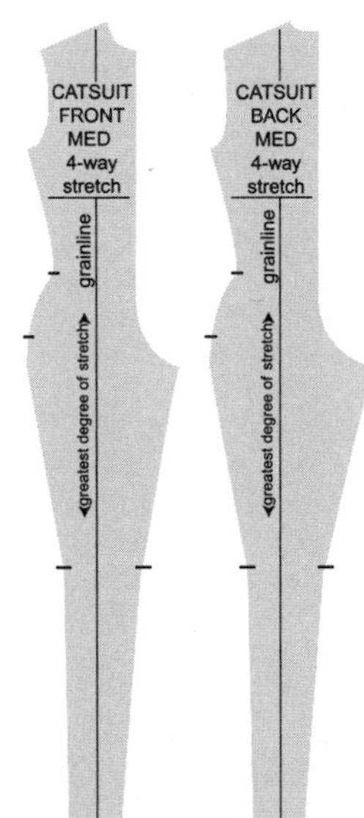

Catsuits, bodysuits, leotards, or any other garment that is anchored by the crotch should have the greatest degree of stretch going up and down the body, so that when the customer raises her arms, there is no discomfort in the crotch area.

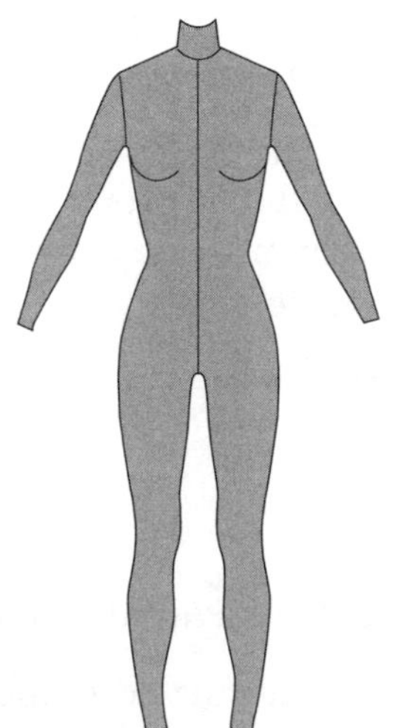

CATSUIT WITH MOCK NECK AND INVISIBLE ZIPPER

This basic catsuit should be drafted, sewn, and fitted to complete the sloper draft.

It will have a simple mock neck with an invisible zipper in the center back.

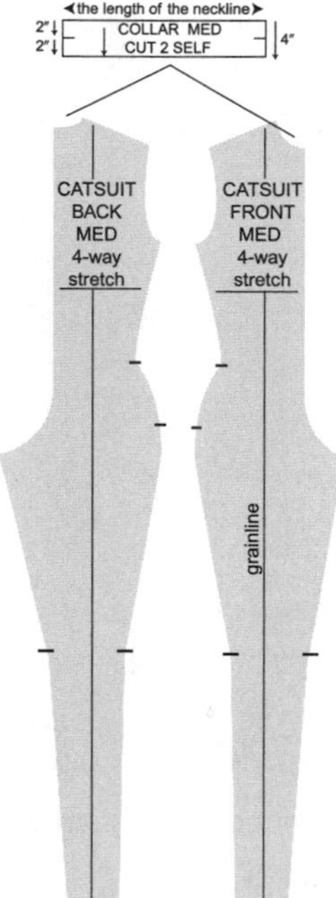

To create the mock neck collar:

Double the height, because the collar will be folded in half and all three layers sewn together.

Illustrated at 4″ for a 2″ finished collar.

To determine the length, measure the front and back necklines and double that measurement, as you've only measured half of the total neckline.

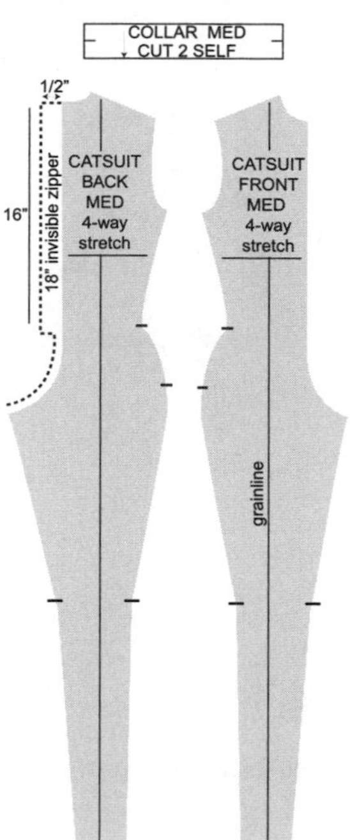

This pattern requires a zipper to get the garment on. Use a ½″ seam allowance the length of the zipper, excluding the distance that the zipper will go up into the collar.

The zipper extension is ½″ by 16″ for an 18″ zipper with a 2″ collar.

Add ¼″ seam allowances for the three-thread serge or ⅜″ seam allowances for the four-thread serge.

The three-thread serge is much stretchier.

Square up a 1″ hem allowance.

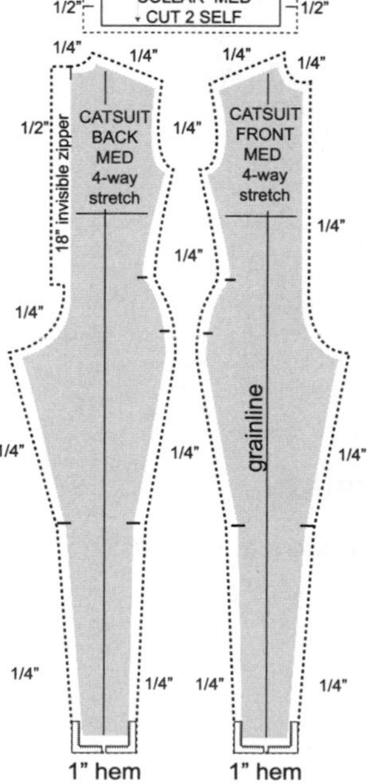

	Extra Extra Small	Extra Small	Small	Medium	Large	Extra Large	Extra Extra Large
Neck	14½	14⅝	14¾	14⅞	15	15⅛	15¼

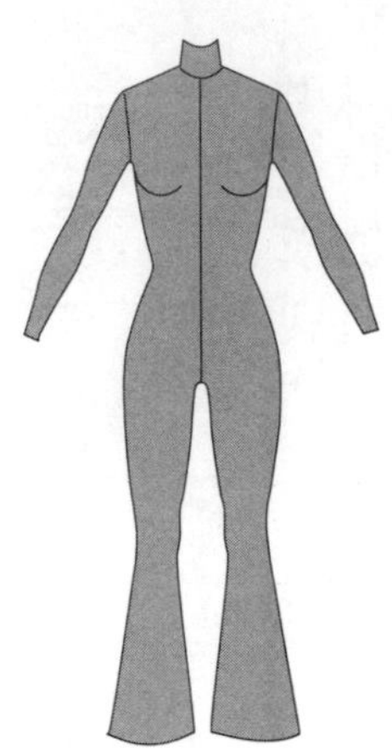

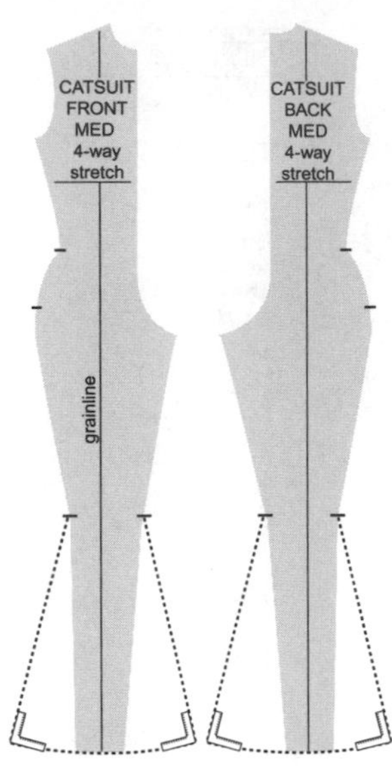

FLARED-LEG CATSUIT

Create a flared or bell-bottom leg on the catsuit.

Widen the circumference of the hem as much as required.

You can start the flare at any point on the leg that you wish.

Remember that whatever amount you add to one side of the leg must be equal on the other side of the leg.

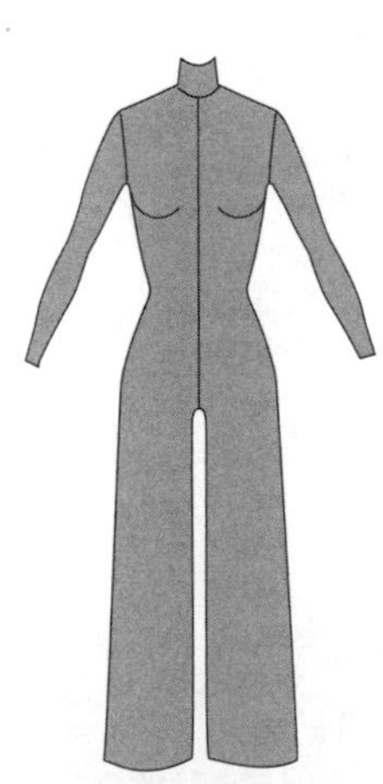

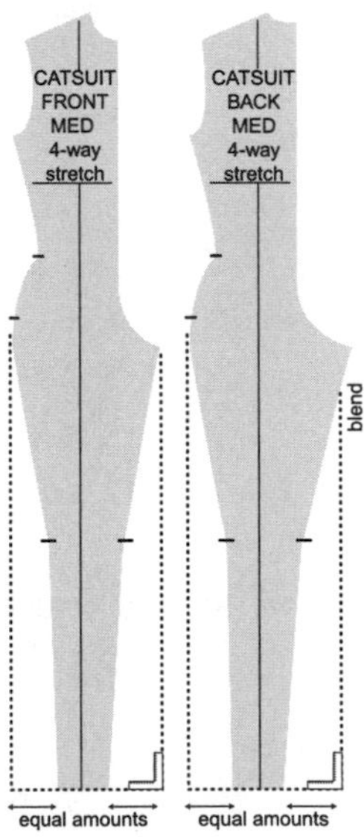

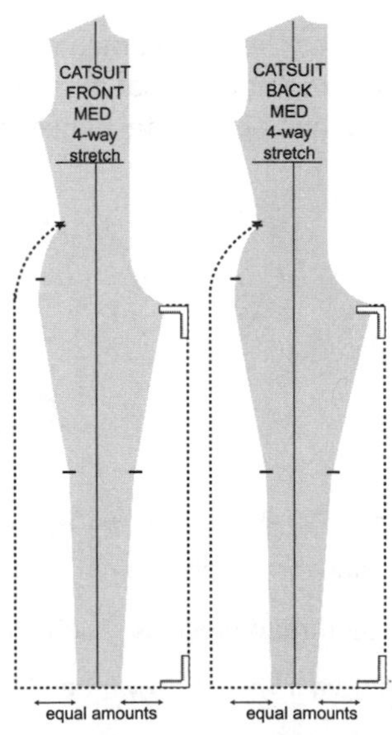

WIDE-LEG CATSUIT

You can easily create a wide-leg catsuit.

Decide on the width you require at the hem of the pants and square a line up to the hip.

Make sure that whatever amount you add to one side of the leg is the same on the other side of the leg, as well as the front and back.

Blend the back inseam if required.

For a wider leg, you must increase the length of the crotch seam and blend into the waist.

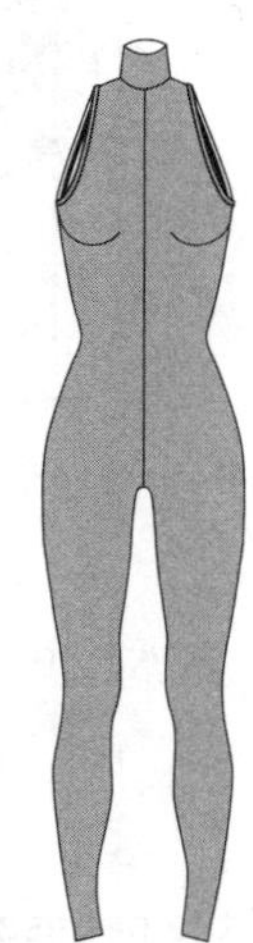

HALTER

This type of halter catsuit is often used in active sportswear, as it allows complete freedom of movement of the arms.

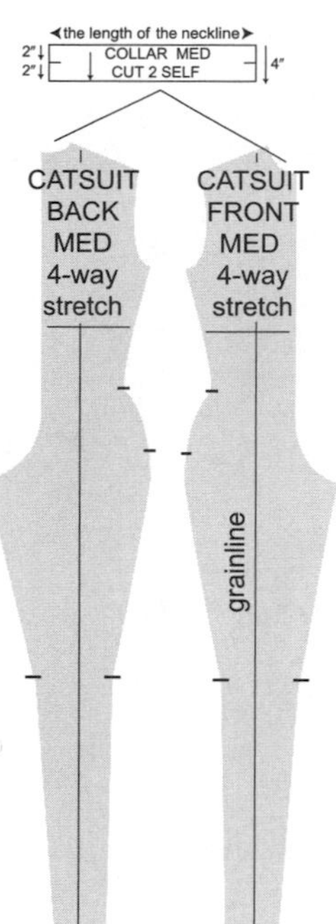

Draft the collar to fit the sloper neckline.

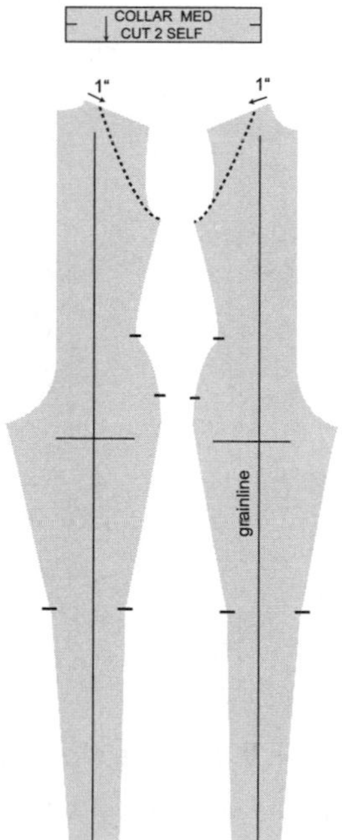

Draw in the halter style lines anywhere you wish.

Remember to cover the bust area completely.

This draft will have a 1″ shoulder seam.

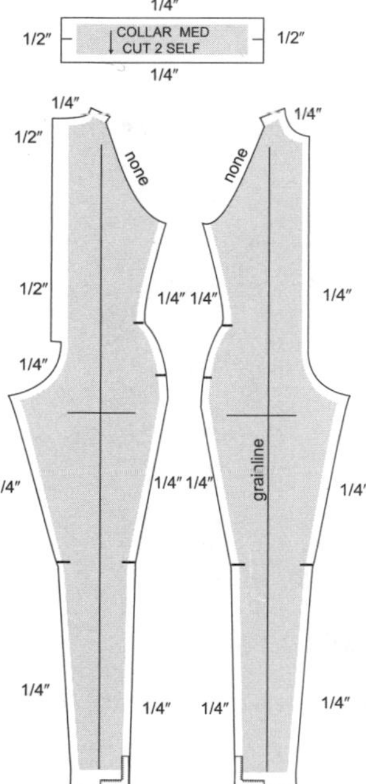

Add the necessary seam allowances as illustrated.

The halter style lines do not have any seam allowances, as they will be finished with 3/8″ binding; for other finishes, you may have to include seam allowances.

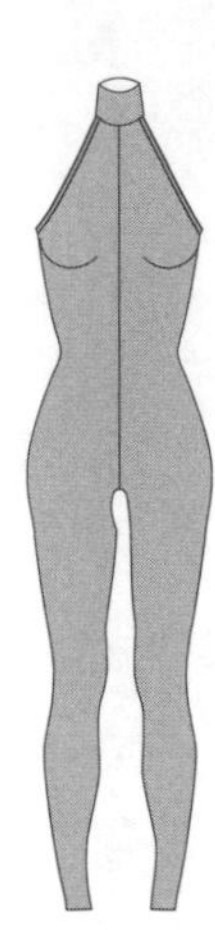

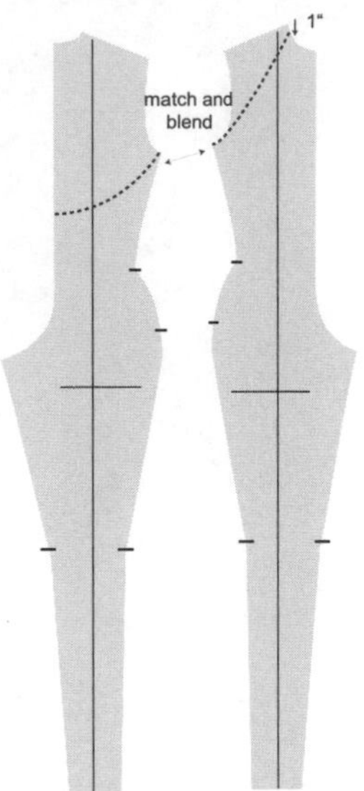

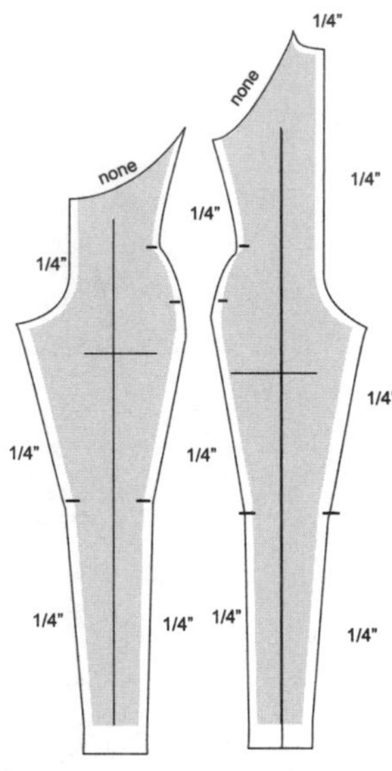

BACKLESS HALTER

This halter style is backless with a collar.

Draw in the style lines as you wish, remembering to cover the bust area completely.

The back may be lower or higher, as you require.

Add the necessary seam allowances as illustrated.

Draft the collar to fit the original catsuit sloper.

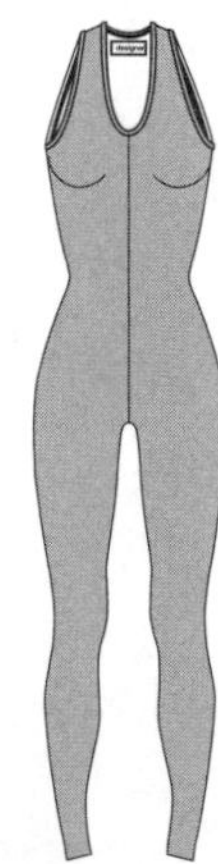

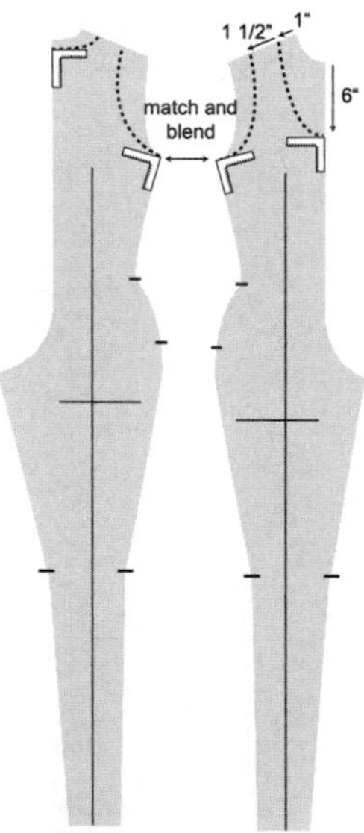

TANK NECKLINE CATSUIT

Catsuits with tank necklines are often used in active sportswear.

Draw any style of tank top on the slopers.

Raise the underarm ½″ and take in ½″, unless some binding, banding, or elastic will eventually raise and tighten the underarm.

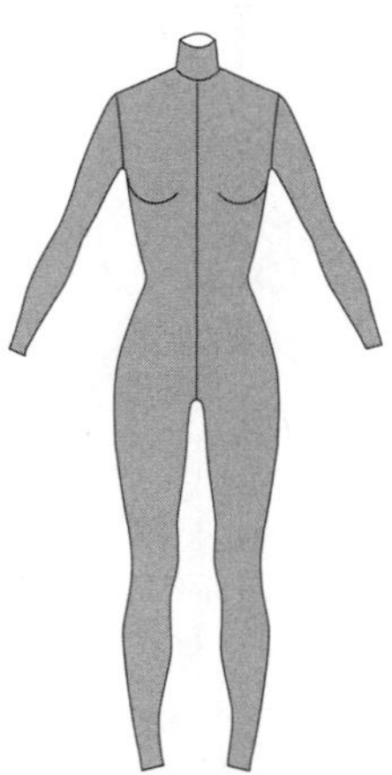

CATSUIT WITHOUT SIDE SEAMS

A catsuit may be developed without any side seam, which makes it very easy to draft color blocked designs.

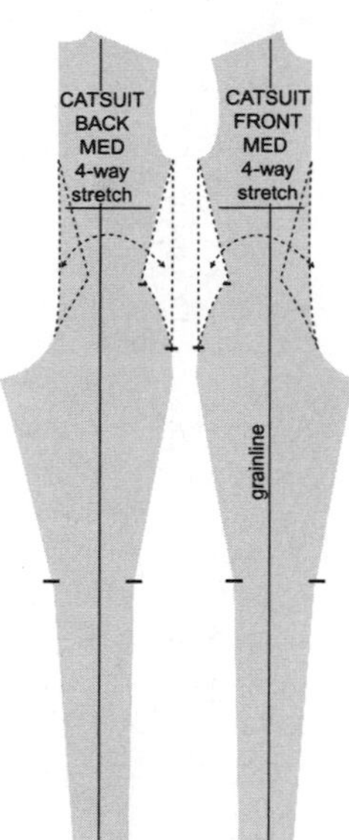

Place the front and back slopers beside each other.

Remove the extra volume from the center front and center back areas.

Try to keep the volume exactly the same and balanced.

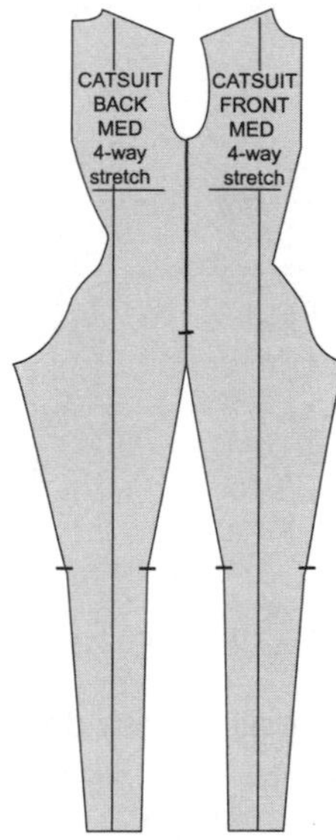

Illustration shows how the draft should appear once the waist volume has been moved from the sides to the front and back.

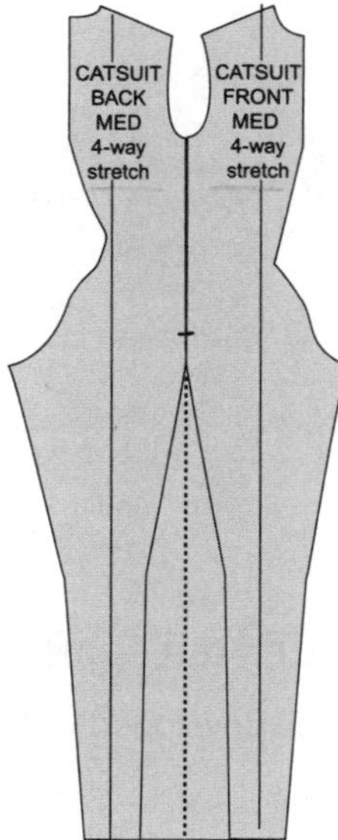

Draw a guideline from the waist to the ankle of the draft.

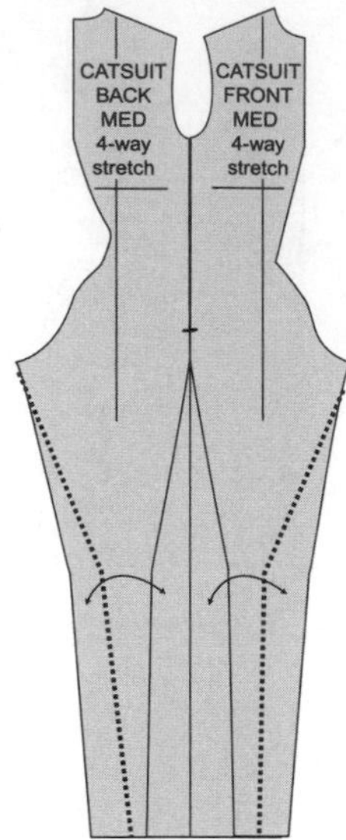

Remove the extra volume gained from the inseams.

Remember to keep the new leg balanced and even.

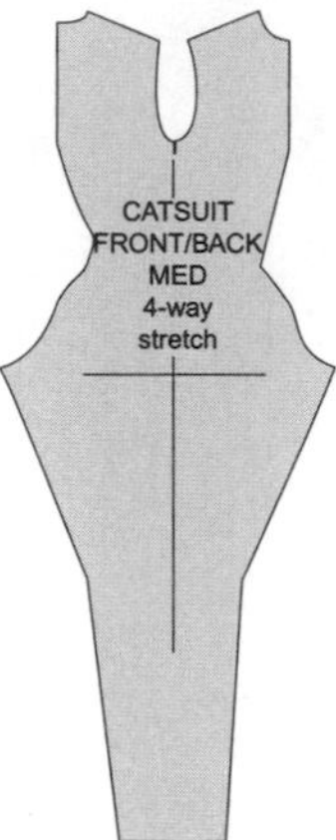

The illustration shows the final sloper, without any side seams.

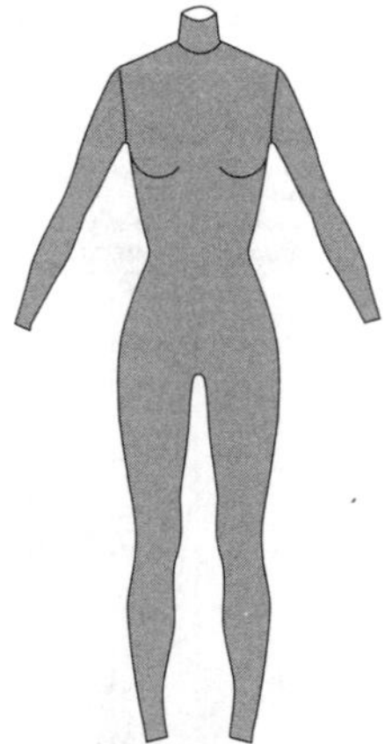

CATSUIT WITHOUT CENTER FRONT SEAM

The catsuit may also be developed without a center front seam.

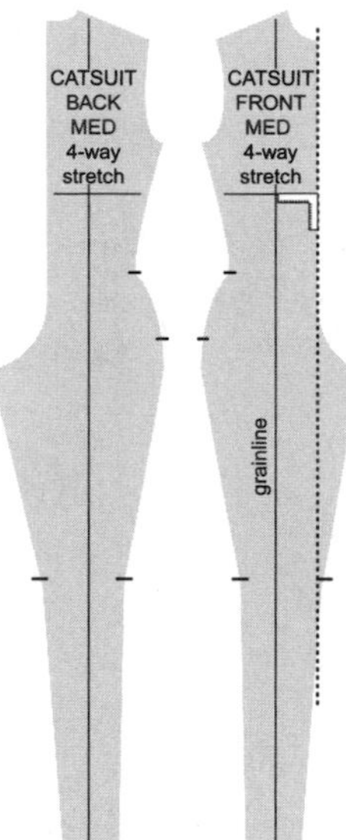

Extend the center front all the way down to the hem.

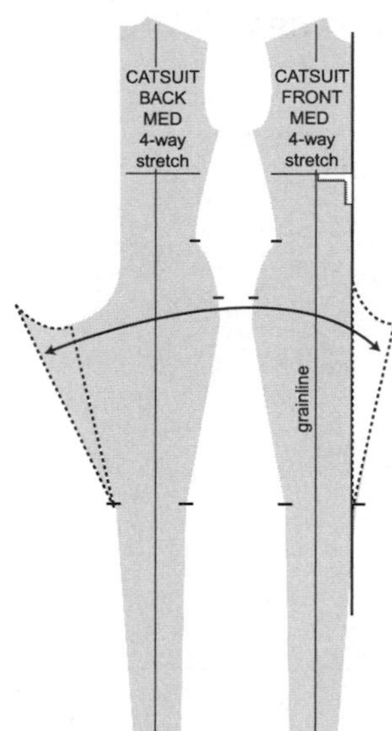

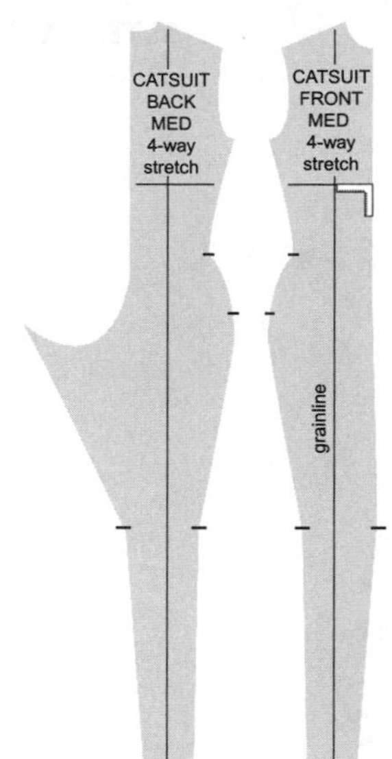

Take the amount of volume that will be lost at the front and move it to the back using tracing paper.

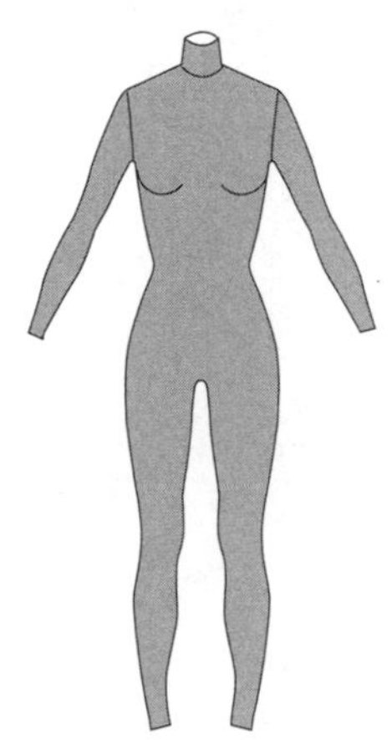

CATSUIT WITHOUT SIDE SEAM OR CENTER FRONT SEAM

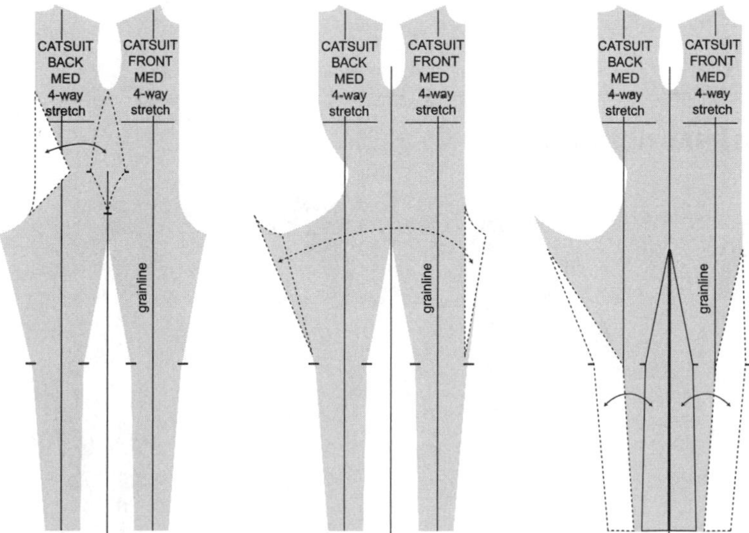

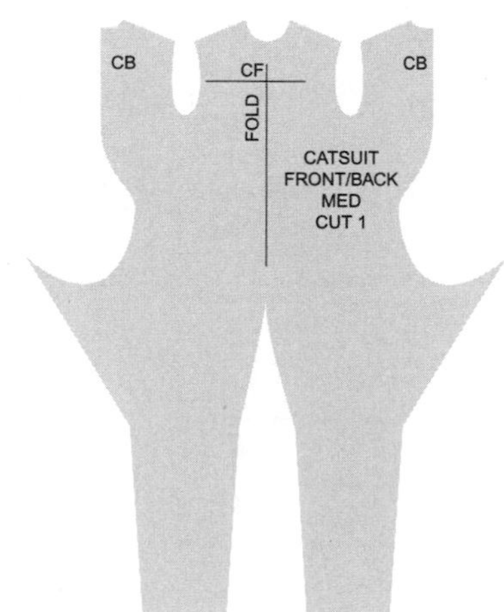

By combining the previous drafts, you can create a catsuit without side seams—or a center front seam. This is useful for color-blocked styles, whereby yoy wouldn't want the seams intersecting.

HALTER WITHOUT SIDE SEAMS OR CENTER FRONT SEAMS

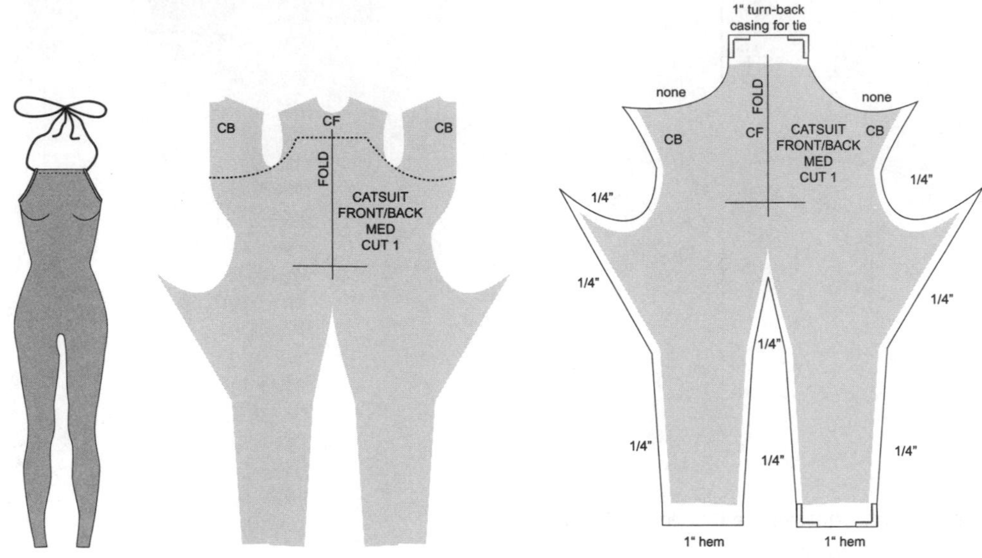

COLOR BLOCKED CATSUIT

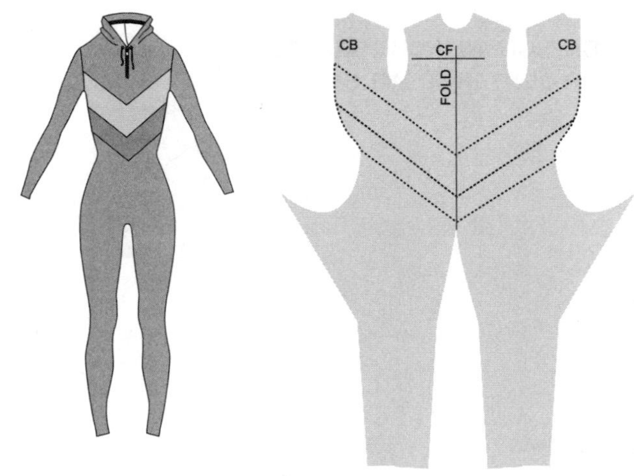

SOME PRACTICE STYLES

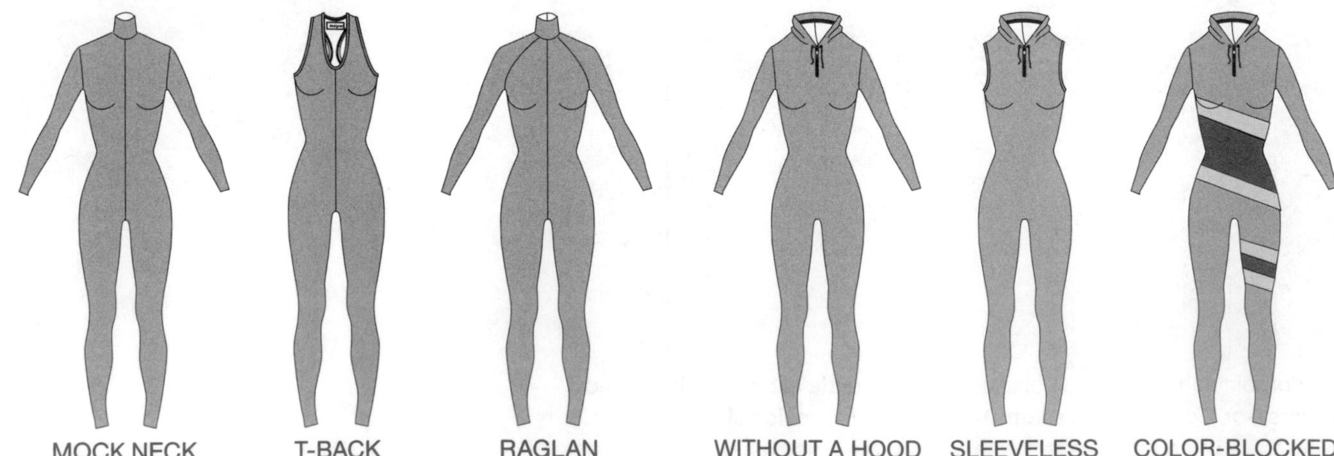

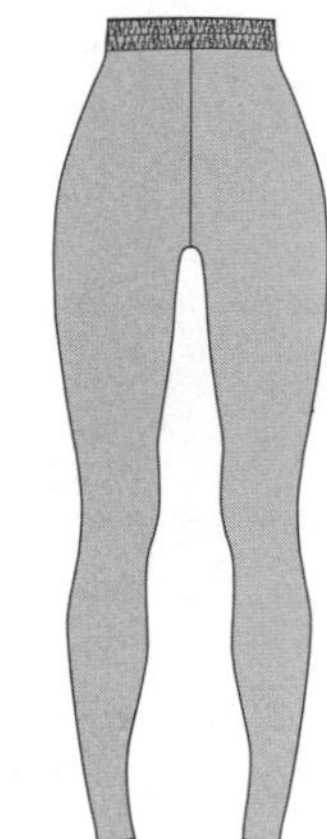

TIGHTS WITH SIDE SEAMS

In this section, we develop tights slopers with side seams and without.

In order to prevent the tights from riding down at the waist when the customer bends over, we must raise the back waist. This is only necessary when the crotch of the pant is really high and tight and doesn't have extra fabric to allow for bending over.

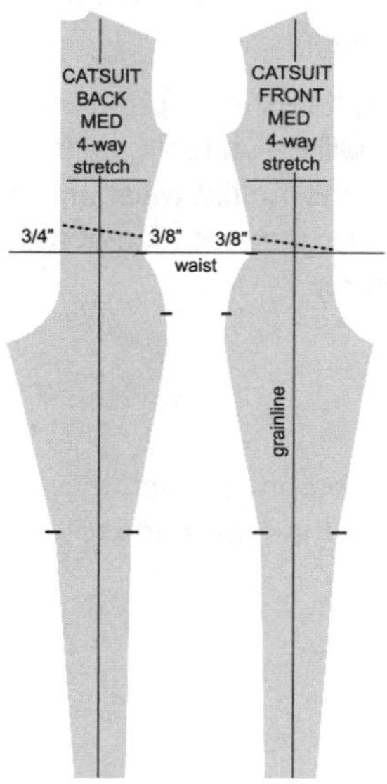

Raise center back waist 3/4″.

Side-seam 3/8″.

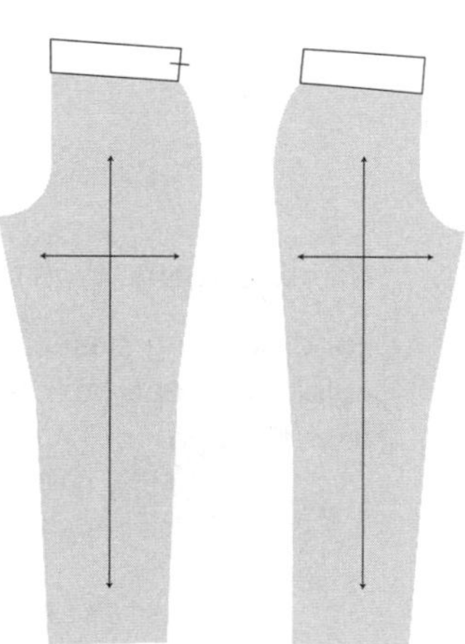

Create an elastic casing the same as for one-way-stretch pants.

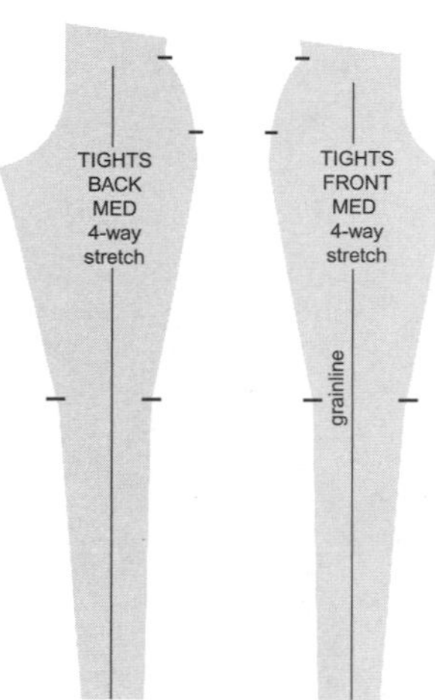

Add nothing at the center front.

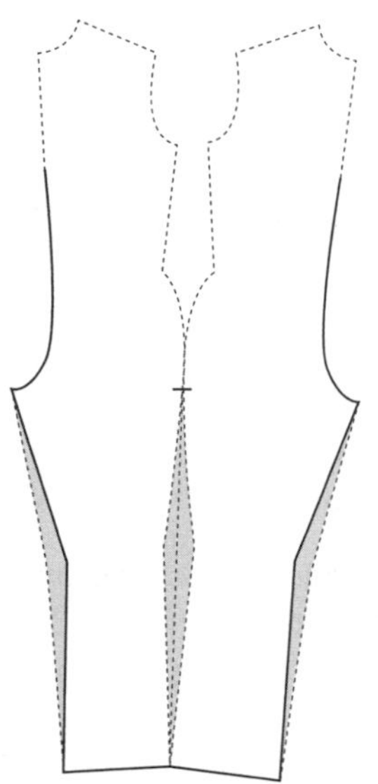

TIGHTS WITHOUT SIDE SEAMS

Place front and back slopers on paper.

Match at the hip and the ankle.

Trace around the slopers to about 3″ above the waist.

Remove slopers.

Measure the amount of the gap between the front and back outseams.

Take in each of the inseams an amount equal to half of the gap.

Follow the shape of the gap exactly.

Remove exactly the same shape from each leg.

Keep the widths identical.

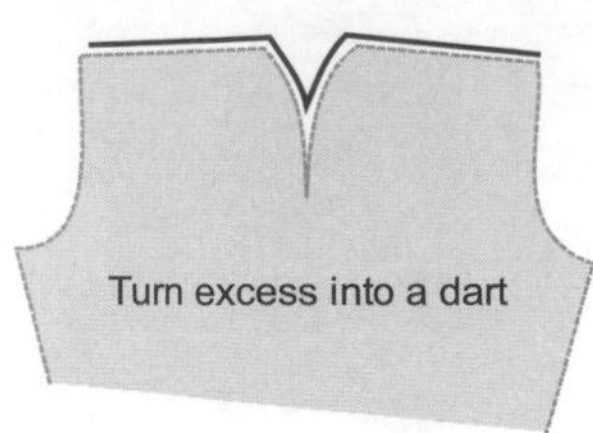

DART INTAKE

Option #1

Add seam allowances and turn the waist excess into a dart. This is sometimes the option a designer wants.

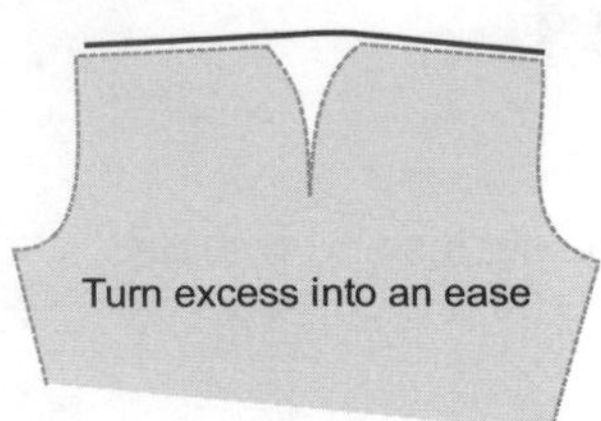

Option #2

Change the entire waist excess into ease by drawing a straight line across the waist and ignoring the dart.

This will create a lot of gathers when elastic is inserted, and may not be the desired look.

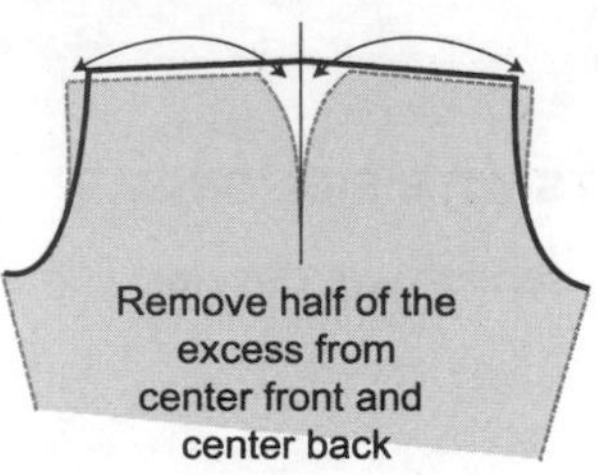

Option #3

No ease.

Remove half of the excess from the center front and half from the center back, the same way as with the legs.

In this case, the waist will be smaller than the elastic, causing it to look odd on the hanger.

However, if this is for dancers or gymnasts, it will be suitable, as they would prefer a smooth flat waist and don't require the garment to look attractive in the store.

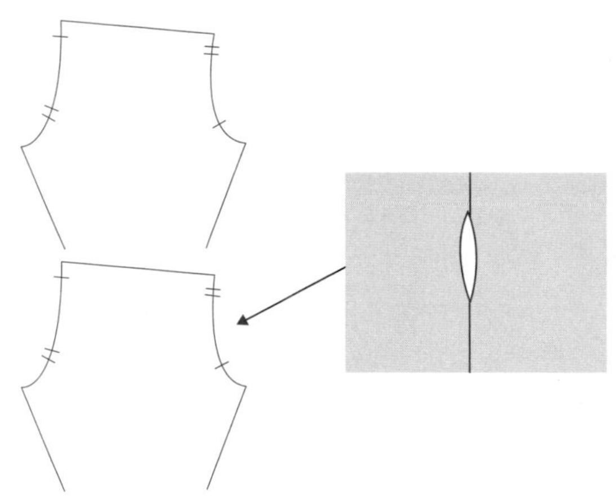

DRAWSTRING WAIST TIGHTS

For drawstring elastic, replace the front notch with two notches ½″ apart to create an opening for the drawstring to pass through.

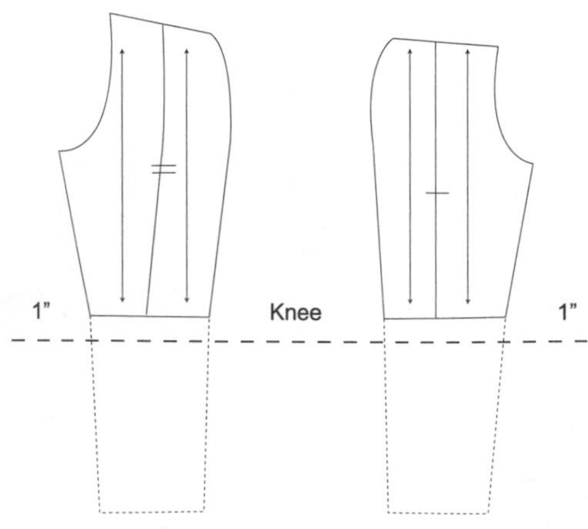

EIGHT-PANEL BICYCLE SHORTS

To create eight-panel bicycle shorts:

Trace out the tights to 1″ above the knee level.

Create a princess seam.

Notch and separate the pattern pieces.

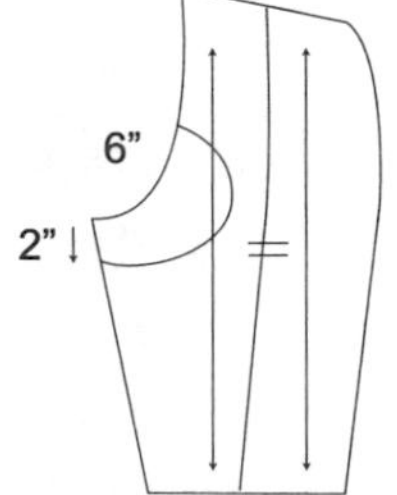

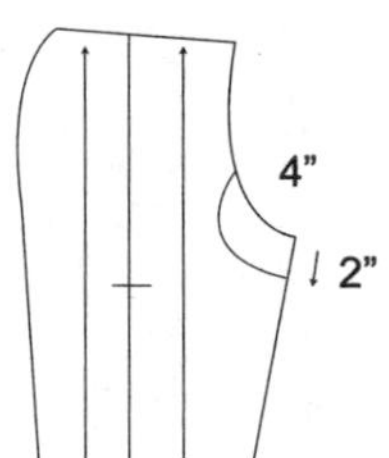

BICYCLE SHORT SHAMMY

Create the shammy as illustrated and cut out in a light leather to soften the crotch area for riding.

Test Your Knowledge of the Material in This Chapter

1. What is a one-way stretch?
2. What is a two-way stretch?
3. What is a four-way stretch?
4. When should you use a four-way stretch sloper?
5. Must four-way stretch fabrics only be used for active wear?
6. What is the difference between the front armhole and the back armhole?
7. Which serger should be used for four-way stretch fabrics?
8. What it "the greatest degree of stretch"?
9. When creating tops, dresses, pants, skirts, and sweaters, which direction should use the "greatest degree of stretch"?
10. When creating catsuits, bodysuits, leotards or any garment that is anchored by the crotch, which direction should use the "greatest degree of stretch"?

CHAPTER 13

Bodysuits, Leotards, and One- and Two-Piece Swimsuits

About this Chapter

This chapter covers development of patterns for bodysuits, leotards, and one-piece and two-piece swimsuits. The slopers may be created from scratch or developed from the catsuit sloper. The leotard sloper may be used to create leotards, bodysuits, or any top with panty attached, as well as one-piece swimsuits. Panties and swimsuit bottoms are also covered in this chapter, but will need a separate sloper. Since there is nothing anchoring the top of the swimsuit, it behaves like a one-way stretch. Note that the catsuit sleeve will also fit this sloper, or you can follow the sleeve instructions in Chapter 8.

Four-Way-Stretch Reductions

Rule of thumb: 10% smaller in crosswise direction without any reductions in lengthwise direction; 10% smaller in the lengthwise direction.

Use these measurements when drafting slopers for fabrics that stretch 100 percent in both directions.

Four-way-stretch slopers are only used for garments that pass through the crotch and shoulders, in order to utilize the lengthwise as well as the horizontal stretch. They may also be used for two-way-stretch fabrics, but there will be no memory in the garment, so it will tend to sag and stretch out of shape on the body after wearing.

FOUR-WAY-STRETCH REDUCTIONS

			Extra Extra Small	Extra Small	Small	Medium	Large	Extra Large	Extra Extra Large
		Multiply by	**0**	**2**	**6**	**10**	**14**	**18**	**20**
1	Bust	× 0.90	28 3/8	29 1/4	30 1/8	31	32	33 1/4	34 5/8
2	Waist	× 0.90	21 1/8	22	23	23 5/8	24 3/4	26 1/8	27 1/2
3	Hip	× 0.90	31	32	32 7/8	33 3/4	34 5/8	36	37 3/8
4	Crotch depth	× 0.90	9	9 1/8	9 1/4	9 3/8	9 1/2	9 5/8	9 5/8
5	Waist to knee	× 0.90	20 3/4	20 7/8	22 1/8	22 1/4	22 3/8	22 1/2	22 5/8
6	Waist to ankle	× 0.90	34 5/8	34 7/8	37	37 1/4	37 1/2	37 3/4	38
7	Ankle	× 0.90	7	7 1/8	7 1/4	7 3/8	7 3/8	7 1/2	7 5/8
8	Knee	× 0.90	12	12 1/4	12 1/2	12 3/4	13	13 1/8	13 3/8
9	Front crotch	× 0.90	2	2	2	2 1/8	2 1/8	2 1/4	2 3/8
10	Back crotch	× 0.90	2 7/8	3	3	3 1/8	3 1/4	3 3/8	3 1/2
11	Crotch angle	× 0.90	1	1	1	1	1 1/8	1 1/8	1 1/8
12	Nape to waist	× 0.90	14 1/8	14 1/4	15 3/8	15 1/2	15 3/4	16	16 1/4
13	Back neck	no reduction	2 3/8	2 3/8	2 1/2	2 1/2	2 1/2	2 1/2	2 1/2
14	Back neck rise	no reduction	3/4	3/4	7/8	7/8	7/8	7/8	7/8
15	Shoulder length	no reduction	5 1/8	5 1/4	5 1/2	5 3/4	6	6 1/4	6 1/2
16	Across back	no reduction	7	7 1/8	7 1/4	7 3/8	7 1/2	7 5/8	7 3/4
17	Sleeve length	no reduction	22 3/4	22 7/8	23	23 1/8	23 1/4	23 3/8	23 1/2
18	Shoulder pitch	no reduction	1 3/8	1 1/2	1 1/2	1 1/2	1 1/2	1 1/2	1 1/2
19	Bicep	× 0.90	9 3/8	9 5/8	10	10 3/8	10 3/4	11	11 3/8
20	Wrist	× 0.90	5	5 1/4	5 5/8	6	6 1/4	6 5/8	7
21	Neck	no reduction	14 1/2	14 5/8	14 3/4	14 7/8	15	15 1/8	15 1/4
22	Bust span	× 0.90	5 7/8	6	6 1/8	6 1/4	6 3/8	6 1/2	6 3/4
23	Bust level	× 0.90	9	9 1/8	9 3/4	9 7/8	10	10 1/8	10 1/4

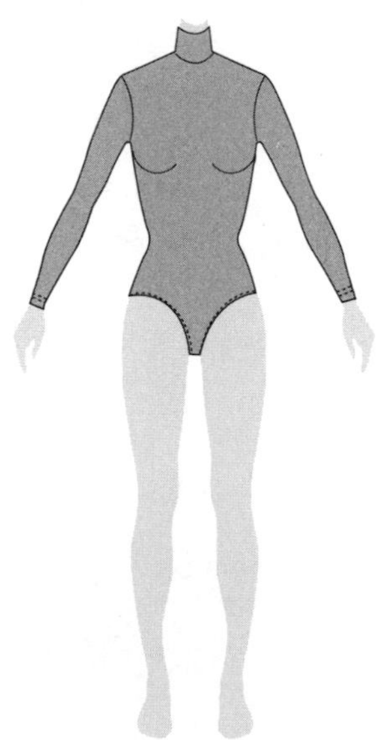

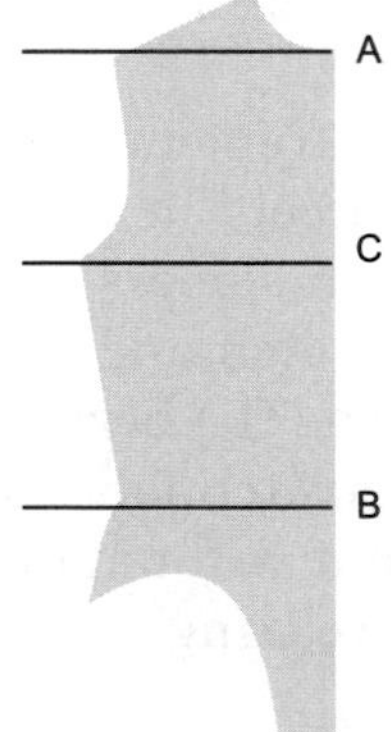

LEOTARD SLOPER

The leotard sloper may be used to create leotards, bodysuits, or any top with panty attached, as well as one-piece swimsuits.

A-B = nape to waist

A-C = half of A-B

A, B, C = square out lines

	Extra Extra Small	Extra Small	Small	Medium	Large	Extra Large	Extra Extra Large
Nape to waist	14 1/8	14 1/4	15 3/8	15 1/2	15 3/4	16	16 1/4
Half-way	7	7 1/8	7 5/8	7 3/4	7 7/8	8	8 1/8

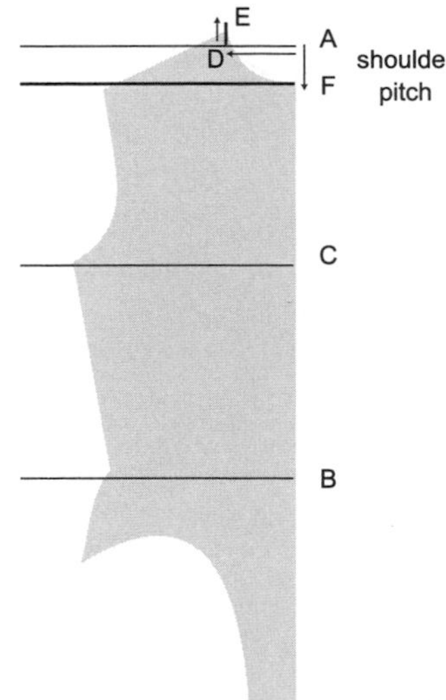

A-D = back neck measurement

D-E = back neck rise

E-F = shoulder pitch

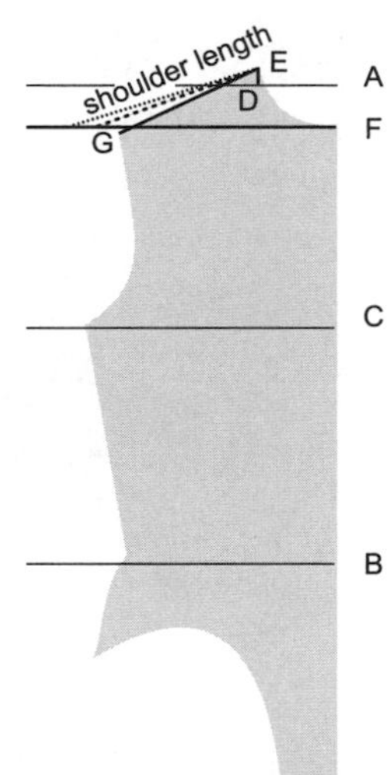

E-G = shoulder length measurement goes from point E to wherever that measurement lines up on the shoulder pitch line, line F.

	Extra Extra Small	Extra Small	Small	Medium	Large	Extra Large	Extra Extra Large
Shoulder pitch	1 3/8	1 1/2	1 1/2	1 1/2	1 1/2	1 1/2	1 1/2
Back neck	2 3/8	2 3/8	2 1/2	2 1/2	2 1/2	2 1/2	2 1/2
Back neck rise	3/4	3/4	7/8	7/8	7/8	7/8	7/8
Shoulder	5 1/8	5 1/4	5 1/2	5 3/4	6	6 1/4	6 1/2

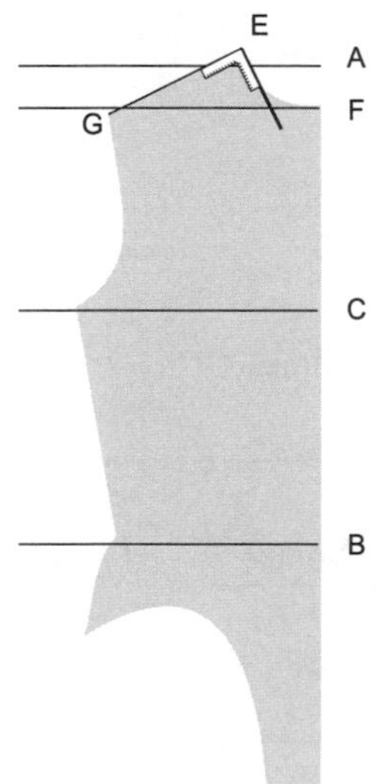

At E, square a line towards line F.

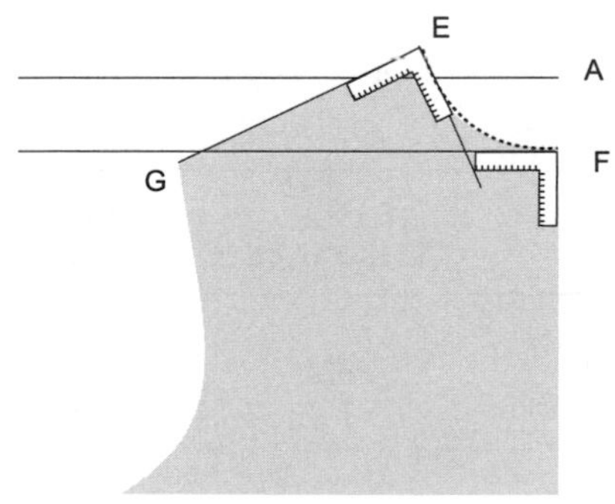

Draw a curved front neckline as illustrated.

Remember to square for ½″ at E and ½″ at F.

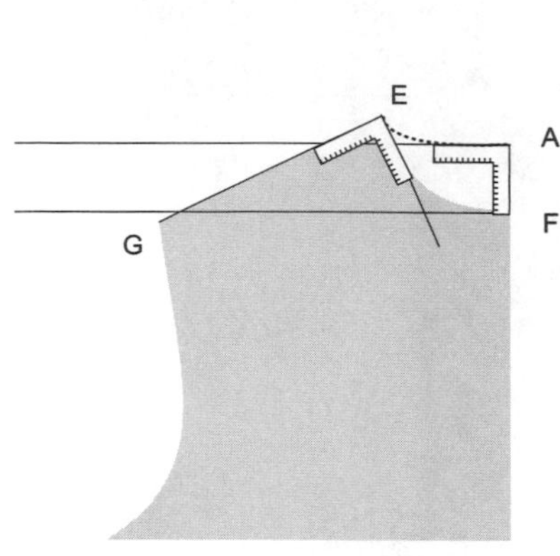

Draw a curved back neckline as illustrated.

Remember to square for ½″ at E and ½″ at A.

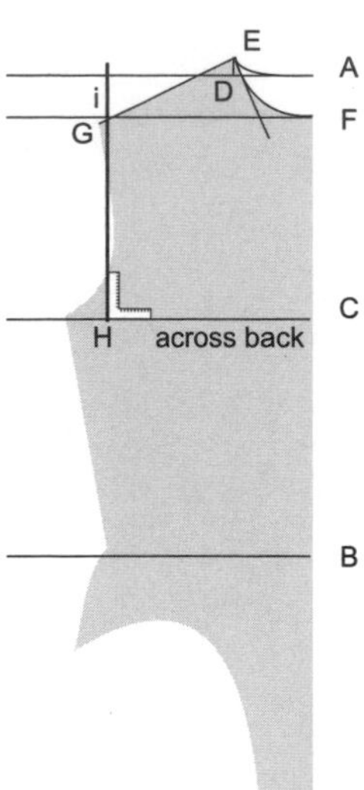

C-H = across back: square up to the shoulder line and label I, note that it may not line up with point G.

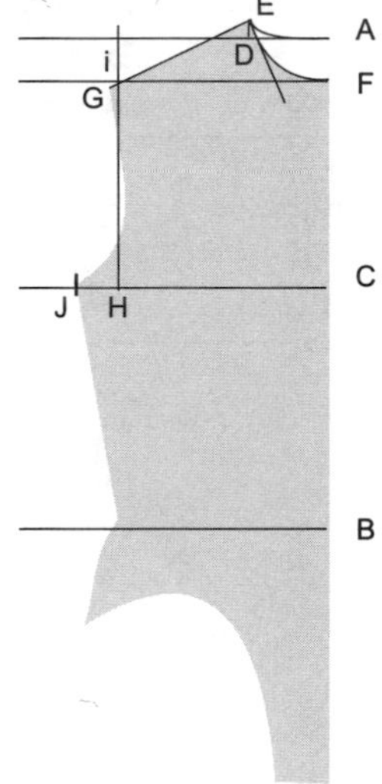

C-J = bust measurement

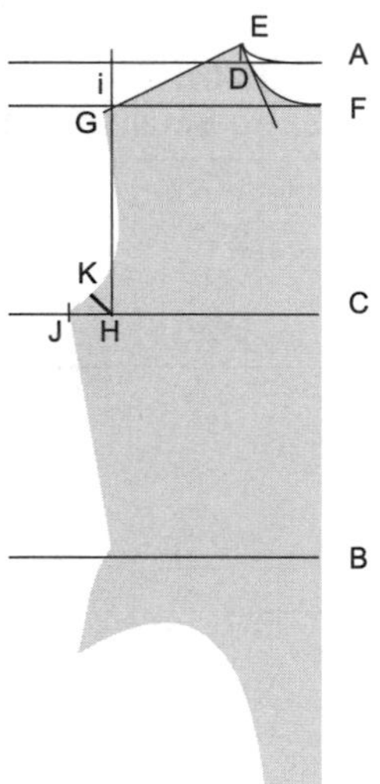

H-K = ½″ on bias angle.

	Extra Extra Small	Extra Small	Small	Medium	Large	Extra Large	Extra Extra Large
Across back	7	7⅛	7¼	7⅜	7½	7⅝	7¾
Bust	28⅜	29¼	30⅛	31	32	33¼	34⅝
¼ of bust	7⅛	7⅜	7½	7¾	8	8⅜	8⅝

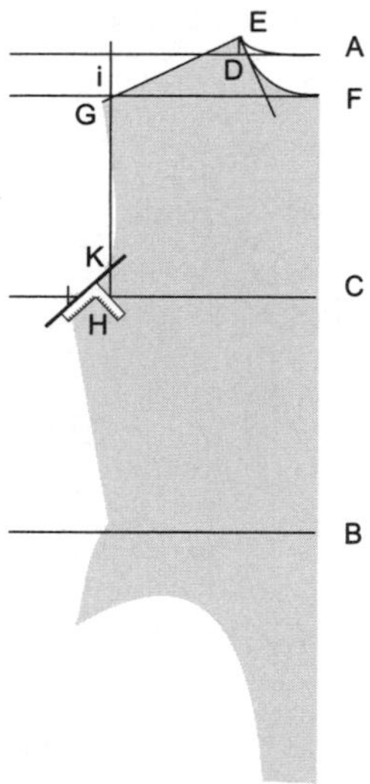

At K, square a guideline in both directions.

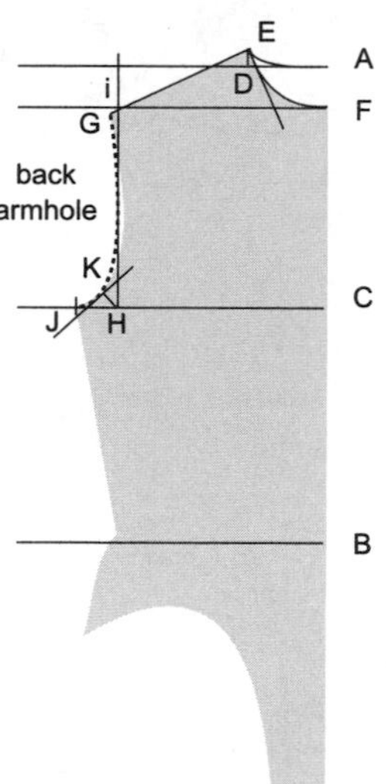

Draw the back armhole from point G-K-I.

Square the line for ½″ at G and at I.

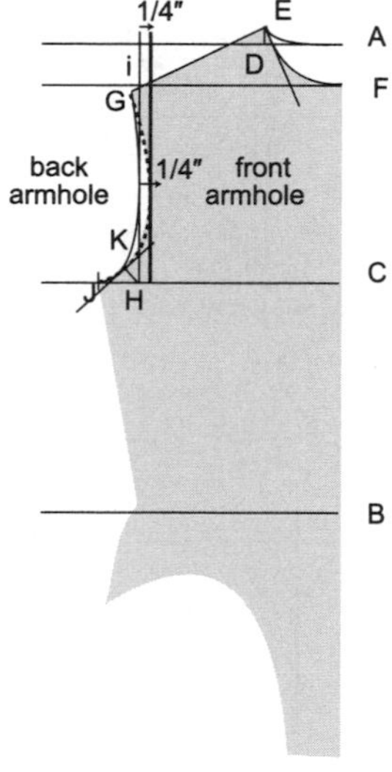

Draw a guideline ½″ in from the back armhole.

Because the sleeve will be drafted on the fold, with no difference between the front and the back, you must include that difference in the body portion of the garment.

Draw the front armhole from point G-K-I, at the inside guideline.

Square the line for ½″ at G and at I.

Note that because the sleeve is drafted on the fold, with no difference between the front and back curves, you must exaggerate the difference in the body of the garment; this way, you can eliminate any notches on the sleeve and armhole, reducing the chances of getting holes in the garment.

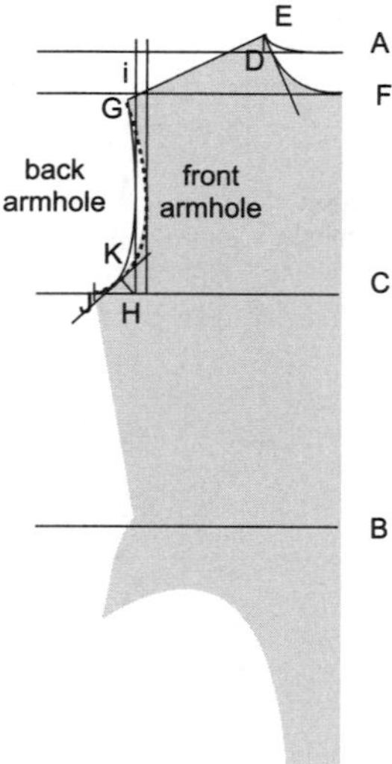

Extend the center front the amount of the crotch depth.

	Extra Extra Small	Extra Small	Small	Medium	Large	Extra Large	Extra Extra Large
Crotch depth	9	9⅛	9¼	9⅜	9½	9⅝	9⅝

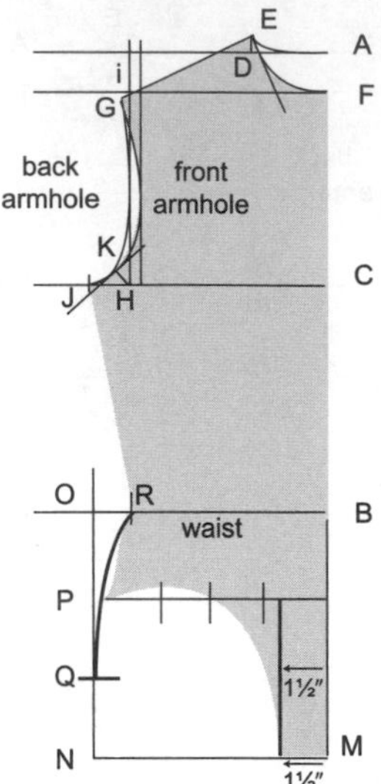

Draw a guideline equal to the hip measurement.

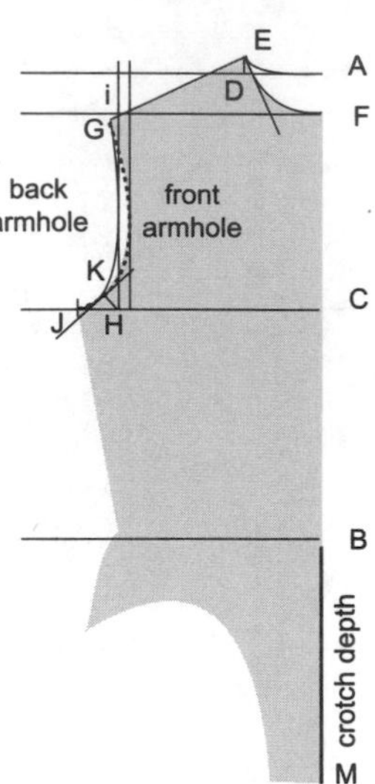

Divide the line, waist to crotch, into three equal sections.

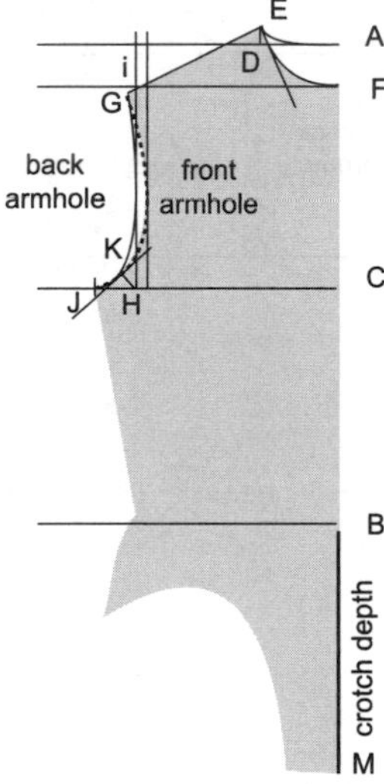

On B-O, measure and mark the waist measurement.

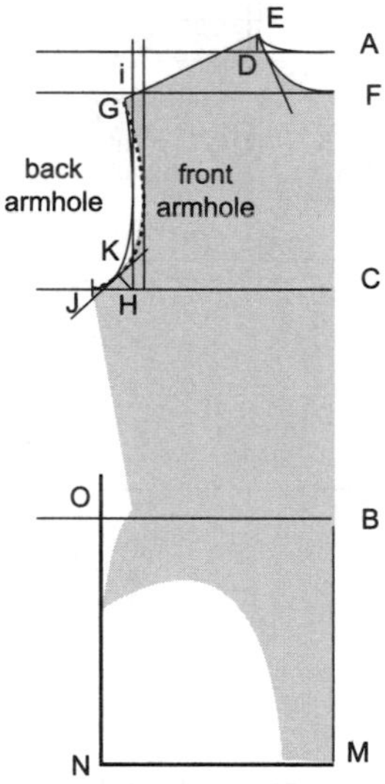

To draw the hip curve, line up #4 of the variform curve with the waist and blend as well as possible into point Q.

	Extra Extra Small	Extra Small	Small	Medium	Large	Extra Large	Extra Extra Large
Hip	7 3/4	8	8 1/4	8 1/2	8 5/8	9	9 3/8
Crotch depth	9	9 1/8	9 1/4	9 3/8	9 1/2	9 5/8	9 5/8
Thirds	3	3	3 1/8	3 1/8	3 1/8	3 1/4	3 1/4
Waist	5 1/4	5 1/2	5 3/4	6	6 1/4	6 1/2	6 7/8

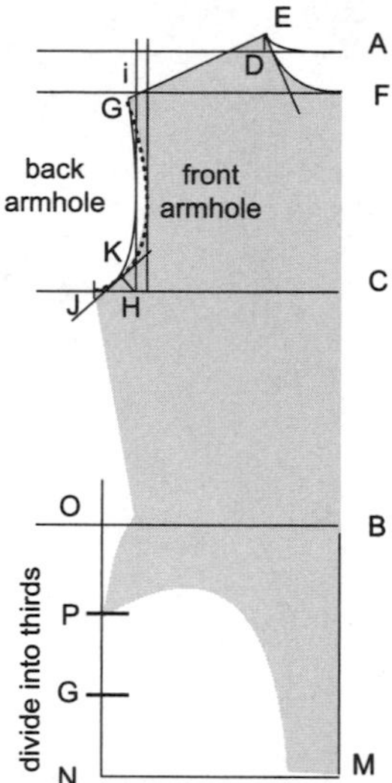

Divide line P into four sections.

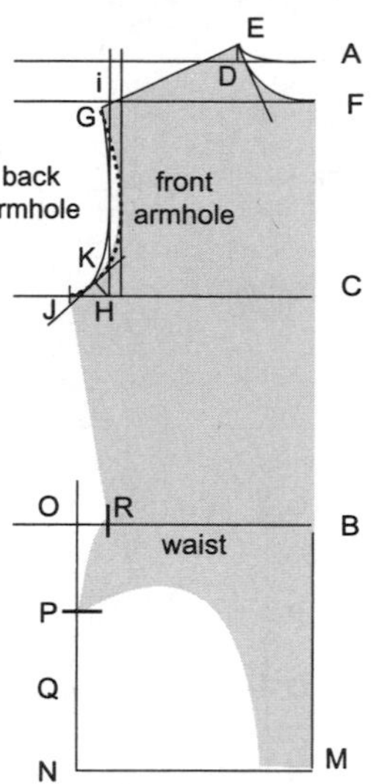

Draw a guideline 1½″ in from the center front. This will be the width of the crotch.

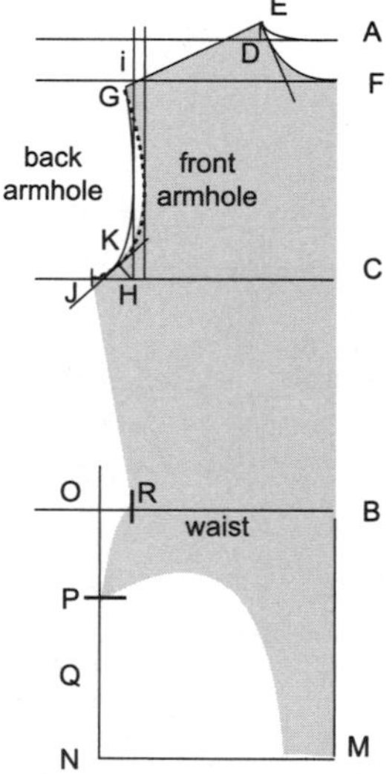

At the intersection of the upper hip, the new front guideline, and the bias angle, draw a 1⅜″ line.

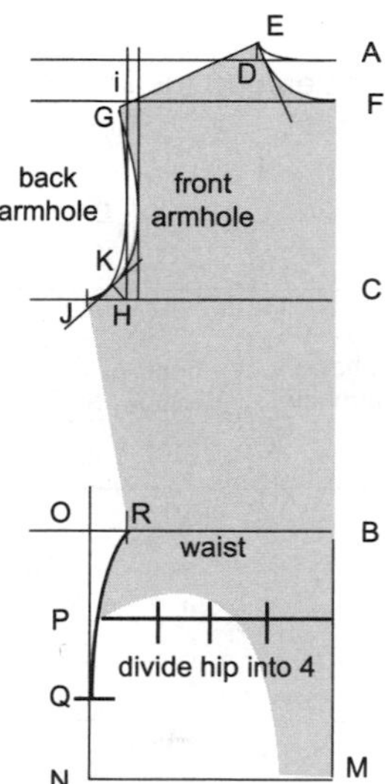

At the mark closest to the side seam, raise ½″.

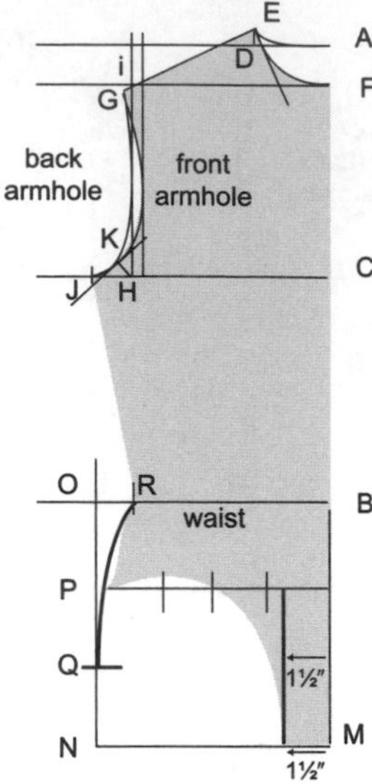

Draw in the front leg opening by connecting the points from 1 to 5.

Make a smooth, continuously curved line that blends into the front crotch line.

Draw freehand, then clean up the lines with the curved ruler.

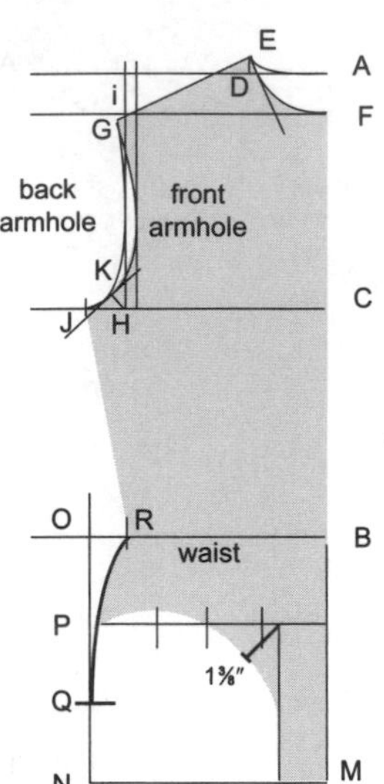

Blend into the center front.

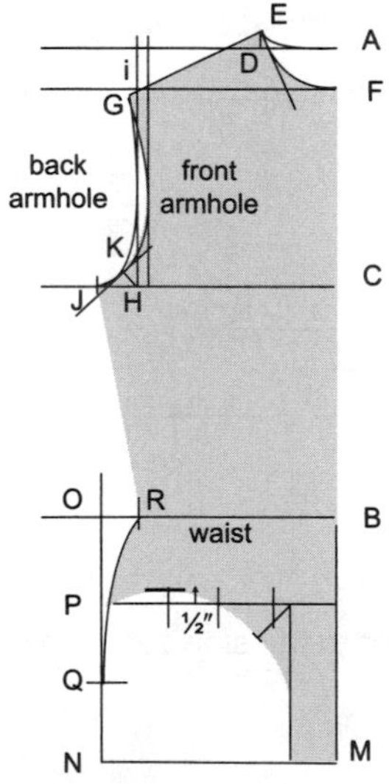

For the back, connect a straight line from point P to the front crotch line.

Find the center of that line and mark out ½" + ½" + ½".

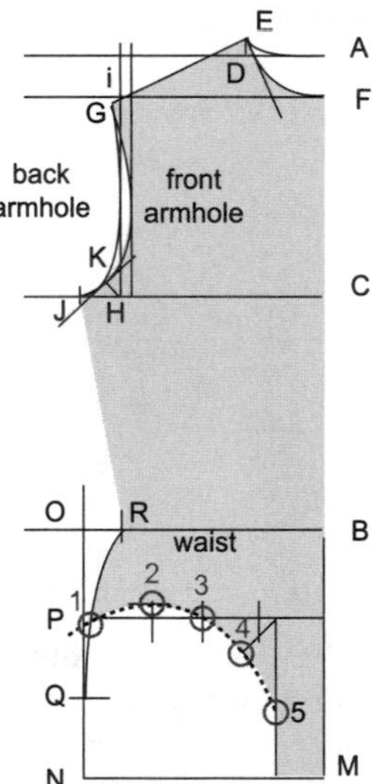

Redraw with curved lines. These lines are for the different sizes of bottoms. Some medium customers have larger or smaller bottoms, and it will depend on your target market which curved line you incorporate.

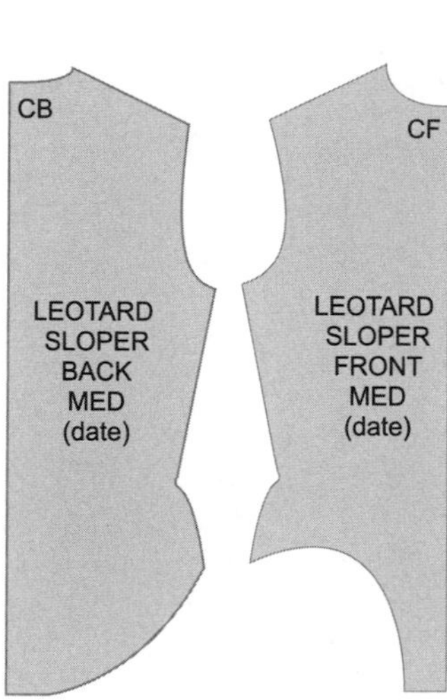

Trace and separate the leotard sloper as illustrated.

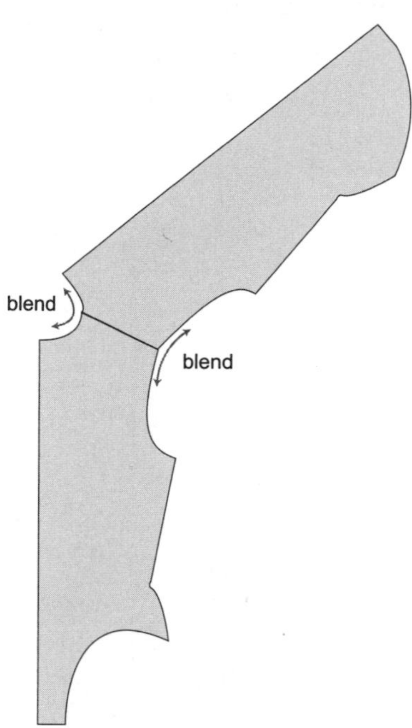

TRUEING THE LEOTARD SLOPERS

To true the neckline and armholes, line up the slopers as illustrated, as if they had been sewn and pressed open.

Make sure that the curves blend in a smooth and continuous manner and that there are NO points in the blend.

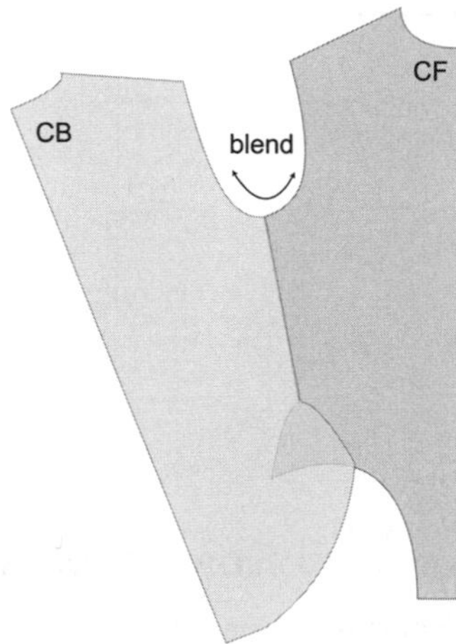

Match the underarms and blend the armhole curves into smooth and continuously curved lines.

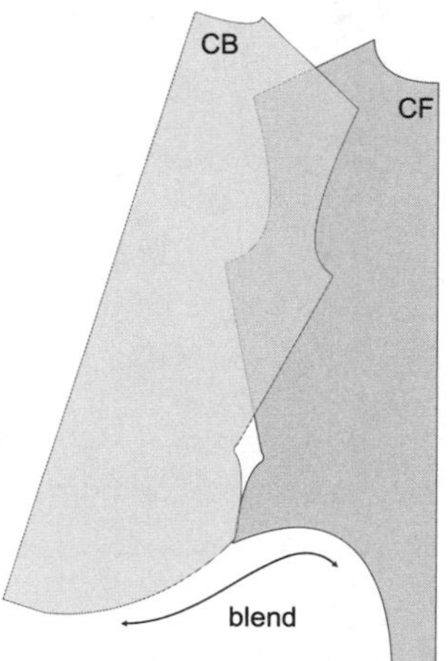

Blend the leg opening at the side seam by matching the waist notches and walking the side seams.

Blend the leg opening into a smooth and continuously curved line.

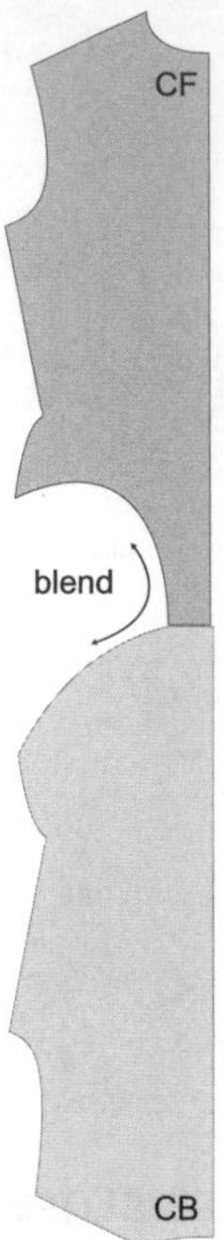

Blend the crotch into a smooth and continuously curved line.

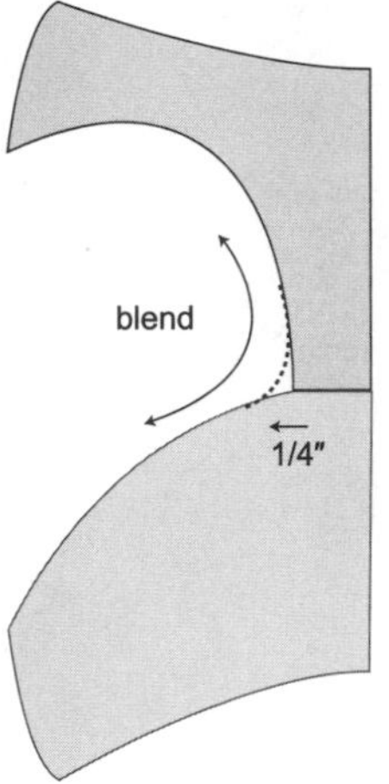

You will have to add an additional 1/4″ to the crotch seams in order to make the curve smooth enough to attach elastic.

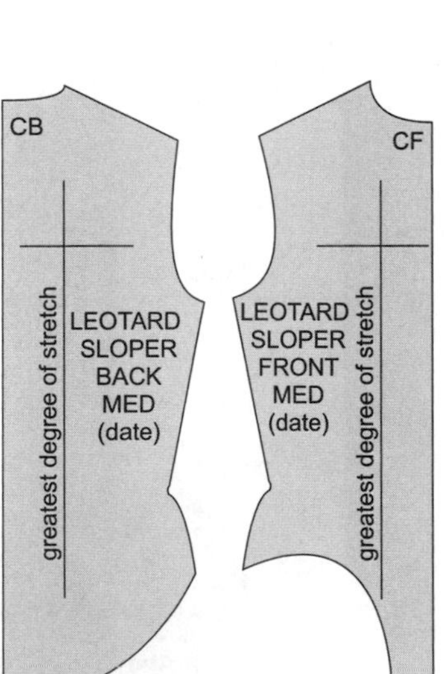

Label the slopers as indicated.

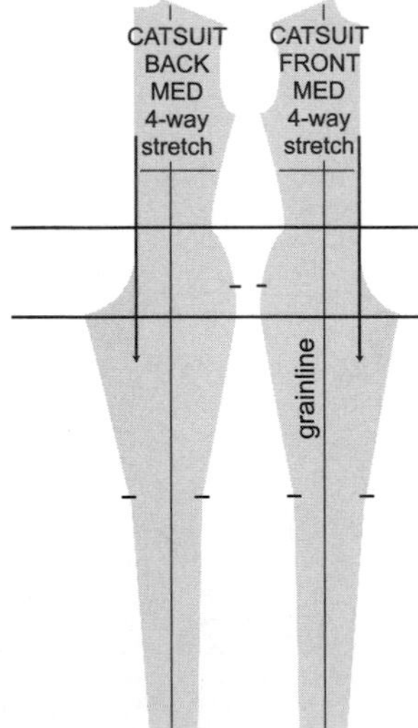

CREATING A LEOTARD SLOPER FROM A CATSUIT

Trace the upper part of the catsuit to just below the crotch.

Draw a guideline at the waist.

Extend the center front to below the crotch.

Square a line in at the crotch.

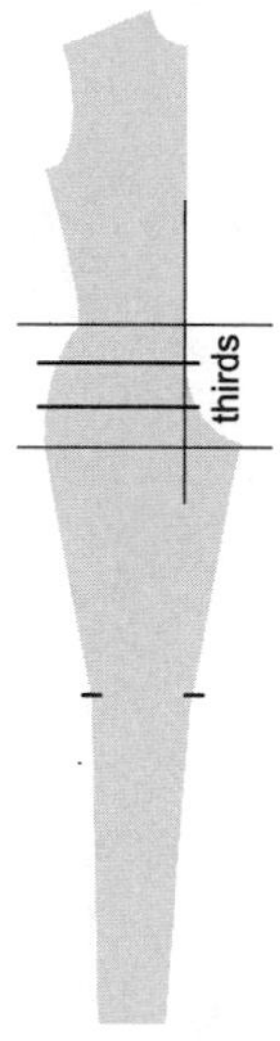

Divide the waist to crotch into three equal parts.

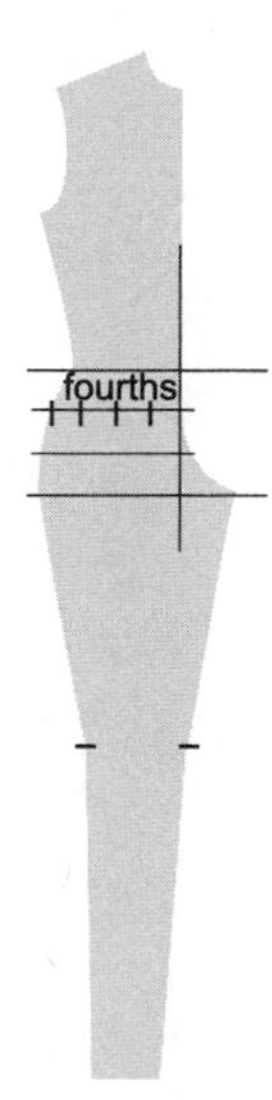

Divide the top line into four parts.

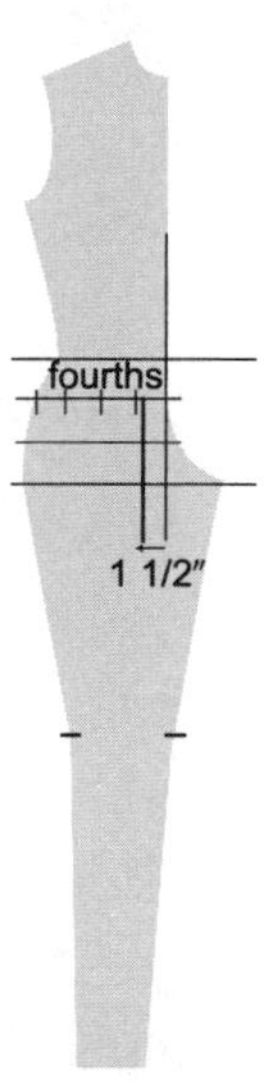

Draw a guideline 1½″ away from the center front crotch line. Note this line may not line up with points on upper hip line.

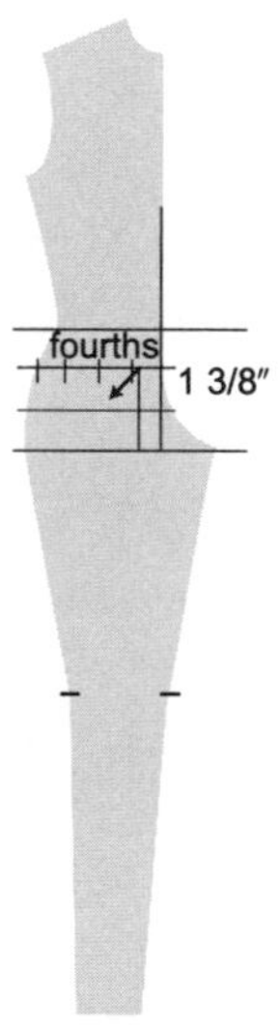

At the intersection, find the bias and draw a guideline.

Mark 1⅜″ on the guideline.

At the mark closest to the side seam, measure up ½″.

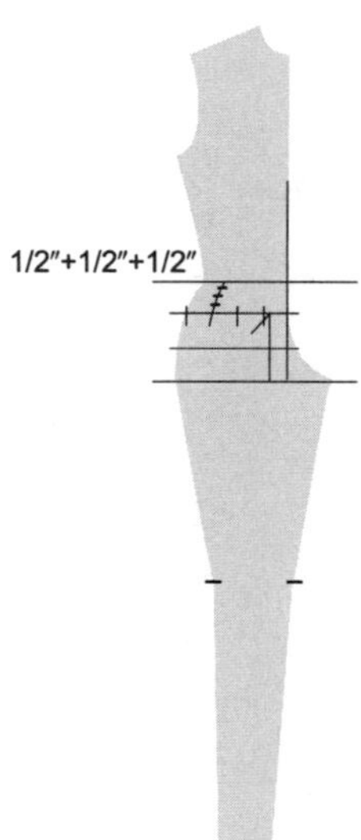

Draw a guideline parallel to the side seams from the first mark. Follow the exact hip curve.

Mark the line ½″ + ½″ + ½″.

Use these marks when drafting higher-cut, sexier swimsuits and leotards.

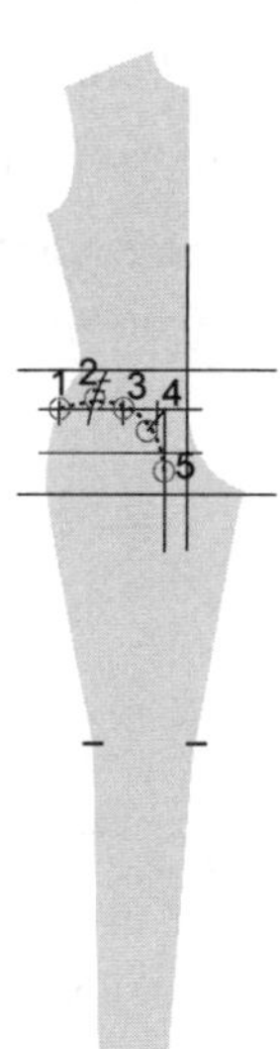

Draw a curved line from the side seam to the ½″ mark to the bias line, and blend into the crotch.

Create one smooth and continuously curved line.

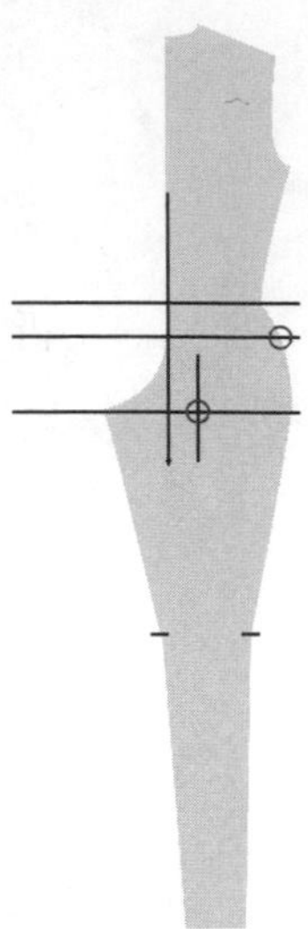

LEOTARD SLOPER BACK

Trace the upper part of the catsuit sloper to just below the crotch.

Draw a guideline at the waist.

Extend the center front to below the crotch.

Square a line from the center back at crotch level.

Place the front leotard draft onto the back draft and trace the upper hip guideline and crotch guidelines.

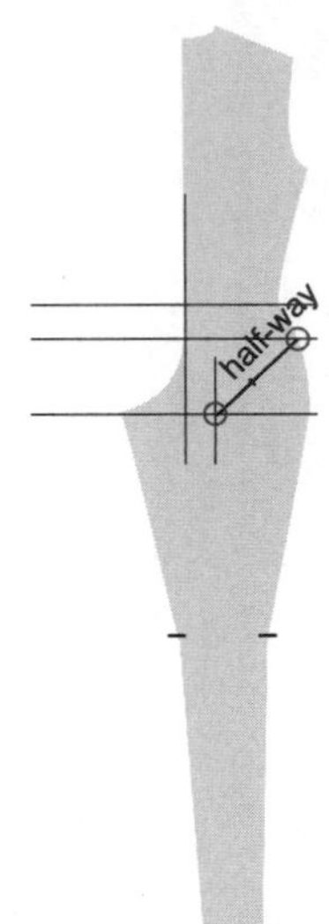

Connect the points with a straight line.

Find the middle of the line.

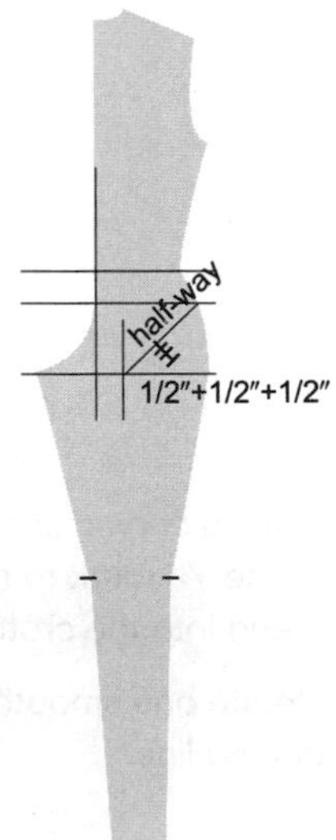

At the middle, measure out:

½″ for small;

1″ for medium;

1½″ for large buttocks.

Note: the customer may still be Small or Medium, but with large buttocks.

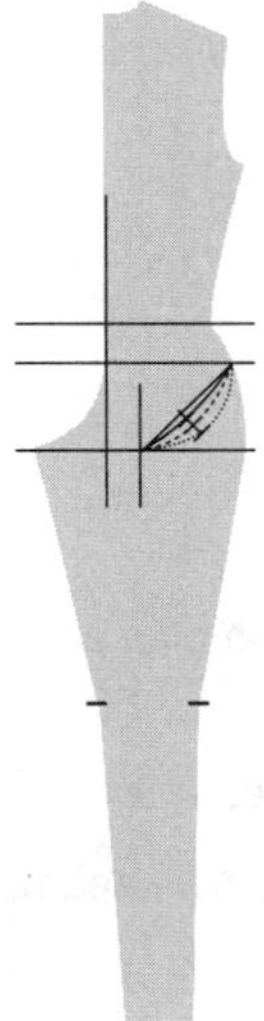

Draw the back leg opening from the crotch to the hip, with a continuously smooth line.

Elastic Reductions

Elastic is of crucial importance when designing and creating swimsuits. Elastic will help keep the garment snug in the crucial areas of the leg openings, the armholes, and even necklines.

The reductions for elastic depend on two variables. The first variable depends on where the elastic is placed on the body. Some areas demand tightness, and other areas require the elastic to be slightly looser. The other variable is the width of the elastic, since wider elastic is much stronger than thin elastic.

In the past, we would reduce 1″ from the front-leg-opening elastic measurement, with no reduction for the back opening, but now most of the industry uses an elastic metering device to attach the elastic, which stretches the elastic evenly all the way around. Since the device cannot tell whether you are sewing the front or the back, the industry has changed practices to reduce the elastic to an even 2″ all the way around the leg opening.

The seam allowances for elastic are usually 1⁄16″ more than the width of the elastic. If you have several layers of fabric wrapping over the elastic (not a very good idea), you may want to allow a little more, about 1⁄32″ extra, per layer of fabric being wrapped with the elastic.

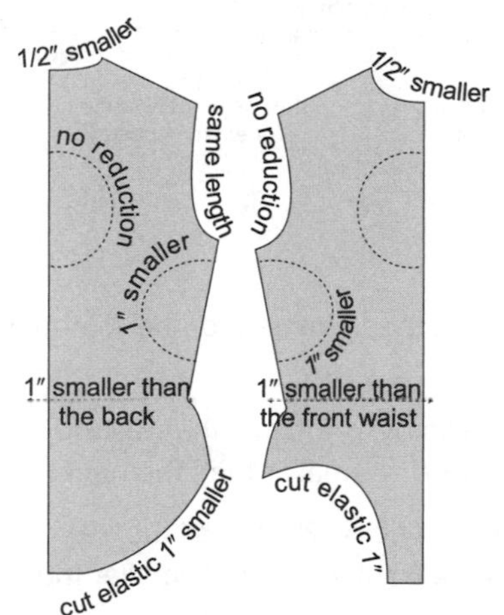

FRONT LEG OPENING

Cut the elastic 1″ smaller than the front leg opening measurement.

BACK LEG OPENING

Cut the elastic 1″ smaller than the back leg opening measurement.

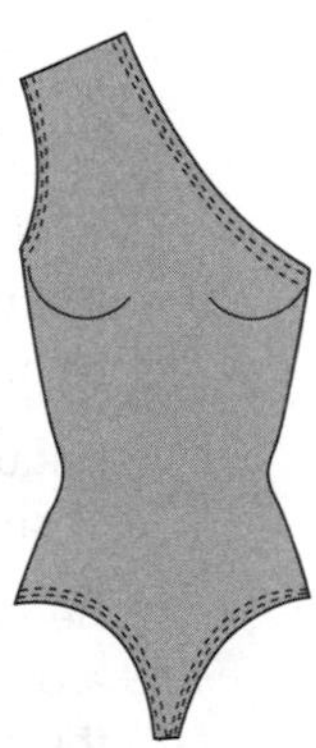

ARMHOLE, NECKLINE, AND LEG OPENING OPTIONS

To create cover-stitched legs, arms, and neckline:

While it is possible to simply cover-stitch hem the arm, neck, and leg openings, if you do, they will not be very snug or tight to the body; they will gape and sit away from the body.

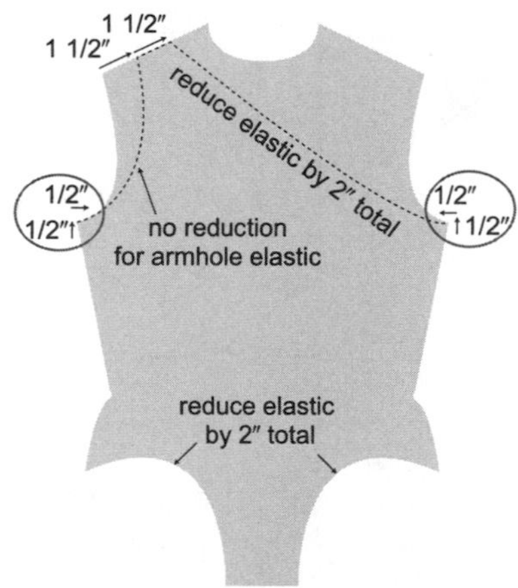

You must raise and take in the underarm for a cover-stitched armhole and neckline. However, if you intend to use elastic, binding, or some type of reducing trim, this is not necessary.

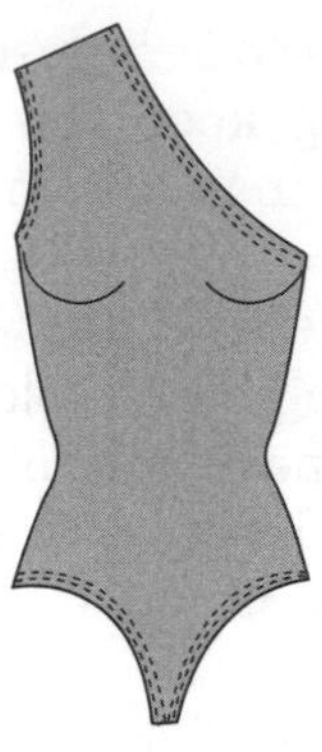

ASYMMETRICAL BODYSUIT WITH ELASTIC LEGS, ARMS, AND NECKLINE

To draft the asymmetrical bodysuit, the pattern must be traced open, full, not on the fold.

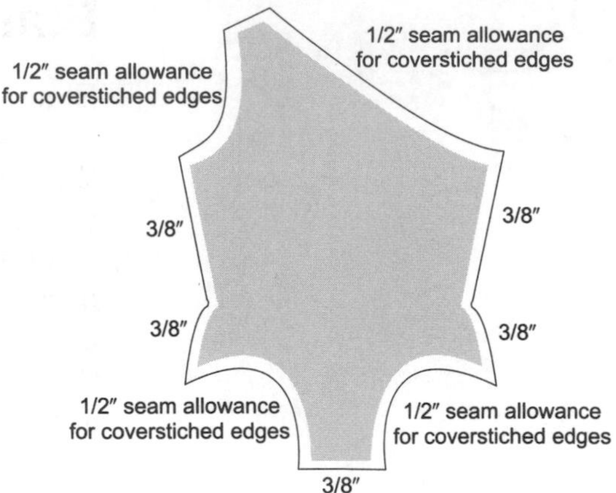

Add seam allowances as illustrated, ³⁄₈″ for seams that will be sewn to other seams, and ½″ for cover-stitched hems.

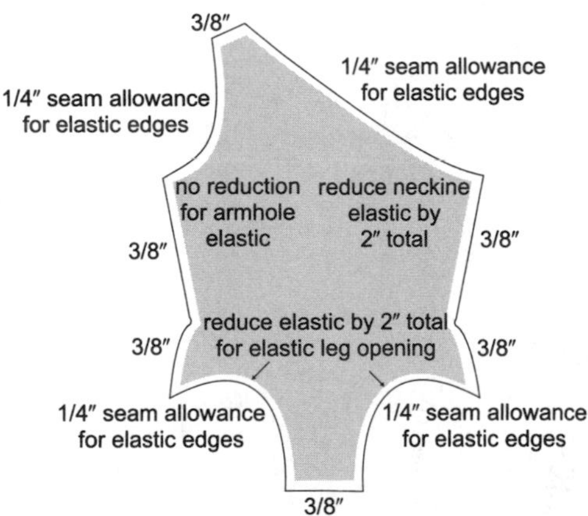

Cut the elastic to the exact measurement of the armhole, without any reductions.

Reduce the neckline elastic by 2″ total all the way around, 1″ smaller than the front and 1″ smaller than the back.

Reduce the leg opening elastic by 2″ total all the way around, 1″ smaller than the front leg and 1″ smaller than the back leg.

Add ¼″ seam allowance for elastic.

Serge the elastic to the "wrong" side of the opening, flip once, and then cover-set.

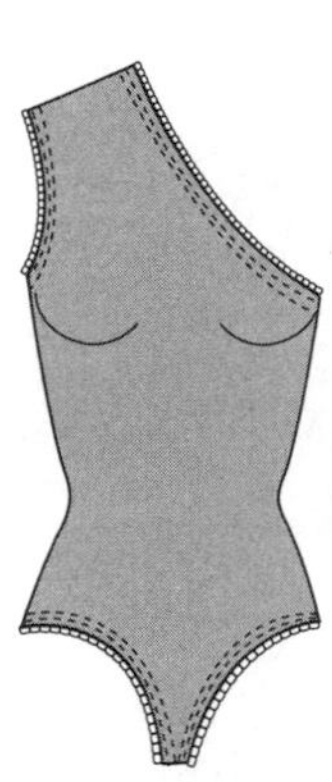

ASYMMETRICAL BODYSUIT WITH PICOT ELASTIC ARMHOLE

Picot elastic is the same as regular elastic except that it has a fine lacy edge on one side that helps reduce panty lines.

Serge the elastic to the outside of the leg openings, flip once, and then cover-stitch to expose the lace.

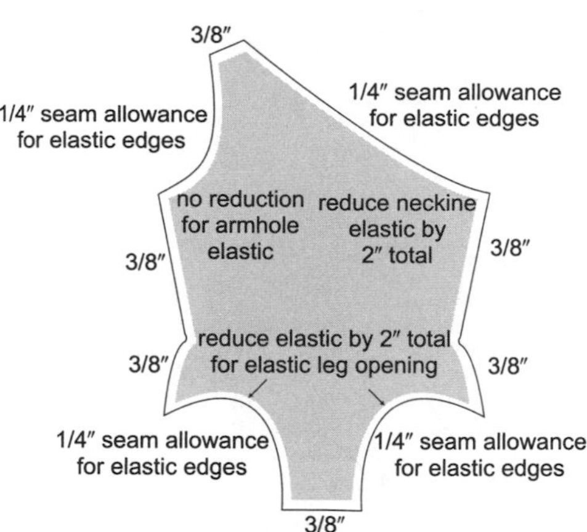

Cut the elastic to the exact measurement of the armhole, without any reductions.

Reduce the neckline elastic by 2″ total all the way around, 1″ smaller than the front and 1″ smaller than the back.

Reduce the leg opening elastic by 2″ total all the way around, 1″ smaller than the front leg and 1″ smaller than the back leg.

Add 1/4″ seam allowance for elastic.

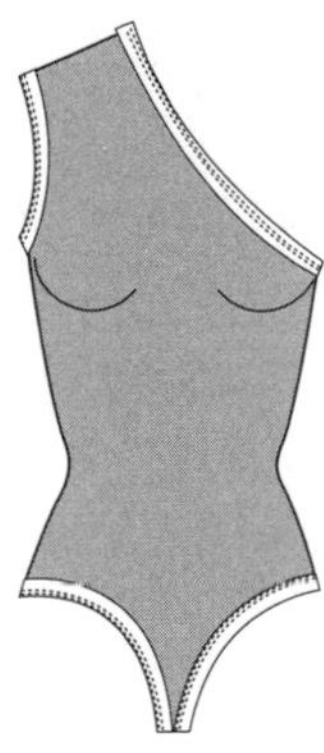

ASYMMETRICAL BODYSUIT WITH BINDING

Cut the binding one-sixth smaller than the armhole.

Don't add any seam allowance to the armhole or neckline when applying binding.

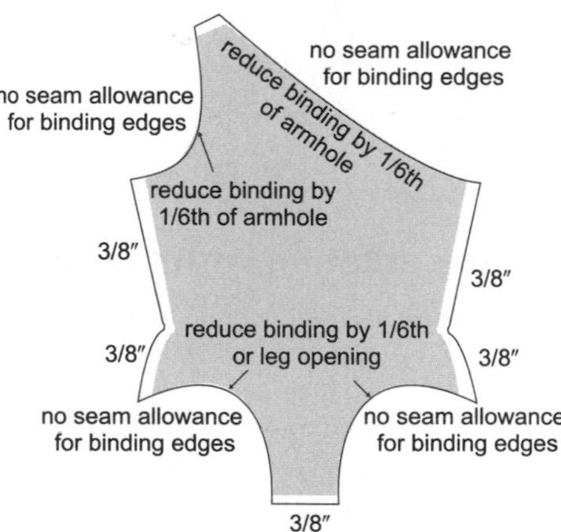

Do add the normal construction seam allowances to the areas that will have binding.

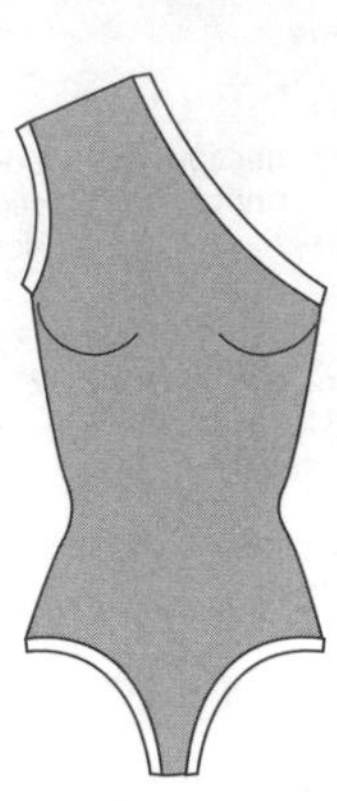

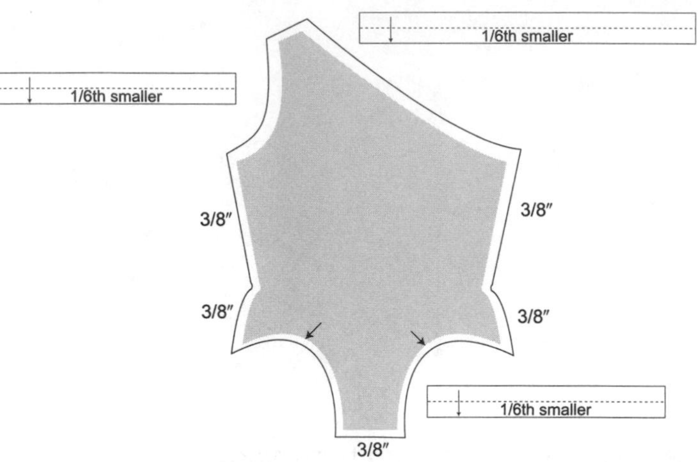

ASYMMETRICAL BODYSUIT WITH BANDING

Banding is another method of finishing the armhole and neck edges.

Cut the banding one-sixth smaller than the armhole.

Add seam allowances to the armhole and neckline when banding will be attached, as determined by the type of fabric and serger used.

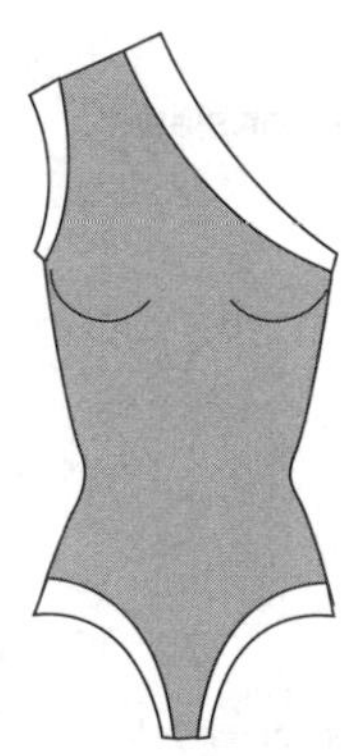

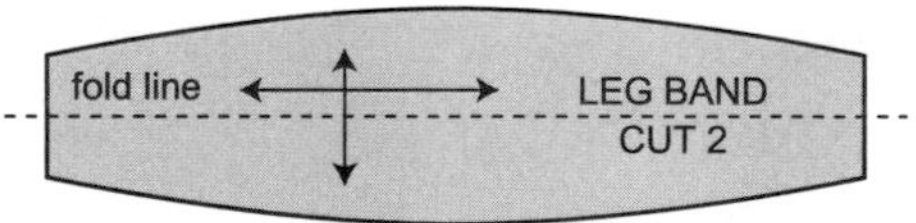

ASYMMETRICAL BODYSUIT WITH SHAPED BANDING

The banding may be shaped for any design.

Shape the banding as required.

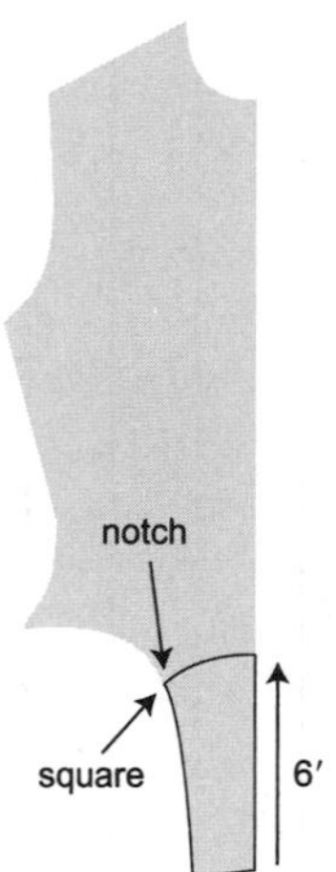

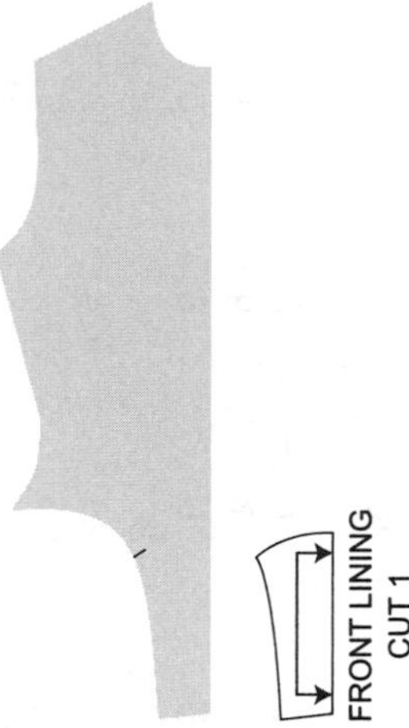

Lining

CROTCH LINING

Measure up 6″.

Square in from the leg opening.

Make the top edge of the lining curved so that it is less likely to show a ridge on the right side of the garment.

Cut this lining in self.

Serge the top edge unless you're working in nylon spandex or a fabric that will not fray or unravel, in which case the edge should be left raw to reduce read-through.

Leave the top of the lining loose, attaching the lining only at the sides and crotch.

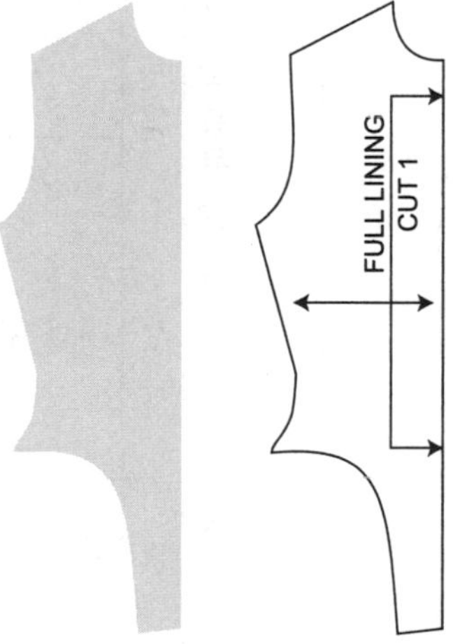

FULL LINING

Cut a full lining in nude tricot lining.

Bikini Tops

ADDING A BUST DART TO THE TOP SLOPER

Use the one-way-stretch top sloper to create the bikini top sloper. Because there is nothing stretching the bikini top, it will act almost like a woven fabric; in fact, these slopers may be used with some woven fabrics.

You must create a dart in the bikini sloper because when knit fabrics stretch, they tend to do so evenly, with even tension; this means they will tend to flatten the bust shape. The dart can be disguised or hidden later, but must be included in the sloper.

The basic top slopers do not have any bust darts built in, so you will need to modify them to create a bust dart in order to draft the bikini top.

CUP DIFFERENCE CHART

You must first determine the cup size by selecting the measurements from this chart.

BUST													
U	inches	30½	31½	32½	33½	34½	35½	37	38½	40	41½	43½	45½
P	30	½	1½	2½	3½	4½	5½	7	8½	10	11½	13½	15½
P	31	–½	½	1½	2½	3½	4½	6	7½	9	10½	12½	14½
E	32	–1½	–½	½	1½	2½	3½	5	6½	8	9½	11½	13½
R	33	–2½	–1½	–½	½	1½	2½	4	5½	7	8½	10½	12½
	34	–3½	–2½	–1½	–½	½	1½	3	4½	6	7½	9½	11½
C	35	–4½	–3½	–2½	–1½	–½	½	2	3½	5	6½	8½	10½
H	36½	–36½	–36½	–36½	–36½	–36½	–36½	–36½	–36½	–36½	–36½	–36½	–36½
E	38	–37½	–36½	–35½	–34½	–33½	–32½	–31	–29½	–28	–26½	–24½	–22½
S	39½	–40	–39	–38	–37	–36	–35	–33½	–32	–30½	–29	–27	–25
T	41	–42½	–41½	–40½	–39½	–38½	–37½	–36	–34½	–33	–31½	–29½	–27½
	43	–45½	–44½	–43½	–42½	–41½	–40½	–39	–37½	–36	–34½	–32½	–30½

CUP SIZES

Cup size is determined by the difference between the bust measurement and the upper bust measurement. This chart is demonstrated with different bust measurements.

Difference	Up to ½″	½″ to 1¼	1½ to 2¼	2½ to 3¼	3½ to 4¼	4½ to 5¼	5½ to 6¼	6½ to 7¼	7½ to 8¼	8½ to 9¼
Cup size	AA	A	B	C	D	DD/E	DDD/F	G	H	I

CUP AMOUNTS

This chart shows the amount needed to increase at the side seam by slashing and spreading.

Cup Size	**8**	**10**	**12**	**14**	**16**	**Small**	**Medium**	**Large**
B	¼	⅜	⅝	¾	1	¼	⅝	⅞
C	⅝	¾	1	¾	1⅜	¾	1	1¼
D	1	1⅛	1⅜	1¾	1¾	1⅛	1⅜	1⅞
DD/e	1⅜	1⅝	1¾	2	2⅛	1½	1¾	2⅛
G								
H								
I								

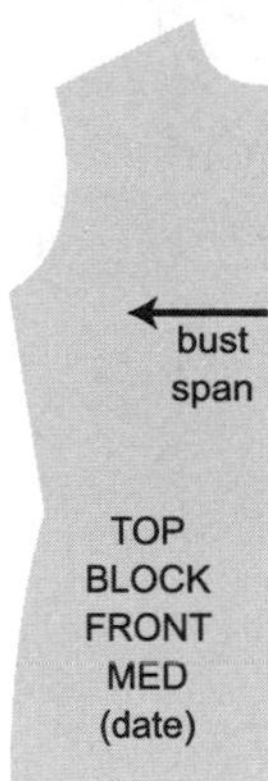

First, find the apex of the bust.

Draw a guideline parallel to the center that is half the bust span away from the center front.

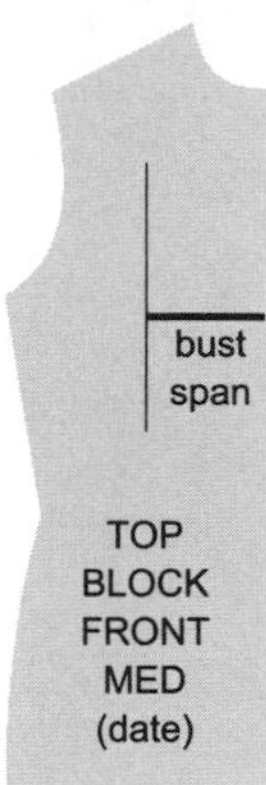

Draw a guideline, parallel to the center front but away from the front, half of the bust span amount.

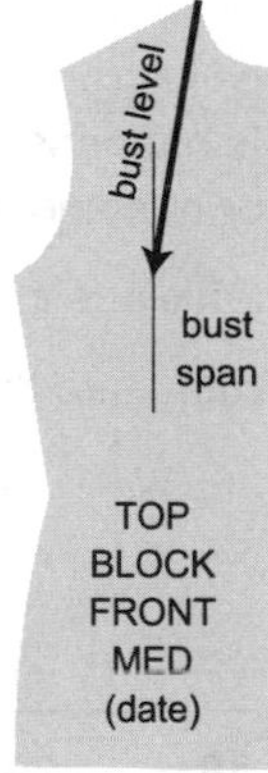

Measure the bust level to wherever it lands on the guideline; this is your apex.

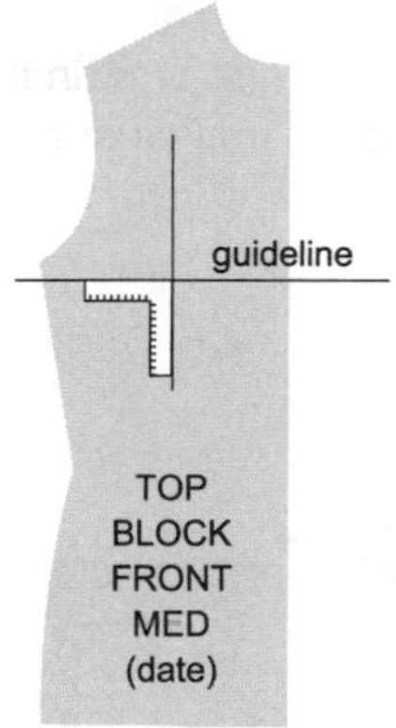

From the apex, draw a guideline that extends from the center front to the side seam. This is the line that you will slash and spread to add extra length for the bust.

	Extra Extra Small	Extra Small	Small	Medium	Large	Extra Large	Extra Extra Large
Stable	6 1/2	6 5/8	6 7/8	7 1/8	7 1/2	7 7/8	8 3/8
Moderate	6 3/8	6 1/2	6 3/4	7 1/8	7 1/2	7 7/8	6 3/8
Stretchy	6 3/8	6 1/2	6 3/4	7	7 3/8	7 7/8	8 1/8
Super-stretch	6 1/4	6 3/8	6 5/8	6 7/8	7 1/4	7 5/8	7 7/8
Rib	5 7/8	6	6 1/4	6 1/2	6 7/8	7 1/4	7 1/2
Bust level	9 7/8	10	10 1/4	10 1/2	10 3/4	11	11 1/4

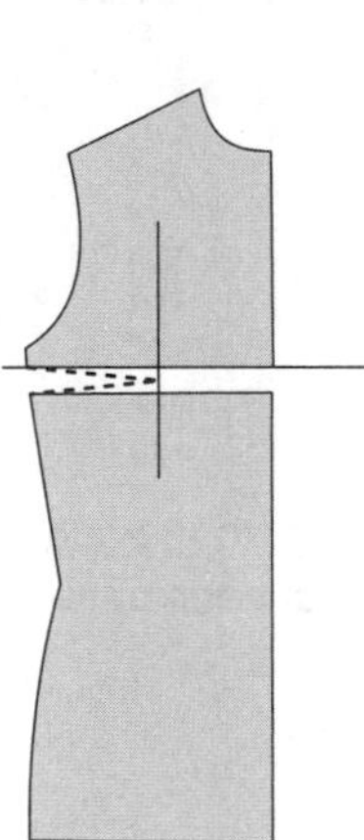

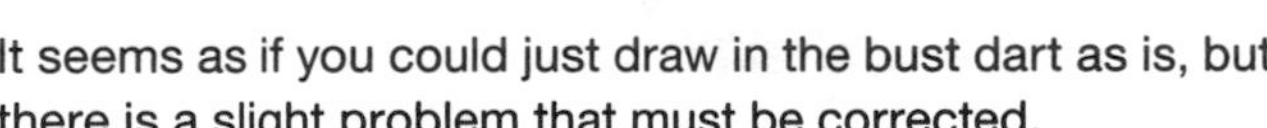

It seems as if you could just draw in the bust dart as is, but there is a slight problem that must be corrected.

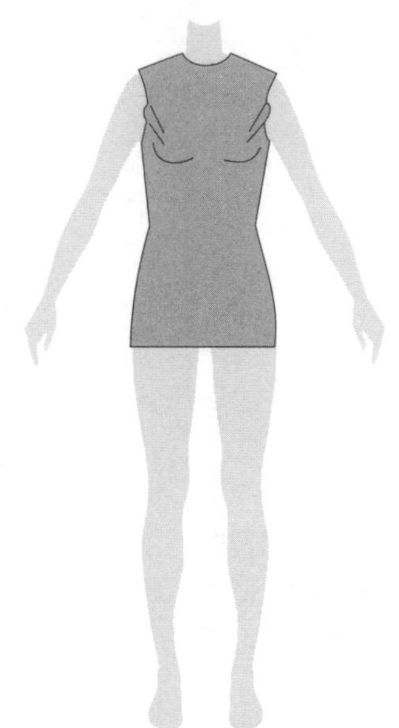

CUP CORRECTIONS

Note how the fabric in the illustration creates ripples pulling from the armhole. This happens with any large bust, whether a dart is added or not, and must be corrected.

Place another small dart, this one in the armhole.

Note: This dart will be pivoted into the bust dart and will not show.

ARMHOLE DART

Remove this amount as an armhole dart to correct the fit noted previously.

Cup Size	2	4	6	8	10	12	14	16	18	20
B	0	0	0	0	0	0	0	0	0	0
C	0	0	¼	½	¾	1	1¼	1½	1¾	2
D	0	0	½	1	1½	2	2½	3	3½	4
DD	0	½	1	1½	2	2½	3	3½	4	4½
DDD/F	0	½	1	1½	2	2½	3	3½	4	4½
G	0	½	1	1½	2	2½	3	3½	4	4½
H	0	½	1	1½	2	2½	3	3½	4	4½
I	0	½	1	1½	2	2½	3	3½	4	4½

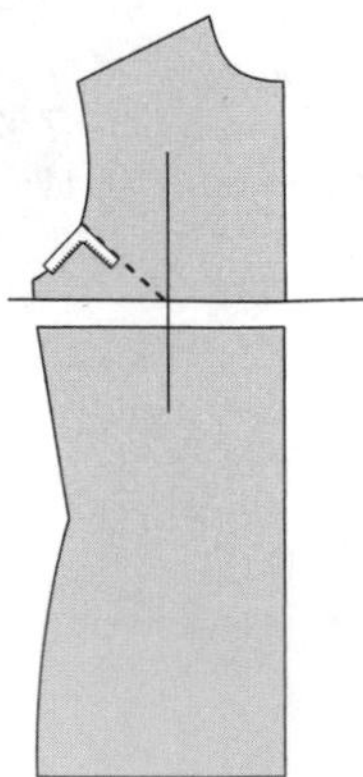

Once you have determined the amount of the armhole dart, square a guideline from the armhole to the apex.

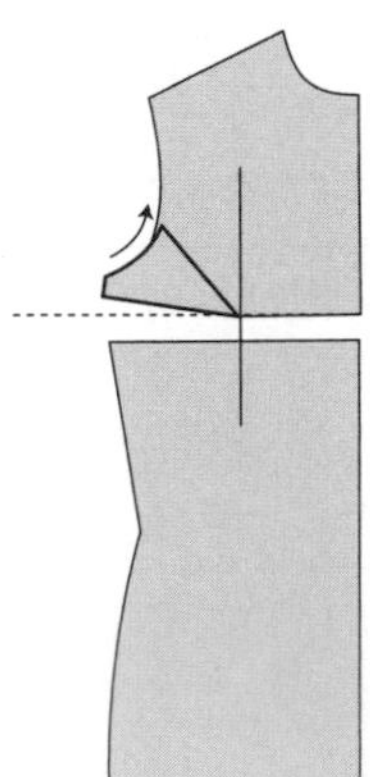

Slash and overlap the armhole dart as illustrated; note how the bust dart gets slightly larger, also.

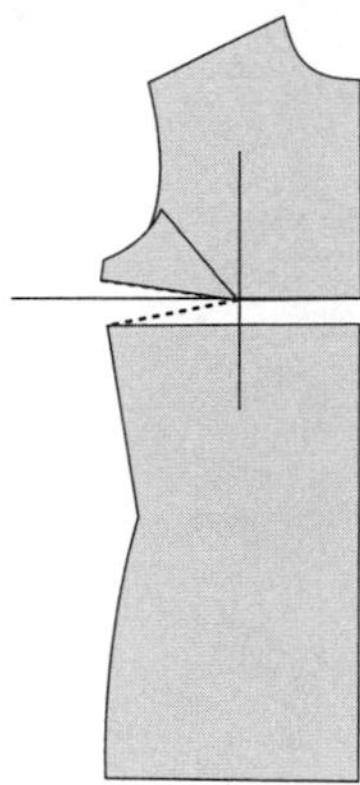

Draw in the bust dart as illustrated.

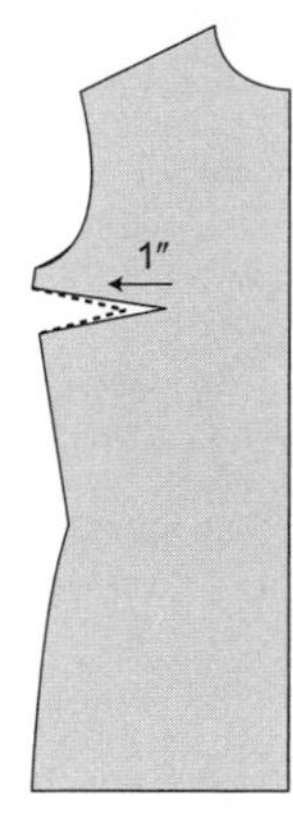

The bust dart cannot be used as is and must be shortened; otherwise it will go right to the apex.

Shorten the dart by 1″ up to 1½″; when pivoting the dart to another position to bring the apex back to the original point, remember to shorten the dart again.

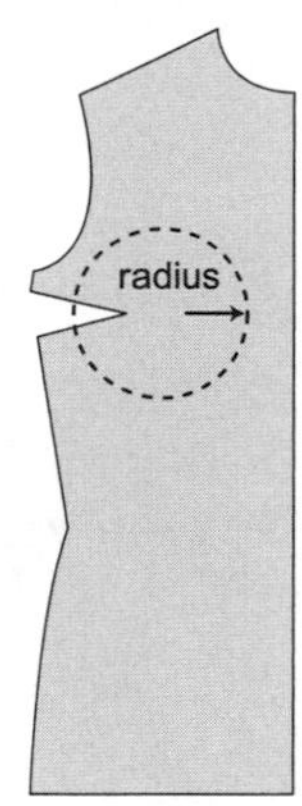

To determine the bust radius, use the chart below.

From the original bust apex, draw in the bust radius, using a compass.

	Extra Extra Small	Extra Small	Small	Medium	Large	Extra Large	Extra Extra Large
Stable	2 1/8	2 1/4	2 3/8	2 1/2	2 5/8	2 3/4	2 7/8
Moderate	2 1/8	2 1/4	2 3/8	2 1/2	2 5/8	2 3/4	2 7/8
Stretchy	2	2 1/8	2 1/4	2 3/8	2 1/2	2 5/8	2 3/4
Super	1 7/8	2	2 1/8	2 1/4	2 3/8	2 1/2	2 5/8
Rib	1 3/4	1 7/8	1 7/8	2	2 1/8	2 1/4	2 3/8

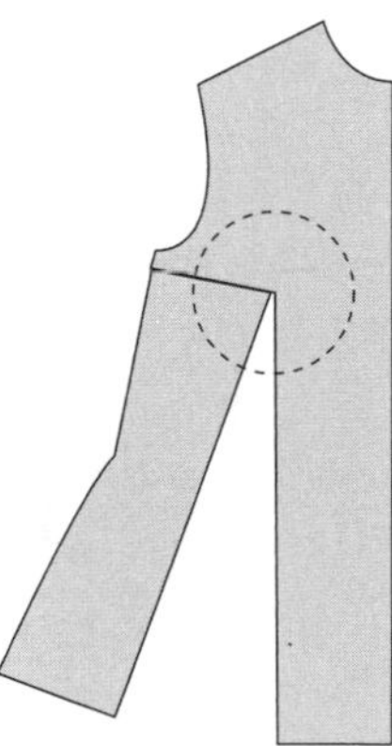

Slash and spread to move the dart to the hem area.

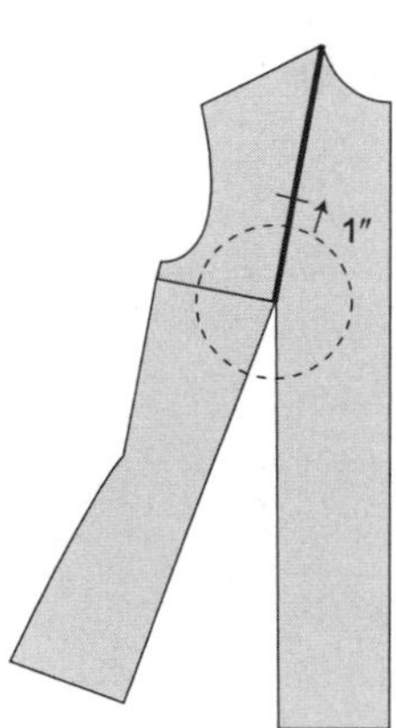

Draw a line from the bust apex to the shoulder/neck intersection as illustrated.

Measure up the line 1″.

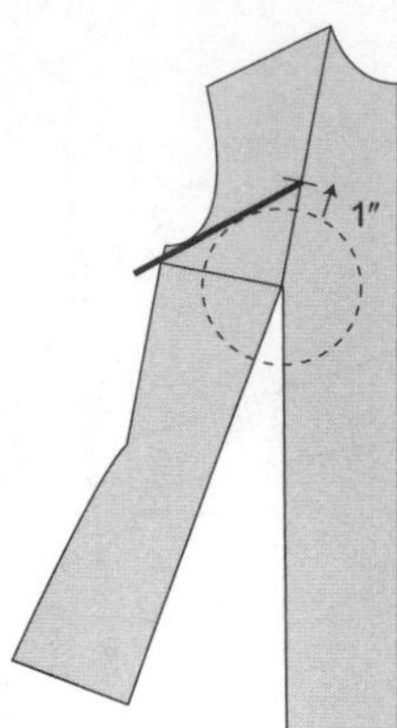

Line your ruler up with the 1″ point and swing it until it touches, tangent to the curve of the bust radius.

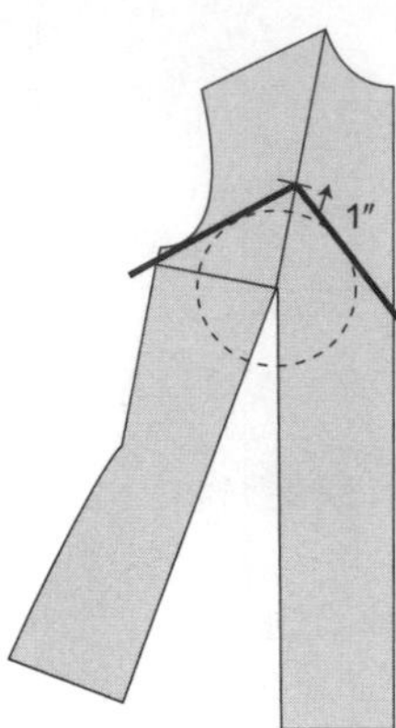

Repeat for the other side.

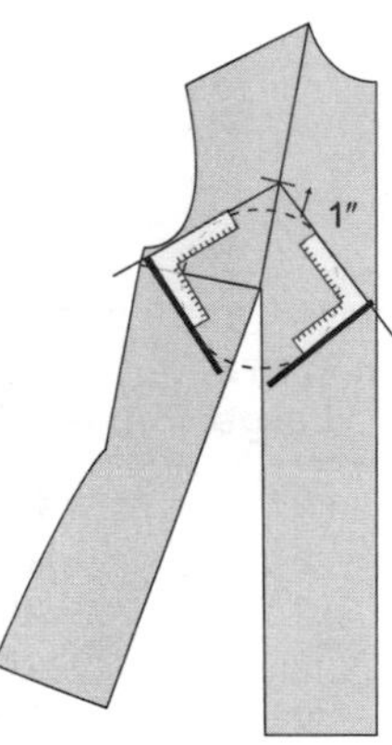

Using an L-square ruler, draw a line that is square to the other guideline and touches the curve of the bust radius.

Repeat for the other side.

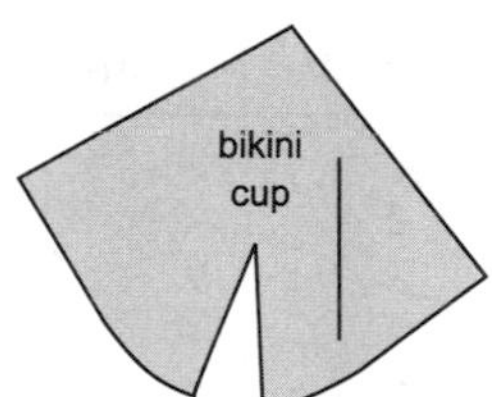

Trace out the cup, and separate.

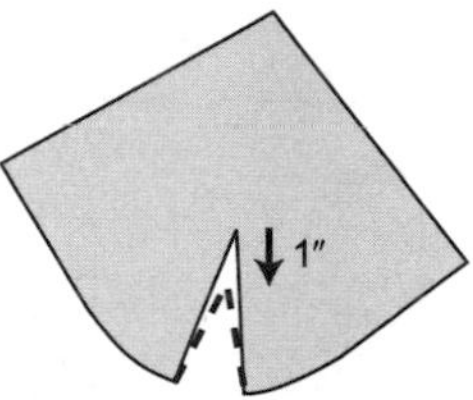

In order to use the cup with the dart, you must shorten the dart lengths; otherwise, the cup becomes too pointy.

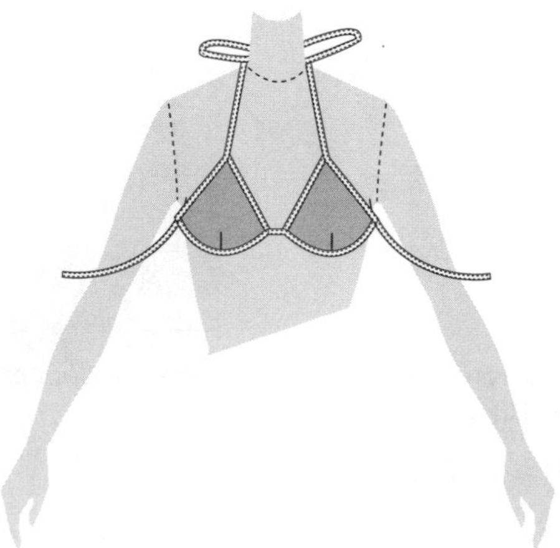

BIKINI WITH DART AND BINDING

This bikini top is finished with self-binding, using the collarette machine.

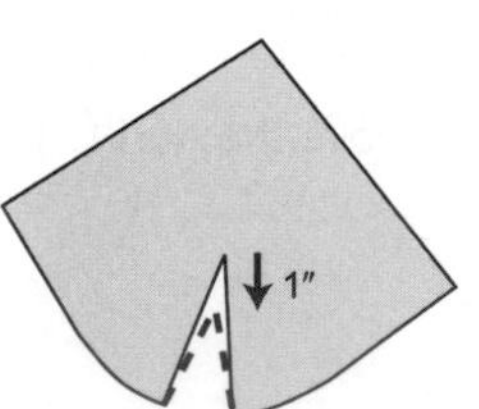

In order to use the cup with the dart, you must shorten the dart lengths; otherwise, the cup becomes too pointy.

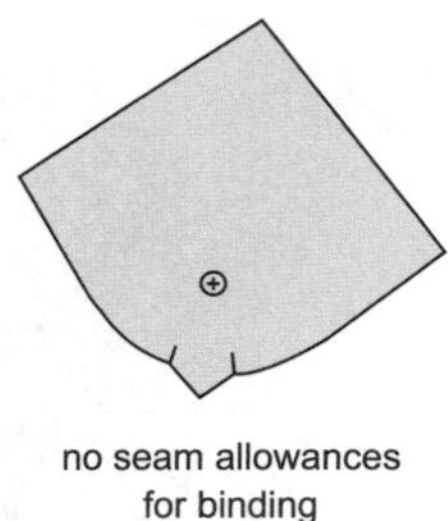

No seam allowances are required for this style; 3/8″ finished binding doesn't need any.

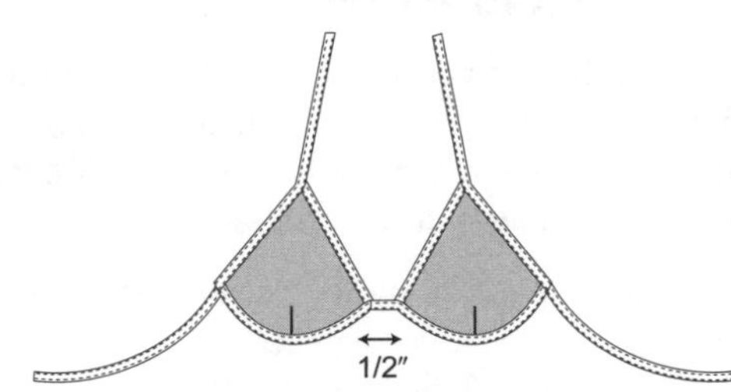

The gap between the cups should be a minimum of 1/2″ for breasts that are very close together, and a maximum of 1″ for breasts that are far apart.

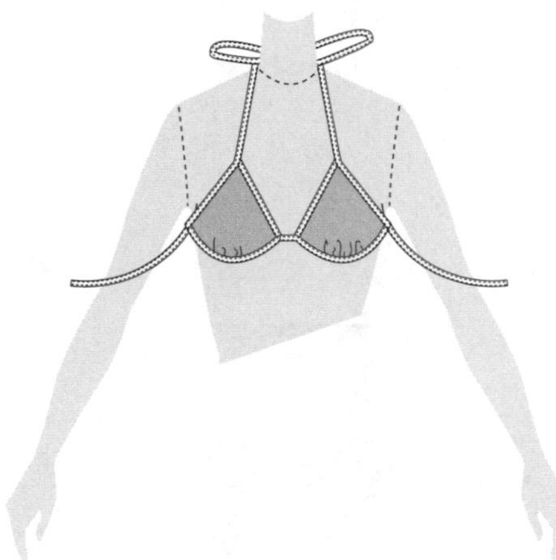

BIKINI WITH EASE AND BINDING

This bikini converts the dart into ease under the bust.

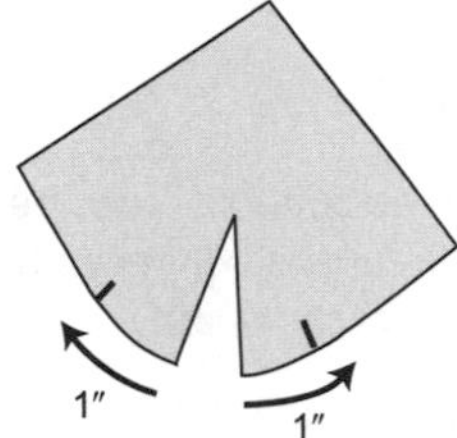

Mark a notch 1″ away from the dart legs, one on each side.

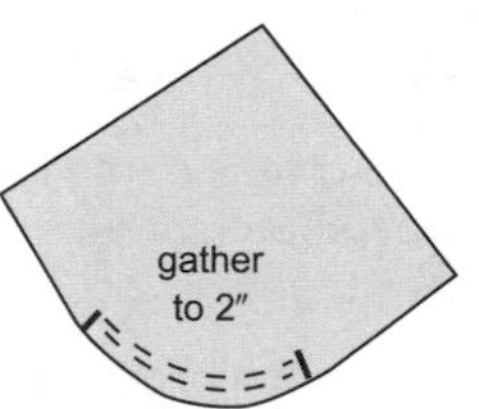

Remove the dart and blend a curve.

Label the pattern to indicate that you must gather between the two notches to a final measurement of 2″.

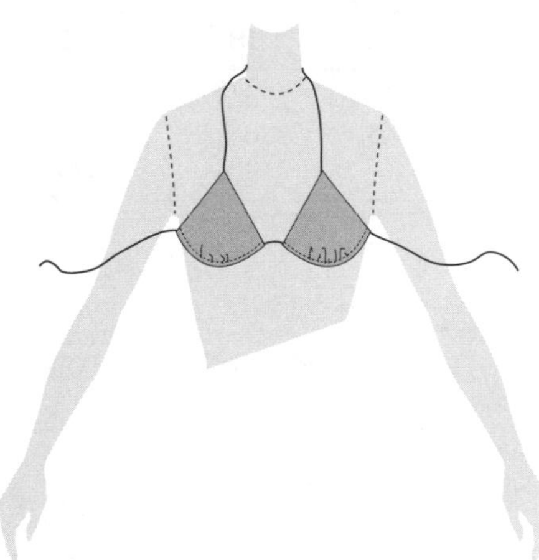

BIKINI WITH A CHANNEL FOR A DRAWSTRING

This bikini top is lined with a spaghetti strap inserted between the self and the lining to create the tie at the top.

The bottom of the bikini has a casing with a string inserted inside.

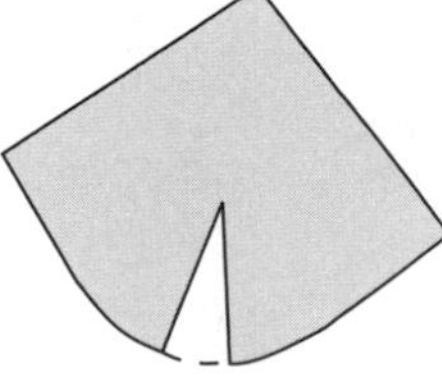

Fill in the dart by drawing a smooth-curved line along the bottom of the draft.

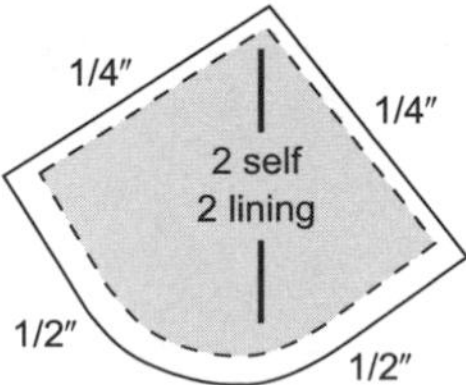

Add 1/4″ seam allowances to the sides to sew to the lining and a 1/2″ seam allowance to the lower edge for a casing.

BIKINI BOTTOMS AND PANTIES

You may expect that you can just cut off the leotard to create a panty bottom, but remember, the length measurements were reduced to accommodate the lengthwise stretch of the fabric. Once the leotard is cut, it will spring back and be lower down on the body.

You must create a separate panty sloper that does not have as much lengthwise reduction.

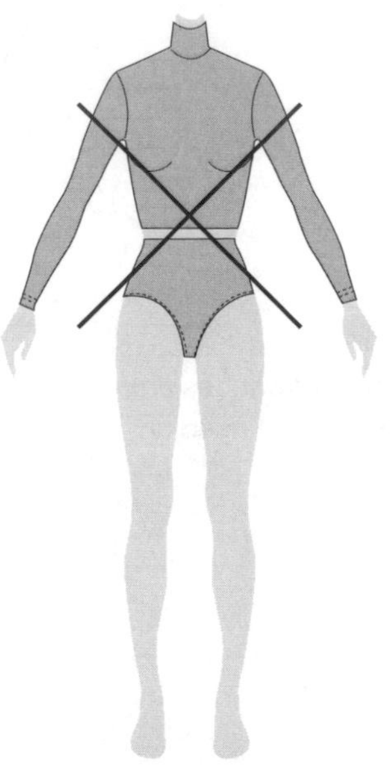

FOUR-WAY-STRETCH REDUCTIONS

Note that the crotch depth is multiplied × 0.95, a reduction of 5%, because the four-way-stretch reduction of 10% is too much, and a 0% reduction, as in one-way-stretch, is too little and will cause the crotch to sag.

This draft is for the bikini panty bottom, and should be used with four-way-stretch fabrics.

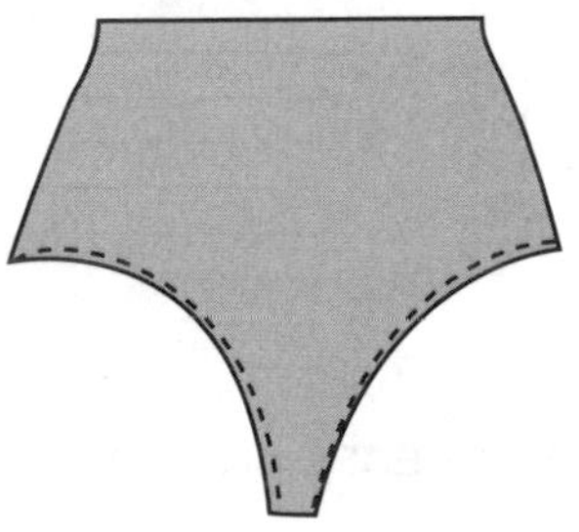

		Multiply by	Extra Extra Small	Extra Small	Small	Medium	Large	Extra Large	Extra Extra Large
			0	2	6	10	14	18	20
2	Waist	× 0.90	21 1/8	22	23	23 7/8	24 3/4	26 1/8	27 1/2
3	Hip	× 0.90	31	32	32 7/8	33 3/4	34 5/8	36	37 3/8
4	Crotch depth	× 0.95	9	9 1/8	9 1/4	9 3/8	9 1/2	9 5/8	9 5/8

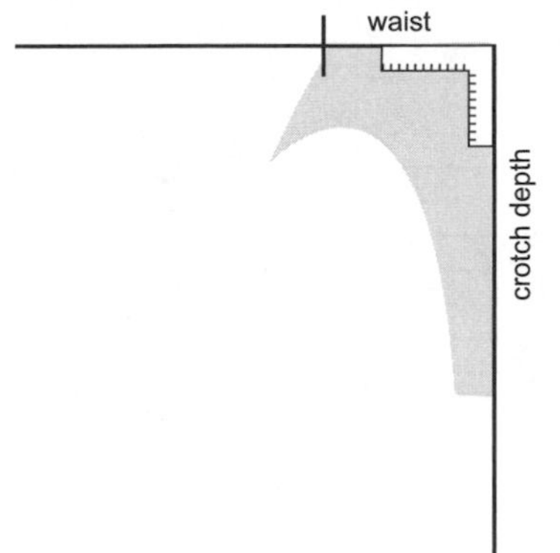

Draw intersecting lines, and measure the waist amount and the crotch depth amount.

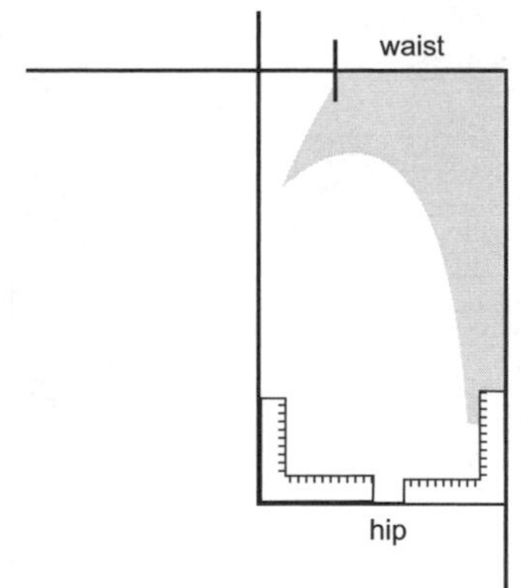

Square a line at the crotch depth, mark with the hip measurement, and square a guideline up to the waist.

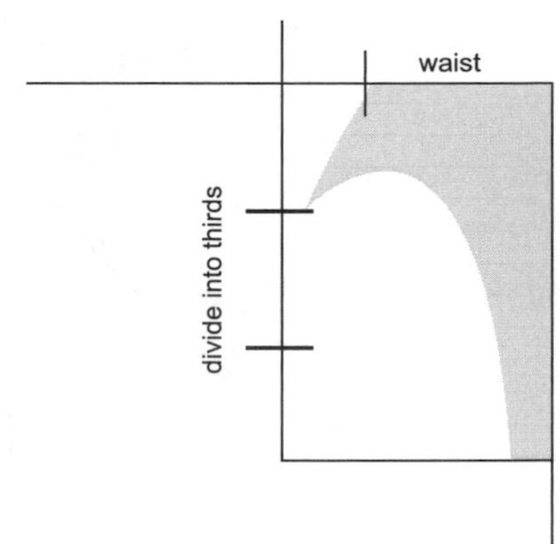

Divide the guideline into thirds.

	Extra Extra Small	Extra Small	Small	Medium	Large	Extra Large	Extra Extra Large
Waist	21 1/8	22	23	23 7/8	24 3/4	26 1/8	27 1/2
Quarter of waist	5 1/4	5 1/2	5 3/4	6	6 1/4	6 1/2	6 7/8
Crotch depth	9	9 1/8	9 1/4	9 3/8	9 1/2	9 5/8	9 5/8
Hip	31	32	32 7/8	33 3/4	34 5/8	36	37 3/8
Quarter of hip	7 3/4	8	8 1/4	8 1/2	8 5/8	9	9 3/8
Crotch depth	9	9 1/8	9 1/4	9 3/8	9 1/2	9 5/8	9 5/8
Thirds	3	3	3 1/8	3 1/8	3 1/8	3 1/4	3 1/4

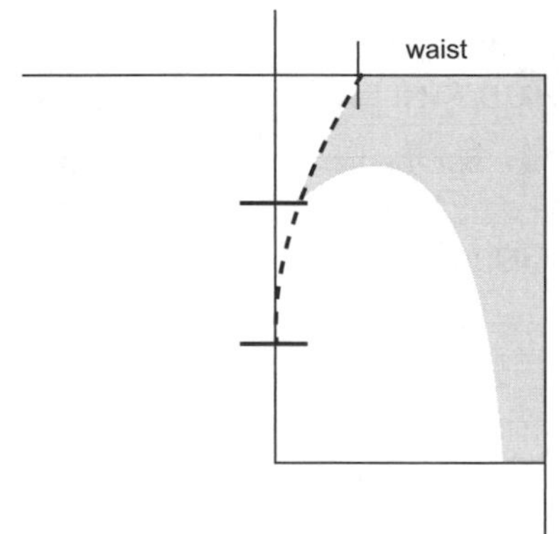

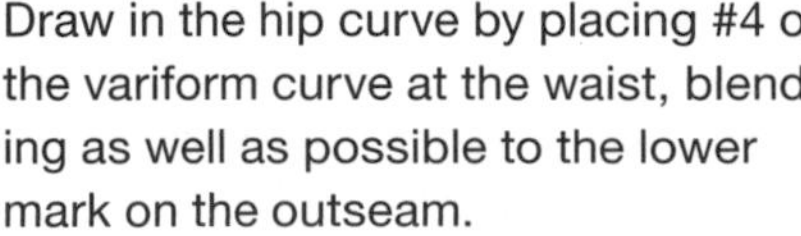

Draw in the hip curve by placing #4 of the variform curve at the waist, blending as well as possible to the lower mark on the outseam.

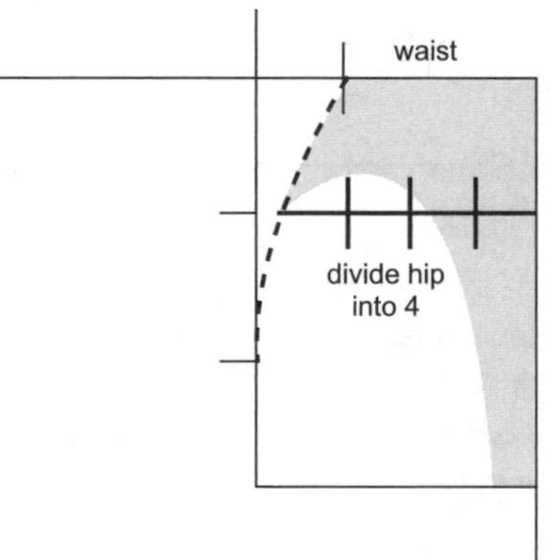

Divide the upper hip line into four equal sections.

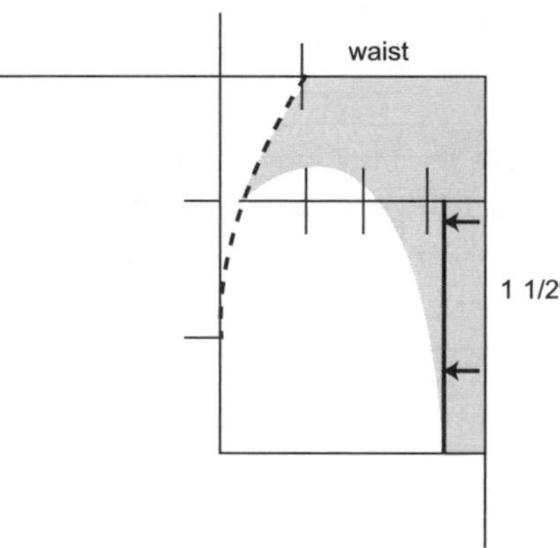

Mark a guideline 1 1/2″ from the center front.

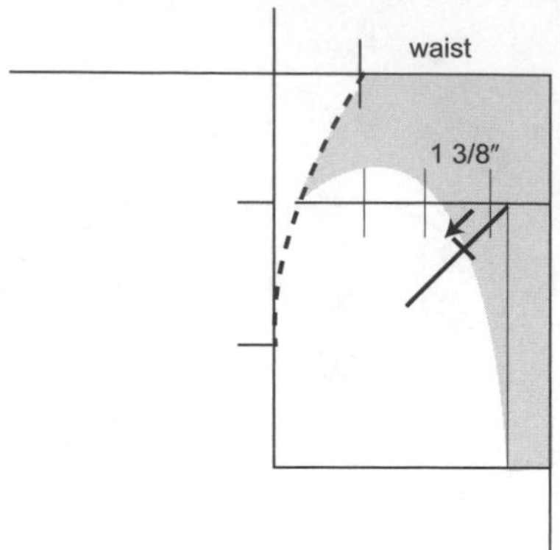

Find the bias in the intersection and measure down 1⅜″.

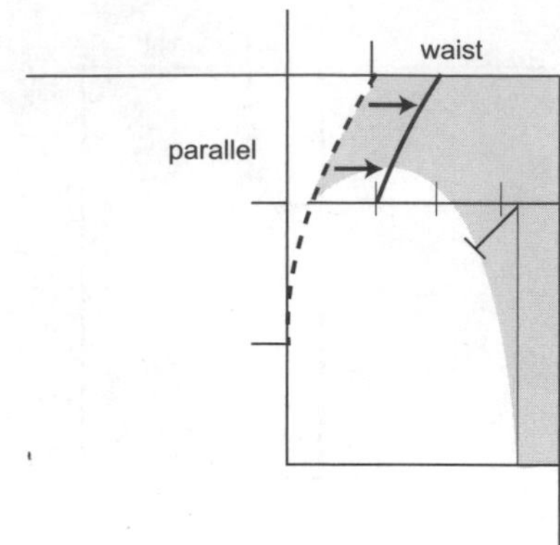

Draw guideline parallel to the side seam that lines up with the mark on the horizontal guideline.

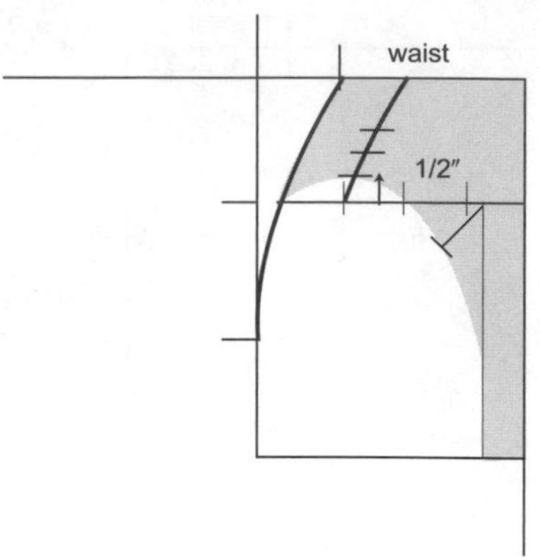

Measure up the guideline ½″ + ½″ + ½″.

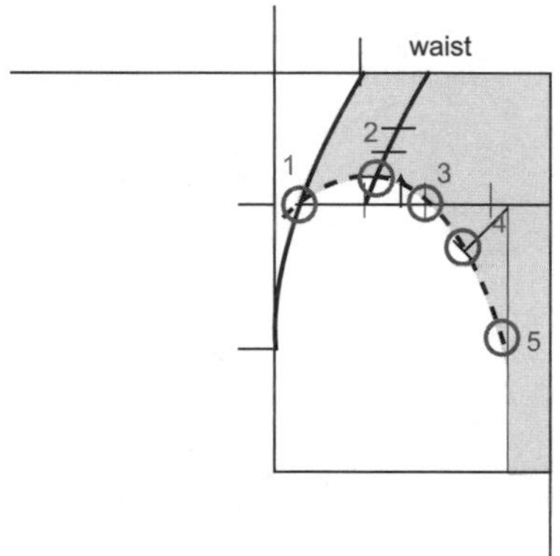

Draw in the front leg, using connection points 1-2-3-4-5, with a smooth and continuous line.

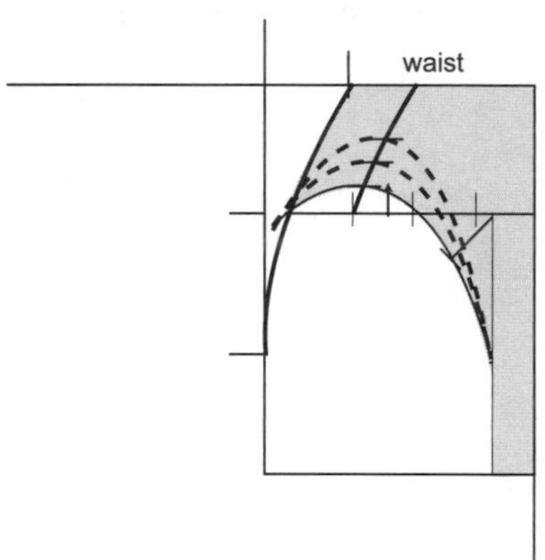

For higher, sexier front legs, use the higher points.

Students and new designers often mistakenly raise the side seams to create a higher leg opening. This will cause the back of the swimsuit to collapse into the buttocks.

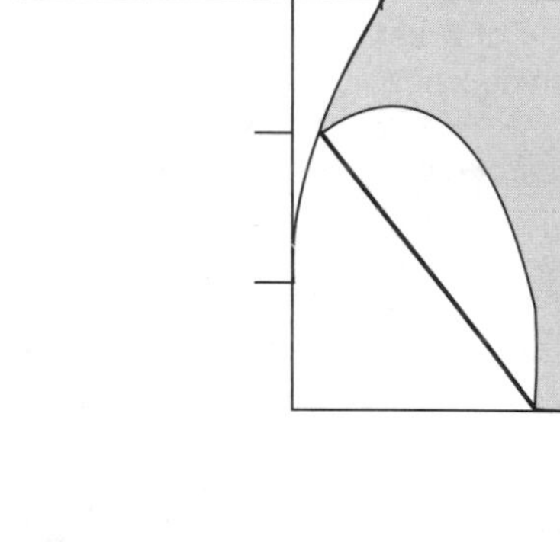

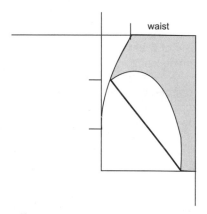

THE BIKINI BACK

Trace out the front draft and connect the crotch point to the hip point with a straight line.

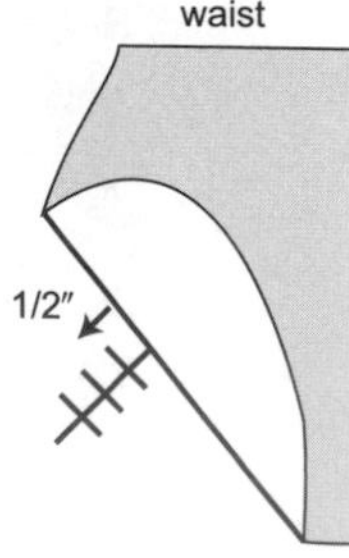

Find the middle of the line and measure out ½″ + ½″ + ½″.

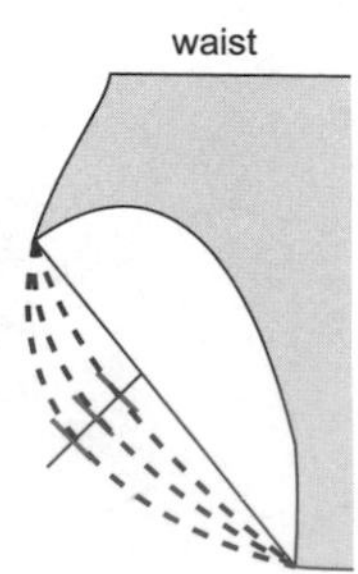

Draw a smooth curve for each of the marks, as illustrated.

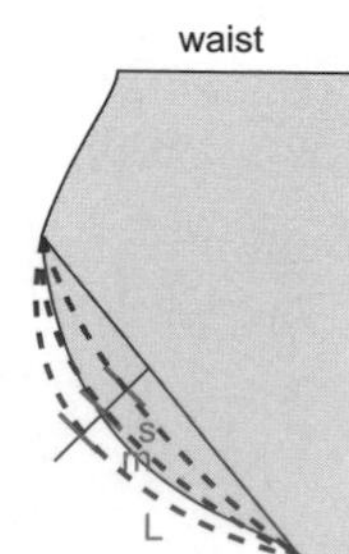

Label the lines as Small, Medium, and Large.

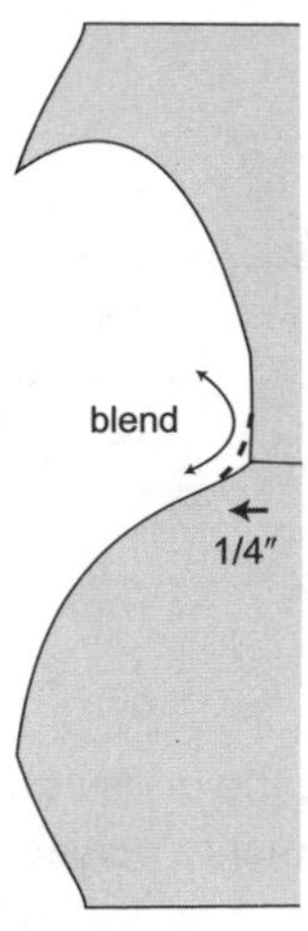

BLENDING AND TRUEING

Line up the crotch seams across from each other and blend the curve.

You will have to increase the size of the crotch by 1/4″ to make the curve smooth enough for elastic.

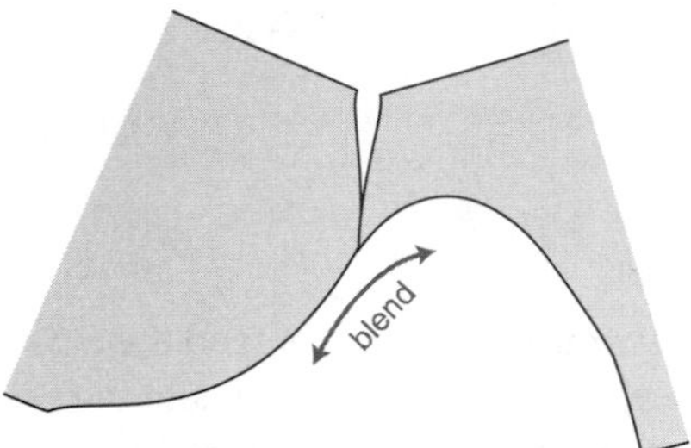

Place the front and back beside each other and walk the side seams down from the waist.

Blend a smooth and continuous sexy line.

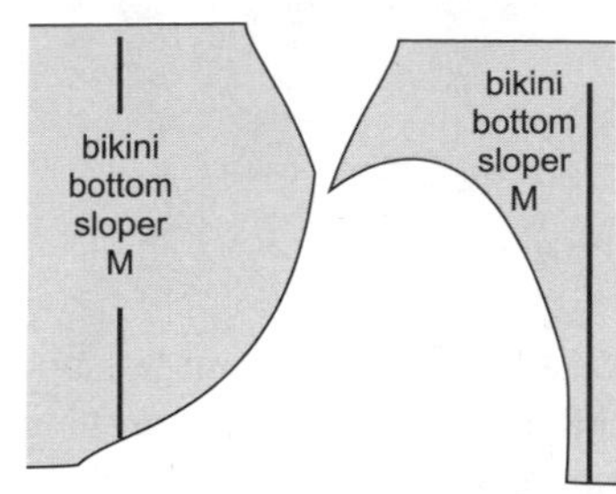

Label the slopers as illustrated.

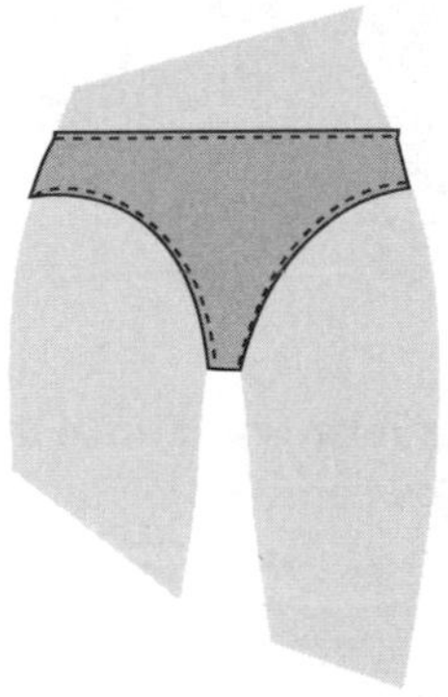

BIKINI WITH LOWERED WAIST

This draft illustrates a lowered waist bikini bottom.

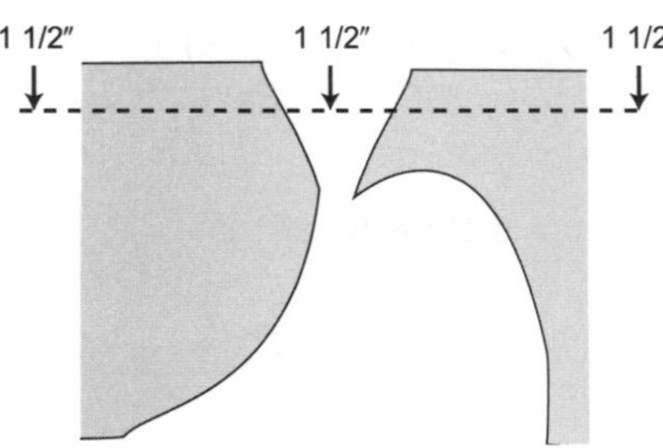

Lower the waist by as much as your design requires, illustrated here at 1½″.

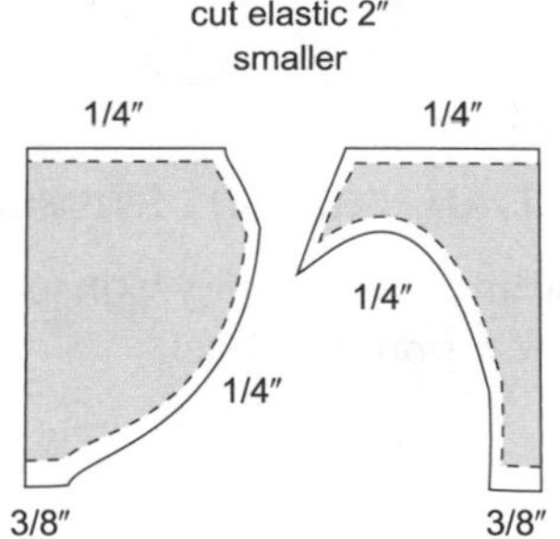

Add the necessary seam allowances.

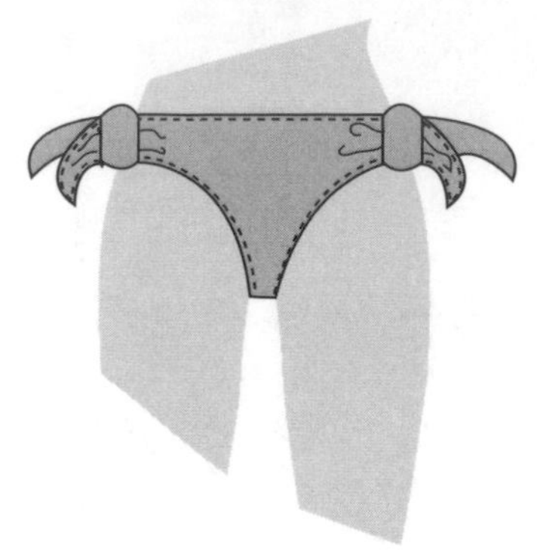

Create a bikini bottom that ties on the side by following these drafting instructions:

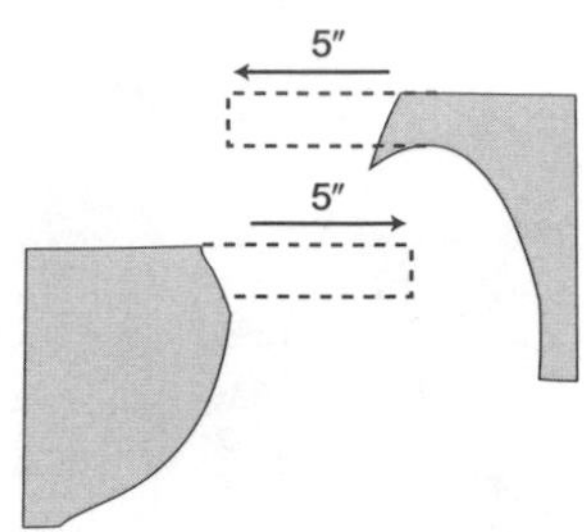

Lower the waist, and extend the side seams 5″ on all sides to create the tie extension.

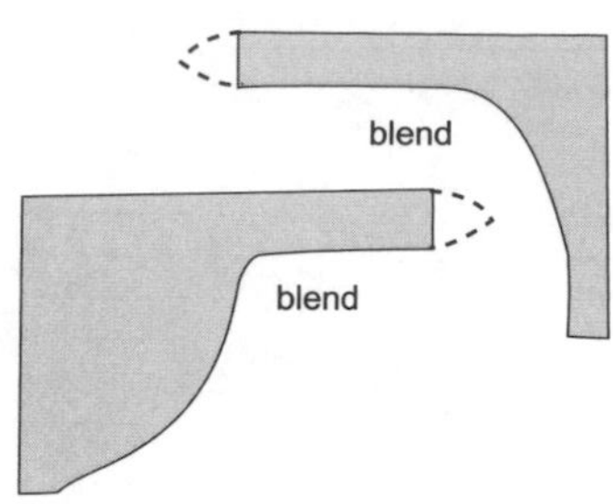

You can leave the ends squared or you can blend them into curves.

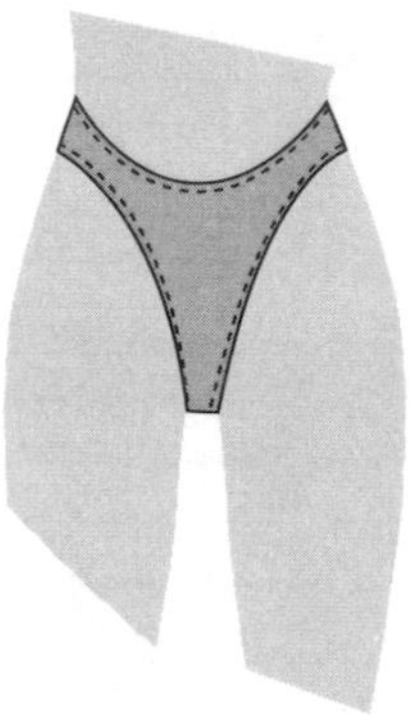

BRAZILIAN HIGH-CUT SWIMSUIT

This swimsuit has a very high leg, with a very low front and back.

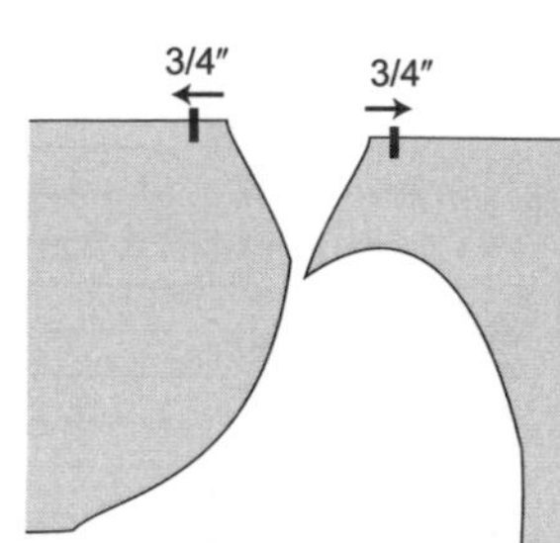

Measure in at the waist ¾″.

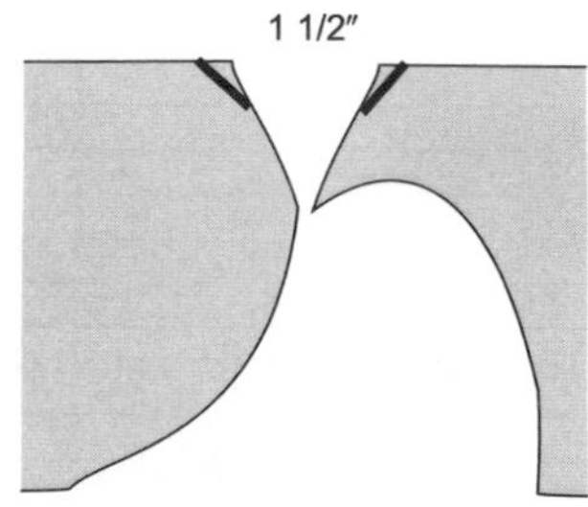

Take your ruler, line it up at the waist, and mark wherever 1½″ lands on the side seam.

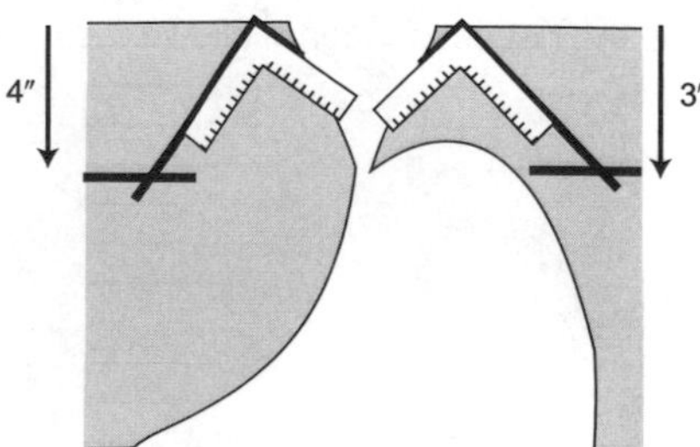

Square a line from the new side seam, the 1½″ mark. Do not concern yourself with the length yet; just make it long enough to reach the front that you will draw in next.

Measure down the front 3″.

Measure down the back 4″.

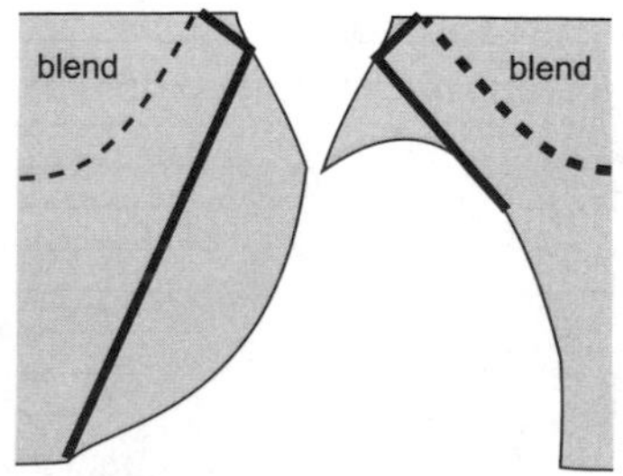

Blend a smooth-curved waist.

Connect the front to the curved portion of the front leg opening.

Connect the back with a straight line.

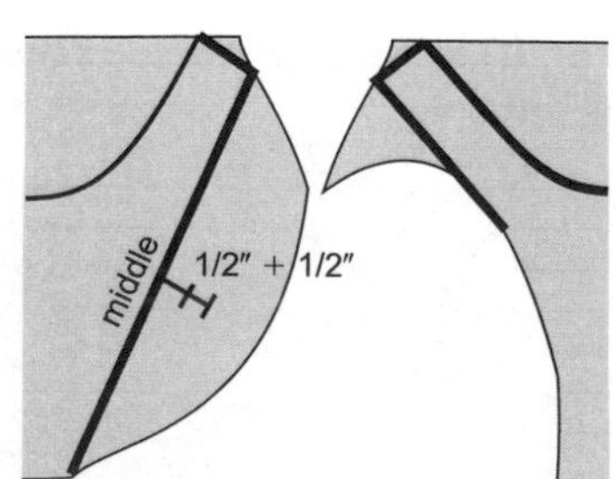

Find the center of the back line and measure ½″ + ½″.

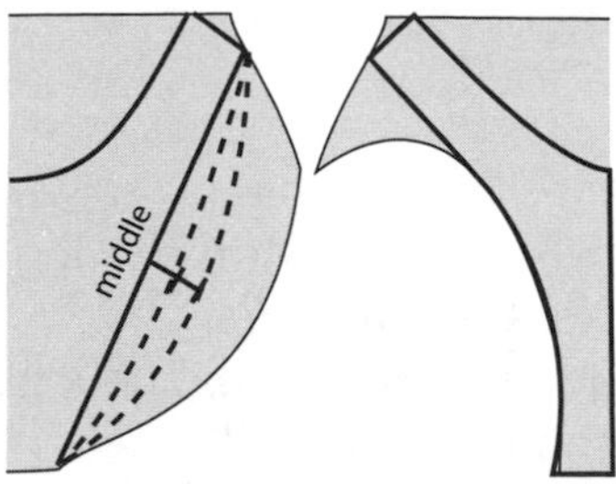

Draw a curved back leg.

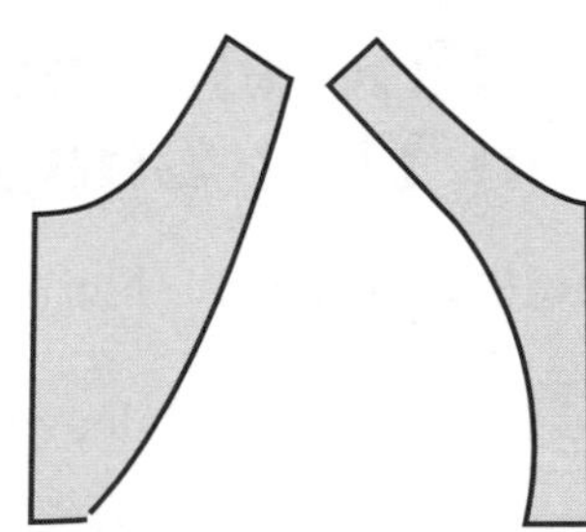

Trace the new bikini bottom.

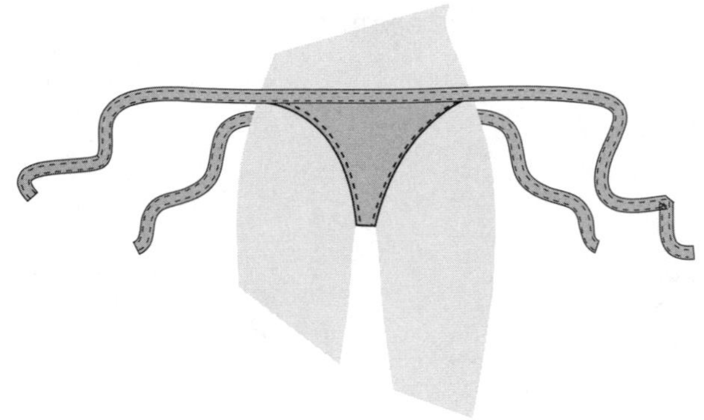

STRING BIKINI

A bikini that ties at the side is easy to draft.

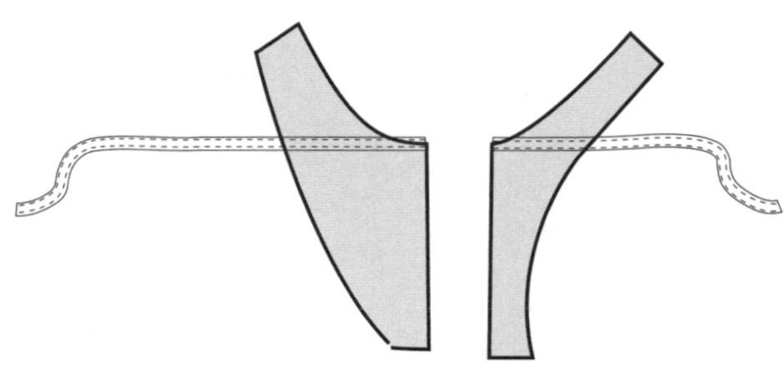

Create the Brazilian high-cut swimsuit bottom draft as shown previously. Simply cut the pattern lower and finish the waist edges with binding ties.

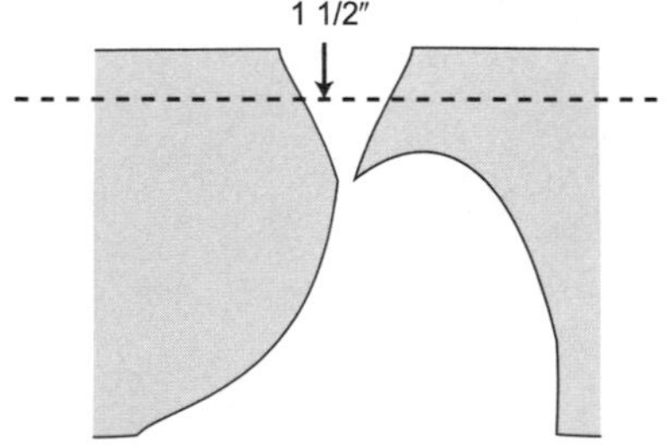

THONG, G-STRING, AND T-BACKS

For the thong, T-back, or G-string, lower the waist 1½″.

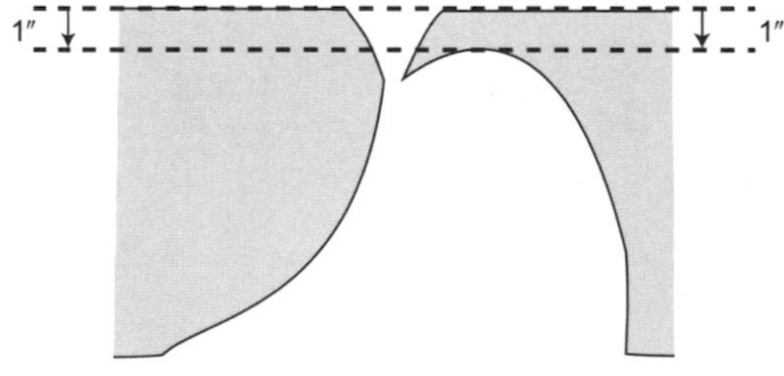

Draw a line parallel to the new waist, 1″ lower.

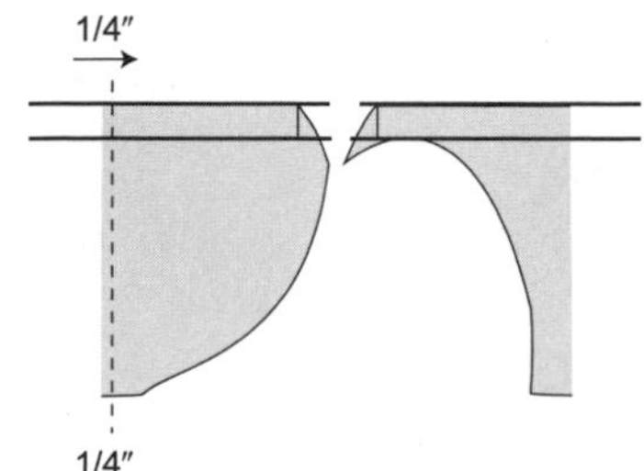

Square the ends of the sides, using the smallest waist.

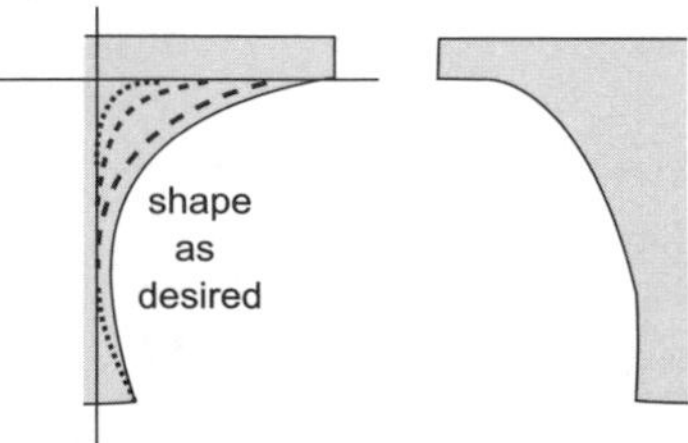

The thong has a center strap that measures ½″ total, ¼″ for each side, and uses 2 × ¼″ elastic on each side

Shape the center back as required.

Test Your Knowledge of the Material in This Chapter

1. When should you use the leotard/bodysuit sloper?
2. How should you true the sleeve to ensure that it fits the armhole?
3. Should the sleeve fit exactly into the armhole?
4. What is the difference between the front and back of the sleeve?
5. How long should you cut the elastic for a leg opening on a bodysuit?
6. How much smaller than the leg opening should the binding be?
7. How much smaller than the leg opening should the banding be?
8. How much should you take in the bodysuit at the side seam when creating a sleeveless style?
9. How should you create a style with shirring on one side seam?

CHAPTER 14

Fitting and Corrections

About This Chapter

This chapter teaches how to improve the fit and style of simple garments, and how to turn an ordinary garment into a "designer" garment. Fitting is part of the patternmaking process, and a pattern cannot be completed until after the fitting and all corrections have been done to the final patterns.

Fitting and Corrections

When doing the fitting on a customer, put the garment on *right side out.* When doing the fitting on a dress-form, you may put the garment on *inside out,* which makes it a little easier to pin the seam allowances. However, a customer might think you don't know what you're doing if you make them put on garments inside out.

When the fitting is complete, remove the pinned garment from the dress form, or model, and trace all of the corrections to the sloper if it is a sloper fitting, or onto the pattern if it is a pattern fitting. Knit garments must always be removed from the dress-form in order to trace out the corrections, since the fabric is stretched out when on the body and needs to relax for you to get an accurate correction.

Label the corrections in a contrast marker and note the fabrication. Many companies require all first corrections to be done in red marker, with second correction in blue, etc. This way everybody in the company can tell where each garment is in the fitting and patternmaking process, and whether a pattern is ready for production.

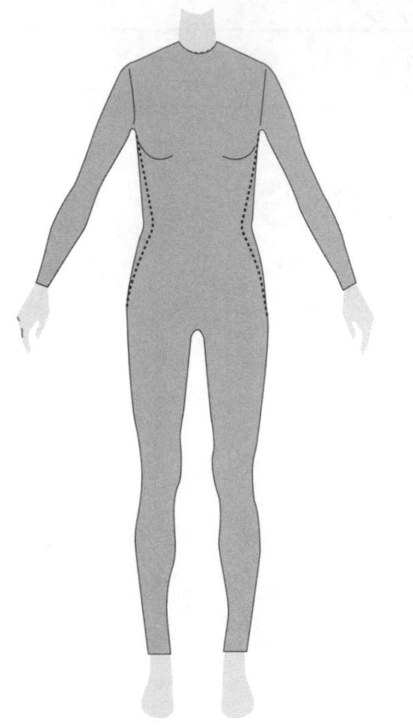

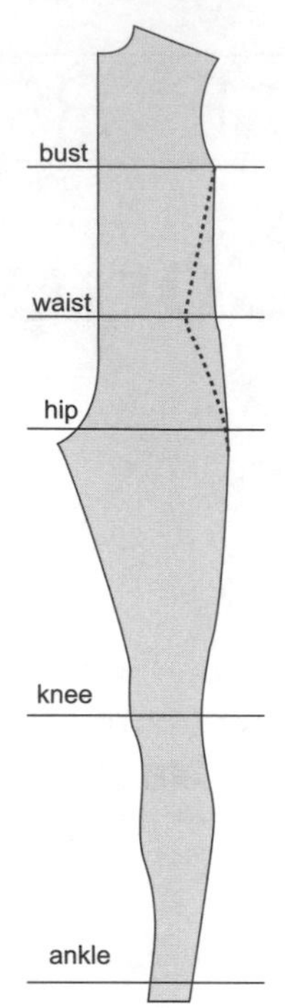

Re-Shaping the Waist

The waist is the most common correction made to garments. Everybody wants a smaller waist, and demand garments that fit correctly in this area. However, do not make the garment too tight in this area or it becomes uncomfortable, and the customer will begin to think she has gained weight. Too tight garments wear out a lot faster than loosely fit garments.

Pin out the excess fabric at the hip and reshape the pattern accordingly.

Do not make the hips too tight or the fabric will strain and wear out prematurely.

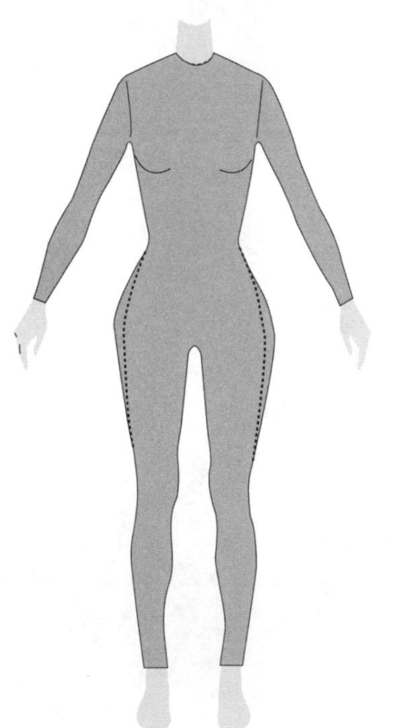

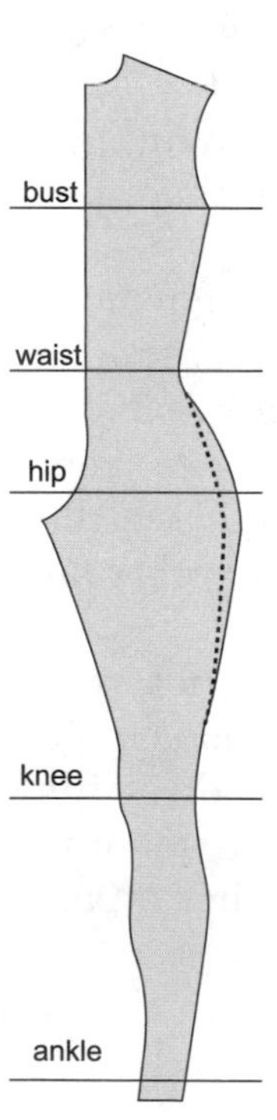

Hip Fittings and Corrections

The hip of pants and skirts often needs to be fitted and corrected. You must pin out the excess fabric and reshape the hip. Don't make the pants too tight, because even though the fabric will stretch to accommodate a larger body, this causes strain on the fabric and causes it to wear out quickly.

Re-Shaping The Legs

Pin out equal amount on both sides of the legs and correct the pattern as indicated.

Make sure to focus on the areas around the knee, to ensure that they fit accurately.

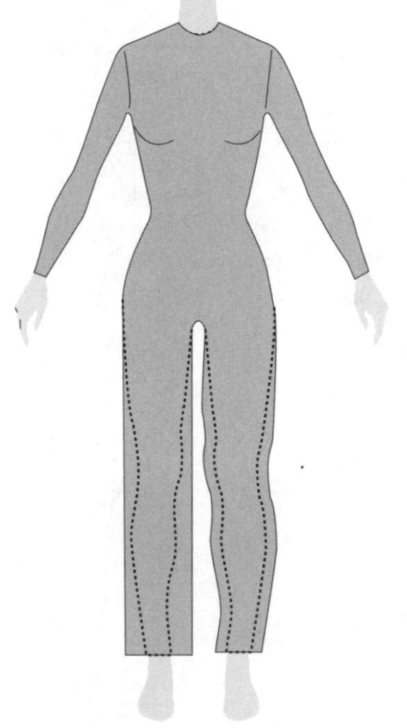

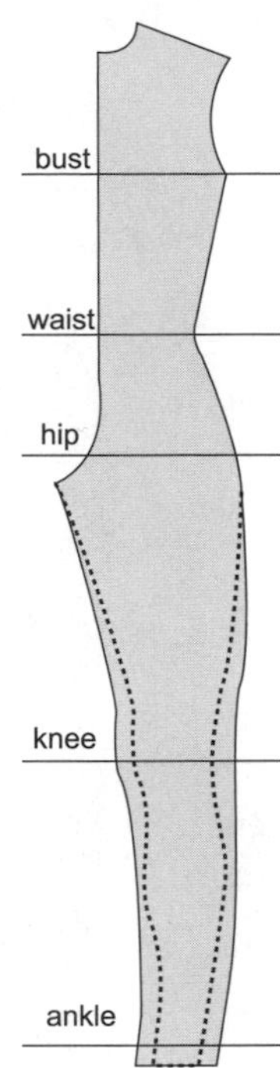

Shoulder is Too Big

The shoulder seam should line up exactly with the shoulder.

If the shoulder is too big, remove the excess from the shoulder of the pattern.

If the shoulder is too small, add extra to the shoulder of the pattern.

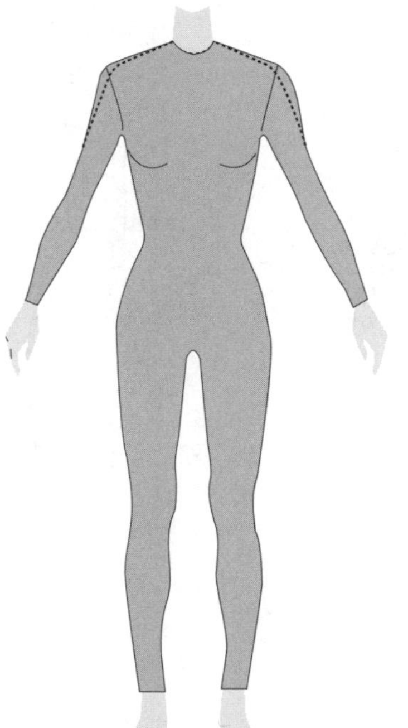

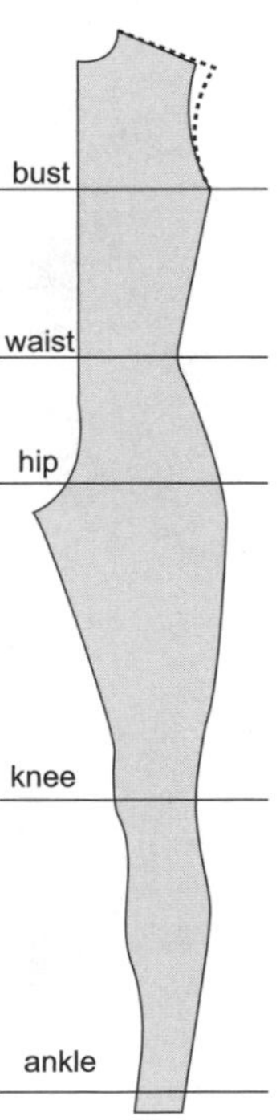

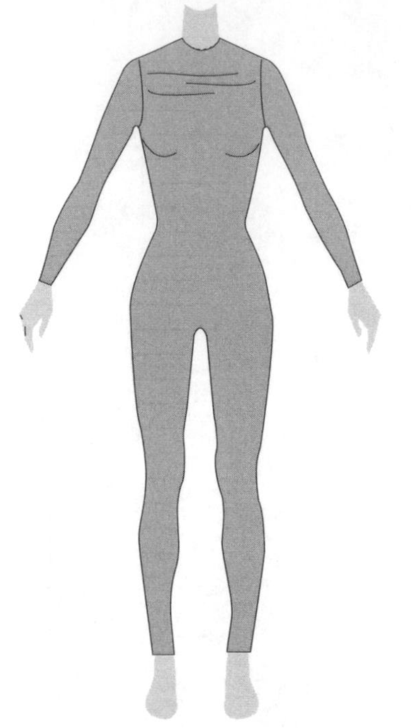

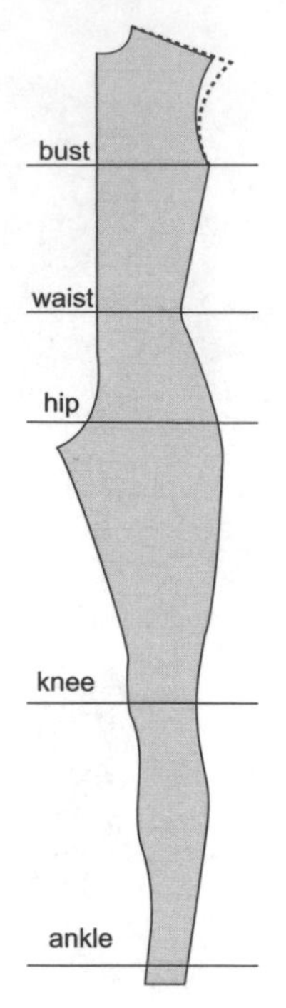

Shoulder is Too Small

If the shoulder is too tight, you will get horizontal lines pulling across the upper chest area.

To correct shoulders that are too narrow, extend the shoulder and armhole outwards increasing the size.

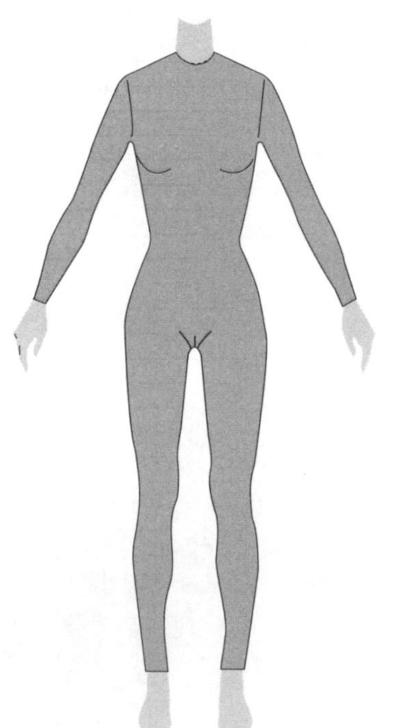

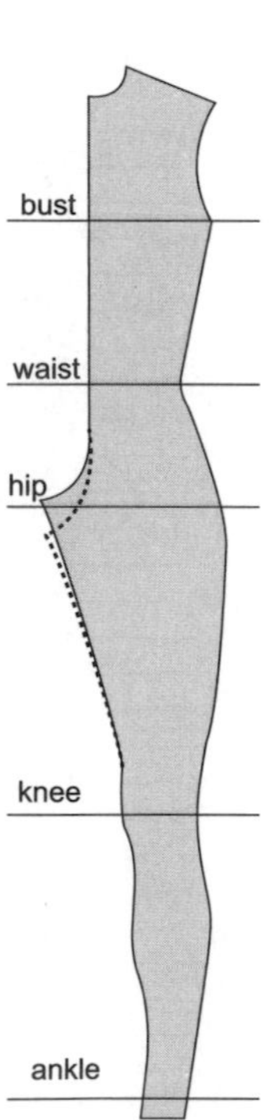

Crotch is Too High

If the model has a longer waist, it may be necessary to lower the crotch.

Lower the crotch as indicated and make corrections to the blocks.

Crotch is Too Shallow

Reshape the crotch as indicated.

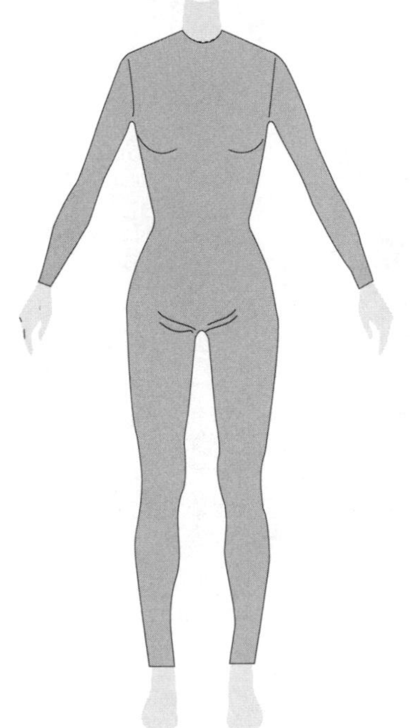

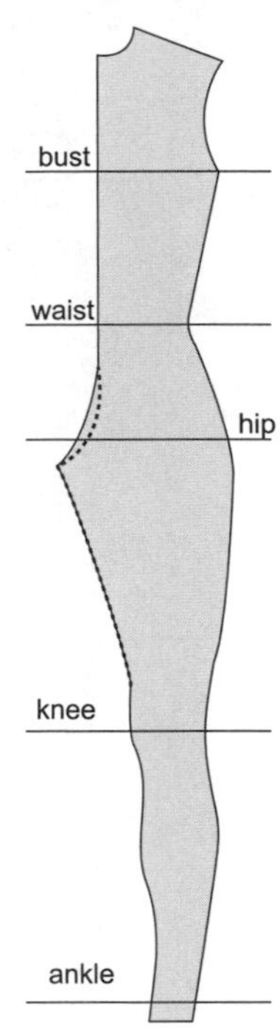

Crotch is Too Low

If the model has a short waist, it may be necessary to raise the crotch. Reshape as necessary.

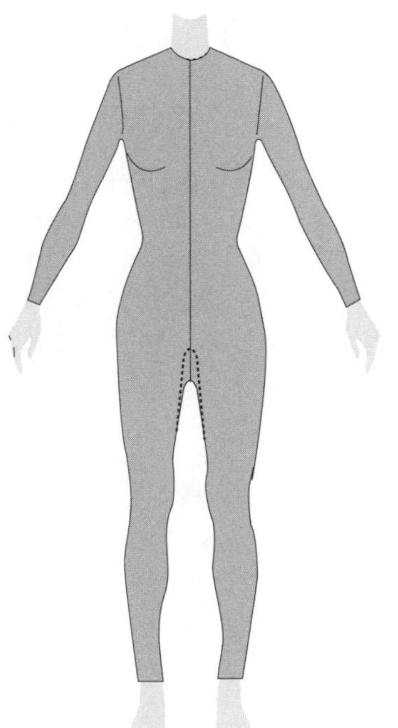

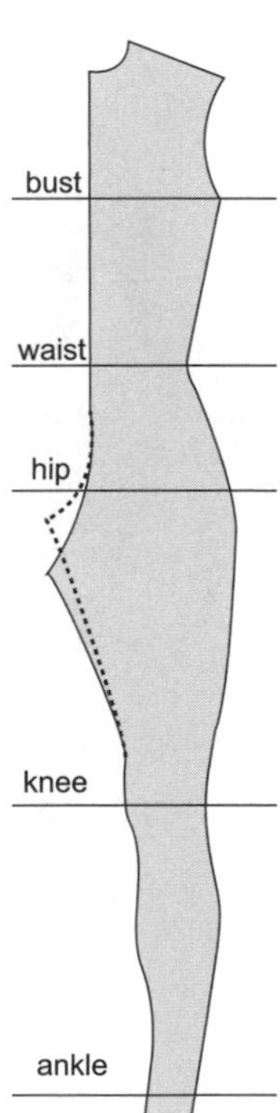

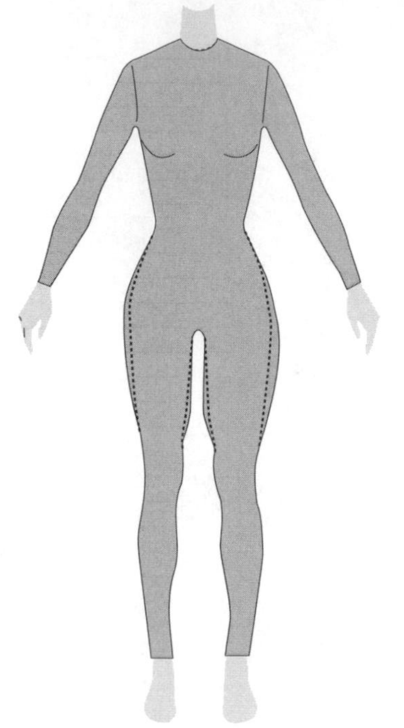

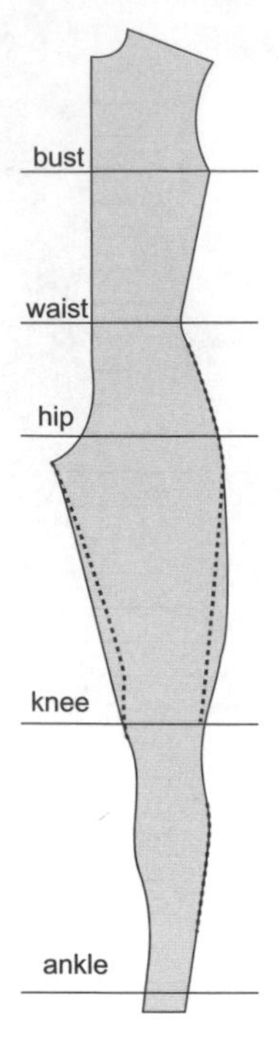

Thigh is Too Wide

Pin out excess fabric and remove from pattern accordingly.

Keep both sides even and equal.

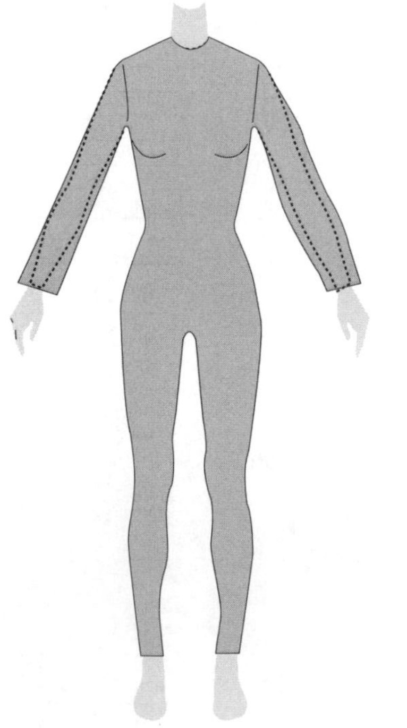

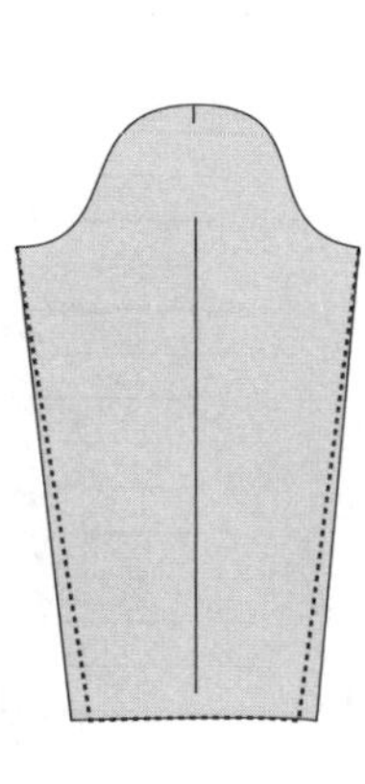

Reshaping the Sleeve

Since most dress-forms don't have any arms, the sleeves must be fit on a live model.

Pin out the excess fabric and correct the pattern and blocks as illustrated.

Correcting the Ease of a Sleeve

The sleeve ease should be minimum 1/8″ and maximim 3/4″. Slash and spread to correct.

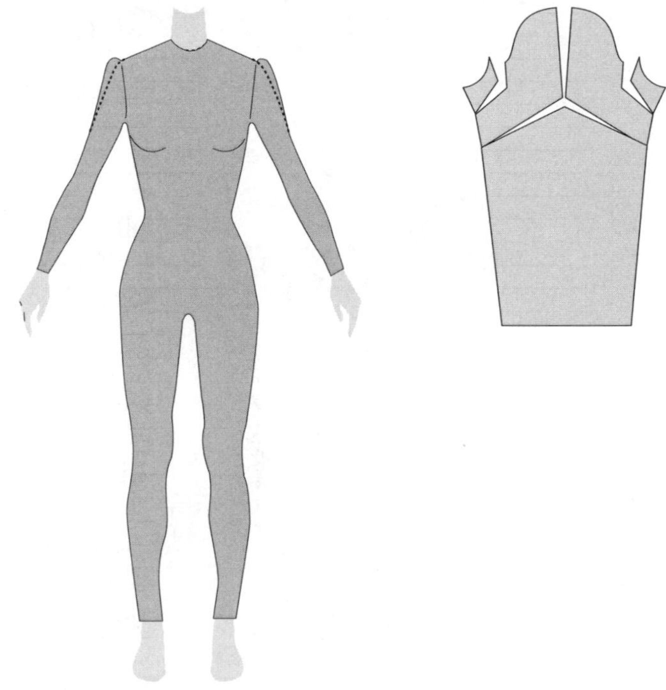

Reshaping the Neckline

Reshape the neckline to ensure that it follows the neck accurately.

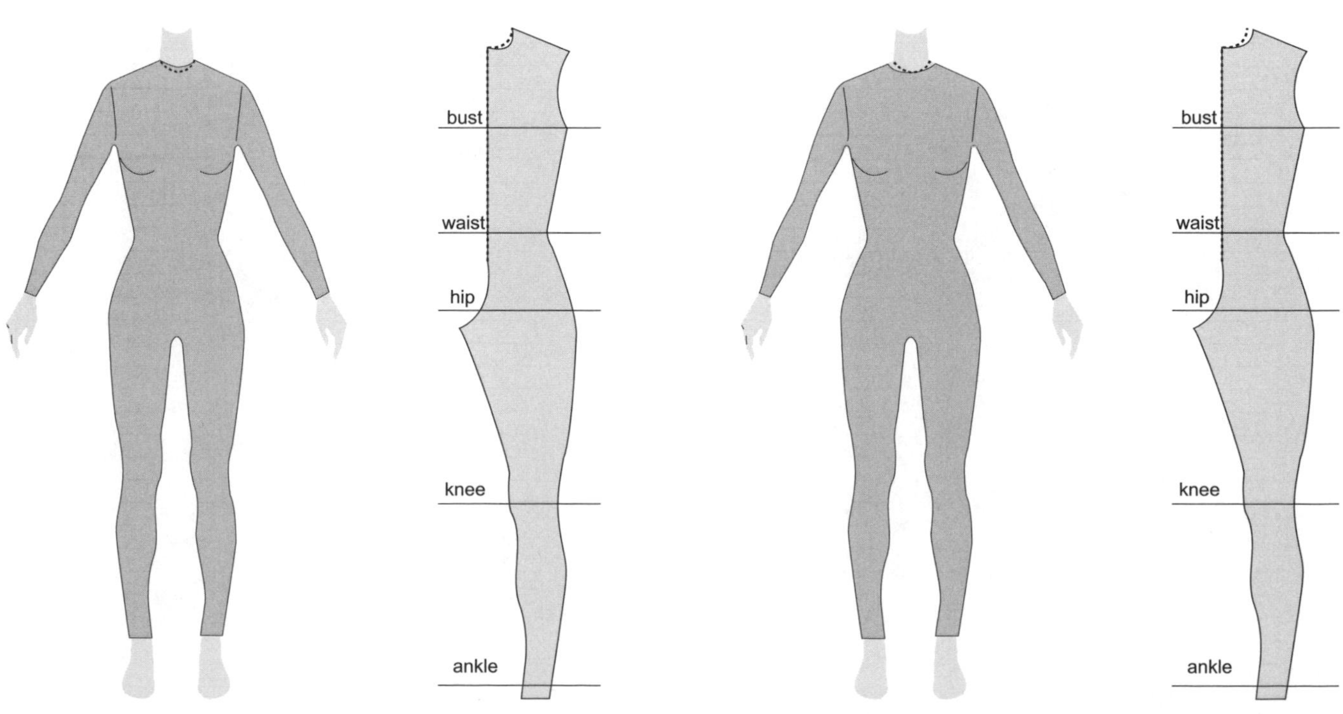

Collar is Too Big

The collar should fit snugly around the neck.

If the collar is too big, pin out the excess amount and correct the pattern.

Remove half the amount of the excess from each end of the collar pattern at the center back.

The neck edge will stretch to fit the neckline, while the folded edge of the collar will fit snugly against the neck.

Because the neck of the customer is wider at the base than at the top, using the exact neckline measurement from the draft will create a collar that gapes at the top, and stands away from the neck. You can leave the draft as is, or make a slight correction to the fit.

To correct this, pinch out the extra amount, measure it, and remove that amount from the pattern as illustrated.

Or simply remove approximately ½″ from each end of the collar pattern.

The top of the collar is now smaller and will fit snug to the neckline.

The edge that attaches to the sweater is also smaller and must be stretched to fit into the neckline of the sweater.

Add seam allowances and label the pattern as in Chapter 9.

The seam of the collar should line up with either the center back or the neckline, or preferably the left shoulder seam (always the left), where it is less noticeable.

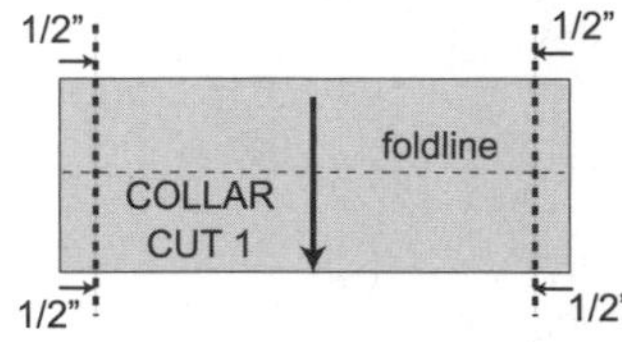

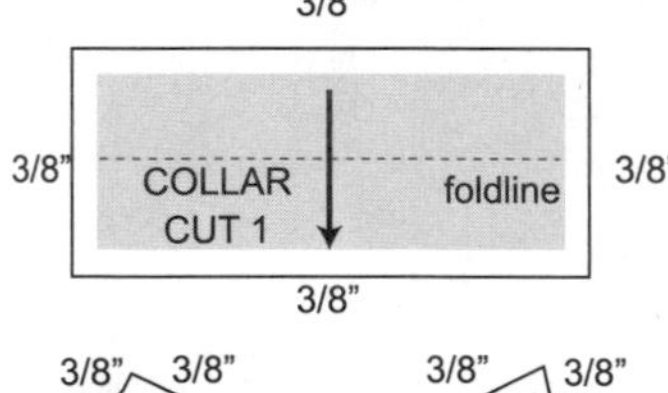

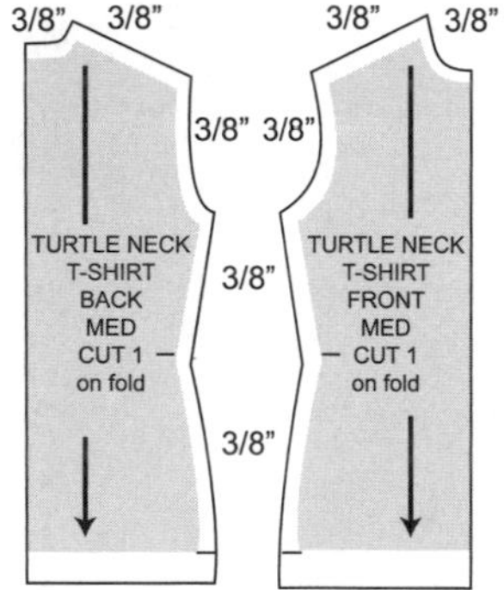

1" hem allowance

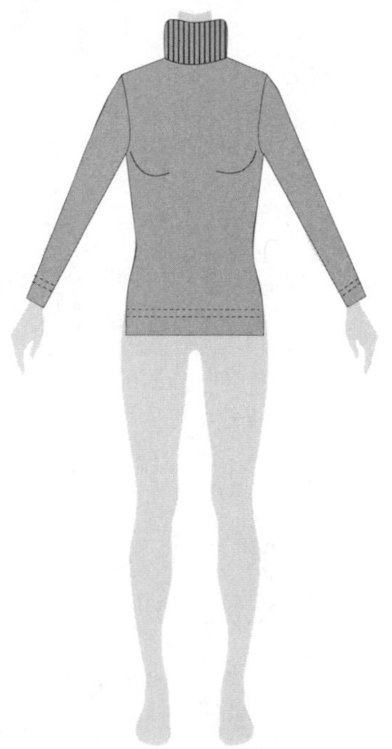

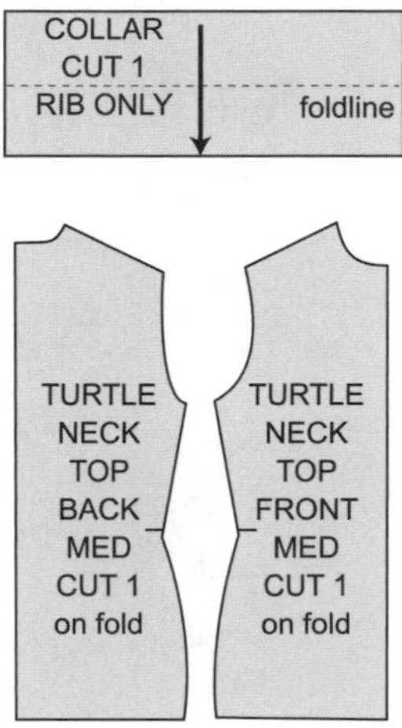

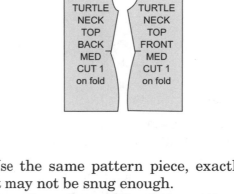

Other Collar Options

If your fabric does not stretch enough for the collar to pull on over the head, then you have several options to correct the collar. Use whichever method your collar demands.

Use a matching rib fabric, so that the rib fabric will stretch enough to fit over the head.

Use the same pattern piece, exactly as is, but it may not be snug enough.

Or reduce the width of the pattern by 10 percent for a snug fit.

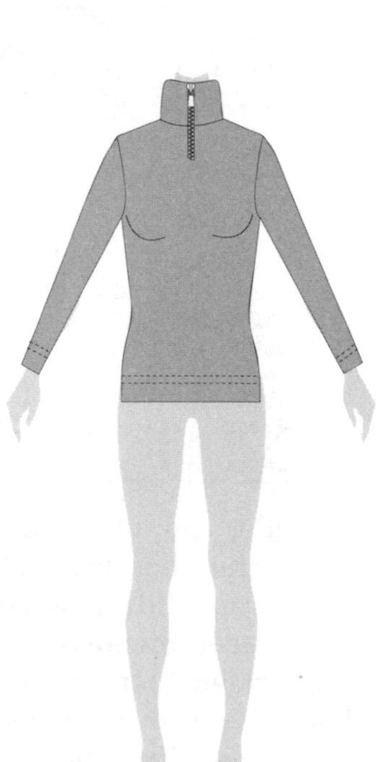

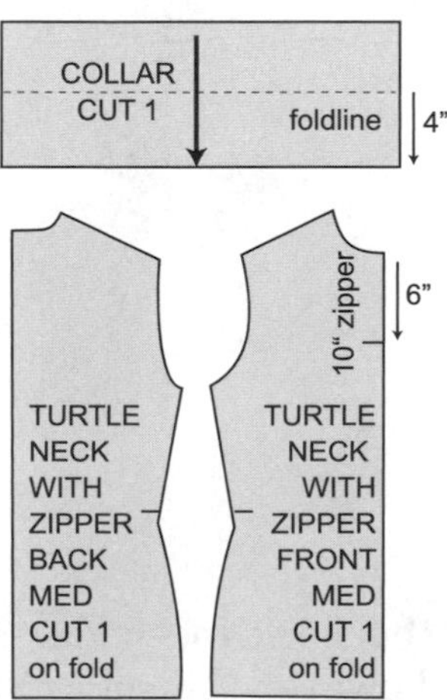

Insert a zipper or other closure in the collar so that the neckline can be opened to take the garment on and off the body.

The zipper should be a total of 10″ with 4″ inserted into the collar, and 6″ inserted into the front of the top.

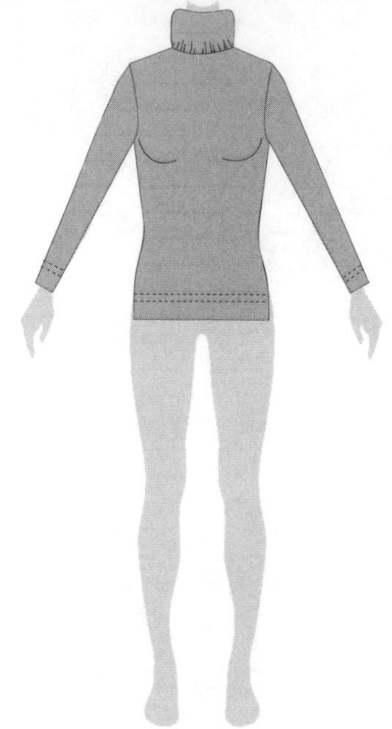

Enlarge the collar and ease it into the neckline for very small amounts only to avoid causing the collar seam to pucker.

This will also depend on your fabric, as some knits, especially shiny ones, will visually exaggerate even the slightest amount of ease.

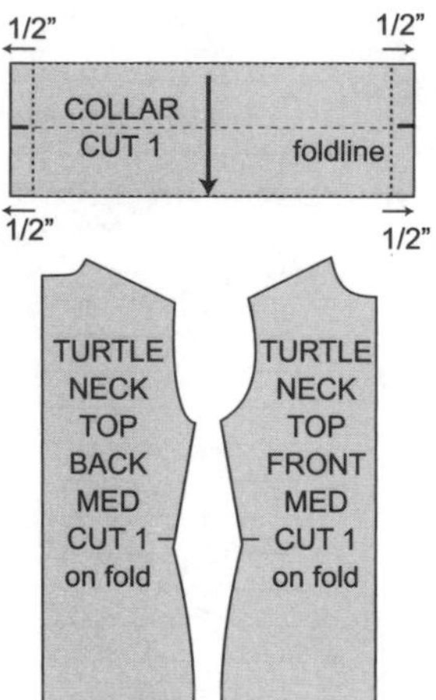

Enlarge the width of the collar, a maximum of ½″ on each side, for a maximum of 1″ wider.

If you make the collar any wider, it may not ease into the neckline without showing gathers and puckers.

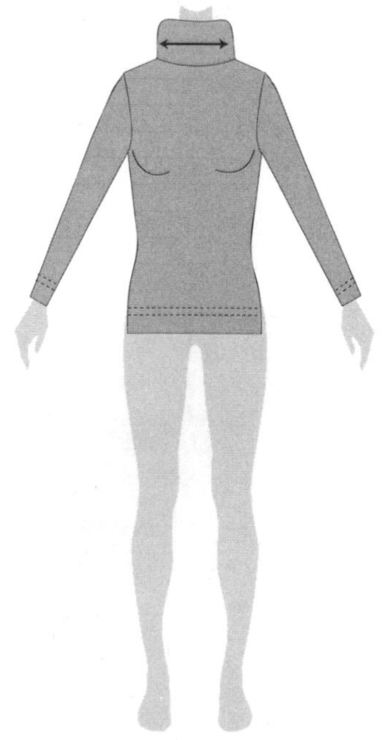

Enlarge the neckline wider and the collar accordingly; however the collar will sit slightly away from the neck.

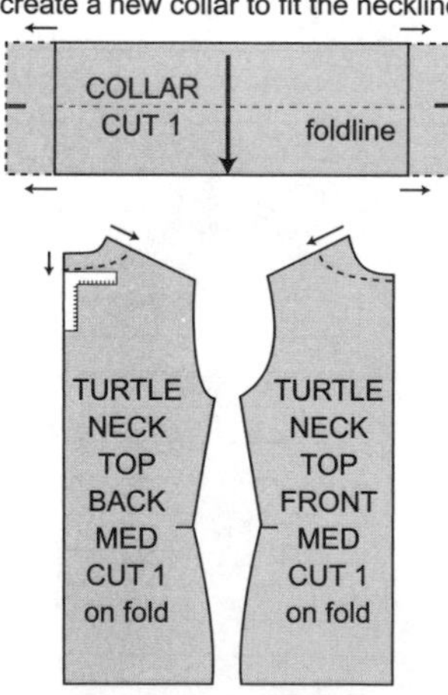

Widen the collar as much as necessary, however, having a shoulder seam of at least ½″ to prevent the top from sliding off the shoulders of the customer is recommended.

Note that in order to maintain a smooth curve on the back neckline, it may be necessary to lower the back neckline, but remember to keep the center back neckline square.

Create a new collar to fit the new widened neckline.

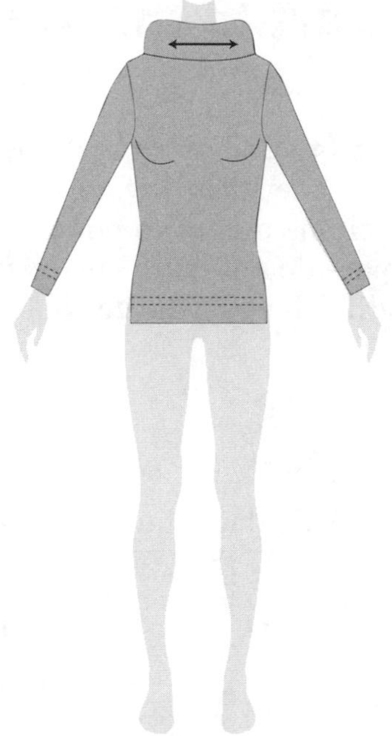

An extremely wide neckline can be created to make the top very easy to get on and off, or as a design feature.

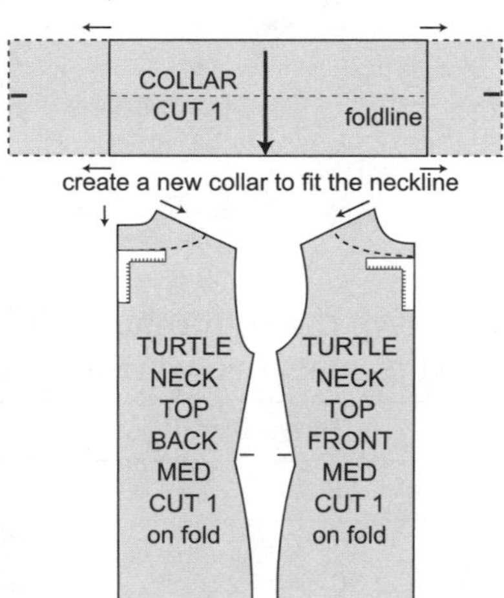

Widen the collar as much as necessary, however, having a shoulder seam of at least ½″ to prevent the top from sliding off the shoulders of the customer is recommended.

Note that, in order to maintain a smooth curve on the back and the front neckline, it may be necessary to lower the necklines, but remember to keep the center back and center front necklines square.

Create a new collar to fit the new widened neckline.

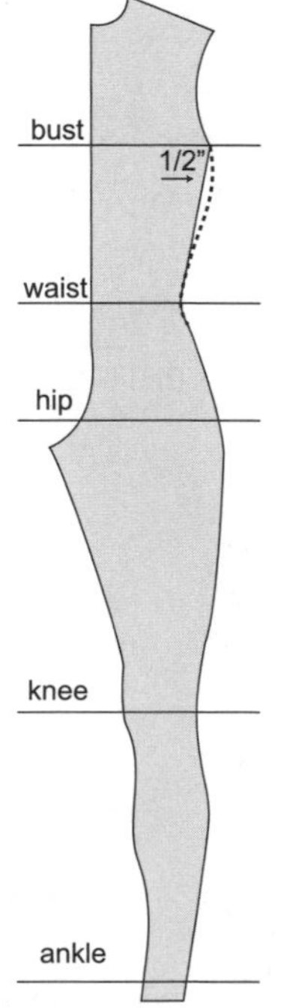

Slightly Enlarging the Bust

Sometimes the customer's bust is too large for the garment, and stretch fabrics tend to flatten out the bust. Therefore, it may be necessary to increase the amount of fabric in the bust area.

Increase the bust area of the front of the garment up to ½″.

For large bust sizes, it may be necessary to add a dart to the sloper.

Adding a Bust Dart to the Top Sloper

Even though knit fabrics stretch, they try to do so evenly, with even tension, which means they will try to flatten the bust shape. To build in a bust shape and even out the tension, use bust darts. The basic slopers do not have any bust darts built in so you will need to modify them for larger bust sizes.

Darts

This chart shows the difference in cup sizes based on a 36″ chest.
You will need to measure your model's bust and upper chest and calculate the differences.

	Extra Small		Small		Medium		Large		Extra Large	
	2	4	6	8	10	12	14	16	18	20
Bra	36½	37	38	39	40	41	42	43	44	45
Upper chest	36	36	36	36	36	36	36	36	36	36
Difference	½	1	2	3	4	5	6	7	8	9

Bust Dart Amount

This chart illustrates how large your bust dart should be at the side seams.

Cup Size	8	10	12	14	16
B	3/16	3/8	9/16	13/16	1
C	9/16	1 3/16	1	1 3/16	1 3/8
D	1	1 3/16	1 3/8	1 3/4	1 3/4
DD	1 3/8	1 9/16	1 3/4	1 15/16	2 3/16

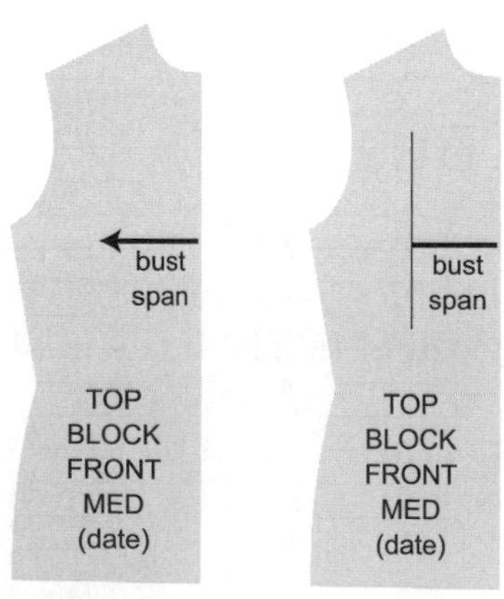

The first step is to find the apex of the bust.

Draw a guideline parallel to the center that is half the bust span away from the center front.

	Extra Extra Small	Extra Small	Small	Medium	Large	Extra Large	Extra Extra Large
Stable	6½	6 5/8	6 7/8	7 1/8	7½	7 7/8	8 3/8
Moderate	6 3/8	6½	6¾	7 1/8	7½	7 7/8	6 3/8
Stretchy	6 3/8	6½	6¾	7	7 3/8	7 7/8	8 1/8
Super-stretch	6¼	6 3/8	6 5/8	6 7/8	7 2/8	7 5/8	7 7/8
Rib	5 7/8	6	6¼	6½	6 7/8	7¼	7½

	Extra Extra Small	Extra Small	Small	Medium	Large	Extra Large	Extra Extra Large
Bust level	9 7/8	10	10 2/8	10 4/8	10 6/8	11	11 2/8

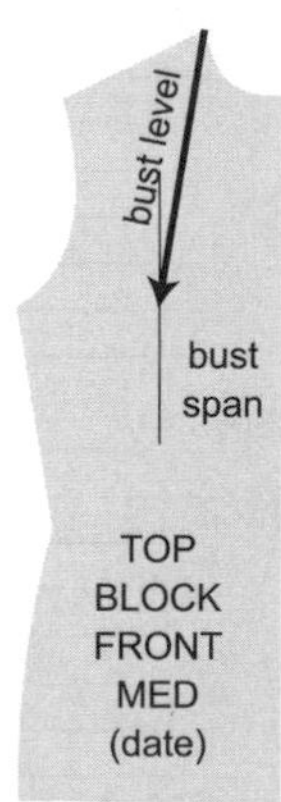

Measure the bust level to wherever it lands on the guideline. This is your apex.

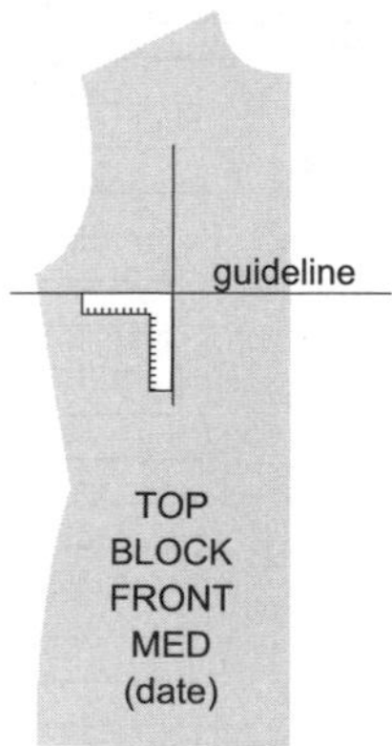

From the apex, draw a guideline that extends from the center front to the side seam.

This is the line that you will slash and spread to add extra length for the bust.

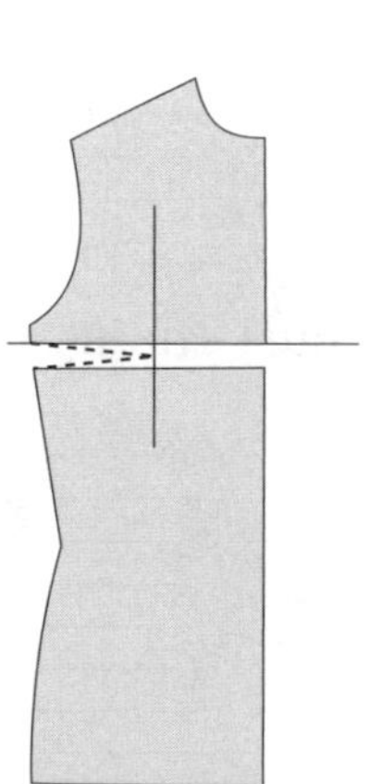

At first it seems as if you could just draw in the bust dart. However, there is another slight problem that must also be corrected.

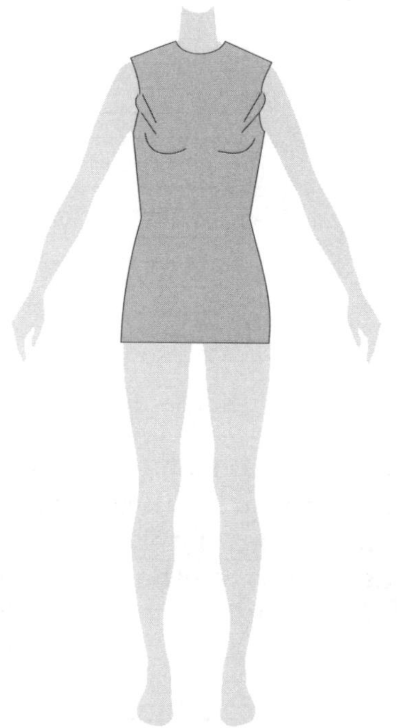

Note how the fabric in the illustration creates ripples pulling from the armhole. This happens with any large bust, whether a dart is added or not, so you must place a small dart in the armhole also. This dart will be pivoted into the bust dart and will not show.

Armhole Dart

Cup Size	8	10	12	14	16
B	0	0	0	0	0
C	3/16	5/16	3/8	1/2	9/16
D	3/8	9/16	13/16	1	1 3/16
DD	9/16	13/16	1	1 3/16	1 3/8

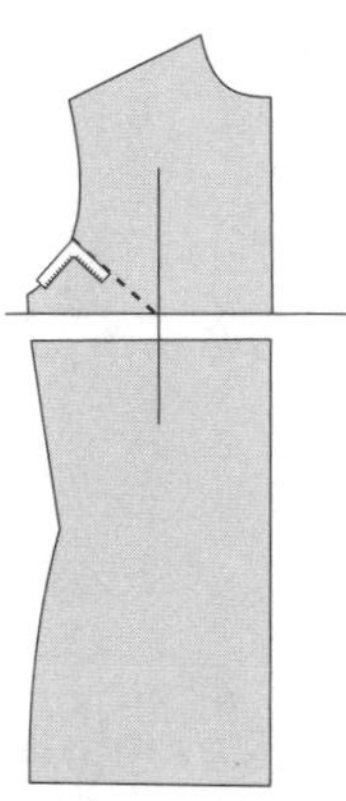

Once you have determined the amount of the armhole dart, square a guideline from the armhole to the apex.

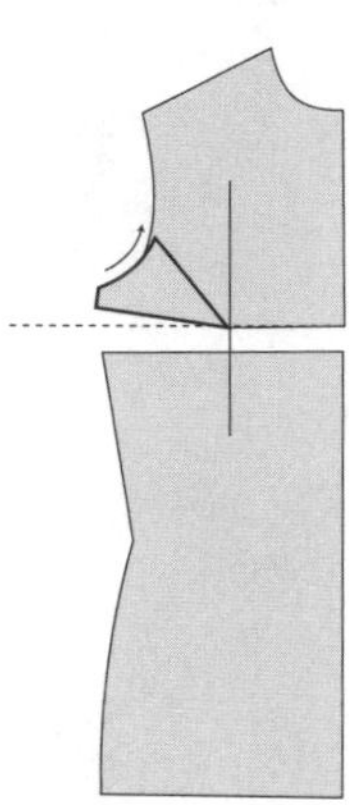

Slash and overlap the armhole dart as illustrated. Note how the bust dart gets slightly larger also.

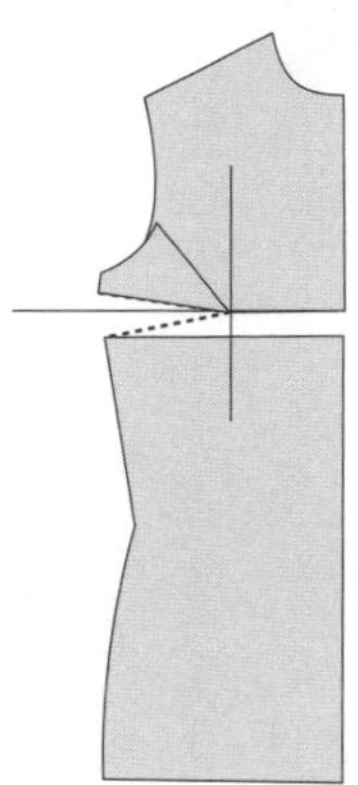

Draw in the bust dart as illustrated.

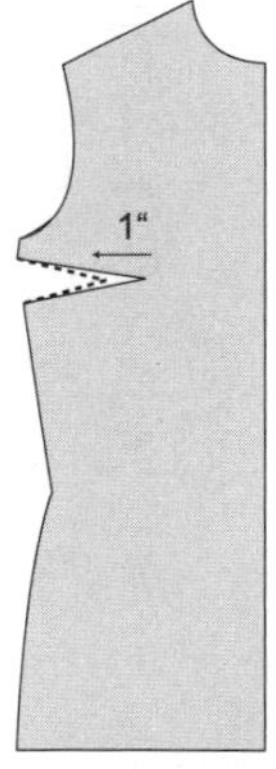

The bust dart cannot be used as is; it must be shortened, otherwise it will go right to the apex.

Shorten the dart by 1", up to 1½". When pivoting the dart to another position, bring the apex back to the original point and then shorten the dart again.

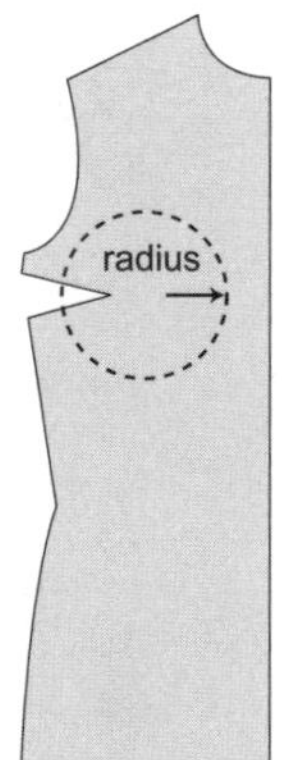

To illustrate the bust radius, use the following chart.

	Extra Extra Small	Extra Small	Small	Medium	Large	Extra Large	Extra Extra Large
Stable	2 1/8	2 1/4	2 3/8	2 1/2	2 5/8	2 3/4	2 7/8
Moderate	2 1/8	2 1/4	2 3/8	2 1/2	2 5/8	2 3/4	2 7/8
Stretchy	2	2 1/8	2 1/4	2 3/8	2 1/2	2 5/8	2 3/4
Super	1 7/8	2	2 1/8	2 1/4	2 3/8	2 1/2	2 5/8
Rib	1 3/4	1 7/8	1 7/8	2	2 1/8	2 1/4	2 3/8

Other Tricks and Corrections to Make a Better Fitting Garment

When most students think of knit garments, they imagine men's $10 garments from a department store, but this isn't always the case. Although knit garments are inexpensive and readily available, you can still create a versatile and attractive designer garment by refining the fit, changing the amount of ease, choosing quality fabrics, altering the neckline, shaping it to flatter different figure types, and adding custom details. This section will show you some subtle pattern-making tricks and techniques to create a more flattering designer-priced garment. The principle example in this section can be used for any stretch project.

Special Fabrics For Knit Garments

Search for fine quality fabrics with unusual or special features. It's also possible to use knit fabrics not always thought of as knit garment fabrics, such as stretch velour, panne velvet, wool jersey, cashmere, and fleece. For fall garments, use slightly heavier knits, like wool jersey, velour, sweater knits, or thermal cottons. It's not always necessary to find matching or coordinated rib knits—quality garments can be made using self-fabrics:

- Bound necklines
- Mock necks
- Turtlenecks
- Bound V-necks
- Self-facing
- Hoods

Fit Corrections

If possible, measure a favorite garment, noting the width, amount of ease, length, and any other key measurements. By comparing this garment with your slopers, it's easy to judge and correct any changes. Creating the perfect garment takes a little time and patience, but is well worth the extra effort.

Ease

In order to make the new garment fit like the original, you must calculate and allow for the same amount of ease. Calculate the ease intended for the garment style by measuring the pattern from side seam to side seam across the front and back at the bust and hip, and then compare the total measurement with your personal measurements. For example, if the original garment measures 34″ around, and if your bust measurement is 32″, then you can conclude that the original garment has 2″ of ease. So, if your sloper measures 33″, you will need to add 1″ of ease to create the same fit as the original. Then you must decide if that amount of ease should be in the shoulder area or the underarm area. Measure the shoulders of the original garment, and compare to the sloper. If the shoulder measurements are the same, then all of the ease must be in the underarm. Often a designer will divide the amount of ease equally between the shoulder and the underarm, but occasionally may need to add ease to only the shoulder area, or only to the underarm area.

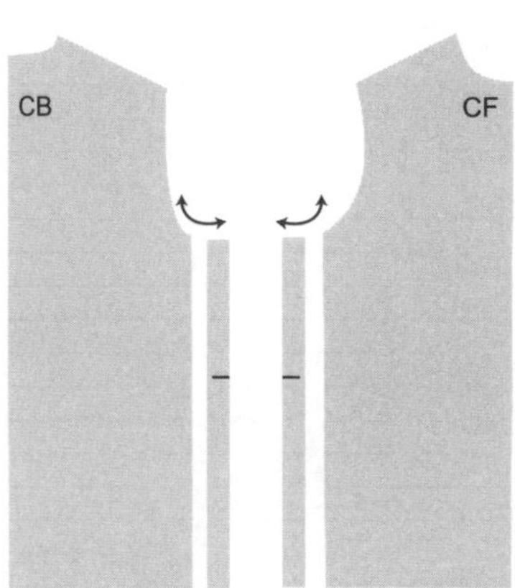

Body Ease

Slash and spread at the underarm to add more ease around the body. Remember to correct your sleeve so that it also fits into the new armhole. Since the ease is placed at the sides of the body, it will not change the fit of the shoulder area or the neck area.

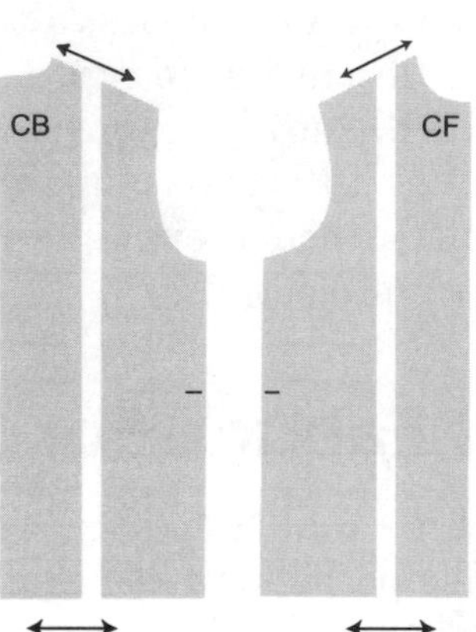

Shoulder Ease

Slash and spread at the underarm to add more ease at the shoulder. Since the ease is placed at the shoulder area, it will not change the silhouette of the garment.

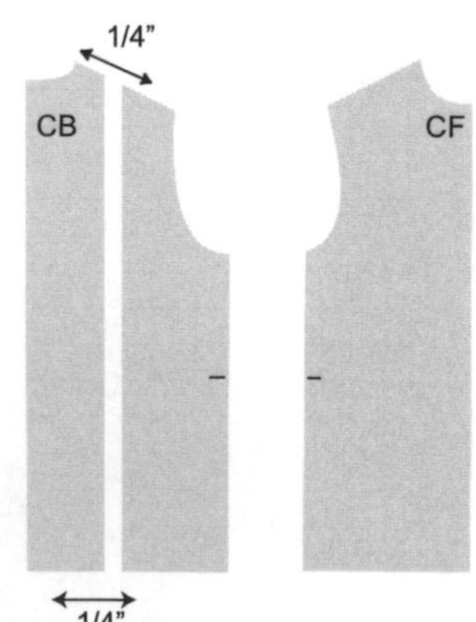

Back Shoulder Ease

Determine your best shoulder width by measuring favorite garments and adjusting the pattern.

For older or larger and stoop-shouldered bodies, you'll get a better fit across the shoulders if the back-shoulder seam is 1/4" longer than the front. The extra 1/4" of the back seam will be eased onto the front seam when serging to the front shoulder, and will be held in place with twill tape.

Slash and spread to create 1/4" ease in the back shoulder.

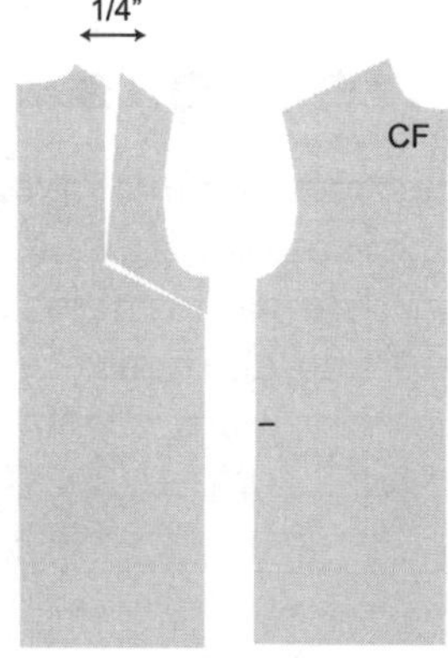

Or:

Slash and spread to create ease in the back shoulder seam without increasing the overall size of the body.

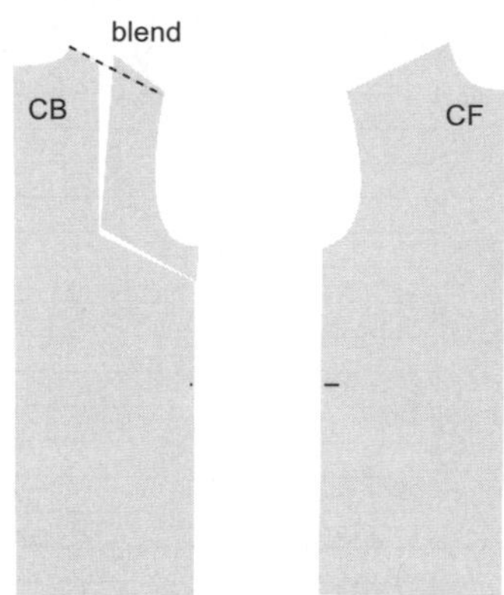

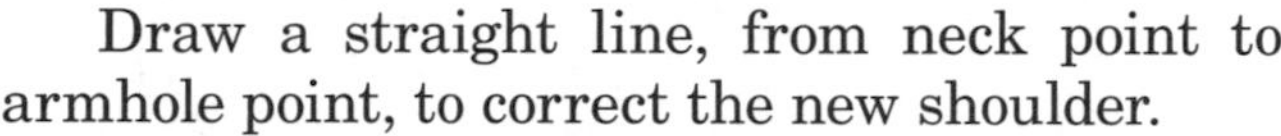
Draw a straight line, from neck point to armhole point, to correct the new shoulder.

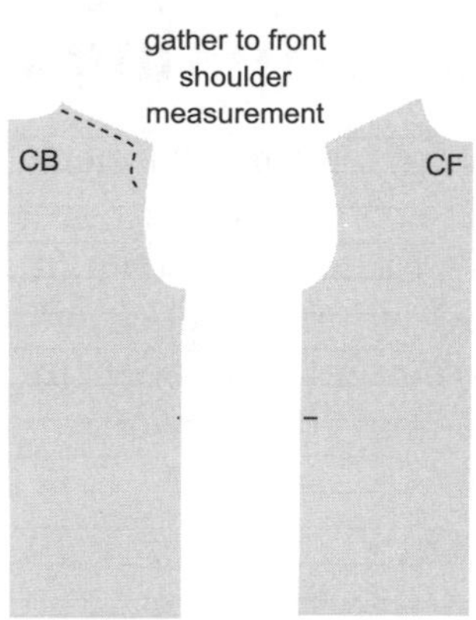

Label the shoulder with dash lines to indicate gathering.

Shoulder Placement

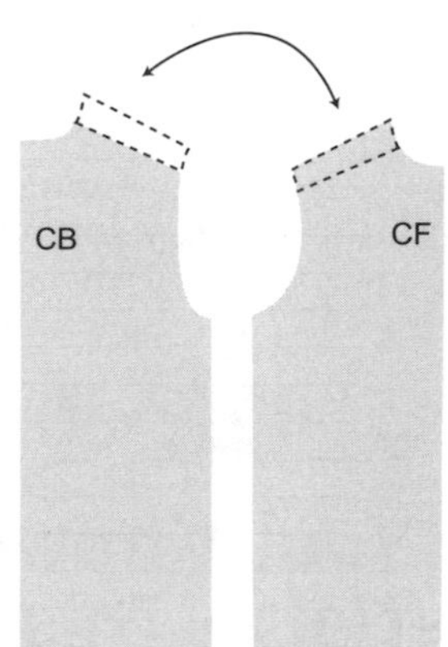

Balance the front and back armhole depths. Then check your slopers. If the front and back armhole depths are exactly the same, you may want to rebalance the armhole by adding extra to the back, and trimming from the front and moving the shoulder seam line forward as illustrated. This correction will prevent garments with lots of ease from falling backward off of the shoulders.

Remove ½″ to 1″, or even as much as 2″, from the front shoulder.

Add that amount to the back shoulder.

Correcting the Neckline

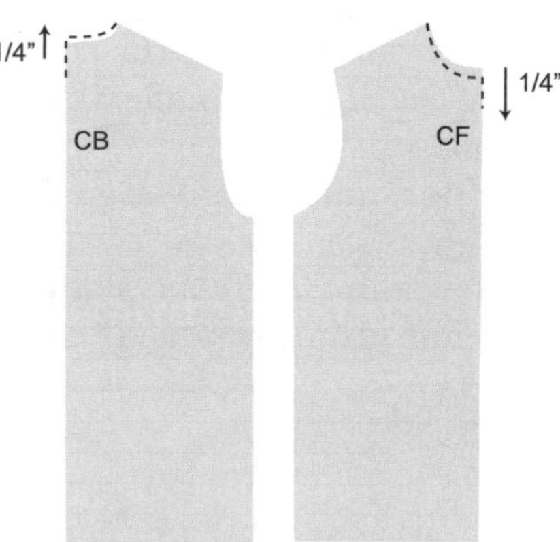

It may be a good idea to raise the back neck, especially for stoop-shouldered and older customers. Raise the back by as much as ½″ and lower the front by the same amount, so the neck circumference, or neck measurement, doesn't change—it is just redistributed.

Raise the back neck for a more flattering fit, and for stooped shoulders.

Lower the front neck as illustrated, so the overall neckline measurement does not change but is simply redistributed. Work in small increments to find the most flattering neck width for your face and body.

Define a Flattering Neckline

There are many options for neck shaping. If your customer's face is very round, you may prefer the contrast of a v-neck, or if you have an angular face, a round neck might be a good choice. If you want a v-neck, mark the depth on the dress form as low you wish the neckline to be, and convert to a v as shown in the next illustration.

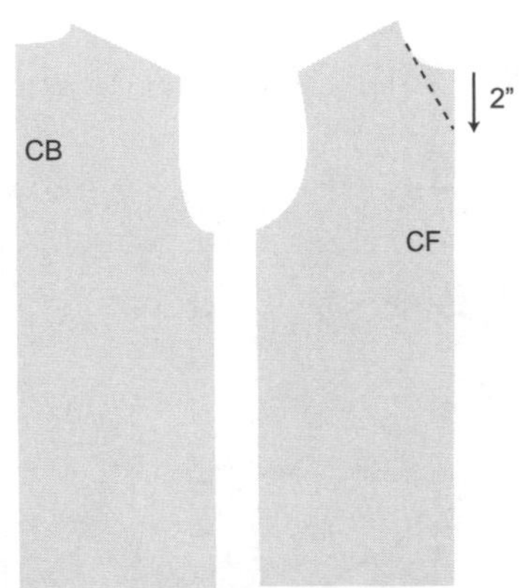

This is a slightly lowered v-neck.

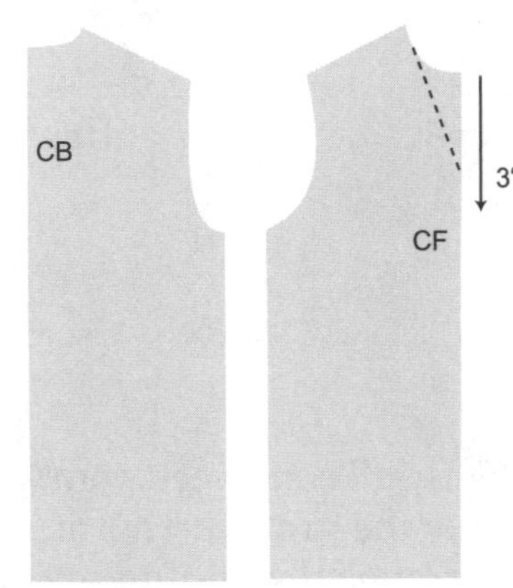

This is a more lowered v-neck.

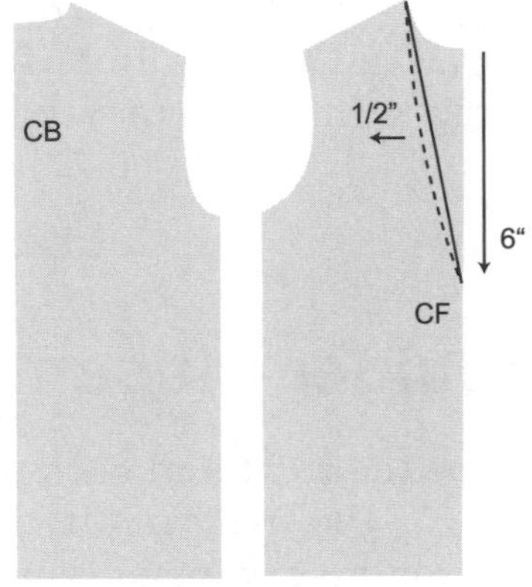

Shape a v-neck to soften the straight line by shaping the line in by ½″.

Test Your Knowledge of the Material in This Chapter

1. Should you place the garment on inside out when doing a fitting?
2. Can you measure the corrections while on the model to transfer the corrections to the patterns?
3. What happens if you make a garment too tight?
4. How can you fit the sleeves of a garment?
5. What should you do if the collar is too big?
6. What can you do if the fabric does not stretch enough for the collar to pull on over the head?
7. How can you slightly increase the bust area?
8. How can you correct the pattern for older or larger and stoop shouldered bodies?

Appendix: Costing Sheets

About This Appendix

This appendix will introduce the reader to the principles of costing and how to fill out and complete a costing sheet for a garment. Remember that the most important part of a garment is the price tag; without it, the garment is worthless. There is no point in creating a garment if it is not for sale. This appendix will also explain pattern cards, their uses, and how to fill them out correctly.

Total Cost and Key Factor Pricing

Total cost pricing works well if the customer would pay whatever you charge for the garment; while this is ideal, it is not very often the case. Competition and the marketplace demand that you sell your garment for a lower price than is calculated by total cost pricing. In this case, use the key factor pricing—subtract the cost of goods from the actual selling price and divide by labor hours. This will result in a "Key" number. Understand that it may appear better to sell the garment at the highest possible price, but in fact, it is not. For example, you might sell one skirt for $10.00, or you can sell 10 skirts for $7.00. If it costs you $5.00 to make the skirts, then you will have made $5.00 profit on the single skirt and $20.00 profit on the 10 skirts. Key factor pricing helps you determine whether a style is worth including in your line or if it is profitable.

Costing Sheets

The following explains how to fill out a costing sheet. Note that the costing sheet may differ for the company you eventually work for.

Complete the following information to obtain the "Cost of Goods."

Name: Include the name of the person who filled out the cost sheet.

Style #: Every style should have a number identifying it from other garments in the collection.

Size Range: You should list the sizes that the garment will eventually be graded to.

Description: Write a short description of the garment; for example, a fleece skirt with elastic casing, a single back patch pocket, and side seam slits. This is important in case someone outside the company uses any of your patterns and won't understand your numbering system.

Fabric: List the name of the fabric that will be used to create this garment. For example, fleece, 12 oz interlock, etc.

Supplier: List where you purchased the fabric used to sample the garment. Later, if you find a cheaper or better version of the same fabric for production, then you can update the pattern card.

Content: List the fiber content, including the blends of fabric used for the garment. Remember that by law you must include this information on the label of every garment.

Care: List any laundry or dry cleaning instruction required for this garment. New designers often believe that they can simply label the garments "Dry Clean Only"; however, there are many stores that refuse to buy "Dry Clean Only" garments, because many customers refuse to buy those garments.

Self: List the total yardage needed to make a single garment. Next, list the price and multiply to find the total cost of self.

Contrast: Contrast is any secondary color or fabric required to make the garment.

Lining: List any linings needed.

Fusing: List any fusing needed.

Zipper: List the length of the zipper, the size of the teeth, and whether it is separating or closed.

Sh/pads: List any shoulder pads required.

Other: List any other notions needed to create the garment, including elastic, buttons, and buttonholes if sent out. Do not list thread, since that will be accounted for in the overhead costs; it is nearly impossible to calculate how much thread is used for each garment.

Total: Add all of the materials together to get the "Cost of Materials."

Cutting: List the cost of cutting; remember that, in the industry, many garments are cut hundreds at a time, so the cost of a single garment will be a lot higher than for someone who is cutting hundreds at a time. If you are working for a large manufacturer, simply take the garment to the cutter and get a cost estimate. Oftentimes, contractors include the cost of cutting in the estimate, so it may not always be necessary to record this cost. It is always a good idea to have a thorough record of the labor costs when hiring a contractor and it will also help you manage time when making duplicate samples.

Sewing: List the time it takes to sew a complete garment. Remember that you will sew a lot slower than in most factories, so as a guide, charge the garment $10/hr for an estimate.

Finishing: List any screen printing, embellishment, decoration, button sewing, or other finishes that the garment requires.

Pressing: List the time it takes to give the garment a final press. Some manufacturers will send out the pressing so it is important to know the costs.

Total: Add all of the construction costs together to get the "Total Cost of Labor."

Subtotal: Add the "Total Cost of Material" and the "Total Cost of Labor" together for the subtotal.

Overhead: Overhead is any other costs required to create the garment: thread, twill tape, electricity, rent, etc. To find an accurate "Overhead Burden," you need to add up all of the expenses your company will incur over the next year, and divide them by the total labor hours the operators have available. You will end up charging an amount to each garment based on the time it takes to construct. So if the overhead burden is $1/hr and the garment takes two hours, you will add $2/garment.

Faulting: Faulting is used to account and allow for any damaged goods and processes. For example, if your fabric arrives with a large hole in the center, or a cone of thread arrives tangled up, then it should be accounted for in the cost of the garment. The industry standard may be anywhere from 2%–3% of the subtotal.

Total Cost: To find the total costs, add the cost of materials, cost of labor, overhead, and faulting.

Wholesale: To find the wholesale price, multiply the total cost times 2. Some manufacturers may multiply by 2½. This is the price at which you will sell the garment to stores.

Retail: To find the retail price, multiply the total cost times two. Some retailers may multiply by 2½. This is the price at which the garment will be sold to the customers.

TOTAL COST PRICING

Name			Style #		
Size			Description		
Fabric			Supplier		
Content			Care		
Self	Yards	@	$	=	$
Contrast	Yards	@	$	=	$
Lining	Yards	@	$	=	$
Fusing	Yards	@	$	=	$
Zipper	Inches	@	$	=	$
Sh/pads	Pair	@	$	=	$
Other		@	$	=	$
Total Cost of Materials					$

Cutting	Hours	@10.00/hr	=	$
Sewing	Hours	@10.00/hr	=	$
Finishing	Hours	@10.00/hr	=	$
Pressing	Hours	@10.00/hr	=	$
Cost of Labor				$

Subtotal	Total labor + total materials	$
Overhead	Overhead burden per construction hour ($1.00 per hour of labor)	$
Faulting	3% of subtotal	$
Total cost	Subtotal + overhead + faulting	$
Wholesale	2 × total cost	$
Retail	2 × wholesale	$

KEY FACTOR PRICING

Name				Style #		
Size				Description		
Fabric				Supplier		
Content				Care		
Self		Yards	@	$	=	$
Contrast	Yards @	$ =	$			
Lining		Yards	@	$	=	$
Fusing		Yards	@	$	=	$
Zipper		Inches	@	$	=	$
Sh/pads		Pair	@	$	=	$
Other			@	$	=	$
Total	Cost of Materials					$

Cutting		Hours	@10.00/hr	=	$
Sewing		Hours	@10.00/hr	=	$
Finishing		Hours	@10.00/hr	=	$
Pressing		Hours	@10.00/hr	=	$
Total	Cost of Labor				$

Market Price	List the price that garment must stay at to remain competitive.
Profit	Subtract the cost of labor from the market price.
Key Factor	Divide the profit by the total labor hours.

Pattern Card

A "pattern card" or "pattern must" lists all the pieces that must be cut in order to make a garment and should be included with every pattern. It helps the cutter, who may not speak the same language as you, understand which pieces to cut out. It also assists the production manager by ensuring that there are enough supplies to make up the garments. Imagine if your factory cut out 100 garments and there were not enough zippers in stock to complete them—all the operators would just sit around with nothing to do till the zippers arrived. Wouldn't it be better to first cut out a style that you already have all the supplies for?

PATTERN CARD

Style #		Date			
Description					
Season		Sizes			
Fabric		Content			
Care					
FRONT VIEW		BACK VIEW			
Piece #	Garment piece	Self	Contrast	Trim/elastic	Fuse
1					
2					
3					
4					
5					
6					
7					
8					
9					
10					
11					
12					
13					
Spec Sheet					
Name					
Style #		Date			
Description					
Season		Sizes		Med	
Fabric		Content			
Care					

HOW TO REDUCE THE MEASUREMENTS FOR EACH PARTICULAR STRETCH RATIO

Each knit fabric has a different stretch ratio and each garment must be drafted by utilizing the stretch ratio accordingly. The charts below illustrate the measurements needed to draft slopers and eventually patterns for each fabric.

Stable knits	5 inches stretches to 6 1/4″	18% to 25% stretch	Reduce by 0%	Use the measurements exactly as recorded
Moderate knits	5 inches stretches to 7 1/2″	26% to 50% stretch	Reduce by 2%	Multiply your across measurements by .98
Stretchy knits	5 inches stretches to 8 3/4″	51% to 75% stretch	Reduce by 3%	Multiply your across measurements by .97
Super stretch	5 inches stretches to 10″	76% to 100% stretch	Reduce by 5%	Multiply your across measurements by .95
Rib	5 inches stretches over 10″	Over 100% stretch	Reduce by 10%	Multiply your across measurements by .90
four-way-stretch	5 inches stretches to 10″ in both directions	100% stretch in both directions	Reduce by 5% across Reduce by 10% lengthwise	Multiply your measurements by .90 in both directions

Any fabric that stretches less than 18% should be treated as woven stretch.

MISSES STABLE KNIT REDUCTIONS

Zero percent smaller in crosswise direction without any reductions in lengthwise direction.
Use these measurements when drafting slopers for fabrics that stretch from 0% to 25%.
Note: All fractions are rounded off to the nearest 1/8th for ease of drafting.

		Multiply Your Across Measurements By	Extra Extra Small	Extra Small	Small	Medium	Large	Extra Large	Extra Extra Large
1	Bust	1 for stable knits	30 1/2	31 1/2	33 1/2	35 1/2	38 1/2	41 1/2	45 1/2
2	Waist	1 for stable knits	22 1/2	23 1/2	25 1/2	27 1/2	30 1/2	33 1/2	37 1/2
3	Hip	1 for stable knits	33 1/2	34 1/2	36 1/2	38 1/2	41 1/2	44 1/2	48 1/2
4	Crotch depth	No reduction	9 7/8	10	10 1/4	10 1/2	10 3/4	11	11 1/4
5	Waist to knee	No reduction	20 1/8	23	23 1/4	23 1/2	23 3/4	24	24 1/4
6	Waist to ankle	No reduction	38 1/4	38 1/2	39	39 1/2	40	40 1/2	41
7	Ankle	1 for stable knits	7 5/8	7 3/4	8	8 1/4	8 1/2	8 3/4	9
8	Knee	1 for stable knits	13 1/8	13 3/8	13 7/8	14 3/8	14 7/8	15 3/8	15 7/8
9	Front crotch	1 for stable knits	2	2 1/8	2 1/4	2 3/8	2 5/8	2 3/4	3
10	Back crotch	1 for stable knits	2 3/4	2 7/8	3	3 1/4	3 1/2	3 3/4	4
11	Crotch angle	1 for stable knits	1	1	1 1/8	1 1/4	1 1/4	1 3/8	1 1/2
12	Nape to waist	No reduction	15 3/8	15 5/8	16 1/8	16 5/8	17 1/8	17 5/8	18 1/8
13	Back neck	No reduction	2 3/8	2 3/8	2 1/2	2 1/2	2 1/2	2 5/8	2 5/8
14	Back neck rise	1 for stable knits	3/4	3/4	7/8	7/8	7/8	7/8	7/8
15	Shoulder length	No reduction	5	5 1/8	5 1/2	6	6 1/2	7	7 1/2
16	Across back	1 for stable knits	6 7/8	7	7 1/4	7 1/2	7 3/4	8	8 3/8
17	Sleeve length	No reduction	22 5/8	22 3/4	23	23 1/4	23 1/2	23 3/4	24
18	Shoulder pitch	1 for stable knits	1 3/8	1 3/8	1 1/2	1 1/2	1 1/2	1 5/8	1 5/8
19	Bicep	1 for stable knits	10	10 3/8	11 1/8	11 7/8	12 5/8	13 3/8	14 1/8
20	Wrist	1 for stable knits	5 1/8	5 1/2	6 1/4	7	7 3/4	8 1/2	9 1/4
21	Neck	1 for stable knits	14 3/8	14 1/2	14 3/4	15	15 1/4	15 1/2	15 3/4
22	Bust span	1 for stable knits	6 1/2	6 5/8	6 7/8	7	7 1/2	7 7/8	8 3/8
23	Bust level	No reduction	9 7/8	10	10 1/4	10 1/2	10 3/4	11	11 1/4

MISSES MODERATE REDUCTIONS

Two percent smaller in crosswise direction without any reductions in lengthwise direction.
Use these measurements when drafting slopers for fabrics that stretch from 25% to 50%.
Multiply your across measurements by .98, 2% smaller, except for the shoulder measurement, since the final garment will have twill tape to stabilize the seam and prevent it from stretching.

		Multiply Your Across Measurements By	Extra Extra Small	Extra Small	Small	Medium	Large	Extra Large	Extra Extra Large
			0	2	6	10	14	18	22
1	Bust	× .98	30 7/8	31 7/8	33 3/4	36 1/4	39 1/4	42 5/8	44 5/8
2	Waist	× .98	23	24	26	28 3/8	31 3/8	34 3/4	36 3/4
3	Hip	× .98	33 3/4	34 3/4	36 3/4	39 1/4	42 1/8	45 5/8	47 1/2
4	Crotch depth	No reduction	10	10 1/8	10 3/8	10 5/8	10 7/8	11 1/8	11 1/4
5	Waist to knee	No reduction	23	23 1/8	23 3/8	23 5/8	23 7/8	24 1/8	24 1/4
6	Waist to ankle	No reduction	38 1/2	38 3/4	39 1/4	39 3/4	40 1/4	40 3/4	41
7	Ankle	× .98	7 5/8	7 3/4	8	8 1/4	8 1/2	8 3/4	8 7/8
8	Knee	× .98	13 1/8	13 3/8	13 7/8	14 3/8	14 7/8	15 3/8	15 4/8
9	Front crotch	× .98	2 1/8	2 1/8	2 1/4	2 1/2	2 5/8	2 7/8	3
10	Back crotch	× .98	2 7/8	2 7/8	3	3 1/4	3 1/2	3 6/8	4
11	Crotch angle	× .98	1	1	1 1/8	1 1/4	1 3/8	1 3/8	1 1/2
12	Nape to waist	No reduction	15 5/8	15 7/8	16 3/8	16 7/8	17 3/8	17 7/8	18 1/8
13	Back neck	No reduction	2 3/8	2 3/8	2 1/2	2 1/2	2 4/8	2 5/8	2 5/8
14	Back neck rise	× .98	3/4	3/4	7/8	7/8	7/8	7/8	7/8
15	Shoulder length	No reduction	5 1/8	5 1/4	5 3/4	6 1/4	6 3/4	7 1/4	7 1/2
16	Across back	× .98	7	7	7 1/3	7 5/8	7 7/8	8	8 3/8
17	Sleeve length	No reduction	22 3/4	22 7/8	23 1/8	23 3/8	23 5/8	23 7/8	24
18	Shoulder pitch	× .98	1 3/8	1 3/8	1 1/2	1 1/2	1 1/2	1 5/8	1 5/8
19	Bicep	× .98	10 1/8	10 1/2	11 1/4	12	12 3/4	13 1/2	13 7/8
20	Wrist	× .98	5 3/8	5 3/4	6 1/2	7 1/4	8	8 3/4	9
21	Neck	× .98	14 1/8	14 1/4	14 1/2	14 3/4	15	15 1/4	15 3/8
22	Bust span	× .98	6 3/8	6 1/2	6 3/4	7 1/8	7 1/2	8	8 1/8
23	Bust level	No reduction	9 3/4	10	10 1/8	10 3/8	10 5/8	11	11

MISSES STRETCHY REDUCTIONS

Three percent smaller in crosswise direction without any reductions in lengthwise direction.
Use these measurements when drafting slopers for fabrics that stretch from 50% to 75%.
Multiply your across measurements by .97, 3% smaller, except for the shoulder measurement, since the final garment will have twill tape to stabilize the seam and prevent it from stretching.

		Multiply Your Across Measurements By	Extra Extra Small	Extra Small	Small	Medium	Large	Extra Large	Extra Extra Large
			0	2	6	10	14	18	20
1	Bust	× .97	30 1/2	31 1/2	33 1/2	35 7/8	38 3/4	42 1/4	44 1/8
2	Waist	× .97	22 3/4	23 3/4	25 3/4	28 1/8	31	34 3/8	36 3/8
3	Hip	× .97	33 1/2	34 3/8	36 3/8	38 3/4	41 3/4	45 1/8	47
4	Crotch depth	No reduction	10	10 1/8	10 3/8	10 5/8	10 7/8	11 1/8	11 1/4
5	Waist to knee	No reduction	23	23 1/8	23 3/8	23 5/8	23 7/8	24 1/8	24 1/4
6	Waist to ankle	No reduction	38 1/2	38 3/4	39 1/4	39 3/4	40 1/4	40 3/4	41
7	Ankle	× .97	7 1/2	7 5/8	7 7/8	8 1/8	8 3/8	8 5/8	8 3/4
8	Knee	× .97	13	13 1/4	13 3/4	14 1/8	14 5/8	15 1/8	15 3/8
9	Front crotch	× .97	2	2 1/8	2 1/4	2 3/8	2 5/8	2 7/8	3
10	Back crotch	× .97	2 6/8	2 7/8	3	3 1/4	3 1/2	3 3/4	4
11	Crotch angle	× .97	1	1	1 1/8	1 1/4	1 1/4	1 3/8	1 1/2
12	Nape to waist	No reduction	15 5/8	15 7/8	16 3/8	16 7/8	17 3/8	17 7/8	18 1/8
13	Back neck	No reduction	2 3/8	2 3/8	2 1/2	2 1/2	2 1/2	2 5/8	2 5/8
14	Back neck rise	× .97	3/4	3/4	7/8	7/8	7/8	7/8	7/8
15	Shoulder length	No reduction	5 1/8	5 1/4	5 3/4	6 1/4	6 3/4	7 1/4	7 1/2
16	Across back	× .97	7	7	7 3/8	7 5/8	7 7/8	8	8 3/8
17	Sleeve length	No reduction	22 3/4	22 7/8	23 1/8	23 3/8	23 5/8	23 7/8	24
18	Shoulder pitch	× .97	1 3/8	1 3/8	1 1/2	1 1/2	1 1/2	1 5/8	1 5/8
19	Bicep	× .97	10	10 3/8	11 1/8	11 7/8	12 5/8	13 3/8	13 3/4
20	Wrist	× .97	5 3/8	5 3/4	6 3/8	7 1/7	7 7/8	8 5/8	9
21	Neck	× .97	14	14 1/8	14 3/8	14 5/8	14 7/8	15	15 1/4
22	Bust span	× .97	6 3/8	6 1/2	6 3/4	7	7 3/8	7 7/8	8
23	Bust level	No reduction	9 3/4	9 7/8	10	10 1/4	10 1/2	10 3/4	11

MISSES SUPER-STRETCH REDUCTIONS

Five percent smaller in crosswise direction without any reductions in lengthwise direction.
Use these measurements when drafting slopers for fabrics that stretch from 75% to 100%.
Multiply your across measurements by .95, 5% smaller, except for the shoulder measurement, since the final garment will have twill tape to stabilize the seam and prevent it from stretching.

		Multiply Your Across Measurements By	Extra Extra Small	Extra Small	Small	Medium	Large	Extra Large	Extra Extra Large
			0	2	6	10	14	18	20
1	Bust	× .95	30	30 7/8	32 3/4	35 1/8	38	41 3/8	43 1/4
2	Waist	× .95	22 3/8	23 2/8	25 1/8	27 1/2	30 3/8	33 3/4	35 5/8
3	Hip	× .95	32 6/8	33 6/8	35 5/8	38	40 7/8	44 1/8	46
4	Crotch depth	No reduction	10	10 1/8	10 3/8	10 5/8	10 7/8	11 1/8	11 1/4
5	Waist to knee	No reduction	23	23 1/8	23 3/8	23 5/8	23 7/8	24 1/8	24 1/4
6	Waist to ankle	No reduction	38 1/2	38 3/4	39 1/4	39 3/4	40 1/4	40 3/4	41
7	Ankle	× .95	7 3/8	7 1/2	7 3/4	8	8 1/4	8 3/8	8 1/2
8	Knee	× .95	12 3/4	13	13 3/8	13 7/8	14 3/8	14 7/8	15
9	Front crotch	× .95	2	2 1/8	2 1/4	2 3/8	2 1/2	2 3/4	2 7/8
10	Back crotch	× .95	2 3/4	2 3/4	3	3 1/8	3 3/8	3 5/8	3 7/8
11	Crotch angle	× .95	1	1	1 1/8	1 1/4	1 2/8	1 3/8	1 1/2
12	Nape to waist	No reduction	15 5/8	15 7/8	16 3/8	16 7/8	17 3/8	17 7/8	18 1/8
13	Back neck	No reduction	2 3/8	2 3/8	2 1/2	2 1/2	2 1/2	2 5/8	2 5/8
14	Back neck rise	× .95	3/4	3/4	7/8	7/8	7/8	7/8	7/8
15	Shoulder length	No reduction	5 1/8	5 1/4	5 3/4	6 1/4	6 3/4	7 1/4	7 1/2
16	Across back	× .95	7	7	7 3/8	7 5/8	7 7/8	8	8 3/8
17	Sleeve length	No reduction	22 3/4	22 7/8	23 1/8	23 3/8	23 5/8	23 7/8	24
18	Shoulder pitch	× .95	1 3/8	1 3/8	1 3/8	1 1/2	1 1/2	1 1/2	1 5/8
19	Bicep	× .95	9 7/8	10 1/4	11	11 5/8	12 3/8	13	13 3/8
20	Wrist	× .95	5 1/4	5 5/8	6 1/4	7	7 3/4	8 3/8	8 3/4
21	Neck	× .95	13 3/4	13 7/8	14	14 1/4	14 1/2	14 3/4	15
22	Bust span	× .95	6 1/4	6 3/8	6 5/8	6 7/8	7 1/4	7 5/8	7 7/8
23	Bust level	No reduction	9 1/2	9 5/8	9 7/8	10	10 1/3	10 4/7	10 3/4

MISSES RIB REDUCTIONS

Ten percent smaller in crosswise direction without any reductions in lengthwise direction.
Use these measurements when drafting slopers for fabrics that stretch 100% and over.
Multiply your across measurements by .90, 10% smaller, except for the shoulder measurement, since the final garment will have twill tape to stabilize the seam and prevent it from stretching.

		Multiply Your Across Measurements By	Extra Extra Small	Extra Small	Small	Medium	Large	Extra Large	Extra Extra Large
			0	2	6	10	14	18	20
1	Bust	× .90	28 3/8	29 1/4	31	33 1/4	36	39 1/8	41
2	Waist	× .90	21 1/8	22	23 7/8	26 1/8	28 3/4	32	33 3/4
3	Hip	× .90	31	32	33 3/4	36	38 3/4	41 7/8	43 5/8
4	Crotch depth	No reduction	10	10 1/8	10 3/8	10 5/8	10 7/8	11 1/8	11 1/4
5	Waist to knee	No reduction	23	23 1/8	23 3/8	23 5/8	23 7/8	24 1/8	24 1/4
6	Waist to ankle	No reduction	38 1/2	38 3/4	39 1/4	39 3/4	40 1/4	40 3/4	41
7	Ankle	× .90	7	7	7 3/8	7 1/2	7 3/4	8	8
8	Knee	× .90	12	12 1/4	12 3/4	13 1/8	13 5/8	14	14 1/4
9	Front crotch	× .90	2	2	2 1/8	2 1/4	2 3/8	2 5/8	2 3/4
10	Back crotch	× .90	2 5/8	2 5/8	2 7/8	3	3 1/4	3 1/2	3 5/8
11	Crotch angle	× .90	1	1	1	1 1/8	1 1/4	1 1/4	1 3/8
12	Nape to waist	No reduction	15 5/8	15 7/8	16 3/8	16 7/8	17 3/8	17 7/8	18 1/8
13	Back neck	No reduction	2 3/8	2 3/8	2 1/2	2 1/2	2 1/2	2 5/8	2 5/8
14	Back neck rise	× .90	3/4	3/4	7/8	7/8	7/8	7/8	7/8
15	Shoulder length	No reduction	5 1/8	5 1/4	5 3/4	6 1/4	6 3/4	7 1/4	7 1/2
16	Across back	× .90	7	7	7 3/8	7 5/8	7 7/8	8	8 3/8
17	Sleeve length	No reduction	22 3/4	22 7/8	23 1/8	23 3/8	23 5/8	23 7/8	24
18	Shoulder pitch	× .90	1 1/4	1 1/4	1 3/8	1 3/8	1 3/8	1 1/2	1 1/2
19	Bicep	× .90	9 3/8	9 5/8	10 3/8	11	11 3/4	12 3/8	12 3/4
20	Wrist	× .90	5	5 1/4	6	6 5/8	7 3/8	8	8 3/8
21	Neck	× .90	13	13 1/8	13 3/8	13 1/2	13 3/4	14	14 1/8
22	Bust span	× .90	6	6	6 1/4	6 1/2	6 7/8	7 1/4	7 1/2
23	Bust level	No reduction	9	9 1/8	9 3/8	9 5/8	9 3/4	10	10 1/8

MISSES FOUR-WAY-STRETCH REDUCTIONS

Ten percent smaller in crosswise direction and 10% smaller in the lengthwise direction.
Use these measurements when drafting slopers for fabrics that stretch 100% in both directions.
Multiply your measurements by .90, 10% smaller, in both directions except for the shoulder measurement, since the final garment will have twill tape to stabilize the seam and prevent it from stretching.
Note that four-way-stretch has memory, and will return to the original shape and twill tape is not necessary to stabilize the shoulders.

		Multiply Your Across Measurements By	Extra Extra Small	Extra Small	Small	Medium	Large	Extra Large	Extra Extra Large
			0	2	6	10	14	18	20
1	Bust	× .90	28 3/8	29 1/4	30 1/8	31	32	33 1/4	34 5/8
2	Waist	× .90	21 1/8	22	23	23 7/8	24 3/4	26 1/8	27 1/2
3	Hip	× .90	31	32	32 7/8	33 3/4	34 5/8	36	37 3/8
4	Crotch depth	× .90	9	9 1/8	9 1/4	9 3/8	9 1/2	9 5/8	9 5/8
5	Waist to knee	× .90	20 3/4	20 7/8	22	22 1/4	22 3/8	22 1/2	22 5/8
6	Waist to ankle	× .90	34 5/8	34 7/8	37	37 1/4	37 1/2	37 3/4	38
7	Ankle	× .90	7	7	7 1/4	7 3/8	7 3/8	7 1/2	7 5/8
8	Knee	× .90	12	12 1/4	12 1/2	12 3/4	13	13 1/8	13 3/8
9	Front crotch	× .90	2	2	2	2 1/8	2 1/8	2 1/4	2 3/8
10	Back crotch	× .90	2 7/8	3	3	3 1/8	3 1/4	3 1/3	3 1/2
11	Crotch angle	× .90	1	1	1	1	1	1 1/8	1 1/8
12	Nape to waist	× .90	14	14 1/4	15 3/8	15 1/2	15 3/4	16	16 1/4
13	Back neck	No reduction	2 3/8	2 3/8	2 1/2	2 1/2	2 1/2	2 1/2	2 1/2
14	Back neck rise	No reduction	3/4	3/4	7/8	7/8	7/8	7/8	7/8
15	Shoulder length	No reduction	5 1/8	5 1/4	5 1/2	5 3/4	6	6 1/4	6 1/2
16	Across back	No reduction	7	7	7 2/8	7 3/8	7 4/8	7 5/8	7 3/4
17	Sleeve length	No reduction	22 3/4	22 7/8	23	23 1/8	23 1/4	23 3/8	23 1/2
18	Shoulder pitch	No reduction	1 3/8	1 1/2	1 1/2	1 1/2	1 1/2	1 1/2	1 4/8
19	Bicep	× .90	9 3/8	9 5/8	10	10 3/8	10 3/4	11	11 3/8
20	Wrist	× .90	5	5 2/8	5 5/8	6	6 1/4	6 5/8	7
21	Neck	No reduction	14 1/2	14 5/8	14 3/4	14 7/8	15	15	15 2/8
22	Bust span	× .90	6	6	6 1/8	6 1/4	6 3/8	6 1/2	6 3/4
23	Bust level	× .90	9	9 1/8	9 3/4	9 7/8	10	10	10 1/4

JUNIOR SIZE STABLE KNIT REDUCTIONS

Zero percent smaller in crosswise direction without any reductions in lengthwise direction.
Use these measurements when drafting slopers for fabrics that stretch from 0% to 25% and exactly as recorded without any reductions.

		Multiply Your Across Measurements By	Extra Extra Small	Extra Small	Small	Medium	Large	Extra Large	Extra Extra Large
			0	2	6	10	14	18	20
1	Bust	× 1	32	32	34	36	39	42	43 1/2
2	Waist	× 1	25	25	27	29	32	35	36 1/2
3	Hip	× 1	35	35	37	39	42	45	46 1/2
4	Crotch depth	No reduction	10 1/4	10 1/4	10 1/2	10 3/4	11	11 1/4	11 3/8
5	Waist to knee	No reduction	22 7/8	22 7/8	23 1/8	23 3/8	23 5/8	23 7/8	24
6	Waist to ankle	No reduction	38 1/4	38 1/4	38 3/4	39 1/4	39 3/4	40 1/4	40 1/2
7	Ankle	× 1	7 7/8	7 7/8	8 3/8	8 7/8	9 3/8	9 7/8	10 1/8
8	Knee	× 1	13 5/8	13 5/8	14 1/8	14 5/8	15 1/8	15 5/8	15 7/8
9	Front crotch	× 1	2 1/4	2 1/4	2 3/8	2 1/2	2 5/8	2 7/8	2 7/8
10	Back crotch	× 1	3	3	3	3 1/4	3 1/2	3 3/4	3 7/8
11	Crotch angle	× 1	1	1	1 1/8	1 1/4	1 3/8	1 3/8	1 4/8
12	Nape to waist	No reduction	15 3/8	15 3/8	15 7/8	16 3/8	16 7/8	17 3/8	17 5/8
13	Back neck	No reduction	2 3/8	2 3/8	2 5/8	2 3/4	2 7/8	3 1/2	0
14	Back neck rise	× 1	3/4	3/4	7/8	1	1	1 1/8	0
15	Shoulder length	No reduction	4 7/8	4 7/8	5	5 3/8	5 5/8	5 7/8	6
16	Across back	× 1	7 1/4	7 1/4	7 5/8	8	8 3/8	8 6/8	8 7/8
17	Sleeve length	No reduction	23 3/8	23 3/8	23 5/8	23 7/8	24 1/8	24 3/8	24 1/2
18	Shoulder pitch	× 1	1 3/8	1 3/8	1 4/8	1 1/2	1 1/2	1 5/8	1 5/8
19	Bicep	× 1	10 3/4	10 3/4	11 1/2	12 1/4	13	13 3/4	14 1/8
20	Wrist	× 1	5 7/8	5 7/8	6 1/8	6 3/8	6 5/8	6 7/8	7
21	Neck	× 1	14 5/8	14 5/8	15 1/4	15 7/8	16 1/2	17	17 3/8
22	Bust span	× 1	6 5/8	6 5/8	6 7/8	7	7 3/8	7 5/8	7 3/4
23	Bust level	No reduction	9 7/8	9 7/8	10 3/8	10 7/8	11 3/8	11 7/8	12 1/8

JUNIOR SIZE MODERATE REDUCTIONS

Two percent smaller in crosswise direction without any reductions in lengthwise direction.
Use these measurements when drafting slopers for fabrics that stretch from 25% to 50%.
Multiply your across measurements by .98, 2% smaller, except for the shoulder measurement, since the final garment will have twill tape to stabilize the seam and prevent it from stretching.

		Multiply Your Across Measurements By	Extra Extra Small	Extra Small	Small	Medium	Large	Extra Large	Extra Extra Large
			0	2	6	10	14	18	20
1	Bust	× .98	31 3/8	32 3/8	33 3/8	34 1/4	35 1/4	36 3/4	38 2/9
2	Waist	× .98	23 1/2	24 1/2	25 1/2	26 1/2	27 4/9	28 3/8	29 7/8
3	Hip	× .98	34 1/4	35 1/4	36 1/4	37 1/4	38 1/4	39 3/4	41 1/8
4	Crotch depth	No reduction	10	10 1/8	10 1/4	10 3/8	10 1/2	10 5/8	10 6/8
5	Waist to knee	No reduction	22 3/8	22 1/2	22 5/8	22 3/4	22 7/8	23	23 1/8
6	Waist to ankle	No reduction	37 1/2	37 3/4	38	38 1/4	38 4/8	38 3/4	39
7	Ankle	× .98	7 3/4	8	8 1/4	8 1/2	8 3/4	9	9 1/4
8	Knee	× .98	13 3/8	13 5/8	13 7/8	14 1/8	14 3/8	14 5/8	14 7/8
9	Front crotch	× .98	2 1/8	2 1/4	2 1/4	2 3/8	2 3/8	2 1/2	2 5/8
10	Back crotch	× .98	2 7/8	3	3	3 1/8	3 1/8	3 1/4	3 3/8
11	Crotch angle	× .98	1 1/8	1 1/8	1 1/8	1 1/8	1 1/4	1 1/4	1 2/8
12	Nape to waist	No reduction	15 1/8	15 3/8	15 1/2	15 3/4	16	16 1/4	16 1/2
13	Back neck	No reduction	2 3/8	2 1/2	2 5/8	2 5/8	2 5/8	2 3/4	2 3/4
14	Back neck rise	× .98	3/4	7/8	7/8	7/8	7/8	7/8	7/8
15	Shoulder length	No reduction	4 3/4	4 7/8	5	5 1/8	5 1/4	5 3/8	5 1/2
16	Across back	× .98	7 1/8	7 1/4	7 3/8	7 5/8	7 3/4	8	8 1/8
17	Sleeve length	No reduction	22 7/8	23	23 1/8	23 1/4	23 3/8	23 4/8	23 5/8
18	Shoulder pitch	× .98	1 3/8	1 3/8	1 3/8	1 3/8	1 1/2	1 1/2	1 1/2
19	Bicep	× .98	10 1/2	10 7/8	11 1/4	11 5/8	12	12 3/8	12 3/4
20	Wrist	× .98	5 3/4	5 7/8	6	6 1/8	6 1/4	6 3/8	6 1/2
21	Neck	× .98	14 1/4	14 5/8	14 7/8	15 1/4	15 4/8	15 3/4	16 1/8
22	Bust span	× .98	6 3/8	6 1/2	6 5/8	6 3/4	6 7/8	7	7 1/8
23	Bust level	No reduction	9 5/8	9 7/8	10 1/8	10 3/8	10 5/8	10 7/8	11 1/8

JUNIOR SIZE STRETCHY KNIT REDUCTIONS

Three percent smaller in crosswise direction without any reductions in lengthwise direction.
Use these measurements when drafting slopers for fabrics that stretch from 50% to 75%.
Multiply your across measurements by .97, 3% smaller, except for the shoulder measurement, since the final garment will have twill tape to stabilize the seam and prevent it from stretching.

		Multiply Your Across Measurements By	Extra Extra Small	Extra Small	Small	Medium	Large	Extra Large
			0	2	6	10	14	18
1	Bust	× .97	31	32	33	35	37 7/8	40 3/4
2	Waist	× .97	23 1/4	24 1/4	26 1/4	28 1/8	31	34
3	Hip	× .97	34	35	35 7/8	37 7/8	40 3/4	43 5/8
4	Crotch depth	No reduction	10	10	10 1/2	10 3/4	11	11 1/4
5	Waist to knee	No reduction	22 1/4	22 1/4	23 1/8	23 3/8	23 5/8	23 7/8
6	Waist to ankle	No reduction	37 1/8	37 1/4	38 3/4	39 1/4	39 3/4	40 1/4
7	Ankle	× .97	7 2/3	7 7/8	8 1/8	8 5/8	9	9 5/8
8	Knee	× .97	13 1/4	13 1/2	13 3/4	14 1/8	14 5/8	15 1/8
9	Front crotch	× .97	2 1/8	2 1/4	2 1/4	2 3/8	2 1/2	2 3/4
10	Back crotch	× .97	2 3/4	3	3	3 1/8	3 3/8	3 5/8
11	Crotch angle	× .97	1	1	1 1/8	1 1/4	1 1/4	1 3/8
12	Nape to waist	No reduction	15	15 1/8	15 7/8	16 3/8	16 7/8	17 3/8
13	Back neck	No reduction	2 1/4	2 1/2	2 5/8	2 3/4	2 7/8	3 1/2
14	Back neck rise	× .97	3/4	7/8	7/8	1	1	1 1/8
15	Shoulder length	No reduction	4 3/4	4 3/4	5	5 3/8	5 5/8	5 7/8
16	Across back	× .97	7	7 1/8	7 5/8	8	8 3/8	8 3/4
17	Sleeve length	No reduction	22 5/8	22 3/4	23 5/8	23 7/8	24 1/8	24 3/8
18	Shoulder pitch	× .97	1 1/4	1 3/8	1 3/8	1 1/2	1 1/2	1 1/2
19	Bicep	× .97	10 3/8	10 3/4	11 1/8	11 7/8	12 5/8	13 3/8
20	Wrist	× .97	5 3/4	5 7/8	6	6 1/8	6 3/8	6 5/8
21	Neck	× .97	14 1/8	14 3/8	14 3/4	15 3/8	16	16 1/2
22	Bust span	× .97	6 3/8	6 1/2	6 5/8	6 7/8	7	7 3/8
23	Bust level	No reduction	9 5/8	9 7/8	10	10 1/2	11	11 1/2

JUNIOR SIZE SUPER-STRETCH REDUCTIONS

Five percent smaller in crosswise direction without any reductions in lengthwise direction.
Use these measurements when drafting slopers for fabrics that stretch from 75% to 100%.
Multiply your across measurements by .95, 5% smaller, except for the shoulder measurement, since the final garment will have twill tape to stabilize the seam and prevent it from stretching.

		Multiply Your Across Measurements By	Extra Extra Small	Extra Small	Small	Medium	Large	Extra Large
			0	2	6	10	14	18
1	Bust	× .95	30 3/8	31 3/8	32 1/4	34 1/4	37	39 7/8
2	Waist	× .95	22 3/4	23 3/4	25 5/8	27 1/2	30 3/8	33 1/4
3	Hip	× .95	33 1/4	34 2/8	35 1/8	37	39 7/8	42 3/4
4	Crotch depth	No reduction	9 3/4	9 7/8	10 1/2	10 3/4	11	11 1/4
5	Waist to knee	No reduction	21 3/4	21 7/8	23 1/8	23 3/8	23 5/8	23 7/8
6	Waist to ankle	No reduction	36 3/8	36 5/8	38 3/4	39 1/4	39 3/4	40 1/4
7	Ankle	× .95	7 1/2	7 3/4	8	8 3/8	9	9 3/8
8	Knee	× .95	13	13 1/8	13 3/8	13 7/8	14 3/8	14 7/8
9	Front crotch	× .95	2 1/8	2 1/8	2 1/4	2 3/8	2 1/2	2 5/8
10	Back crotch	× .95	2 3/4	2 7/8	3	3	3 3/8	3 5/8
11	Crotch angle	× .95	1	1 1/8	1	1 1/8	1 1/4	1 3/8
12	Nape to waist	No reduction	14 5/8	14 7/8	15 7/8	16 3/8	16 7/8	17 3/8
13	Back neck	No reduction	2 1/4	2 4/8	2 5/8	2 3/4	2 7/8	3 1/2
14	Back neck rise	× .95	3/4	7/8	7/8	1	1	1 1/8
15	Shoulder length	No reduction	4 5/8	4 6/8	5	5 3/8	5 5/8	5 7/8
16	Across back	× .95	6 7/8	7	7 5/8	8	8 3/8	8 3/4
17	Sleeve length	No reduction	22 1/4	22 3/8	23 5/8	23 7/8	24 1/8	24 3/8
18	Shoulder pitch	× .95	1 3/8	1 3/8	1 3/8	1 3/8	1 1/2	1 1/2
19	Bicep	× .95	10 1/4	10 5/8	11	11 5/8	12 3/8	13
20	Wrist	× .95	5 5/8	5 3/4	5 7/8	6	6 1/4	6 1/2
21	Neck	× .95	13 7/8	14 1/8	14 3/8	15	15 5/8	16 1/4
22	Bust span	× .95	6 1/4	6 3/8	6 1/2	6 3/4	7	7 1/8
23	Bust level	No reduction	9 3/8	9 5/8	9 7/8	10 3/8	10 3/4	11 1/4

JUNIOR SIZE RIB REDUCTIONS

Ten percent smaller in crosswise direction without any reductions in lengthwise direction.
Use these measurements when drafting slopers for fabrics that stretch 100% and over.
Multiply your across measurements by .90, 10% smaller, except for the shoulder measurement, since the final garment will have twill tape to stabilize the seam and prevent it from stretching.

		Multiply Your Across Measurements By	Extra Extra Small	Extra Small	Small	Medium	Large	Extra Large
			0	2	6	10	14	18
1	Bust	× .90	28 3/4	29 3/4	30 5/8	32 3/8	35 1/8	37 3/4
2	Waist	× .90	21 1/2	22 1/2	24 1/4	26 1/8	28 3/4	31 1/2
3	Hip	× .90	31 1/2	32 1/2	33 1/4	35 1/8	37 3/4	40 1/2
4	Crotch depth	No reduction	9 1/4	9 1/4	10 1/2	10 3/4	11	11 1/4
5	Waist to knee	No reduction	20 1/2	20 3/4	23 1/8	23 3/8	23 5/8	23 7/8
6	Waist to ankle	No reduction	34 1/2	34 3/4	38 3/4	39 1/4	39 3/4	40 1/4
7	Ankle	× .90	7	7 1/4	7 1/2	8	8 1/2	8 7/8
8	Knee	× .90	12 1/4	12 1/2	12 3/4	13 1/8	13 5/8	14
9	Front crotch	× .90	2	2	2	2 1/4	2 3/8	2 1/2
10	Back crotch	× .90	2 3/4	2 3/4	2 3/4	3	3 1/8	3 3/8
11	Crotch angle	× .90	1	1	1	1	1 1/6	1 1/4
12	Nape to waist	No reduction	13 3/4	14	15 7/8	16 3/8	16 7/8	17 3/8
13	Back neck	No reduction	2 1/4	2 1/4	2 5/8	2 3/4	2 7/8	3 1/2
14	Back neck rise	× .90	3/4	3/4	7/8	1	1	1 1/6
15	Shoulder length	No reduction	4 1/4	4 1/2	5	5 3/8	5 5/8	5 7/8
16	Across back	× .90	6 1/2	6 3/4	7 5/8	8	8 1/3	8 3/4
17	Sleeve length	No reduction	21	21 1/4	23 5/8	23 7/8	24 1/8	24 3/8
18	Shoulder pitch	× .90	1 1/4	1 1/4	1 2/7	1 1/3	1 3/8	1 3/7
19	Bicep	× .90	9 3/4	10	10 3/8	11	11 3/4	12 3/8
20	Wrist	× .90	5 1/4	5 1/2	5 1/2	5 3/4	6	6 2/8
21	Neck	× .90	13	13 1/2	13 5/8	14 1/4	14 3/4	15 3/8
22	Bust span	× .90	6	6	6 1/8	6 3/8	6 5/8	6 3/4
23	Bust level	No reduction	9	9	9 3/8	9 3/4	10 1/4	10 3/4

JUNIOR SIZE FOUR-WAY-STRETCH REDUCTIONS

Ten percent smaller in crosswise direction and 10% smaller in the lengthwise direction.
Use these measurements when drafting slopers for fabrics that stretch 100% in both directions.
Multiply your measurements by .90, 10% smaller, in both directions except for the shoulder measurement, since the final garment will have twill tape to stabilize the seam and prevent it from stretching.

		Multiply Your Across Measurements By	Extra Extra Small	Extra Small	Small	Medium	Large	Extra Large
			0	2	6	10	14	18
1	Bust	× .90	28 3/4	29 3/4	29 3/4	30 5/8	31 1/2	32 3/8
2	Waist	× .90	21 1/2	22 1/2	23 3/8	24 1/4	25 1/4	26 1/8
3	Hip	× .90	31 1/2	32 1/2	32 3/8	33 1/4	34 1/4	35 1/8
4	Crotch depth	× .90	9 1/4	9 1/4	9 7/8	10	10	10 2/8
5	Waist to knee	× .90	20 1/2	20 3/4	21 7/8	22	22	22 1/4
6	Waist to ankle	× .90	34 1/2	34 3/4	36 5/8	36 7/8	37	37 1/4
7	Ankle	× .90	7	7 1/4	7 3/8	7 1/2	7 3/4	8
8	Knee	× .90	12 1/4	12 1/2	12 1/2	12 3/4	13	13 1/8
9	Front crotch	× .90	2	2	2	2	2 1/8	2 1/4
10	Back crotch	× .90	2 3/4	2 3/4	3	3	3 1/8	3 1/4
11	Crotch angle	× .90	1	1	1 1/8	1 1/8	1 1/4	1 1/4
12	Nape to waist	× .90	13 3/4	14	14 7/8	15	15 3/8	15 1/2
13	Back neck	No reduction	2 1/4	2 1/4	2 5/8	2 5/8	2 3/4	2 3/4
14	Back neck rise	No reduction	3/4	3/4	7/8	7/8	7/8	1
15	Shoulder length	No reduction	4 1/4	4 1/2	5	5	5 1/4	5 3/8
16	Across back	No reduction	6 1/2	6 3/4	7 3/8	7 5/8	7 3/4	8
17	Sleeve length	No reduction	21	21 1/4	23 1/2	23 5/8	23 3/4	23 7/8
18	Shoulder pitch	No reduction	1 1/4	1 1/4	1 3/8	1 1/2	1 1/2	1 1/2
19	Bicep	× .90	9 3/4	10	10	10 3/8	10 3/4	11
20	Wrist	× .90	5 1/4	5 1/2	5 3/8	5 1/2	5 5/8	5 3/4
21	Neck	No reduction	13	13 1/2	14 7/8	15 1/4	15 1/2	15 7/8
22	Bust span	× .90	6	6	6	6 1/8	6 1/4	6 3/8
23	Bust level	× .90	9	9	9 5/8	9 7/8	10	10 3/8

PETITE SIZE STABLE KNITS REDUCTIONS

Zero percent smaller in crosswise direction without any reductions in lengthwise direction.
Use these measurements when drafting slopers for fabrics that stretch from 0% to 25%.
Multiply your across measurements by 1, 0% smaller, except for the shoulder measurement, since the final garment will have twill tape to stabilize the seam and prevent it from stretching.

		Multiply Your Across Measurements By	Extra Small	Small	Medium	Large	Extra Large
			2	6	10	14	18
1	Bust	× 1	31 1/2	33 1/2	35 1/2	38 1/2	41 1/2
2	Waist	× 1	23 1/2	25 1/2	27 1/2	30 1/2	33 1/2
3	Hip	× 1	34 1/2	36 1/2	38 1/2	41 1/2	44 1/2
4	Crotch depth	No reduction	10 1/8	10 3/8	10 5/8	10 7/8	11 1/8
5	Waist to knee	No reduction	21 3/8	21 5/8	21 7/8	22 1/8	22 3/8
6	Waist to ankle	No reduction	36 5/8	37 1/8	37 5/8	38 1/8	38 5/8
7	Ankle	× 1	6 5/8	6 7/8	7 1/8	7 3/8	7 5/8
8	Knee	× 1	13 1/4	13 3/4	14 1/4	14 3/4	15 1/4
9	Front crotch	× 1	2 1/8	2 1/4	2 3/8	2 5/8	2 3/4
10	Back crotch	× 1	2 7/8	3	3 1/4	3 1/2	3 3/4
11	Crotch angle	× 1	1	1 1/8	1 1/4	1 2/8	1 3/8
12	Nape to waist	No reduction	14 3/4	15 1/4	15 3/4	16 1/4	16 3/4
13	Back neck	No reduction	2 1/4	2 3/8	2 3/8	2 3/8	2 1/2
14	Back neck rise	× 1	3/4	3/4	6/8	3/4	7/8
15	Shoulder length	No reduction	4 7/8	5	5 1/8	5 3/8	5 5/8
16	Across back	× 1	7 1/4	7 4/8	7 3/4	8	8 1/4
17	Sleeve length	No reduction	21 1/4	21 1/2	21 3/4	22	22 1/4
18	Shoulder pitch	× 1	1 3/8	1 3/8	1 3/8	1 1/2	1 1/2
19	Bicep	× 1	10 3/8	11 1/8	11 7/8	12 5/8	13 3/8
20	Wrist	× 1	5 3/4	6 1/2	7 1/4	8	8 3/4
21	Neck	× 1	13 3/4	14	14 1/4	14 1/2	14 3/4
22	Bust span	× 1	6 5/8	6 7/8	7	7 4/8	7 7/8
23	Bust level	No reduction	9 3/8	9 5/8	9 7/8	10 1/8	10 3/8

PETITE SIZE MODERATE REDUCTIONS

Two percent smaller in crosswise direction without any reductions in lengthwise direction.
Use these measurements when drafting slopers for fabrics that stretch from 25% to 50%.
Multiply your across measurements by .98, 2% smaller, except for the shoulder measurement, since the final garment will have twill tape to stabilize the seam and prevent it from stretching.

		Multiply Your Across Measurements By	Extra Small	Small	Medium	Large	Extra Large
			2	6	10	14	18
1	Bust	× .98	30 7/8	32 7/8	34 3/4	37 3/4	40 5/8
2	Waist	× .98	23	25	27	29 7/8	32 7/8
3	Hip	× .98	33 3/4	35 3/4	37 3/4	40 5/8	43 5/8
4	Crotch depth	No reduction	10 1/8	10 3/8	10 5/8	10 7/8	11 1/8
5	Waist to knee	No reduction	21 3/8	21 5/8	21 7/8	22 1/8	22 3/8
6	Waist to ankle	No reduction	36 5/8	37 1/8	37 5/8	38 1/8	38 5/8
7	Ankle	× .98	6 1/2	6 3/4	7	7 2/8	7 1/2
8	Knee	× .98	13	13 3/8	14	14 3/8	14 7/8
9	Front crotch	× .98	2 1/8	2 1/4	2 1/4	2 1/2	2 3/4
10	Back crotch	× .98	2 7/8	3	3 1/8	3 3/8	3 5/8
11	Crotch angle	× .98	1	1 1/8	1 1/8	1 1/4	1 3/8
12	Nape to waist	No reduction	14 3/4	15 1/4	15 3/4	16 1/4	16 3/4
13	Back neck	No reduction	2 1/4	2 3/8	2 3/8	2 3/8	2 1/2
14	Back neck rise	× .98	3/4	3/4	3/4	3/4	7/8
15	Shoulder length	No reduction	4 7/8	5	5 1/8	5 3/8	5 5/8
16	Across back	× .98	7 1/4	7 1/2	7 6/8	8	8 1/4
17	Sleeve length	No reduction	21 1/4	21 1/2	21 3/4	22	22 1/4
18	Shoulder pitch	× .98	1 3/8	1 3/8	1 3/8	1 1/2	1 1/2
19	Bicep	× .98	10 1/8	11	11 5/8	12 3/8	13 1/8
20	Wrist	× .98	5 5/8	6 3/8	7 1/8	7 7/8	8 5/8
21	Neck	× .98	13 1/2	13 3/4	14	14 1/4	14 1/2
22	Bust span	× .98	6 3/8	6 5/8	7	7 1/4	7 5/8
23	Bust level	No reduction	9 1/4	9 3/8	9 5/8	10	10 1/8

PETITE SIZE STRETCHY REDUCTIONS

Three percent smaller in crosswise direction without any reductions in lengthwise direction.
Use these measurements when drafting slopers for fabrics that stretch from 50% to 75%.
Multiply your across measurements by .97, 3% smaller, except for the shoulder measurement, since the final garment will have twill tape to stabilize the seam and prevent it from stretching.

		Multiply Your Across Measurements By	Extra Small	Small	Medium	Large	Extra Large
			2	6	10	14	18
1	Bust	× .97	30 1/2	32 1/2	34 3/8	37 3/8	40 1/4
2	Waist	× .97	22 3/4	24 3/4	26 5/8	29 5/8	32 1/2
3	Hip	× .97	33 1/2	35 3/8	37 3/8	40 1/4	43 1/8
4	Crotch depth	No reduction	10 1/8	10 3/8	10 5/8	10 7/8	11 1/8
5	Waist to knee	No reduction	21 3/8	21 5/8	21 7/8	22 1/8	22 3/8
6	Waist to ankle	No reduction	36 5/8	37 1/8	37 5/8	38 1/8	38 5/8
7	Ankle	× .97	6 3/8	6 5/8	7	7 1/8	7 3/8
8	Knee	× .97	12 3/4	13 1/4	13 3/4	14 1/4	14 3/4
9	Front crotch	× .97	2	2 1/4	2 3/8	2 1/2	2 3/4
10	Back crotch	× .97	2 3/4	3	3 1/8	3 3/8	3 5/8
11	Crotch angle	× .97	1	1 1/8	1 1/8	1 1/4	1 3/8
12	Nape to waist	No reduction	14 3/4	15 1/4	15 3/4	16 1/4	16 3/4
13	Back neck	No reduction	2 1/4	2 1/4	2 3/8	2 3/8	2 1/2
14	Back neck rise	× .97	3/4	3/4	3/4	3/4	7/8
15	Shoulder length	No reduction	4 7/8	5	5 1/8	5 3/8	5 5/8
16	Across back	× .97	7 1/4	7 4/8	7 3/4	8	8 1/4
17	Sleeve length	No reduction	21 1/4	21 1/2	21 3/4	22	22 1/4
18	Shoulder pitch	× .97	1 1/4	1 3/8	1 3/8	1 3/8	1 1/2
19	Bicep	× .97	10	10 3/4	11 1/2	12 1/4	13
20	Wrist	× .97	5 5/8	6 1/4	7	7 3/4	8 1/2
21	Neck	× .97	13 3/8	13 5/8	13 7/8	14	14 1/4
22	Bust span	× .97	6 3/8	6 5/8	6 7/8	7 1/4	7 5/8
23	Bust level	No reduction	9	9 3/8	9 5/8	9 7/8	10

PETITE SIZE SUPER-STRETCH REDUCTIONS

Five percent smaller in crosswise direction without any reductions in lengthwise direction.
Use these measurements when drafting slopers for fabrics that stretch from 75% to 100%.
Multiply your across measurements by .95, 5% smaller, except for the shoulder measurement since the final garment will have twill tape to stabilize the seam and prevent it from stretching.

		Multiply Your Across Measurements By	Extra Small	Small	Medium	Large	Extra Large
			2	6	10	14	18
1	Bust	× .95	30	31 7/8	33 3/4	36 5/8	39 3/8
2	Waist	× .95	22 3/8	24 1/4	26 1/8	29	31 7/8
3	Hip	× .95	32 3/4	34 5/8	36 5/8	39 3/8	42 1/4
4	Crotch depth	No reduction	10 1/8	10 3/8	10 5/8	10 7/8	11 1/8
5	Waist to knee	No reduction	21 3/8	21 5/8	21 7/8	22 1/8	22 3/8
6	Waist to ankle	No reduction	36 5/8	37 1/8	37 5/8	38 1/8	38 5/8
7	Ankle	× .95	6 1/4	6 1/2	6 3/4	7	7 1/4
8	Knee	× .95	12 1/2	13	13 1/2	14	14 3/7
9	Front crotch	× .95	2	2 1/8	2 1/4	2 1/2	2 5/8
10	Back crotch	× .95	2 3/4	2 7/8	3	3 2/8	3 1/2
11	Crotch angle	× .95	1	1	1 1/8	1 1/4	1 3/8
12	Nape to waist	No reduction	14 3/4	15 1/4	15 3/4	16 1/4	16 3/4
13	Back neck	No reduction	2 1/4	2 3/8	2 3/8	2 3/8	2 1/2
14	Back neck rise	× .95	3/4	3/4	3/4	3/4	7/8
15	Shoulder length	No reduction	4 7/8	5	5 1/8	5 3/8	5 5/8
16	Across back	× .95	7 1/4	7 1/2	7 3/4	8	8 1/4
17	Sleeve length	No reduction	21 1/4	21 1/2	21 3/4	22	22 1/4
18	Shoulder pitch	× .95	1 1/4	1 3/8	1 3/8	1 3/8	1 1/2
19	Bicep	× .95	9 7/8	10 5/8	11 2/8	12	12 3/4
20	Wrist	× .95	5 1/2	6 1/8	6 7/8	7 5/8	8 3/8
21	Neck	× .95	13	13 1/4	13 1/2	13 3/4	14
22	Bust span	× .95	6 1/4	6 1/2	6 3/4	7	7 3/8
23	Bust level	No reduction	9	9 1/8	9 3/8	9 5/8	9 7/8

PETITE SIZE RIB REDUCTIONS

Ten percent smaller in crosswise direction without any reductions in lengthwise direction.
Use these measurements when drafting slopers for fabrics that stretch 100% and over.
Multiply your across measurements by .90, 10% smaller, except for the shoulder measurement, since the final garment will have twill tape to stabilize the seam and prevent it from stretching.

		Multiply Your Across Measurements By	Extra Small	Small	Medium	Large	Extra Large
			2	6	10	14	18
1	Bust	× .90	28 3/8	30 1/8	32	34 5/8	37 3/8
2	Waist	× .90	21 1/8	23	24 3/4	27 1/2	30 1/8
3	Hip	× .90	31	32 7/8	34 5/8	37 3/8	40
4	Crotch depth	No reduction	10 1/8	10 3/8	10 5/8	10 7/8	11 1/8
5	Waist to knee	No reduction	21 3/8	21 5/8	21 7/8	22 1/8	22 3/8
6	Waist to ankle	No reduction	36 5/8	37 1/8	37 5/8	38 1/8	38 5/8
7	Ankle	× .90	6	6 1/4	6 3/8	6 5/8	6 7/8
8	Knee	× .90	11 7/8	12 3/8	12 3/4	13 1/4	13 5/8
9	Front crotch	× .90	2	2	2 1/8	2 3/8	2 1/2
10	Back crotch	× .90	2 5/8	2 3/4	2 7/8	3 1/8	3 3/8
11	Crotch angle	× .90	1	1	1	1 1/6	1 1/4
12	Nape to waist	No reduction	14 3/4	15 1/4	15 3/4	16 1/4	16 3/4
13	Back neck	No reduction	2 1/4	2 3/8	2 3/8	2 3/8	2 1/2
14	Back neck rise	× .90	3/4	3/4	3/4	3/4	7/8
15	Shoulder length	No reduction	4 7/8	5	5 1/8	5 3/8	5 5/8
16	Across back	× .90	7 1/4	7 1/2	7 3/4	8	8 1/4
17	Sleeve length	No reduction	21 1/4	21 1/2	21 3/4	22	22 1/4
18	Shoulder pitch	× .90	1 1/4	1 1/4	1 1/4	1 3/8	1 3/8
19	Bicep	× .90	9 3/8	10	10 3/4	11 3/8	12
20	Wrist	× .90	5 1/8	5 7/8	6 1/2	7 1/4	7 7/8
21	Neck	× .90	12 3/8	12 5/8	12 7/8	13	13 1/4
22	Bust span	× .90	6	6 1/8	6 3/8	6 3/4	7
23	Bust level	No reduction	8 1/2	8 5/8	8 7/8	9 1/8	9 3/8

PETITE SIZE FOUR-WAY-STRETCH REDUCTIONS

Ten percent smaller in crosswise direction and 10% smaller in the lengthwise direction.
Use these measurements when drafting slopers for fabrics that stretch 100% in both directions.
Multiply your across measurements by .90, 1% smaller, except for the shoulder measurement, since the final garment will have twill tape to stabilize the seam and prevent it from stretching.

		Multiply Your Across Measurements By	Extra Small	Small	Medium	Large	Extra Large
			2	6	10	14	18
1	Bust	× .90	28 3/8	29 1/4	30 1/8	31	32
2	Waist	× .90	21 1/8	22	23	23 7/8	24 3/4
3	Hip	× .90	31	32	32 7/8	33 3/4	34 5/8
4	Crotch depth	× .90	9 5/8	9 3/4	9 7/8	10	10
5	Waist to knee	× .90	20 1/4	20 3/8	20 1/2	20 5/8	20 3/4
6	Waist to ankle	× .90	34 3/4	35	35 1/4	35 1/2	35 3/4
7	Ankle	× .90	6	6	6 1/4	6 1/4	6 3/8
8	Knee	× .90	11 7/8	12	12 3/8	12 1/2	12 3/4
9	Front crotch	× .90	2	2	2	2 1/8	2 1/8
10	Back crotch	× .90	2 7/8	3	3	3 1/8	3 1/4
11	Crotch angle	× .90	1	1 1/8	1 1/8	1 1/8	1 2/8
12	Nape to waist	× .90	14	14 1/4	14 1/2	14 3/4	15
13	Back neck	No reduction	2 1/4	2 3/8	2 3/8	2 3/8	2 3/8
14	Back neck rise	No reduction	3/4	3/4	3/4	3/4	3/4
15	Shoulder length	No reduction	4 7/8	5	5	5	5 1/8
16	Across back	No reduction	7 1/4	7 3/8	7 1/2	7 5/8	7 3/4
17	Sleeve length	No reduction	21 1/4	21 3/8	21 1/2	21 5/8	21 3/4
18	Shoulder pitch	No reduction	1 3/8	1 3/8	1 3/8	1 3/8	1 3/8
19	Bicep	× .90	9 3/8	9 5/8	10	10 3/8	10 6/8
20	Wrist	× .90	5 1/8	5 1/2	5 7/8	6 1/4	6 1/2
21	Neck	No reduction	13 3/4	13 7/8	14	14 1/8	14 1/4
22	Bust span	× .90	6	6	6 1/8	6 1/4	6 3/8
23	Bust level	× .90	9	9	9 1/8	9 1/4	9 3/8

MISSES TALL STABLE KNIT REDUCTIONS

Zero percent smaller in crosswise direction without any reductions in lengthwise direction.
Use these measurements when drafting slopers for fabrics that stretch from 0% to 25%.
Multiply your across measurements by 1, 0% smaller, except for the shoulder measurement, since the final garment will have twill tape to stabilize the seam and prevent it from stretching.

		Multiply Your Across Measurements By	Extra Small	Small	Medium	Large	Extra Large
			2	6	10	14	18
1	Bust	× 1	32 1/2	34 1/2	36 1/2	39 1/2	42 1/2
2	Waist	× 1	24 1/2	26 1/2	28 1/2	31 1/2	34 1/2
3	Hip	× 1	35 1/2	37 1/2	39 1/2	42 1/2	45 1/2
4	Crotch depth	No reduction	11 1/4	11 1/2	11 3/4	12	12 1/4
5	Waist to knee	No reduction	24 5/8	24 7/8	25 1/8	25 3/8	25 5/8
6	Waist to ankle	No reduction	40 7/8	41 3/8	41 7/8	42 3/8	42 7/8
7	Ankle	× 1	7 7/8	8 1/8	8 3/8	8 5/8	8 7/8
8	Knee	× 1	13 5/8	14 1/8	14 5/8	15 1/8	15 5/8
9	Front crotch	× 1	2 1/4	2 3/8	2 1/2	2 5/8	2 7/8
10	Back crotch	× 1	3	3 1/8	3 1/4	3 1/2	3 3/4
11	Crotch angle	× 1	1 1/8	1 1/8	1 1/4	1 3/8	1 3/8
12	Nape to waist	No reduction	16 7/8	17 3/8	17 7/8	18 3/8	18 7/8
13	Back neck	No reduction	2 4/8	2 1/2	2 1/2	2 5/8	2 5/8
14	Back neck rise	× 1	7/8	7/8	7/8	7/8	7/8
15	Shoulder length	No reduction	4 7/8	5	5 1/8	5 3/8	5 5/8
16	Across back	× 1	7 1/2	7 3/4	8 1/8	8 1/2	8 7/8
17	Sleeve length	No reduction	24 3/8	24 5/8	24 7/8	25 1/8	25 3/8
18	Shoulder pitch	× 1	1 1/2	1 5/8	1 5/8	1 5/8	1 3/4
19	Bicep	× 1	10 5/8	11 3/8	12 1/8	12 7/8	13 5/8
20	Wrist	× 1	5 7/8	6 5/8	7 3/8	8 1/8	8 7/8
21	Neck	× 1	14 5/8	15	15 1/8	15 3/8	15 5/8
22	Bust span	× 1	6 3/4	7	7 1/4	7 5/8	8
23	Bust level	No reduction	10 3/4	11	11 1/4	11 1/2	11 3/4

MISSES TALL MODERATE REDUCTIONS

Two percent smaller in crosswise direction without any reductions in lengthwise direction.
Use these measurements when drafting slopers for fabrics that stretch from 25% to 50%.
Multiply your across measurements by .98, 2% smaller, except for the shoulder measurement, since the final garment will have twill tape to stabilize the seam and prevent it from stretching.

		Multiply Your Across Measurements By	Extra Small	Small	Medium	Large	Extra Large
			2	6	10	14	18
1	Bust	× .98	31 7/8	33 3/4	35 3/4	38 3/4	41 5/8
2	Waist	× .98	24	26	28	30 7/8	33 3/4
3	Hip	× .98	34 3/4	36 3/4	38 3/4	41 5/8	44 5/8
4	Crotch depth	No reduction	11 1/4	11 1/2	11 3/4	12	12 1/4
5	Waist to knee	No reduction	24 5/8	24 7/8	25 1/8	25 3/8	25 5/8
6	Waist to ankle	No reduction	40 7/8	41 3/8	41 7/8	42 3/8	42 7/8
7	Ankle	× .98	7 3/4	8	8 1/4	8 1/2	8 3/4
8	Knee	× .98	13 3/8	13 7/8	14 3/8	14 7/8	15 3/8
9	Front crotch	× .98	2 1/8	2 1/4	2 3/8	2 5/8	2 3/4
10	Back crotch	× .98	2 7/8	3	3 1/4	3 1/2	3 3/4
11	Crotch angle	× .98	1	1 1/8	1 1/4	1 1/4	1 3/8
12	Nape to waist	No reduction	16 7/8	17 3/8	17 7/8	18 3/8	18 7/8
13	Back neck	No reduction	2 1/2	2 1/2	2 1/2	2 5/8	2 5/8
14	Back neck rise	× .98	7/8	7/8	7/8	7/8	7/8
15	Shoulder length	No reduction	4 7/8	5	5 1/8	5 3/8	5 5/8
16	Across back	× .98	7 1/2	7 3/4	8 1/8	8 1/2	8 7/8
17	Sleeve length	No reduction	24 3/8	24 5/8	24 7/8	25 1/8	25 3/8
18	Shoulder pitch	× .98	1 1/2	1 1/2	1 5/8	1 5/8	1 5/8
19	Bicep	× .98	10 3/8	11 1/8	11 8/9	12 5/8	13 3/8
20	Wrist	× .98	5 3/4	6 1/2	7 1/4	8	8 3/4
21	Neck	× .98	14 3/8	14 5/8	14 7/8	15 1/8	15 3/8
22	Bust span	× .98	6 1/2	6 3/4	7	7 3/8	7 3/4
23	Bust level	No reduction	10 1/2	10 3/4	11	11 1/4	11 1/2

MISSES TALL STRETCHY REDUCTIONS

Three percent smaller in crosswise direction without any reductions in lengthwise direction.
Use these measurements when drafting slopers for fabrics that stretch from 50% to 75%.
Multiply your across measurements by .97, 3% smaller, except for the shoulder measurement, since the final garment will have twill tape to stabilize the seam and prevent it from stretching.

		Multiply Your Across Measurements By	Extra Small	Small	Medium	Large	Extra Large
			2	6	10	14	18
1	Bust	× .97	31 1/2	33 1/2	35 3/8	38 3/8	41 1/4
2	Waist	× .97	23 3/4	25 3/4	27 5/8	30 1/2	33 1/2
3	Hip	× .97	34 3/8	36 3/8	38 3/8	41 1/4	44 1/8
4	Crotch depth	No reduction	11 1/4	11 1/2	11 3/4	12	12 1/4
5	Waist to knee	No reduction	24 5/8	24 7/8	25 1/8	25 3/8	25 5/8
6	Waist to ankle	No reduction	40 7/8	41 3/8	41 7/8	42 3/8	42 7/8
7	Ankle	× .97	7 5/8	7 7/8	8 1/8	8 3/8	8 5/8
8	Knee	× .97	13 1/4	13 3/4	14 1/8	14 5/8	15 1/8
9	Front crotch	× .97	2 1/8	2 1/4	2 3/8	2 5/8	2 3/4
10	Back crotch	× .97	2 7/8	3	3 1/4	3 3/8	3 5/8
11	Crotch angle	× .97	1	1 1/8	1 1/4	1 1/4	1 3/8
12	Nape to waist	No reduction	16 7/8	17 3/8	17 7/8	18 3/8	18 7/8
13	Back neck	No reduction	2 1/2	2 1/2	2 1/2	2 5/8	2 5/8
14	Back neck rise	× .97	7/8	7/8	7/8	7/8	7/8
15	Shoulder length	No reduction	4 7/8	5	5 1/8	5 3/8	5 5/8
16	Across back	× .97	7 1/2	7 3/4	8 1/8	8 1/2	8 7/8
17	Sleeve length	No reduction	24 3/8	24 5/8	24 7/8	25 1/8	25 3/8
18	Shoulder pitch	× .97	1 1/2	1 1/2	1 5/8	1 5/8	1 5/8
19	Bicep	× .97	10 1/4	11	11 3/4	12 1/2	13 1/4
20	Wrist	× .97	5 3/4	6 3/8	7 1/8	7 7/8	8 5/8
21	Neck	× .97	14 1/4	14 1/2	14 3/4	15	15 1/4
22	Bust span	× .97	6 1/2	6 3/4	7	7 3/8	7 3/4
23	Bust level	No reduction	10 3/8	10 5/8	10 7/8	11	11 3/8

MISSES TALL SUPER-STRETCH REDUCTIONS

Five percent smaller in crosswise direction without any reductions in lengthwise direction.
Use these measurements when drafting slopers for fabrics that stretch from 75% to 100%.
Multiply your across measurements by .95, 5% smaller, except for the shoulder measurement, since the final garment will have twill tape to stabilize the seam and prevent it from stretching.

		Multiply Your Across Measurements By	Extra Small	Small	Medium	Large	Extra Large
			2	6	10	14	18
1	Bust	× .95	30 7/8	32 3/4	34 5/8	37 1/2	40 3/8
2	Waist	× .95	23 1/4	25 1/8	27	30	32 3/4
3	Hip	× .95	33 3/4	35 5/8	37 1/2	40 3/8	43 1/4
4	Crotch depth	No reduction	11 1/4	11 1/2	11 3/4	12	12 1/4
5	Waist to knee	No reduction	24 5/8	24 7/8	25 1/8	25 3/8	25 5/8
6	Waist to ankle	No reduction	40 7/8	41 3/8	41 7/8	42 3/8	42 7/8
7	Ankle	× .95	7 1/2	7 3/4	8	8 1/4	8 3/8
8	Knee	× .95	13	13 3/8	13 7/8	14 3/8	14 7/8
9	Front crotch	× .95	2 1/8	2 1/4	2 3/8	2 1/2	2 3/4
10	Back crotch	× .95	2 3/4	3	3 1/8	3 3/8	3 5/8
11	Crotch angle	× .95	1	1 1/8	1 1/8	1 1/4	1 3/8
12	Nape to waist	No reduction	16 7/8	17 3/8	17 7/8	18 3/8	18 7/8
13	Back neck	No reduction	2 1/2	2 1/2	2 1/2	2 5/8	2 5/8
14	Back neck rise	× .95	7/8	7/8	7/8	7/8	7/8
15	Shoulder length	No reduction	4 7/8	5	5 1/8	5 3/8	5 5/8
16	Across back	× .95	7 1/2	7 3/4	8 1/8	8 1/2	8 7/8
17	Sleeve length	No reduction	24 3/8	24 5/8	24 7/8	25 1/8	25 3/8
18	Shoulder pitch	× .95	1 1/2	1 1/2	1 1/2	1 3/5	1 5/8
19	Bicep	× .95	10	10 3/4	11 1/2	12 1/4	13
20	Wrist	× .95	5 5/8	6 1/4	7	7 3/4	8 3/8
21	Neck	× .95	14	14 1/8	14 3/8	14 5/8	14 7/8
22	Bust span	× .95	6 3/8	6 5/8	6 7/8	7 1/8	7 1/2
23	Bust level	No reduction	10 1/8	10 3/8	10 5/8	10 7/8	11 1/8

MISSES TALL RIB REDUCTIONS

Ten percent smaller in crosswise direction without any reductions in lengthwise direction.
Use these measurements when drafting slopers for fabrics that stretch 100% and over.
Multiply your across measurements by .90, 10% smaller, except for the shoulder measurement, since the final garment will have twill tape to stabilize the seam and prevent it from stretching.

		Multiply Your Across Measurements By	Extra Small	Small	Medium	Large	Extra Large
			2	6	10	14	18
1	Bust	× .90	29 1/4	31	32 7/8	35 1/2	38 1/4
2	Waist	× .90	22	23 7/8	25 5/8	28 1/3	31
3	Hip	× .90	32	33 3/4	35 1/2	38 1/4	41
4	Crotch depth	No reduction	11 1/4	11 1/2	11 3/4	12	12 1/4
5	Waist to knee	No reduction	24 5/8	24 7/8	25 1/8	25 3/8	25 5/8
6	Waist to ankle	No reduction	40 7/8	41 3/8	41 7/8	42 3/8	42 7/8
7	Ankle	× .90	7	7 3/8	7 1/2	7 3/4	8
8	Knee	× .90	12 1/4	12 3/4	13 1/8	13 5/8	14
9	Front crotch	× .90	2	2 1/8	2 1/4	2 3/8	2 1/2
10	Back crotch	× .90	2 5/8	2 7/8	3	3 1/4	3 3/8
11	Crotch angle	× .90	1	1	1 1/8	1 1/4	1 1/4
12	Nape to waist	No reduction	16 7/8	17 3/8	17 7/8	18 3/8	18 7/8
13	Back neck	No reduction	2 1/2	2 1/2	2 1/2	2 5/8	2 5/8
14	Back neck rise	× .90	7/8	7/8	7/8	7/8	7/8
15	Shoulder length	No reduction	4 7/8	5	5 1/8	5 3/8	5 5/8
16	Across back	× .90	7 1/2	7 3/4	8 1/8	8 1/2	8 7/8
17	Sleeve length	No reduction	24 3/8	24 5/8	24 7/8	25 1/8	25 3/8
18	Shoulder pitch	× .90	1 3/8	1 3/8	1 1/2	1 1/2	1 1/2
19	Bicep	× .90	9 5/8	10 1/4	11	11 5/8	12 1/4
20	Wrist	× .90	5 1/4	6	6 5/8	7 3/8	8
21	Neck	× .90	13 1/4	13 3/8	13 5/8	13 7/8	14
22	Bust span	× .90	6	6 1/4	6 1/2	6 3/4	7 1/8
23	Bust level	No reduction	9 5/8	9 7/8	10	10 1/4	10 1/2

MISSES TALL FOUR-WAY REDUCTIONS

Ten percent smaller in crosswise direction and 10% smaller in the lengthwise direction.
Use these measurements when drafting slopers for fabrics that stretch 100% in both directions.
Multiply your measurements by .90, 10% smaller, in both directions.

		Multiply Your Across Measurements By	Extra Small	Small	Medium	Large	Extra Large
			2	6	10	14	18
1	Bust	× .90	29 1/4	30 1/8	31	32	32 7/8
2	Waist	× .90	22	23	23 7/8	24 3/4	25 5/8
3	Hip	× .90	32	32 7/8	33 3/4	34 5/8	35 1/2
4	Crotch depth	× .90	10 3/4	10 3/4	11	11	11 1/8
5	Waist to knee	× .90	23 3/8	23 1/2	23 5/8	23 3/4	23 7/8
6	Waist to ankle	× .90	38 7/8	39	39 1/4	39 1/2	39 3/4
7	Ankle	× .90	7	7 1/4	7 3/8	7 3/8	7 1/2
8	Knee	× .90	12 1/4	12 1/2	12 3/4	13	13 1/8
9	Front crotch	× .90	2	2	2 1/8	2 1/8	2 2/8
10	Back crotch	× .90	3	3	3 1/8	3 1/4	3 2/8
11	Crotch angle	× .90	1 1/8	1 1/8	1 1/8	1 1/4	1 1/4
12	Nape to waist	× .90	16	16 1/4	16 1/2	16 3/4	17
13	Back neck	No reduction	2 1/2	2 1/2	2 1/2	2 1/2	2 1/2
14	Back neck rise	No reduction	7/8	7/8	7/8	7/8	7/8
15	Shoulder length	No reduction	4 7/8	5	5	5	5 1/8
16	Across back	No reduction	7 1/2	7 5/8	7 3/4	8	8 1/8
17	Sleeve length	No reduction	24 3/8	24 1/2	24 5/8	24 3/4	24 7/8
18	Shoulder pitch	No reduction	1 1/2	1 1/2	1 5/8	1 5/8	1 5/8
19	Bicep	× .90	9 5/8	10	10 1/4	10 5/8	11
20	Wrist	× .90	5 1/4	5 5/8	6	6 1/4	6 5/8
21	Neck	No reduction	14 5/8	14 3/4	15	15	15 1/8
22	Bust span	× .90	6	6 1/8	6 1/4	6 3/8	6 1/2
23	Bust level	× .90	10 1/8	10 1/4	10 3/8	10 1/2	10 5/8

WOMEN'S SIZE STABLE KNITS REDUCTIONS

Zero percent smaller in crosswise direction without any reductions in lengthwise direction.
Use these measurements when drafting slopers for fabrics that stretch from 0% to 25%.
Multiply your across measurements by 1, 0% smaller, except for the shoulder measurement, since the final garment will have twill tape to stabilize the seam and prevent it from stretching.

		Multiply Your Across Measurements By	Extra Small	Small	Medium	Large	Extra Large
			2	6	10	14	18
1	Bust	× 1	43	47	51	55	59
2	Waist	× 1	35	39	43	47	51
3	Hip	× 1	46	50	54	58	62
4	Crotch depth	No reduction	11 3/4	15 3/4	19 3/4	23 3/4	27 3/4
5	Waist to knee	No reduction	24	24 1/4	24 1/2	24 3/4	25
6	Waist to ankle	No reduction	38 5/8	38 7/8	39 1/8	39 3/8	39 5/8
7	Ankle	× 1	10	10 1/2	11	11 1/2	12
8	Knee	× 1	18 1/8	18 3/8	18 5/8	18 7/8	19 1/8
9	Front crotch	× 1	2 7/8	3 3/8	3 7/8	4 3/8	4 7/8
10	Back crotch	× 1	3 7/8	4 1/8	4 1/2	4 7/8	5 1/8
11	Crotch angle	× 1	1 1/2	1 3/8	1 5/8	2	2 3/8
12	Nape to waist	No reduction	16 5/8	17 1/8	17 5/8	18 1/8	18 5/8
13	Back neck	No reduction	3	3 1/2	4	4 1/2	5
14	Back neck rise	× 1	1	1 3/8	1 3/7	1 1/2	1 1/2
15	Shoulder length	No reduction	5 5/8	5 3/4	5 7/8	6	6 1/8
16	Across back	× 1	8 5/8	8 7/8	9	9 3/8	9 5/8
17	Sleeve length	No reduction	23 7/8	24 1/8	24 3/8	24 5/8	24 7/8
18	Shoulder pitch	× 1	1 1/2	1 3/4	2	2 1/4	2 1/2
19	Bicep	× 1	14 1/2	15 1/4	16	16 3/4	17 1/2
20	Wrist	× 1	7 1/8	7 7/8	8 5/8	9 3/8	10 1/8
21	Neck	× 1	17 1/4	18	18 3/4	19 1/2	20 1/4
22	Bust span	× 1	8	8 1/4	8 1/2	8 3/4	9
23	Bust level	No reduction	12 1/4	12 3/4	13 1/4	13 3/4	14 1/4

WOMEN'S SIZE MODERATE REDUCTIONS

Two percent smaller in crosswise direction without any reductions in lengthwise direction.
Use these measurements when drafting slopers for fabrics that stretch from 25% to 50%.
Multiply your across measurements by .98, 2% smaller, except for the shoulder measurement, since the final garment will have twill tape to stabilize the seam and prevent it from stretching.

		Multiply Your Across Measurements By	Extra Small	Small	Medium	Large	Extra Large
			2	6	10	14	18
1	Bust	× .98	42 1/8	46	50	53 7/8	57 7/8
2	Waist	× .98	34 1/4	38 1/4	42 1/8	46	50
3	Hip	× .98	45	49	53	56 7/8	60 3/4
4	Crotch depth	No reduction	11 3/4	15 3/4	19 3/4	23 3/4	27 3/4
5	Waist to knee	No reduction	24	24 1/4	24 1/2	24 3/4	25
6	Waist to ankle	No reduction	38 5/8	38 7/8	39 1/8	39 3/8	39 5/8
7	Ankle	× .98	9 3/4	10 1/4	10 3/4	11 1/4	11 3/4
8	Knee	× .98	17 3/4	18	18 1/4	18 1/2	18 3/4
9	Front crotch	× .98	2 7/8	3 1/4	3 3/4	4 1/4	4 3/4
10	Back crotch	× .98	3 3/4	4	4 3/8	4 3/4	5
11	Crotch angle	× .98	1 3/8	1 1/4	1 5/8	2	2 1/4
12	Nape to waist	No reduction	16 5/8	17 1/8	17 5/8	18 1/8	18 5/8
13	Back neck	No reduction	3	3 1/2	4	4 1/2	5
14	Back neck rise	× .98	1	1 3/8	1 3/8	1 1/2	1 1/2
15	Shoulder length	No reduction	5 5/8	5 3/4	5 7/8	6	6 1/8
16	Across back	× .98	8 5/8	8 7/8	9	9 3/8	9 5/8
17	Sleeve length	No reduction	23 7/8	24 1/8	24 3/8	24 5/8	24 7/8
18	Shoulder pitch	× .98	1 1/2	1 3/4	2	2 1/4	2 1/2
19	Bicep	× .98	14 1/4	15	15 5/8	16 3/8	17 1/8
20	Wrist	× .98	7	7 3/4	8 1/2	9 1/4	10
21	Neck	× .98	16 7/8	17 5/8	18 3/8	19	19 3/4
22	Bust span	× .98	7 7/8	8	8 3/8	8 5/8	8 7/8
23	Bust level	No reduction	12	12 3/8	13	13 3/8	14

WOMEN'S SIZE STRETCHY REDUCTIONS

Three percent smaller in crosswise direction without any reductions in lengthwise direction.
Use these measurements when drafting slopers for fabrics that stretch from 50% to 75%.
Multiply your across measurements by .97, 3% smaller, except for the shoulder measurement, since the final garment will have twill tape to stabilize the seam and prevent it from stretching.

		Multiply Your Across Measurements By	Extra Small	Small	Medium	Large	Extra Large
			2	6	10	14	18
1	Bust	× .97	41 3/4	45 5/8	49 1/2	53 3/8	57 1/4
2	Waist	× .97	34	37 7/8	41 3/4	45 5/8	49 1/2
3	Hip	× .97	44 5/8	48 1/2	52 3/8	56 1/4	60 1/8
4	Crotch depth	No reduction	11 3/4	15 3/4	19 3/4	23 3/4	27 3/4
5	Waist to knee	No reduction	24	24 1/4	24 1/2	24 3/4	25
6	Waist to ankle	No reduction	38 5/8	38 7/8	39 1/8	39 3/8	39 5/8
7	Ankle	× .97	9 3/4	10 1/8	10 5/8	11 1/8	11 5/8
8	Knee	× .97	17 5/8	17 7/8	18	18 1/4	18 1/2
9	Front crotch	× .97	2 3/4	3 1/4	3 3/4	4 1/4	4 3/4
10	Back crotch	× .97	3 3/4	4	4 3/8	4 3/4	5
11	Crotch angle	× .97	1 3/8	1 1/4	1 5/8	2	2 1/4
12	Nape to waist	No reduction	16 5/8	17 1/8	17 5/8	18 1/8	18 5/8
13	Back neck	No reduction	3	3 1/2	4	4 1/2	5
14	Back neck rise	× .97	1	1 3/8	1 3/8	1 1/2	1 1/2
15	Shoulder length	No reduction	5 5/8	5 3/4	5 7/8	6	6 1/8
16	Across back	× .97	8 5/8	8 7/8	9	9 3/8	9 5/8
17	Sleeve length	No reduction	23 7/8	24 1/8	24 3/8	24 5/8	24 7/8
18	Shoulder pitch	× .97	1 1/2	1 3/4	2	2 1/4	2 1/2
19	Bicep	× .97	14	14 3/4	15 1/2	16 1/4	17
20	Wrist	× .97	7	7 5/8	8 3/8	9	9 7/8
21	Neck	× .97	16 5/8	17 3/8	18 1/8	18 7/8	19 5/8
22	Bust span	× .97	7 3/4	8	8 1/4	8 1/2	8 3/4
23	Bust level	No reduction	11 7/8	12 1/4	12 3/4	13 1/4	13 3/4

WOMEN'S SIZE SUPER-STRETCH REDUCTIONS

Five percent smaller in crosswise direction without any reductions in lengthwise direction.
Use these measurements when drafting slopers for fabrics that stretch from 75% to 100%.
Multiply your across measurements by .95, 5% smaller, except for the shoulder measurement, since the final garment will have twill tape to stabilize the seam and prevent it from stretching.

		Multiply Your Across Measurements By	Extra Small	Small	Medium	Large	Extra Large
			2	6	10	14	18
1	Bust	× .95	40 7/8	44 5/8	48 1/2	52 1/4	56
2	Waist	× .95	33 1/4	37	40 7/8	44 5/8	48 1/2
3	Hip	× .95	43 3/4	47 1/2	51 1/4	55	58 7/8
4	Crotch depth	No reduction	11 3/4	15 3/4	19 3/4	23 3/4	27 3/4
5	Waist to knee	No reduction	24	24 1/4	24 1/2	24 3/4	25
6	Waist to ankle	No reduction	38 5/8	38 7/8	39 1/8	39 3/8	39 5/8
7	Ankle	× .95	9 1/2	10	10 1/2	11	11 3/8
8	Knee	× .95	17 1/4	17 1/2	17 3/4	18	18 1/8
9	Front crotch	× .95	2 3/4	3 1/4	3 5/8	4 1/8	4 5/8
10	Back crotch	× .95	3 5/8	4	4 1/4	4 5/8	5
11	Crotch angle	× .95	1 3/8	1 1/4	1 5/8	1 7/8	2 1/4
12	Nape to waist	No reduction	16 5/8	17 1/8	17 5/8	18 1/8	18 5/8
13	Back neck	No reduction	3	3 1/2	4	4 1/2	5
14	Back neck rise	× .95	1	1 3/8	1 3/8	1 1/2	1 1/2
15	Shoulder length	No reduction	5 5/8	5 3/4	5 7/8	6	6 1/8
16	Across back	× .95	8 5/8	8 7/8	9	9 3/8	9 5/8
17	Sleeve length	No reduction	23 7/8	24 1/8	24 3/8	24 5/8	24 7/8
18	Shoulder pitch	× .95	1 1/2	1 3/4	2	2 1/8	2 3/8
19	Bicep	× .95	13 3/4	14 1/2	15 1/4	16	16 5/8
20	Wrist	× .95	6 3/4	7 1/2	8 1/4	9	9 5/8
21	Neck	× .95	16 3/8	17	17 3/4	18 1/2	19 1/8
22	Bust span	× .95	7 5/8	7 7/8	8	8 3/8	8 1/2
23	Bust level	No reduction	11 5/8	12	12 1/2	13	13 1/2

WOMEN'S SIZE RIB REDUCTIONS

Ten percent smaller in crosswise direction without any reductions in lengthwise direction.
Use these measurements when drafting slopers for fabrics that stretch 100% and over.
Multiply your across measurements by .90, 10% smaller, except for the shoulder measurement, since the final garment will have twill tape to stabilize the seam and prevent it from stretching.

		Multiply Your Across Measurements By	Extra Small	Small	Medium	Large	Extra Large
			2	6	10	14	18
1	Bust	× .90	38 3/4	42 1/4	45 7/8	49 1/2	53 1/8
2	Waist	× .90	31 1/2	35 1/8	38 3/4	42 1/4	45 7/8
3	Hip	× .90	41 3/8	45	48 5/8	52 1/4	55 3/4
4	Crotch depth	No reduction	11 3/4	15 3/4	19 3/4	23 3/4	27 3/4
5	Waist to knee	No reduction	24	24 1/4	24 1/2	24 3/4	25
6	Waist to ankle	No reduction	38 5/8	38 7/8	39 1/8	39 3/8	39 5/8
7	Ankle	× .90	9	9 1/2	10	10 3/8	10 3/4
8	Knee	× .90	16 3/8	16 1/2	16 3/4	17	17 1/4
9	Front crotch	× .90	2 5/8	3	3 1/2	4	4 3/8
10	Back crotch	× .90	3 1/2	3 3/4	4	4 3/8	4 5/8
11	Crotch angle	× .90	1 1/4	1 1/8	1 1/2	1 3/4	2
12	Nape to waist	No reduction	16 5/8	17 1/8	17 5/8	18 1/8	18 5/8
13	Back neck	No reduction	3	3 1/2	4	4 1/2	5
14	Back neck rise	× .90	1	1 3/8	1 3/8	1 1/2	1 1/2
15	Shoulder length	No reduction	5 5/8	5 3/4	5 7/8	6	6 1/8
16	Across back	× .90	8 5/8	8 7/8	9	9 3/8	9 5/8
17	Sleeve length	No reduction	23 7/8	24 1/8	24 3/8	24 5/8	24 7/8
18	Shoulder pitch	× .90	1 3/8	1 5/8	1 7/8	2	2 1/4
19	Bicep	× .90	13	13 3/4	14 3/8	15	15 3/4
20	Wrist	× .90	6 3/8	7	7 3/4	8 1/2	9 1/8
21	Neck	× .90	15 1/2	16 1/8	16 7/8	17 1/2	18 1/8
22	Bust span	× .90	7 1/4	7 3/8	7 5/8	7 7/8	8
23	Bust level	No reduction	11	11 3/8	11 7/8	12 3/8	12 3/4

WOMEN'S SIZE FOUR-WAY REDUCTIONS

Ten percent smaller in crosswise direction and 10% smaller in the lengthwise direction.
Use these measurements when drafting slopers for fabrics that stretch 100% in both directions.
Multiply your measurements by .90, 10% smaller, in both directions.

		Multiply Your Across Measurements By	Extra Small	Small	Medium	Large	Extra Large
			2	6	10	14	18
1	Bust	× .90	38 3/4	40 1/2	42 1/4	44 1/8	45 7/8
2	Waist	× .90	31 1/2	33 1/4	35 1/8	36 7/8	38 3/4
3	Hip	× .90	41 3/8	43 1/4	45	46 3/4	48 5/8
4	Crotch depth	× .90	11 1/8	13	15	16 7/8	18 3/4
5	Waist to knee	× .90	22 3/4	23	23	23 1/8	23 1/4
6	Waist to ankle	× .90	36 3/4	36 7/8	37	37	37 1/8
7	Ankle	× .90	9	9 1/4	9 1/2	9 5/8	10
8	Knee	× .90	16 3/8	16 3/8	16 1/2	16 5/8	16 3/4
9	Front crotch	× .90	2 5/8	2 7/8	3	3 1/4	3 1/2
10	Back crotch	× .90	3 7/8	4	4 1/8	4 3/8	4 1/2
11	Crotch angle	× .90	1 1/2	1 1/7	1 3/8	1 1/2	1 5/8
12	Nape to waist	× .90	15 3/4	16	16 1/4	16 1/2	16 3/4
13	Back neck	No reduction	3	3 1/4	3 1/2	3 3/4	4
14	Back neck rise	No reduction	1	1 3/8	1 3/8	1 3/8	1 3/8
15	Shoulder length	No reduction	5 5/8	5 3/4	5 3/4	5 7/8	5 7/8
16	Across back	No reduction	8 5/8	8 3/4	8 7/8	9	9
17	Sleeve length	No reduction	23 7/8	24	24 1/8	24 1/4	24 3/8
18	Shoulder pitch	No reduction	1 1/2	1 5/8	1 3/4	2	2
19	Bicep	× .90	13	13 3/8	13 3/4	14	14 3/8
20	Wrist	× .90	6 3/8	6 3/4	7	7 3/8	7 3/4
21	Neck	No reduction	17 1/4	17 5/8	18	18 3/8	18 3/4
22	Bust span	× .90	7 1/4	7 3/8	7 3/8	7 1/2	7 5/8
23	Bust level	× .90	11 5/8	11 7/8	12	12 2/8	12 1/2

PLUS SIZES STABLE KNITS REDUCTIONS

Zero percent smaller in crosswise direction without any reductions in lengthwise direction.
Use these measurements when drafting slopers for fabrics that stretch from 0% to 25%.
Use your measurements exactly as recorded without any reductions.

		Multiply Your Across Measurements By	1X	2X	3X	4X	5X
			16	20	24	28	32
1	Bust	× 1	41	45	49	53	57
2	Waist	× 1	33	37	41	45	49
3	Hip	× 1	44	48	52	56	60
4	Crotch depth	No reduction	11 5/8	15 5/8	19 5/8	23 5/8	27 5/8
5	Waist to knee	No reduction	24	24 1/4	24 1/2	24 3/4	25
6	Waist to ankle	No reduction	39 5/8	39 7/8	40 1/8	40 3/8	40 5/8
7	Ankle	× 1	9 5/8	10 1/8	10 5/8	11 1/8	11 5/8
8	Knee	× 1	18 1/8	18 3/8	18 5/8	18 7/8	19 1/8
9	Front crotch	× 1	2 3/4	3 1/4	3 3/4	4 1/4	4 3/4
10	Back crotch	× 1	3 5/8	4	4 3/8	4 5/8	5
11	Crotch angle	× 1	1	1 1/4	1 5/8	2	2 1/4
12	Nape to waist	No reduction	17	15 3/4	16 1/4	16 3/4	17 1/4
13	Back neck	No reduction	2 3/4	3 1/4	3 3/4	4 1/4	4 3/4
14	Back neck rise	× 1	1	1 3/8	1 3/8	1 3/8	1 1/2
15	Shoulder length	No reduction	5 1/2	5 5/8	5 3/4	5 7/8	6
16	Across back	× 1	8 3/8	8 5/8	8 7/8	9 1/8	9 3/8
17	Sleeve length	No reduction	32 1/8	32 3/8	32 5/8	32 7/8	33 1/8
18	Shoulder pitch	× 1	1 1/2	1 3/4	2	2 1/4	2 1/2
19	Bicep	× 1	13 3/4	14 1/2	15 1/4	16	16 3/4
20	Wrist	× 1	6 3/4	7 1/2	8 1/4	9	9 3/4
21	Neck	× 1	16 3/4	17 1/2	18 1/4	19	19 3/4
22	Bust span	× 1	7 3/4	8	8 1/4	8 1/2	8 3/4
23	Bust level	No reduction	11 7/8	12 3/8	12 7/8	13 3/8	13 7/8

PLUS SIZES MODERATE REDUCTIONS

Two percent smaller in crosswise direction without any reductions in lengthwise direction.
Use these measurements when drafting slopers for fabrics that stretch from 25% to 50%.
Multiply your across measurements by .98, 2% smaller, except for the shoulder measurement, since the final garment will have twill tape to stabilize the seam and prevent it from stretching.

		Multiply Your Across Measurements By	1X	2X	3X	4X	5X
			16	20	24	28	32
1	Bust	× .98	40 1/8	44 1/8	48	52	55 7/8
2	Waist	× .98	32 3/8	36 1/4	40 1/8	44 1/8	48
3	Hip	× .98	43 1/8	47	51	54 7/8	58 3/4
4	Crotch depth	No reduction	11 5/8	15 5/8	19 5/8	23 5/8	27 5/8
5	Waist to knee	No reduction	24	24 1/4	24 1/2	24 3/4	25
6	Waist to ankle	No reduction	39 5/8	39 7/8	40 1/8	40 3/8	40 5/8
7	Ankle	× .98	9 3/8	10	10 3/8	11	11 3/8
8	Knee	× .98	17 3/4	18	18 1/4	18 1/2	18 3/4
9	Front crotch	× .98	2 3/4	3 1/8	3 5/8	4 1/8	4 5/8
10	Back crotch	× .98	3 5/8	4	4 1/4	4 5/8	5
11	Crotch angle	× .98	1	1 1/4	1 5/8	2	2 1/4
12	Nape to waist	No reduction	17	15 3/4	16 1/4	16 3/4	17 1/4
13	Back neck	No reduction	2 3/4	3 1/4	3 3/4	4 1/4	4 3/4
14	Back neck rise	× .98	1	1 3/8	1 3/8	1 3/8	1 1/2
15	Shoulder length	No reduction	5 1/2	5 5/8	5 3/4	5 7/8	6
16	Across back	× .98	8 3/8	8 5/8	8 7/8	9 1/8	9 3/8
17	Sleeve length	No reduction	32 1/8	32 3/8	32 5/8	32 7/8	33 1/8
18	Shoulder pitch	× .98	1 1/2	1 3/4	2	2 1/4	2 1/2
19	Bicep	× .98	13 1/2	14 1/5	15	15 5/8	16 3/8
20	Wrist	× .98	6 5/8	7 3/8	8	8 7/8	9 1/2
21	Neck	× .98	16 3/8	17 1/8	17 7/8	18 5/8	19 3/8
22	Bust span	× .98	7 5/8	7 7/8	8	8 3/8	8 5/8
23	Bust level	No reduction	11 5/8	12 1/8	12 5/8	13 1/8	13 5/8

PLUS SIZES STRETCHY REDUCTIONS

Three percent smaller in crosswise direction without any reductions in lengthwise direction.
Use these measurements when drafting slopers for fabrics that stretch from 50% to 75%.
Multiply your across measurements by .97, 3% smaller, except for the shoulder measurement, since the final garment will have twill tape to stabilize the seam and prevent it from stretching.

		Multiply Your Across Measurements By	1X	2X	3X	4X	5X
			16	20	24	28	32
1	Bust	× .97	39 3/4	43 5/8	47 1/2	51 3/8	55 1/4
2	Waist	× .97	32	35 7/8	39 3/4	43 5/8	47 1/2
3	Hip	× .97	42 5/8	46 1/2	50 1/2	54 1/3	58 1/4
4	Crotch depth	No reduction	11 5/8	15 5/8	19 5/8	23 5/8	27 5/8
5	Waist to knee	No reduction	24	24 1/4	24 1/2	24 3/4	25
6	Waist to ankle	No reduction	39 5/8	39 7/8	40 1/8	40 3/8	40 5/8
7	Ankle	× .97	9 3/8	9 7/8	10 1/4	10 3/4	11 1/4
8	Knee	× .97	17 5/8	17 7/8	18	18 1/4	18 1/2
9	Front crotch	× .97	2 5/8	3 1/8	3 5/8	4 1/8	4 5/8
10	Back crotch	× .97	3 1/2	3 7/8	4 1/4	4 1/2	4 7/8
11	Crotch angle	× .97	1	1 1/4	1 5/8	2	2 1/4
12	Nape to waist	No reduction	17	15 3/4	16 1/4	16 3/4	17 1/4
13	Back neck	No reduction	2 3/4	3 1/4	3 3/4	4 1/4	4 3/4
14	Back neck rise	× .97	1	1 3/8	1 3/8	1 3/8	1 1/2
15	Shoulder length	No reduction	5 1/2	5 5/8	5 3/4	5 7/8	6
16	Across back	× .97	8 3/8	8 5/8	8 7/8	9 1/8	9 3/8
17	Sleeve length	No reduction	32 1/8	32 3/8	32 5/8	32 7/8	33 1/8
18	Shoulder pitch	× .97	1 1/2	1 3/4	2	2 1/4	2 1/2
19	Bicep	× .97	13 3/8	14	14 3/4	15 1/2	16 1/4
20	Wrist	× .97	6 1/2	7 1/4	8	8 3/4	9 1/2
21	Neck	× .97	16 1/4	17	17 3/4	18 3/8	19 1/8
22	Bust span	× .97	7 1/2	7 3/4	8	8 1/4	8 1/2
23	Bust level	No reduction	11 1/2	12	12 1/2	13	13 1/2

PLUS SIZES SUPER-STRETCH REDUCTIONS

Five percent smaller in crosswise direction without any reductions in lengthwise direction.
Use these measurements when drafting slopers for fabrics that stretch from 75% to 100%.
Multiply your across measurements by .95, 5% smaller, except for the shoulder measurement, since the final garment will have twill tape to stabilize the seam and prevent it from stretching.

		Multiply Your Across Measurements By	1X	2X	3X	4X	5X
			2	6	10	14	18
1	Bust	× .95	39	42 3/4	46 1/2	50 3/8	54 1/8
2	Waist	× .95	31 3/8	35 1/8	39	42 3/4	46 4/8
3	Hip	× .95	41 3/4	45 5/8	49 3/8	53 1/4	57
4	Crotch depth	No reduction	11 5/8	15 5/8	19 5/8	23 5/8	27 5/8
5	Waist to knee	No reduction	24	24 1/4	24 1/2	24 3/4	25
6	Waist to ankle	No reduction	39 5/8	39 7/8	40 1/8	40 3/8	40 5/8
7	Ankle	× .95	9 1/8	9 5/8	10	10 5/8	11
8	Knee	× .95	17 1/4	17 1/2	17 3/4	18	18 1/8
9	Front crotch	× .95	2 5/8	3	3 5/8	4	4 1/2
10	Back crotch	× .95	3 1/2	3 3/4	4 1/8	4 3/8	4 3/4
11	Crotch angle	× .95	1	1 1/4	1 1/2	1 7/8	2 1/8
12	Nape to waist	No reduction	17	15 3/4	16 1/4	16 3/4	17 1/4
13	Back neck	No reduction	2 3/4	3 1/4	3 3/4	4 1/4	4 3/4
14	Back neck rise	× .95	1	1 3/8	1 3/8	1 3/8	1 1/2
15	Shoulder length	No reduction	5 1/2	5 5/8	5 3/4	5 7/8	6
16	Across back	× .95	8 3/8	8 5/8	8 7/8	9 1/8	9 3/8
17	Sleeve length	No reduction	32 1/8	32 3/8	32 5/8	32 7/8	33 1/8
18	Shoulder pitch	× .95	1 1/2	1 3/4	2	2 1/8	2 3/8
19	Bicep	× .95	13	13 3/4	14 1/2	15 1/5	16
20	Wrist	× .95	6 3/8	7 1/8	7 7/8	8 1/2	9 1/4
21	Neck	× .95	16	16 5/8	17 3/8	18	18 3/4
22	Bust span	× .95	7 3/8	7 5/8	7 7/8	8	8 3/8
23	Bust level	No reduction	11 1/4	11 3/4	12 1/4	12 3/4	13 1/8

PLUS SIZES RIB REDUCTIONS

Ten percent smaller in crosswise direction without any reductions in lengthwise direction.
Use these measurements when drafting slopers for fabrics that stretch 100% and over.
Multiply your across measurements by .90, 10% smaller, except for the shoulder measurement, since the final garment will have twill tape to stabilize the seam and prevent it from stretching.

		Multiply Your Across Measurements By	1X	2X	3X	4X	5X
			2	6	10	14	18
1	Bust	× .90	36 7/8	40 1/2	44 1/8	47 3/4	51 1/4
2	Waist	× .90	29 3/4	33 1/4	36 7/8	40 1/2	44 1/8
3	Hip	× .90	39 5/8	43 1/4	46 3/4	50 3/8	54
4	Crotch depth	No reduction	11 5/8	15 5/8	19 5/8	23 5/8	27 5/8
5	Waist to knee	No reduction	24	24 1/4	24 1/2	24 3/4	25
6	Waist to ankle	No reduction	39 5/8	39 7/8	40 1/8	40 3/8	40 5/8
7	Ankle	× .90	8 5/8	9 1/8	9 5/8	10	10 1/2
8	Knee	× .90	16 3/8	16 1/2	16 3/4	17	17 1/4
9	Front crotch	× .90	2 1/2	3	3 3/8	3 7/8	4 1/4
10	Back crotch	× .90	3 1/4	3 5/8	3 7/8	4 1/4	4 1/2
11	Crotch angle	× .90	7/8	1 1/8	1 1/2	1 3/4	2
12	Nape to waist	No reduction	17	15 3/4	16 1/4	16 3/4	17 1/4
13	Back neck	No reduction	2 3/4	3 1/4	3 3/4	4 1/4	4 3/4
14	Back neck rise	× .90	1	1 3/8	1 3/8	1 3/8	1 1/2
15	Shoulder length	No reduction	5 1/2	5 5/8	5 3/4	5 7/8	6
16	Across back	× .90	8 3/8	8 5/8	8 7/8	9 1/8	9 3/8
17	Sleeve length	No reduction	32 1/8	32 3/8	32 5/8	32 7/8	33 1/8
18	Shoulder pitch	× .90	1 3/8	1 5/8	1 7/8	2	2 1/4
19	Bicep	× .90	12 3/8	13	13 3/4	14 3/8	15
20	Wrist	× .90	6	6 3/4	7 3/8	8	8 3/4
21	Neck	× .90	15	15 3/4	16 3/8	17 1/8	17 3/4
22	Bust span	× .90	7	7 1/4	7 3/8	7 5/8	7 7/8
23	Bust level	No reduction	10 3/4	11 1/8	11 5/8	12	12 1/2

PLUS SIZES FOUR-WAY REDUCTIONS

Ten percent smaller in crosswise direction and 10% smaller in the lengthwise direction.
Use these measurements when drafting slopers for fabrics that stretch 100% in both directions.
Multiply your across measurements by .90, 10% smaller, in both directions.

		Multiply Your Across Measurements By	1X	2X	3X	4X	5X
			2	6	10	14	18
1	Bust	× .90	36 7/8	38 3/4	40 1/2	42 1/4	44 1/8
2	Waist	× .90	29 3/4	31 1/2	33 1/4	35 1/8	36 7/8
3	Hip	× .90	39 5/8	41 3/8	43 1/4	45	46 6/8
4	Crotch depth	× .90	11	13	14 7/8	16 3/4	18 5/8
5	Waist to knee	× .90	22 3/4	23	23	23 1/8	23 1/4
6	Waist to ankle	× .90	37 5/8	37 3/4	37 7/8	38	38 1/8
7	Ankle	× .90	8 5/8	8 7/8	9 1/8	9 1/3	9 5/8
8	Knee	× .90	16 3/8	16 3/8	16 1/2	16 5/8	16 3/4
9	Front crotch	× .90	2 1/2	2 3/4	3	3 1/8	3 3/8
10	Back crotch	× .90	3 5/8	3 7/8	4	4 1/8	4 3/8
11	Crotch angle	× .90	1	1 1/8	1 1/4	1 1/2	1 5/8
12	Nape to waist	× .90	16 1/8	14 3/4	15	15 1/4	15 1/2
13	Back neck	No reduction	2 3/4	3	3 1/4	3 1/2	3 3/4
14	Back neck rise	No reduction	1	1 3/8	1 3/8	1 3/8	1 3/8
15	Shoulder length	No reduction	5 1/2	5 5/8	5 5/8	5 3/4	5 3/4
16	Across back	No reduction	8 3/8	8 1/2	8 5/8	8 3/4	8 7/8
17	Sleeve length	No reduction	32 1/8	32 1/4	32 3/8	32 1/2	32 5/8
18	Shoulder pitch	No reduction	1 1/2	1 5/8	1 3/4	2	2
19	Bicep	× .90	12 3/8	12 3/4	13	13 3/8	13 3/4
20	Wrist	× .90	6	6 3/8	6 3/4	7	7 3/8
21	Neck	No reduction	16 3/4	17 1/8	17 1/2	17 7/8	18 1/4
22	Bust span	× .90	7	7	7 1/4	7 3/8	7 3/7
23	Bust level	× .90	11 1/4	11 1/2	11 3/4	12	12 1/4

Half Sizes

HALF SIZES STABLE KNITS REDUCTIONS

Ten percent smaller in crosswise direction without any reductions in lengthwise direction.
Use these measurements when drafting slopers for fabrics that stretch from 0% to 25%.
Use your measurements as recorded without any reductions.

		Multiply Your Across Measurements By	Extra Small	Small	Medium	Large	Extra Large
			14 1/2	18 1/2	22 1/2	26 1/2	30 1/2
1	Bust	× 1	41	45	49	53	57
2	Waist	× 1	32 1/2	36 1/2	40 1/2	44 1/2	48 1/2
3	Hip	× 1	44	48	52	56	60
4	Crotch depth	No reduction	11 1/8	15 1/8	19 1/8	23 1/8	27 1/8
5	Waist to knee	No reduction	22 3/8	22 5/8	22 7/8	23 1/8	23 3/8
6	Waist to ankle	No reduction	37 1/4	37 1/2	37 3/4	38	38 1/4
7	Ankle	× 1	9 5/8	10 1/8	10 5/8	11 1/8	11 5/8
8	Knee	× 1	17 1/4	17 1/2	17 3/4	18	18 1/4
9	Front crotch	× 1	2 3/4	3 1/4	3 3/4	4 1/4	4 3/4
10	Back crotch	× 1	3 5/8	4	4 3/8	4 5/8	5
11	Crotch angle	× 1	1 3/8	1 1/4	1 3/5	2	2 1/4
12	Nape to waist	No reduction	15 1/2	16	16 1/2	17	17 1/2
13	Back neck	No reduction	2 3/4	3 1/4	3 3/4	4 1/4	4 3/4
14	Back neck rise	× 1	1	1 3/8	1 3/8	1 3/8	1 1/2
15	Shoulder length	No reduction	5 1/2	5 5/8	5 3/4	5 7/8	6
16	Across back	× 1	8 3/8	8 5/8	8 7/8	9 1/8	9 3/8
17	Sleeve length	No reduction	22 1/4	22 1/2	22 3/4	23	23 1/4
18	Shoulder pitch	× 1	1 3/8	1 5/8	2	2 1/8	2 3/8
19	Bicep	× 1	13 3/4	14 1/2	15 1/4	16	16 3/4
20	Wrist	× 1	6 3/4	7 1/2	8 1/4	9	9 3/4
21	Neck	× 1	16 3/4	17 1/2	18 1/4	19	19 3/4
22	Bust span	× 1	7 3/4	8	8 1/4	8 1/2	8 3/4
23	Bust level	No reduction	11 3/8	11 7/8	12 3/8	12 7/8	13 3/8

HALF SIZES MODERATE REDUCTIONS

Two percent smaller in crosswise direction without any reductions in lengthwise direction.
Use these measurements when drafting slopers for fabrics that stretch from 25% to 50%.
Multiply your across measurements by .98, 2% smaller, except for the shoulder measurement, since the final garment will have twill tape to stabilize the seam and prevent it from stretching.

		Multiply Your Across Measurements By	Extra Small	Small	Medium	Large	Extra Large
			14 1/2	18 1/2	22 1/2	26 1/2	30 1/2
1	Bust	× .98	40 1/8	44 1/8	48	52	55 7/8
2	Waist	× .98	31 7/8	35 3/4	39 3/4	43 5/8	47 1/2
3	Hip	× .98	43 1/8	47	51	54 7/8	58 3/4
4	Crotch depth	No reduction	11 1/8	15 1/8	19 1/8	23 1/8	27 1/8
5	Waist to knee	No reduction	22 3/8	22 5/8	22 7/8	23 1/8	23 3/8
6	Waist to ankle	No reduction	37 1/4	37 1/2	37 3/4	38	38 1/4
7	Ankle	× .98	9 3/8	10	10 3/8	11	11 3/8
8	Knee	× .98	17	17 1/8	17 3/8	17 5/8	17 7/8
9	Front crotch	× .98	2 3/4	3 1/8	3 5/8	4 1/8	4 5/8
10	Back crotch	× .98	3 5/8	4	4 1/4	4 5/8	5
11	Crotch angle	× .98	1 3/8	1 1/4	1 1/2	1 7/8	2 1/4
12	Nape to waist	No reduction	15 1/2	16	16 1/2	17	17 1/2
13	Back neck	No reduction	2 3/4	3 1/4	3 3/4	4 1/4	4 3/4
14	Back neck rise	× .98	1	1 3/8	1 3/8	1 3/8	1 1/2
15	Shoulder length	No reduction	5 1/2	5 5/8	5 3/4	5 7/8	6
16	Across back	× .98	8 3/8	8 5/8	8 7/8	9 1/8	9 3/8
17	Sleeve length	No reduction	22 1/4	22 1/2	22 3/4	23	23 1/4
18	Shoulder pitch	× .98	1 3/8	1 5/8	1 7/8	2 1/8	2 3/8
19	Bicep	× .98	13 1/2	14 1/4	15	15 5/8	16 3/8
20	Wrist	× .98	6 5/8	7 3/8	8	8 7/8	9 1/2
21	Neck	× .98	16 3/8	17 1/8	17 7/8	18 5/8	19 3/8
22	Bust span	× .98	7 5/8	7 7/8	8	8 3/8	8 5/8
23	Bust level	No reduction	11 1/8	11 5/8	12 1/8	12 5/8	13 1/8

HALF SIZES STRETCHY REDUCTIONS

Three percent smaller in crosswise direction without any reductions in lengthwise direction.
Use these measurements when drafting slopers for fabrics that stretch from 50% to 75%.
Multiply your across measurements by .97, 3% smaller, except for the shoulder measurement, since the final garment will have twill tape to stabilize the seam and prevent it from stretching.

		Multiply Your Across Measurements By	Extra Small	Small	Medium	Large	Extra Large
			14 1/2	18 1/2	22 1/2	26 1/2	30 1/2
1	Bust	× .97	39 3/4	43 5/8	47 1/2	51 3/8	55 1/4
2	Waist	× .97	31 1/2	35 3/8	39 2/8	43 1/8	47
3	Hip	× .97	42 5/8	46 1/2	50 1/2	54 3/8	58 1/4
4	Crotch depth	No reduction	11 1/8	15 1/8	19 1/8	23 1/8	27 1/8
5	Waist to knee	No reduction	22 3/8	22 5/8	22 7/8	23 1/8	23 3/8
6	Waist to ankle	No reduction	37 1/4	37 1/2	37 3/4	38	38 1/4
7	Ankle	× .97	9 3/8	9 7/8	10 1/4	10 3/4	11 1/4
8	Knee	× .97	16 3/4	17	17 1/4	17 1/2	17 3/4
9	Front crotch	× .97	2 5/8	3 1/8	3 5/8	4 1/8	4 5/8
10	Back crotch	× .97	3 1/2	3 7/8	4 1/4	4 1/2	4 7/8
11	Crotch angle	× .97	1 3/8	1 1/4	1 1/2	1 7/8	2 1/4
12	Nape to waist	No reduction	15 1/2	16	16 1/2	17	17 1/2
13	Back neck	No reduction	2 3/4	3 1/4	3 3/4	4 1/4	4 3/4
14	Back neck rise	× .97	1	1 3/8	1 3/8	1 3/8	1 1/2
15	Shoulder length	No reduction	5 1/2	5 5/8	5 3/4	5 7/8	6
16	Across back	× .97	8 3/8	8 5/8	8 7/8	9 1/8	9 3/8
17	Sleeve length	No reduction	22 1/4	22 1/2	22 3/4	23	23 1/4
18	Shoulder pitch	× .97	1 3/8	1 5/8	1 7/8	2 1/8	2 3/8
19	Bicep	× .97	13 3/8	14	14 3/4	15 1/2	16 1/4
20	Wrist	× .97	6 1/2	7 1/4	8	8 3/4	9 1/2
21	Neck	× .97	16 1/4	17	17 3/4	18 3/7	19 1/8
22	Bust span	× .97	7 1/2	7 3/4	8	8 1/4	8 1/2
23	Bust level	No reduction	11	11 1/2	12	12 1/2	13

HALF SIZES SUPER-STRETCH REDUCTIONS

Five percent smaller in crosswise direction without any reductions in lengthwise direction.
Use these measurements when drafting slopers for fabrics that stretch from 75% to 100%.
Multiply your across measurements by .95, 5% smaller, except for the shoulder measurement, since the final garment will have twill tape to stabilize the seam and prevent it from stretching.

		Multiply Your Across Measurements By	Extra Small	Small	Medium	Large	Extra Large
			14 1/2	18 1/2	22 1/2	26 1/2	30 1/2
1	Bust	× .95	39	42 3/4	46 1/2	50 3/8	54 1/8
2	Waist	× .95	30 7/8	34 5/8	38 1/2	42 1/4	46
3	Hip	× .95	41 3/4	45 5/8	49 3/8	53 1/4	57
4	Crotch depth	No reduction	11 1/8	15 1/8	19 1/8	23 1/8	27 1/8
5	Waist to knee	No reduction	22 3/8	22 5/8	22 7/8	23 1/8	23 3/8
6	Waist to ankle	No reduction	37 1/4	37 1/2	37 3/4	38	38 1/4
7	Ankle	× .95	9 1/8	9 5/8	10	10 5/8	11
8	Knee	× .95	16 3/8	16 5/8	16 7/8	17	17 3/8
9	Front crotch	× .95	2 5/8	3	3 5/8	4	4 1/2
10	Back crotch	× .95	3 1/2	3 3/4	4 1/8	4 3/8	4 3/4
11	Crotch angle	× .95	1 1/4	1 1/4	1 1/2	1 7/8	2 1/8
12	Nape to waist	No reduction	15 1/2	16	16 1/2	17	17 1/2
13	Back neck	No reduction	2 3/4	3 1/4	3 3/4	4 1/4	4 3/4
14	Back neck rise	× .95	1	1 3/8	1 3/8	1 3/7	1 1/2
15	Shoulder length	No reduction	5 1/2	5 5/8	5 3/4	5 7/8	6
16	Across back	× .95	8 3/8	8 5/8	8 7/8	9 1/8	9 3/8
17	Sleeve length	No reduction	22 1/4	22 1/2	22 3/4	23	23 1/4
18	Shoulder pitch	× .95	1 3/8	1 5/8	1 7/8	2	2 1/4
19	Bicep	× .95	13	13 3/4	14 1/2	15 1/4	16
20	Wrist	× .95	6 3/8	7 1/8	7 7/8	8 1/2	9 1/4
21	Neck	× .95	16	16 5/8	17 3/8	18	18 3/4
22	Bust span	× .95	7 3/8	7 5/8	7 7/8	8	8 3/8
23	Bust level	No reduction	10 3/4	11 1/4	11 3/4	12 1/4	12 3/4

HALF SIZES RIB REDUCTIONS

Ten percent smaller in crosswise direction without any reductions in lengthwise direction.
Use these measurements when drafting slopers for fabrics that stretch 100% and over.
Multiply your across measurements by .90, 10% smaller, except for the shoulder measurement, since the final garment will have twill tape to stabilize the seam and prevent it from stretching.

		Multiply Your Across Measurements By	Extra Small	Small	Medium	Large	Extra Large
			14 1/2	18 1/2	22 1/2	26 1/2	30 1/2
1	Bust	× .90	36 7/8	40 1/2	44 1/8	47 3/4	51 1/4
2	Waist	× .90	29 1/4	32 7/8	36 1/2	40	43 5/8
3	Hip	× .90	39 5/8	43 1/4	46 3/4	50 3/8	54
4	Crotch depth	No reduction	11 1/8	15 1/8	19 1/8	23 1/8	27 1/8
5	Waist to knee	No reduction	22 3/8	22 5/8	22 7/8	23 1/8	23 3/8
6	Waist to ankle	No reduction	37 1/4	37 1/2	37 3/4	38	38 1/4
7	Ankle	× .90	8 5/8	9 1/8	9 4/7	10	10 1/2
8	Knee	× .90	15 1/2	15 3/4	16	16 1/4	16 3/8
9	Front crotch	× .90	2 1/2	3	3 3/8	3 7/8	4 1/4
10	Back crotch	× .90	3 1/4	3 5/8	3 7/8	4 1/4	4 1/2
11	Crotch angle	× .90	1 1/4	1 1/7	1 3/8	1 3/4	2
12	Nape to waist	No reduction	15 1/2	16	16 1/2	17	17 1/2
13	Back neck	No reduction	2 3/4	3 1/4	3 3/4	4 1/4	4 3/4
14	Back neck rise	× .90	1	1 3/8	1 3/8	1 3/8	1 1/2
15	Shoulder length	No reduction	5 1/2	5 5/8	5 3/4	5 7/8	6
16	Across back	× .90	8 3/8	8 5/8	8 7/8	9 1/8	9 3/8
17	Sleeve length	No reduction	22 1/4	22 1/2	22 3/4	23	23 1/4
18	Shoulder pitch	× .90	1 1/4	1 1/2	1 3/4	2	2 1/4
19	Bicep	× .90	12 3/8	13	13 3/4	14 3/8	15
20	Wrist	× .90	6	6 3/4	7 3/8	8	8 3/4
21	Neck	× .90	15	15 3/4	16 3/8	17 1/8	17 3/4
22	Bust span	× .90	7	7 1/4	7 3/8	7 5/8	7 7/8
23	Bust level	No reduction	10 1/4	10 3/4	11 1/8	11 5/8	12

HALF SIZES FOUR-WAY REDUCTIONS

Ten percent smaller in crosswise direction and 10% smaller in the lengthwise direction.
Use these measurements when drafting slopers for fabrics that stretch 100% in both directions.
Multiply your measurements by .90, 10% smaller, in both directions.

		Multiply Your Across Measurements By	Extra Small	Small	Medium	Large	Extra Large
			14 1/2	18 1/2	22 1/2	26 1/2	30 1/2
1	Bust	× .90	36 7/8	38 3/4	40 1/2	42 1/4	44 1/8
2	Waist	× .90	29 1/4	31	32 7/8	34 5/8	36 1/2
3	Hip	× .90	39 5/8	41 3/8	43 2/8	45	46 3/4
4	Crotch depth	× .90	10 5/8	12 1/2	14 3/8	16 1/4	18 1/8
5	Waist to knee	× .90	21 1/4	21 3/8	21 1/2	21 5/8	21 3/4
6	Waist to ankle	× .90	35 3/8	35 1/2	35 5/8	35 3/4	35 7/8
7	Ankle	× .90	8 5/8	8 7/8	9 1/8	9 3/8	9 5/8
8	Knee	× .90	15 1/2	15 5/8	15 3/4	15 7/8	16
9	Front crotch	× .90	2 1/2	2 3/4	3	3 1/7	3 3/8
10	Back crotch	× .90	3 5/8	3 7/8	4	4 1/8	4 3/8
11	Crotch angle	× .90	1 3/8	1	1 1/4	1 3/8	1 5/8
12	Nape to waist	× .90	14 3/4	15	15 1/4	15 1/2	15 5/8
13	Back neck	No reduction	2 3/4	3	3 1/4	3 1/2	3 6/8
14	Back neck rise	No reduction	1	1 3/8	1 3/8	1 3/8	1 3/8
15	Shoulder length	No reduction	5 1/2	5 5/8	5 5/8	5 3/4	5 3/4
16	Across back	No reduction	8 3/8	8 1/2	8 5/8	8 3/4	8 7/8
17	Sleeve length	No reduction	22 1/4	22 3/8	22 1/2	22 5/8	22 3/4
18	Shoulder pitch	No reduction	1 3/8	1 1/2	1 5/8	1 3/4	2
19	Bicep	× .90	12 3/8	12 3/4	13	13 3/8	13 3/4
20	Wrist	× .90	6	6 3/8	6 3/4	7	7 3/8
21	Neck	No reduction	16 3/4	17 1/8	17 1/2	17 7/8	18 1/4
22	Bust span	× .90	7	7	7 1/4	7 1/3	7 3/8
23	Bust level	× .90	10 3/4	11	11 1/4	11 1/2	11 3/4

MEN'S REGULAR SIZE STABLE KNITS REDUCTIONS

Zero percent smaller in crosswise direction without any reductions in lengthwise direction.
Use these measurements when drafting slopers for fabrics that stretch from 0% to 25%.
Use your measurements exactly as recorded, without any reductions.

		Multiply Your Across Measurements By	Extra Small	Small	Medium	Large	Extra Large
			32	36	40	44	48
1	Chest	× 1	32	36	40	44	48
2	Waist	× 1	26	30	34	38	42
3	Hip	× 1	32	36	40	44	48
4	Crotch depth	No reduction	9	9 1/4	9 1/2	9 3/4	10
5	Waist to knee	No reduction	20 1/2	20 3/4	21	21 1/4	21 1/2
6	Waist to ankle	No reduction	36	36 1/2	37	37 1/2	38
7	Ankle	× 1	8	14	14 1/2	15	15 1/2
8	Knee	× 1	13 5/8	14 1/8	14 5/8	15 1/8	15 5/8
9	Front crotch	× 1	2	2 1/4	2 1/2	2 3/4	3
10	Back crotch	× 1	2 5/8	3	3 3/8	3 5/8	4
11	Crotch angle	× 1	1	1 1/8	1 1/4	1 3/8	1 1/2
12	Nape to waist	No reduction	18 1/8	18 5/8	19 1/8	19 5/8	20 1/8
13	Back neck	No reduction	2 1/4	2 1/4	2 3/8	2 3/8	2 3/8
14	Back neck rise	× 1	3/4	3/4	7/9	4/5	4/5
15	Shoulder length	No reduction	5 7/8	6 1/8	6 3/8	6 5/8	6 7/8
16	Across back	× 1	8	8 1/2	9	9 1/2	10
17	Sleeve length	No reduction	23	23 1/4	23 1/2	23 3/4	24
18	Shoulder pitch	× 1	1 5/8	1 3/4	1 3/4	1 3/4	1 7/8
19	Bicep	× 1	10 1/2	11 1/4	12	12 3/4	13 1/2
20	Wrist	× 1	6 1/4	7	7 3/4	8 1/2	9 1/4
21	Neck	× 1	13 1/2	13 3/4	14	14 1/4	14 1/2
22	Chest span	× 1	5	5 3/8	6	6 3/8	7
23	Chest level	No reduction	9 1/2	9 3/4	10	10 1/4	10 1/2

MEN'S REGULAR SIZE MODERATE REDUCTIONS

Two percent smaller in crosswise direction without any reductions in lengthwise direction.
Use these measurements when drafting slopers for fabrics that stretch from 25% to 50%.
Multiply your across measurements by .98, 2% smaller, except for the shoulder measurement, since the final garment will have twill tape to stabilize the seam and prevent it from stretching.

		Multiply Your Across Measurements By	Extra Small	Small	Medium	Large	Extra Large
			32	36	40	44	48
1	Chest	× .98	31 3/8	35 1/4	39 1/4	43 1/8	47
2	Waist	× .98	25 1/2	29 3/8	33 3/8	37 1/4	41 1/8
3	Hip	× .98	31 3/8	35 1/4	39 1/4	43 1/8	47
4	Crotch depth	No reduction	9	9 1/4	9 1/2	9 3/4	10
5	Waist to knee	No reduction	20 1/2	20 3/4	21	21 1/4	21 1/2
6	Waist to ankle	No reduction	36	36 1/2	37	37 1/2	38
7	Ankle	× .98	8	13 3/4	14 1/4	14 3/4	15 1/4
8	Knee	× .98	13 3/8	13 7/8	14 3/8	14 7/8	15 3/8
9	Front crotch	× .98	2	2 1/4	2 1/2	2 3/4	3
10	Back crotch	× .98	2 5/8	3	3 1/4	3 5/8	4
11	Crotch angle	× .98	1	1 1/8	1 1/4	1 3/8	1 1/2
12	Nape to waist	No reduction	18 1/8	18 5/8	19 1/8	19 5/8	20 1/8
13	Back neck	No reduction	2 1/4	2 1/4	2 3/8	2 3/8	2 3/8
14	Back neck rise	× .98	3/4	3/4	3/4	3/4	3/4
15	Shoulder length	No reduction	5 7/8	6 1/8	6 3/8	6 5/8	6 7/8
16	Across back	× .98	8	8 1/2	9	9 1/2	10
17	Sleeve length	No reduction	23	23 1/4	23 1/2	23 3/4	24
18	Shoulder pitch	× .98	1 5/8	1 5/8	1 3/4	1 3/4	1 3/4
19	Bicep	× .98	10 1/4	11	11 3/4	12 1/2	13 1/4
20	Wrist	× .98	6 1/8	6 7/8	7 5/8	8 3/8	9
21	Neck	× .98	13 1/4	13 1/2	13 3/4	14	14 1/4
22	Chest span	× .98	4 3/4	5 1/4	5 3/4	6 1/4	6 3/4
23	Chest level	No reduction	9 1/4	9 1/2	9 3/4	10	10 1/4

MEN'S REGULAR SIZE STRETCHY REDUCTIONS

Three percent smaller in crosswise direction without any reductions in lengthwise direction.
Use these measurements when drafting slopers for fabrics that stretch from 50% to 75%.
Multiply your across measurements by .97, 3% smaller, except for the shoulder measurement, since the final garment will have twill tape to stabilize the seam and prevent it from stretching.

		Multiply Your Across Measurements By	Extra Small	Small	Medium	Large	Extra Large
			32	36	40	44	48
1	Chest	× .97	31	35	38 3/4	42 5/8	46 1/2
2	Waist	× .97	25 2/8	29	33	36 7/8	40 3/4
3	Hip	× .97	31	35	38 3/4	42 5/8	46 1/2
4	Crotch depth	No reduction	9	9 1/4	9 1/2	9 3/4	10
5	Waist to knee	No reduction	20 1/2	20 3/4	21	21 1/4	21 1/2
6	Waist to ankle	No reduction	36	36 1/2	37	37 1/2	38
7	Ankle	× .97	7 7/8	13 5/8	14	14 1/2	15
8	Knee	× .97	13 1/4	13 3/4	14 1/8	14 5/8	15 1/8
9	Front crotch	× .97	2	2 1/8	2 3/8	2 5/8	3
10	Back crotch	× .97	2 5/8	3	3 1/4	3 1/2	3 7/8
11	Crotch angle	× .97	1	1	1 1/4	1 3/8	1 1/2
12	Nape to waist	No reduction	18 1/8	18 5/8	19 1/8	19 5/8	20 1/8
13	Back neck	No reduction	2 1/4	2 1/4	2 3/8	2 3/8	2 3/8
14	Back neck rise	× .97	3/4	3/4	3/4	3/4	3/4
15	Shoulder length	No reduction	5 7/8	6 1/8	6 3/8	6 5/8	6 7/8
16	Across back	× .97	8	8 1/2	9	9 1/2	10
17	Sleeve length	No reduction	23	23 1/4	23 1/2	23 3/4	24
18	Shoulder pitch	× .97	1 5/8	1 5/8	1 5/8	1 3/4	1 3/4
19	Bicep	× .97	10 1/8	11	11 5/8	12 3/8	13
20	Wrist	× .97	6	6 3/4	7 1/2	8 1/4	9
21	Neck	× .97	13	13 3/8	13 5/8	13 7/8	14
22	Chest span	× .97	4 3/4	5 1/4	5 3/4	6 1/4	6 3/4
23	Chest level	No reduction	9 1/4	9 1/2	9 3/4	10	10 1/8

MEN'S REGULAR SIZE SUPER-STRETCH REDUCTIONS

Five percent smaller in crosswise direction without any reductions in lengthwise direction.
Use these measurements when drafting slopers for fabrics that stretch from 75% to 100%.
Multiply your across measurements by .95, 5% smaller, except for the shoulder measurement, since the final garment will have twill tape to stabilize the seam and prevent it from stretching.

		Multiply Your Across Measurements By	Extra Small	Small	Medium	Large	Extra Large
			32	36	40	44	48
1	Chest	× .95	30 3/8	34 1/4	38	41 3/4	45 5/8
2	Waist	× .95	24 3/4	28 1/2	32 1/4	36 1/8	39 7/8
3	Hip	× .95	30 3/8	34 1/4	38	41 3/4	45 5/8
4	Crotch depth	No reduction	9	9 1/4	9 1/2	9 3/4	10
5	Waist to knee	No reduction	20 1/2	20 3/4	21	21 1/4	21 1/2
6	Waist to ankle	No reduction	36	36 1/2	37	37 1/2	38
7	Ankle	× .95	7 5/8	13 1/4	13 3/4	14 1/4	14 3/4
8	Knee	× .95	13	13 3/8	13 7/8	14 3/8	14 7/8
9	Front crotch	× .95	1 7/8	2 1/8	2 3/8	2 5/8	2 7/8
10	Back crotch	× .95	2 1/2	2 7/8	3 1/8	3 1/2	3 3/4
11	Crotch angle	× .95	1	1	1 1/4	1 1/3	1 3/8
12	Nape to waist	No reduction	18 1/8	18 5/8	19 1/8	19 5/8	20 1/8
13	Back neck	No reduction	2 1/4	2 1/4	2 3/8	2 3/8	2 3/8
14	Back neck rise	× .95	3/4	3/4	3/4	3/4	3/4
15	Shoulder length	No reduction	5 7/8	6 1/8	6 3/8	6 5/8	6 7/8
16	Across back	× .95	8	8 1/2	9	9 1/2	10
17	Sleeve length	No reduction	23	23 1/4	23 1/2	23 3/4	24
18	Shoulder pitch	× .95	1 5/8	1 5/8	1 5/8	1 3/4	1 3/4
19	Bicep	× .95	10	10 3/4	11 3/8	12 1/8	12 7/8
20	Wrist	× .95	6	6 5/8	7 3/8	8	8 3/4
21	Neck	× .95	12 7/8	13	13 1/4	13 1/2	13 3/4
22	Chest span	× .95	4 5/8	5 1/8	5 5/8	6 1/8	6 1/2
23	Chest level	No reduction	9	9 1/4	9 1/2	9 3/4	10

MEN'S REGULAR SIZE RIB REDUCTIONS

Ten percent smaller in crosswise direction without any reductions in lengthwise direction.
Use these measurements when drafting slopers for fabrics that stretch 100% and over.
Multiply your across measurements by .90, 10% smaller, except for the shoulder measurement, since the final garment will have twill tape to stabilize the seam and prevent it from stretching.

		Multiply Your Across Measurements By	Extra Small	Small	Medium	Large	Extra Large
			32	36	40	44	48
1	Chest	× .90	28 3/4	32 3/8	36	39 5/8	43 1/4
2	Waist	× .90	23 3/8	27	30 5/8	34 2/8	37 3/4
3	Hip	× .90	28 3/4	32 3/8	36	39 5/8	43 1/4
4	Crotch depth	No reduction	9	9 1/4	9 1/2	9 3/4	10
5	Waist to knee	No reduction	20 1/2	20 3/4	21	21 1/4	21 1/2
6	Waist to ankle	No reduction	36	36 1/2	37	37 1/2	38
7	Ankle	× .90	7 1/4	12 5/8	13	13 1/2	14
8	Knee	× .90	12 1/4	12 3/4	13 1/8	13 5/8	14
9	Front crotch	× .90	1 3/4	2	2 1/4	2 1/2	2 3/4
10	Back crotch	× .90	2 3/8	2 3/4	3	3 1/4	3 5/8
11	Crotch angle	× .90	7/8	1	1 1/8	1 1/4	1 3/8
12	Nape to waist	No reduction	18 1/8	18 5/8	19 1/8	19 5/8	20 1/8
13	Back neck	No reduction	2 1/4	2 1/4	2 3/8	2 3/8	2 3/8
14	Back neck rise	× .90	3/4	3/4	3/4	3/4	3/4
15	Shoulder length	No reduction	5 7/8	6 1/8	6 3/8	6 5/8	6 7/8
16	Across back	× .90	8	8 1/2	9	9 1/2	10
17	Sleeve length	No reduction	23	23 1/4	23 1/2	23 3/4	24
18	Shoulder pitch	× .90	1 1/2	1 1/2	1 5/8	1 5/8	1 5/8
19	Bicep	× .90	9 1/2	10 1/8	10 3/4	11 1/2	12 1/8
20	Wrist	× .90	5 5/8	6 1/4	7	7 5/8	8 3/8
21	Neck	× .90	12 1/8	12 3/8	12 5/8	12 7/8	13
22	Chest span	× .90	4 3/8	5	5 3/8	5 3/4	6 1/4
23	Chest level	No reduction	8 1/2	8 3/4	9	9 1/4	9 1/2

MEN'S REGULAR SIZE FOUR-WAY REDUCTIONS

Ten percent smaller in crosswise direction and 10% smaller in the lengthwise direction.
Use these measurements when drafting slopers for fabrics that stretch 100% in both directions.
Multiply your measurements by .90, 10% smaller, in both directions.

		Multiply Your Across Measurements By	Extra Small	Small	Medium	Large	Extra Large
			32	36	40	44	48
1	Chest	× .90	28 3/4	30 5/8	32 3/8	34 1/4	36
2	Waist	× .90	23 3/8	25 1/4	27	28 3/4	30 5/8
3	Hip	× .90	28 3/4	30 5/8	32 3/8	34 1/4	36
4	Crotch depth	× .90	8 1/2	8 5/8	8 3/4	9	9
5	Waist to knee	× .90	19 1/2	19 5/8	19 3/4	19 7/8	20
6	Waist to ankle	× .90	34 1/4	34 1/2	34 5/8	35	35 1/8
7	Ankle	× .90	7 1/4	12 3/8	12 5/8	12 7/8	13
8	Knee	× .90	12 1/4	12 1/2	12 3/4	13	13 1/8
9	Front crotch	× .90	1 6/8	2	2	2 1/8	2 1/4
10	Back crotch	× .90	2 5/8	2 7/8	3	3 1/8	3 3/8
11	Crotch angle	× .90	1	1	1 1/8	1 1/4	1 1/4
12	Nape to waist	× .90	17 1/4	17 1/2	17 3/4	18	18 1/8
13	Back neck	No reduction	2 1/4	2 1/4	2 1/4	2 3/8	2 3/8
14	Back neck rise	No reduction	3/4	3/4	3/4	3/4	3/4
15	Shoulder length	No reduction	5 7/8	6	6 1/8	6 1/4	6 3/8
16	Across back	No reduction	8	8 1/4	8 1/2	8 3/4	9
17	Sleeve length	No reduction	23	23 1/8	23 1/4	23 3/8	23 1/2
18	Shoulder pitch	No reduction	1 5/8	1 5/8	1 3/4	1 3/4	1 3/4
19	Bicep	× .90	9 1/2	9 3/4	10 1/8	10 1/2	10 3/4
20	Wrist	× .90	5 5/8	6	6 1/4	6 5/8	7
21	Neck	No reduction	13 1/2	13 5/8	13 3/4	13 7/8	14
22	Chest span	× .90	4 3/8	4 3/4	5	5 1/8	5 3/8
23	Chest level	× .90	9	9 1/8	9 1/4	9 3/8	9 1/2

MEN'S SHORT SIZE STABLE KNITS REDUCTIONS

Zero percent smaller in crosswise direction without any reductions in lengthwise direction.
Use these measurements when drafting slopers for fabrics that stretch from 0% to 25%.
Use your measurements exactly as recorded without any reductions.

		Multiply Your Across Measurements By	Extra Small	Small	Medium	Large	Extra Large
			32 S	36 S	40 S	44 S	48 S
1	Chest	× 1	32	36	40	44	48
2	Waist	× 1	26	30	34	38	42
3	Hip	× 1	34	38	42	46	50
4	Crotch depth	No reduction	9 5/8	9 7/8	10 1/8	10 3/8	10 5/8
5	Waist to knee	No reduction	21 7/8	22 1/8	22 3/8	22 5/8	22 7/8
6	Waist to ankle	No reduction	39 1/8	39 5/8	40 1/8	40 5/8	41 1/8
7	Ankle	× 1	8 3/8	14 3/8	14 7/8	15 3/8	15 7/8
8	Knee	× 1	14	14 1/2	15	15 1/2	16
9	Front crotch	× 1	2 1/8	2 3/8	2 5/8	2 7/8	3 1/8
10	Back crotch	× 1	2 7/8	3 1/8	3 1/2	3 7/8	4 1/8
11	Crotch angle	× 1	1	1 1/4	1 3/8	1 1/2	1 5/8
12	Nape to waist	No reduction	19 1/4	19 3/4	20 1/4	20 3/4	21 1/4
13	Back neck	No reduction	2 3/8	2 3/8	2 3/8	2 1/2	2 1/2
14	Back neck rise	× 1	3/4	3/4	3/4	7/8	7/8
15	Shoulder length	No reduction	6	6 1/4	6 1/2	6 3/4	7
16	Across back	× 1	8 1/4	8 3/4	9 1/4	9 3/4	10 1/4
17	Sleeve length	No reduction	24 5/8	24 7/8	25 1/8	25 3/8	25 5/8
18	Shoulder pitch	× 1	1 3/4	1 3/4	1 7/8	1 7/8	2
19	Bicep	× 1	11 1/4	12	12 3/4	13 1/2	14 1/4
20	Wrist	× 1	6 1/2	7 1/4	8	8 3/4	9 1/2
21	Neck	× 1	14	14 1/4	14 1/2	14 3/4	15
22	Chest span	× 1	5	6	6 3/8	7	7 3/8
23	Chest level	No reduction	9 7/8	9 7/8	9 7/8	9 7/8	9 7/8

MEN'S SHORT SIZE MODERATE REDUCTIONS

Two percent smaller in crosswise direction without any reductions in lengthwise direction.
Use these measurements when drafting slopers for fabrics that stretch from 25% to 50%.
Multiply your across measurements by .98, 2% smaller, except for the shoulder measurement, since the final garment will have twill tape to stabilize the seam and prevent it from stretching.

		Multiply Your Across Measurements By	Extra Small	Small	Medium	Large	Extra Large
			32 S	36 S	40 S	44 S	48 S
1	Chest	× .98	31 3/8	35 1/4	39 1/4	43 1/8	47
2	Waist	× .98	25 1/2	29 3/8	33 3/8	37 1/4	41 1/8
3	Hip	× .98	33 3/8	37 1/4	41 1/8	45	49
4	Crotch depth	No reduction	9 5/8	9 7/8	10 1/8	10 3/8	10 5/8
5	Waist to knee	No reduction	21 7/8	22 1/8	22 3/8	22 5/8	22 7/8
6	Waist to ankle	No reduction	39 1/8	39 5/8	40 1/8	40 5/8	41 1/8
7	Ankle	× .98	8 1/4	14	14 5/8	15	15 1/2
8	Knee	× .98	13 3/4	14 2/8	14 3/4	15 1/4	15 5/8
9	Front crotch	× .98	2	2 3/8	2 5/8	2 7/8	3
10	Back crotch	× .98	2 3/4	3 1/8	3 3/8	3 3/4	4
11	Crotch angle	× .98	1	1 1/8	1 1/4	1 3/8	1 1/2
12	Nape to waist	No reduction	19 1/4	19 3/4	20 1/4	20 3/4	21 1/4
13	Back neck	No reduction	2 3/8	2 3/8	2 3/8	2 1/2	2 1/2
14	Back neck rise	× .98	3/4	3/4	3/4	7/8	7/8
15	Shoulder length	No reduction	6	6 1/4	6 1/2	6 3/4	7
16	Across back	× .98	8 1/4	8 3/4	9 1/4	9 3/4	10 1/4
17	Sleeve length	No reduction	24 5/8	24 7/8	25 1/8	25 3/8	25 5/8
18	Shoulder pitch	× .98	1 3/4	1 3/4	1 3/4	1 7/8	1 7/8
19	Bicep	× .98	11	11 3/4	12 1/2	13 1/4	14
20	Wrist	× .98	6 3/8	7 1/8	7 7/8	8 5/8	9 1/4
21	Neck	× .98	13 3/4	14	14 1/4	14 1/2	14 3/4
22	Chest span	× .98	4 3/4	5 1/4	5 3/4	6 1/4	6 3/4
23	Chest level	No reduction	9 5/8	9 5/8	9 5/8	9 5/8	9 5/8

MEN'S SHORT SIZE STRETCHY REDUCTIONS

Three percent smaller in crosswise direction without any reductions in lengthwise direction.
Use these measurements when drafting slopers for fabrics that stretch from 50% to 75%.
Multiply your across measurements by .97, 3% smaller, except for the shoulder measurement, since the final garment will have twill tape to stabilize the seam and prevent it from stretching.

		Multiply Your Across Measurements By	Extra Small	Small	Medium	Large	Extra Large
			32 S	36 S	40 S	44 S	48 S
1	Chest	× .97	31	35	38 3/4	42 5/8	46 1/2
2	Waist	× .97	25 1/4	29	33	36 7/8	40 3/4
3	Hip	× .97	33	36 7/8	40 3/4	44 5/8	48 1/2
4	Crotch depth	No reduction	9 5/8	9 7/8	10 1/8	10 3/8	10 5/8
5	Waist to knee	No reduction	21 7/8	22 1/8	22 3/8	22 5/8	22 7/8
6	Waist to ankle	No reduction	39 1/8	39 5/8	40 1/8	40 5/8	41 1/8
7	Ankle	× .97	8 1/8	14	14 3/8	15	15 3/8
8	Knee	× .97	13 5/8	14	14 1/2	15	15 1/2
9	Front crotch	× .97	2	2 1/4	2 1/2	2 3/4	3
10	Back crotch	× .97	2 3/4	3	3 3/8	3 3/4	4
11	Crotch angle	× .97	1	1 1/8	1 1/4	1 3/8	1 1/2
12	Nape to waist	No reduction	19 1/4	19 3/4	20 1/4	20 3/4	21 1/4
13	Back neck	No reduction	2 3/8	2 3/8	2 3/8	2 1/2	2 1/2
14	Back neck rise	× .97	3/4	3/4	3/4	7/8	7/8
15	Shoulder length	No reduction	6	6 1/4	6 1/2	6 3/4	7
16	Across back	× .97	8 1/4	8 3/4	9 1/4	9 3/4	10 1/4
17	Sleeve length	No reduction	24 5/8	24 7/8	25 1/8	25 3/8	25 5/8
18	Shoulder pitch	× .97	1 3/4	1 3/4	1 3/4	1 7/8	1 7/8
19	Bicep	× .97	11	11 5/8	12 3/8	13	13 7/8
20	Wrist	× .97	6 1/4	7	7 3/4	8 1/2	9 1/4
21	Neck	× .97	13 5/8	13 7/8	14	14 1/4	14 1/2
22	Chest span	× .97	4 3/4	5 3/4	6 3/4	7 5/8	8 5/8
23	Chest level	No reduction	9 1/2	9 1/2	9 1/2	9 1/2	9 1/2

MEN'S SHORT SIZE SUPER-STRETCH REDUCTIONS

Five percent smaller in crosswise direction without any reductions in lengthwise direction.
Use these measurements when drafting slopers for fabrics that stretch from 75% to 100%.
Multiply your across measurements by .95, 5% smaller, except for the shoulder measurement, since the final garment will have twill tape to stabilize the seam and prevent it from stretching.

		Multiply Your Across Measurements By	Extra Small	Small	Medium	Large	Extra Large
			32 S	36 S	40 S	44 S	48 S
1	Chest	× .95	30 3/8	34 1/4	38	41 3/4	45 5/8
2	Waist	× .95	24 3/4	28 1/2	32 1/4	36 1/8	39 7/8
3	Hip	× .95	32 1/4	36 1/8	39 7/8	43 3/4	47 1/2
4	Crotch depth	No reduction	9 5/8	9 7/8	10 1/8	10 3/8	10 5/8
5	Waist to knee	No reduction	21 7/8	22 1/8	22 3/8	22 5/8	22 7/8
6	Waist to ankle	No reduction	39 1/8	39 5/8	40 1/8	40 5/8	41 1/8
7	Ankle	× .95	8	13 5/8	14 1/8	14 5/8	15
8	Knee	× .95	13 1/4	13 3/4	14 1/4	14 3/4	15 1/4
9	Front crotch	× .95	2	2 1/4	2 1/2	2 3/4	3
10	Back crotch	× .95	2 3/4	3	3 3/8	3 5/8	4
11	Crotch angle	× .95	1	1 1/8	1 1/4	1 3/8	1 1/2
12	Nape to waist	No reduction	19 1/4	19 3/4	20 1/4	20 3/4	21 1/4
13	Back neck	No reduction	2 3/8	2 3/8	2 3/8	2 1/2	2 1/2
14	Back neck rise	× .95	3/4	3/4	3/4	7/8	7/8
15	Shoulder length	No reduction	6	6 1/4	6 1/2	6 3/4	7
16	Across back	× .95	8 1/4	8 3/4	9 1/4	9 3/4	10 1/4
17	Sleeve length	No reduction	24 5/8	24 7/8	25 1/8	25 3/8	25 5/8
18	Shoulder pitch	× .95	1 5/8	1 3/4	1 3/4	1 3/4	1 7/8
19	Bicep	× .95	10 3/4	11 3/8	12 1/8	12 7/8	13 1/2
20	Wrist	× .95	6 1/8	6 7/8	7 5/8	8 3/8	9
21	Neck	× .95	13 1/4	13 1/2	13 3/4	14	14 1/4
22	Chest span	× .95	4 5/8	5 5/8	6 1/2	7 1/2	8 1/2
23	Chest level	No reduction	9 3/8	9 1/2	9 1/4	9 3/8	9 3/8

MEN'S SHORT SIZE RIB REDUCTIONS

Ten percent smaller in crosswise direction without any reductions in lengthwise direction.
Use these measurements when drafting slopers for fabrics that stretch 100% and over.
Multiply your across measurements by .90, 10% smaller, except for the shoulder measurement, since the final garment will have twill tape to stabilize the seam and prevent it from stretching.

		Multiply Your Across Measurements By	Extra Small	Small	Medium	Large	Extra Large
			28 3/4	32 3/8	36	39 5/8	43 1/4
1	Chest	× .90	23 3/8	27	30 5/8	34 1/4	37 3/4
2	Waist	× .90	30 5/8	34 1/4	37 3/4	41 3/8	45
3	Hip	× .90	9 5/8	9 7/8	10 1/8	10 3/8	10 5/8
4	Crotch depth	No reduction	21 7/8	22 1/8	22 3/8	22 5/8	22 7/8
5	Waist to knee	No reduction	39 1/8	39 5/8	40 1/8	40 5/8	41 1/8
6	Waist to ankle	No reduction	7 1/2	13	13 3/8	13 7/8	14 1/4
7	Ankle	× .90	12 5/8	13	13 1/2	14	14 3/8
8	Knee	× .90	2	2 1/8	2 3/8	2 5/8	2 7/8
9	Front crotch	× .90	2 1/2	2 7/8	3 1/8	3 1/2	3 3/4
10	Back crotch	× .90	1	1	1 1/8	1 1/4	1 3/8
11	Crotch angle	× .90	19 1/4	19 3/4	20 1/4	20 3/4	21 1/4
12	Nape to waist	No reduction	2 3/8	2 3/8	2 3/8	2 1/2	2 1/2
13	Back neck	No reduction	3/4	3/4	3/4	7/8	7/8
14	Back neck rise	× .90	6	6 1/4	6 1/2	6 3/4	7
15	Shoulder length	No reduction	8 1/4	8 3/4	9 1/4	9 3/4	10 1/4
16	Across back	× .90	24 5/8	24 7/8	25 1/8	25 3/8	25 5/8
17	Sleeve length	No reduction	1 5/8	1 5/8	1 5/8	1 3/4	1 3/4
18	Shoulder pitch	× .90	10 1/8	10 6/8	11 1/2	12 1/8	12 7/8
19	Bicep	× .90	5 7/8	6 1/2	7 1/4	7 7/8	8 1/2
20	Wrist	× .90	12 5/8	12 7/8	13	13 1/4	13 1/2
21	Neck	× .90	4 3/8	5 1/2	6 1/4	7 1/8	8
22	Chest span	× .90	8 7/8	8 7/8	8 3/4	8 7/8	8 7/8
23	Chest level	No reduction	28 3/4	32 3/8	36	39 5/8	43 1/4

MEN'S SHORT SIZE FOUR-WAY REDUCTIONS

Ten percent smaller in crosswise direction and 10% smaller in the lengthwise direction.
Use these measurements when drafting slopers for fabrics that stretch 100% in both directions.
Multiply your measurements by .90, 10% smaller, in both directions.

		Multiply Your Across Measurements By	Extra Small	Small	Medium	Large	Extra Large
			32 S	36 S	40 S	44 S	48 S
1	Chest	× .90	28 3/4	30 5/8	32 3/8	34 1/4	36
2	Waist	× .90	23 3/8	25 1/4	27	28 6/8	30 5/8
3	Hip	× .90	30 5/8	32 3/8	34 1/4	36	37 6/8
4	Crotch depth	× .90	9 1/8	9 1/4	9 3/8	9 1/2	9 5/8
5	Waist to knee	× .90	20 3/4	20 7/8	21	21 1/8	21 1/4
6	Waist to ankle	× .90	37 1/8	37 3/8	37 5/8	37 7/8	38 1/8
7	Ankle	× .90	7 1/2	12 3/4	13	13 1/8	13 3/8
8	Knee	× .90	12 5/8	12 7/8	13	13 1/4	13 1/2
9	Front crotch	× .90	2	2	2 1/8	2 1/4	2 3/8
10	Back crotch	× .90	2 7/8	3	3 1/8	3 3/8	3 1/2
11	Crotch angle	× .90	1	1 1/8	1 1/4	1 1/4	1 1/3
12	Nape to waist	× .90	18 1/4	18 1/2	18 3/4	19	19 1/4
13	Back neck	No reduction	2 3/8	2 3/8	2 3/8	2 3/8	2 3/8
14	Back neck rise	No reduction	3/4	3/4	3/4	3/4	3/4
15	Shoulder length	No reduction	6	6 1/8	6 1/4	6 3/8	6 1/2
16	Across back	No reduction	8 1/4	8 1/2	8 3/4	9	9 1/4
17	Sleeve length	No reduction	24 5/8	24 3/4	24 7/8	25	25 1/8
18	Shoulder pitch	No reduction	1 3/4	1 3/4	1 3/4	1 7/8	1 7/8
19	Bicep	× .90	10 1/8	10 1/2	10 3/4	11 1/8	11 1/2
20	Wrist	× .90	5 7/8	6 1/4	6 1/2	6 7/8	7 1/4
21	Neck	No reduction	14	14 1/8	14 1/4	14 3/8	14 1/2
22	Chest span	× .90	4 3/8	4 3/4	5 1/4	5 3/4	6 1/4
23	Chest level	× .90	9 3/8	9 1/4	9 1/4	9 3/8	9 1/4

MEN'S TALL SIZE STABLE KNITS REDUCTIONS

Zero percent smaller in crosswise direction without any reductions in lengthwise direction.
Use these measurements when drafting slopers for fabrics that stretch from 0% to 25%.
Use the measurements exactly as recorded without any reductions.

		Multiply Your Across Measurements By	Extra Small	Small	Medium	Large	Extra Large
			32 T	36 T	40 T	44 T	48 T
1	Chest	× 1	32	36	40	44	48
2	Waist	× 1	27	31	35	39	43
3	Hip	× 1	32	36	40	44	48
4	Crotch depth	No reduction	10	10 1/4	10 1/2	10 3/4	11
5	Waist to knee	No reduction	23 1/8	23 3/8	23 5/8	23 7/8	24 1/8
6	Waist to ankle	No reduction	40	40 1/2	41	41 1/2	42
7	Ankle	× 1	8	14	14 1/2	15	15 1/2
8	Knee	× 1	13 5/8	14 1/8	14 5/8	15 1/8	15 5/8
9	Front crotch	× 1	2	2 1/4	2 1/2	2 3/4	3
10	Back crotch	× 1	2 5/8	3	3 3/8	3 5/8	4
11	Crotch angle	× 1	1	1 1/8	1 1/4	1 3/8	1 1/2
12	Nape to waist	No reduction	20 1/8	20 5/8	21 1/8	21 5/8	22 1/8
13	Back neck	No reduction	2 1/4	2 1/4	2 3/8	2 3/8	2 3/8
14	Back neck rise	× 1	3/4	3/4	3/4	3/4	3/4
15	Shoulder length	No reduction	5 7/8	6 1/8	6 3/8	6 5/8	6 7/8
16	Across back	× 1	8	8 1/2	9	9 1/2	10
17	Sleeve length	No reduction	26	26 1/4	26 1/2	26 3/4	27
18	Shoulder pitch	× 1	1 7/8	1 7/8	2	2	2
19	Bicep	× 1	10 1/2	11 1/4	12	12 3/4	13 1/2
20	Wrist	× 1	6 1/4	7	7 3/4	8 1/2	9 1/4
21	Neck	× 1	13 1/2	13 3/4	14	14 1/4	14 1/2
22	Chest span	× 1	5	5 3/8	6	6 3/8	7
23	Chest level	No reduction	9 3/4	10	10 1/4	10 1/2	10 3/4

MEN'S TALL SIZE MODERATE REDUCTIONS

Two percent smaller in crosswise direction without any reductions in lengthwise direction.
Use these measurements when drafting slopers for fabrics that stretch from 25% to 50%.
Multiply your across measurements by .98, 2% smaller, except for the shoulder measurement, since the final garment will have twill tape to stabilize the seam and prevent it from stretching.

		Multiply Your Across Measurements By	Extra Small	Small	Medium	Large	Extra Large
			32 T	36 T	40 T	44 T	48 T
1	Chest	× .98	31 3/8	35 1/4	39 1/4	43 1/8	47
2	Waist	× .98	26 1/2	30 3/8	34 1/4	38 1/4	42 1/8
3	Hip	× .98	31 3/8	35 1/4	39 1/4	43 1/8	47
4	Crotch depth	No reduction	10	10 1/4	10 1/2	10 3/4	11
5	Waist to knee	No reduction	23 1/8	23 3/8	23 5/8	23 7/8	24 1/8
6	Waist to ankle	No reduction	40	40 1/2	41	41 1/2	42
7	Ankle	× .98	8	13 3/4	14 1/4	14 3/4	15 1/4
8	Knee	× .98	13 3/8	13 7/8	14 3/8	14 7/8	15 3/8
9	Front crotch	× .98	2	2 1/4	2 1/2	2 3/4	3
10	Back crotch	× .98	2 5/8	3	3 1/4	3 5/8	4
11	Crotch angle	× .98	1	1 1/8	1 1/4	1 3/8	1 1/2
12	Nape to waist	No reduction	20 1/8	20 5/8	21 1/8	21 5/8	22 1/8
13	Back neck	No reduction	2 1/4	2 2/8	2 3/8	2 3/8	2 3/8
14	Back neck rise	× .98	3/4	3/4	6/8	6/8	6/8
15	Shoulder length	No reduction	5 7/8	6 1/8	6 3/8	6 5/8	6 7/8
16	Across back	× .98	8	8 1/2	9	9 1/2	10
17	Sleeve length	No reduction	26	26 1/4	26 1/2	26 3/4	27
18	Shoulder pitch	× .98	1 3/4	1 7/8	1 7/8	2	2
19	Bicep	× .98	10 1/4	11	11 3/4	12 1/2	13 1/4
20	Wrist	× .98	6 1/8	6 7/8	7 5/8	8 3/8	9
21	Neck	× .98	13 1/4	13 1/2	13 3/4	14	14 1/4
22	Chest span	× .98	4 3/4	5 1/4	5 3/4	6 1/4	6 3/4
23	Chest level	No reduction	9 1/2	9 3/4	10	10 1/4	10 1/2

MEN'S TALL SIZE STRETCHY REDUCTIONS

Three percent smaller in crosswise direction without any reductions in lengthwise direction.
Use these measurements when drafting slopers for fabrics that stretch from 50% to 75%.
Multiply your across measurements by .97, 3% smaller, except for the shoulder measurement, since the final garment will have twill tape to stabilize the seam and prevent it from stretching.

		Multiply Your Across Measurements By	Extra Small	Small	Medium	Large	Extra Large
			32 T	36 T	40 T	44 T	48 T
1	Chest	× .97	31	35	38 3/4	42 5/8	46 1/2
2	Waist	× .97	26 1/4	30	34	37 7/8	41 6/8
3	Hip	× .97	31	35	38 3/4	42 5/8	46 1/2
4	Crotch depth	No reduction	10	10 1/4	10 1/2	10 3/4	11
5	Waist to knee	No reduction	23 1/8	23 3/8	23 5/8	23 7/8	24 1/8
6	Waist to ankle	No reduction	40	40 1/2	41	41 1/2	42
7	Ankle	× .97	7 7/8	13 5/8	14	14 1/2	15
8	Knee	× .97	13 1/4	13 3/4	14 1/8	14 5/8	15 1/8
9	Front crotch	× .97	2	2 1/8	2 3/8	2 5/8	3
10	Back crotch	× .97	2 5/8	3	3 1/4	3 1/2	3 7/8
11	Crotch angle	× .97	1	1	1 1/4	1 3/8	1 1/2
12	Nape to waist	No reduction	20 1/8	20 5/8	21 1/8	21 5/8	22 1/8
13	Back neck	No reduction	2 1/4	2 1/4	2 3/8	2 3/8	2 3/8
14	Back neck rise	× .97	3/4	3/4	3/4	3/4	3/4
15	Shoulder length	No reduction	5 7/8	6 1/8	6 3/8	6 5/8	6 7/8
16	Across back	× .97	8	8 1/2	9	9 1/2	10
17	Sleeve length	No reduction	26	26 1/4	26 1/2	26 3/4	27
18	Shoulder pitch	× .97	1 3/4	1 7/8	1 7/8	2	2
19	Bicep	× .97	10 1/8	11	11 5/8	12 3/8	13
20	Wrist	× .97	6	6 3/4	7 1/2	8 1/4	9
21	Neck	× .97	13	13 3/8	13 5/8	13 7/8	14
22	Chest span	× .97	4 3/4	5 1/4	5 3/4	6 1/4	6 3/4
23	Chest level	No reduction	9 1/2	9 3/4	10	10 1/8	10 3/8

MEN'S TALL SIZE SUPER-STRETCH REDUCTIONS

Five percent smaller in crosswise direction without any reductions in lengthwise direction.
Use these measurements when drafting slopers for fabrics that stretch from 75% to 100%.
Multiply your across measurements by .95, 5% smaller, except for the shoulder measurement, since the final garment will have twill tape to stabilize the seam and prevent it from stretching.

		Multiply Your Across Measurements By	Extra Small	Small	Medium	Large	Extra Large
			32 T	36 T	40 T	44 T	48 T
1	Chest	× .95	30 3/8	34 1/4	38	41 3/4	45 5/8
2	Waist	× .95	25 5/8	29 1/2	33 1/4	37	40 7/8
3	Hip	× .95	30 3/8	34 1/5	38	41 3/4	45 5/8
4	Crotch depth	No reduction	10	10 1/4	10 1/2	10 3/4	11
5	Waist to knee	No reduction	23 1/8	23 3/8	23 5/8	23 7/8	24 1/8
6	Waist to ankle	No reduction	40	40 1/2	41	41 1/2	42
7	Ankle	× .95	7 5/8	13 1/4	13 3/4	14 1/4	14 3/4
8	Knee	× .95	13	13 3/8	13 7/8	14 3/8	14 7/8
9	Front crotch	× .95	1 7/8	2 1/8	2 3/8	2 5/8	2 7/8
10	Back crotch	× .95	2 1/2	2 7/8	3 1/6	3 1/2	3 6/8
11	Crotch angle	× .95	1	1	1 1/4	1 1/4	1 3/8
12	Nape to waist	No reduction	20 1/8	20 5/8	21 1/8	21 5/8	22 1/8
13	Back neck	No reduction	2 1/4	2 1/4	2 3/8	2 3/8	2 3/8
14	Back neck rise	× .95	3/4	3/4	3/4	3/4	3/4
15	Shoulder length	No reduction	5 7/8	6 1/8	6 3/8	6 5/8	6 7/8
16	Across back	× .95	8	8 1/2	9	9 1/2	10
17	Sleeve length	No reduction	26	26 1/4	26 1/2	26 3/4	27
18	Shoulder pitch	× .95	1 3/4	1 3/4	1 7/8	1 7/8	2
19	Bicep	× .95	10	10 3/4	11 3/8	12 1/8	12 7/8
20	Wrist	× .95	6	6 5/8	7 3/8	8	8 3/4
21	Neck	× .95	12 7/8	13	13 1/4	13 1/2	13 3/4
22	Chest span	× .95	4 5/8	5 1/8	5 5/8	6	6 1/2
23	Chest level	No reduction	9 1/4	9 1/2	9 3/4	10	10 1/4

MEN'S TALL SIZE RIB REDUCTIONS

Ten percent smaller in crosswise direction without any reductions in lengthwise direction.
Use these measurements when drafting slopers for fabrics that stretch 100% and over.
Multiply your across measurements by .90, 10% smaller, except for the shoulder measurement, since the final garment will have twill tape to stabilize the seam and prevent it from stretching.

		Multiply Your Across Measurements By	Extra Small	Small	Medium	Large	Extra Large
			32 T	36 T	40 T	44 T	48 T
1	Chest	× .90	28 3/4	32 3/8	36	39 5/8	43 1/4
2	Waist	× .90	24 1/4	28	31 1/2	35 1/8	38 3/4
3	Hip	× .90	28 3/4	32 3/8	36	39 5/8	43 1/4
4	Crotch depth	No reduction	10	10 1/4	10 1/2	10 3/4	11
5	Waist to knee	No reduction	23 1/8	23 3/8	23 5/8	23 7/8	24 1/8
6	Waist to ankle	No reduction	40	40 1/2	41	41 1/2	42
7	Ankle	× .90	7 1/4	12 5/8	13	13 1/2	14
8	Knee	× .90	12 1/4	12 3/4	13 1/8	13 5/8	14
9	Front crotch	× .90	1 3/4	2	2 1/4	2 1/2	2 3/4
10	Back crotch	× .90	2 3/8	2 3/4	3	3 1/4	3 5/8
11	Crotch angle	× .90	7/8	1	1 1/8	1 1/4	1 3/8
12	Nape to waist	No reduction	20 1/8	20 5/8	21 1/8	21 5/8	22 1/8
13	Back neck	No reduction	2 1/4	2 1/4	2 3/8	2 3/8	2 3/8
14	Back neck rise	× .90	3/4	3/4	3/4	3/4	3/4
15	Shoulder length	No reduction	5 7/8	6 1/8	6 3/8	6 5/8	6 7/8
16	Across back	× .90	8	8 1/2	9	9 1/2	10
17	Sleeve length	No reduction	26	26 1/4	26 1/2	26 3/4	27
18	Shoulder pitch	× .90	1 5/8	1 3/4	1 3/4	1 3/4	1 3/4
19	Bicep	× .90	9 1/2	10 1/8	10 3/4	11 1/2	12 1/8
20	Wrist	× .90	5 5/8	6 1/4	7	7 5/8	8 3/8
21	Neck	× .90	12 1/8	12 3/8	12 5/8	12 7/8	13
22	Chest span	× .90	4 3/8	4 7/8	5 3/8	5 3/4	6 1/4
23	Chest level	No reduction	8 3/4	9	9 1/4	9 1/2	9 5/8

MEN'S TALL SIZE FOUR-WAY REDUCTIONS

Ten percent smaller in crosswise direction and 10% smaller in the lengthwise direction.
Use these measurements when drafting slopers for fabrics that stretch 100% in both directions.
Multiply your measurements by .90, 10% smaller, in both directions.

		Multiply Your Across Measurements By	Extra Small	Small	Medium	Large	Extra Large
			32 T	36 T	40 T	44 T	48 T
1	Chest	× .90	28 3/4	30 5/8	32 3/8	34 1/4	36
2	Waist	× .90	24 1/4	26 1/8	28	29 3/4	31 1/2
3	Hip	× .90	28 3/4	30 5/8	32 3/8	34 1/4	36
4	Crotch depth	× .90	9 1/2	9 5/8	9 3/4	9 7/8	10
5	Waist to knee	× .90	22	22	22 1/4	22 1/3	22 1/2
6	Waist to ankle	× .90	38	38 1/4	38 1/2	38 3/4	39
7	Ankle	× .90	7 1/4	12 3/8	12 5/8	12 7/8	13
8	Knee	× .90	12 1/4	12 1/2	12 3/4	13	13 1/8
9	Front crotch	× .90	1 3/4	2	2	2 1/8	2 1/4
10	Back crotch	× .90	2 5/8	2 7/8	3	3 1/8	3 3/8
11	Crotch angle	× .90	1	1	1 1/8	1 1/4	1 1/4
12	Nape to waist	× .90	19 1/8	19 3/8	19 5/8	19 7/8	20
13	Back neck	No reduction	2 1/4	2 1/4	2 1/4	2 3/8	2 3/8
14	Back neck rise	No reduction	3/4	3/4	3/4	3/4	3/4
15	Shoulder length	No reduction	5 7/8	6	6 1/8	6 1/4	6 3/8
16	Across back	No reduction	8	8 1/4	8 1/2	8 3/4	9
17	Sleeve length	No reduction	26	26 1/8	26 1/4	26 3/8	26 1/2
18	Shoulder pitch	No reduction	1 7/8	1 7/8	1 7/8	1 7/8	2
19	Bicep	× .90	9 1/2	9 3/4	10 1/8	10 1/2	10 3/4
20	Wrist	× .90	5 5/8	6	6 1/4	6 5/8	7
21	Neck	No reduction	13 1/2	13 5/8	13 3/4	13 7/8	14
22	Chest span	× .90	4 3/8	4 5/8	4 7/8	5	5 3/8
23	Chest level	× .90	9 1/4	9 3/8	9 1/2	9 5/8	9 3/4